Essential Readings in World Politics

FOURTH EDITION

THE NORTON SERIES IN WORLD POLITICS
Jack L. Snyder, General Editor

Essentials of International Relations, Fifth Edition
Karen A. Mingst and Ivan M. Arreguín-Toft

From Voting to Violence: Democratization and Nationalist Conflict
Jack L. Snyder

Prosperity and Violence: The Political Economy of Development
Robert H. Bates

Triangulating Peace: Democracy, Interdependence, and International Organizations
Bruce Russett and John Oneal

The Tragedy of Great Power Politics
John J. Mearsheimer

Lenses of Analysis (website)
Richard Harknett

Essential Readings in World Politics

FOURTH EDITION

EDITED BY

Karen A. Mingst and Jack L. Snyder

W. W. NORTON & COMPANY

NEW YORK • LONDON

W. W. Norton & Company has been independent since its founding in 1923, when William Warder Norton and Mary D. Herter Norton first published lectures delivered at the People's Institute, the adult education division of New York City's Cooper Union. The firm soon expanded its program beyond the Institute, publishing books by celebrated academics from America and abroad. By mid-century, the two major pillars of Norton's publishing program—trade books and college texts—were firmly established. In the 1950s, the Norton family transferred control of the company to its employees, and today—with a staff of four hundred and a comparable number of trade, college, and professional titles published each year—W. W. Norton & Company stands as the largest and oldest publishing house owned wholly by its employees.

The text of this book is composed in New Aster with the display set in Gotham.

Composition and project management by Westchester Book Group

Manufacturing by Maple—York, PA
Editor: Ann Shin
Editorial Assistant: Jake Schindel
Project Editor: Kathleen Feighery
Production Manager: Benjamin Reynolds
E-media Editor: Lorraine Klimowich
Book design by Guenet Abraham
Design director: Hope Miller Goodell

Library of Congress Cataloging-in-Publication Data

Essential readings in world politics / edited by Karen A. Mingst and Jack L. Snyder.—4th ed.
    p. cm.—(The Norton series in world politics)
  Includes bibliographical references.
  ISBN 978-0-393-93534-9 (pbk.)
 1. International relations. 2. World politics.
I. Mingst, Karen A., 1947– II. Snyder, Jack L.
  JZ1305.E85 2011
  327—dc22   2010033300

W. W. Norton & Company, Inc., 500 Fifth Avenue, New York, N.Y. 10110-0017
www.wwnorton.com
W. W. Norton & Company Ltd., Castle House, 75/76 Wells Street, London W1T 3QT

1 2 3 4 5 6 7 8 9 0

Contents

Preface   **ix**

1 **Approaches**   **1**

One World, Rival Theories   **2**
Jack Snyder

Melian Dialogue   **10**
Thucydides

To Perpetual Peace: A Philosophical Sketch   **12**
Immanuel Kant

2 **History**   **16**

The Fourteen Points   **17**
Woodrow Wilson

The Sources of Soviet Conduct   **19**
George F. Kennan ("X")

3 **Contending Perspectives**   **25**

A Realist Theory of International Politics and Political Power   **26**
Hans J. Morgenthau

Anarchy and the Struggle for Power   **31**
John J. Mearsheimer

Liberalism and World Politics   **50**
Michael W. Doyle

Anarchy Is What States Make of It: The Social Construction
of Power Politics   **64**
Alexander Wendt

Man, the State, and War: Gendered Perspectives on National
Security   **89**
J. Ann Tickner

4   The International System   98

The Balance of Power, Different Methods of the Balance of Power,
and Evaluation of the Balance of Power   **99**
Hans J. Morgenthau

Does Order Exist in World Politics?   **105**
Hedley Bull

Unipolarity, State Behavior, and Systemic Consequences   **110**
G. John Ikenberry, Michael Mastanduno, and William C. Wohlforth

5   The State   130

Sharing Sovereignty: New Institutions for Collapsed
and Failing States   **131**
Stephen D. Krasner

The Five Wars of Globalization   **151**
Moisés Naím

The Clash of Civilizations?   **159**
Samuel P. Huntington

From *Global Rebellion: Religious Challenges to the Secular State,
from Christian Militias to al Qaeda*   **166**
Mark Juergensmeyer

6   The Individual   191

Hypotheses on Misperception   **192**
Robert Jervis

Transformative Choices: Leaders and the Origins of Intervention
Strategy   **206**
Elizabeth N. Saunders

7   IGOs, NGOs, and International Law   222

From *Does Peacekeeping Work?*   **224**
Virginia Page Fortna

Bystanders to Genocide: Why the United States Let the Rwandan
Tragedy Happen   **233**
Samantha Power

Transnational Advocacy Networks in International Politics and
Human Rights Advocacy Networks in Latin America   **253**
Margaret E. Keck and Kathryn Sikkink

The Pitfalls of Universal Jurisdiction   **265**
Henry A. Kissinger

The Case for Universal Jurisdiction   **270**
Kenneth Roth

Is Peace in the Interests of Justice? The Case for Broad Prosecutorial
Discretion at the International Criminal Court   **274**
Kenneth A. Rodman

From *After Hegemony: Cooperation and Discord in the World Political
Economy*   **292**
Robert O. Keohane

The False Promise of International Institutions   **308**
John J. Mearsheimer

8   War and Strife   320

War as an Instrument of Policy   **322**
Carl von Clausewitz

The Diplomacy of Violence   **326**
Thomas C. Schelling

Cooperation under the Security Dilemma   **335**
Robert Jervis

Rationalist Explanations for War   **349**
James D. Fearon

A Nuclear-Armed Iran: A Difficult but Not Impossible Policy
Problem   **375**
Barry R. Posen

Containment Breach   **390**
Robert J. Lieber and Amatzia Baram

The Strategies of Terrorism   **392**
Andrew H. Kydd and Barbara F. Walter

From *The Accidental Guerrilla: Fighting Small Wars in the Midst
of a Big One*   **416**
David Kilcullen

When Is It Right to Fight?   **444**
Gareth Evans

From *The Purpose of Intervention: Changing Beliefs about the Use of Force* **459**
Martha Finnemore

9 International Political Economy 484

The Nature of Political Economy **485**
Robert Gilpin

Globalization, Development, and International Institutions: Normative and Positive Perspectives **493**
Helen V. Milner

From *Why Globalization Works* **516**
Martin Wolf

What Is the Problem with Natural Resource Wealth? **542**
Macartan Humphreys, Jeffrey D. Sachs, and Joseph E. Stiglitz

From *Freefall: America, Free Markets, and the Sinking of the World Economy* **554**
Joseph E. Stiglitz

10 Transnational Issues 574

The Healers: Triumph and Tragedy **575**
William Easterly

Universal Truths: Human Rights and the Westernizing Illusion **592**
Amartya Sen

Trials and Errors: Principle and Pragmatism in Strategies of International Justice **596**
Jack Snyder and Leslie Vinjamuri

The Tragedy of the Commons **616**
Garrett Hardin

Credits **627**

Preface

This reader is a quintessential collaborative effort between the two co-editors. For each of the editions, the co-editors suggested articles for inclusion, traced the sources, and rejected or accepted them, defending choices to skeptical colleagues. This interaction was completed in a flurry of emails and conversations. The final product reflects the fact that while the co-editors are both international relations scholars, they read very different literatures. This book represents a product of that collaborative process and is all the better for the differences.

The articles have been selected to meet several criteria. First, the collection is designed to augment and amplify the core text, *Essentials of International Relations*, Fifth Edition, by Karen Mingst and Ivan Arreguín-Toft. The chapters in this book follow those in the text. Second, the selections are purposefully eclectic; that is, key theoretical articles are paired with contemporary pieces found in the popular literature. When possible, articles have been chosen to reflect diverse theoretical perspectives and policy viewpoints. Finally, the articles are intended to be both readable and engaging to undergraduates. The co-editors struggled to maintain the integrity of the challenging pieces while making them accessible to undergraduates at a variety of colleges and universities.

Special thanks go to those individuals who provided reviews of this book and offered suggestions and reflections based on teaching experience. Our product benefited greatly from these evaluations, although had we included all the suggestions, the book would have been thousands of pages! Our W. W. Norton editor, Ann Shin, and Jake Schindel, assistant editor, orchestrated the process, compiling thorough evaluations from users of earlier editions, mediating our differences, and keeping us "on task" despite other obligations. Their professionalism and understanding made this process much more rewarding. We also thank W. W. Norton's copyediting and production staff for their careful work on this book.

1 Approaches

In Essentials of International Relations, *Fifth Edition, Karen A. Mingst and Ivan M. Arreguín-Toft introduce theories and approaches used to study international relations. The readings in this section of* Essential Readings in World Politics *complement that introduction. Jack Snyder provides an overview of rival critical theories and suggests how theories guide decision makers at times.*

Both historical analysis and philosophical discourse contribute to the study of international relations. In his history of the Peloponnesian War, Thucydides (460 BCE–c. 395 BCE) presents a classic realist/idealist dilemma in the Melian dialogue. The leaders of Melos ponder the fate of the island, deciding whether to fight their antagonists, the Athenians, or to rely on the gods and the enemy of Athens, the Lacedaemonians (also known as Spartans), for their safety.

In a key work from philosophical discourse, the philosopher Immanuel Kant (1724–1804) posited that a group of republican states with representative forms of government that were accountable to their citizens would be able to form an effective league of peace. That observation has generated a huge amount of theoretical and empirical research known as the democratic peace debate, discussed in more detail in Chapter 5 of Essentials of International Relations.

JACK SNYDER

One World, Rival Theories

The U.S. government has endured several painful rounds of scrutiny as it tries to figure out what went wrong on Sept. 11, 2001. The intelligence community faces radical restructuring; the military has made a sharp pivot to face a new enemy; and a vast new federal agency has blossomed to coordinate homeland security. But did September 11 signal a failure of theory on par with the failures of intelligence and policy? Familiar theories about how the world works still dominate academic debate. Instead of radical change, academia has adjusted existing theories to meet new realities. Has this approach succeeded? Does international relations theory still have something to tell policymakers?

Six years ago, political scientist Stephen M. Walt published a much-cited survey of the field in these pages ("One World, Many Theories," Spring 1998). He sketched out three dominant approaches: realism, liberalism, and an updated form of idealism called "constructivism." Walt argued that these theories shape both public discourse and policy analysis. Realism focuses on the shifting distribution of power among states. Liberalism highlights the rising number of democracies and the turbulence of democratic transitions. Idealism illuminates the changing norms of sovereignty, human rights, and international justice, as well as the increased potency of religious ideas in politics.

The influence of these intellectual constructs extends far beyond university classrooms and tenure committees. Policymakers and public commentators invoke elements of all these theories

From *Foreign Policy* (Nov./Dec. 2004): 53–62.

when articulating solutions to global security dilemmas. President George W. Bush promises to fight terror by spreading liberal democracy to the Middle East and claims that skeptics "who call themselves 'realists' . . . have lost contact with a fundamental reality" that "America is always more secure when freedom is on the march." Striking a more eclectic tone, National Security Advisor Condoleezza Rice, a former Stanford University political science professor, explains that the new Bush doctrine is an amalgam of pragmatic realism and Wilsonian liberal theory. During the recent presidential campaign, Sen. John Kerry sounded remarkably similar: "Our foreign policy has achieved greatness," he said, "only when it has combined realism and idealism."

International relations theory also shapes and informs the thinking of the public intellectuals who translate and disseminate academic ideas. During the summer of 2004, for example, two influential framers of neoconservative thought, columnist Charles Krauthammer and political scientist Francis Fukuyama, collided over the implications of these conceptual paradigms for U.S. policy in Iraq. Backing the Bush administration's Middle East policy, Krauthammer argued for an assertive amalgam of liberalism and realism, which he called "democratic realism." Fukuyama claimed that Krauthammer's faith in the use of force and the feasibility of democratic change in Iraq blinds him to the war's lack of legitimacy, a failing that "hurts both the realist part of our agenda, by diminishing our actual power, and the idealist portion of it, by undercutting our appeal as the embodiment of certain ideas and values."

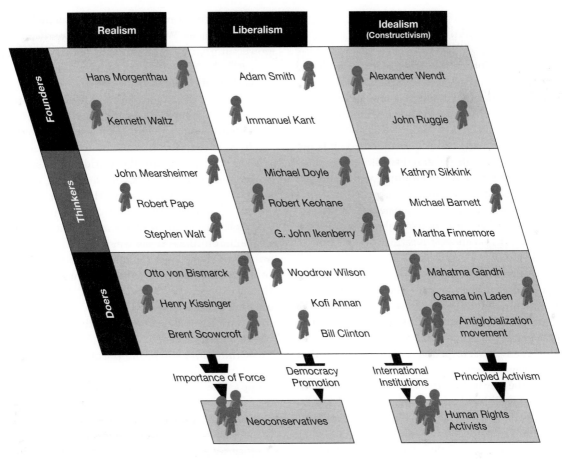

Figure 1.1. From Theory to Practice

Indeed, when realism, liberalism, and idealism enter the policymaking arena and public debate, they can sometimes become intellectual window dressing for simplistic worldviews. Properly understood, however, their policy implications are subtle and multifaceted. Realism instills a pragmatic appreciation of the role of power but also warns that states will suffer if they overreach. Liberalism highlights the cooperative potential of mature democracies, especially when working together through effective institutions, but it also notes democracies' tendency to crusade against tyrannies and the propensity of emerging democracies to collapse into violent ethnic turmoil. Idealism stresses that a consensus on values must underpin any stable political order, yet it also recognizes that forging such a consensus often requires an ideological struggle with the potential for conflict.

Each theory offers a filter for looking at a complicated picture. As such, they help explain the assumptions behind political rhetoric about foreign policy. Even more important, the theories act as a powerful check on each other. Deployed effectively, they reveal the weaknesses in arguments that can lead to misguided policies.

Is Realism Still Realistic?

At realism's core is the belief that international affairs is a struggle for power among self-interested states. Although some of realism's leading lights, notably the late University of Chicago political scientist Hans J. Morgenthau, are deeply pessimistic about human nature, it is not a theory of despair. Clearsighted states can mitigate the causes of war by finding ways to reduce the danger they pose to each other. Nor is realism necessarily amoral; its advocates emphasize that a ruthless pragmatism about power can actually yield a more peaceful world, if not an ideal one.

In liberal democracies, realism is the theory that everyone loves to hate. Developed largely by European émigrés at the end of World War II, realism claimed to be an antidote to the naive belief that international institutions and law alone can preserve peace, a misconception that this new generation of scholars believed had paved the way to war. In recent decades, the realist approach has been most fully articulated by U.S. theorists, but it still has broad appeal outside the United States as well. The influential writer and editor Josef Joffe articulately comments on Germany's strong realist traditions. (Mindful of the overwhelming importance of U.S. power to Europe's development, Joffe once called the United States "Europe's pacifier.") China's current foreign policy is grounded in realist ideas that date back millennia. As China modernizes its economy and enters international institutions such as the World Trade Organization, it behaves in a way that realists understand well: developing its military slowly but surely as its economic power grows, and avoiding a confrontation with superior U.S. forces.

Realism gets some things right about the post-9/11 world. The continued centrality of military strength and the persistence of conflict, even in this age of global economic interdependence, does not surprise realists. The theory's most obvious success is its ability to explain the United States'

forceful military response to the September 11 terrorist attacks. When a state grows vastly more powerful than any opponent, realists expect that it will eventually use that power to expand its sphere of domination, whether for security, wealth, or other motives. The United States employed its military power in what some deemed an imperial fashion in large part because it could.

It is harder for the normally state-centric realists to explain why the world's only superpower announced a war against al Qaeda, a non-state terrorist organization. How can realist theory account for the importance of powerful and violent individuals in a world of states? Realists point out that the central battles in the "war on terror" have been fought against two states (Afghanistan and Iraq), and that states, not the United Nations or Human Rights Watch, have led the fight against terrorism.

Even if realists acknowledge the importance of nonstate actors as a challenge to their assumptions, the theory still has important things to say about the behavior and motivations of these groups. The realist scholar Robert A. Pape, for example, has argued that suicide terrorism can be a rational, realistic strategy for the leadership of national liberation movements seeking to expel democratic powers that occupy their homelands. Other scholars apply standard theories of conflict in anarchy to explain ethnic conflict in collapsed states. Insights from political realism—a profound and wide-ranging intellectual tradition rooted in the enduring philosophy of Thucydides, Niccolò Machiavelli, and Thomas Hobbes—are hardly rendered obsolete because some nonstate groups are now able to resort to violence.

Post-9/11 developments seem to undercut one of realism's core concepts: the balance of power. Standard realist doctrine predicts that weaker states will ally to protect themselves from stronger ones and thereby form and reform a balance of power. So, when Germany unified in the late 19th century and became Europe's leading military and industrial power, Russia and France (and later, Britain) soon aligned to counter its power. Yet no combination of states or other powers can challenge the United States militarily, and no balancing coalition is imminent. Realists are scrambling to find a way to fill this hole in the center of their theory. Some theorists speculate that the United States' geographic distance and its relatively benign intentions have tempered the balancing instinct. Second-tier powers tend to worry more about their immediate neighbors and even see the United States as a helpful source of stability in regions such as East Asia. Other scholars insist that armed resistance by U.S. foes in Iraq, Afghanistan, and elsewhere, and foot-dragging by its formal allies actually constitute the beginnings of balancing against U.S. hegemony. The United States' strained relations with Europe offer ambiguous evidence: French and German opposition to recent U.S. policies could be seen as classic balancing, but they do not resist U.S. dominance militarily. Instead, these states have tried to undermine U.S. moral legitimacy and constrain the superpower in a web of multilateral institutions and treaty regimes—not what standard realist theory predicts.

These conceptual difficulties notwithstanding, realism is alive, well, and creatively reassessing how its root principles relate to the post-9/11 world. Despite changing configurations of power, realists remain steadfast in stressing that policy must be based on positions of real strength, not on either empty bravado or hopeful illusions about a world without conflict. In the run-up to the recent Iraq war, several prominent realists signed a public letter criticizing what they perceived as an exercise in American hubris. And in the continuing aftermath of that war, many prominent thinkers called for a return to realism. A group of scholars and public intellectuals (myself included) even formed the Coalition for a Realistic Foreign Policy, which calls for a more modest and prudent approach. Its statement of principles argues that "the move toward empire must be halted immediately." The coalition, though politically diverse, is largely inspired by realist theory. Its membership of seemingly odd bedfellows—including former Democratic Sen. Gary Hart and Scott McConnell, the executive editor of the

American Conservative magazine—illustrates the power of international relations theory to cut through often ephemeral political labels and carry debate to the underlying assumptions.

The Divided House of Liberalism

The liberal school of international relations theory, whose most famous proponents were German philosopher Immanuel Kant and U.S. President Woodrow Wilson, contends that realism has a stunted vision that cannot account for progress in relations between nations. Liberals foresee a slow but inexorable journey away from the anarchic world the realists envision, as trade and finance forge ties between nations, and democratic norms spread. Because elected leaders are accountable to the people (who bear the burdens of war), liberals expect that democracies will not attack each other and will regard each other's regimes as legitimate and nonthreatening. Many liberals also believe that the rule of law and transparency of democratic processes make it easier to sustain international cooperation, especially when these practices are enshrined in multilateral institutions.

Liberalism has such a powerful presence that the entire U.S. political spectrum, from neoconservatives to human rights advocates, assumes it as largely self-evident. Outside the United States, as well, the liberal view that only elected governments are legitimate and politically reliable has taken hold. So it is no surprise that liberal themes are constantly invoked as a response to today's security dilemmas. But the last several years have also produced a fierce tug-of-war between disparate strains of liberal thought. Supporters and critics of the Bush administration, in particular, have emphasized very different elements of the liberal canon.

For its part, the Bush administration highlights democracy promotion while largely turning its back on the international institutions that most liberal theorists champion. The U.S.

National Security Strategy of September 2002, famous for its support of preventive war, also dwells on the need to promote democracy as a means of fighting terrorism and promoting peace. The Millennium Challenge program allocates part of U.S. foreign aid according to how well countries improve their performance on several measures of democratization and the rule of law. The White House's steadfast support for promoting democracy in the Middle East—even with turmoil in Iraq and rising anti-Americanism in the Arab world—demonstrates liberalism's emotional and rhetorical power.

In many respects, liberalism's claim to be a wise policy guide has plenty of hard data behind it. During the last two decades, the proposition that democratic institutions and values help states cooperate with each other is among the most intensively studied in all of international relations, and it has held up reasonably well. Indeed, the belief that democracies never fight wars against each other is the closest thing we have to an iron law in social science.

But the theory has some very important corollaries, which the Bush administration glosses over as it draws upon the democracy-promotion element of liberal thought. Columbia University political scientist Michael W. Doyle's articles on democratic peace warned that, though democracies never fight each other, they are prone to launch messianic struggles against warlike authoritarian regimes to "make the world safe for democracy." It was precisely American democracy's tendency to oscillate between self-righteous crusading and jaded isolationism that prompted early Cold War realists' call for a more calculated, prudent foreign policy.

Countries transitioning to democracy, with weak political institutions, are more likely than other states to get into international and civil wars. In the last 15 years, wars or large-scale civil violence followed experiments with mass electoral democracy in countries including Armenia, Burundi, Ethiopia, Indonesia, Russia, and the former Yugoslavia. In part, this violence is caused by ethnic groups' competing demands for national self-determination, often a problem in new, multiethnic democracies. More fundamental, emerging democracies often have nascent political institutions that cannot channel popular demands in constructive directions or credibly enforce compromises among rival groups. In this setting, democratic accountability works imperfectly, and nationalist politicians can hijack public debate. The violence that is vexing the experiment with democracy in Iraq is just the latest chapter in a turbulent story that began with the French Revolution.

Contemporary liberal theory also points out that the rising democratic tide creates the presumption that all nations ought to enjoy the benefits of self-determination. Those left out may undertake violent campaigns to secure democratic rights. Some of these movements direct their struggles against democratic or semidemocratic states that they consider occupying powers—such as in Algeria in the 1950s, or Chechnya, Palestine, and the Tamil region of Sri Lanka today. Violence may also be directed at democratic supporters of oppressive regimes, much like the U.S. backing of the governments of Saudi Arabia and Egypt. Democratic regimes make attractive targets for terrorist violence by national liberation movements precisely because they are accountable to a cost-conscious electorate.

Nor is it clear to contemporary liberal scholars that nascent democracy and economic liberalism can always cohabitate. Free trade and the multifaceted globalization that advanced democracies promote often buffet transitional societies. World markets' penetration of societies that run on patronage and protectionism can disrupt social relations and spur strife between potential winners and losers. In other cases, universal free trade can make separatism look attractive, as small regions such as Aceh in Indonesia can lay claim to lucrative natural resources. So far, the trade-fueled boom in China has created incentives for improved relations with the advanced democracies, but it has also set the stage for a possible showdown between the relatively wealthy

Theories:	Realism	Liberalism	Idealism (Constructivism)
Core Beliefs	Self-interested states compete for power and security	Spread of democracy, global economic ties, and international organizations will strengthen peace	International politics is shaped by persuasive ideas, collective values, culture, and social identities
Key Actors in International Relations	States, which behave similarly regardless of their type of government	States, international institutions, and commercial interests	Promoters of new ideas, transnational activist networks, and nongovernmental organizations
Main Instruments	Military power and state diplomacy	International institutions and global commerce	Ideas and values
Theory's Intellectual Blind Spots	Doesn't account for progress and change in international relations or understanding that legitimacy can be a source of military power	Fails to understand that democratic regimes survive only if they safeguard military power and security; some liberals forget that transitions to democracy are sometimes violent	Does not explain which power structures and social conditions allow for changes in values
What the Theory Explains about the Post-9/11 World	Why the United States responded aggressively to terrorist attacks; the inability of international institutions to restrain military superiority	Why spreading democracy has become such an integral part of current U.S. international security strategy	The increasing role of polemics about values; the importance of transnational political networks (whether terrorists or human rights advocates)
What the Theory Fails to Explain about the Post-9/11 World	The failure of smaller powers to militarily balance the United States; the importance of non-state actors such as al Qaeda; the intense U.S. focus on democratization	Why the United States has failed to work with other democracies through international organizations	Why human rights abuses continue, despite intense activism for humanitarian norms and efforts for international justice

Figure 1.2. The Leading Brands

coastal entrepreneurs and the still impoverished rural masses.

While aggressively advocating the virtues of democracy, the Bush administration has shown little patience for these complexities in liberal thought—or for liberalism's emphasis on the importance of international institutions. Far from trying to assure other powers that the United States would adhere to a constitutional order, Bush "unsigned" the International Criminal Court statute, rejected the Kyoto environmental agreement, dictated take-it-or-leave-it arms control changes to Russia, and invaded Iraq despite opposition at the United Nations and among close allies.

Recent liberal theory offers a thoughtful challenge to the administration's policy choices. Shortly before September 11, political scientist G. John Ikenberry studied attempts to establish international order by the victors of hegemonic struggles in 1815, 1919, 1945, and 1989. He argued that even the most powerful victor needed to gain the willing cooperation of the vanquished and other weak states by offering a mutually attractive bargain, codified in an international constitutional order. Democratic victors, he found, have the best chance of creating a working constitutional order, such as the Bretton Woods system after World War II, because their transparency and legalism make their promises credible.

Does the Bush administration's resistance to institution building refute Ikenberry's version of liberal theory? Some realists say it does, and that recent events demonstrate that international institutions cannot constrain a hegemonic power if its preferences change. But international institutions can nonetheless help coordinate outcomes that are in the long-term mutual interest of both the hegemon and the weaker states. Ikenberry did not contend that hegemonic democracies are immune from mistakes. States can act in defiance of the incentives established by their position in the international system, but they will suffer the consequences and probably learn to correct course. In response to Bush's unilateralist stance, Ikenberry wrote that the incentives for the United States to take the lead in establishing a multilateral constitutional order remain powerful. Sooner or later, the pendulum will swing back.

Idealism's New Clothing

Idealism, the belief that foreign policy is and should be guided by ethical and legal standards, also has a long pedigree. Before World War II forced the United States to acknowledge a less pristine reality, Secretary of State Henry Stimson denigrated espionage on the grounds that "gentlemen do not read each other's mail." During the Cold War, such naive idealism acquired a bad name in the Kissingerian corridors of power and among hardheaded academics. Recently, a new version of idealism—called constructivism by its scholarly adherents—returned to a prominent place in debates on international relations theory. Constructivism, which holds that social reality is created through debate about values, often echoes the themes that human rights and international justice activists sound. Recent events seem to vindicate the theory's resurgence; a theory that emphasizes the role of ideologies, identities, persuasion, and transnational networks is highly relevant to understanding the post-9/11 world.

The most prominent voices in the development of constructivist theory have been American, but Europe's role is significant. European philosophical currents helped establish constructivist theory, and the *European Journal of International Relations* is one of the principal outlets for constructivist work. Perhaps most important, Europe's increasingly legalistic approach to international relations, reflected in the process of forming the European Union out of a collection of sovereign states, provides fertile soil for idealist and constructivist conceptions of international politics.

Whereas realists dwell on the balance of power and liberals on the power of international trade and democracy, constructivists believe that debates about ideas are the fundamental building blocks of international life. Individuals and groups become powerful if they can convince others to adopt their ideas. People's understanding of their interests depends on the ideas they hold. Constructivists find absurd the idea of some identifiable and immutable "national interest," which some realists cherish. Especially in liberal societies, there is overlap between constructivist and liberal approaches, but the two are distinct. Constructivists contend that their theory is deeper than realism and liberalism because it explains the origins of the forces that drive those competing theories.

For constructivists, international change results from the work of intellectual entrepreneurs who proselytize new ideas and "name and shame" actors whose behavior deviates from accepted standards. Consequently, constructivists often study the role of transnational activist networks—such as Human Rights Watch or the International Campaign to Ban Landmines—in promoting change. Such groups typically uncover and publicize information about violations of legal or moral standards at least rhetorically supported by powerful democracies, including "disappearances" during the Argentine military's rule in the late 1970s, concentration camps in Bosnia, and the huge number of civilian deaths from land mines. This publicity is then used to press governments to adopt specific remedies, such as the establishment of a war crimes tribunal or the adoption of a landmine treaty. These movements often make pragmatic arguments as well as idealistic ones, but their distinctive power comes from the ability to highlight deviations from deeply held norms of appropriate behavior.

Progressive causes receive the most attention from constructivist scholars, but the theory also helps explain the dynamics of illiberal transnational forces, such as Arab nationalism or Islamist extremism. Professor Michael N. Barnett's 1998 book *Dialogues in Arab Politics: Negotiations in Regional Order* examines how the divergence between state borders and transnational Arab political identities requires vulnerable leaders to contend for legitimacy with radicals throughout the Arab world—a dynamic that often holds moderates hostage to opportunists who take extreme stances.

Constructivist thought can also yield broader insights about the ideas and values in the current international order. In his 2001 book, *Revolutions in Sovereignty: How Ideas Shaped Modern International Relations*, political scientist Daniel Philpott demonstrates how the religious ideas of the Protestant Reformation helped break down the medieval political order and provided a conceptual basis for the modern system of secular sovereign states. After September 11, Philpott focused on the challenge to the secular international order posed by political Islam. "The attacks and the broader resurgence of public religion," he says, ought to lead international relations scholars to "direct far more energy to understanding the impetuses behind movements across the globe that are reorienting purposes and policies." He notes that both liberal human rights movements and radical Islamic movements have transnational structures and principled motivations that challenge the traditional supremacy of self-interested states in international politics. Because constructivists believe that ideas and values helped shape the modern state system, they expect intellectual constructs to be decisive in transforming it—for good or ill.

When it comes to offering advice, however, constructivism points in two seemingly incompatible directions. The insight that political orders arise from shared understanding highlights the need for dialogue across cultures about the appropriate rules of the game. This prescription dovetails with liberalism's emphasis on establishing an agreed international constitutional order. And, yet, the notion of cross-cultural dialogue sits awkwardly with many idealists' view that they already know right and wrong. For these idealists, the essential task is to shame rights abusers and cajole powerful actors into promoting proper values and holding perpetrators accountable to international (generally Western) standards. As with realism and liberalism, constructivism can be many things to many people.

Stumped by Change

None of the three theoretical traditions has a strong ability to explain change—a significant weakness in such turbulent times. Realists failed to predict the end of the Cold War, for example. Even after it happened, they tended to assume that the new system would become multipolar ("back to the future," as the scholar John J. Mearsheimer put it). Likewise, the liberal theory of democratic peace is stronger on what happens after states become democratic than in predicting the timing of democratic transitions, let alone prescribing how to make transitions happen peacefully. Constructivists are good at describing changes in norms and ideas, but they are weak on the material and institutional circumstances necessary to support the emergence of consensus about new values and ideas.

With such uncertain guidance from the theoretical realm, it is no wonder that policymakers, activists, and public commentators fall prey to simplistic or wishful thinking about how to effect change by, say, invading Iraq or setting up an International Criminal Court. In lieu of a good theory of change, the most prudent course is to use the insights of each of the three theoretical traditions as a check on the irrational exuberance of the others. Realists should have to explain whether policies based on calculations of power have sufficient legitimacy to last. Liberals should consider whether nascent democratic institutions can fend off powerful interests that oppose them, or how international institutions can bind a hegemonic power inclined to go its own way. Idealists should be asked about the strategic, institutional, or material conditions in which a set of ideas is likely to take hold.

Theories of international relations claim to explain the way international politics works, but each of the currently prevailing theories falls well short of that goal. One of the principal contributions that international relations theory can make is not predicting the future but providing the vocabulary and conceptual framework to ask hard questions of those who think that changing the world is easy.

THUCYDIDES

Melian Dialogue

adapted by Suresht Bald

It was the sixteenth year of the Peloponnesian War, but for the last six years the two great feuding empires headed by Athens and Sparta (Lacedaemon) had avoided open hostile action against each other. Ten years into the war they had signed a treaty of peace and friendship; however, this treaty did not dissipate the distrust that existed between them. Each feared the other's hegemonic designs on the Peloponnese and sought to increase its power to thwart the other's ambitions. Without openly attacking the other, each used persuasion, coercion, and subversion to strengthen itself and weaken its rival. This struggle for hegemony by Athens and Sparta was felt most acutely by small, hitherto "independent" states who were now being forced to take sides in the bipolar Greek world of the fifth century B.C. One such state was Melos.

From Thucydides, *Complete Writings: The Peloponnesian War*, trans. Richard Crawley (New York: Modern Library, 1951), adapted by Suresht Bald, Willamette University.

Despite being one of the few island colonies of Sparta, Melos had remained neutral in the struggle between Sparta and Athens. Its neutrality, however, was unacceptable to the Athenians, who, accompanied by overwhelming military and naval power, arrived in Melos to pressure it into submission. After strategically positioning their powerful fleet, the Athenian generals sent envoys to Melos to negotiate the island's surrender.

The commissioners of Melos agreed to meet the envoys in private. They were afraid the Athenians, known for their rhetorical skills, might sway the people if allowed a public forum. The envoys came with an offer that if the Melians submitted and became part of the Athenian empire, their people and their possessions would not be harmed. The Melians argued that by the law of nations they had the right to remain neutral, and no nation had the right to attack without provocation. Having been a free state for seven hundred years they were not ready to give up that freedom. Thucydides captures the exchange between the Melian commissioners and the Athenian envoys:

MELIANS: . . . All we can reasonably expect from this negotiation is war, if we prove to have right on our side and refuse to submit, and in the contrary case, slavery.

ATHENIANS: . . . We shall not trouble you with specious pretenses—either of how we have a right to our empire because we overthrew the Mede, or are now attacking you because of the wrong that you have done us—and make a long speech that would not be believed; and in return we hope that you, instead of thinking to influence us by saying that you did not join the Lacedaemonians, although their colonists, or that you have done us no wrong, will aim at what is feasible, . . . since you know as well as we do that right, as the world goes, is only in question between equals in power, while the strong do what they can and the weak suffer what they want. (331)

The Melians pointed out that it was in the interest of all states to respect the laws of nations: "you should not destroy what is our common protection, the privilege of being allowed in danger to invoke what is fair and right. . . ." (331) They reminded the Athenians that a day might come when the Athenians themselves would need such protection.

But the Athenians were not persuaded. To them, Melos' submission was in the interest of their empire, and Melos.

MELIANS: And how pray, could it turn out as good for us to serve as for you to rule?

ATHENIANS: Because you would have the advantage of submitting before suffering the worst, and we should gain by not destroying you.

MELIANS: So you would not consent to our being neutral, friends instead of enemies, but allies of neither side.

ATHENIANS: No; for your hostility cannot so much hurt us as your friendship will be an argument to our subjects of our weakness, and your enmity of our power. (332)

When the Melians asked if that was their "idea of equity," the Athenians responded,

As far as right goes . . . one has as much of it as the other, and if any maintain their independence it is because they are strong, and that if we do not molest them it is because we are afraid. . . . (332)

By subjugating the Melians the Athenians hoped not only to extend their empire but also to improve their image and thus their security. To allow the weaker Melians to remain free, according to the Athenians, would reflect negatively on Athenian power.

Aware of their weak position the Melians hoped that the justice of their cause would gain them the support of the gods, "and what we want in power will be made up by the alliance with the Lacedaemonians, who are bound, if only for very shame, to come to the aid of their kindred."

ATHENIANS: . . . Of the gods we believe, and of men we know, that by a necessary law of their nature they rule wherever they can. And it is not as if we were the first to make this law, or to act upon it when made: we found it existing before us, and will leave it to exist for ever after us; all we do is to make use of it, knowing that you and everybody else having the same power as we have, would do the same as we do. Thus, as far as the gods are concerned we have no fear and no reason to fear that we shall be at a disadvantage. But . . . your notion about the Lacedaemonians, which leads you to believe that shame will make them help you, here we bless your simplicity but do not envy your folly. The Lacedaemonians . . . are conspicuous in considering what is agreeable honourable, and what is expedient just. . . . Your strongest arguments depend upon hope and the future, and your actual resources are too scanty as compared to those arrayed against you, for you to come out victorious. You will therefore show great blindness of judgment, unless, after allowing us to retire you can find some counsel more prudent than this. (334–36)

The envoys then left the conference, giving the Melians the opportunity to deliberate on the

Athenian offer and decide the best course for them to follow.

The Melians decided to stand by the position they had taken at the conference with the Athenian envoys. They refused to submit, placing their faith in the gods and the Lacedaemonians. Though they asked the Athenians to accept their neutrality and leave Melos, the Athenians started preparations for war.

In the war that ensued the Melians were soundly defeated. The Athenians showed no mercy, killing all the adult males and selling the women and children as slaves. Subsequently, they sent out five hundred colonists to settle in Melos, which became an Athenian colony.

* * *

IMMANUEL KANT

To Perpetual Peace: A Philosophical Sketch

* * *

The state of peace among men living in close proximity is not the natural state * * * ; instead, the natural state is a one of war, which does not just consist in open hostilities, but also in the constant and enduring threat of them. The state of peace must therefore be *established*, for the suspension of hostilities does not provide the security of peace, and unless this security is pledged by one neighbor to another (which can happen only in a state of *lawfulness*), the latter, from whom such security has been requested, can treat the former as an enemy.

First Definitive Article of Perpetual Peace: The Civil Constitution of Every Nation Should Be Republican

The sole established constitution that follows from the idea of an original contract, the one on which all of a nation's just legislation must be based, is republican. For, first, it accords with the principles of the *freedom* of the members of a society (as men), second, it accords with the principles of the *dependence* of everyone on a single, common [source of] legislation (as subjects), and third, it accords with the law of the equality of them all (as citizens). Thus, so far as [the matter of] right is concerned, republicanism is the original foundation of all forms of civil constitution. Thus, the only question remaining is this, does it also provide the only foundation for perpetual peace?

Now in addition to the purity of its origin, a purity whose source is the pure concept of right, the republican constitution also provides for this desirable result, namely, perpetual peace, and the reason for this is as follows: If (as must inevitably be the case, given this form of constitution) the consent of the citizenry is required in order to determine whether or not there will be war, it is natural that they consider all its calamities before committing themselves to so risky a game. (Among these are doing the fighting themselves, paying the costs of war from their own resources, having to repair at great sacrifice the war's devastation, and, finally, the ultimate evil that would make peace itself better, never being able—because of new and constant wars—to expunge the burden of debt.) By contrast, under a nonrepublican constitution, where subjects are not citizens, the easiest thing in the world to do is to declare war. Here the ruler is not a fellow citizen, but the nation's owner, and war does not affect his table, his hunt, his places of pleasure, his court festivals, and so on. Thus, he can decide to go to war for the most meaningless of reasons, as if it were a kind of pleasure party, and he can blithely leave its justification (which decency requires) to his diplomatic corps, who are always prepared for such exercises.

The following comments are necessary to prevent confusing (as so often happens) the republican form of constitution with the democratic one: The forms of a nation (*civitas*) can be analyzed either on the basis of the persons who possess the highest political authority or on the basis of the way the people are *governed* by their ruler, whoever he may be. The first is called the form of sovereignty * * *, of which only three kinds are possible, specifically, where either *one*, or *several* in association, or *all* those together who make up civil society possess the sovereign power (Autocracy, Aristocracy and Democracy, the power of a monarch, the power of a nobility, the power of a people). The second is the form of government (*forma regiminis*) and concerns the way in which a nation, based on its constitution (the act of the general will whereby a group becomes a people), exercises its authority. In this regard, government is either *republican* or *despotic*. *Republicanism* is that political principle whereby executive power (the government) is separated from legislative

power. In a despotism the ruler independently executes laws that it has itself made; here rulers have taken hold of the public will and treated it as their own private will. Among the three forms of government, *democracy*, in the proper sense of the term, is necessarily a *despotism*, because it sets up an executive power in which all citizens make decisions about and, if need be, against one (who therefore does not agree); consequently, all, who are not quite all, decide, so that the general will contradicts both itself and freedom.

Every form of government that is not *representative* is properly speaking *without form*, because one and the same person can no more be at one and the same time the legislator and executor of his will (than the universal proposition can serve as the major premise in a syllogism and at the same time be the subsumption of the particular under it in the minor premise). And although the other two forms of political constitution are defective inasmuch as they always leave room for a democratic form of government, it is nonetheless possible that they assume a form of government that accords with the *spirit* of a representative system: As Friederick II at least *said*, "I am merely the nation's highest servant." The democratic system makes this impossible, for everyone wants to rule. One can therefore say, the smaller the number of persons who exercise the power of the nation (the number of rulers), the more they represent and the closer the political constitution approximates the possibility of republicanism, and thus, the constitution can hope through gradual reforms finally to become republican. For this reason, attaining this state that embodies a completely just constitution is more difficult in an aristocracy than in a monarchy, and, except by violent revolution, there is no possibility of attaining it in a democracy. Nonetheless, the people are incomparably more concerned with the form of government than with the form of constitution (although a great deal depends on the degree to which the latter is suited to the goals of the former). But if the form of government is to cohere with the concept of right, it must include the representative system, which is

From Immanuel Kant, *Perpetual Peace, and Other Essays on Politics, History, and Morals*, trans. Ted Humphrey (Indianapolis: Hackett Publishing, 1983), 110–118. Both the author's and the translator's notes have been omitted. Bracketed editorial insertions are the translator's.

possible only in a republican form of government and without which (no matter what the constitution may be) government is despotic and brutish. None of the ancient so-called republics were aware of this, and consequently they inevitably degenerated into despotism; still, this is more bearable under a single person's rulership than other forms of government are.

Second Definitive Article for a Perpetual Peace: The Right of Nations Shall Be Based on a Federation of Free States

As nations, peoples can be regarded as single individuals who injure one another through their close proximity while living in the state of nature (i.e., independently of external laws). For the sake of its own security, each nation can and should demand that the others enter into a contract resembling the civil one and guaranteeing the rights of each. This would be a federation *of nations*, but it must not be a nation consisting of nations. The latter would be contradictory, for in every nation there exists the relation of *ruler* (legislator) to *subject* (those who obey, the people); however, many nations in a single nation would constitute only a single nation, which contradicts our assumption (since we are here weighing the rights of *nations* in relation to one another, rather than fusing them into a single nation).

Just as we view with deep disdain the attachment of savages to their lawless freedom—preferring to scuffle without end rather than to place themselves under lawful restraints that they themselves constitute, consequently preferring a mad freedom to a rational one—and consider it barbarous, rude, and brutishly degrading of humanity, so also should we think that civilized peoples (each one united into a nation) would hasten as quickly as possible to escape so similar a state of abandonment. Instead, however, each *nation* sees its majesty (for it is absurd to speak of the majesty of a people) to consist in not being subject to any external legal constraint, and the glory of its ruler consists in being able, without endangering himself, to command many thousands to sacrifice themselves for a matter that does not concern them. The primary difference between European and American savages is this, that while many of the latter tribes have been completely eaten by their enemies, the former know how to make better use of those they have conquered than to consume them: they increase the number of their subjects and thus also the quantity of instruments they have to wage even more extensive wars.

Given the depravity of human nature, which is revealed and can be glimpsed in the free relations among nations (though deeply concealed by governmental restraints in law governed civil-society), one must wonder why the word *right* has not been completely discarded from the politics of war as pedantic, or why no nation has openly ventured to declare that it should be. For while Hugo Grotius, Pufendorf, Vattel, and others whose philosophically and diplomatically formulated codes do not and cannot have the slightest legal force (since nations do not stand under any common external constraints), are always piously cited in justification of a war of aggression (and who therefore provide only cold comfort), no example can be given of a nation having foregone its intention [of going to war] based on the arguments provided by such important men. The homage that every nation pays (at least in words) to the concept of right proves, nonetheless, that there is in man a still greater, though presently dormant, moral aptitude to master the evil principle in himself (a principle he cannot deny) and to hope that others will also overcome it. For otherwise the word *right* would never leave the mouths of those nations that want to make war on one another, unless it were used mockingly, as when that Gallic prince declared, "Nature has given the strong the prerogative of making the weak obey them."

Nations can press for their rights only by waging war and never in a trial before an independent tribunal, but war and its favorable consequence, victory, cannot determine the right. And although a *treaty of peace* can put an end to some particular war, it cannot end the state of war (the tendency always to find a new pretext for war). (And this situation cannot straightforwardly be declared unjust, since in this circumstance each nation is judge of its own case.) Nor can one say of nations as regards their rights what one can say concerning the natural rights of men in a state of lawlessness, to wit, that "they should abandon this state." (For as nations they already have an internal, legal constitution and therefore have outgrown the compulsion to subject themselves to another legal constitution that is subject to someone else's concept of right.) Nonetheless, from the throne of its moral legislative power, reason absolutely condemns war as a means of determining the right and makes seeking the state of peace a matter of unmitigated duty. But without a contract among nations peace can be neither inaugurated nor guaranteed. A league of a special sort must therefore be established, one that we can call a *league of peace* (*foedus pacificum*), which will be distinguished from a *treaty of peace* (*pactum pacis*) because the latter seeks merely to stop *one* war, while the former seeks to end *all* wars forever. This league does not seek any power of the sort possessed by nations, but only the maintenance and security of each nation's own freedom, as well as that of the other nations leagued with it, without their having thereby to subject themselves to civil laws and their constraints (as men in the state of nature must do). It can be shown that this *idea of federalism* should eventually include all nations and thus lead to perpetual peace. For if good fortune should so dispose matters that a powerful and enlightened people should form a republic (which by its nature must be inclined to seek perpetual peace), it will provide a focal point for a federal association among other nations that will join it in order to guarantee a state of peace among nations that is in accord with the idea of the right of nations, and through several associations of this sort such a federation can extend further and further.

That a people might say, "There should be no war among us, for we want to form ourselves into a nation, i.e., place ourselves under a supreme legislative, executive, and judicial power to resolve our conflicts peacefully," is understandable. But when a nation says, "There should be no war between me and other nations, though I recognize no supreme legislative power to guarantee me my rights and him his," then if there does not exist a surrogate of the union in a civil society, which is a free federation, it is impossible to understand what the basis for so entrusting my rights is. Such a federation is necessarily tied rationally to the concept of the right of nations, at least if this latter notion has any meaning.

The concept of the right of nations as a right to go to war is meaningless (for it would then be the right to determine the right not by independent, universally valid laws that restrict the freedom of everyone, but by one-sided maxims backed by force). Consequently, the concept of the right of nations must be understood as follows: that it serves justly those men who are disposed to seek one another's destruction and thus to find perpetual peace in the grave that covers all the horrors of violence and its perpetrators. Reason can provide related nations with no other means for emerging from the state of lawlessness, which consists solely of war, than that they give up their savage (lawless) freedom, just as individual persons do, and, by accommodating themselves to the constraints of common law, establish a *nation of peoples* (*civitas gentium*) that (continually growing) will finally include all the people of the earth. But they do not will to do this because it does not conform to their idea of the right of nations, and consequently they discard in *hypothesis* what is true in *thesis*. So (if everything is not to be lost) in place of the positive idea of *a world republic* they put only the *negative* surrogate of an enduring, ever expanding *federation* that prevents war and curbs the tendency of that hostile inclination to defy the law, though there will always be constant danger of their breaking loose. * * *

* * *

2 History

Core ideas about international relations, introduced in Chapter 1 and elaborated in Chapter 3 of Essentials of International Relations, *Fifth Edition, have emerged as responses to historic diplomatic challenges. The two selections in this chapter provide insight into key events and trends that spawned many of the ideas that still shape debates about contemporary international politics.*

The post–World War I peace process led to a clear statement of the liberal perspective. U.S. President Woodrow Wilson's "Fourteen Points," in an address to Congress in January 1918, summarizes some of the key ideas emerging from liberal theory. Wilson blames power politics, secret diplomacy, and autocratic leaders for the devastating world war. He suggests that with the spread of democracy and the creation of a "league of nations" aggression would be stopped.

The Cold War also provides the historical setting for the realist/liberal perspective. George F. Kennan, then director of the State Department's Policy Planning Staff, published his famous "X" article in Foreign Affairs *in 1947. He assesses Soviet conduct and provides the intellectual justification for Cold War containment policy. Using realist logic, he suggests that counterpressure must be applied to prevent Soviet expansion.*

WOODROW WILSON

The Fourteen Points

It will be our wish and purpose that the processes of peace, when they are begun, shall be absolutely open and that they shall involve and permit henceforth no secret understandings of any kind. The day of conquest and aggrandizement is gone by; so is also the day of secret covenants entered into in the interest of particular governments and likely at some unlooked-for moment to upset the peace of the world. It is this happy fact, now clear to the view of every public man whose thoughts do not still linger in an age that is dead and gone, which makes it possible for every nation whose purposes are consistent with justice and the peace of the world to avow now or at any other time the objects it has in view.

We entered this war because violations of right had occurred which touched us to the quick and made the life of our own people impossible unless they were corrected and the world secured once and for all against their recurrence. What we demand in this war, therefore, is nothing peculiar to ourselves. It is that the world be made fit and safe to live in; and particularly that it be made safe for every peace-loving nation which, like our own, wishes to live its own life, determine its own institutions, be assured of justice and fair dealing by the other people of the world as against force and selfish aggression. All the peoples of the world are in effect partners in this interest, and for our own part we see very clearly that unless justice be done to others it will not be done to us. The program of the world's peace, therefore, is our program; and that program, the only possible program, as we see it, is this:

From Woodrow Wilson's address to the U.S. Congress, January 8, 1918.

I. Open covenants of peace, openly arrived at, after which there shall be no private international understandings of any kind but diplomacy shall proceed always frankly and in the public view.

II. Absolute freedom of navigation upon the seas, outside territorial waters, alike in peace and in war, except as the seas may be closed in whole or in part by international action for the enforcement of international covenants.

III. The removal, so far as possible, of all economic barriers and the establishment of an equality of trade conditions among all the nations consenting to the peace and associating themselves for its maintenance.

IV. Adequate guarantees given and taken that national armaments will be reduced to the lowest point consistent with domestic safety.

V. A free, open-minded, and absolutely impartial adjustment of all colonial claims, based upon a strict observance of the principle that in determining all such questions of sovereignty the interests of the populations concerned must have equal weight with the equitable claims of the government whose title is to be determined.

VI. The evacuation of all Russian territory and such a settlement of all questions affecting Russia as will secure the best and freest cooperation of the other nations of the world in obtaining for her an unhampered and unembarrassed opportunity for the independent determination of her own political development and national policy and assure her of a sincere welcome into the society of free nations under institutions of her own choosing; and, more than a welcome, assistance also of every kind that she may need and may herself desire. The treatment accorded Russia by her sister nations in the months to come will be the acid test of their good will, of their comprehension of her needs as distinguished from their own interests, and of their intelligent and unselfish sympathy.

VII. Belgium, the whole world will agree, must be evacuated and restored, without any attempt to limit the sovereignty which she enjoys in common with all other free nations. No other single act will serve as this will serve to restore confidence among the nations in the laws which they have themselves set and determined for the government of their relations with one another. Without this healing act the whole structure and validity of international law is forever impaired.

VIII. All French territory should be freed and the invaded portions restored, and the wrong done to France by Prussia in 1871 in the matter of Alsace-Lorraine, which has unsettled the peace of the world for nearly fifty years, should be righted, in order that peace may once more be made secure in the interest of all.

IX. A readjustment of the frontiers of Italy should be effected along clearly recognizable lines of nationality.

X. The peoples of Austria-Hungary, whose place among the nations we wish to see safeguarded and assured, should be accorded the freest opportunity of autonomous development.

XI. Rumania, Serbia, and Montenegro should be evacuated; occupied territories restored; Serbia accorded free and secure access to the sea; and the relations of the several Balkan states to one another determined by friendly counsel along historically established lines of allegiance and nationality; and international guarantees of the political and economic independence and territorial integrity of the several Balkan states should be entered into.

XII. The Turkish portions of the present Ottoman Empire should be assured a secure sovereignty, but the other nationalities which are now under Turkish rule should be assured an undoubted security of life and an absolutely unmolested opportunity of autonomous development, and the Dardanelles should be permanently opened as a free passage to the ships and commerce of all nations under international guarantees.

XIII. An independent Polish state should be erected which should include the territories inhabited by indisputably Polish populations, which should be assured a free and secure access to the sea, and whose political and economic independence and territorial integrity should be guaranteed by international covenant.

XIV. A general association of nations must be formed under specific covenants for the purpose of affording mutual guarantees of political independence and territorial integrity to great and small states alike.

In regard to these essential rectifications of wrong and assertions of right we feel ourselves to be intimate partners of all the governments and peoples associated together against the imperialists. We cannot be separated in interest or divided in purpose. We stand together until the end.

For such arrangements and covenants we are willing to fight and to continue to fight until they are achieved; but only because we wish the right to prevail and desire a just and stable peace such as can be secured only by removing the chief provocations to war, which this program does remove. We have no jealousy of German greatness, and there is nothing in this program that impairs it. We grudge her no achievement or distinction of learning or of pacific enterprise such as have made her record very bright and very enviable. We do not wish to injure her or to block in any way her legitimate influence or power. We do not wish to fight her either with arms or with hostile arrangements of trade if she is willing to associate herself with us and the other peace-loving nations of the world in covenants of justice and law and fair dealing. We wish her only to accept a place of equality among the peoples of the world—the new world in which we now live—instead of a place of mastery.

Neither do we presume to suggest to her any alteration or modification of her institutions. But it is necessary, we must frankly say, and necessary as a preliminary to any intelligent dealings with her on our part, that we should know whom her spokesmen speak for when they speak to us, whether for the Reichstag majority or for the military party and the men whose creed is imperial domination.

We have spoken now, surely, in terms too concrete to admit of any further doubt or question. An evident principle runs through the whole program I have outlined. It is the principle of justice to all peoples and nationalities, and their right to live on equal terms of liberty and safety with one another, whether they be strong or weak. Unless this principle be made its foundation no part of the structure of international justice can stand. The people of the United States could act upon no other principle; and to the vindication of this principle they are ready to devote their lives, their honor, and everything that they possess. The moral climax of this the culminating and final war for human liberty has come, and they are ready to put their own strength, their own highest purpose, their own integrity and devotion to the test.

GEORGE F. KENNAN ("X")

The Sources of Soviet Conduct

I

The political personality of Soviet power as we know it today is the product of ideology and circumstances: ideology inherited by the present Soviet leaders from the movement in which they had their political origin, and circumstances of the power which they now have exercised for nearly three decades in Russia. There can be few tasks of psychological analysis more difficult than to try to trace the interaction of these two forces and the relative role of each in the determination of official Soviet conduct. Yet the attempt must be made if that

conduct is to be understood and effectively countered.

It is difficult to summarize the set of ideological concepts with which the Soviet leaders came into power. Marxian ideology, in its Russian-Communist projection, has always been in process of subtle evolution. The materials on which it bases itself are extensive and complex. But the outstanding features of Communist thought as it existed in 1916 may perhaps be summarized as follows: (*a*) that the central factor in the life of man, the fact which determines the character of public life and the "physiognomy of society," is the system by which material goods are produced and exchanged; (*b*) that the capitalist system of production is a nefarious one which inevitably

From *Foreign Affairs* 25, no. 4 (July 1947): 566–582.

leads to the exploitation of the working class by the capital-owning class and is incapable of developing adequately the economic resources of society or of distributing fairly the material goods produced by human labor; (c) that capitalism contains the seeds of its own destruction and must, in view of the inability of the capital-owning class to adjust itself to economic change, result eventually and inescapably in a revolutionary transfer of power to the working class; and (d) that imperialism, the final phase of capitalism, leads directly to war and revolution.

* * *

Now it must be noted that through all the years of preparation for revolution, the attention of these men, as indeed of Marx himself, had been centered less on the future form which Socialism[1] would take than on the necessary overthrow of rival power which, in their view, had to precede the introduction of Socialism. Their views, therefore, on the positive program to be put into effect, once power was attained, were for the most part nebulous, visionary and impractical. Beyond the nationalization of industry and the expropriation of large private capital holdings there was no agreed program. The treatment of the peasantry, which according to the Marxist formulation was not of the proletariat, had always been a vague spot in the pattern of Communist thought; and it remained an object of controversy and vacillation for the first ten years of Communist power.

The circumstances of the immediate post-Revolution period—the existence in Russia of civil war and foreign intervention, together with the obvious fact that the Communists represented only a tiny minority of the Russian people—made the establishment of dictatorial power a necessity. The experiment with "war Communism" and the abrupt attempt to eliminate private production and trade had unfortunate economic consequences and caused further bitterness against the new revolutionary regime. While the temporary relaxation of the effort to communize Russia, represented by the New Economic Policy, alleviated some of this economic distress and thereby served its purpose, it also made it evident that the "capitalistic sector of society" was still prepared to profit at once from any relaxation of governmental pressure, and would, if permitted to continue to exist, always constitute a powerful opposing element to the Soviet regime and a serious rival for influence in the country. Somewhat the same situation prevailed with respect to the individual peasant who, in his own small way, was also a private producer.

Lenin, had he lived, might have proved a great enough man to reconcile these conflicting forces to the ultimate benefit of Russian society, though this is questionable. But be that as it may, Stalin, and those whom he led in the struggle for succession to Lenin's position of leadership, were not the men to tolerate rival political forces in the sphere of power which they coveted. Their sense of insecurity was too great. Their particular brand of fanaticism, unmodified by any of the Anglo-Saxon traditions of compromise, was too fierce and too jealous to envisage any permanent sharing of power. From the Russian-Asiatic world out of which they had emerged they carried with them a skepticism as to the possibilities of permanent and peaceful coexistence of rival forces. Easily persuaded of their own doctrinaire "rightness," they insisted on the submission or destruction of all competing power. Outside of the Communist Party, Russian society was to have no rigidity. There were to be no forms of collective human activity or association which would not be dominated by the Party. No other force in Russian society was to be permitted to achieve vitality or integrity. Only the Party was to have structure. All else was to be an amorphous mass.

And within the Party the same principle was to apply. The mass of Party members might go through the motions of election, deliberation, decision and action; but in these motions they were to be animated not by their own individual wills but by the awesome breath of the Party leadership and the overbrooding presence of "the world."

Let it be stressed again that subjectively these men probably did not seek absolutism for its own sake. They doubtless believed—and found it easy to believe—that they alone knew what was good for society and that they would accomplish that good once their power was secure and unchallengeable. But in seeking that security of their own rule they were prepared to recognize no restrictions, either of God or man, on the character of their methods. And until such time as that security might be achieved, they placed far down on their scale of operational priorities the comforts and happiness of the peoples entrusted to their care.

Now the outstanding circumstance concerning the Soviet regime is that down to the present day this process of political consolidation has never been completed and the men in the Kremlin have continued to be predominantly absorbed with the struggle to secure and make absolute the power which they seized in November 1917. They have endeavored to secure it primarily against forces at home, within Soviet society itself. But they have also endeavored to secure it against the outside world. For ideology, as we have seen, taught them that the outside world was hostile and that it was their duty eventually to overthrow the political forces beyond their borders. The powerful hands of Russian history and tradition reached up to sustain them in this feeling. Finally, their own aggressive intransigence with respect to the outside world began to find its own reaction; and they were soon forced, to use another Gibbonesque phrase [from Edward Gibbon, *The Decline and Fall of the Roman Empire*], "to chastise the contumacy" which they themselves had provoked. It is an undeniable privilege of every man to prove himself right in the thesis that the world is his enemy; for if he reiterates it frequently enough and makes it the background of his conduct he is bound eventually to be right.

Now it lies in the nature of the mental world of the Soviet leaders, as well as in the character of

their ideology, that no opposition to them can be officially recognized as having any merit or justification whatsoever. Such opposition can flow, in theory, only from the hostile and incorrigible forces of dying capitalism. As long as remnants of capitalism were officially recognized as existing in Russia, it was possible to place on them, as an internal element, part of the blame for the maintenance of a dictatorial form of society. But as these remnants were liquidated, little by little, this justification fell away; and when it was indicated officially that they had been finally destroyed, it disappeared altogether. And this fact created one of the most basic of the compulsions which came to act upon the Soviet regime: since capitalism no longer existed in Russia and since it could not be admitted that there could be serious or widespread opposition to the Kremlin springing spontaneously from the liberated masses under its authority, it became necessary to justify the retention of the dictatorship by stressing the menace of capitalism abroad.

*   *   *

Now the maintenance of this pattern of Soviet power, namely, the pursuit of unlimited authority domestically, accompanied by the cultivation of the semi-myth of implacable foreign hostility, has gone far to shape the actual machinery of Soviet power as we know it today. Internal organs of administration which did not serve this purpose withered on the vine. Organs which did serve this purpose became vastly swollen. The security of Soviet power came to rest on the iron discipline of the Party, on the severity and ubiquity of the secret police, and on the uncompromising economic monopolism of the state. The "organs of suppression," in which the Soviet leaders had sought security from rival forces, became in large measure the masters of those whom they were designed to serve. Today the major part of the structure of Soviet power is committed to the perfection of the dictatorship and to the maintenance of the concept of Russia as in a state of siege, with the enemy lowering beyond the walls. And the millions of human beings who form that part of the structure of power must defend at all costs this concept of Russia's position, for without it they are themselves superfluous.

As things stand today, the rulers can no longer dream of parting with these organs of suppression. The quest for absolute power, pursued now for nearly three decades with a ruthlessness unparalleled (in scope at least) in modern times, has again produced internally, as it did externally, its own reaction. The excesses of the police apparatus have fanned the potential opposition to the regime into something far greater and more dangerous than it could have been before those excesses began.

But least of all can the rulers dispense with the fiction by which the maintenance of dictatorial power has been defended. For this fiction has been canonized in Soviet philosophy by the excesses already committed in its name; and it is now anchored in the Soviet structure of thought by bonds far greater than those of mere ideology.

II

So much for the historical background. What does it spell in terms of the political personality of Soviet power as we know it today?

Of the original ideology, nothing has been officially junked. Belief is maintained in the basic badness of capitalism, in the inevitability of its destruction, in the obligation of the proletariat to assist in that destruction and to take power into its own hands. But stress has come to be laid primarily on those concepts which relate most specifically to the Soviet regime itself: to its position as the sole truly Socialist regime in a dark and misguided world, and to the relationships of power within it.

The first of these concepts is that of the innate antagonism between capitalism and Socialism. We have seen how deeply that concept has become imbedded in foundations of Soviet power. It has profound implications for Russia's conduct as a member of international society. It means that there can never be on Moscow's side any sincere assumption of a community of aims between the Soviet Union and powers which are regarded as capitalism. It must invariably be assumed in Moscow that the aims of the capitalist world are antagonistic to the Soviet regime and, therefore, to the interests of the peoples it controls. If the Soviet Government occasionally sets its signature to documents which would indicate the contrary, this is to be regarded as a tactical maneuver permissible in dealing with the enemy (who is without honor) and should be taken in the spirit of *caveat emptor* [let the buyer beware]. Basically, the antagonism remains. It is postulated. And from it flow many of the phenomena which we find disturbing in the Kremlin's conduct of foreign policy: the secretiveness, the lack of frankness, the duplicity, the war suspiciousness, and the basic unfriendliness of purpose. These phenomena are there to stay, for the foreseeable future. There can be variations of degree and of emphasis. When there is something the Russians want from us, one or the other of these features of their policy may be thrust temporarily into the background; and when that happens there will always be Americans who will leap forward with gleeful announcements that "the Russians have changed," and some who will even try to take credit for having brought about such "changes." But we should not be misled by tactical maneuvers. These characteristics of Soviet policy, like the postulate from which they flow, are basic to the internal nature of Soviet power, and will be with us, whether in the foreground or the background, until the internal nature of Soviet power is changed.

This means that we are going to continue for a long time to find the Russians difficult to deal with. It does not mean that they should be considered as embarked upon a do-or-die program to overthrow our society by a given date. The theory of the inevitability of the eventual fall of capitalism has the fortunate connotation that there is no hurry about it. * * *

*   *   *

* * * [T]he Kremlin is under no ideological compulsion to accomplish its purposes in a hurry. Like the Church, it is dealing in ideological concepts which are of long-term validity, and it can afford to be patient. It has no right to risk the existing achievements of the revolution for the sake of vain baubles of the future. The very teachings of Lenin himself require great caution and flexibility in the pursuit of Communist purposes. Again, these precepts are fortified by the lessons of Russian history: of centuries of obscure battles between nomadic forces over the stretches of a vast unfortified plain. Here caution, circumspection, flexibility and deception are the valuable qualities; and their value finds natural appreciation in the Russian or the oriental mind. Thus the Kremlin has no compunction about retreating in the face of superior force. And being under the compulsion of no timetable, it does not get panicky under the necessity for such retreat. Its political action is a fluid stream which moves constantly, wherever it is permitted to move, toward a given goal. Its main concern is to make sure that it has filled every nook and cranny available to it in the basin of world power. But if it finds unassailable barriers in its path, it accepts these philosophically and accommodates itself to them. The main thing is that there should always be pressure, increasing constant pressure, toward the desired goal. There is no trace of any feeling in Soviet psychology that that goal must be reached at any given time.

These considerations make Soviet diplomacy at once easier and more difficult to deal with than the diplomacy of individual aggressive leaders like Napoleon and Hitler. On the one hand it is more sensitive to contrary force, more ready to yield on individual sectors of the diplomatic front when that force is felt to be too strong, and thus more rational in the logic and rhetoric of power. On the other hand it cannot be easily defeated or discouraged by a single victory on the part of its opponents. And the patient persistence by which it is animated means that it can be effectively countered not by sporadic acts which represent the momentary whims of democratic opinion but only by intelligent long-range policies on the part of Russia's adversaries— policies no less steady in their purpose, and no less variegated and resourceful in their application, than those of the Soviet Union itself.

In these circumstances it is clear that the main element of any United States policy toward the Soviet Union must be that of a long-term, patient but firm and vigilant containment of Russian expansive tendencies. It is important to note, however, that such a policy has nothing to do with outward histrionics: with threats or blustering or superfluous gestures of outward "toughness." While the Kremlin is basically flexible in its reaction to political realities, it is by no means unamenable to considerations of prestige. Like almost any other government, it can be placed by tactless and threatening gestures in a position where it cannot afford to yield even though this might be dictated by its sense of realism. The Russian leaders are keen judges of human psychology, and as such they are highly conscious that loss of temper and of self-control is never a source of strength in political affairs. They are quick to exploit such evidences of weakness. For these reasons, it is a *sine qua non* of successful dealing with Russia that the foreign government in question should remain at all times cool and collected and that its demands on Russian policy should be put forward in such a manner as to leave the way open for a compliance not too detrimental to Russian prestige.

III

In the light of the above, it will be clearly seen that the Soviet pressure against the free institutions of the Western world is something that can be contained by the adroit and vigilant application of counter-force at a series of constantly shifting geographical and political points, corresponding to the shifts and maneuvers of Soviet policy, but which cannot be charmed or talked out of existence. * * *

* * *

IV

* * *

But in actuality the possibilities for American policy are by no means limited to holding the line and hoping for the best. It is entirely possible for the United States to influence by its actions the internal developments, both within Russia and throughout the international Communist movement, by which Russian policy is largely determined. This is not only a question of the modest measure of informational activity which this government can conduct in the Soviet Union and elsewhere, although that, too, is important. It is rather a question of the degree to which the United States can create among the peoples of the world generally the impression of a country which knows what it wants, which is coping successfully with the problems of its internal life and with the responsibilities of a World Power, and which has a spiritual vitality capable of holding its own among the major ideological currents of the time. To the extent that such an impression can be created and maintained, the aims of Russian Communism must appear sterile and quixotic, the hopes and enthusiasm of Moscow's supporters must wane, and added strain must be imposed on the Kremlin's foreign policies. For the palsied decrepitude of the capitalist world is the keystone of Communist philosophy. Even the failure of the United States to experience the early economic depression which the ravens of the Red Square have been predicting with such complacent confidence since hostilities ceased would have deep and important repercussions throughout the Communist world.

By the same token, exhibitions of indecision, disunity and internal disintegration within this country have an exhilarating effect on the whole Communist movement. * * *

* * * [T]he United States has it in its power to increase enormously the strains under which Soviet policy must operate, to force upon the Kremlin a far greater degree of moderation and circumspection than it has had to observe in recent years, and in this way to promote tendencies which must eventually find their outlet in either the break-up or the gradual mellowing of Soviet power. For no mystical, Messianic movement—and particularly not that of the Kremlin—can face frustration indefinitely without eventually adjusting itself in one way or another to the logic of that state of affairs.

* * *

NOTE

1. Here and elsewhere in this paper "Socialism" refers to Marxist or Leninist Communism. * * *

3 Contending Perspectives

Over the past century, the most prominent perspectives for understanding the basic nature of international politics have been realism, liberalism, radicalism, and more recently constructivism. These viewpoints have vied for influence both in public debates and in academic arguments.

The readings in this chapter constitute some of the most concise and important statements of each theoretical tradition. Hans J. Morgenthau, the leading figure in the field of international relations in the period after World War II and at that time a professor at the University of Chicago, presents a realist view of power politics. His influential book Politics among Nations *(1948), excerpted below, played a central role in intellectually preparing Americans to exercise global power in the Cold War period and to reconcile power politics with the idealistic ethics that had often dominated American discussions about foreign relations.*

In The Tragedy of Great Power Politics *(2001), John J. Mearsheimer offers a contemporary interpretation of international politics that he calls "offensive realism." The chapter reprinted here describes clearly and concisely international anarchy and its implications. States operate in a self-help system; to ensure their survival in that system, states must strive to become as powerful as possible. This competitive striving for security makes conflict the enduring and dominant feature of international relations, in Mearsheimer's view.*

Michael W. Doyle, a professor at Columbia University, advances the liberal theory of the democratic peace. His 1986 article in the American Political Science Review *points out that no two democracies had ever fought a war against each other. This sparked an ongoing debate among academics and public commentators on why this was the case, and whether it meant that the United States and other democracies should place efforts to promote the further spreading of democracy at the head of their foreign policy agendas.*

Whereas realists like Mearsheimer argued that the situation of anarchy necessarily causes insecurity and fear among states, social constructivists such as Alexander Wendt insisted that behavior in anarchy depends on the ideas, cultures, and identities that people and their states bring to the anarchical situation. The excerpt below is drawn from the seminal piece in that debate, which has spawned influential research on such topics as the taboo against using nuclear weapons, changing norms of humanitarian military intervention, and the rise of powerful transnational human rights networks.

The final selection illustrates currents in the study of international politics that fundamentally challenge the realist, liberal, and radical perspectives. Arguing from a feminist perspective, J. Ann Tickner of the University of Southern California, in an excerpt from Gender in International Relations *(1992), suggests that much of the warlike behavior realists attribute to the situation of international anarchy is better understood as a consequence of the way male identity has been constructed.*

HANS J. MORGENTHAU

A Realist Theory of International Politics

This book purports to present a theory of international politics. The test by which such a theory must be judged is not *a priori* and abstract but empirical and pragmatic. The theory, in other words, must be judged not by some preconceived abstract principle or concept unrelated to reality, but by its purpose: to bring order and meaning to a mass of phenomena which without it would remain disconnected and unintelligible. It must meet a dual test, an empirical and a logical one: Do the facts as they actually are lend themselves to the interpretation the theory has put upon them, and do the conclusions at which the theory arrives follow with logical necessity from its premises? In short, is the theory consistent with the facts and within itself?

The issue this theory raises concerns the nature of all politics. The history of modern political thought is the story of a contest between two schools that differ fundamentally in their conceptions of the nature of man, society, and politics. One believes that a rational and moral political order, derived from universally valid abstract principles, can be achieved here and now. It assumes the essential goodness and infinite malleability of human nature, and blames the failure of the social order to measure up to the rational standards on lack of knowledge and understanding, obsolescent social institutions, or the depravity of certain isolated individuals or groups. It trusts in education, reform, and the sporadic use of force to remedy these defects.

The other school believes that the world, imperfect as it is from the rational point of view, is the result of forces inherent in human nature. To improve the world one must work with those forces, not against them. This being inherently a world of opposing interests and of conflict among them, moral principles can never be fully realized, but must at best be approximated through the ever temporary balancing of inter-

From Hans J. Morganthau, *Politics among Nations: The Struggle for Power and Peace* (1948; reprint, New York: Knopf, 1960), Chap. 1. The author's notes have been omitted.

ests and the ever precarious settlement of conflicts. This school, then, sees in a system of checks and balances a universal principle for all pluralist societies. It appeals to historic precedent rather than to abstract principles, and aims at the realization of the lesser evil rather than of the absolute good.

* * *

* * * Principles of Political Realism

Political realism believes that politics, like society in general, is governed by objective laws that have their roots in human nature. In order to improve society it is first necessary to understand the laws by which society lives. The operation of these laws being impervious to our preferences, men will challenge them only at the risk of failure.

Realism, believing as it does in the objectivity of the laws of politics, must also believe in the possibility of developing a rational theory that reflects, however imperfectly and one-sidedly, these objective laws. It believes also, then, in the possibility of distinguishing in politics between truth and opinion—between what is true objectively and rationally, supported by evidence and illuminated by reason, and what is only a subjective judgment, divorced from the facts as they are and informed by prejudice and wishful thinking.

* * *

For realism, theory consists in ascertaining facts and giving them meaning through reason. It assumes that the character of a foreign policy can be ascertained only through the examination of the political acts performed and of the foreseeable consequences of these acts. Thus, we can find out what statesmen have actually done, and from the foreseeable consequences of their acts we can surmise what their objectives might have been.

Yet examination of the facts is not enough. To give meaning to the factual raw material of foreign policy, we must approach political reality with a kind of rational outline, a map that suggests to us the possible meanings of foreign policy. In other words, we put ourselves in the position of a statesman who must meet a certain problem of foreign policy under certain circumstances, and we ask ourselves what the rational alternatives are from which a statesman may choose who must meet this problem under these circumstances (presuming always that he acts in a rational manner), and which of these rational alternatives this particular statesman, acting under these circumstances, is likely to choose. It is the testing of this rational hypothesis against the actual facts and their consequences that gives meaning to the facts of international politics and makes a theory of politics possible.

The main signpost that helps political realism to find its way through the landscape of international politics is the concept of interest defined in terms of power. This concept provides the link between reason trying to understand international politics and the facts to be understood. * * *

We assume that statesmen think and act in terms of interest defined as power, and the evidence of history bears that assumption out. That assumption allows us to retrace and anticipate, as it were, the steps a statesman—past, present, or future—has taken or will take on the political scene. We look over his shoulder when he writes his dispatches; we listen in on his conversation with other statesmen; we read and anticipate his very thoughts. Thinking in terms of interest defined as power, we think as he does, and as disinterested observers we understand his thoughts and actions perhaps better than he, the actor on the political scene, does himself.

* * *

Political realism is aware of the moral significance of political action. It is also aware of the ineluctable tension between the moral command and the requirements of successful political action. And it is unwilling to gloss over and obliterate that tension and thus to obfuscate both the moral and the political issue by making it appear as though the stark facts of politics were morally more satisfying than they actually are, and the moral law less exacting than it actually is.

Realism maintains that universal moral principles cannot be applied to the actions of states in their abstract universal formulation, but that they must be filtered through the concrete circumstances of time and place. The individual may say for himself: *"Fiat justitia, pereat mundus* (Let justice be done, even if the world perish)," but the state has no right to say so in the name of those who are in its care. Both individual and state must judge political action by universal moral principles, such as that of liberty. Yet while the individual has a moral right to sacrifice himself in defense of such a moral principle, the state has no right to let its moral disapproval of the infringement of liberty get in the way of successful political action, itself inspired by the moral principle of national survival. There can be no political morality without prudence; that is, without consideration of the political consequences of seemingly moral action. Realism, then, considers prudence—the weighing of the consequences of alternative political actions—to be the supreme virtue in politics. Ethics in the abstract judges action by its conformity with the moral law; political ethics judges action by its political consequences. * * *

Political Power

What Is Political Power?

* * *

International politics, like all politics, is a struggle for power. Whatever the ultimate aims of international politics, power is always the immediate aim. Statesmen and peoples may ultimately seek freedom, security, prosperity, or power itself. They may define their goals in terms of a religious, philosophic, economic, or social ideal. They may hope that this ideal will materialize through its own inner force, through divine intervention, or through the natural development of human affairs. They may also try to further its realization through nonpolitical means, such as technical co-operation with other nations or international organizations. But whenever they strive to realize their goal by means of international politics, they do so by striving for power. The Crusaders wanted to free the holy places from domination by the Infidels; Woodrow Wilson wanted to make the world safe for democracy; the Nazis wanted to open Eastern Europe to German colonization, to dominate Europe, and to conquer the world. Since they all chose power to achieve these ends, they were actors on the scene of international politics.

* * *

* * * When we speak of power, we mean man's control over the minds and actions of other men. By political power we refer to the mutual relations of control among the holders of public authority and between the latter and the people at large.

Political power, however, must be distinguished from force in the sense of the actual exercise of physical violence. The threat of physical violence in the form of police action, imprisonment, capital punishment, or war is an intrinsic element of politics. When violence becomes an actuality, it signifies the abdication of political power in favor of military or pseudo-military power. In international politics in particular, armed strength as a threat or a potentiality is the most important material factor making for the political power of a nation. If it becomes an actuality in war, it signifies the substitution of military for political power. The actual exercise of physical violence substitutes for the psychological relation between two minds, which is of the essence of political power, the physical relation between two bodies, one of which is strong enough to dominate the other's movements. It is for this reason that in the exercise of physical violence the psychological element of the political relationship is lost, and that we must distinguish between military and political power.

Political power is a psychological relation between those who exercise it and those over whom it is exercised. It gives the former control over certain actions of the latter through the influence which the former exert over the latter's minds. That influence derives from three sources: the expectation of benefits, the fear of disadvantages, the respect or love for men or institutions. It may be exerted through orders, threats, persuasion, the authority or charisma of a man or of an office, or a combination of any of these.

While it is generally recognized that the interplay of these factors, in ever changing combinations, forms the basis of all domestic politics, the importance of these factors for international politics is less obvious, but no less real. There has been a tendency to reduce political power to the actual application of force or at least to equate it with successful threats of force and with persuasion, to the neglect of charisma. That neglect * * * accounts in good measure for the neglect of prestige as an independent element in international politics. * * *

* * *

An economic, financial, territorial, or military policy undertaken for its own sake is subject to evaluation in its own terms. Is it economically or financially advantageous? * * *

When, however, the objectives of these policies serve to increase the power of the nation pursuing them with regard to other nations, these policies and their objectives must be judged primarily from the point of view of their contribution to national power. An economic policy that cannot be justified in purely economic terms might nevertheless be undertaken in view of the political policy pursued. The insecure and unprofitable character of a loan to a foreign nation may be a valid argument against it on purely financial grounds. But the argument is irrelevant if the loan, however unwise it may be from a banker's point of view, serves the political policies of the nation. It may of course be that the economic or financial losses involved in such policies will weaken the nation in its international position to such an extent as to outweigh the political advantages to be expected. On these grounds such policies might be rejected. In such a case, what decides the issue is not purely economic and financial considerations but a comparison of the political changes and risks involved; that is, the probable effect of these policies upon the power of the nation.

The Depreciation of Political Power

The aspiration for power being the distinguishing element of international politics, as of all politics, international politics is of necessity power politics. While this fact is generally recognized in the practice of international affairs, it is frequently denied in the pronouncements of scholars, publicists, and even statesmen. Since the end of the Napoleonic Wars, ever larger groups in the Western world have been persuaded that the struggle for power on the international scene is a temporary phenomenon, a historical accident that is bound to disappear once the peculiar historic conditions that have given rise to it have been eliminated. * * * During the nineteenth century, liberals everywhere shared the conviction that power politics and war were residues of an obsolete system of government, and that with the victory of democracy and constitutional government over absolutism and autocracy international harmony and permanent peace would win out over power politics and war. Of this liberal school of thought, Woodrow Wilson was the most eloquent and most influential spokesman.

In recent times, the conviction that the struggle for power can be eliminated from the international scene has been connected with the great attempts at organizing the world, such as the League of Nations and the United Nations. * * *

* * * [In fact,] the struggle for power is universal in time and space and is an undeniable fact of experience. It cannot be denied that throughout historic time, regardless of social, economic, and political conditions, states have met each other in contests for power. Even though anthropologists have shown that certain primitive peoples seem to be free from the desire for power, nobody has yet shown how their state of mind and the conditions under which they live can be recreated on a worldwide scale so as to eliminate the struggle for power from the international scene[1] It would be useless and even self-destructive to free one or the other of the peoples of the earth from the desire for power while leaving it extant in others. If the desire for power cannot be abolished everywhere in the world, those who might be cured would simply fall victims to the power of others.

The position taken here might be criticized on the ground that conclusions drawn from the past are unconvincing, and that to draw such conclusions has always been the main stock in trade of the enemies of progress and reform. Though it is true that certain social arrangements and institutions have always existed in the past, it does not necessarily follow that they must always exist in the future. The situation is, however, different when we deal not with social arrangements and institutions created by man, but with those elemental biopsychological drives by which in turn society is created. The drives to live, to propagate, and to dominate are common to all men.[2] Their relative strength is dependent upon social conditions that may favor one drive and tend to repress another, or that may withhold social approval from certain manifestations of these drives while they encourage others. Thus, to take examples only from the sphere of power, most societies condemn killing as a means of attaining power within society, but all societies encourage the killing of enemies in that struggle for power which is called war. * * *

NOTES

1. For an illuminating discussion of this problem, see Malcolm Sharp, "Aggression: A Study of Values and Law," *Ethics*, Vol. 57, No. 4, Part II (July 1947).
2. Zoologists have tried to show that the drive to dominate is found even in animals, such as chickens and monkeys, who create social hierarchies on the basis of the will and the ability to dominate. See, e.g., Warder Allee, *Animal Life and Social Growth* (Baltimore: The Williams and Wilkins Company, 1932), and *The Social Life of Animals* (New York: W. W. Norton and Company, Inc., 1938).

JOHN J. MEARSHEIMER

Anarchy and the Struggle for Power

Great powers, I argue, are always searching for opportunities to gain power over their rivals, with hegemony as their final goal. This perspective does not allow for status quo powers, except for the unusual state that achieves preponderance. Instead, the system is populated with great powers that have revisionist intentions at their core.[1] This chapter presents a theory that explains this competition for power. Specifically, I attempt to show that there is a compelling logic behind my claim that great powers seek to maximize their share of world power. I do not, however, test offensive realism against the historical record in this chapter. That important task is reserved for later chapters.

Why States Pursue Power

My explanation for why great powers vie with each other for power and strive for hegemony is derived from five assumptions about the international system. None of these assumptions alone mandates that states behave competitively. Taken together, however, they depict a world in which states have considerable reason to think and sometimes behave aggressively. In particular, the system encourages states to look for opportunities to maximize their power vis-à-vis other states.

How important is it that these assumptions be realistic? Some social scientists argue that

From *The Tragedy of Great Power Politics* (New York: Norton, 2001): 29–54. Some of the author's notes have been edited.

the assumptions that underpin a theory need not conform to reality. Indeed, the economist Milton Friedman maintains that the best theories "will be found to have assumptions that are wildly inaccurate descriptive representations of reality, and, in general, the more significant the theory, the more unrealistic the assumptions."[2] According to this view, the explanatory power of a theory is all that matters. If unrealistic assumptions lead to a theory that tells us a lot about how the world works, it is of no importance whether the underlying assumptions are realistic or not.

I reject this view. Although I agree that explanatory power is the ultimate criterion for assessing theories, I also believe that a theory based on unrealistic or false assumptions will not explain much about how the world works.[3] Sound theories are based on sound assumptions. Accordingly, each of these five assumptions is a reasonably accurate representation of an important aspect of life in the international system.

Bedrock Assumptions

The first assumption is that the international system is anarchic, which does not mean that it is chaotic or riven by disorder. It is easy to draw that conclusion, since realism depicts a world characterized by security competition and war. By itself, however, the realist notion of anarchy has nothing to do with conflict; it is an ordering principle, which says that the system comprises independent states that have no central authority above them.[4] Sovereignty, in other words, inheres in states because there is no higher ruling body in the international system.[5] There is no "government over governments."[6]

The second assumption is that great powers inherently possess some offensive military capability, which gives them the wherewithal to hurt and possibly destroy each other. States are potentially dangerous to each other, although some states have more military might than others and are therefore more dangerous. A state's military power is usually identified with the particular weaponry at its disposal, although even if there were no weapons, the individuals in those states could still use their feet and hands to attack the population of another state. After all, for every neck, there are two hands to choke it.

The third assumption is that states can never be certain about other states' intentions. Specifically, no state can be sure that another state will not use its offensive military capability to attack the first state. This is not to say that states necessarily have hostile intentions. Indeed, all of the states in the system may be reliably benign, but it is impossible to be sure of that judgment because intentions are impossible to divine with 100 percent certainty.[7] There are many possible causes of aggression, and no state can be sure that another state is not motivated by one of them.[8] Furthermore, intentions can change quickly, so a state's intentions can be benign one day and hostile the next. Uncertainty about intentions is unavoidable, which means that states can never be sure that other states do not have offensive intentions to go along with their offensive capabilities.

The fourth assumption is that survival is the primary goal of great powers. Specifically, states seek to maintain their territorial integrity and the autonomy of their domestic political order. Survival dominates other motives because, once a state is conquered, it is unlikely to be in a position to pursue other aims. Soviet leader Josef Stalin put the point well during a war scare in 1927: "We can and must build socialism in the [Soviet Union]. But in order to do so we first of all have to exist."[9] States can and do pursue other goals, of course, but security is their most important objective.

The fifth assumption is that great powers are rational actors. They are aware of their external environment and they think strategically about how to survive in it. In particular, they consider the preferences of other states and how their own behavior is likely to affect the behavior of those other states, and how the behavior of those other states is likely to affect their own strategy for survival. Moreover, states pay attention to the long term as well as the immediate consequences of their actions.

As emphasized, none of these assumptions alone dictates that great powers as a general rule *should* behave aggressively toward each other. There is surely the possibility that some state might have hostile intentions, but the only assumption dealing with a specific motive that is common to all states says that their principal objective is to survive, which by itself is a rather harmless goal. Nevertheless, when the five assumptions are married together, they create powerful incentives for great powers to think and act offensively with regard to each other. In particular, three general patterns of behavior result: fear, self-help, and power maximization.

State Behavior

Great powers fear each other. They regard each other with suspicion, and they worry that war might be in the offing. They anticipate danger. There is little room for trust among states. For sure, the level of fear varies across time and space, but it cannot be reduced to a trivial level. From the perspective of any one great power, all other great powers are potential enemies. This point is illustrated by the reaction of the United Kingdom and France to German reunification at the end of the Cold War. Despite the fact that these three states had been close allies for almost forty-five years, both the United Kingdom and France immediately began worrying about the potential dangers of a united Germany.[10]

The basis of this fear is that in a world where great powers have the capability to attack each other and might have the motive to do so, any state bent on survival must be at least suspicious of other states and reluctant to trust them.

Add to this the "911" problem—the absence of a central authority to which a threatened state can turn for help—and states have even greater incentive to fear each other. Moreover, there is no mechanism, other than the possible self-interest of third parties, for punishing an aggressor. Because it is sometimes difficult to deter potential aggressors, states have ample reason not to trust other states and to be prepared for war with them.

The possible consequences of falling victim to aggression further amplify the importance of fear as a motivating force in world politics. Great powers do not compete with each other as if international politics were merely an economic marketplace. Political competition among states is a much more dangerous business than mere economic intercourse; the former can lead to war, and war often means mass killing on the battlefield as well as mass murder of civilians. In extreme cases, war can even lead to the destruction of states. The horrible consequences of war sometimes cause states to view each other not just as competitors, but as potentially deadly enemies. Political antagonism, in short, tends to be intense, because the stakes are great.

States in the international system also aim to guarantee their own survival. Because other states are potential threats, and because there is no higher authority to come to their rescue when they dial 911, states cannot depend on others for their own security. Each state tends to see itself as vulnerable and alone, and therefore it aims to provide for its own survival. In international politics, God helps those who help themselves. This emphasis on self-help does not preclude states from forming alliances.[11] But alliances are only temporary marriages of convenience: today's alliance partner might be tomorrow's enemy, and today's enemy might be tomorrow's alliance partner. For example, the United States fought with China and the Soviet Union against Germany and Japan in World War II, but soon thereafter flip-flopped enemies and partners and allied with West Germany and Japan against China and the Soviet Union during the Cold War.

States operating in a self-help world almost always act according to their own self-interest and do not subordinate their interests to the interests of other states, or to the interests of the so-called international community. The reason is simple: it pays to be selfish in a self-help world. This is true in the short term as well as in the long term, because if a state loses in the short run, it might not be around for the long haul.

Apprehensive about the ultimate intentions of other states, and aware that they operate in a self-help system, states quickly understand that the best way to ensure their survival is to be the most powerful state in the system. The stronger a state is relative to its potential rivals, the less likely it is that any of those rivals will attack it and threaten its survival. Weaker states will be reluctant to pick fights with more powerful states because the weaker states are likely to suffer military defeat. Indeed, the bigger the gap in power between any two states, the less likely it is that the weaker will attack the stronger. Neither Canada nor Mexico, for example, would countenance attacking the United States, which is far more powerful than its neighbors. The ideal situation is to be the hegemon in the system. As Immanuel Kant said, "It is the desire of every state, or of its ruler, to arrive at a condition of perpetual peace by conquering the whole world, if that were possible."[12] Survival would then be almost guaranteed.[13]

Consequently, states pay close attention to how power is distributed among them, and they make a special effort to maximize their share of world power. Specifically, they look for opportunities to alter the balance of power by acquiring additional increments of power at the expense of potential rivals. States employ a variety of means—economic, diplomatic, and military—to shift the balance of power in their favor, even if doing so makes other states suspicious or even hostile. Because one state's gain in power is another state's loss, great powers tend to have a zero-sum mentality when dealing with each other. The trick, of course, is to be the winner in this competition and to dominate the other states in the system. Thus, the claim that states maximize relative power is tantamount to arguing that states are disposed to think offensively toward other states, even though their ultimate motive is simply to survive. In short, great powers have aggressive intentions.[14]

Even when a great power achieves a distinct military advantage over its rivals, it continues looking for chances to gain more power. The pursuit of power stops only when hegemony is achieved. The idea that a great power might feel secure without dominating the system, provided it has an "appropriate amount" of power, is not persuasive, for two reasons.[15] First, it is difficult to assess how much relative power one state must have over its rivals before it is secure. Is twice as much power an appropriate threshold? Or is three times as much power the magic number? The root of the problem is that power calculations alone do not determine which side wins a war. Clever strategies, for example, sometimes allow less powerful states to defeat more powerful foes.

Second, determining how much power is enough becomes even more complicated when great powers contemplate how power will be distributed among them ten or twenty years down the road. The capabilities of individual states vary over time, sometimes markedly, and it is often difficult to predict the direction and scope of change in the balance of power. Remember, few in the West anticipated the collapse of the Soviet Union before it happened. In fact, during the first half of the Cold War, many in the West feared that the Soviet economy would eventually generate greater wealth than the American economy, which would cause a marked power shift against the United States and its allies. What the future holds for China and Russia and what the balance of power will look like in 2020 is difficult to foresee.

Given the difficulty of determining how much power is enough for today and tomorrow, great powers recognize that the best way to ensure their security is to achieve hegemony now, thus eliminating any possibility of a challenge by another great power. Only a misguided state would pass up an opportunity to be the hegemon in the system because it thought it already had sufficient power to survive.[16] But even if a great power does not have the wherewithal to achieve hegemony (and that is usually the case), it will still act offensively to amass as much power as it can, because states are almost always better off with more rather than less power. In short, states do not become status quo powers until they completely dominate the system.

All states are influenced by this logic, which means that not only do they look for opportunities to take advantage of one another, they also work to ensure that other states do not take advantage of them. After all, rival states are driven by the same logic, and most states are likely to recognize their own motives at play in the actions of other states. In short, states ultimately pay attention to defense as well as offense. They think about conquest themselves, and they work to check aggressor states from gaining power at their expense. This inexorably leads to a world of constant security competition, where states are willing to lie, cheat, and use brute force if it helps them gain advantage over their rivals. Peace, if one defines that concept as a state of tranquility or mutual concord, is not likely to break out in this world.

The "security dilemma," which is one of the most well-known concepts in the international relations literature, reflects the basic logic of offensive realism. The essence of the dilemma is that the measures a state takes to increase its own security usually decrease the security of other states. Thus, it is difficult for a state to increase its own chances of survival without threatening the survival of other states. John Herz first introduced the security dilemma in a 1950 article in the journal *World Politics*.[17] After discussing the anarchic nature of international politics, he writes, "Striving to attain security from . . . attack, [states] are driven to acquire more and more power in order to escape the impact of the power of others. This, in turn, renders the others more insecure and compels them to prepare for the worst. Since none can ever feel entirely secure in such a world of competing units, power competition ensues, and the vicious circle of security and power accumulation is on."[18] The implication of Herz's analysis is clear: the best way for a state to survive in anarchy is to take advantage of other states and gain power at their expense. The best defense is a good offense. Since this message is widely understood, ceaseless security competition ensues. Unfortunately, little can be done to ameliorate the security dilemma as long as states operate in anarchy.

It should be apparent from this discussion that saying that states are power maximizers is tantamount to saying that they care about relative power, not absolute power. There is an important distinction here, because states concerned about relative power behave differently than do states interested in absolute power.[19] States that maximize relative power are concerned primarily with the distribution of material capabilities. In particular, they try to gain as large a power advantage as possible over potential rivals, because power is the best means to survival in a dangerous world. Thus, states motivated by relative power concerns are likely to forgo large gains in their own power, if such gains give rival states even greater power, for smaller national gains that nevertheless provide them with a power advantage over their rivals.[20] States that maximize absolute power, on the other hand, care only about the size of their own gains, not those of other states. They are not motivated by balance-of-power logic but instead are concerned with amassing power without regard to how much power other states control. They would jump at the opportunity for large gains, even if a rival gained more in the deal. Power, according to this logic, is not a means to an end (survival), but an end in itself.[21]

Calculated Aggression

There is obviously little room for status quo powers in a world where states are inclined to look for opportunities to gain more power. Nevertheless, great powers cannot always act on their offensive intentions, because behavior is influenced not only by what states want, but also by their capacity to realize these desires. Every state might want to be king of the hill, but not every state has the wherewithal to compete for that lofty position, much less achieve it. Much depends on how military might is distributed among the great powers. A great power that has a marked power advantage over its rivals is likely to behave more aggressively, because it has the capability as well as the incentive to do so.

By contrast, great powers facing powerful opponents will be less inclined to consider offensive action and more concerned with defending the existing balance of power from threats by their more powerful opponents. Let there be an opportunity for those weaker states to revise the balance in their own favor, however, and they will take advantage of it. Stalin put the point well at the end of World War II: "Everyone imposes his own system as far as his army can reach. It cannot be otherwise."[22] States might also have the capability to gain advantage over a rival power but nevertheless decide that the perceived costs of offense are too high and do not justify the expected benefits.

In short, great powers are not mindless aggressors so bent on gaining power that they charge headlong into losing wars or pursue Pyrrhic victories. On the contrary, before great powers take offensive actions, they think carefully about the balance of power and about how other states will react to their moves. They weigh the costs and risks of offense against the likely benefits. If the benefits do not outweigh the risks, they sit tight and wait for a more propitious moment. Nor do states start arms races that are unlikely to improve their overall position. As discussed at greater length in Chapter 3, states sometimes limit defense spending either because spending more would bring no strategic advantage or because spending more would weaken the economy and undermine the state's power in the long run.[23] To paraphrase Clint Eastwood, a state has to know its limitations to survive in the international system.

Nevertheless, great powers miscalculate from time to time because they invariably make important decisions on the basis of imperfect information. States hardly ever have complete information about any situation they confront. There are two dimensions to this problem. Potential adversaries have incentives to misrepresent their own strength or weakness, and to conceal their true aims.[24] For example, a weaker state trying to deter a stronger state is likely to exaggerate its own power to discourage the potential aggressor from attacking. On the other hand, a state bent on aggression is likely to emphasize its peaceful goals while exaggerating its military weakness, so that the potential victim does not build up its own arms and thus leaves itself vulnerable to attack. Probably no national leader was better at practicing this kind of deception than Adolf Hitler.

But even if disinformation was not a problem, great powers are often unsure about how their own military forces, as well as the adversary's, will perform on the battlefield. For example, it is sometimes difficult to determine in advance how new weapons and untested combat units will perform in the face of enemy fire. Peacetime maneuvers and war games are helpful but imperfect indicators of what is likely to happen in actual combat. Fighting wars is a complicated business in which it is often difficult to predict outcomes. Remember that although the United States and its allies scored a stunning and remarkably easy victory against Iraq in early 1991, most experts at the time believed that Iraq's military would be a formidable foe and put up stubborn resistance before finally succumbing to American military might.[25]

Great powers are also sometimes unsure about the resolve of opposing states as well as allies. For example, Germany believed that if it went to war against France and Russia in the summer of 1914, the United Kingdom would probably stay out of the fight. Saddam Hussein expected the United States to stand aside when he invaded Kuwait in August 1990. Both aggressors guessed wrong, but each had good reason to think that its initial judgment was correct. In the 1930s, Adolf Hitler believed that his great-

power rivals would be easy to exploit and isolate because each had little interest in fighting Germany and instead was determined to get someone else to assume that burden. He guessed right. In short, great powers constantly find themselves confronting situations in which they have to make important decisions with incomplete information. Not surprisingly, they sometimes make faulty judgments and end up doing themselves serious harm.

Some defensive realists go so far as to suggest that the constraints of the international system are so powerful that offense rarely succeeds, and that aggressive great powers invariably end up being punished.[26] As noted, they emphasize that 1) threatened states balance against aggressors and ultimately crush them, and 2) there is an offense-defense balance that is usually heavily tilted toward the defense, thus making conquest especially difficult. Great powers, therefore, should be content with the existing, balance of power and not try to change it by force. After all, it makes little sense for a state to initiate a war that it is likely to lose; that would be self-defeating behavior. It is better to concentrate instead on preserving the balance of power.[27] Moreover, because aggressors seldom succeed, states should understand that security is abundant, and thus there is no good strategic reason for wanting more power in the first place. In a world where conquest seldom pays, states should have relatively benign intentions toward each other. If they do not, these defensive realists argue, the reason is probably poisonous domestic politics, not smart calculations about how to guarantee one's security in an anarchic world.

There is no question that systemic factors constrain aggression, especially balancing by threatened states. But defensive realists exaggerate those restraining forces.[28] Indeed, the historical record provides little support for their claim that offense rarely succeeds. One study estimates that there were 63 wars between 1815 and 1980, and the initiator won 39 times, which translates into about a 60 percent success rate.[29] Turning to specific cases, Otto von Bismarck unified Germany by winning military victories against Denmark in 1864, Austria in 1866, and France in 1870, and the United States as we know it today was created in good part by conquest in the nineteenth century. Conquest certainly paid big dividends in these cases. Nazi Germany won wars against Poland in 1939 and France in 1940, but lost to the Soviet Union between 1941 and 1945. Conquest ultimately did not pay for the Third Reich, but if Hitler had restrained himself after the fall of France and had not invaded the Soviet Union, conquest probably would have paid handsomely for the Nazis. In short, the historical record shows that offense sometimes succeeds and sometimes does not. The trick for a sophisticated power maximizer is to figure out when to raise and when to fold.[30]

Hegemony's Limits

Great powers, as I have emphasized, strive to gain power over their rivals and hopefully become hegemons. Once a state achieves that exalted position, it becomes a status quo power. More needs to be said, however, about the meaning of hegemony.

A hegemon is a state that is so powerful that it dominates all the other states in the system.[31] No other state has the military wherewithal to put up a serious fight against it. In essence, a hegemon is the only great power in the system. A state that is substantially more powerful than the other great powers in the system is not a hegemon, because it faces, by definition, other great powers. The United Kingdom in the mid-nineteenth century, for example, is sometimes called a hegemon. But it was not a hegemon, because there were four other great powers in Europe at the time—Austria, France, Prussia, and Russia—and the United Kingdom did not dominate them in any meaningful way. In fact, during that period, the United Kingdom considered France to be a serious threat to the balance of power. Europe in the nineteenth century was multipolar, not unipolar.

Hegemony means domination of the system, which is usually interpreted to mean the entire world. It is possible, however, to apply the concept of a system more narrowly and use it to describe particular regions, such as Europe, Northeast Asia, and the Western Hemisphere. Thus, one can distinguish between *global hegemons*, which dominate the world, and *regional hegemons*, which dominate distinct geographical areas. The United States has been a regional hegemon in the Western Hemisphere for at least the past one hundred years. No other state in the Americas has sufficient military might to challenge it, which is why the United States is widely recognized as the only great power in its region.

My argument, which I develop at length in subsequent chapters, is that except for the unlikely event wherein one state achieves clear-cut nuclear superiority, it is virtually impossible for any state to achieve global hegemony. The principal impediment to world domination is the difficulty of projecting power across the world's oceans onto the territory of a rival great power. The United States, for example, is the most powerful state on the planet today. But it does not dominate Europe and Northeast Asia the way it does the Western Hemisphere, and it has no intention of trying to conquer and control those distant regions, mainly because of the stopping power of water. Indeed, there is reason to think that the American military commitment to Europe and Northeast Asia might wither away over the next decade. In short, there has never been a global hegemon, and there is not likely to be one anytime soon.

The best outcome a great power can hope for is to be a regional hegemon and possibly control another region that is nearby and accessible over land. The United States is the only regional hegemon in modern history, although other states have fought major wars in pursuit of regional hegemony: imperial Japan in Northeast Asia, and Napoleonic France, Wilhelmine Germany, and Nazi Germany in Europe. But none succeeded. The Soviet Union, which is located in Europe and Northeast Asia, threatened to dominate both of those regions during the Cold War. The Soviet Union might also have attempted to conquer the oil-rich Persian Gulf region, with which it shared a border. But even if Moscow had been able to dominate Europe, Northeast Asia, and the Persian Gulf, which it never came close to doing, it still would have been unable to conquer the Western Hemisphere and become a true global hegemon.

States that achieve regional hegemony seek to prevent great powers in other regions from duplicating their feat. Regional hegemons, in other words, do not want peers. Thus the United States, for example, played a key role in preventing imperial Japan, Wilhelmine Germany, Nazi Germany, and the Soviet Union from gaining regional supremacy. Regional hegemons attempt to check aspiring hegemons in other regions because they fear that a rival great power that dominates its own region will be an especially powerful foe that is essentially free to cause trouble in the fearful great power's backyard. Regional hegemons prefer that there be at least two great powers located together in other regions, because their proximity will force them to concentrate their attention on each other rather than on the distant hegemon.

Furthermore, if a potential hegemon emerges among them, the other great powers in that region might be able to contain it by themselves, allowing the distant hegemon to remain safely on the sidelines. Of course, if the local great powers were unable to do the job, the distant hegemon would take the appropriate measures to deal with the threatening state. The United States, as noted, has assumed that burden on four separate occasions in the twentieth century, which is why it is commonly referred to as an "offshore balancer."

In sum, the ideal situation for any great power is to be the only regional hegemon in the world. That state would be a status quo power, and it would go to considerable lengths to preserve the existing distribution of power. The United States is in that enviable position today; it dominates the Western Hemisphere and there is no hegemon in any other area of the world. But if a regional hegemon is confronted with a peer competitor, it would no longer be a status quo power. Indeed, it would go to considerable lengths to weaken and maybe even destroy its distant rival. Of course, both regional hegemons would be motivated by that logic, which would make for a fierce security competition between them.

Power and Fear

That great powers fear each other is a central aspect of life in the international system. But as noted, the level of fear varies from case to case. For example, the Soviet Union worried much less about Germany in 1930 than it did in 1939. How much states fear each other matters greatly, because the amount of fear between them largely determines the severity of their security competition, as well as the probability that they will fight a war. The more profound the fear is, the more intense is the security competition, and the more likely is war. The logic is straightforward: a scared state will look especially hard for ways to enhance its security, and it will be disposed to pursue risky policies to achieve that end. Therefore, it is important to understand what causes states to fear each other more or less intensely.

Fear among great powers derives from the fact that they invariably have some offensive military capability that they can use against each other, and the fact that one can never be certain that other states do not intend to use that power against oneself. Moreover, because states operate in an anarchic system, there is no night watchman to whom they can turn for help if another great power attacks them. Although anarchy and uncertainty about other states' intentions create an irreducible level of fear among states that leads to power-maximizing behavior, they cannot account for why sometimes that level of fear is greater than at other times. The reason is that anarchy and the difficulty of discerning state intentions are constant facts of life, and constants cannot explain variation. The capability that states have to threaten each other, however, varies from case to case, and it is the key factor that drives fear levels up and down. Specifically, the more power a state possesses, the more fear it generates among its rivals. Germany, for example, was much more powerful at the end of the 1930s than it was at the decade's beginning, which is why the Soviets became increasingly fearful of Germany over the course of that decade.

This discussion of how power affects fear prompts the question, What is power? It is important to distinguish between potential and actual power. A state's potential power is based on the size of its population and the level of its wealth. These two assets are the main building blocks of military power. Wealthy rivals with large populations can usually build formidable military forces. A state's actual power is embedded mainly in its army and the air and naval forces that directly support it. Armies are the central ingredient of military power, because they are the principal instrument for conquering and controlling territory—the paramount political objective in a world of territorial states. In short, the key component of military might, even in the nuclear age, is land power.

Power considerations affect the intensity of fear among states in three main ways. First, rival states that possess nuclear forces that can survive a nuclear attack and retaliate against it are likely to fear each other less than if these same states had no nuclear weapons. During the Cold War, for example, the level of fear between the superpowers probably would have been substantially greater if nuclear weapons had not been invented. The logic here is simple: because nuclear weapons can inflict devastating destruction on a rival state in a short period of time, nuclear-armed rivals are going to be reluctant to fight with each other, which means that each side will have less reason to fear the other than would otherwise be the case. But as the Cold War demonstrates, this does not mean that war between nuclear powers is no longer thinkable; they still have reason to fear each other.

Second, when great powers are separated by large bodies of water, they usually do not have much offensive capability against each other, regardless of the relative size of their armies. Large bodies of water are formidable obstacles that cause significant power-projection problems for attacking armies. For example, the stopping power of water explains in good part why the United Kingdom and the United States (since becoming a great power in 1898) have never been invaded by another great power. It also explains why the United States has never tried to conquer territory in Europe or Northeast Asia, and why the United Kingdom has never attempted to dominate the European continent. Great powers located on the same landmass are in a much better position to attack and conquer each other. That is especially true of states that share a common border. Therefore, great powers separated by water are likely to fear each other less than great powers that can get at each other over land.

Third, the distribution of power among the states in the system also markedly affects the levels of fear.[32] The key issue is whether power is distributed more or less evenly among the great powers or whether there are sharp power asymmetries. The configuration of power that generates the most fear is a multipolar system that contains a potential hegemon—what I call "unbalanced multipolarity."

A potential hegemon is more than just the most powerful state in the system. It is a great power with so much actual military capability and so much potential power that it stands a good chance of dominating and controlling all of the other great powers in its region of the world. A potential hegemon need not have the wherewithal to fight all of its rivals at once, but it must have excellent prospects of defeating each opponent alone, and good prospects of defeating some of them in tandem. The key relationship, however, is the power gap between the potential hegemon and the second most powerful state in the system: there must be a marked gap between them. To qualify as a potential hegemon, a state must have—by some reasonably large margin—the most formidable army as well as the most latent power among all the states located in its region.

Bipolarity is the power configuration that produces the least amount of fear among the great powers, although not a negligible amount by any means. Fear tends to be less acute in bipolarity, because there is usually a rough balance of power between the two major states in the system. Multipolar systems without a potential hegemon, what I call "balanced multipolarity," are still likely to have power asymmetries among their members, although these asymmetries will not be as pronounced as the gaps created by the presence of an aspiring hegemon. Therefore, balanced multipolarity is likely to generate less fear than unbalanced multipolarity, but more fear than bipolarity.

This discussion of how the level of fear between great powers varies with changes in the distribution of power, not with assessments about each other's intentions, raises a related point. When a state surveys its environment to determine which states pose a threat to its survival, it focuses mainly on the offensive *capabilities* of potential rivals, not their intentions. As emphasized earlier, intentions are ultimately unknowable, so states worried about their survival must make worst-case assumptions about their rivals' intentions. Capabilities, however, not only can be measured but also determine whether or not a rival state is a serious threat. In short, great powers balance against capabilities, not intentions.[33]

Great powers obviously balance against states with formidable military forces, because that offensive military capability is the tangible threat to their survival. But great powers also pay careful attention to how much latent power rival states control, because rich and populous states usually can and do build powerful armies. Thus, great powers tend to fear states with large populations and rapidly expanding economies, even if these states have not yet translated their wealth into military might.

The Hierarchy of State Goals

Survival is the number one goal of great powers, according to my theory. In practice, however, states pursue non-security goals as well. For example, great powers invariably seek greater economic prosperity to enhance the welfare of their citizenry. They sometimes seek to promote a particular ideology abroad, as happened during the Cold War when the United States tried to spread democracy around the world and the Soviet Union tried to sell communism. National unification is another goal that sometimes motivates states, as it did with Prussia and Italy in the nineteenth century and Germany after the Cold War. Great powers also occasionally try to foster human rights around the globe. States might pursue any of these, as well as a number of other non-security goals.

Offensive realism certainly recognizes that great powers might pursue these non-security goals, but it has little to say about them, save for one important point: states can pursue them as long as the requisite behavior does not conflict with balance-of-power logic, which is often the case.[34] Indeed, the pursuit of these non-security goals sometimes complements the hunt for relative power. For example, Nazi Germany expanded into eastern Europe for both ideological and realist reasons, and the superpowers competed with each other during the Cold War for similar reasons. Furthermore, greater economic prosperity invariably means greater wealth, which has significant implications for security, because wealth is the foundation of military power. Wealthy states can afford powerful military forces, which enhance a state's prospects for survival. As the political economist Jacob Viner noted more than fifty years ago, "there is a long-run harmony" between wealth and power.[35] National unification is another goal that usually complements the pursuit of power. For example, the unified German state that emerged in 1871 was more powerful than the Prussian state it replaced.

Sometimes the pursuit of non-security goals has hardly any effect on the balance of power, one way or the other. Human rights interventions usually fit this description, because they tend to be small-scale operations that cost little and do not detract from a great power's prospects for survival. For better or for worse, states are rarely willing to expend blood and treasure to protect foreign populations from gross abuses, including genocide. For instance, despite claims that American foreign policy is infused with moralism, Somalia (1992–93) is the only instance during the past one hundred years in which U.S. soldiers were killed in action on a humanitarian mission. And in that case, the loss of a mere eighteen soldiers in an infamous firefight in October 1993 so traumatized American policymakers that they immediately pulled all U.S. troops out of Somalia and then refused to intervene in Rwanda in the spring of 1994, when ethnic Hutu went on a genocidal rampage against their Tutsi neighbors.[36] Stopping that genocide would have been relatively easy and it would have had virtually no effect on the position of the United States in the balance of power.[37] Yet nothing was done. In short, although realism does not prescribe human rights interventions, it does not necessarily proscribe them.

But sometimes the pursuit of non-security goals conflicts with balance-of-power logic, in which case states usually act according to the dictates of realism. For example, despite the U.S. commitment to spreading democracy across the globe, it helped overthrow democratically elected governments and embraced a number of authoritarian regimes during the Cold War, when American policymakers felt that these actions would help contain the Soviet Union.[38] In World War II, the liberal democracies put aside their antipathy for communism and formed an alliance with the Soviet Union against Nazi Germany. "I can't take communism," Franklin Roosevelt emphasized, but to defeat Hitler "I would hold hands with the Devil."[39] In the same way, Stalin repeatedly demonstrated that when his ideological preferences clashed with power considerations, the latter won out. To take the most blatant example of his realism, the Soviet Union formed a non-aggression pact with Nazi Germany in August 1939—the infamous Molotov-Ribbentrop Pact—in hopes that the agreement would at least temporarily satisfy Hitler's territorial ambitions in eastern Europe and turn the Wehrmacht toward France and the United Kingdom.[40] When great powers confront a serious threat, in short, they pay little attention to ideology as they search for alliance partners.[41]

Security also trumps wealth when those two goals conflict, because "defence," as Adam Smith wrote in *The Wealth of Nations*, "is of much more importance than opulence."[42] Smith provides a good illustration of how states behave when forced to choose between wealth and relative power. In 1651, England put into effect the famous Navigation Act, protectionist legislation designed to damage Holland's commerce and ultimately cripple the Dutch economy. The legislation mandated that all goods imported into England be carried either in English ships or ships owned by the country that originally produced the goods. Since the Dutch produced few goods themselves, this measure would badly damage their shipping, the central ingredient in their economic success. Of course, the Navigation Act would hurt England's economy as well, mainly because it would rob England of the benefits of free trade. "The act of navigation," Smith wrote, "is not favorable to foreign commerce, or to the growth of that opulence that can arise from it." Nevertheless, Smith considered the legislation "the wisest of all the commercial regulations of England" because it did more damage to the Dutch economy than to the English economy, and in the mid-seventeenth century Holland was "the only naval power which could endanger the security of England."[43]

Creating World Order

The claim is sometimes made that great powers can transcend realist logic by working together to build an international order that fosters peace and justice. World peace, it would appear, can only enhance a state's prosperity and security. America's political leaders paid considerable lip service to this line of argument over the course of the twentieth century. President Clinton, for example, told an audience at the United Nations in September 1993 that "at the birth of this organization 48 years ago . . . a generation of gifted leaders from many nations stepped forward to organize the world's efforts on behalf of security and prosperity. . . . Now history has granted to us a moment of even greater opportunity. . . . Let us resolve that we will dream larger. . . . Let us ensure that the world we pass to our children is healthier, safer and more abundant than the one we inhabit today."[44]

This rhetoric notwithstanding, great powers do not work together to promote world order for its own sake. Instead, each seeks to maximize its own share of world power, which is likely to clash with the goal of creating and sustaining stable international orders.[45] This is not to say that great powers never aim to prevent wars and keep the peace. On the contrary, they work hard to deter wars in which they would be the likely victim. In such cases, however, state behavior is driven largely by narrow calculations about relative power, not by a commitment to build a world order independent of a state's own interests. The United States, for example, devoted enormous resources to deterring the Soviet Union from starting a war in Europe during the Cold War, not because of some deep-seated commitment to promoting peace around the world, but because American leaders feared that a Soviet victory would lead to a dangerous shift in the balance of power.[46]

The particular international order that obtains at any time is mainly a by-product of the self-interested behavior of the system's great powers. The configuration of the system, in other words, is the unintended consequence of great-power security competition, not the result of states acting together to organize peace. The establishment of the Cold War order in Europe illustrates this point. Neither the Soviet Union nor the United States intended to establish it, nor did they work together to create it. In fact, each superpower worked hard in the early years of the Cold War to gain power at the expense of the other, while preventing the other from doing likewise.[47] The system that emerged in Europe in the aftermath of World War II was the unplanned consequence of intense security competition between the superpowers.

Although that intense superpower rivalry ended along with the Cold War in 1990, Russia and the United States have not worked together to create the present order in Europe. The United States, for example, has rejected out of hand various Russian proposals to make the Organization for Security and Cooperation in Europe the central organizing pillar of European security (replacing the U.S.-dominated NATO). Furthermore, Russia was deeply opposed to NATO expansion, which it viewed as a serious threat to Russian security. Recognizing that Russia's weakness would preclude any retaliation, however, the United States ignored Russia's concerns and pushed NATO to accept the Czech Republic, Hungary, and Poland as new members. Russia has also opposed U.S. policy in the Balkans over the past decade, especially NATO's 1999 war against Yugoslavia. Again, the United States has paid little attention to Russia's concerns and has taken the steps it deems necessary to bring peace to that volatile region. Finally, it is worth noting that although Russia is dead set against allowing the United States to deploy ballistic missile defenses, it is highly likely that Washington will deploy such a system if it is judged to be technologically feasible.

For sure, great-power rivalry will sometimes produce a stable international order, as happened during the Cold War. Nevertheless, the great powers will continue looking for opportunities to increase their share of world power, and if a favorable situation arises, they will move to undermine that stable order. Consider how hard the United States worked during the late 1980s to weaken the Soviet Union and bring down the stable order that had emerged in Europe during the latter part of the Cold War.[48] Of course, the states that stand to lose power will work to deter aggression and preserve the existing order. But their motives will be selfish, revolving around balance-of-power logic, not some commitment to world peace.

Great powers cannot commit themselves to the pursuit of a peaceful world order for two reasons. First, states are unlikely to agree on a general formula for bolstering peace. Certainly, international relations scholars have never reached a consensus on what the blueprint should look like. In fact, it seems there are about as many theories on the causes of war and peace as there are scholars studying the subject. But more important, policymakers are unable to agree on how to create a stable world. For example, at the Paris Peace Conference after World War I, important differences over how to create stability in Europe divided Georges Clemenceau, David Lloyd George, and Woodrow Wilson.[49] In particular, Clemenceau was determined to impose harsher terms on Germany over the Rhineland than was either Lloyd George or Wilson, while Lloyd George stood out as the hard-liner on German reparations. The Treaty of Versailles, not surprisingly, did little to promote European stability.

Furthermore, consider American thinking on how to achieve stability in Europe in the early days of the Cold War.[50] The key elements for a stable and durable system were in place by the early 1950s. They included the division of Germany, the positioning of American ground forces in Western Europe to deter a Soviet attack, and ensuring that West Germany would not seek to develop nuclear weapons. Officials in the Truman administration, however, disagreed about whether a divided Germany would be a source of peace or war. For example, George Kennan and Paul Nitze, who held important positions in the State Department, believed that a divided Germany would be a source of instability, whereas Secretary of State Dean Acheson disagreed with them. In the 1950s, President Eisenhower sought to end the American commitment to defend Western Europe and to provide West Germany with its own nuclear deterrent. This policy, which was never fully adopted, nevertheless caused significant instability in Europe, as it led directly to the Berlin crises of 1958–59 and 1961.[51]

Second, great powers cannot put aside power considerations and work to promote international peace because they cannot be sure that their efforts will succeed. If their attempt fails, they are likely to pay a steep price for having neglected the balance of power, because if an aggressor appears at the door there will be no answer when they dial 911. That is a risk few states are willing to run. Therefore, prudence dictates that they behave according to realist logic. This line of reasoning accounts for why collective security schemes, which call for states to put aside narrow concerns about the balance of power and instead act in accordance with the broader interests of the international community, invariably die at birth.[52]

Cooperation Among States

One might conclude from the preceding discussion that my theory does not allow for any cooperation among the great powers. But this conclusion would be wrong. States can cooperate, although cooperation is sometimes difficult to achieve and always difficult to sustain. Two factors inhibit cooperation: considerations about relative gains and concern about cheating.[53] Ultimately, great powers live in a fundamentally competitive world where they view each other as real, or at least potential, enemies, and they therefore look to gain power at each other's expense.

Any two states contemplating cooperation must consider how profits or gains will be distributed between them. They can think about the division in terms of either absolute or relative gains (recall the distinction made earlier between pursuing either absolute power or relative power; the concept here is the same). With absolute gains, each side is concerned with maximizing its own profits and cares little about how much the other side gains or loses in the deal. Each side cares about the other only to the extent that the other side's behavior affects its own prospects for achieving maximum profits. With relative gains, on the other hand, each side considers not only its own individual gain, but also how well it fares compared to the other side.

Because great powers care deeply about the balance of power, their thinking focuses on relative gains when they consider cooperating with other states. For sure, each state tries to maximize its absolute gains; still, it is more important for a state to make sure that it does no worse, and perhaps better, than the other state in any agreement. Cooperation is more difficult to achieve, however, when states are attuned to relative gains rather than absolute gains.[54] This is because states concerned about absolute gains have to make sure that if the pie is expanding, they are getting at least some portion of the increase, whereas states that worry about relative gains must pay careful attention to how the pie is divided, which complicates cooperative efforts.

Concerns about cheating also hinder cooperation. Great powers are often reluctant to enter into cooperative agreements for fear that the other side will cheat on the agreement and gain a significant advantage. This concern is especially acute in the military realm, causing a "special peril of defection," because the nature of military weaponry allows for rapid shifts in the balance of power.[55] Such a development could create a window of opportunity for the state that cheats to inflict a decisive defeat on its victim.

These barriers to cooperation notwithstanding, great powers do cooperate in a realist world. Balance-of-power logic often causes great powers to form alliances and cooperate against common enemies. The United Kingdom, France, and Russia, for example, were allies against Germany before and during World War I. States sometimes cooperate to gang up on a third state, as Germany and the Soviet Union did against Poland in 1939.[56] More recently, Serbia and Croatia

agreed to conquer and divide Bosnia between them, although the United States and its European allies prevented them from executing their agreement.[57] Rivals as well as allies cooperate. After all, deals can be struck that roughly reflect the distribution of power and satisfy concerns about cheating. The various arms control agreements signed by the superpowers during the Cold War illustrate this point.

The bottom line, however, is that cooperation takes place in a world that is competitive at its core—one where states have powerful incentives to take advantage of other states. This point is graphically highlighted by the state of European politics in the forty years before World War I. The great powers cooperated frequently during this period, but that did not stop them from going to war on August 1, 1914.[58] The United States and the Soviet Union also cooperated considerably during World War II, but that cooperation did not prevent the outbreak of the Cold War shortly after Germany and Japan were defeated. Perhaps most amazingly, there was significant economic and military cooperation between Nazi Germany and the Soviet Union during the two years before the Wehrmacht attacked the Red Army.[59] No amount of cooperation can eliminate the dominating logic of security competition. Genuine peace, or a world in which states do not compete for power, is not likely as long as the state system remains anarchic.

Conclusion

In sum, my argument is that the structure of the international system, not the particular characteristics of individual great powers, causes them to think and act offensively and to seek hegemony.[60] I do not adopt Morgenthau's claim that states invariably behave aggressively because they have a will to power hardwired into them. Instead, I assume that the principal motive behind great-power behavior is survival. In anarchy, however, the desire to survive encourages states to behave aggressively. Nor does my theory classify states as more or less aggressive on the basis of their economic or political systems. Offensive realism makes only a handful of assumptions about great powers, and these assumptions apply equally to all great powers. Except for differences in how much power each state controls, the theory treats all states alike.

I have now laid out the logic explaining why states seek to gain as much power as possible over their rivals. * * *

NOTES

1. Most realist scholars allow in their theories for status quo powers that are not hegemons. At least some states, they argue, are likely to be satisfied with the balance of power and thus have no incentive to change it. See Randall L. Schweller, "Neorealism's Status-Quo Bias: What Security Dilemma?" *Security Studies* 5, No. 3 (Spring 1996, special issue on "Realism: Restatements and Renewal," ed. Benjamin Frankel), pp. 98–101; and Arnold Wolfers, *Discord and Collaboration: Essays on International Politics* (Baltimore, MD: Johns Hopkins University Press, 1962), pp. 84–86, 91–92, 125–26.

2. Milton Friedman, *Essays in Positive Economics* (Chicago: University of Chicago Press, 1953), p. 14. Also see Kenneth N. Waltz, *Theory of International Politics* (Reading, MA: Addison-Wesley, 1979), pp. 5–6, 91, 119.

3. Terry Moe makes a helpful distinction between assumptions that are simply useful simplifications of reality (i.e., realistic in themselves but with unnecessary details omitted), and assumptions that are clearly contrary to reality (i.e., that directly violate well-established truths). See Moe, "On the Scientific Status of Rational Models," *American Journal of Political Science* 23, No. 1 (February 1979), pp. 215–43.

4. The concept of anarchy and its consequences for international politics was first articulated by G. Lowes Dickinson, *The European Anarchy* (New York: Macmillan, 1916). For a more recent and more elaborate discussion of anarchy, see Waltz, *Theory of International Politics*, pp. 88–93. Also see Robert J. Art and Robert Jervis, eds., *International Politics: Anarchy, Force, Imperialism* (Boston: Little, Brown, 1973), pt. 1; and Helen Milner, "The Assumption of Anarchy in International Relations Theory: A Critique," *Review of International Studies* 17, No. 1 (January 1991), pp. 67–85.

5. Although the focus in this study is on the state system, realist logic can be applied to other kinds of anarchic systems. After all, it is the absence of central authority, not any special characteristic of states, that causes them to compete for power.

6. Inis L. Claude, Jr., *Swords into Plowshares: The Problems and Progress of International Organization*, 4th ed. (New York: Random House, 1971), p. 14.

7. The claim that states might have benign intentions is simply a starting assumption. I argue subsequently that when you combine the theory's five assumptions, states are put in a position in which they are strongly disposed to having hostile intentions toward each other.

8. My theory ultimately argues that great powers behave offensively toward each other because that is the best way for them to guarantee their security in an anarchic world. The assumption here, however, is that there are many reasons besides security for why a state might behave aggressively toward another state. In fact, it is uncertainty about whether those non-security causes of war are at play, or might come into play, that pushes great powers to worry about their survival and thus act offensively. Security concerns alone cannot cause great powers to act aggressively. The possibility that at least one state might be motivated by non-security calculations is a necessary condition for offensive realism, as well as for any other structural theory of

international politics that predicts security competition.

9. Quoted in Jon Jacobson, *When the Soviet Union Entered World Politics* (Berkeley: University of California Press, 1994), p. 271.

10. See Elizabeth Pond, *Beyond the Wall: Germany's Road to Unification* (Washington, DC: Brookings Institution Press, 1993), chap. 12; Margaret Thatcher, *The Downing Street Years* (New York: HarperCollins, 1993), chaps. 25–26; and Philip Zelikow and Condoleezza Rice, *Germany Unified and Europe Transformed: A Study in Statecraft* (Cambridge, MA: Harvard University Press, 1995), chap. 4.

11. Frederick Schuman introduced the concept of self-help in *International Politics: An Introduction to the Western State System* (New York: McGraw-Hill, 1933), pp. 199–202, 514, although Waltz made the concept famous in *Theory of International Politics*, chap. 6. On realism and alliances, see Stephen M. Walt, *The Origins of Alliances* (Ithaca, NY: Cornell University Press, 1987).

12. Quoted in Martin Wight, *Power Politics* (London: Royal Institute of International Affairs, 1946), p. 40.

13. If one state achieves hegemony, the system ceases to be anarchic and becomes hierarchic. Offensive realism, which assumes international anarchy, has little to say about politics under hierarchy. But as discussed later, it is highly unlikely that any state will become a global hegemon, although regional hegemony is feasible. Thus, realism is likely to provide important insights about world politics for the foreseeable future, save for what goes on inside in a region that is dominated by a hegemon.

14. Although great powers always have aggressive intentions, they are not always *aggressors*, mainly because sometimes they do not have the capability to behave aggressively. I use the term "aggressor" throughout this book to denote great powers that have the material wherewithal to act on their aggressive intentions.

15. Kenneth Waltz maintains that great powers should not pursue hegemony but instead should aim to control an "appropriate" amount of world power. See Waltz, "The Origins of War in Neorealist Theory," in Robert I. Rotberg and Theodore K. Rabb, eds., *The Origin and Prevention of Major Wars* (Cambridge: Cambridge University Press, 1989), p. 40.

16. The following hypothetical example illustrates this point. Assume that American policy-makers were forced to choose between two different power balances in the Western Hemisphere. The first is the present distribution of power, whereby the United States is a hegemon that no state in the region would dare challenge militarily. In the second scenario, China replaces Canada and Germany takes the place of Mexico. Even though the United States would have a significant military advantage over both China and Germany, it is difficult to imagine any American strategist opting for this scenario over U.S. hegemony in the Western Hemisphere.

17. John H. Herz, "Idealist Internationalism and the Security Dilemma," *World Politics* 2, No. 2 (January 1950), pp. 157–80. Although Dickinson did not use the term "security dilemma," its logic is clearly articulated in *European Anarchy*, pp. 20, 88.

18. Herz, "Idealist Internationalism," p. 157.

19. See Joseph M. Grieco, "Anarchy and the Limits of Cooperation: A Realist Critique of the Newest Liberal Institutionalism," *International Organization* 42, No. 3 (Summer 1988), pp. 485–507; Stephen D. Krasner, "Global Communications and National Power: Life on the Pareto Frontier," *World Politics* 43, No. 3 (April 1991), pp. 336–66; and Robert Powell, "Absolute and Relative Gains in International Relations Theory," *American Political Science Review* 85, No. 4 (December 1991), pp. 1303–20.

20. See Michael Mastanduno, "Do Relative Gains Matter? America's Response to Japanese Industrial Policy," *International Security* 16, No. 1 (Summer 1991), pp. 73–113.

21. Waltz maintains that in Hans Morgenthau's theory, states seek power as an end in itself; thus, they are concerned with absolute power, not relative power. See Waltz, "Origins of War," pp. 40–41; and Waltz, *Theory of International Politics*, pp. 126–27.

22. Quoted in Marc Trachtenberg, *A Constructed Peace: The Making of the European Settlement, 1945–1963* (Princeton, NJ: Princeton University Press, 1999), p. 36.

23. In short, the key issue for evaluating offensive realism is not whether a state is constantly trying to conquer other countries or going all out in terms of defense spending, but whether or not great powers routinely pass up promising opportunities to gain power over rivals.

24. See Richard K. Betts, *Surprise Attack: Lessons for Defense Planning* (Washington, DC: Brookings Institution Press, 1982); James D. Fearon, "Rationalist Explanations for War," *International Organization* 49, No. 3 (Summer 1995), pp. 390–401; Robert Jervis, *The Logic of Images in International Relations* (Princeton, NJ: Princeton University Press, 1970); and Stephen Van Evera, *Causes of War: Power and the Roots of Conflict* (Ithaca, NY: Cornell University Press, 1999), pp. 45–51, 83, 137–42.

25. See Joel Achenbach, "The Experts in Retreat: After-the-Fact Explanations for the Gloomy Predictions," *Washington Post*, February 28, 1991; and Jacob Weisberg, "Gulfballs: How the Experts Blew It, Big-Time," *New Republic*, March 25, 1991.

26. Jack Snyder and Stephen Van Evera make this argument in its boldest form. See Jack Snyder, *Myths of Empire: Domestic Politics and International Ambition* (Ithaca, NY: Cornell University Press, 1991), esp. pp. 1, 307–8; and Van Evera, *Causes of War*, esp. pp. 6, 9.

27. Relatedly, some defensive realists interpret the security dilemma to say that the offensive measures a state takes to enhance its own security force rival states to respond in kind, leaving all states no better off than if they had done nothing, and possibly even worse off. See Charles L. Glaser, "The Security Dilemma Revisited," *World Politics* 50, No. 1 (October 1997), pp. 171–201.

28. Although threatened states sometimes balance efficiently against aggressors, they often do not, thereby creating opportunities for successful offense. Snyder appears to be aware of this problem, as he adds the important qualifier "at least in the long run" to his claim that "states typically form balancing alliances to resist aggressors." *Myths of Empire*, p. 11.

29. John Arquilla, *Dubious Battles: Aggression, Defeat, and the International System* (Washington, DC: Crane Russak, 1992), p. 2. Also see Bruce Bueno de Mesquita, *The War Trap* (New Haven, CT: Yale University Press, 1981), pp. 21–22; and Kevin Wang and James Ray, "Beginners and Winners: The Fate of Initiators of Interstate Wars Involving Great Powers since 1495," *International Studies Quarterly* 38, No. 1 (March 1994), pp. 139–54.

30. Although Snyder and Van Evera maintain that conquest rarely pays, both concede in subtle but important ways that aggression sometimes succeeds. Snyder, for example, distinguishes between expansion (successful offense) and overexpansion (unsuccessful offense), which is the behavior that he wants to explain. See, for example, his discussion of Japanese expansion between 1868 and 1945 in *Myths of Empire*, pp. 114–16. Van Evera allows for variation in the offense-defense balance, to include a few periods where conquest is feasible. See *Causes of War*, chap. 6. Of course, allowing for successful aggression contradicts their central claim that offense hardly ever succeeds.

31. See Robert Gilpin, *War and Change in World Politics* (Cambridge: Cambridge University Press, 1981), p. 29; and William C. Wohlforth, *The Elusive Balance: Power and Perceptions during the Cold War* (Ithaca, NY: Cornell University Press, 1993), pp. 12–14.

32. In subsequent chapters, the power-projection problems associated with large bodies of

water are taken into account when measuring the distribution of power (see Chapter 4). Those two factors are treated separately here, however, simply to highlight the profound influence that oceans have on the behavior of great powers.

33. For an opposing view, see David M. Edelstein, "Choosing Friends and Enemies: Perceptions of Intentions in International Relations," Ph.D. diss., University of Chicago, August 2000; Andrew Kydd, "Why Security Seekers Do Not Fight Each Other," *Security Studies* 7, No. 1 (Autumn 1997), pp. 114–54; and Walt, *Origins of Alliances*.

34. See note 8 in this chapter.

35. Jacob Viner, "Power versus Plenty as Objectives of Foreign Policy in the Seventeenth and Eighteenth Centuries," *World Politics* I, No. 1 (October 1948), p. 10.

36. See Mark Bowden, *Black Hawk Down: A Story of Modern War* (London: Penguin, 1999); Alison Des Forges, *"Leave None to Tell the Story": Genocide in Rwanda* (New York: Human Rights Watch, 1999), pp. 623–25; and Gerard Prunier, *The Rwanda Crisis: History of a Genocide* (New York: Columbia University Press, 1995), pp. 274–75.

37. See Scott R. Feil, *Preventing Genocide: How the Early Use of Force Might Have Succeeded in Rwanda* (New York: Carnegie Corporation, 1998); and John Mueller, "The Banality of 'Ethnic War,'" *International Security* 25, No. 1 (Summer 2000), pp. 58–62. For a less sanguine view of how many lives would have been saved had the United States intervened in Rwanda, see Alan J. Kuperman, "Rwanda in Retrospect," *Foreign Affairs* 79, No. 1 (January–February 2000), pp. 94–118.

38. See David F. Schmitz, *Thank God They're on Our Side: The United States and Right-Wing Dictatorships, 1921–1965* (Chapel Hill: University of North Carolina Press, 1999), chaps. 4–6; Gaddis Smith, *The Last Years of the Monroe Doctrine, 1945–1993* (New York: Hill and Wang, 1994); Tony Smith, *America's Mission: The United States and the Worldwide Struggle for Democracy in the Twentieth Century* (Princeton, NJ: Princeton University Press, 1994); and Stephen Van Evera, "Why Europe Matters, Why the Third World Doesn't: American Grand Strategy after the Cold War," *Journal of Strategic Studies* 13, No. 2 (June 1990), pp. 25–30.

39. Quoted in John M. Carroll and George C. Herring, eds., *Modern American Diplomacy*, rev. ed. (Wilmington, DE: Scholarly Resources, 1996), p. 122.

40. Nikita Khrushchev makes a similar point about Stalin's policy toward Chinese nationalist leader Chiang Kai-shek during World War II.

41. See Walt, *Origins of Alliances*, pp. 5, 266–68.

42. Adam Smith, *An Inquiry into the Nature and Causes of the Wealth of Nations*, ed. Edwin Cannan (Chicago: University of Chicago Press, 1976), Vol. 1, p. 487. All the quotes in this paragraph are from pp. 484–87 of that book.

43. For an overview of the Anglo-Dutch rivalry, see Jack S. Levy, "The Rise and Decline of the Anglo-Dutch Rivalry, 1609–1689," in William R. Thompson, ed., *Great Power Rivalries* (Columbia: University of South Carolina Press, 1999), pp. 172–200; and Paul M. Kennedy, *The Rise and Fall of British Naval Mastery* (London: Allen Lane, 1976), chap. 2.

44. William J. Clinton, "Address by the President to the 48th Session of the United Nations General Assembly," United Nations, New York, September 27, 1993. Also see George Bush, "Toward a New World Order: Address by the President to a Joint Session of Congress," September 11, 1990.

45. Bradley Thayer examined whether the victorious powers were able to create and maintain stable security orders in the aftermath of the Napoleonic Wars, World War I, and World War II, or whether they competed among themselves for power, as realism would predict. Thayer concludes that the rhetoric of the triumphant powers notwithstanding, they remained firmly committed to gaining power

at each other's expense. See Bradley A. Thayer, "Creating Stability in New World Orders," Ph.D. diss., University of Chicago, August 1996.

46. See Melvyn P. Leffler, *A Preponderance of Power: National Security, the Truman Administration, and the Cold War* (Stanford, CA: Stanford University Press, 1992).

47. For a discussion of American efforts to undermine Soviet control of Eastern Europe, see Peter Grose, *Operation Rollback: America's Secret War behind the Iron Curtain* (Boston: Houghton Mifflin, 2000); Walter L. Hixson, *Parting the Curtain: Propaganda, Culture, and the Cold War, 1945–1961* (New York: St. Martin's, 1997); and Gregory Mitrovich, *Undermining the Kremlin: America's Strategy to Subvert the Soviet Bloc, 1947–1956* (Ithaca, NY: Cornell University Press, 2000).

48. For a synoptic discussion of U.S. policy toward the Soviet Union in the late 1980s that cites most of the key sources on the subject, see Randall L. Schweller and William C. Wohlforth, "Power Test: Evaluating Realism in Response to the End of the Cold War," *Security Studies* 9, No. 3 (Spring 2000), pp. 91–97.

49. The editors of a major book on the Treaty of Versailles write, "The resulting reappraisal, as documented in this book, constitutes a new synthesis of peace conference scholarship. The findings call attention to divergent peace aims within the American and Allied camps and underscore the degree to which the negotiators themselves considered the Versailles Treaty a work in progress." Manfred F. Boemeke, Gerald D. Feldman, and Elisabeth Glaser, eds., *The Treaty of Versailles: A Reassessment after 75 Years* (Cambridge: Cambridge University Press, 1998), p. 1.

50. This paragraph draws heavily on Trachtenberg, *Constructed Peace*; and Marc Trachtenberg, *History and Strategy* (Princeton, NJ: Princeton University Press, 1991), chaps. 4–5. Also see G. John Ikenberry, "Rethinking the Origins of American Hegemony," *Political Sci-*

ence Quarterly 104, No. 3 (Autumn 1989), pp. 375–400.

51. The failure of American policymakers during the early Cold War to understand where the security competition in Europe was leading is summarized by Trachtenberg, "The predictions that were made pointed as a rule in the opposite direction: that Germany could not be kept down forever; that the Federal Republic would ultimately . . . want nuclear forces of her own; that U.S. troops could not be expected to remain in . . . Europe. . . . Yet all these predictions—every single one—turned out to be wrong." Trachtenberg, *History and Strategy*, pp. 231–32. Also see Trachtenberg, *Constructed Peace*, pp. vii–viii.

52. For more discussion of the pitfalls of collective security, see John J. Mearsheimer, "The False Promise of International Institutions," *International Security* 19, No. 3 (Winter 1994–95), pp. 26–37.

53. See Grieco, "Anarchy and the Limits of Cooperation," pp. 498, 500.

54. For evidence of relative gains considerations thwarting cooperation among states, see Paul W. Schroeder, *The Transformation of European Politics, 1763–1848* (Oxford: Clarendon, 1994), chap. 3.

55. Charles Lipson, "International Cooperation in Economic and Security Affairs," *World Politics* 37, No. 1 (October 1984), p. 14.

56. See Randall L. Schweller, "Bandwagoning for Profit: Bringing the Revisionist State Back In," *International Security* 19, No. 1 (Summer 1994), pp. 72–107. See also the works cited in note 59 in this chapter.

57. See Misha Glenny, *The Fall of Yugoslavia: The Third Balkan War*, 3d rev. ed. (New York: Penguin, 1996), p. 149; Philip Sherwell and Alina Petric, "Tudjman Tapes Reveal Plans to Divide Bosnia and Hide War Crimes," *Sunday Telegraph* (London), June 18, 2000; Laura Silber and Allan Little, *Yugoslavia: Death of a Nation*, rev. ed. (New York: Penguin, 1997), pp. 131–32, 213; and Warren

Zimmerman, *Origins of a Catastrophe: Yugoslavia and Its Destroyers—America's Last Ambassador Tells What Happened and Why* (New York: Times Books, 1996), pp. 116–17.

58. See John Maynard Keynes, *The Economic Consequences of the Peace* (New York: Penguin, 1988), chap. 2; and J. M. Roberts, *Europe, 1880–1945* (London: Longman, 1970), pp. 239–41.

59. For information on the Molotov-Ribbentrop Pact of August 1939 and the ensuing cooperation between those states, see Alan Bullock, *Hitler and Stalin: Parallel Lives* (London: HarperCollins, 1991), chaps. 14–15; I.C.B. Dear, ed., *The Oxford Companion to World War II* (Oxford: Oxford University Press, 1995), pp. 780–82; Anthony Read and David Fisher, *The Deadly Embrace: Hitler, Stalin, and the Nazi-Soviet Pact, 1939–1941* (New York: Norton, 1988); Geoffrey Roberts, *The Unholy Alliance: Stalin's Pact with Hitler* (Bloomington: Indiana University Press, 1989), chaps. 8–10; and Adam B. Ulam, *Expansion and Coexistence: Soviet Foreign Policy, 1917–1973*, 2d ed. (New York: Holt, Rinehart, and Winston, 1974), chap. 6.

60. Waltz maintains that structural theories can explain international outcomes—i.e., whether war is more likely in bipolar or multipolar systems—but that they cannot explain the foreign policy behavior of particular states. A separate theory of foreign policy, he argues, is needed for that task. See *Theory of International Politics*, pp. 71–72, 121–23.

MICHAEL W. DOYLE

Liberalism and World Politics

Promoting freedom will produce peace, we have often been told. In a speech before the British Parliament in June of 1982, President Reagan proclaimed that governments founded on a respect for individual liberty exercise "restraint" and "peaceful intentions" in their foreign policy. He then announced a "crusade for freedom" and a "campaign for democratic development" (Reagan, June 9, 1982).

In making these claims the president joined a long list of liberal theorists (and propagandists) and echoed an old argument: the aggressive instincts of authoritarian leaders and totalitarian ruling parties make for war. Liberal states, founded on such individual rights as equality before the law, free speech and other civil liberties, private property, and elected representation are fundamentally against war this argument asserts. When the citizens who bear the burdens of war elect their governments, wars become impossible. Furthermore, citizens appreciate that the benefits of trade can be enjoyed only under conditions of peace. Thus the very existence of liberal states, such as the U.S., Japan, and our European allies, makes for peace.

Building on a growing literature in international political science, I reexamine the liberal claim President Reagan reiterated for us. I look at three distinct theoretical traditions of liberalism, attributable to three theorists: Schumpeter,

From *American Political Science Review* 80, no. 4 (Dec. 1986): 1151–1169. The author's notes have been omitted.

a brilliant explicator of the liberal pacifism the president invoked; Machiavelli, a classical republican whose glory is an imperialism we often practice; and Kant.

Despite the contradictions of liberal pacifism and liberal imperialism, I find, with Kant and other liberal republicans, that liberalism does leave a coherent legacy on foreign affairs. Liberal states are different. They are indeed peaceful, yet they are also prone to make war, as the U.S. and our "freedom fighters" are now doing, not so covertly, against Nicaragua. Liberal states have created a separate peace, as Kant argued they would, and have also discovered liberal reasons for aggression, as he feared they might. I conclude by arguing that the differences among liberal pacifism, liberal imperialism, and Kant's liberal internationalism are not arbitrary but rooted in differing conceptions of the citizen and the state.

Liberal Pacifism

There is no canonical description of liberalism. What we tend to call *liberal* resembles a family portrait of principles and institutions, recognizable by certain characteristics—for example, individual freedom, political participation, private property, and equality of opportunity—that most liberal states share, although none has perfected them all. Joseph Schumpeter clearly fits within this family when he considers the international effects of capitalism and democracy.

Schumpeter's "Sociology of Imperialisms," published in 1919, made a coherent and sustained argument concerning the pacifying (in the sense of nonaggressive) effects of liberal institutions and principles (Schumpeter, 1955; see also Doyle, 1986, pp. 155–59). Unlike some of the earlier liberal theorists who focused on a single feature such as trade (Montesquieu, 1949, vol. I, bk. 20, chap. 1) or failed to examine critically the arguments they were advancing, Schumpeter saw the interaction of capitalism and democracy as the foundation of

liberal pacifism, and he tested his arguments in a sociology of historical imperialisms.

He defines *imperialism* as "an objectless disposition on the part of a state to unlimited forcible expansion" (Schumpeter, 1955, p. 6). Excluding imperialisms that were mere "catchwords" and those that were "object-ful" (e.g., defensive imperialism), he traces the roots of objectless imperialism to three sources, each an atavism. Modern imperialism, according to Schumpeter, resulted from the combined impact of a "war machine," warlike instincts, and export monopolism.

Once necessary, the war machine later developed a life of its own and took control of a state's foreign policy: "Created by the wars that required it, the machine now created the wars it required" (Schumpeter, 1955, p. 25). Thus, Schumpeter tells us that the army of ancient Egypt, created to drive the Hyksos out of Egypt, took over the state and pursued militaristic imperialism. Like the later armies of the courts of absolutist Europe, it fought wars for the sake of glory and booty, for the sake of warriors and monarchs—wars *gratia* warriors.

A warlike disposition, elsewhere called "instinctual elements of bloody primitivism," is the natural ideology of a war machine. It also exists independently; the Persians, says Schumpeter (1955, pp. 25–32), were a warrior nation from the outset.

Under modern capitalism, export monopolists, the third source of modern imperialism, push for imperialist expansion as a way to expand their closed markets. The absolute monarchies were the last clear-cut imperialisms. Nineteenth-century imperialisms merely represent the vestiges of the imperialisms created by Louis XIV and Catherine the Great. Thus, the export monopolists are an atavism of the absolute monarchies, for they depend completely on the tariffs imposed by the monarchs and their militaristic successors for revenue (Schumpeter, 1955, p. 82–83). Without tariffs, monopolies would be eliminated by foreign competition.

Modern (nineteenth century) imperialism, therefore, rests on an atavistic war machine, militaristic attitudes left over from the days of monarchical wars, and export monopolism, which is nothing more than the economic residue of monarchical finance. In the modern era, imperialists gratify their private interests. From the national perspective, their imperialistic wars are objectless.

Schumpeter's theme now emerges. Capitalism and democracy are forces for peace. Indeed, they are antithetical to imperialism. For Schumpeter, the further development of capitalism and democracy means that imperialism will inevitably disappear. He maintains that capitalism produces an unwarlike disposition; its populace is "democratized, individualized, rationalized" (Schumpeter, 1955, p. 68). The people's energies are daily absorbed in production. The disciplines of industry and the market train people in "economic rationalism"; the instability of industrial life necessitates calculation. Capitalism also "individualizes"; "subjective opportunities" replace the "immutable factors" of traditional, hierarchical society. Rational individuals demand democratic governance.

Democratic capitalism leads to peace. As evidence, Schumpeter claims that throughout the capitalist world an opposition has arisen to "war, expansion, cabinet diplomacy"; that contemporary capitalism is associated with peace parties; and that the industrial worker of capitalism is "vigorously anti-imperialist." In addition, he points out that the capitalist world has developed means of preventing war, such as the Hague Court and that the least feudal, most capitalist society—the United States—has demonstrated the least imperialistic tendencies (Schumpeter, 1955, pp. 95–96). An example of the lack of imperialistic tendencies in the U.S., Schumpeter thought, was our leaving over half of Mexico unconquered in the war of 1846–48.

Schumpeter's explanation for liberal pacifism is quite simple: Only war profiteers and military aristocrats gain from wars. No democracy would pursue a minority interest and tolerate the high costs of imperialism. When free trade prevails, "no class" gains from forcible expansion because

> foreign raw materials and food stuffs are as accessible to each nation as though they were in its own territory. Where the cultural backwardness of a region makes normal economic intercourse dependent on colonization it does not matter, assuming free trade, which of the "civilized" nations undertakes the task of colonization. (Schumpeter, 1955, pp. 75–76)

Schumpeter's arguments are difficult to evaluate. In partial tests of quasi-Schumpeterian propositions, Michael Haas (1974, pp. 464–65) discovered a cluster that associates democracy, development, and sustained modernization with peaceful conditions. However, M. Small and J. D. Singer (1976) have discovered that there is no clearly negative correlation between democracy and war in the period 1816–1965—the period that would be central to Schumpeter's argument (see also Wilkenfeld, 1968, Wright, 1942, p. 841).

* * * A recent study by R. J. Rummel (1983) of "libertarianism" and international violence is the closest test Schumpeterian pacifism has received. "Free" states (those enjoying political and economic freedom) were shown to have considerably less conflict at or above the level of economic sanctions than "nonfree" states. The free states, the partly free states (including the democratic socialist countries such as Sweden), and the nonfree states accounted for 24%, 26%, and 61%, respectively, of the international violence during the period examined.

These effects are impressive but not conclusive for the Schumpeterian thesis. The data are limited, in this test, to the period 1976 to 1980. It includes, for example, the Russo-Afghan War, the Vietnamese invasion of Cambodia, China's invasion of Vietnam, and Tanzania's invasion of Uganda but just misses the U.S., quasi-covert intervention in Angola (1975) and our not so covert war against Nicaragua (1981–). More importantly, it excludes the cold war period, with its numerous interventions, and the long history of colonial wars (the Boer War, the Spanish-American War, the Mexican Intervention, etc.) that marked the history of liberal, including democratic capitalist, states (Doyle, 1983b; Chan, 1984; Weede, 1984).

The discrepancy between the warlike history of liberal states and Schumpeter's pacifistic expectations highlights three extreme assumptions. First, his "materialistic monism" leaves little room for noneconomic objectives, whether espoused by states or individuals. Neither glory, nor prestige, nor ideological justification, nor the pure power of ruling shapes policy. These nonmaterial goals leave little room for positive-sum gains, such as the comparative advantages of trade. Second, and relatedly, the same is true for his states. The political life of individuals seems to have been homogenized at the same time as the individuals were "rationalized, individualized, and democratized." Citizens—capitalists and workers, rural and urban—seek material welfare. Schumpeter seems to presume that ruling makes no difference. He also presumes that no one is prepared to take those measures (such as stirring up foreign quarrels to preserve a domestic ruling coalition) that enhance one's political power, despite deterimental effects on mass welfare. Third, like domestic politics, world politics are homogenized. Materially monistic and democratically capitalist, all states evolve toward free trade and liberty together. Countries differently constituted seem to disappear from Schumpeter's analysis. "Civilized" nations govern "culturally backward" *regions*. These assumptions are not shared by Machiavelli's theory of liberalism.

Liberal Imperialism

Machiavelli argues, not only that republics are not pacifistic, but that they are the best form of state for imperial expansion. Establishing a republic fit for imperial expansion is, moreover, the best way to guarantee the survival of a state.

Machiavelli's republic is a classical mixed republic. It is not a democracy—which he thought would quickly degenerate into a tyranny—but is characterized by social equality, popular liberty, and political participation (Machiavelli, 1950, bk. 1, chap. 2, p. 112; see also Huliung, 1983, chap. 2; Mansfield, 1970; Pocock, 1975, pp. 198–99; Skinner, 1981, chap. 3). The consuls serve as "kings," the senate as an aristocracy managing the state, and the people in the assembly as the source of strength.

Liberty results from "disunion"—the competition and necessity for compromise required by the division of powers among senate, consuls, and tribunes (the last representing the common people). Liberty also results from the popular veto. The powerful few threaten the rest with tyranny, Machiavelli says, because they seek to dominate. The mass demands not to be dominated, and their veto thus preserves the liberties of the state (Machiavelli, 1950, bk. 1, chap. 5, p. 122). However, since the people and the rulers have different social characters, the people need to be "managed" by the few to avoid having their recklessness overturn or their fecklessness undermine the ability of the state to expand (Machiavelli, 1950, bk. 1, chap. 53, pp. 249–50). Thus the senate and the consuls plan expansion, consult oracles, and employ religion to manage the resources that the energy of the people supplies.

Strength, and then imperial expansion, results from the way liberty encourages increased population and property, which grow when the citizens know their lives and goods are secure from arbitrary seizure. Free citizens equip large armies and provide soldiers who fight for public glory and the common good because these are, in fact, their own (Machiavelli, 1950, bk. 2, chap. 2, pp. 287–90). If you seek the honor of having your state expand, Machiavelli advises, you should organize it as a free and popular republic like Rome, rather than as an aristocratic republic like Sparta or Venice. Expansion thus calls for a free republic.

"Necessity"—political survival—calls for expansion. If a stable aristocratic republic is forced by foreign conflict "to extend her territory, in such a case we shall see her foundations give way and herself quickly brought to ruin"; if, on the other hand, domestic security prevails, "the continued tranquility would enervate her, or provoke internal disensions, which together, or either of them separately, will apt to prove her ruin" (Machiavelli, 1950, bk. 1, chap. 6, p. 129). Machiavelli therefore believes it is necessary to take the constitution of Rome, rather than that of Sparta or Venice, as our model.

Hence, this belief leads to liberal imperialism. We are lovers of glory, Machiavelli announces. We seek to rule or, at least, to avoid being oppressed. In either case, we want more for ourselves and our states than just material welfare (materialistic monism). Because other states with similar aims thereby threaten us, we prepare ourselves for expansion. Because our fellow citizens threaten us if we do not allow them either to satisfy their ambition or to release their political energies through imperial expansion, we expand.

There is considerable historical evidence for liberal imperialism. Machiavelli's (Polybius's) Rome and Thucydides' Athens both were imperial republics in the Machiavellian sense (Thucydides, 1954, bk. 6). The historical record of numerous U.S. interventions in the postwar period supports Machiavelli's argument (* * * Barnet, 1968, chap. 11), but the current record of liberal pacifism, weak as it is, calls some of his insights into question. To the extent that the modern populace actually controls (and thus unbalances) the mixed republic, its diffidence may outweigh elite ("senatorial") aggressiveness.

We can conclude either that (1) liberal pacifism has at least taken over with the further development of capitalist democracy, as Schumpeter predicted it would or that (2) the mixed record of liberalism—pacifism and imperialism—indicates that some liberal states are Schumpeterian democracies while others are Machiavellian republics. Before we accept either conclusion, however, we must consider a third apparent regularity of modern world politics.

Liberal Internationalism

Modern liberalism carries with it two legacies. They do not affect liberal states separately, according to whether they are pacifistic or imperialistic, but simultaneously.

The first of these legacies is the pacification of foreign relations among liberal states. * * *

Beginning in the eighteenth century and slowly growing since then, a zone of peace, which Kant called the "pacific federation" or "pacific union," has begun to be established among liberal societies. More than 40 liberal states currently make up the union. Most are in Europe and North America, but they can be found on every continent, as Appendix 1 indicates.

Here the predictions of liberal pacifists (and President Reagan) are borne out: liberal states do exercise peaceful restraint, and a separate peace exists among them. This separate peace provides a solid foundation for the United States' crucial alliances with the liberal powers, e.g., the North Atlantic Treaty Organization and our Japanese alliance. This foundation appears to be impervious to the quarrels with our allies that bedeviled the Carter and Reagan administrations. It also offers the promise of a continuing peace among liberal states, and as the number of liberal states increases, it announces the possibility of global peace this side of the grave or world conquest.

Of course, the probability of the outbreak of war in any given year between any two given states is low. The occurrence of a war between any two adjacent states, considered over a long period of time, would be more probable. The apparent absence of war between liberal states, whether adjacent or not, for almost 200 years thus may have significance. Similar claims cannot be made for feudal, fascist, communist, authoritarian, or totalitarian forms of rule (Doyle, 1983a, pp. 222), nor for pluralistic or merely similar societies. More significant perhaps is that when states are forced to decide on which side of an impending world war they will fight, liberal states all wind up on the same side despite the complexity of the paths that take them there. These characteristics do not prove that the peace among liberals is statistically significant nor that liberalism is the sole valid explanation for the peace. They do suggest that we consider the possibility that liberals have indeed established a separate peace—but only among themselves.

Liberalism also carries with it a second legacy: international "imprudence" (Hume, 1963, pp. 346–47). Peaceful restraint only seems to work in liberals' relations with other liberals. Liberal states have fought numerous wars with nonliberal states. (For a list of international wars since 1816 see Appendix 2.)

Many of these wars have been defensive and thus prudent by necessity. Liberal states have been attacked and threatened by nonliberal states that do not exercise any special restraint in their dealings with the liberal states. Authoritarian rulers both stimulate and respond to an international political environment in which conflicts of prestige, interest, and pure fear of what other states might do all lead states toward war. War and conquest have thus characterized the careers of many authoritarian rulers and ruling parties, from Louis XIV and Napoleon to Mussolini's fascists, Hitler's Nazis, and Stalin's communists.

Yet we cannot simply blame warfare on the authoritarians or totalitarians, as many of our more enthusiastic politicians would have us do. Most wars arise out of calculations and miscalculations of interest, misunderstandings, and mutual suspicions, such as those that characterized the origins of World War I. However, aggression by the liberal state has also characterized a large number of wars. Both France and Britain fought expansionist colonial wars throughout the nineteenth century. The United States fought a similar war with Mexico from 1846 to 1848, waged a war of annihilation against the American Indians, and intervened militarily against sovereign states many times before and after World War II. Liberal states invade weak nonliberal states and display striking distrust in dealings with powerful nonliberal states (Doyle, 1983b).

Neither realist (statist) nor Marxist theory accounts well for these two legacies. While they can account for aspects of certain periods of international stability (* * * Russett, 1985), neither the logic of the balance of power nor the logic of international hegemony explains the separate peace maintained for more than 150 years among states sharing one particular form of governance—liberal principles and institutions. Balance-of-power theory expects—indeed is premised upon—flexible arrangements of geostrategic rivalry that include preventive war. Hegemonies wax and wane, but the liberal peace holds. Marxist "ultra-imperialists" expect a form of peaceful rivalry among capitalists, but only liberal capitalists maintain peace. Leninists expect liberal capitalists to be aggressive toward nonliberal states, but they also (and especially) expect them to be imperialistic toward fellow liberal capitalists.

Kant's theory of liberal internationalism helps us understand these two legacies. * * * *Perpetual Peace*, written in 1795 (Kant, 1970, pp. 93–130), helps us understand the interactive nature of international relations. Kant tries to teach us methodologically that we can study neither the systemic relations of states nor the varieties of state behavior in isolation from each other. Substantively, he anticipates for us the ever-widening pacification of a liberal pacific union, explains this pacification, and at the same time suggests why liberal states are not pacific in their relations with nonliberal states. Kant argues that perpetual peace will be guaranteed by the ever-widening acceptance of three "definitive articles" of peace. When all nations have accepted the definitive articles in a metaphorical "treaty" of perpetual peace he asks them to sign, perpetual peace will have been established.

The First Definitive Article requires the civil constitution of the state to be republican. By *republican* Kant means a political society that has solved the problem of combining moral autonomy, individualism, and social order. A private property and market-oriented economy partially addressed that dilemma in the private sphere. The public, or political, sphere was more troubling. His answer was a republic that preserved juridical freedom—the legal equality of citizens as subjects—on the basis of a representative government with a separation of powers. Juridical freedom is preserved because the morally autonomous individual is by means of representation a self-legislator making laws that apply to all citizens equally, including himself or herself. Tyranny is avoided because the individual is subject to laws he or she does not also administer (Kant, *PP* [*Perpetual Peace*], pp. 99–102 * * *).

Liberal republics will progressively establish peace among themselves by means of the pacific federation, or union (*foedus pacificum*), described in Kant's Second Definitive Article. The pacific union will establish peace within a federation of free states and securely maintain the rights of each state. The world will not have achieved the "perpetual peace" that provides the ultimate guarantor of republican freedom until "a late stage and after many unsuccessful attempts" (Kant, *UH* [*The Idea for a Universal History with a Cosmopolitan Purpose*], p. 47). At that time, all nations will have learned the lessons of peace through right conceptions of the appropriate constitution, great and sad experience, and good will. Only then will individuals enjoy perfect republican rights or the full guarantee of a global and just peace. In the meantime, the "pacific federation" of liberal republics—"an enduring and gradually expanding federation likely to prevent war"—brings within it more and more republics—despite republican collapses, backsliding, and disastrous wars—creating an ever-expanding separate peace (Kant, *PP*, p. 105). Kant emphasizes that

> it can be shown that this idea of federalism, extending gradually to encompass all states and thus leading to perpetual peace, is practicable and has objective reality. For if by good fortune one powerful and enlightened nation can form a republic (which is by nature inclined to seek peace), this

will provide a focal point for federal association among other states. These will join up with the first one, thus securing the freedom of each state in accordance with the idea of international right, and the whole will gradually spread further and further by a series of alliances of this kind. (Kant, *PP*, p. 104)

The pacific union is not a single peace treaty ending one war, a world state, nor a state of nations. Kant finds the first insufficient. The second and third are impossible or potentially tyrannical. National sovereignty precludes reliable subservience to a state of nations; a world state destroys the civic freedom on which the development of human capacities rests (Kant, *UH*, p. 50). Although Kant obliquely refers to various classical interstate confederations and modern diplomatic congresses, he develops no systematic organizational embodiment of this treaty and presumably does not find institutionalization necessary (Riley, 1983, chap. 5; Schwarz, 1962, p. 77). He appears to have in mind a mutual nonaggression pact, perhaps a collective security agreement, and the cosmopolitan law set forth in the Third Definitive Article.

The Third Definitive Article establishes a cosmopolitan law to operate in conjunction with the pacific union. The cosmopolitan law "shall be limited to conditions of universal hospitality." In this Kant calls for the recognition of the "right of a foreigner not to be treated with hostility when he arrives on someone else's territory." This "does not extend beyond those conditions which make it possible for them [foreigners] to attempt to enter into relations [commerce] with the native inhabitants" (Kant, *PP*, p. 106). Hospitality does not require extending to foreigners either the right to citizenship or the right to settlement, unless the foreign visitors would perish if they were expelled. Foreign conquest and plunder also find no justification under this right. Hospitality does appear to include the right of access and the obligation of maintaining the opportunity for citizens to exchange goods and ideas without imposing the obligation to trade (a voluntary act in all cases under liberal constitutions).

Perpetual peace, for Kant, is an epistemology, a condition for ethical action, and, most importantly, an explanation of how the "mechanical process of nature visibly exhibits the purposive plan of producing concord among men, even against their will and indeed by means of their very discord" (Kant, *PP*, p. 108; *UH*, pp. 44–45). Understanding history requires an epistemological foundation, for without a teleology, such as the promise of perpetual peace, the complexity of history would overwhelm human understanding (Kant, *UH*, pp. 51–53). Perpetual peace, however, is not merely a heuristic device with which to interpret history. It is guaranteed, Kant explains in the "First Addition" to *Perpetual Peace* ("On the Guarantee of Perpetual Peace"), to result from men fulfilling their ethical duty or, failing that, from a hidden plan. Peace is an ethical duty because it is only under conditions of peace that all men can treat each other as ends, rather than means to an end (Kant, *UH*, p. 50; Murphy, 1970, chap. 3). * * *

In the end, however, our guarantee of perpetual peace does not rest on ethical conduct. * * * The guarantee thus rests, Kant argues, not on the probable behavior of moral angels, but on that of "devils, so long as they possess understanding" (*PP*, p. 112). In explaining the sources of each of the three definitive articles of the perpetual peace, Kant then tells us how we (as free and intelligent devils) could be motivated by fear, force, and calculated advantage to undertake a course of action whose outcome we could reasonably anticipate to be perpetual peace. Yet while it is possible to conceive of the Kantian road to peace in these terms, Kant himself recognizes and argues that social evolution also makes the conditions of moral behavior less onerous and hence more likely (*CF* [*The Contest of Faculties*], pp. 187–89; Kelly, 1969, pp. 106–13). In tracing the effects of both political and moral development, he builds an account of why liberal states do maintain peace among themselves and of how it will (by implication, has) come

about that the pacific union will expand. He also explains how these republics would engage in wars with nonrepublics and therefore suffer the "sad experience" of wars that an ethical policy might have avoided.

* * *

Kant shows how republics, once established, lead to peaceful relations. He argues that once the aggressive interests of absolutist monarchies are tamed and the habit of respect for individual rights engrained by republican government, wars would appear as the disaster to the people's welfare that he and the other liberals thought them to be. The fundamental reason is this:

> If, as is inevitability the case under this constitution, the consent of the citizens is required to decide whether or not war should be declared, it is very natural that they will have a great hesitation in embarking on so dangerous an enterprise. For this would mean calling down on themselves all the miseries of war, such as doing the fighting themselves, supplying the costs of the war from their own resources, painfully making good the ensuing devastation, and, as the crowning evil, having to take upon themselves a burden of debts which will embitter peace itself and which can never be paid off on account of the constant threat of new wars. But under a constitution where the subject is not a citizen, and which is therefore not republican, it is the simplest thing in the world to go to war. For the head of state is not a fellow citizen, but the owner of the state, and war will not force him to make the slightest sacrifice so far as his banquets, hunts, pleasure palaces and court festivals are concerned. He can thus decide on war, without any significant reason, as a kind of amusement, and unconcernedly leave it to the diplomatic corps (who are always ready for such proposes) to justify the war for the sake of propriety. (Kant, *PP*, p. 100).

Yet these domestic republican restraints do not end war. If they did, liberal states would not be warlike, which is far from the case. They do introduce republican caution—Kant's "hesitation"—in place of monarchical caprice. Liberal wars are only fought for popular, liberal purposes. The historical liberal legacy is laden with popular wars fought to promote freedom, to protect private property, or to support liberal allies against nonliberal enemies. Kant's position is ambiguous. He regards these wars as unjust and warns liberals of their susceptibility to them (Kant, *PP*, p. 106). At the same time, Kant argues that each nation "can and ought to" demand that its neighboring nations enter into the pacific union of liberal states (*PP*, p. 102). * * *

* * *

* * * As republics emerge (the first source) and as culture progresses, an understanding of the legitimate rights of all citizens and of all republics comes into play; and this, now that caution characterizes policy, sets up the moral foundations for the liberal peace. Correspondingly, international law highlights the importance of Kantian publicity. Domestically, publicity helps ensure that the officials of republics act according to the principles they profess to hold just and according to the interests of the electors they claim to represent. Internationally, free speech and the effective communication of accurate conceptions of the political life of foreign peoples is essential to establishing and preserving the understanding on which the guarantee of respect depends. Domestically just republics, which rest on consent, then presume foreign republics also to be consensual, just, and therefore deserving of accommodation. * * * Because nonliberal governments are in a state of aggression with their own people, their foreign relations become for liberal governments deeply suspect. In short, fellow liberals benefit from a presumption of amity; nonliberals suffer from a presumption of enmity. Both presumptions may be accurate; each, however, may also be self-confirming.

Lastly, cosmopolitan law adds material incentives to moral commitments. The cosmopolitan right to hospitality permits the "spirit of commerce" sooner or later to take hold of every nation, thus impelling states to promote peace and to try to avert war. Liberal economic theory holds that these cosmopolitan ties derive from a cooperative international division of labor and free trade according to comparative advantage. Each economy is said to be better off than it would have been under autarky; each thus acquires an incentive to avoid policies that would lead the other to break these economic ties. Because keeping open markets rests upon the assumption that the next set of transactions will also be determined by prices rather than coercion, a sense of mutual security is vital to avoid security-motivated searches for economic autarky. Thus, avoiding a challenge to another liberal state's security or even enhancing each other's security by means of alliance naturally follows economic interdependence.

A further cosmopolitan source of liberal peace is the international market's removal of difficult decisions of production and distribution from the direct sphere of state policy. A foreign state thus does not appear directly responsible for these outcomes, and states can stand aside from, and to some degree above, these contentious market rivalries and be ready to step in to resolve crises. The interdependence of commerce and the international contacts of state officials help create crosscutting transnational ties that serve as lobbies for mutual accommodation. According to modern liberal scholars, international financiers and transnational and transgovernmental organizations create interests in favor of accommodation. Moreover, their variety has ensured that no single conflict sours an entire relationship by setting off a spiral of reciprocated retaliation * * *. Conversely, a sense of suspicion, such as that characterizing relations between liberal and nonliberal governments, can lead to restrictions on the range of contacts between societies, and this can increase the prospect that a single conflict will determine an entire relationship.

No single constitutional, international, or cosmopolitan source is alone sufficient, but together (and only together) they plausibly connect the characteristics of liberal polities and economies with sustained liberal peace. Alliances founded on mutual strategic interest among liberal and nonliberal states have been broken; economic ties between liberal and nonliberal states have proven fragile; but the political bonds of liberal rights and interests have proven a remarkably firm foundation for mutual nonaggression. A separate peace exists among liberal states.

In their relations with nonliberal states, however, liberal states have not escaped from the insecurity caused by anarchy in the world political system considered as a whole. Moreover, the very constitutional restraint, international respect for individual rights, and shared commercial interests that establish grounds for peace among liberal states establish grounds for additional conflict in relations between liberal and nonliberal societies.

Conclusion

Kant's liberal internationalism, Machiavelli's liberal imperialism, and Schumpeter's liberal pacifism rest on fundamentally different views of the nature of the human being, the state, and international relations. Schumpeter's humans are rationalized, individualized, and democratized. They are also homogenized, pursuing material interests "monistically." Because their material interests lie in peaceful trade, they and the democratic state that these fellow citizens control are pacifistic. Machiavelli's citizens are splendidly diverse in their goals but fundamentally unequal in them as well, seeking to rule or fearing being dominated. Extending the rule of the dominant elite or avoiding the political collapse of their state, each calls for imperial expansion.

Kant's citizens, too, are diverse in their goals and individualized and rationalized, but most importantly, they are capable of appreciating the moral equality of all individuals and of treating other individuals as ends rather than as means. The Kantian state thus is governed publicly according to law, as a republic. Kant's is the state that solves the problem of governing individualized equals, whether they are the "rational devils" he says we often find ourselves to be or the ethical agents we can and should become. Republics tell us that

> in order to organize a group of rational beings who together require universal laws for their survival, but of whom each separate individual is secretly inclined to exempt himself from them, the constitution must be so designed so that, although the citizens are opposed to one another in their private attitudes, these opposing views may inhibit one another in such a way that the public conduct of the citizens will be the same as if they did not have such evil attitudes. (Kant, *PP*, p. 113)

Unlike Machiavelli's republics, Kant's republics are capable of achieving peace among themselves because they exercise democratic caution and are capable of appreciating the international rights of foreign republics. These international rights of republics derive from the representation of foreign individuals, who are our moral equals. Unlike Schumpeter's capitalist democracies, Kant's republics—including our own—remain in a state of war with nonrepublics. Liberal republics see themselves as threatened by aggression from nonrepublics that are not constrained by representation. Even though wars often cost more than the economic return they generate, liberal republics also are prepared to protect and promote—sometimes forcibly—democracy, private property, and the rights of individuals overseas against nonrepublics, which, because they do not authentically represent the rights of individuals, have no rights to noninterference. These wars may liberate oppressed individuals overseas; they also can generate enormous suffering.

* * *

Perpetual peace, Kant says, is the end point of the hard journey his republics will take. The promise of perpetual peace, the violent lessons of war, and the experience of a partial peace are proof of the need for and the possibility of world peace. They are also the grounds for moral citizens and statesmen to assume the duty of striving for peace.

APPENDIX 1		
LIBERAL REGIMES AND THE PACIFIC UNION, 1700–1982		
Period	*Period*	*Period*
18th Century	Argentina, 1880–	Mexico, 1928–
Swiss Cantons[a]	Chile, 1891–	Lebanon, 1944–
French Republie, 1790–	Total=13	Total=29
1795		
United States,[a] 1776–	1900–1945	1945–[b]
Total=3	Switzerland	Switzerland
	United States	United States
1800–1850	Great Britain	Great Britain
Swiss Confederation	Sweden	Sweden
United States	Canada	Canada
France, 1830–1849	Greece, –1911; 1928–1936	Australia
Belgium, 1830–	Italy, –1922	New Zealand
1800–1850 (cont.)	Belgium, –1940	Finland
Great Britain,	Netherlands, –1940	Ireland
1832–	Argentina, –1943	Mexico
Netherlands, 1848–	France, –1940	Uruguay, –1973
Piedmont, 1848–	Chile, –1924; 1932–	Chile, –1973
Denmark, 1849–	Australia, 1901	Lebanon, –1975
Total=8	Norway, 1905–1940	Costa Rica, –1948; 1953–
	New Zealand, 1907–	Iceland, 1944–
1850–1900	Colombia, 1910–1949	France, 1945–
Switzerland	Denmark, 1914–1940	Denmark, 1945
United States	Poland, 1917–1935	Norway, 1945
Belgium	Latvia, 1922–1934	Austria, 1945–
Great Britain	Germany, 1918–1932	Brazil, 1945–1954; 1955–1964
Netherlands	Austria, 1918–1934	Belgium, 1946–
Piedmont, –1861	Estonia, 1919–1934	Luxembourg, 1946–
Italy, 1861–	Finland, 1919–	Netherlands, 1946–
Denmark, –1866	Uruguay, 1919–	Italy, 1946–
Sweden, 1864–	Costa Rica, 1919–	Philippines, 1946–1972
Greece, 1864–	Czechosovakia,	India, 1947–1975; 1977–
Canada, 1867–	1920–1939	Sri Lanka, 1948–1961;
France, 1871–	Ireland, 1920–	1963–1971; 1978–

(continued)

APPENDIX 1 *(continued)*

1945–(cont.)
  Ecuador, 1948–1963; 1979–
  Israel, 1949–
  West Germany, 1949–
  Greece, 1950–1967; 1975–
  Peru, 1950–1962; 1963–
    1968; 1980–
  El Salvador, 1950–1961
  Turkey, 1950–1960;
    1966–1971

Japan, 1951–
Bolivia, 1956–1969; 1982–
Colombia, 1958–
Venezuela, 1959–
Nigeria, 1961–1964;
1979–1984
Jamaica, 1962–
Trinidad and Tobago, 1962–
Senegal, 1963–

Malaysia, 1963–
Botswana, 1966–
Singapore, 1965–
Portugal, 1976–
Spain, 1978–
Dominican Republic, 1978–
Honduras, 1981–
Papua New Guinea, 1982–
  Total=50

NOTE: I have drawn up this approximate list of "Liberal Regimes" according to the four institutions Kant described as essential: market and private property economies; politics that are externally sovereign; citizens who possess juridical rights; and "republican" (whether republican or parliamentary monarchy), representative government. This latter includes the requirement that the legislative branch have an effective role in public policy and be formally and competitively (either inter- or intra-party) elected. Furthermore, I have taken into account whether male suffrage is wide (i.e., 30%) or, as Kant (*MM* [*The Metaphysics of Morals*], p. 139) would have had it, open by "achievement" to inhabitants of the national or metropolitan territory (e.g., to poll-tax payers or householders). This list of liberal regimes is thus more inclusive than a list of democratic regimes, or polyarchies (Powell, 1982, p. 5). Other conditions taken into account here are that female suffrage is granted within a generation of its being demanded by an extensive female suffrage movement and that representative government is internally sovereign (e.g., including, and especially over military and foreign affairs) as well as stable (in existence for at least three years). Sources for these data are Banks and Overstreet (1983), Gastil (1985), *The Europa Yearbook, 1985* (1985), Langer (1968), U.K. Foreign and Commonwealth Office (1980), and U.S. Department of State (1981). Finally, these lists exclude ancient and medieval "republics," since none appears to fit Kant's commitment to liberal individualism (Holmes, 1979).

[a]There are domestic variations within these liberal regimes: Switzerland was liberal only in certain cantons; the United States was liberal only north of the Mason-Dixon line until 1865, when it became liberal throughout.

[b]Selected list, excludes liberal regimes with populations less than one million. These include all states categorized as "free" by Gastil and those "partly free" (four-fifths or more free) states with a more pronounced capitalist orientation.

APPENDIX 2

INTERNATIONAL WARS LISTED CHRONOLOGICALLY

British-Maharattan (1817–1818)
Greek (1821–1828)
Franco-Spanish (1823)
First Anglo-Burmese (1823–1826)
Javanese (1825–1830)
Russo-Persian (1826–1828)
Russo-Turkish (1828–1829)
First Polish (1831)

First Syrian (1831–1832)
Texas (1835–1836)
First British-Afghan (1838–1842)
Second Syrian (1839–1940)
Franco-Algerian (1839–1847)
Peruvian-Bolivian (1841)
First British-Sikh (1845–1846)
Mexican-American (1846–1848)

(continued)

APPENDIX 2 *(continued)*

Austro-Sardinian (1848–1849)
First Schleswig-Holstein (1848–1849)
Hungarian (1848–1849)
Second British-Sikh (1848–1849)
Roman Republic (1849)
La Plata (1851–1852)
First Turco-Montenegran (1852–1853)
Crimean (1853–1856)
Anglo-Persian (1856–1857)
Sepoy (1857–1859)
Second Turco-Montenegran (1858–1859)
Italian Unification (1859)
Spanish-Moroccan (1859–1860)
Italo-Roman (1860)
Italo-Sicilian (1860–1861)
Franco-Mexican (1862–1867)
Ecuadorian-Colombian (1863)
Second Polish (1863–1864)
Spanish-Santo Dominican (1863–1865)
Second Schleswig-Holstein (1864)
Lopez (1864–1870)
Spanish-Chilean (1865–1866)
Seven Weeks (1866)
Ten Years (1868–1878)
Franco-Prussian (1870–1871)
Dutch-Achinese (1873–1878)
Balkan (1875–1877)
Russo-Turkish (1877–1878)
Bosnian (1878)
Second British-Afghan (1878–1880)
Pacific (1879–1883)
British-Zulu (1879)
Franco-Indochinese (1882–1884)
Mahdist (1882–1885)
Sino-French (1884–1885)
Central American (1885)
Serbo-Bulgarian (1885)
Sino-Japanese (1894–1895)
Franco-Madagascan (1894–1895)
Cuban (1895–1898)
Italo-Ethiopian (1895–1896)
First Philippine (1896–1898)
Greco-Turkish (1897)
Spanish-American (1898)
Second Philippine (1899–1902)
Boer (1899–1902)

Boxer Rebellion (1900)
Ilinden (1903)
Vietnamese-Cambodian (1975–)
Timor (1975–)
Saharan (1975–)
Ogaden (1976–)
Russo-Japanese (1904–1905)
Central American (1906)
Central American (1907)
Spanish-Moroccan (1909–1910)
Italo-Turkish (1911–1912)
First Balkan (1912–1913)
Second Balkan (1913)
World War I (1914–1918)
Russian Nationalities (1917–1921)
Russo-Polish (1919–1920)
Hungarian-Allies (1919)
Greco-Turkish (1919–1922)
Riffian (1921–1926)
Druze (1925–1927)
Sino-Soviet (1929)
Manchurian (1931–1933)
Chaco (1932–1935)
Italo-Ethiopian (1935–1936)
Sino-Japanese (1937–1941)
Changkufeng (1938)
Nomohan (1939)
World War II (1939–1945)
Russo-Finnish (1939–1940)
Franco-Thai (1940–1941)
Indonesian (1945–1946)
Indochinese (1945–1954)
Madagascan (1947–1948)
First Kashmir (1947–1949)
Palestine (1948–1949)
Hyderabad (1948)
Korean (1950–1953)
Algerian (1954–1962)
Russo-Hungarian (1956)
Sinai (1956)
Tibetan (1956–1959)
Sino-Indian (1962)
Vietnamese (1965–1975)
Second Kashmir (1965)
Six Day (1967)
Israeli-Egyptian (1969–1970)

(continued)

APPENDIX 2 *(continued)*	
Football (1969)	Ethiopian-Eritrean (1974–)
Bangladesh (1971)	Ugandan-Tanzanian (1978–1979)
Philippine-MNLF (1972–)	Sino-Vietnamese (1979)
Yom Kippur (1973)	Russo-Afghan (1979–)
Turco-Cypriot (1974)	Iran-Iraqi (1980–)

NOTE: This table is taken from Melvin Small and J. David Singer (1982, pp. 79–80). This is a partial list of international wars fought between 1816 and 1980. In Appendices A and B, Small and Singer identify a total of 575 wars during this period, but approximately 159 of them appear to be largely domestic, or civil wars.

This list excludes covert interventions, some of which have been directed by liberal regimes against other liberal regimes—for example, the United States' effort to destabilize the Chilean election and Allende's government. Nonetheless, it is significant that such interventions are not pursued publicly as acknowledged policy. The covert destabilization campaign against Chile is recounted by the Senate Select Committee to Study Governmental Operations with Respect to Intelligence Activities (1975, *Covert Action in Chile, 1963–73*).

Following the argument of this article, this list also excludes civil wars. Civil wars differ from international wars, not in the ferocity of combat, but in the issues that engender them. Two nations that could abide one another as independent neighbors separated by a border might well be the fiercest of enemies if forced to live together in one state, jointly deciding how to raise and spend taxes, choose leaders, and legislate fundamental questions of value. Notwithstanding these differences, no civil wars that I recall upset the argument of liberal pacification.

REFERENCES

Banks, Arthur, and William Overstreet, eds. 1983. *A Political Handbook of the World; 1982–1983*. New York: McGraw Hill.

Barnet, Richard. 1968. *Intervention and Revolution*. Cleveland: World Publishing Co.

Chan, Steve. 1984. Mirror, Mirror on the Wall . . . : Are Freer Countries More Pacific? *Journal of Conflict Resolution*, 28:617–48.

Doyle, Michael W. 1983a. Kant, Liberal Legacies, and Foreign Affairs: Part 1. *Philosophy and Public Affairs*, 12:205–35.

Doyle, Michael W. 1983b. Kant, Liberal Legacies, and Foreign Affairs: Part 2. *Philosophy and Public Affairs*, 12:323–53.

Doyle, Michael W. 1986. *Empires*. Ithaca: Cornell University Press.

The Europa Yearbook for 1985. 1985. 2 vols. London: Europa Publications.

Gastil, Raymond. 1985. The Comparative Survey of Freedom 1985. *Freedom at Issue*, 82:3–16.

Haas, Michael. 1974. *International Conflict*. New York: Bobbs-Merrill.

Holmes, Stephen. 1979. Aristippus in and out of Athens. *American Political Science Review*, 73:113–28.

Huliung, Mark. 1983. *Citizen Machiavelli*. Princeton: Princeton University Press.

Hume, David. 1963. Of the Balance of Power. *Essays: Moral, Political, and Literary*. Oxford: Oxford University Press.

Kant, Immanuel. 1970. *Kant's Political Writings*. Hans Reiss, ed. H. B. Nisbet, trans. Cambridge: Cambridge University Press.

Kelly, George A. 1969. *Idealism, Politics, and History*. Cambridge: Cambridge University Press.

Langer, William L., ed. 1968. *The Encyclopedia of World History*. Boston: Houghton Mifflin.

Machiavelli, Niccolo. 1950. *The Prince and the Discourses*. Max Lerner, ed. Luigi Ricci and Christian Detmold, trans. New York: Modern Library.

Mansfield, Harvey C. 1970. Machiavelli's New Regime. *Italian Quarterly*, 13:63–95.

Montesquieu, Charles de. 1949. *Spirit of the Laws*. New York: Hafner. (Originally published in 1748.)

Murphy, Jeffrie. 1970. *Kant: The Philosophy of Right*. New York: St. Martins.

Pocock, J. G. A. 1975. *The Machiavellian Moment*. Princeton: Princeton University Press.

Powell, G. Bingham. 1982. *Contemporary Democracies*. Cambridge, MA: Harvard University Press.

Reagan, Ronald. June 9, 1982. Address to Parliament. *New York Times*.

Riley, Patrick. 1983. *Kant's Political Philosophy*. Totowa, NJ: Rowman and Littlefield.

Rummel, Rudolph J. 1983. Libertarianism and International Violence. *Journal of Conflict Resolution*, 27:27–71.

Russett, Bruce. 1985. The Mysterious Case of Vanishing Hegemony. *International Organization*, 39:207–31.

Schumpeter, Joseph. 1955. The Sociology of Imperialism. In *Imperialism and Social Classes*. Cleveland: World Publishing Co. (Essay originally published in 1919.)

Schwarz, Wolfgang. 1962. Kant's Philosophy of Law and International Peace. *Philosophy and Phenomenonological Research*, 23:71–80.

Skinner, Quentin. 1981. *Machiavelli*. New York: Hill and Wang.

Small, Melvin, and J. David Singer. 1976. The War-Proneness of Democratic Regimes. *The Jerusalem Journal of International Relations*, 1(4):50–69.

Small, Melvin, and J. David Singer. 1982. *Resort to Arms*. Beverly Hills: Sage Publications.

Thucydides. 1954. *The Peloponnesian War*. Rex Warner, ed. and trans. Baltimore: Penguin.

U.K. Foreign and Commonwealth Office. 1980. *A Yearbook of the Commonwealth 1980*. London: HMSO.

U.S. Congress. Senate. Select Committee to Study Governmental Operations with Respect to Intelligence Activities. 1975. *Covert Action in Chile, 1963–74*. 94th Cong., 1st sess., Washington, D.C.: U.S. Government Printing Office.

U.S. Department of State. 1981. *Country Reports on Human Rights Practices*. Washington, D.C.: U.S. Government Printing Office.

Weede, Erich. 1984. Democracy and War Involvement. *Journal of Conflict Resolution*, 28:649–64.

Wilkenfeld, Jonathan. 1968. Domestic and Foreign Conflict Behavior of Nations. *Journal of Peace Research*, 5:56–69.

Wright, Quincy. 1942. *A Study of History*. Chicago: Chicago University Press.

ALEXANDER WENDT

Anarchy Is What States Make of It: The Social Construction of Power Politics

The debate between realists and liberals has reemerged as an axis of contention in international relations theory.[1] Revolving in the past

From *International Organization* 46, no. 2 (Spring 1992): 391–425. Some of the author's notes have been omitted.

around competing theories of human nature, the debate is more concerned today with the extent to which state action is influenced by "structure" (anarchy and the distribution of power) versus "process" (interaction and learning) and institutions. Does the absence of centralized political authority force states to play competitive power politics? Can international regimes overcome this logic, and under what conditions? What in anarchy is given and immutable, and what is amenable to change?

* * *

* * * I argue that self-help and power politics do not follow either logically or causally from anarchy and that if today we find ourselves in a self-help world, this is due to process, not structure. There is no "logic" of anarchy apart from the practices that create and instantiate one structure of identities and interests rather than another; structure has no existence or causal powers apart from process. Self-help and power politics are institutions, not essential features of anarchy. *Anarchy is what states make of it.*

* * *

Anarchy and Power Politics

Classical realists such as Thomas Hobbes, Reinhold Niebuhr, and Hans Morgenthau attributed egoism and power politics primarily to human nature, whereas structural realists or neorealists emphasize anarchy. The difference stems in part from different interpretations of anarchy's causal powers. Kenneth Waltz's work is important for both. In *Man, the State, and War,* he defines anarchy as a condition of possibility for or "permissive" cause of war, arguing that "wars occur because there is nothing to prevent them."[2] It is the human nature or domestic politics of predator states, however, that provide the initial impetus or "efficient" cause of conflict which forces other states to respond in kind.[3] Waltz is not entirely consistent about this, since he slips without justification from the permissive causal claim that in anarchy war is always possible to the active

causal claim that "war may at any moment occur."[4] But despite Waltz's concluding call for third-image theory, the efficient causes that initialize anarchic systems are from the first and second images. This is reversed in Waltz's *Theory of International Politics,* in which first- and second-image theories are spurned as "reductionist," and the logic of anarchy seems by itself to constitute self-help and power politics as necessary features of world politics.[5]

This is unfortunate, since whatever one may think of first- and second-image theories, they have the virtue of implying that practices determine the character of anarchy. In the permissive view, only if human or domestic factors cause A to attack B will B have to defend itself. Anarchies may contain dynamics that lead to competitive power politics, but they also may not, and we can argue about when particular structures of identity and interest will emerge. In neorealism, however, the role of practice in shaping the character of anarchy is substantially reduced, and so there is less about which to argue: self-help and competitive power politics are simply given exogenously by the structure of the state system.

I will not here contest the neorealist description of the contemporary state system as a competitive, self-help world;[6] I will only dispute its explanation. I develop my argument in three stages. First, I disentangle the concepts of self-help and anarchy by showing that self-interested conceptions of security are not a constitutive property of anarchy. Second, I show how self-help and competitive power politics may be produced causally by processes of interaction between states in which anarchy plays only a permissive role. In both of these stages of my argument, I self-consciously bracket the first- and second-image determinants of state identity, not because they are unimportant (they are indeed important), but because like Waltz's objective, mine is to clarify the "logic" of anarchy. Third, I reintroduce first- and second-image determinants to assess their effects on identity-formation in different kinds of anarchies.

Anarchy, Self-Help, and Intersubjective Knowledge

Waltz defines political structure on three dimensions: ordering principles (in this case, anarchy), principles of differentiation (which here drop out), and the distribution of capabilities.[7] By itself, this definition predicts little about state behavior. It does not predict whether two states will be friends or foes, will recognize each other's sovereignty, will have dynastic ties, will be revisionist or status quo powers, and so on. These factors, which are fundamentally intersubjective, affect states' security interests and thus the character of their interaction under anarchy. In an important revision of Waltz's theory, Stephen Walt implies as much when he argues that the "balance of threats," rather than the balance of power, determines state action, threats being socially constructed.[8] Put more generally, without assumptions about the structure of identities and interests in the system, Waltz's definition of structure cannot predict the content or dynamics of anarchy. Self-help is one such intersubjective structure and, as such, does the decisive explanatory work in the theory. The question is whether self-help is a logical or contingent feature of anarchy. In this section, I develop the concept of a "structure of identity and interest" and show that no particular one follows logically from anarchy.

A fundamental principle of constructivist social theory is that people act toward objects, including other actors, on the basis of the meanings that the objects have for them.[9] States act differently toward enemies than they do toward friends because enemies are threatening and friends are not. Anarchy and the distribution of power are insufficient to tell us which is which. U.S. military power has a different significance for Canada than for Cuba, despite their similar "structural" positions, just as British missiles have a different significance for the United States than do Soviet missiles. The distribution of power may always affect states' calculations, but how it does so depends on the intersubjective understandings and expectations, on the "distribution of knowledge," that constitute their conceptions of self and other.[10] If society "forgets" what a university is, the powers and practices of professor and student cease to exist; if the United States and Soviet Union decide that they are no longer enemies, "the cold war is over." It is collective meanings that constitute the structures which organize our actions.

Actors acquire identities—relatively stable, role-specific understandings and expectations about self—by participating in such collective meanings.[11] Identities are inherently relational: "Identity, with its appropriate attachments of psychological reality, is always identity within a specific, socially constructed world," Peter Berger argues.[12] Each person has many identities linked to institutional roles, such as brother, son, teacher, and citizen. Similarly, a state may have multiple identities as "sovereign," "leader of the free world," "imperial power," and so on.[13] The commitment to and the salience of particular identities vary, but each identity is an inherently social definition of the actor grounded in the theories which actors collectively hold about themselves and one another and which constitute the structure of the social world.

Identities are the basis of interests. Actors do not have a "portfolio" of interests that they carry around independent of social context; instead, they define their interests in the process of defining situations.[14] As Nelson Foote puts it: "Motivation . . . refer[s] to the degree to which a human being, as a participant in the ongoing social process in which he necessarily finds himself, defines a problematic situation as calling for the performance of a particular act, with more or less anticipated consummations and consequences, and thereby his organism releases the energy appropriate to performing it."[15] Sometimes situations are unprecedented in our experience, and in these cases we have to construct their meaning, and thus our interests, by analogy or invent them de novo. More often they have routine qualities in which we assign meanings on the basis of institutionally defined roles. When we say that professors have an "interest" in teaching, research, or going on leave, we are saying that to function in the role identity of "professor," they have to define certain situations as calling for certain actions. This does not mean that they will necessarily do so (expectations and competence do not equal performance), but if they do not, they will not get tenure. The absence or failure of roles makes defining situations and interests more difficult, and identity confusion may result. This seems to be happening today in the United States and the former Soviet Union: without the cold war's mutual attributions of threat and hostility to define their identities, these states seem unsure of what their "interests" should be.

An institution is a relatively stable set or "structure" of identities and interests. Such structures are often codified in formal rules and norms, but these have motivational force only in virtue of actors' socialization to and participation in collective knowledge. Institutions are fundamentally cognitive entities that do not exist apart from actors' ideas about how the world works.[16] This does not mean that institutions are not real or objective, that they are "nothing but" beliefs. As collective knowledge, they are experienced as having an existence "over and above the individuals who happen to embody them at the moment."[17] In this way, institutions come to confront individuals as more or less coercive social facts, but they are still a function of what actors collectively "know." Identities and such collective cognitions do not exist apart from each other; they are "mutually constitutive."[18] On this view, institutionalization is a process of internalizing new identities and interests, not something occurring outside them and affecting only behavior; socialization is a cognitive process, not just a behavioral one. Conceived in this way, institutions may be cooperative or conflictual, a point sometimes lost in scholarship on international regimes, which tends to equate institutions with cooperation. There are important differences between conflictual and cooperative institutions to be sure, but all relatively stable self-other relations—even those of "enemies"—are defined intersubjectively.

Self-help is an institution, one of various structures of identity and interest that may exist under anarchy. Processes of identity-formation under anarchy are concerned first and foremost with preservation or "security" of the self. Concepts of security therefore differ in the extent to which and the manner in which the self is identified cognitively with the other,[19] and, I want to suggest, it is upon this cognitive variation that the meaning of anarchy and the distribution of power depends. Let me illustrate with a standard continuum of security systems.[20]

At one end is the "competitive" security system, in which states identify negatively with each other's security so that ego's gain is seen as alter's loss. Negative identification under anarchy constitutes system of "realist" power politics: risk-averse actors that infer intentions from capabilities and worry about relative gains and losses. At the limit—in the Hobbesian war of all against all—collective action is nearly impossible in such a system because each actor must constantly fear being stabbed in the back.

In the middle is the "individualistic" security system, in which states are indifferent to the relationship between their own and others' security. This constitutes "neoliberal" systems: states are still self-regarding about their security but are concerned primarily with absolute gains rather than relative gains. One's position in the distribution of power is less important, and collective action is more possible (though still subject to free riding because states continue to be "egoists").

Competitive and individualistic systems are both "self-help" forms of anarchy in the sense that states do not positively identify the security of self with that of others but instead treat security as the individual responsibility of each. Given the lack of a positive cognitive identification on the basis of which to build security regimes, power politics within such systems will necessarily consist of efforts to manipulate others to satisfy self-regarding interests.

This contrasts with the "cooperative" security system, in which states identify positively with one another so that the security of each is perceived as the responsibility of all. This is not self-help in any interesting sense, since the "self" in terms of which interests are defined is the community; national interests are international interests.[21] In practice, of course, the extent to which states' identification with the community varies, from the limited form found in "concerts" to the full-blown form seen in "collective security" arrangements.[22] Depending on how well developed the collective self is, it will produce security practices that are in varying degrees altruistic or prosocial. This makes collective action less dependent on the presence of active threats and less prone to free riding.[23] Moreover, it restructures efforts to advance one's objectives, or "power politics," in terms of shared norms rather than relative power.[24]

On this view, the tendency in international relations scholarship to view power and institutions as two opposing explanations of foreign policy is therefore misleading, since anarchy and the distribution of power only have meaning for state action in virtue of the understandings and expectations that constitute institutional identities and interests. Self-help is one such institution, constituting one kind of anarchy but not the only kind. Waltz's three-part definition of structure therefore seems underspecified. In order to go from structure to action, we need to add a fourth: the intersubjectively constituted structure of identities and interests in the system.

This has an important implication for the way in which we conceive of states in the state of nature before their first encounter with each other. Because states do not have conceptions of self and other, and thus security interests, apart from or prior to interaction, we assume too much about the state of nature if we concur with Waltz that, in virtue of anarchy, "international political systems, like economic markets, are formed by the coaction of self-regarding units."[25] We also assume too much if we argue that, in virtue of anarchy, states in the state of nature necessarily face a "stag hunt" or "security dilemma."[26] These claims presuppose a history of interaction in which actors have acquired "selfish" identities

and interests; before interaction (and still in abstraction from first- and second-image factors) they would have no experience upon which to base such definitions of self and other. To assume otherwise is to attribute to states in the state of nature qualities that they can only possess in society.[27] Self-help is an institution, not a constitutive feature of anarchy.

What, then, *is* a constitutive feature of the state of nature before interaction? Two things are left if we strip away those properties of the self which presuppose interaction with others. The first is the material substrate of agency, including its intrinsic capabilities. For human beings, this is the body; for states, it is an organizational apparatus of governance. In effect, I am suggesting for rhetorical purposes that the raw material out of which members of the state system are constituted is created by domestic society before states enter the constitutive process of international society,[28] although this process implies neither stable territoriality nor sovereignty, which are internationally negotiated terms of individuality (as discussed further below). The second is a desire to preserve this material substrate, to survive. This does not entail "self-regardingness," however, since actors do not have a self prior to interaction with an other; how they view the meaning and requirements of this survival therefore depends on the processes by which conceptions of self evolve.

This may all seem very arcane, but there is an important issue at stake: are the foreign policy identities and interests of states exogenous or endogenous to the state system? The former is the answer of an individualistic or undersocialized systemic theory for which rationalism is appropriate; the latter is the answer of a fully socialized systemic theory. Waltz seems to offer the latter and proposes two mechanisms, competition and socialization, by which structure conditions state action.[29] The content of his argument about this conditioning, however, presupposes a self-help system that is not itself a constitutive feature of anarchy. As James Morrow points out, Waltz's two mechanisms condition behavior, not identity and interest.[30] This explains how Waltz can be accused of both "individualism" and "structuralism."[31] He is the former with respect to systemic constitutions of identity and interest, the latter with respect to systemic determinations of behavior.

Anarchy and the Social Construction of Power Politics

If self-help is not a constitutive feature of anarchy, it must emerge causally from processes in which anarchy plays only a permissive role.[32] This reflects a second principle of constructivism: that the meanings in terms of which action is organized arise out of interaction.[33] This being said, however, the situation facing states as they encounter one another for the first time may be such that only self-regarding conceptions of identity can survive; if so, even if these conceptions are socially constructed, neorealists may be right in holding identities and interests constant and thus in privileging one particular meaning of anarchic structure over process. In this case, rationalists would be right to argue for a weak, behavioral conception of the difference that institutions make, and realists would be right to argue that any international institutions which are created will be inherently unstable, since without the power to transform identities and interests they will be "continuing objects of choice" by exogenously constituted actors constrained only by the transaction costs of behavioral change.[34] Even in a permissive causal role, in other words, anarchy may decisively restrict interaction and therefore restrict viable forms of systemic theory. I address these causal issues first by showing how self-regarding ideas about security might develop and then by examining the conditions under which a key efficient cause—predation—may dispose states in this direction rather than others.

Conceptions of self and interest tend to "mirror" the practices of significant others over time. This principle of identity-formation is captured by the symbolic interactionist notion of the "looking-glass self," which asserts that the self is a reflection of an actor's socialization.

Consider two actors—ego and alter—encountering each other for the first time.[35] Each wants to survive and has certain material capabilities, but neither actor has biological or domestic imperatives for power, glory, or conquest (still bracketed), and there is no history of security or insecurity between the two. What should they do? Realists would probably argue that each should act on the basis of worst-case assumptions about the other's intentions, justifying such an attitude as prudent in view of the possibility of death from making a mistake. Such a possibility always exists, even in civil society; however, society would be impossible if people made decisions purely on the basis of worst-case possibilities. Instead, most decisions are and should be made on the basis of probabilities, and these are produced by interaction, by what actors *do*.

In the beginning is ego's gesture, which may consist, for example, of an advance, a retreat, a brandishing of arms, a laying down of arms, or an attack.[36] For ego, this gesture represents the basis on which it is prepared to respond to alter. This basis is unknown to alter, however, and so it must make an inference or "attribution" about ego's intentions and, in particular, given that this is anarchy, about whether ego is a threat.[37] The content of this inference will largely depend on two considerations. The first is the gesture's and ego's physical qualities, which are in part contrived by ego and which include the direction of movement, noise, numbers, and immediate consequences of the gesture.[38] The second consideration concerns what alter would intend by such qualities were it to make such a gesture itself. Alter may make an attributional "error" in its inference about ego's intent, but there is also no reason for it to assume a priori—before the gesture—that ego is threatening, since it is only through a process of signaling and interpreting that the costs and probabilities of being wrong can be determined.[39] Social threats are constructed, not natural.

Consider an example. Would we assume, a priori, that we were about to be attacked if we are ever contacted by members of an alien civilization? I think not. We would be highly alert, of course, but whether we placed our military forces on alert or launched an attack would depend on how we interpreted the import of their first gesture for our security—if only to avoid making an immediate enemy out of what may be a dangerous adversary. The possibility of error, in other words, does not force us to act on the assumption that the aliens are threatening: action depends on the probabilities we assign, and these are in key part a function of what the aliens do; prior to their gesture, we have no systemic basis for assigning probabilities. If their first gesture is to appear with a thousand spaceships and destroy New York, we will define the situation as threatening and respond accordingly. But if they appear with one spaceship, saying what seems to be "we come in peace," we will feel "reassured" and will probably respond with a gesture intended to reassure them, even if this gesture is not necessarily interpreted by them as such.[40]

This process of signaling, interpreting, and responding completes a "social act" and begins the process of creating intersubjective meanings. It advances the same way. The first social act creates expectations on both sides about each other's future behavior: potentially mistaken and certainly tentative, but expectations nonetheless. Based on this tentative knowledge, ego makes a new gesture, again signifying the basis on which it will respond to alter, and again alter responds, adding to the pool of knowledge each has about the other, and so on over time. The mechanism here is reinforcement; interaction rewards actors for holding certain ideas about each other and discourages them from holding others. If repeated long enough, these "reciprocal typifications" will create relatively stable concepts of self and other regarding the issue at stake in the interaction.[41]

It is through reciprocal interaction, in other words, that we create and instantiate the relatively enduring social structures in terms of which we define our identities and interests. Jeff Coulter sums up the ontological dependence of structure on process this way: "The parameters

of social organization themselves are reproduced only in and through the orientations and practices of members engaged in social interactions over time. . . . Social configurations are not 'objective' like mountains or forests, but neither are they 'subjective' like dreams or flights of speculative fancy. They are, as most social scientists concede at the theoretical level, intersubjective constructions."[42]

The simple overall model of identity- and interest-formation proposed in Figure 3.1 applies to competitive institutions no less than to cooperative ones. Self-help security systems evolve from cycles of interaction in which each party acts in ways that the other feels are threatening to the self, creating expectations that the other is not to be trusted. Competitive or egoistic identities are caused by such insecurity; if the other is threatening, the self is forced to "mirror" such behavior in its conception of the self's relationship to that other.[43] Being treated as an object for the gratification of others precludes the positive identification with others necessary for collective security; conversely, being treated by others in ways that are empathic with respect to the security of the self permits such identification.[44]

Competitive systems of interaction are prone to security "dilemmas," in which the efforts of actors to enhance their security unilaterally threatens the security of the others, perpetuating distrust and alienation. The forms of identity and interest that constitute such dilemmas, however, are themselves ongoing effects of, not exogenous to, the interaction; identities are produced in and through "situated activity."[45] We do not *begin* our relationship with the aliens in a security dilemma; security dilemmas are not given by anarchy or nature. Of course, once institutionalized such a dilemma may be hard to change (I return to this below), but the point remains: identities and interests are constituted by collective meanings that are always in process. As Sheldon Stryker emphasizes, "The social process is one of constructing and reconstructing self and social relationships."[46] If states find themselves in a self-help system, this is because their practices made it that way. Chang-

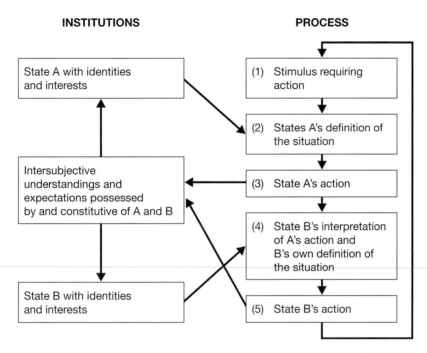

Figure 3.1. The Codetermination of Institutions and Process

ing the practices will change the intersubjective knowledge that constitutes the system.

Predator States and Anarchy as Permissive Cause

The mirror theory of identity-formation is a crude account of how the process of creating identities and interests might work, but it does not tell us why a system of states—such as, arguably, our own—would have ended up with self-regarding and not collective identities. In this section, I examine an efficient cause, predation, which, in conjunction with anarchy as a permissive cause, may generate a self-help system. In so doing, however, I show the key role that the structure of identities and interests plays in mediating anarchy's explanatory role.

The predator argument is straightforward and compelling. For whatever reasons—biology, domestic politics, or systemic victimization— some states may become predisposed toward aggression. The aggressive behavior of these predators or "bad apples" forces other states to engage in competitive power politics, to meet fire with fire, since failure to do so may degrade or destroy them. One predator will best a hundred pacifists because anarchy provides no guarantees. This argument is powerful in part because it is so weak: rather than making the strong assumption that all states are inherently power-seeking (a purely reductionist theory of power politics), it assumes that just one is power-seeking and that the others have to follow suit because anarchy permits the one to exploit them.

In making this argument, it is important to reiterate that the possibility of predation does not in itself force states to anticipate it a priori with competitive power politics of their own. The possibility of predation does not mean that "war may at any moment occur"; it may in fact be extremely unlikely. Once a predator emerges, however, it may condition identity- and interest-formation in the following manner.

In an anarchy of two, if ego is predatory, alter must either define its security in self-help terms or pay the price. This follows directly from the above argument, in which conceptions of self mirror treatment by the other. In an anarchy of many, however, the effect of predation also depends on the level of collective identity already attained in the system. If predation occurs right after the first encounter in the state of nature, it will force others with whom it comes in contact to defend themselves, first individually and then collectively *if* they come to perceive a common threat. The emergence of such a defensive alliance will be seriously inhibited if the structure of identities and interests has already evolved into a Hobbesian world of maximum insecurity, since potential allies will strongly distrust each other and face intense collective action problems; such insecure allies are also more likely to fall out amongst themselves once the predator is removed. If collective security identity is high, however, the emergence of a predator may do much less damage. If the predator attacks any member of the collective, the latter will come to the victim's defense on the principle of "all for one, one for all," even if the predator is not presently a threat to other members of the collective. If the predator is not strong enough to withstand the collective, it will be defeated and collective security will obtain. But if it is strong enough, the logic of the two-actor case (now predator and collective) will activate, and balance-of-power politics will reestablish itself.

The timing of the emergence of predation relative to the history of identity-formation in the community is therefore crucial to anarchy's explanatory role as a permissive cause. Predation will always lead victims to defend themselves, but whether defense will be collective or not depends on the history of interaction within the potential collective as much as on the ambitions of the predator. Will the disappearance of the Soviet threat renew old insecurities among the members of the North Atlantic Treaty Organization? Perhaps, but not if they have reasons independent of that threat for identifying their

security with one another. Identities and interests are relationship-specific, not intrinsic attributes of a "portfolio"; states may be competitive in some relationships and solidary in others. "Mature" anarchies are less likely than "immature" ones to be reduced by predation to a Hobbesian condition, and maturity, which is a proxy for structures of identity and interest, is a function of process.[47]

The source of predation also matters. If it stems from unit-level causes that are immune to systemic impacts (causes such as human nature or domestic politics taken in isolation), then it functions in a manner analogous to a "genetic trait" in the constructed world of the state system. Even if successful, this trait does not select for other predators in an evolutionary sense so much as it teaches other states to respond in kind, but since traits cannot be unlearned, the other states will continue competitive behavior until the predator is either destroyed or transformed from within. However, in the more likely event that predation stems at least in part from prior systemic interaction—perhaps as a result of being victimized in the past (one thinks here of Nazi Germany or the Soviet Union)—then it is more a response to a learned identity and, as such, might be transformed by future social interaction in the form of appeasement, reassurances that security needs will be met, systemic effects on domestic politics, and so on. In this case, in other words, there is more hope that process can transform a bad apple into a good one.

The role of predation in generating a self-help system, then, is consistent with a systematic focus on process. Even if the source of predation is entirely exogenous to the system, it is what states *do* that determines the quality of their interactions under anarchy. In this respect, it is not surprising that it is classical realists rather than structural realists who emphasize this sort of argument. The former's emphasis on unit-level causes of power politics leads more easily to a permissive view of anarchy's explanatory role (and therefore to a processual view of international relations) than does the latter's emphasis on anarchy as a "structural cause";[48] neorealists do not need predation because the system is given as self-help.

This raises anew the question of exactly how much and what kind of role human nature and domestic politics play in world politics. The greater and more destructive this role, the more significant predation will be, and the less amenable anarchy will be to formation of collective identities. Classical realists, of course, assumed that human nature was possessed by an inherent lust for power or glory. My argument suggests that assumptions such as this were made for a reason: an unchanging Hobbesian man provides the powerful efficient cause necessary for a relentless pessimism about world politics that anarchic structure alone, or even structure plus intermittent predation, cannot supply. One can be skeptical of such an essentialist assumption, as I am, but it does produce determinate results at the expense of systemic theory. A concern with systemic process over structure suggests that perhaps it is time to revisit the debate over the relative importance of first-, second-, and third-image theories of state identity-formation.[49]

Assuming for now that systemic theories of identity-formation in world politics are worth pursuing, let me conclude by suggesting that the realist-rationalist alliance "reifies" self-help in the sense of treating it as something separate from the practices by which it is produced and sustained. Peter Berger and Thomas Luckmann define reification as follows: "[It] is the apprehension of the products of human activity *as if* they were something else than human products—such as facts of nature, results of cosmic laws, or manifestations of divine will. Reification implies that man is capable of forgetting his own authorship of the human world, and further, that the dialectic between man, the producer, and his products is lost to consciousness. The reified world is . . . experienced by man as a strange facticity, an *opus alienum* over which he has no control rather than as the *opus proprium* of his own productive activity."[50] By denying or bracketing states' collective authorship of their identities and interests,

in other words, the realist-rationalist alliance denies or brackets the fact that competitive power politics help create the very "problem of order" they are supposed to solve—that realism is a self-fulfilling prophecy. Far from being exogenously given, the intersubjective knowledge that constitutes competitive identities and interests is constructed every day by processes of "social will formation."[51] It is what states have made of themselves.

Institutional Transformations of Power Politics

Let us assume that processes of identity- and interest-formation have created a world in which states do not recognize rights to territory or existence—a war of all against all. In this world, anarchy has a "realist" meaning for state action: be insecure and concerned with relative power. Anarchy has this meaning only in virtue of collective, insecurity-producing practices, but if those practices are relatively stable, they do constitute a system that may resist change. The fact that worlds of power politics are socially constructed, in other words, does not guarantee they are malleable, for at least two reasons.

The first reason is that once constituted, any social system confronts each of its members as an objective social fact that reinforces certain behaviors and discourages others. Self-help systems, for example, tend to reward competition and punish altruism. The possibility of change depends on whether the exigencies of such competition leave room for actions that deviate from the prescribed script. If they do not, the system will be reproduced and deviant actors will not.[52]

The second reason is that systemic change may also be inhibited by actors' interests in maintaining relatively stable role identities. Such interests are rooted not only in the desire to minimize uncertainty and anxiety, manifested in efforts to confirm existing beliefs about the social world, but also in the desire to avoid the expected costs of breaking commitments made to others—notably domestic constituencies and foreign allies in the case of states—as part of past practices. The level of resistance that these commitments induce will depend on the "salience" of particular role identities to the actor.[53] The United States, for example, is more likely to resist threats to its identity as "leader of anticommunist crusades" than to its identity as "promoter of human rights." But for almost any role identity, practices and information that challenge it are likely to create cognitive dissonance and even perceptions of threat, and these may cause resistance to transformations of the self and thus to social change.[54]

For both systemic and "psychological" reasons, then, intersubjective understandings and expectations may have a self-perpetuating quality, constituting path-dependencies that new ideas about self and other must transcend. This does not change the fact that through practice agents are continuously producing and reproducing identities and interests, continuously "choosing now the preferences [they] will have later."[55] But it does mean that choices may not be experienced with meaningful degrees of freedom. This could be a constructivist justification for the realist position that only simple learning is possible in self-help systems. The realist might concede that such systems are socially constructed and still argue that after the corresponding identities and interests have become institutionalized, they are almost impossible to transform.

In the remainder of this article, I examine three institutional transformations of identity and security interest through which states might escape a Hobbesian world of their own making. In so doing, I seek to clarify what it means to say that "institutions transform identities and interests," emphasizing that the key to such transformations is relatively stable practice.

Sovereignty, Recognition, and Security

In a Hobbesian state of nature, states are individuated by the domestic processes that constitute them as states and by their material capacity to deter threats from other states. In this world, even if free momentarily from the predations of others, state security does not have any basis in social recognition—in intersubjective understandings or norms that a state has a right to its existence, territory, and subjects. Security is a matter of national power, nothing more.

The principle of sovereignty transforms this situation by providing a social basis for the individuality and security of states. Sovereignty is an institution, and so it exists only in virtue of certain intersubjective understandings and expectations; there is no sovereignty without an other. These understandings and expectations not only constitute a particular kind of state—the "sovereign" state—but also constitute a particular form of community, since identities are relational. The essence of this community is a mutual recognition of one another's right to exercise exclusive political authority within territorial limits. These reciprocal "permissions"[56] constitute a spatially rather than functionally differentiated world—a world in which fields of practice constitute and are organized around "domestic" and "international" spaces rather than around the performance of particular activities.[57] The location of the boundaries between these spaces is of course sometimes contested, war being one practice through which states negotiate the terms of their individuality. But this does not change the fact that it is only in virtue of mutual recognition that states have "territorial property rights."[58] This recognition functions as a form of "social closure" that disempowers nonstate actors and empowers and helps stabilize interaction among states.[59]

Sovereignty norms are now so taken for granted, so natural, that it is easy to overlook the extent to which they are both presupposed by and an ongoing artifact of practice. When states tax "their" "citizens" and not others, when they "protect" their markets against foreign "imports," when they kill thousands of Iraqis in one kind of war and then refuse to "intervene" to kill even one person in another kind, a "civil" war, and when they fight a global war against a regime that sought to destroy the institution of sovereignty and then give Germany back to the Germans, they are acting against the background of, and thereby reproducing, shared norms about what it means to be a sovereign state.

If states stopped acting on those norms, their identity as "sovereigns" (if not necessarily as "states") would disappear. The sovereign state is an ongoing accomplishment of practice, not a once-and-for-all creation of norms that somehow exist apart from practice.[60] Thus, saying that "the institution of sovereignty transforms identities" is shorthand for saying that "regular practices produce mutually constituting sovereign identities (agents) and their associated institutional norms (structures)." Practice is the core of constructivist resolutions of the agent-structure problem. This ongoing process may not be politically problematic in particular historical contexts and, indeed, once a community of mutual recognition is constituted, its members—even the disadvantaged ones[61]—may have a vested interest in reproducing it. In fact, this is part of what having an identity means. But this identity and institution remain dependent on what actors do: removing those practices will remove their intersubjective conditions of existence.

This may tell us something about how institutions of sovereign states are reproduced through social interaction, but it does not tell us why such a structure of identity and interest would arise in the first place. Two conditions would seem necessary for this to happen: (1) the density and regularity of interactions must be sufficiently high and (2) actors must be dissatisfied with preexisting forms of identity and interaction. Given these conditions, a norm of mutual recognition is relatively undemanding in terms of social trust, having the form of an assurance game in which a player will acknowledge the sovereignty of the others as long as they will in turn acknowledge that player's own sovereignty. Articulating international legal principles such as those embodied in the Peace of Augsburg

(1555) and the Peace of Westphalia (1648) may also help by establishing explicit criteria for determining violations of the nascent social consensus.[62] But whether such a consensus holds depends on what states do. If they treat each other as if they were sovereign, then over time they will institutionalize that mode of subjectivity; if they do not, then that mode will not become the norm.

Practices of sovereignty will transform understandings of security and power politics in at least three ways. First, states will come to define their (and our) security in terms of preserving their "property rights" over particular territories. We now see this as natural, but the preservation of territorial frontiers is not, in fact, equivalent to the survival of the state or its people. Indeed, some states would probably be more secure if they would relinquish certain territories—the "Soviet Union" of some minority republics, "Yugoslavia" of Croatia and Slovenia, Israel of the West Bank, and so on. The fact that sovereignty practices have historically been oriented toward producing distinct territorial spaces, in other words, affects states' conceptualization of what they must "secure" to function in that identity, a process that may help account for the "hardening" of territorial boundaries over the centuries.[63]

Second, to the extent that states successfully internalize sovereignty norms, they will be more respectful toward the territorial rights of others.[64] This restraint is *not* primarily because of the costs of violating sovereignty norms, although when violators do get punished (as in the Gulf War) it reminds everyone of what these costs can be, but because part of what it means to be a "sovereign" state is that one does not violate the territorial rights of others without "just cause." A clear example of such an institutional effect, convincingly argued by David Strang, is the markedly different treatment that weak states receive within and outside communities of mutual recognition.[65] What keeps the United States from conquering the Bahamas, or Nigeria from seizing Togo, or Australia from occupying Vanuatu?

Clearly, power is not the issue, and in these cases even the cost of sanctions would probably be negligible. One might argue that great powers simply have no "interest" in these conquests, and this might be so, but this lack of interest can only be understood in terms of their recognition of weak states' sovereignty. I have no interest in exploiting my friends, not because of the relative costs and benefits of such action but because they are my friends. The absence of recognition, in turn, helps explain the Western states' practices of territorial conquest, enslavement, and genocide against Native American and African peoples. It is in *that* world that only power matters, not the world of today.

Finally, to the extent that their ongoing socialization teaches states that their sovereignty depends on recognition by other states, they can afford to rely more on the institutional fabric of international society and less on individual national means—especially military power—to protect their security. The intersubjective understandings embodied in the institution of sovereignty, in other words, may redefine the meaning of others' power for the security of the self. In policy terms, this means that states can be less worried about short-term survival and relative power and can thus shift their resources accordingly. Ironically, it is the great powers, the states with the greatest national means, that may have the hardest time learning this lesson; small powers do not have the luxury of relying on national means and may therefore learn faster that collective recognition is a cornerstone of security.

None of this is to say that power becomes irrelevant in a community of sovereign states. Sometimes states *are* threatened by others that do not recognize their existence or particular territorial claims, that resent the externalities from their economic policies, and so on. But most of the time, these threats are played out within the terms of the sovereignty game. The fates of Napoleon and Hitler show what happens when they are not.

Cooperation among Egoists and Transformations of Identity

We began this section with a Hobbesian state of nature. Cooperation for joint gain is extremely difficult in this context, since trust is lacking, time horizons are short, and relative power concerns are high. Life is "nasty, brutish, and short." Sovereignty transforms this system into a Lockean world of (mostly) mutually recognized property rights and (mostly) egoistic rather than competitive conceptions of security, reducing the fear that what states already have will be seized at any moment by potential collaborators, thereby enabling them to contemplate more direct forms of cooperation. A necessary condition for such cooperation is that outcomes be positively interdependent in the sense that potential gains exist which cannot be realized by unilateral action. States such as Brazil and Botswana may recognize each other's sovereignty, but they need further incentives to engage in joint action. One important source of incentives is the growing "dynamic density" of interaction among states in a world with new communications technology, nuclear weapons, externalities from industrial development, and so on.[66] Unfortunately, growing dynamic density does not ensure that states will in fact realize joint gains; interdependence also entails vulnerability and the risk of being "the sucker," which if exploited will become a source of conflict rather than cooperation.

This is the rationale for the familiar assumption that egoistic states will often find themselves facing prisoners' dilemma, a game in which the dominant strategy, if played only once, is to defect. As Michael Taylor and Robert Axelrod have shown, however, given iteration and a sufficient shadow of the future, egoists using a tit-for-tat strategy can escape this result and build cooperative institutions.[67] The story they tell about this process on the surface seems quite similar to George Herbert Mead's constructivist analysis of interaction, part of which is also told in terms of "games."[68] Cooperation is a gesture indicating ego's willingness to cooperate; if alter defects, ego does likewise, signaling its unwillingness to be exploited; over time and through reciprocal play, each learns to form relatively stable expectations about the other's behavior, and through these, habits of cooperation (or defection) form. Despite similar concerns with communication, learning, and habit-formation, however, there is an important difference between the game-theoretic and constructivist analysis of interaction that bears on how we conceptualize the causal powers of institutions.

In the traditional game-theoretic analysis of cooperation, even an iterated one, the structure of the game—of identities and interests—is exogenous to interaction and, as such, does not change.[69] A "black box" is put around identity- and interest-formation, and analysis focuses instead on the relationship between expectations and behavior. The norms that evolve from interaction are treated as rules and behavioral regularities which are external to the actors and which resist change because of the transaction costs of creating new ones. The game-theoretic analysis of cooperation among egoists is at base behavioral.

A constructivist analysis of cooperation, in contrast, would concentrate on how the expectations produced by behavior affect identities and interests. The process of creating institutions is one of internalizing new understandings of self and other, of acquiring new role identities, not just of creating external constraints on the behavior of exogenously constituted actors.[70] Even if not intended as such, in other words, the process by which egoists learn to cooperate is at the same time a process of reconstructing their interests in terms of shared commitments to social norms. Over time, this will tend to transform a positive interdependence of *outcomes* into a positive interdependence of *utilities* or collective interest organized around the norms in question. These norms will resist change because they are tied to actors' commitments to their identities and interests, not merely because of transaction costs. A constructivist analysis of "the cooperation problem," in other words, is at base cognitive rather than behavioral, since it treats the intersubjective knowledge that defines the structure of identities and interests, of the "game," as endogenous to and instantiated by interaction itself.

The debate over the future of collective security in Western Europe may illustrate the significance of this difference. A weak liberal or rationalist analysis would assume that the European states' "portfolio" of interests has not fundamentally changed and that the emergence of new factors, such as the collapse of the Soviet threat and the rise of Germany, would alter their cost-benefit ratios for pursuing current arrangements, thereby causing existing institutions to break down. The European states formed collaborative institutions for good, exogenously constituted egoistic reasons, and the same reasons may lead them to reject those institutions; the game of European power politics has not changed. A strong liberal or constructivist analysis of this problem would suggest that four decades of cooperation may have transformed a positive interdependence of outcomes into a collective "European identity" in terms of which states increasingly define their "self"-interests.[71] Even if egoistic reasons were its starting point, the process of cooperating tends to redefine those reasons by reconstituting identities and interests in terms of new intersubjective understandings and commitments. Changes in the distribution of power during the late twentieth century are undoubtedly a challenge to these new understandings, but it is not as if West European states have some inherent, exogenously given interest in abandoning collective security if the price is right. Their identities and security interests are continuously in process, and if collective identities become "embedded," they will be as resistant to change as egoistic ones.[72] Through participation in new forms of social knowledge, in other words, the European states of 1990 might no longer be the states of 1950.

Critical Strategic Theory and Collective Security

The transformation of identity and interest through an "evolution of cooperation" faces two important constraints. The first is that the process is incremental and slow. Actors' objectives in such a process are typically to realize joint gains within what they take to be a relatively stable context, and they are therefore unlikely to engage in substantial reflection about how to change the parameters of that context (including the structure of identities and interests) and unlikely to pursue policies specifically designed to bring about such changes. Learning to cooperate may change those parameters, but this occurs as an unintended consequence of policies pursued for other reasons rather than as a result of intentional efforts to transcend existing institutions.

A second, more fundamental, constraint is that the evolution of cooperation story presupposes that actors do not identify negatively with one another. Actors must be concerned primarily with absolute gains; to the extent that antipathy and distrust lead them to define their security in relativistic terms, it will be hard to accept the vulnerabilities that attend cooperation.[73] This is important because it is precisely the "central balance" in the state system that seems to be so often afflicted with such competitive thinking, and realists can therefore argue that the possibility of cooperation within one "pole" (for example, the West) is parasitic on the dominance of competition between poles (the East–West conflict). Relations between the poles may be amenable to some positive reciprocity in areas such as arms control, but the atmosphere of distrust leaves little room for such cooperation and its transformative consequences.[74] The conditions of negative identification that make an "evolution of cooperation" most needed work precisely against such a logic.

This seemingly intractable situation may nevertheless be amenable to quite a different logic of transformation, one driven more by self-conscious efforts to change structures of identity and interest than by unintended consequences. Such voluntarism may seem to contradict the spirit of constructivism, since would-be revolutionaries are presumably themselves effects of socialization to structures of identity and interest. How can they think about changing that to which they owe their identity? The possibility lies in the distinction between the social determination of the self and the personal determination of choice, between what Mead called the "me" and the "I."[75] The "me" is that part of subjectivity which is defined in terms of others; the character and behavioral expectations of a person's role identity as "professor," or of the United States as "leader of the alliance," for example, are socially constituted. Roles are not played in mechanical fashion according to precise scripts, however, but are "taken" and adapted in idiosyncratic ways by each actor.[76] Even in the most constrained situations, role performance involves a choice by the actor. The "I" is the part of subjectivity in which this appropriation and reaction to roles and its corresponding existential freedom lie.

The fact that roles are "taken" means that, in principle, actors always have a capacity for "character planning"—for engaging in critical self-reflection and choices designed to bring about changes in their lives.[77] But when or under what conditions can this creative capacity be exercised? Clearly, much of the time it cannot: if actors were constantly reinventing their identities, social order would be impossible, and the relative stability of identities and interests in the real world is indicative of our propensity for habitual rather than creative action. The exceptional, conscious choosing to transform or transcend roles has at least two preconditions. First, there must be a reason to think of oneself in novel terms. This would most likely stem from the presence of new social situations that cannot be managed in terms of preexisting self-conceptions. Second, the expected costs of intentional role change—the sanctions imposed by others with whom one interacted in previous roles—cannot be greater than its rewards.

When these conditions are present, actors can engage in self-reflection and practice specifically designed to transform their identities and interests and thus to "change the games" in which they are embedded. Such "critical" strategic theory and practice has not received the attention it merits from students of world politics (another legacy of exogenously given interests perhaps), particularly given that one of the most important phenomena in contemporary world politics, Mikhail Gorbachev's policy of "New Thinking," is arguably precisely that.[78] Let me therefore use this policy as an example of how states might transform a competitive security system into a cooperative one, dividing the transformative process into four stages.

The first stage in intentional transformation is the breakdown of consensus about identity commitments. In the Soviet case, identity commitments centered on the Leninist theory of imperialism, with its belief that relations between capitalist and socialist states are inherently conflictual, and on the alliance patterns that this belief engendered. In the 1980s, the consensus within the Soviet Union over the Leninist theory broke down for a variety of reasons, principal among which seem to have been the state's inability to meet the economic-technological-military challenge from the West, the government's decline of political legitimacy at home, and the reassurance from the West that it did not intend to invade the Soviet Union, a reassurance that reduced the external costs of role change.[79] These factors paved the way for a radical leadership transition and for a subsequent "unfreezing of conflict schemas" concerning relations with the West.[80]

The breakdown of consensus makes possible a second stage of critical examination of old ideas about self and other and, by extension, of the structures of interaction by which the ideas have been sustained. In periods of relatively stable role identities, ideas and structures may become reified and thus treated as things that exist independently of social action. If so, the second stage is one of denaturalization, of identifying the practices that reproduce seemingly inevitable ideas about self and other; to that extent, it is a form of "critical" rather than "problem-solving" theory.[81] The result of such a critique should be an identification of new "possible selves" and aspirations.[82] New Thinking embodies such critical theorizing. Gorbachev wants to free the Soviet Union from the coercive social logic of the cold war and engage the West in far-reaching cooperation. Toward this end, he has rejected the Leninist belief in the inherent conflict of interest between socialist and capitalist states and, perhaps more important, has recognized the crucial role that Soviet aggressive practices played in sustaining that conflict.

Such rethinking paves the way for a third stage of new practice. In most cases, it is not enough to rethink one's own ideas about self and other, since old identities have been sustained by systems of interaction with *other* actors, the practices of which remain a social fact for the transformative agent. In order to change the self, then, it is often necessary to change the identities and interests of the others that help sustain those systems of interaction. The vehicle for inducing such change is one's own practice and, in particular, the practice of "altercasting"—a technique of interactor control in which ego uses tactics of self-presentation and stage management in an attempt to frame alter's definitions of social situations in ways that create the role which ego desires alter to play.[83] In effect, in altercasting ego tries to induce alter to take on a new identity (and thereby enlist alter in ego's effort to change itself) by treating alter *as if* it already had that identity. The logic of this follows directly from the mirror theory of identity-formation, in which alter's identity is a reflection of ego's practices; change those practices and ego begins to change alter's conception of itself.

What these practices should consist of depends on the logic by which the preexisting identities were sustained. Competitive security systems are sustained by practices that create insecurity and distrust. In this case, transformative practices should attempt to teach other states that one's own state can be trusted and should not be viewed as a threat to their security. The fastest way to do this is to make unilateral initiatives and self-binding commitments of sufficient significance that another state is faced with "an offer it cannot refuse."[84] Gorbachev has tried to do this by withdrawing from Afghanistan and Eastern Europe, implementing asymmetric cuts in nuclear and conventional forces, calling for "defensive defense," and so on. In addition, he has skillfully cast the West in the role of being morally required to give aid and comfort to the Soviet Union, has emphasized the bonds of common fate between the Soviet Union and the West, and has indicated that further progress in East–West relations is contingent upon the West assuming the identity being projected onto it. These actions are all dimensions of altercasting, the intention of which is to take away the Western "excuse" for distrusting the Soviet Union, which, in Gorbachev's view, has helped sustain competitive identities in the past.

Yet by themselves such practices cannot transform a competitive security system, since if they are not reciprocated by alter, they will expose ego to a "sucker" payoff and quickly wither on the vine. In order for critical strategic practice to transform competitive identities, it must be "rewarded" by alter, which will encourage more such practice by ego, and so on.[85] Over time, this will institutionalize a positive rather than a negative identification between the security of self and other and will thereby provide a firm intersubjective basis for what were initially tentative commitments to new identities and interests.[86]

Notwithstanding today's rhetoric about the end of the cold war, skeptics may still doubt whether Gorbachev (or some future leader) will succeed in building an intersubjective basis for a new Soviet (or Russian) role identity. There are important domestic, bureaucratic, and cognitive-ideological sources of resistance in both East and West to such a change, not the least of which is the shakiness of the democratic forces' domestic position. But if my argument about the role of intersubjective knowledge in creating competi-

tive structures of identity and interest is right, then at least New Thinking shows a greater appreciation—conscious or not—for the deep structure of power politics than we are accustomed to in international relations practice.

Conclusion

All theories of international relations are based on social theories of the relationship between agency, process, and social structure. Social theories do not determine the content of our international theorizing, but they do structure the questions we ask about world politics and our approaches to answering those questions. The substantive issue at stake in debates about social theory is what kind of foundation offers the most fruitful set of questions and research strategies for explaining the revolutionary changes that seem to be occurring in the late twentieth century international system. Put simply, what should systemic theories of international relations look like? How should they conceptualize the relationship between structure and process? Should they be based exclusively on "microeconomic" analogies in which identities and interests are exogenously given by structure and process is reduced to interactions within those parameters? Or should they also be based on "sociological" and "social psychological" analogies in which identities and interests and therefore the meaning of structure are endogenous to process? Should a behavioral-individualism or a cognitive-constructivism be the basis for systemic theories of world politics?

This article notwithstanding, this question is ultimately an empirical one in two respects. First, its answer depends in part on how important interaction among states is for the constitution of their identities and interests. On the one hand, it may be that domestic or genetic factors, which I have systematically bracketed, are in fact much more important determinants of states' identities and interests than are systemic factors.

To the extent that this is true, the individualism of a rationalist approach and the inherent privileging of structure over process in this approach become more substantively appropriate for systemic theory (if not for first- and second-image theory), since identities and interests are *in fact* largely exogenous to interaction among states. On the other hand, if the bracketed factors are relatively unimportant or if the importance of the international system varies historically (perhaps with the level of dynamic density and interdependence in the system), then such a framework would not be appropriate as an exclusive foundation for general systemic theory.

Second, the answer to the question about what systemic theories should look like also depends on how easily state identities and interests can change as a result of systemic interaction. Even if interaction is initially important in constructing identities and interests, once institutionalized its logic may make transformation extremely difficult. If the meaning of structure for state action changes so slowly that it becomes a de facto parameter within which process takes place, then it may again be substantively appropriate to adopt the rationalist assumption that identities and interests are given (although again, this may vary historically).

We cannot address these empirical issues, however, unless we have a framework for doing systemic research that makes state identity and interest an issue for both theoretical and empirical inquiry. Let me emphasize that this is *not* to say we should never treat identities and interests as given. The framing of problems and research strategies should be question-driven rather than method-driven, and if we are not interested in identity- and interest-formation, we may find the assumptions of a rationalist discourse perfectly reasonable. Nothing in this article, in other words, should be taken as an attack on rationalism per se. By the same token, however, we should not let this legitimate analytical stance become a de facto ontological stance with respect to the content of third-image theory, at least not until after we have determined that systemic interaction does not play an important role in processes of state identity- and interest-formation. We should not choose our philosophical anthropologies and social theories prematurely. By arguing that we cannot derive a self-help structure of identity and interest from the principle of anarchy alone—by arguing that anarchy is what states make of it—this article has challenged one important justification for ignoring processes of identity- and interest-formation in world politics. As such, it helps set the stage for inquiry into the empirical issues raised above and thus for a debate about whether communitarian or individualist assumptions are a better foundation for systemic theory.

I have tried to indicate by crude example what such a research agenda might look like. Its objective should be to assess the causal relationship between practice and interaction (as independent variable) and the cognitive structures at the level of individual states and of systems of states which constitute identities and interests (as dependent variable)—that is, the relationship between what actors *do* and what they *are*. We may have some a priori notion that state actors and systemic structures are "mutually constitutive," but this tells us little in the absence of an understanding of how the mechanics of dyadic, triadic, and *n*-actor interaction shape and are in turn shaped by "stocks of knowledge" that collectively constitute identities and interests and, more broadly, constitute the structures of international life. Particularly important in this respect is the role of practice in shaping attitudes toward the "givenness" of these structures. How and why do actors reify social structures, and under what conditions do they denaturalize such reifications?

The state-centrism of this agenda may strike some, particularly postmodernists, as "depressingly familiar."[87] The significance of states relative to multinational corporations, new social movements, transnationals, and intergovernmental organizations is clearly declining, and "postmodern" forms of world politics merit more research attention than they have received. But I also believe, with realists, that in the medium run sovereign states will remain the dominant political actors in the international system. Any transition to new structures of global political authority and identity—to "postinternational" politics—will be mediated by and path-dependent on the particular institutional resolution of the tension between unity and diversity, or particularism and universality, that is the sovereign state.[88] In such a world there should continue to be a place for theories of anarchic interstate politics, alongside other forms of international theory; to that extent, I am a statist and a realist. I have argued in this article, however, that statism need not be bound by realist ideas about what "state" must mean. State identities and interests can be collectively transformed within an anarchic context by many factors—individual, domestic, systemic, or transnational—and as such are an important dependent variable. Such a reconstruction of state-centric international theory is necessary if we are to theorize adequately about the emerging forms of transnational political identity that sovereign states will help bring into being. To that extent, I hope that statism, like the state, can be historically progressive.

* * *

NOTES

1. See, for example, Joseph Grieco, "Anarchy and the Limits of Cooperation: A Realist Critique of the Newest Liberal Institutionalism," *International Organization* 42 (Summer 1988), pp. 485–507; Joseph Nye, "Neorealism and Neoliberalism," *World Politics* 40 (January 1988), pp. 235–51; Robert Keohane, "Neoliberal Institutionalism: A Perspective on World Politics," in his collection of essays entitled *International Institutions and State Power* (Boulder, Colo.: Westview Press, 1989), pp. 1–20; John Mearsheimer, "Back to the Future: Instability in Europe after the Cold War," *International Security* 13 (Summer 1990), pp. 5–56.

2. Kenneth Waltz, *Man, the State, and War* (New York: Columbia University Press, 1959), p. 232.

3. Ibid., pp. 169–70.

4. Ibid., p. 232. This point is made by Hidemi Suganami in "Bringing Order to the Causes of War Debates," *Millennium* 19 (Spring 1990), p. 34, fn. 11.

5. Kenneth Waltz, *Theory of International Politics* (Boston: Addison-Wesley, 1979).

6. The neorealist description is not unproblematic. For a powerful critique, see David Lumsdaine, [*Moral Vision in International Politics:*] *The Foreign Aid Regime, 1949–1989* (Princeton, N.J.: Princeton University Press, [1993]).

7. Waltz, *Theory of International Politics*, pp. 79–101.

8. Stephen Walt, *The Origins of Alliances* (Ithaca, N.Y.: Cornell University Press, 1987).

9. See, for example, Herbert Blumer, "The Methodological Position of Symbolic Interactionism," in his *Symbolic Interactionism: Perspective and Method* (Englewood Cliffs, N.J.: Prentice-Hall, 1969), p. 2. Throughout this article, I assume that a theoretically productive analogy can be made between individuals and states.

10. The phrase "distribution of knowledge" is Barry Barnes's, as discussed in his work *The Nature of Power* (Cambridge: Polity Press, 1988); see also Peter Berger and Thomas Luckmann, *The Social Construction of Reality* (New York: Anchor Books, 1966).

11. For an excellent short statement of how collective meanings constitute identities, see Peter Berger, "Identity as a Problem in the Sociology of Knowledge," *European Journal of Sociology*, vol. 7, no. 1, 1966, pp. 32–40.

12. Berger, "Identity as a Problem in the Sociology of Knowledge," p. 111.

13. While not normally cast in such terms, foreign policy scholarship on national role conceptions could be adapted to such identity language. See Kal Holsti, "National Role Conceptions in the Study of Foreign Policy," *International Studies Quarterly* 14 (Septem-

ber 1970), pp. 233–309; and Stephen Walker, ed., *Role Theory and Foreign Policy Analysis* (Durham, N.C.: Duke University Press, 1987). For an important effort to do so, see Stephen Walker, "Symbolic Interactionism and International Politics: Role Theory's Contribution to International Organization," in C. Shih and Martha Cottam, eds., *Contending Dramas: A Cognitive Approach to Post-War International Organizational Processes* (New York: Praeger, [1992]).

14. On the "portfolio" conception of interests, see Barry Hindess, *Political Choice and Social Structure* (Aldershot, U.K.: Edward Elgar, 1989), pp. 2–3. The "definition of the situation" is a central concept in interactionist theory.

15. Nelson Foote, "Identification as the Basis for a Theory of Motivation," *American Sociological Review* 16 (February 1951), p. 15. Such strongly sociological conceptions of interest have been criticized, with some justice, for being "oversocialized"; see Dennis Wrong, "The Oversocialized Conception of Man in Modern Sociology," *American Sociological Review* 26 (April 1961), pp. 183–93. For useful correctives, which focus on the activation of presocial but nondetermining human needs within social contexts, see Turner, *A Theory of Social Interaction*, pp. 23–69; and Viktor Gecas, "The Self-Concept as a Basis for a Theory of Motivation," in Judith Howard and Peter Callero, eds., *The Self-Society Dynamic* (Cambridge: Cambridge University Press, 1991), pp. 171–87.

16. In neo-Durkheimian parlance, institutions are "social representations." See Serge Moscovici, "The Phenomenon of Social Representations," in Rob Farr and Serge Moscovici, eds., *Social Representations* (Cambridge: Cambridge University Press, 1984), pp. 3–69.

17. Berger and Luckmann, *The Social Construction of Reality*, p. 58.

18. See Giddens, *Central Problems in Social Theory*; and Alexander Wendt and Raymond Duvall, "Institutions and International Order," in Ernst-Otto Czempiel and James Rosenau, eds., *Global Changes and Theoretical Challenges* (Lexington, Mass.: Lexington Books, 1989), pp. 51–74.

19. Proponents of choice theory might put this in terms of "interdependent utilities."

20. Security systems might also vary in the extent to which there is a functional differentiation or a hierarchical relationship between patron and client, with the patron playing a hegemonic role within its sphere of influence in defining the security interests of its clients. I do not examine this dimension here; for preliminary discussion, see Alexander Wendt, "The States System and Global Militarization," Ph.D. diss., University of Minnesota, Minneapolis, 1989; and Alexander Wendt and Michael Barnett, "The International System and Third World Militarization," unpublished manuscript, 1991.

21. This amounts to an "internationalization of the state." For a discussion of this subject, see Raymond Duvall and Alexander Wendt, "The International Capital Regime and the Internationalization of the State," unpublished manuscript, 1987. See also R. B. J. Walker, "Sovereignty, Identity, Community: Reflections on the Horizons of Contemporary Political Practice," in R. B. J. Walker and Saul Mendlovitz, eds., *Contending Sovereignties* (Boulder, Colo.: Lynne Rienner, 1990), pp. 159–85.

22. On the spectrum of cooperative security arrangements, see Charles Kupchan and Clifford Kupchan, "Concerts, Collective Security, and the Future of Europe," *International Security* 16 (Summer 1991), pp. 114–61; and Richard Smoke, "A Theory of Mutual Security," in Richard Smoke and Andrei Kortunov, eds., *Mutual Security* (New York: St. Martin's Press, 1991), pp. 59–111. These may be usefully set alongside Christopher Jencks' "Varieties of Altruism," in Jane Mansbridge, ed., *Beyond Self-Interest* (Chicago: University of Chicago Press, 1990), pp. 53–67.

23. On the role of collective identity in reducing collective action problems, see Bruce Fireman

and William Gamson, "Utilitarian Logic in the Resource Mobilization Perspective," in Mayer Zald and John McCarthy, eds., *The Dynamics of Social Movements* (Cambridge, Mass.: Winthrop, 1979), pp. 8–44; Robyn Dawes et al., "Cooperation for the Benefit of Us—Not Me, or My Conscience," in Mansbridge, *Beyond Self-Interest*, pp. 97–110; and Craig Calhoun, "The Problem of Identity in Collective Action," in Joan Huber, ed., *Macro-Micro Linkages in Sociology* (Beverly Hills, Calif.: Sage, 1991), pp. 51–75.

24. See Thomas Risse-Kappen, "Are Democratic Alliances Special?" unpublished manuscript, Yale University, New Haven, Conn., 1991.

25. Waltz, *Theory of International Politics*, p. 91.

26. See Waltz, *Man, the State, and War;* and Robert Jervis, "Cooperation Under the Security Dilemma," *World Politics* 30 (January 1978), pp. 167–214.

27. My argument here parallels Rousseau's critique of Hobbes. For an excellent critique of realist appropriations of Rousseau, see Michael Williams, "Rousseau, Realism, and Realpolitik," *Millennium* 18 (Summer 1989), pp. 188–204. Williams argues that far from being a fundamental starting point in the state of nature, for Rousseau the stag hunt represented a stage in man's fall. On p. 190, Williams cites Rousseau's description of man prior to leaving the state of nature: "Man only knows himself; he does not see his own well-being to be identified with or contrary to that of anyone else; he neither hates anything nor loves anything; but limited to no more than physical instinct, he is no one, he is an animal." For another critique of Hobbes on the state of nature that parallels my constructivist reading of anarchy, see Charles Landesman, "Reflections on Hobbes: Anarchy and Human Nature," in Peter Caws, ed., *The Causes of Quarrel* (Boston: Beacon, 1989), pp. 139–48.

28. Empirically, this suggestion is problematic, since the process of decolonization and the subsequent support of many Third World states by international society point to ways in which even the raw material of "empirical statehood" is constituted by the society of states. See Robert Jackson and Carl Rosberg, "Why Africa's Weak States Persist: The Empirical and the Juridical in Statehood," *World Politics* 35 (October 1982), pp. 1–24.

29. Waltz, *Theory of International Politics*, pp. 74–77.

30. See James Morrow, "Social Choice and System Structure in World Politics," *World Politics* 41 (October 1988), p. 89. Waltz's behavioral treatment of socialization may be usefully contrasted with the more cognitive approach taken by Ikenberry and the Kupchans in the following articles: G. John Ikenberry and Charles Kupchan, "Socialization and Hegemonic Power," *International Organization* 44 (Summer 1989), pp. 283–316; and Kupchan and Kupchan, "Concerts, Collective Security, and the Future of Europe." Their approach is close to my own, but they define socialization as an elite strategy to induce value change in others, rather than as a ubiquitous feature of interaction in terms of which all identities and interests get produced and reproduced.

31. Regarding individualism, see Richard Ashley, "The Poverty of Neorealism," *International Organization* 38 (Spring 1984), pp. 225–86; Wendt, "The Agent-Structure Problem in International Relations Theory"; and David Dessler, "What's at Stake in the Agent-Structure Debate?" *International Organization* 43 (Summer 1989), pp. 441–74. Regarding structuralism, see R. B. J. Walker, "Realism, Change, and International Political Theory," *International Studies Quarterly* 31 (March 1987), pp. 65–86; and Martin Hollis and Steven Smith, *Explaining and Understanding International Relations* (Oxford: Clarendon Press, 1989).

32. The importance of the distinction between constitutive and causal explanations is not sufficiently appreciated in constructivist discourse. See Wendt, "The Agent-Structure Problem in International Relations Theory,"

pp. 362–65; Wendt, "The States System and Global Militarization," pp. 110–13; and Wendt, "Bridging the Theory/Meta-Theory Gap in International Relations," *Review of International Studies* 17 (October 1991), p. 390.

33. See Blumer, "The Methodological Position of Symbolic Interactionism," pp. 2–4.

34. See Robert Grafstein, "Rational Choice: Theory and Institutions," in Kristen Monroe, ed., *The Economic Approach to Politics* (New York: Harper Collins, 1991), pp. 263–64. A good example of the promise and limits of transaction cost approaches to institutional analysis is offered by Robert Keohane in his *After Hegemony* (Princeton, N.J.: Princeton University Press, 1984).

35. This situation is not entirely metaphorical in world politics, since throughout history states have "discovered" each other, generating an instant anarchy as it were.

36. Mead's analysis of gestures remains definitive. See Mead's *Mind, Self, and Society*. See also the discussion of the role of signaling in the "mechanics of interaction" in Turner's *A Theory of Social Interaction*, pp. 74–79 and 92–115.

37. On the role of attribution processes in the interactionist account of identity-formation, see Sheldon Stryker and Avi Gottlieb, "Attribution Theory and Symbolic Interactionism," in John Harvey et al., eds., *New Directions in Attribution Research*, vol. 3 (Hillsdale, N.J.: Lawrence Erlbaum, 1981), pp. 425–58; and Kathleen Crittenden, "Sociological Aspects of Attribution," *Annual Review of Sociology*, vol. 9, 1983, pp. 425–46. On attributional processes in international relations, see Shawn Rosenberg and Gary Wolfsfeld, "International Conflict and the Problem of Attribution," *Journal of Conflict Resolution* 21 (March 1977), pp. 75–103.

38. On the "stagecraft" involved in "presentations of self," see Erving Goffman, *The Presentation of Self in Everyday Life* (New York: Doubleday, 1959). On the role of appearance in definitions of the situation, see Gregory Stone, "Appearance and the Self," in Arnold Rose, ed., *Human Behavior and Social Processes* (Boston: Houghton Mifflin, 1962), pp. 86–118.

39. This discussion of the role of possibilities and probabilities in threat perception owes much to Stewart Johnson's comments on an earlier draft of my article.

40. On the role of "reassurance" in threat situations, see Richard Ned Lebow and Janice Gross Stein, "Beyond Deterrence," *Journal of Social Issues*, vol. 43, no. 4, 1987, pp. 5–72.

41. On "reciprocal typifications," see Berger and Luckmann, *The Social Construction of Reality*, pp. 54–58.

42. Jeff Coulter, "Remarks on the Conceptualization of Social Structure," *Philosophy of the Social Sciences* 12 (March 1982), pp. 42–43.

43. The following articles by Noel Kaplowitz have made an important contribution to such thinking in international relations: "Psychopolitical Dimensions of International Relations: The Reciprocal Effects of Conflict Strategies," *International Studies Quarterly* 28 (December 1984), pp. 373–406; and "National Self-Images, Perception of Enemies, and Conflict Strategies: Psychopolitical Dimensions of International Relations," *Political Psychology* 11 (March 1990), pp. 39–82.

44. These arguments are common in theories of narcissism and altruism. See Heinz Kohut, *Self-Psychology and the Humanities* (New York: Norton, 1985); and Martin Hoffmann, "Empathy, Its Limitations, and Its Role in a Comprehensive Moral Theory," in William Kurtines and Jacob Gewirtz, eds., *Morality, Moral Behavior, and Moral Development* (New York: Wiley, 1984), pp. 283–302.

45. See C. Norman Alexander and Mary Glenn Wiley, "Situated Activity and Identity Formation," in Morris Rosenberg and Ralph Turner, eds., *Social Psychology: Sociological Perspectives* (New York: Basic Books, 1981), pp. 269–89.

46. Sheldon Stryker, "The Vitalization of Symbolic Interactionism," *Social Psychology Quarterly* 50 (March 1987), p. 93.

47. On the "maturity" of anarchies, see Barry Buzan, *People, States, and Fear* (Chapel Hill: University of North Carolina Press, 1983).

48. A similar intuition may lie behind Ashley's effort to reappropriate classical realist discourse for critical international relations theory. See Richard Ashley, "Political Realism and Human Interests," *International Studies Quarterly* 38 (June 1981), pp. 204–36.

49. Waltz has himself helped open up such a debate with his recognition that systemic factors condition but do not determine state actions. See Kenneth Waltz, "Reflections on *Theory of International Politics:* A Response to My Critics," in Robert Keohane, ed., *Neorealism and Its Critics* (New York: Columbia University Press, 1986), pp. 322–45. The growing literature on the observation that "democracies do not fight each other" is relevant to this question, as are two other studies that break important ground toward a "reductionist" theory of state identity: William Bloom's *Personal Identity, National Identity and International Relations* (Cambridge: Cambridge University Press, 1990) and Lumsdaine's *Ideals and Interests.*

50. See Berger and Luckmann, *The Social Construction of Reality*, p. 89. See also Douglas Maynard and Thomas Wilson, "On the Reification of Social Structure," in Scott McNall and Gary Howe, eds., *Current Perspectives in Social Theory*, vol. 1 (Greenwich, Conn.: JAI Press, 1980), pp. 287–322.

51. See Richard Ashley, "Social Will and International Anarchy," in Hayward Alker and Richard Ashley, eds., *After Realism*, work in progress, Massachusetts Institute of Technology, Cambridge, and Arizona State University, Tempe, 1992.

52. See Ralph Turner, "Role-Taking: Process Versus Conformity," in Rose, *Human Behavior and Social Processes*, pp. 20–40; and Judith Howard, "From Changing Selves toward Changing Society," in Howard and Callero, *The Self-Society Dynamic*, pp. 209–37.

53. On the relationship between commitment and identity, see Foote, "Identification as the Basis for a Theory of Motivation"; Howard Becker, "Notes on the Concept of Commitment," *American Journal of Sociology* 66 (July 1960), pp. 32–40; and Stryker, *Symbolic Interactionism*. On role salience, see Stryker, ibid.

54. On threats to identity and the types of resistance that they may create, see Glynis Breakwell, *Coping with Threatened Identities* (London: Methuen, 1986); and Terrell Northrup, "The Dynamic of Identity in Personal and Social Conflict," in Louis Kreisberg et al., eds., *Intractable Conflicts and Their Transformation* (Syracuse, N.Y.: Syracuse University Press, 1989), pp. 55–82. For a broad overview of resistance to change, see Timur Kuran, "The Tenacious Past: Theories of Personal and Collective Conservatism," *Journal of Economic Behavior and Organization* 10 (September 1988), pp. 143–71.

55. James March, "Bounded Rationality, Ambiguity, and the Engineering of Choice," *Bell Journal of Economics* 9 (Autumn 1978), p. 600.

56. Haskell Fain, *Normative Politics and the Community of Nations* (Philadelphia: Temple University Press, 1987).

57. This is the intersubjective basis for the principle of functional nondifferentiation among states, which "drops out" of Waltz's definition of structure because the latter has no explicit intersubjective basis. In international relations scholarship, the social production of territorial space has been emphasized primarily by poststructuralists. See, for example, Richard Ashley, "The Geopolitics of Geopolitical Space: Toward a Critical Social Theory of International Politics," *Alternatives* 12 (October 1987), pp. 403–34; and Simon Dalby, *Creating the Second Cold War* (London: Pinter, 1990). But the idea of space as both product and constituent of practice is also prominent in structurationist discourse. See Giddens, *Central Problems in Social Theory;* and Derek Gregory and John Urry, eds.,

Social Relations and Spatial Structures (London: Macmillan, 1985).

58. See John Ruggie, "Continuity and Transformation in the World Polity: Toward a Neorealist Synthesis," *World Politics* 35 (January 1983), pp. 261–85.

59. For a definition and discussion of "social closure," see Raymond Murphy, *Social Closure* (Oxford: Clarendon Press, 1988).

60. See Richard Ashley, "Untying the Sovereign State: A Double Reading of the Anarchy Problematique," *Millennium* 17 (Summer 1988), pp. 227–62.

61. See, for example, Mohammed Ayoob, "The Third World in the System of States: Acute Schizophrenia or Growing Pains?" *International Studies Quarterly* 33 (March 1989), pp. 67–80.

62. See William Coplin, "International Law and Assumptions about the State System," *World Politics* 17 (July 1965), pp. 615–34.

63. See Anthony Smith, "States and Homelands: The Social and Geopolitical Implications of National Territory," *Millennium* 10 (Autumn 1981), pp. 187–202.

64. This assumes that there are no other, competing, principles that organize political space and identity in the international system and coexist with traditional notions of sovereignty; in fact, of course, there are. On "spheres of influence" and "informal empires," see Jan Triska, ed., *Dominant Powers and Subordinate States* (Durham, N.C.: Duke University Press, 1986); and Ronald Robinson, "The Excentric Idea of Imperialism, With or Without Empire," in Wolfgang Mommsen and Jurgen Osterhammel, eds., *Imperialism and After: Continuities and Discontinuities* (London: Allen & Unwin, 1986), pp. 267–89. On Arab conceptions of sovereignty, see Michael Barnett, "Sovereignty, Institutions, and Identity: From Pan-Arabism to the Arab State System," unpublished manuscript, University of Wisconsin, Madison, 1991.

65. David Strang, "Anomaly and Commonplace in European Expansion: Realist and Institutional Accounts," *International Organization* 45 (Spring 1991), pp. 143–62.

66. On "dynamic density," see Ruggie, "Continuity and Transformation in the World Polity"; and Waltz, "Reflections on *Theory of International Politics*." The role of interdependence in conditioning the speed and depth of social learning is much greater than the attention to which I have paid it. On the consequences of interdependence under anarchy, see Helen Milner, "The Assumption of Anarchy in International Relations Theory: A Critique," *Review of International Studies* 17 (January 1991), pp. 67–85.

67. See Michael Taylor, *Anarchy and Cooperation* (New York: Wiley, 1976); and Robert Axelrod, *The Evolution of Cooperation* (New York: Basic Books, 1984).

68. Mead, *Mind, Self, and Society.*

69. Strictly speaking, this is not true, since in iterated games the addition of future benefits to current ones changes the payoff structure of the game at T1, in this case from prisoners' dilemma to an assurance game. This transformation of interest takes place entirely within the actor, however, and as such is not a function of interaction with the other.

70. In fairness to Axelrod, he does point out that internalization of norms is a real possibility that may increase the resilience of institutions. My point is that this important idea cannot be derived from an approach to theory that takes identities and interests as exogenously given.

71. On "European identity," see Barry Buzan et al., eds., *The European Security Order Recast* (London: Pinter, 1990), pp. 45–63.

72. On "embeddedness," see John Ruggie, "International Regimes, Transactions, and Change: Embedded Liberalism in a Postwar Economic Order," in Krasner, *International Regimes*, pp. 195–232.

73. See Grieco, "Anarchy and the Limits of Cooperation."

74. On the difficulties of creating cooperative security regimes given competitive interests,

see Robert Jervis, "Security Regimes," in Krasner, *International Regimes,* pp. 173–94; and Charles Lipson, "International Cooperation in Economic and Security Affairs," *World Politics* 37 (October 1984), pp. 1–23.

75. See Mead, *Mind, Self, and Society.*

76. Turner, "Role-Taking."

77. On "character planning," see Jon Elster, *Sour Grapes: Studies in the Subversion of Rationality* (Cambridge: Cambridge University Press, 1983), p. 117.

78. For useful overviews of New Thinking, see Mikhail Gorbachev, *Perestroika: New Thinking for Our Country and the World* (New York: Harper & Row, 1987); and Allen Lynch, *Gorbachev's International Outlook: Intellectual Origins and Political Consequences* (New York: Institute for East–West Security Studies, 1989).

79. For useful overviews of these factors, see Jack Snyder, "The Gorbachev Revolution: A Waning of Soviet Expansionism?" *World Politics* 12 (Winter 1987–88), pp. 93–121; and Stephen Meyer, "The Sources and Prospects of Gorbachev's New Political Thinking on Security," *International Security* 13 (Fall 1988), pp. 124–63.

80. See Daniel Bar-Tal et al., "Conflict Termination: An Epistemological Analysis of International Cases," *Political Psychology* 10 (June 1989), pp. 233–55.

81. See Robert Cox, "Social Forces, States and World Orders: Beyond International Relations Theory," in Keohane, *Neorealism and Its Critics,* pp. 204–55. See also Brian Fay, *Critical Social Science* (Ithaca, N.Y.: Cornell University Press, 1987).

82. Hazel Markus and Paula Nurius, "Possible Selves," *American Psychologist* 41 (September 1986), pp. 954–69.

83. See Goffman, *The Presentation of Self in Everyday Life;* Eugene Weinstein and Paul Deutschberger, "Some Dimensions of Altercasting," *Sociometry* 26 (December 1963), pp. 454–66; and Walter Earle, "International Relations and the Psychology of Control: Alternative Control Strategies and Their Consequences," *Political Psychology* 7 (June 1986), pp. 369–75.

84. See Volker Boge and Peter Wilke, "Peace Movements and Unilateral Disarmament: Old Concepts in a New Light," *Anns Control* 7 (September 1986), pp. 156–70; Zeev Maoz and Daniel Felsenthal, "Self-Binding Commitments, the Inducement of Trust, Social Choice, and the Theory of International Cooperation," *International Studies Quarterly* 31 (June 1987), pp. 177–200; and V. Sakamoto, "Unilateral Initiative as an Alternative Strategy," *World Futures,* vol. 24, nos. 1–4, 1987, pp. 107–34.

85. On rewards, see Thomas Milburn and Daniel Christie, "Rewarding in International Politics," *Political Psychology* 10 (December 1989), pp. 625–45.

86. The importance of reciprocity in completing the process of structural transformation makes the logic in this stage similar to that in the "evolution of cooperation." The difference is one of prerequisites and objective: in the former, ego's tentative redefinition of self enables it to try and change alter by acting "as if" both were already playing a new game; in the latter, ego acts only on the basis of given interests and prior experience, with transformation emerging only as an unintended consequence.

87. Yale Ferguson and Richard Mansbach, "Between Celebration and Despair: Constructive Suggestions for Future International Theory," *International Studies Quarterly* 35 (December 1991), p. 375.

88. For excellent discussions of this tension, see Walker, "Sovereignty, Identity, Community"; and R. B. J. Walker, "Security, Sovereignty, and the Challenge of World Politics," *Alternatives* 15 (Winter 1990), pp. 3–27. On institutional path dependencies, see Stephen Krasner, "Sovereignty: An Institutional Perspective," *Comparative Political Studies* 21 (April 1988), pp. 66–94.

J. ANN TICKNER

Man, the State, and War: Gendered Perspectives on National Security

> It is not in giving life but in risking life that man is raised above the animal: that is why superiority has been accorded in humanity not to the sex that brings forth but to that which kills.
>
> —Simone de Beauvoir

> If we do not redefine manhood, war is inevitable.
>
> —Paul Fussell

In the face of what is generally perceived as a dangerous international environment, states have ranked national security high in terms of their policy priorities. According to international relations scholar Kenneth Waltz, the state conducts its affairs in the "brooding shadow of violence," and therefore war could break out at any time.[1] In the name of national security, states have justified large defense budgets, which take priority over domestic spending, military conscription of their young adult male population, foreign invasions, and the curtailment of civil liberties. The security of the state is perceived as a core value that is generally supported unquestioningly by most citizens, particularly in time of war. While the role of the state in the twentieth century has expanded to include the provision of domestic social programs, national security often takes precedence over the social security of individuals.

When we think about the provision of national security we enter into what has been, and continues to be, an almost exclusively male domain.

While most women support what they take to be legitimate calls for state action in the interests of international security, the task of defining, defending, and advancing the security interests of the state is a man's affair, a task that, through its association with war, has been especially valorized and rewarded in many cultures throughout history. As Simone de Beauvoir's explanation for male superiority suggests, giving one's life for one's country has been considered the highest form of patriotism, but it is an act from which women have been virtually excluded. While men have been associated with defending the state and advancing its international interests as soldiers and diplomats, women have typically been engaged in the "ordering" and "comforting" roles both in the domestic sphere, as mothers and basic needs providers, and in the caring professions, as teachers, nurses, and social workers.[2] The role of women with respect to national security has been ambiguous: defined as those whom the state and its men are protecting, women have had little control over the conditions of their protection.

* * *

From J. Ann Tickner, *Gender in International Relations: Feminist Perspectives on Achieving Global Security* (New York: Columbia University Press, 1992), 27–66.

A Gendered Perspective on National Security

Morgenthau, Waltz, and other realists claim that it is possible to develop a rational, objective theory of international politics based on universal laws that operate across time and space. In her feminist critique of the natural sciences, Evelyn Fox Keller points out that most scientific communities share the "assumption that the universe they study is directly accessible, represented by concepts shaped not by language but only by the demands of logic and experiment." The laws of nature, according to this view of science, are beyond the relativity of language.[3] Like most contemporary feminists, Keller rejects this positivist view of science that, she asserts, imposes a coercive, hierarchical, and conformist pattern on scientific inquiry. Since most contemporary feminist scholars believe that knowledge is socially constructed, they are skeptical of finding an unmediated foundation for knowledge that realists claim is possible. Since they believe that it is language that transmits knowledge, many feminists suggest that the scholarly claims about the neutral uses of language and about objectivity must continually be questioned.[4]

I shall now investigate the individual, the state, and the international system—the three levels of analysis that realists use in their analysis of war and national security—and examine how they have been constructed in realist discourse. I shall argue that the language used to describe these concepts comes out of a Western-centered historical worldview that draws almost exclusively on the experiences of men. Underneath its claim to universality this worldview privileges a view of security that is constructed out of values associated with hegemonic masculinity.

"Political Man"

In his *Politics Among Nations*, a text rich in historical detail, Morgenthau has constructed a world almost entirely without women. Morgenthau claims that individuals are engaged in a struggle for power whenever they come into contact with one another, for the tendency to dominate exists at all levels of human life: the family, the polity, and the international system; it is modified only by the conditions under which the struggle takes place.[5] Since women rarely occupy positions of power in any of these arenas, we can assume that, when Morgenthau talks about domination, he is talking primarily about men, although not all men.[6] His "political man" is a social construct based on a partial representation of human nature abstracted from the behavior of men in positions of public power.[7] Morgenthau goes on to suggest that, while society condemns the violent behavior that can result from this struggle for power within the polity, it encourages it in the international system in the form of war.

While Morgenthau's "political man" has been criticized by other international relations scholars for its essentializing view of human nature, the social construction of hegemonic masculinity and its opposition to a devalued femininity have been central to the way in which the discourse of international politics has been constructed more generally. In Western political theory from the Greeks to Machiavelli, traditions upon which contemporary realism relies heavily for its analysis, this socially constructed type of masculinity has been projected onto the international behavior of states. The violence with which it is associated has been legitimated through the glorification of war.

* * *

The International System: The War of Everyman Against Everyman

According to Richard Ashley, realists have privileged a higher reality called "the sovereign state" against which they have posited anarchy understood in a negative way as difference, ambiguity, and contingency—as a space that is external and dangerous.[8] All these characteristics have also been attributed to women. Anarchy is an actual or potential site of war. The most common metaphor that realists employ to describe the anarchical international system is that of the seventeenth-century English philosopher Thomas Hobbes's depiction of the state of nature. Although Hobbes did not write much about international politics, realists have applied his description of individuals' behavior in a hypothetical precontractual state of nature, which Hobbes termed the war of everyman against everyman, to the behavior of states in the international system.[9]

Carole Pateman argues that, in all contemporary discussions of the state of nature, the differentiation between the sexes is generally ignored, even though it was an important consideration for contract theorists themselves.[10] Although Hobbes did suggest that women as well as men could be free and equal individuals in the state of nature, his description of human behavior in this environment refers to that of adult males whose behavior is taken as constitutive of human nature as a whole by contemporary realist analysis. According to Jane Flax, the individuals that Hobbes described in the state of nature appeared to come to full maturity without any engagement with one another; they were solitary creatures lacking any socialization in interactive behavior. Any interactions they did have led to power struggles that resulted in domination or submission. Suspicion of others' motives led to behavior characterized by aggression, self-interest, and the drive for autonomy.[11] In a similar vein, Christine Di Stephano uses feminist psychoanalytic theory to support her claim that the masculine dimension of atomistic egoism is powerfully underscored in Hobbes's state of nature, which, she asserts, is built on the foundation of denied maternity. "Hobbes' abstract man is a creature who is self-possessed and radically solitary in a crowded and inhospitable world, whose relations with others are unavoidably contractual and whose freedom consists in the absence of impediments to the attainment of privately generated and understood desires."[12]

As a model of human behavior, Hobbes's depiction of individuals in the state of nature is partial at best; certain feminists have argued that such behavior could be applicable only to adult males, for if life was to go on for more than one generation in the state of nature, women must have been involved in activities such as reproduction and child rearing rather than in warfare. Reproductive activities require an environment that can provide for the survival of infants and behavior that is interactive and nurturing.

* * *

* * * [W]ar is central to the way we learn about international relations. * * * War is a time when male and female characteristics become polarized; it is a gendering activity at a time when the discourse of militarism and masculinity permeates the whole fabric of society.[13]

As Jean Elshtain points out, war is an experience to which women are exterior; men have inhabited the world of war in a way that women have not.[14] The history of international politics is therefore a history from which women are, for the most part, absent. Little material can be found on women's roles in wars; generally they are seen as victims, rarely as agents. While war can be a time of advancement for women as they step in to do men's jobs, the battlefront takes precedence, so the hierarchy remains and women are urged to step aside once peace is restored. When women themselves engage in violence, it is often portrayed as a mob or a food riot that is out of control.[15] Movements for peace, which are also part of our history, have not been central to the conventional way in which the evolution of the Western state system has been presented to us. International relations scholars of the early twentieth century, who wrote positively about the possibilities of international law and the collective security system of the League of Nations, were labeled "idealists" and not taken seriously by the more powerful realist tradition.

Metaphors, such as Hobbes's state of nature, are primarily concerned with representing conflictual relations between great powers. The images used to describe nineteenth-century imperialist projects and contemporary great power relations with former colonial states are somewhat different. Historically, colonial people were often described in terms that drew on characteristics associated with women in order to place them lower in a hierarchy that put their white male colonizers on top. As the European state system expanded outward to conquer much of the world in the nineteenth century, its "civilizing" mission was frequently described in stereotypically gendered terms. Colonized peoples were often described as being effeminate, masculinity was an attribute of the white man, and colonial order depended on Victorian standards of manliness. Cynthia Enloe suggests that the concept of "ladylike behavior" was one of the mainstays of imperialist civilization. Like sanitation and Christianity, feminine respectability was meant to convince colonizers and colonized alike that foreign conquest was right and necessary. Masculinity denoted protection of the respectable lady; she stood for the civilizing mission that justified the colonization of benighted peoples.[16] Whereas the feminine stood for danger and disorder for Machiavelli, the European female, in contrast to her colonial counterpart, came to represent a stable, civilized order in nineteenth-century representations of British imperialism.

An example of the way in which these gender identities were manipulated to justify Western policy with respect to the rest of the world can also be seen in attitudes toward Latin America prevalent in the United States in the nineteenth century. According to Michael Hunt, nineteenth-century American images of Latin society depicted a (usually black) male who was lazy, dishonest, and corrupt. A contrary image that was more positive—a Latin as redeemable—took the form of a fair-skinned senorita living in a marginalized society, yet escaping its degrading effects. Hunt suggests that Americans entered the twentieth century with three images of Latin America fostered through legends brought back by American merchants and diplomats. These legends, perpetuated through school texts, cartoons, and political rhetoric, were even incorporated into the views of policymakers. The three images pictured the Latin as a half-breed brute, feminized, or infantile. In each case, Americans stood superior; the first image permitted a predatory aggressiveness, the second allowed the United States to assume the role of ardent suitor, and the third justified America's need to provide tutelage and discipline. All these images are profoundly gendered: the United States as a civilizing warrior, a suitor, or a father, and Latin America as a lesser male, a female, or a child.[17]

Such images, although somewhat muted, remain today and are particularly prevalent in the thinking of Western states when they are dealing with the Third World. * * *

＊   ＊   ＊

Feminist Perspectives on National Security

Women Define Security

It is difficult to find definitions by women of national security. While it is not necessarily the case that women have not had ideas on this subject, they are not readily accessible in the literature of international relations. When women speak or write about national security, they are often dismissed as being naive or unrealistic. An example of this is the women in the United States and Europe who spoke out in the early years of the century for a more secure world order. Addressing the International Congress of Women at the Hague during World War I, Jane Addams spoke of the need for a new internationalism to replace the self-destructive nationalism that contributed so centrally to the outbreak and mass destruction of that war. Resolutions adopted at the close of the congress questioned the assumption that women, and civilians more generally, could be protected during modern war. The conference concluded that assuring security through military means was no longer possible owing to the indiscriminate nature of modern warfare, and it called for disarmament as a more appropriate course for ensuring future security.[18]

At the Women's International Peace Conference in Halifax, Canada, in 1985, a meeting of women from all over the world, participants defined security in various ways depending on the most immediate threats to their survival; security meant safe working conditions and freedom from the threat of war or unemployment or the economic squeeze of foreign debt. Discussions of the meaning of security revealed divisions between Western middle-class women's concerns with nuclear war, concerns that were similar to those of Jane Addams and her colleagues, and Third World women who defined insecurity more broadly in terms of the structural violence associated with imperialism, militarism, racism, and sexism. Yet all agreed that security meant nothing if it was built on others' insecurity.[19]

The final document of the World Conference to Review and Appraise the Achievements of the United Nations Decade for Women, held in Nairobi in 1985, offered a similarly multidimensional definition of security. The introductory chapter of the document defined peace as "not only the absence of war, violence and hostilities at the national and international levels but also the enjoyment of economic and social justice."[20] All these definitions of security take issue with realists' assumptions that security is zero-sum and must therefore be built on the insecurity of others.

*   *   *

Citizenship Redefined

Building on the notion of hegemonic masculinity, the notion of the citizen-warrior depends on a devalued femininity for its construction. In international relations, this devalued femininity is bound up with myths about women as victims in need of protection; the protector/protected myth contributes to the legitimation of a milita-

rized version of citizenship that results in unequal gender relations that can precipitate violence against women. Certain feminists have called for the construction of an enriched version of citizenship that would depend less on military values and more on an equal recognition of women's contributions to society. Such a notion of citizenship cannot come about, however, until myths that perpetuate views of women as victims rather than agents are eliminated.

One such myth is the association of women with peace, an association that has been invalidated through considerable evidence of women's support for men's wars in many societies.[21] In spite of a gender gap, a plurality of women generally support war and national security policies; Bernice Carroll suggests that the association of women and peace is one that has been imposed on women by their disarmed condition.[22] In the West, this association grew out of the Victorian ideology of women's moral superiority and the glorification of motherhood. This ideal was expressed by feminist Charlotte Perkins Gilman whose book *Herland* was first serialized in *The Forerunner* in 1915. Gilman glorified women as caring and nurturing mothers whose private sphere skills could benefit the world at large.[23] Most turn-of-the-century feminists shared Gilman's ideas. But if the implication of this view was that women were disqualified from participating in the corrupt world of political and economic power by virtue of their moral superiority, the result could only be the perpetuation of male dominance. Many contemporary feminists see dangers in the continuation of these essentializing myths that can only result in the perpetuation of women's subordination and reinforce dualisms that serve to make men more powerful. The association of femininity with peace lends support to an idealized masculinity that depends on constructing women as passive victims in need of protection. It also contributes to the claim that women are naive in matters relating to international politics. An enriched, less militarized notion of citizenship cannot be built on such a weak foundation.

While women have often been willing to support men's wars, many women are ambivalent about fighting in them, often preferring to leave that task to men. Feminists have also been divided on this issue; some argue, on the grounds of equality, that women must be given equal access to the military, while others suggest that women must resist the draft in order to promote a politics of peace. * * *

* * *

In spite of many women's support for men's wars, a consistent gender gap in voting on defense-related issues in many countries suggests that women are less supportive of policies that rest on the use of direct violence. Before the outbreak of the Persian Gulf War in 1990, women in the United States were overwhelmingly against the use of force and, for the first time, women alone turned the public opinion polls against opting for war.[24] During the 1980s, when the Reagan administration was increasing defense budgets, women were less likely to support defense at the expense of social programs, a pattern that, in the United States, holds true for women's behavior more generally.

Explanations for this gender gap, which in the United States appears to be increasing as time goes on, range from suggestions that women have not been socialized into the practice of violence to claims that women are increasingly voting their own interests. While holding down jobs, millions of women also care for children, the aged, and the sick—activities that usually take place outside the economy. When more resources go to the military, additional burdens are placed on such women as public sector resources for social services shrink. While certain women are able, through access to the military, to give service to their country, many more are serving in these traditional care-giving roles. A feminist challenge to the traditional definition of patriotism should therefore question the meaning of service to one's country.[25] In contrast to a citizenship that rests on the assumption that it is

more glorious to die than to live for one's state, Wendy Brown suggests that a more constructive view of citizenship could center on the courage to sustain life.[26] In similar terms, Jean Elshtain asserts the need to move toward a politics that shifts the focus of political loyalty and identity from sacrifice to responsibility.[27] Only when women's contributions to society are seen as equal to men's can these reconstructed visions of citizenship come about.

Feminist Perspectives on States' Security-Seeking Behavior

Realists have offered us an instrumental version of states' security-seeking behavior, which, I have argued, depends on a partial representation of human behavior associated with a stereotypical hegemonic masculinity. Feminist redefinitions of citizenship allow us to envisage a less militarized version of states' identities, and feminist theories can also propose alternative models for states' international security-seeking behavior, extrapolated from a more comprehensive view of human behavior.

Realists use state-of-nature stories as metaphors to describe the insecurity of states in an anarchical international system. I shall suggest an alternative story, which could equally be applied to the behavior of individuals in the state of nature. Although frequently unreported in standard historical accounts, it is a true story, not a myth, about a state of nature in early nineteenth-century America. Among those present in the first winter encampment of the 1804–1806 Lewis and Clark expedition into the Northwest territories was Sacajawea, a member of the Shoshone tribe. Sacajawea had joined the expedition as the wife of a French interpreter; her presence was proving invaluable to the security of the expedition's members, whose task it was to explore uncharted territory and establish contact with the native inhabitants to inform them of claims to these territories by the United States. Although unanticipated by its leaders, the presence of a woman served to assure the native inhabitants that the expedition was peaceful since the Native Americans assumed that war parties would not include women: the expedition was therefore safer because it was not armed.[28]

This story demonstrates that the introduction of women can change the way humans are assumed to behave in the state of nature. Just as Sacajawea's presence changed the Native American's expectations about the behavior of intruders into their territory, the introduction of women into our state-of-nature myths could change the way we think about the behavior of states in the international system. The use of the Hobbesian analogy in international relations theory is based on a partial view of human nature that is stereotypically masculine; a more inclusive perspective would see human nature as both conflictual and cooperative, containing elements of social reproduction and interdependence as well as domination and separation. Generalizing from this more comprehensive view of human nature, a feminist perspective would assume that the potential for international community also exists and that an atomistic, conflictual view of the international system is only a partial representation of reality. Liberal individualism, the instrumental rationality of the marketplace, and the defector's self-help approach in Rousseau's stag hunt [see p. 344] are all, in analagous ways, based on a partial masculine model of human behavior.[29]

* * *

Feminist perspectives on national security take us beyond realism's statist representations. They allow us to see that the realist view of national security is constructed out of a masculinized discourse that, while it is only a partial view of reality, is taken as universal. Women's definitions of security are multilevel and multidimensional. Women have defined security as the absence of violence whether it be military, economic, or sexual. Not until the hierarchical social relations, including gender relations, that have been hidden by realism's frequently depersonalized discourse are brought to light can we begin to construct a language of national security that speaks out of the multiple experiences of both women and men. * * *

NOTES

I owe the title of this chapter to Kenneth Waltz's book *Man, the State, and War*.

De Beauvoir epigraph from *The Second Sex* [New York: Knopf, 1972], p. 72. De Beauvoir's analysis suggests that she herself endorsed this explanation for male superiority; * * * Fussell epigraph quoted by Anna Quindlen in the *New York Times*, February 7, 1991, p. A25.

1. [Kenneth N.] Waltz, *Theory of International Politics* [Boston: Addison-Wesley, 1979], p. 102.
2. While heads of state, all men, discussed the "important" issues in world politics at the Group of Seven meeting in London in July 1991, Barbara Bush and Princess Diana were pictured on the "CBS Evening News" (July 17, 1991) meeting with British AIDS patients.
3. [Evelyn Fox] Keller, *Reflections on Gender and Science* [New Haven: Yale University Press 1985], p. 130.
4. For example, see [Donna] Haraway, *Primate Visions* [New York: Routledge, 1989], ch. 1. Considering scientific practice from the perspective of the way its factual findings are narrated, Haraway provocatively explores how scientific theories produce and are embedded in particular kinds of stories. This allows her to challenge the neutrality and objectivity of scientific facts. She suggests that texts about primates can be read as science fictions about race, gender, and nature.
5. [Hans J.] Morgenthau, *Politics among Nations* [New York: Knopf, 1973], p. 34.
6. Morgenthau does talk about dominating mothers-in-law, but as feminist research has suggested, it is generally men, legally designated as heads of households in most societies, who hold the real power even in the family

and certainly with respect to the family's interaction with the public sphere.

7. For an extended discussion of Morgenthau's "political man," see [J. Ann] Tickner, "Hans Morgenthau's Principles of Political Realism" [*Millennium* 17(3):429–440]. In neorealism's depersonalized structural analysis, Morgenthau's depiction of human nature slips out of sight.

8. [Richard K.] Ashley, "Untying the Sovereign State" [*Millennium* 17(2) (1988)], p. 230.

9. Hobbes, *Leviathan*, part 1, ch. 13, quoted in Vasquez, ed., *Classics of International Relations*, pp. 213–215.

10. [Carole] Pateman, *The Sexual Contract* [Stanford: Stanford University Press, 1988], p. 41.

11. [Jane] Flax, "Political Philosophy and the Patriarchal Unconscious: A Psychoanalytic Perspective on Epistemology and Metaphysics," in Harding and Hintikka, eds., *Discovering Reality* [Dordrecht, Holland: D. Reidel, 1983], pp. 245–281.

12. [Christine] Di Stephano, "Masculinity as Ideology in Political Theory" [Women's Studies International Forum 6(6) (1983):633–644]. Carole Pateman has disputed some of Di Stephano's assumptions about Hobbes's characterizations of women and the family in the state of nature. But this does not deny the fact that Di Stephano's characterization of men is the one used by realists in their depiction of the international system. See Pateman, "'God Hath Ordained to Man a Helper': Hobbes, Patriarchy, and Conjugal Right."

13. [Margaret Randolph] Higonnet et al., *Behind the Lines* [New Haven: Yale University Press, 1987], introduction.

14. [Jean Bethke] Elshtain, *Women and War* [New York: Basic Books, 1987], p. 194.

15. Ibid., p. 168.

16. [Cynthia] Enloe, *Bananas, Beaches, and Bases* [Berkeley: University of California Press, 1990], pp. 48–49.

17. [Michael H.] Hunt, *Ideology and U.S. Foreign Policy* [New Haven: Yale University Press, 1987], pp. 58–62.

18. [Jane] Addams et al., *Women at The Hague* [New York: Macmillan, 1916], pp. 150ff.

19. [Anne Sisson] Runyan, "Feminism, Peace, and International Politics" [Ph.D. diss., American University, 1988], ch. 6.

20. "Forward-looking Strategies for the Advancement of Women towards the Year 2000." Quoted in [Hilkka] Pietilä and [Jeanne] Vickers, *Making Women Matter* [London: Zed Books, 1990], pp. 46–47.

21. See Elshtain, *Women and War*, ch. 3.

22. Carroll, "Feminism and Pacifism: Historical and Theoretical Connections," in [Ruth Roach] Pierson, ed., *Women and Peace* [London: Croom Helm, 1987], pp. 2–28.

23. Margaret Hobbs, "The Perils of 'Unbridled Masculinity': Pacifist Elements in the Feminist and Socialist Thought of Charlotte Perkins Gilman," in Pierson, ed., *Women and Peace*, pp. 149–169.

24. The *New York Times* of December 12, 1990 (p. A35) reported that while men were about evenly split on attacking Iraqi forces in Kuwait, women were 73 percent against and 22 percent in favor.

25. Suzanne Gordon, "Another Enemy," *Boston Globe*, March 8, 1991, p. 15.

26. [Wendy] Brown, *Manhood and Politics* [Totowa, N.J.: Rowman and Littlefield, 1988], p. 206.

27. Elshtain, "Sovereignty, Identity, Sacrifice," in [V. Spike] Peterson, ed., *Gendered States* [Boulder: Lynne Rienner, 1992].

28. I am grateful to Michael Capps, historian at the Lewis and Clark Museum in St. Louis, Missouri, for this information. The story of Sacajawea is told in one of the museum's exhibits.

29. In *Man, the State, and War* [New York: Columbia University Press, 1959], [Kenneth N.] Waltz argues that "in the stag-hunt example, the will of the rabbit-snatcher was rational and predictable from his own point of view" (p. 183), while "in the early state of nature, men were sufficiently dispersed to make any pattern of cooperation unnecessary" (p. 167).

Neorealist revisionists, such as Snidal [see "Relative Gains and the Pattern of International Cooperation"] do not question the masculine bias of the stag hunt metaphor. Like Waltz and Rousseau, they also assume the autonomous, adult male (unparented and in an environment without women or children) in their discussion of the stag hunt; they do not question the rationality of the rabbit-snatching defector or the restrictive situational descriptions implied by their payoff matrices. Transformations in the social nature of an interaction are very hard to represent using such a model. Their reformulation of Waltz's position is instead focused on the exploration of different specifications of the game payoff in less conflictual ways (i.e., as an assurance game) and on inferences concerning the likely consequences of relative gain-seeking behavior in a gamelike interaction with more than two (equally autonomous and unsocialized) players.

4 The International System

Liberals, realists, and radicals offer different conceptions of the international system. Realist Hans J. Morgenthau writes in Politics among Nations *(4th ed., 1967) that the international system is characterized by the desire of state actors to maximize power. For international stability to be achieved, a balance-of-power system is necessary. In this selection, Morgenthau discusses what states can do to ensure the balance.*

One prominent strand of liberal thinking conceives the international system as an "international society." Hedley Bull's The Anarchical Society *(2d ed., 1977), a major statement of the so-called English School of international relations, argues that states in the international society, no matter how competitive, have nonetheless had common interests, developed common rules, and participated in common institutions. According to this variant of liberal thinking, these commonalities represent elements of order that regulate competition in the international system.*

What are the characteristics of the contemporary international system? John Ikenberry, Michael Mastanduno, and William C. Wohlforth argue that the United States has emerged from the 1990s as the unrivaled global power in a unipolar international system. What, they ask, are the policy and theoretical implications of unipolarity? Are constraints on the United States really removed with unipolarity? What are the implications for balance of power or power transition theories? The authors suggest the need to rethink not only balance of power and alliances but also the logic of international economic cooperation and the relationship between power and legitimacy in light of unipolarity.

HANS J. MORGENTHAU

The Balance of Power[1]

The aspiration for power on the part of several nations, each trying either to maintain or overthrow the status quo, leads of necessity to a configuration that is called the balance of power and to policies that aim at preserving it. We say "of necessity" advisedly. For here again we are confronted with the basic misconception that has impeded the understanding of international politics and has made us the prey of illusions. This misconception asserts that men have a choice between power politics and its necessary outgrowth, the balance of power, on the other hand, and a different, better kind of international relations on the other. It insists that a foreign policy based on the balance of power is one among several possible foreign policies and that only stupid and evil men will choose the former and reject the latter.

It will be shown * * * that the international balance of power is only a particular manifestation of a general social principle to which all societies composed of a number of autonomous units owe the autonomy of their component parts; that the balance of power and policies aiming at its preservation are not only inevitable but are an essential stabilizing factor in a society of sovereign nations; and that the instability of the international balance of power is due not to the faultiness of the principle but to the particular conditions under which the principle must operate in a society of sovereign nations.

From Hans J. Morgenthau, *Politics among Nations: The Struggle for Power and Peace*, 4th ed. (New York: Knopf, 1967), Chaps. 11, 12, 14. Some of the author's notes have been omitted.

Social Equilibrium

Balance of Power as Universal Concept

The concept of "equilibrium" as a synonym for "balance" is commonly employed in many sciences—physics, biology, economics, sociology, and political science. It signifies stability within a system composed of a number of autonomous forces. Whenever the equilibrium is disturbed either by an outside force or by a change in one or the other elements composing the system, the system shows a tendency to re-establish either the original or a new equilibrium. Thus equilibrium exists in the human body. While the human body changes in the process of growth, the equilibrium persists as long as the changes occurring in the different organs of the body do not disturb the body's stability. This is especially so if the quantitative and qualitative changes in the different organs are proportionate to each other. When, however, the body suffers a wound or loss of one of its organs through outside interference, or experiences a malignant growth or a pathological transformation of one of its organs, the equilibrium is disturbed, and the body tries to overcome the disturbance by reestablishing the equilibrium either on the same or a different level from the one that obtained before the disturbance occurred.[2]

The same concept of equilibrium is used in a social science, such as economics, with reference to the relations between the different elements of the economic system, e.g., between savings and investments, exports and imports, supply and demand, costs and prices. Contemporary capitalism itself has been described as a system of "countervailing power."[3] It also applies to society as a whole. Thus we search for a proper balance between different geographical regions, such as the East and the West, the North and the South; between different kinds of activities, such as agriculture and industry, heavy and light industries, big and small businesses, producers and consumers, management and labor, between different functional groups, such as city and country, the old, the middle-aged, and the young, the economic and the political sphere, the middle classes and the upper and lower classes.

Two assumptions are at the foundation of all such equilibriums: first, that the elements to be balanced are necessary for society or are entitled to exist and, second, that without a state of equilibrium among them one element will gain ascendancy over the others, encroach upon their interests and rights, and may ultimately destroy them. Consequently, it is the purpose of all such equilibriums to maintain the stability of the system without destroying the multiplicity of the elements composing it. If the goal were stability alone, it could be achieved by allowing one element to destroy or overwhelm the others and take their place. Since the goal is stability plus the preservation of all the elements of the system, the equilibrium must aim at preventing any element from gaining ascendancy over the others. The means employed to maintain the equilibrium consist in allowing the different elements to pursue their opposing tendencies up to the point where the tendency of one is not so strong as to overcome the tendency of the others, but strong enough to prevent the others from overcoming its own. * * *

* * *

Different Methods of the Balance of Power

The balancing process can be carried on either by diminishing the weight of the heavier scale or by increasing the weight of the lighter one.

Divide and Rule

The former method has found its classic manifestation, aside from the imposition of onerous conditions in peace treaties and the incitement to treason and revolution, in the maxim "divide and rule." It has been resorted to by nations who tried to make or keep their competitors weak by dividing them or keeping them divided. The most consistent and important policies of this kind in modern times are the policy of France with respect to Germany and the policy of the Soviet Union with respect to the rest of Europe. From the seventeenth century to the end of the Second World War, it has been an unvarying principle of French foreign policy either to favor the division of the German Empire into a number of small independent states or to prevent the coalescence of such states into one unified nation. * * * Similarly, the Soviet Union from the twenties to the present has consistently opposed all plans for the unification of Europe, on the assumption that the pooling of the divided strength of the European nations into a "Western bloc" would give the enemies of the Soviet Union such power as to threaten the latter's security.

The other method of balancing the power of several nations consists in adding to the strength of the weaker nation. This method can be carried out by two different means: Either B can increase its power sufficiently to offset, if not surpass, the power of A, and vice versa; or B can pool its power with the power of all the other nations that pursue identical policies with regard to A, in which case A will pool its power with all the nations pursuing identical policies with respect to B. The former alternative is exemplified by the policy of compensations and the armament race as well as by disarmament; the latter, by the policy of alliances.

Compensations

Compensations of a territorial nature were a common device in the eighteenth and nineteenth centuries for maintaining a balance of power which had been, or was to be, disturbed by the territorial acquisitions of one nation. The Treaty of Utrecht of 1713, which terminated the War of the Spanish Succession, recognized for the first time expressly the principle of the balance of power by way of territorial compensations. It provided for the division of most of the Spanish possessions, European and colonial, between the Hapsburgs and the Bourbons *"ad conservandum in Europa equilibrium,"* as the treaty put it.

* * *

In the latter part of the nineteenth and the beginning of the twentieth century, the principle of compensations was again deliberately applied to the distribution of colonial territories and the delimitation of colonial or semicolonial spheres of influence. Africa, in particular, was during that period the object of numerous treaties delimiting spheres of influence for the major colonial powers. Thus the competition between France, Great Britain, and Italy for the domination of Ethiopia was provisionally resolved * * * by the treaty of 1906, which divided the country into three spheres of influence for the purpose of establishing in that region a balance of power among the nations concerned. * * *

Even where the principle of compensations is not deliberately applied, however, * * * it is nowhere absent from political arrangements, territorial or other, made within a balance-of-power system. For, given such a system, no nation will agree to concede political advantages to another nation without the expectation, which may or may not be well founded, of receiving proportionate advantages in return. The bargaining of diplomatic negotiations, issuing in political compromise, is but the principle of compensations in its most general form, and as such it is organically connected with the balance of power.

Armaments

The principal means, however, by which a nation endeavors with the power at its disposal to maintain or re-establish the balance of power are armaments. The armaments race in which Nation A tries to keep up with, and then to outdo, the armaments of Nation B, and vice versa, is the typical instrumentality of an unstable, dynamic balance of power. The necessary corollary of the armaments race is a constantly increasing burden of military preparations devouring an ever greater portion of the national budget and making for ever deepening fears, suspicions, and insecurity. The situation preceding the First World War, with the naval competition between Germany and Great Britain and the rivalry of the French and German armies, illustrates this point.

It is in recognition of situations such as these that, since the end of the Napoleonic Wars, repeated attempts have been made to create a stable balance of power, if not to establish permanent peace, by means of the proportionate disarmament of competing nations. The technique of stabilizing the balance of power by means of a proportionate reduction of armaments is somewhat similar to the technique of territorial compensations. For both techniques require a quantitative evaluation of the influence that the arrangement is likely to exert on the respective power of the individual nations. The difficulties in making such a quantitative evaluation—in correlating, for instance, the military strength of the

French army of 1932 with the military power represented by the industrial potential of Germany—have greatly contributed to the failure of most attempts at creating a stable balance of power by means of disarmament. The only outstanding success of this kind was the Washington Naval Treaty of 1922, in which Great Britain, the United States, Japan, France, and Italy agreed to a proportionate reduction and limitation of naval armaments. Yet it must be noted that this treaty was part of an over-all political and territorial settlement in the Pacific which sought to stabilize the power relations in that region on the foundation of Anglo-American predominance.

Alliances

The historically most important manifestation of the balance of power, however, is to be found not in the equilibrium of two isolated nations but in the relations between one nation or alliance of nations and another alliance.

* * *

Alliances are a necessary function of the balance of power operating within a multiple-state system. Nations A and B, competing with each other, have three choices in order to maintain and improve their relative power positions. They can increase their own power, they can add to their own power the power of other nations, or they can withhold the power of other nations from the adversary. When they make the first choice, they embark upon an armaments race. When they choose the second and third alternatives, they pursue a policy of alliances.

Whether or not a nation shall pursue a policy of alliances is, then, a matter not of principle but of expediency. A nation will shun alliances if it believes that it is strong enough to hold its own unaided or that the burden of the commitments resulting from the alliance is likely to outweigh the advantages to be expected. It is for one or the other or both of these reasons that, throughout the better part of their history, Great Britain and the United States have refrained from entering into peacetime alliances with other nations.

* * *

The "Holder" of the Balance

Whenever the balance of power is to be realized by means of an alliance—and this has been generally so throughout the history of the Western world—two possible variations of this pattern have to be distinguished. To use the metaphor of the balance, the system may consist of two scales, in each of which are to be found the nation or nations identified with the same policy of the status quo or of imperialism. The continental nations of Europe have generally operated the balance of power in this way.

The system may, however, consist of two scales plus a third element, the "holder" of the balance or the "balancer." The balancer is not permanently identified with the policies of either nation or group of nations. Its only objective within the system is the maintenance of the balance, regardless of the concrete policies the balance will serve. In consequence, the holder of the balance will throw its weight at one time in this scale, at another time in the other scale, guided only by one consideration—the relative position of the scales. Thus it will put its weight always in the scale that seems to be higher than the other because it is lighter. The balancer may become in a relatively short span of history consecutively the friend and foe of all major powers, provided they all consecutively threaten the balance by approaching predominance over the others and are in turn threatened by others about to gain such predominance. To paraphrase a statement of Palmerston: while the holder of the balance has no permanent friends, it has no permanent enemies either; it has only the permanent interest of maintaining the balance of power itself.

The balancer is in a position of "splendid isolation." It is isolated by its own choice; for, while the two scales of the balance must vie with each other to add its weight to theirs in order to gain the overweight necessary for success, it must refuse to enter into permanent ties with either side. The holder of the balance waits in the middle in watchful detachment to see which scale is likely to sink. Its isolation is "splendid"; for, since its support or lack of support is the decisive factor in the struggle for power, its foreign policy, if cleverly managed, is able to extract the highest price from those whom it supports. But since this support, regardless of the price paid for it, is always uncertain and shifts from one side to the other in accordance with the movements of the balance, its policies are resented and subject to condemnation on moral grounds. Thus it has been said of the outstanding balancer in modern times, Great Britain, that it lets others fight its wars, that it keeps Europe divided in order to dominate the continent, and that the fickleness of its policies is such as to make alliances with Great Britain impossible. "Perfidious Albion" has become a byword in the mouths of those who either were unable to gain Great Britain's support, however

hard they tried, or else lost it after they had paid what seemed to them too high a price.

The holder of the balance occupies the key position in the balance-of-power system, since its position determines the outcome of the struggle for power. It has, therefore, been called the "arbiter" of the system, deciding who will win and who will lose. By making it impossible for any nation or combination of nations to gain predominance over the others, it preserves its own independence as well as the independence of all the other nations, and is thus a most powerful factor in international politics.

The holder of the balance can use this power in three different ways. It can make its joining one or the other nation or alliance dependent upon certain conditions favorable to the maintenance or restoration of the balance. It can make its support of the peace settlement dependent upon similar conditions. It can, finally, in either situation see to it that the objectives of its own national policy, apart from the maintenance of the balance of power, are realized in the process of balancing the power of others.

* * *

Evaluation of the Balance of Power

* * *

The Unreality of the Balance of Power

[The] uncertainty of all power calculations not only makes the balance of power incapable of practical application but leads also to its very negation in practice. Since no nation can be sure

that its calculation of the distribution of power at any particular moment in history is correct, it must at least make sure that, whatever errors it may commit, they will not put the nation at a disadvantage in the contest for power. In other words, the nation must try to have at least a margin of safety which will allow it to make erroneous calculations and still maintain the balance of power. To that effect, all nations actively engaged in the struggle for power must actually aim not at a balance—that is, equality—of power, but at superiority of power in their own behalf. And since no nation can foresee how large its miscalculations will turn out to be, all nations must ultimately seek the maximum of power obtainable under the circumstances. Only thus can they hope to attain the maximum margin of safety commensurate with the maximum of errors they might commit. The limitless aspiration for power, potentially always present * * * in the power drives of nations, finds in the balance of power a mighty incentive to transform itself into an actuality.

Since the desire to attain a maximum of power is universal, all nations must always be afraid that their own miscalculations and the power increases of other nations might add up to an inferiority for themselves which they must at all costs try to avoid. Hence all nations who have gained an apparent edge over their competitors tend to consolidate that advantage and use it for changing the distribution of power permanently in their favor. This can be done through diplomatic pressure by bringing the full weight of that advantage to bear upon the other nations, compelling them to make the concessions that will consolidate the temporary advantage into a permanent superiority. It can also be done by war. Since in a balance-of-power system all nations live in constant fear lest their rivals deprive them, at the first opportune moment, of their power position, all nations have a vital interest in anticipating such a development and doing unto the others what they do not want the others to do unto them. * * *

NOTES

1. The term "balance of power" is used in the text with four different meanings: (1) as a policy aimed at a certain state of affairs, (2) as an actual state of affairs, (3) as an approximately equal distribution of power, (4) as any distribution of power. Whenever the term is used without qualification, it refers to an actual state of affairs in which power is distributed among several nations with approximate equality. * * *

2. Cf., for instance, the impressive analogy between the equilibrium in the human body and in society in Walter B. Cannon, *The Wisdom of the Body* (New York: W. W. Norton and Company, 1932), pp. 293, 294: "At the outset it is noteworthy that the body politic itself exhibits some indications of crude automatic stabilizing processes. In the previous chapter I expressed the postulate that a certain degree of constancy in a complex system is itself evidence that agencies are acting or are ready to act to maintain that constancy. And moreover, that when a system remains steady it does so because any tendency towards change is met by increased effectiveness of the factor or factors which resist the change. Many familiar facts prove that these statements are to some degree true for society even in its present unstabilized condition. A display of conservatism excites a radical revolt and that in turn is followed by a return to conservatism. Loose government and its consequences bring the reformers into power, but their tight reins soon provoke restiveness and the desire for release. The noble enthusiasms and sacrifices of war are succeeded by moral apathy and orgies of self-indulgence. Hardly any strong tendency in a nation continues to the stage of disaster; before that extreme is reached corrective forces arise which check the tendency and they commonly prevail to such an excessive degree as themselves to cause a reaction. A study of the nature of these social swings and their reversal might lead to valuable understanding and possibly to means of more narrowly limiting the disturbances. At this point, however, we merely note that the disturbances are roughly limited, and that this limitation suggests, perhaps, the early stages of social homeostasis." (Reprinted by permission of the publisher. Copyright 1932, 1939, by Walter B. Cannon.)

3. John K. Galbraith, *American Capitalism, the Concept of Countervailing Power* (Boston: Houghton Mifflin, 1952).

HEDLEY BULL

Does Order Exist in World Politics?

* * *

The Idea of International Society

Throughout the history of the modern states system there have been three competing traditions of thought: the Hobbesian or realist tradition, which views international politics as a state of war; the Kantian or universalist tradition, which sees at work in international politics a potential community of mankind; and the Grotian or internationalist tradition, which views international politics as taking place within an international society.[1] Here I shall state what is essential to the Grotian or internationalist idea of international society, and what divides it from the Hobbesian or realist tradition on the one hand, and from the Kantian or universalist tradition on the other. Each of these traditional patterns of thought embodies a description of the nature of international politics and a set of prescriptions about international conduct.

The Hobbesian tradition describes international relations as a state of war of all against all, an arena of struggle in which each state is pitted against every other. International relations, on the Hobbesian view, represent pure conflict between states and resemble a game that is wholly distributive or zero-sum: the interests of each state exclude the interests of any other. The particular

From Hedley Bull, *The Anarchical Society: A Study of Order in World Politics*, 2d ed. (New York: Columbia University Press, 1977), Chap. 2.

international activity that, on the Hobbesian view, is most typical of international activity as a whole, or best provides the clue to it, is war itself. Thus peace, on the Hobbesian view, is a period of recuperation from the last war and preparation for the next.

The Hobbesian prescription for international conduct is that the state is free to pursue its goals in relation to other states without moral or legal restrictions of any kind. Ideas of morality and law, on this view, are valid only in the context of a society, but international life is beyond the bounds of any society. If any moral or legal goals are to be pursued in international politics, these can only be the moral or legal goals of the state itself. Either it is held (as by Machiavelli) that the state conducts foreign policy in a kind of moral and legal vacuum, or it is held (as by Hegel and his successors) that moral behaviour for the state in foreign policy lies in its own self-assertion. The only rules or principles which, for those in the Hobbesian tradition, may be said to limit or circumscribe the behaviour of states in their relations with one another are rules of prudence or expediency. Thus agreements may be kept if it is expedient to keep them, but may be broken if it is not.

The Kantian or universalist tradition, at the other extreme, takes the essential nature of international politics to lie not in conflict among states, as on the Hobbesian view, but in the transnational social bonds that link the individual human beings who are the subjects or citizens of states. The dominant theme of international relations, on the Kantian view, is only apparently the relationship among states, and is really the relationship among all men in the community of mankind—which exists potentially, even if it does not exist actually, and which when it comes into being will sweep the system of states into limbo.[2]

Within the community of all mankind, on the universalist view, the interests of all men are one and the same; international politics, considered from this perspective, is not a purely distributive or zero-sum game, as the Hobbesians maintain, but a purely cooperative or non-zero-sum game. Conflicts of interest exist among the ruling cliques of states, but this is only at the superficial or transient level of the existing system of states; properly understood, the interests of all peoples are the same. The particular international activity which, on the Kantian view, most typifies international activity as a whole is the horizontal conflict of ideology that cuts across the boundaries of states and divides human society into two camps—the trustees of the immanent community of mankind and those who stand in its way, those who are of the true faith and the heretics, the liberators and the oppressed.

The Kantian or universalist view of international morality is that, in contrast to the Hobbesian conception, there are moral imperatives in the field of international relations limiting the action of states, but that these imperatives enjoin not coexistence and co-operation among states but rather the overthrow of the system of states and its replacement by a cosmopolitan society. The community of mankind, on the Kantian view, is not only the central reality in international politics, in the sense that the forces able to bring it into being are present; it is also the end or object of the highest moral endeavour. The rules that sustain coexistence and social intercourse among states should be ignored if the imperatives of this higher morality require it. Good faith with heretics has no meaning, except in terms of tactical convenience; between the elect and the damned, the liberators and the oppressed, the question of mutual acceptance of rights to sovereignty or independence does not arise.

What has been called the Grotian or internationalist tradition stands between the realist tradition and the universalist tradition. The Grotian tradition describes international politics in terms of a society of states or international society.[3] As against the Hobbesian tradition, the Grotians contend that states are not engaged in simple struggle, like gladiators in an arena, but are limited in their conflicts with one another by common rules and institutions. But as against the Kantian or universalist perspective the Grotians accept the Hobbesian premise that sovereigns or states are the principal reality in international politics; the immediate members of international society are states rather than individual human beings. International politics, in the Grotian understanding, expresses neither complete conflict of interest between states nor complete identity of interest; it resembles a game that is partly distributive but also partly productive. The particular international activity which, on the Grotian view, best typifies international activity as a whole is neither war between states, nor horizontal conflict cutting across the boundaries of states, but trade—or, more generally, economic and social intercourse between one country and another.

The Grotian prescription for international conduct is that all states, in their dealings with one another, are bound by the rules and institutions of the society they form. As against the view of the Hobbesians, states in the Grotian view are bound not only by rules of prudence or expediency but also by imperatives of morality and law. But, as against the view of the universalists, what these imperatives enjoin is not the overthrow of the system of states and its replacement by a universal community of mankind, but rather acceptance of the requirements of coexistence and co-operation in a society of states.

Each of these traditions embodies a great variety of doctrines about international politics, among which there exists only a loose connection. In different periods each pattern of thought appears in a different idiom and in relation to different issues and preoccupations. This is not the place to explore further the connections and distinctions within each tradition. Here we have only to take account of the fact that the Grotian idea of international society has always been present in thought about the states system, and to indicate in broad terms the metamorphoses which, in the last three to four centuries, it has undergone.

Christian International Society

In the fifteenth, sixteenth and seventeenth centuries, when the universal political organisation of Western Christendom was still in process of disintegration, and modern states in process of articulation, the three patterns of thought purporting to describe the new international politics, and to prescribe conduct within it, first took shape. On the one hand, thinkers like Machiavelli, Bacon and Hobbes saw the emerging states as confronting one another in the social and moral vacuum left by the receding *respublica Christiana*. On the other hand Papal and Imperialist writers fought a rearguard action on behalf of the ideas of the universal authority of Pope and Emperor. As against these alternatives there was asserted by a third group of thinkers, relying upon the tradition of natural law, the possibility that the princes now making themselves supreme over local rivals and independent of outside authorities were nevertheless bound by common interests and rules. * * *

* * *

European International Society

In the eighteenth and nineteenth centuries, when the vestiges of Western Christendom came almost to disappear from the theory and practice of international politics, when the state came to be fully articulated, first in its dynastic or absolutist phase, then in its national or popular phase, and when a body of modern inter-state

practice came to be accumulated and studied, the idea of international society assumed a different form. * * *

The international society conceived by theorists of this period was identified as European rather than Christian in its values or culture. References to Christendom or to divine law as cementing the society of states declined and disappeared, as did religious oaths in treaties. References to Europe took their place, for example in the titles of their books: in the 1740s the Abbe de Mably published his *Droit public de l'Europe*, in the 1770s J. J. Moser his *Versuch des neuesten Europaischen Volkerrechts*, in the 1790s Burke denounced the regicide Directory of France for having violated "the public law of Europe."[4]

As the sense grew of the specifically European character of the society of states, so also did the sense of its cultural differentiation from what lay outside: the sense that European powers in their dealings with one another were bound by a code of conduct that did not apply to them in their dealings with other and lesser societies. * * *

* * *

World International Society

* * *

In the twentieth century international society ceased to be regarded as specifically European and came to be considered as global or world wide. * * *

Today, when non-European states represent the great majority in international society and the United Nations is nearly universal in its membership, the doctrine that this society rests upon a specific culture or civilisation is generally rejected. * * *

In the twentieth century, * * * there has been a retreat from the confident assertions, made in the age of Vattel [France, eighteenth century], that the members of international society were states and nations, towards the ambiguity and imprecision on this point that characterised the era of Grotius [Holland, seventeenth century]. The state as a bearer of rights and duties, legal and moral, in international society today is widely thought to be joined by international organisations, by non-state groups of various kinds operating across frontiers, and—as implied by the Nuremberg and Tokyo War Crimes Tribunals, and by the Universal Declaration of Human Rights—by individuals. There is no agreement as to the relative importance of these different kinds of legal and moral agents, or on any general scheme of rules that would relate them one to another, but Vattel's conception of a society simply of states has been under attack from many different directions.

* * *

The twentieth-century emphasis upon ideas of a reformed or improved international society, as distinct from the elements of society in actual practice, has led to a treatment of the League of Nations, the United Nations and other general international organisations as the chief institutions of international society, to the neglect of those institutions whose role in the maintenance of international order is the central one. Thus there has developed the Wilsonian rejection of the balance of power, the denigration of diplomacy and the tendency to seek to replace it by international administration, and a return to the tendency that prevailed in the Grotian era to confuse international law with international morality or international improvement.

* * *

The Element of Society

My contention is that the element of a society has always been present, and remains present, in the modern international system, although only as one of the elements in it, whose survival is sometimes precarious. The modern international system in fact reflects all three of the elements singled out, respectively, by the Hobbesian, the Kantian and the Grotian traditions: the element of war and struggle for power among states, the element of transnational solidarity and conflict, cutting across the divisions among states, and the element of cooperation and regulated intercourse among states. In different historical phases of the states system, in different geographical theatres of its operation, and in the policies of different states and statesmen, one of these three elements may predominate over the others.

* * *

Because international society is no more than one of the basic elements at work in modern international politics, and is always in competition with the elements of a state of war and of transnational solidarity or conflict, it is always erroneous to interpret international events as if international society were the sole or the dominant element. This is the error committed by those who speak or write as if the Concert of Europe, the League of Nations or the United Nations were the principal factors in international politics in their respective times; as if international law were to be assessed only in relation to the function it has of binding states together, and not also in relation to its function as an instrument of state interest and as a vehicle of transnational purposes; as if attempts to maintain a balance of power were to be interpreted only as endeavours to preserve the system of states, and not also as manoeuvres on the part of particular powers to gain ascendancy; as if great powers were to be viewed only as "great responsibles" or "great indispensables," and not also as great predators; as if wars were to be construed only as attempts to violate the law or to uphold it, and not also simply as attempts to advance the interests of particular states or of transnational groups. The element of international society is real, but the elements of a state of war and of transnational loyalties and divisions are real also, and to reify the first element, or to speak as if it annulled the second and third, is an illusion.

Moreover, the fact that international society provides some element of order in international politics should not be taken as justifying an attitude of complacency about it, or as showing that the arguments of those who are dissatisfied with the order provided by international society are without foundation. The order provided within modern international society is precarious and imperfect. To show that modern international society has provided some degree of order is not to have shown that order in world politics could not be provided more effectively by structures of a quite different kind.

NOTES

1. This threefold division derives from Martin Wight. The best published account of it is his "Western Values in International Relations," in *Diplomatic Investigations*, ed. Herbert Butterfield and Martin Wight (London: Allen & Unwin, 1967). The division is further discussed in my "Martin Wight and the Theory of International Relations. The Second Martin Wight Memorial Lecture," *British Journal of International Studies*, vol. II, no. 2 (1976).

2. In Kant's own doctrine there is of course ambivalence as between the universalism of *The Idea of Universal History from a Cosmopolitical Point of View* (1784) and the position taken up in *Perpetual Peace* (1795), in which Kant accepts the substitute goal of a league of "republican" states.

3. I have myself used the term "Grotian" in two senses: (i) as here, to describe the broad doctrine that there is a society of states; (ii) to describe the solidarist form of this doctrine, which united Grotius himself and the twentieth-century neo-Grotians, in opposition to the pluralist conception of international society entertained by Vattel and later positivist writers. See "The Grotian Conception of International Society," in *Diplomatic Investigations*.

4. See "Third Letter on the Proposals for Peace with the Regicide Directory of France," in *The Works of the Right Honourable Edmund Burke*, ed. John C. Nimmo (London: Bohn's British Classics, 1887).

G. JOHN IKENBERRY, MICHAEL MASTANDUNO, AND WILLIAM C. WOHLFORTH

Unipolarity, State Behavior, and Systemic Consequences

American primacy in the global distribution of capabilities is one of the most salient features of the contemporary international system. The end of the cold war did not return the world to multipolarity. Instead the United States—already materially preeminent—became more so. We currently live in a one superpower world, a circumstance unprecedented in the modern era. No other great power has enjoyed such advantages in material capabilities—military, economic, technological, and geographical. Other states rival the United States in one area or another, but the multifaceted character of American power places it in a category of its own. The sudden collapse of the Soviet Union and its empire, slower economic growth in Japan and Western Europe during the 1990s, and America's outsized military spending have all enhanced these disparities. While in most historical eras the distribution of capabilities among major states has tended to be multipolar or bipolar—with several major states of roughly equal size and capability—the United States emerged from the 1990s as an unrivaled global power. It became a "unipolar" state.

Not surprisingly, this extraordinary imbalance has triggered global debate. Governments, including that of the United States, are struggling to respond to this peculiar international environment. What is the character of domination in a unipolar distribution? If world politics is always a mixture of force and consent, does unipolarity remove restraints and alter the mix

in favor of force? Is a unipolar world likely to be built around rules and institutions or based more on the unilateral exercise of unipolar power? To what extent and in what ways can a unipolar state translate its formidable capabilities into meaningful political influence? These questions have been asked in the context of a global debate over the projection of power by the Bush administration. To what extent has America's foreign policy after 2001 been a reflection simply of the idiosyncratic and provocative strategies of the Bush administration itself, rather than a manifestation of the deeper structural features of the global system of power? These concerns over how a unipolar world operates—and how the unipolar state itself behaves—are the not-so-hidden subtext of world politics at the turn of the twenty-first century.

Classic questions of international relations theory are at stake in the debate over unipolarity. The most obvious question concerns balance of power theory, which predicts that states will respond to concentrated power by counterbalancing.[1] Some are puzzled by what they see as the absence of a balancing response to American unipolar power, whereas others argue, to the contrary, that incipient or specific types of balancing behavior are in fact occurring.[2] A related debate concerns power transition theory, which focuses on the specific forms of conflict that are generated between rising and declining hegemonic states.[3] The abrupt shift in the distribution of capabilities that followed the end of the cold war and the rise of China after the cold war raise

From *World Politics* 61, no. 1 (Jan. 2009): 1–27.

questions about the character of conflict between dominant and challenger states as they move along trajectories of rise and decline. A unipolar distribution also raises issues that scholars grappled with during the cold war, namely, about the structure and dynamics of different types of polar systems. Here the questions concern the ways in which the features of polarity affect the durability and war proneness of the state system.[4] Likewise, scholarly debates about threat perception, the impact of regime characteristics on foreign policy, the propensity of dominant states to provide collective goods, and the ability of a state to translate preponderant capabilities into effective influence are also at stake in the debate over unipolarity.[5]

This [essay introduces] systematic inquiry into the logic and dynamics of unipolarity. Its starting point is the distinctive distribution of capabilities among states in the contemporary global system. The central question driving our inquiry is straightforward: to what extent—and how—does this distribution of capabilities matter for patterns of international politics?

In their initial efforts to make sense of an American-dominated international system, scholars and observers have invoked a wide array of grand terms such as empire, hegemony, unipolarity, imperium, and "uni-multipolarity."[6] Scholars are searching for a conceptual language to depict and place in historical and comparative perspective the distinctive political formation that has emerged after the cold war. But this multiplicity of terms obscures more than it reveals. In this project unipolarity refers narrowly to the underlying material distribution of capabilities and not to the political patterns or relationships depicted by terms such as empire, imperium, and hegemony. What makes the global system unipolar is the distinctive distribution of material resources. An important research question is whether and in what ways this particular distribution of capabilities affects patterns of international politics to create outcomes that are different from what one might expect under conditions of bipolarity or multipolarity.

Setting up the inquiry in this manner requires a basic distinction between power as material resources and power as influence. Power resources refer to the distribution of material capabilities among states. The global system today—seen in comparative historical perspective—has concentrated power capabilities unprecedented in the modern era. But this observation should not prejudge questions about the extent and character of influence or about the logic of political relationships within the global system. Nor should this observation prejudge the question of whether the global system is coercive, consensual, legitimate, or illegitimate. Describing the system as unipolar leaves unanswered the Weberian questions about the logic and character of the global political system that is organized around unipolarity.[7]

In [this essay] we develop a framework for analyzing unipolarity[,] highlight the arguments of * * * hypotheses[,] and explore the impact of unipolarity on the behavior of the dominant state, on the reactions of other states, and on the properties of the international system. Collectively, we find that unipolarity does have a profound impact on international politics. International relations under conditions of unipolarity force us to rethink conventional and received understandings about the operation of the balance of power, the meaning of alliance partnerships, the logic of international economic cooperation, the relationship between power and legitimacy, and the behavior of satisfied and revisionist states. A unipolar distribution of capabilities will eventually give way to other distributions. The argument advanced here is not that unipolarity will last indefinitely but rather that as long as it does last, it will constitute a critical factor in understanding patterns of foreign policy and world politics.

Definition and Measurement

Scholars use the term unipolarity to distinguish a system with one extremely capable state from systems with two or more great powers (bi-, tri-, and multipolarity). Unipolarity should also be distinguished from hegemony and empire, terms that refer to political relationships and degrees of influence rather than to distributions of material capability. The adjective unipolar describes something that has a single pole. International relations scholars have long defined a pole as a state that (1) commands an especially large share of the resources or capabilities states can use to achieve their ends and that (2) excels in all the component elements of state capability, conventionally defined as size of population and territory, resource endowment, economic capacity, military might, and organizational-institutional "competence."[8]

A unipolar system is one whose structure is defined by the fact of only one state meeting these criteria. The underpinnings of the concept are familiar to international relations scholars. They flow from the massive literature on polarity, especially from Waltz's seminal treatment. The core contention is that polarity structures the horizon of states' probable actions and reactions, narrowing the range of choice and providing subtle incentives and disincentives for certain types of behavior. An appreciation of polarity yields important insights about patterns of behavior in international politics over the long term. Even for those scholars most persuaded of its analytical utility, polarity is at best a necessary part of an explanation rather than a sufficient explanation.[9] The distribution of capabilities may be a place to begin an explanation, but it is rarely enough to complete one.

Polarity is a theoretical construct; real international systems only approximate various polar ideal types. The polarity concept implies a threshold value of the distribution of capabilities. The more unambiguously the poles in a real international system pass the threshold, the more confident analysts can be that the properties attributed to a given system structure in theory will obtain in practice. The more unambiguously the capabilities of the great powers in a multipolar system clearly stand apart from all other states and are comparable to each other, the more relevant are the insights from the theoretical literature on multipolarity. Waltz often discussed the logic of a bipolar system as if it were a two-actor system. The more dominant the superpowers were in reality, the more confidence analysts could have that those logical deductions actually applied. In reality, the cold war international system was never "perfectly" bipolar. Analysts used to speak of loose versus tight bipolarity and debated whether the Soviet Union had the full complement of capabilities to measure up as a pole.

How do we know whether or to what degree an international system has passed the unipolar threshold? Using the conventional definition of a pole, an international system can be said to be unipolar if it contains one state whose overall share of capabilities places it unambiguously in a class by itself compared to all other states. This reflects the fact that poles are defined not on an absolute scale but relative to each other and to other states. In addition, preponderance must characterize all the relevant categories of state capabilities.[10] To determine polarity, one has to examine the distribution of capabilities and identify the states whose shares of overall resources obviously place them into their own class.

There will doubtless be times in which polarity cannot be determined, but now does not appear to be one of them. Scholars largely agree that there were four or more states that qualified as poles before 1945; that by 1950 or so only two measured up; and that by the 1990s one of these two poles was gone. They largely agree, further, that no other power—not Japan, China, India, or Russia, not any European country and not the EU—has increased its overall portfolio of capabilities sufficiently to transform its standing.[11] This leaves a single pole.

There is widespread agreement, moreover, that any plausible index aggregating the relevant dimensions of state capabilities would place the United States in a separate class by a large margin.[12] The most widely used measures of capability are GDP and military spending. As of 2006 the United States accounted for roughly one-quarter

TABLE 4.1

ECONOMIC INDICATORS FOR THE MAJOR POWERS, 2006[a]

	GDP Current Prices ($ Billion)	% Great Power GDP, Current Prices	% World GDP, Current Prices	% World GDP, PPP	GDP per Capita, Current Prices	Public Debt (% GDP)	Productivity ($ GDP per Hour Worked)
United States	13,245	46.1	27.5	22.5	44,190	64.7	48.3
China	2,630	9.2	5.5	9.7	2,001	22.1	n.a.
Japan	4,367	15.2	9.1	7.4	34,188	176.2	34.4
Germany	2,897	10.1	6	4.6	35,204	66.8	44
Russia	979	3.4	2	3.1	6,856	8	n.a.
France	2,232	7.8	4.6	3.4	35,404	64.7	49
Britain	2,374	8.3	4.9	3.5	39,213	42.2	40.1

[a] % World GDP, PPP is World Bank estimate for 2005; differences between PPP and market exchange rate measures are discussed in Brooks and Wohlforth (n. 10), chap. 2. Data for United States public debt are from 2005. Productivity estimates are from 2005.

SOURCES: *International Monetary Fund, World Economic Outlook Database, April 2007,* at http://www.imf.org/external/pubs/ft/weo/2007/01/data/index.aspx (accessed November 7, 2007); World Bank, *2005 International Comparison Program, Preliminary Results,* at http://siteresources.world bank.org/ICPINT/Resources/ICPre-portprelim.pdf (accessed December 12, 2007); Central Intelligence Agency, *CIA World Factbook,* at https:// www.cia.gov/library/publications/the-world-factbook/ (accessed November 8, 2007); Organization for Economic Development and Cooperation, *OECD Employment Outlook 2007, Statistical Annex,* at http://www.oecd.org/document/26/0,3343,en_2649_33927_38551002_1_1_1,00.html (accessed November 8, 2007); Organization for Economic Development and Cooperation, *OECD Compendium of Productivity Indicators 2006.*

of global GDP and nearly 50 percent of GDP among the conventionally defined great powers (see Table 4.1). This surpasses the relative economic size of any leading state in modern history, with the sole exception of the United States itself in the early cold war years, when World War II had temporarily depressed every other major economy. By virtue of the size and wealth of the United States economy, its massive military capabilities represented only about 4 percent of its GDP in 2006 (Table 4.2), compared with the nearly 10 percent it averaged over the peak years of the cold war—1950–70—as well as with the burdens borne by most of the major powers of the past.[13]

The United States now likely spends more on defense than the rest of the world combined (Table 4.2). Military research and development (R&D) may best capture the scale of the long-term investments that now give the United States its dramatic qualitative edge over other states. As Table 4.2 shows, in 2004 U.S. military expenditures on R&D were more than six times greater than those of Germany, Japan, France, and Britain combined. By some estimates over half of the military R&D

expenditures in the world are American, a disparity that has been sustained for decades: over the past thirty years, for example, the United States invested more than three times what the EU countries combined invested in military R&D. Hence, on any composite index featuring these two indicators the United States obviously looks like a unipole. That perception is reinforced by a snapshot of science and technology indicators for the major powers (see Table 4.3).

These vast commitments do not make the United States omnipotent, but they do facilitate a preeminence in military capabilities vis-à-vis all other major powers that is unique in the post-seventeenth-century experience. While other powers can contest U.S. forces operating in or very near their homelands, especially over issues that involve credible nuclear deterrence, the United States is and will long remain the only state capable of projecting major military power globally.[14] This dominant position is enabled by what Barry Posen calls "command of the commons"—that is, unassilable military dominance over the sea, air, and space. The result is an international system

TABLE 4.2					
DEFENSE EXPENDITURES FOR THE MAJOR POWERS, 2006[a]					
	Defense Expenditures ($ Billion)	*% Great Power Defense Expenditures*	*% World Defense Expenditures*	*Defense Expenditures % of GDP*	*Defense R&D Expenditures ($ Billion)*
United States	528.6	65.6	46	4.1	75.5
China	49.5	6.1	4	2	n.a.
Japan	43.9	5.4	4	1	1.1
Germany	36.9	4.6	3	1.4	1.1
Russia	34.7	4.3	3	4.1	n.a.
France	53	6.6	5	2.5	3.9
Britain	59.2	7.3	5	2.7	4.4

[a]Defense expenditures as % GDP are 2005 estimates; R&D expenditures are for 2004.

SOURCES: Stockholm International Peace Research Institute, "The 15 Major Spending Countries in 2006," at http://www.sipri.org/contents/milap/milex/mex_data_index.html (accessed November 8, 2007); Stockholm International Peace Research Institute Military Expenditures Database, at http://www.sipri.org/contents/milap/milex/mex_database1.html (accessed November 8, 2007); Organization for Economic Development and Cooperation, *OECD Main Science and Technology Indicators* 2006, no. 2 (Paris: OECD, 2006), 49.

TABLE 4.3

SCIENCE AND TECHNOLOGY INDICATORS FOR THE MAJOR POWERS, 2003-6

	High Tech Production ($ Millions (2003))[a]	% World High Tech Production (2003)	Gross Domestic Expenditure R&D ($ Million PPP) (2006)	# of Triadic Patent Families (2005)[b]	Science and Engineering Doctoral Degrees (2003)[c]	PCs per 1000 People (2004)	Internet Access per 1000 People (2005)	Secure Internet Servers[e] per Million People (2006)
United States	1,351,048.7	39	343,747.5	16,368	26,891	762.2	630.1[d]	869.2
China	423,825.9	12	115,196.9	433	8,153	40.9	85.1	0.4
Japan	376,250.1	11	130,745.4	15,239	7,581	541.6	667.5	331.9
Germany	146,494	4	62,493.2	6,266	10,796	545.3	454.7	348.6
Russia	n.a.	n.a.	16,668.7	49	10,409	104.3	152.3	3.2
France	136,665.7	4	40,392	2,463	6,890	495.7	429.6	96.5
Britain	116,200.2	3	35,171.10	1,588	8,810	599.8	473.5	561.5

[a]In 1997 dollars.
[b]Triadic patents families represent attempt to receive patents for an invention in the United States, Europe, and Japan.
[c]The data for China are from 2001; the data for France are from 2002; and the data for Russia are from 2000.
[d]Data are from 2005, with the exception of the U.S. data, which are from 2004.
[e]Secure Internet servers use encryption technology in Internet transactions; see www.netcraft.com.

SOURCES: World Bank, *World Development Indicators 2007*, at http://go.worldbank.org/3JU2HA60D0 (accessed November 8, 2007); Organization for Economic Development and Cooperation, *OECD Main Science and Technology Indicators*, 2007, vol. 1, at http://www.oecd.org/document/33/0,3343,en_2694_34455l_1901082_1_1_1,00.html (accessed November 8, 2007); National Science Board, "Science and Engineering Indicators 2006, Volume 2," at http://nsf.gov/statistics/seind06/pdf/colume2.pdf (accessed November 8, 2007).

FIGURE 4.1

DISTRIBUTION (PERCENTAGE) OF ECONOMIC AND MILITARY CAPABILITIES AMONG THE MAJOR POWERS (17TH–21ST CENTURIES)[a]

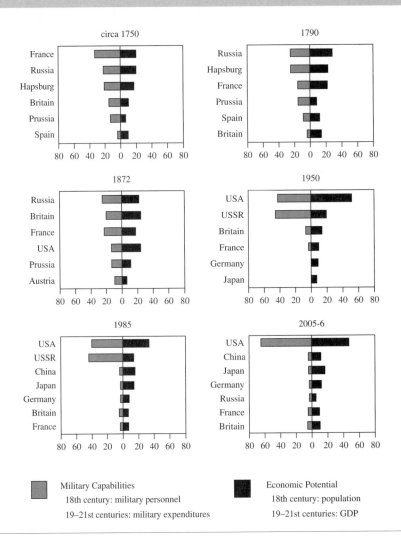

[a]Germany=FRG, and Russia=USSR in 1950 and 1985; Maddison's estimates are based on states' modern territories. For 1872, Austria, Hungary, and Czechoslovakia are combined, as are Russia and Finland.

SOURCES: This figure is reproduced from Brooks and Wohlforth (n. 10), 30. Eighteenth-century data: Paul M. Kennedy, *The Rise and Fall of the Great Powers* (New York: Random House, 1987). GDP, 1870–1985: Angus Maddison, *Monitoring the World Economy, 1829–1992* (Paris: OECD, 1995); GDP, 2005–6: sources from Table 4.1; military expenditures, 1872–1985: National Material Capabilities data set v. 3.02, at http://www.correlatesofwar.org. The construction of these data is discussed in J. David Singer, Stuart Bremer, and John Stuckey, "Capability Distribution, Uncertainty, and Major Power War, 1820–1965," in Bruce Russett, ed., *Peace, War, and Numbers* (Beverly Hills, Calif.: Sage, 1972), 19–48.

that contains only one state with the capability to organize major politico-military action any-where in the system.[15] No other state or even combination of states is capable of mounting and deploying a major expeditionary force outside its own region, except with the assistance of the United States.

Conventional measures thus suggest that the concentration of military and overall economic potential in the United States distinguishes the current international system from its predecessors over the past four centuries (see Figure 4.1). As historian Paul Kennedy observed: "Nothing has ever existed like this disparity of power; nothing, . . . I have returned to all of the comparative defense spending and military personnel statistics over the past 500 years that I compiled in *The Rise and Fall of the Great Powers*, and no other nation comes close."[16]

The bottom line is that if we adopt conventional definitions of polarity and standard measures of capabilities, then the current international system is as unambiguously unipolar as past systems were multipolar and bipolar.

Unipolarity and Its Consequences

* * * [T]he effects of unipolarity are potentially widespread. For purposes of analytical clarity it is possible to consider these effects in three ways, in terms of (1) the behavior of the unipole, (2) the actions of other states, and (3) the properties of the international system itself.

Behavior of the Unipole

The specific characteristics and dynamics of any unipolar system will obviously depend on how the unipolar state behaves. But the unipole's behavior might be affected by incentives and constraints associated with its structural position in the international system. Indeed, even the unipole's domestic politics and institutions—

the immediate well-springs of its behavior on the international scene—might themselves change profoundly under the influence of its position of primacy in the international system. * * * [H]ypotheses concerning four general behavioral patterns [follow].

UNIPOLARITY AND REVISIONISM: IS THE UNIPOLE A SATISFIED STATE? The stability of any international system depends significantly on the degree to which the major powers are satisfied with the status quo.[17] In *War and Change in World Politics*, Robert Gilpin argued that leading states "will attempt to change the international system if the expected benefits exceed the expected costs."[18] In the quarter century since that book's publication, international relations scholars have never seriously debated whether the "expected net gain" of systemic revisionism might be positive for the United States. It is hardly surprising that scholars set aside the question of revising the territorial status quo—it is hard to imagine plausible arguments for the utility of large-scale conquest in an age of nuclear weapons and economic globalization. But the territorial status quo is only a part of what Gilpin meant by "international system." The other part comprises the rules, institutions, and standards of legitimacy that frame daily interactions. Why has there been no scholarly debate on whether the United States might seek to revise that aspect of the system? In the 1980s, to be sure, the question did not seem relevant. Scholars believed that the United States was in relative decline, so the costs of changing the system were simply assumed to be high, and a U.S. preference for the status quo appeared obvious.

The transition from bipolarity to unipolarity arguably represented a dramatic power shift in favor of the United States, altering Gilpin's equation toward revisionism. Yet the question of whether, as a new unipole, the United States might adopt a more revisionist stance has not figured centrally in international relations research. The reason was a key assumption built into almost all research on hegemonic stability and power transition theory: that the leading state in any international system is bound to be satisfied. Hence, research on the origins of satisfaction and revisionism is overwhelmingly about subordinate states, not the dominant state.[19]

Robert Jervis ["Unipolarity: A Structural Perspective," *World Politics* 61, no. 1 (January 2009): 188–213] * * * demonstrates that this assumption is no longer tenable. While the case can be made that a unipole—particularly one that achieved this status in an international system already strongly shaped by its power and preferences—might rationally opt for conservatism,[20] international relations scholarship is rich with hypotheses proposing that the opposite is equally if not more likely. Jervis argues that unipolarity offers powerful structural incentives for the leading state to be revisionist. These include the absence of countervailing power, the tendency for both the interests and the fears of the leading state to increase as its relative capabilities increase, and the psychological tendency to worry more about the future to the extent the present situation is desirable. Jervis also suggests that these structural incentives are reinforced by particular features of the American approach to unipolarity—the sense after the attacks of September 11, 2001, that the world could and must be transformed and the enduring and widespread belief that international peace and cooperation will be sustained only when all other important states are democratic. The structural and contingent features of contemporary unipolarity point plausibly in the direction of a revisionist unipole, one simultaneously powerful, fearful, and opportunistic.

UNIPOLARITY AND THE PROVISION OF PUBLIC GOODS Public or collective goods may be consumed by multiple actors without those actors necessarily having to pay the full costs of producing them. The classic theoretical insight is that if enough actors follow their rational self-interest and choose to free ride on the efforts of others, public goods will be underproduced or not produced at all.[21] Overcoming the free-rider problem therefore requires cooperation among self-interested actors.[22] A good part of the IR literature, in particular that associated with hegemonic stability theory, hypothesizes that cooperation in international relations requires the leadership of a dominant state.[23] Given its preponderance of economic and military resources, the dominant state has the ability to bear a disproportionate share of the costs of providing international collective goods such as an open world economy or a stable security order. The dominant state has an interest in bearing those costs because it benefits disproportionately from promoting systemwide outcomes that reflect its values and interests.

During the cold war the United States took on the responsibilities that Kindleberger argued were needed to promote international economic stability, such as serving as an open market of last resort and allowing the use of its currency for exchange and reserve purposes. International economic stability among the Western powers reinforced their security alliance against the Soviet Union. The United States also bore a disproportionate share of the direct costs of Western alliance security. The Soviet Union, on its side of the international divide, ultimately shouldered disproportionate alliance costs as well.[24] Waltz took the argument a step further, arguing that in the bipolar system the United States and the Soviet Union may have been adversaries but, as the two dominant powers, shared a mutual interest in system stability, an interest that prompted them to cooperate in providing public goods such as nuclear nonproliferation.[25] Hedley Bull makes a similar point in his classic study of the international system as a society of states.[26]

How might the shift from a bipolar to a unipolar system affect the inclination of the now singularly dominant state to provide international public goods? Two hypotheses arise, with contradictory behavioral expectations. First, we might expect a unipole to take on an even greater responsibility for the provision of international public goods. The capabilities of a unipole relative to other major states are greater than those of either dominant power in a bipolar structure. The unipole's incentive should be stronger as well, since it now has the opportunity to influence international outcomes globally, not just in its particular subsystem. We should expect the unipole to try to "lock in" a durable international order that reflects its interests and values.[27]

A second hypothesis, however, suggests the opposite. We should expect a unipolar power to underproduce public goods despite its preponderant capabilities. The fact that it is unthreatened by peer competitors and relatively unconstrained by other states creates incentives for the unipole to pursue more parochial interests even at the expense of a stable international order. The fact that it is extraordinarily powerful means that the unipole will be more inclined to force adjustment costs on others, rather than bear disproportionate burdens itself.

* * * Michael Mastanduno's analysis of the global political economy ["System Maker and Privilege Taker: U.S. Power and the International Political Economy," pp. 121–154] shows that the dominant state will be both system maker and privilege taker—it will seek simultaneously to provide public goods and to exploit its advantageous structural position for parochial gain. It enlists the cooperation of other states and seeks, with varying degrees of success, to force adjustment burdens upon them. Jervis suggests that because the unipole has wide discretion in determining the nature and the extent of the goods provided, its efforts are likely to be perceived by less powerful states as hypocritical attempts to mask the actual pursuit of private goods.

UNIPOLARITY AND CONTROL OVER OUTCOMES

It has long been an axiom of social science that resources (or capabilities as defined herein) do not translate automatically into power (control over outcomes or over the behavior of other actors).[28] Yet most observers regard it as similarly axiomatic that there is some positive relationship between a state's relative capability to help or harm others and its ability to get them to do what it wants. Even if the relationship is complex, more capabilities relative to others ought to translate generally into more power and influence. By this commonsense logic, a unipole should be expected to have more influence than either of the two great powers in a bipolar system.

* * * Some articles in the *World Politics* 2009 special issue on unipolarity argue that the shift from bipolarity to unipolarity may not be an unambiguous benefit for the unipole's ability to wield influence. On the contrary, a unipolar state may face the paradoxical situation of being simultaneously more capable and more constrained. Two distinct theoretical logics suggest that a unipole might enjoy less power to shape the international system than a superpower in bipolarity. First is the logic of balancing, alliance, and opposition, [as] discussed * * * by Stephen Walt and Mastanduno. The increased concentration of capabilities in the unipole may elicit increased opposition from other states—in the form of either traditional counterbalancing or subtler soft balancing. Even if such resistance falls short of offering a real counterweight, it may materially hamstring the unipole's ability to exercise influence. As Walt ["Alliances in a Unipolar World," pp. 86–120] argues, the structural shift to unipolarity removed one of the major motivations for the middle-ranked great powers to defer to the United States. Mastanduno offers a similar argument: the collapse of a unifying central threat signifies that in this post–cold war era the United States has less control over adjustment struggles with its principal economic partners, because it can no longer leverage their security dependence to dictate international economic outcomes. Globalization reinforces this U.S. predicament by expanding the number of relevant players in the world economy and by offering them alternatives to economic reliance on the United States. While under bipolarity the propensity of other middle powers to defer to the United States was structurally favored, under unipolarity the opposite may obtain. Even if observable balancing behavior

reminiscent of bipolarity or multipolarity never occurs, a structurally induced tendency of the middle-ranked great powers to withhold cooperation may sap the unipole's effective power.

Second is a social logic of legitimacy, analyzed by Martha Finnemore ["Legitimacy, Hypocrisy, and the Social Structure of Unipolarity: Why Being a Unipole Isn't All It's Cracked Up to Be," pp. 58–85]. To use capabilities effectively, she argues, a unipole must seek to legitimate its role. But any system of legitimation imposes limits on the unipole's ability to translate capabilities into power. Finnemore stresses that the legitimation strategy followed by the United States after World War II—institutionalization—imposes especially severe constraints on the use of its material capabilities in pursuit of power. The rules, norms, and institutions that constitute the current international order are thus especially resistant to the unilateral use of superior capabilities to drive outcomes. Hence, for reasons Finnemore spells out in detail, the shift from bipolarity to unipolarity may well have diminished the effective utility of the preponderant capabilities of the United States.

UNIPOLARITY AND DOMESTIC POLITICS The impact of domestic politics on foreign policy is of long-standing interest in the study of politics. In his classic appraisal of the United States, Tocqueville concluded that the U.S. political system was "decidedly inferior" to other types in the conduct of foreign policy, with a tendency to "obey impulse rather than prudence" and to "abandon a mature design for the gratification of a momentary passion."[29] During the cold war Theodore Lowi, Stephen Krasner, and others reinforced the idea that American political institutions create disadvantages in external policy.[30] More recent literature has reversed the presumption and argues that democracy offers distinctive advantages in foreign policy, including legitimacy, transparency, the ability to mobilize the public for war fighting efforts, and the poten-

tial to use competition among branches of government to gain advantage in diplomacy and negotiations.[31]

Political scientists have placed greater emphasis on the impact of regime type on foreign policy than on how changes in the relative international position of a country affect the role domestic politics play in its foreign policy.[32] Nonetheless, conventional wisdom during the cold war suggested that the bipolar structure had a double disciplining effect on the conduct of U.S. foreign policy. The external threat disciplined American society, leading interest groups and the public generally to defer to central decision makers on the definition of national interest and how best to achieve it. Domestic politics stopped at the "water's edge" because the international stakes were so high. The cold war constrained American decision makers as well, forcing them to exercise caution in the international arena and to assure that public opinion or interest groups did not capture or derail foreign policy for parochial reasons.

Under unipolarity, the double disciplining effect is no longer operative, with neither publics nor central decision makers as constrained as in a bipolar context. The consequent impact of domestic politics on foreign policy will depend in part on which party is more inclined to take the initiative: central decision makers or societal actors. One hypothesis is that under unipolarity the line between domestic and foreign policy will blur and domestic politics will no longer stop at the water's edge. With less at stake in foreign policy, it is harder for leaders to discipline societal actors and easier for societal actors to capture aspects of the foreign policy agenda to suit their parochial needs. The likely results are a less coherent foreign policy and a tendency for the state to underperform in the international arena, missing opportunities to exercise influence commensurate with its preponderant capabilities. A second hypothesis is that central decision makers will exploit the lack of constraint to manipulate a public—one that no longer has clear guiding principles in foreign policy—to respond to a wide array of possible threats and opportunities. As Jervis suggests, for the unipole threats may be nowhere—or everywhere.

* * * Jack Snyder, Robert Shapiro, and Yaeli Bloch-Elkon ["Free Hand Abroad, Divide and Rule at Home," pp. 155–187] [take] up the impact of domestic politics under unipolarity. They find that the Bush administration has taken advantage of the structural discretion offered by unipolarity to conduct a far more active and risky foreign policy than would be possible under the constraints of bipolarity. Developments in American politics such as political polarization have not only encouraged this effort by leaders but have also enabled interest groups to tie their particular domestic concerns to the more activist foreign policy agenda, and they have encouraged opportunistic leaders to use foreign policy as a salient issue in domestic political debate.

Unipolarity and the Behavior of Secondary States

Unipolarity may present secondary states with dramatically different incentives and constraints than would bipolar or multipolar settings. * * * [T]hree general behavioral patterns * * * may be shaped by the unipolar stucture: strategies of resistance to or insulation from the unipole's overweening capabilities, alliances and alignments, and the use of international institutions.

BALANCING AND OTHER FORMS OF RESISTANCE

The proposition that great concentrations of capabilities generate countervailing tendencies toward balance is among the oldest and best known in international relations.[33] Applying this balancing proposition to a unipolar system is complex, however, for even as unipolarity increases the incentives for counterbalancing it also raises the costs. Walt and Finnemore each analyze the interplay between these incentives. They agree on the basic proposition that the current unipolar order pushes secondary states away from traditional hard counterbalancing—formal military alliances and/or military buildups meant to create a global counterweight to the unipole—and toward other, often subtler strategies, such as soft balancing, hiding, binding, delegitimation, or norm entrapment. These analyses lead to the general expectation that a shift from a multipolar or bipolar to a unipolar structure would increase the relative salience of such subtler balancing/resistance strategies.

Walt argues that standard neorealist balance of power theory predicts the absence of counterbalancing under unipolarity. Yet he contends that the core causal mechanisms of balance-of-threat theory remain operative in a unipolar setting. Walt develops a modification of the theory that highlights the role of soft balancing and other subtler strategies of resistance as vehicles to overcome the particular challenges unipolarity presents to counterbalancing. He contends that balancing dynamics remain latent within a unipolar structure and can be brought forth if the unipole acts in a particularly threatening manner.

Finnemore develops a contrasting theoretical architecture for explaining secondary state behavior. For her, both the absence of balancing and the presence of other patterns of resistance can be explained only by reference to the social, as opposed to the material, structure of international politics. In particular, secondary state strategies that have the effect of reining in the unipole cannot be understood as the result of standard security-maximizing incentives. Rather, they are partially the outgrowth of the secondary states' internalization of the norms and rules of the institutional order. If the unipole acts in accordance with those rules, the tendency of other states to resist or withhold cooperation will be muted. Finnemore establishes three social mechanisms that constrain the unipole: legitimation, institutionalization, and incentives for hypocrisy. Each of these entails a logic of resistance to actions by the unipole that violate certain socially defined boundaries.

ALLIANCES AND ALIGNMENT Scholars have long recognized that the dynamics of alliance and alignment transcend the imperative of counterhegemonic balancing.[34] Aggregating capabilities against a potentially dominant state is thus only one of the many purposes alliances serve. States may also choose to ally with a dominant power either to shield themselves from its capabilities or to seek to influence its policies. In addition, secondary states may ally with each other for purposes not directly connected to resistance to the dominant state, such as influencing each other's domestic or foreign policies or coordinating policies on regional or functional issues.

Larger patterns of such alliance behavior may be systematically related to the international system's structure. Scholars contend that in classic multipolar systems, especially those with no clear hegemon in sight, a large proportion of alliance behavior was unconnected to systemic balancing imperatives.[35] Under bipolarity, the proportion of alliance dynamics that was an outgrowth of systemic balancing increased, yet the rivalry between the two superpowers also created opportunities for secondary states to use alliance choices as leverage, playing each superpower off against the other. Walt argues that in a unipolar system nearly all significant alliance behavior will in one way or another be a reaction to the unipole—to contain, influence, or exploit it. As a result, independent alliances focused on other threats will be relatively rare, compared to bipolar or multipolar systems. Walt also contends that under unipolarity leverage opportunities dramatically decline compared to bipolarity, and he specifies the conditions under which secondary states will tend to opt for alignments with the unipole, neutrality, or resistance.

USE OF INTERNATIONAL INSTITUTIONS Although their relative power affords opportunities to go it alone, dominant states find a variety of reasons to use international institutions. Institutions may be helpful in coalition building. They facilitate the exercise of power by creating patterns of behavior that reflect the interests and values of the dominant state. Institutions can conceal or soften the exercise of power, and they can lock in a hegemonic order and enable it to persist "after hegemony."[36]

Weaker states in a unipolar structure similarly have incentives to utilize institutions. Two types of motivation are relevant. First, weaker states may engage a unipole by enlisting its participation in new or modified institutional arrangements in order to constrain or tie it down. Since a unipolar state may be powerful enough to follow its own rules, possibly to the detriment of weaker states, those states may appeal within an institutional context to the unipole's concern for its reputation as a member of the international community or to its need for cooperating partners, in order to persuade it to engage in rule-based order even if it cannot simply determine the rules unilaterally. The dispute between the United States and some of its allies over U.S. participation in the International Criminal Court reflects the attempt by weaker states to tie the unipole down and the unipole's effort in turn to remain a free agent in the event it cannot define the institutional rules. Second, weaker states may create or strengthen international institutions that exclude the unipolar state. These institutions might be designed or intended to foster a common identity (for example, the European Union, the East Asian Economic Caucus), build capacity to withstand influence attempts by the unipole (for example, the European common currency), or create the potential to act independently of the unipole or at cross-purposes with it (for example, Shanghai Cooperation Organization, European Rapid Reaction Force).

In bipolarity, weaker states tend to participate in institutional arrangements defined and dominated by one or the other of the major players. The nonaligned movement during the cold war was distinctive precisely because it sought—though not necessarily with success—to institutionalize a path independent of either superpower. Under conditions of unipolarity, we can hypothesize that weaker states, lacking the capacity to balance the unipole, will turn to a variety of institutional initiatives intended to constrain the unipolar state or to enhance their own autonomy in the face of its power. The use of international institutions by weaker states is highlighted in the articles by Walt and Finnemore [discussed earlier].

Systemic Properties: How Peaceful Is Unipolarity, and Will It Endure?

The classical systems theorists were preoccupied with two dependent variables: peacefulness and stability.[37] Scholars today have reason to be less optimistic that deterministic laws of stability or peacefulness can be derived from the structural characteristics of any international system.[38] Nonetheless, the questions of whether some types of international systems are more prone to conflict than others and whether some types are more likely to endure than others remain critical and take on added significance in the context of the more novel international system of unipolarity.

UNIPOLARITY AND GREAT POWER CONFLICT

Two major theoretical traditions deal with causes of war in ways that may relate to system structure: neorealism and power transition theory. Applying these in the context of unipolarity yields the general proposition that military conflicts involving the unipole and other major powers (that is, great power wars) are less likely in unipolar systems than in either bipolar or multipolar systems. According to neorealist theory, bipolarity is less war prone than multipolarity because each superpower knows that only the other can threaten it, realizes that it cannot pass the buck to third parties, and recognizes it can balance accretions to the other's capabilities by internal rather than external means. Bipolarity blocks or at least complicates three common paths to war in neorealism: uncertainty, free riding, and fear of allied defection. The first and second operated during the 1930s and the third operated prior to World War I. By the same logic, unipolarity is even less war prone: none of these causal mechanisms is relevant to a unipole's interactions with other great powers. Power transition and hegemonic theories predict that major war involving the leading state and a challenger becomes more likely as their relative capabilities approach parity.[39] Under unipolarity, parity is beyond the reach of a would-be challenger, so this mechanism does not operate. In any event, many scholars question whether these traditional theories of war remain relevant in a world in which the declining benefits of conquest, nuclear deterrence among most major powers, the spread of democracy, and changing collective norms and ideas reduce the probability of major war among great powers to a historically low level.[40] The absence of major conflicts among the great powers may thus be overdetermined or have little to do with unipolarity.

[William] Wohlforth ["Unipolarity, Status Competition, and Great Power War," pp. 28–57] develops an alternative theoretical framework for assessing the consequences of unipolarity for great power conflict, one that focuses on status or prestige seeking as opposed to security as the core preference for major states. From a diverse theoretical literature he derives a single hypothesis on the relationship between unipolar capability distributions and great power conflict. He tests it in the current international system and historically, and he derives further implications for relationships between the unipole and secondary states. He supplies theoretical reasons and initial empirical support for the proposition that unipolarity itself helps to explain low levels of militarized interactions among great powers since 1991. The same logic and evidence, however, suggest that the route back to bipolarity or multipolarity may be more prone to great power conflict than many scholars now suppose.

THE DURABILITY OF A UNIPOLAR SYSTEM

The current unipolar system has already lasted longer than some scholars were anticipating at the end of the cold war.[41] How much longer it will persist before transforming itself into the more "normal" systemic pattern of multipolarity or perhaps into to a new bipolarity remains to be seen. Durability will depend primarily on developments in the capabilities and behavior of the unipole and other major powers. Because the unipole is such a disproportionately powerful actor in this system, the evolution of its own capabilities and behavior is likely to carry the greatest weight. Other actors are more likely to react to the unipole than to trigger system-transforming processes on their own.

The evolution of relative *capabilities* is obviously a crucial variable, and there is no clear theoretical presumption. One hypothesis is that unipolarity is self-reinforcing. The unipole is so far ahead militarily that it finds it relatively easy to maintain and even widen its capability lead over that of would-be peers—especially if, as some scholars argue, the contemporary U.S. defense industry benefits from increasing returns to scale.[42] Given massive investments in the military requirements of unipolar status over many years, other states face formidable barriers to entry—technological, economic, and domestic political—in any effort to become peer competitors.

The contrary hypothesis can be drawn from Gilpin's work, which highlights the tendency of dominant powers to plant the seeds of their own demise. Dominant states may not maintain or widen their capability lead because they fall prey to overextension abroad and/or the corrupting influences of affluence at home.[43] Similarly, the very success of their order may inadvertently encourage or develop challengers to their dominant role within it.[44] The U.S.-centered system promotes openness and globalization; the diffusion of the benefits of these processes strengthens states on the periphery that can outpace the United States economically and eventually translate their economic strength into political influence and military capacity.

The *behavior* of the unipole matters as well, again with potentially divergent effects. A unipole may discourage peer competition by reassuring states already inclined toward the status quo and by providing the benefits of system integration to those with ambivalent intentions.[45] Through its behavior, the unipole may encourage would-be challengers to accept subordinate but beneficial roles. Alternatively, and because it has the capability and discretion to act as a revisionist state itself, the unipole's behavior might heighten the insecurity of other states and prompt them to contemplate individual or collective challenges to its dominance.

The impact of developments across capabilities and behavior may be reinforcing or contradictory. A unipole might successfully reassure other states while simultaneously maintaining its capability lead over them. It might alarm other states while dissipating its relative advantages. Or its behavior might point in one direction while its capabilities point in another.

Conclusion

One of the oldest insights in the study of international relations is that power, in the form of material capabilities, has a decisive impact on relations among states. Thucydides famously recorded the frank and brutal observation that "the strong do what they can and the weak suffer what they must." In a world of states, power disparities generate both security and insecurity and have an impact on what states want and what they can get. Few scholars embrace theories of world politics that rely exclusively on the structural circumstances created by material capabilities of states and its distribution within the international system. But it is also widely agreed that one ignores such factors at one's explanatory peril.

For most of modern world history, the distribution of material capabilities has been best characterized as multipolar or bipolar. The contemporary structure is extraordinary and has the potential to endure beyond a historical "moment." One of the great theoretical challenges in the study of international relations is to identify the extent to which and the various ways in which a unipolar distribution of power influences how states act and generates patterns of conflict and cooperation. In broad terms, the articles in this issue are concerned with how a unipolar international order differs in its character and functioning from a bipolar or multipolar order. In more operational terms, we are interested in how the shift from the cold war bipolar system to the current American-centered unipolar system matters for the behavior of states and the character of international rule and order.

There are obvious limitations on our ability to validate hypotheses or subject theoretical claims to rigorous empirical tests. Precisely because a unipolar distribution of power has not appeared routinely in earlier eras, we do not possess multiple historical cases for systematic comparisons. It is equally difficult to draw inferences about the impact of unipolarity because we are still living through it. In effect, we are in the midst of a historical cycle. Patterns of foreign policy and international outcomes will be better discerned after unipolarity has given way to bipolarity or multipolarity. What this [essay] does accomplish, however, is to lay out the questions, categories, and hypotheses that should continue to guide inquiry and to offer initial empirical determinations of our claims. The set of hypotheses we develop collectively in three categories—the behavior of the unipole, the reactions of secondary states, and the overall functioning of the international system—constitutes a rich agenda for future theoretical and empirical research. Three aspects of that agenda strike us as sufficiently salient to merit emphasis in closing.

First, scholarship needs to untangle and clarify three related but distinct manifestations of unipolarity that easily become confused in the process of making causal arguments. One is the unipolar distribution of power as an ideal type across time, the second is unipolarity in the particular international circumstances of the early twenty-first century (for example, including the existence of nuclear weapons and a security community among some of the leading powers), and the third is American unipolarity, or unipolarity with the United States as the dom-

inant state with its particular institutional and ideological features. In making causal claims, it is exceedingly difficult to determine how deeply rooted cause and effect are in the distribution of power. Do the foreign policy patterns of the Bush administration follow in a relatively straightforward way from conditions of unipolarity or are they much more circumstantial? Would other states—were they to emerge as a unipolar power—act in a similar way, or is behavior more contingent on the character of the state or the peculiarities of its leaders? [There are] various answers to these questions of causation, but [scholars] tend to agree that there remains considerable contingency in a unipolar system. Constraints and opportunities—as well as threats and interests—do shift when the global system moves from bipolarity to unipolarity, but the linkages between the structure of power and the actions of states are not straightforward. Future research will want to specify these linkages and the way in which circumstance modifies and mediates the structural impact of unipolarity.

A second research agenda concerns the nature and character of constraints on the unipolar state. One of the defining features of unipolarity is that the power of the leading state is not balanced by other major states. Yet in the absence of this classic mechanism of power constraint it remains unclear what, if anything, in fact disciplines and restrains unipolar power. Finnemore looks closely at the role of legitimacy as a constraint on state power and provides some evidence that this so-called soft mechanism of constraint does matter. It is plausible to expect that a unipolar state, any unipolar state, would prefer to lead and operate in an international order that is seen as normatively acceptable— that is, legitimate—to other states. Legitimate domination is more desirable than coercive domination. But questions remain about how powerful this incentive is for the leaders of a dominant state and how costly it actually becomes to the unipole, in the short and longer term, when its behavior and the system associated with its power are perceived by others as less legitimate.

A third research area concerns how unipolarity affects the logic of hegemonic behavior. As noted earlier, there are two lines of argument regarding how a unipolar state might act in regard to the provisioning of public goods, rules, and institutions. One suggests that the leading state has a clear incentive to commit itself to leadership in the establishment and management of a cooperative, rule-based system. It receives a flow of material rewards and enjoys reduced costs of enforcement according to this logic. But the theoretical and policy-relevant question is whether the shift from cold war bipolarity to unipolarity has altered hegemonic leadership incentives. One possibility is that the decline in a shared security threat makes it harder to strike bargains: the leading state's offerings of security are less needed by other states and it is less dependent on the frontline support of weaker and secondary states. Another possibility is that unipolarity increases the incentives for free riding by subordinate states while at the same time reducing the willingness of the lead state to bear the disproportionate costs of public goods provision. Hegemonic leadership may also hinge on judgments about the overall life cycle of unipolarity. If a unipolar state assumes that its dominance is semipermanent, it may be willing to suffer lost legitimacy or the costs of enforcement—costs that are seen as less consequential than the freedom of action that is achieved by reducing its hegemonic responsibilities. But if the leading state judges that its unipolar position will decline in the years ahead, the value of rules and institutions may increase to the extent those rules and institutions are "sticky" and can help protect the leading state's interests and lock in its preferred international order during the days when it inevitably becomes relatively less capable.

The hypotheses and findings * * * ultimately take us back to basic questions in the study of international relations. The surprising onset of unipolarity encourages us to revisit questions about how the international structure of capabilities shapes, encourages, and constrains state behavior. In attempting to make sense of this new type of global structure, we are forced to grapple with the enduring issue of how the powerful and the weak make their way in a changing international environment.

NOTES

1. See Jack S. Levy, "Balances and Balancing: Concepts, Propositions and Research Design," in John A. Vasquez and Colin Elman, eds., *Realism and the Balancing of Power: A New Debate* (Saddle River, N.J.: Prentice-Hall, 2003).

2. G. John Ikenberry, ed., *America Unrivaled: The Future of the Balance of Power* (Ithaca, N.Y.: Cornell University Press, 2002); and T. V. Paul, James J. Wirtz, and Michel Fortman, eds., *Balance of Power: Theory and Practice in the 21st Century* (Stanford, Calif.: Stanford University Press, 2004). On incipient balancing, see Kenneth Waltz, "Structural Realism after the Cold War," *International Security* 24 (Summer 2000); Christopher Layne, "The Unipolar Illusion: Why New Great Powers Will Arise," *International Security* 17 (Spring 1993); Robert Pape, "Soft Balancing against the United States," *International Security* 30 (Summer 2005); and Keir Lieber and Gerard Alexander, "Waiting for Balancing: Why the World Is Not Pushing Back," *International Security* 30 (Summer 2005).

3. Robert Gilpin, *War and Change in World Politics* (New York: Cambridge University Press, 1981); A. F. K. Organski, *World Politics* (New York: Alfred A. Knopf, 1958); and A. F. K. Organski and Jacek Kugler, *The War Ledger* (Chicago: University of Chicago Press, 1980).

4. See Karl W. Deutsch and J. David Singer, "Multipolar Power Systems and International Stability," *World Politics* 16 (April 1964); Richard N. Rosecrance, "Bipolarity, Mutilpolarity and the Future," *Journal of Conflict Resolution* 10 (September 1966); Kenneth N. Waltz, "The Stability of a Bipolar World," *Daedalus* 93 (Summer 1964); and Morton A. Kaplan,

System and Process in International Politics (New York: John Wiley, 1957).

5. For example, Stephen Walt, *Taming American Power: The Global Responses to American Primacy* (New York: Norton, 2006); Robert Jervis, "The Remaking of a Unipolar World," *Washington Quarterly* 29 (Summer 2006).

6. A huge literature has emerged—or returned—depicting America as an empire. See, for example, Charles Maier, *Among Empires: American Ascendancy and Its Predecessors* (Cambridge: Harvard University Press, 2006); Niall Ferguson, *Colossus: The Price of America's Empire* (New York: Penguin, 2004); Chalmers Johnson, *The Sorrows of Empire: Militarism, Secrecy, and the End of the Republic* (New York: Metropolitan Books, 2004). On hegemony, see G. John Ikenberry, *After Victory: Institutions, Strategic Restraint, and the Rebuilding of Order after Major War* (Princeton: Princeton University Press, 2001). On imperium, see Peter Katzenstein, *A World of Regions: Asia and Europe in the American Imperium* (Ithaca, N.Y.: Cornell University Press, 2006). On uni-multipolarity, see Samuel Huntington, "The Lonely Superpower," *Foreign Affairs* 78 (March–April 1999).

7. In this way, we are following a basic distinction made in the power theory literature. See, in particular, David A. Baldwin, *Paradoxes of Power* (New York: Basil Blackwell, 1989).

8. Kenneth Waltz, *Theory of International Politics* (Reading, Mass.: Addison-Wesley 1979), 131.

9. For a comprehensive critical review of the polarity literature, see Barry Buzan, *The United States and the Great Powers: World Politics in the Twenty-first Century* (Cambridge: Polity Press, 2004).

10. [William] Wohlforth, "The Stability of a Unipolar World," *International Security* 21 (Summer 1999); idem, "U.S. Strategy in a Unipolar World," in Ikenberry (n. 2); Stephen G. Brooks and William Wohlforth, *World Out of Balance: International Relations and the Challenge of American Primacy* (Princeton: Princeton University Press, 2008).

11. Some scholars argue that bipolarity or multipolarity might characterize international politics in certain regional settings. See, for example, Robert Ross, "The Geography of the Peace: East Asia in the Twenty-first Century," *International Security* 23 (Spring 1999); and Andrew Moravcsik, "The Quiet Superpower," *Newsweek*, June 17 2002.

12. See, for example, Ethan B. Kapstein, "Does Unipolarity Have a Future?" in Kapstein and Michael Mastanduno, eds., *Unipolar Politics: Realism and State Strategies after the Cold War* (New York: Columbia University Press, 1999); Birthe Hansen, *Unipolarity and the Middle East* (New York: St. Martin's, 2000); Wohlforth (n. 10, 1999, 2002); Brooks and Wohlforth (n. 10); William E. Odom and Robert Dujarric, *America's Inadvertent Empire* (New Haven: Yale University Press, 2004); and Arvind Virmani, "Global Power from the 18th to the 21st Century: Power Potential (VIP2), Strategic Assets and Actual Power (VIP)," Working Paper no. 175 (New Delhi: Indian Council for Research on International Economic Relations, 2005). The most comprehensive contrarian view is Michael Mann, whose main arguments are that the United States is weaker economically that it seems (a claim mainly about the future) and that U.S. military capability is comparatively ineffective at achieving favorable outcomes (a claim about utility); Mann, *Incoherent Empire* (London: Verso, 2003).

13. Calculated from *Budget of the United States Government Fiscal Year 2005: Historical Tables* (Washington, D.C.: United States Government Printing Office, 2005).

14. Sustained U.S. investment in nuclear capabilities, against the backdrop of Russian decline and Chinese stasis, have even led some to question the existence of stable deterrence between these countries. See Keir A. Lieber and Daryl G. Press, "The End of MAD? The

Nuclear Dimension of U.S. Primacy," *International Security* 30 (Spring 2006).

15. David Wilkinson, "Unipolarity without Hegemony," *International Studies Review* 1 (Spring 1999); Hansen (n. 12); Stuart Kaufman, Richard Little, and William Wohlforth, eds., *The Balance of Power in World History* (London: Palgrave Macmillan, 2007); and Posen, "Command of the Commons: The Military Foundations of U.S. Hegemony," *International Security* 28 (Fall 2003).

16. "The Eagle Has Landed: The New U.S. Global Military Position," *Financial Times Weekend*, February 1, 2002.

17. E. H. Carr, *The Twenty Years' Crisis* (London: Macmillan and Company, 1939); Organski [and Kugler] (n. 3); Randall L. Schweller, "Bandwagoning for Profit: Bringing the Revisionist State Back In," *International Security* 19 (Summer 1994); and Robert Powell, "Stability and the Distribution of Power," *World Politics* 48 (January 1996).

18. Gilpin (n. 3), chap. 2.

19. See, for example, Ronald L. Tammen, Jacek Kugler, Douglas Lemke, Carole Alsharabati, Brian Efird, Alan C. Stam III, and A. F. K. Organski, *Power Transitions: Strategies for the 21st Century* (New York: Chatham House, 2000); Jonathan M. DiCicco and Jack S. Levy, "Power Shifts and Problem Shifts," *Journal of Conflict Resolution* 43 (December 1999); and Jason Davidson, *The Origins of Revisionist and Status-quo States* (New York: Palgrave Macmillan, 2006).

20. Josef Joffe, "Bismarck or Britain? Toward an American Grand Strategy after Unipolarity," *International Security* 19 (Spring 1995); and Michael Mastanduno, "Preserving the Unipolar Moment: Realist Theories and U.S. Grand Strategy after the Cold War," *International Security* 21 (Spring 1997).

21. See Robert O. Keohane, *After Hegemony: Cooperation and Discord in the World Political Economy* (Princeton: Princeton University Press, 1984), and the literature discussed therein.

22. Kenneth Oye, ed., *Cooperation under Anarchy* (Princeton: Princeton University Press, 1986).

23. This literature is vast, and its claims have been subject to considerable critical scrutiny. Key statements include Charles P. Kindleberger, *The World in Depression, 1929–1939* (Berkeley: University of California Press, 1973); Robert O. Keohane, "The Theory of Hegemonic Stability and Changes in International Economic Regimes," in Alexander L. George, Ole R. Holsti, and Randolph M. Siverson, *Change in the International System* (Boulder, Colo.: Westview Press, 1980); Stephen D. Krasner, "State Power and the Structure of International Trade," *World Politics* 28 (April 1976); Bruce Russett, "The Mysterious Case of Vanishing Hegemony," *International Organization* 39 (Spring 1985); Duncan Snidal, "The Limits of Hegemonic Stability Theory," *International Organization* 39 (Autumn 1985); David A. Lake, "Leadership, Hegemony and the International Economy: Naked Emperor or Tattered Monarch with Potential?" *International Studies Quarterly* 37 (December 1993); and Joanne Gowa, "Rational Hegemons, Excludable Goods, and Small Groups: An Epitaph for Hegemonic Stability Theory?" *World Politics* 41 (April 1989).

24. See Valerie Bunce, "The Empire Strikes Back: The Evolution of the Eastern Bloc from Soviet Asset to Liability," *International Organization* 39 (Winter 1985); and Randall Stone, *Satellites and Commissars: Strategy and Conflict in the Politics of Soviet-Bloc Trade* (Princeton: Princeton University Press, 1996).

25. Waltz (n. 8).

26. Hedley Bull, *The Anarchical Society: A Study of Order in World Politics* (New York: Columbia University Press, 1977).

27. Ikenberry (n. 6).

28. Robert Dahl, "The Concept of Power," *Behavioral Science* 2 (July 1957); Baldwin (n. 7).

29. Alexis de Tocqueville, *Democracy in America*, trans. Henry Reeve (Cambridge: Sever and Francis, 1863), 1: 299–300.

30. Theodore Lowi, "Making Democracy Safe for the World," in G. John Ikenberry, ed., *American Foreign Policy: Theoretical Essays* (New York: Harper Collins 1989); and Stephen Krasner, "United States Commercial and Monetary Policy: Unravelling the Paradox of Internal Weakness and External Strength," in Peter Katzenstein, ed., *Between Power and Plenty* (Madison: University of Wisconsin Press, 1978).

31. For example, David Lake, "Powerful Pacifists: Democratic States and War," *American Political Science Review* 86 (March 1992); Dan Reiter and Allan C. Stam, *Democracies at War* (Princeton: Princeton University Press, 2002); and Robert Pastor, "The President vs. Congress," in Robert Art and Seyom Brown, eds., *U.S. Foreign Policy: The Search for a New Role* (New York: Macmillan, 1993).

32. See Otto Hintze, "Military Organization and the Organization of States," in Felix Gilbert, ed., *The Historical Essays of Otto Hintze* (New York: Oxford University Press, 1975); and Peter Alexis Gourevitch, "The Second Image Reversed," *International Organization* 32 (Autumn 1978).

33. See the reviews and discussion in Jack S. Levy, "Balances and Balancing: Concepts, Propositions, and Research Design," in John A. Vasquez and Colin Elman, eds., *Realism and the Balancing of Power: A New Debate* (Englewood Cliffs, N.J.: Prentice-Hall, 2003); and Jack S. Levy and William R. Thompson, "Hegemonic Threats and Great-Power Balancing in Europe, 1495–1999," *Security Studies* 14 (January–March 2005).

34. See, for example, Glen H. Snyder, *Alliance Politics* (Ithaca, N.Y.: Cornell University Press, 1997); Stephen M. Walt, "Alliances in Theory and Practice: What Lies Ahead?" *Journal of International Affairs* 43 (Summer–Fall 1989); idem, "Why Alliances Endure or Collapse," *Survival* 39 (Spring 1997); and Paul W. Schroeder, "Historical Reality versus Neorealist Theory," *International Security* 19 (Winter 1994).

35. See Schroeder (n. 34); and R. Harrison Wagner, "What Was Bipolarity?" *International Organization* 47 (Winter 1993).

36. Keohane (n. 21); Ikenberry (n. 6).

37. See the discussion in Jervis, *System Effects: Complexity in Political and Social Life* (Princeton: Princeton University Press 1997), chap. 3; and idem, "Unipolarity: A Structural Perspective," [*World Politics* 61, no. 1 (January 2009)].

38. See Robert Powell, *In the Shadow of Power: States and Strategies in International Politics* (Princeton: Princeton University Press, 1999); and Alexander Wendt, *Social Theory of International Politics* (Cambridge: Cambridge University Press, 1999).

39. See Gilpin (n. 3); Tammen et al. (n. 19); and * * * DiCiccio [and Levy] (n. 19).

40. Robert Jervis, *American Foreign Policy in a New Era* (London: Routledge, 2005), 31.

41. See Christopher Layne, "The Unipolar Illusion: Why New Great Powers Will Arise," *International Security* 14 (Spring 1993); Kenneth N. Waltz, "The Emerging Structure of International Politics," *International Security* 18 (Fall 1993); and idem, "Structural Realism after the Cold War," in Ikenberry (n. 2). See also the retrospective in Christopher Layne, "The Unipolar Illusion Revisited," *International Security* 31 (Winter 2006).

42. See Jonathan Caverley, "United States Hegemony and the New Economics of Defense," *Security Studies* 16 (October 2007).

43. Gilpin (n. 3).

44. Ibid., 75.

45. Michael Mastanduno, "Preserving the Unipolar Moment: Realist Theories and U.S. Grand Strategy after the Cold War," in Kapstein and Mastanduno (n. 12).

5 The State

The state remains the key actor in international relations, although challenges to the state are increasing, as explained in Chapter 5 of Essentials of International Relations. The selections in this chapter examine issues concerning the state, its strength, and challenges to it. Stanford University professor Stephen D. Krasner discusses the principles of sovereignty but finds that they do not work for many parts of the world. Alternatives to state failure must entail new options, including shared sovereignty and de facto trusteeships. Economic globalization may also challenge the state and sovereignty in unanticipated ways. Foreign Policy editor Moisés Naím discusses how open borders and new technologies have led to illegal markets in people, drugs, weapons, and financial flows, undermining the state power and authority.

The state is challenged in other ways as well. Transnational religious and ideological movements are threats to states and state sovereignty. Samuel P. Huntington, a Harvard University political scientist, predicts that the future international system will be characterized by a clash between Western and Islamic civilizations. The article included here and the book that elaborates the thesis, The Clash of Civilizations and the Remaking of World Order (1996), have been widely discussed and criticized. Among the potent critiques is the argument that Islam is a more diverse "opponent" than Huntington suggests and that the real threat comes from religious fundamentalism more generally.

Sociologist Mark Juergensmeyer of the University of California, Santa Barbara, in excerpts from his comprehensive book Global Rebellion: Religious Challenges to the Secular State, from Christian Militias to al Qaeda (2008), navigates the complex interplay between politics and religion. He helps us understand the roots of both religious and secular nationalism, drawing on examples from the Middle East to Asia. Rather than labeling movements fundamentalist, he calls for examining religious activists who have both religious and political goals.

STEPHEN D. KRASNER

Sharing Sovereignty: New Institutions for Collapsed and Failing States

Conventional sovereignty assumes a world of autonomous, internationally recognized, and well-governed states. Although frequently violated in practice, the fundamental rules of conventional sovereignty—recognition of juridically independent territorial entities and nonintervention in the internal affairs of other states—have rarely been challenged in principle. But these rules no longer work, and their inadequacies have had deleterious consequences for the strong as well as the weak. The policy tools that powerful and well-governed states have available to "fix" badly governed or collapsed states—principally governance assistance and transitional administration (whether formally authorized by the United Nations or engaged in by a coalition of the willing led by the United States)—are inadequate. In the future, better domestic governance in badly governed, failed, and occupied polities will require the transcendence of accepted rules, including the creation of shared sovereignty in specific areas. In some cases, decent governance may require some new form of trusteeship, almost certainly de facto rather than de jure.[1]

Many countries suffer under failed, weak, incompetent, or abusive national authority structures. The best that people living in such countries can hope for is marginal improvement in their material well-being; limited access to social services, including health care and education; and a moderate degree of individual physical security. At worst they will confront endemic violence,

exploitative political leaders, falling life expectancy, declining per capita income, and even state-sponsored genocide. In the Democratic Republic of Congo (formerly Zaire), for example, civil wars that have persisted for more than two decades have resulted in millions of deaths. In Zimbabwe the policies of President Robert Mugabe, who was determined to stay in office regardless of the consequences for his country's citizens, led to an economic debacle that began in 2000 with falling per capita income, inflation above 500 percent, and the threat of mass starvation. In Colombia much of the territory is controlled by the Revolutionary Armed Forces of Colombia (FARC), a Marxist rebel group that derives most of its income from drug trafficking. In Rwanda more than 700,000 people were slaughtered in a matter of weeks in 1994 as a result of a government-organized genocide.

The consequences of failed and inadequate governance have not been limited to the societies directly affected. Poorly governed societies can generate conflicts that spill across international borders. Transnational criminal and terrorist networks can operate in territories not controlled by the internationally recognized government. Humanitarian disasters not only prick the conscience of political leaders in advanced democratic societies but also leave them with no policy options that are appealing to voters.

Challenges related to creating better governance also arise where national authority structures have collapsed because of external invasion and occupation rather than internal conflict. The availability of weapons of mass destruction

From *International Security* 29, no. 2 (Fall 2004): 85–120. Some of the author's notes have been omitted.

and the presence of transnational terrorism have created a historically unprecedented situation in which polities with very limited material capability can threaten the security of much more powerful states. These polities can be conquered and occupied with relative ease, leaving the occupying power with the more challenging task of establishing an acceptable domestic governing structure. Contemporary Afghanistan and Iraq are the obvious cases in point.

Left to their own devices, collapsed and badly governed states will not fix themselves because they have limited administrative capacity, not least with regard to maintaining internal security.[2] Occupying powers cannot escape choices about what new governance structures will be created and sustained. To reduce international threats and improve the prospects for individuals in such polities, alternative institutional arrangements supported by external actors, such as de facto trusteeships and shared sovereignty, should be added to the list of policy options.

The current menu of policy instruments for dealing with collapsed and failing states is paltry, consisting primarily of transitional administration and foreign assistance to improve governance, both of which assume that in more or less short order, targeted states can function effectively on their own. Nation-building or state-building efforts are almost always described in terms of empowering local authorities to assume the responsibilities of conventional sovereignty. The role of external actors is understood to be limited with regard to time, if not scope, in the case of transitional administration exercising full executive authority. Even as the rules of conventional sovereignty are de facto violated if not de jure challenged, and it is evident that in many cases effective autonomous national government is far in the future, the language of diplomacy, the media, and the street portrays nothing other than a world of fully sovereign states.

The next section of this article describes the basic elements that constitute the conventional understanding of sovereignty and provides a taxonomy of alternative institutional forms. It is followed by a discussion of the ways in which conventional sovereignty has failed in some states, threatening the well-being of their own citizens and others. The inadequacy of the current repertoire of policy options for dealing with collapsed, occupied, and badly governed states—governance assistance and transitional administration—is then assessed. The possibilities for new institutional forms—notably shared sovereignty and some de facto form of trusteeship—are examined. Included is a discussion of why such arrangements might be accepted by political leaders in target as well as intervening states.

Conventional Sovereignty and Some Alternatives

Conventional sovereignty has three elements: international legal sovereignty, Westphalian/Vatellian sovereignty, and domestic sovereignty.[3] The basic rule of international legal sovereignty is to recognize juridically independent territorial entities. These entities then have the right to freely decide which agreements or treaties they will enter into. In practice, this rule has been widely but not universally honored. Some entities that are not juridically independent have been recognized (e.g., Byelorussia and the Ukraine during the Cold War), and some entities that are juridically independent have not been recognized (e.g., the People's Republic of China from 1949 to the 1970s).

The fundamental rule of Westphalian/Vatellian sovereignty is to refrain from intervening in the internal affairs of other states. Each state has the right to determine its own domestic authority structures. In practice, Westphalian/Vatellian sovereignty has frequently been violated.

Domestic sovereignty does not involve a norm or a rule, but is rather a description of the nature of domestic authority structures and the extent to which they are able to control activities within a state's boundaries. Ideally, authority structures would ensure a society that is peaceful, protects human rights, has a consultative mechanism, and honors a rule of law based on a shared understanding of justice.

In the ideal sovereign state system, international legal sovereignty, Westphalian/Vatellian sovereignty, and domestic sovereignty are mutually supportive. Recognized authorities within territorial entities regulate behavior, enjoy independence from outside interference, and enter into mutually beneficial contractual relations (treaties) with other recognized entities. This is the conventional world of international politics in which state-to-state relations are what count. One of the most striking aspects of the contemporary world is the extent to which domestic sovereignty has faltered so badly in states that still enjoy international legal, and sometimes even Westphalian/Vatellian, sovereignty. Somalia, for instance, is still an internationally recognized entity, even though it has barely any national institutions; and external actors have not, in recent years, tried to do much about Somalia's domestic sovereignty, or the lack thereof.

Conventional sovereignty was not always the hegemonic structure for ordering political life. Obviously, the basic rules of medieval Europe or the pre-nineteenth-century Sinocentric world were very different. But even in the nineteenth century, by which time conventional sovereignty had become a well-recognized structure, there were also legitimated and accepted alternatives. Protectorates were one alternative to conventional sovereignty; the rulers of a protectorate relinquished control over foreign policy to a more powerful state but retained authority over domestic affairs. For instance, in 1899 the ruler of Kuwait signed an agreement that gave Britain control of most elements of his country's foreign policy because he needed external support against threats from both Iraq and members of his own family.[4] In nineteenth-century China the major powers established treaty ports where British, French, German, and Japanese authorities regulated commerce and exercised extraterritorial authority over their own citizens and sometimes Chinese as well.[5] Within the British

Empire, Australia, Canada, and South Africa became dominions that enjoyed almost complete control over their domestic affairs, recognized the British ruler as the head of state, but to some extent deferred to Britain in matters of foreign policy. Finally, colonization was a legitimated practice in the nineteenth century that allowed powerful states to assume international legal sovereignty and regulate the domestic authority structures of far-flung territories.

Conventional sovereignty is currently the only fully legitimated institutional form, but unfortunately, it does not always work. Honoring Westphalian/Vatellian sovereignty (and sometimes international legal sovereignty as well) makes it impossible to secure decent and effective domestic sovereignty, because the autochthonous political incentives facing political leaders in many failed, failing, or occupied states are perverse. These leaders are better able to enhance their own power and wealth by making exclusionist ethnic appeals or undermining even the limited legal routinized administrative capacity that might otherwise be available.

To secure decent domestic governance in failed, failing, and occupied states, new institutional forms are needed that compromise Westphalian/Vatellian sovereignty for an indefinite period. Shared sovereignty, arrangements under which individuals chosen by international organizations, powerful states, or ad hoc entities would share authority with nationals over some aspects of domestic sovereignty, would be a useful addition to the policy repertoire. Ideally, shared sovereignty would be legitimated by a contract between national authorities and an external agent. In other cases, external interveners may conclude that the most attractive option would be the establishment of a de facto trusteeship or protectorate. Under such an arrangement, the Westphalian/Vatellian sovereignty of the target polity would be violated, executive authority would be vested primarily with external actors, and international legal sovereignty would be suspended. There will not, however, be any effort to formalize through an international

TABLE 5.1							
ALTERNATIVE INSTITUTIONAL ARRANGEMENTS							
	International Legal Sovereignty		*Westphalian/Vatellian Sovereignty*			*Duration of Rule Violation*		
	No	Yes	None	Some	Full	Short	Medium	Long
Conventional sovereignty		X			X	n/a	n/a	n/a
Colony	X		X					X
Transitional administration with full foreign executive authority	X		X			X		
Trusteeship	X		X or X			X	X	
Shared sovereignty		X		X				X
Nineteenth-century protectorate	X			X				X

convention or treaty a general set of principles for such an option.[6] (For a summary of these different institutional possibilities, see Table 5.1.)

Failures of Conventional Sovereignty

Failed, inadequate, incompetent, or abusive national authority structures have sabotaged the economic well-being, violated the basic human rights, and undermined the physical security of their countries' populations. In some cases, state authority has collapsed altogether for an extended period, although such instances are rare. Afghanistan in the early 1990s before the Taliban consolidated power, Liberia for much of the 1990s, and the Democratic Republic of Congo and Sierra Leone in the late 1990s are just a few of the examples. Governance challenges have also arisen in Afghanistan and Iraq, where authority structures collapsed as a result of external invasion rather than internal conflict. The occupying powers, most obviously the United States, were then confronted with the challenge of fashioning decent governance structures in both countries.

In some parts of the world, disorder (including civil war) has become endemic. For the period 1955 to 1998, the State Failure Task Force identified 136 occurrences of state failure in countries with populations larger than 500,000. The task force operationalized state failure as one of four kinds of internal political crisis: revolutionary war, ethnic war, "adverse regime change," or genocide. In 1955 fewer than 6 percent of the countries were in failure. In the early 1990s the figure had risen to almost 30 percent, falling to about 20 percent in 1998, the last year of the study. Adverse regime change was the most common form of state failure, followed by ethnic war, revolutionary war, and genocide. The task force identified partial democracy, trade closure, and low levels of economic well-being as indicated by high infant mortality rates as the primary causes of state failure. James Fearon and David Laitin show that internal strife is more likely in countries suffering from poverty, recent decolonization, high population, and mountainous terrain. These conditions allow even relatively small guerrilla bands to operate successfully because recognized governments do not have the administrative competence to engage in effective rural policing and counter-insurgency operations.[7]

States that experience failure or poor governance more generally are beset by many problems. In such states, infrastructure deteriorates; corruption is widespread; borders are unregulated; gross domestic product is declining or stagnant; crime is rampant; and the national currency is not widely accepted. Armed groups operate within the state's boundaries but outside the control of the government. The writ of the central government, the entity that exercises the prerogatives of international legal sovereignty (e.g., signing treaties and sending delegates to international meetings), may not extend to the whole country; in some cases, it may not extend beyond the capital. Authority may be exercised by local entities in other parts of the country, or by no one at all.

Political leaders operating in an environment in which material and institutional resources are limited have often chosen policies that make a bad situation even worse. For some leaders, disorder and uncertainty are more attractive than order and stability because they are better able to extract resources from a disorderly society. Decisions affecting the distribution of wealth are based on personal connections rather than bureaucratic regulations or the rule of law. Leaders create multiple armed units that they can play off against each other. They find it more advantageous to take a bigger piece of a shrinking pie than a smaller piece of a growing pie.

The largest number of poorly governed states is found on the continent of Africa. Since the mid-1950s about a third of African states have been in failure.[8] In constant 1995 U.S. dollars, gross domestic product per capita for all of sub-Saharan Africa fell from $660 in 1980 to $587 in 1990 to $563 in 2000. Out of the sub-Saharan states for which data are available from the World Bank, eighteen had increases in their per capita gross domestic product from 1990 to 2000, seven had decreases of less than 5 percent, and seventeen experienced decreases of more than 5 percent. With the exception of the former Soviet Union, no other area of the world fared so badly with regard to economic performance.[9]

* * *

Thus, for many countries domestic sovereignty is not working, and the situation is not improving in any substantive way. Although the number and percentage of countries suffering from civil war declined during the 1990s, the per capita gross national income in current U.S. dollars of the least developed countries continued to drop, falling by 9 percent from 1990 to 2000, a period of robust growth for the world as a whole.

Why Sovereignty Failures Matter

In the contemporary world, powerful states have not been able to ignore governance failures. Polities where domestic authority has collapsed or been inadequate have threatened the economic and security interests of these states. Humanitarian crises have engaged electorates in advanced democracies and created no-win situations for political leaders who are damned if they intervene and damned if they do not. And, most obviously, when a state has been invaded, the occupiers have been confronted with the problem of establishing effective domestic sovereignty.

The availability of weapons of mass destruction, the ease of movement across borders, and the emergence of terrorist networks have attenuated the relationship between the underlying capabilities of actors and the ability to kill large numbers of people. In the past, state and nonstate actors with limited resources could not threaten the security of states with substantial resources. The killing power of a nation's military depended on the underlying wealth of the country. Nonstate actors such as anarchist groups in the nineteenth century could throw bombs that might kill fifty or even several hundred people, but not more. This is no longer true. States with limited means can procure chemical and biological weapons. Nuclear weapons demand more resources, but they are not out of reach of even a dismally poor country such as North Korea. Weapons of mass destruction can be delivered in myriad ways, not only by missiles but also by commercial ships, trucks, planes, and even envelopes. Failed or weak states may provide terrorists with territory in which they can operate freely.

Moreover, political leaders who have effective control within their borders but limited resources to defend or deter an invasion present a tempting target if they adopt policies that threaten the core security interests of powerful states. For instance, throughout his rule Saddam Hussein sought and sometimes used weapons of mass destruction, and even when faced with invasion, failed to fully cooperate with UN inspectors. In Afghanistan the Taliban supported al-Qa'ida, which had already demonstrated that it could strike core targets in the United States. Neither Iraq nor Afghanistan could defend itself against, or deter, a U.S. attack. When the threat is high and invasion is easy, powerful states are likely to use military force to bring down a menacing regime. When, however, the old regime has collapsed, the occupiers confront the challenge of creating effective and decent domestic sovereignty.

Sovereignty failures may also present problems in the area of transnational criminality. Drug trafficking is difficult to control under any circumstances, but such activities are more likely to flourish where domestic sovereignty is inadequate. About 95 percent of illicit drug production takes place in areas of civil strife. Colombia, where the FARC controls a large part of the territory, has been one of the major sources of such drugs for the United States. In the late 1990s Afghanistan cultivated 75 percent of the world's opium poppies, and despite a ban by the Taliban at the end of its rule, production revived after the regime was overthrown because the new government in Kabul had only limited control over much of the country. Transnational trafficking in persons is more likely, although not limited to, countries where domestic authority and control are weak or ineffective. A 2004 State Department report lists ten countries—Bangladesh, Burma, Cuba, Ecuador, Equatorial Guinea, Guyana, North Korea, Sierra Leone, Sudan, and Venezuela—that have not met minimum efforts to control trafficking in persons. Most of the ten are failed or badly governed states.[10] In addition, it is more difficult to trace and punish the perpetrators of transnational financial fraud in countries where the police and judiciary do not function well.

Finally, gross violations of human rights present unpleasant political choices for democratic leaders in powerful states. There have been a number of humanitarian catastrophes in recent years, with the killings in Rwanda in the mid-1990s being one of the most appalling and most widely reported. Millions of people have died in other countries as well at the hands of their own government or rival political groups. These and other humanitarian disasters have engaged attentive elites. The Canadian ministry of foreign affairs, for instance, organized the International Commission on Intervention and State Sovereignty in 2000 in response to UN Secretary-General Kofi Annan's appeal for a new consensus on the right of humanitarian intervention. The commission, composed of twelve eminent persons, produced a widely circulated report entitled *The Responsibility to Protect*. The report defends the principle of humanitarian intervention when governments abuse or fail to protect their own citizens. Samantha Power's book, *A Problem from Hell: America and the Age of Genocide*, which describes the failure of the United States to act either to prevent or to mitigate a number of genocides throughout the twentieth century, won a Pulitzer Prize in 2003.[11]

＊　＊　＊

Humanitarian crises, then, present decision-makers in democratic countries with a no-win situation. If they fail to intervene and a humanitarian disaster occurs, they may lose the votes of citizens who are attentive to and care about the fate of particular countries, regions, ethnic groups, or principled issues in general. On the other hand, if a political leader does intervene, the costs in terms of soldiers killed will be readily apparent, but the number of lives saved can never be demonstrated with certainty.

The Existing Institutional Repertoire: Governance Assistance and Transitional Administration

Political leaders in powerful and weak states have been reluctant to challenge the conventional norms of sovereignty. The policy options currently available to repair occupied or badly governed states—governance assistance and transitional administration—are consistent with these norms. They have made some limited contribution to improving governance in badly run and collapsed states, but policymakers would be better served if they had a wider repertoire of policy choices.

Governance Assistance

For the last decade international organizations, the United States, and other donor countries have devoted substantial resources to promoting better governance. U.S. foreign aid has been given to train judges, rewrite criminal codes, increase fiscal transparency, professionalize the police, encourage an open media, strengthen political parties, and monitor elections. In 2004 President George W. Bush's administration launched a new foreign aid initiative, the Millennium Challenge Account (MCA), which, if fully funded, will increase U.S. foreign assistance by 50 percent and provide these resources to a relatively small number of poor countries that have demonstrated good governance in the areas of promoting economic freedom, governing justly, and investing in people.[12]

Since the 1950s, international financial institutions have been involved in questions of policy and sometimes institutional reform in borrowing countries. The conditions attached to lending by the World Bank and the International Monetary Fund (IMF) have covered a wide range of issues such as aggregate credit expansion, subsidies, number of government employees, indexation of salaries, tariffs, tax rates, and institution building. International financial institutions have placed their own personnel in key bureaus.[13] In the mid-1990s the managing director of the IMF and the president of the World Bank committed themselves to a more aggressive attack on corruption in developing states.[14] In 1997 the World Bank subtitled its world development report *The State in a Changing World*. The report declares that the "clamor for greater government effectiveness has reached crisis proportions in many developing countries where the state has failed to deliver even such fundamental public goods as property rights, roads, and basic health and education."[15] Further, it lists basic tasks for the state, including establishing a foundation of law, protecting the environment, and shielding the vulnerable; chastises governments for spending too much on rich and middle-class students in universities while neglecting primary education; and urges these governments to manage ethnic and social differences. Finally, and most ambitiously, the 1991 Agreement Establishing the European Bank for Reconstruction and Development explicitly includes a commitment to democracy as a condition of membership.

Foreign assistance to improve governance in weak states does not usually contradict the rules of conventional sovereignty. Governments contract with external agencies (e.g., countries, multilateral organizations, and nongovernmental organizations [NGOs]) to provide training in various areas. Such contracting is a manifestation of international legal sovereignty and is consistent with Westphalian/Vatellian sovereignty, so long as the influence of external actors on domestic authority structures is limited to specific policies or improvements in the capabilities of government employees. When bargaining power is highly asymmetric, as may be the case in some conditionality agreements between international financial institutions and borrowing countries, Westphalian/Vatellian sovereignty can be compromised. External actors can influence not just policies but also institutional arrangements in target states. The borrowing country is better off with the agreement, conditions or no, than it would have been without it; otherwise it would not have signed. Nevertheless, political leaders may accept undesired and intrusive engagement from external actors because the alternative is loss of access to international capital markets.

The effectiveness of governance assistance will always be limited. Some leaders will find the exploitation of their own populations more advantageous than the introduction of reforms. The leverage of external actors will usually be constrained. International financial institutions are in the business of lending money; they cannot put too stringent restrictions on their loans lest their customers disappear. Many IMF agreements are renegotiated, sometimes several times. Small social democratic countries in Europe have been committed, because of the views of their electorates, to assisting the poor; they will be loath to allow their funding levels to drop below the generally recognized target of 0.7 percent of national income. The wealthier countries also routinely provide humanitarian assistance, regardless of the quality of governance in a particular country.

Moreover, those providing governance assistance are likely to adopt formulas that reflect their own domestic experience and that may be ill suited to the environments of particular target countries. The United States, for instance, has emphasized elections and independent legislatures. Interest groups have been regarded as independent of the state, whereas in European social democratic countries, they are legitimated by and sometimes created by the state.

Transitional Administration

Transitional administration is the one recognized alternative to conventional sovereignty that exists in the present international environment, but it is explicitly not meant as a challenge to the basic norms of sovereignty. The scope of transitional administration or peacekeeping and peacebuilding operations has ranged from the full assertion of executive authority by the UN for some period of time, East Timor being an example, to more modest efforts involving monitoring the implementation of peace agreements, as was the case in Guatemala in the 1990s. Transitional administration, usually authorized by the UN Security Council, has always been seen as a temporary, transitional measure designed to create the conditions under which conventional sovereignty can be restored. The U.S. occupation of Iraq has followed the same script, albeit without any UN endorsement of the occupation itself, although the Security Council did validate the restoration of international legal sovereignty in June 2004. Westphalian/Vatellian sovereignty and sometimes international legal sovereignty are violated in the short term so that they can be restored in the longer term; at least that is the standard explanation.

The record of peacebuilding efforts since World War II has been mixed. One recent study identified 124 cases of peacebuilding by the international community. Of these, 43 percent were judged to be successful based on the absence of hostilities. If progress toward democracy is added as a measure of success, only 35 percent were successful.[16]

More extensive peacekeeping operations, those that might accurately be called "transitional administration" because they involve the assertion of wide-ranging or full executive authority by the UN (or the United States), are difficult: the demands are high; advance planning, which must prejudge outcomes, is complicated, especially for the UN; and resources—economic, institutional, and military—are often limited. UN missions have run monetary systems, enforced laws, appointed officials, created central banks, decided property claims, regulated businesses, and operated public utilities. The resources to undertake these tasks have rarely been adequate. Each operation has been ad hoc; no cadres of bureaucrats, police, soldiers, or judges permanently committed to transitional administration exist; and there is a tension between devolving authority to local actors and having international actors assume responsibility for all governmental functions because, at least at the outset, this latter course is seen as being more efficient.[17]

Transitional administration is particularly problematic in situations where local actors disagree about basic objectives among themselves and with external actors. Under these circumstances, as opposed to situations in which local actors agree on goals but need external monitoring to provide reassurances about the behavior of their compatriots, the inherently temporary character of transitional administration increases the difficulty of creating stable institutions. If indigenous groups disagree about the distribution of power and the constitutional structure of the new state, then the optimal strategy for their political leaders is to strengthen their own position in anticipation of the departure of external actors. They do so by maximizing support among their followers rather than backing effective national institutions. Alternatively, local leaders who become dependent on external actors during a transitional administration, but who lack support within their own country, do not have

an incentive to invest in the development of new institutional arrangements that would allow their external benefactors to leave at an earlier date.[18]

Multiple external actors with varying interests and little reason to coordinate their activities have exacerbated the problems associated with transitional administration. The bureaucratic and financial interests of international organizations are not necessarily complementary. NGOs need to raise money and make a mark. The command structures for security and civilian activities have been separated. The permanent members of the Security Council, to whom UN peacekeeping authorities are ultimately responsible, have not always had the same interests.[19]

* * *

Transitional administration has been most effective when the level of violence in a country has been low, where there has been involvement by major powers, and where the contending parties within the country have reached a mutually acceptable agreement. The key role for the transitional administration is then to monitor the implementation of the agreement. For instance, in Namibia the contact group, comprising Canada, France, Germany, Great Britain, and the United States, was involved in UN discussions about the constitutional structure for an independent Namibia beginning in 1978. All of the major contending parties consented to the UN Transition Assistance Group (UNTAG) that was sent in 1989, allowing the lightly armed mission to play a neutral role between South Africa and Namibia. The strength of the major potential spoilers, hard-line whites, was undermined by the collapse of apartheid in South Africa. The major responsibility of UNTAG was to supervise the elections for the government that assumed power when Namibia secured international legal sovereignty.[20]

There were also successful missions in Central America in the 1990s. In both Guatemala and Nicaragua, government and rebel groups had reached a mutually acceptable settlement. Peacekeeping missions contributed to stability by supervising elections, helping to demobilize combatants, and training police.[21]

In sum, transitional administration has worked best for the easiest cases, those where the key actors have already reached a mutually acceptable agreement. In these situations, the transitional administration plays a monitoring role. It can be truly neutral among the contending parties. The mission does not have to be heavily armed. Transitional administration, however, is much more difficult in cases such as Bosnia, Kosovo, Afghanistan, and Iraq—that is, where local leaders have not reached agreement on what the ultimate outcome for their polity should be and where they must think about positioning themselves to win support from parochial constituencies when transitional administration, along with its large foreign military force, comes to an end.

New Institutional Options: De Facto Trusteeships and Shared Sovereignty

Given the limitations of governance assistance and transitional administration, other options for dealing with countries where international legal sovereignty and Westphalian/Vatellian sovereignty are inconsistent with effective and responsible domestic sovereignty need to be explored. At least two such arrangements would add to the available tool kit of policy options. The first would be to revive the idea of trusteeship or protectorate, probably de facto rather than de jure. The second would be to explore possibilities for shared sovereignty in which national rulers would use their international legal sovereignty to legitimate institutions within their states in which authority was shared between internal and external actors.

De Facto Trusteeships

In a prescient article published in 1993, Gerald Helman and Steven Ratner argued that in extreme cases of state failure, the establishment of trusteeships under the auspices of the UN Security Council would be necessary. By the end of the 1990s, such suggestions had become more common. Analysts have noted that de facto trusteeships have become a fact of international life. In a monograph published in 2002, Richard Caplan argues, "An idea that once enjoyed limited academic currency at best—international trusteeship for failed states and contested territories—has become a reality in all but name." Martin Indyk, an assistant secretary of state during President Bill Clinton's administration, has argued that the most attractive path to permanent peace in the Middle East would be to establish a protectorate in Palestine, legitimated by the United Nations and with the United States playing a key role in security and other areas. Even if final status talks were completed, the trusteeship would remain in place until a responsible Palestinian government was established.[22]

Despite these recent observations, developing an alternative to conventional sovereignty, one that explicitly recognizes that international legal sovereignty will be withdrawn and that external actors will control many aspects of domestic sovereignty for an indefinite period of time, will not be easy. To date there has been no effort, for instance, to produce a treaty or convention that would define and embody in international law a new form of trusteeship. Just the opposite. The rhetorical commitment of all significant actors, including the United States, has been to restore authority to local actors at the soonest possible moment, a stance exemplified by the decision to give what U.S. officials insisted was full sovereignty to Iraq in June 2004.[23]

Codifying a general set of principles and rules for some new kind of trusteeship or protectorate would involve deciding who would appoint the authority and oversee its activities: the UN

Security Council? A regional organization such as the European Union? A coalition of the willing? A single state? A treaty or convention would have to define the possible scope of authority of the governing entity: all activities of the state including security and international affairs? Only matters related to the provision of public goods such as roads, but not those related to the private sphere such as marriage? Given that there would be no fixed date for ending a trusteeship or protectorate, how would the appropriate moment for transferring authority to local actors be determined? What intermediate steps would be taken? Could a trusteeship, for instance, be granted international legal recognition and sovereignty, while some aspects of domestic governance remained under the control of the trustee or conservator?

The most substantial barrier to a general international treaty codifying a new form of trusteeship or protectorate is that it will not receive support from either the powerful, who would have to implement it, or the weak, who might be subject to it. There is widespread sentiment for the proposition that Westphalian/Vatellian sovereignty is not absolute and can be breached in cases of massive human rights violations. UN Secretary-General Annan expressed this view in 1999 to widespread international acclaim.[24] But arguing that Westphalian/Vatellian sovereignty is not absolute is quite different from codifying an explicit alternative that would deprive states of their international legal sovereignty as well as control over their domestic affairs.

An explicit and legitimated alternative to sovereignty would require, at minimum, agreement among the major powers. An arrangement supported by leading states that are not members of the OECD such as Brazil, China, India, Indonesia, Nigeria, and South Africa would be even better. Best of all would be an agreement endorsed by the Security Council and the General Assembly. There is no indication, however, that such widespread support would be given. None of the actors has a clear interest in doing so. The major

powers, those with the capacity to create a trusteeship, want to be able to pick and choose not only where they intervene but also the policies they would follow. The endorsement of a new institutional arrangement would provide a new choice on the menu, but this option might make it difficult to engage in ad hoc arrangements better suited to specific circumstances. For states in the third world, any successor to the mandate system of the League of Nations, or the trusteeship system of the UN, would smell if not look too much like colonialism.[25]

Shared Sovereignty

Shared sovereignty would involve the engagement of external actors in some of the domestic authority structures of the target state for an indefinite period of time. Such arrangements would be legitimated by agreements signed by recognized national authorities. National actors would use their international legal sovereignty to enter into agreements that would compromise their Westphalian/Vatellian sovereignty with the goal of improving domestic sovereignty. One core element of sovereignty—voluntary agreements—would be preserved, while another core element—the principle of autonomy—would be violated.

National leaders could establish shared sovereignty through either treaties or unilateral commitments. To be effective, such arrangements would have to create self-enforcing equilibria involving either domestic players alone or some combination of domestic and international actors. Political elites in the target state would have to believe that they would be worse off if the shared sovereignty arrangement were violated.

For policy purposes, it would be best to refer to shared sovereignty as "partnerships." This would more easily let policymakers engage in organized hypocrisy, that is, saying one thing and doing another. Shared sovereignty or partnerships would allow political leaders to embrace sovereignty, because these arrangements would be legitimated by the target state's international legal sovereignty, even though they violate the core principle of Westphalian/Vatellian sovereignty: autonomy. Organized hypocrisy is not surprising in an environment such as the international system where there are competing norms (e.g., human rights vs. Westphalian/Vatellian sovereignty), power differentials that allow strong actors to pursue policies that are inconsistent with recognized rules, and exceptional complexity that makes it impossible to write any set of rules that could provide optimal outcomes under all conditions. Shared sovereignty or partnerships would make no claim to being an explicit alternative to conventional sovereignty. It would allow actors to obfuscate the fact that their behavior would be inconsistent with their principles.

HISTORICAL EXAMPLES OF SHARED SOVEREIGNTY Shared sovereignty agreements have been used in the past. There are several late nineteenth-century shared sovereignty arrangements in which external actors assumed control over part of the revenue-generating stream of a state that had defaulted on its debt. The state wanted renewed access to international capital markets. The lenders wanted assurance that they would be repaid. Direct control over the collection of specific taxes provided greater confidence than other available measures.

For example, a shared sovereignty arrangement between external lenders and the Porte (the government of the Ottoman Empire) was constructed for some parts of the revenue system of the empire during the latter part of the nineteenth century. The empire entered international capital markets in the 1850s to fund military expenditures associated with the Crimean War. By 1875, after receiving more than a dozen new loans, the empire was unable to service its foreign debt. To again secure access to international capital markets, the Ottomans agreed in 1881 to create, through government decree, the Council of the Public Debt. The members of the council—two from France; one each from Austria, Germany, Italy, and the Ottoman Empire itself; and one from Britain and the Netherlands together—were selected by foreign creditors. Until the debt was liquidated, the Porte gave control of several major sources of revenue to the council and authorized it to take initiatives that would increase economic activity. The council promoted, for instance, the export of salt (the tax on which it controlled) to India and introduced new technologies for the silk and wine industries. It increased the confidence of foreign investors in the empire's railways by collecting revenues that the government had promised to foreign companies. In the decade before World War I, the council controlled about one-quarter of the empire's revenue. It was disbanded after the war.[26]

Unlike classic gunboat diplomacy, where the governments of foreign creditors took over control of customs houses to secure repayment of loans, in the case of the Ottoman Council of the Public Debt, the norm of international legal sovereignty was honored, at least in form. The council was established by an edict issued by the Ottoman Empire at the behest of foreign creditors. International legal sovereignty was honored; Westphalian/Vatellian sovereignty was ignored. This arrangement was durable because if the empire had revoked its decree, it would have lost access to international capital markets.

The relationship of the Soviet Union to the satellite states of Eastern Europe during the Cold War is another example of shared sovereignty. For more than forty years, Soviet penetration of domestic regimes, close oversight of officials, and policy direction from Moscow kept communist regimes in power. During the 1950s the Polish secret police, for instance, reported directly to Moscow. The militaries of the satellites were integrated into the Soviet command structure and unable to operate independently. The communist regimes that Moscow had put in place and sustained by violating Westphalian/Vatellian sovereignty dutifully signed off on the security arrangements that their overlord preferred. Except in a few instances, such as the invasion of

Czechoslovakia in 1968, Soviet behavior was consistent with international legal sovereignty. The implicit and sometimes explicit use of force, however, was necessary to support these regimes because many of the citizens of the satellite states were alienated from their rulers.

The shared sovereignty arrangements established by the United States after World War II were more successful. Germany is the prime example. The Western allies wanted to internationally legitimate the Federal Republic of Germany (FRG or West Germany) but at the same time constrain its freedom of action. The Bonn agreements, signed in 1952 by the FRG, France, the United Kingdom, and the United States and revised in Paris in 1954, gave West Germany full authority over its internal and external affairs but with key exceptions in the security area. Not only did the FRG renounce its right to produce chemical, biological, and nuclear weapons; it also signed a status of forces agreement that gave the allies expansive powers. These included exclusive jurisdiction over the members of their armed forces and the right to patrol public areas including roads, railways, and restaurants. Allied forces could take any measures necessary to ensure order and discipline.[27] West Germany's military was fully integrated into NATO. Article 5(2) of the Convention on Relations gave the Western powers the right to declare a state of emergency until FRG officials obtained adequate powers enabling them to take effective action to protect the security of the foreign forces.[28] Without a clear definition of these adequate powers, the Western allies formally retained the right to resume their occupation of the Federal Republic until 1990, when the 1990 Treaty on the Final Settlement with Respect to Germany terminated the Bonn agreements.

The United States succeeded in the West German case because most Germans supported democracy, a market economy, and constraints on the FRG's security policies. Obviously the strength of this support reflected many factors, including the long-term economic success of the West relative to the Soviet bloc. Shared sovereignty arrangements for security in the FRG contributed to effective domestic governance by taking a potentially explosive issue off the table both within and, more important, without West Germany. Security dilemmas that might have strengthened undemocratic forces in the FRG never occurred because the Bonn government did not have exclusive control of the country's defense.

* * *

INCENTIVES FOR SHARED SOVEREIGNTY Shared sovereignty arrangements can work only if they create a self-enforcing equilibrium, which might include external as well as domestic players. There are at least four circumstances that might make shared sovereignty arrangements attractive for political decision-makers, those who hold international legal sovereignty, in target states: avarice, postconflict occupation, desperation, and elections.

NATURAL RESOURCES AND AVARICE Rulers salivate at the wealth and power that natural resources, most notably oil, can bring them. Their bargaining position, however, depends on the acceptance of the precepts of conventional sovereignty: the state owns the oil and has the right to sign contracts and set rules governing its exploitation. Neither companies, nor consuming states, nor international organizations have challenged the property rights of the state. No one, at least no one in a position of authority, has suggested, for instance, that oil in badly governed states ought to be declared part of the common heritage of mankind and placed under the control of perhaps the World Bank.

For poorly governed countries, however, natural resources, especially oil, have been a curse that has feathered the nests of rulers and undermined democracy and economic growth. Oil concentrates resources in the hands of the state. The road to wealth and power for any ambitious individual leads through the offices of the central government, not through individual enterprise or productive economic activity. With oil wealth, the state can buy off dissenters and build military machines that can be used to repress those who cannot be bought off.[29]

Shared sovereignty arrangements for extractive industries would offer an alternative to conventional practices that would provide better governance in oil-abundant states, more benefits for their people, and fewer incentives for corruption and conflict. Such arrangements would depend on the willingness of wealthier democratic states to constrain the options available to political leaders in poorly governed resource-rich states. Conventional sovereignty would not be challenged in principle but would be compromised in practice. Political leaders in host countries would then be confronted with a choice between nothing and something, although much less than they might have at their private disposal under conventional practices.

A shared sovereignty arrangement for natural resources could work in the following way. An agreement between the host country and, say, the World Bank would create a trust. The trust would be domiciled in an advanced industrialized country with effective rule of law. All funds generated by the natural resources project would be placed in an international escrow account controlled by the trust. All disbursements from the account would have to be approved by a majority of the directors of the trust. Half of the board of directors of the trust would be appointed by the host government, the other half by the World Bank; the bank could name directors from any country but would not designate its own employees. Directors would have to believe that their success depended on the success of the trust.

The trust agreement would stipulate that a large part of these funds would be used for social welfare programs, although specific allocations for, say, health care or education would be left to the host government. The trust would refuse to dispense funds that did not conform with these commitments. The trust might even be charged with implementing programs using

the resources of the escrow account if the government failed to act expeditiously.

The laws of the advanced democracy in which the trust was incorporated would hold accountable the directors of the trust. Legislation enacted by the country in which the trust was domiciled would back the firms' responsibility to pay revenues into the escrow account, and only the escrow account.

No doubt the leaders of oil-rich or other natural resource–rich countries would cringe at such arrangements. They would have much more difficulty putting billions of dollars in foreign bank accounts, as did Sani Abacha, the late Nigerian military dictator. It would be hard to spend half a billion dollars on a European vacation as did some members of the Saudi royal family in 2002. But if the major democracies passed legislation requiring that any imported oil be governed by a trust arrangement, avarice might induce political leaders in resource-rich countries to accept shared sovereignty, because without shared sovereignty they would get nothing.[30]

POSTCONFLICT OCCUPATION Postconflict occupation might also be conducive to creating shared sovereignty arrangements. When there is military intervention and occupation, local leaders have limited choice. In Afghanistan, Bosnia, East Timor, Iraq, and Kosovo, the local leaders have been dependent to some extent on external actors. They have had to accept the presence of nonnationals. Foreigners have been running many of the ministries in Bosnia. In Kosovo joint implementation for administrative structures has been the norm: there are twenty administrative departments and four independent agencies, all of which are codirected by a Kosovar and a senior UNMIK staff person.[31] In Afghanistan and Iraq, security has been provided in part by foreign forces.

Shared sovereignty contracts would make such arrangements permanent, not transitional. The presence of external actors would not be the result of a unilateral decision by an external administrator but rather of a contract between external and domestic actors who would be granted international legal sovereignty. Because the contract would have no termination date, local actors could no longer assume that they could simply wait for the foreigners to leave. Some local leaders might still decide that acting as a spoiler might maximize their interests, but others would see cooperation as more likely to enhance their long-term prospects.

Such arrangements could be successful in the long run only if they were supported by a winning coalition in the host country. Unlike oil trusts, external enforcement mechanisms would be difficult to create. External actors might bolster domestic agents committed to shared sovereignty or threaten to impose sanctions or cut foreign assistance if the agreement were violated, but there could not be an ironclad guarantee of success.

Still, shared sovereignty arrangements would be more promising than constitution writing, which has been the center of attention in recent occupations. The problem with relying on a constitution or any other legal commitments made under pressure at a particular moment in time is that once the occupying power leaves, the incentives for domestic actors to honor their earlier commitments can radically change. Shared sovereignty, in contrast, could generate a self-enforcing equilibrium if it provided benefits to a large enough group of domestic actors.

Monetary policy is one area where shared sovereignty might work in a postconflict or even a more benign environment. Controlling inflation can be a daunting problem. A few countries, East Timor being one example, have simply resorted to using the U.S. dollar. Others have tried to engineer credible commitments through domestic institutions, such as independent central banks. Appointment of the governors of the central bank by both government and external actors could enhance the credibility of such arrangements. In this regard, the IMF might be the right partner. Nonnational governors could be of any nationality. They would not be IMF employees. The fund would sign a contract with the host country setting up shared sovereignty on a permanent basis or until both parties agreed to end the arrangement. If the national government unilaterally abrogated the arrangement, it would be a clear signal to external actors that the government was abandoning the path of monetary responsibility. If the central bank were successful in constraining inflation, the arrangement would generate support from domestic actors. Like oil trusts, one major attraction of such an agreement is that it would not be costly for the IMF or any other external actor.

Commercial courts might be another area where shared sovereignty could be productive. Again, the opportunities in this area would not be limited to postconflict situations. In a state where the rule of law has been sketchy, the international legal sovereign would conclude a contract with an external entity—for instance, a regional organization such as the EU or the Organization of American States—to establish a separate commercial court system. The judges in these courts would be appointed by both the national government and its external partner. The expectation would be that local business interests would find this court system attractive. It would provide a venue in which they could resolve disagreements more effectively than would be the case within existing national institutions. The presence of such a court system might even attract higher levels of foreign investment. Like oil trusts and central banks, such an arrangement would not involve substantial costs for the external actor. The national government, or even to some extent the litigants, could fund commercial courts.

DESPERATION Aside from the avarice associated with natural resources and the pressures arising from occupation, desperation for external resources might also motivate national authorities to enter into shared sovereignty arrangements. For countries that have spiraled into the abyss because of civil war or misgovernance, and that do not have easily exploited natural resources, foreign assistance might be a major potential source of revenue. The bargaining leverage of political leaders under such circumstances would be limited. The ability of external actors to negotiate shared sovereignty arrangements would be high.

As in the case of occupation, the most promising spheres for shared sovereignty, such as monetary policy and commercial courts, would not require substantial resources from external actors but would generate adequate domestic support. In collapsed or near-collapsed states, however, external actors would have to provide resources at least for some period of time. This would open additional possibilities for shared sovereignty for activities funded by external donors. A committee composed of national officials and individuals appointed by the education ministries of major donor countries might make, for instance, decisions about educational curriculum. A system of health care facilities administered by external aid workers or NGOs could be created separate from the national ministry of health. Because donors are not likely to be willing to provide aid on a quasi-permanent basis, however, such arrangements could be sustained only if a large enough domestic coalition were willing to support them even after foreign funding had been withdrawn.

ELECTIONS   Finally, in badly governed illiberal democracies, elections might provide an incentive for shared sovereignty contracts. Political candidates might make such policies part of their electoral platform. Illiberal democracies are polities that hold competitive elections but are deficient with regard to rule of law, an active civil society, and a free press. In illiberal democracies, government does not work very well. Public officials are disconnected from the citizenry. Individuals or parties might change, but policies remain more or less the same. Voters become cynical, and even potentially progressive political candidates have no way to make their campaign pledges credible. Shared sovereignty contracts could be an appealing political strategy for a dissident candidate. Such a political platform could

win votes by signaling to the electorate that a politician would make a decisive break with the past by engaging external actors in domestic decisionmaking processes.

The long-term credibility of a shared sovereignty arrangement concluded by a successful dissident candidate in an illiberal democracy would depend both on the extent to which such practices have been internationally legitimated and on their effectiveness. The more common shared sovereignty agreements are, the easier it would be for any one leader to defend his actions against opponents who might claim that he had compromised the state's sovereignty. The greater the improvement in governance associated with shared sovereignty arrangements, the greater the likelihood that they would be honored over the long term.

Thus some form of de facto protectorate and, more promising, shared sovereignty are policy tools that could be added to the meager selection of options currently available to deal with bad governance or to create effective institutions following military occupations. Legitimacy for shared sovereignty would be provided by the agreement of those exercising the target state's international legal sovereignty.

Conclusion

During the twentieth century, the norms of international legal sovereignty and Westphalian/Vatellian sovereignty became universally accepted. It has often been tacitly assumed that these norms would be accompanied by effective domestic sovereignty, that is, by governance structures that exercised competent and ideally constructive control over their countries' populations and territory. This assumption has proven false. Poor, even malevolent, governance is a widespread problem. Badly governed states have become a threat to the interests of much more powerful actors: weapons of mass destruction have broken the connection between resources and the ability to do grievous harm; genocides leave political leaders in democratic polities with uncomfortable choices; and transnational disease and crime are persistent challenges.

The policy tools available to external actors—governance assistance and transitional administration—are inadequate, even when foreign powers have militarily occupied a country. Governance assistance can have positive results in occupied or badly governed states, but the available evidence suggests that the impact is weak. Transitional administration, which aims to restore conventional sovereignty in a relatively short time frame, can be effective only if indigenous political leaders believe that they will be better off allying with external actors not only while these actors are present but also after they leave.

The menu of options to deal with failing and collapsed states could be expanded in at least two ways. First, major states or regional or international organizations could assume some form of de facto trusteeship or protectorate responsibility for specific countries, even if there is no general international convention defining such arrangements. In a trusteeship, international actors would assume control over local functions for an indefinite period of time. They might also eliminate the international legal sovereignty of the entity or control treaty-making powers in whole or in part (e.g., in specific areas such as security or trade). There would be no assumption of a withdrawal in the short or medium term.

Second, domestic sovereignty in collapsed or poorly governed states could be improved through shared sovereignty contracts. These contracts would create joint authority structures in specific areas. They would not involve a direct assault on sovereignty norms because they would be formally consistent with international legal sovereignty, even though they would violate Westphalian/Vatellian sovereignty. Natural resources trusts, whose directors were appointed by national and nonnational entities, would be one possibility; central banks whose boards of governors comprised citizens and noncitizens would be another.

Political leaders in target states might accept such arrangements to secure external resources, either payments for raw materials' exploitation or foreign assistance, to encourage the departure of occupying forces or to attract voters. To be durable, shared sovereignty institutions either would require external enforcement, something that would be possible for natural resources trusts, or would have to create adequate domestic support, which would depend on the results delivered.

For external signatories—international organizations, regional organizations, and states—the most attractive shared sovereignty arrangements would be ones that did not require any significant commitment of resources over the long term. Natural resources trusts and central bank administration would meet this condition. In cases of states recovering from collapse, or something near to it, where foreign aid is the incentive for national leaders to accept shared sovereignty, resources commitments by external actors would be unavoidable for the short and medium terms. Over the longer term, though, shared sovereignty institutions could survive only if the services they provided were funded from internal sources of revenue.

De facto trusteeships or protectorates and shared sovereignty hardly exhaust the possibilities for improving domestic sovereignty in poorly governed states. Leaders in some polities have already used private firms to carry out some activities that have traditionally been in the hands of state officials. Indonesia, for instance, used a Swiss firm to collect its customs for more than eleven years. Other governments have hired private military companies (PMCs). Perhaps with stronger accountability mechanisms enforced by advanced industrial states, such as the ability to prosecute PMCs and their employees for abuses, the results might be more consistently salutary.

There is no panacea for domestic sovereignty failures. Even with the best of intentions and substantial resources, external actors cannot quickly eliminate the causes of these failures: poverty, weak indigenous institutions, insecurity, and the raw materials curse. But the instruments currently available to policy-makers to deal with places such as Congo, Liberia, and Iraq are woefully inadequate. De facto trusteeships, and especially shared sovereignty, would offer political leaders a better chance of bringing peace and prosperity to the populations of badly governed states and reduce the threat that such polities present to the wider international community.

NOTES

1. For a discussion of the requirements for successful international engagement that complements many of the points made in this article, see James D. Fearon and David D. Laitin, "Neotrusteeship and the Problem of Weak States," *International Security*, Vol. 28, No. 4 (Spring 2004), pp. 5–43.

2. See ibid., especially pp. 36–37.

3. Although the principle of nonintervention is traditionally associated with the Peace of Westphalia of 1648, the doctrine was not explicitly articulated until a century later by the Swiss jurist Emmerich de Vattel in his *The Law of Nations or Principles of the Law of Nature Applied to the Conduct and Affairs of Nations and Sovereigns*, originally published in French in 1758.

4. Mary Ann Tetreault, "Autonomy, Necessity, and the Small State: Ruling Kuwait in the Twentieth Century," *International Organization*, Vol. 45, No. 4 (Autumn 1991), pp. 565–591.

5. In Shanghai, for instance, the British established a municipal council that regulated the activities of Chinese living within Shanghai as well as non-Chinese. See Jean Chesneaux, Marianne Bastid, and Marie-Claire Bergere, *China from the Opium Wars to the 1911 Revolution* (Hassocks, Sussex, U.K.: Harvester, 1977), pp. 61–68.

6. For two very similar analyses, see Robert O. Keohane, "Political Authority after Intervention: Gradations in Sovereignty," in J.L. Holzgrefe and Keohane, eds., *Humanitarian Intervention: Ethical, Legal, and Political Dilemmas* (Cambridge: Cambridge University Press, 2003), pp. 276–277; and Gerald B. Helman and Steven R. Ratner, "Saving Failed States," *Foreign Policy*, No. 89 (Winter 1993), pp. 3–21. Keohane argues that there should be gradations of sovereignty. Helman and Ratner suggest that there are three forms of what they call "guardianship": governance assistance, the delegation of government authority, and trusteeship. They also suggest the term "conservatorship" as an alternative to trusteeship.

7. James D. Fearon and David D. Laitin, "Ethnicity, Insurgency, and Civil War," *American Political Science Review*, Vol. 97, No. 1 (March 2003), pp. 1–17; and Fearon and Laitin, "Neotrusteeship and the Problem of Weak States," pp. 36–37.

8. Goldstone et al., *State Failure Task Force Report*, p. 21.

9. These figures are derived from data found at World Bank, *WDI Online*, http://devdata.worldbank.org/dataonline/.

10. U.S. Department of State, *Trafficking in Persons Report* (Washington, D.C.: U.S. Department of State, June 2004), http://www.state.gov/documents/organization/33614.pdf.

11. International Commission on Intervention and State Sovereignty, *The Responsibility to Protect* (Ottawa: International Development Research Centre, 2001), http://www.dfait-maeci.gc.ca/icissciise/pdf/Commission-Report.pdf. See also Gareth Evans and Mohamed Sahnoun, "The Responsibility to Protect," *Foreign Affairs*, Vol. 81, No. 6 (November/December 2002), pp. 99–110.

12. For the White House description of the MCA, see http://www.whitehouse.gov/infocus/developingnations/millenium.html. For a list of the first set of countries to receive funding from the MCA, see MCA, press release, "The Millennium Challenge Corporation Names MCA Eligible Countries," May 6, 2004, http://www.usaid.gov/mca/Documents/PR_

Eligible.pdf. For a discussion of the World Bank's governance assistance programs, see http://www.worldbank.org/wbi/governance/about.html. See also Arthur A. Goldsmith, "Foreign Aid and Statehood in Africa," *International Organization*, Vol. 55, No. 1 (Winter 2000), pp. 135–136.

13. International Monetary Fund, Fiscal Affairs Department, *Fund-Supported Programs, Fiscal Policy, and Income Distribution*, Occasional Paper No. 46 (Washington, D.C.: International Monetary Fund, 1986), p. 40; and Robin Broad, *Unequal Alliance: The World Bank, the International Monetary Fund, and the Philippines* (Berkeley: University of California Press, 1988), pp. 51–53, Table 12.

14. Paul Lewis, "Global Lenders Use Leverage to Combat Corruption," *New York Times*, late ed., August 11, 1997, p. 4; and James C. McKinley Jr., "Kenyan Who Charged 4 Officials with Graft Is Suspended," *New York Times*, late ed., July 31, 1998, p. 4.

15. World Bank, *World Development Report, 1997: The State in a Changing World* (Washington, D.C.: World Bank, 1997), p. 2.

16. Michael W. Doyle and Nicholas Sambanis, "International Peacebuilding: A Theoretical and Quantitative Analysis," *American Political Science Review*, Vol. 94, No. 4 (December 2000), pp. 779–802. For a second study with a different database but comparable findings, see George Downs and Stephen John Stedman, "Evaluating Issues in Peace Implementation," in Stedman, Donald Rothchild, and Elizabeth M. Cousens, eds., *Ending Civil Wars: The Implementation of Peace Agreements* (Boulder, Colo.: Lynne Rienner, 2002), pp. 50–52.

17. Richard Caplan, *A New Trusteeship? The International Administration of War-torn Territories* (London: International Institute for Strategic Studies, 2002), pp. 8–9, 50–51; United Nations, *Report of the Panel on United Nations Peace Operations* (Brahimi report) (New York: United Nations, 2000), pp. 7, 14. In June 2003 Secretary of Defense Donald Rumsfeld discussed the possibility of a standing international peacekeeping force under the leadership of the United States. Ester Schrader, "U.S. Looks at Organizing Global Peacekeeping Force," *Los Angeles Times*, June 27, 2003, p. A1.

18. Fearon and Laitin, "Neotrusteeship and the Problem of Weak States," p. 37. See also David M. Edelstein, "Occupational Hazards: Why Military Occupations Succeed or Fail," *International Security*, Vol. 29, No. 1 (Summer 2004), pp. 49–81.

19. Michael Ignatieff points to the possibly negative consequences of competition among NGOs. Ignatieff, "State Failure and Nation-Building," p. 27.

20. For Namibia, see Downs and Stedman, "Evaluating Issues in Peace Implementation," pp. 59–61; and Roland Paris, *At War's End? Building Peace after Civil Conflict* (Cambridge: Cambridge University Press, 2004), chap. 8.

21. Downs and Stedman, "Evaluating Issues in Peace Implementation," pp. 62–63; and Paris, *At War's End*, chap. 7.

22. Helman and Ratner, "Saving Failed States," pp. 3–21; Caplan, *A New Trusteeship?* p. 7; Ignatieff, "State Failure and Nation-Building," p. 308; and Martin Indyk, "A Trusteeship for Palestine?" *Foreign Affairs*, Vol. 82, No. 3 (May/June 2003), pp. 51–66.

23. At least one way to interpret the strategy of U.S. decisionmakers is to understand the June transfer as one that gives Iraq international legal sovereignty. With this international legal sovereignty, the new Iraqi government will be able to legitimate agreements with external agents. Given the dependence of the new government on the United States for security and revenue, such agreements will allow the United States to continue to pursue its core interests.

24. Kofi Annan, "The Legitimacy to Intervene: International Action to Uphold Human Rights Requires a New Understanding of State and Individual Sovereignty," *Financial Times*, December 31, 1999.

25. Fearon and Laitin have suggested that "neo-trusteeship" is the most appropriate term for arrangements that could cope with the post-conflict security problems afflicting states suffering from weak administrative capacity, poverty, and rough terrain. Because such states are unlikely to be able to conduct effective policing and counterinsurgency operations on their own, maintaining security will require the engagement of external actors for an extended period of time. The authors do not, however, argue that neotrusteeship would involve a loss of international legal sovereignty. See Fearon and Laitin, "Neotrusteeship and the Problem of Weak States," especially pp. 24–41.

26. Donald C. Blaisdell, *European Financial Control in the Ottoman Empire: A Study of the Establishment, Activities, and Significance of the Administration of the Ottoman Public Debt* (New York: Columbia University Press, 1929), pp. 90–120, 124–130; Herbert Feis, *Europe, the World's Banker, 1870–1914: An Account of European Foreign Investment and the Connection of World Finance with Diplomacy before World War I* (New York: W. W. Norton, 1965), pp. 332–341; Bernard Lewis, *The Middle East: A Brief History of the Last 2,000 Years* (New York: Scribner, 1995), pp. 298–299; and Roger Owen, *The Middle East in the World Economy, 1800–1914* (Cambridge: Cambridge University Press, 1981), p. 101.

27. "Revised NATO SOFA Supplementary Agreement," articles 19, 22, 28. The full text of the agreement is available at http://www.oxc.army.mil/others/Gca/files%5Cgermany.doc.

28. "Convention on Relations between the Three Powers and the Federal Republic of Germany," *American Journal of International Law*, Vol. 49, No. 3 (July 1955), pp. 57–69. For a detailed examination of the retained rights of the Western powers, see Joseph W. Bishop Jr., "The 'Contractual Agreements' with the Federal Republic of Germany," *American Journal of International Law*, Vol. 49, No. 2 (April 1955), pp. 125–147. For a general analysis of Germany's situation after World War II, see Peter J. Katzenstein, *Policy and Politics in West Germany: The Growth of a Semisovereign State* (Philadelphia: Temple University Press, 1987).

29. Michael Lewin Ross, "Does Oil Hinder Democracy?" *World Politics*, Vol. 53, No. 3 (April 2001), pp. 325–361.

30. This proposal assumes that oil could be exploited only by companies domiciled in advanced democratic polities interested in supporting good governance and that these countries cooperate with each other. Absent these conditions, the host country could play one oil company off against another and avoid the constraints that would come with a shared sovereignty trust.

31. Caplan, *A New Trusteeship?* p. 39.

MOISÉS NAÍM

The Five Wars of Globalization

The persistence of al Qaeda underscores how hard it is for governments to stamp out stateless, decentralized networks that move freely, quickly, and stealthily across national borders to engage in terror. The intense media coverage devoted to the war on terrorism, however, obscures five other similar global wars that pit governments against agile, well-financed networks of highly dedicated individuals. These are the fights against the illegal international trade in drugs, arms, intellectual property, people, and money. Religious zeal or political goals drive terrorists, but the promise of enormous financial gain motivates those who battle governments in these five wars. Tragically, profit is no less a motivator for murder, mayhem, and global insecurity than religious fanaticism.

In one form or another, governments have been fighting these five wars for centuries. And losing them. Indeed, thanks to the changes spurred by globalization over the last decade, their losing streak has become even more pronounced. To be sure, nation-states have benefited from the information revolution, stronger political and economic linkages, and the shrinking importance of geographic distance. Unfortunately, criminal networks have benefited even more. Never fettered by the niceties of sovereignty, they are now increasingly free of geographic constraints. Moreover, globalization has not only expanded illegal markets and boosted the size and the resources of criminal networks, it has also imposed more burdens on govern-

ments: Tighter public budgets, decentralization, privatization, deregulation, and a more open environment for international trade and investment all make the task of fighting global criminals more difficult. Governments are made up of cumbersome bureaucracies that generally cooperate with difficulty, but drug traffickers, arms dealers, alien smugglers, counterfeiters, and money launderers have refined networking to a high science, entering into complex and improbable strategic alliances that span cultures and continents.

Defeating these foes may prove impossible. But the first steps to reversing their recent dramatic gains must be to recognize the fundamental similarities among the five wars and to treat these conflicts not as law enforcement problems but as a new global trend that shapes the world as much as confrontations between nation-states did in the past. Customs officials, police officers, lawyers, and judges alone will never win these wars. Governments must recruit and deploy more spies, soldiers, diplomats, and economists who understand how to use incentives and regulations to steer markets away from bad social outcomes. But changing the skill set of government combatants alone will not end these wars. Their doctrines and institutions also need a major overhaul.

From *Foreign Policy* no. 134 (Jan./Feb. 2003): 28–37.

The Five Wars

Pick up any newspaper anywhere in the world, any day, and you will find news about illegal migrants, drug busts, smuggled weapons, laundered money, or counterfeit goods. The global nature of these five wars was unimaginable just a decade ago. The resources—financial, human, institutional, technological—deployed by the combatants have reached unfathomable orders of magnitude. So have the numbers of victims. The tactics and tricks of both sides boggle the mind. Yet if you cut through the fog of daily headlines and orchestrated photo ops, one inescapable truth emerges: The world's governments are fighting a qualitatively new phenomenon with obsolete tools, inadequate laws, inefficient bureaucratic arrangements, and ineffective strategies. Not surprisingly, the evidence shows that governments are losing.

Drugs

The best known of the five wars is, of course, the war on drugs. In 1999, the United Nations' "Human Development Report" calculated the annual trade in illicit drugs at $400 billion, roughly the size of the Spanish economy and about 8 percent of world trade. Many countries are reporting an increase in drug use. Feeding this habit is a global supply chain that uses everything from passenger jets that can carry shipments of cocaine worth $500 million in a single trip to custom-built submarines that ply the waters between Colombia and Puerto Rico. To foil eavesdroppers, drug smugglers use "cloned" cell phones and broadband radio receivers while also relying on complex financial structures that blend legitimate and illegitimate enterprises with [elaborate] fronts and structures of cross-ownership.

The United States spends between $35 billion and $40 billion each year on the war on drugs; most of this money is spent on interdiction and intelligence. But the creativity and boldness of drug cartels has routinely outstripped steady increases in government resources. Responding to tighter security at the U.S.-Mexican border, drug smugglers built a tunnel to move tons of drugs and billions of dollars in cash until

authorities discovered it in March 2002. Over the last decade, the success of the Bolivian and Peruvian governments in eradicating coca plantations has shifted production to Colombia. Now, the U.S.-supported Plan Colombia is displacing coca production and processing labs back to other Andean countries. Despite the heroic efforts of these Andean countries and the massive financial and technical support of the United States, the total acreage of coca plantations in Peru, Colombia, and Bolivia has increased in the last decade from 206,200 hectares in 1991 to 210,939 in 2001. Between 1990 and 2000, according to economist Jeff DeSimone, the median price of a gram of cocaine in the United States fell from $152 to $112.

Even when top leaders of drug cartels are captured or killed, former rivals take their place. Authorities have acknowledged, for example, that the recent arrest of Benjamin Arellano Felix, accused of running Mexico's most ruthless drug cartel, has done little to stop the flow of drugs to the United States. As Arellano said in a recent interview from jail, "They talk about a war against the Arellano brothers. They haven't won. I'm here, and nothing has changed."

Arms Trafficking

Drugs and arms often go together. In 1999, the Peruvian military parachuted 10,000 AK-47s to the Revolutionary Armed Forces of Colombia, a guerrilla group closely allied to drug growers and traffickers. The group purchased the weapons in Jordan. Most of the roughly 80 million AK-47s in circulation today are in the wrong hands. According to the United Nations, only 18 million (or about 3 percent) of the 550 million small arms and light weapons in circulation today are used by government, military, or police forces. Illic[i]t trade accounts for almost 20 percent of the total small arms trade and generates more than $1 billion a year. Small arms helped fuel 46 of the 49 largest conflicts of the last decade and in 2001 were estimated to be responsible for 1,000 deaths a day; more than 80 percent of those victims were women and children.

Small arms are just a small part of the problem. The illegal market for munitions encompasses top-of-the-line tanks, radar systems that detect Stealth aircraft, and the makings of the deadliest weapons of mass destruction. The International Atomic Energy Agency has confirmed more than a dozen cases of smuggled nuclear-weapons-usable material, and hundreds more cases have been reported and investigated over the last decade. The actual supply of stolen nuclear-, biological-, or chemical-weapons materials and technology may still be small. But the potential demand is strong and growing from both would-be nuclear powers and cause prices to rise and create enormous incentives for illegal activities. More than one fifth of the 120,000 workers in Russia's former "nuclear cities"—where more than half of all employees earn less than $50 a month—say they would be willing to work in the military complex of another country.

Governments have been largely ineffective in curbing either supply or demand. In recent years, two countries, Pakistan and India, joined the declared nuclear power club. A U.N. arms embargo failed to prevent the reported sale to Iraq of jet fighter engine parts from Yugoslavia and the Kolchuga anti-Stealth radar system from Ukraine. Multilateral efforts to curb the manufacture and distribution of weapons are faltering, not least because some powers are unwilling to accept curbs on their own activities. In 2001, for example, the United States blocked a legally binding global treaty to control small arms in part because it worried about restrictions on its own citizens' rights to own guns. In the absence of effective international legislation and enforcement, the laws of economics dictate the sale of more weapons at cheaper prices: In 1986, an AK-47 in Kolowa, Kenya, cost 15 cows. Today, it costs just four.

OTHER FRONTS

Drugs, arms, intellectual property, people, and money are not the only commodities traded illegally for huge profits by international networks. They also trade in human organs, endangered species, stolen art, and toxic waste. The illegal global trades in all these goods share several fundamental characteristics: Technological innovations and political changes open new markets, globalization is increasing both the geographical reach and the profit opportunities for criminal networks, and governments are on the losing end of the fight to stop them. Some examples:

Human organs: Corneas, kidneys, and livers are the most commonly traded human parts in a market that has boomed thanks to technology, which has improved preservation techniques and made transplants less risky. In the United States, 70,000 patients are on the waiting list for major organ transplants while only 20,000 of them succeed in getting the organ they need. Unscrupulous "organ brokers" partly meet this demand by providing, for a fee, organs and transplant services. Some of the donors, especially of kidneys, are desperately poor. In India, an estimated 2,000 people a year sell their organs. Many organs, however, come from nonconsenting donors forced to undergo operations or from cadavers in police morgues. For example, medical centers in Germany and Austria were recently found to have used human heart valves taken without consent from the cadavers of poor South Africans.

Endangered species: From sturgeon for caviar in gourmet delicatessens to tigers or elephants for private zoos, the trade in endangered animals and plants is worth billions of dollars and includes hundreds of millions of plant and animal types. This trade ranges from live animals and plants to all kinds of wildlife products derived from them, including food products, exotic leather goods, wooden musical instruments, timber, tourist curiosities, and medicines.

Stolen art: Paintings and sculptures taken from museums, galleries, and private homes, from

Holocaust victims, or from "cultural artifacts" poached from archeological digs and other ancient ruins are also illegally traded internationally in a market worth an estimated $2 billion to $6 billion each year. The growing use of art-based transactions in money laundering has spurred demand over the last decade. The supply has boomed because the Soviet Union's collapse flooded the world's market with art that had been under state control. The Czech Republic, Poland, and Russia are three of the five countries most affected by art crime worldwide.

Toxic waste: Innovations in maritime transport, tighter environmental regulations in industrialized countries coupled with increased integration of poor countries to the global economy and better telecommunications have created a market where waste is traded internationally. Greenpeace estimates that during the 20 years prior to 1989, just 3.6 million tons of hazardous waste were exported; in the five years after 1989, the trade soared to about 6.7 billion tons. The environmental organization also reckons that 86 to 90 percent of all hazardous waste shipments destined for developing countries—purportedly for recycling, reuse, recovery, or humanitarian uses—are toxic waste.

Intellectual Property

In 2001, two days after recording the voice track of a movie in Hollywood, actor Dennis Hopper was in Shanghai where a street vendor sold him an excellent pirated copy of the movie with his voice already on it. "I don't know how they got my voice into the country before I got here," he wondered. Hopper's experience is one tiny slice of an illicit trade that cost the United States an estimated $9.4 billion in 2001. The piracy rate of business software in Japan and France is 40 percent, in Greece and South Korea it is about 60 percent, and in Germany and Britain it hovers around 30 percent. Forty percent of Procter & Gamble shampoos and 60 percent of Honda motorbikes sold in China in 2001 were pirated. Up to 50 percent of medical drugs in Nigeria and Thailand are bootleg copies. This problem is not limited to consumer products: Italian makers of industrial valves worry that their $2 billion a year export market is eroded by counterfeit Chinese valves sold in world markets at prices that are 40 percent cheaper.

The drivers of this bootlegging boom are complex. Technology is obviously boosting both the demand and the supply of illegally copied products. Users of Napster, the now defunct Internet company that allowed anyone, anywhere to download and reproduce copyrighted music for free, grew from zero to 20 million in just one year. Some 500,000 film files are traded daily through file-sharing services such as Kazaa and Morpheus; and in late 2002, some 900 million music files could be downloaded for free on the Internet—that is, almost two and a half times more files than those available when Napster reached its peak in February 2001.

Global marketing and branding are also playing a part, as more people are attracted to products bearing a well-known brand like Prada or Cartier. And thanks to the rapid growth and integration into the global economy of countries, such as China, with weak central governments and ineffective laws, producing and exporting near perfect knockoffs are both less expensive and less risky. In the words of the CEO of one of the best known Swiss watchmakers: "We now compete with a product manufactured by Chinese prisoners. The business is run by the Chinese military, their families and friends, using roughly the same machines we have, which they purchased at the same industrial fairs we go to. The way we have rationalized this problem is by assuming that their customers and ours are different. The person that buys a pirated copy of one of our $5,000 watches for less than $100 is not a client we are losing. Perhaps it is a future client that some day will want to own the real thing instead of a fake. We may be wrong and we do spend money to fight the piracy of our products. But given that our efforts do not seem to protect us much, we close our eyes and hope for the better." This posture stands in contrast to that of companies that sell cheaper products such as garments, music, or videos, whose revenues are directly affected by piracy.

Governments have attempted to protect intellectual property rights through various means, most notably the World Trade Organization's Agreement on Trade-Related Aspects of Intellectual Property Rights (TRIPS). Several other organizations such as the World Intellectual Property Organization, the World Customs Union, and Interpol are also involved. Yet the large and growing volume of this trade, or a simple stroll in the streets of Manhattan or Madrid, show that governments are far from winning this fight.

Alien Smuggling

The man or woman who sells a bogus Hermes scarf or a Rolex watch in the streets of Milan is likely to be an illegal alien. Just as likely, he or she was transported across several continents by a trafficking network allied with another network that specializes in the illegal copying, manufacturing, and distributing of high-end, brand-name products.

Alien smuggling is a $7 billion a year enterprise and according to the United Nations is the fastest growing business of organized crime. Roughly 500,000 people enter the United States illegally each year—about the same number as illegally enter the European Union, and part of the approximately 150 million who live outside their countries of origin. Many of these back-door travelers are voluntary migrants who pay smugglers up to $35,000, the top-dollar fee for passage from China to New York. Others, instead, are trafficked—that is, bought and sold internationally—as commodities. The U.S. Congressional Research Service reckons that each year between 1 million and 2 million people are trafficked across borders, the majority of whom

are women and children. A woman can be "bought" in Timisoara, Romania, for between $50 and $200 and "resold" in Western Europe for 10 times that price. The United Nations Children's Fund estimates that cross-border smugglers in Central and Western Africa enslave 200,000 children a year. Traffickers initially tempt victims with job offers or, in the case of children, with offers of adoption in wealthier countries, and then keep the victims in subservience through physical violence, debt bondage, passport confiscation, and threats of arrest, deportation, or violence against their families back home.

Governments everywhere are enacting tougher immigration laws and devoting more time, money, and technology to fight the flow of illegal aliens. But the plight of the United Kingdom's government illustrates how tough that fight is. The British government throws money at the problem, plans to use the Royal Navy and Royal Air Force to intercept illegal immigrants, and imposes large fines on truck drivers who (generally unwittingly) transport stowaways. Still, 42,000 of the 50,000 refugees who have passed through the Sangatte camp (a main entry point for illegal immigration to the United Kingdom) over the last three years have made it to Britain. At current rates, it will take 43 years for Britain to clear its asylum backlog. And that country is an island. Continental nations such as Spain, Italy, or the United States face an even greater challenge as immigration pressures overwhelm their ability to control the inflow of illegal aliens.

Money Laundering

The Cayman Islands has a population of 36,000. It also has more than 2,200 mutual funds, 500 insurance companies, 60,000 businesses, and 600 banks and trust companies with almost $800 billion in assets. Not surprisingly, it figures prominently in any discussion of money laundering. So does the United States, several of whose major banks have been caught up in investigations of money laundering, tax evasion, and fraud. Few, if any, countries can claim to be free of the practice of helping individuals and companies hide funds from governments, creditors, business partners, or even family members, including the proceeds of tax evasion, gambling, and other crimes. Estimates of the volume of global money laundering range between 2 and 5 percent of the world's annual gross national product, or between $800 billion and $2 trillion.

Smuggling money, gold coins, and other valuables is an ancient trade. Yet in the last two decades, new political and economic trends coincided with technological changes to make this ancient trade easier, cheaper, and less risky. Political changes led to the deregulation of financial markets that now facilitate cross-border money transfers, and technological changes made distance less of a factor and money less "physical." Suitcases full of banknotes are still a key tool for money launderers, but computers, the Internet, and complex financial schemes that combine legal and illegal practices and institutions are more common. The sophistication of technology, the complex web of financial institutions that crisscross the globe, and the ease with which "dirty" funds can be electronically morphed into legitimate assets make the regulation of international flows of money a daunting task. In Russia, for example, it is estimated that by the mid-1990s organized crime groups had set up 700 legal and financial institutions to launder their money.

Faced with this growing tide, governments have stepped up their efforts to clamp down on rogue international banking, tax havens, and money laundering. The imminent, large-scale introduction of e-money—cards with microchips that can store large amounts of money and thus can be easily transported outside regular channels or simply exchanged among individuals—will only magnify this challenge.

Why Governments Can't Win

The fundamental changes that have given the five wars new intensity over the last decade are likely to persist. Technology will continue to spread widely; criminal networks will be able to exploit these technologies more quickly than governments that must cope with tight budgets, bureaucracies, media scrutiny, and electorates. International trade will continue to grow, providing more cover for the expansion of illicit trade. International migration will likewise grow, with much the same effect, offering ethnically based gangs an ever growing supply of recruits and victims. The spread of democracy may also help criminal cartels, which can manipulate weak public institutions by corrupting police officers or tempting politicians with offers of cash for their increasingly expensive election campaigns. And ironically, even the spread of international law—with its growing web of embargoes, sanctions, and conventions—will offer criminals new opportunities for providing forbidden goods to those on the wrong side of the international community.

These changes may affect each of the five wars in different ways, but these conflicts will continue to share four common characteristics:

They Are Not Bound by Geography

Some forms of crime have always had an international component: The Mafia was born in Sicily and exported to the United States, and smuggling has always been by definition international. But the five wars are truly global. Where is the theater or front line of the war on drugs? Is it Colombia or Miami? Myanmar (Burma) or Milan? Where are the battles against money launderers being fought? In Nauru or in London? Is China the main theater in the war against the infringement of intellectual property, or are the trenches of that war on the Internet?

They Defy Traditional Notions of Sovereignty

Al Qaeda's members have passports and nationalities—and often more than one—but they are truly stateless. Their allegiance is to their cause, not to any nation. The same is also true of the criminal networks engaged in the five wars. The same, however, is patently *not* true of government employees—police officers, customs agents, and judges—who fight them. This asymmetry is a crippling disadvantage for governments waging these wars. Highly paid, hypermotivated, and resource-rich combatants on one side of the wars (the criminal gangs) can seek refuge in and take advantage of national borders, but combatants of the other side (the governments) have fewer resources and are hampered by traditional notions of sovereignty. A former senior CIA official reported that international criminal gangs are able to move people, money, and weapons globally faster than he can move resources inside his own agency, let alone worldwide. Coordination and information sharing among government agencies in different countries has certainly improved, especially after September 11. Yet these tactics fall short of what is needed to combat agile organizations that can exploit every nook and cranny of an evolving but imperfect body of international law and multilateral treaties.

They Pit Governments against Market Forces

In each of the five wars, one or more government bureaucracies fight to contain the disparate, uncoordinated actions of thousands of independent, stateless organizations. These groups are motivated by large profits obtained by exploiting international price differentials, an unsatisfied demand, or the cost advantages produced by theft. Hourly wages for a Chinese cook are far higher in Manhattan than in Fujian. A gram of cocaine in Kansas City is 17,000 percent more expensive than in Bogotá. Fake Italian valves are 40 percent cheaper because counterfeiters don't have to cover the costs of developing the product. A well-funded guerrilla group will pay anything to get the weapons it needs. In each of these five wars, the incentives to successfully overcome government-imposed limits to trade are simply enormous.

They Pit Bureaucracies against Networks

The same network that smuggles East European women to Berlin may be involved in distributing opium there. The proceeds of the latter fund the purchase of counterfeit Bulgari watches made in China and often sold on the streets of Manhattan by illegal African immigrants. Colombian drug cartels make deals with Ukrainian arms traffickers, while Wall Street brokers controlled by the U.S.-based Mafia have been known to front for Russian money launderers. These highly decentralized groups and individuals are bound by strong ties of loyalty and common purpose and organized around semiautonomous clusters or "nodes" capable of operating swiftly and flexibly. John Arquilla and David Ronfeldt, two of the best known experts on these types of organizations, observe that networks often lack central leadership, command, or headquarters, thus "no precise heart or head that can be targeted. The network as a whole (but not necessarily each node) has little to no hierarchy; there may be multiple leaders. . . . Thus the [organization's] design may sometimes appear acephalous (headless), and at other times polycephalous (Hydra-headed)." Typically, governments respond to these challenges by forming interagency task forces or creating new bureaucracies. Consider the creation of the new Department of Homeland Security in the United States, which encompasses 22 former federal agencies and their 170,000 employees and is responsible for, among other things, fighting the war on drugs.

Rethinking the Problem

Governments may never be able to completely eradicate the kind of international trade involved in the five wars. But they can and should do better. There are at least four areas where efforts can yield better ideas on how to tackle the problems posed by these wars:

Develop More Flexible Notions of Sovereignty

Governments need to recognize that restricting the scope of multilateral action for the sake of protecting their sovereignty is often a moot point. Their sovereignty is compromised daily, not by nation-states but by stateless networks that break laws and cross borders in pursuit of trade. In May 1999, for example, the Venezuelan government denied U.S. planes authorization to fly over Venezuelan territory to monitor air routes commonly used by narcotraffickers. Venezuelan authorities placed more importance on the symbolic value of asserting sovereignty over air space than on the fact that drug traffickers' planes regularly violate Venezuelan territory. Without new forms of codifying and "managing" sovereignty, governments will continue to face a large disadvantage while fighting the five wars.

Strengthen Existing Multilateral Institutions

The global nature of these wars means no government, regardless of its economic, political, or military power, will make much progress acting alone. If this seems obvious, then why does Interpol, the multilateral agency in charge of fighting international crime, have a staff of 384, only 112 of whom are police officers, and an annual budget of $28 million, less than the price of some boats or planes used by drug traffickers? Similarly, Europol, Europe's Interpol equivalent, has a staff of 240 and a budget of $51 million.

One reason Interpol is poorly funded and staffed is because its 181 member governments don't trust each other. Many assume, and perhaps rightly so, that the criminal networks they are fighting have penetrated the police departments of other countries and that sharing information with such compromised officials would not be prudent. Others fear today's allies will become tomorrow's enemies. Still others face legal impediments to sharing intelligence with fellow nation-states or have intelligence services and law enforcement agencies with organiza-tional cultures that make effective collabouration almost impossible. Progress will only be made if the world's governments unite behind stronger, more effective multilateral organizations.

Devise New Mechanisms and Institutions

These five wars stretch and even render obsolete many of the existing institutions, legal frameworks, military doctrines, weapons systems, and law enforcement techniques on which governments have relied for years. Analysts need to rethink the concept of war "fronts" defined by geography and the definition of "combatants" according to the Geneva Convention. The functions of intelligence agents, soldiers, police officers, customs agents, or immigration officers need rethinking and adaptation to the new realities. Policymakers also need to reconsider the notion that ownership is essentially a physical reality and not a "virtual" one or that only sovereign nations can issue money when thinking about ways to fight the five wars.

Move from Repression to Regulation

Beating market forces is next to impossible. In some cases, this reality may force governments to move from repressing the market to regulating it. In others, creating market incentives may be better than using bureaucracies to curb the excesses of these markets. Technology can often accomplish more than government policies can. For example, powerful encryption techniques can better protect software or CDs from being copied in Ukraine than would making the country enforce patents and copyrights and trademarks.

In all of the five wars, government agencies fight against networks motivated by the enormous profit opportunities created by other government agencies. In all cases, these profits can be traced to some form of government intervention that creates a major imbalance between demand and supply and makes prices and profit margins skyrocket. In some cases, these government interventions are often justified and it would be imprudent to eliminate them—governments can't simply walk away from the fight against trafficking in heroin, human beings, or weapons of mass destruction. But society can better deal with other segments of these kinds of illegal trade through regulation, not prohibition. Policymakers must focus on opportunities where market regulation can ameliorate problems that have defied approaches based on prohibition and armed interdiction of international trade.

Ultimately, governments, politicians, and voters need to realize that the way in which the world is conducting these five wars is doomed to fail—not for lack of effort, resources, or political will but because the collective thinking that guides government strategies in the five wars is rooted in wrong ideas, false assumptions, and obsolete institutions. Recognizing that governments have no chance of winning unless they change the ways they wage these wars is an indispensable first step in the search for solutions.

SAMUEL P. HUNTINGTON

The Clash of Civilizations?

The Next Pattern of Conflict

World politics is entering a new phase, and intellectuals have not hesitated to proliferate visions of what it will be—the end of history, the return of traditional rivalries between nation states, and the decline of the nation state from the conflicting pulls of tribalism and globalism, among others. Each of these visions catches aspects of the emerging reality. Yet they all miss a crucial, indeed a central, aspect of what global politics is likely to be in the coming years.

It is my hypothesis that the fundamental source of conflict in this new world will not be primarily ideological or primarily economic. The great divisions among humankind and the dominating source of conflict will be cultural. Nation states will remain the most powerful actors in world affairs, but the principal conflicts of global politics will occur between nations and

groups of different civilizations. The clash of civilizations will dominate global politics. The fault lines between civilizations will be the battle lines of the future.

Conflict between civilizations will be the latest phase in the evolution of conflict in the modern world. For a century and a half after the emergence of the modern international system with the Peace of Westphalia, the conflicts of the Western world were largely among princes—emperors, absolute monarchs and constitutional monarchs attempting to expand their bureaucracies, their armies, their mercantilist economic strength and, most important, the territory they ruled. In the process they created nation states, and beginning with the French Revolution the principal lines of conflict were between nations rather than princes. * * * [A]s a result of the Russian Revolution and the reaction against it, the conflict of nations yielded to the conflict of ideologies, first among communism, fascism-Nazism and liberal democracy, and then between communism and liberal democracy. During the Cold

From *Foreign Affairs* 72, no. 3 (Summer 1993): 22–49.

War, this latter conflict became embodied in the struggle between the two superpowers, neither of which was a nation state in the classical European sense and each of which defined its identity in terms of its ideology.

* * * With the end of the Cold War, international politics moves out of its Western phase, and its centerpiece becomes the interaction between the West and non-Western civilizations and among non-Western civilizations. In the politics of civilizations, the peoples and governments of non-Western civilizations no longer remain the objects of history as targets of Western colonialism but join the West as movers and shapers of history.

The Nature of Civilizations

During the Cold War the world was divided into the First, Second and Third Worlds. Those divisions are no longer relevant. It is far more meaningful now to group countries not in terms of their political or economic systems or in terms of their level of economic development but rather in terms of their culture and civilization.

What do we mean when we talk of a civilization? A civilization is a cultural entity. Villages, regions, ethnic groups, nationalities, religious groups, all have distinct cultures at different levels of cultural heterogeneity. The culture of a village in southern Italy may be different from that of a village in northern Italy, but both will share in a common Italian culture that distinguishes them from German villages. European communities, in turn, will share cultural features that distinguish them from Arab or Chinese communities. Arabs, Chinese and Westerners, however, are not part of any broader cultural entity. They constitute civilizations. A civilization is thus the highest cultural grouping of people and the broadest level of cultural identity people have short of that which distinguishes humans from other species. It is defined both by common objective elements, such as language,

history, religion, customs, institutions, and by the subjective self-identification of people. * * *

* * * Civilizations are nonetheless meaningful entities, and while the lines between them are seldom sharp, they are real. Civilizations are dynamic; they rise and fall; they divide and merge. And, as any student of history knows, civilizations disappear and are buried in the sands of time.

Westerners tend to think of nation states as the principal actors in global affairs. They have been that, however, for only a few centuries. The broader reaches of human history have been the history of civilizations. In *A Study of History*, Arnold Toynbee identified 21 major civilizations; only six of them exist in the contemporary world.

Why Civilizations Will Clash

Civilization identity will be increasingly important in the future, and the world will be shaped in large measure by the interactions among seven or eight major civilizations. These include Western, Confucian, Japanese, Islamic, Hindu, Slavic-Orthodox, Latin American and possibly African civilization. The most important conflicts of the future will occur along the cultural fault lines separating these civilizations from one another.

Why will this be the case?

First, differences among civilizations are not only real; they are basic. Civilizations are differentiated from each other by history, language, culture, tradition and, most important, religion. The people of different civilizations have different views on the relations between God and man, the individual and the group, the citizen and the state, parents and children, husband and wife, as well as differing views of the relative importance of rights and responsibilities, liberty and authority, equality and hierarchy. These differences are the product of centuries. They will not soon disappear. * * *

Second, the world is becoming a smaller place. The interactions between peoples of different civilizations are increasing; these increasing interactions intensify civilization consciousness and awareness of differences between civilizations and commonalities within civilizations. * * *

Third, the processes of economic modernization and social change throughout the world are separating people from longstanding local identities. They also weaken the nation state as a source of identity. In much of the world religion has moved in to fill this gap, often in the form of movements that are labeled "fundamentalist." Such movements are found in Western Christianity, Judaism, Buddhism and Hinduism, as well as in Islam. * * * The "unsecularization of the world," George Weigel has remarked, "is one of the dominant social facts of life in the late twentieth century." * * *

Fourth, the growth of civilization-consciousness is enhanced by the dual role of the West. On the one hand, the West is at a peak of power. At the same time, however, and perhaps as a result, a return to the roots phenomenon is occurring among non-Western civilizations. Increasingly one hears references to trends toward a turning inward and "Asianization" in Japan, the end of the Nehru legacy and the "Hinduization" of India, the failure of Western ideas of socialism and nationalism and hence "re-Islamization" of the Middle East, and now a debate over Westernization versus Russianization in Boris Yeltsin's country. A West at the peak of its power confronts non-Wests that increasingly have the desire, the will and the resources to shape the world in non-Western ways.

* * *

Fifth, cultural characteristics and differences are less mutable and hence less easily compromised and resolved than political and economic ones. In the former Soviet Union, communists can become democrats, the rich can become poor and the poor rich, but Russians cannot become Estonians and Azeris cannot become Armenians. * * * Even more than ethnicity, religion discriminates sharply and exclusively among people. A person can be half-French and half-Arab and simultaneously even a citizen of two countries. It is more difficult to be half-Catholic and half-Muslim.

Finally, economic regionalism is increasing. * * * On the one hand, successful economic regionalism will reinforce civilization-consciousness. On the other hand, economic regionalism may succeed only when it is rooted in a common civilization. The European Community rests on the shared foundation of European culture and Western Christianity. The success of the North American Free Trade Area depends on the convergence now underway of Mexican, Canadian and American cultures. Japan, in contrast, faces difficulties in creating a comparable economic entity in East Asia because Japan is a society and civilization unique to itself. * * *

* * *

As people define their identity in ethnic and religious terms, they are likely to see an "us" versus "them" relation existing between themselves and people of different ethnicity or religion. The end of ideologically defined states in Eastern Europe and the former Soviet Union permits traditional ethnic identities and animosities to come to the fore. Differences in culture and religion create differences over policy issues, ranging from human rights to immigration to trade and commerce to the environment. * * * Most important, the efforts of the West to promote its values of democracy and liberalism as universal values, to maintain its military predominance and to advance its economic interests engender countering responses from other civilizations. * * *

The clash of civilizations thus occurs at two levels. At the micro-level, adjacent groups along the fault lines between civilizations struggle, often violently, over the control of territory and each other. At the macro-level, states from different civilizations compete for relative military and economic power, struggle over the control of international institutions and third parties, and competitively promote their particular political and religious values.

The Fault Lines between Civilizations

The fault lines between civilizations are replacing the political and ideological boundaries of the Cold War as the flash points for crisis and bloodshed. The Cold War began when the Iron Curtain divided Europe politically and ideologically. The Cold War ended with the end of the Iron Curtain. As the ideological division of Europe has disappeared, the cultural division of Europe between Western Christianity, on the one hand, and Orthodox Christianity and Islam, on the other, has reemerged. The most significant dividing line in Europe, as William Wallace has suggested, may well be the eastern boundary of Western Christianity in the year 1500. This line runs along what are now the boundaries between Finland and Russia and between the Baltic states and Russia, cuts through Belarus and Ukraine separating the more Catholic western Ukraine from Orthodox eastern Ukraine, swings westward separating Transylvania from the rest of Romania, and then goes through Yugoslavia almost exactly along the line now separating Croatia and Slovenia from the rest of Yugoslavia. In the Balkans this line, of course, coincides with the historic boundary between the Hapsburg and Ottoman empires. The peoples to the north and west of this line are Protestant or Catholic; they shared the common experiences of European history—feudalism, the Renaissance, the Reformation, the Enlightenment, the French Revolution, the Industrial Revolution; they are generally economically better off than the peoples to the east; and they may now look forward to increasing involvement in a common European economy and to the consolidation of democratic political systems. The peoples to the east and south of this line are Orthodox or Muslim; they historically belonged to the Ottoman or Tsarist empires and were only lightly touched by the shaping events in the rest of Europe; they are generally less advanced economically; they seem much less likely to develop stable democratic political systems. The Velvet Curtain of culture has replaced the Iron Curtain of ideology as the most significant dividing line in Europe. As the events in Yugoslavia show, it is not only a line of difference; it is also at times a line of bloody conflict.

Conflict along the fault line between Western and Islamic civilizations has been going on for 1,300 years. * * *

* * *

This centuries-old military interaction between the West and Islam is unlikely to decline. It could become more virulent. The Gulf War left some Arabs feeling proud that Saddam Hussein had attacked Israel and stood up to the West. It also left many feeling humiliated and resentful of the West's military presence in the Persian Gulf, the West's overwhelming military dominance, and their apparent inability to shape their own destiny. Many Arab countries, in addition to the oil exporters, are reaching levels of economic and social development where autocratic forms of government become inappropriate and efforts to introduce democracy become stronger. Some openings in Arab political systems have already occurred. The principal beneficiaries of these openings have been Islamist movements. * * *

Those relations are also complicated by demography. The spectacular population growth in Arab countries, particularly in North Africa, has led to increased migration to Western Europe. The movement within Western Europe toward minimizing internal boundaries has sharpened political sensitivities with respect to this development. * * *

* * *

Historically, the other great antagonistic interaction of Arab Islamic civilization has been with the pagan, animist, and now increasingly Christian black peoples to the south. In the past, this antagonism was epitomized in the image of Arab slave dealers and black slaves. It has been reflected in the on-going civil war in the Sudan between Arabs and blacks, the fighting in Chad between Libyan-supported insurgents and the government, the tensions between Orthodox Christians and Muslims in the Horn of Africa, and the political conflicts, recurring riots and communal violence between Muslims and Christians in Nigeria. The modernization of Africa and the spread of Christianity are likely to enhance the probability of violence along this fault line. Symptomatic of the intensification of this conflict was the Pope John Paul II's speech in Khartoum in February 1993 attacking the actions of the Sudan's Islamist government against the Christian minority there.

On the northern border of Islam, conflict has increasingly erupted between Orthodox and Muslim peoples, including the carnage of Bosnia and Sarajevo, the simmering violence between Serb and Albanian, the tenuous relations between Bulgarians and their Turkish minority, the violence between Ossetians and Ingush, the unremitting slaughter of each other by Armenians and Azeris, the tense relations between Russians and Muslims in Central Asia. * * *

The conflict of civilizations is deeply rooted elsewhere in Asia. The historic clash between Muslim and Hindu in the subcontinent manifests itself now not only in the rivalry between Pakistan and India but also in intensifying religious strife within India between increasingly militant Hindu groups and India's substantial Muslim minority. The destruction of the Ayodhya mosque in December 1992 brought to the fore the issue of whether India wll remain a secular democratic state or become a Hindu one. * * *

*   *   *

Groups or states belonging to one civilization that become involved in war with people from a different civilization naturally try to rally support from other members of their own civilization. * * *

*   *   *

Civilization rallying to date has been limited, but it has been growing, and it clearly has the potential to spread much further. As the conflicts in the Persian Gulf, the Caucasus and Bosnia continued, the positions of nations and the cleavages between them increasingly were along civilizational lines. Populist politicians, religious leaders and the media have found it a potent means of arousing mass support and of pressuring hesitant governments. In the coming years, the local conflicts most likely to escalate into major wars will be those, as in Bosnia and the Caucasus, along the fault lines between civilizations. The next world war, if there is one, will be a war between civilizations.

The West versus the Rest

The West is now at an extraordinary peak of power in relation to other civilizations. Its superpower opponent has disappeared from the map. Military conflict among Western states is unthinkable, and Western military power is unrivaled. Apart from Japan, the West faces no economic challenge. It dominates international political and security institutions and with Japan international economic institutions. Global political and security issues are effectively settled by a directorate of the United States, Britain and France, world economic issues by a directorate of the United States, Germany and Japan, all of which maintain extraordinarily close relations with each other to the exclusion of lesser and largely non-Western countries. Decisions made at the U.N. Security Council or in the International Monetary Fund that reflect the interests of the West are presented to the world as reflecting the desires of the world community. The very phrase "the world community" has become the euphemistic collective noun (replacing "the Free World") to give global legitimacy to actions reflecting the interests of the United States and other Western powers.[1] * * *

* * *

* * * V. S. Naipaul has argued that Western civilization is the "universal civilization" that "fits all men." At a superficial level much of Western culture has indeed permeated the rest of the world. At a more basic level, however, Western concepts differ fundamentally from those prevalent in other civilizations. Western ideas of individualism, liberalism, constitutionalism, human rights, equality, liberty, the rule of law, democracy, free markets, the separation of church and state often have little resonance in Islamic, Confucian, Japanese, Hindu, Buddhist or Orthodox cultures. Western efforts to propagate such ideas produce instead a reaction against "human rights imperialism" and a reaffirmation of indigenous values, as can be seen in the support for religious fundamentalism by the younger generation in non-Western cultures. The very notion that there could be a "universal civilization" is a Western idea, directly at odds with the particularism of most Asian societies and their emphasis on what distinguishes one people from another. Indeed, the author of a review of 100 comparative studies of values in different societies concluded that "the values that are most important in the West are least important worldwide."[2] In the political realm, of course, these differences are most manifest in the efforts of the United States and other Western powers to induce other peoples to adopt Western ideas concerning democracy and human rights. Modern democratic government originated in the West. When it has developed in non-Western societies it has usually been the product of Western colonialism or imposition.

The central axis of world politics in the future is likely to be, in Kishore Mahbubani's phrase, the conflict between "the West and the Rest" and the responses of non-Western civilizations to Western power and values.[3] Those responses generally take one or a combination of three forms. At one extreme, non-Western states can, like Burma and North Korea, attempt to pursue a course of isolation, to insulate their societies from penetration or "corruption" by the West, and, in effect, to opt out of participation in the Western-dominated global community. The costs of this course, however, are high, and few states have pursued it exclusively. A second alternative, the equivalent of "band-wagoning" in international relations theory, is to attempt to join the West and accept its values and institutions. The third alternative is to attempt to "balance" the West by developing economic and military power and cooperating with other non-Western societies against the West, while preserving indigenous values and institutions; in short, to modernize but not to Westernize.

* * *

Implications for the West

This article does not argue that civilization identities will replace all other identities, that nation states will disappear, that each civilization will become a single coherent political entity, that groups within a civilization will not conflict with and even fight each other. This paper does set forth the hypotheses that differences between civilizations are real and important; civilization-consciousness is increasing; conflict between civilizations will supplant ideological and other forms of conflict as the dominant global form of conflict; international relations, historically a game played out within Western civilization, will increasingly be de-Westernized and become a game in which non-Western civilizations are actors and not simply objects; successful political, security and economic international institutions are more likely to develop within civilizations than across civilizations; conflicts between groups in different civilizations will be more frequent, more sustained and more violent than conflicts between groups in the same civilization; violent conflicts between groups in different civilizations are the most likely and most dangerous source of escalation that could lead to global wars; the paramount axis of world politics will be the relations between "the West and the Rest"; the elites in some torn non-Western countries will try to make their countries part of the West, but in most cases face major obstacles to accomplishing this; a central focus of conflict for the immediate future will be between the West and several Islamic-Confucian states.

This is not to advocate the desirability of conflicts between civilizations. It is to set forth descriptive hypotheses as to what the future may be like. If these are plausible hypotheses, however, it is necessary to consider their implications for Western policy. These implications should be divided between short-term advantage and long-term accommodation. In the short term it is clearly in the interest of the West to promote greater cooperation and unity within its own civilization, particularly between its European and North American components; to incorporate into the West societies in Eastern Europe, and Latin America whose cultures are close to those of the West; to promote and maintain cooperative relations with Russia and Japan; to prevent escalation of local inter-civilization conflicts into major inter-civilization wars; to limit the expansion of the military strength of Confucian and Islamic states; to moderate the reduction of Western military capabilities and maintain military superiority in East and Southwest Asia; to exploit differences and conflicts among Confucian and Islamic states; to support in other civilizations groups sympathetic to Western values and interests; to strengthen international institutions that reflect and legitimate Western interests and values and to promote the involvement of non-Western states in those institutions.

In the longer term other measures would be called for. Western civilization is both Western and modern. Non-Western civilizations have attempted to become modern without becoming Western. To date only Japan has fully succeeded in this quest. Non-Western civilizations will continue to attempt to acquire the wealth, technology, skills, machines and weapons that are part of being modern. They will also attempt to reconcile this modernity with their traditional culture and values. Their economic and military strength relative to the West will increase. Hence the West will increasingly have to accommodate these non-Western modern civilizations whose power approaches that of the West but whose values and interests differ significantly from those of the West. This will require the West to maintain the economic and military power necessary to protect its interests in relation to these civilizations. It will also, however, require the West to develop a more profound understanding of the basic religious and philosophical assumptions underlying other civilizations and the ways in which people in those civilizations see their interests. It will require an effort to identify elements of commonality between Western and other civilizations. For the relevant future, there will be no universal civilization, but instead a world of different civilizations, each of which will have to learn to coexist with the others.

NOTES

1. Almost invariably Western leaders claim they are acting on behalf of "the world community." One minor lapse occurred during the run-up to the Gulf War. In an interview on "Good Morning America," Dec. 21, 1990, British Prime Minister John Major referred to the actions "the West" was taking against Saddam Hussein. He quickly corrected himself and subsequently referred to "the world community." He was, however, right when he erred.

2. Harry C. Triandis, *The New York Times*, Dec. 25, 1990, p. 41, and "Cross-Cultural Studies

of Individualism and Collectivism," *Nebraska Symposium on Motivation*, vol. 37, 1989, pp. 41–133.

3. Kishore Mahbubani, "The West and the Rest," *The National Interest*, Summer 1992, pp. 3–13.

MARK JUERGENSMEYER

From *Global Rebellion: Religious Challenges to the Secular State, from Christian Militias to al Qaeda*

The Religious Challenge to the Secular State

One of the more puzzling features of the *fatweh* in which Osama bin Laden proclaimed war on the American and European West in 1996 was his comparison of Western presence in the Middle East with the Crusades and colonialism. This may have surprised many Westerners who were not used to hearing issues of international relations expressed in cultural terms—especially not in images derived from the Middle Ages and the colonial era. Most Americans and Europeans thought that this kind of cultural oppression was buried in the unhappy past.

To many in the non-Western world, however, these images aptly characterized the present. When the Ayatollah Khomeini railed against American and European influence in Iran, what he had in mind was a new kind of colonialism. Though Iran had never been colonized by European powers, the domination of Western cultural and economic control seemed like colonialism all the same.

From Mark Juergensmeyer, *Global Rebellion: Religious Challenges to the Secular State, from Christian Militias to al Qaeda* (Berkeley: University of California Press, 2008), Chaps. 1, 2, 5. Some of the author's notes have been omitted.

The ayatollah and many other leaders of what used to be known as the "third world" of Africa, Asia, Latin America, and the Middle East regarded Western influence as an intrusion that did not end with European political and military retreat in the mid-twentieth century. They regarded it as having continued for the next forty years of the Cold War era under the guise of political ideology and economic control and into the twenty-first century in the form of American-orchestrated globalization. The new secular nationalism that was Europe's legacy in the developing world began to be perceived by many in those regions as morally vacuous and politically corrupt—the wors[t] features of the colonial past.

The Loss of Faith in Secular Nationalism

In the celebrations following the first stages of elections that threatened to bring Islamic nationalists to power in Algeria in the 1990s, a jubilant supporter of the Islamic Front spied a foreigner on the streets of Algiers and grabbed her by the arm. "Please give my condolences to President Mitterrand," the Algerian said.[1] Behind this amusing bit of sarcasm is an impression shared by many Muslims in Algeria: that the nation's ruling party, the National Front, which came to power during the war of independence with France and which controlled the country afterward, was, in a cultural sense, an extension of French colonial rule. Independent Algeria was seen as not entirely independent, but rather a vestige of a past that was itself in need of liberation. An Islamic Algeria would finally mark the country's true freedom from colonialization.

In the middle of the twentieth century, when Algeria and many other former colonies in the developing world gained political independence, Europeans and Americans often wrote with an almost religious fervor about what they regarded as these new nations' freedom—by which they meant the spread of nationalism throughout the world. Invariably, they meant a secular nationalism: new nations that elicited loyalties forged entirely from a sense of territorial citizenship. These secular-nationalist loyalties were based on the idea that the legitimacy of the state was rooted in the will of the people in a particular geographic region and divorced from any religious sanction.

The secular nationalism of the day was defined by what it was—and what it was not. It distanced itself especially from the old ethnic and religious identities that had made nations parochial and quarrelsome in the past. The major exception was the creation of the state of Israel in 1948 as a safe haven for Jews, but even in this case the nation's constitution was firmly secular, and Israeli citizenship was open to people of all religious backgrounds—not only Jews but also Christians and Muslims. In general, mid-twentieth-century scholars viewed the spread of secular nationalism in a hopeful, almost eschatological, light: it was ushering in a new future. It meant, in essence, the emergence of mini-Americas all over the world.

Hans Kohn, his generation's best-known historian of nationalism, observed in 1955 that the twentieth century was unique: "It is the first period in history in which the whole of mankind has accepted one and the same political attitude, that of nationalism."[2] In his telling, the concept had its origins in antiquity. It was presaged by ancient Hebrews and fully enunciated by ancient Greeks. Inexplicably, however, the concept stagnated for almost two thousand years, according

to Kohn's account, until suddenly it took off in earnest in England, "the first modern nation," during the seventeenth century.[3] By the time of his writing, in the mid-twentieth century, he cheerfully observed that the whole world had responded to "the awakening of nationalism and liberty."[4]

Not only Western academics but also a good number of new leaders—especially those in the emerging nations created out of former colonial empires—were swept up by the vision of a world of free and equal secular nations. The concept of secular nationalism gave them an ideological justification for being, and the electorate that subscribed to it provided them power bases from which they could vault into positions of leadership ahead of traditional ethnic and religious figures. But secularism was more than just a political issue; it was also a matter of personal identity. A new kind of person had come into existence—the "Indian nationalist" or "Ceylonese nationalist" who had an abiding faith in a secular nationalism identified with his or her homeland. Perhaps none exemplified this new spirit more than Gamal Abdel Nasser of Egypt and Jawaharlal Nehru of India. According to Nehru, "there is no going back" to a past full of religious identities, for the modern, secular "spirit of the age" will inevitably triumph throughout the world.[5]

* * *

Leaders of minority religious communities—such as Hindu Tamils in Ceylon and Coptic Christians in Egypt—seemed especially eager to embrace secular nationalism because a secular nation-state would ensure that the public life of the country would not be dominated completely by the majority religious community. In India, where the Congress Party became the standard-bearer of Nehru's vision, the party's most reliable supporters were those at the margins of Hindu society—untouchables and Muslims—who had the most to fear from an intolerant religious majority.

The main carriers of the banner of secular nationalism in these newly independent countries, however, were not members of any religious community at all, at least in a traditional sense. Rather, they were members of the urban educated elite. For many of them, embracing a secular form of nationalism was a way of promoting its major premise—freedom from the parochial identities of the past—and thereby avoiding the obstacles that religious loyalties create for a country's political goals. By implication, political power based on religious values and traditional communities held no authority.

The problem, however, was that in asserting that the nationalism of their country was secular, the new nationalists had to have faith in a secular culture that was at least as compelling as a sacred one. That meant, on a social level, believing that secular nationalism could triumph over religion. It could also mean making secular nationalism a suprareligion of its own, which a society could aspire to beyond any single religious allegiance. In India, for example, political identity based on religious affiliation was termed *communalism*. In the view of Nehru and other secular nationalists, religion was the chief competitor of an even higher object of loyalty: secular India. * * *

The secular nationalists' attempts to give their ideologies an antireligious or a suprareligious force were encouraged, perhaps unwittingly, by their Western mentors. The words used to define *nationalism* by Western political leaders and such scholars as Kohn always implied not only that it was secular but that it was competitive with religion and ultimately superior to it. "Nationalism [by which he meant secular nationalism] is a state of mind," Kohn wrote, "in which the *supreme loyalty* of the individual is felt to be due the nation-state."[6] And he boldly asserted that secular nationalism had replaced religion in its influence: "An understanding of nationalism and its implications for modern history and for our time appears as fundamental today as an understanding of religion would have been for thirteenth century Christendom."[7]

Rupert Emerson's influential *From Empire to Nation*, written several years later, shared the same exciting vision of a secular nationalism that "sweeps out [from Europe] to embrace the whole wide world."[8] Emerson acknowledged, however, that although in the European experience "the rise of nationalism [again, secular nationalism] coincided with a decline in the hold of religion," in other parts of the world, such as Asia, as secular nationalism "moved on" and enveloped these regions, "the religious issue pressed more clearly to the fore again."[9] * * *

When Kohn and Emerson used the term *nationalism* they had in mind not just a secular political ideology and a religiously neutral national identity but a particular form of political organization: the modern European and American nation-state. In such an organization, individuals are linked to a centralized, all-embracing democratic political system that is unaffected by any other affiliations, be they ethnic, cultural, or religious. That linkage is sealed by an emotional sense of identification with a geographical area and a loyalty to a particular people, an identity that is part of the feeling of nationalism. This affective dimension of nationalism is important to keep in mind, especially in comparing secular nationalism with religion. * * *

Secular nationalism as we know it today—as the ideological ally of the nation-state—began to appear in England and America in the eighteenth century. Only by then had the idea of a nation-state taken root deeply enough to nurture a loyalty of its own, unassisted by religion or tradition, and only by then had the political and military apparatus of the nation-state expanded sufficiently to encompass a large geographic region. * * *

The changes of the late eighteenth and nineteenth centuries included boundaries; the development of the technical capacity to knit a country together through roads, rivers, and other means of transportation and communication; the construction of the economic capacity to do so, through an increasingly integrated market structure; the emergence of a world economic system based on the building blocks of nation-states;[10] the formation of mass education, which socialized each generation of youth into a homogeneous society; and the rise of parliamentary democracy as a system of representation and an expression of the will of the people. The glue that held all these changes together was a new form of nationalism: the notion that individuals naturally associate with the people and place of their ancestral birth (or an adopted homeland such as the United States) in an economic and political system identified with a secular nation-state. Secular nationalism was thought to be not only natural but also universally applicable and morally right.

Although it was regarded almost as a natural law, secular nationalism was ultimately viewed as an expression of neither God nor nature but of the will of citizens.[11] It was the political manifestation of the Enlightenment view of humanity. John Locke's ideas of the origins of a civil community[12] and Jean-Jacques Rousseau's social-contract theories required little commitment to religious belief.[13] * * * Their secular concepts of nation and state had the effect of taking religion—at least church religion—out of public life.

* * *

At the same time that religion in the West was becoming less political, its secular nationalism was becoming more religious. It became clothed in romantic and xenophobic images that would have startled its Enlightenment forebears. The French Revolution, the model for much of the nationalist fervor that developed in the nineteenth century, infused a religious zeal into revolutionary democracy; the revolution took on the trappings of church religion in the priestly power meted out to its demagogic leaders and in the slavish devotion to what it called the temple of reason. According to Alexis de Tocqueville, the French Revolution "assumed many of the aspects of a religious revolution."[14] The American Revolution also had a religious side: many of

its leaders had been influenced by eighteenth-century deism, a religion of science and natural law that was "devoted to exposing [church] religion to the light of knowledge."[15] As in France, American nationalism developed its own religious characteristics, blending the ideals of secular nationalism and the symbols of Christianity into what has been called "civil religion."[16]

The nineteenth century saw the fulfillment of Tocqueville's prophecy that the "strange religion" of secular nationalism would, "like Islam, overrun the whole world with its apostles, militants, and martyrs."[17] It spread throughout the world with an almost missionary zeal and was shipped to the newly colonized areas of Asia, Africa, and Latin America as part of the ideological freight of colonialism. * * * As it had in the West during previous centuries, secular nationalism in the colonized countries during the nineteenth and twentieth centuries came to represent one side of a great encounter between two vastly different ways of perceiving the sociopolitical order and the relationship of the individual to the state: one informed by religion, the other by a notion of a secular compact.

* * *

* * * Contemporary religious politics, then, is the result of an almost Hegelian dialectic between two competing frameworks of social order: secular nationalism (allied with the nation-state) and religion (allied with large ethnic communities, some of them transnational). The clashes between the two have often been destructive, but, as we shall see, they have also offered possibilities for accommodation. In some cases these encounters have given birth to a synthesis in which religion has become the ally of a new kind of nation-state. At the same time, other liaisons with contemporary political trends have led to a different vision: religious versions of a transnationalism that would supplant the nation-state world.

* * *

The Mutual Rejection of Religion and Secularism

In places like the United States and Europe, where secular nationalism, rather than religion, has become the dominant paradigm in society, religion has been shunted to the periphery. This transposition is most dramatically illustrated by the clublike church religion that is common in the United States. Yet, even there, attempts have been made to assimilate some aspects of religion into the national consensus. The reasons for doing so are varied: coopting elements of religion into nationalism keeps religion from building its own antinational power base; it provides religious legitimacy for the state; and it helps give nationalism a religious aura. To accomplish these goals, national leaders have borrowed various elements of a society's religious culture. The secular nationalism of the United States is to some extent colored by a religiosity such as this, as Bellah has pointed out in his analysis of the "civil religion" sprinkled throughout the inaugural addresses of American presidents and the rhetoric of other public speakers.[18]

* * *

* * * But if accommodating religion has been difficult for the West, efforts to bridle religion in the new nations in Africa, Asia, and the Middle East have been a thousand times more problematic. * * * Given religious histories that are part of national heritages, religious institutions that are sometimes the nations' most effective systems of communication, and religious leaders who are often more socially devoted, efficient, and intelligent than government officials, religion cannot be ignored. The attempts to accommodate it, however, have not always been successful. * * *

* * *

In India, three generations of prime ministers in the Nehru dynasty—Jawaharlal, his daughter Indira Gandhi, and her son Rajiv—all tried to accommodate religion as little as possible. Yet at times they were forced to make concessions to religious groups almost against their wills. Nehru seemed virtually allergic to religion, putting secularism alongside socialism as his great political goal. Nonetheless the Indian constitution and subsequent parliamentary actions have given a great deal of public support to religious entities.[19] Special seats have been reserved in the legislature for Muslims and members of other minority communities; religious schools have been affiliated with the state; and temples and mosques have received direct public support. In general the Indian government has not been indifferent to religion but has attempted to treat—and foster—each religion in the country equally. As Ainslie Embree puts it, "Advocates of secularism in India always insisted . . . that far from being hostile to religion, they valued it."[20]

* * *

* * * Attempts to accommodate religion in secular nationalism lead to a double frustration: those who make these compromises are sometimes considered traitors from both a spiritual and a secular point of view. Moreover, these compromises imply that spiritual and political matters are separate—an idea that most religious activists reject and see as a capitulation to secularism. They sense that behind the compromises is a basic allegiance not to religion but to the secular state.

This suspicion about secularism's competition with religion has led to the conclusion that secular nationalism is "a kind of religion," as one of the leaders of the Iranian revolution put it. The Iranian leader, Abolhassan Bani-Sadr, wrote this in a matter-of-fact manner that indicated that what he said was taken as an obvious truth by most of his readers.[21] Bani-Sadr went on to explain that it was not only a religion but one peculiar to the West, a point echoed by one of the leaders of the Muslim Brotherhood in Egypt.[22] Behind his statement was the assumption that secular nationalism responds to the same needs for collective identity, ultimate loyalty, and moral authority that religion has traditionally responded to and that this similar response makes secular nationalism de facto a religion. * * *

* * *

Behind this charge is a certain vision of social reality, one that involves a series of concentric circles. The smallest circles are families and clans; then come ethnic groups and nations; the largest, and implicitly most important, are global civilizations. Among the global civilizations are Islam, Buddhism, and what some who hold this view call "Christendom" or simply "Western civilization."[23] Particular nations such as Germany, France, and the United States, in this conceptualization, stand as subsets of Christendom/Western civilization; similarly, Egypt, Iran, Pakistan, and other nations are subsets of Islamic civilization.

From this vantage point, it is a serious error to suggest that Egypt or Iran should be thrust into a Western frame of reference. In this view of the world they are intrinsically part of Islamic, not Western, civilization, and it is an act of imperialism to think of them in any other way. Even before the idea of a "clash of civilizations" gained popularity, religious activists around the world asserted that their views about religious politics reflected basic differences in worldviews. They were anticipating the controversial thesis that the Harvard political scientist Samuel Huntington propounded in the mid-1990s.[24]

One notable pre-Huntington adherent of the "clash of civilization" thesis was the Ayatollah Khomeini, who lamented what in prerevolutionary Iran he and others referred to as "Westoxification" or "West-omania."[25] According to Khomeini, Islamic peoples have been stricken with Westomania since the eighth century, and partly for that reason they readily accepted the cultural and political postures of the shah. More recent attempts to capitalize on Westomania, he maintained, have come from the insidious efforts of Western imperialists.[26] The goal of the Islamic revolution in Iran, then, was not only to free Iranians politically from the shah but also to liberate them conceptually from Western ways of thinking.

* * *

Islamic revolutionaries in Iran have also regarded the secular government under the shah as a form of Western colonialism, even though Iran was never a colony in the same sense that many Middle Eastern and South Asian countries were. The heavy-handed role of the U.S. Central Intelligence Agency in Iranian politics and the force-feeding of Western ideas by the shah were regarded as forms of colonialism all the same. * * *

These leaders regard as especially pernicious the fact that the cultural colonialism of Western ideas erodes confidence in traditional values. For that matter, they maintain, it also undermines traditional religious constructs of society and the state. Concerns over both these matters and over the erosion of religion's influence in public life unite religious activists from Egypt to Sri Lanka, even those who bitterly oppose one another. A leader of the religious right in Israel and a spokesperson for the Islamic movement in Palestine, for instance, used exactly the same words to describe their sentiments: "Secular government is the enemy."[27]

* * *

One of the reasons secular ideas and institutions are so firmly rejected by some religious leaders is that they hold these ideas and institutions accountable for the moral decline within their own countries. The moral impact of Western secularism in Sri Lanka was devastating, according to the calculations of some leaders of Buddhist monastic organizations. One of them, in discussing this matter, carefully identified the evils of the society around him and then laid them fully at the feet of the secular government.

"We live in an immoral world," the bhikkhu (monk) stated, giving as his examples of immorality gambling, slaughtering animals for meat, and drinking *arrack* (a locally produced alcohol that is popular in the countryside).[28] In each case the government was implicated: the state lottery promoted gambling, the state encouraged animal husbandry, and it licensed liquor shops. The institutions of government were all suspect, the bhikkhu implied: "People in public office are not to be trusted."[29]

*   *   *

Secular nationalists within developing countries are thought to be enemies in part because they are in league with a more global enemy, the secular West. To some religious nationalists' way of thinking, there is a global conspiracy against religion, orchestrated by the United States. For this reason virtually anything the United States does that involves non-Western societies, even when its stated intentions are positive, is viewed as part of a plot to destroy or control them. * * *

At the extreme of this critique of secular power is the notion that the United States is not just power-hungry but evil. The Palestinian Islamic movement Hamas issued a communiqué stating that the United States "commands all the forces hostile to Islam and the Muslims." It singled out George H. W. Bush, who, it claimed, was not only "the leader of the forces of evil" but also "the chief of the false gods."[30] As the communiqué indicates, this line of reasoning often leads down a slippery slope, for once secular institutions and authorities begin to loom larger than life and are seen as forces of evil, the conclusion rushes on, inevitably and irretrievably, that secular enemies are more than mortal foes: they are mythic entities and satanic forces.

*   *   *

The process of satanization indicates that secular nationalism is seen as a religious entity, albeit a sinister one, and this view can be explained, in part, by the "fallen-angel" syndrome: the higher the expectations, the more severe the recriminations when expectations are not met.[31] Many members of formerly colonized countries had maintained such high expectations of secular nationalism, and put such great faith in it, that their disappointment in its failure was also extreme. Where anticipation of secularism's performance had assumed messianic proportions, the anger at the lack of performance reached satanic depths.

Hence the loss of faith in secular nationalism is part of a profound disappointment: the perception that secular institutions have failed to perform. In many parts of the world the secular state has not lived up to its own promises of political freedom, economic prosperity, and social justice. Some of the most poignant cases of disenchantment with secularism have been found among educated members of the middle class who were raised with the high expectations propagated by secular-nationalist political leaders. Some of them were propelled toward religious nationalism after trying to live as secular nationalists and feeling betrayed, or at least unfulfilled. Many of them also felt that Western societies betrayed themselves: the government scandals, persistent social inequities, and devastating economic difficulties of the United States and the former Soviet Union made both democracy and socialism less appealing as political models than they had been during the more innocent 1940s and 1950s. The global mass media, in their exaggerated way, brought to religious leaders in non-Western nations the message that there was a deep malaise in the United States caused by the social failures of unwed mothers, divorce, racism, and drug addiction, the political failures of various political scandals, and the economic failures associated with trade imbalances and the mounting deficit.

But mass media or no, religious leaders in the new nations did not need to look any further than their own national backyards for evidence that the high expectations raised by secular nationalists in their own countries were not being met. "It is an economic, social, and moral failure," a Muslim leader in Egypt said, speaking of the policies of his nation's secular state.[32] Other new religious revolutionaries were disturbed not so much by the failure of the experiment in secular nationalism as by the failure to fully implement religious nationalism, except in Iran and Afghanistan.

*   *   *

In many parts of the world, the profound disappointment in secular nationalism has led to disillusionment. Many have lost faith in its relevance and its vision for the future. In their own way, these critics of secular nationalism have experienced what Jürgen Habermas has dubbed a modern "crisis of legitimation," in which the public's respect for political and social institutions has been deflated.[33] * * * Secular nationalism came to be seen as alien, the expression of only a small, educated, and privileged few within non-Western societies. As both capitalist and formerly socialist governments wrestled with their own constituencies over the moral purpose of their nations and the directions they might take, their old, tired forms of nationalism seemed less appealing elsewhere.

Yet even though secular nationalism does not easily accommodate religion and religion does not accept the ideology of secular nationalism, religion can sometimes be hospitable to the institution of the nation-state—albeit on religion's terms. Religious activists are well aware that if a nation is based from the start on the premise of secular nationalism, religion is often made marginal to the political order. This outcome is especially unfortunate from many radical religious perspectives—including Jihadi militants, messianic Jewish Zionists, and Christian militias—because they regard the two ideologies as unequal: the religious one is far superior. Rather than starting with secular nationalism, they prefer to begin with religion.

According to one Sinhalese writer, whose tract *The Revolt in the Temple* was published shortly after Sri Lankan independence and was influential in spurring on the Buddhist national cause, "it is clear that the unifying, healing, progressive principle" that held together the entity known as Ceylon throughout the years has always been "the Buddhist faith."[34] The writer goes on to say that religion in Sri Lanka continues to provide the basis for a "liberating nationalism" and that Sinhalese Buddhism is "the only patriotism worthy of the name," worth fighting for or dying for.[35] * * *

The implication of this way of speaking is not that religion is antithetical to nationalism, but that religious rather than secular nationalism is the appropriate premise on which to build a nation—even a modern nation-state. In fact, most references to nationhood used by religious activists assume that the modern nation-state is the only way in which a nation can be construed. (The major exception is the global jihad movement, which envisages a transnational Islamic state.) The term *religious nationalism* refers to the contemporary attempt to link religion and the nation-state. This is a new development in the history of nationalism, and it immediately raises the question of whether such a linkage is possible: whether what we in the West think of as a modern secular nation—a unified, democratically controlled system of economic and political administration—can in fact be accommodated within religion.

*   *   *

The Front Line of Religious Rebellion: The Middle East

Iran's Paradigmatic Revolution

Muslim activists in Iran have achieved what for many of their colleagues in other parts of the world is still an elusive goal: a successful revolution and the establishment of a religious state. Even so, Shi'a Muslim politics are different from

Sunni politics, and Egyptian activists have been influenced far more by Arab and Pakistani ideas than by Iranian ones.[36] Despite their common goals there is little connection between radical religious leaders in Sunni and Shi'a areas. "They have their political problems," a member of the Muslim Brotherhood in Cairo told me, "and we have ours.[37] * * *

Some of the early movements of Muslim activism in Iran were influenced by Egyptian ideas—the thinking of al-Banna and Qutb, for example—and by Egypt's radical religious organizations.* * * By the time the Iranian Islamic movement gathered steam in the 1970s, however, the motives and the organization were distinctly Iranian.

"An entire population has risen up against the Shah," the Ayatollah Khomeini announced to a professor from the University of California who visited him in France during the declining days of the Pahlavi regime.[38] This "revolutionary movement," as Khomeini described it, was an "explosion" that occurred as a direct result of American intervention and the repression of Islam over the preceding fifty years. At the time of the interview, 1978, Khomeini remarked that the situation had "intensified to an extraordinary degree."[39] A few days later, he was bound for Iran and his headquarters in Qom, where he presided over the new regime until his death on June 4, 1989.

* * * This regime and the remarkable transfer of power that inaugurated it can be seen as the paradigm of religious revolution. The demon of the revolution was the secular nationalism patterned on the West that was ineptly promoted by the shah. The critique of the shah's Westernized regime was couched in religious terms, the rebellion was led by religious figures, and the new order was fashioned as a utopian religious state. It was not simply a revival of an earlier form of Muslim rule, but a new form of Islamic politics. In a curious way, it provided a unified political system for the country and made the shah's vision of an Iranian nationalism come true.

The new politics of the Iranian revolution were fundamentally Muslim—and particularly Shi'ite. Politics of various kinds have always been part and parcel of Islam. The Prophet Muhammad himself was a military as well as a spiritual leader, and there have been strong Muslim rulers virtually from the tradition's inception. In classical Islam, as in most traditional religious societies, there was no distinction between church and state, and the concept of secularism was alien to Islam—as it was to most religious traditions—until quite recently.[40] All aspects of social and personal behavior were subject to divine guidance, and all political authority ultimately derived from sacred authority. This continues to be a general principle in Islamic societies. What is novel about the new Islamic movements is their struggle to infuse—in a distinctively modern way—this religious authority into the institution of the nation-state.

* * *

THE SHI'A TRADITION OF STRUGGLE Shi'ism was born in conflict, in the struggle for power immediately after the death of the Prophet Muhammad. The term *shi'a* means "partisans," followers of a particular religious and political position. The dispute was between those who felt that the spiritual and temporal authority of Islam resided in the caliphs who came after him and those who believed that it dwelled in the members of the Prophet's own family—specifically in the descendants of Ali—the Prophet's cousin and son-in-law. The critical moment in this conflict came in 680 C.E., with the assassination of Ali's son, Hussain, who led the Shi'ite community in Karbala (in present-day Iraq). The assassin, Yazid, was a caliph of the Sunni's Umayyad dynasty. To this day, that event is recognized as the tragic turning point in Shi'ite history—rather as the Crucifixion is regarded in Christian history.

The assassination of Hussain is commemorated annually in massive parades throughout

Shi'ite communities. Men stripped to the waist march down city streets, flagellating themselves with whips and barbed wire until their backs become raw and bloody. On these occasions—the Ashura celebrations held every year during the first ten days of the Islamic month of Muharram—the faithful remember the suffering of Hussain and grieve for his death and their own vicarious guilt for not having stood by him in his time of trial.

In Iran, from the early 1960s on, the Ashura took a political turn. The Ayatollah Khomeini and his colleagues began to alter the emphasis from personal mourning to collective outrage against oppression. They had in mind especially the shah's oppression of Islam, and they likened him to Yazid, Hussain's assassin. * * *

THE POLITICAL POWER OF THE CLERGY Islam is primarily a layperson's religion, and although political leaders are expected to adhere to its precepts and to use the state's apparatus to administer Muslim law, the clergy in most parts of the Muslim world has little political influence. In such predominantly Sunni societies as Egypt and Syria, for instance, the clergy has been relatively uninvolved in radical Islamic politics.[41] The Shi'a tradition is different, in part for theological reasons. The idea of an imam, a great leader who shapes world history, has conditioned Shi'ites to expect strong leadership in what we would regard as both secular and religious spheres. During a period of history when an imam is not physically present—such as the contemporary period, when the imam is supposedly "hidden"—his power resides in the mullahs, the Shi'a clergy. Another source for the power of certain religious leaders is their ancestral ties to the family of Ali and hence to the Prophet himself. The Ayatollah Khomeini could claim such ties, and even the modern Iraqi leader, Saddam Hussein, let it be known that he had such connections. * * *

* * *

MESSIANIC AND UTOPIAN EXPECTATIONS In the Shi'a view of history, the hidden imam will return again at the end of history in the form of the Mahdi, the Messiah who will overthrow the evil forces and institute a realm of justice and freedom. It would have been heresy to suggest that the Ayatollah Khomeini was the Mahdi and that the Iranian revolution was that realm, and no Shi'ite dared do so.[42] * * *

These three aspects of Shi'ite Islam—its history of struggle against oppression, the political power it has traditionally vested in the clergy, and its tradition of messianic and utopian expectations—made Islam in Iran ripe for revolutionary political exploitation. That the revolution happened so easily was due in part to the vulnerability of its adversaries. Few characters in the Shi'ite drama of the forces of good struggling against the forces of evil have been so effectively thrust into the role of evil as the members of the Pahlavi dynasty—Riza Shah, who established a military dictatorship in 1921, and his son Muhammad Riza Shah, who succeeded him in 1941. The Pahlavi reign was interrupted from 1951 to 1953 by a democratically elected prime minister, Mohammed Mossadegh (Musaddiq), who attempted to nationalize the oil industry and, with the help of the U.S. Central Intelligence Agency, was promptly overthrown.

When the shah returned, he attempted to mollify the mullahs by giving them free rein in developing their organizations and helping them to finance Islamic schools. To some extent this policy was successful, and even Khomeini's predecessor, Ayatollah Hosain Burujirdi, supported the shah in the 1950s; at this time the clergy was accused of being a "pillar of the Pahlavi state."[43] This accommodation of the mullahs changed in the 1960s, however, when the shah sought to institute land reforms that threatened religious institutions and extended the right to vote to women—acts that many of the mullahs regarded as threatening. * * * Although they tried publicly to appear to be good Muslims, the Pahlavis were faulted for destroying traditional Muslim schools and seminaries, Westernizing the universities, and creating a modern secular bureaucracy to administer the state. Women were forbidden to wear the veil (although the shah later relaxed that rule). In Teheran and other cities Western culture began to thrive, bringing in its wake not only Coca-Cola and Western movies but also discos, girlie magazines, and gay bars. It was not the Islamic utopia the mullahs had in mind. The mullahs described it, in fact, as "a satanic rule."[44]

The government's control of the media and the presence of the sinister SAVAK, the secret police, made opposition difficult. According to one observer, it was "impossible to breathe freely in Iran."[45] The group that was most difficult to contain and had the largest capacity to organize was the clergy, which found a natural leader in Ruhullah al-Musavi al-Khomeini. * * * It is probably not a coincidence that Khomeini's increasingly outspoken public pronouncements against the shah at that time were concomitant with his rising popularity and the solidification of his power within the Shi'ite community. In any event, the protest, and Khomeini's leadership of it, surfaced in a massive demonstration in Qom in the spring of 1963. The demonstration led to Khomeini's imprisonment, followed by his release in 1964, and re-imprisonment again in that year, and then his expulsion from the country. Khomeini continued to live in exile—first in Turkey, then in Iraq, and finally in France—until after the revolution was completed in 1979. * * *

To the surprise of everyone, the end came quite suddenly. Perhaps most caught off guard were the Americans, who had great difficulty even conceiving the possibility that a band of bearded, black-robed rural mullahs might pose a serious threat to the poised and urbane shah, with all his worldly connections and military power.[46] Even more inconceivable was that the power of the shah should crumble so effortlessly. Only a few months before, U.S. president Jimmy Carter had praised the shah for creating an "island of stability" in the region.

Although the new revolutionary regime did not live up to its utopian promises, it introduced radical changes in Iran's government and culture. After the revolution, Islamic law became the law of the land, and most marks of "Westoxification" were systematically erased. These reforms have not always been introduced with subtlety—some seven thousand people were executed for purported "crimes" as varied as homosexuality and believing in the Baha'i faith—and the revolutionary spirit has not been easily contained. For a time bands of young people in the Hizbollah (Party of God) roamed the streets, attacking anyone or anything that appeared anti-Islamic, and a group of rowdy youths, without government authorization (at least at the beginning), precipitated a foreign-policy crisis by taking hostages at the American Embassy in Teheran.[47]

Following the revolution and the establishment of an Islamic Republic of Iran in 1979, the regime has gone through several stages. It began as a moderate, secular rule led first by Mehdi Bazargan and then by Abolhassan Bani-Sadr, until Khomeini used the hostage crisis as a means of forcing out the moderates.[48] After Bani-Sadr fled the country in 1981, a period of repression set in, during which thousands were killed, moderate and leftist political forces were destroyed, and the power of the clergy was consolidated.[49] In 1985, the revolutionary regime began something of a Thermidorean return, for a time, to a more pragmatic and moderate rule. From 1980 to 1988, the resources of the country were drained by a war with Iraq. The Iraqi military forces of Saddam Hussein were supported by the United States, which at the time considered Iran the greater evil.

After the death of the Ayatollah Khomeini on June 4, 1989, his son, Ahmad Khomeini, remained virtually the only radical member of the clergy in the government's inner circles; the new president of Iran, Ali-Akbar H[a]shemi-Rafsanjani, continued to steer a pragmatic course. During the Gulf War, Rafsanjani refused to side with Iraq and his criticism of the United States was relatively restrained, to the disappointment of the conservative clergy.[50] At the end of 1991, Iranian leaders negotiated the release of American hostages held for years in Lebanon. In the first months of 1992, apparently to impress upon the conservative clergy that he had not capitulated to the Americans, Rafsanjani denounced the American-sponsored Arab-Israeli peace talks and described the United States as "an arrogant power."[51] Although the April 1992 election was a triumph for the moderates, its reforms were largely economic. The nation's radical political posture persisted, and in 1993 Iran greatly increased its financial aid to Islamic political movements in Algeria, Bosnia, Lebanon, Pakistan, Tajikistan, and elsewhere.[52]

The elections of 1997 swept a reform politician, Seyyed Mohammad Khatami, into power. Khatami was supported by intellectuals and urban youth, and his presidency was accompanied by expectations of social reform that would mitigate the harsher aspects of Islamic rule. Internationally, Khatami called for a "dialogue of civilizations" to replace the clash of civilizations, a sentiment that was supported by the United Nations General Assembly, which designated the year 2001 as the year of the Dialogue of Civilizations. In skirmishes with the Guardian Council appointed by the Supreme Leader, Ali Khamenei, Khatami was regularly defeated and his authority undermined. By the 2005 elections, even his own followers had become disillusioned.

This struggle between reformists and the hard-line Muslim clergy was a central issue in the 2005 Iranian presidential elections. Though the moderate former president, Ali-Akbar Hashemi-Rafsanjani, was favored, an upset victory resulted in the ascension to power of Tehran's former mayor, Mahmoud Ahmadinejad, who was supported by Khamenei and was popular among disaffected villagers and the urban poor. He also benefited from his anti-Americanism, a position that was popular in part because of the inclusion of Iran in the "axis of evil" by U.S. president George W. Bush in his State of Union address in 2002. After the election, Ahmadinejad, who is said to be an adherent of an unusually conservative and apocalyptic Shi'a sect, the Hojjatieh, consolidated his political control, indirectly challenged Khamenei's authority, and presented himself as the spokesman for the conservative political wing of the Muslim world. He took a hard line against Israel, wrote an open letter to U.S. president George W. Bush criticizing America's foreign policy, and antagonized the United States and much of the world through his defense of Iran's nuclear program. Domestically, he stepped up the enforcement of Islamic customs and purged the universities in an attempt to Islamicize the curriculum. * * *

During the 2006 Israeli incursion into Lebanon, Ahm[a]dinejad supported the Hizbollah leader Sheik Hassan Nasrallah, whom the U.S. government had dubbed an Iranian puppet. There is some evidence to support the contention that for many years prior to the 2006 clashes between Israel and Lebanon's Hizbollah, Iran had been building up the Lebanese militant Shi'ite movement and arming its militia. Iran also supported the regime of Hafez al-Assad and his son Bashar in Syria, members of the small but powerful Shi'a religious movement known as Alawites.

On the eastern side of the country, Iran has long supported the Shi'a Hazara tribal group in Afghanistan; and it has had ties to Tajiks, the Persian ethnic communities in Afghanistan and Central Asia that are largely Sunni. Iran supported the Tajik Afghan leader Ahmed Shah Massoud and his Northern Alliance militia in their resistance to the Pashtun's Taliban movement. After Massoud was killed by operatives close to Osama bin Laden shortly before the September 11, 2001, attacks on the World Trade Center and the Pentagon, Iran favored the destruction of the Taliban. Iran also has had ties to other Tajik communities in Tajikistan, Uzbekistan, Pakistan, and the Xinjiang province of China. Many of these have been involved in militant religious movements of their own.

Perhaps the most enduring legacies of the Islamic revolution in Iran are the constitutional privileges granted to religion in Iran's public life and the creation of an Iranian nationalism that the shah tried but failed to achieve.[53] Iranian nationalist goals have become fused with Shi'ite political ideology, the Muslim clergy has substantial political authority, and religion plays a leading role in the country's administration. The extent of the religious leadership's political authority is particularly interesting, for the architects of the revolution have taken the concept of the just ruler (*al-sultan al-'adil*) in Shi'ite Islam and transformed it into a political position—an elder statesman who guides and advises the president and other governmental officials.[54] During Khomeini's lifetime, he himself played that role, and after his death he was succeeded by the Ayatollah Ali Khamenei. The extent of the Supreme Leader's authority is ambiguous, for, as Khomeini explained, "the religious leaders do not wish to be the government, but neither are they separate from the government."[55] Separate or not, Khomeini warned that the clergy would be prepared to "intervene" if the secular leaders of the government make "a false step."[56] Religious revolutionaries in other parts of the world would give almost anything to acquire this remarkable political leverage.

Israel's Militant Zionism

Though Israel's religious rebels are Jewish rather than Muslim, their situation is not unlike that of many Muslim activists. But they are more like the Muslim rebels in Egypt than Iran. Rather than confronting entirely secular rulers like the shah, they oppose moderate leaders who are more than nominally committed to their nation's dominant religion—in this case, Judaism. While extreme Jewish activists view the state of Israel as a largely secular entity, for many (including its Arab opponents), Israel is an example of religious nationalism achieved. Muslim nationalism in the Middle East has been fueled in part by a kind of religious competition, since many Muslim political observers feel that they deserve what the Jews have—their own state. * * *

However, within Israel itself a large contingent of politically active Jews regard their homeland as the expression of an incomplete form of religious nationalism, at best. Although Israel is hospitable to Jewish refugees, it is essentially a secular state, informed by the rules and mores of European and American society, and that leaves many Jewish religious nationalists deeply dissatisfied.

One of the most vocal of these Jewish nationalists was Rabbi Meir Kahane, the spokesman for the radical Kach ("Thus!") Party. Not surprisingly, perhaps, he had a certain admiration for the Ayatollah Khomeini.[57] He told me that he felt closer to Khomeini and other militant Muslims than he did to such framers of secular political thought as John Locke or even to secular Jews.[58] The reason, he explained, was that Khomeini believed in the relevance of religion to everyday life and especially in the importance of religion in shaping a nation's morality and communal identity. * * * Kahane's views on Jewish nationalism are not entirely unprecedented. Tensions between the religious and secular dimensions of the state have been a persistent theme in the recent struggle for Israeli nationhood. * * *

∗   ∗   ∗

These and other groups continued their assaults on secular Israel after the establishment of an independent state in 1948, even though significant compromises had been made to accommodate their positions. Jewish religious courts created during the British Mandate from 1943 to 1947 became integrated into the new legal system, and a "status quo agreement" between the religious parties and the prestate administration, the Jewish Agency, called for religious concessions that included the government's observance of dietary laws and maintenance of religious schools.

∗   ∗   ∗

More recently, a movement has formed in Israel based on the idea that the present secular Jewish state is the precursor of an ideal religious

Israel.[59] It is the revival of an old idea, one advocated by Rabbi Avraham Yitzhak ha-Kohen Kuk, the chief rabbi of pre-Israeli Palestine. According to Kuk (and his son and successor, Z. Y. Kuk), the secular state of Israel prepares the way for a nation based explicitly on faith; it contains a "hidden spark" of the sacred.[60] The implications of this position are that the coming of the Messiah is likely to happen soon, and the religious purification of the state of Israel could help make that arrival occur more quickly.

Kuk's ideas ignited the religious imaginations of many Israelis after the Six-Day War in 1967. The war had two results that affected the growth of Jewish nationalist movements. The success of the military engagement led to widespread national euphoria, a feeling that Israel was suddenly moving in an expansive and triumphant direction. * * *

Jewish nationalists who were impressed with the theology of Rabbi Kuk felt strongly that history was leading to the moment of divine redemption and the re-creation of the biblical state of Israel. This meant that the Palestinians living in the West Bank were in the way: at best they were an annoyance to be controlled, at worst an enemy to be destroyed. The *intifada*, or "rebellion," that erupted in the Arab areas of Gaza, Jerusalem, and the West Bank in December 1987 only inflamed the sentiments of the Kukists. The influx of Soviet and Ethiopian Jews increased the pressure on living space and visibly supported the claim that Jews throughout the world are looking toward Israel as a redemptive nation.

One of the most vocal of the Jewish nationalists in the Kuk lineage was Meir Kahane. Kahane, an American who had a long history of Jewish political activism in Brooklyn, formed the Jewish Defense League (JDL) in the 1960s to counter acts of anti-Semitism.[61] In 1971 he came to Israel and turned to a more messianic vision of Jewish politics; in 1974 he created the Kach party, whose main platform was that Israel should be ruled according to a strict construction of Jewish law; non-Jews—for that matter, even secular Jews—had no place in this sacred order. * * *

* * *

* * * In Kahane's view, the coming of the Messiah was imminent, and the Arabs were simply in the wrong place at the wrong time. He told me that he did not hate the Arabs; he "respected them" and felt that they "should not live in disgrace in an occupied land."[62] For that reason, they should leave. The problem, for Kahane, was not that they were Arabs but that they were non-Jews living in a place designated by God for Jewish people since biblical times.[63] From a biblical point of view, Kahane argued, the true Israel is the West Bank of the Jordan River and the hills around Jerusalem—not the plains where Israel's largest city, Tel Aviv, is located.[64] The desire to reclaim the West Bank was therefore not simply irredentism: it was a part of a sacred plan of redemption. * * *

Although most Jewish settlers do not agree with what Ehud Sprinzak describes as Kahane's "catastrophic messianism" and subscribe instead to Kuk's incremental theory of messianic history, they view their occupation of the West Bank not only as a social experiment but as a religious act.[65] Rabbi Moshe Levinger, a leader of the Gush Emunim—an organization that encourages the new settlements and claims Rabbi Kuk as its founder—told me that the settlers' "return to the land is the first aspect of the return of the Messiah."[66] The religious settlers are by no means the majority of those who have established residential colonies on the West Bank—they are only a small percentage—but their presence colors the entire movement. Many of them regard the Palestinian Arabs around them with contempt. Hostility from the Arabs—and, for that matter, from many secular Jews—has hardened many of the members of the Gush Emunim and turned what began as a romantic venture into a militant cult.[67]

Much the same can be said about those who long for the rebuilding of the Temple in Jerusalem. According to Kuk's theology, the event that will trigger the return of the Messiah and the start of the messianic age is the reconstruction of the Temple on Temple Mount.[68] Again, like the

Jewish conquest of biblical lands, it is an act of God that invites human participation: Jewish activists can join this act of redemption by helping to rebuild the Temple. The main practical constraint against doing so is the fact that Judaism's holiest place is simultaneously one of Islam's most sacred sites. * * *

* * *

Another Jewish nationalist who laments the absence of the temple is Gershon Salomon. He heads a small group known as the Faithful of Temple Mount—one of several groups committed to rebuilding the Temple. Salomon explained to me that the construction of the Temple will precipitate an "awakening" of the Jewish people and the advent of the messianic age.[69] * * *

* * *

In September 1993, when many Israelis were celebrating the mutual recognition of Israel and the PLO, leaders of Kahane's Kach party denounced the historic accord, calling it a fraud. They joined members of opposition parties, the Gush Emunim, and West Bank settlers in launching a campaign of civil disobedience against the accord, and vowed to fight by "any means." The passion of their protest—reminiscent of the style of Rabbi Kahane, whom they considered a martyr—came from the conviction that an Israeli retreat from the biblical lands of the West Bank was not only bad politics but bad religion. In their view, a religious state ruled by Jewish law and located on the site of biblical Israel was essential for the redemption of the entire cosmos. For this reason, not long after the accord was signed, a follower of Kahane slaughtered a group of Arabs as they worshipped in the mosque at Hebron's Tomb of the Prophets.

* * *

An even greater demon in the eyes of most Israelis is the Jewish activist Yigal Amir, who thought he was helping save Israel's honor when he assassinated the country's prime minister, Yitzhak Rabin. * * *

* * * Amir, a student from Tel Aviv's conservative Bar-Ilan University, aimed his pistol and shot the prime minister at point-blank range. As Rabin lay dying on the sidewalk next to the car, Amir was apprehended by the police. He was quoted as saying that he had no regrets for what he had done, adding that he had "acted alone and on orders from God."[70]

Amir, a former combat soldier who had studied Jewish law, said that his decision to assassinate the prime minister was not a casual one and that he had attempted to carry out the act on two previous occasions. At those times, however, the conditions had not been right. His decision to kill the prime minister was influenced by the opinions of militant rabbis that such an assassination would be justified by the "pursuer's decree" of Jewish legal precedent.[71] The principle morally obligates a Jew to halt someone who presents "a mortal danger" to Jews. Such a danger, Amir reasoned, was created by Rabin in allowing the Palestinian Authority to expand on the West Bank.

The assassination of Rabin did not deter succeeding Israeli governments from selectively withdrawing from some areas of Palestinian control, including Gaza and parts of the West Bank. In August 2005, over 9,500 settlers and the troops that supported them were required to leave the area. By September, Israel had withdrawn support from all Jewish settlements in Gaza, despite the fierce opposition of extreme religious opponents who felt that any withdrawal of Jewish control over what they regarded as the biblical lands of Israel was an act of treason and a violation of the faith. Some protestors threw eggs, bottles, and paint at the soldiers who were sent to evacuate the area; others barricaded themselves in synagogues. Many of the protestors were young people from religious settlements in the West Bank who claimed that God had given the land to the Jews and considered allowing any piece of it to be given away a violation of divine will.

Jewish settlers on the West Bank were even more resistant to relinquishing territory in areas that they claimed had been occupied by Jews in biblical times. But in fact only a few isolated Jewish settlements in the West Bank were dismantled by the Israeli government. Many of the settlements around the city of Jerusalem were simply absorbed into redefined boundaries of the city limits. Settlements in other parts of the West Bank were incorporated into Israeli territory by the construction of a network of controlled highways that was begun in 2004. Many of the settlements were protected by a controversial barrier, described by the Israeli government as a security fence and by most Palestinians as a wall. Construction of the 420-mile barrier began in 2002 and continued for some years. In many sections it was indeed a metal fence; in other areas, including the city of Jerusalem, it was a thirty-foot-tall concrete wall. Opposition to the barrier included concerns not only about the divisive nature of the barrier but also about its location. The barrier created a de facto demarcation of boundaries that absorbed an estimated 40 percent of formerly Palestinian-controlled areas. Though Jewish extremists were still unhappy with what they thought were unnecessary compromises with the Palestinians, the protected settlements, the network of highways, and the extensive barrier created a significant expansion of direct Israeli control over what had been regarded as Palestinian territory. The dream of incorporating into the Jewish state of Israel the biblical land on the West Bank had largely been fulfilled.

* * *

Insurgents in Iraq

The Israeli attack in 2004 that killed the Palestinian Hamas leader Sheik Ahmed Yassin had repercussions in a different part of the Arab world: the al-Anbar province of post-Saddam Iraq. At the time that Sheik Yassin was killed, Sunni activists in Iraq were beginning to mobilize protests against the U.S. occupation of their country that began with the American-led military coalition that toppled Saddam Hussein's government in April 2003.

"We hated Saddam," a Sunni Muslim cleric told me, indicating that he and his colleagues in the Sunni triangle of al-Anbar and adjacent provinces had no use for the secular dictator.[72] Nonetheless, he and his allies regarded the American coalition authority that replaced Saddam's government as an even worse choice. They saw the U.S. occupation as a repressive force, imposing a Western-style government on Muslim territory, much as America's ally, Israel, imposed itself on the Middle East. For this reason they saw parallels to their own experience in Iraq with Hamas and the Muslim struggle in Palestine.

The killing of Sheik Yassin had an impact especially on the insurgency in Fallujah during the critical month of March 2004. The Iraqis in Fallujah had identified themselves with the Palestinians, and Sheik Yassin had been widely revered in Iraq's Sunni stronghold. Televised scenes of the site of the crippled leader's death outraged Muslims in Fallujah, who poured out into the streets in a spontaneous demonstration. The U.S. military used a show of force to control the demonstration, but the American presence reinforced the idea that the politics of the United States and Israel were essentially identical. It was a common belief among Iraqis that the United States supported what was regarded as Israel's oppression of Palestinian freedom. Thus the anger against Israel's control over Palestine became merged with the hatred of the U.S. occupation of Iraq. In the eyes of many in Fallujah, the Palestinian and Iraqi cause was the same. One of the city's main streets, which ended in a square metal bridge over the Euphrates River—was renamed in honor of the fallen Sheik Yassin.

For over a week tension mounted. On March 31, several American-made sport-utility vehicles came hurtling through Fallujah on the newly named Sheik Yassin Street. The passengers in the vehicles were security staff employed by a North Carolina firm, Blackwater Security Consulting, but from the Iraqi point of view these armed Americans were either soldiers or spies. The vehicles were ambushed.[73] Soon the stalled vehicles burst into flames with the occupants caught inside.[74]

* * *

This was a critical moment in the increasing intensity of the insurgency and in the militancy of the U.S. occupation authority's response. Against the advice of the American generals on the scene, orders came from the Pentagon to quell the insurgency by directly attacking Fallujah. A major military assault ensued in the following month, and after a difficult ceasefire during the summer, the city was virtually emptied by a U.S. military campaign in November 2004 that was determined to rid the city of insurgents. The intensity of the American assault, however, hardened the opposition and created a more dedicated resistance. * * *

The fall of Fallujah marked a turning point in jihadi influence on the insurgency. * * * The destruction of Fallujah's social network by the U.S. military weakened those ties, however, and scattered the insurgents. Increasingly they came under the influence of the more radical activists. Before the fall of Fallujah, the jihad outsiders had been mistrusted; the destruction of Fallujah provided evidence in the eyes of many that the jihadi rhetoric of cosmic war was real.

When I was in Baghdad in 2004, my interviews with clerics associated with the Sunni resistance convinced me that at that time their main concern had been the religious consequences of the U.S. occupation of Iraq, not global jihad. One of them told me that he was certain that the purpose of the U.S. invasion and occupation of his country was to coopt an Islamic revolution against the secular government; he regarded the U.S.-supported regime in Baghdad as simply a continuation of the anti-Islamic secular policies of Saddam Hussein.[75] * * *

The jihadi elements that came into Iraq in the months following the U.S. military invasion were different from these local insurgents—they were more strident, more expansive in their vision of global religious struggle. They were transnationalists. The jihadi warriors from Jordan, Syria, and elsewhere in the Middle East saw Iraq as a new battleground in the global confrontation between Islam and what they regarded as the anti-Islamic forces of the secular West. One of the leaders of these new jihadi soldiers who helped to transform the Iraqi resistance was the Jordanian militant Abu Musab al-Zarqawi.

Al-Zarqawi's lasting impact on Iraq's civil strife was his effort to create religious conflict between Arab Sunnis and Shi'ites. In March 2004, his group launched an attack on Shi'a shrines in Karbala and Baghdad. In December 2004 the group attacked the leading Shi'a shrine in Najaf and again bombed the Karbala mosque. Perhaps the most destructive attack was the February 2006 bombing of the al-Asqari mosque in Samarra—one of Shi'a Islam's holiest sites—destroying its striking golden dome and killing 165 people. Al-Zarqawi had publicly proclaimed his intention to foment Sunni-Shi'a animosity, and the destruction of the shrine was clearly meant to accomplish that goal.

Al-Zarqawi's goal of sectarian strife indeed came to fruition, and these hostilities outlived al-Zarqawi himself. On June 7, 2006, U.S. military intelligence received information regarding al-Zarqawi's location near the city of Baquba, and attacked the location with a missile strike that killed him, along with one of his wives and one of his children. * * *

In the meantime, the momentum of sectarian strife had taken on a life of its own. Soon after the February 2006 bombing of the Samarra mosque, over a hundred Sunni mosques were attacked and ten Sunni imams were killed. Fifteen more were kidnapped. A tit-for-tat litany of reprisal killings between Shi'a and Sunni neighborhoods intensified during the following year.

Much of the fervor of Shi'a retaliation against Sunnis was urged on by the radical Shi'a cleric Muqtada al-Sadr. Though relatively young and undistinguished among Shi'a clergy in Iraq,

Muqtada had imposing family ties. He was the son of one of Iraq's most famous clerics, the late Grand Ayatollah Mohammad Sadeq al-Sadr, and son-in-law of another distinguished cleric, the Grand Ayatollah Mohammad Baqir as-Sadr. Perhaps more important, he had set up something of a theocratic rule in one of Baghdad's most crowded districts, Sadr City, which consisted almost entirely of poor Shi'a immigrants. Moreover, Muqtada served as the commander of a large paramilitary force, the Mahdi Army, that drew its manpower from former units of the disbanded Iraqi army and was said to have received covert support from Iran.

Muqtada had no use for the American-led coalition government, which sought his arrest in 2004. At the same time he despised al-Zarqawi's forces, whose terrorists attacks were directed at Shi'a targets. After the destruction of the Samarra mosque, rogue elements related to the Muqtada camp undertook unusually savage acts of terrorism, aimed at the Sunni population in retaliation for car bomb assaults in Shi'a neighborhoods, many of them in Sadr City. The Shi'a reprisals were equally brutal. Groups of ordinary Sunni citizens were rounded up, tortured, and murdered, their bodies mutilated by electric drills and dumped in the Tigris River or in fields outside of the city of Baghdad.

Though the sectarian violence in Iraq was often described as Sunni-Shi'a civil war, there was little support for the violence from moderates and mainstream religious leaders on either side. On the Sunni side, the Sunni Association of Muslim Clerics resisted the attempts of the al-Tawhid jihadis to coopt it, and the association often played a positive role in helping to moderate the violence. I spoke with one Sunni cleric who told me that he had sought to mediate between extremist insurgents and the Iraqi government for the sake of Iraqi unity.[76] The jihadi extremists became increasingly impatient with what they regarded as compromises by the nationalistic-minded Sunni leaders.

By 2007 the tensions between moderate Iraqi Sunni leaders and the jihadi outsiders had erupted into dissention and violence between their factions. Sunni militia in al-Anbar Province—who had worked with the foreign jihadis in attacks on the U.S. and Iraqi military—were now colluding with U.S. forces in apprehending their former allies and in some instances torturing and killing them. On the Shi'a side, the Shi'a-dominated Iraq government pledged to control Muqtada's gangs, and leading clerics such as Grand Ayatollah Sayyid Ali Husaini al-Sistani distanced themselves from Shi'a extremists. Sistani carried considerable political weight, not only because of his religious authority but also because of his relationship with the leading Shi'a political party, the Supreme Council for the Islamic Revolution in Iraq, led by Abdul Aziz al-Hakim.

* * *

Global Jihad

* * *

Global Jihad after September 11, 2001

After 2001, and especially after the U.S. invasion of Iraq in 2003, a resurgence of jihadi activism erupted around the world. Groups of self-proclaimed jihadi activists emerged in the Middle East, Southeast Asia, North Africa, Europe and the United Kingdom, though it is doubtful that they were orchestrated by central command. These new jihadi groups were stimulated by at least three factors: One was the dramatic character of the 2001 attacks, which had an impact around the world. To many Muslims it was a hideous crime unworthy of being associated with Islam. To others, however, it was impressive: it showed that Muslim activists could successfully undertake a mission of this magnitude, and do it with audacity and conviction. The jihadi videos that were compiled after 2001 as recruitment aids emphasize the courage of the nineteen hijackers.

A second factor in the growth of jihadi sympathy was related to U.S. foreign policy after 2001. The American military incursions in Afghanistan and especially in Iraq were perceived as motivated in large part by efforts to "control Muslim politics," as a mullah in Baghdad put it in a conversation with me after the U.S. invasion of Iraq.[77] Because the United States' stance during the administration of President George W. Bush was widely perceived in the Muslim world as being uncritically in favor of Israel, U.S. policies in the Middle East were often construed as being calculated to oppose Islam either directly or indirectly.

A third factor was the advent of new forms of communication that provided instant and intimate access to large numbers of young Muslims around the world. Internet sites provided both chat rooms for conversations and websites for information. Short propaganda and recruitment videos were produced that could easily be accessed through the Internet and downloaded on iPods and home computers. The theme of these jihadi videos was invariably valor in the face of repression. * * *

Behind these three factors was a fourth: * * * the loss of faith in the secular nation-state. Though this theme runs through all of the cases I have described, it has been exacerbated in the twenty-first century by globalization. The rise of the global jihad movement coincides with the increased pace of global social, economic, and cultural changes in the first decade of this century and the weakening of political authority in many parts of the world. Protests against what are perceived to be the moral failures of the state often take religious forms, and in the Muslim world they are easily fused with the rhetoric of global jihad. * * *

One of the first examples of this decentralized phase of the global jihad movement came in 2002, when a series of car bombs in Bali leveled nightclubs and killed more than two hundred people, many of them young Australians on holiday. The Indonesian Jemaah Islamiyah leader Riduan Isamuddin (popularly known as Hambali), who was implicated in the attacks, was said to have been a colleague of Khalid Sheik Mohammed and had met two of the September 2001 hijackers before they undertook their mission.[78] But the Indonesian activist and his co-conspirators had their own anti-Western momentum, encouraged by the radical Indonesian cleric Abu Bakar Bashir. For some years the Indonesian Muslim militants had condemned the secular authorities in Jakarta for pandering to the interests of the West.

This pattern of local anti-authoritarian Islamic activism that is loosely tied to the international jihadi movement also appears in other post-2001 terrorist incidents. It applies to attacks in India in the disputed northern region of Kashmir and Kashmir-related terrorist assaults in Delhi and Mumbai, including the December 2001 attack on India's parliament and the July 2006 train bombs in Mumbai, in which over two hundred were killed. In both cases local pro-Kashmiri Muslim activists were implicated and alleged to have received support from global jihadi connections in Pakistan and the Middle East.

A critical turning point in the post-2001 growth of the global jihad movement came as a result of the war that followed the downfall of Saddam Hussein's regime by an American-led military coalition in March 2003. Iraq was important for the jihad movement in two ways. It presented a clear example of the jihadi claim that the United States was determined to control Muslim countries, and it provided a new center for global struggle, attracting jihadi activists from around the world. * * *

The central figure in the Iraq theater of the global jihadi war was Musab al-Zarqawi. * * * Later in life he became a convert to militant jihad and traveled to Afghanistan in 1989 to join the last stages of the *mujahadin* struggle against the Soviet-supported government. * * * It was there that al-Zarqawi most likely met Osama bin Laden, Ayman al-Zawahiri, Khalid Sheik Mohammed, and other expatriate jihadis who were forming a global activist coalition. Though bin Laden is said to have been wary of the coarse and thuggish al-Zarqawi—and for his part al-Zarqawi was said to have resisted paying obeisance to bin Laden or anyone else—bin Laden reportedly provided him some monetary support.[79]

After the September 11, 2001, attacks and the subsequent U.S.-led military invasion of Afghanistan, al-Zarqawi for a time supported the remnants of the Taliban in their resistance struggle against the new government in Kabul. In 2002 he was in Iraq—according to some reports, for medical treatment of injuries sustained in the Afghan struggles.[80] He settled in the north, in the Kurdish region, which enjoyed semi-autonomous status with American military support. Al-Zarqawi joined an Islamic guerrilla movement, Ansar al-Islam, that aimed at resisting Kurdish nationalism. Hence at the time of the U.S.-led military coalition's invasion of Iraq in March 2003, al-Zarqawi and his cadre were well poised to join the resistance movement and to try to bend it in a transnational jihadi direction.

Al-Zarqawi's forces, organized under the banner of the al-Tawhid group, targeted a wide range of individuals and public institutions in order to destabilize and discredit the embryonic Iraqi government that was being established by U.S.-led reconstruction efforts. One of their first acts was a well-orchestrated suicide truck-bombing that demolished the United Nations headquarters in Baghdad on August 19, 2003, killing twenty-two, including U.N. special envoy Sérgio Vieira de Mello. The group found that their acts of violence drew more attention if they were performed in a particularly gruesome manner—hence the rash of televised beheadings, beginning with a young American, Nicholas Berg, in May 2004, and including British hostage Ken Bigley, who was kidnapped in Baghdad's upscale al-Mansour district and beheaded in September 2004. * * *

Al-Zarqawi provided a model for ad-hoc acts of antiauthoritarian struggle that could be conducted by jihadi activists anywhere. In some cases he helped promote these acts; in other cases he served as an inspiration for makeshift terrorism. Increasingly small groups of jihadi activists—often young men—were involved in vicious attacks that were related both to local issues and global concerns. * * *

* * *

Attacks in 2005 in the Egyptian resort of Sharm el-Sheik at the southern end of the Sinai Peninsula were also aimed at removing the presence of foreigners. In this case the bombs were directed at tourist hotels and restaurants visited by Israelis. An Egyptian group was implicated in the attack. * * *

The perpetrators of a similar group of attacks on tourist hotels in Amman, Jordan in 2005—the Grand Hyatt, the Radisson SAS and the Days Inn—had ties to the international jihadi network, and in this case they were directly associated with al-Zarqawi. The Radisson explosion targeted a wedding party and was conducted by a husband-and-wife team of suicide bombers that al-Zarqawi had recruited from Iraq.

The jihadi-related attacks in Europe in the post-2001 anti-American climate have also been motivated by both local and transnational issues: disgruntled members of Muslim minorities in European nations have identified their local causes with that of global jihad, particularly with the role of the United States and European nations in the occupation of Iraq and the support for Israeli policies. In Madrid in March 2004, a cadre of expatriate Moroccans, supporters of the group that had been involved in the Casablanca blasts the year before, were implicated in a series of bombing attacks on commuter trains that were widely interpreted as a reprisal for Spain's support of the U.S. position in Iraq. Almost two hundred were killed. In London on July 7, 2005, three bombs exploded within a minute of one another on three underground subway trains, and a fourth was ignited an hour later on a double-decker bus. Over fifty commuters were killed. After the bombing, the Al-Jazeera television network aired a videotape in which one of the bombers professed his defense of Islam against the purported global aggression of the United Kingdom, the United States, and European nations.[81]

Though the al Qaeda headquarters in Afghanistan were destroyed soon after the U.S.-supported coup that toppled the Taliban government in 2001, bin Laden and al-Zawahiri survived. From secret hiding places along the Afghanistan-Pakistan border, they continued to send out a stream of audio and video messages to the wider world.[82] Al-Zawahiri wrote a book stating the al Qaeda position *Knights under the Prophet's Banner,* and issued written proclamations.[83] What is not clear is whether anyone was listening to the messages.

* * *

The relationship between al-Zarqawi and the al Qaeda leaders indicates how tenuous were the ties within the global jihadi movement. According to some reports, Osama bin Laden took an immediate dislike to the crude, brash al-Zarqawi.[84] Bin Laden regarded the green tattoos on al-Zarqawi's hand as contrary to Islamic practice and was disturbed by al-Zarqawi's almost visceral hatred of Shi'ites. Bin Laden's own mother could be described as a Shi'ite, since she was from Syria and was most likely Alawite, a movement that is an offshoot of Shi'ite Islam. Bin Laden was raised in the Sunni tradition, but he had no particular animus against Shi'ism; moreover, he regarded internal squabbles as distractions from his jihad's principal target: American and Israeli influence in the Middle East. Nonetheless, al-Zarqawi was said to have received several hundred thousand dollars in funding from al Qaeda to set up jihadi training camps in Afghanistan, and in 2005 bin Laden and al-Zarqawi forged a kind of alliance that helped to promote the idea of al Qaeda as a centrally administered international organization.

This was a misleading impression, however. It seems likely that the global jihadi movement which spread rapidly throughout the world after September 11, 2001, was much like the earlier jihadi movement in lacking a unified organization. Ideological differences, internal power struggles, and competing groups weakened what otherwise might have been a significant political force. Yet as a social movement it was quite remarkable. Through the Internet and personal networks, a sizable number of Muslim youth throughout the world became excited by the notion that they could at least vicariously participate in a great struggle between the forces of good and evil, exemplified by the jihadi confrontation with the secular state. In the United States and Europe, an influential element of the political leadership saw the struggle in equally vaunted terms. Thus the global jihadi encounter with secular political authority has revived the idea of ideological enemies that propelled the Cold War between capitalism and communism over many decades in the twentieth century. It would be an almost poignant recapitulation of the crusty old global encounter of the Cold War—if the new religious incarnation of ideological confrontation had not been so bitterly violent.

NOTES

1. Quoted in Kim Murphy, "Islamic Party Wins Power in Algeria," *Los Angeles Times*, December 28, 1991, A1. * * *
2. Hans Kohn, *Nationalism: Its Meaning and History* (Princeton: D. Van Nostrand, 1955), 89.
3. Ibid., 16.
4. Ibid.
5. Jawaharlal Nehru, *The Discovery of India* (New York: John Day, 1946), 531–32.
6. Kohn, *Nationalism*, 9 (italics supplied).
7. Ibid., 4.
8. Rupert Emerson, *From Empire to Nation: The Rise to Self-Assertion of Asian and African Peoples* (Boston: Beacon Press, 1960), 158.
9. Ibid.
10. Anthony Giddens, *The Nation-State and Violence*, volume 2 of *A Contemporary Critique of*

Historical Materialism (Berkeley: University of California Press, 1985), 25ff. This world economic pattern, which Immanuel Wallerstein calls the "modern world-system," has its roots in the sixteenth century. * * *

11. Challenges to the divine right to rule in Europe reach back at least to the twelfth century, when John of Salisbury, who is sometimes regarded as the first modern political philosopher, held that rulers should be subject to charges of treason and could be overthrown—violently if necessary—if they violated their public trust. * * *

12. Because humans are "equal and independent" before God, Locke argued, they have the sole right to exercise the power of the Law of Nature, and the only way in which an individual can be deprived of his or her liberty is "by agreeing with other Men to joyn and unite into a community, for their comfortable, safe, and peacable living one amongst another." John Locke, "Of the Beginnings of Political Societies," chap. 8 of *The Second Treatise on Government* (New York: Cambridge University Press, 1960), 375.

13. According to Rousseau, a *social contract* is a tacit admission by the people that they need to be ruled and an expression of their willingness to relinquish some of their rights and freedoms to the state in exchange for its administrative protection. It is an exchange of what Rousseau calls one's "natural liberty" for the security and justice provided through "civil liberty." Rousseau implied that the state does not need the church to grant it moral legitimacy: the people grant it a legitimacy on their own through a divine right that is directly invested in them as a part of the God-given natural order. Jean-Jacques Rousseau, "On the Civil State," chap. 8 of *The Social Contract* (New York: Pocket Books, 1967), 23.

14. Alexis de Tocqueville, *The Old Regime and the French Revolution*, translated by Stuart Gilbert (New York: Doubleday, Anchor Books, 1955), 11. See also John McManners, *The French Revolution and the Church* (Westport, Conn.: Greenwood Press, 1969).

15. Ernst Cassirer, *The Philosophy of the Enlightenment* (Boston: Beacon Press, 1955), 171. Among the devotees of deism were Thomas Jefferson, Benjamin Franklin, and other founding fathers of the United States.

16. Robert Bellah, "Civil Religion in America," *Daedalus* 96, no. 1 (Winter 1967): 1–22.

17. Tocqueville, *The Old Régime*, 13.

18. Robert N. Bellah, "Civil Religion in America," *Daedalus* 96, no. 1 (Winter 1967): 1–21, reprinted in Robert N. Bellah, *Beyond Belief* (New York: Harper & Row, 1970).

19. See Donald Eugene Smith, *India as a Secular State* (Princeton: Princeton University Press, 1963), which details the many concessions the government has made.

20. Ainslie T. Embree, *Utopias in Conflict: Religion and Nationalism in Modern India* (Berkeley: University of California Press, 1990), 88.

21. Abolhassan Bani-Sadr, *The Fundamental Principles and Precepts of Islamic Government*, translated by Mohammed R. Ghanoonparvar (Lexington, Ky.: Mazda Publishers, 1981), 40.

22. Interview with Essam el-Arian, medical doctor, member of the National Assembly, and member of the Muslim Brotherhood, in Cairo, January 11, 1989.

23. To some, including Ibrahim Shitta, professor of Persian literature at Cairo University, *Christendom* and *Western civilization* are interchangeable terms.

24. Samuel Huntington, "The Clash of Civilizations?" *Foreign Affairs* (Summer 1993): 22–49. The essay was revised, expanded, and published as a book, *The Clash of Civilizations and the Remaking of World Order* (New York: Simon and Schuster, 1996).

25. The terms *Westomania* and *West-toxification* (and also sometimes *Occidentosis*) are translations of the Farsi word *gharbzadegi*, coined by Jalal Al-e Ahmad. It is discussed in Michael C. Hillmann's introduction to Jalal Al-e Ahmad, *The School Principal*, translated

by John K. Newton (Minneapolis: Bibliotheca Islamica), 1974.

26. Imam [Ayatollah] Khomeini, "Anniversary of the Uprising of Khurdad 15," in Khomeini, *Islam and Revolution: Writings and Declarations*, translated and annotated by Hamid Algar (Berkeley: Mizan Press, 1981; London: Routledge & Kegan Paul, 1985), 270.

27. Interview with Rabbi Meir Kahane, former member, Knesset, and leader, Kach Party, in Jerusalem, January 18, 1989; and an article by an anonymous author in the pamphlet *Islam and Palestine*, Leaflet 5 (Limassol, Cyprus, June 1988).

28. Interview with Uduwawala Chandananda Thero, Kandy, Sri Lanka, February 2, 1988.

29. Ibid.

30. Hamas communiqué, January 22, 1991, quoted in Jean-François Legrain, "A Defining Moment: Palestinian Islamic Fundamentalism," in James P. Piscatori, ed., *Islamic Fundamentalisms and the Gulf Crisis* (Chicago: Fundamentalism Project, American Academy of Arts and Sciences, 1991), 76.

31. I explore further this process of satanization in my *Terror in the Mind of God* (Berkeley: University of California Press, 2003), 174–89.

32. Interview with el-Arian, January 11, 1989.

33. Jürgen Habermas, *Legitimation Crisis*, translated by Thomas McCarthy (Boston: Beacon Press, 1975), passim.

34. D. C. Vejayavardhana, *The Revolt in the Temple: Composed to Commemorate 2,500 Years of the Land, the Race, and the Faith* (Colombo: Sinha Publications, 1953), reprinted in Donald Eugene Smith, *Religion, Politics and Social Change in the Third World: A Sourcebook* (New York: Free Press, 1971), 105.

35. Ibid.

36. Shahrough Akhavi, "The Impact of the Iranian Revolution on Egypt," in John L, Esposito, ed., *The Iranian Revolution: Its Global Impact* (Miami: Florida International University Press, 1990), 138. For a comprehensive analysis of the separation between Sunni and Shi'a radical groups, see [Emmanuel] Sivan, "Sunni Radicalism [in the Middle East and the Iranian Revolution,]" [*International Journal for Middle East Studies* 21 (1989)].

37. Interview with el-Arian, Cairo, January 11, 1989.

38. Interview with Ayatollah Khomeini by Hamid Algar on December 29, 1978, at Neauphle-le-Chateau, France, in Khomeini, *Islam and Revolution*, 323.

39. Ibid.

40. [Bernard] Lewis, [*The*] *Political Language of Islam* [Chicago: University of Chicago Press, 1988], 2.

41. Sivan, "Sunni Radicalism," 8–11 and 29, n. 11.

42. Hamid Algar, foreword to Khomeini, *Islam and Revolution*, 10.

43. A. Ali-Babai, "An Open Letter to Khomeini, *Iranshahr*, June 15–July 16, 1982, quoted in Ervand Abrahamian, *Radical Islam: The Iranian Mojahedin* (London: I. B. Tauris, 1989), 19.

44. Khomeini, *Islam and Revolution*, 334.

45. Ibid., 335.

46. For the U.S. State Department's perspective on the crisis, see the revealing study by [Gary] Sick, *All Fall Down*[: *America's Tragic Encounter with Iran*, rev. ed. (New York: Penguin, 1986)].

47. Ibid., 229–30.

48. The early years of the revolution and the mullahs' ascension to power are chronicled in Shaul Bakhash, *The Reign of the Ayatollahs: Iran and the Islamic Revolution* (New York: Basic Books, 1984).

49. Supporters of the moderate Islamic revolutionary movement, the Mojahedin, were especially targeted for repression because of the considerable power and popularity they had gained after the revolution. See Abrahamian, *Radical Islam*.

50. Said Amir Arjomand, "A Victory for the Pragmatists: The Islamic Fundamentalist Reaction in Iran," in Piscatori, *Islamic Fundamentalisms*, 52.

51. Nick B. Williams Jr., "Iran's Rafsanjani, Guarding His Political Flanks, Steers a More

Militant Course," *Los Angeles Times*, January 13, 1992.

52. Robin Wright, "Iran Extends Reach of Its Aid to Islamic Groups," *Los Angeles Times*, April 6, 1993.

53. For interesting accounts of life in postrevolutionary Iran, see Robin Wright, *In the Name of God: The Khomeini Decade* (New York: Simon & Schuster, 1989); John Simpson, *Inside Iran: Life under Khomeini's Regime* (New York: St. Martin's Press, 1988); and Roy P. Mottahedeh, *The Mantle of the Prophet* (New York: Pantheon, 1986).

54. For the theological history of the concept, see Abdulaziz Abdul-Hussein Sachedina, *The Just Ruler (al-sultan al-'adil) in Shi'ite Islam: The Comprehensive Authority of the Jurist in Imamite Jurisprudence* (New York: Oxford University Press, 1988).

55. Khomeini, *Islam and Revolution*, 342.

56. Ibid., 343.

57. Interview with Kahane, Jerusalem, January 18, 1989.

58. Ibid. See also an interview with Kahane published in Raphael Mergui and Philippe Simonnot, *Israel's Ayatollahs: Meir Kahane and the Far Right in Israel* (London: Saqi Books, 1987), 40–41.

59. The best analysis of the new religious politics in Israel may be found in Ehud Sprinzak, *The Ascendance of Israel's Radical Right* (New York: Oxford University Press, 1991). See also Ian S. Lustick, *For the Land and the Lord: Jewish Fundamentalism in Israel* (New York: Council on Foreign Relations, 1989).

60. Alter B. Z. Metzger, *Rabbi Kook's Philosophy of Repentance: A Translation of "Orot Ha-Teshuvah,"* Studies in Torah Judaism 11 (New York: Yeshiva University Press, 1968), 111. See also Jacob B. Agus, *Banner of Jerusalem: The Life, Times, and Thought of Rabbi Abraham Isaac Kuk* (New York: Bloch, 1946).

61. There have been several biographies of Kahane, including Robert Friedman, *The False Prophet: Rabbi Meir Kahane—From FBI Informant to Knesset Member* (London: Faber & Faber, 1990). For a comprehensive study of the religious right in Israel that puts Kahane's movement in context, see Sprinzak, *The Ascendance of Israel's Radical Right*.

62. Interview with Kahane, Jerusalem, January 18, 1989.

63. According to Sprinzak (*The Ascendance of Israel's Radical Right*, 225), Kahane did not make the usual nationalist argument that the Jews deserved the land because it was their ancient birthplace; rather, the Jews *"expropriated* it in the name of God and his sovereign will" (italics in the original).

64. Kahane made this point during a function proclaiming a new state of Judea—one that would be established on the West Bank if and when the Israeli army retreated from those areas (from my notes taken at the event in Jerusalem, January 18, 1989).

65. Sprinzak, *The Ascendance of Israel's Political Right*, 220.

66. Interview with Rabbi Moshe Levinger, Jerusalem, January 16, 1989.

67. See Ehud Sprinzak, "Fundamentalism, Terrorism, and Democracy: The Case of Gush Emunim Underground" (Colloquium paper given at the Woodrow Wilson International Center for Scholars, Washington, D.C., September 16, 1986), published in revised and expanded form as "From Messianic Pioneering to Vigilante Terrorism: The Case of Gush Emunim Underground," *Journal of Strategic Studies* 10, no. 4 (December 1987): 194–216 (a special issue titled "Inside Terrorist Organizations," edited by David C. Rapoport) and reissued as a book: David C. Rapoport, ed., *Inside Terrorist Organizations* (New York: Columbia University Press, 1988).

68. The idea that the rebuilding of the Temple will be a part of the messianic age is a common theme in Jewish history. See, for example, George W. Buchanan, *Revelation and Redemption: Jewish Documents of Deliverance from the Fall of Jerusalem to the Death of Nahmanides* (Dillsboro: Western North Carolina Press, 1978); and Jonathan Frankel, ed., *Jews*

and Messianism in the Modern Era: Metaphor and Meaning, Studies in Contemporary Jewry 7 (New York: Oxford University Press, and Jerusalem: Institute of Contemporary Jewry, Hebrew University of Jerusalem, 1991), 197–213 and 34–67. I am grateful to Richard Hecht of the University of California, Santa Barbara, for bringing to my attention these and other references on Jewish nationalism.

69. Interview with Gersho[n] Salomon, head, Faithful of Temple Mount, in Jerusalem, May 25, 1990.

70. Yigal Amir, quoted in Joel Greenberg, "Rabin's Assassin," *New York Times,* November 5, 1995, A1.

71. [Serge] Schmemann, "Rabin Assassinated in Jerusalem," *New York Times,* November 11, 1995, A1.

72. Interview with Muhammad al-Kubaisi, Association of Muslim Clerics, in Baghdad, May 6, 2004.

73. Jeffrey Gettleman, "Enraged Mob in Falluja Kills Four American Contractors," *New York Times,* March 31, 2004.

74. David Barstow, "Killed Contractors Were Ambushed," *New York Times,* April 10, 2004.

75. Interview with Muhammad al-Kubaisi, Baghdad, May 6, 2004. I discuss this theory further in my article "Dateline Baghdad: The Saddam Conspiracy Theory," *The Globalist,* September 24, 2004.

76. Interview with Dr. Isam Al-Rawi, professor of geology at Baghdad University and member of the Association of Muslim Clerics, Iraq, in Cairo, March 12, 2005. In 2007 an unknown assassin killed Dr. Al-Rawi on the grounds of the university.

77. Interview with Sheik Muhammad al-Kubaisi, deputy secretary general, Association of Muslim Clerics, at the Mother of All Battles Mosque, Baghdad, May 6, 2004.

78. [Report of the National Commission on Terrorist Attacks upon the United States ("] *9/11 Commission Report*["), September 24, 2004 (www.9-11commission.gov/)], chap. 5, sec. 1.

79. Mary Ann Weaver, "Inventing al-Zarqawi," *Atlantic Monthly* (July/August 2006).

80. Ibid.

81. Statement of Mohammad Sidique Kahn broadcast on Al-Jazeera television, September 1, 2005.

82. [Bruce] Lawrence, *Messages to the World,* [the Statements of Osama bin Laden (London: Verso, 2005)], 100–275.

83. Al-Zawahiri, *Knights under the Prophet's Banner,* serialized in *Al-Sharq al-Awsat,* a London-based Saudi-owned daily newspaper, in 2001.

84. Weaver, "Inventing al-Zarqawi."

6 The Individual

Individual psychology is also important in shaping international relations. Individuals include not only foreign policy elites—the leaders who move the world—but also the diplomats, warriors, activists, and voters whose attitudes and perceptions animate the politics of international issues. In a now-classic piece originally published in 1968, Robert Jervis articulates hypotheses on the origins of misperceptions. Drawing heavily on psychology, he suggests strategies for decision makers to mitigate the effects of misperception.

While Jervis emphasizes psychological biases that many people share, Elizabeth N. Saunders looks at beliefs that are distinctive to particular leaders. She finds that different attitudes on the nature of international threats that John F. Kennedy and Lyndon B. Johnson held before they became U.S. presidents explain why they adopted different approaches to military intervention in foreign conflicts, with Kennedy stessing the need to transform war-torn societies and LBJ relying only on military coercion of the enemy. In this way, the outlooks of individual leaders do matter.

ROBERT JERVIS

Hypotheses on Misperception

In determining how he will behave, an actor must try to predict how others will act and how their actions will affect his values. The actor must therefore develop an image of others and of their intentions. This image may, however, turn out to be an inaccurate one; the actor may, for a number of reasons, misperceive both others' actions and their intentions. * * * I wish to discuss the types of misperceptions of other states' intentions which states tend to make. * * *

* * *

Theories—Necessary and Dangerous

* * * The evidence from both psychology and history overwhelmingly supports the view (which may be labeled Hypothesis 1) that decision-makers tend to fit incoming information into their existing theories and images. Indeed, their theories and images play a large part in determining what they notice. In other words, actors tend to perceive what they expect. Furthermore (Hypothesis 1a), a theory will have greater impact on an actor's interpretation of data (a) the greater the ambiguity of the data and (b) the higher the degree of confidence with which the actor holds the theory.[1]

* * *

From *World Politics* 20, no. 3 (Apr. 1968): 454–479. Some of the author's notes have been omitted.

* * * Hypothesis 2: scholars and decision-makers are apt to err by being too wedded to the established view and too closed to new information, as opposed to being too willing to alter their theories. Another way of making this point is to argue that actors tend to establish their theories and expectations prematurely. In politics, of course, this is often necessary because of the need for action. But experimental evidence indicates that the same tendency also occurs on the unconscious level. * * *

However, when we apply these and other findings to politics and discuss kinds of misperception, we should not quickly apply the label of cognitive distortion. We should proceed cautiously for two related reasons. The first is that the evidence available to decision-makers almost always permits several interpretations. It should be noted that there are cases of visual perception in which different stimuli can produce exactly the same pattern on an observer's retina. Thus, for an observer using one eye the same pattern would be produced by a sphere the size of a golf ball which was quite close to the observer, by a baseball-sized sphere that was further away, or by a basketball-sized sphere still further away. Without other clues, the observer cannot possibly determine which of these stimuli he is presented with, and we would not want to call his incorrect perceptions examples of distortion. Such cases, relatively rare in visual perception, are frequent in international relations. The evidence available to decision-makers is almost always very ambiguous since accurate clues to others' intentions are surrounded by noise[2] and deception. In most cases, no matter how long, deeply, and "objectively" the evidence is analyzed, people can differ in their interpretations, and there are no general rules to indicate who is correct.

The second reason to avoid the label of cognitive distortion is that the distinction between perception and judgment, obscure enough in individual psychology, is almost absent in the making of inferences in international politics. Decision-makers who reject information that contradicts their views—or who develop complex interpretations of it—often do so consciously and explicitly. Since the evidence available contains contradictory information, to make any inferences requires that much information be ignored or given interpretations that will seem tortuous to those who hold a different position.

Indeed, if we consider only the evidence available to a decision-maker at the time of decision, the view later proved incorrect may be supported by as much evidence as the correct one—or even by more. Scholars have often been too unsympathetic with the people who were proved wrong. On closer examination, it is frequently difficult to point to differences between those who were right and those who were wrong with respect to their openness to new information and willingness to modify their views. Winston Churchill, for example, did not open-mindedly view each Nazi action to see if the explanations provided by the appeasers accounted for the data better than his own beliefs. Instead, like Chamberlain, he fitted each bit of ambiguous information into his own hypotheses. That he was correct should not lead us to overlook the fact that his methods of analysis and use of theory to produce cognitive consistency did not basically differ from those of the appeasers.

A consideration of the importance of expectations in influencing perception also indicates that the widespread belief in the prevalence of "wishful thinking" may be incorrect, or at least may be based on inadequate data. The psychological literature on the interaction between affect and perception is immense and cannot be treated here, but it should be noted that phenomena that at first were considered strong evidence for the impact of affect on perception

often can be better treated as demonstrating the influence of expectations.[3] Thus, in international relations, cases like the United States' misestimation of the political climate in Cuba in April 1961, which may seem at first glance to have been instances of wishful thinking, may instead be more adequately explained by the theories held by the decision-makers (e.g., Communist governments are unpopular). Of course, desires may have an impact on perception by influencing expectations, but since so many other factors affect expectations, the net influence of desires may not be great.

There is evidence from both psychology[4] and international relations that when expectations and desires clash, expectations seem to be more important. The United States would like to believe that North Vietnam is about to negotiate or that the USSR is ready to give up what the United States believes is its goal of world domination, but ambiguous evidence is seen to confirm the opposite conclusion, which conforms to the United States' expectations. Actors are apt to be especially sensitive to evidence of grave danger if they think they can take action to protect themselves against the menace once it has been detected.

Safeguards

Can anything then he said to scholars and decision-makers other than "Avoid being either too open or too closed, but be especially aware of the latter danger"? Although decision-makers will always be faced with ambiguous and confusing evidence and will be forced to make inferences about others which will often be inaccurate, a number of safeguards may be suggested which could enable them to minimize their errors. First, and most obvious, decision-makers should be aware that they do not make "unbiased" interpretations of each new bit of incoming information, but rather are inevitably heavily influenced by the theories they expect to be verified. They should know that what may appear to them as a self-evident and unambiguous inference often seems so only because of their preexisting beliefs. To someone with a different theory the same data may appear to be unimportant or to support another explanation. Thus many events provide less independent support for the decision-makers' images than they may at first realize. Knowledge of this should lead decision-makers to examine more closely evidence that others believe contradicts their views.

Second, decision-makers should see if their attitudes contain consistent or supporting beliefs that are not logically linked. These may be examples of true psycho-logic. While it is not logically surprising nor is it evidence of psychological pressures to find that people who believe that Russia is aggressive are very suspicious of any Soviet move, other kinds of consistency are more suspect. For example, most people who feel that it is important for the United States to win the war in Vietnam also feel that a meaningful victory is possible. And most people who feel defeat would neither endanger U.S. national security nor be costly in terms of other values also feel that we cannot win. Although there are important logical linkages between the two parts of each of these views (especially through theories of guerrilla warfare), they do not seem strong enough to explain the degree to which the opinions are correlated. Similarly, in Finland in the winter of 1939, those who felt that grave consequences would follow Finnish agreement to give Russia a military base also believed that the Soviets would withdraw their demand if Finland stood firm. And those who felt that concessions would not lead to loss of major values also believed that Russia would fight if need be.[5] In this country, those who favored a nuclear test ban tended to argue that fallout was very harmful, that only limited improvements in technology would flow from further testing, and that a test ban would increase the chances for peace and security. Those who opposed the test ban were apt to disagree on all three points. This does not mean, of course, that the people holding such sets of supporting views were necessarily wrong in

any one element. The Finns who wanted to make concessions to the USSR were probably correct in both parts of their argument. But decision-makers should be suspicious if they hold a position in which elements that are not logically connected support the same conclusion. This condition is psychologically comfortable and makes decisions easier to reach (since competing values do not have to be balanced off against each other). The chances are thus considerable that at least part of the reason why a person holds some of these views is related to psychology and not to the substance of the evidence.

Decision-makers should also be aware that actors who suddenly find themselves having an important shared interest with other actors have a tendency to overestimate the degree of common interest involved. This tendency is especially strong for those actors (e.g., the United States, at least before 1950) whose beliefs about international relations and morality imply that they can cooperate only with "good" states and that with those states there will be no major conflicts. On the other hand, states that have either a tradition of limited cooperation with others (e.g., Britain) or a strongly held theory that differentiates occasional from permanent allies[6] (e.g., the Soviet Union) find it easier to resist this tendency and need not devote special efforts to combating its danger.

A third safeguard for decision-makers would be to make their assumptions, beliefs, and the predictions that follow from them as explicit as possible. An actor should try to determine, before events occur, what evidence would count for and against his theories. By knowing what to expect he would know what to be surprised by, and surprise could indicate to that actor that his beliefs needed reevaluation.[7]

A fourth safeguard is more complex. The decision-maker should try to prevent individuals and organizations from letting their main task, political future, and identity become tied to specific theories and images of other actors.[8] If this occurs, subgoals originally sought for their contribution to higher ends will take on value of their own, and information indicating possible alternative routes to the original goals will not be carefully considered. For example, the U.S. Forest Service was unable to carry out its original purpose as effectively when it began to see its distinctive competence not in promoting the best use of lands and forests but rather in preventing all types of forest fires.[9]

Organizations that claim to be unbiased may not realize the extent to which their definition of their role has become involved with certain beliefs about the world. Allen Dulles is a victim of this lack of understanding when he says, "I grant that we are all creatures of prejudice, including CIA officials, but by entrusting intelligence coordination to our central intelligence service, which is excluded from policy-making and is married to no particular military hardware, we can avoid, to the greatest possible extent, the bending of facts obtained through intelligence to suit a particular occupational viewpoint."[10] This statement overlooks the fact that the CIA has developed a certain view of international relations and of the cold war which maximizes the importance of its information-gathering, espionage, and subversive activities. Since the CIA would lose its unique place in the government if it were decided that the "back alleys" of world politics were no longer vital to U.S. security, it is not surprising that the organization interprets information in a way that stresses the continued need for its techniques.

Fifth, decision-makers should realize the validity and implications of Roberta Wohlstetter's argument that "a willingness to play with material from different angles and in the context of unpopular as well as popular hypotheses is an essential ingredient of a good detective, whether the end is the solution of a crime or an intelligence estimate."[11] However, it is often difficult, psychologically and politically, for any one person to do this. Since a decision-maker usually cannot get "unbiased" treatments of data, he should instead seek to structure conflicting biases into the decision-making process. The decision-maker, in other words, should have devil's advocates around. Just as, as Neustadt points out,[12] the decision-maker will want to create conflicts among his subordinates in order to make appropriate choices, so he will also want to ensure that incoming information is examined from many different perspectives with many different hypotheses in mind. To some extent this kind of examination will be done automatically through the divergence of goals, training, experience, and information that exists in any large organization. But in many cases this divergence will not be sufficient. The views of those analyzing the data will still be too homogeneous, and the decision-maker will have to go out of his way not only to cultivate but to create differing viewpoints.

While all that would be needed would be to have some people examining the data trying to validate unpopular hypotheses, it would probably be more effective if they actually believed and had a stake in the views they were trying to support. If in 1941 someone had had the task of proving the view that Japan would attack Pearl Harbor, the government might have been less surprised by the attack. And only a person who was out to show that Russia would take objectively great risks would have been apt to note that several ships with especially large hatches going to Cuba were riding high in the water, indicating the presence of a bulky but light cargo that was not likely to be anything other than strategic missiles. And many people who doubt the wisdom of the administration's Vietnam policy would be somewhat reassured if there were people in the government who searched the statements and actions of both sides in an effort to prove that North Vietnam was willing to negotiate and that the official interpretation of such moves as the Communist activities during the Têt truce of 1967 was incorrect.

Of course all these safeguards involve costs. They would divert resources from other tasks and would increase internal dissension. Determining whether these costs would be worth the gains would depend on a detailed analysis of how the suggested safeguards might be implemented. Even if they were adopted by a government, of course, they would not eliminate the chance of misperception. However, the safeguards would make it more likely that national decision-makers would make conscious choices about the way data were interpreted rather than merely assuming that they can be seen in only one way and can mean only one thing. Statesmen would thus be reminded of alternative images of others just as they are constantly reminded of alternative policies.

These safeguards are partly based on Hypothesis 3: actors can more easily assimilate into their established image of another actor information contradicting that image if the information is transmitted and considered bit by bit than if it comes all at once. In the former case, each piece of discrepant data can be coped with as it arrives and each of the conflicts with the prevailing view will be small enough to go unnoticed, to be dismissed as unimportant, or to necessitate at most a slight modification of the image (e.g., addition of exceptions to the rule). When the information arrives in a block, the contradiction between it and the prevailing view is apt to be much clearer and the probability of major cognitive reorganization will be higher.

Sources of Concepts

An actor's perceptual thresholds—and thus the images that ambiguous information is apt to produce—are influenced by what he has experienced and learned about.[13] If one actor is to perceive that another fits in a given category he must first have, or develop, a concept for that category. We can usefully distinguish three levels at which a concept can be present or absent. First, the concept can be completely missing. The actor's cognitive structure may not include anything corresponding to the phenomenon he is encountering. This situation can occur not only in science fiction, but also in a world of rapid change or in the meeting of two dissimilar systems. Thus China's image of the Western world was extremely

inaccurate in the mid-nineteenth century, her learning was very slow, and her responses were woefully inadequate. The West was spared a similar struggle only because it had the power to reshape the system it encountered. Once the actor clearly sees one instance of the new phenomenon, he is apt to recognize it much more quickly in the future.[14] Second, the actor can know about a concept but not believe that it reflects an actual phenomenon. Thus Communist and Western decision-makers are each aware of the other's explanation of how his system functions, but do not think that the concept corresponds to reality. Communist elites, furthermore, deny that anything *could* correspond to the democracies' description of themselves. Third, the actor may hold a concept, but not believe that another actor fills it at the present moment. Thus the British and French statesmen of the 1930's held a concept of states with unlimited ambitions. They realized that Napoleons were possible, but they did not think Hitler belonged in that category. Hypothesis 4 distinguishes these three cases: misperception is most difficult to correct in the case of a missing concept and least difficult to correct in the case of a recognized but presumably unfilled concept. All other things being equal (e.g., the degree to which the concept is central to the actor's cognitive structure), the first case requires more cognitive reorganization than does the second, and the second requires more reorganization than the third.

However, this hypothesis does not mean that learning will necessarily be slowest in the first case, for if the phenomena are totally new the actor may make such grossly inappropriate responses that he will quickly acquire information clearly indicating that he is faced with something he does not understand. And the sooner the actor realizes that things are not—or may not be—what they seem, the sooner he is apt to correct his image.[15]

Three main sources contribute to decision-makers' concepts of international relations and of other states and influence the level of their perceptual thresholds for various phenomena.

First, an actor's beliefs about his own domestic political system are apt to be important. In some cases, like that of the USSR, the decision-makers' concepts are tied to an ideology that explicitly provides a frame of reference for viewing foreign affairs. Even where this is not the case, experience with his own system will partly determine what the actor is familiar with and what he is apt to perceive in others. Louis Hartz claims, "It is the absence of the experience of social revolution which is at the heart of the whole American dilemma. . . . In a whole series of specific ways it enters into our difficulty of communication with the rest of the world. We find it difficult to understand Europe's 'social question'. . . . We are not familiar with the deeper social struggles of Asia and hence tend to interpret even reactionary regimes as 'democratic.'"[16] Similarly, George Kennan argues that in World War I the Allied, powers, and especially America, could not understand the bitterness and violence of others' internal conflicts: ". . . The inability of the Allied statesmen to picture to themselves the passions of the Russian civil war [was partly caused by the fact that] we represent . . . a society in which the manifestations of evil have been carefully buried and sublimated in the social behavior of people, as in their very consciousness. For this reason, probably, despite our widely traveled and outwardly cosmopolitan lives, the mainsprings of political behavior in such a country as Russia tend to remain concealed from our vision."[17]

Second, concepts will be supplied by the actor's previous experiences. An experiment from another field illustrates this. Dearborn and Simon presented business executives from various divisions (e.g., sales, accounting, production) with the same hypothetical data and asked them for an analysis and recommendations from the standpoint of what would be best for the company as a whole. The executives' views heavily reflected their departmental perspectives.[18] William W. Kaufmann shows how the perceptions of Ambassador Joseph Kennedy were affected by his past: "As befitted a former chairman of the Securities Exchange and Maritime Commissions, his primary interest lay in economic matters. . . . The revolutionary character of the Nazi regime was not a phenomenon that he could easily grasp. . . . It was far simpler, and more in accord with his own premises, to explain German aggressiveness in economic terms. The Third Reich was dissatisfied, authoritarian, and expansive largely because her economy was unsound."[19] Similarly it has been argued that Chamberlain was slow to recognize Hitler's intentions partly because of the limiting nature of his personal background and business experiences. The impact of training and experience seems to be demonstrated when the background of the appeasers is compared to that of their opponents. One difference stands out: "A substantially higher percentage of the anti-appeasers (irrespective of class origins) had the kind of knowledge which comes from close acquaintance, mainly professional, with foreign affairs."[20] Since members of the diplomatic corps are responsible for meeting threats to the nation's security before these grow to major proportions and since they have learned about cases in which aggressive states were not recognized as such until very late, they may be prone to interpret ambiguous data as showing that others are aggressive. It should be stressed that we cannot say that the professionals of the 1930's were more apt to make accurate judgments of other states. Rather, they may have been more sensitive to the chance that others were aggressive. They would then rarely take an aggressor for a status-quo power, but would more often make the opposite error. Thus in the years before World War I the permanent officials in the British Foreign Office overestimated German aggressiveness.[21]

A parallel demonstration in psychology of the impact of training on perception is presented by an experiment in which ambiguous pictures were shown to both advanced and beginning police-administration students. The advanced group perceived more violence in the pictures than did the beginners. The probable explanation is that "the law enforcer may come to accept crime as a familiar personal experience, one which he himself is not surprised to encounter. The acceptance of crime as a familiar experience in turn increases the ability or readiness to perceive violence where clues to it are potentially available."[22] This experiment lends weight to the view that the British diplomats' sensitivity to aggressive states was not totally a product of personnel selection procedures.

A third source of concepts, which frequently will be the most directly relevant to a decision-maker's perception of international relations, is international history. As Henry Kissinger points out, one reason why statesmen were so slow to recognize the threat posed by Napoleon was that previous events had accustomed them only to actors who wanted to modify the existing system, not overthrow it.[23] The other side of the coin is even more striking: historical traumas can heavily influence future perceptions. They can either establish a state's image of the other state involved or can be used as analogies. An example of the former case is provided by the fact that for at least ten years after the Franco-Prussian War most of Europe's statesmen felt that Bismarck had aggressive plans when in fact his main goal was to protect the status quo. Of course the evidence was ambiguous. The post-1871 Bismarckian maneuvers, which were designed to keep peace, looked not unlike the pre-1871 maneuvers designed to set the stage for war. But that the post-1871 maneuvers were seen as indicating aggressive plans is largely attributable to the impact of Bismarck's earlier actions on the statesmen's image of him.

A state's previous unfortunate experience with a type of danger can sensitize it to other examples of that danger. While this sensitivity may lead the state to avoid the mistake it committed in the past, it may also lead it mistakenly to believe that the present situation is like the past one. Santayana's maxim could be turned around: "Those who remember the past are condemned to make the opposite mistakes." As Paul Kecskemeti shows, both defenders and critics of the unconditional surrender plan of the Second World War thought in terms of the conditions of World War I.[24] Annette Baker Fox found that

the Scandinavian countries' neutrality policies in World War II were strongly influenced by their experiences in the previous war, even though vital aspects of the two situations were different. Thus "Norway's success [during the First World War] in remaining non-belligerent though pro-Allied gave the Norwegians confidence that their country could again stay out of war."[25] And the lesson drawn from the unfortunate results of this policy was an important factor in Norway's decision to join NATO.

The application of the Munich analogy to various contemporary events has been much commented on, and I do not wish to argue the substantive points at stake. But it seems clear that the probabilities that any state is facing an aggressor who has to be met by force are not altered by the career of Hitler and the history of the 1930's. Similarly the probability of an aggressor's announcing his plans is not increased (if anything, it is decreased) by the fact that Hitler wrote *Mein Kampf.* Yet decision-makers are more sensitive to these possibilities, and thus more apt to perceive ambiguous evidence as indicating they apply to a given case, than they would have been had there been no Nazi Germany.

Historical analogies often precede, rather than follow, a careful analysis of a situation (e.g., Truman's initial reaction to the news of the invasion of South Korea was to think of the Japanese invasion of Manchuria). Noting this precedence, however, does not show us which of many analogies will come to a decision-maker's mind. Truman could have thought of nineteenth-century European wars that were of no interest to the United States. Several factors having nothing to do with the event under consideration influence what analogies a decision-maker is apt to make. One factor is the number of cases similar to the analogy with which the decision-maker is familiar. Another is the importance of the past event to the political system of which the decision-maker is a part. The more times such an event occurred and the greater its consequences were, the more a decision-maker will be sensitive to the particular danger involved and the more he will be apt to see ambiguous stimuli as indicating another instance of this kind of event. A third factor is the degree of the decision-maker's personal involvement in the past case—in time, energy, ego, and position. The last-mentioned variable will affect not only the event's impact on the decision-maker's cognitive structure, but also the way he perceives the event and the lesson he draws. Someone who was involved in getting troops into South Korea after the attack will remember the Korean War differently from someone who was involved in considering the possible use of nuclear weapons or in deciding what messages should be sent to the Chinese. Greater personal involvement will usually give the event greater impact, especially if the decision-maker's own views were validated by the event. One need not accept a total application of learning theory to nations to believe that "nothing fails like success."[26] It also seems likely that if many critics argued at the time that the decision-maker was wrong, he will be even more apt to see other situations in terms of the original event. For example, because Anthony Eden left the government on account of his views and was later shown to have been correct, he probably was more apt to see as Hitlers other leaders with whom he had conflicts (e.g., Nasser). A fourth factor is the degree to which the analogy is compatible with the rest of his belief system. A fifth is the absence of alternative concepts and analogies. Individuals and states vary in the amount of direct or indirect political experience they have had which can provide different ways of interpreting data. Decision-makers who are aware of multiple possibilities of states' intentions may be less likely to seize on an analogy prematurely. The perception of citizens of nations like the United States which have relatively little history of international politics may be more apt to be heavily influenced by the few major international events that have been important to their country.

The first three factors indicate that an event is more apt to shape present perceptions if it occurred in the recent rather than the remote past. If it occurred recently, the statesman will then know about it at first hand even if he was not involved in the making of policy at the time. Thus if generals are prepared to fight the last war, diplomats may be prepared to avoid the last war. Part of the Anglo-French reaction to Hitler can be explained by the prevailing beliefs that the First World War was to a large extent caused by misunderstandings and could have been avoided by farsighted and nonbelligerent diplomacy. And part of the Western perception of Russia and China can be explained by the view that appeasement was an inappropriate response to Hitler.[27]

The Evoked Set

The way people perceive data is influenced not only by their cognitive structure and theories about other actors but also by what they are concerned with at the time they receive the information. Information is evaluated in light of the small part of the person's memory that is presently active—the "evoked set." My perceptions of the dark streets I pass walking home from the movies will be different if the film I saw had dealt with spies than if it had been a comedy. If I am working on aiding a country's education system and I hear someone talk about the need for economic development in that state, I am apt to think he is concerned with education, whereas if I had been working on, say, trying to achieve political stability in that country, I would have placed his remarks in that framework.[28]

Thus Hypothesis 5 states that when messages are sent from a different background of concerns and information than is possessed by the receiver, misunderstanding is likely. Person A and person B will read the same message quite differently if A has seen several related messages that B does not know about. This difference will be compounded if, as is frequently the case, A and B each assume that the other has the same background he does. This means that misperception can occur even when deception is neither intended nor expected. Thus Roberta Wohlstetter found not only that different parts of the United States government had different perceptions of data about Japan's intentions and messages partly because they saw the incoming information in very different contexts, but also that officers in the field misunderstood warnings from Washington: "Washington advised General Short [in Pearl Harbor] on November 27 to expect 'hostile action' at any moment, by which it meant 'attack on American possessions from without,' but General Short understood this phrase to mean 'sabotage.'"[29] Washington did not realize the extent to which Pearl Harbor considered the danger of sabotage to be primary, and furthermore it incorrectly believed that General Short had received the intercepts of the secret Japanese diplomatic messages available in Washington which indicated that surprise attack was a distinct possibility. Another implication of this hypothesis is that if important information is known to only part of the government of state A and part of the government of state B, international messages may be misunderstood by those parts of the receiver's government that do not match, in the information they have, the part of the sender's government that dispatched the message.[30]

Two additional hypotheses can be drawn from the problems of those sending messages. Hypothesis 6 states that when people spend a great deal of time drawing up a plan or making a decision, they tend to think that the message about it they wish to convey will be clear to the receiver.[31] Since they are aware of what is to them the important pattern in their actions, they often feel that the pattern will be equally obvious to others, and they overlook the degree to which the message is apparent to them only because they know what to look for. Those who have not participated in the endless meetings may not understand what information the sender is trying to convey. George Quester has shown how the German and, to a lesser extent, the British desire to maintain target limits on bombing in the first eighteen months of World War II was undermined partly by the fact that each side knew the limits it was seeking and its own reasons for any

apparent "exceptions" (e.g., the German attack on Rotterdam) and incorrectly felt that these limits and reasons were equally clear to the other side.[32]

Hypothesis 7 holds that actors often do not realize that actions intended to project a given image may not have the desired effect because the actions themselves do not turn out as planned. Thus even without appreciable impact of different cognitive structures and backgrounds, an action may convey an unwanted message. For example, a country's representatives may not follow instructions and so may give others impressions contrary to those the home government wished to convey. The efforts of Washington and Berlin to settle their dispute over Samoa in the late 1880's were complicated by the provocative behavior of their agents on the spot. These agents not only increased the intensity of the local conflict, but led the decision-makers to become more suspicious of the other state because they tended to assume that their agents were obeying instructions and that the actions of the other side represented official policy. In such cases both sides will believe that the other is reading hostility into a policy of theirs which is friendly. Similarly, Quester's study shows that the attempt to limit bombing referred to above failed partly because neither side was able to bomb as accurately as it thought it could and thus did not realize the physical effects of its actions.[33]

Further Hypotheses from the Perspective of the Perceiver

From the perspective of the perceiver several other hypotheses seem to hold. Hypothesis 8 is that there is an overall tendency for decision-makers to see other states as more hostile than they are.[34] There seem to be more cases of statesmen incorrectly believing others are planning major acts against their interest than of statesmen being lulled by a potential aggressor. There are many reasons for this which are too complex to be treated here (e.g., some parts of the bureaucracy feel it is their responsibility to be suspicious of all other states; decision-makers often feel they are "playing it safe" to believe and act as though the other state were hostile in questionable cases; and often, when people do not feel they are a threat to others, they find it difficult to believe that others may see them as a threat). It should be noted, however, that decision-makers whose perceptions are described by this hypothesis would not necessarily further their own values by trying to correct for this tendency. The values of possible outcomes as well as their probabilities must be considered, and it may be that the probability of an unnecessary arms-tension cycle arising out of misperceptions, multiplied by the costs of such a cycle, may seem less to decision-makers than the probability of incorrectly believing another state is friendly, multiplied by the costs of this eventuality.

Hypothesis 9 states that actors tend to see the behavior of others as more centralized, disciplined, and coordinated than it is. This hypothesis holds true in related ways. Frequently, too many complex events are squeezed into a perceived pattern. Actors are hesitant to admit or even see that particular incidents cannot be explained by their theories.[35] Those events not caused by factors that are important parts of the perceiver's image are often seen as though they were. Further, actors see others as more internally united than they in fact are and generally overestimate the degree to which others are following a coherent policy. The degree to which the other side's policies are the product of internal bargaining,[36] internal misunderstandings, or subordinates' not following instructions is underestimated. This is the case partly because actors tend to be unfamiliar with the details of another state's policy-making processes. Seeing only the finished product, they find it simpler to try to construct a rational explanation for the policies, even though they know that such an analysis could not explain their own policies.[37]

Familiarity also accounts for Hypothesis 10: because a state gets most of its information about the other state's policies from the other's foreign office, it tends to take the foreign office's position for the stand of the other government as a whole. In many cases this perception will be an accurate one, but when the other government is divided or when the other foreign office is acting without specific authorization, misperception may result. For example, part of the reason why in 1918 Allied governments incorrectly thought "that the Japanese were preparing to take action [in Siberia], if need be, with agreement with the British and French alone, disregarding the absence of American consent,"[38] was that Allied ambassadors had talked mostly with Foreign Minister Motono, who was among the minority of the Japanese favoring this policy. Similarly, America's NATO allies may have gained an inaccurate picture of the degree to which the American government was committed to the MLF because they had greatest contact with parts of the government that strongly favored the MLF. And states that tried to get information about Nazi foreign policy from German diplomats were often misled because these officials were generally ignorant of or out of sympathy with Hitler's plans. The Germans and the Japanese sometimes purposely misinformed their own ambassadors in order to deceive their enemies more effectively.

Hypothesis 11 states that actors tend to overestimate the degree to which others are acting in response to what they themselves do when the others behave in accordance with the actor's desires; but when the behavior of the other is undesired, it is usually seen as derived from internal forces. If the *effect* of another's action is to injure or threaten the first side, the first side is apt to believe that such was the other's *purpose*. An example of the first part of the hypothesis is provided by Kennan's account of the activities of official and unofficial American representatives who protested to the new Bolshevik government against several of its actions. When the Soviets changed their position, these representatives felt it was largely because of their influence.[39] This sort of interpretation can be explained not only by the fact that it is gratifying to the individual making it, but also, taking the other side of the coin mentioned in Hypothesis 9, by the fact that the actor is most familiar with his own input into the other's decision and has less knowledge of other influences. The second part of Hypothesis 11 is illustrated by the tendency of actors to believe that the hostile behavior of others is to be explained by the other side's motives and not by its reaction to the first side. Thus Chamberlain did not see that Hitler's behavior was related in part to his belief that the British were weak. More common is the failure to see that the other side is reacting out of fear of the first side, which can lead to self-fulfilling prophecies and spirals of misperception and hostility.

This difficulty is often compounded by an implication of Hypothesis 12: when actors have intentions that they do not try to conceal from others, they tend to assume that others accurately perceive these intentions. Only rarely do they believe that others may be reacting to a much less favorable image of themselves than they think they are projecting.[40]

For state A to understand how state B perceives A's policy is often difficult because such understanding may involve a conflict with A's image of itself. Raymond Sontag argues that Anglo-German relations before World War I deteriorated partly because "the British did not like to think of themselves as selfish, or unwilling to tolerate 'legitimate' German expansion. The Germans did not like to think of themselves as aggressive, or unwilling to recognize 'legitimate' British vested interest."[41]

Hypothesis 13 suggests that if it is hard for an actor to believe that the other can see him as a menace, it is often even harder for him to see that issues important to him are not important to others. While he may know that another actor is on an opposing team, it may be more difficult for him to realize that the other is playing an entirely different game. This is especially true when the game he is playing seems vital to him.[42]

The final hypothesis, Hypothesis 14, is as follows: actors tend to overlook the fact that evidence consistent with their theories may also be consistent with other views. When choosing

between two theories we have to pay attention only to data that cannot be accounted for by one of the theories. But it is common to find people claiming as proof of their theories data that could also support alternative views. This phenomenon is related to the point made earlier that any single bit of information can be interpreted only within a framework of hypotheses and theories. And while it is true that "we may without a vicious circularity accept some datum as a fact because it conforms to the very law for which it counts as another confirming instance, and reject an allegation of fact because it is already excluded by law,"[43] we should be careful lest we forget that a piece of information seems in many cases to confirm a certain hypothesis only because we already believe that hypothesis to be correct and that the information can with as much validity support a different hypothesis. For example, one of the reasons why the German attack on Norway took both that country and England by surprise, even though they had detected German ships moving toward Norway, was that they expected not an attack but an attempt by the Germans to break through the British blockade and reach the Atlantic. The initial course of the ships was consistent with either plan, but the British and Norwegians took this course to mean that their predictions were being borne out.[44] This is not to imply that the interpretation made was foolish, but only that the decision-makers should have been aware that the evidence was also consistent with an invasion and should have had a bit less confidence in their views.

The longer the ships would have to travel the same route whether they were going to one or another of two destinations, the more information would be needed to determine their plans. Taken as a metaphor, this incident applies generally to the treatment of evidence. Thus as long as Hitler made demands for control only of ethnically German areas, his actions could be explained either by the hypothesis that he had unlimited ambitions or by the hypothesis that he wanted to unite all the Germans. But actions against non-Germans (e.g., the takeover of Czechoslovakia in

March 1938) could not be accounted for by the latter hypothesis. And it was this action that convinced the appeasers that Hitler had to be stopped. It is interesting to speculate on what the British reaction would have been had Hitler left Czechoslovakia alone for a while and instead made demands on Poland similar to those he eventually made in the summer of 1939. The two paths would then still not have diverged, and further misperception could have occurred.

NOTES

1. Floyd Allport, *Theories of Perception and the Concept of Structure* (New York 1955), 382; Ole Holsti, "Cognitive Dynamics and Images of the Enemy," in David Finlay, Ole Holsti, and Richard Fagen, *Enemies in Politics* (Chicago 1967), 70.
2. For a use of this concept in political communication, see Roberta Wohlstetter, *Pearl Harbor* (Stanford 1962).
3. See, for example, Donald Campbell, "Systematic Error on the Part of Human Links in Communications Systems," *Information and Control*, I (1958), 346–50; and Leo Postman, "The Experimental Analysis of Motivational Factors in Perception," in Judson S. Brown, ed., *Current Theory and Research in Motivation* (Lincoln, Neb., 1953), 59–108.
4. Dale Wyatt and Donald Campbell, "A Study of Interviewer Bias as Related to Interviewer's Expectations and Own Opinions," *International Journal of Opinion and Attitude Research*, IV (Spring 1950), 77–83.
5. Max Jacobson, *The Diplomacy of the Winter War* (Cambridge, Mass., 1961), 136–39.
6. Raymond Aron, *Peace and War* (Garden City 1966), 29.
7. Cf. Kuhn, *The Structure of Scientific Revolution*, 65. A fairly high degree of knowledge is needed before one can state precise expectations. One indication of the lack of international relations theory is that most of us are not sure what "naturally" flows from our the-

ories and what constitutes either "puzzles" to be further explored with the paradigm or "anomalies" that cast doubt on the basic theories.
8. See Philip Selznick, *Leadership in Administration* (Evanston 1957).
9. Ashley Schiff, *Fire and Water: Scientific Heresy in the Forest Service* (Cambridge, Mass., 1962). Despite its title, this book is a fascinating and valuable study.
10. *The Craft of Intelligence* (New York 1963), 53.
11. P. 302. See Beveridge, 93, for a discussion of the idea that the scientist should keep in mind as many hypotheses as possible when conducting and analyzing experiments.
12. *Presidential Power* (New York 1960).
13. Most psychologists argue that this influence also holds for perception of shapes. For data showing that people in different societies differ in respect to their predisposition to experience certain optical illusions and for a convincing argument that this difference can be explained by the societies' different physical environments, which have led their people to develop different patterns of drawing inferences from ambiguous visual cues, see Marshall Segall, Donald Campbell, and Melville Herskovits, *The Influence of Culture on Visual Perceptions* (Indianapolis 1966).
14. Thus when Bruner and Postman's subjects first were presented with incongruous playing cards (i.e., cards in which symbols and colors of the suits were not matching, producing red spades or black diamonds), long exposure times were necessary for correct identification. But once a subject correctly perceived the card and added this type of card to his repertoire of categories, he was able to identify other incongruous cards much more quickly. For an analogous example—in this case, changes in the analysis of aerial reconnaissance photographs of an enemy's secret weapons-testing facilities produced by the belief that a previously unknown object may be present—see David Irving, *The Mare's Nest* (Boston 1964), 66–67, 274–75.

15. Bruner and Postman, 220.

16. *The Liberal Tradition in America* (New York 1955), 306.

17. *Russia and the West Under Lenin and Stalin* (New York 1962), 142–43.

18. DeWitt Dearborn and Herbert Simon, "Selective Perception: A Note on the Departmental Identification of Executives," *Sociometry*, XXI (June 1958), 140–44.

19. "Two American Ambassadors: Bullitt and Kennedy," in Craig and Gilbert, 358–59.

20. Donald Lammer, *Explaining Munich* (Stanford 1966), 15.

21. George Monger, *The End of Isolation* (London 1963). I am also indebted to Frederick Collignon for his unpublished manuscript and several conversations on this point.

22. Hans Toch and Richard Schulte, "Readiness to Perceive Violence as a Result of Police Training," *British Journal of Psychology*, LII (November 1961), 392 (original italics omitted). It should be stressed that one cannot say whether or not the advanced police students perceived the pictures "accurately." The point is that their training predisposed them to see violence in ambiguous situations. Whether on balance they would make fewer perceptual errors and better decisions is very hard to determine. For an experiment showing that training can lead people to "recognize" an expected stimulus even when that stimulus is in fact not shown, see Israel Goldiamond and William F. Hawkins, "Vexierversuch: The Log Relationship between Word-Frequency and Recognition Obtained in the Absence of Stimulus Words," *Journal of Experimental Psychology*, LVI (December 1958), 457–63.

23. *A World Restored* (New York 1964), 2–3.

24. *Strategic Surrender* (New York 1964), 215–41.

25. *The Power of Small States* (Chicago 1959), 81.

26. William Inge, *Outspoken Essays*, First Series (London 1923), 88.

27. Of course, analogies themselves are not "unmoved movers." The interpretation of past events is not automatic and is informed by general views of international relations and complex judgments. And just as beliefs about the past influence the present, views about the present influence interpretations of history. It is difficult to determine the degree to which the United States' interpretation of the reasons it went to war in 1917 influenced American foreign policy in the 1920's and 1930's and how much the isolationism of that period influenced the histories of the war.

28. For some psychological experiments on this subject, see Jerome Bruner and A. Leigh Minturn, "Perceptual Identification and Perceptual Organization" *Journal of General Psychology*, LIII (July 1955), 22–28; Seymour Feshbach and Robert Singer, "The Effects of Fear Arousal and Suppression of Fear upon Social Perception," *Journal of Abnormal and Social Psychology*, LV (November 1957), 283–88; and Elsa Sippoal, "A Group Study of Some Effects of Preparatory Sets," *Psychology Monographs*, XLVI, No. 210 (1935), 27–28. For a general discussion of the importance of the perceiver's evoked set, see Postman, 87.

29. Pp. 73–74.

30. For example, Roger Hilsman points out, "Those who knew of the peripheral reconnaissance flights that probed Soviet air defenses during the Eisenhower administration and the U-2 flights over the Soviet Union itself . . . were better able to understand some of the things the Soviets were saying and doing than people who did not know of these activities" (*To Move a Nation* [Garden City 1967], 66). But it is also possible that those who knew about the U-2 flights at times misinterpreted Soviet messages by incorrectly believing that the sender was influenced by, or at least knew of, these flights.

31. I am grateful to Thomas Schelling for discussion on this point.

32. *Deterrence before Hiroshima* (New York 1966), 105–22.

33. *Ibid.*

34. For a slightly different formulation of this view, see Holsti, 27.

35. The Soviets consciously hold an extreme version of this view and seem to believe that nothing is accidental. See the discussion in Nathan Leites, *A Study of Bolshevism* (Glencoe 1953), 67–73.

36. A. W. Marshall criticizes Western explanations of Soviet military posture for failing to take this into account. See his "Problems of Estimating Military Power," a paper presented at the 1966 Annual Meeting of the American Political Science Association, 16.

37. It has also been noted that in labor-management disputes both sides may be apt to believe incorrectly that the other is controlled from above, either from the international union office or from the company's central headquarters (Robert Blake, Herbert Shepard, and Jane Mouton, *Managing Intergroup Conflict in Industry* [Houston 1964], 182). It has been further noted that both Democratic and Republican members of the House tend to see the other party as the one that is more disciplined and united (Charles Clapp, *The Congressman* [Washington 1963], 17–19).

38. George Kennan, *Russia Leaves the War* (New York 1967), 484.

39. *Ibid.*, 404, 408, 500.

40. Herbert Butterfield notes that these assumptions can contribute to the spiral of "Hobbesian fear. . . . You yourself may vividly feel the terrible fear that you have of the other party, but you cannot enter into the other man's counter-fear, or even understand why he should be particularly nervous. For you know that you yourself mean him no harm, and that you want nothing from him save guarantees for your own safety; and it is never possible for you to realize or remember properly that since he cannot see the inside of your mind, he can never have the same assurance of your intentions that you have" (*History and Human Conflict* [London 1951], 20).

41. *European Diplomatic History 1871–1932* (New York 1933), 125. It takes great mental effort to realize that actions which seem only the natural consequence of defending your vital interests can look to others as though you are refusing them any chance of increasing their influence. In rebutting the famous Crowe "balance of power" memorandum of 1907, which justified a policy of "containing" Germany on the grounds that she was a threat to British national security, Sanderson, a former permanent undersecretary in the Foreign Office, wrote, "It has sometimes seemed to me that to a foreigner reading our press the British Empire must appear in the light of some huge giant sprawling all over the globe, with gouty fingers and toes stretching in every direction, which cannot be approached without eliciting a scream" (quoted in Monger, 315). But few other Englishmen could be convinced that others might see them this way.

42. George Kennan makes clear that in 1918 this kind of difficulty was partly responsible for the inability of either the Allies or the new Bolshevik government to understand the motivations of the other side: "There is . . . nothing in nature more egocentrical than the embattled democracy. . . . It . . . tends to attach to its own cause an absolute value which distorts its own vision of everything else. . . . It will readily be seen that people who have got themselves into this frame of mind have little understanding for the issues of any contest other than the one in which they are involved. The idea of people wasting time and substance on any *other* issue seems to them preposterous" (*Russia and the West*, 11–12).

43. Kaplan, 89.

44. Johan Jorgen Holst, "Surprise, Signals, and Reaction: The Attack on Norway," *Cooperation and Conflict*, No. 1 (1966), 34. The Germans made a similar mistake in November 1942 when they interpreted the presence of an Allied convoy in the Mediterranean as confirming their belief that Malta would be resupplied. They thus were taken by surprise when landings took place in North Africa (William Langer, *Our Vichy Gamble* [New York 1966], 365).

ELIZABETH N. SAUNDERS

Transformative Choices: Leaders and the Origins of Intervention Strategy

One of the most contentious issues in U.S. foreign policy has been the use of military force to intervene in the domestic affairs of other states. U.S. military interventions since 1945 have varied significantly, however, in how deeply they intrude on the domestic institutions of target states. Some interventions involved significant interference in other states' domestic affairs (from the Vietnam War to the operations in Haiti and the Balkans in the 1990s); in other cases, the United States rejected such interference (as in the 1991 Persian Gulf War). More generally, some great power military interventions explicitly try to transform the domestic institutions of the states they target, whereas others do not, attempting only to reverse foreign policies or resolve disputes without trying to reshape the internal landscape of the target state.

The choice of intervention strategy is crucial not only for the target state but also for the intervening state itself. Choosing a strategy ill-suited to the conflict or for which the intervening state is ill-prepared can have disastrous consequences for both intervener and target. The choice of strategy is likely to remain central to future intervention debates, even after Iraq. Indeed, Richard Haass, president of the Council on Foreign Relations, asserts that choices such as whether to pursue democracy or stability—one manifestation of the debate over intervention strategy—lie along the "single most important fault line in American foreign policy today."[1]

From *International Security* 34, no. 2 (Fall 2009): 119–161. Some of the author's notes have been omitted.

This article argues that it is impossible to fully understand both when and how states intervene without exploring a crucial but often-overlooked factor in international relations: the role of individual leaders. Even among U.S. interventions, successive American presidents have approached the same conflict differently. For example, George H.W. Bush limited the U.S. intervention in Somalia to humanitarian aid, whereas Bill Clinton at least initially allowed the mission to expand to address underlying internal problems. Although leaders frequently profess otherwise, most great power military interventions in smaller powers are "wars of choice"—that is, they do not result from a direct or existential threat to the state. Leaders play a critical role in choosing where and how states respond to other, more indirect threats with intervention. Furthermore, theories relying on relatively stable or slow-changing factors such as the structure of the international system or regime type cannot fully account for changes in a state's intervention choices over time. Moving the focus of the analysis to individual leaders can help to address this variation.

In the last few decades, however, international relations theorists—with the notable exception of those who take a psychological approach—have rarely focused on leaders. Some scholars do not expect leaders to play a significant role independent of the domestic or international setting; others recognize that leaders matter, but despair of making parsimonious, generalizable predictions about individuals.[2]

This article charts a middle course between the two extremes of studying leaders as a series of "great men," on the one hand, and excluding them by assuming that they respond to domestic or international conditions in similar ways, on the other. The article contributes to a recent revival of interest in the role of leaders in international relations by providing a simple but powerful typology of leaders that addresses changes in how states intervene over time. The critical variable centers on how leaders perceive threats: Do they believe that the internal characteristics of other states are the ultimate source of threats? This variation in leaders' causal beliefs about the origin of threats yields two ideal-typical ways to assess and prioritize the many threats states confront. "Internally focused" leaders see a causal connection between threatening foreign and security policies and the internal organization of states, and thus are more willing to undertake "transformative" interventions, in which the intervening state is deeply involved in the building or rebuilding of domestic institutions in the target state. In contrast, "externally focused" leaders diagnose threats directly from the foreign and security policies of other states, and thus are more likely to pursue "nontransformative" strategies that aim only to resolve a given conflict with minimal involvement in domestic affairs.

These different causal beliefs about the origin of threats shape the cost-benefit calculation leaders make when they confront intervention decisions, in two ways. First, causal beliefs influence the value leaders place on transforming target states. Second, causal beliefs affect how leaders allocate scarce resources that influence preparedness for different intervention strategies. * * * Thus leaders' causal beliefs about the origin of threats have profound consequences for the decision to intervene and for the choice of intervention strategy, as well as implications for the probability of intervention success.

Intuitively leaders seem crucial to understanding the choice of intervention strategy. Yet demonstrating how their beliefs act as an independent influence on the way states intervene is a challenge. To isolate the effect of leaders, I examine two U.S. presidents during the Cold War—John F. Kennedy and Lyndon B. Johnson—allowing me to hold constant domestic institutions, great power status, and the structure of the international system. The Kennedy-Johnson comparison provides strong analytical leverage. To avoid several problems in studying beliefs, I measure leaders' causal beliefs in the period before they arrive in office, using archival and historical sources. As Henry Kissinger put it, "The convictions that leaders have formed before reaching high office are the intellectual capital they will consume as long as they continue in office."[3] The empirical discussion illustrates one manifestation of the argument: leaders confronting the same conflict may arrive at different diagnoses of threat, and thus choose different strategies. I examine how Kennedy and Johnson approached Vietnam, a difficult case for the theory. Kennedy chose a transformative strategy of deep interference in South Vietnamese affairs, whereas Johnson pursued a nontransformative strategy that concentrated on defeating aggression from the North. Illustrating that leaders differed on a question as fundamental as the nature of a threat to national security, and that this difference affected how they intervened, helps to demonstrate that leaders systematically influence how states use force.

* * *

Transformative versus Nontransformative Strategies

* * *

I distinguish between two ideal-typical strategies. A transformative strategy explicitly aims to interfere in or actively determine the target state's domestic institutions (most notably political institutions but also economic, social, or military institutions). National-level institutions are an obvious source of change, but transformation may occur through local-level institutions, either in tandem with national-level change or as a way to spur national-level change or bolster an existing regime. As John Owen points out, changing institutions is distinct from changing only the leader (or a small group of elites),[4] and thus the distinction between transformative and nontransformative strategies holds even at the level of regime change. Leadership change that occurs along with institutional change would qualify as transformative. But interventions that result in regime change might change only the leadership of the target state (in what might be termed a "decapitation") without fundamentally altering its domestic institutions. Similarly, interventions to shore up existing governments may interfere with domestic institutions or attempt to stop institutional change that would otherwise occur, but they may also try to protect the status quo with limited or no institutional interference.

A transformative strategy may also aim to change local-level institutions, usually as a means of achieving national-level change, but with most of the institution building occurring at the local level. Examples of local-level transformative strategies include nation building and postconflict reconstruction. Some forms of counterinsurgency, particularly population-centered counterinsurgency, explicitly incorporate institution building into the warfighting strategy, and thus can also be considered transformative.[5] * * *

* * *

In contrast, a nontransformative strategy seeks to resolve an international or civil conflict or crisis, or restrain or roll back a foreign policy action, without the explicit intention to alter domestic institutions at any level. Examples include interventions designed to liberate territory or protect local allies from outside aggression (as in the 1991 Gulf War). Leaders can also choose a nontransformative strategy in humanitarian interventions, as in George H.W. Bush's limited approach in Somalia. For a civil conflict,

a nontransformative strategy would focus on stopping the fighting or preventing international consequences such as conflict spillover, but without nation building. Of course, a nontransformative strategy may have a dramatic effect on civilians and institutions, and it is possible that internal change may occur as a by-product. Furthermore, nontransformative interventions, particularly in internal crises, usually involve some treading on the state's internal affairs. But the coding is intended to distinguish limited or collateral involvement (which may even be brutal or highly destructive) from deliberate institutional interference. * * *

Notwithstanding gradations within each class of intervention, it makes sense to treat the distinction between transformative and nontransformative strategies as dichotomous. Actively involving the military in the internal affairs of the target is fundamentally different from a more conventional battle that seeks no such interference.

Explaining Intervention Strategy

This section formulates potential alternative explanations drawn from the existing literature on intervention, and argues for a focus on the individual level.

Potential Alternative Explanations

* * * Most existing approaches do not address how states choose among different intervention strategies, or the specific issue of how deeply intervention interferes in the domestic institutions of target states.

Several theories could potentially be extended to address the choice of intervention strategy. Many formulations, however, are not well suited to explaining variation in intervention choices within states over time because they rely on international or domestic factors that are either stable or slow to change. Furthermore, although they differ widely on the specifics, many explanations suggest that states with given international or domestic characteristics respond to intervention opportunities in similar ways, leaving no independent role for leaders. For example, most realist theories share the assumption that states respond to threats in the international system—the structure of which changes rarely—in ways that depend primarily on power, regardless of who is in charge.[6] * * * Constructivists often emphasize the social or shared nature of ideas, and thus also tend to focus on long-term trends. Finnemore, for example, details how shared understandings of the purpose of intervention have evolved. But within a given time period such as the Cold War, most states share one understanding of the purpose of intervention.[7] Thus, while many of these analysts highlight important tendencies and continuities, there remain short-term changes in the way states use intervention that can provoke fierce debate.

Certain variants of existing approaches are better suited to addressing changes in intervention strategy over time, and thus form the principal alternative explanations I explore. One simple explanation is that states choose intervention strategies through a cost-benefit analysis that is independent of individual leaders. Under this structural/material conditions hypothesis, all leaders should make the same cost-benefit calculation in the face of similar situations and existing capabilities. Leaders determine strategy based on factors such as available capabilities in the intervening state or the characteristics of a given intervention opportunity (e.g., terrain).

Another set of alternative explanations involves competition among domestic actors. Here, domestic political actors, including leaders, may vary in the way they view the benefits of intervening with a given strategy. But under this domestic competition hypothesis, it is the political struggle among these actors that accounts for variation in intervention decisions. A model that focuses on how leaders vary in their interactions with bureaucracies, or how much they defer to or override organizations such as the military, could account for variation over time. Intervention

decisions might also result from interactions or logrolling among advisers, other elites, or domestic groups. Examining the behavior of different leaders who confront similar bureaucratic preferences or interact with similar advisory groups can help to sort out the relative role of leaders.

* * *

Causal Beliefs: Two Paths to Threat Perception

* * *

* * * Two different ideal-typical causal beliefs lead to perceptions of threat. One belief—held by internally focused leaders—is that the smaller power's foreign and security policies, including its alliances, are intimately connected to its internal institutions. Leaders who hold this causal belief care about threatening foreign and security policies or outcomes, but they also view the smaller power's domestic order as a genuine source of threat, in several ways. Internally focused leaders are concerned about the risk that a regional ally or friendly state will be attacked, or in the Cold War context, that a client state will fall under the other superpower's sphere of influence. But an internally focused leader would blame the smaller power's internal institutions for leaving it vulnerable to either external attack or takeover from within. Internally focused leaders may see another state's domestic institutions as more directly threatening, linking aggressive behavior to internal institutions. Institutions themselves may also be sufficient to trigger threat perception. In a democracy, for example, internally focused leaders might subscribe to the liberal proposition that nondemocracies are inherently threatening.[8] * * *

In contrast, externally focused leaders diagnose threats from other states' foreign and security policies or international orientation, and do not see a causal connection between these outcomes and the domestic institutions of smaller powers. * * * Externally focused leaders treat smaller powers relatively similarly, because in this view, any state might engage in such behavior regardless of its internal organization. Any concern an externally focused leader has about domestic crises within other states centers on the international dimensions of those crises, such as whether civil strife results in conflict spill-over, produces a change in the state's alliances, or threatens a state's ability to meet its international economic obligations. * * *

In this framework leaders may hold either causal belief. It is important to note that both leader types are usually concerned with other states' foreign and security policies and position in the international system; the difference arises from how the two types diagnose the source of those policies and outcomes. Internally focused leaders, while concerned with international behavior and outcomes, pay additional attention to domestic organization. Internally focused leaders may have a longer time horizon, perhaps expecting that over time, a government with a favorable internal order will moderate any unacceptable foreign policies. Internally focused leaders might also see more total potential threats, given that the very nature of a smaller power's domestic order could be considered an embryonic threat. These two leader types are, of course, ideal types; in reality, leaders may have a more complex understanding of the nature of threats.

* * *

Leaders form these causal beliefs before they arrive in office. The theory is agnostic about how leaders acquire beliefs. The varied pathways—which may include psychological mechanisms (such as learning from past experience), work on policy issues, self-education, or contact with groups that hold shared beliefs—show that causal beliefs are not reducible to a single alternative explanation.

* * *

How Causal Beliefs Influence Intervention Decisions

There are two mechanisms through which causal beliefs shape the way leaders confront intervention decisions. The leader's type directly shapes the cost-benefit calculus of intervention decisions by influencing how the leader values the benefits of successfully transforming target states. Externally focused leaders place relatively more weight on the international aspects of crisis outcomes. If forced to choose, they rank obtaining favorable foreign and security policies from the target state over achieving the "right" domestic institutions. * * *

In contrast, when considering conflict or crisis outcomes, internally focused leaders prioritize favorable domestic outcomes within target states. * * * But knowing that it may take time for policies to evolve, internally focused leaders may be willing to sacrifice favorable foreign policies in the short term in exchange for long-term institutional success. Thus internally focused leaders see greater benefits from achieving internally successful outcomes, which in turn contribute more to these leaders' expected utility calculation for a transformative intervention.

Leaders' causal beliefs also influence the cost-benefit calculus of interventions through a second, indirect mechanism: by influencing how leaders allocate scarce resources to confront threats. * * * Policy investments provide an observable implication of beliefs, because leaders in effect declare in advance what threats they believe are most important. Policy investments occur through several mechanisms, including changes in staffing, overall strategy and the defense posture, budgetary allocations, institutional creation and change (particularly within the bureaucracy), and contingency planning. These mechanisms affect the distribution of resources—including not only material capabilities but also bureaucratic and intellectual capabilities—available for transformative and nontransformative strategies. * * *

* * *

When leaders face a decision to intervene, they must evaluate the expected utility of the strategy they may employ (as well as the expected utility of not intervening at all). The theory does not predict that leaders blindly follow their beliefs; rather, it argues that structural and material factors and domestic competition are not sufficient to explain the choice of strategy, and that leaders' causal beliefs have an effect on decisions independent of structural and material conditions or domestic competition. The most direct way that causal beliefs influence the expected utility of a given intervention strategy is through the valuation of benefits. The effect of causal beliefs is also channeled indirectly through policy investments, which affect estimates of both costs and the probability of success through the mechanism of preparedness. Thus internally focused leaders are more likely to pursue transformative strategies, whereas externally focused leaders are more likely to pursue nontransformative strategies.

* * *

Research Design: Isolating and Measuring Causal Beliefs

This section outlines the research design I use to examine two U.S. presidents—Kennedy and Johnson—who agreed that the conflict in Vietnam merited intervention, but viewed the nature of the threat differently and thus chose different intervention strategies. To isolate the effect of leaders' beliefs, I concentrate on a single state within a single international system: the United States during the Cold War. Holding constant not only the bipolar structure of the international environment but also the democratic institutions of the United States helps to show that neither regime type nor a consistent tendency within American foreign policy fully determines the choice of intervention strategy. Examining the United States provides a hard test for the role of leaders, who might be expected to play a greater role in autocracies; furthermore, the public and elite groups have more access to policymaking than in other systems. Additionally, one might expect a strong "threat consensus" during the Cold War. Yet despite a shared commitment to fighting communism, Cold War presidents varied in how they viewed the threat and in how they pursued containment, especially in the third world.[9] * * *

* * *

To measure causal beliefs, I investigate the future president's views on the nature of threats; how the future president viewed states in the third world (where most Cold War military interventions occurred), especially whether he focused on third world states' internal institutions or their external alignment; and the nature and purpose of foreign aid, a useful measure of how the future president saw the nature of threats that is not necessarily correlated with an intervention strategy. These indicators probe threat perception (independent of intervention decisions), and not simply a belief in the efficacy of a particular strategy, which would risk a tautological explanation. I also examine any views the future president expressed on strategy and policy investments. Understanding how a leader's causal beliefs translated into positions on strategy and the use of force in his prepresidential years is helpful evidence because it is separated in time from the future leader's intervention decisions, and it helps establish whether his views changed over time. Finally, I examine policy investments made early in each administration.

* * *

The Vietnam War is arguably a difficult case for the theory. Conflicts such as Vietnam attracted American interest in part because the nature of the government was at stake amid the super-power struggle; all presidents who confronted the conflict hoped to keep South Vietnam non-communist. Successive presidents also feared that the loss of Vietnam would damage U.S. credibility. Given this consensus, any differences in how presidents viewed the nature of the conflict are particularly instructive; furthermore, in the particular case of Vietnam, Johnson felt pressure to continue Kennedy's policies. Yet even if one assumes that presidents agreed that the loss of Vietnam would harm U.S. interests in the Cold War, the theory still implies that leaders might view a conflict such as Vietnam differently. The theory expects an internally focused leader to identify the domestic institutions of states such as South Vietnam as the source of their vulnerability to a communist takeover, and thus focus on building up those institutions as part of his intervention strategy. In contrast, an externally focused leader would be expected to limit his concern primarily to ensuring a non-communist government, paying less attention to the nature of that government and concentrating more on the international or outside sources of vulnerability.

* * * Given that Vietnam is a difficult case for the theory, and that the theory identifies ideal types that, by definition, cannot perfectly match reality, I make a limited claim: that Kennedy and Johnson approached the conflict in Vietnam through different prisms that reflected their different causal beliefs, and these different approaches left a discernible imprint on their choices.

John F. Kennedy: Beliefs and Policy Investments

John F. Kennedy arrived in office with a strong interest in transformative strategies, the product of a consistent focus on the developing world's internal problems throughout his congressional career. Like most U.S. politicians during the Cold War, Kennedy was concerned about the advance of communism in the third world, and he was not immune from the tendency to see the Kremlin's hand everywhere. But he also believed that the domestic conditions of third world states were an important risk factor for communist takeovers, and thus directly affected U.S. national security. * * * Yet during his years in Congress, Kennedy devoted considerable time to domestic conditions in the third world.

Kennedy displayed an early tendency to diagnose crises and threats in terms of other states' domestic problems. For example, in a speech discussing the 1951 crisis over British oil interests in Iran, Kennedy argued that the crisis was "not over oil alone," citing a litany of internal problems in countries such as Iran, including "corrupt and ineffient bureacrac[ies]."[10] * * *

Kennedy also displayed an internal focus in his approach to the problem of building and maintaining the United States' alliances and sphere of influence. Kennedy emphasized the priority of internal issues over short-term external alignment, and stressed that the United States should not require new nations to pick sides in the superpower contest. He was therefore tolerant of neutral states such as India: as long as other states' institutions developed along favorable lines, foreign policies might follow. On his 1951 tour, he talked with Indian Prime Minister Jawaharlal Nehru about nonalignment and the problems of newly independent nations and came away with a more sympathetic view of neutralism.[11] * * *

Kennedy saw foreign aid as an important tool for defending U.S. interests. In contrast to Eisenhower, and later Johnson, Kennedy emphasized the form that aid should take and the necessity of responding to each country's needs,[12] with an eye toward investing in long-term institutional development. In a major speech on India in March 1958, he argued that only through "programs of real economic improvement" could developing states "find the political balance and social stability which provide the true defense against Communist penetration."[13] Kennedy also advocated moving away from Eisenhower's emphasis on military aid and toward internal political and economic aid, while using the military for local development programs.[14]

Finally, Kennedy's views on strategy and the use of force in his prepresidential career show how his internal diagnosis of threats translated into policy prescriptions in these years. One of the most striking and well documented aspects of Kennedy's prepresidential views on strategy was his deep interest in guerrilla warfare. Kennedy was exposed to the brand of counterinsurgency theory that emphasized transformative elements such as modernization and institution building. On his 1951 trip, he saw up close the British counterinsurgency strategy in Malaya, known as the "Briggs plan," which involved a large-scale population resettlement program and institution building.[15] * * * He seemed to understand the local nature of the conflict, noting that much of the Chinese population was "sitting on [the] fence as [they] don't want to pick [the] wrong side," and was "subject to threats and intimidation" by guerrillas.[16] * * *

Kennedy also expressed views on the conflict in Indochina. He connected the nature of the communist threat to domestic issues. During his visit to Vietnam on his 1951 trip, he recorded in his travel journal that the communists were "preaching" issues such as independence, reform, and development, and thus "we will lose if all we offer is merely a defense of [the] status quo."[17] During the 1954 debate over whether to intervene in Indochina to save the collapsing French position at Dien Bien Phu, Kennedy argued that "the war in Indo-China is an internal one . . . military guarantees of assistance from surrounding countries in case of outright aggression by the Chinese will be of little value in a war that is primarily civil."[18] * * *

Kennedy carried these views to the White House. He recruited many academic theorists of development as advisers, though they largely confirmed his preexisting views. His overall strategy gave significant weight to internal threats within other states, and he invested heavily in programs designed to shape the internal order of other states. A major focus of his policy investments was a top-down effort to increase counterinsurgency capabilities, to which he devoted considerable personal attention. * * *

Kennedy also worked to institutionalize his strategy within the bureaucracy. He created a White House–based monitoring committee, the "Special Group (CI)," to oversee interagency efforts on counterinsurgency. In addition to the Agency for International Development and the Peace Corps, he launched the Alliance for Progress. Despite their limitations, all had a transformative character. He also began to shift the emphasis of U.S. aid away from military aid and toward economic development assistance. He told Congress in 1961 that failing to meet the United States' moral, economic, and political obligations in the world would be, "in the long run, more expensive," because it risked a "collapse of existing political and social structures which would inevitably invite the advance of totalitarianism into every weak and unstable area. Thus our own security would be endangered."[19] * * *

Lyndon B. Johnson: Beliefs and Policy Investments

*   *   *

Johnson's view of threats in the international environment homed in on the risk that the communist bloc would engage in aggression, either directly through an attack or through subversion that was still directed from the outside. He therefore emphasized drawing lines against aggressors, but unlike Kennedy, he paid little attention to exactly where the line was drawn or whether the domestic characteristics of the states on the front line might make them less vulnerable to communism. Amid the 1947 debate on the

Truman Doctrine, for example, Johnson wrote one of his mentors that he thought Truman should say, "'This is it. We will not tolerate prima donna, high-handed, sulking, thieving forces who seek to gobble up helpless peoples in order to become the dominant power and rule the world.' As you well said, Truman chose to say that the place is Greece, the time is now."[20] * * *

Johnson's somewhat complex views on foreign aid also displayed a tendency to separate the domestic institutions of third world states from their place in the Cold War struggle. He had genuine concern for the world's poor; indeed, some scholars see a connection between Johnson's transformative vision for the United States (through his commitment to the New Deal and, later, the Great Society) and his view of the developing world. But for Johnson, internal problems were largely separate from Cold War threats, whereas for Kennedy, they were intertwined. Johnson wrote a constituent in June 1958 that he was "uncertain as to how far we should go in spending money for this program," but that foreign aid might help "as a means of battling for the cooperation of the one-third of the world's population that is not at present committed to the United States or Russia."[21] But his version of a "hearts and minds" campaign did not have much depth with regard to its long-term commitment to the development of other states' institutions. * * *

These externally oriented views translated into a nontransformative view of strategy and a focus on conventional preparedness in Johnson's prepresidential years. In 1948, for example, he peppered his staff with inquiries about the U.S. military's manpower strength, the stockpiling of raw materials, and particularly air power.[22] In July 1950 Johnson persuaded his colleagues to name him chairman of a new watchdog subcommittee for preparedness. Over the next few years, the subcommittee investigated many of the same themes of conventional preparedness that Johnson raised in 1948, with no discernible interest in unconventional warfare.[23] * * * Thus in the period when Kennedy began to focus on the

third world's internal problems as a source of threat, Johnson simply saw territory that might be grabbed by the Soviets and prepared to defend it accordingly.

Kennedy's assassination, as well as Johnson's desire to convey a sense of continuity, meant that Johnson had less flexibility than most new presidents to make policy investments. Nonetheless, his choices are illuminating. Although there was much continuity in the advisory circle, there were shifts: in particular, midlevel officials who favored a politically oriented approach to third world conflicts became increasingly peripheral. In terms of policy, Johnson de-emphasized development-oriented aid and demanded support for U.S. anti communist goals in return for aid. Although he promised to continue the Alliance for Progress—which Kennedy himself, by the time of his death, recognized as problematic—Johnson shifted the program's emphasis away from gradually transforming Latin American countries. Johnson also did not sustain the top-down pressure to build counterinsurgency forces. He allowed the Special Group (CI) to wither. * * *

Kennedy, Johnson, and Vietnam

This section discusses how Presidents Kennedy and Johnson intervened in Vietnam, focusing on the choice of strategy. I also discuss possible alternative explanations. * * *

Kennedy and Vietnam

Kennedy's approach to Vietnam reflected the tight link he saw between the political situation within South Vietnam and the war effort. In a January 1961 meeting, for example, he "asked whether the situation was not basically one of politics and morale."[24] At a November 1961 National Security Council (NSC) meeting, the president noted that whereas Korea had been a "case of clear aggression," the "conflict in Viet

Nam is more obscure and less flagrant." Kennedy "described it as being more a political issue, of different magnitude and (again) less defined than the Korean War."[25] Although he often referred to the problem of insurgency as "Communist-directed" or a form of "indirect aggression,"[26] Kennedy located the source of the conflict within Vietnam.

* * * From the early days of his tenure, Kennedy repeatedly resisted recommendations for a conventional deployment in Vietnam and instead asked for more counterinsurgency options that would address underlying internal issues. In February 1961, for example, he asked Joint Chiefs of Staff (JCS) Chairman Lyman Lemnitzer whether troops in South Vietnam could be redistributed for "anti-guerilla activities," even if it meant taking troops away from defending the border.[27] In May 1961 he resisted a JCS recommendation for a deployment intended, among other purposes, to deter a potential invasion from North Vietnam or China, and to signal "firmness."[28] In the fall of 1961, Kennedy sent Deputy National Security Adviser Walt Rostow and Gen. Maxwell Taylor to Vietnam, specifically instructing Taylor to examine political, social, and economic issues as closely as military considerations.

Despite repeated recommendations from his advisers (including Rostow and Taylor) to send troops, however, Kennedy opposed a conventional deployment and pushed for a counterinsurgency alternative. He expressed not only skepticism about intervening at all but also displeasure with his advisers' strategy for intervention. * * *

Finally, in early 1962 such a strategy began to come together. Passing over many of his top advisers, Kennedy relied on the State Department's Roger Hilsman, who had experience with guerrilla warfare. * * * The Hilsman-Thompson strategy had become the basis for U.S. policy in South Vietnam by March 1962.

At the heart of this policy was the "Strategic Hamlet Program," which, on paper at least, aimed at local-level transformation through civic action designed to change the national government's relationship to its people. The Hilsman report's "Strategic Concept" section listed as its first principle that the "problem presented by the Viet Cong is a political and not a military problem." In addition to the physical creation of strategic hamlets for the purpose of providing security to the population (a key to the population-centered counterinsurgency approach), the plan called for civic action teams "to assist locals in the construction of strategic villages and to build the essential socio-political base. . . . The public administration members will set up village government and tie it into the district and national levels assuring the flow of information on village needs and problems upward and the flow of government services downward."[29]

Thus the intended U.S. strategy—which is of primary interest here—was transformative, in the sense that the aim was to build local-level institutions, interact with the population, and integrate nonmilitary issues with the overall military strategy. The Strategic Hamlet Program itself was ultimately a failure, for complex reasons, including flawed assumptions, poor implementation on the U.S. side, and the refusal of President Diem, a leader aiming to retain power, to reform his corrupt regime. The rural population suffered terrible dislocation, further diminishing support for the government (which used the program to increase Diem's power). * * *

* * *

Although he vacillated, Kennedy sympathized with the view that the problem in Vietnam was political and that Diem was an obstacle to military progress. In instructions to McNamara before a mission to Saigon in September 1963, for example, Kennedy wrote that "events in South Vietnam since May have now raised serious questions . . . about the future effectiveness of this effort unless there can be important political improvement in the country." He went on to argue, "It is obvious that the overall political situation and the military and paramilitary effort are closely interconnected in all sorts of ways."[30] Kennedy was under no illusions that there was a logical, much less desirable, successor to Diem. The president's willingness to entertain a change in government in South Vietnam is even more surprising in the face of such potential uncertainty and instability.

The move against Diem was motivated neither by moral outrage against Diem's repressive policies nor by the impulse to democratize Vietnam for its own sake, but rather by the link many in the administration saw between the political situation and the war effort. Indeed, at the NSC meeting on October 2, 1963, Kennedy explicitly argued that U.S. policy should be based "on the harm which Diem's political actions are causing to the effort against the Viet Cong rather than on our moral opposition to the kind of government Diem is running."[31] The goal was not necessarily a democratic government in South Vietnam, but rather a government that at least had a broader base of support. One need not assume, therefore, that Kennedy was motivated by an idealist impulse to conclude that he connected military success with some form of political change. For its proponents, at least, the coup was a component of a transformative strategy, rather than an operation that would simply swap one leader for another. Despite his awareness of the hazards of removing Diem—a U.S. ally—Kennedy was willing to risk destabilizing Vietnam to transform it. Ironically, the fears of those who opposed the coup proved correct: Diem's death on November 2, 1963 (a surprise to Kennedy, who thought Diem would go into exile), left internal instability in South Vietnam that would preoccupy Johnson.

* * *

Johnson and Vietnam

Johnson faced different and arguably more difficult circumstances in Vietnam, in addition to the burden of taking over for Kennedy. But as Dallek summarizes, Johnson was a "different man facing different circumstances" and "charted his own course."[32] * * *

* * * Johnson sat in on many Kennedy administration meetings, and had exposure to debates about the nature of the war and the counterinsurgency approach that Kennedy favored. Yet Johnson fit more naturally with those who placed less emphasis on the political aspects of the war, and thus opposed a coup against Diem, or even pushing Diem to reform. After traveling—very reluctantly—to Vietnam as vice president in 1961, Johnson told the House Foreign Affairs Committee, "This certainly is no time for nit-picking where Diem is concerned." He argued, "We either decide that we are going to support him and support him zealously or that we are going to let South Vietnam fall."[33] In August 1963, amid the debate over the coup against Diem, Johnson argued in a high-level meeting that he "recognized the evils of Diem but has seen no alternative to him. Certainly we can't pull out. We must reestablish ourselves and stop playing cops and robbers."[34] * * *

When Johnson assumed the presidency, he publicly pledged to continue Kennedy's policies. But behind the scenes, he quickly demonstrated a key difference on Vietnam policy: he was less interested in domestic issues within Vietnam or in nation building. According to Central Intelligence Agency Director John McCone, in his first group meeting with advisers on Vietnam on November 24, 1963, Johnson said "he wanted to make it abundantly clear that he did not think we had to reform every Asian into our own image. He said that he felt all too often when we engaged in the affairs of a foreign country we wanted to immediately transform that country into our image and this, in his opinion, was a mistake. He was anxious to get along, win the war—he didn't want as much effort placed on so-called social reforms."[35] * * *

In late 1964 and early 1965, Johnson wrestled with governance problems in South Vietnam, and did show a persistent interest in finding stability.

During this period, Johnson (like Kennedy before him) rejected several military suggestions for escalating the U.S. response in Vietnam using conventional force, including options to take the war to the North. * * * In early March 1965 (even as he considered escalation), Johnson "expressed concern and understandable frustration" about the pacification effort, and "[kept] wondering if we are doing all we can."[36] * * *

* * *

More significantly, in this same period, even as Johnson discussed political and other nonmilitary measures to shore up the South, his analysis of the problem in Vietnam was consistent with an external focus. Johnson diagnosed the source of South Vietnam's vulnerability to a communist takeover in terms of external aggression from the North. On November 2, 1964, the day before his landslide general election victory, Johnson ordered a new NSC working group to study options in Vietnam, setting the escalation in motion in earnest and culminating in the choice of a limited bombing campaign against the North. In his analysis of Johnson's decisionmaking, Khong argues that the president found the analogy with the Korean War persuasive and thus saw the problem in terms of external aggression, a key factor in his acceptance of a limited bombing campaign (the so-called Option C).[37] The salience of the Korean analogy in Johnson's thinking, in turn, may have arisen from his causal beliefs. In contrast, as Khong notes, Kennedy rejected the Korean analogy, and had been far more inclined to draw on the Greek and Malayan analogies.

In this period Johnson also displayed a tendency to separate the military aspects of the war from Vietnamese domestic issues. * * * Even in 1964 Johnson's focus began to shift to North Vietnam. On May 13, 1964, in a call with National Security advisor McGeorge Bundy, he argued that "we've got to have some program out there from the Joint Chiefs, to start stepping that thing up and do some winning and do a little

stuff up in the North some way or other. We just can't sit idly by and do nothing there."[38] * * *

* * *

In the fateful escalation decisions from February through July 1965, Johnson focused primarily on hurting the North and stopping the Vietcong using conventional force, with few connections between the military strategy and changing the internal situation in the South. In the debate over ground strategy, for example, one option was to deploy troops along the coast in "enclaves," with a primary focus on defense and local security—not necessarily transformative, but with some of the spirit of population-oriented counterinsurgency. The alternative was to use U.S. troops to seek and kill insurgents in what would become the "search and destroy" strategy, which the army favored. This preference long preceded Johnson, but unlike Kennedy, Johnson showed little inclination to challenge the conventional attrition strategy (which was not inevitable). * * *

I do not claim that Johnson bears sole responsibility for choosing the attrition strategy, although many studies emphasize the dominance of Johnson himself, rather than his advisers, in the Vietnam deliberations. The key point is that he was exposed to arguments for an alternative strategy, yet did not question the nature of the war. Despite his attention to South Vietnam's internal problems, his decisions after the election fit more naturally with the pattern of his prepresidential beliefs, the way those beliefs translated into views about strategy in his prepresidential career (including his vice presidential years), and his early pronouncements about "do-gooding" in the immediate aftermath of Kennedy's death. Yet the administration officials who advocated concentration on reforming South Vietnam or on pacification highlight the alternative thinking on precisely how to escalate in Vietnam.

Thus Johnson employed what can be considered a nontransformative strategy in Vietnam. To be sure, the mere presence of half a million troops was deeply and destructively transformative, and the U.S. strategy sometimes involved deliberately devastating effects on villages and civilians. But in the sense that the strategy did not integrate military and nonmilitary measures or focus on local institution building—U.S. soldiers rarely stayed long enough in an area even to provide security—it was nontransformative. * * *

* * *

Discussion

Under difficult circumstances for the theory, Johnson's approach to Vietnam revealed a different emphasis that had consequences for the way the Vietnam intervention unfolded. Logevall, who emphasizes the role of individuals in understanding Vietnam, concludes that "Kennedy was more cognizant than Johnson of the need for genuine political reforms in South Vietnam if there were to be long-term success in the war effort."[39] Other factors, of course, played a role in the Vietnam decisions. But while this discussion is not the place to disentangle the puzzle of Vietnam, it illustrates that other factors, though important, are insufficient to explain the choice of strategy.

The evolving circumstances within South Vietnam undoubtedly affected Johnson's decisionmaking, but they are not sufficient to explain the evolution of U.S. strategy. * * *

Other structural and material conditions are also insufficient to explain the choice of strategy. Internationally, both presidents faced pressure to compete with Moscow in the third world and to signal resolve. Yet the prepresidential record shows that Kennedy's attention to guerrilla warfare long predated Nikita Khrushchev's 1961 "Wars of National Liberation" speech declaring Soviet support for third world revolutions. Credibility concerns weighed on both presidents, but are insufficient to explain how they intervened. * * *

In terms of capabilities, as John Lewis Gaddis argues, Kennedy and Johnson spent liberally on defense; the increased capabilities may have made them more likely to see areas such as Southeast Asia as vital.[40] But their choices in terms of resource allocation and strategy differed. As vice president, Johnson was dismissive of Kennedy's efforts to alter the distribution of capabilities; as president, he might have channeled spending into alternative capabilities but did not, at least until the escalation was well under way.

It is possible to argue that domestic and international politics shaped the form of both Kennedy's and Johnson's strategies, because each chose a middle course that would not invite Soviet or Chinese counterintervention, overwhelm the U.S. public, or endanger domestic programs (in Johnson's case, the Great Society). Yet these arguments say more about the speed and size of the escalation—gradual and, while large, ultimately limited by Johnson's refusal to call up reserves. Even though both presidents hoped to do just enough in Vietnam to avoid defeat, they still approached the conflict differently and faced advisers advocating different strategies, suggesting there was no single, obvious middle way. * * *

Turning to the domestic competition hypothesis, both Kennedy and Johnson faced electoral pressures and (particularly in Johnson's case) feared looking weak, yet chose different strategies. Both presidents also faced a military that preferred conventional warfare, a significant factor in the ultimate outcome of the Vietnam intervention. But both presidents were willing to override the military, and they confronted the military's specific preference for conventional warfare differently. Kennedy consistently questioned the conventional approach (although his failure to ensure that the military carried out his wishes for more emphasis on counterinsurgency left a gap between the intended strategy and the actual policy), whereas Johnson did not question the nature of the war. Both presidents were also willing to overrule their advisers (most of whom, in turn, owed their influence to the president himself), suggesting that executive leadership, rather than shared ideas, is crucial.

Finally, one might object that the Vietnam case does not provide a complete picture of Kennedy's and Johnson's intervention choices. Indeed, Kennedy used covert operations to try to undermine or even "decapitate" regimes. But the theory identifies ideal types and outlines their preferences over different intervention outcomes. These preferences are only one aspect of the cost-benefit calculus of intervention, and thus threat perceptions will not perfectly correlate with intervention choices. * * *

Conclusion

* * *

For international relations theory, the article helps to show that variation in the attributes of individual leaders cannot be left out of explanations for how states use military force, and that it is possible to make arguments about leaders that yield generalizable propositions about how leaders matter and rely on variables that are measurable ex ante. * * *

Future analysis of military interventions must do more than pay lip service to the role of leaders. Leaders have fundamentally—but systematically—different views about the nature of threats. These beliefs, as well as the choices leaders make at the outset of their tenure, are an independent source of variation in how states define and confront threats, and ultimately choose where and how to use force.

NOTES

1. Quoted in David E. Sanger, "Tug of War over Foreign Policy Approach," *New York Times*, September 5, 2008.

2. For a summary of these arguments and a strong rebuttal, see Daniel L. Byman and Kenneth M. Pollack, "Let Us Now Praise Great Men: Bringing the Statesman Back In," *International Security*, Vol. 25, No. 4 (Spring 2001), pp. 110–114. The neglect of leaders can be traced partly to Kenneth N. Waltz's dismissal of individual-level explanations based on human nature. See Waltz, *Man, the State, and War: A Theoretical Analysis* (New York: Columbia University Press, 1959), p. 33.

3. Henry Kissinger, *White House Years* (Boston: Little, Brown, 1979), p. 54. See also Robert Jervis, *Perception and Misperception in International Politics* (Princeton, N.J.: Princeton University Press, 1976), pp. 146–147.

4. John M. Owen IV, "The Foreign Imposition of Domestic Institutions," *International Organization*, Vol. 56, No. 2 (Spring 2002), p. 377.

5. For a useful summary of this approach to counterinsurgency, see Andrew F. Krepinevich Jr., *The Army and Vietnam* (Baltimore: Johns Hopkins University Press, 1986), pp. 7–16.

6. Such logic underpins structural realist approaches such as that of Kenneth N. Waltz, although this approach is not a theory of foreign policy. See Waltz, *Theory of International Politics* (Reading, Mass.: Addison-Wesley, 1979).

7. Martha Finnemore, *The Purpose of Intervention: Changing Beliefs about the Use of Force* (Ithaca, N.Y.: Cornell University Press, 2003), pp. 124–129. * * *

8. See, for example, Michael W. Doyle, "Liberalism and World Politics," *American Political Science Review*, Vol. 80, No. 4 (December 1986), p. 1161.

9. See John Lewis Gaddis, *Strategies of Containment: A Critical Appraisal of American National Security Policy during the Cold War*, rev. and exp. ed. (Oxford: Oxford University Press, 2005). See also Yuen Foong Khong, *Analogies at War: Korea, Munich, Dien Bien Phu, and the Vietnam Decisions of 1965* (Princeton, N.J.: Princeton University Press, 1992), pp. 71–73.

10. JFK, speech to Massachusetts Federation of Taxpayers Associations, April 21, 1951, John F. Kennedy Pre-Presidential Papers, House

Files, Box 95, "Middle East, Mass. Federation of Taxpayers, 4/21/51" folder, John F. Kennedy Library (JFKL), pp. 3–6.

11. See, for example, JFK, speech to Boston Chamber of Commerce, November 19, 1951, Pre-Presidential Papers, Campaign Files, Box 102, "Speeches—Middle & Far East Trip" folder, JFKL, pp. 4–5.

12. See, for example, JFK to Dean Erwin N. Griswold of Harvard Law School, June 7, 1957, PPP-SF, Box 667, "Foreign Aid, 5/3/57–6/7/57" folder, JFKL.

13. JFK, "The Choice in Asia—Democratic Development in India," March 25, 1958, in John Fitzgerald Kennedy, *A Compilation of Statements and Speeches Made during His Service in the United States Senate and House of Representatives* (Washington, D.C.: U.S. Government Printing Office, 1964), p. 607.

14. See JFK, "Remarks to the Fifth National Conference on International Economic and Social Development," February 26, 1958, PPP-SF, Box 561, "Foreign Aid, 10/20/57-2/24/59" folder, JFKL, pp. 4–5.

15. The institution building aspects of the British approach are emphasized in the writings of Sir Robert G.K. Thompson, who worked on the Briggs Plan and later served as an adviser in Vietnam. See Thompson, *Defeating Communist Insurgency: The Lessons of Malaya and Vietnam* (New York: Praeger, 1966), pp. 50–55, chap. 6.

16. JFK Travel Journal, Personal Papers, Box 11, "1951 Travel Journal Book 2, October–November, 1951" folders (four folders in total), JFKL, pp. 137–140.

17. JFK Travel Journal, pp. 133–134.

18. JFK, Speech Materials for Speech to Cook County Democrats, Chicago, April 20, 1954 (labeled "KS-3 1954" in the "Doodles" series), Personal Papers, Box 40, "1954—KS3" folder, JFKL, p. 9.

19. JFK, "Special Message to the Congress on Foreign Aid," March 22, 1961, in John T. Woolley and Gerhard Peters, *The American Presidency Project* (Santa Barbara: University of California), http://www.presidency.ucsb.edu/ws/?pid?8545.

20. LBJ to Alvin J. Wirtz, April 29, 1947, Lyndon B. Johnson Pre-Presidential Papers, LBJA Selected Names File, Box 37, "Wirtz, A.J., 1944–" folder, Lyndon B. Johnson Library (LBJL).

21. LBJ to William G. Goodrich Jr., March 28, 1958, PPP-SP, Box 601, "Foreign Relations, Aid [4 of 6]" folder, LBJL.

22. See the memos to Johnson (which reference his queries) in Pre-Presidential Papers, House of Representatives Papers, Box 329, "Memos to Johnson" folder, LBJL.

23. See "Summary of First Thirty-Six Reports of the Senate Preparedness Subcommittee," undated, PPP-SP, Box 346, "[Continuance of the Preparedness Subcommittee]" folder, LBJL.

24. Rostow to Bundy (summarizing White House meeting of January 28, 1961), January 30, 1961, *Foreign Relations of the United States, 1961–1963*, Vol. 1, Doc. 4. (*FRUS* documents cited in this article are available online at http://www.state.gov/r/pa/ho/frus).

25. Notes on the National Security Council Meeting, November 15, 1961, *FRUS, 1961–1963*, Vol. 1, Doc. 254.

26. For an example of Kennedy using the "Communist-directed" and "indirect aggression" language, see JFK to McNamara, January 11, 1962, *FRUS, 1961–1963*, Vol. 8, Doc. 67.

27. NSAM No. 12, February 6, 1961, *FRUS 1961–1963*, Vol. 1, Doc. 9.

28. Senator Mike Gravel, ed., *The Pentagon Papers: The Defense Department History of United States Decisionmaking on Vietnam*, Vol. 2 (Boston: Beacon, 1971), p. 49.

29. Hilsman, "A Strategic Concept for South Vietnam," February 2, 1962, *FRUS, 1961–1963*, Vol. 2, Doc. 42. As Michael Latham notes, despite abuses in the program, its supporters believed "that civic action and the organization of a new political culture

could provide the institutional framework and activist values to win the allegiance of a dislocated population." Michael E. Latham, *Modernization as Ideology: American Social Science and "Nation Building" in the Kennedy Era* (Chapel Hill: University of North Carolina Press, 2000), pp. 185–186.

30. JFK to McNamara, September 21, 1963, *FRUS, 1961–1963*, Vol. 4, Doc. 142.

31. Summary record of the 519th Meeting of the National Security Council, October 2, 1963, *FRUS, 1961–1963*, Vol. 4, Doc. 169.

32. Robert Dallek, *Flawed Giant: Lyndon Johnson and His Times, 1961–1973* (New York: Oxford University Press, 1998), p. 99. See also [Fredrik] Logevall, *Choosing War [: The Lost Chance for Peace and the Escalation of the War in Vietnam* (Berkeley: University of California Press, 1999)], p. 78.

33. LBJ, Statement before House Foreign Affairs Committee, June 5, 1961, VPSF, Box 11, "Proposed Statement of VP Before House Foreign Affairs Committee, June 5, 1961" folder, LBJL, p. 14.

34. Memorandum of Conversation (drafted by Hilsman), August 31, 1963, *FRUS, 1961–1963*, Vol. 4, Doc. 37.

35. Memorandum for the Record of Meeting (drafted by McCone), November 24, 1963, *FRUS, 1961–1963*, Vol. 4, Doc. 330.

36. See Cooper to Bundy, March 1, 1965, *FRUS, 1964–1968*, Vol. 2, Doc. 173.

37. Khong, *Analogies at War*, pp. 99–111, 138–143.

38. Transcript of telephone call, LBJ with Bundy, May 13, 1964, in Guian A. McKee, ed., *The Presidential Recordings: Lyndon B. Johnson*, Vol. 6 (New York: W.W. Norton, 2007), p. 684. On Johnson's focus on the North in this period, see [George C.] Herring, *America's Longest War[: The United States and Vietnam, 1950–1975*, 3d ed. (New York: McGraw-Hill, 1996)], p. 131.

39. Logevall, *Choosing War*, p. 398.

40. Gaddis, *Strategies of Containment*, p. 259.

7

IGOs, NGOs, and International Law

International organizations such as the United Nations are major actors in international relations. One of the key tasks of the UN, regional organizations, and ad hoc state coalitions is peacekeeping in countries that are at risk of war. Virginia Page Fortna, in an excerpt from her book Does Peacekeeping Work? Shaping Belligerents' Choices after Civil War *(2008), poses two seemingly simple questions: Does peacekeeping work, and if so, how? Drawing on both statistical data and case studies, she finds not only that peacekeepers deploy to the hardest cases, but that the risk of war resuming is reduced by 55 percent or more when peacekeepers are deployed. While Fortna shows that peacekeeping does work under certain conditions, Samantha Power, in a selection from* The Atlantic, *explains why neither the United Nations and its bureaucracy nor the United States did more to stop the 1994 genocide in Rwanda. According to Power, both American politicians and UN bureaucrats are to blame.*

In addition to intergovernmental organizations (IGOs), research on nongovernmental organizations (NGOs), social movements, and transnational advocacy networks has expanded since the 1990s. Using a constructivist approach, Margaret E. Keck and Kathryn Sikkink, in an excerpt from their award-winning book Activists beyond Borders: Advocacy Networks in International Politics *(1998), show how such networks develop by "building new links among actors in civil societies, states, and international organizations."*

International advocacy networks have been particularly active in the area of legal accountability for war crimes and other atrocities. They successfully advocated for a treaty creating the International Criminal Court, and they have promoted the doctrine of universal jurisdiction in the national courts of any country for such crimes. Henry A. Kissinger, academic and former secretary of state and national security advisor (and himself a possible target of indictment by national courts for allegations arising out of his actions in the Nixon administration), argues against the practice. The tyranny of judges replaces that of governments, he contends, and political disagreements should not be resolved by legal means. Kenneth Roth of Human Rights Watch disagrees. Kenneth A. Rodman, in his excerpted article, places that debate in a broader perspective.

What are the trade-offs between justice and peace? More specifically, should the prosecutor of the International Criminal Court have the discretion to take into account the political context in which international criminal law operates? Using two ICC cases (prosecution of the Lord's Resistance Army of Northern Uganda and Darfur), Rodman argues that international law cannot be isolated from the political context in which it operates.

Transnational cooperation involving states and civil society groups often takes place in an institutional setting shaped by international organizations such as the UN, the ICC, the International Monetary Fund, and the World Trade Organization. Robert O. Keohane, in his highly regarded book After Hegemony: Cooperation and Discord in the World Political Economy *(1984), lays out the theory of liberal institutionalism to explain how such institutions make cooperation possible despite the absence of a sovereign enforcement power standing above states. He explains that international institutions (or "international regimes") establish rules around which expectations converge. Rules reduce the costs of transactions, facilitate bargaining across different issue areas, and provide information that reduces the risk of cheating. By way of contrast, John J. Mearsheimer, the quintessential realist, is skeptical about the impact of international institutions. In his excerpt, he delineates the flaws of liberal institutionalist theory, arguing that international institutions exert no independent influence of their own because they simply reflect the underlying power and interests of states.*

VIRGINIA PAGE FORTNA

From *Does Peacekeeping Work?*

Peacekeeping and the Peacekept * * *

The Questions

In countries wracked by civil war, the international community is frequently called upon to deploy monitors and troops to try to keep the peace. The United Nations, regional organizations, and sometimes ad hoc groups of states have sent peacekeepers to high-profile trouble-spots such as Rwanda and Bosnia and to lesser-known conflicts in places like the Central African Republic, Namibia, and Papua New Guinea. How effective are these international interventions? Does peacekeeping work? Does it actually keep the peace in the aftermath of civil war? And if so, how? How do peacekeepers change things on the ground, from the perspective of the "peacekept," such that war is less likely to resume? These are the questions that motivate this [project].

As a tool for maintaining peace, international peacekeeping was only rarely used in internal conflicts during the Cold War, but the number, size, and scope of missions deployed in the aftermath of civil wars has exploded since 1989. Early optimism about the potential of the UN and regional organizations to help settle internal conflicts after the fall of the Berlin Wall was soon tempered by the initial failure of the mission in Bosnia and the scapegoating of the UN

From Virginia Page Fortna, *Does Peacekeeping Work? Shaping Belligerents' Choices after Civil War* (Princeton and Oxford: Princeton University Press, 2008), Chaps. 1, 7. Some of the author's notes have been omitted.

mission in Somalia.[1] The United States in particular became disillusioned with peacekeeping, objecting to anything more than a minimal international response in war-torn countries (most notoriously in Rwanda). Even in Afghanistan and Iraq, where vital interests are now at stake, the United States has been reluctant to countenance widespread multilateral peacekeeping missions. But the demand for peacekeeping continues apace. In recent years, the UN has taken up an unprecedented number of large, complex peacekeeping missions, in places such as the Congo, Liberia, Haiti, and Sudan.

Through these ups and downs, scholars and practitioners of peacekeeping have debated the merits of the new wave of more "robust" and complex forms of peacekeeping and peace enforcement developed after the Cold War, and even the effectiveness of more traditional forms of peacekeeping.[2] However, this debate is hampered by shortcomings in our knowledge about peacekeeping. Despite a now vast literature on the topic, very little rigorous testing of the effectiveness of peacekeeping has taken place. We do not have a very good idea of whether it really works. Nor do we have an adequate sense of how exactly peacekeeping helps to keep the peace.

Casual observers and many policymakers opposed to a greater peacekeeping role for the international community can point to the dramatic failures that dominate news coverage of peacekeeping, but rarely acknowledge the success stories that make less exciting news. Meanwhile, most analysts of peacekeeping draw lessons from a literature that compares cases and missions, but with few exceptions, examines only cases in which peacekeepers are deployed, not cases in which belligerents are left to their own devices. This literature therefore cannot tell us whether peace is more likely to last when peacekeepers are present than when they are absent. Surprisingly little empirical work has addressed this question. Moreover, the few studies that do address it, at least in passing, come to contradictory findings. Some find that peacekeeping makes peace last longer, some find that it does not, and some find that only some kinds of peacekeeping are effective.[3] A closer look is clearly needed.

The literature on peacekeeping is also surprisingly underdeveloped theoretically. Causal arguments about peacekeeping are therefore often misinformed. Opponents of intervention dismiss peacekeeping as irrelevant, or worse, counterproductive.[4] Proponents, on the other hand, simply list the functions of peacekeeping (monitoring, interposition, electoral oversight, etc.), describing its practices with little discussion of how exactly the presence of peacekeepers might influence the prospects for peace. Little theoretical work has been done to specify what peacekeepers do to help belligerents maintain a cease-fire, or how peacekeepers might shape the choices made by the peacekept about war and peace.

Further, most existing studies of peacekeeping focus almost exclusively on the perspective of the peacekeepers or the international community. In discussions of mandates, equipment and personnel, relations among national contingents or between the field and headquarters, and so on, it is easy to lose track of the fundamental fact that it is the belligerents themselves who ultimately make decisions about maintaining peace or resuming the fight. Only by considering the perspective of the peacekept—their incentives, the information available to them, and their decision making—can we understand whether and how peacekeeping makes a difference.

In short, our current understanding of peacekeeping suffers from three gaps: we know too little about whether or how much peacekeepers contribute empirically to lasting peace, we lack a solid understanding of the causal mechanisms

through which peacekeepers affect the stability of peace, and we know too little about the perspective of the peacekept on these matters. This project aims to rectify these shortcomings. [Discussion] draws on theories of cooperation and bargaining in international relations to develop the causal mechanisms through which peacekeepers might affect the decisions belligerents make about maintaining peace or returning to war. It assesses the empirical effects of peacekeeping by comparing (both quantitatively and qualitatively) civil conflicts in which peacekeeping was used to conflicts in which peacekeepers were not deployed. And it evaluates the causal mechanisms of peacekeeping by drawing on the perspective of the belligerents themselves.

Two simple questions drive this study: does peacekeeping work? And if so, how? Answering these questions is not so simple, however. To know whether peace lasts longer when international personnel are present than when belligerents are left to their own devices, we need to compare both types of cases. But we also need to know something about where peacekeepers tend to be deployed. Unlike treatments in a controlled laboratory experiment, peacekeeping is not "applied" to war-torn states at random. If the international community follows the common policy prescriptions to send peacekeepers when there is strong "political will" for peace and where the chances for success are high (that is, to the easy cases), then a simple comparison of how long peace lasts with and without peacekeeping would misleadingly suggest a very strong effect for peacekeeping. If, on the other hand, peacekeepers are sent where they are most needed—where peace is otherwise hardest to keep, then a simple comparison would lead us to conclude, again incorrectly, that peacekeeping is useless or even counterproductive.[5] To address whether and how peacekeeping works, I must first answer the question of why peacekeepers deploy to some cases and not others. The first empirical step in this project must therefore be to examine where peacekeepers go. The [project] therefore addresses three questions: Where do peacekeepers go? Do they make peace more likely to last? Through what causal mechanisms do they operate?

This project aims to have a direct impact on the policy debates over peacekeeping. It furthers our understanding of why some conflicts draw in international peacekeepers while others do not. It goes on to provide clear evidence that this policy tool is indeed extremely effective at maintaining peace, substantially reducing the risk of another war. And it spells out how peacekeeping works, so that more effective strategies for maintaining peace can be developed by the international community.

* * *

Conclusion and Implications

[The project] asks three empirical questions: Where do peacekeepers go? Does peacekeeping work? And if so, how does it work? This [discussion] summarizes the answers to these questions, drawing out implications for our understanding of the problem of recidivism after civil wars, and especially for policymakers trying to reduce it.

The first question is important for evaluating the other two, but it is also interesting in its own right. While existing studies of this question have focused on choices made by the international community, I argue that choices made by the belligerents themselves are as important, at least for the consent-based missions that make up the bulk of peacekeeping. Not surprisingly, peacekeeping is a matter of both supply and demand. That peacekeeping is unlikely in civil wars within or next door to the permanent five members of the Security Council is testament to a supply-side effect. But the fact that peacekeeping is generally more likely when rebels are relatively strong (but not strong enough to win outright) reflects dynamics on the demand side. The case studies illustrate this point well. Whether or not consent-based peacekeeping happened in Bangladesh, Mozambique, and Sierra Leone was the result of choices made by the belligerents, and particularly by the

relative bargaining strength of rebels and the government.

For the purposes of the rest of the analysis, the most important answer to the question of where peacekeepers go, is that they are much more likely to deploy when the danger of war recurring is particularly high. That is, peacekeepers select into the hardest cases. This finding flies in the face of policy admonitions that peacekeepers should only go where the chances of "success" are relatively good. A policy of sending peacekeepers only to the easy cases would help international organizations avoid embarrassment, but would ensure that peacekeeping was less useful than it could be. If peacekeepers only went where peace is likely to last in any case, they would render themselves irrelevant. Fortunately, however, this policy advice has apparently been ignored. As both the quantitative and qualitative evidence * * * makes clear, the higher the risk of recidivism in a particular case, the more likely peacekeepers are to deploy. In particular, peacekeeping is most likely when neither side has won outright, where mistrust is high, and where refugee flows threaten regional peace. Chapter VI consent-based peacekeeping is more likely where rebel groups are relatively strong and in countries with lower living standards. Chapter VII enforcement missions are more likely in less democratic states and where the war involves multiple fighting factions. In short, peacekeepers are most likely to be sent where they are most needed, where the job of maintaining peace is most difficult.

The answer to the question of whether peacekeeping works is a clear and resounding yes. To see this, it is crucial to control for the fact that peacekeepers select into the difficult cases. But once this selection is accounted for, the statistical evidence is overwhelming. [Even analyzing] the data in many different ways, * * * the conclusion is always the same; the risk of war resuming is much lower when peacekeepers are present than when belligerents are left to their own devices. Estimates of the size of this effect depend on how conservative one wants to be. If one sets up a particularly difficult test, in which peacekeepers are only given credit for keeping peace while they are actually deployed, not for peace that lasts after they leave, peacekeepers reduce the risk of another war by 55%–60%, all else equal. If peacekeepers are given credit for cases in which peace survives even after they go home (which, after all, is their main goal) estimates of the beneficial effects of peacekeeping are much more dramatic, suggesting that the risk of recidivism falls by at least 75%–85% relative to nonpeacekeeping cases. The evidence from interviews with rebel and government decision makers also supports this general conclusion that peacekeeping works. The belligerents themselves view peacekeeping as an important and effective tool that has helped them maintain peace.

Several other findings emerge from the analysis of peacekeeping's effects. One of the most important for peacekeeping policy is that Chapter VI consent-based missions are empirically just as effective as the militarily more robust Chapter VII enforcement missions. Much of the discussion within policy circles in the last several years has been about the importance of beefing up the mandates of peacekeeping missions. There are certainly cases in which an enforcement mandate may be necessary. More robust military capabilities can help peacekeepers protect themselves and others if peace begins to falter. And if the aim is to deter aggression militarily, then a Chapter VII mandate is needed. But it is not enough. Only enforcement missions that prove their willingness to fight, as missions that intervene to create a cease-fire by force have done, can deter effectively. Otherwise, a Chapter VII mandate does not a credible deterrent make. Thus, UNAMSIL's [United Nations Mission in Sierra Leone] Chapter VII mandate meant little until British intervention and a robust force posture convinced the RUF [Revolutionary Unified Front (Sierra Leone)] that the international community was serious about enforcing peace.

However, the findings of this study show that peacekeeping is worthwhile even under consent-based mandates. Large and relatively well armed troop deployments are not necessarily essential for peacekeeping to work; even small, unarmed or very lightly armed missions significantly reduce the likelihood that peace will break down. Given that consent-based missions are typically much less expensive, and that it may be easier to find countries willing and able to contribute troops for them, this is an important finding. Robust Chapter VII–mandated peacekeeping may be the safest option, but the international community should not shy away from smaller, less robust Chapter VI peacekeeping if that is all that is possible politically. In other words, we should not conclude that the mission's mandate does not matter, but rather that even peacekeeping missions with limited mandates and constrained military power can be extremely effective. This is because many of the mechanisms through which peacekeepers have an effect are political and economic in nature and do not depend on robust mandates or strong military force (more on this below).

Among consent-based operations, multidimensional missions are most effective. The dearth of cases in each category makes it harder to reach strong conclusions about the relative effects of different types of Chapter VI missions, so this finding should be treated with some caution. But the available evidence suggests that the civilian aspects of peacekeeping that go into multidimensional missions—election monitoring, human rights training, police reform, and so on—do contribute to its general effectiveness. More of the causal mechanisms through which peacekeeping operates, particularly those relating to political exclusion, are at play in these multidimensional missions than in other types of peacekeeping.

Peacekeeping is not a cure-all. Beyond the task of maintaining peace, the international community increasingly aims to foster democracy in the war-torn societies in which it intervenes. While stable peace may be a requisite for the growth of democracy, and as we have seen here, peacekeeping promotes stable peace, outside intervention may in other ways undermine or crowd out democratization. So, while peace-keeping is clearly effective at maintaining peace, it has not necessarily left significantly more democratic societies in its wake.[6] Nonetheless, if the aim is simply to keep the peace, to keep civil war from recurring, then peacekeeping is an extremely effective policy tool.

While the answers to the first two questions addressed in this [project] can be summarized quickly—peacekeepers go where peace is hardest to keep, and yes, peacekeeping works to keep peace—the answer to the third question, how does peacekeeping work, is a bit more compli-cated. Peacekeeping works along multiple causal pathways. To understand the causal mechanisms of peacekeeping, we must consider the reasons belligerents who have recently been fighting each other might return to war. This work identified four analytically distinct, but in practice overlap-ping pathways: aggression, fear and mistrust, accident or the actions of rogue groups within either side, and political exclusion. I hypothesized particular ways that the presence of peacekeepers might block these potential causal pathways; that is, ways peacekeepers might (1) change the incen-tives for aggression relative to maintaining peace, (2) alleviate fear and mistrust so as to reduce security dilemmas, (3) prevent or control acci-dents or "involuntary defection" by hard-liners, and (4) dissuade either side (and particularly the government) from excluding the other from the political process.

An empirical evaluation of the specific causal mechanisms through which peacekeepers might achieve these results requires paying attention to the perspective of the peacekept. The peace-keeping literature tends to be a bit narcissistic. It pays attention mostly to the peacekeepers, to their functions, the particulars of mandates, troop deployments, command and control, rela-tionships between headquarters and the field, "best practices," and so, while largely ignoring the peacekept. But it is the peacekept who must choose between war and peace. Only if peace-keepers change something for the peacekept can they have a causal impact on this choice. This project has tried to rectify this shortcoming in the literature by examining how the belligerents themselves viewed the situation they faced, and particularly how they thought the presence or absence of peacekeepers mattered in their case.

The evidence from interviews with the peacekept (or not peacekept in the Bangladeshi case) indicates a number of ways in which the presence of peacekeepers can shape belliger-ents' choices. In large enforcement missions, this shift can entail military deterrence, although, as stressed above, to be effective, a deterrent force must establish the credibility that all deterrence entails. Where peacekeeping will depend on mil-itary deterrence, the international community must expect to have to prove its credibility on the ground. Enforcement missions may actu-ally have to fight to convince the peacekept that peacekeepers are willing to use force. Smaller missions and consent-based peacekeeping might serve as a trip wire for more robust intervention, but again, would-be spoilers must believe that the international community really will respond with a large-scale intervention. The conditions under which peacekeeping has a strong military effect are therefore fairly narrow. But many of the ways in which peacekeeping changes bellig-erents' incentives are nonmilitary in nature.

Peacekeepers can have a causal impact by changing economic incentives. For rank-and-file soldiers, this generally entails the material benefits of going through a demobilization, dis-armament, and reintegration (DDR) process. For leaders, it can entail the general boost to the economy that a peacekeeping mission brings, a boost that political elites are often in a position to capitalize on. Or it may entail more direct forms of co-option. The Mozambique case pro-vides examples of both. Co-option can happen without peacekeepers, of course. But as the CHT [Chittagons Hill Tracts] examples show, if one side buys off the other, as the Bangladeshi gov-ernment did the PCJSS [Parbatya Chattagram Jana Samhati Saniti (Chittagong Hill Tracts

United Peoples' Party)] by granting control of local budgets (and the opportunities for corruption that go with it), this leaves the co-opted open to charges of selling out. Co-option done by a peacekeeping mission, as a more neutral and acceptable body, is less likely to strengthen hardliners at the expense of moderates than is co-option among the belligerents themselves.

Because altering economic incentives can be crucial to maintaining stable peace, contraband financing for rebels is not only a powerful factor in civil war recidivism, it also reduces peacekeepers' leverage. As shown * * *, peacekeeping still helps when parties have independent and illegal sources of funding, but its effect is diminished. Co-option will be more expensive, perhaps prohibitively so, in these cases. Alternatively, as was the case in Sierra Leone, attempts to alter economic incentives may work in conjunction with military deterrence when contraband financing is an issue.

Beyond economics, peacekeepers can influence the incentives of the peacekept by influencing perceptions of the parties' legitimacy, both internationally and domestically. In many civil wars, recognition as a legitimate political actor is itself a valuable and sought-after good, as well as one that may translate into international economic or other aid. Internally, pronouncements by peacekeepers about who is or is not cooperating with a peace process may affect parties' electoral prospects.

In short, while peacekeeping may deter aggression through military means in some cases, its effects on the incentives facing belligerents are largely economic and political. There are policy implications of this for peacekeepers. Peacekeeping strategy should focus at least as much on identifying the points of economic and political influence in a particular case that will provide the most leverage over belligerents' decision making as on beefing up the mission's military strength. Similarly, the allocation of scarce resources (money, personnel, etc.) should be directed at least as much to making peace profit-

able and politically viable for the peacekept as to the creation of militarily effective peacekeeping forces. Where possible, an attempt should be made to control or eliminate contraband sources of funding for belligerents.[7]

By alleviating fear and mistrust, peacekeeping also increases the chances that belligerents will maintain peace. It does this, in part, by helping erstwhile deadly enemies to communicate with one another. Thus, as the inevitable problems and glitches in the peace process arise, peacekeeping missions should emphasize ongoing mediation. They can also support peace by monitoring each side's compliance with a ceasefire. It is here, perhaps, that the military nature of peacekeeping is most important. Peacekeeping missions should include military personnel, not because they can fight (in fact, unarmed military observers may be most effective in some cases), but because they have the expertise to monitor demobilization and disarmament, and because they can garner the respect of the soldiers they monitor and the commanders they work with.

Peacekeepers also alleviate fear and mistrust, to some degree, merely by existing. To the extent that agreeing to peacekeeping allows the parties to signal their intentions to each other, it is less what peacekeepers actually do than whether the parties have asked for them or not that makes a difference. But for this signaling mechanism to work, it has to be credible, and to be credible, it has to be costly. Specifically, it has to be costly for a party that intends to resume fighting. Peacekeeping missions should thus be designed to be as intrusive as possible as a way of testing the credibility of this signal. Peacekeeping, particularly UN peacekeeping, traditionally proceeded on an assumption of good faith on the part of the belligerents. Lessons learned, usually the hard way, during the 1990s have tempered this assumption, with more attention now paid to the possibility of spoilers. But the signaling function of peacekeeping should be used proactively. Peacekeeping strategy should focus on identifying and insisting on things that those intending to go back to war or renege on a political deal would object to, but that those committed to peace would not necessarily mind. And because intentions can shift over time, peacekeepers should be intrusive not just when they first deploy, but over the life of the mission. This is not to say that they should go out of their way to antagonize the parties to the conflict, but rather that missions should be designed so as to maximize the clarity of the signal that consent and ongoing cooperation with peacekeeping provides to the other side.

Peacekeeping can make the resumption of war less likely by preventing hard-liners or rogue factions from inciting violence, and by helping to prevent or control accidents from sparking renewed conflict. Peacekeepers should work with moderates on each side to identify hard-liners within their own group who might pose a threat to peace. Peacekeeping strategy should determine whether these would-be spoiler splinter groups can be deterred militarily (something even relatively weak peacekeeping forces may be capable of), and how they can be weakened politically. By facilitating communication, peacekeeping can nip accidental conflagrations in the bud. This provides another reason peacekeepers should spend time and energy on continuing mediation between the parties, both among leaders and among local commanders, dealing with problems on the spot.

Providing security or basic law and order can help accidents from starting in the first place, so peacekeeping missions should continue to invest in policing, perhaps especially in identity conflicts where the actions of the general population might provide sparks for the fire. Similarly, providing security in particularly tense phases of the peace process (such as disarmament) or in particularly contested territory (diamond-mining areas, for example) can forestall problems that could easily escalate. Finally, peacekeeping missions should establish a formal mechanism for handling disputes over compliance. This gives both sides an

alternative to, on the one hand, doing nothing in the face of perceived violations by their antagonists, and on the other, responding in kind and risking escalation. These dispute resolution mechanisms can appear irrelevant. Their formal findings may not tell either side anything it does not already know. But often it is not their role in providing information to the various parties that is important, but rather their existence as a political mechanism that allows the parties to save face by taking nonescalatory action in response to alleged violations.

Last, but certainly not least, peacekeepers can make peace more likely to endure by preventing either side from shutting the other out of a political process in a way that makes the political loser choose war. In most cases this entails pressuring the government, which can use the trappings of state power to influence political outcomes, not to abuse its position. There is a stark contrast in this regard between the Chittagong Hill Tracts conflict, where the absence of peacekeepers has given the Bangladeshi government a relatively free hand to disregard key elements of the peace deal, and Mozambique and Sierra Leone, where considerable pressure was brought to bear on the government to be inclusive. Beyond general political pressure (with international aid and legitimacy providing leverage), peacekeepers can minimize abuse by monitoring security forces and by monitoring or running electoral processes. They can help military groups (especially rebels) transform themselves into viable political parties, sometimes with the expenditure of relatively small amounts of money or other resources. (In some cases, computers and new suits can go a long way.) After some conflicts, peacekeepers may temporarily take over the entire administration of the country to prevent either side from dominating the political process during the most dangerous phases of the transition to peace. Again, peacekeeping strategy should be formed with an eye toward these mechanisms.

In short, peacekeeping intervenes in the most difficult cases, dramatically increases the chances that peace will last, and does so by altering the incentives of the peacekept, by alleviating their fear and mistrust of each other, by preventing and controlling accidents and misbehavior by hard-line factions, and by encouraging political inclusion.

Beyond its answers to these questions about peacekeeping and its effects, this study also makes both theoretical and empirical contributions. It builds on a theory of international cooperation developed for interstate conflict, extending it to the realm of internal warfare.[8] It provides further support for the notion that while cooperation is often extremely difficult, perhaps nowhere more so than among deadly enemies who have just fought a war, deliberate efforts by the belligerents themselves and by outsiders can often overcome the obstacles to peace.

It also helps us to understand the more general issue of recurrent civil war. Interstate war has, thankfully, become relatively rare since the end of the Cold War. This has left internal conflicts as arguably the greatest security problem facing the world as a whole.[9] Countries that have been torn apart by civil war face a significant recidivism problem—those who have had a civil war are especially likely to have another. The empirical findings of this study help us understand the nature of that problem. They point to particular factors (such as military outcomes, or contraband financing for rebels) that make civil wars particularly likely to recur. But they also show that this "conflict trap" is not inevitable.[10] The conclusions of this project are therefore fundamentally optimistic. The problem of maintaining peace in the aftermath of civil war is a serious one, but it is not a hopeless one. Parties to civil war, together with the international community, can use the tool of peacekeeping to reduce dramatically the risk of another war.

Peacekeeping is not free. It costs money and personnel on the part of the international community and the countries that contribute troops. It also entails political costs for the peacekept, not least of which is the infringement on a coun-

try's sovereignty. Policymakers may decide peacekeeping is not worth these costs in a particular instance. But relative to the cost of recurrent warfare, peacekeeping is an extremely good investment. Peacekeeping is not a panacea, nor a silver bullet. It cannot guarantee that peace will last. But contrary to the views of many who think only of well-publicized failures, peacekeeping is an extremely effective tool for maintaining peace—a tool that the findings of this study will, I hope, make even more useful.

NOTES

1. Note that the U.S. led and UN missions in Somalia (UNITAF [Unified Task Force on Somalia] and UNOSOM [UN Operation in Somalia], respectively) were not peacekeeping missions as defined here, but rather humanitarian assistance missions (see definitions below). This distinction was lost, however, in the debates over the merits of peacekeeping after the fiasco in Mogadishu.
2. On this debate see, for example, Tharoor 1995–96 and Luttwak 1999.
3. See Hartzell, Hoddie, and Rothchild 2001; Dubey 2002; and Doyle and Sambanis 2000, respectively. See also Doyle and Sambanis 2006; Gilligan and Sergenti 2007. For studies of the effects of international involvement on peace after interstate (as opposed to civil) wars, see Diehl, Reifschneider, and Hensel 1996; and Fortna 2004.
4. Luttwak 1999; Weinstein 2005.
5. Peacekeeping is thus endogenous to processes that affect the duration of peace. The selection of peacekeeping must be accounted for before we can assess its effects.
6. See Fortna 2008.
7. The Kimberly Process Certification Scheme to combat the trafficking of "blood diamonds" from conflict zones is an important step in this direction.
8. Fortna 2003, 2004.

9. Other threats, such as terrorism or the proliferation of nuclear weapons, may be of greater concern to particular countries at particular moments. Civil wars may also be on the decline, but continue to pose a significant threat to the lives and livelihoods of millions.

10. See Collier et al. 2003.

REFERENCES

Collier, Paul, V. L. Elliot, Håvard Hegre, Anke Hoeffler, Marta Reynal-Querol, and Nicholas Sambanis. 2003. *Breaking the Conflict Trap: Civil War and Development Policy.* Washington, DC: World Bank and Oxford University Press.

Diehl, Paul F., Jennifer Reifschneider, and Paul R. Hensel. 1996. United Nations Intervention and Recurring Conflict. *International Organization* 50 (4): 683–700.

Doyle, Michael W., and Nicholas Sambanis. 2000. International Peacebuilding: A Theoretical and Quantitative Analysis. *American Political Science Review* 94 (4): 779–801.

———. 2006. *Making War and Building Peace: United Nations Peace Operations.* Princeton: Princeton University Press.

Dubey, Amitabh. 2002. Domestic Institutions and the Duration of Civil War Settlements. Paper presented at Annual Meeting of the International Studies Association, New Orleans.

Fortna, Virginia Page. 2003. Scraps of Paper? Agreements and the Durability of Peace. *International Organization* 57 (2): 337–72

Fortna, Virginia Page. 2004. *Peace Time: Cease-Fire Agreements and the Durability of Peace.* Princeton: Princeton University Press.

Fortna, Virginia Page. 2008. Peacekeeping and Democratization. In *From War to Democracy: Dilemmas of Peacebuilding,* edited by A. Jarstad and T. Sisk. Cambridge: Cambridge University Press.

Gilligan, Michael J., and Ernest J. Sergenti. 2007. Does Peacekeeping Keep Peace? Using Matching to Improve Causal Inference. Unpublished paper, New York University and Harvard University.

Hartzell, Caroline, Mathew Hoddie, and Donald Rothchild. 2001. Stabilizing the Peace after Civil War. *International Organization* 55 (1): 183–208.

Luttwak, Edward N. 1999. Give War a Chance. *Foreign Affairs* 78 (4): 36–44.

Tharoor, Shashi. 1995–96. Should UN Peacekeeping Go 'Back to Basics'? *Survival* 37 (4): 52–64.

Weinstein, Jeremy M. 2005. Autonomous Recovery and International Intervention in Comparative Perspective. Unpublished paper. Center for Global Development, Washington, DC.

———. 2007. *Inside Rebellion: The Politics of Insurgent Violence.* New York: Cambridge University Press.

SAMANTHA POWER

Bystanders to Genocide: Why the United States Let the Rwandan Tragedy Happen

I. People Sitting in Offices

In the course of a hundred days in 1994 the Hutu government of Rwanda and its extremist allies very nearly succeeded in exterminating the country's Tutsi minority. Using firearms, machetes, and a variety of garden implements, Hutu militiamen, soldiers, and ordinary citizens murdered some 800,000 Tutsi and politically moderate Hutu. It was the fastest, most efficient killing spree of the twentieth century.

A few years later, in a series in *The New Yorker*, Philip Gourevitch recounted in horrific detail the story of the genocide and the world's failure to stop it. President Bill Clinton, a famously avid reader, expressed shock. He sent copies of Gourevitch's articles to his second-term national-security adviser, Sandy Berger. The articles bore confused, angry, searching queries in the margins. "Is what he's saying true?" Clinton wrote with a thick black felt-tip pen beside heavily underlined paragraphs. "How did this happen?" he asked, adding, "I want to get to the bottom of this." The President's urgency and outrage were oddly timed. As the terror in Rwanda had unfolded, Clinton had shown virtually no interest in stopping the genocide, and his Administration had stood by as the death toll rose into the hundreds of thousands.

Why did the United States not do more for the Rwandans at the time of the killings? Did the President really not know about the genocide, as

From *The Atlantic* (Sept. 2001), 84–108.

his marginalia suggested? Who were the people in his Administration who made the life-and-death decisions that dictated U.S. policy? Why did they decide (or decide not to decide) as they did? Were any voices inside or outside the U.S. government demanding that the United States do more? If so, why weren't they heeded? And most crucial, what could the United States have done to save lives?

So far people have explained the U.S. failure to respond to the Rwandan genocide by claiming that the United States didn't know what was happening, that it knew but didn't care, or that regardless of what it knew there was nothing useful to be done. The account that follows is based on a three-year investigation involving sixty interviews with senior, mid-level, and junior State Department, Defense Department, and National Security Council officials who helped to shape or inform U.S. policy. It also reflects dozens of interviews with Rwandan, European, and United Nations officials and with peacekeepers, journalists, and nongovernmental workers in Rwanda. Thanks to the National Security Archive (www.nsarchive.org), a nonprofit organization that uses the Freedom of Information Act to secure the release of classified U.S. documents, this account also draws on hundreds of pages of newly available government records. This material provides a clearer picture than was previously possible of the interplay among people, motives, and events. It reveals that the U.S. government knew enough about the genocide early on to save lives, but passed up countless opportunities to intervene.

In March of 1998, on a visit to Rwanda, President Clinton issued what would later be known as the "Clinton apology," which was actually a carefully hedged acknowledgment. He spoke to the crowd assembled on the tarmac at Kigali Airport: "We come here today partly in recognition of the fact that we in the United States and the world community did not do as much as we could have and should have done to try to limit what occurred" in Rwanda.

This implied that the United States had done a good deal but not quite enough. In reality the United States did much more than fail to send troops. It led a successful effort to remove most of the UN peacekeepers who were already in Rwanda. It aggressively worked to block the subsequent authorization of UN reinforcements. It refused to use its technology to jam radio broadcasts that were a crucial instrument in the coordination and perpetuation of the genocide. And even as, on average, 8,000 Rwandans were being butchered each day, U.S. officials shunned the term "genocide," for fear of being obliged to act. The United States in fact did virtually nothing "to try to limit what occurred." Indeed, staying out of Rwanda was an explicit U.S. policy objective.

With the grace of one grown practiced at public remorse, the President gripped the lectern with both hands and looked across the dais at the Rwandan officials and survivors who surrounded him. Making eye contact and shaking his head, he explained, "It may seem strange to you here, especially the many of you who lost members of your family, but all over the world there were people like me sitting in offices, day after day after day, who *did not fully appreciate* [pause] the depth [pause] and the speed [pause] with which you were being engulfed by this *unimaginable* terror."

Clinton chose his words with characteristic care. It was true that although top U.S. officials could not help knowing the basic facts—thousands of Rwandans were dying every day—that were being reported in the morning papers, many did not "fully appreciate" the meaning. In the first three weeks of the genocide the most influential American policymakers portrayed (and, they insist, perceived) the deaths not as astrocities or the components and symptoms of genocide but as wartime "casualties"—the deaths of combatants or those caught between them in a civil war.

Yet this formulation avoids the critical issue of whether Clinton and his close advisers might reasonably have been expected to "fully appreciate" the true dimensions and nature of the massacres. During the first three days of the killings U.S. diplomats in Rwanda reported back to Washington that well-armed extremists were intent on eliminating the Tutsi. And the American press spoke of the door-to-door hunting of unarmed civilians. By the end of the second week informed nongovernmental groups had already begun to call on the Administration to use the term "genocide," causing diplomats and lawyers at the State Department to begin debating the word's applicability soon thereafter. In order not to appreciate that genocide or something close to it was under way, U.S. officials had to ignore public reports and internal intelligence and debate.

The story of U.S. policy during the genocide in Rwanda is not a story of willful complicity with evil. U.S. officials did not sit around and conspire to allow genocide to happen. But whatever their convictions about "never again," many of them did sit around, and they most certainly did allow genocide to happen. In examining how and why the United States failed Rwanda, we see that without strong leadership the system will incline toward risk-averse policy choices. We also see that with the possibility of deploying U.S. troops to Rwanda taken off the table early on—and with crises elsewhere in the world unfolding—the slaughter never received the top-level attention it deserved. Domestic political forces that might have pressed for action were absent. And most U.S. officials opposed to American involvement in Rwanda were firmly convinced that they were doing all they could—and, most important, all they *should*—in light of competing

American interests and a highly circumscribed understanding of what was "possible" for the United States to do.

One of the most thoughtful analyses of how the American system can remain predicated on the noblest of values while allowing the vilest of crimes was offered in 1971 by a brilliant and earnest young foreign-service officer who had just resigned from the National Security Council to protest the 1970 U.S. invasion of Cambodia. In an article in *Foreign Policy*, "The Human Reality of Realpolitik," he and a colleague analyzed the process whereby American policymakers with moral sensibilities could have waged a war of such immoral consequence as the one in Vietnam. They wrote,

> The answer to that question begins with a basic intellectual approach which views foreign policy as a lifeless, bloodless set of abstractions. "Nations," "interests," "influence," "prestige"—all are disembodied and dehumanized terms which encourage easy inattention to the real people whose lives our decisions affect or even end.

Policy analysis excluded discussion of human consequences. "It simply is not *done*," the authors wrote. "Policy—good, steady policy—is made by the 'tough-minded.' To talk of suffering is to lose 'effectiveness,' almost to lose one's grip. It is seen as a sign that one's 'rational' arguments are weak."

In 1994, fifty years after the Holocaust and twenty years after America's retreat from Vietnam, it was possible to believe that the system had changed and that talk of human consequences had become admissible. Indeed, when the machetes were raised in Central Africa, the White House official primarily responsible for the shaping of U.S. foreign policy was one of the authors of that 1971 critique: Anthony Lake, President Clinton's first-term national-security adviser. The genocide in Rwanda presented Lake and the rest of the Clinton team with an opportunity to prove that "good, steady policy" could be made in the interest of saving lives.

II. The Peacekeepers

Rwanda was a test for another man as well: Romeo Dallaire, then a major general in the Canadian army who at the time of the genocide was the commander of the UN Assistance Mission in Rwanda. If ever there was a peacekeeper who believed wholeheartedly in the promise of humanitarian action, it was Dallaire. A broad-shouldered French-Canadian with deep-set sky-blue eyes, Dallaire has the thick, calloused hands of one brought up in a culture that prizes soldiering, service, and sacrifice. He saw the United Nations as the embodiment of all three.

Before his posting to Rwanda Dallaire had served as the commandant of an army brigade that sent peacekeeping battalions to Cambodia and Bosnia, but he had never seen actual combat himself. "I was like a fireman who has never been to a fire, but has dreamed for years about how he would fare when the fire came," the fifty-five-year-old Dallaire recalls. When, in the summer of 1993, he received the phone call from UN headquarters offering him the Rwanda posting, he was ecstatic. "It was answering the aim of my life," he says. "It's *all* you've been waiting for."

Dallaire was sent to command a UN force that would help to keep the peace in Rwanda, a nation the size of Vermont, which was known as "the land of a thousand hills" for its rolling terrain. Before Rwanda achieved independence from Belgium, in 1962, the Tutsi, who made up 15 percent of the populace, had enjoyed a privileged status. But independence ushered in three decades of Hutu rule, under which Tutsi were systematically discriminated against and periodically subjected to waves of killing and ethnic cleansing. In 1990 a group of armed exiles, mainly Tutsi, who had been clustered on the Ugandan border, invaded Rwanda. Over the next several years the rebels, known as the Rwandan Patriotic Front, gained ground against Hutu government forces. In 1993 Tanzania brokered peace talks, which resulted in a power-sharing agreement known as the Arusha Accords. Under its terms the Rwandan government agreed to share power with Hutu opposition parties and the Tutsi minority. UN peacekeepers would be deployed to patrol a cease-fire and assist in demilitarization and demobilization as well as to help provide a secure environment, so that exiled Tutsi could return. The hope among moderate Rwandans and Western observers was that Hutu and Tutsi would at last be able to coexist in harmony.

Hutu extremists rejected these terms and set out to terrorize Tutsi and also those Hutu politicians supportive of the peace process. In 1993 several thousand Rwandans were killed, and some 9,000 were detained. Guns, grenades, and machetes began arriving by the planeload. A pair of international commissions—one sent by the United Nations, the other by an independent collection of human-rights organizations—warned explicitly of a possible genocide.

But Dallaire knew nothing of the precariousness of the Arusha Accords. When he made a preliminary reconnaissance trip to Rwanda, in August of 1993, he was told that the country was committed to peace and that a UN presence was essential. A visit with extremists, who preferred to eradicate Tutsi rather than cede power, was not on Dallaire's itinerary. Remarkably, no UN officials in New York thought to give Dallaire copies of the alarming reports from the international investigators.

The sum total of Dallaire's intelligence data before that first trip to Rwanda consisted of one encyclopedia's summary of Rwandan history, which Major Brent Beardsley, Dallaire's executive assistant, had snatched at the last minute from his local public library. Beardsley says, "We flew to Rwanda with a Michelin road map, a copy of the Arusha agreement, and that was it. We were under the impression that the situation was quite straightforward: there was one cohesive government side and one cohesive rebel side, and they had come together to sign the peace agreement and had then requested that we come in to help them implement it."

Though Dallaire gravely underestimated the tensions brewing in Rwanda, he still felt that he would need a force of 5,000 to help the parties implement the terms of the Arusha Accords. But when his superiors warned him that the United States would never agree to pay for such a large deployment, Dallaire reluctantly trimmed his written request to 2,500. He remembers, "I was told, 'Don't ask for a brigade, because it ain't there.'"

Once he was actually posted to Rwanda, in October of 1993, Dallaire lacked not merely intelligence data and manpower but also institutional support. The small Department of Peacekeeping Operations in New York, run by the Ghanaian diplomat Kofi Annan, now the UN secretary general, was overwhelmed. Madeleine Albright, then the U.S. ambassador to the UN, recalls, "The global nine-one-one was always either busy or nobody was there." At the time of the Rwanda deployment, with a staff of a few hundred, the UN was posting 70,000 peacekeepers on seventeen missions around the world. Amid these widespread crises and logistical headaches the Rwanda mission had a very low status.

Life was not made easier for Dallaire or the UN peacekeeping office by the fact that American patience for peacekeeping was thinning. Congress owed half a billion dollars in UN dues and peacekeeping costs. It had tired of its obligation to foot a third of the bill for what had come to feel like an insatiable global appetite for mischief and an equally insatiable UN appetite for missions. The Clinton Administration had taken office better disposed toward peacekeeping than any other Administration in U.S. history. But it felt that the Department of Peacekeeping Operations needed fixing and demanded that the UN "learn to say no" to chancy or costly missions.

Every aspect of the UN Assistance Mission in Rwanda was run on a shoestring. UNAMIR (the acronym by which it was known) was equipped with hand-me-down vehicles from the UN's Cambodia mission, and only eighty of the 300 that turned up were usable. When the medical supplies ran out, in March of 1994, New York said there was no cash for resupply. Very little could be procured locally, given that Rwanda was one of Africa's poorest nations. Replacement spare parts, batteries, and even ammunition could rarely be found. Dallaire spent some 70 percent of his time battling UN logistics.

Dallaire had major problems with his personnel, as well. He commanded troops, military observers, and civilian personnel from twenty-six countries. Though multinationality is meant to be a virtue of UN missions, the diversity yielded grave discrepancies in resources. Whereas Belgian troops turned up well armed and ready to perform the tasks assigned to them, the poorer contingents showed up "bare-assed," in Dallaire's words, and demanded that the United Nations suit them up. "Since nobody else was offering to send troops, we had to take what we could get," he says. When Dallaire expressed concern, he was instructed by a senior UN official to lower his expectations. He recalls, "I was told, 'Listen, General, you are NATO-trained. This is not NATO.'" Although some 2,500 UNAMIR personnel had arrived by early April of 1994, few of the soldiers had the kit they needed to perform even basic tasks.

The signs of militarization in Rwanda were so widespread that even without much of an intelligence-gathering capacity, Dallaire was able to learn of the extremists' sinister intentions. In January of 1994 an anonymous Hutu informant, said to be high up in the inner circles of the Rwandan government, had come forward to describe the rapid arming and training of local militias. In what is now referred to as the "Dallaire fax," Dallaire relayed to New York the informant's claim that Hutu extremists "had been ordered to register all the Tutsi in Kigali." "He suspects it is for their extermination," Dallaire wrote. "Example he gave was that in 20 minutes his personnel could kill up to 1000 Tutsis." "Jean-Pierre," as the informant became known, had said that the militia planned first to provoke and murder a number of Belgian peacekeepers, to "thus guarantee Belgian withdrawal from Rwanda." When Dallaire notified Kofi Annan's office that UNAMIR was poised to raid Hutu arms caches, Annan's deputy forbade him to do

so. Instead Dallaire was instructed to notify the Rwandan President, Juvénal Habyarimana, and the Western ambassadors of the informant's claims. Though Dallaire battled by phone with New York, and confirmed the reliability of the informant, his political masters told him plainly and consistently that the United States in particular would not support aggressive peacekeeping. (A request by the Belgians for reinforcements was also turned down.) In Washington, Dallaire's alarm was discounted. Lieutenant Colonel Tony Marley, the U.S. military liaison to the Arusha process, respected Dallaire but knew he was operating in Africa for the first time. "I thought that the neophyte meant well, but I questioned whether he knew what he was talking about," Marley recalls.

III. The Early Killings

On the evening of April 6, 1994, Romeo Dallaire was sitting on the couch in his bungalow residence in Kigali, watching CNN with Brent Beardsley. Beardsley was preparing plans for a national Sports Day that would match Tutsi rebel soldiers against Hutu government soldiers in a soccer game. Dallaire said, "You know, Brent, if the shit ever hit the fan here, none of this stuff would really matter, would it?" The next instant the phone rang. Rwandan President Habyarimana's Mystère Falcon jet, a gift from French President François Mitterrand, had just been shot down, with Habyarimana and Burundian President Cyprien Ntaryamira aboard. Dallaire and Beardsley raced in their UN jeep to Rwandan army headquarters, where a crisis meeting was under way.

Back in Washington, Kevin Aiston, the Rwanda desk officer, knocked on the door of Deputy Assistant Secretary of State Prudence Bushnell and told her that the Presidents of Rwanda and Burundi had gone down in a plane crash. "Oh, shit," she said. "Are you sure?" In fact nobody was sure at first, but Dallaire's forces supplied confirmation within the hour. The Rwandan authorities quickly announced a curfew, and Hutu militias and government soldiers erected roadblocks around the capital.

Bushnell drafted an urgent memo to Secretary of State Warren Christopher. She was concerned about a probable outbreak of killing in both Rwanda and its neighbor Burundi. The memo read,

> If, as it appears, both Presidents have been killed, there is a strong likelihood that widespread violence could break out in either or both countries, particularly if it is confirmed that the plane was shot down. Our strategy is to appeal for calm in both countries, both through public statements and in other ways.

A few public statements proved to be virtually the only strategy that Washington would muster in the weeks ahead.

Lieutenant General Wesley Clark, who later commanded the NATO air war in Kosovo, was the director of strategic plans and policy for the Joint Chiefs of Staff at the Pentagon. On learning of the crash, Clark remembers, staff officers asked, "Is it Hutu and Tutsi or Tutu and Hutsi?" He frantically called for insight into the ethnic dimension of events in Rwanda. Unfortunately, Rwanda had never been of more than marginal concern to Washington's most influential planners.

America's best-informed Rwanda observer was not a government official but a private citizen, Alison Des Forges, a historian and a board member of Human Rights Watch, who lived in Buffalo, New York. Des Forges had been visiting Rwanda since 1963. She had received a Ph.D. from Yale in African history, specializing in Rwanda, and she could speak the Rwandan language, Kinyarwanda. Half an hour after the plane crash Des Forges got a phone call from a close friend in Kigali, the human-rights activist Monique Mujawamariya. Des Forges had been worried about Mujawamariya for weeks, because the Hutu extremist radio station, Radio Mille Collines, had branded her "a bad patriot who

deserves to die." Mujawamariya had sent Human Rights Watch a chilling warning a week earlier: "For the last two weeks, all of Kigali has lived under the threat of an instantaneous, carefully prepared operation to eliminate all those who give trouble to President Habyarimana."

Now Habyarimana was dead, and Mujawamariya knew instantly that the hardline Hutu would use the crash as a pretext to begin mass killing. "This is it," she told Des Forges on the phone. For the next twenty-four hours Des Forges called her friend's home every half hour. With each conversation Des Forges could hear the gunfire grow louder as the militia drew closer. Finally the gunmen entered Mujawamariya's home. "I don't want you to hear this," Mujawamariya said softly. "Take care of my children." She hung up the phone.

Mujawamariya's instincts were correct. Within hours of the plane crash Hutu militiamen took command of the streets of Kigali. Dallaire quickly grasped that supporters of the Arusha peace process were being targeted. His phone at UNAMIR headquarters rang constantly as Rwandans around the capital pleaded for help. Dallaire was especially concerned about Prime Minister Agathe Uwilingiyimana, a reformer who with the President's death had become the titular head of state. Just after dawn on April 7 five Ghanaian and ten Belgian peacekeepers arrived at the Prime Minister's home in order to deliver her to Radio Rwanda, so that she could broadcast an emergency appeal for calm.

Joyce Leader, the second-in-command at the U.S. embassy, lived next door to Uwilingiyimana. She spent the early hours of the morning behind the steel-barred gates of her embassy-owned house as Hutu killers hunted and dispatched their first victims. Leader's phone rang. Uwilingiyimana was on the other end. "Please hide me," she begged.

Minutes after the phone call a UN peacekeeper attempted to hike the Prime Minister over the wall separating their compounds. When Leader heard shots fired, she urged the peacekeeper to abandon the effort. "They can see you!"

she shouted. Uwilingiyimana managed to slip with her husband and children into another compound, which was occupied by the UN Development Program. But the militiamen hunted them down in the yard, where the couple surrendered. There were more shots. Leader recalls, "We heard her screaming and then, suddenly, after the gunfire the screaming stopped, and we heard people cheering." Hutu gunmen in the Presidential Guard that day systematically tracked down and eliminated Rwanda's moderate leadership.

The raid on Uwilingiyimana's compound not only cost Rwanda a prominent supporter of the Arusha Accords; it also triggered the collapse of Dallaire's mission. In keeping with the plan to target the Belgians which the informant Jean-Pierre had relayed to UNAMIR in January, Hutu soldiers rounded up the peacekeepers at Uwilingiyimana's home, took them to a military camp, led the Ghanaians to safety, and then killed and savagely mutilated the ten Belgians. In Belgium the cry for either expanding UNAMIR's mandate or immediately withdrawing was prompt and loud.

In response to the initial killings by the Hutu government, Tutsi rebels of the Rwandan Patriotic Front—stationed in Kigali under the terms of the Arusha Accords—surged out of their barracks and resumed their civil war against the Hutu regime. But under the cover of that war were early and strong indications that systematic genocide was taking place. From April 7 onward the Hutu-controlled army, the gendarmerie, and the militias worked together to wipe out Rwanda's Tutsi. Many of the early Tutsi victims found themselves specifically, not spontaneously, pursued: lists of targets had been prepared in advance, and Radio Mille Collines broadcast names, addresses, and even license-plate numbers. Killers often carried a machete in one hand and a transistor radio in the other. Tens of thousands of Tutsi fled their homes in panic and were snared and butchered at checkpoints. Little care was given to their disposal. Some were shoveled into landfills. Human flesh rotted in the sunshine. In churches bodies mingled with scattered hosts.

If the killers had taken the time to tend to sanitation, it would have slowed their "sanitization" campaign.

IV. The "Last War"

The two tracks of events in Rwanda—simultaneous war and genocide—confused policymakers who had scant prior understanding of the country. Atrocities are often carried out in places that are not commonly visited, where outside expertise is limited. When country-specific knowledge is lacking, foreign governments become all the more likely to employ faulty analogies and to "fight the last war." The analogy employed by many of those who confronted the outbreak of killing in Rwanda was a peacekeeping intervention that had gone horribly wrong in Somalia.

On October 3, 1993, ten months after President Bush had sent U.S. troops to Somalia as part of what had seemed a low-risk humanitarian mission, U.S. Army Rangers and Delta special forces in Somalia attempted to seize several top advisers to the warlord Mohammed Farah Aideed. Aideed's faction had ambushed and killed two dozen Pakistani peacekeepers, and the United States was striking back. But in the firefight that ensued the Somali militia killed eighteen Americans, wounded seventy-three, and captured one Black Hawk helicopter pilot. Somali television broadcast both a video interview with the trembling, disoriented pilot and a gory procession in which the corpse of a U.S. Ranger was dragged through a Mogadishu street.

On receiving word of these events, President Clinton cut short a trip to California and convened an urgent crisis-management meeting at the White House. When an aide began recapping the situation, an angry President interrupted him. "Cut the bullshit," Clinton snapped. "Let's work this out." "Work it out" meant walk out. Republican Congressional pressure was intense. Clinton appeared on American television the next day, called off the manhunt for Aideed, temporarily reinforced the troop presence, and announced that all U.S. forces would be home within six months. The Pentagon leadership concluded that peacekeeping in Africa meant trouble and that neither the White House nor Congress would stand by it when the chips were down.

Even before the deadly blowup in Somalia the United States had resisted deploying a UN mission to Rwanda. "Anytime you mentioned peacekeeping in Africa," one U.S. official remembers, "the crucifixes and garlic would come up on every door." Having lost much of its early enthusiasm for peacekeeping and for the United Nations itself, Washington was nervous that the Rwanda mission would sour like so many others. But President Habyarimana had traveled to Washington in 1993 to offer assurances that his government was committed to carrying out the terms of the Arusha Accords. In the end, after strenuous lobbying by France (Rwanda's chief diplomatic and military patron), U.S. officials accepted the proposition that UNAMIR could be the rare "UN winner." On October 5, 1993, two days after the Somalia firefight, the United States reluctantly voted in the Security Council to authorize Dallaire's mission. Even so, U.S. officials made it clear that Washington would give no consideration to sending U.S. troops to Rwanda. Somalia and another recent embarrassment in Haiti indicated that multilateral initiatives for humanitarian purposes would likely bring the United States all loss and no gain.

Against this backdrop, and under the leadership of Anthony Lake, the national-security adviser, the Clinton Administration accelerated the development of a formal U.S. peacekeeping doctrine. The job was given to Richard Clarke, of the National Security Council, a special assistant to the President who was known as one of the most effective bureaucrats in Washington. In an interagency process that lasted more than a year, Clarke managed the production of a presidential decision directive, PDD-25, which listed sixteen factors that policymakers needed to consider when deciding whether to support peacekeeping activities: seven factors if the United States was

to vote in the UN Security Council on peace operations carried out by non-American soldiers, six additional and more stringent factors if U.S. forces were to participate in UN peacekeeping missions, and three final factors if U.S. troops were likely to engage in actual combat. In the words of Representative David Obey, of Wisconsin, the restrictive checklist tried to satisfy the American desire for "zero degree of involvement, and zero degree of risk, and zero degree of pain and confusion." The architects of the doctrine remain its strongest defenders. "Many say PDD-25 was some evil thing designed to kill peacekeeping, when in fact it was there to save peacekeeping," Clarke says. "Peacekeeping was almost dead. There was no support for it in the U.S. government, and the peacekeepers were not effective in the field." Although the directive was not publicly released until May 3, 1994, a month into the genocide, the considerations encapsulated in the doctrine and the Administration's frustration with peacekeeping greatly influenced the thinking of U.S. officials involved in shaping Rwanda policy.

V. The Peace Processors

Each of the American actors dealing with Rwanda brought particular institutional interests and biases to his or her handling of the crisis. Secretary of State Warren Christopher knew little about Africa. At one meeting with his top advisers, several weeks after the plane crash, he pulled an atlas off his shelf to help him locate the country. Belgian Foreign Minister Willie Claes recalls trying to discuss Rwanda with his American counterpart and being told, "I have other responsibilities." Officials in the State Department's Africa Bureau were, of course, better informed. Prudence Bushnell, the deputy assistant secretary, was one of them. The daughter of a diplomat, Bushnell had joined the foreign service in 1981, at the age of thirty-five. With her agile mind and sharp tongue, she had earned the attention of George Moose when she served under him at the U.S. embassy in Senegal. When Moose was named the assistant secretary of state for African affairs, in 1993, he made Bushnell his deputy. Just two weeks before the plane crash the State Department had dispatched Bushnell and a colleague to Rwanda in an effort to contain the escalating violence and to spur the stalled peace process.

Unfortunately, for all the concern of the Americans familiar with Rwanda, their diplomacy suffered from three weaknesses. First, ahead of the plane crash diplomats had repeatedly threatened to pull out UN peacekeepers in retaliation for the parties' failure to implement Arusha. These threats were of course counterproductive, because the very Hutu who opposed power-sharing wanted nothing more than a UN withdrawal. One senior U.S. official remembers, "The first response to trouble is 'Let's yank the peacekeepers.' But that is like believing that when children are misbehaving, the proper response is 'Let's send the baby-sitter home.'"

Second, before and during the massacres U.S. diplomacy revealed its natural bias toward states and toward negotiations. Because most official contact occurs between representatives of states, U.S. officials were predisposed to trust the assurances of Rwandan officials, several of whom were plotting genocide behind the scenes. Those in the U.S. government who knew Rwanda best viewed the escalating violence with a diplomatic prejudice that left them both institutionally oriented toward the Rwandan government and reluctant to do anything to disrupt the peace process. An examination of the cable traffic from the U.S. embassy in Kigali to Washington between the signing of the Arusha agreement and the downing of the presidential plane reveals that setbacks were perceived as "dangers to the peace process" more than as "dangers to Rwandans." American criticisms were deliberately and steadfastly leveled at "both sides," though Hutu government and militia forces were usually responsible.

The U.S. ambassador in Kigali, David Rawson, proved especially vulnerable to such bias.

Rawson had grown up in Burundi, where his father, an American missionary, had set up a Quaker hospital. He entered the foreign service in 1971. When, in 1993, at age fifty-two, he was given the embassy in Rwanda, his first, he could not have been more intimate with the region, the culture, or the peril. He spoke the local language—almost unprecedented for an ambassador in Central Africa. But Rawson found it difficult to imagine the Rwandans who surrounded the President as conspirators in genocide. He issued pro forma demarches over Habyarimana's obstruction of power-sharing, but the cable traffic shows that he accepted the President's assurances that he was doing all he could. The U.S. investment in the peace process gave rise to a wishful tendency to see peace "around the corner." Rawson remembers, "We were naive policy optimists, I suppose. The fact that negotiations can't work is almost not one of the options open to people who care about peace. We were looking for the hopeful signs, not the dark signs. In fact, we were looking away from the dark signs . . . One of the things I learned and should have already known is that once you launch a process, it takes on its own momentum. I had said, 'Let's try this, and then if it doesn't work, we can back away.' But bureaucracies don't allow that. Once the Washington side buys into a process, it gets pursued, almost blindly." Even after the Hutu government began exterminating Tutsi, U.S. diplomats focused most of their efforts on "re-establishing a cease-fire" and "getting Arusha back on track."

The third problematic feature of U.S. diplomacy before and during the genocide was a tendency toward blindness bred by familiarity: the few people in Washington who were paying attention to Rwanda before Habyarimana's plane was shot down were those who had been tracking Rwanda for some time and had thus come to expect a certain level of ethnic violence from the region. And because the U.S. government had done little when some 40,000 people had been killed in Hutu-Tutsi violence in Burundi in October of 1993, these officials also knew that Washington was prepared to tolerate substantial bloodshed. When the massacres began in April, some U.S. regional specialists initially suspected that Rwanda was undergoing "another flare-up" that would involve another "acceptable" (if tragic) round of ethnic murder.

Rawson had read up on genocide before his posting to Rwanda, surveying what had become a relatively extensive scholarly literature on its causes. But although he expected internecine killing, he did not anticipate the scale at which it occurred. "Nothing in Rwandan culture or history could have led a person to that forecast," he says. "Most of us thought that if a war broke out, it would be quick, that these poor people didn't have the resources, the means, to fight a sophisticated war. I couldn't have known that they would do each other in with the most economic means." George Moose agrees: "We were psychologically and imaginatively too limited."

*   *   *

VII. Genocide? What Genocide?

Just when did Washington know of the sinister Hutu designs on Rwanda's Tutsi? Writing in *Foreign Affairs* last year [2000], Alan Kuperman argued that President Clinton "could not have known that a nationwide genocide was under way" until about two weeks into the killing. It is true that the precise nature and extent of the slaughter was obscured by the civil war, the withdrawal of U.S. diplomatic sources, some confused press reporting, and the lies of the Rwandan government. Nonetheless, both the testimony of U.S. officials who worked the issue day to day and the declassified documents indicate that plenty was known about the killers' intentions.

A determination of genocide turns not on the numbers killed, which is always difficult to ascertain at a time of crisis, but on the perpetrators' intent: Were Hutu forces attempting to destroy Rwanda's Tutsi? The answer to this question was available early on. "By eight A.M. the morning after the plane crash we knew what was happening, that there was systematic killing of Tutsi," Joyce Leader recalls. "People were calling me and telling me who was getting killed. I knew they were going door to door." Back at the State Department she explained to her colleagues that three kinds of killing were going on: war, politically motivated murder, and genocide. Dallaire's early cables to New York likewise described the armed conflict that had resumed between rebels and government forces, and also stated plainly that savage "ethnic cleansing" of Tutsi was occurring. U.S. analysts warned that mass killings would increase. In an April 11 memo prepared for Frank Wisner, the undersecretary of defense for policy, in advance of a dinner with Henry Kissinger, a key talking point was "Unless both sides can be convinced to return to the peace process, a massive (hundreds of thousands of deaths) bloodbath will ensue."

Whatever the inevitable imperfections of U.S. intelligence early on, the reports from Rwanda were severe enough to distinguish Hutu killers from ordinary combatants in civil war. And they certainly warranted directing additional U.S. intelligence assets toward the region—to snap satellite photos of large gatherings of Rwandan civilians or of mass graves, to intercept military communications, or to infiltrate the country in person. Though there is no evidence that senior policy-makers deployed such assets, routine intelligence continued to pour in. On April 26 an unattributed intelligence memo titled "Responsibility for Massacres in Rwanda" reported that the ringleaders of the genocide, Colonel Théoneste Bagosora and his crisis committee, were determined to liquidate their opposition and exterminate the Tutsi populace. A May 9 Defense Intelligence Agency report stated plainly that the Rwandan violence was not spontaneous but was directed by the government, with lists of victims prepared well in advance. The DIA observed that an "organized parallel effort of *genocide* [was] being implemented by the army to destroy the leadership of the Tutsi community."

From April 8 onward media coverage featured eyewitness accounts describing the widespread targeting of Tutsi and the corpses piling up on Kigali's streets. American reporters relayed stories of missionaries and embassy officials who had been unable to save their Rwandan friends and neighbors from death. On April 9 a front-page *Washington Post* story quoted reports that the Rwandan employees of the major international relief agencies had been executed "in front of horrified expatriate staffers." On April 10 a *New York Times* front-page article quoted the Red Cross claim that "tens of thousands" were dead, 8,000 in Kigali alone, and that corpses were "in the houses, in the streets, everywhere." The *Post* the same day led its front-page story with a description of "a pile of corpses six feet high" outside the main hospital. On April 14 the *New York Times* reported the shooting and hacking to death of nearly 1,200 men, women, and children in the church where they had sought refuge. On April 19 Human Rights Watch, which had excellent sources on the ground in Rwanda, estimated the number of dead at 100,000 and called for use of the term "genocide." The 100,000 figure (which proved to be a gross underestimate) was picked up immediately by the Western media, endorsed by the Red Cross, and featured on the front page of the *Washington Post*. On April 24 the *Post* reported how "the heads and limbs of victims were sorted and piled neatly, a bone-chilling order in the midst of chaos that harked back to the Holocaust." President Clinton certainly could have known that a genocide was under way, if he had wanted to know.

Even after the reality of genocide in Rwanda had become irrefutable, when bodies were shown choking the Kagera River on the nightly news, the brute fact of the slaughter failed to influence U.S. policy except in a negative way. American officials, for a variety of reasons, shunned the use of what became known as "the g-word." They felt that using it would have obliged the United States to act, under the terms of the 1948 Genocide Convention. They also believed, understandably, that it would harm U.S. credi-

bility to name the crime and then do nothing to stop it. A discussion paper on Rwanda, prepared by an official in the Office of the Secretary of Defense and dated May 1, testifies to the nature of official thinking. Regarding issues that might be brought up at the next interagency working group, it stated,

> 1. Genocide Investigation: Language that calls for an international investigation of human rights abuses and possible violations of the genocide convention. *Be Careful. Legal at State was worried about this yesterday—Genocide finding could commit [the U.S. government] to actually "do something."* [Emphasis added.]

At an interagency teleconference in late April, Susan Rice, a rising star on the NSC who worked under Richard Clarke, stunned a few of the officials present when she asked, "If we use the word 'genocide' and are seen as doing nothing, what will be the effect on the November [congressional] election?" Lieutenant Colonel Tony Marley remembers the incredulity of his colleagues at the State Department. "We could believe that people would wonder that," he says, "but not that they would actually voice it." Rice does not recall the incident but concedes, "If I said it, it was completely inappropriate, as well as irrelevant."

The genocide debate in U.S. government circles began the last week of April, but it was not until May 21, six weeks after the killing began, that Secretary Christopher gave his diplomats permission to use the term "genocide"—sort of. The UN Human Rights Commission was about to meet in special session, and the U.S. representative, Geraldine Ferraro, needed guidance on whether to join a resolution stating that genocide had occurred. The stubborn U.S. stand had become untenable internationally.

The case for a label of genocide was straightforward, according to a May 18 confidential analysis prepared by the State Department's assistant secretary for intelligence and research, Toby Gati: lists of Tutsi victims' names and addresses had reportedly been prepared; Rwandan government troops and Hutu militia and youth squads were the main perpetrators; massacres were reported all over the country; humanitarian agencies were now "claiming from 200,000 to 500,000 lives" lost. Gati offered the intelligence bureau's view: "We believe 500,000 may be an exaggerated estimate, but no accurate figures are available. Systematic killings began within hours of Habyarimana's death. Most of those killed have been Tutsi civilians, including women and children." The terms of the Genocide Convention had been met. "We weren't quibbling about these numbers," Gati says. "We can never know precise figures, but our analysts had been reporting huge numbers of deaths for weeks. We were basically saying, 'A rose by any other name . . .'"

Despite this straightforward assessment, Christopher remained reluctant to speak the obvious truth. When he issued his guidance, on May 21, fully a month after Human Rights Watch had put a name to the tragedy, Christopher's instructions were hopelessly muddied.

> The delegation is authorized to agree to a resolution that states that "acts of genocide" have occurred in Rwanda or that "genocide has occurred in Rwanda." Other formulations that suggest that some, but not all of the killings in Rwanda are genocide . . . e.g. "genocide is taking place in Rwanda"—are authorized. Delegation is not authorized to agree to the characterization of any specific incident as genocide or to agree to any formulation that indicates that all killings in Rwanda are genocide.

Notably, Christopher confined permission to acknowledge full-fledged genocide to the upcoming session of the Human Rights Commission. Outside that venue State Department officials were authorized to state publicly only that *acts* of genocide had occurred.

Christine Shelly, a State Department spokesperson, had long been charged with publicly articulating the U.S. position on whether events in Rwanda counted as genocide. For two months she had avoided the term, and as her June 10 exchange with the Reuters correspondent Alan Elsner reveals, her semantic dance continued.

ELSNER: How would you describe the events taking place in Rwanda?

SHELLY: Based on the evidence we have seen from observations on the ground, we have every reason to believe that acts of genocide have occurred in Rwanda.

ELSNER: What's the difference between "acts of genocide" and "genocide"?

SHELLY: Well, I think the—as you know, there's a legal definition of this . . . clearly not all of the killings that have taken place in Rwanda are killings to which you might apply that label . . . But as to the distinctions between the words, we're trying to call what we have seen so far as best as we can; and based, again, on the evidence, we have every reason to believe that acts of genocide have occurred.

ELSNER: How many acts of genocide does it take to make genocide?

SHELLY: Alan, that's just not a question that I'm in a position to answer.

The same day, in Istanbul, Warren Christopher, by then under severe internal and external pressure, relented: "If there is any particular magic in calling it genocide, I have no hesitancy in saying that."

VIII. "Not Even a Sideshow"

Once the Americans had been evacuated, Rwanda largely dropped off the radar of most senior Clinton Administration officials. In the situation room on the seventh floor of the State Department a map of Rwanda had been hurriedly pinned to the wall in the aftermath of the plane crash, and eight banks of phones had rung off the hook. Now, with U.S. citizens safely home, the State Department chaired a daily interagency meeting, often by teleconference, designed to coordinate mid-level diplomatic and humanitarian responses. Cabinet-level officials focused on crises elsewhere. Anthony Lake recalls, "I was obsessed with Haiti and Bosnia during that period, so Rwanda was, in William Shawcross's words, a 'sideshow,' but not even a sideshow—a no-show." At the NSC the person who managed Rwanda policy was not Lake, the national-security adviser, who happened to know Africa, but Richard Clarke, who oversaw peacekeeping policy, and for whom the news from Rwanda only confirmed a deep skepticism about the viability of UN deployments. Clarke believed that another UN failure could doom relations between Congress and the United Nations. He also sought to shield the President from congressional and public criticism. Donald Steinberg managed the Africa portfolio at the NSC and tried to look out for the dying Rwandans, but he was not an experienced infighter and, colleagues say, he "never won a single argument" with Clarke.

*　*　*

During the entire three months of the genocide Clinton never assembled his top policy advisers to discuss the killings. Anthony Lake likewise never gathered the "principals"—the Cabinet-level members of the foreign-policy team. Rwanda was never thought to warrant its own top-level meeting. When the subject came up, it did so along with, and subordinate to, discussions of Somalia, Haiti, and Bosnia. Whereas these crises involved U.S. personnel and stirred some public interest, Rwanda generated no sense of urgency and could safely be avoided by Clinton at no political cost. The editorial boards of the major American newspapers discouraged U.S. intervention during the genocide. They, like the Administration, lamented the killings but believed, in the words of an April 17 *Washington Post* editorial, "The United States has no recognizable national interest in taking a role, certainly not a leading role." Capitol Hill was quiet. Some in Congress were glad to be free of the expense of another flawed UN mission. Others, including a few members of the Africa subcommittees and the Congressional Black Caucus, eventually appealed tamely for the United States to play a role in ending the violence—but again,

they did not dare urge U.S. involvement on the ground, and they did not kick up a public fuss. Members of Congress weren't hearing from their constituents. Pat Schroeder, of Colorado, said on April 30, "There are some groups terribly concerned about the gorillas . . . But—it sounds terrible—people just don't know what can be done about the people." Randall Robinson, of the nongovernmental organization TransAfrica, was preoccupied, staging a hunger strike to protest the U.S. repatriation of Haitian refugees. Human Rights Watch supplied exemplary intelligence and established important one-on-one contacts in the Administration, but the organization lacks a grassroots base from which to mobilize a broader segment of American society.

IX. The UN Withdrawal

When the killing began, Romeo Dallaire expected and appealed for reinforcements. Within hours of the plane crash he had cabled UN headquarters in New York: "Give me the means and I can do more." He was sending peacekeepers on rescue missions around the city, and he felt it was essential to increase the size and improve the quality of the UN's presence. But the United States opposed the idea of sending reinforcements, no matter where they were from. The fear, articulated mainly at the Pentagon but felt throughout the bureaucracy, was that what would start as a small engagement by foreign troops would end as a large and costly one by Americans. This was the lesson of Somalia, where U.S. troops had gotten into trouble in an effort to bail out the beleaguered Pakistanis. The logical outgrowth of this fear was an effort to steer clear of Rwanda entirely and be sure others did the same. Only by yanking Dallaire's entire peacekeeping force could the United States protect itself from involvement down the road.

One senior U.S. official remembers, "When the reports of the deaths of the ten Belgians came in, it was clear that it was Somalia redux, and the sense was that there would be an expectation everywhere that the U.S. would get involved. We thought leaving the peacekeepers in Rwanda and having them confront the violence would take us where we'd been before. It was a foregone conclusion that the United States wouldn't intervene and that the concept of UN peacekeeping could not be sacrificed again."

A foregone conclusion. What is most remarkable about the American response to the Rwandan genocide is not so much the absence of U.S. military action as that during the entire genocide the possibility of U.S. military intervention was never even debated. Indeed, the United States resisted intervention of any kind.

The bodies of the slain Belgian soldiers were returned to Brussels on April 14. One of the pivotal conversations in the course of the genocide took place around that time, when Willie Claes, the Belgian Foreign Minister, called the State Department to request "cover." "We are pulling out, but we don't want to be seen to be doing it alone," Claes said, asking the Americans to support a full UN withdrawal. Dallaire had not anticipated that Belgium would extract its soldiers, removing the backbone of his mission and stranding Rwandans in their hour of greatest need. "I expected the excolonial white countries would stick it out even if they took casualties," he remembers. "I thought their pride would have led them to stay to try to sort the place out. The Belgian decision caught me totally off guard. I was truly stunned."

Belgium did not want to leave ignominiously, by itself. Warren Christopher agreed to back Belgian requests for a full UN exit. Policy over the next month or so can be described simply: no U.S. military intervention, robust demands for a withdrawal of all of Dallaire's forces, and no support for a new UN mission that would challenge the killers. Belgium had the cover it needed.

On April 15 Christopher sent one of the most forceful documents to be produced in the entire three months of the genocide to Madeleine Albright at the UN—a cable instructing her to demand a full UN withdrawal. The cable, which was heavily influenced by Richard Clarke at the NSC, and which bypassed Donald Steinberg and was never seen by Anthony Lake, was unequivocal about the next steps. Saying that he had "fully" taken into account the "humanitarian reasons put forth for retention of UNAMIR elements in Rwanda," Christopher wrote that there was "insufficient justification" to retain a UN presence.

> The international community must give highest priority to full, orderly withdrawal of all UNAMIR personnel as soon as possible . . . We will oppose any effort at this time to preserve a UNAMIR presence in Rwanda . . . Our opposition to retaining a UNAMIR presence in Rwanda is firm. It is based on our conviction that the Security Council has an obligation to ensure that peacekeeping operations are viable, that they are capable of fulfilling their mandates, and that UN peacekeeping personnel are not placed or retained, knowingly, in an untenable situation.

"Once we knew the Belgians were leaving, we were left with a rump mission incapable of doing anything to help people," Clarke remembers. "They were doing nothing to stop the killings."

But Clarke underestimated the deterrent effect that Dallaire's very few peacekeepers were having. Although some soldiers hunkered down, terrified, others scoured Kigali, rescuing Tutsi, and later established defensive positions in the city, opening their doors to the fortunate Tutsi who made it through roadblocks to reach them. One Senegalese captain saved a hundred or so lives single-handedly. Some 25,000 Rwandans eventually assembled at positions manned by UNAMIR personnel. The Hutu were generally reluctant to massacre large groups of Tutsi if foreigners (armed or unarmed) were present. It did not take many UN soldiers to dissuade the Hutu from attacking. At the Hotel des Mille Collines ten peacekeepers and four UN military observers helped to protect the several hundred civilians sheltered there for the duration of the crisis. About 10,000 Rwandans gathered at the Amohoro Stadium under light UN cover. Brent

Beardsley, Dallaire's executive assistant, remembers, "If there was any determined resistance at close quarters, the government guys tended to back off." Kevin Aiston, the Rwanda desk officer at the State Department, was keeping track of Rwandan civilians under UN protection. When Prudence Bushnell told him of the U.S. decision to demand a UNAMIR withdrawal, he turned pale. "We can't," he said. Bushnell replied, "The train has already left the station."

On April 19 the Belgian Colonel Luc Marchal delivered his final salute and departed with the last of his soldiers. The Belgian withdrawal reduced Dallaire's troop strength to 2,100. More crucially, he lost his best troops. Command and control among Dallaire's remaining forces became tenuous. Dallaire soon lost every line of communication to the countryside. He had only a single satellite phone link to the outside world.

The UN Security Council now made a decision that sealed the Tutsi's fate and signaled the militia that it would have free rein. The U.S. demand for a full UN withdrawal had been opposed by some African nations, and even by Madeleine Albright; so the United States lobbied instead for a dramatic drawdown in troop strength. On April 21, amid press reports of some 100,000 dead in Rwanda, the Security Council voted to slash UNAMIR's forces to 270 men. Albright went along, publicly declaring that a "small, skeletal" operation would be left in Kigali to "show the will of the international community."

After the UN vote Clarke sent a memorandum to Lake reporting that language about "the safety and security of Rwandans under UN protection had been inserted by US/UN at the end of the day to prevent an otherwise unanimous UNSC from walking away from the at-risk Rwandans under UN protection as the peacekeepers drew down to 270." In other words, the memorandum suggested that the United States was *leading* efforts to ensure that the Rwandans under UN protection were not abandoned. The opposite was true.

Most of Dallaire's troops were evacuated by April 25. Though he was supposed to reduce the size of his force to 270, he ended up keeping 503 peacekeepers. By this time Dallaire was trying to deal with a bloody frenzy. "My force was standing knee-deep in mutilated bodies, surrounded by the guttural moans of dying people, looking into the eyes of children bleeding to death with their wounds burning in the sun and being invaded by maggots and flies," he later wrote. "I found myself walking through villages where the only sign of life was a goat, or a chicken, or a songbird, as all the people were dead, their bodies being eaten by voracious packs of wild dogs."

Dallaire had to work within narrow limits. He attempted simply to keep the positions he held and to protect the 25,000 Rwandans under UN supervision while hoping that the member states on the Security Council would change their minds and send him some help while it still mattered.

By coincidence Rwanda held one of the rotating seats on the Security Council at the time of the genocide. Neither the United States nor any other UN member state ever suggested that the representative of the genocidal government be expelled from the council. Nor did any Security Council country offer to provide safe haven to Rwandan refugees who escaped the carnage. In one instance Dallaire's forces succeeded in evacuating a group of Rwandans by plane to Kenya. The Nairobi authorities allowed the plane to land, sequestered it in a hangar, and, echoing the American decision to turn back the *S.S. St. Louis* during the Holocaust, then forced the plane to return to Rwanda. The fate of the passengers is unknown.

Throughout this period the Clinton Administration was largely silent. The closest it came to a public denunciation of the Rwandan government occurred after personal lobbying by Human Rights Watch, when Anthony Lake issued a statement calling on Rwandan military leaders by name to "do everything in their power to end the violence immediately." When I spoke with Lake six years later, and informed him that human-rights groups and U.S. officials point to this statement as the sum total of official public attempts to shame the Rwandan government in this period, he seemed stunned. "You're kidding," he said. "That's truly pathetic."

At the State Department the diplomacy was conducted privately, by telephone. Prudence Bushnell regularly set her alarm for 2:00 A.M. and phoned Rwandan government officials. She spoke several times with Augustin Bizimungu, the Rwandan military chief of staff. "These were the most bizarre phone calls," she says. "He spoke in perfectly charming French. 'Oh, it's so nice to hear from you,' he said. I told him, 'I am calling to tell you President Clinton is going to hold you accountable for the killings.' He said, 'Oh, how nice it is that your President is thinking of me.'"

X. The Pentagon "Chop"

The daily meeting of the Rwanda interagency working group was attended, either in person or by teleconference, by representatives from the various State Department bureaus, the Pentagon, the National Security Council, and the intelligence community. Any proposal that originated in the working group had to survive the Pentagon "chop." "Hard intervention," meaning U.S. military action, was obviously out of the question. But Pentagon officials routinely stymied initiatives for "soft intervention" as well.

The Pentagon discussion paper on Rwanda, referred to earlier, ran down a list of the working group's six short-term policy objectives and carped at most of them. The fear of a slippery slope was persuasive. Next to the seemingly innocuous suggestion that the United States "support the UN and others in attempts to achieve a cease-fire" the Pentagon official responded, "Need to change 'attempts' to 'political efforts'—without 'political' there is a danger of signing up to troop contributions."

The one policy move the Defense Department supported was a U.S. effort to achieve an arms embargo. But the same discussion paper acknowledged the ineffectiveness of this step: "We do not envision it will have a significant impact on the killings because machetes, knives and other hand implements have been the most common weapons."

Dallaire never spoke to Bushnell or to Tony Marley, the U.S. military liaison to the Arusha process, during the genocide, but they all reached the same conclusions. Seeing that no troops were forthcoming, they turned their attention to measures short of full-scale deployment which might alleviate the suffering. Dallaire pleaded with New York, and Bushnell and her team recommended in Washington, that something be done to "neutralize" Radio Mille Collines.

The country best equipped to prevent the genocide planners from broadcasting murderous instructions directly to the population was the United States. Marley offered three possibilities. The United States could destroy the antenna. It could transmit "counter-broadcasts" urging perpetrators to stop the genocide. Or it could jam the hate radio station's broadcasts. This could have been done from an airborne platform such as the Air Force's Commando Solo airplane. Anthony Lake raised the matter with Secretary of Defense William Perry at the end of April. Pentagon officials considered all the proposals non-starters. On May 5 Frank Wisner, the undersecretary of defense for policy, prepared a memo for Sandy Berger, then the deputy national-security adviser. Wisner's memo testifies to the unwillingness of the U.S. government to make even financial sacrifices to diminish the killing.

> We have looked at options to stop the broadcasts within the Pentagon, discussed them interagency and concluded jamming is an ineffective and expensive mechanism that will not accomplish the objective the NSC Advisor seeks.
>
> International legal conventions complicate airborne or ground based jamming and the mountainous terrain reduces the effectiveness of either option. Commando Solo, an Air National Guard asset, is the only suitable DOD jamming platform. It costs approximately $8500 per flight hour and

requires a semi-secure area of operations due to its vulnerability and limited self-protection.

I believe it would be wiser to use air to assist in Rwanda in the [food] relief effort . . .

The plane would have needed to remain in Rwandan airspace while it waited for radio transmissions to begin. "First we would have had to figure out whether it made sense to use Commando Solo," Wisner recalls. "Then we had to get it from where it was already and be sure it could be moved. Then we would have needed flight clearance from all the countries nearby. And then we would need the political go-ahead. By the time we got all this, weeks would have passed. And it was not going to solve the fundamental problem, which was one that needed to be addressed militarily." Pentagon planners understood that stopping the genocide required a military solution. Neither they nor the White House wanted any part in a military solution. Yet instead of undertaking other forms of intervention that might have at least saved some lives, they justified inaction by arguing that a military solution was required.

Whatever the limitations of radio jamming, which clearly would have been no panacea, most of the delays Wisner cites could have been avoided if senior Administration officials had followed through. But Rwanda was not their problem. Instead justifications for standing by abounded. In early May the State Department Legal Advisor's Office issued a finding against radio jamming, citing international broadcasting agreements and the American commitment to free speech. When Bushnell raised radio jamming yet again at a meeting, one Pentagon official chided her for naiveté: "Pru, radios don't kill people. *People* kill people!"

* * *

However significant and obstructionist the role of the Pentagon in April and May, Defense Department officials were stepping into a vacuum. As one U.S. official put it, "Look, nobody senior was paying any attention to this mess. And in the absence of any political leadership from the top, when you have one group that feels pretty strongly about what *shouldn't* be done, it is extremely likely they are going to end up shaping U.S. policy." Lieutenant General Wesley Clark looked to the White House for leadership. "The Pentagon is always going to be the last to want to intervene," he says. "It is up to the civilians to tell us they want to do something and we'll figure out how to do it."

* * *

XI. PDD-25 in Action

No sooner had most of Dallaire's forces been withdrawn, in late April, than a handful of non-permanent members of the Security Council, aghast at the scale of the slaughter, pressed the major powers to send a new, beefed-up force (UNAMIR II) to Rwanda.

When Dallaire's troops had first arrived, in the fall of 1993, they had done so under a fairly traditional peacekeeping mandate known as a Chapter VI deployment—a mission that assumes a cease-fire and a desire on both sides to comply with a peace accord. The Security Council now had to decide whether it was prepared to move from peacekeeping to peace *enforcement*—that is, to a Chapter VII mission in a hostile environment. This would demand more peacekeepers with far greater resources, more-aggressive rules of engagement, and an explicit recognition that the UN soldiers were there to protect civilians.

Two proposals emerged. Dallaire submitted a plan that called for joining his remaining peacekeepers with about 5,000 well-armed soldiers he hoped could be gathered quickly by the Security Council. He wanted to secure Kigali and then fan outward to create safe havens for Rwandans who had gathered in large numbers at churches and schools and on hillsides around the country. The United States was one of the few countries that could supply the rapid airlift and logistic support needed to move reinforcements to the region. In a meeting with UN Secretary General Boutros Boutros-Ghali on May 10, Vice President Al Gore pledged U.S. help with transport.

Richard Clarke, at the NSC, and representatives of the Joint Chiefs challenged Dallaire's plan. "How do you plan to take control of the airport in Kigali so that the reinforcements will be able to land?" Clarke asked. He argued instead for an "outside-in" strategy, as opposed to Dallaire's "inside-out" approach. The U.S. proposal would have created protected zones for refugees at Rwanda's borders. It would have kept any U.S. pilots involved in airlifting the peacekeepers safely out of Rwanda. "Our proposal was the most feasible, doable thing that could have been done in the short term," Clarke insists. Dallaire's proposal, in contrast, "could not be done in the short term and could not attract peacekeepers." The U.S. plan—which was modeled on Operation Provide Comfort, for the Kurds of northern Iraq— seemed to assume that the people in need were refugees fleeing to the border, but most endangered Tutsi could not make it to the border. The most vulnerable Rwandans were those clustered together, awaiting salvation, deep inside Rwanda. Dallaire's plan would have had UN soldiers move to the Tutsi in hiding. The U.S. plan would have required civilians to move to the safe zones, negotiating murderous roadblocks on the way. "The two plans had very different objectives," Dallaire says. "My mission was to save Rwandans. Their mission was to put on a show at no risk."

America's new peacekeeping doctrine, of which Clarke was the primary architect, was unveiled on May 3, and U.S. officials applied its criteria zealously. PDD-25 did not merely circumscribe U.S. participation in UN missions; it also limited U.S. support for other states that hoped to carry out UN missions. Before such missions could garner U.S. approval, policymakers had to answer certain questions: Were U.S. interests at stake? Was there a threat to world peace? A clear mission goal? Acceptable costs? Congressional, public, and allied support? A working cease-fire?

A clear command-and-control arrangement? And, finally, what was the exit strategy?

The United States haggled at the Security Council and with the UN Department of Peacekeeping Operations for the first two weeks of May. U.S. officials pointed to the flaws in Dallaire's proposal without offering the resources that would have helped him to overcome them. On May 13 Deputy Secretary of State Strobe Talbott sent Madeleine Albright instructions on how the United States should respond to Dallaire's plan. Noting the logistic hazards of airlifting troops into the capital, Talbott wrote, "The U.S. is not prepared at this point to lift heavy equipment and troops into Kigali." The "more manageable" operation would be to create the protected zones at the border, secure humanitarian-aid deliveries, and "promot[e] restoration of a cease-fire and return to the Arusha Peace Process." Talbott acknowledged that even the minimalist American proposal contained "many unanswered questions":

> Where will the needed forces come from; how will they be transported . . . where precisely should these safe zones be created; . . . would UN forces be authorized to move out of the zones to assist affected populations not in the zones . . . will the fighting parties in Rwanda agree to this arrangement . . . what conditions would need to obtain for the operation to end successfully?

Nonetheless, Talbott concluded, "We would urge the UN to explore and refine this alternative and present the Council with a menu of at least two options in a formal report from the [Secretary General] along with cost estimates before the Security Council votes on changing UNAMIR's mandate." U.S. policymakers were asking valid questions. Dallaire's plan certainly would have required the intervening troops to take risks in an effort to reach the targeted Rwandans or to confront the Hutu militia and government forces. But the business-as-usual tone of the American inquiry did not seem appropriate to the unprecedented and utterly unconventional crisis that was under way.

On May 17, by which time most of the Tutsi victims of the genocide were already dead, the United States finally acceded to a version of Dallaire's plan. However, few African countries stepped forward to offer troops. Even if troops had been immediately available, the lethargy of the major powers would have hindered their use. Though the Administration had committed the United States to provide armored support if the African nations provided soldiers, Pentagon stalling resumed. On May 19 the UN formally requested fifty American armored personnel carriers. On May 31 the United States agreed to send the APCs from Germany to Entebbe, Uganda. But squabbles between the Pentagon and UN planners arose. Who would pay for the vehicles? Should the vehicles be tracked or wheeled? Would the UN buy them or simply lease them? And who would pay the shipping costs? Compounding the disputes was the fact that Department of Defense regulations prevented the U.S. Army from preparing the vehicles for transport until contracts had been signed. The Defense Department demanded that it be reimbursed $15 million for shipping spare parts and equipment to and from Rwanda. In mid-June the White House finally intervened. On June 19, a month after the UN request, the United States began transporting the APCs, but they were missing the radios and heavy machine guns that would be needed if UN troops came under fire. By the time the APCs arrived, the genocide was over—halted by Rwandan Patriotic Front forces under the command of the Tutsi leader, Paul Kagame.

XII. The Stories We Tell

It is not hard to conceive of how the United States might have done things differently. Ahead of the plane crash, as violence escalated, it could have agreed to Belgian pleas for UN reinforcements. Once the killing of thousands of Rwandans a day had begun, the President could have deployed U.S. troops to Rwanda. The United States could have joined Dallaire's beleaguered UNAMIR forces or, if it feared associating with shoddy UN peacekeeping, it could have intervened unilaterally with the Security Council's backing, as France eventually did in late June. The United States could also have acted without the UN's blessing, as it did five years later in Kosovo. Securing congressional support for U.S. intervention would have been extremely difficult, but by the second week of the killing Clinton could have made the case that something approximating genocide was under way, that a supreme American value was imperiled by its occurrence, and that U.S. contingents at relatively low risk could stop the extermination of a people.

Alan Kuperman wrote in *Foreign Affairs* that President Clinton was in the dark for two weeks; by the time a large U.S. force could deploy, it would not have saved "even half of the ultimate victims." The evidence indicates that the killers' intentions were known by mid-level officials and knowable by their bosses within a week of the plane crash. Any failure to fully appreciate the genocide stemmed from political, moral, and imaginative weaknesses, not informational ones. As for what force could have accomplished, Kuperman's claims are purely speculative. We cannot know how the announcement of a robust or even a limited U.S. deployment would have affected the perpetrators' behavior. It is worth noting that even Kuperman concedes that belated intervention would have saved 75,000 to 125,000—no small achievement. A more serious challenge comes from the U.S. officials who argue that no amount of leadership from the White House would have overcome congressional opposition to sending U.S. troops to Africa. But even if that highly debatable point was true, the United States still had a variety of options. Instead of leaving it to mid-level officials to communicate with the Rwandan leadership behind the scenes, senior officials in the Administration could have taken control of the process. They could have publicly and frequently denounced the slaughter. They could have branded the crimes "genocide" at a far earlier stage. They could have called for the expulsion of the Rwandan delegation from the Security Council. On the telephone, at the UN, and on the Voice of America they could have threatened to prosecute those complicit in the genocide, naming names when possible. They could have deployed Pentagon assets to jam—even temporarily—the crucial, deadly radio broadcasts.

Instead of demanding a UN withdrawal, quibbling over costs, and coming forward (belatedly) with a plan better suited to caring for refugees than to stopping massacres, U.S. officials could have worked to make UNAMIR a force to contend with. They could have urged their Belgian allies to stay and protect Rwandan civilians. If the Belgians insisted on withdrawing, the White House could have done everything within its power to make sure that Dallaire was immediately reinforced. Senior officials could have spent U.S. political capital rallying troops from other nations and could have supplied strategic airlift and logistic support to a coalition that it had helped to create. In short, the United States could have led the world.

Why did none of these things happen? One reason is that all possible sources of pressure—U.S. allies, Congress, editorial boards, and the American people—were mute when it mattered for Rwanda. American leaders have a circular and deliberate relationship to public opinion. It is circular because public opinion is rarely if ever aroused by foreign crises, even genocidal ones, in the absence of political leadership, and yet at the same time, American leaders continually cite the absence of public support as grounds for inaction. The relationship is deliberate because American leadership is not absent in such circumstances: it was present regarding Rwanda, but devoted mainly to suppressing public outrage and thwarting UN initiatives so as to avoid acting.

Strikingly, most officials involved in shaping U.S. policy were able to define the decision not to stop genocide as ethical and moral. The Administration employed several devices to keep down enthusiasm for action and to preserve the pub-

lic's sense—and, more important, its own—that U.S. policy choices were not merely politically astute but also morally acceptable. First, Administration officials exaggerated the extremity of the possible responses. Time and again U.S. leaders posed the choice as between staying out of Rwanda and "getting involved everywhere." In addition, they often presented the choice as one between doing nothing and sending in the Marines. On May 25, at the Naval Academy graduation ceremony, Clinton described America's relationship to ethnic trouble spots: "We cannot turn away from them, but our interests are not sufficiently at stake in so many of them to justify a commitment of our folks."

Second, Administration policymakers appealed to notions of the greater good. They did not simply frame U.S. policy as one contrived in order to advance the national interest or avoid U.S. casualties. Rather, they often argued against intervention from the standpoint of people committed to protecting human life. Owing to recent failures in UN peacekeeping, many humanitarian interventionists in the U.S. government were concerned about the future of America's relationship with the United Nations generally and peacekeeping specifically. They believed that the UN and humanitarianism could not afford another Somalia. Many internalized the belief that the UN had more to lose by sending reinforcements and failing than by allowing the killings to proceed. Their chief priority, after the evacuation of the Americans, was looking after UN peacekeepers, and they justified the withdrawal of the peacekeepers on the grounds that it would ensure a future for humanitarian intervention. In other words, Dallaire's peacekeeping mission in Rwanda had to be destroyed so that peacekeeping might be saved for use elsewhere.

A third feature of the response that helped to console U.S. officials at the time was the sheer flurry of Rwanda-related activity. U.S. officials with a special concern for Rwanda took their solace from mini-victories—working on behalf of specific individuals or groups (Monique Mujawamariya; the Rwandans gathered at the hotel). Government officials involved in policy met constantly and remained "seized of the matter"; they neither appeared nor felt indifferent. Although little in the way of effective intervention emerged from midlevel meetings in Washington or New York, an abundance of memoranda and other documents did.

Finally, the almost willful delusion that what was happening in Rwanda did not amount to genocide created a nurturing ethical framework for inaction. "War" was "tragic" but created no moral imperative.

What is most frightening about this story is that it testifies to a system that in effect worked.

President Clinton and his advisers had several aims. First, they wanted to avoid engagement in a conflict that posed little threat to American interests, narrowly defined. Second, they sought to appease a restless Congress by showing that they were cautious in their approach to peacekeeping. And third, they hoped to contain the political costs and avoid the moral stigma associated with allowing genocide. By and large, they achieved all three objectives. The normal operations of the foreign-policy bureaucracy and the international community permitted an illusion of continual deliberation, complex activity, and intense concern, even as Rwandans were left to die.

MARGARET E. KECK AND KATHRYN SIKKINK

Transnational Advocacy Networks in International Politics

World politics at the end of the twentieth century involves, alongside states, many nonstate actors that interact with each other, with states, and with international organizations. These interactions are structured in terms of networks, and transnational networks are increasingly visible in international politics. [Networks are forms of organization characterized by voluntary, reciprocal, and horizontal patterns of communication and exchange.] Some involve economic actors and firms. Some are networks of scientists and experts whose professional ties and shared causal ideas underpin their efforts to

From Margaret E. Keck and Kathryn Sikkink, *Activists beyond Borders: Advocacy Networks in International Politics* (Ithaca, N.Y.: Cornell University Press, 1998), Chaps. 1, 3.

influence policy.[1] Others are networks of activists, distinguishable largely by the centrality of principled ideas or values in motivating their formation.[2] We will call these *transnational advocacy networks*. [A transnational advocacy network includes those relevant actors working internationally on an issue who are bound together by shared values, a common discourse, and dense exchanges of information and services.]

Advocacy networks are significant transnationally and domestically. By building new links among actors in civil societies, states, and international organizations, they multiply the channels of access to the international system. In such issue areas as the environment and human rights, they also make international resources available to new actors in domestic political and social struggles. By thus blurring the boundaries between a state's relations with its own nationals and the recourse both citizens and states have to the international system, advocacy networks are helping to transform the practice of national sovereignty.

*   *   *

Transnational advocacy networks are proliferating, and their goal is to change the behavior of states and of international organizations. Simultaneously principled and strategic actors, they "frame" issues to make them comprehensible to target audiences, to attract attention and encourage action, and to "fit" with favorable institutional venues.[3] Network actors bring new ideas, norms, and discourses into policy debates, and serve as sources of information and testimony. * * *

They also promote norm implementation, by pressuring target actors to adopt new policies, and by monitoring compliance with international standards. Insofar as is possible, they seek to maximize their influence or leverage over the target of their actions. In doing so they contribute to changing perceptions that both state and societal actors may have of their identities, interests, and preferences, to transforming their discursive positions, and ultimately to changing procedures, policies, and behavior.[4]

Networks are communicative structures. To influence discourse, procedures, and policy, activists may engage and become part of larger policy communities that group actors working on an issue from a variety of institutional and value perspectives. Transnational advocacy networks must also be understood as political spaces, in which differently situated actors negotiate— formally or informally—the social, cultural, and political meanings of their joint enterprise.

*   *   *

Major actors in advocacy networks may include the following: (1) international and domestic nongovernmental research and advocacy organizations; (2) local social movements; (3) foundations;

(4) the media; (5) churches, trade unions, consumer organizations, and intellectuals; (6) parts of regional and international intergovernmental organizations; and (7) parts of the executive and/or parliamentary branches of governments. Not all these will be present in each advocacy network. Initial research suggests, however, that international and domestic NGOs play a central role in all advocacy networks, usually initiating actions and pressuring more powerful actors to take positions. NGOs introduce new ideas, provide information, and lobby for policy changes.

Groups in a network share values and frequently exchange information and services. The flow of information among actors in the network reveals a dense web of connections among these groups, both formal and informal. The movement of funds and services is especially notable between foundations and NGOs, and some NGOs provide services such as training for other NGOs in the same and sometimes other advocacy networks. Personnel also circulate within and among networks, as relevant players move from one to another in a version of the "revolving door."

*   *   *

We cannot accurately count transnational advocacy networks to measure their growth over time, but one proxy is the increase in the number of international NGOs committed to social change. Because international NGOs are key components of any advocacy network, this increase suggests broader trends in the number, size, and density of advocacy networks generally. Table 7.1 suggests that the number of international nongovernmental social change groups has increased across all issues, though to varying degrees in different issue areas. There are five times as many organizations working primarily on human rights as there were in 1950, but proportionally human rights groups have remained roughly a quarter of all such groups. Similarly, groups working on women's rights accounted for 9 percent of all groups in 1953 and in 1993. Transnational environmental organiza-

TABLE 7.1				
INTERNATIONAL NONGOVERNMENTAL SOCIAL CHANGE ORGANIZATIONS (CATEGORIZED BY THE MAJOR ISSUE FOCUS OF THEIR WORK)				
Issue area (N)	*1953* (N=110)	*1963* (N=141)	*1973* (N=183)	*1983* (N=348)	*1993* (N=631)
Human rights	33 30.0%	38 27.0%	41 22.4%	79 22.7%	168 26.6%
World order	8 7.3	4 2.8	12 6.6	31 8.9	48 7.6
International law	14 12.7	19 13.4	25 13.7	26 7.4	26 4.1
Peace	11 10.0	20 14.2	14 7.7	22 6.3	59 9.4
Women's rights	10 9.1	14 9.9	16 8.7	25 7.2	61 9.7
Environment	2 1.8	5 3.5	10 5.5	26 7.5	90 14.3
Development	3 2.7	3 2.1	7 3.8	13 3.7	34 5.4
Ethnic unity/Group rts.	10 9.1	12 8.5	18 9.8	37 10.6	29 4.6
Esperanto	11 10.0	18 12.8	28 15.3	41 11.8	54 8.6

SOURCE: Union of International Associations, *Yearbook of International Organizations* (1953, 1963, 1973, 1983, 1993). We are indebted to Jackie Smith, University of Notre Dame, for the use of her data from 1983 and 1993, and the use of her coding form and codebook for our data collection for the period 1953–73.

tions have grown most dramatically in absolute and relative terms, increasing from two groups in 1953 to ninety in 1993, and from 1.8 percent of total groups in 1953 to 14.3 percent in 1993. The percentage share of groups in such issue areas as international law, peace, ethnic unity, and Esperanto, has declined.[5]

* * *

How Do Transnational Advocacy Networks Work?

Transnational advocacy networks seek influence in many of the same ways that other political groups or social movements do. Since they are not powerful in a traditional sense of the word, they must use the power of their information, ideas, and strategies to alter the information and value contexts within which states make policies. The bulk of what networks do might be termed persuasion or socialization, but neither process is devoid of conflict. Persuasion and socialization often involve not just reasoning with opponents, but also bringing pressure, arm-twisting, encouraging sanctions, and shaming. * * *

Our typology of tactics that networks use in their efforts at persuasion, socialization, and pressure includes (1) *information politics*, or the ability to quickly and credibly generate politically usable information and move it to where it will have the most impact; (2) *symbolic politics*, or the ability to call upon symbols, actions, or stories that make sense of a situation for an audience that is frequently far away;[6] (3) *leverage politics*, or the ability to call upon powerful actors to affect a situation where weaker members of a network are unlikely to have influence; and (4) *accountability politics*, or the effort to hold powerful actors to their previously stated policies or principles.

A single campaign may contain many of these elements simultaneously. For example, the human rights network disseminated information about human rights abuses in Argentina in the period 1976–83. The Mothers of the Plaza de Mayo marched in circles in the central square in Buenos Aires wearing white handkerchiefs to draw symbolic attention to the plight of their missing children. The network also tried to use both material and moral leverage against the Argentine regime, by pressuring the United States and other governments to cut off military and economic aid, and by efforts to get the UN and the Inter-American Commission on Human Rights to condemn Argentina's human rights practices. Monitoring is a variation on information politics, in which activists use information strategically to ensure accountability with public statements, existing legislation and international standards.

* * *

Network members actively seek ways to bring issues to the public agenda by framing them in innovative ways and by seeking hospitable venues. Sometimes they create issues by framing old problems in new ways; occasionally they help transform other actors' understanding of their identities and their interests. Land use rights in the Amazon, for example, took on an entirely different character and gained quite different allies viewed in a deforestation frame than they did in either social justice or regional development frames. In the 1970s and 1980s many states decided for the first time that promotion of human rights in other countries was a

legitimate foreign policy goal and an authentic expression of national interest. This decision came in part from interaction with an emerging global human rights network. We argue that this represents not the victory of morality over self-interest, but a transformed understanding of national interest, possible in part because of structured interactions between state components and networks. * * *

* * *

Under What Conditions Do Advocacy Networks Have Influence?

To assess the influence of advocacy networks we must look at goal achievement at several different levels. We identify the following types or stages of network influence: (1) issue creation and agenda setting; (2) influence on discursive positions of states and international organizations; (3) influence on institutional procedures; (4) influence on policy change in "target actors" which may be states, international organizations like the World Bank, or private actors like the Nestlé Corporation; and (5) influence on state behavior.

Networks generate attention to new issues and help set agendas when they provoke media attention, debates, hearings, and meetings on issues that previously had not been a matter of public debate. Because values are the essence of advocacy networks, this stage of influence may require a modification of the "value context" in which policy debates takes place. The UN's theme years and decades, such as International Women's Decade and the Year of Indigenous Peoples, were international events promoted by networks that heightened awareness of issues.

Networks influence discursive positions when they help persuade states and international organizations to support international declarations or to change stated domestic policy positions. The role environmental networks played in shaping state positions and conference declarations at the 1992 "Earth Summit" in Rio de Janeiro is an example of this kind of impact. They may also pressure states to make more binding commitments by signing conventions and codes of conduct.

The targets of network campaigns frequently respond to demands for policy change with changes in procedures (which may affect policies in the future). The multilateral bank campaign is largely responsible for a number of changes in internal bank directives mandating greater NGO and local participation in discussions of projects. It also opened access to formerly restricted information, and led to the establishment of an independent inspection panel for World Bank projects. Procedural changes can greatly increase the opportunity for advocacy organizations to develop regular contact with other key players on an issue, and they sometimes offer the opportunity to move from outside to inside pressure strategies.

A network's activities may produce changes in policies, not only of the target states, but also of other states and/or international institutions. Explicit policy shifts seem to denote success, but even here both their causes and meanings may be elusive. We can point with some confidence to network impact where human rights network pressures have achieved cutoffs of military aid to repressive regimes, or a curtailment of repressive practices. Sometimes human rights activity even affects regime stability. But we must take care to distinguish between policy change and change in behavior; official policies regarding timber extraction in Sarawak, Malaysia, for example, may say little about how timber companies behave on the ground in the absence of enforcement.

We speak of stages of impact, and not merely types of impact, because we believe that increased attention, followed by changes in discursive positions, make governments more vulnerable to the claims that networks raise. (Discursive changes can also have a powerfully divisive effect on networks themselves, splitting insiders from outsiders, reformers from radicals.[7]) A government that claims to be protecting indigenous areas or ecological reserves is potentially more vulnerable to charges that such areas are endangered than one that makes no such claim. At that point the effort is not to make governments change their position but to hold them to their word. Meaningful policy change is thus more likely when the first three types or stages of impact have occurred.

Both issue characteristics and actor characteristics are important parts of our explanation of how networks affect political outcomes and the conditions under which networks can be effective. Issue characteristics such as salience and resonance within existing national or institutional agendas can tell us something about where networks are likely to be able to insert new ideas and discourses into policy debates. Success in influencing policy also depends on the strength and density of the network and its ability to achieve leverage. * * *

* * *

Toward a Global Civil Society?

Many other scholars now recognize that "the state does not monopolize the public sphere,"[8] and are seeking, as we are, ways to describe the sphere of international interactions under a variety of names: transnational relations, international civil society, and global civil society.[9] In these views, states no longer look unitary from the outside. Increasingly dense interactions among individuals, groups, actors from states, and international institutions appear to involve much more than representing interests on a world stage.

We contend that the advocacy network concept cannot be subsumed under notions of transnational social movements or global civil society. In particular, theorists who suggest that a global civil society will inevitably emerge from economic globalization or from revolutions in communication and transportation technologies ignore the issues of agency and political opportunity that we find central for understanding the evolution of new international institutions and relationships.

* * *

We lack convincing studies of the sustained and specific processes through which individuals and organizations create (or resist the creation of) something resembling a global civil society. Our research leads us to believe that these interactions involve much more agency than a pure diffusionist perspective suggests. Even though the implications of our findings are much broader than most political scientists would admit, the findings themselves do not yet support the strong claims about an emerging global civil society.[10] We are much more comfortable with a conception of transnational civil society as an arena of struggle, a fragmented and contested area where "the politics of transnational civil society is centrally about the way in which certain groups emerge and are legitimized (by governments, institutions, and other groups)."[11]

* * *

Human Rights Advocacy Networks in Latin America

Argentina

Even before the military coup of March 1976, international human rights pressures had influenced the Argentine military's decision to cause political opponents to "disappear," rather than imprisoning them or executing them publicly.[12] (The technique led to the widespread use of the verb "to disappear" in a transitive sense.) The Argentine military believed they had "learned" from the international reaction to the human rights abuses after the Chilean coup. When the Chilean military executed and imprisoned large numbers of people, the ensuing uproar led to the international isolation of the regime of Augusto Pinochet. Hoping to maintain a moderate international image, the Argentine military decided to secretly kidnap, detain, and execute its victims, while denying any knowledge of their whereabouts.[13]

Although this method did initially mute the international response to the coup, Amnesty International and groups staffed by Argentine political exiles eventually were able to document and condemn the new forms of repressive practices. To counteract the rising tide of criticism, the Argentina junta invited AI for an on-site visit in 1976. In March 1977, on the first anniversary of the military coup, AI published the report on its visit, a well-documented denunciation of the abuses of the regime with emphasis on the problem of the disappeared. Amnesty estimated that the regime had taken six thousand political prisoners, most without specifying charges, and had abducted between two and ten thousand people. The report helped demonstrate that the disappearances were part of a deliberate government policy by which the military and the police kidnapped perceived opponents, took them to secret detention centers where they tortured, interrogated, and killed them, then secretly disposed of their bodies.[14] Amnesty International's denunciations of the Argentine regime were legitimized when it won the Nobel Peace Prize later that year.

Such information led the Carter administration and the French, Italian, and Swedish governments to denounce rights violations by the junta. France, Italy, and Sweden each had citizens who had been victims of Argentine repression, but their concerns extended beyond their own citizens. Although the Argentine government claimed that such attacks constituted unacceptable intervention in their internal affairs and violated Argentine sovereignty, U.S. and European officials persisted. In 1977 the U.S. government reduced the planned level of military aid for Argentina because of human rights abuses. Congress later passed a bill eliminating all military assistance to Argentina, which went into effect on 30 September 1978.[15] A number of high-level U.S. delegations met with junta members during this period to discuss human rights.

Early U.S. action on Argentina was based primarily on the human rights documentation provided by AI and other NGOs, not on information received through official channels at the embassy or the State Department.[16] For example, during a 1977 visit, Secretary of State Cyrus Vance carried a list of disappeared people prepared by human rights NGOs to present to members of the junta.[17] When Patricia Derian met with junta member Admiral Emilio Massera during a visit in 1977, she brought up the navy's use of torture. In response to Massera's denial, Derian said she had seen a rudimentary map of a secret detention center in the Navy Mechanical School, where their meeting was being held, and asked whether perhaps under their feet someone was being tortured. Among Derian's key sources of information were NGOs and especially the families of the disappeared, with whom she met frequently during her visits to Buenos Aires.[18]

Within a year of the coup, Argentine domestic human rights organizations began to develop significant external contacts. Their members traveled frequently to the United States and Europe, where they met with human rights organizations, talked to the press, and met with parliamentarians and government officials. These groups sought foreign contacts to publicize the human rights situation, to fund their activities, and to help protect themselves from further repression by their government, and they provided evidence to U.S. and European policymakers. Much of their funding came from European and U.S.-based foundations.[19]

Two key events that served to keep the case of Argentine human rights in the minds of U.S. and European policymakers reflect the impact of transnational linkages on policy. In 1979 the Argentine authorities released Jacobo Timerman, whose memoir describing his disappearance and torture by the Argentine military helped human rights organizations, members of the U.S. Jewish community, and U.S. journalists to make his case a cause célèbre in U.S. policy circles.[20] Then in 1980 the Nobel Peace Prize was awarded to an Argentine human rights activist, Adolfo Pérez Esquivel. Peace and human rights groups in the United States and Europe helped sponsor Pérez Esquivel's speaking tour to the United States exactly at the time that the OAS was considering the IACHR report on Argentina and Congress was debating the end of the arms embargo to Argentina.

The Argentine military government wanted to avoid international human rights censure. Scholars have long recognized that even authoritarian regimes depend on a combination of coercion and consent to stay in power. Without the legitimacy conferred by elections, they rely heavily on claims about their political efficacy and on nationalism.[21] Although the Argentine military mobilized nationalist rhetoric against foreign criticism, a sticking point was that Argentines, especially the groups that most supported the military regime, thought of themselves as the most European of Latin American countries. The military junta claimed to be carrying out the repression in the name of "our Western and Christian civilization."[22] But the military's intent to integrate Argentina more fully into the liberal global economic order was being jeopardized by deteriorating relations with countries most identified with that economic order, and with "Western and Christian civilization."

The junta adopted a sequence of responses to international pressures. From 1976 to 1978 the military pursued an initial strategy of denying the legitimacy of international concern over human rights in Argentina. At the same time it took actions that appear to have contradicted this strategy, such as permitting the visit of the Amnesty International mission to Argentina in 1976. The "failure" of the Amnesty visit, from the military point of view, appeared to reaffirm the junta's resistance to human rights pressures. This strategy was most obvious at the UN, where the Argentine government worked to silence international condemnation in the UN Commission on Human Rights. Ironically, the rabidly anticommunist Argentine regime found a diplomatic ally in the Soviet Union, an importer of Argentine wheat, and the two countries collaborated to block UN consideration of the Argentine human rights situation.[23] Concerned states circumvented this blockage by creating the UN Working Group on Disappearances in 1980. Human rights NGOs provided information, lobbied government delegations, and pursued joint strategies with sympathetic UN delegations.

By 1978 the Argentine government recognized that something had to be done to improve its international image in the United States and Europe, and to restore the flow of military and economic aid.[24] To these ends the junta invited the Inter-American Commission on Human Rights for an on-site visit, in exchange for a U.S. commitment to release Export-Import Bank funds and otherwise improve U.S.-Argentine relations.[25] During 1978 the human rights situation in Argentina improved significantly. [T]he practice of disappearance as a tool of state policy was curtailed only after 1978, when the government began to take the "international variable" seriously.[26]

The value of the network perspective in the Argentine case is in highlighting the fact that international pressures did not work independently, but rather in coordination with national actors. Rapid change occurred because strong domestic human rights organizations documented abuses and protested against repression, and international pressures helped protect domestic monitors and open spaces for their protest. International groups amplified both information

and symbolic politics of domestic groups and projected them onto an international stage, from which they echoed back into Argentina. This classic boomerang process was executed nowhere more skillfully than in Argentina, in large part due to the courage and ability of domestic human rights organizations.

Some argue that repression stopped because the military had finally killed all the people that they thought they needed to kill. This argument disregards disagreements within the regime about the size and nature of the "enemy." International pressures affected particular factions within the military regime that had differing ideas about how much repression was "necessary." Although by the military's admission 90 percent of the *armed* opposition had been eliminated by April 1977, this did not lead to an immediate change in human rights practices.[27] By 1978 there were splits within the military about what it should do in the future. One faction was led by Admiral Massera, a right-wing populist, another by Generals Carlos Suarez Mason and Luciano Menéndez, who supported indefinite military dictatorship and unrelenting war against the left, and a third by Generals Jorge Videla and Roberto Viola, who hoped for eventual political liberalization under a military president. Over time, the Videla-Viola faction won out, and by late 1978 Videla had gained increased control over the Ministry of Foreign Affairs, previously under the influence of the navy.[28] Videla's ascendancy in the fall of 1978, combined with U.S. pressure, helps explain his ability to deliver on his promise to allow the Inter-American Commission on Human Rights visit in December.

The Argentine military government thus moved from initial refusal to accept international human rights interventions, to cosmetic cooperation with the human rights network, and eventually to concrete improvements in response to increased international pressures. Once it had invited IACHR and discovered that the commission could not be co-opted or confused, the government ended the practice of disappearance, released political prisoners, and restored some semblance of political participation. Full restoration of human rights in Argentina did not come until after the Malvinas War and the transition to democracy in 1983, but after 1980 the worst abuses had been curtailed.

In 1985, after democratization, Argentina tried the top military leaders of the juntas for human rights abuses, and a number of key network members testified: Theo Van Boven and Patricia Derian spoke about international awareness of the Argentine human rights situation, and a member of the IACHR delegation to Argentina discussed the OAS report. Clyde Snow and Eric Stover provided information about the exhumation of cadavers from mass graves. Snow's testimony, corroborated by witnesses, was a key part of the prosecutor's success in establishing that top military officers were guilty of murder.[29] A public opinion poll taken during the trials showed that 92 percent of Argentines were in favor of the trials of the military juntas.[30] The tribunal convicted five of the nine defendants, though only two—ex-president Videla, and Admiral Massera—were given life sentences. The trials were the first of their kind in Latin America, and among the very few in the world ever to try former leaders for human rights abuses during their rule. In 1990 President Carlos Menem pardoned the former officers. By the mid-1990s, however, democratic rule in Argentina was firmly entrenched, civilian authority over the military was well established, and the military had been weakened by internal disputes and severe cuts in funding.[31]

The Argentine case set important precedents for other international and regional human rights action, and shows the intricate interactions of groups and individuals within the network and the repercussions of these interactions. The story of the Grandmothers of the Plaza de Mayo is an exemplar of network interaction and unanticipated effects. The persistence of the Grandmothers helped create a new profession—what one might call "human rights forensic science." (The scientific skills existed before, but they had never been put to the service of human

rights.) Once the Argentine case had demonstrated that forensic science could illuminate mass murder and lead to convictions, these skills were diffused and legitimized. Eric Stover, Clyde Snow, and the Argentine forensic anthropology team they helped create were the prime agents of international diffusion. The team later carried out exhumations and training in Chile, Bolivia, Brazil, Venezuela, and Guatemala.[32] Forensic science is being used to prosecute mass murderers in El Salvador, Honduras, Rwanda, and Bosnia. By 1996 the UN International Criminal Tribunal for the former Yugoslavia had contracted with two veterans of the Argentine forensic experiment, Stover and Dr. Robert Kirschner, to do forensic investigations for its war crimes tribunal. "'A war crime creates a crime scene,' said Dr. Kirschner, 'That's how we treat it. We recover forensic evidence for prosecution and create a record which cannot be successfully challenged in court.'"[33]

* * *

Conclusions

A realist approach to international relations would have trouble attributing significance either to the network's activities or to the adoption and implementation of state human rights policies. Realism offers no convincing explanation for why relatively weak nonstate actors could affect state policy, or why states would concern themselves with the internal human rights practices of other states even when doing so interferes with the pursuit of other goals. For example, the U.S. government's pressure on Argentina on human rights led Argentina to defect from the grain embargo of the Soviet Union. Raising human rights issues with Mexico could have undermined the successful completion of the free trade agreement and cooperation with Mexico on antidrug operations. Human rights pressures have costs, even in strategically less important countries of Latin America.

In liberal versions of international relations theory, states and nonstate actors cooperate to realize joint gains or avoid mutually undesirable outcomes when they face problems they cannot resolve alone. These situations have been characterized as cooperation or coordination games with particular payoff structures.[34] But human rights issues are not easily modeled as such. Usually states can ignore the internal human rights practices of other states without incurring undesirable economic or security costs.

In the issue of human rights it is primarily principled ideas that drive change and cooperation. We cannot understand why countries, organizations, and individuals are concerned about human rights or why countries respond to human rights pressures without taking into account the role of norms and ideas in international life. Jack Donnelly has argued that such moral interests are as real as material interests, and that a sense of moral interdependence has led to the emergence of human rights regimes.[35] For human rights * * * the primary movers behind this form of principled international action are international networks.

NOTES

1. Peter Haas has called these "knowledge-based" or "epistemic communities." See Peter Haas, "Introduction: Epistemic Communities and International Policy Coordination," *Knowledge, Power and International Policy Coordination,* special issue, *International Organization* 46 (Winter 1992), pp. 1–36.

2. Ideas that specify criteria for determining whether actions are right and wrong and whether outcomes are just or unjust are shared principled beliefs or values. Beliefs about cause-effect relationships are shared casual beliefs. Judith Goldstein and Robert Keohane, eds., *Ideas and Foreign Policy: Beliefs, Institutions, and Political Change* (Ithaca: Cornell University Press, 1993), pp. 8–10.

3. David Snow and his colleagues have adapted Erving Goffman's concept of framing. We use it to mean "conscious strategic efforts by groups of people to fashion shared understandings of the world and of themselves that legitimate and motivate collective action." Definition from Doug McAdam, John D. McCarthy, and Mayer N. Zald, "Introduction," *Comparative Perspectives on Social Movements: Political Opportunities, Mobilizing Structures, and Cultural Framings,* ed. McAdam, McCarthy, and Zald (New York: Cambridge University Press, 1996), p. 6. See also Frank Baumgartner and Bryan Jones, "Agenda Dynamics and Policy Subsystems," *Journal of Politics* 53:4 (1991): 1044–74.

4. With the "constructivists" in international relations theory, we take actors and interests to be constituted in interaction. See Martha Finnemore, *National Interests in International Society* (Ithaca: Cornell University Press, 1996), who argues that "states are embedded in dense networks of transnational and international social relations that shape their perceptions of the world and their role in that world. States are *socialized* to want certain things by the international society in which they and the people in them live" (p. 2).

5. Data from a collaborative research project with Jackie G. Smith. We thank her for the use of her data from the period 1983–93, whose results are presented in Jackie G. Smith, "Characteristics of the Modern Transnational Social Movement Sector," in Jackie G. Smith, et al., eds. *Transnational Social Movements and World Politics: Solidarity beyond the State* (Syracuse: Syracuse University Press, forthcoming 1997), and for permission to use her coding form and codebook for our data collection for the period 1953–73. All data were coded from Union of International Associations, *The Yearbook of International Organizations,* 1948–95 (published annually).

6. Alison Brysk uses the categories "information politics" and "symbolic politics" to discuss strategies of transnational actors, especially networks around Indian rights. See "Acting Globally: Indian Rights and International Politics in Latin America," in *Indigenous Peoples and Democracy in Latin America,* ed. Donna Lee Van Cott (New York: St. Martin's Press/Inter-American Dialogue, 1994), pp. 29–51; and "Hearts and Minds: Bringing Symbolic Politics Back In," *Polity* 27 (Summer 1995): 559–85.

7. We thank Jonathan Fox for reminding us of this point.

8. M. J. Peterson, "Transnational Activity, International Society, and World Politics," *Millennium* 21:3 (1992): 375–76.

9. See, for example, Ronnie Lipschutz, "Reconstructing World Politics: The Emergence of Global Civil Society," *Millennium* 21:3 (1992): 389–420; Paul Wapner, "Politics beyond the State: Environmental Activism and World Civic Politics," *World Politics* 47 (April 1995): 311–40; and the special issue of *Millennium* on social movements and world politics, 23:3 (Winter 1994).

10. Sidney Tarrow, *Power in Movement: Social Movements and Contentious Politics,* rev. ed. (Cambridge: Cambridge University Press, forthcoming 1998), Chapter 11. An earlier version appeared as "Fishnets, Internets and Catnets: Globalization and Transnational Collective Action," Instituto Juan March de Estudios e Investigaciones, Madrid: Working Papers 1996/78, March 1996; and Peterson, "Transnational Activity."

11. Andrew Hurrell and Ngaire Woods, "Globalisation and Inequality," *Millennium* 24:3 (1995), p. 468.

12. This section draws upon some material from an earlier co-authored work: Lisa L. Martin and Kathryn Sikkink, "U.S. Policy and Human Rights in Argentina and Guatemala, 1973–1980," in *Double-Edged Diplomacy: International Bargaining and Domestic Politics,* ed., Peter B. Evans, Harold K. Jacobson, and Robert D. Putnam (Berkeley: University of California Press, 1993), pp. 330–62.

13. See Emilio Mignone, *Derechos humanos y sociedad: el caso argentino* (Buenos Aires: Ediciones del Pensamiento Nacional and Centro de Estudios Legales y Sociales, 1991), p. 66; Claudio Uriarte, *Almirante Cero: Biografía No Autorizada de Emilio Eduardo Massera* (Buenos Aires: Planeta, 1992), p. 97; and Carlos H. Acuña and Catalina Smulovitz, "Adjusting the Armed Forces to Democracy: Successes, Failures, and Ambiguities in the Southern Cone," in *Constructing Democracy: Human Rights, Citizenship, and Society in Latin America,* ed. Elizabeth Jelin and Eric Hershberg (Boulder, Colo.: Westview, 1993), p. 15.

14. Amnesty International, *Report of an Amnesty International Mission to Argentina* (London: Amnesty International, 1977).

15. Congressional Research Service, Foreign Affairs and National Defense Division, *Human Rights and U.S. Foreign Assistance: Experiences and Issues in Policy Implementation (1977–1978),* report prepared for U.S. Senate Committee on Foreign Relations, November 1979, p. 106.

16. After the 1976 coup, Argentine political exiles set up branches of the Argentine Human Rights Commission (CADHU) in Paris, Mexico, Rome, Geneva, and Washington, D.C. In October two of its members testified on human rights abuses before the U.S. House Subcommittee on Human Rights and International Organization. Iain Guest, *Behind the Disappearances: Argentina's Dirty War against Human Rights and the United Nations* (Philadelphia: University of Pennsylvania Press, 1990), pp. 66–67.

17. Interview with Robert Pastor, Wianno, Massachusetts, 28 June 1990.

18. Testimony given by Patricia Derian to the National Criminal Appeals Court in Buenos Aires during the trials of junta members. "Massera sonrió y me dijo: Sabe qué pasó con Poncio Pilatos . . . ?" *Diario del Juicio,* 18 June 1985, p. 3; Guest, *Behind the Disappearances,*

pp. 161–63. Later it was confirmed that the Navy Mechanical School was one of the most notorious secret torture and detention centers. *Nunca Más: The Report of the Argentine National Commission for the Disappeared* (New York: Farrar Straus & Giroux, 1986), pp. 79–84.

19. The Mothers of the Plaza de Mayo received grants from Dutch churches and the Norwegian Parliament, and the Ford Foundation provided funds for the Center for Legal and Social Studies (CELS) and the Grandmothers of the Plaza de Mayo.

20. Jacobo Timerman, *Prisoner without a Name, Cell without a Number* (New York: Random House, 1981).

21. See Guillermo O'Donnell, "Tensions in the Bureaucratic Authoritarian State and the Question of Democracy," in *The New Authoritarianism in Latin America*, ed. David Collier (Princeton: Princeton University Press, 1979), pp. 288, 292–94.

22. Daniel Frontalini and Maria Cristina Caiati, *El Mito de la Guerra Sucia* (Buenos Aires: Centro de Estudios Legales y Sociales, 1984), p. 24.

23. Guest, *Behind the Disappearances*, pp. 118–19, 182–83.

24. *Carta Política*, a news magazine considered to reflect the junta's views concluded in 1978 that "the principal problem facing the Argentine State has now become the international siege (*cerco internacional*)." "Cuadro de Situación," *Carta Política* 57 (August 1978): 8.

25. Interviews with Walter Mondale, Minneapolis, Minnesota, 20 June 1989, and Ricardo Yofre, Buenos Aires, 1 August 1990.

26. See Asamblea Permanente por los Derechos Humanos, *Las Cifras de la Guerra Sucia* (Buenos Aires, 1988), pp. 26–32.

27. According to a memorandum signed by General Jorge Videla, the objectives of the military government "go well beyond the simple defeat of subversion." The memorandum called for a continuation and intensification of the "general offensive against subversion," including "intense military action." "Directivo 504," 20 April 1977, in "La orden secreta de Videla," *Diario del Juicio* 28 (3 December 1985): 5–8.

28. David Rock, *Argentina, 1516–1987: From Spanish Colonization to Alfonsín* (Berkeley: University of California Press, 1985), pp. 370–71; Timerman, *Prisoner without a Name*, p. 163.

29. *Diario del Juicio* 1 (27 May 1985), and 9 (23 July 1985).

30. *Diario del Juicio* 25 (12 November 1985).

31. Acuña and Smulovitz, "Adjusting the Armed Forces to Democracy," pp. 20–21.

32. Cohen Salama, *Tumbas anónimas [informe sobre la identificación de restos de víctimas de la represión* (Buenos Aires: Catálogos Editora, 1992)], p. 275.

33. Mike O'Connor, "Harvesting Evidence in Bosnia's Killing Fields," *New York Times*, 7 April 1996, p. E3.

34. See, e.g., Arthur A. Stein, "Coordination and Collaboration: Regimes in an Anarchic World," *International Organization* 36:2 (Spring 1982): 299–324.

35. Donnelly, *Universal Human Rights [in Theory and Practice* (Ithaca: Cornell University Press, 1989)], pp. 211–12.

HENRY A. KISSINGER

The Pitfalls of Universal Jurisdiction

Risking Judicial Tyranny

In less than a decade, an unprecedented move-ment has emerged to submit international politics to judicial procedures. It has spread with extraor-dinary speed and has not been subjected to sys-tematic debate, partly because of the intimidating passion of its advocates. To be sure, human rights violations, war crimes, genocide, and torture have so disgraced the modern age and in such a variety of places that the effort to interpose legal norms to prevent or punish such outrages does credit to its advocates. The danger lies in pushing the effort to extremes that risk substituting the tyranny of judges for that of governments; historically, the dictatorship of the virtuous has often led to inqui-sitions and even witch-hunts.

The doctrine of universal jurisdiction asserts that some crimes are so heinous that their per-petrators should not escape justice by invoking doctrines of sovereign immunity or the sacro-sanct nature of national frontiers. Two specific approaches to achieve this goal have emerged recently. The first seeks to apply the procedures of domestic criminal justice to violations of uni-versal standards, some of which are embodied in United Nations conventions, by authorizing national prosecutors to bring offenders into their jurisdictions through extradition from third countries. The second approach is the Interna-tional Criminal Court (ICC), the founding treaty for which was created by a conference in Rome in July 1998 and signed by 95 states, including

From *Foreign Affairs* 80, no. 4 (July/Aug. 2001): 86–96.

most European countries. It has already been ratified by 30 nations and will go into effect when the total reaches 60. On December 31, 2000, President Bill Clinton signed the ICC treaty with only hours to spare before the cutoff date. But he indicated that he would neither submit it for Senate approval nor recommend that his succes-sor do so while the treaty remains in its present form.

The very concept of universal jurisdiction is of recent vintage. The sixth edition of *Black's Law Dictionary*, published in 1990, does not contain even an entry for the term. The closest analogous concept listed is *hostes humani generis* ("enemies of the human race"). Until recently, the latter term has been applied to pirates, hijackers, and similar outlaws whose crimes were typically committed outside the territory of any state. The notion that heads of state and senior public officials should have the same standing as outlaws before the bar of justice is quite new.

In the aftermath of the Holocaust and the many atrocities committed since, major efforts have been made to find a judicial standard to deal with such catastrophes: the Nuremberg trials of 1945–46, the Universal Declaration of Human Rights of 1948, the genocide convention of 1948, and the antitorture convention of 1988. The Final Act of the Conference on Security and Coopera-tion in Europe, signed in Helsinki in 1975 by President Gerald Ford on behalf of the United States, obligated the 35 signatory nations to observe certain stated human rights, subjecting violators to the pressures by which foreign policy commitments are generally sustained. In the hands of courageous groups in Eastern Europe, the Final Act became one of several weapons by which communist rule was delegitimized and eventually undermined. In the 1990s, international tribunals to punish crimes committed in the former Yugoslavia and Rwanda, established ad hoc by the U.N. Security Council, have sought to provide a system of accountability for specific regions ravaged by arbitrary violence.

But none of these steps was conceived at the time as instituting a "universal jurisdiction." It is unlikely that any of the signatories of either the U.N. conventions or the Helsinki Final Act thought it possible that national judges would use them as a basis for extradition requests regarding alleged crimes committed outside their jurisdictions. The drafters almost certainly believed that they were stating general principles, not laws that would be enforced by national courts. For example, Eleanor Roosevelt, one of the drafters of the Universal Declaration of Human Rights, referred to it as a "common standard." As one of the negotiators of the Final Act of the Helsinki conference, I can affirm that the administration I represented considered it primarily a diplomatic weapon to use to thwart the communists' attempts to pressure the Soviet and captive peoples. Even with respect to binding undertakings such as the genocide convention, it was never thought that they would subject past and future leaders of one nation to prosecution by the national magistrates of another state where the violations had not occurred. Nor, until recently, was it argued that the various U.N. declarations subjected past and future leaders to the possibility of prosecution by national magistrates of third countries without either due process safeguards or institutional restraints.

Yet this is in essence the precedent that was set by the 1998 British detention of former Chilean President Augusto Pinochet as the result of an extradition request by a Spanish judge seeking to try Pinochet for crimes committed against Spaniards on Chilean soil. For advocates of universal jurisdiction, that detention—

lasting more than 16 months—was a landmark establishing a just principle. But any universal system should contain procedures not only to punish the wicked but also to constrain the righteous. It must not allow legal principles to be used as weapons to settle political scores. Questions such as these must therefore be answered: What legal norms are being applied? What are the rules of evidence? What safeguards exist for the defendant? And how will prosecutions affect other fundamental foreign policy objectives and interests?

A Dangerous Precedent

It is decidedly unfashionable to express any degree of skepticism about the way the Pinochet case was handled. For almost all the parties of the European left, Augusto Pinochet is the incarnation of a right-wing assault on democracy because he led a coup d'état against an elected leader. At the time, others, including the leaders of Chile's democratic parties, viewed Salvador Allende as a radical Marxist ideologue bent on imposing a Castro-style dictatorship with the aid of Cuban-trained militias and Cuban weapons. This was why the leaders of Chile's democratic parties publicly welcomed—yes, welcomed—Allende's overthrow. (They changed their attitude only after the junta brutally maintained its autocratic rule far longer than was warranted by the invocation of an emergency.)

Disapproval of the Allende regime does not exonerate those who perpetrated systematic human rights abuses after it was overthrown. But neither should the applicability of universal jurisdiction as a policy be determined by one's view of the political history of Chile. The appropriate solution was arrived at in August 2000 when the Chilean Supreme Court withdrew Pinochet's senatorial immunity, making it possible to deal with the charges against him in the courts of the country most competent to judge this history and to relate its decisions to the stability and vitality of its democratic institutions.

On November 25, 1998, the judiciary committee of the British House of Lords (the United Kingdom's supreme court) concluded that "international law has made it plain that certain types of conduct . . . are not acceptable conduct on the part of anyone." But that principle did not oblige the lords to endow a Spanish magistrate—and presumably other magistrates elsewhere in the world—with the authority to enforce it in a country where the accused had committed no crime, and then to cause the restraint of the accused for 16 months in yet another country in which he was equally a stranger. It could have held that Chile, or an international tribunal specifically established for crimes committed in Chile on the model of the courts set up for heinous crimes in the former Yugoslavia and Rwanda, was the appropriate forum.

The unprecedented and sweeping interpretation of international law in *Ex parte Pinochet* would arm any magistrate anywhere in the world with the power to demand extradition, substituting the magistrate's own judgment for the reconciliation procedures of even incontestably democratic societies where alleged violations of human rights may have occurred. It would also subject the accused to the criminal procedures of the magistrate's country, with a legal system that may be unfamiliar to the defendant and that would force the defendant to bring evidence and witnesses from long distances. Such a system goes far beyond the explicit and limited mandates established by the U.N. Security Council for the tribunals covering war crimes in the former Yugoslavia and Rwanda as well as the one being negotiated for Cambodia.

Perhaps the most important issue is the relationship of universal jurisdiction to national reconciliation procedures set up by new democratic governments to deal with their countries' questionable pasts. One would have thought that a Spanish magistrate would have been sensitive to the incongruity of a request by Spain, itself haunted by transgressions committed during the Spanish Civil War and the regime of General Francisco Franco, to try in Spanish courts alleged crimes against humanity committed elsewhere.

The decision of post-Franco Spain to avoid wholesale criminal trials for the human rights violations of the recent past was designed explicitly to foster a process of national reconciliation that undoubtedly contributed much to the present vigor of Spanish democracy. Why should Chile's attempt at national reconciliation not have been given the same opportunity? Should any outside group dissatisfied with the reconciliation procedures of, say, South Africa be free to challenge them in their own national courts or those of third countries?

It is an important principle that those who commit war crimes or systematically violate human rights should be held accountable. But the consolidation of law, domestic peace, and representative government in a nation struggling to come to terms with a brutal past has a claim as well. The instinct to punish must be related, as in every constitutional democratic political structure, to a system of checks and balances that includes other elements critical to the survival and expansion of democracy.

Another grave issue is the use in such cases of extradition procedures designed for ordinary criminals. If the Pinochet case becomes a precedent, magistrates anywhere will be in a position to put forward an extradition request without warning to the accused and regardless of the policies the accused's country might already have in place for dealing with the charges. The country from which extradition is requested then faces a seemingly technical legal decision that, in fact, amounts to the exercise of political discretion—whether to entertain the claim or not.

Once extradition procedures are in train, they develop a momentum of their own. The accused is not allowed to challenge the substantive merit of the case and instead is confined to procedural issues: that there was, say, some technical flaw in the extradition request, that the judicial system of the requesting country is incapable of providing a fair hearing, or that the crime for which the extradition is sought is not treated as a crime in the country from which extradition has been requested—thereby conceding much of the merit of the charge. Meanwhile, while these claims are being considered by the judicial system of the country from which extradition is sought, the accused remains in some form of detention, possibly for years. Such procedures provide an opportunity for political harassment long before the accused is in a position to present any defense. It would be ironic if a doctrine designed to transcend the political process turns into a means to pursue political enemies rather than universal justice.

The Pinochet precedent, if literally applied, would permit the two sides in the Arab-Israeli conflict, or those in any other passionate international controversy, to project their battles into the various national courts by pursuing adversaries with extradition requests. When discretion on what crimes are subject to universal jurisdiction and whom to prosecute is left to national prosecutors, the scope for arbitrariness is wide indeed. So far, universal jurisdiction has involved the prosecution of one fashionably reviled man of the right while scores of East European communist leaders—not to speak of Caribbean, Middle Eastern, or African leaders who inflicted their own full measures of torture and suffering—have not had to face similar prosecutions.

Some will argue that a double standard does not excuse violations of international law and that it is better to bring one malefactor to justice than to grant immunity to all. This is not an argument permitted in the domestic jurisdictions of many democracies—in Canada, for example, a charge can be thrown out of court merely by showing that a prosecution has been selective enough to amount to an abuse of process. In any case, a universal standard of justice should not be based on the proposition that a just end warrants unjust means, or that political fashion trumps fair judicial procedures.

An Indiscriminate Court

The ideological supporters of universal jurisdiction also provide much of the intellectual compass for the emerging International Criminal Court. Their goal is to criminalize certain types of military and political actions and thereby bring about a more humane conduct of international relations. To the extent that the ICC replaces the claim of national judges to universal jurisdiction, it greatly improves the state of international law. And, in time, it may be possible to negotiate modifications of the present statute to make the ICC more compatible with U.S. constitutional practice. But in its present form of assigning the ultimate dilemmas of international politics to unelected jurists—and to an international judiciary at that—it represents such a fundamental change in U.S. constitutional practice that a full national debate and the full participation of Congress are imperative. Such a momentous revolution should not come about by tacit acquiescence in the decision of the House of Lords or by dealing with the ICC issue through a strategy of improving specific clauses rather than as a fundamental issue of principle.

The doctrine of universal jurisdiction is based on the proposition that the individuals or cases subject to it have been clearly identified. In some instances, especially those based on Nuremberg precedents, the definition of who can be prosecuted in an international court and in what circumstances is self-evident. But many issues are much more vague and depend on an understanding of the historical and political context. It is this fuzziness that risks arbitrariness on the part of prosecutors and judges years after the event and that became apparent with respect to existing tribunals.

For example, can any leader of the United States or of another country be hauled before international tribunals established for other purposes? This is precisely what Amnesty International implied when, in the summer of 1999, it supported a "complaint" by a group of European and Canadian law professors to Louise Arbour, then the prosecutor of the International Criminal Tribunal for the Former Yugoslavia (ICTY). The complaint alleged that crimes against humanity had been committed during the NATO air campaign in Kosovo. Arbour ordered an internal staff review, thereby implying that she did have jurisdiction if such violations could, in fact, be demonstrated. Her successor, Carla Del Ponte, in the end declined to indict any NATO official because of a general inability "to pinpoint individual responsibilities," thereby implying anew that the court had jurisdiction over NATO and American leaders in the Balkans and would have issued an indictment had it been able to identify the particular leaders allegedly involved.

Most Americans would be amazed to learn that the ICTY, created at U.S. behest in 1993 to deal with Balkan war criminals, had asserted a right to investigate U.S. political and military leaders for allegedly criminal conduct—and for the indefinite future, since no statute of limitations applies. Though the ICTY prosecutor chose not to pursue the charge—on the ambiguous ground of an inability to collect evidence—some national prosecutor may wish later to take up the matter as a valid subject for universal jurisdiction.

The pressures to achieve the widest scope for the doctrine of universal jurisdiction were demonstrated as well by a suit before the European Court of Human Rights in June 2000 by families of Argentine sailors who died in the sinking of the Argentine cruiser *General Belgano* during the Falklands War. The concept of universal jurisdiction has moved from judging alleged political crimes against humanity to second-guessing, 18 years after the event, military operations in which neither civilians nor civilian targets were involved.

Distrusting national governments, many of the advocates of universal jurisdiction seek to place politicians under the supervision of magistrates and the judicial system. But prosecutorial discretion without accountability is precisely one of the flaws of the International Criminal Court. Definitions of the relevant crimes are vague and highly susceptible to politicized application. Defendants will not enjoy due process as understood in the United States. Any signatory state has the right to trigger an investigation. As the U.S. experience with the special prosecutors investigating the executive branch shows, such a procedure is likely to develop its own momentum without time limits and can turn into an instrument of political warfare. And the extraordinary attempt of the ICC to assert jurisdiction over Americans even in the absence of U.S. accession to the treaty has already triggered legislation in Congress to resist it.

The independent prosecutor of the ICC has the power to issue indictments, subject to review only by a panel of three judges. According to the Rome statute, the Security Council has the right to quash any indictment. But since revoking an indictment is subject to the veto of any permanent Security Council member, and since the prosecutor is unlikely to issue an indictment without the backing of at least one permanent member of the Security Council, he or she has virtually unlimited discretion in practice. Another provision permits the country whose citizen is accused to take over the investigation and trial. But the ICC retains the ultimate authority on whether that function has been adequately exercised and, if it finds it has not, the ICC can reassert jurisdiction. While these procedures are taking place, which may take years, the accused will be under some restraint and certainly under grave public shadow.

The advocates of universal jurisdiction argue that the state is the basic cause of war and cannot be trusted to deliver justice. If law replaced politics, peace and justice would prevail. But even a cursory examination of history shows that there is no evidence to support such a theory. The role of the statesman is to choose the best option when seeking to advance peace and justice, realizing that there is frequently a tension between the two and that any reconciliation is likely to be partial. The choice, however, is not simply between universal and national jurisdictions.

Modest Proposals

The precedents set by international tribunals established to deal with situations where the enormity of the crime is evident and the local judicial system is clearly incapable of administering justice, as in the former Yugoslavia and Rwanda, have shown that it is possible to punish without removing from the process all political judgment and experience. In time, it may be possible to renegotiate the ICC statute to avoid its shortcomings and dangers. Until then, the United States should go no further toward a more formal system than one containing the following three provisions. First, the U.N. Security Council would create a Human Rights Commission or a special subcommittee to report whenever systematic human rights violations seem to warrant judicial action. Second, when the government under which the alleged crime occurred is not authentically representative, or where the domestic judicial system is incapable of sitting in judgment on the crime, the Security Council would set up an ad hoc international tribunal on the model of those of the former Yugoslavia or Rwanda. And third, the procedures for these international tribunals as well as the scope of the prosecution should be precisely defined by the Security Council, and the accused should be entitled to the due process safeguards accorded in common jurisdictions.

In this manner, internationally agreed procedures to deal with war crimes, genocide, or other crimes against humanity could become institutionalized. Furthermore, the one-sidedness of the current pursuit of universal jurisdiction would be avoided. This pursuit could threaten the very purpose for which the concept has been developed. In the end, an excessive reliance on universal jurisdiction may undermine the political will to sustain the humane norms of international behavior so necessary to temper the violent times in which we live.

KENNETH ROTH

The Case for Universal Jurisdiction

Behind much of the savagery of modern history lies impunity. Tyrants commit atrocities, including genocide, when they calculate they can get away with them. Too often, dictators use violence and intimidation to shut down any prospect of domestic prosecution. Over the past decade, however, a slowly emerging system of international justice has begun to break this pattern of impunity in national courts.

From *Foreign Affairs* 80, no. 5 (Sept./Oct. 2001): 150–154.

The United Nations Security Council established international war crimes tribunals for the former Yugoslavia in 1993 and Rwanda in 1994 and is now negotiating the creation of mixed national-international tribunals for Cambodia and Sierra Leone. In 1998, the world's governments gathered in Rome to adopt a treaty for an International Criminal Court (ICC) with potentially global jurisdiction over genocide, war crimes, and crimes against humanity.

With growing frequency, national courts operating under the doctrine of universal jurisdiction are prosecuting despots in their custody for atrocities committed abroad. Impunity may still be the norm in many domestic courts, but international justice is an increasingly viable option, promising a measure of solace to victims and their families and raising the possibility that would-be tyrants will begin to think twice before embarking on a barbarous path.

In "The Pitfalls of Universal Jurisdiction" (July/August 2001), former Secretary of State Henry Kissinger catalogues a list of grievances against the juridical concept that people who commit the most severe human rights crimes can be tried wherever they are found. But his objections are misplaced, and the alternative he proposes is little better than a return to impunity.

Kissinger begins by suggesting that universal jurisdiction is a new idea, at least as applied to heads of state and senior public officials. However, the exercise by U.S. courts of jurisdiction over certain heinous crimes committed overseas is an accepted part of American jurisprudence, reflected in treaties on terrorism and aircraft hijacking dating from 1970. Universal jurisdiction was also the concept that allowed Israel to try Adolf Eichmann in Jerusalem in 1961.

Kissinger says that the drafters of the Helsinki Accords—the basic human rights principles adopted by the Conference on Security and Cooperation in Europe in 1975—and the U.N.'s 1948 Universal Declaration of Human Rights never intended to authorize universal jurisdiction. But this argument is irrelevant, because these hortatory declarations are not legally binding treaties of the sort that could grant such powers.

As for the many formal treaties on human rights, Kissinger believes it "unlikely" that their signatories "thought it possible that national judges would use them as a basis for extradition requests regarding alleged crimes committed outside their jurisdictions." To the contrary, the Torture Convention of 1984, ratified by 124 governments including the United States, requires states either to prosecute any suspected torturer found on their territory, regardless of where the torture took place, or to extradite the suspect to a country that will do so. Similarly, the Geneva Conventions of 1949 on the conduct of war, ratified by 189 countries including the United States, require each participating state to "search for" persons who have committed grave breaches of the conventions and to "bring such persons, regardless of nationality, before its own courts." What is new is not the concept of extraterritorial jurisdiction but the willingness of some governments to fulfill this duty against those in high places.

Order and the Court

Kissinger's critique of universal jurisdiction has two principal targets: the soon-to-be-formed International Criminal Court and the exercise of universal jurisdiction by national courts. (Strictly speaking, the ICC will use not universal jurisdiction but, rather, a delegation of states' traditional power to try crimes committed on their own territory.) Kissinger claims that the crimes detailed in the ICC treaty are "vague and highly susceptible to politicized application." But the treaty's definition of war crimes closely resembles that found in the Pentagon's own military manuals and is derived from the widely ratified Geneva Conventions and their Additional Protocols adopted in 1977. Similarly, the ICC treaty's definition of genocide is borrowed directly from the Genocide Convention of 1948, which the United States and 131 other governments have ratified and pledged to uphold, including by prose-cuting offenders. The definition of crimes against humanity is derived from the Nuremberg Charter, which, as Kissinger acknowledges, proscribes conduct that is "self-evident[ly]" wrong.

Kissinger further asserts that the ICC prosecutor will have "discretion without accountability," going so far as to raise the specter of Independent Counsel Kenneth Starr and to decry "the tyranny of judges." In fact, the prosecutor can be removed for misconduct by a simple majority of the governments that ratify the ICC treaty, and a two-thirds vote can remove a judge. Because joining the court means giving it jurisdiction over crimes committed on the signatory's territory, the vast majority of member states will be democracies, not the abusive governments that self-protectively flock to U.N. human rights bodies, where membership bears no cost.

Kissinger criticizes the "extraordinary attempt of the ICC to assert jurisdiction over Americans even in the absence of U.S. accession to the treaty." But the United States itself asserts such jurisdiction over others' citizens when it prosecutes terrorists or drug traffickers, such as Panamanian dictator Manuel Noriega, without the consent of the suspect's government. Moreover, the ICC will assert such power only if an American commits a specified atrocity on the territory of a government that has joined the ICC and has thus delegated its prosecutorial authority to the court.

Kissinger claims that ICC defendants "will not enjoy due process as understood in the United States"—an apparent allusion to the lack of a jury trial in a court that will blend civil and common law traditions. But U.S. courts martial also do not provide trials by jury. Moreover, U.S. civilian courts routinely approve the constitutionality of extradition to countries that lack jury trials, so long as their courts otherwise observe basic due process. The ICC clearly will provide such due process, since its treaty requires adherence to the full complement of international fair-trial standards.

Of course, any court's regard for due process is only as good as the quality and temperament of its judges. The ICC's judges will be chosen by the governments that join the court, most of which, as noted, will be democracies. Even without ratifying the ICC treaty, the U.S. government could help shape a culture of respect for due process by quietly working with the court, as it has done successfully with the international war crimes tribunals for Rwanda and the former Yugoslavia. Regrettably, ICC opponents in Wash-

ington are pushing legislation—the misnamed American Servicemembers Protection Act—that would preclude such cooperation.

The experience of the Yugoslav and Rwandan tribunals, of which Kissinger speaks favorably, suggests that international jurists, when forced to decide the fate of a particular criminal suspect, do so with scrupulous regard for fair trial standards. Kissinger's only stated objection to these tribunals concerns the decision of the prosecutor of the tribunal for the former Yugoslavia to pursue a brief inquiry into how NATO conducted its air war against the new Yugoslavia—an inquiry that led her to exonerate NATO.

It should be noted, in addition, that the jurisdiction of the Yugoslav tribunal was set not by the prosecutor but by the U.N. Security Council, with U.S. consent. The council chose to grant jurisdiction without prospective time limit, over serious human rights crimes within the territory of the former Yugoslavia committed by anyone—not just Serbs, Croats, and Bosnian Muslims. In light of that mandate, the prosecutor would have been derelict in her duties not to consider NATO's conduct; according to an extensive field investigation by Human Rights Watch, roughly half of the approximately 500 civilian deaths caused by NATO's bombs could be attributed to NATO's failure, albeit not criminal, to abide by international humanitarian law.

Kissinger claims that the ICC would violate the U.S. Constitution if it asserted jurisdiction over an American. But the court is unlikely to prosecute an American because the Rome treaty deprives the ICC of jurisdiction if, after the court gives required notice of its intention to examine a suspect, the suspect's government conducts its own good-faith investigation and, if appropriate, prosecution. It is the stated policy of the U.S. government to investigate and prosecute its own war criminals.

Moreover, the ICC's assertion of jurisdiction over an American for a crime committed abroad poses no greater constitutional problem than the routine practice under status-of-forces agreements of allowing foreign prosecution of American military personnel for crimes committed overseas, such as Japan's arrest in July of a U.S. Air Force sergeant for an alleged rape on Okinawa. An unconstitutional delegation of U.S. judicial power would arguably take place only if the United States ratified the ICC treaty; then an American committed genocide, war crimes, or crimes against humanity on U.S. soil; and then U.S. authorities did not prosecute the offender. Yet that remote possibility would signal a constitutional crisis far graver than one spawned by an ICC prosecution.

No Place to Hide

National courts come under Kissinger's fire for selectively applying universal jurisdiction. He characterizes the extradition request by a Spanish judge seeking to try former Chilean President Augusto Pinochet for crimes against Spanish citizens on Chilean soil as singling out a "fashionably reviled man of the right." But Pinochet was sought not, as Kissinger writes, "because he led a coup d'état against an elected leader" who was a favorite of the left. Rather, Pinochet was targeted because security forces under his command murdered and forcibly "disappeared" some 3,000 people and tortured thousands more.

Furthermore, in recent years national courts have exercised universal jurisdiction against a wide range of suspects: Bosnian war criminals, Rwandan *génocidaires*, Argentine torturers, and Chad's former dictator. It has come to the point where the main limit on national courts empowered to exercise universal jurisdiction is the availability of the defendant, not questions of ideology.

Kissinger also cites the Pinochet case to argue that international justice interferes with the choice by democratic governments to forgive rather than prosecute past offenders. In fact,

Pinochet's imposition of a self-amnesty at the height of his dictatorship limited Chile's democratic options. Only after 16 months of detention in the United Kingdom diminished his power was Chilean democracy able to begin prosecution. Such imposed impunity is far more common than democratically chosen impunity.

Kissinger would have had a better case had prosecutors sought, for example, to overturn the compromise negotiated by South Africa's Nelson Mandela, widely recognized at the time as the legitimate representative of the victims of apartheid. Mandela agreed to grant abusers immunity from prosecution if they gave detailed testimony about their crimes. In an appropriate exercise of prosecutorial discretion, no prosecutor has challenged this arrangement, and no government would likely countenance such a challenge.

Kissinger legitimately worries that the nations exercising universal jurisdiction could include governments with less-entrenched traditions of due process than the United Kingdom's. But his fear of governments robotically extraditing suspects for sham or counterproductive trials is overblown. Governments regularly deny extradition to courts that are unable to ensure high standards of due process. And foreign ministries, including the U.S. State Department, routinely deny extradition requests for reasons of public policy.

If an American faced prosecution by an untrustworthy foreign court, the United States undoubtedly would apply pressure for his or her release. If that failed, however, it might prove useful to offer the prosecuting government the face-saving alternative of transferring the suspect to the ICC, with its extensive procedural protections, including deference to good-faith investigations and prosecutions by a suspect's own government. Unfortunately, the legislation being pushed by ICC opponents in Washington would preclude that option.

Until the ICC treaty is renegotiated to avoid what Kissinger sees as its "short-comings and dangers," he recommends that the U.N. Security Council determine which cases warrant an international tribunal. That option was rejected during the Rome negotiations on the ICC because it would allow the council's five permanent members, including Russia and China as well as the United States, to exempt their nationals and those of their allies by exercising their vetoes.

As a nation committed to human rights and the rule of law, the United States should be embracing an international system of justice, even if it means that Americans, like everyone else, might sometimes be scrutinized.

KENNETH A. RODMAN

Is Peace in the Interests of Justice? The Case for Broad Prosecutorial Discretion at the International Criminal Court

On 4 June 2007 Stephen Rapp, the Prosecutor of the Special Court for Sierra Leone, described the civil war in that country as among "the ugliest scenes of viciousness in recent memory."

> Human beings, young and old, mutilated. Rebels chopping off arms and legs, gouging out eyes, chopping at ears. Girls and women enslaved and sexually violated. Children committing some of the most awful crimes. The exploitation of the resources of Sierra Leone used not for the benefit of its citizens but to maim and kill its citizens. The very worst that human beings are capable of doing to one another.[1]

This was the opening statement in the trial of Charles Taylor, the former president of Liberia. Although Taylor had never set foot in Sierra Leone, he was accused of having supported the Revolutionary United Front (RUF), a rebel group that had committed these atrocities to control the country's diamond resources. The trial—

which is the first of an African head of state before an international tribunal—has been hailed as an important step in ending the culture of impunity in which tyrants and rebel leaders believe they will never be held accountable for their crimes. As Rapp noted in an interview with the *Christian Science Monitor*, "The world has turned a page in the wake of Taylor's arrest . . . The days are gone when leaders accused of atrocities could escape into exile."[2]

An attempt to turn that page had been made four years earlier by David Crane, the first Prosecutor for the Special Court, when he unsealed the indictment of Taylor while the latter was still president of Liberia. He had just arrived in Accra for a meeting with other west African leaders in an attempt to negotiate an end to Liberia's civil war by persuading him to step down and accept asylum in Nigeria. Crane's goal was to put the participants on notice that they should not negotiate with a war criminal but, instead, extradite him to the Special Court. His hosts, however, were committed to the negotiations and were unwilling to hand over a fellow head of state. Not taking any chances,

From *Leiden Journal of International Law* 22 (2009): 99–126. Some of the author's notes have been omitted.

Taylor returned to Liberia as soon as he learned of the indictment, triggering the collapse of the peace talks.[3] While Taylor's departure was secured two months later, an opportunity to end the violence earlier was effectively vetoed by the Prosecutor. Roughly 1,000 people died in stepped-up political violence between the breakdown of the talks in Accra and Taylor's eventual resignation.[4]

These two episodes in the Taylor case illustrate one of the central conflicts confronting the International Criminal Court (ICC), namely the tension between the legal goal of enforcing the rule of law to end impunity and the political requirements of negotiating an end to armed conflicts. Should the Prosecutor hold back from criminal proceedings if he is persuaded that prosecution could interfere with negotiated transitions? Article 53 of the ICC's founding Rome Statute allows the Prosecutor to exercise his discretion not to investigate or prosecute if it would not serve "the interests of justice." Should that phrase be construed sufficiently broadly to include the interests of peace?

* * *

This article challenges the empirical premises that underlie the policy argument against factoring peace processes into prosecutorial discretion. Legalists assume that law can and should be separated from politics, and that in doing so, it can transform politics. This reverses the actual relationship between politics and law evident in the history of international war crimes tribunals and the cases currently under review by the ICC. Those episodes demonstrate that political factors—most notably the power of the perpetrators relative to the forces arrayed against them and the political strategies of the latter to address the conflict—determine when a criminal law approach is effective and whether it contributes to peace. Hence the Prosecutor should construe his discretion broadly in order to assess the political context in which international criminal law has to operate.

1. The Rome Statute: Can the Prosecutor Exercise Discretion in the Interests of Peace?

The establishment of the ICC is the most ambitious step the international community has taken in introducing criminal accountability into the culture of international relations. Its founding Rome Statute was negotiated in July 1998, building on the precedents of the UN-created International Criminal Tribunals for the former Yugoslavia (ICTY) and for Rwanda (ICTR) by creating a permanent court that would have its own legal personality independent of the United Nations. The Court currently has jurisdiction over genocide, crimes against humanity, and war crimes committed after the treaty came into force on 1 July 2002. It can exercise universal jurisdiction if the Security Council refers a case. Otherwise, ICC jurisdiction requires some nexus to state consent, either through ratification of the Rome Statute, which subjects the nationals and territory of states parties to ICC oversight, or the voluntary consent of non-parties to the ICC's jurisdiction on an ad hoc basis. One of the ICC's most distinctive features is the principle of complementarity. Unlike the UN-created tribunals for the former Yugoslavia and Rwanda, primary jurisdiction resides with national courts and the Prosecutor must defer to them if they are doing their job. The ICC can only step in when national systems of justice are unwilling or unable to investigate or prosecute.

Does the ICC Prosecutor have a duty to prosecute crimes of sufficient gravity within the jurisdiction of the Court if national criminal justice systems do not? This is an important question, because states have often chosen alternatives to prosecution in a transition from dictatorship or armed conflict, particularly when those accused of criminal violence retain significant power and negotiation is the most viable strategy of political change. As a result, the leaders of abusive regimes and rebel movements are often granted formal or de facto amnesties or allowed to accept exile abroad in order to advance the bargaining process. These instruments are often accompanied by non-penal forms of justice, such as truth commissions, reparations, or lustration.[5] The best-known example is South Africa's Truth and Reconciliation Commission (TRC), under which amnesty was conditioned on the public confession of political crimes committed by all sides.[6] Amnesties also played a crucial role in several UN-brokered peace agreements, such as Mozambique, El Salvador, and Haiti.[7]

Even without formal amnesties, conflict resolution often involves subordinating trials to expedient bargaining when the leaders whom a prosecutor might want to put in the dock are still in power and their cooperation is necessary to end violent conflicts.[8] This was the U.S. led NATO strategy in engaging the Serbian president Slobodan Milošević to negotiate the Dayton Accords which ended the war in Bosnia and Herzegovina.[9] It was also the premise behind inviting Charles Taylor to the peace talks in Accra.

Should the Prosecutor hold back from criminal proceedings if the parties believe that alternatives to criminal justice are necessary for a transition from repressive rule or armed conflict? Should he make an independent judgment of their political legitimacy or assess whether they are necessary for peace processes or democratization?

The text of the Rome Statute creates a presumption against making such determinations. Its preamble lays out the ICC's mission, which is to ensure prosecution of "the most serious crimes of concern to the international community" in order to "put an end to impunity for the perpetrators of these crimes and thus to contribute to the prevention of such crimes." Its only reference to peace is that "such grave crimes threaten the peace, security and well-being of the world." The implication is that peace is more likely to come from a consistent policy of prosecution than from deferring prosecution to political negotiations. As Darryl Robinson notes, "the very pur-

pose of the ICC was to ensure the investigation and punishment of serious international crimes, and to prompt states to overcome the considerations of expedience and *realpolitik* that had so often led them to trade away justice in the past."[10]

* * *

* * * Article 53(1)(c) allows the Prosecutor to decline to investigate crimes that satisfy the Rome Statute's jurisdictional and admissibility criteria if, "[t]aking into account the gravity of the crime and the interests of victims, there are nonetheless substantial reasons to believe that an investigation would not serve the interests of justice." Under Article 53(2)(c), the Prosecutor can decline to move from investigation to prosecution if it "is not in the interests of justice, taking into account all the circumstances, including the gravity of the crime, the interests of the victims and the age or infirmity of the alleged perpetrator, and his or her role in the alleged crime." The phrase "interests of justice" is not defined in the Rome Statute. Some commentators interpreted it as a form of "creative ambiguity" which could encompass alternative justice mechanisms such as the TRC.[11] Others argued that it was intended to grant the Prosecutor broad political discretion to "arbitrate between the imperatives of justice and the imperatives of peace."[12] While the Prosecutor is required to justify his decision to the Pre-Trial Chamber, which would review and possibly reverse it, it theoretically provides the Prosecutor with a means of holding back from criminal proceedings or considering alternative justice mechanisms when demanding prosecution might prolong an armed conflict or dissuade a tyrant from stepping down.

* * *

2. The Duty to Prosecute and the Case for Narrow Prosecutorial Discretion

The suggestion that Article 53 could be used to defer to peace negotiations provoked a sharp challenge from many of the human rights lawyers and NGOs [non-governmental organizations] that have been most supportive of the Court. Human Rights Watch and Amnesty International each drafted policy papers that argued that the Prosecutor's duties under the Rome Statute required a narrow construction of the "interests of justice" test. Citing the Vienna Convention on the Law of Treaties, Human Rights Watch argued that the phrase can only be understood in the light of the "object and purpose" of the Rome Statute, which is to end impunity by holding perpetrators criminally accountable, not to assist peace negotiations.[13] Hence "the prosecutor may not fail to initiate an investigation or decide not to go from investigation to trial because of developments at the national level such as truth commissions, national amnesties, or the implementation of traditional reconciliation methods, or because of concerns regarding an ongoing peace process."[14]

Should the Prosecutor decide otherwise, he would be making political judgments about peace negotiations or the legitimacy of alternative reconciliation methods, which are inappropriate for a judicial institution whose mission and expertise are in international criminal law. Amnesty argues that the consultations necessary to make such determinations would violate the Prosecutor's legal duties, citing Article 42(1) on the independence of the Prosecutor, who "shall not seek or act on instructions from any external source."[15] Both reports also warned that adopting an expansive view of discretion would set a dangerous precedent, subjecting the Court to manipulation by warring factions and interested parties. This, in turn, would "undermine the perception and reality of the prosecutor as independent and beyond political influence."[16]

Deferring prosecution to political negotiations would be incompatible with the Court's legal obligations not only under the Rome Statute, but also more generally under international law. Most of the crimes subject to the ICC—genocide, crimes against humanity, grave breaches of the Geneva Conventions, torture—involve an international duty to prosecute as the result of treaty or custom that pre-dates the Rome Statute.[17] Human Rights Watch notes that this has resulted in a growing trend in international law to reject amnesties for such crimes, citing as evidence the reservation from the UN Special Representative to the 1999 Lomé Peace Accords, that there would be no international recognition of the blanket amnesty granted to all parties in the civil war in Sierra Leone if they involved serious international crimes—a marked contrast to the United Nations' approach to peace negotiations earlier in the decade.[18] In such cases a decision to hold back from prosecution would place the Court outside the very legal developments that gave rise to the drafting of the Rome Statute in the first place.

Finally, such an approach would be an abrogation of a duty to the victims, for whom the Court was created. Human Rights Watch notes that Article 53(2)(c) mentions the "interests of victims" in the same phrase as the "interests of justice," and that the latter should only be understood in terms of the former's need for criminal justice.[19] This would preclude amnesties, which are incompatible not only with international law but also with the rights of victims. As Ben Chigara put it in his moral critique of amnesties,

> They treat victims as if they did not have predetermined rights at the moment of abuse . . . what matters is whether there is sufficient threat of disruption of the incoming government's agenda by those that committed the alleged crimes against humanity.[20]

The Court would also be defaulting on its duty to victims if it merely suspended criminal proceedings. As the Amnesty letter put it,

> The suspension would create a sense of helplessness as the one court of last resort when no state was able or willing to investigate the most horrendous crimes informed them that it had suspended indefinitely the investigation that had given them hope of justice, truth, and full reparations.[21]

The only approach consistent with a duty to victims is to act in line with the old adage, "justice delayed is justice denied," and ignore the political consequences of that choice.[22]

Both papers concede that if the international community is genuinely concerned about the impact of prosecution on peace negotiations, the only legitimate place to make that call is the Security Council, as prescribed by the Rome Statute. Under Article 16 the Security Council has the authority to suspend any investigation or prosecution for renewable 12-month periods through passage of a resolution under Chapter VII of the UN Charter. Both NGOs opposed this provision at Rome, fearing that it would serve as a conduit for politicization, and their policy papers continue to express reservations about its use. Nonetheless, Amnesty argues that the decision to subordinate prosecution to peace must be made by "a political power that the drafters intended to be exercised only by a political body."[23] The logic, as one scholar put it, is that "political institutions should do politics and policy; judicial institutions should do justice."[24]

Moreover, pursuing justice untainted by politics is not just a matter of legal duty; it also has superior policy consequences in terms of making and consolidating peace. First, legalists challenge what Amnesty calls the "false premise that international justice was incompatible with political negotiations to end armed conflicts."[25] Despite warnings from the UN Secretary-General and from international mediators, the ICTY's indictments of Bosnian Serb President Radovan Karadžić and General Ratko Mladić in July 1995 did not derail the successful conclusion of the Dayton Peace Accords. Nor did the indictment of Slobodan Milošević in the middle of the Kosovo war prevent a settlement that allowed the refugees to return to their homes.[26]

Second, as the Human Rights Watch paper observes, justice can "have a tremendous value in contributing to peace and stability" by stigmatizing disruptive actors, such as Milošević or Taylor, thereby "undermin[ing] the political weight of those individuals and marginaliz[ing] them from political life in their former countries."[27] This is likely to happen even if those indicted are not apprehended, as was the case with Karadžić and Mladić. Richard Goldstone, the ICTY Prosecutor who obtained those indictments, subsequently wrote that they made a positive contribution to the peace process, by making it "legally and politically possible for the international community to insist on excluding Karadžić from the Dayton peace talks," without which the Bosnian government would not have participated. They also isolated the two most virulent ethnic extremists from post-war politics, thereby minimizing their disruptive influence on the implementation of Dayton.[28]

Third, criminal justice can contribute to peace by individualizing guilt in criminal leaders rather than allowing the victims to collectivize it in entire groups. This, in turn, is necessary to break the cycle of violence and revenge that keeps many ethnic conflicts going, particularly if it assigns guilt to criminal behavior on all sides. This is why Antonio Cassese, the first president of the ICTY, referred to the tribunal as an "instrument of reconciliation" rather than a "means of revenge."[29]

Finally, anti-impunity advocates see criminal accountability as necessary to establish the rule of law and deter a return to political violence in post-conflict societies. "Impunity for atrocities committed in the past," by contrast, "sends the message that such crimes may be tolerated in the future."[30] Some proponents of the duty to prosecute contend that the decision to negotiate with Milošević at Dayton, despite his complicity in ethnic cleansing campaigns in Croatia and Bosnia and Herzegovina, emboldened him to believe that he could return to criminal violence in Kosovo three years later without any legal repercussions.[31] The Lomé amnesty, which included a power-sharing agreement that made RUF leader Foday Sankoh vice-president and minister of mines, produced a similar outcome in Sierra Leone. In less than a year the RUF violated the agreement by attacking UN peacekeepers and taking them hostage, thereby demonstrating the tenuousness of peace without justice.[32]

3. The Consequentialist Case for Broad Prosecutorial Discretion

The consequentialist case for a duty to prosecute is most persuasive in a relatively stable post-conflict environment in which alleged war criminals are no longer in power and can be apprehended without a serious risk of violent backlash. It is on shakier ground during ongoing conflicts or fragile peace processes in which those accused of war crimes still command substantial power. Some of the advocacy by NGOs and legal scholars seems to imply that in such situations pursuing justice over impunity is a matter of making the right legal choice regardless of the political choices used to address existing power realities. * * *

* * *

In Bosnia and Herzegovina * * * the Security Council authorized the creation of the ICTY in 1993 at time when NATO and the United Nations were unwilling to deploy anything more than a neutral peacekeeping force with no mandate to stop the violence. Even when that mandate was augmented to enforce "safe areas," there was a reluctance to implement it because of the risks for peacekeepers it would impose.[33] In such a political vacuum it is unlikely that a more aggressive judicial strategy could have had a meaningful impact on ethnic cleansing. In fact, the worst single atrocity of the Bosnian war—the Srebrenica massacre—was perpetrated by forces under the command of General Mladić two years after the creation of the ICTY and three months after Goldstone had asked the Bosnian courts to defer to his investigation of Mladić for crimes against humanity.[34] The use of criminal violence with impunity was effectively challenged only after NATO was willing to use force—both directly through Operation Deliberate Force and indirectly through assisting Croatian and Bosnian military offensives—in order to convince Belgrade to rein in its Bosnian Serb allies.[35] This, in turn, was a prerequisite for the ability of the ICTY to prosecute anyone of significance and make a contribution to the peace process by removing criminal spoilers from the political scene.

In Sierra Leone it is clear that engaging the RUF was a mistake, as was releasing Sankoh from prison to lead the RUF delegation in Lomé after he had been prosecuted in Freetown and sentenced to death for treason. However, keeping Sankoh in prison and issuing indictments of rebel leaders still at large would not have ended the RUF's reign of terror since it had not been defeated on the battlefield. More importantly, Nigeria, which led the West African peacekeeping force that had kept the RUF at bay, was no longer willing to keep its troops in Sierra Leone and the United Nations was only willing to replace them with a neutral peacekeeping force.[36] Therefore the alternative to peace with amnesty was not peace with justice, but the continuation of the civil war—without foreign military assistance—against a rebel group that was still being armed by Charles Taylor's Liberia. Impunity was a symptom of these political realities that no justice and accountability mechanism could have erased. And as in Bosnia and Herzegovina, it only ended with military intervention, in this case from the United Kingdom, in response to a plea from UN Secretary-General

Kofi Annan after the RUF had returned to criminal violence and taken 500 UN peacekeepers hostage. This strengthened what had been a neutral (and up to that point, ineffectual) peacekeeping operation into an enforcement mission that eventually defeated the RUF.[37]

Moreover, the feasibility of prosecution and its contribution to peaceful transitions are dependent upon the political or military strategies designed to bring a conflict to an end. If the perpetrators' forces have been defeated or weakened to a point where negotiations are unnecessary, criminal leaders could be put on trial without a serious risk of violent backlash. This was the historical experience after the Second World War with the Nuremberg and Tokyo War Crimes Tribunals, which were made possible by the unconditional surrender of Nazi Germany and imperial Japan.[38] In Rwanda, the defeat of the genocidal Hutu regime by the Rwandan Patriotic Front meant that the architects of the genocide could face national and international prosecution without destabilizing the post-conflict transition. Similarly, the RUF's surrender to a more robust international force made possible the creation of the Special Court for Sierra Leone and the prosecution of RUF leaders, who were no longer in a position to disrupt a peace settlement. Prosecutions under these circumstances entail the risk of partisan justice in which the losers are prosecuted and the victors are immune.[39] Nonetheless, defeating criminal actors, or weakening them to the point where their cooperation is not needed to end a conflict, is a prerequisite for discounting the potential impact of criminal justice on peace.

If, by contrast, the perpetrators are not defeated and retain significant power, conflict resolution will have to be based on a bargaining paradigm that involves some compromises with criminal justice. This most clearly applies when the United Nations or other mediators adopt an impartial Chapter VI approach to conflict resolution. As explained by Haile Menkerios, the former head of the African division of the UN Department of Peacekeeping Affairs,

So many leaders of these conflicts have committed abuses, crimes, and the killing and the suffering of innocent civilians continues as long as the conflict continues. So you have two choices. You can consider them criminals, bring them to face justice, and get them out of the way, or invite them to negotiate for a peaceful settlement. When there is neither the internal capacity nor the external will to do the first, there is no other choice but to invite them to negotiate, often for power sharing in a transitional arrangement to stop the wars.[40]

These arrangements are often problematical in terms of human rights, since those implicated in war crimes are allowed to enter the political arena. If, however, the international community is unwilling or unable to take enforcement actions against them, then there is no choice but to engage them in peace negotiations, and it is difficult simultaneously to criminalize them and to try to solicit their voluntary cooperation.

* * *

The reason why indicting Milošević was impractical in 1995 was because his cooperation was necessary both to negotiate and to maintain Dayton, given the political–military constraints under which NATO and the United Nations were operating. This changed with the Kosovo war in 1999. When Belgrade did not withdraw after the first few weeks of bombing, the United States and NATO concluded that Milošević was not only no longer the key to the peace process, he was now the main source of instability in the region.[41] Moreover, unlike Dayton, NATO's war aims did not require Belgrade's continuing cooperation to stabilize the post-conflict environment. Given NATO's political strategy, the ICTY's indictment of Milošević—which was encouraged by U.S. and UK officials, who released previously classified information to the ICTY Prosecutor[42]—did not interfere with NATO's strategies of war termination and post-conflict nation-building.

4. Peace-versus-Justice Dilemmas Facing the International Criminal Court

The lesson that should be drawn from the cases described above is that the feasibility of prosecution and its impact on peace are shaped and constrained by the political strategies designed to end a conflict. This is relevant to the first three situations under investigation by the ICC, since each is taking place in the context of ongoing political violence, creating tensions between international criminal justice and conflict resolution. As a result, the Prosecutor will need to find some means of injecting political prudence into his discretion in order to be effective without foreclosing negotiated solutions or disrupting fragile peace processes.

4.1. Northern Uganda

The LRA case has presented the ICC with its most overt controversy regarding the impact of prosecution on peace. Its strongest critics have been Acholi civil society leaders, who opposed its involvement from the start because they feared it would drive the LRA [Lord's Resistance Army] from peace talks.[43] When negotiations resumed in the south Sudanese capital of Juba in July 2006, they asked the Prosecutor to withdraw the arrest warrants, which were seen as an obstacle to their completion—a view that persisted even after the Juba process collapsed in April 2008 when [LRA leader Joseph] Kony refused to sign the peace accords.[44] Their alternative was to extend the 2000 Amnesty Act to the indicted LRA leaders if they agreed to end the war. Instead of prosecution, they advocated a traditional reconciliation ritual, the *mato oput*, in which a wrongdoer drinks a potion made from a bitter root, confesses to his victims, and makes amends.[45]

The reason why most Acholi leaders have prioritized peace over prosecution is because the war has been the principal source of humanitarian problems in the region. When the arrest warrants were unsealed in October 2005, 1.7 million people, or roughly 90 percent of the population in the three most war-ravaged districts, had been relocated to internally displaced persons (IDP) camps, where the Uganda People's Defence Force (UPDF) have provided inadequate protection from the LRA. In addition, local and international NGOs have documented military abuses against civilians, including torture, rape, arbitrary detention, and extortion.[46] The health and sanitary conditions in the camps have also had devastating social consequences. According to a study conducted by the Ugandan Ministry of Health in collaboration with UN agencies, roughly 1,000 people were dying each week from preventable disease and malnutrition.[47]

Despite these concerns, Human Rights Watch and Amnesty International have consistently opposed trading justice for peace. They were joined by several international lawyers during the Juba negotiations when [Uganda's President Yoweri] Museveni and other government officials suggested that they might offer an amnesty to the indicted LRA leaders in exchange for a genuine commitment to end the war.[48] As for the conditions in the IDP camps, both NGOs have called on the OTP [Office of the Prosecutor] to investigate Ugandan military and civilian leaders for the forcible relocation of civilians—a crime under the Rome Statute—and for the abuses in the camps.[49] In other words, human rights are best promoted not by compromising justice in the interests of peace, but by applying criminal law even-handedly.

For his part, [ICC Prosecutor Luis] Moreno-Ocampo claimed jurisdiction to evaluate allegations against all parties in Northern Uganda, including the government and the military. He justified the current focus on the LRA rather than the UPDF because his investigations found that "the crimes committed by the LRA are of dramatically higher gravity."[50] As to Museveni's statements that he would protect Kony from the

ICC, Moreno-Ocampo held that the arrest warrants cannot be withdrawn and that Uganda, as a party to the Rome Statute, has a duty to execute them. While acknowledging Uganda's right to adopt alternative justice mechanisms, he insisted on prosecuting those who bore the greatest responsibility and refused to use his discretion to suspend the arrest warrants.[51] Nonetheless, the ICC chose to maintain a low profile to minimize interference with the peace process from the initiation of the Juba talks in July 2006 to their breakdown in April 2008.[52]

* * *

During the negotiations the ICC and its NGO supporters made a persuasive case that the referral contributed positively to the peace process.[53] First, it concentrated the attention and resources of the United Nations, the African Union (AU), and Western donors on what had been a neglected humanitarian crisis. Second, the criminalization of the LRA isolated it from external assistance, particularly from Sudan, which had provided it with sanctuary and arms in a proxy war with Uganda in response to Kampala's support for the Sudan People's Liberation Army (SPLA) in its rebellion against Khartoum.[54] Finally, the reduction of outside support, combined with the threat of prosecution, increased the pressure on the LRA to negotiate its own safety.[55]

Therein, however, lies the conundrum for any possible resumption of the peace process. While the arrest warrants might serve as a prod to negotiations, insisting on their execution is likely to prevent their completion. It is implausible that Kony would sign a peace agreement that would leave him vulnerable to trial either in Kampala or The Hague—unless his forces have been so weakened that the likely alternative is being killed or captured by the UPDF. Moreover, some analysts attributed the problems at Juba to the unrepresentative nature of the LRA delegation, given the unwillingness of the indicted LRA leaders to

attend for fear of being arrested.[56] Any prospective negotiations will consequently require at least some temporary compromises with criminal justice, such as guarantees of safe passage to attend peace talks or an arrangement to provide Kony and his commanders with asylum in a state that has not ratified the Rome Statute.

Given the nature and scale of the LRA's crimes, most proponents of international criminal justice would object to such arrangements as condoning impunity and weakening the ICC's deterrent impact elsewhere.[57] Others argue that such compromises are likely to be futile, since the LRA remains a spoiler and is using the negotiations as breathing space to regroup and return to violence, particularly if the Sudanese peace agreement collapses and its former patron in Khartoum once again sees it as a useful proxy against the SPLA.[58] Kony's refusal to sign the peace agreement and reports of the LRA's return to the forced conscription of abducted children lend support to this view.[59]

If one accepts these arguments, the logical consequence is to dismiss the possibility of meaningful negotiations and prepare for a military solution. Many supporters of prosecution seem to elide this dilemma by using * * * domestic law enforcement, calling for the execution of arrest warrants.[60] However, apprehending the leaders of a well-armed rebel movement that has not been defeated requires something more than a police operation, as is demonstrated by the inability of the UPDF for two decades to capture Kony. This also explains why the Prosecutor's agreements with neighboring states and the United Nations to bring Kony to justice have not yet led to his arrest. * * *

Another option is allowing the UPDF to enter the DRC [Democratic Republic of the Congo]. Some analysts believe that Museveni's ulterior motive for going to the ICC was to legitimize such an intervention by having the LRA branded as international criminals.[61] Yet during the Congolese civil war this was the part of the DRC that Uganda had occupied, both directly and through ethnic militias, in order to control its resources. As a result, attempts by Uganda to persuade the Security Council to grant it authority for such an intervention have been rebuffed.[62] * * *

Military solutions, however, have not worked in the past, and will involve risks not only to the interveners, but also to victim communities in Northern Uganda. It could have the unintended consequence of intensifying violence in the north—repeating the experience of Operation Iron Fist in 2002 when the UPDF attacked LRA bases in southern Sudan—and reversing improvements to the humanitarian situation since the ceasefire. It could also jeopardize the lives of abducted children whose families want them returned—an outcome more likely to be achieved through negotiation than through force.[63] Prosecution, on the other hand, requires a commitment by international and regional actors to assume those risks because the threat posed by the LRA is proportionately greater. Absent that commitment—either because of the lack of will or because the risks to peace and other values are too high—the alternatives are either to live with and contain the LRA threat or to try again to end it diplomatically. If there ever is a return to the latter option, the ICC's role will likely be as a source of leverage in negotiations, whose successful completion will probably require compromises with criminal justice.

* * *

4.3. Darfur

The Darfur case was referred to the ICC on 31 March 2005—approximately two years after the outbreak of a civil war that involved an ethnic cleansing campaign against the region's African population by government forces and government-supported Arab militias known as *janjaweed*, which has left several hundred thousand people dead and more than two million displaced. The referral required authorization by the UN Security Council because, unlike Uganda and the DRC, Sudan is not a party to the Rome Statute. In fact, it was made despite the opposition of the Sudanese government, which has blocked any meaningful cooperation with the ICC. The Prosecutor nonetheless moved forward. On 27 February 2007 he identified a former interior minister and a militia leader as his first cases and on 2 May the Pre-Trial Chamber issued warrants for their arrest.[64] After more than a year of non-compliance—including the appointment of one of the indictees as minister of humanitarian affairs—the Prosecutor reported to the Security Council that the atrocities were part of a "criminal plan" involving "the entire Sudanese state apparatus."[65] On 14 July 2008 he applied for an arrest warrant for Sudan's president, Omar Hassan al-Bashir, on charges of genocide.[66]

Anti-impunity advocates contend that by indicting the sitting head of state, the ICC can have an impact on ending criminal violence in Darfur.[67] That will only happen if the judicial process serves as a catalyst to a change in the political strategies of conflict resolution used by powerful states and intergovernmental organizations.

It has been the mismatch between legal and political strategies that explains the limited impact of the ICC up to this point. The ICC referral, like the creation of the ICTY in the early phases of the Bosnian war, created a criminal justice process unaccompanied by enforcement actions against behavior deemed to be criminal. Although the Security Council had passed several resolutions under Chapter VII calling for Khartoum to disarm the *janjaweed* and end the violence, no meaningful sanctions were imposed for non-compliance or explicitly linked to future compliance. The only international presence on the ground was an underfunded and understaffed AU [African Union] force that had been deployed a year earlier to monitor a non-existent ceasefire. When the Security Council authorized a more robust civilian protection force in August 2006, it never moved beyond what amounted to a pacific settlement approach in which deployment would depend on Sudanese consent. No penalties were imposed or threatened when that consent was declined, or when it subsequently accepted deployment of a hybrid UN–AU Mission in Darfur (UN-AMID), but imposed conditions that amounted to obstruction.[68]

Given the unwillingness of the Security Council to authorize enforcement, the principal instrument of conflict resolution has been impartial mediation through the good offices of the United Nations and the AU. This is incompatible with the ICC referral because one cannot simultaneously subject the government to criminal scrutiny and non-coercively seek its cooperation. It is also incongruent with conditions on the ground. For such an approach to succeed in ending a civil war, all parties must be in a "mutually hurting stalemate"[69] in which they recognize that they cannot achieve their objectives militarily and that the continuation of the war will make them all worse off. The ruling party in Khartoum, however, believes that maintaining its power is better served by the continuation of the war than by a negotiated settlement, which the International Crisis Group pinpoints as one of the central reasons for the failure of the peace process.[70] In fact, the most significant outcome of the mediation effort, the Darfur Peace Agreement, signed on 5 May 2006 by Khartoum and one faction of the two main rebel groups, resulted in increased fighting and the deterioration of the humanitarian situation as the faction that signed joined government forces in escalating attacks on rebel-controlled areas.[71] As in Bosnia and Herzegovina, a pacific settlement approach to large-scale ethnic cleansing is incompatible with both criminal justice and conflict resolution.

For the Bashir indictment to be something more than naming and shaming, it will have to provoke the Security Council into moving from pacific to some form of coercive conflict resolution. This could involve the use of sanctions targeted at Sudan's leadership or its oil revenues, followed possibly by a credible threat of force—actions that so far have been blocked by China's threatened veto, given its economic and strategic relationship with Sudan.[72] The publicity surrounding the indictments—augmented by civil society groups—could increase the reputational costs to China in playing this role, dissuading it from vetoing sanctions resolutions or encouraging it to put pressure on Sudan to comply with Security Council mandates.[73] It could also cause Western governments to press the matter more forcefully in the Security Council or even to take action outside it. In fact, some ICC supporters have suggested that the Bashir indictment itself could be used as a source of leverage to get Sudan to end the conflict, or at least allow greater humanitarian access and a more robust peacekeeping presence.[74]

If the indictment does indeed serve either as a prod to enforcement or as a source of leverage, success will almost certainly require compromises with criminal justice. That is because the purpose of pressure is to change regime behavior—that is, to increase the costs and risks of the war for Khartoum to a point where ending it serves its interests. A principled approach to criminal justice, however, amounts to a demand for regime change, since the Prosecutor and major UN and NGO studies have attributed responsibility not only to President Bashir, but also to Sudan's most influential political and military officials.[75] Moreover, as with Dayton, the successful deployment of an effective peacekeeping force will probably require the continuing cooperation of the Sudanese government to negotiate and maintain a ceasefire and to disarm the militias, which the UN peacekeepers would monitor rather than enforce. If this is ever a realistic prospect, it will require some short-to-medium-term compromises on criminal justice, such as the use of Article 16 by the Security Council to suspend criminal proceedings on renewable 12-month periods, restrictions on UN peacekeepers in enforcing arrest warrants, or the Prosecutor exercising his discretion and lowering his profile if genuine progress is being made. A more aggressive criminal law approach would only be feasible if international intervention resulted in the removal of the regime—either directly or by triggering a leadership change—or if the civilian protection mandate does not require the active cooperation of the Sudanese government, as was the case with the Milošević regime after the Kosovo war.

4.4. Implications for Prosecutorial Discretion

Since there is a potential "peace versus justice" dilemma in each of the cases under his purview, the ICC Prosecutor will have to exercise political prudence in deciding when and how to proceed. The NGO studies are correct that the OTP is not ideally suited to play this role, since it is a legal institution whose mandate and expertise are in the law, not in diplomacy. Preferably, these calls should be made by the Security Council, a political body responsible for maintaining peace and security. If, for example, the Ugandan government believes that amnesty is needed to end the war with the LRA or mediators view the ICC as an obstacle to negotiations in Darfur, the proper venue for making such an appeal is the Security Council, not the Prosecutor's office. As a former ICC Deputy Prosecutor, Serge Brammertz, put it, "The priority of the Rome Statute is to prosecute[;] it's not here for political stability."[76]

The problem with establishing such a categorical division of labor is that it is not clear that the Security Council will play its designated role when there is a genuine conflict. While the Security Council is a political institution, its resolutions often reflect a least-common-denominator compromise of national interests rather than a coherent political strategy. Article 16 is also a blunt instrument, suspending the entire criminal process for renewable 12-month periods, and is only likely to be invoked after a peace deal has been finalized and at the request of the parties or of international mediators. Given the fluidity of negotiations during ongoing conflicts, most of the cases in which an aggressive prosecutorial strategy might have destabilizing consequences will fall below the Security Council's radar screen.

* * *

The Prosecutor will consequently have to act as both lawyer and diplomat in exercising his discretion, evaluating not only the gravity of the crime and the admissibility of the case, but also the likely impact of an investigation or prosecution on prolonging a conflict or undermining a political transition. In doing so, he should consult with a wide variety of stakeholders likely to be affected by criminal proceedings, as well as the United Nations, regional organizations, and governments and NGOs involved in mediation efforts. This does not make the Prosecutor a political actor who takes instructions from others. While he should maintain his independence as a legal officer, he also needs to acknowledge the interdependence of politics and law, the boundaries the former sets for the latter, and the risks of trespassing across them. Hence one OTP analyst wrote that, to be effective, a prosecutor should "pursue a process of consultation and a sufficient degree of international consensus-building" to "operate in co-ordination with, rather than in opposition to, international efforts to address conflicts."[77] If he instead emulates David Crane's indictment of Charles Taylor through the aggressive pursuit of cases that could undermine peace processes, he is likely to dry up the capital he has with political actors, thereby weakening the Court as an institution.[78]

The final question is whether Article 53 is the best means of reconciling legal duty with political constraint, and there is a case to be made that it is not. The OTP's interpretation of the "interests of justice" test has moved closer to the legalist position since the LRA controversy in 2005. A September 2007 policy paper stated that it should not be "conceived of so broadly as to embrace all issues related to peace and security" and that "the broader matter of peace and security is not the responsibility of the Prosecutor."[79] In fact, it implicitly rejects the need to adapt prosecution to peace processes when it asserts that any "political or security initiative" must conform to "the new legal framework and this framework necessarily impacts on conflict management efforts."[80] In other words, the Court should follow its legal duty to identify those responsible for criminal violence without political considerations and this should constrain political actors from offering amnesty or exile as instruments of peacemaking.

Nonetheless, the document suggests more flexibility than the NGO papers when it acknowledges that Article 53's reference to "the interests of victims" could include interests other than prosecution, such as their security and protection.[81] This, in turn, requires an "ongoing risk assessment" and a dialogue with victims and their representatives, which could influence the timing and profile of investigations and indictments. Such an approach, broadly defined, could be the rough equivalent of factoring peace processes into prosecutorial discretion since their destabilization would almost inevitably lead to further victimization. Nonetheless, Article 53 is unlikely to be the vehicle for exercising such discretion. It could limit the OTP's flexibility, since any deferral would have to be submitted to the Pre-Trial Chamber, which could overturn the decision, and a decision to resume criminal proceedings would require the submission of new evidence. Moreover, the publicity surrounding the submission could subject it to political controversy and compromise its appearance of impartiality.

* * *

5. Conclusion

The central philosophical question underlying this legal controversy is whether justice in the aftermath of war and atrocity requires the application of criminal justice to its sponsors. In a book that takes politicians, diplomats, and even the ICTY Prosecutor to task for subordinating justice to accommodation during the Bosnian war, Paul Williams and Michael Scharf answer that question affirmatively and support that claim with a passage from Michael Walzer's classic work on just war theory:

> [T]he assignment of responsibility is the critical test of the argument for justice . . . If there are recognizable war crimes there must be recognizable criminals . . . The theory of justice should point us to the men and women from whom we can rightly demand an accounting, and it should shape and control the judgments we make of the excuses they offer (or are offered on their behalf) . . . There can be no justice in war if there are not, ultimately, responsible men and women.[82]

This, however, is an incomplete reading of Walzer's treatment of the subject. Following the excerpted quote, he explains that he is discussing moral responsibility rather than guilt or innocence as determined by judges, and he goes on to argue that considerations of proportionality mean that there are "often prudential reasons for not calling judges."[83] That is because the apprehension of criminal leaders requires something different from domestic law enforcement and that difference is more potentially threatening to the rights and lives of innocent civilians. Walzer illustrates this point through a quote from U.S. Secretary of State Dean Acheson defending the U.S. decision to cross the 38th parallel during the Korean War as necessary to "round up the people who were putting on the aggression." This, however, required military escalation rather than police work, and it inflicted harm "far beyond the people who are rounded up."[84] Walzer is prepared to accept those costs on proportionality grounds in order to remove from power and try the leaders of a radically evil regime, such as Hitler's Germany, but not for lesser despotisms, such as imperial Japan or communist North Korea. Whether or not one agrees with this position, the argument forces us to consider the humanitarian costs that would have to be accepted to bring to justice leaders who have not yet been defeated.

Yet many of the arguments marshalled by NGOs and international lawyers ignore these trade-offs by using the language of domestic law enforcement as if what is needed is the simple execution of arrest warrants. To illustrate, the former ICTY Prosecutor Richard Goldstone attributed Milošević's belief in his own impunity to "the failure of the international community to prosecute Pol Pot, Idi Amin, Saddam Hussein and Mohammed Aidid."[85] But bringing any of these malefactors to justice would have involved something more than executing arrest warrants. Take Goldstone's last two examples. With Saddam Hussein, it would have required a decision in 1991 to march to Baghdad, with all of the attendant costs and risks that have been made evident by the second Iraq war. With Aidid, one could argue that the Security Council issued its first arrest warrant when it passed Resolution 837 (1993), which called for the bringing to justice of those who ambushed and murdered 24 Pakistani peacekeepers serving in the UN mission in Somalia. The attempt to apprehend Aidid led to an escalation of conflict between U.S. and international forces and Aidid's clan, culminating in the tragic battle of Mogadishu, which precipitated the withdrawal of those forces.[86]

Similarly, executing an arrest warrant against Kony, a yet-to-be-defeated rebel leader, is a military operation, not a police action, and involves a much broader set of political and moral calculations than does law enforcement. As Walzer notes, "war affects more people than domestic crime and punishment, and it is the rights of these people that force us to limit its purpose."[87] If military escalation is necessary to apprehend the criminal actors and one cannot justify the ensuing loss of innocent life on proportionality grounds, then the perpetrators cannot be "removed from the (moral) world of bargaining and accommodation."[88]

Allowing criminal actors to enter this world rather than the world of crime and punishment is likely to be challenged by many within the human rights community as compromising accountability. Bassiouni put the issue starkly in a way that informs much of the anti-impunity movement:

The human rights arena is defined by a constant tension between the attraction of *realpolitik* and the demand for accountability. *Realpolitik* involves the pursuit of political settlements unencumbered by moral and ethical limitations. As such, this approach often runs directly counter to the interests of justice, particularly as understood from the perspective of victims of gross violations of human rights.[89]

The goal of institutions like the ICC is to insulate international criminal law from politics as much as possible, so as to make justice less vulnerable to the compromises imposed on it by diplomacy and statecraft: "Compromise is the art of politics, not of justice."[90]

This formulation creates a false dichotomy between realpolitik and justice. As Gary Jonathan Bass notes, "legal justice is one good among many . . . not a duty that trumps all others."[91] Ethical decision-making requires that it be weighed and balanced against other values, such as stability and peace, particularly since war creates the license for the worst abuses of human rights. Factoring power realities into this equation is not necessarily surrendering to realpolitik; it is indispensable in determining what kinds of justice and accountability mechanisms are possible and assessing their consequences for other values. Pursuing justice in ways that are blind to power realities will either be futile exercises in high-mindedness or counterproductive to political settlements that are necessary to end violent conflicts. International law cannot be isolated from the political context in which it has to operate.

* * *

NOTES

1. *The Prosecutor of the Special Court v. Charles Gankay Taylor,* Prosecution Opening Statement, 4 June 2007, at 28, available at www.sc-sl.org/Transcripts/Taylor/4june2007.pdf.

2. T. McConnell, "Charles Taylor's Trial Puts Dictators on Notice," *Christian Science Monitor*, 4 June 2007, 1.

3. K. C. Moghalu, *Global Justice: The Politics of War Crimes Trials* (2006), 109–11.

4. U.S. Department of State, Bureau of Democracy, Human Rights and Labor, "Country Reports on Human Rights 2003—Liberia," 25 February 2004.

5. R. G. Teitel, *Transitional Justice* (2000), 51–9.

6. P. B. Hayner, *Unspeakable Truths: Confronting State Terror and Atrocity* (2001), 154–9.

7. E. Skaar, "Truth Commissions, Trials—or Nothing? Policy Options in Democratic Transitions," (1999) 20 *Third World Quarterly* 1109.

8. See J. Snyder and L. Vinjamuri, "Trials and Errors: Principle and Pragmatism in Strategies of International Justice," (2003) 28 *International Security* 5.

9. See [G. J.] Bass, [*Stay the Hand of Vigilance: The Politics of War Crime Tribunals* (2000),] 227–31.

10. D. Robinson, "Serving the Interests of Justice: Amnesties, Truth Commissions and the International Criminal Court," (2003) 14 EJIL 481, at 483.

11. See the statement by P. Kirsch in [M. P.] Scharf, ["The Amnesty Exception to the Jurisdiction of the International Criminal Court," (1999) 32 *Cornell International Law Journal* 507,] at 522; see also [J.] Dugard, ["Possible Conflicts of Justices with Truth Commissions," in A. Cassese, P. Gaeta, and J. R. W. D. Jones (eds.), *The Rome Statute of the International Criminal Court: A Commentary* (2002),] 702; [M. R.] Brubacher, ["Prosecutorial Discretion within the International Criminal Court," (2004) 2 *Journal of International Criminal Justice* 71,] at 81, and R. J. Goldstone and N. Fritz, "'In the Interests of Justice' and Independent Referral: The ICC Prosecutor's Unprecedented Powers," (2000) 13 LJIL 655.

12. See the statement from W. Bourdon in L. Côté, "Reflections on the Exercise of Prosecutorial Discretion in International Criminal Law," (2005) 3 *Journal of International Criminal Justice* 162, at 178.

13. [Human Rights Watch (HRW), "The Meaning of the 'Interests of Justice' in Article 53 of the Rome Statute," Policy Paper, June 2005,] 3–4.

14. Ibid., at 2.

15. See Amnesty [International, "Open Letter to the Chief Prosecutor of the International Criminal Court: Comments on the Concept of the Interests of Justice, Drafted by Martin Macpherson, Senior Director of the International Law and Organizations Program," 17 June 2005,] 4. The letter on Amnesty's website mistakenly cites Article 43(1).

16. See HRW, *supra* note 13, at 8; see also Amnesty, *supra* note 15, at 6–8.

17. See HRW, *supra* note 13, at 9–11.

18. Ibid., at 12.

19. Ibid., at 19–20.

20. B. Chigara, *Amnesty in International Law: The Legality under International Law of National Amnesty Laws* (2002), 4.

21. See Amnesty, *supra* note 15, at 3.

22. Ibid, at 1.

23. Ibid., at 1; see also HRW, *supra* note 13, at 7–9.

24. E. Blumenson, "The Challenge of a Global Standard of Justice: Peace, Pluralism, and Punishment at the International Criminal Court," (2006) 44 *Columbia Journal of Transnational Law* 797, at 820.

25. Amnesty, *supra* note 15, at 2.

26. See the comments by R. Goldstone in Amnesty, *supra* note 15, at 7–8.

27. See HRW, *supra* note 13, at 15.

28. R. Goldstone, "Bringing War Criminals to Justice in an Ongoing War," in J. Moore (ed.), *Hard Choices: Moral Dilemmas in Humanitarian Intervention* (1998), 205–6.

29. Cited in P. R. Williams and M. P. Scharf, *Peace with Justice? War Crimes and Accountability in the Former Yugoslavia* (2002), 17; see also Goldstone, *supra* note 28, at 201–4.

30. Testimony of C. Dufka, Human Rights Watch, in U.S. Congress, House Committee

on International Relations, Subcommittee on Africa, *Confronting War Crimes in Africa*, Hearings, 24 June 2004, at 54.

31. See Williams and Scharf, *supra* note 29, at 159.

32. See Dufka Testimony, *supra* note 30, at 55–6.

33. N. J. Wheeler, *Saving Strangers: Humanitarian Intervention in International Society* (2000), 253–5.

34. See Bass, *supra* note 9, at 229–31.

35. S. L. Burg, "Coercive Diplomacy in the Balkans: The Use of Force in Bosnia and Kosovo," in R. J. Art and P. M. Cronin, *The United States and Coercive Diplomacy* (2003), 65–6.

36. J. Traub, *The Best Intentions: Kofi Annan and the UN in the Era of American World Power* (2006), 117–20.

37. P. Hirsh, "Sierra Leone," in D. M. Malone (ed.), *The UN Security Council: From the Cold War to the 21st Century* (2004), 528–30.

38. In both Germany and Japan, the United States confronted the risk of a political backlash against the trials on the part of politicians and elites that Washington saw as the most reliable allies in the Cold War confrontation with the Soviet Union. This eventually led the United States to back off from war crimes prosecutions in both countries. See P. Maguire, *Law and War: An American Story* (2000), ch. 5.

39. For an analysis of the degree to which the replacement of national trials with international tribunals can change this dynamic, see V. Peskin, "Beyond Victor's Justice: The Challenge of Prosecuting the Winners at the International Criminal Tribunals for the Former Yugoslavia and Rwanda," (2005) 4 *Journal of Human Rights*, at 213–31.

40. Quoted in A. Lebor, *"Complicity with Evil": The United Nations in the Age of Modern Genocide* (2006), 233.

41. See Burg, *supra* note 35, at 94–6.

42. Williams and Scharf, *supra* note 29, at 206–7; see also the remarks of D. Owen in P. Hazan, *Justice in a Time of War: The True Story Behind the International Criminal Tribunal for the Former Yugoslavia* (2004), 61–2.

43. See [T.] Allen, [*Trial Justice: The International Criminal Court and the Lord's Resistance Army* (2006),] 117–22.

44. See E. K. Baines, "The Haunting of Alice: Local Approaches to Justice and Reconciliation in Northern Uganda," (2007) I *International Journal of Transitional Justice* 797, at 103. For post-Juba attitudes see B. Oketch, "Negotiators Try Again: Northern Ugandans Say They Prefer Talk of Peace to Talk of War," 11 July 2008, Institute of War & Peace Reporting (IWPR), available at www.iwpr. net/?p=acr&s=f&0=345650&apc_state= henh.

45. M. Lacey, "Victims of Uganda Atrocities Choose a Path of Forgiveness," *New York Times*, 18 April 2005, A1. For contrasting views of this advocacy, see Allen, *supra* note 43, ch. 5; and A. Branch, "Uganda's Civil War and the Politics of ICC Intervention," 2007 (June) 21 *Ethics & International Affair* 179.

46. See Allen, *supra* note 43, at 185.

47. ICG, "Peace in Northern Uganda?" African Briefing No. 41, 13 September 2006, 9.

48. See A. Kakaire, "Amnesty Offer Blow for Rebel Chief Arrest Plans" IWPR, 6 July 2006, available at www.iwpr.net/?p=acr&s=f&o= 322105&apc_state=henh; K. Glassborow, "Peace versus Justice in Uganda" IWPR, 27 September 2006, available at www.iwpr.net/ ?p=acr&s=f&o=324160&apc_state=henh; and C. McGreal, "Museveni Refuses to Hand Over Rebel Leaders to War Crimes Court" *Guardian*, 13 March 2008, 18.

49. Allen, *supra* note 43, at 185–91.

50. Statement by L. Moreno-Ocampo, Informal Meeting of Legal Advisers of Ministries of Foreign Affairs, 24 October 2005, at 7. Left unsaid is the virtual certainty that meaningful assistance from Kampala ends if formal investigations of senior political and military officials were opened, given the dependence of the ICC on voluntary state cooperation.

51. See F. Osike, "ICC Prosecutor Luis Ocampo at His Office in The Hague," *New Vision* (Uganda), 13 July 2007.

52. L. Clifford, "Uganda: ICC Policy under Scrutiny," IWPR, 13 April 2007, available at www.iwpr.net/?p=acr&s=f&o=334879&apc_state=henh. Moreno-Ocampo has been more outspoken in his criticism of the peace process since the talks collapsed. See P. Eichstaedt, "ICC Chief Prosecutor Talks Tough," IWPR, 28 April 2008, available at www.iwpr.net/?p=acr&s=f&o=344364&apc_state=henh.

53. ICC, L. Moreno-Ocampo, Opening Remarks, Fifth Session of the Assembly of States Parties, 23 November 2006, at 2, available at www.icc-cpi.int/library/organs/otp/LMO_20061123_En.pdf.

54. The central reason for Sudan's official cooperation was the Comprehensive Peace Agreement (CPA) that ended the Sudan's north–south civil war, although there are reports of Sudanese support for the LRA. However, the ICC's simultaneous investigation of Sudan over Darfur complicates this cooperation. Spillover from Darfur or a breakdown of the CPA could lead Khartoum to arm the LRA to destabilize the government in Juba or to put Uganda on the defensive.

55. ICG, "Northern Uganda: Seizing the Opportunity for Peace," Africa Report No. 124, 26 April 2007, at 15.

56. Ibid., at 10–11.

57. See M. Ssenyonjo, "How Joseph Kony Is Keeping His Options Open," Guardian, 26 March 2008.

58. See P. Eichstaedt, "The Kony Problem," IWPR, 2 June 2008, available at www.iwpr.net/?p=acr&s=f&o=344912&apc_state=henh; and R. Dicker, "When Peace Talks Undermine Justice," International Herald Tribune, 5 July 2008, 6.

59. See K. Glassborow and P. Eichstaedt, "LRA Prepares for War, Not Peace," 24 April 2008, IWPR, available at www.iwpr.net/?p=acr&apc_state=henh&s=f&o=344252.

60. See the comments by C. Hall of Amnesty International and M. Ellis of the International Bar Association in Clifford, supra note 52.

61. See Branch, supra note 45, at 184.

62. See ICG, supra note 55, at 7.

63. E. Mutaizibwa, "Plan[n]ed Attack on LRA 'Reckless,'" IWPR, 24 January 2008, available at www.iwpr.net/?p=acr&s=f&o=342181&apc_state=henh.

64. L. Clifford, "ICC Issues Sudan Arrest Warrants," IWPR, 2 May 2007, available at www.iwpr.net/?p=acr&s=f&o=335266&apc_state=henh.

65. Statement to the United Nations Security Council pursuant to UNSCR 1593 (2005), 5 June 2008, 6.

66. Prosecutor's Application for Warrant of Arrest under Article 58 against Omar Hassan Ahmad AL BASHIR, 14 July 2008.

67. See R. Goldstone, "Catching a War Criminal in the Act," New York Times, 15 July 2008, A19.

68. K. A. Rodman, "Darfur and the Limits of Legal Deterrence," (2008) 30 Human Rights Quarterly 529, at 543–8.

69. I. W. Zartman, Ripe for Resolution: Conflict and Intervention in Africa (1989), 268.

70. ICG, "Darfur's New Security Reality," Africa Report No. 134, 26 November 2007, 8–11.

71. Ibid., at 21–3.

72. See J. Holslag, "China's Diplomatic Maneuvering on the Question of Darfur," (2008) 17 Journal of Contemporary China 71.

73. See J. Prendergast and C. Thomas-Jensen, "Blowing the Horn," (2007) Foreign Affairs 59, at 72–3.

74. J. Norris, D. Sullivan, and J. Prendergast, "The Merits of Justice," (2008) 35 Center for American Progress, Enough Strategy Paper.

75. International Commission of Inquiry on Darfur, Report to the Secretary-General, 25 January 2005, at 133–43; Human Rights Watch, "Entrenching Impunity: Government Responsibility for International Crimes in Darfur," December 2005, 58–63; Statement to the United Nations Security Council pursuant to UNSCR 1593 (2005), 6.

76. Quoted in Blumenson, supra note 24, at 821.

77. M. Brubacher, "The Development of Prosecutorial Discretion in International Criminal

Courts," in E. Hughes, W. A. Schabas, and R. Thakur (eds.), *Atrocities and International Accountability: Beyond Transitional Justice* (2007), 142, 153.

78. One could argue that the application to indict Bashir entails precisely these kinds of risk. While it comports with the formal international consensus in Security Council Resolution 1593 (2005), it depends upon enforcement actions that the international community has so far been unwilling to take. Since the ICC is currently receiving no real backing from the Security Council, it is unlikely to jeopardize the cooperation needed for its Darfur investigation, and it may have the benefit of shaking the status quo of Security Council inaction. Nonetheless, the decision is incompatible with the existing policy of impartial mediation, neutral peacekeeping, and humanitarian relief, all of which depend upon the consent of the government, whose leader may be branded an international criminal. It is therefore fraught with risk for the Court given Khartoum's threat to expel the UN peacekeepers if the Pre-Trial Chamber issues the arrest warrant. If the end result is increasing political violence and decreasing humanitarian access, this could poison the ICC's future relationship with the Security Council and the AU.

79. ICC-OTP, [Policy Paper on the Interests of Justice, September 2007,] 8–9; this should be contrasted with a 2004 memorandum which equated "the interests of justice" with the impact "on the stability and security of the country concerned." Cited in M. Delmas-Marty, "Interactions between National and International Criminal Law in the Preliminary Phase of Trial at the ICC," (2005) 3 *Journal of International Criminal Justice* 2, at 8.

80. ICC-OTP, *supra* note 79, at 4. As one OTP official wrote, "The Rome Statute provides the legal framework in which discussion about the pursuit of peace must be circumscribed. If the pursuit of peace cannot come to an accommodation with the obligations to which states have voluntarily bound themselves, States simply cannot endorse such agreements." P. Seils, "The Impact of the ICC on Peace Negotiations," expert paper, conference on "Building a Future of Peace and Justice," Nuremberg, Germany, 25–27 July 2007, 1.

81. ICC-OTP, *supra* note 79, at 5–6; contrast with HRW, *supra* note 13, at 19–20.

82. M. Walzer, *Just and Unjust Wars: A Moral Argument with Historical Illustrations* (1977), 287–8, cited in Williams and Scharf, *supra* note 29, at 17.

83. Walzer, *supra* note 82, at 288.

84. Ibid., at 119.

85. Cited in M. Scharf, "The Case for a Permanent International Truth Commission," (1999) 7 *Duké Journal of Comparative and International Law* 375, at 398.

86. Wheeler, *supra* note 33, at 194–7.

87. Walzer, *supra* note 82, at 116.

88. Ibid., at 113.

89. M. C. Bassiouni, "Justice and Peace: The Importance of Choosing Accountability over Realpolitik," (2004) 35 *Case Western Reserve Law Journal* 191, at 191.

90. M. C. Bassiouni, "From Versailles to Rwanda in Seventy-Five Years: The Need to Establish a Permanent International Criminal Court," (1997) 10 *Harvard Human Rights Journal* 11, at 12.

91. G. J. Bass, "Jus Post Bellum," (2004) 32 *Philosophy & Public Affairs* 384, at 405.

ROBERT O. KEOHANE

From *After Hegemony: Cooperation and Discord in the World Political Economy*

Realism, Institutionalism, and Cooperation

Impressed with the difficulties of cooperation, observers have often compared world politics to a "state of war." In this conception, international politics is "a competition of units in the kind of state of nature that knows no restraints other than those which the changing necessities of the game and the shallow conveniences of the players impose" (Hoffmann, 1965, p. vii). It is anarchic in the sense that it lacks an authoritative government that can enact and enforce rules of behavior. States must rely on "the means they can generate and the arrangements they can make for themselves" (Waltz, 1979, p. 111). Conflict and war result, since each state is judge in its own cause and can use force to carry out its judgments (Waltz, 1959, p. 159). The discord that prevails is accounted for by fundamental conflicts of interest (Waltz, 1959; Tucker, 1977).

Were this portrayal of world politics correct, any cooperation that occurs would be derivative from overall patterns of conflict. Alliance cooperation would be easy to explain as a result of the operation of a balance of power, but system-wide patterns of cooperation that benefit many countries without being tied to an

From Robert O. Keohane, *After Hegemony: Cooperation and Discord in the World Political Economy* (Princeton, N.J.: Princeton University Press, 1984), Chaps. 1, 6, 7. Some of the author's notes have been omitted.

alliance system directed against an adversary would not. If international politics were a state of war, institutionalized patterns of cooperation on the basis of shared purposes should not exist except as part of a larger struggle for power. The extensive patterns of international agreement that we observe on issues as diverse as trade, financial relations, health, telecommunications, and environmental protection would be absent.

At the other extreme from these "Realists" are writers who see cooperation as essential in a world of economic interdependence, and who argue that shared economic interests create a demand for international institutions and rules (Mitrany, 1975). Such an approach, which I refer to as "Institutionalist" because of its adherents' emphasis on the functions performed by international institutions, runs the risk of being naive about power and conflict. Too often its proponents incorporate in their theories excessively optimistic assumptions about the role of ideals in world politics, or about the ability of statesmen to learn what the theorist considers the "right lessons." But sophisticated students of institutions and rules have a good deal to teach us. They view institutions not simply as formal organizations with headquarters buildings and specialized staffs, but more broadly as "recognized patterns of practice around which expectations converge" (Young, 1980, p. 337). They regard these patterns of practice as significant because they affect state behavior. Sophisticated institutionalists do not expect cooperation always to prevail, but they are aware of the malleability of interests and they argue that interdependence creates interests in cooperation.

During the first twenty years or so after World War II, these views, though very different in their intellectual origins and their broader implications about human society, made similar predictions about the world political economy, and particularly about the subject of this [discussion], the political economy of the advanced market-economy countries. Institutionalists expected successful cooperation in one field to "spill over" into others (Haas, 1958). Realists anticipated a relatively stable international economic order as a result of the dominance of the United States. Neither set of observers was surprised by what happened, although they interpreted events differently.

Institutionalists could interpret the liberal international arrangements for trade and international finance as responses to the need for policy coordination created by the fact of interdependence. These arrangements, which we will call "international regimes," contained rules, norms, principles, and decisionmaking procedures. Realists could reply that these regimes were constructed on the basis of principles espoused by the United States, and that American power was essential for their construction and maintenance. For Realists, in other words, the early postwar regimes rested on the *political hegemony* of the United States. Thus Realists and Institutionalists could both regard early postwar developments as supporting their theories.

After the mid-1960s, however, U.S. dominance in the world political economy was challenged by the economic recovery and increasing unity of Europe and by the rapid economic growth of Japan. Yet economic interdependence continued to grow, and the pace of increased U.S. involvement in the world economy even accelerated after 1970. At this point, therefore, the Institutionalist and Realist predictions began to diverge. From a strict Institutionalist standpoint, the increasing need for coordination of policy, created by interdependence, should have led to more cooperation. From a Realist perspective, by contrast, the diffusion of power should have undermined the ability of anyone to create order.

On the surface, the Realists would seem to have made the better forecast. Since the late 1960s there have been signs of decline in the extent and efficacy of efforts to cooperate in the world political economy. As American power eroded, so did international regimes. The erosion of these regimes after World War II certainly refutes a naive version of the Institutionalist faith in interdependence as a solvent of conflict and a creator of cooperation. But it does not prove that only the Realist emphasis on power as a creator of order is valid. It might be possible, after the decline of hegemonic regimes, for more symmetrical patterns of cooperation to evolve after a transitional period of discord. Indeed, the persistence of attempts at cooperation during the 1970s suggests that the decline of hegemony does not necessarily sound cooperation's death knell.

International cooperation and discord thus remain puzzling. Under what conditions can independent countries cooperate in the world political economy? In particular, can cooperation take place without hegemony and, if so, how? This [project] is designed to help us find answers to these questions. I begin with Realist insights about the role of power and the effects of hegemony. But my central arguments draw more on the Institutionalist tradition, arguing that cooperation can under some conditions develop on the basis of complementary interests, and that institutions, broadly defined, affect the patterns of cooperation that emerge.

Hegemonic leadership is unlikely to be revived in this century for the United States or any other country. Hegemonic powers have historically only emerged after world wars; during peacetime, weaker countries have tended to gain on the hegemon rather than vice versa (Gilpin, 1981). It is difficult to believe that world civilization, much less a complex international economy, would survive such a war in the nuclear age. Certainly no prosperous hegemonic power is likely to emerge from such a cataclysm. As long as a world political economy persists, therefore, its central political dilemma will be how to organize cooperation without hegemony.

* * *

A Functional Theory of International Regimes

* * * [I]nternational regimes could be created and emphasized their value for overcoming what could be called "political market failure." * * * [Following is a] detailed examination of this argument by exploring why political market failure occurs and how international regimes can help to overcome it. This investigation will help us understand both why states often comply with regime rules and why international regimes can be maintained even after the conditions that facilitated their creation have disappeared. The functional theory developed in this chapter will therefore suggest some reasons to believe that even if U.S. hegemonic leadership may have been a crucial factor in the creation of some contemporary international economic regimes, the continuation of hegemony is not necessarily essential for their continued viability.

Political Market Failure and the Coase Theorem

Like imperfect markets, world politics is characterized by institutional deficiencies that inhibit mutually advantageous cooperation. * * * [I]n this self-help system, [there are] conflicts of interest between actors. In economic terms, these conflicts can be regarded as arising in part from the existence of externalities: actors do not bear the full costs, or receive the full benefits, of their own actions.[1] Yet in a famous article Ronald Coase (1960) argued that the presence of externalities alone does not necessarily prevent effective coordination among independent actors.

Under certain conditions, declared Coase, bargaining among these actors could lead to solutions that are Pareto-optimal regardless of the rules of legal liability.

To illustrate the Coase theorem and its counter-intuitive result, suppose that soot emitted by a paint factory is deposited by the wind onto clothing hanging outdoors in the yard of an old-fashioned laundry. Assume that the damage to the laundry is greater than the $20,000 it would cost the laundry to enclose its yard and install indoor drying equipment; so if no other alternative were available, it would be worthwhile for the laundry to take these actions. Assume also, however, that it would cost the paint factory only $10,000 to eliminate its emissions of air pollutants. Social welfare would clearly be enhanced by eliminating the pollution rather than by installing indoor drying equipment, but in the absence of either governmental enforcement or bargaining, the egoistic owner of the paint factory would have no incentive to spend anything to achieve this result.

It has frequently been argued that this sort of situation requires centralized governmental authority to provide the public good of clean air. Thus if the laundry had an enforceable legal right to demand compensation, the factory owner would have an incentive to invest $10,000 in pollution control devices to avoid a $20,000 court judgment. Coase argued, however, that the pollution would be cleaned up equally efficiently even if the laundry had no such recourse. If the law, or the existence of a decentralized self-help system, gave the factory a right to pollute, the laundry owner could simply pay the factory owner a sum greater than $10,000, but less than $20,000, to install anti-soot equipment. Both parties would agree to some such bargain, since both would benefit.

In either case, the externality of pollution would be eliminated. The key difference would not be one of economic efficiency, but of distribution of benefits between the factory and the laundry. In a self-help system, the laundry would have to pay between $10,000 and $20,000 and the factory would reap a profit from its capacity to pollute. But if legal liability rules were based on "the polluter pays principle," the laundry would pay nothing and the factory would have to invest $10,000 without reaping a financial return. Coase did not dispute that rules of liability could be evaluated on grounds of fairness, but insisted that, given his assumptions, efficient arrangements could be consummated even where the rules of liability favored producers of externalities rather than their victims.

The Coase theorem has frequently been used to show the efficacy of bargaining without central authority, and it has occasionally been applied specifically to international relations (Conybeare, 1980). The principle of sovereignty in effect establishes rules of liability that put the burden of externalities on those who suffer from them. The Coase theorem could be interpreted, therefore, as predicting that problems of collective action could easily be overcome in international politics through bargaining and mutual adjustment—that is, through cooperation * * * The further inference could be drawn that the discord observed must be the result of fundamental conflicts of interest rather than problems of coordination. The Coase theorem, in other words, could be taken as minimizing the importance of [Mancur] Olson's [1965] perverse logic of collective action or of the problems of coordination emphasized by game theory. However, such a conclusion would be incorrect for two compelling sets of reasons.

In the first place, Coase specified three crucial conditions for his conclusion to hold. These were: a legal framework establishing liability for actions, presumably supported by governmental authority; perfect information; and zero transaction costs (including organization costs and the costs of making side-payments). It is absolutely clear that none of these conditions is met in world politics. World government does not exist, making property rights and rules of legal liability fragile; information is extremely costly and often held unequally by different actors; transaction costs, including costs of organization and side-payments, are often very high. Thus an *inversion*

of the Coase theorem would seem more appropriate to our subject. In the absence of the conditions that Coase specified, coordination will often be thwarted by dilemmas of collective action.

Second, recent critiques of Coase's argument reinforce the conclusion that it cannot simply be applied to world politics, and suggest further interesting implications about the functions of international regimes. It has been shown on the basis of game theory that, with more than two participants, the Coase theorem cannot necessarily be demonstrated. Under certain conditions, there will be no stable solution: any coalition that forms will be inferior, for at least one of its members, to another possible coalition. The result is an infinite regress. In game-theoretic terminology, the "core" of the game is empty. When the core is empty, the assumption of zero transaction costs means that agreement is hindered rather than facilitated: "in a world of zero transaction costs, the inherent instability of all coalitions could result in endless recontracting among the firms" (Aivazian and Callen, 1981, p. 179; Veljanovski, 1982).

What do Coase and his critics together suggest about the conditions for international cooperation through bargaining? First, it appears that approximating Coase's first two conditions—that is, having a clear legal framework establishing property rights and low-cost information available in a roughly equal way to all parties—will tend to facilitate cooperative solutions. But the implications of reducing transaction costs are more complex. If transaction costs are too high, no bargains will take place; but if they are too low, under certain conditions an infinite series of unstable coalitions may form.

Inverting the Coase theorem allows us to analyze international institutions largely as responses to problems of property rights, uncertainty, and transaction costs. Without consciously designed institutions, these problems will thwart attempts to cooperate in world politics even when actors' interests are complementary. From the deficiency of the "self-help system" (even from the perspective of purely self-interested national actors) we derive a need for international regimes. Insofar as they fill this need, international regimes perform the functions of establishing patterns of legal liability, providing relatively symmetrical information, and arranging the costs of bargaining so that specific agreements can more easily be made. Regimes are developed in part because actors in world politics believe that with such arrangements they will be able to make mutually beneficial agreements that would otherwise be difficult or impossible to attain.

This is to say that the architects of regimes anticipate that the regimes will facilitate cooperation. Within the functional argument being constructed here, these expectations explain the formation of the regimes: the *anticipated effects* of the regimes account for the actions of governments that establish them. Governments believe that *ad hoc* attempts to construct particular agreements, without a regime framework, will yield inferior results compared to negotiations within the framework of regimes. Following our inversion of the Coase theorem, we can classify the reasons for this belief under the categories of legal liability (property rights), transaction costs, and problems of uncertainty. We will consider these issues in turn.

LEGAL LIABILITY Since governments put a high value on the maintenance of their own autonomy, it is usually impossible to establish international institutions that exercise authority over states. This fact is widely recognized by officials of international organizations and their advocates in national governments as well as by scholars. It would therefore be mistaken to regard international regimes, or the organizations that constitute elements of them, as characteristically unsuccessful attempts to institutionalize centralized authority in world politics. They cannot establish patterns of legal liability that are as solid as those developed within well-ordered societies, and their architects are well aware of this limitation.

Of course, the lack of a hierarchical structure of world politics does not prevent regimes from developing bits and pieces of law (Henkin, 1979, pp. 13–22). But the principal significance of international regimes does not lie in their formal legal status, since any patterns of legal liability and property rights established in world politics are subject to being overturned by the actions of sovereign states. International regimes are more like the "quasi-agreements" that William Fellner (1949) discusses when analyzing the behavior of oligopolistic firms than they are like governments. These quasi-agreements are legally unenforceable but, like contracts, help to organize relationships in mutually beneficial ways (Lowry, 1979, p. 276). Regimes also resemble conventions: practices, regarded as common knowledge in a community, that actors conform to not because they are uniquely best, but because others conform to them as well (Hardin, 1982; Lewis, 1969; Young, 1983). What these arrangements have in common is that they are designed not to implement centralized enforcement of agreements, but rather to establish stable mutual expectations about others' patterns of behavior and to develop working relationships that will allow the parties to adapt their practices to new situations. Contracts, conventions, and quasi-agreements provide information and generate patterns of transaction costs: costs of reneging on commitments are increased, and the costs of operating within these frameworks are reduced.

Both these arrangements and international regimes are often weak and fragile. Like contracts and quasi-agreements, international regimes are frequently altered: their rules are changed, bent, or broken to meet the exigencies of the moment. They are rarely enforced automatically, and they are not self-executing. Indeed, they are often matters for negotiation and renegotiation. As [Donald] Puchala has argued, "attempts to enforce EEC regulations open political cleavages up and down the supranational-to-local continuum and spark intense politicking along the cleavage lines" (1975, p. 509).

TRANSACTION COSTS Like oligopolistic quasi-agreements, international regimes alter the relative costs of transactions. Certain agreements are forbidden. Under the provisions of the General Agreement on Tariffs and Trade (GATT), for instance, it is not permitted to make discriminatory trade arrangements except under specific conditions. Since there is no centralized government, states can nevertheless implement such actions, but their lack of legitimacy means that such measures are likely to be costly. Under GATT rules, for instance, retaliation against such behavior is justified. By elevating injunctions to the level of principles and rules, furthermore, regimes construct linkages between issues. No longer does a specific discriminatory agreement constitute merely a particular act without general significance; on the contrary, it becomes a "violation of GATT" with serious implications for a large number of other issues. In the terms of Prisoners' Dilemma, the situation has been transformed from a single-play to an iterated game. In market-failure terms, the transaction costs of certain possible bargains have been increased, while the costs of others have been reduced. In either case, the result is the same: incentives to violate regime principles are reduced. International regimes reduce transaction costs of legitimate bargains and increase them for illegitimate ones.

International regimes also affect transaction costs in the more mundane sense of making it cheaper for governments to get together to negotiate agreements. It is more convenient to make agreements within a regime than outside of one. International economic regimes usually incorporate international organizations that provide forums for meetings and secretariats that can act as catalysts for agreement. Insofar as their principles and rules can be applied to a wide variety of particular issues, they are efficient: establishing the rules and principles at the outset makes it unnecessary to renegotiate them each time a specific question arises.

International regimes thus allow governments to take advantage of potential economics of scale. Once a regime has been established, the marginal cost of dealing with each additional issue will be lower than it would be without a regime. * * * [I]f a policy area is sufficiently dense, establishing a regime will be worthwhile. Up to a point there may even be what economists call "increasing returns to scale." In such a situation, each additional issue could be included under the regime at lower cost than the previous one. As [Paul] Samuelson notes, in modern economies, "increasing returns is the prime case of deviations from perfect competition" (1967, p. 117). In world politics, we should expect increasing returns to scale to lead to more extensive international regimes.

In view of the benefits of economies of scale, it is not surprising that specific agreements tend to be "nested" within regimes. For instance, an agreement by the United States, Japan, and the European Community in the Multilateral Trade Negotiations to reduce a particular tariff will be affected by the rules and principles of GATT—that is, by the trade regime. The trade regime, in turn, is nested within a set of other arrangements, including those for monetary relations, energy, foreign investment, aid to developing countries, and other issues, which together constitute a complex and interlinked pattern of relations among the advance market-economy countries. These, in turn, are related to military-security relations among the major states.[2]

The nesting patterns of international regimes affect transaction costs by making it easier or more difficult to link particular issues and to arrange side-payments, giving someone something on one issue in return for her help on another.[3] Clustering of issues under a regime facilitates side-payments among these issues: more potential *quids* are available for the *quo*. Without international regimes linking clusters of issues to one another, side-payments and linkages would be difficult to arrange in world politics; in the absence of a price system for the exchange of favors, institutional barriers would hinder the construction of mutually beneficial bargains.

Suppose, for instance, that each issue were handled separately from all others, by a different governmental bureau in each country. Since a side-payment or linkage always means that a government must give up something on one dimension to get something on another, there would always be a bureaucratic loser within each government. Bureaus that would lose from proposed side-payments, on issues that matter to them, would be unlikely to bear the costs of these linkages willingly on the basis of other agencies' claims that the national interest required it.

Of course, each issue is not considered separately by a different governmental department or bureau. On the contrary, issues are grouped together, in functionally organized departments such as Treasury, Commerce, and Energy (in the United States). Furthermore, how governments organize themselves to deal with foreign policy is affected by how issues are organized internationally; issues considered by different regimes are often dealt with by different bureaucracies at home. Linkages and side-payments among issues grouped in the same regime thus become easier, since the necessary internal tradeoffs will tend to take place within rather than across bureaus; but linkages among issues falling into different regimes will remain difficult, or even become more so (since the natural linkages on those issues will be with issues within the same regime).

Insofar as issues are dealt with separately from one another on the international level, it is often hard, in simply bureaucratic terms, to arrange for them to be considered together. There are bound to be difficulties in coordinating policies of different international organizations—GATT, the IMF [International Monetary Fund], and the IEA [International Energy Agency] all have different memberships and different operating styles—in addition to the resistance that will appear to such a move within member governments. Within regimes, by contrast, side-payments are facilitated by the fact that regimes bring together negotiators to consider sets of issues that

may well lie within the negotiators' bureaucratic bailiwicks at home. GATT negotiations, as well as deliberations on the international monetary system, have been characterized by extensive bargaining over side-payments and the politics of issue-linkage (Hutton, 1975). The well-known literature on "spillover" in bargaining, relating to the European Community and other integration schemes, can also be interpreted as concerned with side-payments. According to these writings, expectations that an integration arrangement can be expanded to new issue-areas permit the broadening of potential side-payments, thus facilitating agreement (Haas, 1958).

We conclude that international regimes affect the costs of transactions. The value of a potential agreement to its prospective participants will depend, in part, on how consistent it is with principles of legitimacy embodied in international regimes. Transactions that violate these principles will be costly. Regimes also affect bureaucratic costs of transactions: successful regimes organize issue-areas so that productive linkages (those that facilitate agreements consistent with the principles of the regime) are facilitated, while destructive linkages and bargains that are inconsistent with regime principles are discouraged.

UNCERTAINTY AND INFORMATION From the perspective of market-failure theories, the informational functions of regimes are the most important of all. * * * [W]hat Akerlof [1970] called "quality uncertainty" was the crucial problem in [a] "market for lemons" example. Even in games of pure coordination with stable equilibria, this may be a problem. Conventions—commuters meeting under the clock at Grand Central Station, suburban families on a shopping trip "meeting at the car"—become important. But in simple games of coordination, severe information problems are not embedded in the structure of relationships, since actors have incentives to reveal information and their own preferences fully to one another. In these games the problem is to reach some point of agreement; but it may not matter much which of several possible points is chosen (Schelling, 1960/1978). Conventions are important and ingenuity may be required, but serious systemic impediments to the acquisition and exchange of information are lacking (Lewis, 1969; Young, 1983).

Yet as we have seen in * * * discussions of collective action and Prisoners' Dilemma, many situations—both in game theory and in world politics—are characterized by conflicts of interest as well as common interests. In such situations, actors have to worry about being deceived and double-crossed, just as the buyer of a used car has to guard against purchasing a "lemon." The literature on market failure elaborates on its most fundamental contention—that, in the absence of appropriate institutions, some mutually advantageous bargains will not be made because of uncertainty—by pointing to three particularly important sources of difficulty: *asymmetrical information; moral hazard;* and *irresponsibility.*

ASYMMETRICAL INFORMATION Some actors may know more about a situation than others. Expecting that the resulting bargains would be unfair, "outsiders" will be reluctant to make agreements with "insiders" (Williamson, 1975, pp. 31–33). This is essentially the problem of "quality uncertainty" as discussed by Akerlof. Recall that this is a problem not merely of insufficient information, but rather of *systematically biased* patterns of information, which are recognized in advance of any agreement both by the holder of more information (the seller of the used car) and by its less well-informed prospective partner (the potential buyer of the "lemon" or "creampuff," as the case may be). Awareness that others have greater knowledge than oneself, and are therefore capable of manipulating a relationship or even engaging successful deception and double-cross, is a barrier to making agreements. When this suspicion is unfounded—that is, the agreement would be mutually beneficial—it is an obstacle to improving welfare through cooperation.

This problem of asymmetrical information only appears when dishonest behavior is possi-ble. In a society of saints, communication would be open and no one would take advantage of superior information. In our imperfect world, however, asymmetries of information are not rectified simply by communication. Not all communication reduces uncertainty, since communication may lead to asymmetrical or unfair bargaining outcomes as a result of deception. Effective communication is not measured well by the amount of talking that used-car salespersons do to customers or that governmental officials do to one another in negotiating international regimes! The information that is required in entering into an international regime is not merely information about other governments' resources and formal negotiating positions, but also accurate knowledge of their future positions. In part, this is a matter of estimating whether they will keep their commitments. As the "market for lemons" example suggests, and as we will see in more detail below, a government's reputation therefore becomes an important asset in persuading others to enter into agreements with it. International regimes help governments to assess others' reputations by providing standards of behavior against which performance can be measured, by linking these standards to specific issues, and by providing forums, often through international organizations, in which these evaluations can be made.[4] Regimes may also include international organizations whose secretariats act not only as mediators but as providers of unbiased information that is made available, more or less equally to all members. By reducing asymmetries of information through a process of upgrading the general level of available information, international regimes reduce uncertainty. Agreements based on misapprehension and deception may be avoided; mutually beneficial agreements are more likely to be made.

Regimes provide information to members, thereby reducing risks of making agreements. But the information provided by a regime may be insufficiently detailed. A government may require precise information about its prospective partners' internal evaluations of a particular situation, their intentions, the intensity of their preferences, and their willingness to adhere to an agreement even in adverse future circumstances. Governments also need to know whether other participants will follow the spirit as well as the letter of agreements, whether they will share the burden of adjustment to unexpected adverse change, and whether they are likely to seek to strengthen the regime in the future.

The significance of asymmetrical information and quality uncertainty in theories of market failure therefore calls attention to the importance not only of international regimes but also of variations in the degree of closure of different states' decisionmaking processes. Some governments maintain secrecy much more zealously than others. American officials, for example, often lament that the U.S. government leaks information "like a sieve" and claim that this openness puts the United States at a disadvantage vis-à-vis its rivals.

Surely there are disadvantages in openness. The real or apparent incoherence in policy that often accompanies it may lead the open government's partners to view it as unreliable because its top leaders, whatever their intentions, are incapable of carrying out their agreements. A cacophony of messages may render all of them uninterpretable. But some reflection on the problem of making agreements in world politics suggests that there are advantages for the open government that cannot be duplicated by countries with more tightly closed bureaucracies. Governments that cannot provide detailed and reliable information about their intentions—for instance, because their decisionmaking processes are closed to the outside world and their officials are prevented from developing frank informal relationships with their foreign counterparts—may be unable convincingly to persuade their potential partners of their commitment to the contemplated arrangements. Observers from other countries will be uncertain about the genuineness of officials' enthusiasm or the depth of their support for the cooperative scheme under consideration. These potential partners will there-

fore insist on discounting the value of prospective agreements to take account of their uncertainty. As in the "market for lemons," some potential agreements, which would be beneficial to all parties, will not be made because of "quality uncertainty"—about the quality of the closed government's commitment to the accord.[5]

MORAL HAZARD   Agreements may alter incentives in such a way as to encourage less cooperative behavior. Insurance companies face this problem of "moral hazard." Property insurance, for instance, may make people less careful with their property and therefore increase the risk of loss (Arrow, 1974). The problem of moral hazard arises quite sharply in international banking. The solvency of a major country's largest banks may be essential to its financial system, or even to the stability of the entire international banking network. As a result, the country's central bank may have to intervene if one of these banks is threatened. The U.S. Federal Reserve, for instance, could hardly stand idly by while the Bank of America or Citibank became unable to meet its liabilities. Yet this responsibility creates a problem of moral hazard, since the largest banks, in effect, have automatic insurance against disastrous consequences of risky but (in the short-run at least) profitable loans. They have incentives to follow risk-seeking rather than risk-averse behavior at the expense of the central bank (Hirsch, 1977).

IRRESPONSIBILITY   Some actors may be irresponsible, making commitments that they may not be able to carry out. Governments or firms may enter into agreements that they intend to keep, assuming that the environment will continue to be benign; if adversity sets in, they may be unable to keep their commitments. Banks regularly face this problem, leading them to devise standards of creditworthiness. Large governments trying to gain adherents to international agreements may face similar difficulties: countries that are enthusiastic about cooperation are likely to be those that expect to gain more, proportionately, than they contribute. This is a problem of self-selection, as discussed in the market-failure literature. For instance, if rates are not properly adjusted, people with high risks of heart attack will seek life insurance more avidly that those with longer life expectancies; people who purchased "lemons" will tend to sell them earlier on the used-car market than people with "creampuffs" (Akerlof, 1970; Arrow, 1974). In international politics, self-selection means that for certain types of activities—such as sharing research and development information—weak states (with much to gain but little to give) may have more incentive to participate than strong ones, but less incentive actually to spend funds on research and developments.[6] Without the strong states, the enterprise as a whole will fail.

From the perspective of the outside observer, irresponsibility is an aspect of the problem of public goods and free-riding; but from the standpoint of the actor trying to determine whether to rely on a potentially irresponsible partner, it is a problem of uncertainty. Either way, informational costs and asymmetries may prevent mutually beneficial agreement.

REGIMES AND MARKET FAILURE International regimes help states to deal with all of these problems. As the principles and rules of a regime reduce the range of expected behavior, uncertainty declines, and as information becomes more widely available, the asymmetry of its distribution is likely to lessen. Arrangements within regimes to monitor actors' behavior * * * mitigate problems of moral hazard. Linkages among particular issues within the context of regimes raise the costs of deception and irresponsibility, since the consequences of such behavior are likely to extend beyond the issue on which they are manifested. Close ties among officials involved in managing international regimes increase the ability of governments to make mutually beneficial agreements, because intergovernmental relationships characterized by ongoing communication among working-level officials, informal as well as formal, are inherently more conducive to exchange of information than are traditional relationships between closed bureaucracies. In general, regimes make it more sensible to cooperate by lowering the likelihood of being double-crossed. Whether we view this problem through the lens of game theory or that of market failure, the central conclusion is the same: international regimes can facilitate cooperation by reducing uncertainty. Like international law, broadly defined, their function is "to make human actions conform to predictable patterns so that contemplated actions can go forward with some hope of achieving a rational relationship between means and ends" (Barkun, 1968, p. 154).

Thus international regimes are useful to governments. Far from being threats to governments (in which case it would be hard to understand why they exist at all), they permit governments to attain objectives that would otherwise be unattainable. They do so in part by facilitating intergovernmental agreements. Regimes facilitate agreements by raising the anticipated costs of violating others' property rights, by altering transaction costs through the clustering of issues, and by providing reliable information to members. Regimes are relatively efficient institutions, compared with the alternative of having a myriad of unrelated agreements, since their principles, rules, and institutions create linkages among issues that give actors incentives to reach mutually beneficial agreements. They thrive in situations where states have common as well as conflicting interests on multiple, overlapping issues and where externalities are difficult but not impossible to deal with through bargaining. Where these conditions exist, international regimes can be of value to states.

We have seen that it does not follow from this argument that regimes necessarily increase global welfare. They can be used to pursue particularistic and parochial interests as well as more widely shared objectives. Nor should we conclude that all potentially valuable regimes will necessarily be instituted. * * * [E]ven regimes that promise substantial overall benefits may be difficult to invent.

* * *

Bounded Rationality and Redefinitions of Self-Interest

The perfectly rational decisionmaker * * * may face uncertainty as a result of the behavior of others, or the forces of nature, but she is assumed to make her own calculations costlessly. Yet this individual, familiar in textbooks, is not made of human flesh and blood. Even the shrewdest speculator or the most brilliant scientist faces limitations on her capacity for calculation. To imagine that all available information will be used by a decisionmaker is to exaggerate the intelligence of the human species.

Decisionmakers are in practice subject to limitations on their own cognitive abilities, quite apart from the uncertainties inherent in their environments. Herbert Simon has made this point with his usual lucidity (1982, p. 162):

> Particularly important is the distinction between those theories that locate all the conditions and constraints in the environment, outside the skin of the rational actor, and those theories that postulate important constraints arising from the limitations of the actor himself as an information processor. Theories that incorporate constraints on the information-processing capacities of the actor may be called *theories of bounded rationality*.

Actors subject to bounded rationality cannot maximize in the classical sense, because they are not capable of using all the information that is potentially available. They cannot compile exhaustive lists of alternative courses of action, ascertaining the value of each alternative and accurately judging the probability of each possible outcome (Simon, 1955/1979a, p. 10). It is crucial to emphasize that the source of their difficulties in calculation lies not merely in the complexity of the external world, but in their own cognitive limitations. In this respect, behavioral theories of bounded rationality are quite different from recent neoclassical theories, such as the theories of market failure * * *, which retain the assumption of perfect maximization:

> [In new neoclassical theories] limits and costs of information are introduced, not as psychological characteristics of the decision maker, but as part of his technological environment. Hence, the new theories do nothing to alleviate the computational complexities facing the decision maker—do not see him coping with them by heroic approximation, simplifying and satisficing, but simply magnify and multiply them. Now he needs to compute not merely the shapes of his supply and demand curves, but in addition, the costs and benefits of computing those shapes to greater accuracy as well. Hence, to some extent, the impression that these new theories deal with the hitherto ignored phenomena of uncertainty and information transmission is illusory. (Simon, 1979b, p. 504)

In Simon's own theory, people "satisfice" rather than maximize. That is, they economize on information by searching only until they find a course of action that falls above a satisfactory level—their "aspiration level." Aspiration levels are adjusted from time to time in response to new information about the environment (Simon, 1972, p. 168). In view of people's knowledge of their own cognitive limitations, this is often a sensible strategy; it is by no means irrational and may well be the best way to make most decisions.

In ordinary life, we satisfice all the time. We economize on information by developing habits, by devising operating rules to simplify calculation in situations that repeat themselves, and by adopting general principles that we expect, in the long run, to yield satisfactory results. I do not normally calculate whether to brush my teeth in the morning, whether to hit a tennis ball directed at me with my backhand or my fore-hand, or whether to tell the truth when asked on the telephone whether Robert Keohane is home. On the contrary, even apart from any moral scruples I might have (for instance, about lying), I assume that my interests will be furthered bet-ter by habitually brushing my teeth, applying the rule "when in doubt, hit it with your forehand because you have a lousy backhand," and adopt-ing the general principle of telling the truth than by calculating the costs and benefits of every alternative in each case. I do not mean to deny that I might occasionally be advantaged by pur-suing a new idea at my desk rather than brush-ing my teeth, hitting a particular shot with my backhand, or lying to an obnoxious salesman on the telephone. If I could costlessly compute the value of each alternative, it might indeed be pref-erable to make the necessary calculations each time I faced a choice. But since this is not feasi-ble, given the costs of processing information, it is in my long-run interest to eschew calculation in these situations.

Simon's analysis of bounded rationality bears some resemblance to the argument made for rule-utilitarianism in philosophy, which empha-sizes the value of rules in contributing to the gen-eral happiness.[7] Rule-utilitarianism was defined by John Austin in a dictum: "Our rules would be fashioned on utility; our conduct, on our rules" (Mackie, 1977, p. 136). The rule-utilitarian adopts these rules, or "secondary principles," in John Stuart Mill's terms, in the belief that they will lead, in general, to better results than a series of *ad hoc* decisions based each time on first princi-ples.[8] A major reason for formulating and fol-lowing such rules is the limited calculating ability of human beings. In explicating his doctrine of utilitarianism, Mill therefore anticipated much of Simon's argument about bounded rationality (1861/1951, p. 30):

> Nobody argues that the art of navigation is not founded on astronomy, because sailors cannot wait to calculate the Nautical Almanack. Being rational creatures, they go to sea with it ready calculated; and all rational creatures go out upon the sea of life with their minds made up on the common ques-tions of right and wrong, as well as on many of the far more difficult questions of wise and foolish. And this, as long as foresight is a human quality, it is to be presumed they will continue to do.

If individuals typically satisfice rather than maximize, all the more so do governments and other large organizations (Allison, 1971; Stein-bruner, 1974; Snyder and Diesing, 1977). Organi-zational decision-making processes hardly meet the requirements of classical rationality. Orga-nizations have multiple goals, defined in terms of aspiration levels; they search until satisfac-tory courses of action are found; they resort to feedback rather than systematically forecasting future conditions; and they use "standard oper-ating procedures and rules of thumb" to make and implement decisions (Cyert and March, 1963, p. 113; March and Simon, 1958).

The behavioral theory of the firm has made it clear that satisficing does not constitute aberrant behavior that should be rectified where possible; on the contrary, it is intelligent. The leader of a large organization who demanded that the orga-nization meet the criteria of classical rationality would herself be foolish, perhaps irrationally so. An organization whose leaders behaved in this way would become paralyzed unless their subor-dinates found ways to fool them into believing that impossible standards were being met. This assertion holds even more for governments than for business firms, since governments' constitu-encies are more varied, their goals more diverse (and frequently contradictory), and success or failure more difficult to measure. Assumptions of unbounded rationality, however dear they may be to the hearts of classical Realist theorists (Morgenthau, 1948/1966) and writers on foreign policy, are idealizations. A large, complex gov-ernment would tie itself in knots by "keeping its options open," since middle-level bureaucrats would not know how to behave and the top poli-cymakers would be overwhelmed by minor prob-lems. The search for complete flexibility is as quixotic as looking for the Holy Grail or the fountain of youth.

If governments are viewed as constrained by bounded rationality, what are the implications for the functional argument * * * about the value of international regimes? * * * [U]nder rational-choice assumptions, international regimes are valuable to governments because they reduce transaction costs and particularly because they reduce uncertainty in the external environment. Each government is better able, with regimes in place, to predict that its counterparts will follow predictably cooperative policies. According to this theory, governments sacrifice the ability to maximize their myopic self-interest by making calculations on each issue as it arises, in return for acquiring greater certainty about others' behavior.

Under bounded rationality, the inclination of governments to join or support international regimes will be reinforced by the fact that the alternatives to regimes are less attractive than they would be if the assumptions of classical rationality were valid. Actors laboring under bounded rationality cannot calculate the costs and benefits of each alternative course of action on each issue. On the contrary, they need to simplify their own decisionmaking processes in order to function effectively at all. The rules of thumb they devise will not yield better, and will generally yield worse, results (apart from decisionmaking costs) than classically rational action—whether these rules of thumb are adopted unilaterally or as part of an international regime. Thus a comparison between the value of a unilateral rule of thumb and that of a regime rule will normally be more favorable to the regime rule than a comparison between the value of costless, perfectly rational calculation and the regime rule.

When we abandon the assumption of classical rationality, we see that it is not international regimes that deny governments the ability to make classically rational calculations. The obstacle is rather the nature of governments as large, complex organizations composed of human beings with limited problem-solving capabilities. The choice that governments actually face with respect to international regimes is not whether to adhere to regimes at the expense of maximizing utility through continuous calculation, but rather on what rules of thumb to rely. Normally, unilateral rules will fit the individual country's situation better than rules devised multilaterally. Regime rules, however, have the advantage of constraining the actions of others. The question is whether the value of the constraints imposed on others justifies the costs of accepting regime rules in place of the rules of thumb that the country would have adopted on its own.

Thus if we accept that governments must adopt rules of thumb, the costs of adhering to international regimes appear less severe than they would be if classical rationality were a realistic possibility. Regimes merely substitute multilateral rules (presumably somewhat less congenial per se) for unilateral ones, with the advantage that other actors' behavior thereby becomes more predictably cooperative. International regimes neither enforce hierarchical rules on governments nor substitute their own rules for autonomous calculation; instead, they provide rules of thumb in place of those that governments would otherwise adopt.

* * * [W]e can see how different our conception of international regimes is from the self-help system that is often taken as revealing the essence of international politics. In a pure self-help system, each actor calculates its interests on each particular issue, preserving its options until that decision has been made. The rational response to another actor's distress in such a system is to take advantage of it by driving a hard bargain, demanding as much as "the traffic will bear" in return for one's money, one's oil, or one's military support. Many such bargains are in fact struck in world politics, especially among adversaries; but one of the key features of international regimes is that they limit the ability of countries in a particularly strong bargaining position (however transitory) to take advantage of that situation. This limitation, as we have stressed, is not the result of altruism but of the fact that

joining a regime changes calculations of long-run self-interest. To a government that values its ability to make future agreements, reputation is a crucial resource; and the most important aspect of an actor's reputation in world politics is the belief of others that it will keep its future commitments even when a particular situation, myopically viewed, makes it appear disadvantageous to do so. Thus even classically rational governments will sometimes join regimes and comply with their rules. To a government seeking to economize on decisionmaking costs, the regime is also valuable for providing rules of thumb; discarding it would require establishing a new set of rules to guide one's bureaucracy. The convenience of rules of thumb combines with the superiority of long-run calculations of self-interest over myopic ones to reinforce adherence to rules by egoistic governments, particularly when they labor under the constraints of bounded rationality.

* * *

NOTES

1. For an elaborated version of this definition, see Davis and North (1971, p. 16).
2. For the idea of "nesting," I am indebted to Aggarwal (1981). Snidal (1981) also relies on this concept, which was used in a similar context some years ago by Barkun (1968, p. 17).
3. On linkage, see especially the work of Kenneth A. Oye (1979, 1983). See also Stein (1980) and Tollison and Willett (1979).
4. This point was suggested to me by reading Elizabeth Colson's account of how stateless societies reach consensus on the character of individuals: through discussions and gossip that allow people to "apply the standards of performance in particular roles in making an overall judgement about the total person; this in turn allows them to predict future behavior" (1974, p. 53).

5. In 1960 Thomas Schelling made a similar argument about the problem of surprise attack. Asking how we would prove that we were not planning a surprise attack if the Russians suspected we were, he observed that "evidently it is not going to be enough just to tell the truth. . . . There has to be some way of authenticating certain facts, the facts presumably involving the disposition of forces" (p. 247). To authenticate facts requires becoming more open to external monitoring as a way of alleviating what Akerlof [1970] later called "quality uncertainty."
6. Bobrow and Kudrle found evidence of severe problems of collective goods in the IEA's energy research and development program, suggesting that "commercial interests and other national rivalries appear to have blocked extensive international cooperation" (1979, p. 170).
7. In philosophy, utilitarianism refers to an ethical theory that purports to provide generalizable principles for moral human action. Since my argument here is a positive one, seeking to explain the behavior of egoistic actors rather than to develop or criticize an ethical theory, its relationship to rule-utilitarianism in philosophy, as my colleague Susan Okin has pointed out to me, is only tangential.
8. John Mackie argues that even act-utilitarians "regularly admit the use of rules of thumb," and that whether one follows rules therefore does not distinguish act- from rule-utilitarianism (1977, p. 137). Conversely, Joseph Nye has pointed out to me that even rule-utilitarians must depart at some point from their rules for consequentialist reasons. The point here is not to draw a hard-and-fast dichotomy between the two forms of utilitarianism, but rather to point out the similarities between Mill's notion of relying on rules and Simon's conception of bounded rationality. If all utilitarians have to resort to rules of thumb to some extent, this only strengthens the point I am making about the

importance of rules in affecting, but not determining, the behavior of governments. For a succinct discussion of utilitarianism in philosophy, see Urmson (1968).

BIBLIOGRAPHY

* * * Where a date is given for an original as well as a later edition, the latter was used; page references in the text refer to it.

Aggarwal, Vinod, 1981. Hanging by a Thread: International Regime Change in the Textile/Apparel System, 1950–1979 (Ph.D. dissertation. Stanford University).

Aivazian, Varouj A., and Jeffrey L. Callen, 1981. The Coase theorem and the empty core. *Journal of Law and Economics*, vol. 24, no. 1 (April), pp. 175–81.

Akerlof, George A., 1970. The market for "lemons." *Quarterly Journal of Economics*, vol. 84, no. 3 (August), pp. 488–500.

Allison, Graham, 1971. *Essence of Decision: Explaining the Cuban Missile Crisis* (Boston: Little, Brown).

Arrow, Kenneth J., 1974. *Essays in the Theory of Risk-Bearing* (New York: North-Holland/American Elsevier).

Barkun, Michael, 1968. *Law without Sanctions: Order in Primitive Societies and the World Community* (New Haven: Yale University Press).

Bobrow, Davis W., and Robert Kudrle, 1979. Energy R & D: in tepid pursuit of collective goods. *International Organization*, vol. 33, no. 2 (Spring), pp. 149–76.

Coase, Ronald, 1960. The problem of social cost. *Journal of Law and Economics*, vol. 3, pp. 1–44.

Colson, Elizabeth, 1974. *Tradition and Contract: The Problem of Order* (Chicago: Aldine Publishing Company).

Conybeare, John A.C., 1980. International organization and the theory of property rights. *International Organization*, vol. 34, no. 3 (Summer), pp. 307–34.

Cyert, Richard, and James G. March, 1963. *The Behavioral Theory of the Firm* (Englewood Cliffs, N.J.: Prentice-Hall).

Davis, Lance, and Douglass C. North, 1971. *Institutional Change and American Economic Growth* (Cambridge: Cambridge University Press).

Fellner, William, 1949. *Competition among the Few* (New York: Knopf).

Gilpin, Robert, 1981. *War and Change in World Politics* (Cambridge: Cambridge University Press).

Haas, Ernst B., 1958. *The Uniting of Europe* (Stanford: Stanford University Press).

Hardin, Russell, 1982. *Collective Action* (Baltimore: The Johns Hopkins University Press for Resources for the Future).

Henkin, Louis, 1979. *How Nations Behave: Law and Foreign Policy*, 2nd edition (New York: Columbia University Press for the Council on Foreign Relations).

Hirsch, Fred, 1977. The Bagehot problem. *The Manchester School*, vol. 45, no. 3 (September), pp. 241–57.

Hoffmann, Stanley, 1965. *The State of War: Essays on the Theory and Practice of International Politics* (New York: Praeger).

Hutton, Nicholas, 1975. The salience of linkage in international economic negotiations. *Journal of Common Market Studies*, vol. 13, nos. 1–2, pp. 136–60.

Krasner, Stephen D., ed., 1983. *International Regimes* (Ithaca: Cornell University Press).

Lewis, David K., 1969. *Convention: A Philosophical Study* (Cambridge: Harvard University Press).

Lowry, S. Todd. 1979. Bargain and contract theory in law and economics. In Samuels, 1979, pp. 261–82.

Mackie, J. L., 1977. *Ethics: Inventing Right and Wrong* (Harmondsworth, England: Penguin Books).

March, James G., and Herbert Simon, 1958. *Organizations* (New York: John Wiley & Sons).

Mill, John Stuart, 1861/1951. *Utilitarianism* (New York: E. P. Dutton).

Mitrany, David, 1975. *The Functional Theory of Politics* (London: St. Martin's Press for the London School of Economics and Political Science).

Morgenthau, Hans J., 1948/1966. *Politics among Nations*, 4th edition (New York: Knopf).

Olson, Mancur, 1965, *The Logic of Collective Action* (Cambridge: Harvard University Press).

Oye, Kenneth A., 1979. The domain of choice. In Oye et al., 1979, pp. 3–33.

Oye, Kenneth A., 1983 Belief Systems, Bargaining and Breakdown: International Political Economy 1929–1934 (Ph.D. dissertation, Harvard University).

Oye, Kenneth A., Donald Rothchild, and Robert J. Lieber, eds., 1979. *Eagle Entangled: U.S. Foreign Policy in a Complex World* (New York: Longman).

Puchala, Donald J., 1975. Domestic politics and regional harmonization in the European Communities. *World Politics*, vol. 27, no. 4 (July), pp. 496–520.

Samuels, Warren J., 1979. *The Economy as a System of Power* (New Brunswick, N.J.: Transaction Books).

Samuelson, Paul A., 1967. The monopolistic competition revolution. In R. E. Kuenne, ed., *Monopolistic Competition Theory* (New York: John Wiley & Sons).

Schelling, Thomas C., 1960/1980. *The Strategy of Conflict* (Cambridge: Harvard University Press).

Schelling, Thomas C., 1978. *Micromotives and Macrobehavior* (New York: W. W. Norton).

Simon, Herbert A., 1955. A behavioral model of rational choice. *Quarterly Journal of Economics*, vol. 69, no. 1 (February), pp. 99–118. Reprinted in Simon, 1979a, pp. 7–19.

Simon, Herbert A., 1972. Theories of bounded rationality. In Radner and Radner, 1972, pp. 161–76. Reprinted in Simon, 1982, pp. 408–23.

Simon, Herbert A., 1979a. *Models of Thought* (New Haven: Yale University Press).

Simon, Herbert A., 1979b. Rational decision making in business organizations. *American Economic Review*, vol. 69, no. 4 (September), pp. 493–513. Reprinted in Simon, 1982, pp. 474–94.

Simon, Herbert A., 1982. *Models of Bounded Rationality*, 2 vols. (Cambridge: MIT Press).

Snidal, Duncan, 1981. Interdependence, Regimes and International Cooperation (unpublished manuscript).

Snyder, Glenn H., and Paul Diesing, 1977. *Conflict among Nations: Bargaining, Decision making, and System Structure in International Crises* (Princeton: Princeton University Press).

Stein, Arthur A., 1980. The politics of linkage. *World Politics*, vol. 33, no. 1 (October), pp. 62–81.

Steinbruner, John D., 1974. *The Cybernetic Theory of Decision: New Dimensions of Political Analysis* (Princeton: Princeton University Press).

Tollison, Robert D., and Thomas D. Willett, 1979. An economic theory of mutually advantageous issue linkages in international negotiations. *International Organization*, vol. 33, no. 4 (Autumn), pp. 425–49.

Tucker, Robert W., 1977. *The Inequality of Nations* (New York: Basic Books).

Urmson, J. O., 1968. Utilitarianism. *International Encyclopedia of the Social Sciences* (New York: Macmillan), pp. 224–29.

Veljanovski, Cento G., 1982. The Coase theorems and the economic theory of markets and law. *Kyklos*, vol. 35, fasc. 1, pp. 53–74.

Waltz, Kenneth, 1959. *Man, the State and War* (New York: Columbia University Press).

Waltz, Kenneth, 1979. *Theory of World Politics* (Reading, Mass.: Addison-Wesley).

Williamson, Oliver, 1975. *Markets and Hierarchies: Analysis and Anti-Trust Implications* (New York: The Free Press).

Young, Oran R., 1980. International regimes: problems of concept formation. *World Politics*, vol. 32, no. 3 (April), pp. 331–56.

Young, Oran R., 1983. Regime dynamics: the rise and fall of international regimes. In Krasner, 1983, pp. 93–114.

JOHN J. MEARSHEIMER

The False Promise of International Institutions

* * *

What Are Institutions?

There is no widely agreed upon definition of institutions in the international relations literature.[1] The concept is sometimes defined so broadly as to encompass all of international relations, which gives it little analytical bite.[2] For example, defining institutions as "recognized patterns of behavior or practice around which expectations converge" allows the concept to cover almost every regularized pattern of activity between states, from war to tariff bindings negotiated under the General Agreement on Tariffs and Trade (GATT), thus rendering it largely meaningless.[3] Still, it is possible to devise a useful definition that is consistent with how most institutionalist scholars employ the concept.

I define institutions as a set of rules that stipulate the ways in which states should cooperate and compete with each other.[4] They prescribe acceptable forms of state behavior, and proscribe unacceptable kinds of behavior. These rules are negotiated by states, and according to many prominent theorists, they entail the mutual acceptance of higher norms, which are "standards of behavior defined in terms of rights and obligations."[5] These rules are typically formalized in international agreements, and are usually embodied in organizations with their own personnel and budgets.[6] Although rules are usually

From *International Security* 19, no. 3 (Winter 1994/95): 5–49.

incorporated into a formal international organization, it is not the organization *per se* that compels states to obey the rules. Institutions are not a form of world government. States themselves must choose to obey the rules they created. Institutions, in short, call for the "decentralized cooperation of individual sovereign states, without any effective mechanism of command."[7]

* * *

Institutions in a Realist World

Realists * * * recognize that states sometimes operate through institutions. However, they believe that those rules reflect state calculations of self-interest based primarily on the international distribution of power. The most powerful states in the system create and shape institutions so that they can maintain their share of world power, or even increase it. In this view, institutions are essentially "arenas for acting out power relationships."[8] For realists, the causes of war and peace are mainly a function of the balance of power, and institutions largely mirror the distribution of power in the system. In short, the balance of power is the independent variable that explains war; institutions are merely an intervening variable in the process.

NATO provides a good example of realist thinking about institutions. NATO is an institution, and it certainly played a role in preventing World War III and helping the West win the Cold War. Nevertheless, NATO was basically a manifestation of the bipolar distribution of power in Europe during the Cold War, and it was that balance of power, not NATO *per se*, that provided the key to maintaining stability on the continent. NATO was essentially an American tool for managing power in the face of the Soviet threat. Now, with the collapse of the Soviet Union, realists argue that NATO must either disappear or reconstitute itself on the basis of the new distribution of power in Europe.[9] NATO cannot remain as it was during the Cold War.

* * *

Liberal Institutionalism

Liberal institutionalism does not directly address the question of whether institutions cause peace, but instead focuses on the less ambitious goal of explaining cooperation in cases where state interests are not fundamentally opposed.[10] Specifically, the theory looks at cases where states are having difficulty cooperating because they have "mixed" interests; in other words, each side has incentives both to cooperate and not to cooperate.[11] Each side can benefit from cooperation, however, which liberal institutionalists define as "goal-directed behavior that entails mutual policy adjustments so that all sides end up better off than they would otherwise be."[12] The theory is of little relevance in situations where states' interests are fundamentally conflictual and neither side thinks it has much to gain from cooperation. In these circumstances, states aim to gain advantage over each other. They think in terms of winning and losing, and this invariably leads to intense security competition, and sometimes war. But liberal institutionalism does not deal directly with these situations, and thus says little about how to resolve or even ameliorate them.

Therefore, the theory largely ignores security issues and concentrates instead on economic and, to a lesser extent, environmental issues.[13] In fact, the theory is built on the assumption that international politics can be divided into two realms—security and political economy—and that liberal institutionalism mainly applies to the latter, but not the former. * * *

* * *

According to liberal institutionalists, the principal obstacle to cooperation among states with mutual interests is the threat of cheating.[14] The famous "prisoners' dilemma," which is the analytical centerpiece of most of the liberal institutionalist literature, captures the essence of the problem that states must solve to achieve cooperation.[15] Each of two states can either cheat or cooperate with the other. Each side wants to maximize its own gain, but does not care about the size of the other side's gain; each side cares about the other side only so far as the other side's chosen strategy affects its own prospects for maximizing gain. The most attractive strategy for each state is to cheat and hope the other state pursues a cooperative strategy. In other words, a state's ideal outcome is to "sucker" the other side into thinking it is going to cooperate, and then cheat. But both sides understand this logic, and therefore both sides will try to cheat the other. Consequently, both sides will end up worse off than if they had cooperated, since mutual cheating leads to the worst possible outcome. Even though mutual cooperation is not as attractive as suckering the other side, it is certainly better than the outcome when both sides cheat.

The key to solving this dilemma is for each side to convince the other that they have a collective interest in making what appear to be short-term sacrifices (the gain that might result from successful cheating) for the sake of long-term benefits (the substantial payoff from mutual long-term cooperation). This means convincing states to accept the second-best outcome, which is mutual collaboration. The principal obstacle to reaching this cooperative outcome will be fear of getting suckered, should the other side cheat. This, in a nutshell, is the problem that institutions must solve.

To deal with this problem of "political market failure," institutions must deter cheaters and protect victims.[16] Three messages must be sent to potential cheaters: you will be caught, you will be punished immediately, and you will jeopardize future cooperative efforts. Potential victims, on the other hand, need early warning of cheating to avoid serious injury, and need the means to punish cheaters.

Liberal institutionalists do not aim to deal with cheaters and victims by changing fundamental norms of state behavior. Nor do they suggest transforming the anarchical nature of the international system. They accept the assumption that states operate in an anarchic environment and behave in a self-interested manner.[17] * * * Liberal institutionalists instead concentrate on showing how rules can work to counter the cheating problem, even while states seek to maximize their own welfare. They argue that institutions can change a state's calculations about how to maximize gains. Specifically, rules can get states to make the short-term sacrifices needed to resolve the prisoners' dilemma and thus to realize long-term gains. Institutions, in short, can produce cooperation.

Rules can ideally be employed to make four major changes in "the contractual environment."[18] First, rules can increase the number of transactions between particular states over time.[19] This *institutionalized iteration* discourages cheating in three ways. It raises the costs of cheating by creating the prospect of future gains through cooperation, thereby invoking "the shadow of the future" to deter cheating today. A state caught cheating would jeopardize its prospects of benefiting from future cooperation, since the victim would probably retaliate. In addition, iteration gives the victim the opportunity to pay back the cheater: it allows for reciprocation, the tit-for-tat strategy, which works to punish cheaters and not allow them to get away with their transgression. Finally, it rewards states that develop a reputation for faithful adherence to agreements, and punishes states that acquire a reputation for cheating.[20]

Second, rules can tie together interactions between states in different issue areas. *Issue-linkage* aims to create greater interdependence between states, who will then be reluctant to cheat in one issue area for fear that the victim—and perhaps other states as well—will retaliate in another issue area. It discourages cheating in much the same way as iteration: it raises the costs of cheating and provides a way for the victim to retaliate against the cheater.

Third, a structure of rules can increase the amount of *information* available to participants in cooperative agreements so that close monitoring is possible. Raising the level of information discourages cheating in two ways: it increases the likelihood that cheaters will be caught, and more importantly, it provides victims with early warning of cheating, thereby enabling them to take protective measures before they are badly hurt.

Fourth, rules can reduce the *transaction costs* of individual agreements.[21] When institutions perform the tasks described above, states can devote less effort to negotiating and monitoring cooperative agreements, and to hedging against possible defections. By increasing the efficiency of international cooperation, institutions make it more profitable and thus more attractive for self-interested states.

Liberal institutionalism is generally thought to be of limited utility in the security realm, because fear of cheating is considered a much greater obstacle to cooperation when military issues are at stake.[22] There is the constant threat that betrayal will result in a devastating military defeat. This threat of "swift, decisive defection" is simply not present when dealing with international economics. Given that "the costs of betrayal" are potentially much graver in the military than the economic sphere, states will be very reluctant to accept the "one step backward, two steps forward" logic which underpins the tit-for-tat strategy of conditional cooperation. One step backward in the security realm might mean destruction, in which case there will be no next step—backward or forward.[23]

* * * There is an important theoretical failing in the liberal institutionalist logic, even as it applies to economic issues. The theory is correct

as far as it goes: cheating can be a serious barrier to cooperation. It ignores, however, the other major obstacle to cooperation: relative-gains concerns. As Joseph Grieco has shown, liberal institutionalists assume that states are not concerned about relative gains, but focus exclusively on absolute gains.[24] * * *

This oversight is revealed by the assumed order of preference in the prisoners' dilemma game: each state cares about how its opponent's strategy will affect its own (absolute) gains, but not about how much one side gains relative to the other. In other words, each side simply wants to get the best deal for itself, and does not pay attention to how well the other side fares in the process.[25] Nevertheless, liberal institutionalists cannot ignore relative-gains considerations, because they assume that states are self-interested actors in an anarchic system, and they recognize that military power matters to states. A theory that explicitly accepts realism's core assumptions—and liberal institutionalism does that—must confront the issue of relative gains if it hopes to develop a sound explanation for why states cooperate.

One might expect liberal institutionalist to offer the counterargument that relative-gains logic applies only to the security realm, while absolute-gains logic applies to the economic realm. Given that they are mainly concerned with explaining economic and environmental cooperation, leaving relative-gains concerns out of the theory does not matter.

There are two problems with this argument. First, if cheating were the only significant obstacle to cooperation, liberal institutionalists could argue that their theory applies to the economic, but not the military realm. In fact, they do make that argument. However, once relative-gains considerations are factored into the equation, it becomes impossible to maintain the neat dividing line between economic and military issues, mainly because military might is significantly dependent on economic might. The relative size of a state's economy has profound consequences for its standing in the international balance of military power. Therefore, relative-gains concerns must be taken into account for security reasons when looking at the economic as well as military domain. The neat dividing line that liberal institutionalists employ to specify when their theory applies has little utility when one accepts that states worry about relative gains.[26]

Second, there are non-realist (i.e., nonsecurity) logics that might explain why states worry about relative gains. Strategic trade theory, for example, provides a straightforward economic logic for why states should care about relative gains.[27] It argues that states should help their own firms gain comparative advantage over the firms of rival states, because that is the best way to insure national economic prosperity. There is also a psychological logic, which portrays individuals as caring about how well they do (or their state does) in a cooperative agreement, not for material reasons, but because it is human nature to compare one's progress with that of others.[28]

Another possible liberal institutionalist counterargument is that solving the cheating problem renders the relative-gains problem irrelevant. If states cannot cheat each other, they need not fear each other, and therefore, states would not have to worry about relative power. The problem with this argument, however, is that even if the cheating problem were solved, states would still have to worry about relative gains because gaps in gains can be translated into military advantage that can be used for coercion or aggression. And in the international system, states sometimes have conflicting interests that lead to aggression.

There is also empirical evidence that relative-gains considerations mattered during the Cold War even in economic relations among the advanced industrialized democracies in the Organization for Economic Cooperation and Development (OECD). One would not expect realist logic about relative gains to be influential in this case: the United States was a superpower with little to fear militarily from the other OECD states, and those states were unlikely to use a relative-gains advantage to threaten the United States.[29] Furthermore, the OECD states were important American allies during the Cold War, and thus the United States benefited strategically when they gained substantially in size and strength.

Nonetheless, relative gains appear to have mattered in economic relations among the advanced industrial states. Consider three prominent studies. Stephen Krasner considered efforts at cooperation in different sectors of the international communications industry. He found that states were remarkably unconcerned about cheating but deeply worried about relative gains, which led him to conclude that liberal institutionalism "is not relevant for global communications." Grieco examined American and EC efforts to implement, under the auspices of GATT, a number of agreements relating to non-tariff barriers to trade. He found that the level of success was not a function of concerns about cheating but was influenced primarily by concern about the distribution of gains. Similarly, Michael Mastanduno found that concern about relative gains, not about cheating, was an important factor in shaping American policy towards Japan in three cases: the FSX fighter aircraft, satellites, and high-definition television.[30]

I am not suggesting that relative-gains considerations make cooperation impossible; my point is simply that they can pose a serious impediment to cooperation and must therefore be taken into account when developing a theory of cooperation among states. This point is apparently now recognized by liberal institutionalists. Keohane, for example, acknowledges that he "did make a major mistake by underemphasizing distributive issues and the complexities they create for international cooperation."[31]

CAN LIBERAL INSTITUTIONALISM BE REPAIRED?
Liberal institutionalists must address two questions if they are to repair their theory. First,

can institutions facilitate cooperation when states seriously care about relative gains, or do institutions only matter when states can ignore relative-gains considerations and focus instead on absolute gains? I find no evidence that liberal institutionalists believe that institutions facilitate cooperation when states care deeply about relative gains. They apparently concede that their theory only applies when relative-gains considerations matter little or hardly at all.[32] Thus the second question: when do states not worry about relative gains? The answer to this question would ultimately define the realm in which liberal institutionalism applies.

Liberal institutionalists have not addressed this important question in a systematic fashion, so any assessment of their efforts to repair the theory must be preliminary. * * *

＊　＊　＊

PROBLEMS WITH THE EMPIRICAL RECORD
Although there is much evidence of cooperation among states, this alone does not constitute support for liberal institutionalism. What is needed is evidence of cooperation that would not have occurred in the absence of institutions because of fear of cheating, or its actual presence. But scholars have provided little evidence of cooperation of that sort, nor of cooperation failing because of cheating. Moreover, as discussed above, there is considerable evidence that states worry much about relative gains not only in security matters, but in the economic realm as well.

This dearth of empirical support for liberal institutionalism is acknowledged by proponents of that theory.[33] The empirical record is not completely blank, however, but the few historical cases that liberal institutionalists have studied provide scant support for the theory. Consider two prominent examples.

Keohane looked at the performance of the International Energy Agency (IEA) in 1974–81, a period that included the 1979 oil crisis.[34] This case does not appear to lend the theory much support. First, Keohane concedes that the IEA failed outright when put to the test in 1979: "regimeoriented efforts at cooperation do not always succeed, as the fiasco of IEA actions in 1979 illustrates."[35] He claims, however, that in 1980 the IEA had a minor success "under relatively favorable conditions" in responding to the outbreak of the Iran-Iraq War. Although he admits it is difficult to specify how much the IEA mattered in the 1980 case, he notes that "it seems clear that 'it [the IEA] leaned in the right direction,'" a claim that hardly constitutes strong support for the theory.[36] Second, it does not appear from Keohane's analysis that either fear of cheating or actual cheating hindered cooperation in the 1979 case, as the theory would predict. Third, Keohane chose the IEA case precisely because it involved relations among advanced Western democracies with market economies, where the prospects for cooperation were excellent.[37] The modest impact of institutions in this case is thus all the more damning to the theory.

Lisa Martin examined the role that the European Community (EC) played during the Falklands War in helping Britain coax its reluctant allies to continue economic sanctions against Argentina after military action started.[38] She concludes that the EC helped Britain win its allies' cooperation by lowering transaction costs and facilitating issue linkage. Specifically, Britain made concessions on the EC budget and the Common Agricultural Policy (CAP); Britain's allies agreed in return to keep sanctions on Argentina.

This case, too, is less than a ringing endorsement for liberal institutionalism. First, British efforts to maintain EC sanctions against Argentina were not impeded by fears of possible cheating, which the theory identifies as the central impediment to cooperation. So this case does not present an important test of liberal institutionalism, and thus the cooperative outcome does not tell us much about the theory's explanatory

power. Second, it was relatively easy for Britain and her allies to strike a deal in this case. Neither side's core interests were threatened, and neither side had to make significant sacrifices to reach an agreement. Forging an accord to continue sanctions was not a difficult undertaking. A stronger test for liberal institutionalism would require states to cooperate when doing so entailed significant costs and risks. Third, the EC was not essential to an agreement. Issues could have been linked without the EC, and although the EC may have lowered transaction costs somewhat, there is no reason to think these costs were a serious impediment to striking a deal.[39] It is noteworthy that Britain and America were able to cooperate during the Falklands War, even though the United States did not belong to the EC.

There is also evidence that directly challenges liberal institutionalism in issue areas where one would expect the theory to operate successfully. The studies discussed above by Grieco, Krasner, and Mastanduno test the institutionalist argument in a number of different political economy cases, and each finds the theory has little explanatory power. More empirical work is needed before a final judgment is rendered on the explanatory power of liberal institutionalism. Nevertheless, the evidence gathered so far is unpromising at best.

In summary, liberal institutionalism does not provide a sound basis for understanding international relations and promoting stability in the post–Cold War world. It makes modest claims about the impact of institutions, and steers clear of war and peace issues, focusing instead on the less ambitious task of explaining economic cooperation. Furthermore, the theory's causal logic is flawed, as proponents of the theory now admit. Having overlooked the relative-gains problem, they are now attempting to repair the theory, but their initial efforts are not promising. Finally, the available empirical evidence provides little support for the theory.

* * *

Conclusion

*   *   *

The attraction of institutionalist theories for both policymakers and scholars is explained, I believe, not by their intrinsic value, but by their relationship to realism, and especially to core elements of American political ideology. Realism has long been and continues to be an influential theory in the United States.[40] Leading realist thinkers such as George Kennan and Henry Kissinger, for example, occupied key policymaking positions during the Cold War. The impact of realism in the academic world is amply demonstrated in the institutionalist literature, where discussions of realism are pervasive.[41] Yet despite its influence, Americans who think seriously about foreign policy issues tend to dislike realism intensely, mainly because it clashes with their basic values. The theory stands opposed to how most Americans prefer to think about themselves and the wider world.[42]

There are four principal reasons why American elites, as well as the American public, tend to regard realism with hostility. First, realism is a pessimistic theory. It depicts a world of stark and harsh competition, and it holds out little promise of making that world more benign. Realists, as Hans Morgenthau wrote, are resigned to the fact that "there is no escape from the evil of power, regardless of what one does."[43] Such pessimism, of course, runs up against the deep-seated American belief that with time and effort, reasonable individuals can solve important social problems. Americans regard progress as both desirable and possible in politics, and they are therefore uncomfortable with realism's claim that security competition and war will persist despite our best efforts to eliminate them.[44]

Second, realism treats war as an inevitable, and indeed sometimes necessary, form of state activity. For realists, war is an extension of politics by other means. Realists are very cautious in their prescriptions about the use of force: wars

should not be fought for idealistic purposes, but instead for balance-of-power reasons. Most Americans, however, tend to think of war as a hideous enterprise that should ultimately be abolished. For the time being, however, it can only justifiably be used for lofty moral goals, like "making the world safe for democracy"; it is morally incorrect to fight wars to change or preserve the balance of power. This makes the realist conception of warfare anathema to many Americans.

Third, as an analytical matter, realism does not distinguish between "good" states and "bad" states, but essentially treats them like billiard balls of varying size. In realist theory, all states are forced to seek the same goal: maximum relative power.[45] A purely realist interpretation of the Cold War, for example, allows for no meaningful difference in the motives behind American and Soviet behavior during that conflict. According to the theory, both sides must have been driven by concerns about the balance of power, and must have done what was necessary to try to achieve a favorable balance. Most Americans would recoil at such a description of the Cold War, because they believe the United States was motivated by good intentions while the Soviet Union was not.[46]

Fourth, America has a rich history of thumbing its nose at realism. For its first 140 years of existence, geography and the British navy allowed the United States to avoid serious involvement in the power politics of Europe. America had an isolationist foreign policy for most of this period, and its rhetoric explicitly emphasized the evils of entangling alliances and balancing behavior. Even as the United States finally entered its first European war in 1917, Woodrow Wilson railed against realist thinking. America has a long tradition of antirealist rhetoric, which continues to influence us today.

Given that realism is largely alien to American culture, there is a powerful demand in the United States for alternative ways of looking at the world, and especially for theories that square with basic American values. Institutionalist theories nicely meet these requirements, and that is the main source of their appeal to policymakers and scholars. Whatever else one might say about these theories, they have one undeniable advantage in the eyes of their supporters: they are not realism. Not only do institutionalist theories offer an alternative to realism, but they explicitly seek to undermine it. Moreover, institutionalists offer arguments that reflect basic American values. For example, they are optimistic about the possibility of greatly reducing, if not eliminating, security competition among states and creating a more peaceful world. They certainly do not accept the realist stricture that war is politics by other means. Institutionalists, in short, purvey a message that Americans long to hear.

There is, however, a downside for policymakers who rely on institutionalist theories: these theories do not accurately describe the world, hence policies based on them are bound to fail. The international system strongly shapes the behavior of states, limiting the amount of damage that false faith in institutional theories can cause. The constraints of the system notwithstanding, however, states still have considerable freedom of action, and their policy choices can succeed or fail in protecting American national interests and the interests of vulnerable people around the globe. The failure of the League of Nations to address German and Japanese aggression in the 1930s is a case in point. The failure of institutions to prevent or stop the war in Bosnia offers a more recent example. These cases illustrate that institutions have mattered rather little in the past; they also suggest that the false belief that institutions matter has mattered more, and has had pernicious effects. Unfortunately, misplaced reliance on institutional solutions is likely to lead to more failures in the future.

NOTES

1. Regimes and institutions are treated as synonymous concepts in this article. They are also used interchangeably in the institutionalist literature. See Robert O. Keohane, "International Institutions: Two Approaches," *International Studies Quarterly*, Vol. 32, No. 4 (December 1988), p. 384; Robert O. Keohane, *International Institutions and State Power: Essays in International Relations Theory* (Boulder, Colo.: Westview Press, 1989), pp. 3–4; and Oran R. Young, *International Cooperation: Building Regimes for Natural Resources and the Environment* (Ithaca, N.Y.: Cornell University Press, 1989), chaps. 1 and 8. The term "multilateralism" is also virtually synonymous with institutions. To quote John Ruggie, "the term 'multilateral' is an adjective that modifies the noun 'institution.' Thus, multilateralism depicts a *generic institutional form* in international relations. . . . [Specifically,] multilateralism is an institutional form which coordinates relations among three or more states on the basis of 'generalized' principles of conduct." Ruggie, "Multilateralism[: The Anatomy of an Institution]," [*International Organization*, Vol. 46, No. 3 (Summer 1992),] pp. 570–571.

2. For discussion of this point, see Arthur A. Stein, *Why Nations Cooperate: Circumstance and Choice in International Relations* (Ithaca, N.Y.: Cornell University Press, 1990), pp. 25–27. Also see Susan Strange, *"Cave! Hic Dragones:* A Critique of Regime Analysis," in Stephen D. Krasner, ed., *International Regimes*, special issue of *International Organization*, Vol. 36, No. 2 (Spring 1982), pp. 479–496.

3. Oran R. Young, "Regime Dynamics: The Rise and Fall of International Regimes," in Krasner, *International Regimes*, p. 277.

4. See Douglass C. North and Robert P. Thomas, "An Economic Theory of the Growth of the Western World," *The Economic History Review*, 2nd series, Vol. 23, No. 1 (April 1970), p. 5.

5. Krasner, *International Regimes*, p. 186. Nonrealist institutions are often based on higher norms, while few, if any, realist institutions are based on norms. The dividing line between norms and rules is not sharply defined in the institutionalist literature. See Robert O. Keohane, *After Hegemony:*

Cooperation and Discord in the World Political Economy (Princeton, N.J.: Princeton University Press, 1984), pp. 57–58. For example, one might argue that rules, not just norms, are concerned with rights and obligations. The key point, however, is that for many institutionalists, norms, which are core beliefs about standards of appropriate state behavior, are the foundation on which more specific rules are constructed. This distinction between norms and rules applies in a rather straightforward way in the subsequent discussion. Both collective security and critical theory challenge the realist belief that states behave in a self-interested way, and argue instead for developing norms that require states to act more altruistically. Liberal institutionalism, on the other hand, accepts the realist view that states act on the basis of self-interest, and concentrates on devising rules that facilitate cooperation among states.

6. International organizations are public agencies established through the cooperative efforts of two or more states. These administrative structures have their own budget, personnel, and buildings. John Ruggie defines them as "palpable entities with headquarters and letterheads, voting procedures, and generous pension plans." Ruggie, "Multilateralism," p. 573. Once rules are incorporated into an international organization, "they may seem almost coterminous," even though they are "distinguishable analytically." Keohane, *International Institutions and State Power*, p. 5.

7. Charles Lipson, "Is the Future of Collective Security Like the Past?" in George W. Downs, ed., *Collective Security beyond the Cold War* (Ann Arbor: University of Michigan Press), p. 114.

8. Tony Evans and Peter Wilson, "Regime Theory and the English School of International Relations: A Comparison," *Millennium: Journal of International Studies*, Vol. 21, No. 3 (Winter 1992), p. 330.

9. See Gunther Hellmann and Reinhard Wolf, "Neorealism Neoliberal Institutionalism,

and the Future of NATO," *Security Studies*, Vol. 3, No. 1 (Autumn 1993), pp. 3–43.

10. Among the key liberal institutionalist works are: Robert Axelrod and Robert O. Keohane, "Achieving Cooperation under Anarchy: Strategies and Institutions," *World Politics*, Vol. 38, No. 1 (October 1985), pp. 226–254; Keohane, *After Hegemony*; Keohane, "International Institutions: Two Approaches," pp. 379–396; Keohane, *International Institutions and State Power*, chap. 1; Charles Lipson, "International Cooperation in Economic and Security Affairs," *World Politics*, Vol. 37, No. 1 (October 1984), pp. 1–23; Lisa L. Martin, "Institutions and Cooperation: Sanctions during the Falkland Islands Conflict," *International Security*, Vol. 16, No. 4 (Spring 1992), pp. 143–178; Lisa L. Martin, *Coercive Cooperation: Explaining Multilateral Economic Sanctions* (Princeton, N.J.: Princeton University Press, 1992); Kenneth A. Oye, "Explaining Cooperation under Anarchy: Hypotheses and Strategies," *World Politics*, Vol. 38, No. 1 (October 1985), pp. 1–24; and Stein, *Why Nations Cooperate*.

11. Stein, *Why Nations Cooperate*, chap. 2. Also see Keohane, *After Hegemony*, pp. 6–7, 12–13, 67–69.

12. Milner, "International Theories of Cooperation [among Nations: Strengths and Weaknesses]," [*World Politics*, Vol. 44, No. 3 (April 1992),] p. 468.

13. For examples of the theory at work in the environmental realm, see Peter M. Haas, Robert O. Keohane, and Marc A. Levy, eds., *Institutions for the Earth: Sources of Effective International Environmental Protection* (Cambridge, Mass.: MIT Press, 1993), especially chaps. 1 and 9. Some of the most important work on institutions and the environment has been done by Oran Young. See, for example, Young, *International Cooperation*. The rest of my discussion concentrates on economic, not environmental issues, for conciseness, and also because the key theoretical works in the liberal institutionalist literature focus on economic rather than environmental matters.

14. Cheating is basically a "breach of promise." Oye, "Explaining Cooperation under Anarchy," p. 1. It usually implies unobserved noncompliance, although there can be observed cheating as well. Defection is a synonym for cheating in the institutionalist literature.

15. The centrality of the prisoners' dilemma and cheating to the liberal institutionalist literature is clearly reflected in virtually all the works cited in footnote 10. As Helen Milner notes in her review essay on this literature: "The focus is primarily on the role of regimes [institutions] in solving the defection [cheating] problem." Milner, "International Theories of Cooperation," p. 475.

16. The phrase is from Keohane, *After Hegemony*, p. 85.

17. Kenneth Oye, for example, writes in the introduction to an issue of *World Politics* containing a number of liberal institutionalist essays: "Our focus is on non-altruistic cooperation among states dwelling in international anarchy." Oye, "Explaining Cooperation under Anarchy," p. 2. Also see Keohane, "International Institutions: Two Approaches," pp. 380–381; and Keohane, *International Institutions and State Power*, p. 3.

18. Haas, Keohane, and Levy, *Institutions for the Earth*, p. 11. For general discussions of how rules work, which inform my subsequent discussion of the matter, see Keohane, *After Hegemony*, chaps. 5–6; Martin, "Institutions and Cooperation," pp. 143–178; and Milner, "International Theories of Cooperation," pp. 474–478.

19. See Axelrod and Keohane, "Achieving Cooperation under Anarchy," pp. 248–250; Lipson, "International Cooperation," pp. 4–18.

20. Lipson, "International Cooperation," p. 5.

21. See Keohane, *After Hegemony*, pp. 89–92.

22. This point is clearly articulated in Lipson, "International Cooperation," especially pp. 12–18. The subsequent quotations in this paragraph are from ibid. Also see Axelrod and Keohane, "Achieving Cooperation under Anarchy," pp. 232–233.

23. See Roger B. Parks, "What If 'Fools Die'? A Comment on Axelrod," Letter to *American Political Science Review*, Vol. 79, No. 4 (December 1985), pp. 1173–1174.

24. See Grieco, "Anarchy and the Limits of Cooperation[: A Realist Critique of the Newest Liberal Institutionalism,]" [*International Organization*, Vol. 42, No. 3 (Summer 1988)]. Other works by Grieco bearing on the subject include: Joseph M. Grieco, "Realist Theory and the Problem of International Cooperation: Analysis with an Amended Prisoner's Dilemma Model," *Journal of Politics*, Vol. 50, No. 3 (August 1988), pp. 600–624; Grieco, *Cooperation among Nations: Europe, America, and Non-Tariff Barriers to Trade* (Ithaca, N.Y.: Cornell University Press, 1990); and Grieco, "Understanding the Problem of International Cooperation: The Limits of Neoliberal Institutionalism and the Future of Realist Theory," in Baldwin, [ed.,] *Neorealism and Neoliberalism*[: *The Contempory Debate* (New York: Columbia University Press, 1993)], pp. 301–338. The telling effect of Grieco's criticism is reflected in ibid., which is essentially organized around the relative gains vs. absolute gains debate, an issue given little attention before Grieco raised it in his widely cited 1988 article. The matter was briefly discussed by two other scholars before Grieco. See Joanne Gowa, "Anarchy, Egoism, and Third Images: *The Evolution of Cooperation* and International Relations," *International Organization*, Vol. 40, No. 1 (Winter 1986), pp. 172–179; and Oran R. Young, "International Regimes: Toward a New Theory of Institutions," *World Politics*, Vol. 39, No. 1 (October 1986), pp. 118–119.

25. Lipson writes: "The Prisoner's Dilemma, in its simplest form, involves two players. Each is assumed to be a self-interested, self-reliant maximizer of his own utility, an assumption that clearly parallels the Realist conception of sovereign states in international politics." Lipson, "International Cooperation," p. 2. Realists, however, do not accept this conception of

international politics and, not surprisingly, have questioned the relevance of the prisoners' dilemma (at least in its common form) for explaining much of international relations. See Gowa, "Anarchy, Egoism, and Third Images"; Grieco, "Realist Theory and the Problem of International Cooperation"; and Stephen D. Krasner, "Global Communications and National Power: Life on the Pareto Frontier," *World Politics*, Vol. 43, No. 3 (April 1991), pp. 336–366.

26. My thinking on this matter has been markedly influenced by Sean Lynn-Jones, in his June 19, 1994, correspondence with me.

27. For a short discussion of strategic trade theory, see Robert Gilpin, *The Political Economy of International Relations* (Princeton, N.J.: Princeton University Press, 1987), pp. 215–221. The most commonly cited reference on the subject is Paul R. Krugman, ed., *Strategic Trade Policy and the New International Economics* (Cambridge, Mass.: MIT Press, 1986).

28. See Robert Axelrod, *The Evolution of Cooperation* (New York: Basic Books, 1984), pp. 110–113.

29. Grieco maintains in *Cooperation among Nations* that realist logic should apply here. Robert Powell, however, points out that "in the context of negotiations between the European Community and the United States . . . it is difficult to attribute any concern for relative gains to the effects that a relative loss may have on the probability of survival." Robert Powell, "Absolute and Relative Gains in International Relations Theory," *American Political Science Review*, Vol. 85, No. 4 (December 1991), p. 1319, footnote 26. I agree with Powell. It is clear from Grieco's response to Powell that Grieco includes non-military logics like strategic trade theory in the realist tent, whereas Powell and I do not. See Grieco's contribution to "The Relative-Gains Problem for International Relations," *American Political Science Review*, Vol. 87, No. 3 (September 1993), pp. 733–735.

30. Krasner, "Global Communications and National Power," pp. 336–366; Grieco, *Cooperation among Nations*; and Michael Mastanduno, "Do Relative Gains Matter? America's Response to Japanese Industrial Policy," *International Security*, Vol. 16, No. 1 (Summer 1991), pp. 73–113. Also see Jonathan B. Tucker, "Partners and Rivals: A Model of International Collaboration in Advanced Technology," *International Organization*, Vol. 45, No. 1 (Winter 1991), pp. 83–120.

31. Keohane, "Institutional Theory and the Realist Challenge," [in Baldwin, *Neorealism and Neoliberalism*,] p. 292.

32. For example, Keohane wrote after becoming aware of Grieco's argument about relative gains: "Under specified conditions—where mutual interests are low and relative gains are therefore particularly important to states—neoliberal theory expects neorealism to explain elements of state behavior." Keohane, *International Institutions and State Power*, pp. 15–16.

33. For example, Lisa Martin writes that "scholars working in the realist tradition maintain a well-founded skepticism about the empirical impact of institutional factors on state behavior. This skepticism is grounded in a lack of studies that show precisely how and when institutions have constrained state decision-making." According to Oran Young, "One of the more surprising features of the emerging literature on regimes [institutions] is the relative absence of sustained discussions of the significance of . . . institutions, as determinants of collective outcomes at the international level." Martin, "Institutions and Cooperation," p. 144; Young, *International Cooperation*, p. 206.

34. Keohane, *After Hegemony*, chap. 10.

35. Ibid., p. 16.

36. Ibid., p. 236. A U.S. Department of Energy review of the IEA's performance in the 1980 crisis concluded that it had "failed to fulfill its promise." Ethan B. Kapstein, *The Insecure Alliance: Energy Crises and Western Politics*

since 1944 (New York: Oxford University Press, 1990), p. 198.

37. Keohane, *After Hegemony*, p. 7.

38. Martin, "Institutions and Cooperation." Martin looks closely at three other cases in *Coercive Cooperation* to determine the effect of institutions on cooperation. I have concentrated on the Falklands War case, however, because it is, by her own admission, her strongest case. See ibid., p. 96.

39. Martin does not claim that agreement would not have been possible without the EC. Indeed, she appears to concede that even without the EC, Britain still could have fashioned "separate bilateral agreements with each EEC member in order to gain its cooperation, [although] this would have involved much higher transaction costs." Martin, "Institutions and Cooperation," pp. 174–175. However, transaction costs among the advanced industrial democracies are not very high in an era of rapid communications and permanent diplomatic establishments.

40. See Michael J. Smith, *Realist Thought from Weber to Kissinger* (Baton Rouge: Lousiana State University Press, 1986), chap. 1.

41. Summing up the autobiographical essays of 34 international relations scholars, Joseph Kruzel notes that "Hans Morgenthau is more frequently cited than any other name in these memoirs." Joseph Kruzel, "Reflections on the Journeys," in Joseph Kruzel and James N. Rosenau, eds., *Journeys through World Politics: Autobiographical Reflections of Thirty-four Academic Travelers* (Lexington, Mass.: Lexington Books, 1989), p. 505. Although "Morgenthau is often cited, many of the references in these pages are negative in tone. He seems to have inspired his critics even more than his supporters." Ibid.

42. See Keith L. Shimko, "Realism, Neorealism, and American Liberalism," *Review of Politics*, Vol. 54, No. 2 (Spring 1992), pp. 281–301.

43. Hans J. Morgenthau, *Scientific Man vs. Power Politics* (Chicago: University of Chicago Press, 1974), p. 201. Nevertheless, Keith Shimko convincingly argues that the shift within realism, away from Morgenthau's belief that states are motivated by an unalterable will to power, and toward Waltz's view that states are motivated by the desire for security, provides "a residual, though subdued optimism, or at least a possible basis for optimism [about international politics]. The extent to which this optimism is stressed or suppressed varies, but it is there if one wants it to be." Shimko, "Realism, Neorealism, and American Liberalism," p. 297. Realists like Stephen Van Evera, for example, point out that although states operate in a dangerous world, they can take steps to dampen security competition and minimize the danger of war. See Van Evera, *Causes of War* [Vol. II: *National Misperception and the Origins of War*, forthcoming].

44. See Reinhold Niebuhr, *The Children of Light and the Children of Darkness: A Vindication of Democracy and a Critique of Its Traditional Defense* (New York: Charles Scribner's, 1944), especially pp. 153–190. See also Samuel P. Huntington, *The Soldier and the State: The Theory and Politics of Civil-Military Relations* (New York: Vintage Books, 1964).

45. It should be emphasized that many realists have strong moral preferences and are driven by deep moral convictions. Realism is not a normative theory, however, and it provides no criteria for moral judgment. Instead, realism merely seeks to explain how the world works. Virtually all realists would prefer a world without security competition and war, but they believe that goal is unrealistic given the structure of the international system. See, for example, Robert G. Gilpin, "The Richness of the Tradition of Political Realism," in Keohane, [ed.,] *Neorealism and Its Critics*, [New York: Columbia University Press, 1986] p. 321.

46. Realism's treatment of states as billiard balls of different sizes tends to raise the hackles of comparative politics scholars, who believe that domestic political and economic factors matter greatly for explaining foreign policy behavior.

8 War and Strife

Warfare and military intervention continue to be central problems of international relations. Two of the readings in this section address a core issue: the relationship between the use of force and politics. Excerpts from classic books by Carl von Clausewitz, On War (originally published in the 1830s), and Thomas C. Schelling, Arms and Influence (1966), remind us that warfare is not simply a matter of brute force; war needs to be understood as a continuation of political bargaining. In the most influential treatise on warfare ever written, the Prussian general Clausewitz reminded the generation that followed the devastating Napoleonic wars that armed conflict should not be considered a blind, all-out struggle governed by the logic of military operations. Rather, he said, the conduct of war had to be subordinated to its political objectives. These ideas resonated strongly with American strategic thinkers of Schelling's era, who worried that military plans for total nuclear war would outstrip the ability of political leaders to control them. Schelling, a Harvard professor who also advised the U.S. Air Force on its nuclear weapons strategy, explained that political bargaining and risk taking, not military victory, lay at the heart of the use and threat of force in the nuclear era.

Like Schelling, Robert Jervis drew on mathematical game theory and theories of bargaining in his influential 1978 article on the "security dilemma," which explains how war can arise even among states that seek only to defend themselves. Like the realists, these analysts are interested in studying how states' strategies for survival can lead to tragic results. However, they go beyond the realists in examining how differences in bargaining tactics and perceptions can intensify or mitigate the struggle for security.

James D. Fearon's 1995 article, "Rationalist Explanations for War," explores the puzzle of why two rational states would ever fight a costly war rather than settle their dispute more cheaply through peaceful bargaining. He shows that three problems can hinder the achievement of bargains that would benefit both sides: private information that lead the sides to have different estimates of who would prevail in a fight, the inability of one of the sides to convince the other *that it would live up to the agreement in the future, and the impossibility of dividing up the stakes that they are disputing.*

The advent of nuclear weapons has led to a lively debate over the relationship between nuclear proliferation and international system stability. The debate has been fueled by the emergence of nuclear states in South Asia and dangers of nuclearization in both Iran and North Korea. Barry R. Posen examines the policy alternatives should Iran become nuclear: preventive attacks, economic coercion, containment, and coexistence with a nuclear armed Iran. A short article in Foreign Policy *posits that containment of a nuclear armed Iran will not be as effective as Posen suggests. Robert J. Lieber and Amatzia Baram argue that defusing an Israeli–Iranian nuclear confrontation will be much more difficult than was averting a nuclear war during the Cold War.*

While terrorism has long been used as a means of achieving political objectives, the attention of the international community has been drawn to this phenomenon following the September 11, 2001, attacks. Andrew H. Kydd and Barbara F. Walter explore the types of goals that terrorists seek, the strategies terrorists use to achieve those goals, the counterstrategies that can be used against the tactics, and the conditions under which such strategies will or will not work.

How can the post–9/11 security environment best be explained? Is this a backlash against globalization, a global insurgency, a civil war within Islam, or asymmetric warfare? To former military officer and anthropologist David Kilcullen, all four models are appropriate, as examined in his book The Accidental Guerrilla: Fighting Small Wars in the Midst of a Big One *(2009). The war on terrorism is a form of globalized insurgency making use of the tools of globalization, the strategy of guerrilla warfare, and exploiting local grievances, making accidental guerrillas. In that situation, counter-terrorism will not work. As advisor to the U.S. government in Iraq and Afghanistan, Kilcullen conceptualizes these types of war as hybrid wars, necessitating use of both military and nonmilitary aspects of national power.*

Whereas Kilcullen asks how to fight, Gareth Evans, co-chair of the International Commission on Intervention and State Sovereignty in 2001 and author of The Responsibilty to Protect: Ending Mass Atrocity Crimes Once and For All *(2008), asks when is it right to fight. Drawing on international law and the "just war tradition" in philosophy, he suggests five criteria for the UN Security Council to consider: seriousness of threat, proper purpose, last resort, proportional means, and balance of consequences. Yet ideas about when it is right to fight, including when humanitarian intervention is justified, have evolved over time, as explained by Martha Finnemore in her book* The Purpose of Intervention: Changing Beliefs about the Use of Force *(2003). In this constructivist piece, Finnemore shows how changes in international system–level norms explain why states choose to intervene in the affairs of other states, even when no national interests are at stake.*

CARL VON CLAUSEWITZ

War as an Instrument of Policy

* * *

* * * War is only a part of political intercourse, therefore by no means an independent thing in itself.

We know, certainly, that War is only called forth through the political intercourse of Governments and Nations; but in general it is supposed that such intercourse is broken off by War, and that a totally different state of things ensues, subject to no laws but its own.

We maintain, on the contrary, that War is nothing but a continuation of political intercourse, with a mixture of other means. We say mixed with other means in order thereby to maintain at the same time that this political intercourse does not cease by the War itself, is not changed into something quite different, but that, in its essence, it continues to exist, whatever may be the form of the means which it uses, and that the chief lines on which the events of the War progress, and to which they are attached, are only the general features of policy which run all through the War until peace takes place. And how can we conceive it to be otherwise? Does the cessation of diplomatic notes stop the political relations between different Nations and Governments? Is not War merely another kind of writing and language for political thoughts? It has certainly a grammar of its own, but its logic is not peculiar to itself.

From Carl von Clausewitz, *On War* (Harmondsworth: Penguin Books, 1968), Bk. 5, Chap. 6. The author's notes have been omitted.

Accordingly, War can never be separated from political intercourse, and if, in the consideration of the matter, this is done in any way, all the threads of the different relations are, to a certain extent, broken, and we have before us a senseless thing without an object.

This kind of idea would be indispensable even if War was perfect War, the perfectly unbridled element of hostility, for all the circumstances on which it rests, and which determine its leading features, viz. our own power, the enemy's power, Allies on both sides, the characteristics of the people and their Governments respectively, etc.—are they not of a political nature, and are they not so intimately connected with the whole political intercourse that it is impossible to separate them? But this view is doubly indispensable if we reflect that real War is no such consistent effort tending to an extreme, as it should be according to the abstract idea, but a half-and-half thing, a contradiction in itself; that, as such, it cannot follow its own laws, but must be looked upon as a part of another whole—and this whole is policy.

Policy in making use of War avoids all those rigorous conclusions which proceed from its nature; it troubles itself little about final possibilities, confining its attention to immediate probabilities. If such uncertainty in the whole action ensues therefrom, if it thereby becomes a sort of game, the policy of each Cabinet places its confidence in the belief that in this game it will surpass its neighbour in skill and sharp-sightedness.

Thus policy makes out of the all-overpowering element of War a mere instrument, changes the tremendous battle-sword, which should be lifted with both hands and the whole power of the body to strike once for all, into a light handy weapon, which is even sometimes nothing more than a rapier to exchange thrusts and feints and parries.

Thus the contradictions in which man, naturally timid, becomes involved by War may be solved, if we choose to accept this as a solution.

If War belongs to policy, it will naturally take its character from thence. If policy is grand and powerful, so also will be the War, and this may be carried to the point at which War attains to *its absolute form.*

In this way of viewing the subject, therefore, we need not shut out of sight the absolute form of War, we rather keep it continually in view in the background.

Only through this kind of view War recovers unity; only by it can we see all Wars as things of *one* kind; and it is only through it that the judgement can obtain the true and perfect basis and point of view from which great plans may be traced out and determined upon.

It is true the political element does not sink deep into the details of War. Vedettes are not planted, patrols do not make their rounds from political considerations; but small as is its influence in this respect, it is great in the formation of a plan for a whole War, or a campaign, and often even for a battle.

For this reason we were in no hurry to establish this view at the commencement. While engaged with particulars, it would have given us little help, and, on the other hand, would have distracted our attention to a certain extent; in the plan of a War or campaign it is indispensable.

There is, upon the whole, nothing more important in life than to find out the right point of view from which things should be looked at and judged of, and then to keep to that point; for we can only apprehend the mass of events in their unity from *one* standpoint; and it is only the keeping to one point of view that guards us from inconsistency.

If, therefore, in drawing up a plan of a War, it is not allowable to have a two-fold or three-fold point of view, from which things may be looked at, now with the eye of a soldier, then with that of an administrator, and then again with that of a politician, etc., then the next question is, whether *policy* is necessarily paramount and everything else subordinate to it.

That policy unites in itself, and reconciles all the interests of internal administrations, even those of humanity, and whatever else are rational subjects of consideration is presupposed, for it is nothing in itself, except a mere representative and exponent of all these interests towards other States. That policy may take a false direction, and may promote unfairly the ambitious ends, the private interests, the vanity of rulers, does not concern us here; for, under no circumstances can the Art of War be regarded as its preceptor, and we can only look at policy here as the representative of the interests generally of the whole community.

The only question, therefore, is whether in framing plans for a War the political point of view should give way to the purely military (if such a point is conceivable), that is to say, should disappear altogether, or subordinate itself to it, or whether the political is to remain the ruling point of view and the military to be considered subordinate to it.

That the political point of view should end completely when War begins is only conceivable in contests which are Wars of life and death, from pure hatred: as Wars are in reality, they are, as we before said, only the expressions or manifestations of policy itself. The subordination of the political point of view to the military would be contrary to common sense, for policy has declared the War; it is the intelligent faculty, War only the instrument, and not the reverse. The subordination of the military point of view to the political is, therefore, the only thing which is possible.

If we reflect on the nature of real War, and call to mind what has been said, *that every War should be viewed above all things according to the probability of its character, and its leading features as they are to be deduced from the political forces and proportions*, and that often—indeed we may safely affirm, in our days, *almost* always—War is to be regarded as an organic whole, from which the single branches are not to be separated, in which therefore every individual activity flows into the whole, and also has its origin in the idea of this whole, then it becomes certain and palpable to us that the superior standpoint for the conduct of the War, from which its leading lines must proceed, can be no other than that of policy.

From this point of view the plans come, as it were, out of a cast; the apprehension of them and the judgement upon them become easier and more natural, our convictions respecting them gain in force, motives are more satisfying and history more intelligible.

At all events from this point of view there is no longer in the nature of things a necessary conflict between the political and military interests, and where it appears it is therefore to be regarded as imperfect knowledge only. That policy makes demands on the War which it cannot respond to, would be contrary to the supposition that it knows the instrument which it is going to use, therefore, contrary to a natural and indispensable supposition. But if policy judges correctly of the march of military events, it is entirely its affair to determine what are the events and what the direction of events most favourable to the ultimate and great end of the War.

In one word, the Art of War in its highest point of view is policy, but, no doubt, a policy which fights battles instead of writing notes.

According to this view, to leave a great military enterprise or the plan for one, to *a purely military judgement and decision* is a distinction which cannot be allowed, and is even prejudicial; indeed, it is an irrational proceeding to consult professional soldiers on the plan of a War, that they may give a *purely military opinion* upon what

the Cabinet ought to do; but still more absurd is the demand of Theorists that a statement of the available means of War should be laid before the General, that he may draw out a purely military plan for the War or for a campaign in accordance with those means. Experience in general also teaches us that notwithstanding the multifarious branches and scientific character of military art in the present day, still the leading outlines of a War are always determined by the Cabinet, that is, if we would use technical language, by a political not a military organ.

This is perfectly natural. None of the principal plans which are required for a War can be made without an insight into the political relations; and, in reality, when people speak, as they often do, of the prejudicial influence of policy on the conduct of a War, they say in reality something very different to what they intend. It is not this influence but the policy itself which should be found fault with. If policy is right, that is, if it succeeds in hitting the object, then it can only act with advantage on the War. If this influence of policy causes a divergence from the object, the cause is only to be looked for in a mistaken policy.

It is only when policy promises itself a wrong effect from certain military means and measures, an effect opposed to their nature, that it can exercise a prejudicial effect on War by the course it prescribes. Just as a person in a language with which he is not conversant sometimes says what he does not intend, so policy, when intending right, may often order things which do not tally with its own views.

This has happened times without end, and it shows that a certain knowledge of the nature of War is essential to the management of political intercourse.

But before going further, we must guard ourselves against a false interpretation of which this is very susceptible. We are far from holding the opinion that a War Minister smothered in official papers, a scientific engineer, or even a soldier who has been well tried in the field, would, any of them, necessarily make the best Minister of State where the Sovereign does not act for himself; or, in other words, we do not mean to say that this acquaintance with the nature of War is the principal qualification for a War Minister; elevation, superiority of mind, strength of character, these are the principal qualifications which he must possess; a knowledge of War may be supplied in one way or the other. * * *

* * *

We shall now conclude with some reflections derived from history.

In the last decade of the past century, when that remarkable change in the Art of War in Europe took place by which the best Armies found that a part of their method of War had become utterly unserviceable, and events were brought about of a magnitude far beyond what any one had any previous conception of, it certainly appeared that a false calculation of everything was to be laid to the charge of the Art of War. * * *

* * *

But is it true that the real surprise by which men's minds were seized was confined to the conduct of War, and did not rather relate to policy itself? That is: Did the ill success proceed from the influence of policy on the War, or from a wrong policy itself?

The prodigious effects of the French Revolution abroad were evidently brought about much less through new methods and views introduced by the French in the conduct of War than through the changes which it wrought in statecraft and civil administration, in the character of Governments, in the condition of the people, etc. That other Governments took a mistaken view of all these things; that they endeavoured, with their ordinary means, to hold their own against forces of a novel kind and overwhelm-

ing in strength—all that was a blunder in policy.

Would it have been possible to perceive and mend this error by a scheme for the War from a purely military point of view? Impossible. For if there had been a philosophical strategist, who merely from the nature of the hostile elements had foreseen all the consequences, and prophesied remote possibilities, still it would have been practically impossible to have turned such wisdom to account.

If policy had risen to a just appreciation of the forces which had sprung up in France, and of the new relations in the political state of Europe, it might have foreseen the consequences which must follow in respect to the great features of War, and it was only in this way that it could arrive at a correct view of the extent of the means required as well as of the best use to make of those means.

We may therefore say, that the twenty years' victories of the Revolution are chiefly to be ascribed to the erroneous policy of the Governments by which it was opposed.

It is true these errors first displayed themselves in the War, and the events of the War completely disappointed the expectations which policy entertained. But this did not take place because policy neglected to consult its military advisers. That Art of War in which the politician of the day could believe, namely, that derived from the reality of War at that time, that which belonged to the policy of the day, that familiar instrument which policy had hitherto used—*that* Art of War, I say, was naturally involved in the error of policy, and therefore could not teach it anything better. It is true that War itself underwent important alterations both in its nature and forms, which brought it nearer to its absolute form; but these changes were not brought about because the French Government had, to a certain extent, delivered itself from the leading-strings of policy; they arose from an altered policy, produced by the French Revolution, not only in France, but over the rest of Europe as well. This policy had called forth other means and other powers, by which it became possible to conduct War with a degree of energy which could not have been thought of otherwise.

Therefore, the actual changes in the Art of War are a consequence of alterations in policy; and, so far from being an argument for the possible separation of the two, they are, on the contrary, very strong evidence of the intimacy of their connexion.

Therefore, once more: War is an instrument of policy; it must necessarily bear its character, it must measure with its scale: the conduct of War, in its great features, is therefore policy itself, which takes up the sword in place of the pen, but does not on that account cease to think according to its own laws.

THOMAS C. SCHELLING

The Diplomacy of Violence

The usual distinction between diplomacy and force is not merely in the instruments, words or bullets, but in the relation between adversaries— in the interplay of motives and the role of communication, understandings, compromise, and restraint. Diplomacy is bargaining: it seeks outcomes that, though not ideal for either party, are better for both than some of the alternatives. In diplomacy each party somewhat controls what the other wants, and can get more by compromise, exchange, or collaboration than by taking things in his own hands and ignoring the other's wishes. The bargaining can be polite or rude, entail threats as well as offers, assume a status quo or ignore all rights and privileges, and assume mistrust rather than trust. But whether polite or impolite, constructive or aggressive, respectful or vicious, whether it occurs among friends or antagonists and whether or not there is a basis for trust and goodwill, there must be some common interest, if only in the avoidance of mutual damage, and an awareness of the need to make the other party prefer an outcome acceptable to oneself.

With enough military force a country may not need to bargain. Some things a country wants it can take, and some things it has it can keep, by sheer strength, skill and ingenuity. It can do this *forcibly*, accommodating only to opposing strength, skill, and ingenuity and without trying to appeal to an enemy's wishes. Forcibly a country can repel and expel, penetrate and occupy, seize, exterminate, disarm and disable, confine, deny access, and directly frustrate intrusion or attack. It can, that is, if it has enough strength. "Enough" depends on how much an opponent has.

There is something else, though, that force can do. It is less military, less heroic, less impersonal, and less unilateral; it is uglier, and has received less attention in Western military strategy. In addition to seizing and holding, disarming and confining, penetrating and obstructing, and all that, military force can be used *to hurt*. In addition to taking and protecting things of value it can *destroy* value. In addition to weakening an enemy militarily it can cause an enemy plain suffering.

From Thomas C. Schelling, *Arms and Influence* (New Haven, Conn.: Yale University Press, 1966), Chap. 1. Some of the author's notes have been omitted.

Pain and shock, loss and grief, privation and horror are always in some degree, sometimes in terrible degree, among the results of warfare; but in traditional military science they are incidental, they are not the object. If violence can be done incidentally, though, it can also be done purposely. The power to hurt can be counted among the most impressive attributes of military force.

Hurting, unlike forcible seizure or self-defense, is not unconcerned with the interest of others. It is measured in the suffering it can cause and the victims' motivation to avoid it. Forcible action will work against weeds or floods as well as against armies, but suffering requires a victim that can feel pain or has something to lose. To inflict suffering gains nothing and saves nothing directly; it can only make people behave to avoid it. The only purpose, unless sport or revenge, must be to influence somebody's behavior, to coerce his decision or choice. To be coercive, violence has to be anticipated. And it has to be avoidable by accommodation. The power to hurt is bargaining power. To exploit it is diplomacy—vicious diplomacy, but diplomacy.

The Contrast of Brute Force with Coercion

There is a difference between taking what you want and making someone give it to you, between fending off assault and making someone afraid to assault you, between holding what people are trying to take and making them afraid to take it, between losing what someone can forcibly take and giving it up to avoid risk or damage. It is the difference between defense and deterrence, between brute force and intimidation, between conquest and blackmail, between action and threats. It is the difference between the unilateral, "undiplomatic" recourse to strength, and coercive diplomacy based on the power to hurt.

The contrasts are several. The purely "military" or "undiplomatic" recourse to forcible action is concerned with enemy strength, not enemy interests; the coercive use of the power to hurt, though, is the very exploitation of enemy wants and fears. And brute strength is usually measured relative to enemy strength, the one directly opposing the other, while the power to hurt is typically not reduced by the enemy's power to hurt in return. Opposing strengths may cancel each other, pain and grief do not. The willingness to hurt, the credibility of a threat, and the ability to exploit the power to hurt will indeed depend on how much the adversary can hurt in return; but there is little or nothing about an adversary's pain or grief that directly reduces one's own. Two sides cannot both overcome each other with superior strength; they may both be able to hurt each other. With strength they can dispute objects of value; with sheer violence they can destroy them.

And brute force succeeds when it is used, whereas the power to hurt is most successful when held in reserve. It is the *threat* of damage, or of more damage to come, that can make someone yield or comply. It is *latent* violence that can influence someone's choice—violence that can still be withheld or inflicted, or that a victim believes can be withheld or inflicted. The threat of pain tries to structure someone's motives, while brute force tries to overcome his strength. Unhappily, the power to hurt is often communicated by some performance of it. Whether it is sheer terroristic violence to induce an irrational response, or cool premeditated violence to persuade somebody that you mean it and may do it again, it is not the pain and damage itself but its influence on somebody's behavior that matters. It is the expectation of *more* violence that gets the wanted behavior, if the power to hurt can get it at all.

To exploit a capacity for hurting and inflicting damage one needs to know what an adversary treasures and what scares him and one needs the adversary to understand what behavior of his will cause the violence to be inflicted and what will cause it to be withheld. The victim has to know what is wanted, and he may have to be assured of what is not wanted. The pain and suffering have to appear *contingent* on his behavior; it is not alone the threat that is effective—the threat of pain or loss if he fails to comply—but the corresponding assurance, possibly an implicit one, that he can avoid the pain or loss if he does comply. The prospect of certain death may stun him, but it gives him no choice.

Coercion by threat of damage also requires that our interests and our opponent's not be absolutely opposed. If his pain were our greatest delight and our satisfaction his greatest woe, we would just proceed to hurt and to frustrate each other. It is when his pain gives us little or no satisfaction compared with what he can do for us, and the action or inaction that satisfies us costs him less than the pain we can cause, that there is room for coercion. Coercion requires finding a bargain, arranging for him to be better off doing what we want—worse off not doing what we want—when he takes the threatened penalty into account.

It is this capacity for pure damage, pure violence, that is usually associated with the most vicious labor disputes, with racial disorders, with civil uprisings and their suppression, with racketeering. It is also the power to hurt rather than brute force that we use in dealing with criminals; we hurt them afterward, or threaten to, for their misdeeds rather than protect ourselves with cordons of electric wires, masonry walls, and armed guards. Jail, of course, can be either forcible restraint or threatened privation; if the object is to keep criminals out of mischief by confinement, success is measured by how many of them are gotten behind bars, but if the object is to *threaten* privation, success will be measured by how few have to be put behind bars and success then depends on the subject's understanding of the consequences. Pure damage is what a car threatens when it tries to hog the road or to keep its rightful share, or to go first through an intersection. A tank or a bulldozer can force its way regardless of others' wishes; the rest of us have to threaten damage, usually mutual damage, hoping the other driver values his car or his limbs enough to give way, hoping he sees us, and hoping he is in control of his own

car. The threat of pure damage will not work against an unmanned vehicle.

This difference between coercion and brute force is as often in the intent as in the instrument. To hunt down Comanches and to exterminate them was brute force; to raid their villages to make them behave was coercive diplomacy, based on the power to hurt. The pain and loss to the Indians might have looked much the same one way as the other; the difference was one of purpose and effect. If Indians were killed because they were in the way, or somebody wanted their land, or the authorities despaired of making them behave and could not confine them and decided to exterminate them, that was pure unilateral force. If *some* Indians were killed to make *other* Indians behave, that was coercive violence—or intended to be, whether or not it was effective. The Germans at Verdun perceived themselves to be chewing up hundreds of thousands of French soldiers in a gruesome "meat-grinder." If the purpose was to eliminate a military obstacle—the French infantryman, viewed as a military "asset" rather than as a warm human being—the offensive at Verdun was a unilateral exercise of military force. If instead the object was to make the loss of young men—not of impersonal "effectives," but of sons, husbands, fathers, and the pride of French manhood—so anguishing as to be unendurable, to make surrender a welcome relief and to spoil the foretaste of an Allied victory, then it was an exercise in coercion, in applied violence, intended to offer relief upon accommodation. And of course, since any use of force tends to be brutal, thoughtless, vengeful, or plain obstinate, the motives themselves can be mixed and confused. The fact that heroism and brutality can be either coercive diplomacy or a contest in pure strength does not promise that the distinction will be made, and the strategies enlightened by the distinction, every time some vicious enterprise gets launched.

The contrast between brute force and coercion is illustrated by two alternative strategies attributed to Genghis Khan. Early in his career he pursued the war creed of the Mongols: the vanquished can never be the friends of the victors, their death is necessary for the victor's safety. This was the unilateral extermination of a menace or a liability. The turning point of his career, according to Lynn Montross, came later when he discovered how to use his power to hurt for diplomatic ends. "The great Khan, who was not inhibited by the usual mercies, conceived the plan of forcing captives—women, children, aged fathers, favorite sons—to march ahead of his army as the first potential victims of resistance."[1] Live captives have often proved more valuable than enemy dead; and the technique discovered by the Khan in his maturity remains contemporary. North Koreans and Chinese were reported to have quartered prisoners of war near strategic targets to inhibit bombing attacks by United Nations aircraft. Hostages represent the power to hurt in its purest form.

Coercive Violence in Warfare

This distinction between the power to hurt and the power to seize or hold forcibly is important in modern war, both big war and little war, hypothetical war and real war. For many years the Greeks and the Turks on Cyprus could hurt each other indefinitely but neither could quite take or hold forcibly what they wanted or protect themselves from violence by physical means. The Jews in Palestine could not expel the British in the late 1940s but they could cause pain and fear and frustration through terrorism, and eventually influence somebody's decision. The brutal war in Algeria was more a contest in pure violence than in military strength; the question was who would first find the pain and degradation unendurable. The French troops preferred—indeed they continually tried—to make it a contest of strength, to pit military force against the nationalists' capacity for terror, to exterminate or disable the nationalists and to screen off

the nationalists from the victims of their violence. But because in civil war terrorists commonly have access to victims by sheer physical propinquity, the victims and their properties could not be forcibly defended and in the end the French troops themselves resorted, unsuccessfully, to a war of pain.

Nobody believes that the Russians can take Hawaii from us, or New York, or Chicago, but nobody doubts that they might destroy people and buildings in Hawaii, Chicago, or New York. Whether the Russians can conquer West Germany in any meaningful sense is questionable; whether they can hurt it terribly is not doubted. That the United States can destroy a large part of Russia is universally taken for granted; that the United States can keep from being badly hurt, even devastated, in return, or can keep Western Europe from being devastated while itself destroying Russia, is at best arguable; and it is virtually out of the question that we could conquer Russia territorially and use its economic assets unless it were by threatening disaster and inducing compliance. It is the power to hurt, not military strength in the traditional sense, that inheres in our most impressive military capabilities at the present time [1966]. We have a Department of *Defense* but emphasize *retaliation*—"to return evil for evil" (synonyms: requital, reprisal, revenge, vengeance, retribution). And it is pain and violence, not force in the traditional sense, that inheres also in some of the least impressive military capabilities of the present time—the plastic bomb, the terrorist's bullet, the burnt crops, and the tortured farmer.

War appears to be, or threatens to be, not so much a contest of strength as one of endurance, nerve, obstinacy, and pain. It appears to be, and threatens to be, not so much a contest of military strength as a bargaining process—dirty, extortionate, and often quite reluctant bargaining on one side or both—nevertheless a bargaining process.

The difference cannot quite be expressed as one between the *use* of force and the *threat* of force. The actions involved in forcible accomplishment, on the one hand, and in fulfilling a threat, on the other, can be quite different. Sometimes the most effective direct action inflicts enough cost or pain on the enemy to serve as a threat, sometimes not. The United States threatens the Soviet Union with virtual destruction of its society in the event of a surprise attack on the United States; a hundred million deaths are awesome as pure damage, but they are useless in stopping the Soviet attack—especially if the threat is to do it all afterward anyway. So it is worth while to keep the concepts distinct—to distinguish forcible action from the threat of pain—recognizing that some actions serve as both a means of forcible accomplishment and a means of inflicting pure damage, some do not. Hostages tend to entail almost pure pain and damage, as do all forms of reprisal after the fact. Some modes of self-defense may exact so little in blood or treasure as to entail negligible violence; and some forcible actions entail so much violence that their threat can be effective by itself.

The power to hurt, though it can usually accomplish nothing directly, is potentially more versatile than a straightforward capacity for forcible accomplishment. By force alone we cannot even lead a horse to water—we have to drag him—much less make him drink. Any affirmative action, any collaboration, almost anything but physical exclusion, expulsion, or extermination, requires that an opponent or a victim *do* something, even if only to stop or get out. The threat of pain and damage may make him want to do it, and anything he can do is potentially susceptible to inducement. Brute force can only accomplish what requires no collaboration. The principle is illustrated by a technique of unarmed combat: one can disable a man by various stunning, fracturing, or killing blows, but to take him to jail one has to exploit the man's own efforts. "Come-along" holds are those that threaten pain or disablement, giving relief as long as the victim complies, giving him the option of using his own legs to get to jail.

We have to keep in mind, though, that what is pure pain, or the threat of it, at one level of decision can be equivalent to brute force at another level. Churchill was worried, during the early bombing raids on London in 1940, that Londoners might panic. Against people the bombs were pure violence, to induce their undisciplined evasion; to Churchill and the government, the bombs were a cause of inefficiency, whether they spoiled transport and made people late to work or scared people and made them afraid to work. Churchill's decisions were not going to be coerced by the fear of a few casualties. Similarly on the battlefield: tactics that frighten soldiers so that they run, duck their heads, or lay down their arms and surrender represent coercion based on the power to hurt; to the top command, which is frustrated but not coerced, such tactics are part of the contest in military discipline and strength.

The fact that violence—pure pain and damage—can be used or threatened to coerce and to deter, to intimidate and to blackmail, to demoralize and to paralyze, in a conscious process of dirty bargaining, does not by any means imply that violence is not often wanton and meaningless or, even when purposive, in danger of getting out of hand. Ancient wars were often quite "total" for the loser, the men being put to death, the women sold as slaves, the boys castrated, the cattle slaughtered, and the buildings leveled, for the sake of revenge, justice, personal gain, or merely custom. If an enemy bombs a city, by design or by carelessness, we usually bomb his if we can. In the excitement and fatigue of warfare, revenge is one of the few satisfactions that can be savored; and justice can often be construed to demand the enemy's punishment, even if it is delivered with more enthusiasm than justice requires. When Jerusalem fell to the Crusaders in 1099 the ensuing slaughter was one of the bloodiest in military chronicles. "The men of the West literally waded in gore, their march to the church of the Holy Sepulcher being gruesomely likened to 'treading out the wine press'. . . . ," reports Montross (p. 138), who observes that these excesses usually came at the climax of the capture of a fortified post or city. "For long the assailants have endured more punishment than they were able to inflict; then once the walls are breached, pent up emotions find an outlet in murder, rape and plunder, which discipline is powerless to prevent." The same occurred when Tyre fell to Alexander after a painful siege, and the phenomenon was not unknown on Pacific islands in the Second World War. Pure violence, like fire, can be harnessed to a purpose; that does not mean that behind every holocaust is a shrewd intention successfully fulfilled.

But if the occurrence of violence does not always bespeak a shrewd purpose, the absence of pain and destruction is no sign that violence was idle. Violence is most purposive and most successful when it is threatened and not used. Successful threats are those that do not have to be carried out. By European standards, Denmark was virtually unharmed in the Second World War; it was violence that made the Danes submit. Withheld violence—successfully threatened violence—can look clean, even merciful. The fact that a kidnap victim is returned unharmed, against receipt of ample ransom, does not make kidnapping a nonviolent enterprise. * * *

* * *

The Strategic Role of Pain and Damage

Pure violence, nonmilitary violence, appears most conspicuously in relations between unequal countries, where there is no substantial military challenge and the outcome of military engagement is not in question. Hitler could make his threats contemptuously and brutally against Austria; he could make them, if he wished, in a more refined way against Denmark. It is noteworthy that it was Hitler, not his generals, who used this kind of language; proud military establishments do not like to think of themselves as extortionists. Their favorite job is to deliver victory, to dispose of opposing military force and to leave most of the civilian violence to politics and diplomacy. But if there is no room for doubt how a contest in strength will come out, it may be possible to bypass the military stage altogether and to proceed at once to the coercive bargaining.

A typical confrontation of unequal forces occurs at the *end* of a war, between victor and vanquished. Where Austria was vulnerable before a shot was fired, France was vulnerable after its military shield had collapsed in 1940. Surrender negotiations are the place where the threat of civil violence can come to the fore. Surrender negotiations are often so one-sided, or the potential violence so unmistakable, that bargaining succeeds and the violence remains in reserve. But the fact that most of the actual damage was done during the military stage of the war, prior to victory and defeat, does not mean that violence was idle in the aftermath, only that it was latent and the threat of it successful.

Indeed, victory is often but a prerequisite to the exploitation of the power to hurt. When Xenophon was fighting in Asia Minor under Persian leadership, it took military strength to disperse enemy soldiers and occupy their lands; but land was not what the victor wanted, nor was victory for its own sake.

> Next day the Persian leader burned the villages to the ground, not leaving a single house standing, so as to strike terror into the other tribes to show them what would happen if they did not give in. . . . He sent some of the prisoners into the hills and told them to say that if the inhabitants did not come down and settle in their houses to submit to him, he would burn up their villages too and destroy their crops, and they would die of hunger.[2]

Military victory was but the *price of admission*. The payoff depended upon the successful threat of violence.

* * *

The Nuclear Contribution to Terror and Violence

Man has, it is said, for the first time in history enough military power to eliminate his species from the earth, weapons against which there is no conceivable defense. War has become, it is said, so destructive and terrible that it ceases to be an instrument of national power. "For the first time in human history," says Max Lerner in a book whose title, *The Age of Overkill*, conveys the point, "men have bottled up a power . . . which they have thus far not dared to use."[3] And Soviet military authorities, whose party dislikes having to accommodate an entire theory of history to a single technological event, have had to reexamine a set of principles that had been given the embarrassing name of "permanently operating factors" in warfare. Indeed, our era is epitomized by words like "the first time in human history," and by the abdication of what was "permanent."

For dramatic impact these statements are splendid. Some of them display a tendency, not at all necessary, to belittle the catastrophe of earlier wars. They may exaggerate the historical novelty of deterrence and the balance of terror. More important, they do not help to identify just what is new about war when so much destructive energy can be packed in warheads at a price that permits advanced countries to have them in large numbers. Nuclear warheads are incomparably more devastating than anything packaged before. What does that imply about war?

It is not true that for the first time in history man has the capability to destroy a large fraction, even the major part, of the human race. Japan was defenseless by August 1945. With a combination of bombing and blockade, eventually invasion, and if necessary the deliberate spread of disease, the United States could probably have exterminated the population of the Japanese islands without nuclear weapons. It would have been a gruesome, expensive, and mortifying campaign; it would have taken time and demanded persistence. But we had the economic and technical capacity to do it; and, together with the Russians or without them, we could have done the same in many populous parts of the world. Against defenseless people there is not much that nuclear weapons can do that cannot be done with an ice pick. And it would not have strained our Gross National Product to do it with ice picks.

It is a grisly thing to talk about. We did not do it and it is not imaginable that we would have done it. We had no reason; if we had had a reason, we would not have the persistence of purpose, once the fury of war had been dissipated in victory and we had taken on the task of executioner. If we and our enemies might do such a thing to each other now, and to others as well, it is not because nuclear weapons have for the first time made it feasible.

* * *

* * * In the past it has usually been the victors who could do what they pleased to the enemy. War has often been "total war" for the loser. With deadly monotony the Persians, Greeks, or Romans "put to death all men of military age, and sold the women and children into slavery," leaving the defeated territory nothing but its name until new settlers arrived sometime later. But the defeated could not do the same to their victors. The boys could be castrated and sold only after the war had been won, and only on the side that lost it. The power to hurt could be brought to bear only after military strength had achieved victory. The same sequence characterized the great wars of this century; for reasons of technology and geography, military force has usually had to penetrate, to exhaust, or to collapse opposing military force—to achieve military victory—before it could be brought to bear on the enemy nation itself. The Allies in World War I could not inflict coercive pain and suffering directly on the Germans in a decisive way until they could defeat the German army; and the Germans could not coerce the French people with bayonets unless they first beat the Allied troops that stood in their way. With two-dimensional warfare, there is a tendency for troops to confront each other, shielding their own lands while attempting to press into each other's. Small penetrations could not do major damage to the people; large penetrations were so destructive of military organization that they usually ended the military phase of the war.

Nuclear weapons make it possible to do monstrous violence to the enemy without first achieving victory. With nuclear weapons and today's means of delivery, one expects to penetrate an enemy homeland without first collapsing his military force. What nuclear weapons have done, or appear to do, is to promote this kind of warfare to first place. Nuclear weapons threaten to make war less military, and are responsible for the lowered status of "military victory" at the present time. *Victory is no longer a prerequisite for hurting the enemy.* And it is no assurance against being terribly hurt. One need not wait until he has won the war before inflicting "unendurable" damages on his enemy. One need not wait until he has lost the war. There was a time when the assurance of victory—false or genuine assurance—could make national leaders not just willing but sometimes enthusiastic about war. Not now.

Not only *can* nuclear weapons hurt the enemy before the war has been won, and perhaps hurt decisively enough to make the military engagement academic, but it is widely assumed that in a major war that is *all* they can do. Major war is often discussed as though it would be only a contest in national destruction. If this is indeed the case—if the destruction of cities and their populations has become, with nuclear weapons, the primary object in an all-out war—the sequence of war has been reversed. Instead of destroying enemy forces as a prelude to imposing one's will on the enemy nation, one would have to destroy the nation as a means or a prelude to destroying the enemy forces. If one cannot disable enemy forces without virtually destroying the country, the victor does not even have the option of sparing the conquered nation. He has already destroyed it. Even with blockade and strategic bombing

it could be supposed that a country would be defeated before it was destroyed, or would elect surrender before annihilation had gone far. In the Civil War it could be hoped that the South would become too weak to fight before it became too weak to survive. For "all-out" war, nuclear weapons threaten to reverse this sequence.

So nuclear weapons do make a difference, marking an epoch in warfare. The difference is not just in the amount of destruction that can be accomplished but in the role of destruction and in the decision process. Nuclear weapons can change the speed of events, the control of events, the sequence of events, the relation of victor to vanquished, and the relation of homeland to fighting front. Deterrence rests today on the threat of pain and extinction, not just on the threat of military defeat. We may argue about the wisdom of announcing "unconditional surrender" as an aim in the last major war, but seem to expect "unconditional destruction" as a matter of course in another one.

Something like the same destruction always *could* be done. With nuclear weapons there is an expectation that it *would* be done. It is not "over-kill" that is new; the American army surely had enough 30 caliber bullets to kill everybody in the world in 1945, or if it did not it could have bought them without any strain. What is new is plain "kill"—the idea that major war might be just a contest in the killing of countries, or not even a contest but just two parallel exercises in devastation.

That is the difference nuclear weapons make. At least they *may* make that difference. They also may not. If the weapons themselves are vulnerable to attack, or the machines that carry them, a successful surprise might eliminate the opponent's means of retribution. That an enormous explosion can be packaged in a single bomb does not by itself guarantee that the victor will receive deadly punishment. Two gunfighters facing each other in a Western town had an unquestioned capacity to kill one another; that did not guarantee that both would die in a gunfight—only the slower of the two. Less deadly weapons, permitting an injured one to shoot back before he died, might have been more conducive to a restraining balance of terror, or of caution. The very efficiency of nuclear weapons could make them ideal for starting war, if they can suddenly eliminate the enemy's capability to shoot back.

And there is a contrary possibility: that nuclear weapons are not vulnerable to attack and prove not to be terribly effective against each other, posing no need to shoot them quickly for fear they will be destroyed before they are launched, and with no task available but the systematic destruction of the enemy country and no necessary reason to do it fast rather than slowly. Imagine that nuclear destruction *had* to go slowly—that the bombs could be dropped only one per day. The prospect would look very different, something like the most terroristic guerilla warfare on a massive scale. It happens that nuclear war does not have to go slowly; but it may also not have to go speedily. The mere existence of nuclear weapons does not itself determine that everything must go off in a blinding flash, any more than that it must go slowly. Nuclear weapons do not simplify things quite that much.

＊　＊　＊

War no longer looks like just a contest of strength. War and the brink of war are more a contest of nerve and risk-taking, of pain and endurance. Small wars embody the threat of a larger war; they are not just military engagements but "crisis diplomacy." The threat of war has always been somewhere underneath international diplomacy, but for Americans it is now much nearer the surface. Like the threat of a strike in industrial relations, the threat of divorce in a family dispute, or the threat of bolting the party at a political convention, the threat of violence continuously circumscribes international politics. Neither strength nor goodwill procures immunity.

Military strategy can no longer be thought of, as it could for some countries in some eras, as the science of military victory. It is now equally, if not more, the art of coercion, of intimidation and deterrence. The instruments of war are more punitive than acquisitive. Military strategy, whether we like it or not, has become the diplomacy of violence.

NOTES

1. Lynn Montross, *War Through the Ages* (3d ed. New York, Harper and Brothers, 1960), p. 146.
2. Xenophon, *The Persian Expedition*, Rex Warner, transl. (Baltimore, Penguin Books, 1949), p. 272. "The 'rational' goal of the threat of violence," says H. L. Nieburg, "is an accommodation of interests, not the provocation of actual violence. Similarly the 'rational' goal of actual violence is demonstration of the will and capability of action, establishing a measure of the credibility of future threats, not the exhaustion of that capability in unlimited conflict." "Uses of Violence," *Journal of Conflict Resolution*, 7 (1963), 44.
3. New York, Simon and Schuster, 1962, p. 47.

ROBERT JERVIS

Cooperation under the Security Dilemma

I. Anarchy and the Security Dilemma

The lack of an international sovereign not only permits wars to occur, but also makes it difficult for states that are satisfied with the status quo to arrive at goals that they recognize as being in their common interest. Because there are no institutions or authorities that can make and enforce international laws, the policies of cooperation that will bring mutual rewards if others cooperate may bring disaster if they do not. Because states are aware of this, anarchy encourages behavior that leaves all concerned worse off than they could be, even in the extreme case in which all states would like to freeze the status quo. This is true of the men in Rousseau's "Stag Hunt." If they cooperate to trap the stag, they will all eat well. But if one person defects to chase a rabbit—which he likes less than stag—none of the others will get anything. Thus, all actors have the same preference order, and there is a solution that gives each his first choice: (1) cooperate and trap the stag (the international analogue being cooperation and disarmament); (2) chase a rabbit while others remain at their posts (maintain a high level of arms while others are disarmed); (3) all chase rabbits (arms competition and high risk of war); and (4) stay at the original position while another chases a rabbit (being disarmed while others are armed). Unless each person thinks that the others will cooperate, he himself will not. And why might he fear

From *World Politics* 30, no. 2 (Jan. 1978): 167–214. Some of the author's notes have been omitted.

that any other person would do something that would sacrifice his own first choice? The other might not understand the situation, or might not be able to control his impulses if he saw a rabbit, or might fear that some other member of the group is unreliable. If the person voices any of these suspicions, others are more likely to fear that he will defect, thus making them more likely to defect, thus making it more rational for him to defect. Of course in this simple case—and in many that are more realistic—there are a number of arrangements that could permit cooperation. But the main point remains: although actors may know that they seek a common goal, they may not be able to reach it.

Even when there is a solution that is everyone's first choice, the international case is characterized by three difficulties not present in the Stag Hunt. First, to the incentives to defect given above must be added the potent fear that even if the other state now supports the status quo, it may become dissatisfied later. No matter how much decision makers are committed to the status quo, they cannot bind themselves and their successors to the same path. Minds can be changed, new leaders can come to power, values can shift, new opportunities and dangers can arise.

The second problem arises from a possible solution. In order to protect their possessions, states often seek to control resources or land outside their own territory. Countries that are not self-sufficient must try to assure that the necessary supplies will continue to flow in wartime. This was part of the explanation for Japan's drive into China and Southeast Asia before World War II. If there were an international authority that could guarantee access, this motive for control would disappear. But since there is not, even a state that would prefer the status quo to increasing its area of control may pursue the latter policy.

When there are believed to be tight linkages between domestic and foreign policy or between the domestic politics of two states, the quest for security may drive states to interfere preemptively in the domestic politics of others in order to provide an ideological buffer zone. * * *

More frequently, the concern is with direct attack. In order to protect themselves, states seek to control, or at least to neutralize, areas on their borders. But attempts to establish buffer zones can alarm others who have stakes there, who fear that undesirable precedents will be set, or who believe that their own vulnerability will be increased. When buffers are sought in areas empty of great powers, expansion tends to feed on itself in order to protect what is acquired * * *.

Though this process is most clearly visible when it involves territorial expansion, it often operates with the increase of less tangible power and influence. The expansion of power usually brings with it an expansion of responsibilities and commitments; to meet them, still greater power is required. The state will take many positions that are subject to challenge. It will be involved with a wide range of controversial issues unrelated to its core values. And retreats that would be seen as normal if made by a small power would be taken as an index of weakness inviting predation if made by a large one.

The third problem present in international politics but not in the Stag Hunt is the security dilemma: many of the means by which a state tries to increase its security decrease the security of others. In domestic society, there are several ways to increase the safety of one's person and property without endangering others. One can move to a safer neighborhood, put bars on the windows, avoid dark streets, and keep a distance from suspicious-looking characters. Of course these measures are not convenient, cheap, or cer-

tain of success. But no one save criminals need be alarmed if a person takes them. In international politics, however, one state's gain in security often inadvertently threatens others. In explaining British policy on naval disarmament in the interwar period to the Japanese, Ramsey Mac-Donald said that "Nobody wanted Japan to be insecure."[1] But the problem was not with British desires, but with the consequences of her policy. In earlier periods, too, Britain had needed a navy large enough to keep the shipping lanes open. But such a navy could not avoid being a menace to any other state with a coast that could be raided, trade that could be interdicted, or colonies that could be isolated. When Germany started building a powerful navy before World War I, Britain objected that it could only be an offensive weapon aimed at her. As Sir Edward Grey, the Foreign Secretary, put it to King Edward VII: "If the German Fleet ever becomes superior to ours, the German Army can conquer this country. There is no corresponding risk of this kind to Germany; for however superior our Fleet was, no naval victory could bring us any nearer to Berlin." The English position was half correct: Germany's navy was an anti-British instrument. But the British often overlooked what the Germans knew full well: "in every quarrel with England, German colonies and trade were . . . hostages for England to take." Thus, whether she intended it or not, the British Navy constituted an important instrument of coercion.[2]

II. What Makes Cooperation More Likely?

Given this gloomy picture, the obvious question is, why are we not all dead? Or, to put it less starkly, what kinds of variables ameliorate the impact of anarchy and the security dilemma? The working of several can be seen in terms of the Stag Hunt or repeated plays of the Prisoner's Dilemma.[3] The Prisoner's Dilemma differs from the Stag Hunt in that there is no solution that is in the best interests of all the participants; there are offensive as well as defensive incentives to defect from the coalition with the others; and, if the game is to be played only once, the only rational response is to defect [Figure 8.1]. But if the game is repeated indefinitely, the latter characteristic no longer holds and we can analyze the game in terms similar to those applied to the Stag Hunt. It would be in the interest of each actor to have others deprived of the power to defect; each would be willing to sacrifice this ability if others were similarly restrained. But if the others are not, then it is in the actor's interest to retain the power to defect.[4] The game theory matrices for these two situations are given below, with the numbers in the boxes being the order of the actor's preferences.

We can see the logical possibilities by rephrasing our question: "Given either of the above situations, what makes it more or less likely that the players will cooperate and arrive at CC?" The chances of achieving this outcome will be increased by: (1) anything that increases incentives to cooperate by increasing the gains of mutual cooperation (CC) and/or decreasing the costs the actor will pay if he cooperates and the other does not (CD); (2) anything that decreases the incentives for defecting by decreasing the gains of taking advantage of the other (DC) and/or increasing the costs of mutual noncooperation (DD); (3) anything that increases each side's expectation that the other will cooperate.[5]

The Costs of Being Exploited (CD)

The fear of being exploited (that is, the cost of CD) most strongly drives the security dilemma; one of the main reasons why international life is not more nasty, brutish, and short is that states are not as vulnerable as men are in a state of nature. People are easy to kill, but as Adam Smith replied to a friend who feared that the Napoleonic Wars would ruin England, "Sir, there is a great deal of ruin in a nation."[6] The easier it is to destroy a state, the greater the reason for it either to join a larger and more secure unit, or else to be especially suspicious of others, to require a large army, and, if conditions are favorable, to attack at the slightest provocation rather than wait to be attacked. If the failure to eat that day—be it venison or rabbit—means that he will starve, a person is likely to defect in the Stag Hunt even if he really likes venison and has a high level of trust in his colleagues. (Defection is especially likely if the others are also starving or if they know that he is.) By contrast, if the costs of CD are lower, if people are well-fed or states are resilient, they can afford to take a more relaxed view of threats.

A relatively low cost of CD has the effect of transforming the game from one in which both players make their choices simultaneously to one in which an actor can make his choice after the other has moved. He will not have to defect out of fear that the other will, but can wait to see what the other will do. States that can afford to be cheated in a bargain or that cannot be destroyed by a surprise attack can more easily trust others and need not act at the first, and ambiguous, sign of menace. Because they have a margin of time and error, they need not match, or more than match, any others' arms in peacetime. They can mobilize in the prewar period or even at the start of the war itself, and still survive. For example, those who opposed a crash program to develop the H-bomb felt that the U.S. margin of safety was large enough so that even if Russia managed to gain a lead in the race, America

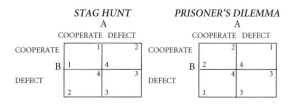

Figure 8.1. Stag Hunt and Prisoner's Dilemma

would not be endangered. The program's advocates disagreed: "If we let the Russians get the super first, catastrophe becomes all but certain."[7]

When the costs of CD are tolerable, not only is security easier to attain but, what is even more important here, the relatively low level of arms and relatively passive foreign policy that a status-quo power will be able to adopt are less likely to threaten others. Thus it is easier for status-quo states to act on their common interests if they are hard to conquer. All other things being equal, a world of small states will feel the effects of anarchy much more than a world of large ones. Defensible borders, large size, and protection against sudden attack not only aid the state, but facilitate cooperation that can benefit all states.

Of course, if one state gains invulnerability by being more powerful than most others, the problem will remain because its security provides a base from which it can exploit others. When the price a state will pay for DD is low, it leaves others with few hostages for its good behavior. Others who are more vulnerable will grow apprehensive, which will lead them to acquire more arms and will reduce the chances of cooperation. The best situation is one in which a state will not suffer greatly if others exploit it, for example, by cheating on an arms control agreement (that is, the costs of CD are low); but it will pay a high long-run price if cooperation with the others breaks down—for example, if agreements cease functioning or if there is a long war (that is, the costs of DD are high). The state's invulnerability is then mostly passive; it provides some protection, but it cannot be used to menace others. As we will discuss below, this situation is approximated when it is easier for states to defend themselves than to attack others, or when mutual deterrence obtains because neither side can protect itself.

The differences between highly vulnerable and less vulnerable states are illustrated by the contrasting policies of Britain and Austria after the Napoleonic Wars. Britain's geographic isolation and political stability allowed her to take a fairly relaxed view of disturbances on the Continent. Minor wars and small changes in territory or in the distribution of power did not affect her vital interests. An adversary who was out to overthrow the system could be stopped after he had made his intentions clear. And revolutions within other states were no menace, since they would not set off unrest within England. Austria, surrounded by strong powers, was not so fortunate; her policy had to be more closely attuned to all conflicts. By the time an aggressor-state had clearly shown its colors, Austria would be gravely threatened. And foreign revolutions, be they democratic or nationalistic, would encourage groups in Austria to upset the existing order. So it is not surprising that Metternich propounded the doctrine summarized earlier, which defended Austria's right to interfere in the internal affairs of others, and that British leaders rejected this view. Similarly, Austria wanted the Congress system to be a relatively tight one, regulating most disputes. The British favored a less centralized system. In other words, in order to protect herself, Austria had either to threaten or to harm others, whereas Britain did not. For Austria and her neighbors the security dilemma was acute; for Britain it was not.

The ultimate cost of CD is of course loss of sovereignty. This cost can vary from situation to situation. The lower it is (for instance, because the two states have compatible ideologies, are similar ethnically, have a common culture, or because the citizens of the losing state expect economic benefits), the less the impact of the security dilemma; the greater the costs, the greater the impact of the dilemma. Here is another reason why extreme differences in values and ideologies exacerbate international conflict.

* * *

SUBJECTIVE SECURITY DEMANDS Decision makers act in terms of the vulnerability they feel, which can differ from the actual situation; we must therefore examine the decision makers' subjective security requirements. Two dimensions are involved. First, even if they agree about the objective situation, people can differ about how much security they desire—or, to put it more precisely, about the price they are willing to pay to gain increments of security. The more states value their security above all else (that is, see a prohibitively high cost in CD), the more they are likely to be sensitive to even minimal threats, and to demand high levels of arms. And if arms are positively valued because of pressures from a military-industrial complex, it will be especially hard for status-quo powers to cooperate. By contrast, the security dilemma will not operate as strongly when pressing domestic concerns increase the opportunity costs of armaments. In this case, the net advantage of exploiting the other (DC) will be less, and the costs of arms races (that is, one aspect of DD) will be greater; therefore the state will behave as though it were relatively invulnerable.

The second aspect of subjective security is the perception of threat (that is, the estimate of whether the other will cooperate). A state that is predisposed to see either a specific other state as an adversary, or others in general as a menace, will react more strongly and more quickly than a state that sees its environment as benign. Indeed, when a state believes that another not only is not likely to be an adversary, but has sufficient interests in common with it to be an ally, then it will actually welcome an increase in the other's power.

* * *

Geography, Commitments, Beliefs, and Security through Expansion

* * * Situations vary in the ease or difficulty with which all states can simultaneously achieve a high degree of security. The influence of military technology on this variable is the subject of the next section. Here we want to treat the impact of beliefs, geography, and commitments (many of which can be considered to be modifications of geography, since they bind states to defend areas

outside their homelands). In the crowded continent of Europe, security requirements were hard to mesh. Being surrounded by powerful states, Germany's problem—or the problem created by Germany—was always great and was even worse when her relations with both France and Russia were bad, such as before World War I. In that case, even a status-quo Germany, if she could not change the political situation, would almost have been forced to adopt something like the Schlieffen Plan. Because she could not hold off both of her enemies, she had to be prepared to defeat one quickly and then deal with the other in a more leisurely fashion. If France or Russia stayed out of a war between the other state and Germany, they would allow Germany to dominate the Continent (even if that was not Germany's aim). They therefore had to deny Germany this ability, thus making Germany less secure. Although Germany's arrogant and erratic behavior, coupled with the desire for an unreasonably high level of security (which amounted to the desire to escape from her geographic plight), compounded the problem, even wise German statesmen would have been hard put to gain a high degree of security without alarming their neighbors.

* * *

III. Offense, Defense, and the Security Dilemma

Another approach starts with the central point of the security dilemma—that an increase in one state's security decreases the security of others—and examines the conditions under which this proposition holds. Two crucial variables are involved: whether defensive weapons and policies can be distinguished from offensive ones, and whether the defense or the offense has the advantage. The definitions are not always clear, and many cases are difficult to judge, but these two variables shed a great deal of light on the question of whether status-quo powers will adopt compatible security policies. All the variables discussed so far leave the heart of the problem untouched. But when defensive weapons differ from offensive ones, it is possible for a state to make itself more secure without making others less secure. And when the defense has the advantage over the offense, a large increase in one state's security only slightly decreases the security of the others, and status-quo powers can all enjoy a high level of security and largely escape from the state of nature.

Offense-Defense Balance

When we say that the offense has the advantage, we simply mean that it is easier to destroy the other's army and take its territory than it is to defend one's own. When the defense has the advantage, it is easier to protect and to hold than it is to move forward, destroy, and take. If effective defenses can be erected quickly, an attacker may be able to keep territory he has taken in an initial victory. Thus, the dominance of the defense made it very hard for Britain and France to push Germany out of France in World War I. But when superior defenses are difficult for an aggressor to improvise on the battlefield and must be constructed during peacetime, they provide no direct assistance to him.

The security dilemma is at its most vicious when commitments, strategy, or technology dictate that the only route to security lies through expansion. Status-quo powers must then act like aggressors; the fact that they would gladly agree to forego the opportunity for expansion in return for guarantees for their security has no implications for their behavior. Even if expansion is not sought as a goal in itself, there will be quick and drastic changes in the distribution of territory and influence. Conversely, when the defense has the advantage, status-quo states can make themselves more secure without gravely endangering others.[8] Indeed, if the defense has enough of an advantage and if the states are of roughly equal size, not only will the security dilemma cease to inhibit status-quo states from cooperating, but aggression will be next to impossible, thus rendering international anarchy relatively unimportant. If states cannot conquer each other, then the lack of sovereignty, although it presents problems of collective goods in a number of areas, no longer forces states to devote their primary attention to self-preservation. Although, if force were not usable, there would be fewer restraints on the use of nonmilitary instruments, these are rarely powerful enough to threaten the vital interests of a major state.

Two questions of the offense-defense balance can be separated. First, does the state have to spend more or less than one dollar on defensive forces to offset each dollar spent by the other side on forces that could be used to attack? If the state has one dollar to spend on increasing its security, should it put it into offensive or defensive forces? Second, with a given inventory of forces, is it better to attack or to defend? Is there an incentive to strike first or to absorb the other's blow? These two aspects are often linked: if each dollar spent on offense can overcome each dollar spent on defense, and if both sides have the same defense budgets, then both are likely to build offensive forces and find it attractive to attack rather than to wait for the adversary to strike.

These aspects affect the security dilemma in different ways. The first has its greatest impact on arms races. If the defense has the advantage, and if the status-quo powers have reasonable subjective security requirements, they can probably avoid an arms race. Although an increase in one side's arms and security will still decrease the other's security, the former's increase will be larger than the latter's decrease. So if one side increases its arms, the other can bring its security back up to its previous level by adding a smaller amount to its forces. And if the first side reacts to this change, its increase will also be smaller than the stimulus that produced it. Thus a stable equilibrium will be reached. Shifting from dynamics to statics, each side can be quite secure with forces roughly equal to those of the other. Indeed, if the defense is much more potent than the offense, each side can be willing to have forces much smaller than the other's, and can be indifferent to a wide range of the other's defense policies.

The second aspect—whether it is better to attack or to defend—influences short-run stability. When the offense has the advantage, a state's reaction to international tension will increase the chances of war. The incentives for pre-emption and the "reciprocal fear of surprise attack" in this situation have been made clear by analyses of the dangers that exist when two countries have first-strike capabilities.[9] There is no way for the state to increase its security without menacing, or even attacking, the other. Even Bismarck, who once called preventive war "committing suicide from fear of death," said that "no government, if it regards war as inevitable even if it does not want it, would be so foolish as to leave to the enemy the choice of time and occasion and to wait for the moment which is most convenient for the enemy."[10] In another arena, the same dilemma applies to the policeman in a dark alley confronting a suspected criminal who appears to be holding a weapon. Though racism may indeed be present, the security dilemma can account for many of the tragic shootings of innocent people in the ghettos.

Beliefs about the course of a war in which the offense has the advantage further deepen the security dilemma. When there are incentives to strike first, a successful attack will usually so weaken the other side that victory will be relatively quick, bloodless, and decisive. It is in these periods when conquest is possible and attractive that states consolidate power internally—for instance, by destroying the feudal barons—and expand externally. There are several consequences that decrease the chance of cooperation among status-quo states. First, war will be profitable for the winner. The costs will be low and the benefits high. Of course, losers will suffer; the fear of losing could induce states to try to

form stable cooperative arrangements, but the temptation of victory will make this particularly difficult. Second, because wars are expected to be both frequent and short, there will be incentives for high levels of arms, and quick and strong reaction to the other's increases in arms. The state cannot afford to wait until there is unambiguous evidence that the other is building new weapons. Even large states that have faith in their economic strength cannot wait, because the war will be over before their products can reach the army. Third, when wars are quick, states will have to recruit allies in advance.[11] Without the opportunity for bargaining and re-alignments during the opening stages of hostilities, peacetime diplomacy loses a degree of the fluidity that facilitates balance-of-power policies. Because alliances must be secured during peacetime, the international system is more likely to become bipolar. It is hard to say whether war therefore becomes more or less likely, but this bipolarity increases tension between the two camps and makes it harder for status-quo states to gain the benefits of cooperation. Fourth, if wars are frequent, statesmen's perceptual thresholds will be adjusted accordingly and they will be quick to perceive ambiguous evidence as indicating that others are aggressive. Thus, there will be more cases of status-quo powers arming against each other in the incorrect belief that the other is hostile.

When the defense has the advantage, all the foregoing is reversed. The state that fears attack does not pre-empt—since that would be a wasteful use of its military resources—but rather prepares to receive an attack. Doing so does not decrease the security of others, and several states can do it simultaneously; the situation will therefore be stable, and status-quo powers will be able to cooperate. * * *

More is involved than short-run dynamics. When the defense is dominant, wars are likely to become stalemates and can be won only at enormous cost. Relatively small and weak states can hold off larger and stronger ones, or can deter attack by raising the costs of conquest to an unacceptable level. States then approach equality in what they can do to each other. Like the .45-caliber pistol in the American West, fortifications were the "great equalizer" in some periods. Changes in the status quo are less frequent and cooperation is more common wherever the security dilemma is thereby reduced.

Many of these arguments can be illustrated by the major powers' policies in the periods preceding the two world wars. Bismarck's wars surprised statesmen by showing that the offense had the advantage, and by being quick, relatively cheap, and quite decisive. Falling into a common error, observers projected this pattern into the future. The resulting expectations had several effects. First, states sought semi-permanent allies. In the early stages of the Franco-Prussian War, Napoleon III had thought that there would be plenty of time to recruit Austria to his side. Now, others were not going to repeat this mistake. Second, defense budgets were high and reacted quite sharply to increases on the other side. * * * Third, most decision makers thought that the next European war would not cost much blood and treasure.[12] That is one reason why war was generally seen as inevitable and why mass opinion was so bellicose. Fourth, once war seemed likely, there were strong pressures to preempt. Both sides believed that whoever moved first could penetrate the other deep enough to disrupt mobilization and thus gain an insurmountable advantage. (There was no such belief about the use of naval forces. Although Churchill made an ill-advised speech saying that if German ships "do not come out and fight in time of war they will be dug out like rats in a hole,"[13] everyone knew that submarines, mines, and coastal fortifications made this impossible. So at the start of the war each navy prepared to defend itself rather than attack, and the short-run destabilizing forces that launched the armies toward each other did not operate.)[14] Furthermore, each side knew that the other saw the situation the same way, thus increasing the perceived danger that the other would attack, and giving each

added reasons to precipitate a war if conditions seemed favorable. In the long and the short run, there were thus both offensive and defensive incentives to strike. This situation casts light on the common question about German motives in 1914: "Did Germany unleash the war deliberately to become a world power or did she support Austria merely to defend a weakening ally," thereby protecting her own position?[15] To some extent, this question is misleading. Because of the perceived advantage of the offense, war was seen as the best route both to gaining expansion and to avoiding drastic loss of influence. There seemed to be no way for Germany merely to retain and safeguard her existing position.

Of course the war showed these beliefs to have been wrong on all points. Trenches and machine guns gave the defense an overwhelming advantage. The fighting became deadlocked and produced horrendous casualties. It made no sense for the combatants to bleed themselves to death. If they had known the power of the defense beforehand, they would have rushed for their own trenches rather than for the enemy's territory. Each side could have done this without increasing the other's incentives to strike. War might have broken out anyway, * * * but at least the pressures of time and the fear of allowing the other to get the first blow would not have contributed to this end. And, had both sides known the costs of the war, they would have negotiated much more seriously. The obvious question is why the states did not seek a negotiated settlement as soon as the shape of the war became clear. Schlieffen had said that if his plan failed, peace should be sought.[16] The answer is complex, uncertain, and largely outside of the scope of our concerns. But part of the reason was the hope and sometimes the expectation that breakthroughs could be made and the dominance of the offensive restored. Without that hope, the political and psychological pressures to fight to a decisive victory might have been overcome.

The politics of the interwar period were shaped by the memories of the previous conflict and the belief that any future war would resemble it. Political and military lessons reinforced each other in ameliorating the security dilemma. Because it was believed that the First World War had been a mistake that could have been avoided by skillful conciliation, both Britain and, to a lesser extent, France were highly sensitive to the possibility that interwar Germany was not a real threat to peace, and alert to the danger that reacting quickly and strongly to her arms could create unnecessary conflict. And because Britain and France expected the defense to continue to dominate, they concluded that it was safe to adopt a more relaxed and non-threatening military posture.[17] Britain also felt less need to maintain tight alliance bonds. The Allies' military posture then constituted only a slight danger to Germany; had the latter been content with the status quo, it would have been easy for both sides to have felt secure behind their lines of fortifications. Of course the Germans were not content, so it is not surprising that they devoted their money and attention to finding ways out of a defense-dominated stalemate. *Blitzkrieg* tactics were necessary if they were to use force to change the status quo.

The initial stages of the war on the Western Front also contrasted with the First World War. Only with the new air arm were there any incentives to strike first, and these forces were too weak to carry out the grandiose plans that had been both dreamed and feared. The armies, still the main instrument, rushed to defensive positions. Perhaps the allies could have successfully attacked while the Germans were occupied in Poland.[18] But belief in the defense was so great that this was never seriously contemplated. Three months after the start of the war, the French Prime Minister summed up the view held by almost everyone but Hitler: on the Western Front there is "deadlock. Two Forces of equal strength and the one that attacks seeing such enormous casualties that it cannot move without endangering the continuation of the war or of the aftermath."[19] The Allies were caught in a dilemma they never fully recognized, let alone solved. On the one hand, they had very high war aims; although unconditional surrender had not yet been adopted, the British had decided from the start that the removal of Hitler was a necessary condition for peace.[20] On the other hand, there were no realistic plans or instruments for allowing the Allies to impose their will on the other side. The British Chief of the Imperial General Staff noted, "The French have no intention of carrying out an offensive for years, if at all"; the British were only slightly bolder.[21] So the Allies looked to a long war that would wear the Germans down, cause civilian suffering through shortages, and eventually undermine Hitler. There was little analysis to support this view—and indeed it probably was not supportable—but as long as the defense was dominant and the numbers on each side relatively equal, what else could the Allies do?

To summarize, the security dilemma was much less powerful after World War I than it had been before. In the later period, the expected power of the defense allowed status-quo states to pursue compatible security policies and avoid arms races. Furthermore, high tension and fear of war did not set off short-run dynamics by which each state, trying to increase its security, inadvertently acted to make war more likely. The expected high costs of war, however, led the Allies to believe that no sane German leader would run the risks entailed in an attempt to dominate the Continent, and discouraged them from risking war themselves.

TECHNOLOGY AND GEOGRAPHY Technology and geography are the two main factors that determine whether the offense or the defense has the advantage. As Brodie notes, "On the tactical level, as a rule, few physical factors favor the attacker but many favor the defender. The defender usually has the advantage of cover. He characteristically fires from behind some form of shelter while his opponent crosses open ground."[22] Anything that increases the amount of ground the attacker has to cross, or impedes his progress across it, or makes him more vulnerable while crossing, increases the advantage accruing to the defense. When states are separated by barriers that produce these effects, the security dilemma is eased, since both can have forces adequate for defense without being able to attack. * * *

Oceans, large rivers, and mountain ranges serve the same function as buffer zones. Being hard to cross, they allow defense against superior numbers. The defender has merely to stay on his side of the barrier and so can utilize all the men he can bring up to it. The attacker's men, however, can cross only a few at a time, and they are very vulnerable when doing so. If all states were self-sufficient islands, anarchy would be much less of a problem. A small investment in shore defenses and a small army would be sufficient to repel invasion. Only very weak states would be vulnerable, and only very large ones could menace others. As noted above, the United States, and to a lesser extent Great Britain, have partly been able to escape from the state of nature because their geographical positions approximated this ideal.

Although geography cannot be changed to conform to borders, borders can and do change to conform to geography. Borders across which an attack is easy tend to be unstable. States living within them are likely to expand or be absorbed. Frequent wars are almost inevitable since attacking will often seem the best way to protect what one has. This process will stop, or at least slow down, when the state's borders reach—by expansion or contraction—a line of natural obstacles. Security without attack will then be possible. Furthermore, these lines constitute salient solutions to bargaining problems and, to the extent that they are barriers to migration, are likely to divide ethnic groups, thereby raising the costs and lowering the incentives for conquest.

Attachment to one's state and its land reinforce one quasi-geographical aid to the defense. Conquest usually becomes more difficult the deeper the attacker pushes into the other's territory. Nationalism spurs the defenders to fight harder; advancing not only lengthens the attacker's supply lines, but takes him through unfamiliar and often devastated lands that require troops for garrison duty. These stabilizing dynamics will not operate, however, if the defender's war materiel is situated near its borders, or if the people do not care about their state, but only about being on the winning side. * * *

* * *

The other major determinant of the offense-defense balance is technology. When weapons are highly vulnerable, they must be employed before they are attacked. Others can remain quite invulnerable in their bases. The former characteristics are embodied in unprotected missiles and many kinds of bombers. (It should be noted that it is not vulnerability *per se* that is crucial, but the location of the vulnerability. Bombers and missiles that are easy to destroy only after having been launched toward their targets do not create destabilizing dynamics.) Incentives to strike first are usually absent for naval forces that are threatened by a naval attack. Like missiles in hardened silos, they are usually well protected when in their bases. Both sides can then simultaneously be prepared to defend themselves successfully.

In ground warfare under some conditions, forts, trenches, and small groups of men in prepared positions can hold off large numbers of attackers. * * *

* * *

Concerning nuclear weapons, it is generally agreed that defense is impossible—a triumph not of the offense, but of deterrence. Attack makes no sense, not because it can be beaten off, but because the attacker will be destroyed in turn. In terms of the questions under consideration here, the result is the equivalent of the primacy of the defense. First, security is relatively cheap. Less than one percent of the G.N.P. is devoted to deterring a direct attack on the United States; most of it is spent on acquiring redundant systems to provide a lot of insurance against the worst conceivable contingencies. Second, both sides can simultaneously gain security in the form of second-strike capability. Third, and related to the foregoing, second-strike capability can be maintained in the face of wide variations in the other side's military posture. There is no purely military reason why each side has to react quickly and strongly to the other's increases in arms. Any spending that the other devotes to trying to achieve first-strike capability can be neutralized by the state's spending much smaller sums on protecting its second-strike capability. Fourth, there are no incentives to strike first in a crisis.

* * *

Offense-Defense Differentiation

The other major variable that affects how strongly the security dilemma operates is whether weapons and policies that protect the state also provide the capability for attack. If they do not, the basic postulate of the security dilemma no longer applies. A state can increase its own security without decreasing that of others. The advantage of the defense can only ameliorate the security dilemma. A differentiation between offensive and defensive stances comes close to abolishing it. Such differentiation does not mean, however, that all security problems will be abolished. If the offense has the advantage, conquest and aggression will still be possible. And if the offense's advantage is great enough, status-quo powers may find it too expensive to protect themselves by defensive forces and decide to procure offensive weapons even though this will menace others. Furthermore, states will still have to worry that even if the other's military posture shows that it is peaceful now, it may develop aggressive intentions in the future.

Assuming that the defense is at least as potent as the offense, the differentiation between them allows status-quo states to behave in ways that are clearly different from those of aggres-

sors. Three beneficial consequences follow. First, status-quo powers can identify each other, thus laying the foundations for cooperation. Conflicts growing out of the mistaken belief that the other side is expansionist will be less frequent. Second, status-quo states will obtain advance warning when others plan aggression. Before a state can attack, it has to develop and deploy offensive weapons. If procurement of these weapons cannot be disguised and takes a fair amount of time, as it almost always does, a status-quo state will have the time to take countermeasures. It need not maintain a high level of defensive arms as long as its potential adversaries are adopting a peaceful posture. * * *

* * *

* * * [I]f all states support the status quo, an obvious arms control agreement is a ban on weapons that are useful for attacking. As President Roosevelt put it in his message to the Geneva Disarmament Conference in 1933: "If all nations will agree wholly to eliminate from possession and use the weapons which make possible a successful attack, defenses automatically will become impregnable, and the frontiers and independence of every nation will become secure."[23] The fact that such treaties have been rare * * * shows either that states are not always willing to guarantee the security of others, or that it is hard to distinguish offensive from defensive weapons.

* * *

IV. Four Worlds

The two variables we have been discussing—whether the offense or the defense has the advantage, and whether offensive postures can be distinguished from defensive ones—can be combined to yield four possible worlds.

The first world is the worst for status-quo states. There is no way to get security without menacing others, and security through defense is terribly difficult to obtain. Because offensive and defensive postures are the same, status-quo states acquire the same kind of arms that are sought by aggressors. And because the offense has the advantage over the defense, attacking is the best route to protecting what you have; status-quo states will therefore behave like aggressors. The situation will be unstable. Arms races are likely. Incentives to strike first will turn crises into wars. Decisive victories and conquests will be common. States will grow and shrink rapidly, and it will be hard for any state to maintain its size and influence without trying to increase them. Cooperation among status-quo powers will be extremely hard to achieve.

	Offense Has the Advantage	Defense Has the Advantage
Offensive Posture Not Distinguishable from Defensive One	1 Doubly dangerous	2 Security dilemma, but security requirements may be compatible.
Offensive Posture Distinguishable from Defensive One	3 No security dilemma, but aggression possible. Status-quo states can follow different policy than aggressors. Warning given.	4 Doubly stable

Figure 8.2.

There are no cases that totally fit this picture, but it bears more than a passing resemblance to Europe before World War I. Britain and Germany, although in many respects natural allies, ended up as enemies. Of course much of the explanation lies in Germany's ill-chosen policy. And from the perspective of our theory, the powers' ability to avoid war in a series of earlier crises cannot be easily explained. Nevertheless, much of the behavior in this period was the product of technology and beliefs that magnified the security dilemma. Decision makers thought that the offense had a big advantage and saw little difference between offensive and defensive military postures. The era was characterized by arms races. And once war seemed likely, mobilization races created powerful incentives to strike first.

In the nuclear era, the first world would be one in which each side relied on vulnerable weapons that were aimed at similar forces and each side understood the situation. In this case, the incentives to strike first would be very high—so high that status-quo powers as well as aggressors would be sorely tempted to pre-empt. And since the forces could be used to change the status quo as well as to preserve it, there would be no way for both sides to increase their security simultaneously. Now the familiar logic of deterrence leads both sides to see the dangers in this world. Indeed, the new understanding of this situation was one reason why vulnerable bombers and missiles were replaced. Ironically, the 1950's would have been more hazardous if the decision makers had been aware of the dangers of their posture and had therefore felt greater pressure to strike first. This situation could be recreated if both sides were to rely on MIRVed ICBMs.

In the second world, the security dilemma operates because offensive and defensive postures cannot be distinguished; but it does not operate as strongly as in the first world because the defense has the advantage, and so an increment in one side's strength increases its security more than it decreases the other's. So, if both sides have reasonable subjective security requirements, are of roughly equal power, and the variables discussed earlier are favorable, it is quite likely that status-quo states can adopt compatible security policies. * * *

This world is the one that comes closest to matching most periods in history. Attacking is usually harder than defending because of the strength of fortifications and obstacles. But purely defensive postures are rarely possible because fortifications are usually supplemented by armies and mobile guns which can support an attack. In the nuclear era, this world would be one in which both sides relied on relatively invulnerable ICBMs and believed that limited nuclear war was impossible. * * *

In the third world there may be no security dilemma, but there are security problems. Because states can procure defensive systems that do not threaten others, the dilemma need not operate. But because the offense has the advantage, aggression is possible, and perhaps easy. If the offense has enough of an advantage, even a status-quo state may take the initiative rather than risk being attacked and defeated. If the offense has less of an advantage, stability and cooperation are likely because the status-quo states will procure defensive forces. They need not react to others who are similarly armed, but can wait for the warning they would receive if others started to deploy offensive weapons. But each state will have to watch the others carefully, and there is room for false suspicions. The costliness of the defense and the allure of the offense can lead to unnecessary mistrust, hostility, and war, unless some of the variables discussed earlier are operating to restrain defection.

* * *

The fourth world is doubly safe. The differentiation between offensive and defensive systems permits a way out of the security dilemma; the advantage of the defense disposes of the problems discussed in the previous paragraphs. There is no reason for a status-quo power to be tempted to procure offensive forces, and aggressors give notice of their intentions by the posture they adopt. Indeed, if the advantage of the defense is great enough, there are no security problems. The loss of the ultimate form of the power to alter the status quo would allow greater scope for the exercise of nonmilitary means and probably would tend to freeze the distribution of values.

* * *

NOTES

1. Quoted in Gerald Wheeler, *Prelude to Pearl Harbor* (Columbia: University of Missouri Press 1963), 167.
2. Quoted in Leonard Wainstein, "The Dreadnought Gap," in Robert Art and Kenneth Waltz, eds., *The Use of Force* (Boston: Little, Brown 1971), 155 * * *.
3. In another article, Jervis says: "International politics sometimes resembles what is called a Prisoner's Dilemma (PD). In this scenario, two men have been caught red-handed committing a minor crime. The district attorney knows that they are also guilty of a much more serious offense. He tells each of them separately that if he confesses and squeals on his buddy, he will go free and the former colleague will go to jail for thirty years. If both of them refuse to give any information, they will be prosecuted for the minor crime and be jailed for thirty days; if they both squeal, plea-bargaining will get them ten years. In other words, as long as each criminal cares only about himself, he will confess to the more serious crime no matter what he thinks his colleague will do. If he confesses and his buddy does not, he will get the best possible outcome (freedom); if he confesses and his buddy also does so, the outcome will not be good (ten years in jail), but it will be better than keeping silent and going to jail for thirty years. Since both can see this, both will confess. Paradoxically, if they had both been irrational and kept quiet, they would have gone to jail for only a month." (Robert Jervis, "A Political Science Perspective on the Balance of Power and the Concert," *American Historical Review* 97, no. 3 (June 1992): 720.)
4. Experimental evidence for this proposition is summarized in James Tedeschi, Barry Schlenker, and Thomas Bonoma, *Conflict, Power, and Games* (Chicago: Aldine 1973), 135–41.

5. The results of Prisoner's Dilemma games played in the labouratory support this argument. See Anatol Rapoport and Albert Chammah, *Prisoner's Dilemma* (Ann Arbor: University of Michigan Press 1965), 33–50. Also see Robert Axelrod, *Conflict of Interest* (Chicago: Markham 1970), 60–70.

6. Quoted in Bernard Brodie, *Strategy in the Missile Age* (Princeton: Princeton University Press 1959), 6.

7. Herbert York, *The Advisors: Oppenheimer, Teller, and the Superbomb* (San Francisco: Freemar, 1976), 56–60.

8. Thus, when Wolfers, [*Discord and Collaboration* (Baltimore: Johns Hopkins Press 1962),] 126, argues that a status-quo state that settles for rough equality of power with its adversary, rather than seeking preponderance, may be able to convince the other to reciprocate by showing that it wants only to protect itself, not menace the other, he assumes that the defense has an advantage.

9. Schelling, [*The Strategy of Conflict* (New York: Oxford University Press 1963),] chap. 9.

10. Quoted in Fritz Fischer, *War of Illusions* (New York: Norton 1975), 377, 461.

11. George Quester, *Offense and Defense in the International System* (New York: John Wiley 1977), 105–06; Sontag [*European Diplomatic History, 1871–1932* (New York: Appleton-Century-Crofts 1933)], 4–5.

12. Some were not so optimistic. Gray's remark is well-known: "The lamps are going out all over Europe; we shall not see them lit again in our life-time." The German Prime Minister, Bethmann Hollweg, also feared the consequences of the war. But the controlling view was that it would certainly pay for the winner.

13. Quoted in Martin Gilbert, *Winston S. Churchill*, III, *The Challenge of War, 1914–1916* (Boston: Houghton Mifflin 1971), 84.

14. Quester (fn. 33), 98–99. Robert Art, *The Influence of Foreign Policy on Seapower*, II (Beverly Hills: Sage Professional Papers in International Studies Series, 1973), 14–18, 26–28.

15. Konrad Jarausch, "The Illusion of Limited War: Chancellor Bethmann Hollweg's Calculated Risk, July 1914," *Central European History*, II (March 1969), 50.

16. Brodie (fn. 6), 58.

17. President Roosevelt and the American delegates to the League of Nations Disarmament Conference maintained that the tank and mobile heavy artillery had re-established the dominance of the offensive, thus making disarmament more urgent (Boggs, [*Attempts to Define and. Limit "Aggressive" Armament in Diplomacy and Strategy* (Columbia: University of Missouri Studies, XVI, No. 1, 1941)], pp. 31, 108), but this was a minority position and may not even have been believed by the Americans. The reduced prestige and influence of the military, and the high pressures to cut government spending throughout this period also contributed to the lowering of defense budgets.

18. Jon Kimche, *The Unfought Battle* (New York: Stein 1968); Nicholas William Bethell, *The War Hitler Won: The Fall of Poland, September 1939* (New York: Holt 1972); Alan Alexandroff and Richard Rosecrance, "Deterrence in 1939," *World Politics*, XXIX (April 1977), 404–24.

19. Roderick Macleod and Denis Kelly, eds., *Time Unguarded: The Ironside Diaries, 1937–1940* (New York: McKay 1962), 173.

20. For a short time, as France was falling, the British Cabinet did discuss reaching a negotiated peace with Hitler. The official history ignores this, but it is covered in P.M.H. Bell, *A Certain Eventuality* (Farnborough, England: Saxon House 1974), 40–48.

21. Macleod and Kelly (fn. 19), 174. In flat contradiction to common sense and almost everything they believed about modern warfare, the Allies planned an expedition to Scandinavia to cut the supply of iron ore to Germany and to aid Finland against the Rus-

sians. But the dominant mood was the one described above.

22. Brodie (fn. 6), 179.

23. Quoted in Merze Tate, *The United States and Armaments* (Cambridge: Harvard University Press 1948), 108.

JAMES D. FEARON

Rationalist Explanations for War

The central puzzle about war, and also the main reason we study it, is that wars are costly but nonetheless wars recur. Scholars have attempted to resolve the puzzle with three types of argument. First, one can argue that people (and state leaders in particular) are sometimes or always irrational. They are subject to biases and pathologies that lead them to neglect the costs of war or to misunderstand how their actions will produce it. Second, one can argue that the leaders who order war enjoy its benefits but do not pay the costs, which are suffered by soldiers and citizens. Third, one can argue that even rational leaders who consider the risks and costs of war may end up fighting nonetheless.

This article focuses on arguments of the third sort, which I will call rationalist explanations.[1] Rationalist explanations abound in the literature on international conflict, assuming a great variety of specific forms. Moreover, for at least two reasons many scholars have given rationalist explanations a certain pride of place. First, historians and political scientists who

have studied the origins of particular wars often have concluded that war can be a rational alternative for leaders who are acting in their states' interest—they find that the expected benefits of war sometimes outweigh the expected costs, however unfortunate this may be. Second, the dominant paradigm in international relations theory, neorealism, is thought to advance or even to depend on rationalist arguments about the causes of war. Indeed, if no rationalist explanation for war is theoretically or empirically tenable, then neither is neorealism. The causes of war would then lie in the defects of human nature or particular states rather than in the international system, as argued by neorealists. What I refer to here as "rationalist explanations for war" could just as well be called "neorealist explanations."[2]

This article attempts to provide a clear statement of what a rationalist explanation for war is and to characterize the full set of rationalist explanations that are both theoretically coherent and empirically plausible. It should be obvious that this theoretical exercise must take place prior to testing rationalist explanations against alternatives—we cannot perform such tests unless we know what a rationalist explanation really is. Arguably, the exercise is also foundational for neorealism. Despite its prominence, neorealist

From *International Organization* 49, no. 3 (Summer 1995): 379–410. Bracketed editorial insertions are the author's and three asterisks (***) are used to mark places where technical material has been omitted. Some notes and a technical appendix have been omitted.

theory lacks a clearly stated and fully conceived explanation for war. As I will argue below, it is not enough to say that under anarchy nothing stops states from using force, or that anarchy forces states to rely on self-help, which engenders mutual suspicion and (through spirals or the security dilemma) armed conflict. Neither do diverse references to miscalculation, deterrence failure because of inadequate forces or incredible threats, preventive and preemptive considerations, or free-riding in alliances amount to theoretically coherent rationalist explanations for war.

My main argument is that on close inspection none of the principal rationalist arguments advanced in the literature holds up as an explanation because none addresses or adequately resolves the central puzzle, namely, that war is costly and risky, so rational states should have incentives to locate negotiated settlements that all would prefer to the gamble of war. The common flaw of the standard rationalist arguments is that they fail either to address or to explain adequately what prevents leaders from reaching *ex ante* (prewar) bargains that would avoid the costs and risks of fighting. A coherent rationalist explanation for war must do more than give reasons why armed conflict might appear an attractive option to a rational leader under some circumstances—it must show why states are unable to locate an alternative outcome that both would prefer to a fight.

To summarize what follows, the article will consider five rationalist arguments accepted as tenable in the literature on the causes of war. Discussed at length below, these arguments are given the following labels: (1) anarchy; (2) expected benefits greater than expected costs; (3) rational preventive war; (4) rational miscalculation due to lack of information; and (5) rational miscalculation or disagreement about relative power. I argue that the first three arguments simply do not address the question of what prevents state leaders from bargaining to a settlement that would avoid the costs of fighting. The fourth and fifth arguments do address the ques-

tion, holding that rational leaders may miss a superior negotiated settlement when lack of information leads them to miscalculate relative power or resolve. However, as typically stated, neither argument explains what prevents rational leaders from using diplomacy or other forms of communication to avoid such costly miscalculations.

If these standard arguments do not resolve the puzzle on rationalist terms, what does? I propose that there are three defensible answers, which take the form of general mechanisms, or causal logics, that operate in a variety of more specific international contexts.[3] In the first mechanism, rational leaders may be unable to locate a mutually preferable negotiated settlement due to *private information* about relative capabilities or resolve and *incentives to misrepresent* such information. Leaders know things about their military capabilities and willingness to fight that other states do not know, and in bargaining situations they can have incentives to misrepresent such private information in order to gain a better deal. I show that given these incentives, communication may not allow rational leaders to clarify relative power or resolve without generating a real risk of war. This is not simply a matter of miscalculation due to poor information but rather of specific strategic dynamics that result from the combination of asymmetric information and incentives to dissemble.

Second, rationally led states may be unable to arrange a settlement that both would prefer to war due to *commitment problems*, situations in which mutually preferable bargains are unattainable because one or more states would have an incentive to renege on the terms. While anarchy (understood as the absence of an authority capable of policing agreements) is routinely cited as a cause of war in the literature, it is difficult to find explanations for exactly why the inability to make commitments should imply that war will sometimes occur. That is, what are the specific, empirically identifiable mechanisms by which the inability to commit makes it impossible for states to strike deals that would avoid the costs of war? I identify three such specific mechanisms, arguing in particular that preventive war between rational states stems from a commitment problem rather than from differential power growth per se.

The third sort of rationalist explanation I find less compelling than the first two, although it is logically tenable. States might be unable to locate a peaceful settlement both prefer due to *issue indivisibilities*. Perhaps some issues, by their very natures, simply will not admit compromise. Though neither example is wholly convincing, issues that might exhibit indivisibility include abortion in domestic politics and the problem of which prince sits on the throne of, say, Spain, in eighteenth- or nineteenth-century international politics. Issue indivisibility could in principle make war rational for the obvious reason that if the issue allows only a finite number of resolutions, it might be that none falls within the range that both prefer to fighting. However, the issues over which states bargain typically are complex and multidimensional; side-payments or linkages with other issues typically are possible; and in principle states could alternate or randomize among a fixed number of possible solutions to a dispute. War-prone international issues may often be *effectively* indivisible, but the cause of this indivisibility lies in domestic political and other mechanisms rather than in the nature of the issues themselves.

In the first section of the article I discuss the puzzle posed by the fact that war is costly. Using a simple formalization of the bargaining problem faced by states in conflict, I show that under very broad conditions bargains will exist that genuinely rational states would prefer to a risky and costly fight. The second section argues that rational miscalculations of relative power and resolve must be due to private information and then considers how war may result from the combination of private information and incentives to misrepresent that information in bargaining. In the third section, I discuss commitment problems as the second class of defensible rationalist explanations for war. Throughout, I specify theoretical arguments with simple game-theoretic representations and assess plausibility with historical examples.

Before beginning, I should make it clear that I am not presenting either commitment problems or private information and incentives to misrepresent as wholly novel explanations for war that are proposed here for the first time. The literature on the causes of war is massive, and these ideas, mixed with myriad others, can be found in it in various guises. The main theoretical task facing students of war is not to add to the already long list of arguments and conjectures but instead to take apart and reassemble these diverse arguments into a coherent theory fit for guiding empirical research. Toward this end, I am arguing that when one looks carefully at the problem of explaining how war could occur between genuinely rational, unitary states, one finds that there are really only two ways to do it. The diverse rationalist or neorealist explanations commonly found in the literature fail for two reasons. First, many do not even address the relevant question–what prevents states from locating a bargain both sides would prefer to a fight? They do not address the question because it is widely but incorrectly assumed that rational states can face a situation of deadlock, wherein no agreements exist that both sides would prefer to a war.[4] Second, the rationalist arguments that do address the question—such as (4) and (5) above—do not go far enough in answering it. When fully developed, they prove to be one of the two major mechanisms developed here, namely, either a commitment problem or a problem arising from private information and incentives to misrepresent. These two mechanisms, I will argue, provide the foundations for a rationalist or neorealist theory of war.

The Puzzle

Most historians and political scientists who study war dismiss as naive the view that all wars must be unwanted because they entail destruction and suffering. Instead, most agree that while a few wars may have been unwanted by the leaders who brought them about—World War I is sometimes given as an example—many or perhaps most wars were simply wanted. The leaders involved viewed war as a costly but worthwhile gamble.[5]

Moreover, many scholars believe that wanted wars are easily explained from a rationalist perspective. Wanted wars are thought to be Pareto-efficient—they occur when no negotiated settlements exist that both sides would prefer to the gamble of military conflict. Conventional wisdom holds that while this situation may be tragic, it is entirely possible between states led by rational leaders who consider the costs and risks of fighting. Unwanted wars, which take place despite the existence of settlements both sides preferred to conflict, are thought to pose more of a puzzle, but one that is resolvable and also fairly rare.

The conventional distinction between wanted and unwanted wars misunderstands the puzzle posed by war. The reason is that the standard conception does not distinguish between two types of efficiency—*ex ante* and *ex post*. As long as both sides suffer some costs for fighting, then war is always inefficient *ex post*—both sides would have been better off if they could have achieved the same final resolution without suffering the costs (or by paying lower costs). This is true even if the costs of fighting are small, or if one or both sides viewed the potential benefits as greater than the costs, since there are still costs. Unless states enjoy the activity of fighting for its own sake, as a consumption good, then war is inefficient *ex post*.

From a rationalist perspective, the central puzzle about war is precisely this *ex post* inefficiency. Before fighting, both sides know that war will entail some costs, and even if they expect offsetting benefits they still have an incentive to avoid the costs. The central question, then, is what prevents states in a dispute from reaching an *ex ante* agreement that avoids the costs they know will be paid *ex post* if they go to war? Giv-

ing a rationalist explanation for war amounts to answering this question.

Three of the most common and widely employed rationalist arguments in the literature do not directly address or answer the question. These are arguments from anarchy, preventive war, and positive expected utility.

Anarchy

Since Kenneth Waltz's influential *Man, the State, and War*, the anarchical nature of the international realm is routinely cited as a root cause of or explanation for the recurrence of war. Waltz argued that under anarchy, without a supranational authority to make and enforce law, "war occurs because there is nothing to prevent it. . . . Among states as among men there is no automatic adjustment of interests. In the absence of a supreme authority there is then the constant possibility that conflicts will be settled by force."[6]

The argument focuses our attention on a fundamental difference between domestic and international politics. Within a well-ordered state, organized violence as a strategy is ruled out—or at least made very dangerous—by the potential reprisals of a central government. In international relations, by contrast, no agency exists that can credibly threaten reprisal for the use of force to settle disputes.[7] The claim is that without such a credible threat, war will sometimes appear the best option for states that have conflicting interests.

While I do not doubt that the condition of anarchy accounts for major differences between domestic and international politics, and that anarchy encourages both fear of and opportunities for military conflict, the standard framing of the argument is not enough to explain why wars occur and recur. Under anarchy, nothing stops states from using force if they wish. But if using force is a costly option regardless of the outcome, then why is it ever employed? How exactly does the lack of a central authority prevent states from negotiating agreements both sides would prefer to fighting? As it is typically stated, the argument that anarchy provides a rationalist explanation for war does not address this question and so does not solve the problem posed by war's *ex post* inefficiency.

Neither, it should be added, do related arguments invoking the security dilemma, the fact that under anarchy one state's efforts to make itself more secure can have the undesired but unavoidable effect of making another state less secure.[8] By itself this fact says nothing about the availability or feasibility of peaceful bargains that would avoid the costs of war. More elaborate arguments are required, and those that are typically given do not envision bargaining and do not address the puzzle of costs. Consider, for instance, a spiral scenario in which an insecure state increases its arms, rendering another so insecure that it decides to attack. If the first state anticipated the reaction producing war, then by itself this is a deadlock argument; I argue against these below. If the first state did not anticipate war and did not want it, then the problem would seem to be miscalculation rather than anarchy, and we need to know why signaling and bargaining could not have solved it. As Robert Jervis has argued, anarchy and the security dilemma may well foster arms races and territorial competition.[9] But with the exception of occasional references to the preemptive war problem, the standard security dilemma arguments do not explicitly address the question of why the inability to make commitments should necessarily make for war between rational states.[10]

Below I will argue that anarchy is indeed implicated as a cause of specific sorts of military conflict (e.g., preventive and preemptive war and in some cases war over strategic territory). In contrast to the standard arguments, however, showing how anarchy figures in a coherent rationalist explanation entails describing the specific mechanism by which states' inability to write enforceable contracts makes peaceful bargains both sides would prefer unattainable.

Preventive War

It frequently is argued that if a declining power expects it might be attacked by a rising power in the future, then a preventive war in the present may be rational. Typically, however, preventive war arguments do not consider whether the rising and declining powers could construct a bargain, perhaps across time, that would leave both sides better off than a costly and risky preventive war would.[11] The incentives for such a deal surely exist. The rising state should not want to be attacked while it is relatively weak, so what stops it from offering concessions in the present and the future that would make the declining state prefer not to attack? Also, if war is inefficient and bargains both sides prefer to a fight will exist, why should the declining power rationally fear being attacked in the future? The standard argument supposes that an anticipated shift in the balance of power can by itself be enough to make war rational, but this is not so.

Positive Expected Utility

Perhaps the most common informal rationalist explanation found in the literature is that war may occur when two states each estimate that the expected benefits of fighting outweigh the expected costs. As Bruce Bueno de Mesquita argued in an influential formalization of this claim, war can be rational if both sides have positive expected utility for fighting; that is, if the expected utility of war (expected benefits less costs) is greater than the expected utility of remaining at peace.[12]

Informal versions of the expected utility argument typically fail to address the question of how or under what conditions it can be possible for two states both to prefer the costly gamble of war to any negotiated settlement. Formal versions have tended to avoid the question by making various restrictive and sometimes nonrationalist assumptions. To support these claims, I need to be more precise about the expected utility argument.

When Will There Exist Bargains Both Sides Prefer to War?

This section considers the question of whether and when two rationally led states could both prefer war to any negotiated settlement.

Consider two states, A and B, who have preferences over a set of issues represented by the interval $X = [0, 1]$. State A prefers issue resolutions closer to 1, while B prefers outcomes closer to 0. For concreteness we might think of x as representing the proportion of all territory between A and B that is controlled by A. [Thus, a point X in the interval represents the situation where state A controls all the territory from ø to X, while state B controls all the territory from X to 1.][13]

In order to say whether the set X contains negotiated settlements that both sides would prefer to conflict, it must be possible to say how the states evaluate the military option versus those outcomes. Almost all analysts of war have stressed that war is a gamble whose outcome may be determined by random or otherwise unforeseeable events.[14] As Bueno de Mesquita argued, this makes expected utility a natural candidate.[15] Suppose that if the states fight a war, state A prevails with probability $p \in [0, 1]$, and that the winner gets to choose its favorite outcome in the issue

space. * * * [Thus, A's expected utility for war is $p - c$, since A gets all the territory, which is worth 1, with probability p, loses everything with probability $1 - p$, and pays a cost for fighting c_A in either event.] Similarly, state B's expected utility for war will be $1 - p - c_B$. Since we are considering rationalist theories for war, we assume that c_A and c_B are both positive. War is thus represented as a costly lottery.[16]

We can now answer the question posed above. The following result is easily demonstrated: given the assumptions stated in the last two paragraphs, there always exists a set of negotiated settlements that both sides prefer to fighting. * * * [For example, in the special case where each state's value for an additional increment of territory is constant, the two states will both prefer any division of territory in the range from $p - c_A$ to $p + c_B$ over fighting a war. This interval represents the bargaining range, with $p - c_A$ and $p + c_B$ as the reservation levels that delimit it. This case of "risk neutral" states is depicted in Figure 8.3.]

This simple but important result is worth belaboring with some intuition. Suppose that two people (or states) are bargaining over the division of $100—if they can agree on a split they can keep what they agree to. However, in contrast to the usual economic scenarios, in this international relations example the players also have an outside option.[17] For a price of $20, they can go to war, in which case each player has a

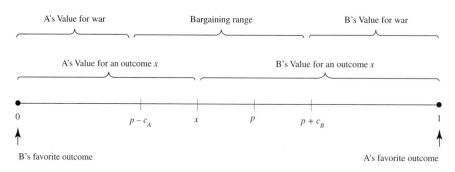

Figure 8.3. The Bargaining Range

50-percent chance of winning the whole $100. This implies that the expected value of the war option is $30 (0.5 · 100 + 0.5 · 0 − 20) for each side, so that if the players are risk-neutral, then neither should be willing to accept less than $30 in the bargaining. But notice that there is still a range of peaceful, bargained outcomes from ($31, $69) to ($69, $31) that make both sides strictly better off than the war option. Risk aversion will tend to increase the range yet further; indeed, even if the leaders pay no costs for war, a set of agreements both sides prefer to a fight will still exist provided both are risk-averse over the issues. In effect, the costs and risks of fighting open up a "wedge" of bargained solutions that risk-neutral or risk-averse states will prefer to the gamble of conflict. The existence of this *ex ante* bargaining range derives from the fact that war is inefficient *ex post*.

Three substantive assumptions are needed for the result, none of which seems particularly strong. First, the states know that there is some true probability p that one state would win in a military contest. As discussed below, it could be that the states have conflicting estimates of the likelihood of victory, and if both sides are optimistic about their chances this can obscure the bargaining range. But even if the states have private and conflicting estimates of what would happen in a war, if they are rational, they should know that there can be only one true probability that one or the other will prevail (perhaps different from their own estimate). Thus rational states should know that there must in fact exist a set of agreements all prefer to a fight.

Second, it is assumed that the states are risk-averse or risk-neutral over the issues. Because risk attitude is defined relative to an underlying metric (such as money in economics), the substantive meaning of this assumption depends on the bargaining context. Loosely, it says that the states prefer a fifty-fifty split or share of whatever is at issue (in whatever metric it comes, if any) to a fifty-fifty chance at all or nothing, where this refers to the value of winning or losing a war. In

effect, the assumption means that leaders do not like gambling when the downside risk is losing at war, which seems plausible given the presumption that state leaders normally wish to retain territory and power. A risk-acceptant leader is analogous to a compulsive gambler—willing to accept a sequence of gambles that has the expected outcome of eliminating the state and regime. Even if we admitted such a leader as rational, it seems doubtful that many have held such preferences (Hitler being a possible exception).

Finally, it was assumed that a continuous range of peaceful settlements (from 0 to 1) exists. In other words, the issues in dispute are perfectly divisible, so that there are always feasible bargains between the states' reservation levels $p - c_A$ and $p + c_B$. This third assumption immediately suggests a tenable rationalist explanation for war. Perhaps something about the nature of some international issues, such as which successor will sit on a throne, does not admit finely graded divisions and compromise. If so, then small costs for fighting and bad luck may make for rational war over such issues.

But we would immediately like to know what about the nature of an issue makes it impossible to divide up. On more thought, this seems empirically implausible. In the first place, most issues states negotiate over are quite complex—they have many dimensions of concern and allow many possible settlements. Second, if states can simply pay each other sums of money or goods (which they can, in principle), or make linkages with other issues, then this should have the effect of making any issues in dispute perfectly divisible. Before the age of nationalism, princes often bought, sold, and partitioned land.[18] In the nineteenth century the United States purchased the Louisiana Territory from France, and Alaska from Russia, and as late as 1898 President McKinley explored the possibility of buying Cuba from Spain in order to avoid a war over it.[19] Third, if something about the nature of an issue means that it can be settled in only, say, two ways, then some sort of random allocation or alternation between the two resolutions could in principle serve to create intermediate bargains. Mafia dons, for example, apparently have avoided costly internal wars by using lotteries to allocate construction contracts among families.[20]

In practice, creating intermediate settlements with cash, with linkages to other issues, or with randomization or alternation often seems difficult or impossible for states engaged in a dispute. For example, the immediate issue that gave rise to the Franco–Prussian war was a dispute over which prince would take the Spanish throne. It doubtless occurred to no one to propose that the two candidates alternate year by year, or three years for the Hapsburg and one for the Hohenzollern, or whatever. In this case as in many others, the issue could in principle have been made more continuous and was not for other reasons—here, alternating kings would have violated so many conventions and norms as to have been domestically unworkable. To give a more realistic example, nineteenth- and twentieth-century leaders cannot divide up and trade territory in international negotiations as easily as could rulers in the seventeenth and eighteenth centuries, due in part to domestic political consequences of the rise of nationalism; contrast, for example, the Congress of Vienna with the negotiations following World War I.

So in principle the indivisibility of the issues that are the subject of international bargaining can provide a coherent rationalist explanation for war. However, the real question in such cases is what prevents leaders from creating intermediate settlements, and the answer is likely to be other mechanisms (often domestic political) rather than the nature of the issues themselves.[21] Both the intrinsic complexity and richness of most matters over which states negotiate and the availability of linkages and side-payments suggest that intermediate bargains typically will exist.

It is thus not sufficient to say that positive expected utility by itself supplies a coherent or compelling rationalist explanation for war. Provided that the issues in dispute are sufficiently divisible, or that side-payments are possible, there should exist a set of negotiated agreements that have greater utility for both sides than the gamble of war does. The reason is that the *ex post* inefficiency of war opens up an *ex ante* bargaining range.

So, to explain how war could occur between rationally led states, we need to answer the following question. Given the existence of an *ex ante* bargaining range, why might states fail either to locate or to agree on an outcome in this range, so avoiding the costs and risks of war?

War Due to Private Information and Incentives to Misrepresent

Two commonly employed rationalist explanations in the literature directly address the preceding question. Both turn on the claim that war can be and often is the product of rational miscalculation. One explanation holds that a state's leaders may rationally overestimate their chance of military victory against an adversary, so producing a disagreement about relative power that only war can resolve. The other argues that rationally led states may lack information about an adversary's willingness to fight over some interest and so may challenge in the mistaken belief that war will not follow.

In this section I argue that while these ideas point toward a tenable rationalist explanation for war, neither goes far enough and neither works by itself. Both neglect the fact that states can in principle communicate with each other and so avoid a costly miscalculation of relative power or will. The cause of war cannot be simply lack of information, but whatever it is that prevents its disclosure. I argue that the fact that states have incentives to misrepresent their positions is crucial here, explaining on rationalist terms why diplomacy may not allow rational states to clarify disagreements about relative power or to avoid the miscalculation of resolve.

The mainstream international relations literature recognizes the existence of both private information and incentives to misrepresent, but typically views them as background conditions to be taken for granted rather than as key elements of an explanation of how rationally led states might end up at war. For example, Jack Levy's impressive review of the literature on the causes of war contains nothing on the role of incentives to misrepresent and discusses private information largely in the context of misperceptions of other states' intentions (which are linked to psychological biases). This is an accurate reflection of where these factors stand in the mainstream literature.[22]

Disagreements about Relative Power

Geoffrey Blainey's well-known and often-cited argument is that "wars usually begin when two nations disagree on their relative strength."[23] It is easy to see how a disagreement about relative strength—understood as conflicting estimates of the likelihood of military victory—can eliminate any *ex ante* bargaining range. Recall the example given above, where two states bargain over the division of $100, and each has the outside option of going to war. If each expects that it surely would prevail at war, then each side's expected value for the war option is $80 $(1 \cdot 100 + 0 \cdot 0 - 20)$. So given these expectations, neither side will accept less than $80 in the bargaining, implying that no negotiated outcome is mutually preferred to war. More generally, suppose that state A expects to win with probability p, state B expects to win with probability r, and p and r sum to greater than one. Such conflicting expectations will certainly shrink and could eliminate any *ex ante* bargaining range.

But how could rationally led states have conflicting expectations about the likely outcome of military conflict? In the extreme case, how could both sides rationally expect to win? The literature barely addresses this question in explicit terms. Blainey, whom the literature

views as advancing a rationalist explanation for war, in fact explains disagreements about relative power as a consequence of human *ir*rationality. He says that mutual optimism about victory in war is the product of "moods which cannot be grounded in fact" and which "permeate what appear to be rational assessments of the relative military strength of two contending powers." Mutual optimism is said to result from a "process by which nations evade reality," which hardly sounds like a rationalist explanation.[24]

Conflicting expectations about the likely outcome of military conflict may be explained in three ways. First, as Blainey suggests, emotional commitments could irrationally bias leaders' military estimates. They might, for instance, come to believe nationalist rhetoric holding that their soldiers are more courageous and spirited than those of the adversary.[25] Second, the world is a very complex place, and for this reason military analysts in different states could reach different conclusions about the likely impact of different technologies, doctrines, and tactics on the expected course of battle. Third, state leaders might have private information about militarily relevant factors—military capabilities, strategy, and tactics; the population's willingness to prosecute a long war; or third-state intentions. If a state has superior (and so private) information about any such factor, then its estimate of the probable course of battle may differ from that of an adversary.

Under a strict but standard definition of rationality, only the third explanation qualifies as an account of how rationally led states could have conflicting estimates of the probability of winning in war. As argued by John Harsanyi, if two rational agents have the same information about an uncertain event, then they should have the same beliefs about its likely outcome.[26] The claim is that given identical information, truly rational agents should reason to the same conclusions about the probability of one uncertain outcome or another. Conflicting estimates should occur only if the agents have different (and so necessarily private) information.[27]

It follows that the second explanation for disagreements about relative power listed above—the complexity of the world—is not a rationalist account. Instead, it is an account that explains conflicting military estimates as a consequence of bounded rationality. In this view, leaders or military analysts with the same information about military technology, strategy, political will, etc., might reason to different conclusions about the likely course of a war because of differential ability to cope with complexity of the problem. This is entirely plausible, but it is a bounded rationality explanation rather than a fully rationalist one.[28]

The rationalist account of how disagreements about the probability of winning might arise also seems empirically plausible. States certainly have private information about factors affecting the likely course of battle—for example, they jealously guard military secrets and often have superior information about what an ally will or will not fight for. Nonetheless, while private information about militarily relevant capabilities provides a first step, it does not provide a coherent rationalist explanation for war. The problem is that even if leaders have such private information, they should understand that their own estimates based on this information are suspect because they do not know the other side's private information. In principle, both sides could gain by sharing information, which would yield a consensus military estimate (absent bounded rationality). And, as shown above, doing so could not help but reveal bargains that both would prefer to a fight.[29]

So the question of how rationally led states can disagree about relative power devolves to the question of what prevents states from sharing private information about factors that might affect the course of battle. Before turning to this question, I will consider the second common explanation for how a rational miscalculation may produce war.

War Due to the Miscalculation of an Opponent's Willingness to Fight

Many wars have been given the following so-called rationalist explanation: state A transgressed some interest of state B in the erroneous belief that B would not fight a war over the matter. Though rationally led, state A lacked information about B's willingness to fight and simply happened to guess wrong, causing a war. Thus, some say that Germany miscalculated Russian and/or British willingness to fight in 1914; Hitler miscalculated Britain and France's willingness to resist his drive to the east; Japanese leaders in 1941 miscalculated U.S. willingness to fight a long war over control in the South Pacific; North Korea miscalculated U.S. willingness to defend South Korea; the United States miscalculated China's willingness to defend North Korea; and so on. In each case, the argument would hold that lack of information led a more-or-less rational actor to guess wrong about the extent of the bargaining range.

Blainey has argued that if states agree on relative power they are very unlikely to go to war against each other.[30] It is worth pointing out that in the preceding argument, war can occur despite complete agreement on relative power across states. To show how and for later use, I will introduce a simple model of international bargaining. As in the empirical examples just mentioned, in the model one state unilaterally chooses some revision of the status quo. The second state can then either acquiesce to the revision or can go to war to reverse it.

Formally, suppose there is a status quo resolution of the issues, [represented as number q between 0 and 1,] and that state A has the opportunity to chose any outcome x [between 0 and 1], presenting state B with a fait accompli. On observing what state A did (which might be nothing, i.e., $x = q$), state B can choose whether to go to war or to acquiesce to A's revision of the status quo.

If neither state has any private information, so that all payoffs are common knowledge, state

A does best to push the outcome just up to B's reservation level $p + c_B$, which makes B just willing to acquiesce rather than go to war. With complete information, then, the states avoid the inefficient outcome of war.[31] On the other hand, if state B has private information about either its capabilities (which affect p) or its value for the issues at stake relative to the costs of conflict (c_B), then state A may not know whether a particular "demand" x will yield war or peace. Lacking this information, state A faces a trade-off in deciding whether and how much territory to "grab": The larger the grab, the greater the risk of war, but the better off A will be if state B acquiesces.

Suppose, for example, that A and B share a common estimate of p—they agree about relative power—but that A is unsure about B's costs for fighting. Under very broad conditions, if A cannot learn B's private information and if A's own costs are not too large, then state A's optimal grab produces a positive chance of war. Intuitively, if A is not too fearful of the costs of war relative to what might be gained in bargaining, it will run some risk of war in hopes of gaining on the ground. So Blainey's suggestion that a disagreement about relative power is necessary for war is incorrect—all that is necessary is that the states in dispute be unable to locate or agree on some outcome in the bargaining range. Since the bargaining range is determined not just by relative power but also by states' values for the issues at stake relative to the costs of fighting, uncertainty about the latter can (and apparently does) produce war.

Once again, it is entirely plausible that state leaders have private information about their value for various international interests relative to their costs of fighting over them.[32] Thus it seems we have a second tenable rationalist explanation for war, again based on the concept of private information. But as in the case of disagreements about relative power, the explanation fails as given because it does not explain why states cannot avoid miscalculating a potential opponent's willingness to fight. In the model, why cannot state A simply ask state B whether it would fight rather than acquiesce to a particular demand? To give a concrete example, why did German leaders in 1914 not simply ask their British and Russian counterparts what they would do if Austria were to attack Serbia? If they could have done so and if the answers could have been believed, the Germans might not have miscalculated concerning Russian and, more importantly, British willingness to fight. In consequence they might have avoided the horrendous costs of World War I.

To recap, I have argued that in a rationalist framework, disagreements about relative power and uncertainty about a potential opponent's willingness to fight must have the same source: leaders' private information about factors affecting the likely course of a war or their resolve to fight over specific interests. In order to avoid war's *ex post* inefficiency, leaders have incentives to share any such private information, which would have the effect of revealing peaceful settlements that lie within the bargaining range. So, to explain how war could occur between states led by rational leaders who consider the costs of fighting, we need to explain what would prevent them from sharing such private information.

Incentives to Misrepresent in Bargaining

Prewar bargaining may fail to locate an outcome in the bargaining range because of strategic incentives to withhold or misrepresent private information. While states have an incentive to avoid the costs of war, they also wish to obtain a favorable resolution of the issues. This latter desire can give them an incentive to exaggerate their true willingness or capability to fight, if by doing so they might deter future challenges or persuade the other side to make concessions. States can also have an incentive to conceal their capabilities or resolve, if they are concerned that revelation would make them militarily (and hence politically) vulnerable or would reduce the chances for a successful first strike. Similarly, states may conceal their true willingness to fight in order to avoid appearing as the aggressor.

Combined with the fact of private information, these various incentives to misrepresent can explain why even rational leaders may be unable to avoid the miscalculations of relative will and power that can cause war. This section first considers why this is so theoretically and then discusses two empirical examples.

A drawback of the simple bargaining model given above was that state B had no opportunity to try to communicate its willingness to fight to state A. It is easy to imagine that if communication were possible—say, if B could announce what interests in X it considered vital enough to fight over—this might at least lower the chance of war by miscalculation. To check this, we give state B an initial opportunity to make a foreign policy announcement f, which can be any statement about its foreign policy or what it considers to be vital or peripheral interests. (Assume as before that A is uncertain about B's capabilities or costs for fighting.)

If the announcement itself has no effect on either side's payoffs, then it can be shown that in any equilibrium in which state A does not choose randomly among demands, A will make the same demand regardless of what state B says, and the *ex ante* risk of war will remain the same as in the game without communication by state B. To gain an intuition for these results, suppose that A conditioned its behavior on f, grabbing more or less depending on what B announced. Then regardless of B's true willingness to fight, B does best to make the announcement that leads to the smallest grab by A—that is, B has an incentive to misrepresent its actual willingness to resist. But then A learns nothing from the announcement.[33]

This conclusion is slightly altered if the leaders of B can render the announcement f costly to make.[34] In practice, five common methods include building weapons, mobilizing troops, signing alliance treaties, supporting troops in a foreign land, and creating domestic political costs that would be paid if the announcement proves false. Of course, signaling by means of domestic political audience costs lies outside a purely unitary rational-actor framework, since this pre-sumes a state run by an agent on behalf of a principal (the "audience") rather than a unitary state with a perfectly secure leadership. In the latter case, leaders may be able to make foreign policy announcements credible only by engaging an international reputation, taking financially costly mobilization measures, or bearing the costs and risks of limited military engagements.[35]

Even when the signal is costly, however, this will not in general completely eliminate all risk of war by miscalculation—indeed, it may even increase it. The reason concerns the nature of the signals that states have incentives to send. To be genuinely informative about a state's actual willingness or ability to fight, a signal must be costly in such a way that a state with lesser resolve or capability might not wish to send it. Actions that generate a real risk of war—for example, troop mobilizations that engage a leadership's reputation before international or domestic audiences—can easily satisfy this constraint, since states with high resolve are less fearful of taking them. In other words, a rational state may choose to run a real risk of (inefficient) war in order to signal that it will fight if not given a good deal in bargaining.[36]

The July crisis of World War I provides several examples of how incentives to misrepresent can make miscalculations of resolve hard to dispel. Soon after German leaders secretly endorsed Austrian plans to crush Serbia, they received both direct and indirect verbal indications from St. Petersburg that Russia would fight rather than acquiesce.[37] For example, on 21 July, the Russian Foreign Minister told the German ambassador that "Russia would not be able to tolerate Austria-Hungary's using threatening language to Serbia or taking military measures."[38] Such verbal statements had little effect on German leaders' beliefs, however, since they knew Russian leaders had a strategic incentive to misrepresent. On 18 July in a cable explaining Berlin's policy to Ambassador Lichnowsky in London, Secretary of State Jagow wrote that "there is certain to be some blustering in St. Petersburg."[39] Similarly, when on 26 July Lichnowsky began to report that Britain might join with France and Russia in the event of war, German Chancellor Bethmann Hollweg told his personal assistant of the "danger that France and England will commit their support to Russia in order not to alienate it, perhaps without really believing that for us mobilization means war, thinking of it as a bluff which they answer with a counterbluff."[40]

At the same time, the Chancellor had an incentive to misrepresent the strength and nature of German support for Austria's plans. Bethmann correctly anticipated that revealing this information would make Germany appear the aggressor, which might undermine Social Democratic support for his policies in Germany as well as turn British public opinion more solidly against his state.[41] This incentive led the Chancellor to avoid making direct or pointed inquiries about England's attitude in case of war. The incentive also led him to pretend to go along with the British Foreign Secretary's proposals for a conference to mediate the dispute.[42] In consequence, Lord Grey may not have grasped the need for a stronger warning to Germany until fairly late in the crisis (on 29 July), by which time diplomatic and military actions had made backing off more difficult for both Austria and Germany.

In July 1914, incentives to misrepresent private information fostered and supported miscalculations of willingness to fight. Miscalculations of relative power can arise from this same source. On the one hand, states at times have an incentive to exaggerate their capabilities in an attempt to do better in bargaining. On the other hand, they can also have the well-known incentive to withhold information about capabilities and strategy. Presumably because of the strongly zero-sum aspect of military engagements, a state that has superior knowledge of an adversary's war plans may do better in war and thus in prewar bargaining—hence, states rarely publicize war plans. While the theoretical logic has not been worked out, it seems plausible that states' incentives to conceal information about capabilities and strategy could help explain some disagreements about relative power.

The 1904 war between Japan and Russia serves to illustrate this scenario. On the eve of the war, Russian leaders believed that their military could almost certainly defeat Japan.[43] In this conviction they differed little from the view of most European observers. By contrast, at the imperial council of 4 February that decided for war, the Japanese chief of staff estimated a fifty-fifty chance of prevailing, if their attack began immediately.[44] Thus Japanese and Russian leaders disagreed about relative power—their estimates of the likelihood of victory summed to greater than 1.

Moreover, historical accounts implicate this disagreement as a major cause of the war: Russia's refusal to compromise despite repeated offers by the Japanese was motivated in large measure by their belief that Japan would not dare attack them. The Japanese Cabinet finally decided for war after the Tsar and his advisers failed to make any real compromises over Korea or Manchuria in a series of proposals exchanged in 1903. The Tsar and his top advisers were hardly eager to fight, not because they expected to lose but because they saw an Asian war as a costly diversion of resources to the wrong theater.[45] Nonetheless, they refused to make concessions from what they viewed as a position of great military strength. They believed that Japan would have to settle for less, given its relative military weakness.[46]

The disagreement arose in substantial part from Japanese private information about their military capabilities and how they compared with Russia's. A far superior intelligence service had provided the Japanese military with a clear picture of Russian strengths and weaknesses in Northeast Asia and enabled them to develop an effective offensive strategy. According to John Albert White, due to this intelligence "the Japanese government apparently faced the war with a far more accurate conception of their task than their enemy had."[47] In addition, compared with the Russians or indeed with any European power, Japanese leaders had much better knowledge of the fighting ability of the relatively untested

Japanese army and of the effect of the reforms, training, and capital development of the previous decade.[48]

If by communicating this private information the Japanese could have led the Russians to see that their chances of victory were smaller than expected, they might have done so. Almost all historians who have carefully examined the case agree that the Japanese government was not bent on war for its own sake—they were willing to compromise if the Russians would as well.[49] However, it was unthinkable for the Japanese to reveal such information or convince the Russians even if they did. In the first place, the Japanese could not simply make announcements about the quality of their forces, since the Russians would have had no reason to believe them. Second, explaining how they planned to win a war might seriously compromise any such attempt by changing the likelihood that they would win; there is a trade-off between revealing information about resolve or capabilities to influence bargaining and reducing the advantages of a first strike.

In sum, the combination of private information about relative power or will and the strategic incentive to misrepresent these afford a tenable rationalist explanation for war. While states always have incentives to locate a peaceful bargain cheaper than war, they also always have incentives to do well in the bargaining. Given the fact of private information about capabilities or resolve, these incentives mean that states cannot always use quiet diplomatic conversations to discover mutually preferable settlements. It may be that the only way to surmount this barrier to communication is to take actions that produce a real risk of inefficient war.

This general mechanism operates in at least two other empirically important ways to produce conflict in specific circumstances. First, private information about the costs of fighting or the value leaders place on international interests can give them an incentive to cultivate a reputation for having lower costs or more far-flung vital interests than they actually do. If cutting a deal in one dispute would lead other states to conclude the leader's costs for using force are high, then the leader might choose a costly war rather than suffer the depredations that might follow from making concessions. The U.S. interventions in Korea and Vietnam are sometimes explained in these terms, and states surely have worried about such inferences drawn by other states for a long time.[50] The same logic operates when a small state or group (for example, Finland or the Chechens) chooses to fight a losing war against a larger one (for example, the Soviet Union or Russia) in order to develop a reputation for being hard to subjugate. In both cases, states employ war itself as a costly signal of privately known and otherwise unverifiable information about willingness to fight.

Second, since incentives to misrepresent military strength can undermine diplomatic signaling, states may be forced to use war as a credible means to reveal private information about their military capabilities. Thus, a rising state may seek out armed conflict in order to demonstrate that it is more powerful than others realize, while a state in apparent decline may fight in hope of revealing that its capabilities remain better than most believe. In both instances, the inefficient outcome of war derives from the fact that states have private information about their capabilities and a strategic incentive to misrepresent it to other states.

War as a Consequence of Commitment Problems

This section considers a second and quite different rationalist mechanism by which war may occur even though the states in dispute share the same assessment of the bargaining range. Even if private information and incentives to misrepresent it do not tempt states into a risky process of discovery or foster costly investments in reputation, states may be unable to settle on an efficient bargained outcome when for structural reasons they cannot trust each other to uphold the deal.

In this class of explanations, the structural condition of anarchy reemerges as a major factor, although for nonstandard reasons. In the conventional argument, anarchy matters because no hegemonic power exists to threaten states with "jail" if they use force. Without this threat, states become suspicious and worried about other states' intentions; they engage in self-help by building weapons; and somehow uncertainty-plus-weapons leads them ultimately to attack each other (the security dilemma or spiral model). Below, I show that anarchy does indeed matter but for more specific reasons and in more specific contexts. Anarchy matters when an unfortunate combination of state preferences and opportunities for action imply that one or both sides in a dispute have incentives to renege on peaceful bargains which, if they were enforceable, would be mutually preferred to war. I will consider three such unfortunate situations that can claim some empirical plausibility.

It should be stressed that in standard security dilemma and spiral model arguments the suspicions and lack of trust engendered by anarchy are understood to originate either from states' inability to observe each other's motivations (that is, from private information about greed or desire for conquest) or from the knowledge that motivations can change.[51] By contrast, in the arguments given below, states have no private information and motivations never change; thus states understand each other's motivations perfectly. This is not to argue that private information about the value a leadership places on expansion is unimportant in international politics—it surely is. Indeed, private information about motivation and various incentives to misrepresent it might exacerbate any of the three specific commitment problems discussed below. However, when they do so this is a matter of an interaction between informational and commitment problems rather than of anarchy per se. Our first task should be to isolate and specify the mechanisms by which anarchy itself might cause war.

Preemptive War and Offensive Advantages

Consider the problem faced by two gunslingers with the following preferences. Each would most prefer to kill the other by stealth, facing no risk of retaliation, but each prefers that both live in peace to a gunfight in which each risks death. There is a bargain here that both sides prefer to "war"—namely, that each leaves the other alone—but without the enforcement capabilities of a third party, such as an effective sheriff, they may not be able to attain it. Given their preferences, neither person can credibly commit not to defect from the bargain by trying to shoot the other in the back. Note that no matter how far the shadow of the future extends, iteration (or repeat play) will not make cooperation possible in strategic situations of this sort. Because being the "sucker" here may mean being permanently eliminated, strategies of conditional cooperation such as tit-for-tat are infeasible.[52] Thus, if we can find a plausible analogy in international relations, this example might afford a coherent rationalist explanation for war.

Preemptive war scenarios provide the analogy. If geography or military technology happened to create large first-strike or offensive advantages, then states might face the same problem as the gunslingers. To demonstrate this theoretically, I consider how offensive advantages affect the bargaining range between two states engaged in a dispute.

There are at least three ways of interpreting offensive advantages in a formal context. First, an offensive advantage might mean that a state's odds of winning are better if it attacks rather than defends. Second, an offensive advantage might mean that the costs of fighting are lower for an attacking state than for a defending state. It can be shown that no commitment problem operates in this second case, although lowering the costs of war for attackers does narrow the de facto bargaining range. Third, offensive advantages might mean that military technology and doctrine increase the variance of battlefield outcomes. That is, technology and doctrine might make total victory or total defeat more likely, while rendering stalemate and small territorial changes less likely. In this case, offensive advantages can actually reduce the expected utility of war for both sides, thus increasing the bargaining range and perhaps making war less rather than more likely. Intuitively, if states care most of all about security (understood as survival), then offensive advantages make war less safe by increasing the risk of total defeat.[53]

A commitment problem of the sort faced by the gunslingers arises only under the first interpretation, in which "offensive advantage" refers to an increase in a state's military prospects if it attacks rather than defends. To demonstrate this, let p_f be the probability that state A wins a war if A attacks; p_s the probability that A wins if A strikes second or defends; and p the chance that A wins if both states mobilize and attack at the same time. Thus, an offensive advantage exists when $p_f > p > p_s$.

Since states can always choose to attack if they wish, a peaceful resolution of the issues is feasible only if neither side has an incentive to defect unilaterally by attacking. * * * [It is easy to show that there will exist stable outcomes both sides prefer to conflict only if there is a de facto bargaining range represented by issue resolutions between $p_f - c_A$ and $p_s + c_B$. One end of the range is determined by A's value for attacking with a first strike advantage, and the other by B's.]

Notice that as p_f increases above p, and p_s decreases below it, this interval shrinks and may even disappear. Thus, first-strike advantages narrow the de facto bargaining range, while second-strike (or defensive) advantages increase it. The reason is that when first-strike advantages are large, both states must be given more from the peacetime bargain in order to allay the greater temptation of unilateral attack.

In the extreme case, [if the first-strike advantage is sufficiently large relative to the total costs of fighting,] no self-enforcing peaceful outcomes exist [$p_f - c_A$ is greater than $p_s + c_B$]. This does not mean that no bargains exist that both sides would prefer to war. Since by definition both states cannot enjoy the advantage of going first, agreements that both sides prefer to fighting are always available in principle. The problem is that under anarchy, large enough first-strike incentives (relative to cost-benefit ratios) can make all of these agreements unenforceable and incredible as bargains.

Does this prisoners' dilemma logic provide an empirically plausible explanation for war? Though I lack the space to develop the point, I would argue that first-strike and offensive advantages probably are an important factor making war more likely in a few cases, but not because they make mobilization and attack a dominant strategy, as in the extreme case above. In the pure preemptive war scenario leaders reason as follows: "The first-strike advantage is so great that regardless of how we resolve any diplomatic issues between us, one side will always want to attack the other in an effort to gain the (huge) advantage of going first." But even in July 1914, a case in which European leaders apparently held extreme views about the advantage of striking first, we do not find leaders thinking in these terms.[54] It would be rather surprising if they did, since they had all lived at peace but with the same military technology prior to July 1914. Moreover, in the crisis itself military first-strike advantages did not become a concern until quite late, and right to the end competed with significant political (and so strategic) disadvantages to striking first.[55]

Rather than completely eliminating enforceable bargains and so causing war, it seems more plausible that first-strike and offensive advantages exacerbate other causes of war by narrowing the bargaining range. If for whatever reason the issues in dispute are hard to divide up, then war will be more likely the smaller the set of enforceable agreements both sides prefer to a fight. Alternatively, the problems posed by private information and incentives to misrepresent may be more intractable when the de facto bargaining range is small.[56] For example, in 1914 large perceived first-strike advantages meant that relatively few costly signals of intent were sufficient to commit both sides to war (chiefly, for Germany/Austria and Russia). Had leaders thought defense had the advantage, the set of enforceable agreements both would have preferred would have been larger, and this may have made costly signaling less likely to have destroyed the bargaining range.

I should note that scholars have sometimes portrayed the preemptive war problem differently, assuming that neither state would want to attack unilaterally but that each would want to attack if the other was expected to also. This is a coordination problem known as "stag hunt" that would seem easily resolved by communication. At any rate, it seems farfetched to think that small numbers of states (typically dyads) would have trouble reaching the efficient solution here, if coordination were really the only problem.[57]

Preventive War as a Commitment Problem

Empirically, preventive motivations seem more prevalent and important than preemptive concerns. In his diplomatic history of Europe from 1848 to 1918, A.J.P. Taylor argued that "every war between the Great Powers [in this period] started as a preventive war, not a war of conquest."[58] In this subsection I argue that within a rationalist framework, preventive war is properly understood as arising from a commitment problem occasioned by anarchy and briefly discuss some empirical implications of this view.[59]

The theoretical framework used above is readily adapted for an analysis of the preventive war problem. Whatever their details, preventive war arguments are necessarily dynamic—they picture state leaders who think about what may happen in the future. So, we must modify the bargaining model to make it dynamic as well. Suppose state A will have the opportunity to choose the resolution of the issues in each of an infinite number of successive periods. For periods $t = 1, 2, \ldots$, state A can attempt a fait accompli to revise the status quo, choosing a demand x_t. On seeing the demand x_t, state B can either acquiesce or go to war, which state A is assumed to win with probability p_t. * * *

This model extends the one-period bargaining game considered above to an infinite-horizon case in which military power can vary over time. An important observation about the multiperiod model is that war remains a strictly inefficient outcome. It is straightforward to show that there will always exist peaceful settlements in X such that both states would prefer to see one of these settlements implemented in every period from t forward rather than go to war.[60]

The strategic dilemma is that without some third party capable of guaranteeing agreements, state A may not be able to commit itself to future foreign policy behavior that makes B prefer not to attack at some point. Consider the simple case in which A's chance of winning a war begins at p_1 and then will increase to $p_2 > p_1$ in the next period, where it will remain for all subsequent periods. Under anarchy, state A cannot commit itself not to exploit the greater bargaining leverage it will have starting in the second period. * * * [At that time, A will choose a resolution of the issues that makes state B just willing to acquiesce, given the new distribution of military power. This means that in the first period, when state B is still relatively strong, B is choosing between going to war and acquiescing to A's first period demand, which gives it some value today plus the issue equivalent of fighting a war at a disadvantage in the next period. The most state A could possibly do for B in the first period would be to cede B's most preferred outcome ($x_1 = 0$). However, if the change in relative military power is large enough, this concession can still be too small to make accepting it worthwhile for state B. B may prefer to "lock in" what it gets from war when it is relatively strong, to one period of concessions followed by a significantly worse deal when it is militarily weaker. In sum,] if B's expected decline in military power is too large relative to B's costs for war, then state A's inability to commit to restrain its foreign policy demands after it gains power makes preventive attack rational for state B.[61] Note also that A's commitment problem meshes with a parallel problem facing B. If B could commit to fight in the second period rather than accept the rising state's increased demands, then B's bargaining power would not fall in the second period, so that preventive war would be unnecessary in the first.

Several points about this rationalist analysis of preventive war are worth stressing. First, preventive war occurs here despite (and in fact partially because of) the states' agreement about relative power. Preventive war is thus another area where Blainey's argument misleads. Second, contrary to the standard formulation, the declining state attacks not because it fears being attacked in the future but because it fears the peace it will have to accept after the rival has grown stronger. To illustrate, even if Iraq had moved from Kuwait to the conquest of Saudi Arabia, invasion of the United States would not have followed. Instead, the war for Kuwait aimed to prevent the development of an oil hegemon that would have had considerable bargaining leverage due to U.S. reliance on oil.[62]

Third, while preventive war arises here from states' inability to trust each other to keep to a bargain, the lack of trust is not due to states' uncertainty about present or future motivations, as in typical security-dilemma and spiral-model accounts. In my argument, states understand each other's motivations perfectly well—there is no private information—and they further understand that each would like to avoid the

costs of war—they are not ineluctably greedy. Lack of trust arises here from the situation, a structure of preferences and opportunities, that gives one party an incentive to renege. For example, regardless of expectations about Saddam Hussein's future motivation or intentions, one could predict with some confidence that decreased competition among sellers of oil would have led to higher prices. My claim is not that uncertainty about intentions is unimportant in such situations—it surely is—but that commitment and informational problems are distinct mechanisms and that a rationalist preventive war argument turns crucially on a commitment problem.

Finally, the commitment problem behind preventive war may be undermined if the determinants of military power can reliably be transferred between states. In the model, the rising state can actually have an incentive to transfer away or otherwise limit the sources of its new strength, since by doing so it may avoid being attacked. While such transfers might seem implausible from a realist perspective, the practice of "compensation" in classical balance-of-power politics may be understood in exactly these terms: states that gained territory by war or other means were expected to (and sometimes did) allow compensating gains in order to reduce the incentive for preventive war against them.[63]

Preventive motivations figured in the origins of World War I and are useful to illustrate these points. One of the reasons that German leaders were willing to run serious risks of global conflict in 1914 was that they feared the consequences of further growth of Russian military power, which appeared to them to be on a dangerous upward trajectory.[64] Even if the increase in Russian power had not led Russia to attack Austria and Germany at some point in the future—war still being a costly option—greater Russian power would have allowed St. Petersburg to pursue a more aggressive foreign policy in the Balkans and the Near East, where Austria and Russia had conflicting interests. Austrian and German leaders greatly feared the consequences of such a (pro-Slav) Russian foreign policy for the domestic stability of the Austro-Hungarian Empire, thus giving them incentives for a preventive attack on Russia.[65]

By the argument made above, the states should in principle have had incentives to cut a multiperiod deal both sides would have preferred to preventive war. For example, fearing preventive attack by Austria and Germany, Russian leaders might have wished to have committed themselves not to push so hard in the Balkans as to endanger the Dual Monarchy. But such a deal would be so obviously unenforceable as to not be worth proposing. Leaving aside the serious monitoring difficulties, once Russia had become stronger militarily, Austria would have no choice but to acquiesce to a somewhat more aggressive Russian policy in the Balkans. And so Russia would be drawn to pursue it, regardless of its overall motivation or desire for conquest of Austria-Hungary.

While German leaders in July 1914 were willing to accept a very serious risk that Russia might go to war in support of Serbia, they seem to have hoped at the start of the crisis that Russia would accept the Austrian demarche.[66] Thus, it is hard to argue that the preventive logic itself produced the war. Rather, as is probably true for other cases in which these concerns appear, the preventive logic may have made war more likely in combination with other causes, such as private information, by making Berlin much more willing to risk war.[67] How preventive concerns impinge on international bargaining with private information is an important topic for future research.

Commitment, Strategic Territory, and the Problem of Appeasement

The objects over which states bargain frequently are themselves sources of military power. Territory is the most important example, since it may

provide economic resources that can be used for the military or be strategically located, meaning that its control greatly increases a state's chances for successful attack or defense. Territory is probably also the main issue over which states fight wars.[68]

In international bargaining on issues with this property, a commitment problem can operate that makes mutually preferable negotiated solutions unattainable. The problem is similar to that underlying preventive war. Here, both sides might prefer some package of territorial concessions to a fight, but if the territory in question is strategically vital or economically important, its transfer could radically increase one side's future bargaining leverage (think of the Golan Heights). In principle, one state might prefer war to the status quo but be unable to commit not to exploit the large increase in bargaining leverage it would gain from limited territorial concessions. Thus the other state might prefer war to limited concessions (appeasement), so it might appear that the issues in dispute were indivisible. But the underlying cause of war in this instance is not indivisibility per se but rather the inability of states to make credible commitments under anarchy.[69]

As an example, the 1939 Winter War between Finland and the Soviet Union followed on the refusal of the Finnish government to cede some tiny islands in the Gulf of Finland that Stalin seems to have viewed as necessary for the defense of Leningrad in the event of a European war. One of the main reasons the Finns were so reluctant to grant these concessions was that they believed they could not trust Stalin not to use these advantages to pressure Finland for more in the future. So it is possible that Stalin's inability to commit himself not to attempt to carry out in Finland the program he had just applied in the Baltic states may have led or contributed to a costly war both sides clearly wished to avoid.[70]

Conclusion

The article has developed two major claims. First, under broad conditions the fact that fighting is costly and risky implies that there should exist negotiated agreements that rationally led states in dispute would prefer to war. This claim runs directly counter to the conventional view that rational states can and often do face a situation of deadlock, in which war occurs because no mutually preferable bargain exists.

Second, essentially two mechanisms, or causal logics, explain why rationally led states are sometimes unable to locate or agree on such a bargain: (1) the combination of private information about resolve or capability and incentives to misrepresent these, and (2) states' inability, in specific circumstances, to commit to uphold a deal. Historical examples were intended to suggest that both mechanisms can claim empirical relevance.

I conclude by anticipating two criticisms. First, I am not saying that explanations for war based on irrationality or "pathological" domestic politics are less empirically relevant. Doubtless they are important, but we cannot say how so or in what measure if we have not clearly specified the causal mechanisms making for war in the "ideal" case of rational unitary states. In fact, a better understanding of what the assumption of rationality really implies for explaining war may actually raise our estimate of the importance of particular irrational and second-image factors.

For example, once the distinction is made clear, bounded rationality may appear a more important cause of disagreements about relative power than private information about military capabilities. If private information about capabilities was often a major factor influencing the odds of victory, then we would expect rational leaders to update their war estimates during international crises; a tough bargaining stand by an adversary would signal that the adversary was militarily stronger than expected. Diplomatic records should then contain evidence of leaders reasoning as follows: "The fact that the other side is not backing down means that we are probably less likely to win at war than we initially thought." I do not know of a single clear instance of this sort of updating in any international crisis, even though updating about an opponent's resolve, or willingness to fight, is very common.

Second, one might argue that since both anarchy and private information plus incentives to misrepresent are constant features of international politics, neither can explain why states fail to strike a bargain preferable to war in one instance but not another. This argument is correct. But the task of specifying the causal mechanisms that explain the occurrence of war must precede the identification of factors that lead the mechanisms to produce one outcome rather than another in particular settings. That is, specific models in which commitment or information problems operate allow one to analyze how different variables (such as power shifts and cost-benefit ratios in the preventive war model) make for war in some cases rather than others.

This is the sense in which these two general mechanisms provide the foundations for a coherent rationalist or neorealist theory of war. A neorealist explanation for war shows how war could occur given the assumption of rational and unitary ("billiard ball") states, the assumption made throughout this article. Consider any particular factor argued in the literature to be a cause of war under this assumption—for example, a failure to balance power, offensive advantages, multipolarity, or shifts in relative power. My claim is that showing how any such factor could cause war between rational states requires showing how the factor can occasion an unresolvable commitment or information problem in specific empirical circumstances. Short of this, the central puzzle posed by war, its costs, has not been addressed.

NOTES

1. Of course, arguments of the second sort may and often do presume rational behavior by

individual leaders; that is, war may be rational for civilian or military leaders if they will enjoy various benefits of war without suffering costs imposed on the population. While I believe that "second-image" mechanisms of this sort are very important empirically, I do not explore them here. A more accurate label for the subject of the article might be "rational unitary-actor explanations," but this is cumbersome.

2. For the founding work of neorealism, see Kenneth Waltz, *Theory of International Politics* (Reading, Mass.: Addison-Wesley, 1979). For examples of theorizing along these lines, see Robert Jervis, "Cooperation Under the Security Dilemma," *World Politics* 30 (January 1978), pp. 167–214; Stephen Walt, *The Origins of Alliances* (Ithaca, N.Y.: Cornell University Press, 1987); John J. Mearsheimer, "Back to the Future: Instability in Europe After the Cold War," *International Security* 15 (Summer 1990), pp. 5–56; and Charles Glaser, "Realists as Optimists: Cooperation as Self-Help," *International Security* 19 (Winter 1994/95), pp. 50–90.

3. The sense of "mechanism" is similar to that proposed by Elster, although somewhat broader. See Jon Elster, *Political Psychology* (Cambridge: Cambridge University Press, 1993), pp. 1–7; and Jon Elster, *Nuts and Bolts for the Social Sciences* (Cambridge: Cambridge University Press, 1989), chap. 1.

4. For an influential example of this common assumption see Glenn Snyder and Paul Diesing, *Conflict among Nations* (Princeton, N.J.: Princeton University Press, 1977).

5. See, for examples, Geoffry Blainey, *The Causes of War* (New York: Free Press, 1973); Michael Howard, *The Causes of Wars* (Cambridge, Mass.: Harvard University Press, 1983), especially chap. 1; and Arthur Stein, *Why Nations Cooperate: Circumstance and Choice in International Relations* (Ithaca, N.Y.: Cornell University Press, 1990), pp. 60–64. Even the case of World War I is contested; an important historical school argues that this was a wanted war. See Fritz Fisher, *Germany's Aims in the First World War* (New York: Norton, 1967).

6. The quotation is drawn from Kenneth Waltz, *Man, the State, and War: A Theoretical Analysis* (New York: Columbia University Press, 1959), p. 188.

7. For a careful analysis and critique of this standard argument on the difference between the international and domestic arenas, see R. Harrison Wagner, "The Causes of Peace," in Roy A. Licklider, ed., *Stopping the Killing: How Civil Wars End* (New York: New York University Press, 1993), pp. 235–68 and especially pp. 251–57.

8. See John H. Herz, "Idealist Internationalism and the Security Dilemma," *World Politics* 2 (January 1950), pp. 157–80; and Jervis, "Cooperation Under the Security Dilemma." Anarchy is implicated in the security dilemma externality by the following logic: but for anarchy, states could commit to use weapons only for nonthreatening, defensive purposes.

9. Jervis, "Cooperation under the Security Dilemma."

10. For an analysis of the security dilemma that takes into account signaling, see Andrew Kydd, "The Security Dilemma, Game Theory, and World War I," paper presented at the annual meeting of the American Political Science Association, Washington, D.C., 2–5 September 1993.

11. The most developed exception I know of is found in Stephen Van Evera, "Causes of War," Ph.D. diss., University of California, Berkeley, 1984, pp. 61–64.

12. See Bruce Bueno de Mesquita, *The War Trap* (New Haven, Conn.: Yale University Press, 1981), and "The War Trap Revisited: A Revised Expected Utility Model," *American Political Science Review* 79 (March 1985), pp. 157–76. For a generalization that introduces the idea of a bargaining range, see James D. Morrow, "A Continuous-Outcome Expected Utility Theory of War," *Journal of Conflict Resolution* 29 (September 1985), pp. 473–502.

Informal versions of the expected utility argument are everywhere. For example, Waltz's statement that "A state will use force to attain its goals if, after assessing the prospects for success, it values those goals more than it values the pleasures of peace" appears in different ways in a great many works on war. See Waltz, *Man, the State, and War,* p. 60.

13. Let the states' utilities for the outcome $x \in X$ be $u_A(x)$ and $u_B(1-x)$, and assume for now that $u_A(\cdot)$ and $u_B(\cdot)$ are continuous, increasing, and weakly concave (that is, risk-neutral or risk-averse). Without losing any generality, we can set $u_i(1) = 1$ and $u_i(0) = 0$ for both states ($i = A, B$).

14. See, for classic examples, Thucydides, *The Peloponnesian War* (New York: Modern Library, 1951), pp. 45 and 48; and Carl von Clausewitz, *On War* (Princeton, N.J.: Princeton University Press, 1984), p. 85.

15. Bueno de Mesquita, *The War Trap.*

16. Note that in this formulation the terms c_A and c_B capture not only the states' values for the costs of war but also the value they place on winning or losing on the issues at stake. That is, c_A reflects state A's costs for war relative to any possible benefits. For example, if the two states see little to gain from winning a war against each other, then c_A and c_B would be large even if neither side expected to suffer much damage in a war.

17. On the theory of bargaining with outside options, see Martin J. Osborne and Ariel Rubinstein, *Bargaining and Markets* (New York: Academic Press, 1990), chap. 3; Motty Perry, "An Example of Price Formation in Bilateral Situations," *Econometrica* 50 (March 1986), pp. 313–21; and Robert Powell, "Bargaining in the Shadow of Power" (University of California, Berkeley, 1993, mimeographed). See also the analyses in R. Harrison Wagner, "Peace, War, and the Balance of Power," *American Political Science Review* 88 (September 1994), pp. 593–607; and Wagner, "The Causes of Peace."

18. See, for example, Evan Luard, *War in International Society* (New Haven, Conn.: Yale University Press, 1992), p. 191. Schroeder notes that "patronage, bribes, and corruption" were "a major element" of eighteenth-century international relations. See Paul Schroeder, *The Transformation of European Politics, 1763–1848* (Oxford: Oxford University Press, 1994), p. 579.

19. On Cuba, see Ernest May, *Imperial Democracy* (New York: Harper and Row, 1961), pp. 149–50. On the Louisiana Purchase, military threats raised in the U.S. Senate apparently made Napoleon more eager to negotiate the sale. See E. Wilson Lyon, *Louisiana in French Diplomacy* (Norman: University of Oklahoma Press, 1934), pp. 179 and 214ff.

20. Diego Gambetta, *The Sicilian Mafia: The Business of Private Protection* (Cambridge, Mass.: Harvard University Press, 1993), p. 214.

21. In one of the only articles on this problem, Morrow proposes a private information explanation for states' failures to link issues in many disputes. See James D. Morrow, "Signaling Difficulties with Linkage in Crisis Bargaining," *International Studies Quarterly* 36 (June 1992), pp. 153–72.

22. See Jack Levy, "The Causes of War: A Review of Theories and Evidence," in Philip E. Tetlock et al., eds., *Behavior, Society, and Nuclear War,* vol. 1 (Oxford: Oxford University Press, 1989), pp. 209–333. Recent work using limited-information game theory to analyze crisis bargaining places the strategic consequences of private information at the center of the analysis. See, for examples, Bruce Bueno de Mesquita and David Lalman, *War and Reason* (New Haven, Conn.: Yale University Press, 1992); James D. Fearon, "Domestic Political Audiences and the Escalation of International Disputes," *American Political Science Review* 88 (September 1994), pp. 577–92; James D. Morrow, "Capabilities, Uncertainty, and Resolve: A Limited Information Model of Crisis Bargaining," *American Journal of Politi-*

cal Science 33 (November 1989), pp. 941–72; Barry Nalebuff, "Brinksmanship and Nuclear Deterrence: The Neutrality of Escalation," *Conflict Management and Peace Science* 9 (Spring 1986), pp. 19–30; and Robert Powell, *Nuclear Deterrence Theory: The Problem of Credibility* (Cambridge: Cambridge University Press, 1990).

23. Blainey, *The Causes of War*, p. 246.

24. Ibid., p. 54. Blainey also blames patriotic and nationalistic fervor, leaders' (irrational) tendency to surround themselves with yes-men, and crowd psychology.

25. See Ralph K. White, *Nobody Wanted War: Misperception in Vietnam and Other Wars* (New York: Doubleday/Anchor), chap. 7; Blainey, *The Causes of War*, p. 54; and Richard Ned Lebow, *Between Peace and War: The Nature of International Crises* (Baltimore, Md.: Johns Hopkins University Press, 1981), p. 247.

26. John C. Harsanyi, "Games with Incomplete Information Played by 'Bayesian' Players, Part III," *Management Science* 14 (March 1968), pp. 486–502.

27. Aumann observed an interesting implication of this doctrine: genuinely rational agents cannot "agree to disagree," in the sense that it cannot be commonly known that they are rational and that they hold different estimates of the likelihood of some uncertain event. See Robert Aumann, "Agreeing to Disagree," *The Annals of Statistics* 4 (November 1976), pp. 1236–39. Emerson Niou, Peter Ordeshook, and Gregory Rose note that this implies that rational states cannot agree to disagree about the probability that one or the other would win in a war in *The Balance of Power: Stability in the International System* (Cambridge: Cambridge University Press, 1989), p. 59.

28. On bounded rationality, see Herbert A. Simon, "A Behavioral Model of Rational Choice," *Quarterly Journal of Economics* 69 (February 1955), pp. 99–118.

29. This analysis runs exactly parallel to work in law and economics on pretrial bargaining in legal disputes. Early studies explained costly litigation as resulting from divergent expectations about the likely trial outcome, while in more recent work such expectations derive from private information about the strength of one's case. For a review and references, see Robert D. Cooter and Daniel L. Rubinfeld, "Economic Analysis of Legal Disputes and Their Resolution," *Journal of Economic Literature* 27 (September 1989), pp. 1067–97.

30. Blainey, *The Causes of War*.

31. This take-it-or-leave-it model of international bargaining is proposed and analyzed under conditions of both complete and incomplete information in James D. Fearon, "Threats to Use Force: The Role of Costly Signals in International Crises," Ph.D. diss., University of California, Berkeley, 1992, chap. 1. Similar results for more elaborate bargaining structures are given in my own work in progress. See James D. Fearon, "Game-Theoretic Models of International Bargaining: An Overview," University of Chicago, 1995. Powell has analyzed an alternative model in which both sides must agree if the status quo is to be revised. See Powell, "Bargaining in the Shadow of Power."

32. For examples and discussion on this point, see Fearon, "Threats to Use Force," chap. 3.

33. * * * Cheap talk announcements can affect outcomes in some bargaining contexts. For an example from economics, see Joseph Farrell and Robert Gibbons, "Cheap Talk Can Matter in Bargaining," *Journal of Economic Theory* 48 (June 1989), pp. 221–37. These authors show how cheap talk might credibly signal a willingness to negotiate seriously that then affects subsequent terms of trade. For an example from international relations, see James D. Morrow, "Modeling the Forms of International Cooperation: Distribution Versus Information," *International Organization* 48 (Summer 1994), pp. 387–423.

34. The conclusion is likewise altered if the possibility of repeated interactions in sufficiently

similar contexts is great enough that reputation building can be supported.

35. On signaling costs in crises and audience costs in particular, see Fearon, "Threats to Use Force," and "Domestic Political Audiences and the Escalation of International Disputes." For an excellent analysis of international signaling in general, see Robert Jervis, *The Logic of Images in International Relations* (Princeton, N.J.: Princeton University Press, 1970).

36. For developed models that make this point, see James Fearon, "Deterrence and the Spiral Model: The Role of Costly Signals in Crisis Bargaining," paper presented at the annual meeting of the American Political Science Association, 30 August–2 September 1990, San Francisco, Calif.; Fearon, "Domestic Political Audiences and the Escalation of International Disputes"; Morrow, "Capabilities, Uncertainty, and Resolve"; Nalebuff, "Brinkmanship and Nuclear Deterrence"; and Powell, *Nuclear Deterrence Theory.*

37. Luigi Albertini, *The Origins of the War of 1914*, vol. 2 (London: Oxford University Press, 1953), pp. 183–87.

38. Ibid., p. 187.

39. Ibid., p. 158. For the full text of the cable, see Karl Kautsky, comp., *German Documents Relating to the Outbreak of the World War* (New York: Oxford University Press, 1924), doc. no. 71, p. 130.

40. Konrad Jarausch, "The Illusion of Limited War: Chancellor Bethmann Hollweg's Calculated Risk," *Central European History* 2 (March 1969), pp. 48–76. The quotation is drawn from p. 65.

41. See L. C. F. Turner, *Origins of the First World War* (New York: Norton, 1970), p. 101; and Jarausch, "The Illusion of Limited War," p. 63. Trachtenberg writes that "one of Bethmann's basic goals was for Germany to avoid coming across as the aggressor." See Marc Trachtenberg, *History and Strategy* (Princeton, N.J.: Princeton University Press, 1991), p. 90.

42. Albertini concludes that "on the evening of the 27th all the Chancellor sought to do was to throw dust in the eyes of Grey and lead him to believe that Berlin was seriously trying to avert a conflict, that if war broke out it would be Russia's fault and that England could therefore remain neutral." See Albertini, *The Origins of the War of 1914*, vol. 1, pp. 444–45. See also Turner, *Origins of the First World War*, p. 99.

43. See J. A. White, *The Diplomacy of the Russo–Japanese War* (Princeton, N.J.: Princeton University Press, 1964), pp. 142–43; and Ian Nish, *The Origins of the Russo–Japanese War* (London: Longman, 1985), pp. 241–42.

44. J. N. Westwood, *Russia against Japan, 1904–5: A New Look at the Russo–Japanese War* (Albany: State University of New York Press, 1986), p. 22. Estimates varied within the Japanese leadership, but with the exception of junior-level officers, few seem to have been highly confident of victory. For example, as the decision for war was taken the Japanese navy requested a two-week delay to allow it to even the odds at sea. See Nish, *The Origins of the Russo–Japanese War*, pp. 197–200 and 206–7.

45. See, for example, David Walder, *The Short Victorious War: The Russo–Japanese Conflict, 1904–5* (London: Hutchinson, 1973), pp. 53–56; and Nish, *The Origins of the Russo–Japanese War*, p. 253.

46. See White, *The Diplomacy of the Russo–Japanese War*, chaps. 6–8; Nish, *The Origins of the Russo–Japanese War*, p. 241; and Lebow, *Between Peace and War*, pp. 244–46.

47. White, *The Diplomacy of the Russo–Japanese War*, p. 139. Nish writes that "many Russians certainly took a view of [the Japanese military] which was derisory in comparison with themselves. It may be that this derived from a deliberate policy of secrecy and concealment which the Japanese army applied because of the historic coolness between the two countries." See Nish, *The Origins of the Russo–Japanese War*, p. 241.

48. The British were the major exception, who as recent allies of Japan had better knowledge of its capabilities and level of organization. See Nish, *The Origins of the Russo–Japanese War*, p. 241.

49. See, for example, William Langer, "The Origins of the Russo–Japanese War," in Carl Schorske and Elizabeth Schorske, eds., *Explorations in Crisis* (Cambridge, Mass.: Harvard University Press, 1969), p. 44.

50. For some examples, see Fearon, "Threats to Use Force," chap. 3. For a formal version of reputational dynamics due to private information, see Barry Nalebuff, "Rational Deterrence in an Imperfect World," *World Politics* 43 (April 1991), pp. 313–35.

51. See, for examples, Robert Jervis, *Perception and Misperception in International Politics* (Princeton, N.J.: Princeton University Press, 1976), pp. 62–67; Barry Posen, *The Sources of Military Doctrine* (Ithaca, N.Y.: Cornell University Press, 1984), pp. 16–17; and Charles Glaser, "The Political Consequences of Military Strategy," *World Politics* 44 (July 1992), p. 506.

52. For dynamic game models that demonstrate this, see Robert Powell, "Absolute and Relative Gains in International Relations Theory," *American Political Science Review* 85 (December 1991), pp. 1303–20; and James D. Fearon, "Cooperation and Bargaining Under Anarchy," (University of Chicago, 1994, mimeographed). On tit-for-tat and the impact of the shadow of the future, see Robert Axelrod, *The Evolution of Cooperation* (New York: Basic Books, 1984); and Kenneth Oye, ed., *Cooperation under Anarchy* (Princeton, N.J.: Princeton University Press, 1986).

53. This argument about military variance runs counter to the usual hypothesis that offensive advantages foster war. For a discussion and an empirical assessment, see James D. Fearon, "Offensive Advantages and War since 1648," paper presented at the annual meeting of the International Studies Association, 21–25 February 1995. On the offense–defense balance and war, see Jervis, "Cooperation under the Security Dilemma"; and Van Evera, "Causes of War," chap. 3.

54. For the argument about leaders' views on first-strike advantages in 1914, see Stephen Van Evera, "The Cult of the Offensive and the Origins of the First World War," *International Security* 9 (Summer 1984), pp. 58–107.

55. See, for example, Trachtenberg, *History and Strategy*, p. 90.

56. This is suggested by results in Roger Myerson and Mark Satterthwaite, "Efficient Mechanisms for Bilateral Trading," *Journal of Economic Theory* 29 (April 1983), pp. 265–81.

57. Schelling suggested that efficient coordination in stag hunt-like preemption problems might be prevented by a rational dynamic of "reciprocal fear of surprise attack." See Thomas Schelling, *The Strategy of Conflict* (Cambridge, Mass.: Harvard University Press, 1960), chap. 9. Powell has argued that no such dynamic exists between rational adversaries. See Robert Powell, "Crisis Stability in the Nuclear Age," *American Political Science Review* 83 (March 1989), pp. 61–76.

58. Taylor, *The Struggle for Mastery in Europe, 1848–1918* (London: Oxford University Press, 1954), p. 166. Carr held a similar view: "The most serious wars are fought in order to make one's own country militarily stronger or, more often, to prevent another country from becoming militarily stronger." See E. H. Carr, *The Twenty Years' Crisis, 1919–1939* (New York: Harper and Row, 1964), pp. 111–12.

59. To my knowledge, Van Evera is the only scholar whose treatment of preventive war analyzes at some length how issues of credible commitment intervene. The issue is raised by both Snyder and Levy. See Van Evera, "Causes of War," pp. 62–64; Jack Snyder, "Perceptions of the Security Dilemma in 1914," in Robert Jervis, Richard Ned Lebow, and Janice Gross Stein, eds., *Psychology and Deterrence* (Baltimore, Md.: Johns Hopkins University Press, 1985), p. 160; and Jack Levy, "Declining Power

and the Preventive Motivation for War," *World Politics* 40 (October 1987), p. 96.

60. If the states go to war in period t, expected payoffs from period t on are $(p_t/(1-\delta)) - c_A$ for state A and $((1-p_t)/(1-\delta)) - c_B$ for state B where δ is the time discount factor that both states apply to payoffs to be received in the next period.

61. The formal condition for preventive war is δ $p_2 - p_1 > c_B (1-\delta)^2$.

62. According to Hiro, President Bush's main concern at the first National Security Council meeting following the invasion of Kuwait was the potential increase in Iraq's economic leverage and its likely influence on an "already gloomy" U.S. economy. See Dilip Hiro, *Desert Shield to Desert Storm: The Second Gulf War* (London: Harper-Collins, 1992), p. 108.

63. On compensation, see Edward V. Gulick, *Europe's Classical Balance of Power* (New York: Norton, 1955), pp. 70–72; and Paul W. Schroeder, *The Transformation of European Politics, 1763–1848*, pp. 6–7.

64. See Trachtenberg, *History and Strategy*, pp. 56–59; Albertini, *The Origins of the War of 1914*, vol. 2, pp. 129–30; Turner, *Origins of the First World War*, chap. 4; James Joll, *The Origins of the First World War* (London: Longman, 1984), p. 87; and Van Evera, "The Cult of the Offensive and the Origins of the First World War," pp. 79–85.

65. Samuel Williamson, "The Origins of World War I," *Journal of Interdisciplinary History* (Spring 1988), pp. 795–818 and pp. 797–805 in particular; and D. C. B. Lieven, *Russia and the Origins of the First World War* (New York: St. Martins, 1983), pp. 38–49.

66. Jack S. Levy, "Preferences, Constraints, and Choices in July 1914," *International Security* 15 (Winter 1990/91), pp. 234–36.

67. Levy argues that preventive considerations are rarely themselves sufficient to cause war. See Levy, "Declining Power and the Preventive Motivation for War."

68. See, for example, Kalevi J. Holsti, *Peace and War: Armed Conflicts and International Order 1648–1989* (Cambridge: Cambridge University Press, 1991); and John Vasquez, *The War Puzzle* (Cambridge: Cambridge University Press, 1993).

69. The argument is formalized in work in progress by the author, where it is shown that the conditions under which war will occur are restrictive: the states must be unable to continuously adjust the odds of victory by dividing up and trading the land. In other words, the smallest feasible territorial transfer must produce a discontinuously large change in a state's military chances for war to be possible. See also Wagner, "Peace, War, and the Balance of Power," p. 598, on this commitment problem.

70. See Max Jakobson, *The Diplomacy of the Winter War: An Account of the Russo-Finnish Conflict, 1939–1940* (Cambridge, Mass.: Harvard University Press, 1961), pp. 135–39; and Van Evera, "Causes of War," p. 63. Private information and incentives to misrepresent also caused problems in the bargaining here. See Fearon, "Threats to Use Force," chap. 3.

BARRY R. POSEN

A Nuclear-Armed Iran: A Difficult but Not Impossible Policy Problem

Introduction

Iran's nuclear energy research and development efforts seem on course to achieve an ability to produce highly enriched uranium, the key element of a nuclear weapon. While the capability itself would not be a violation of the Nuclear Non-Proliferation Treaty (NPT) if it were under the full scope safeguards of the International Atomic Energy Agency (IAEA), Iran's deceptive behavior in the development of this technology, as well as the flimsy economic arguments Iran has used to justify this capability, have produced broad international opposition to the program. Many reasonably fear that Iran's actual purpose is to produce nuclear weapons, though there is no definite proof that it has decided to do so. It should be acknowledged that Iran could insist on its right to enrich uranium for power reactors, but refrain from producing nuclear weapons. France, Germany, and the United Kingdom, acting under the auspices of the European Union, and with the support of the United States, have negotiated intensively with Iran since 2003 to discourage further Iranian nuclear enrichment progress; the United Nations Security Council demanded that Iran suspend enrichment and implement other important arms control measures with Resolution 1696 in July 2006. Nevertheless diplomacy has thus far been unsuccessful, and there is no guarantee of future success.

Barry R. Posen, "A Nuclear-Armed Iran: A Difficult but Not Impossible Policy Problem" (New York: Century Foundation, 2006).

If negotiations fail, interested powers such as the United States, the European Union, and Iran's neighbors will face three alternatives: (1) they could move from diplomacy to economic and political coercion; (2) one or more states (most probably the United States or Israel) could launch a preventive attack to erode or destroy the Iranian nuclear program; or (3) these powers could develop strategies of containment and deterrence to coexist with a nuclear-armed Iran—if Iran achieves weapons capability.

The primary purpose of this [discussion] is to address the third option—to spell out a strategy of containment and deterrence and show how it could work. I systematically review the standard objections to this strategy, and explain why they are misplaced. Summarizing the other options, I then argue that a containment and deterrence strategy is more likely to achieve U.S. strategic goals, and do so at lower risks and costs. Finally, I briefly review the proliferation risks that would arise from an Iranian nuclear program, and argue that these risks can be reduced by a deterrence and containment strategy. That said, containment of a nuclear-armed Iran is not the preferred outcome. It would be better if diplomacy were to succeed. Thus, one implication of this analysis is that the United States and its allies should review their current diplomatic approach to Iran and try to devise a more promising political strategy.

For many reasons, it would be better if Iran had neither nuclear weapons, nor the enabling technologies that would permit it to build nuclear weapons:

- Neither nuclear energy nor nuclear weapons are risk-free technologies—new civil and military nuclear powers run the risks of any novice. These include environmental problems, equipment failures, and unsafe or insecure weapons storage.

- It is natural for the nonnuclear states in the region to fear a nuclear Iran. These fears may cause countermeasures that are fraught with danger—including national nuclear energy or weapons programs of their own—which also would run "novice" risks.

- As other states try to acquire nuclear weapons, they may inadvertently threaten each other, setting off new security competitions.

- Iran and any of its neighbors that chose to deploy nuclear weapons may have problems developing a secure basing method, which could tempt them to adopt "hair trigger," day-to-day alert postures, which in turn could raise the risks of accidental war or preemptive war.

- Iran may be emboldened by its possession of nuclear weapons, and could threaten the security of regional or distant powers.

These are all valid concerns, which should make even Iran wary of nuclear weaponry. These risks have prompted the international diplomatic efforts to induce Iran to refrain from the enrichment of uranium (or the reprocessing of plutonium). If these efforts fail, however, concerned states will need to choose from the three remaining alternative policies—nonmilitary coercion mainly through sanctions, preventive military strikes, or containment and deterrence.

Economic Coercion

Though economic coercion should be attempted if the current round of diplomacy fails, this seems unlikely to work unless it is combined with a new set of incentives. First, it is improbable that a particularly strong international sanctions regime can be organized against Iran. Russia, China, and even many European states fear that the initiation of a strong sanctions policy, blessed by the UN, is the first step on the road to war. Sanctions may not change Iranian behavior, but they will have further committed the international community to do something about Iran's program. Some states also will oppose a strong sanctions policy because they profit from their relationships with Iran, due to its energy resources, or expect to profit even more if they help shield Iran from stern measures. Finally, given tight oil markets and high prices, most states would not support a sanctions regime that embargoed the export of Iranian oil.[1]

Second, though Iran is not a wealthy country, it has a relatively well-rounded economy. Aside from its obvious strengths in oil and gas production, Iran is endowed with abundant raw materials and agricultural land, and has a moderately well developed industrial sector. If a sanctions regime did not close off Iran's oil exports, it seems very likely that, with its own endowments and the cash it raises from energy exports, it could weather any plausible sanctions regime.[2]

If the threat of international economic sanctions were accompanied by more focused diplomacy, it might find more support and be more credible. In particular, the United States would need to assure Iran that it has abandoned any hopes to overthrow the current regime. Some have suggested a "grand bargain" in which the United States would offer Iran a security guarantee, an end to sanctions, and the normalization of diplomatic relations, in exchange for major concessions on Iran's nuclear program and an end to support for terrorism.[3] Such a negotiating offer might reduce the concerns of fence sitters such as Russia and China, who fear that the ultimate U.S. objective is regime change, and that the United States intends to leverage ineffective sanctions into an argument for war. The offer of a grand bargain also would put Iran in a difficult position, insofar as declining the offer would be tantamount to admitting its ambitions to produce a nuclear weapon. Moreover, if such a negotiating gambit fails, and the United States turns to a strategy of containment, states in the region will be even more likely to want U.S. assistance, and will more easily be able to portray a strengthened relationship with the United States as an essential counter to Iranian ambitions.

Preventive Military Action

A military attack on Iran's nuclear infrastructure could set back the program, but probably not prevent its recovery, unless the attack were somehow to topple the Iranian government and bring a very different ruling group to power. A military strike carries significant political and military risks. If time bought by setting back the Iranian program through military strikes would be used to good effect—that is, if in the interim other disputes in which Iran is directly or indirectly involved were solved, or if Iran became a liberal-democratic mirror-image of a Western democracy—a preventive attack might look attractive. But there is no reason to believe that this will be the case, and the reverse is more probable. Small or large attacks on Iran will inject energy into Persian nationalism, strengthen the regime's argument that the West is a threat, and leave Iran with a grudge that it may express by deepening or initiating relationships with other states and groups hostile to U.S. purposes. Even regional states with something to fear from a nuclear armed Iran probably would not welcome a preventive attack, simply because the region is already so roiled with violence, much of it attributed to mistaken U.S. policies.

Published assessments of possible attacks on Iran's nuclear infrastructure necessarily involve some speculation. There are nuclear facilities that we have good public information about, but there is likely a great deal of information that is known by Western intelligence agencies that has not leaked into the public domain, and more information in Iran that has not leaked to anyone. Poor intelligence alone is one factor that might hinder the success of these operations. That said, three types of attack, of increasing strength, have been suggested.

First, some have considered very limited attacks on what seem to be critical nodes in a nuclear weapons production chain—especially Iran's plants at Isfahan to produce uranium hexafluoride gas and its facilities at Natanz to process this gas through centrifuges in order to enrich its fissionable material content. One careful analysis suggests that even Israeli fighter-bombers, armed with precision guided weapons Israel is known to possess, could destroy these facilities, presuming that they could refuel from aerial tankers en route, and fly over Jordan and Iraq, or Saudi Arabia, or Turkey.[4] For the United States, destroying these facilities would be a trivial matter. That said, the rest of the Iranian nuclear research and development effort would survive, and it seems likely that failing a change of government, Iran would persevere, and do so in a way that leaves the program less vulnerable. One might believe that a limited attack, however, would produce a relatively modest Iranian military response.

Second, some have suggested that one should try for maximum damage to the entire Iranian nuclear program. A recent analysis suggests that an attack on the Iranian nuclear infrastructure would involve four hundred aim points. The Pentagon's own intelligence would produce an even bigger target set. The United States easily could strike four hundred aim points with precision guided munitions in a single night.[5] Though no one could guarantee that this would be the end of Iran's program, it seems likely that the setback would be far greater than the limited attack on two critical nodes. An Iranian regime might determine that an attack of this size needed to be answered with a forceful response. The regime would look weak regionally, and domestically, if it simply accepted such an attack without a response. The regime reasonably could fear that failure to respond simply would invite further attacks, because the United States would doubt Iran's capability and will. Insofar as the

United States has made plain that it wants to overthrow the Iranian regime, it is unlikely that Iran would view such a large attack as the final move.

Finally, precisely because civilian and military strategists in the Bush administration seem to have accepted the preceding logic, rumors have surfaced of even larger attack plans. To the target list associated with Iran's nuclear infrastructure, would be added an array of conventional targets—including naval bases, airfields, surface-to-air missile sites, surface-to-surface missiles sites, and so on. During the first three nights of the 1991 Gulf War, coalition aircraft struck nearly three thousand targets of this kind.[6] Such attacks would have the purpose of forestalling an Iranian military retaliation against countries as close as Kuwait and as distant as Israel, U.S. forces in the region including those in Iraq, and oil tanker routes. Attacks of this size may also have the purpose of weakening the Iranian regime, though the precise mechanism is unclear, insofar as attacks of this kind have typically strengthened rather than weakened national cohesion and public support of governments, at least in the first instance. Though such an attack may succeed in reducing Iran's retaliatory options, it is implausible that it can reduce them to zero. U.S. forces in Iraq, and their line of communication, which runs through Shia populated areas where Iran has considerable influence, are quite vulnerable to tactical rocket and commando attacks that U.S. air strikes probably cannot prevent.[7] Beyond these significant immediate local costs, the United States attack will become a significant factor in future Iranian politics, discrediting any political faction that seems remotely associated with the United States or its purposes, and providing a potent political/ideological rationale for violence against the United States and its friends for many years to come.

Given that the odds of nonmilitary coercion achieving a success seem low, and the possible costs of a significant, if partly successful, large military operation seem high, it is reasonable to consider the remaining alternative systematically—containment and deterrence of a nuclear-armed Iran.

"Grand Strategy"—Iran and the United States

Before considering the consequences of a nuclear-armed Iran for both the stability of the Middle East and Persian Gulf region and the security interests of the United States, one ought to consider the objectives that an Iranian nuclear force might be meant to serve. This requires some speculation about Iran's own "grand strategy."

Given that Iran is the most populous and economically developed state in the Persian Gulf area, a realist expects it to have ambitions to expand its power and influence in the region. Indeed, it is reasonable to expect that revolutionary Iran, like Iran under the Shah, has pretensions to regional hegemony. This is a general prediction, however, and much depends on what this means to Iran. For example, though many analysts do believe Iran has hegemonic ambitions, they usually couch this in cultural and political terms, not military terms.[8] Iran is active in expanding its influence, especially among Shia Arab populations in Iraq, in the Gulf region, and in Lebanon. Though Iran does have some disputes about islands, water rights, waterways, and coastal zones, according to the Central Intelligence Agency it has no major territorial claims beyond its borders.[9] The United States is no doubt perceived as an obstacle to Iran's regional ambitions. Iran surely would like to reduce the United States presence in the Gulf region, especially since the Bush administration adopted regime change in Iran as an objective.

Iran uses military force with some calculation, to increase the costs to others who might obstruct its goals, rather than to remove obstacles directly. Iran is not shy about using military assistance to nonstate actors as a way to discomfit those it defines as enemies, such as the United States and Israel. Iran sees some interest in maintaining a plausible capability to disrupt the flow of oil from the Persian Gulf, by leveraging its own limited naval capacity and its geographic control of one side of the narrow Strait of Hormuz to create a threat to Western economies. This threat is probably dissuasive—a retaliatory capability, as Iran cannot disrupt the flow of oil out of the Gulf without losing its own ability to export, which is vital to its economy. On the whole, Iran seems deliberate, unafraid to use violence in limited ways, but cautious as it tries to increase its influence and reduce that of others. The main exception to this description is its inflammatory rhetoric about Israel. I hypothesize, however, that much of this rhetoric is instrumental. Iran faces a major obstacle in expanding its influence—it is a Persian state amidst Arabs, and a Shia state amidst Sunnis. These differences are important and cause most Arab regimes to mistrust Iran. Iran may be using the struggle with Israel to submerge these differences in the face of a common enemy, and so legitimate itself among those not affectively inclined to follow its leadership, and weak enough to fear its power.

The United States pursues an ambitious inter-related complex of economic, security, and political objectives in the Persian Gulf. At this moment, political and security goals loom largest. President [George W.] Bush wishes to transform the politics of the region and bring liberal democracy to the regional states, including Iran. The president identifies the absence of democracy in the region as a cause of terrorism, and terrorism as a danger to the United States. Hence political transformation is a security goal. The president also believes that the West cannot wait for transformation to end terror, so he pursues terrorists, and real and suspected state sponsors, with conventional military power—and is waging two wars to do so. Finally, the president believes that the United States must ensure that

hostile powers, which Iran is deemed to be, do not get their hands on weapons of mass destruction, because the president and his allies do not agree with the analysis I advance below.

The United States also has more traditional economic interests in the Gulf, which also are connected to security interests. Much of the world's internationally traded oil comes from the Gulf, so the United States is interested in the free flow of oil from the region. It also wishes to ensure that the oil resources not come under the control of hostile powers that might use it as a coercive lever. And finally, the United States wants to assure that the earnings from oil exports not end up in mischievous hands. These concerns generate a broad security agenda—including the defense of oil routes, the prevention of the conquest of any oil state by another, and watchful oversight of the internal politics of certain countries to ensure that dangerous elements not come to power. U.S. strategists may also believe that U.S. hegemony in the Gulf region gives them some leverage over oil exports, and thus increases U.S. power in other parts of the world. For all these reasons, the United States must maintain a very large military presence, and remain the predominant military power in the Gulf region.

This brief assessment of Iranian and U.S. goals suggests that these two powers are destined to be in an intensely competitive relationship. Each has cards to play in this competition. Iran knows the region well, has an excellent geographic position, and may be able to find support in Shiite Arab populations in neighboring countries. Though economically and militarily weak compared to the United States, it is the strongest power in the Gulf, and has proven itself capable of mobilizing very large ground forces. The United States has a giant economy and the world's most advanced military. The United States also has two potential political advantages. Historically, most states consider large proximate land powers such as Iran to be more dangerous to them than distant sea powers such as the United States. And, Iran—an Islamic country, with potential Shia domestic allies in many [G]ulf states—poses a more credible threat of domestic destabilization than does the U.S. rhetoric of democratization. However powerful and assertive the United States may be, neighboring Iran poses at least as great a threat—and perhaps a greater threat. Hence, despite the present diplomatic ill effects of its mistakes in Iraq, over time the United States is likely to prove the more attractive ally to most states in the region.

Nuclear weapons would make Iran a somewhat more powerful state, which could allow it to pursue certain interests with greater vigor. Fear of Iranian nuclear weapons may cause other states in the region to want their own nuclear weapons, which may in turn cause still others to want nuclear weapons. This would not only be a problem in its own terms, it could further damage the Nuclear Non-Proliferation Treaty and the institutions that sustain it. The ability of the United States and its allies and friends outside and inside the region to contain and deter Iran will affect whether or not significant nuclear proliferation occurs in the region, so I turn first to the likely U.S. and regional responses to a nuclear Iran.

Nuclear-Armed Iran's Four Threats

Reviewing the debate over Iranian nuclear weapons, one can find four different strategic fears of a nuclear-armed Iran: (1) Iran could be emboldened by the possession of a deterrent force and its foreign policy thus would become more adventurous and more violent; (2) Iran could directly threaten others with nuclear attack unless certain demands were met; (3) Iran could give nuclear weapons to nonstate actors; and (4) Iran simply could attack Israel with nuclear weapons—heedless of the inevitable Israeli nuclear retaliation.

A More Adventurous Iran

During the recent fighting between Israel and Hezbollah, President Bush averred that the event would have been much more dangerous had Iran possessed nuclear weapons, but he did not explain why. His implication was that Iran would have been more inclined to involve itself directly in the crisis. The argument would be that Iran's leadership would shelter behind its nuclear deterrent. Great powers would be afraid to attack Iran directly, especially to invade Iran, if they faced the risk of nuclear escalation. So Iran would be free to do anything from meddling in the internal affairs of other countries to invading them with conventional forces, because it could control its costs. This concern is quite reasonable; Iran's leaders might have this idea, but how much different would the situation be than it is today?

Iran already dabbles in subversion and terror. Its leaders do not seem too concerned about invasion, and overthrow, and with good reason. Iran's population is some 70 million, and its land area is roughly three times the size of France. The United States, with the most capable army in the world, is having a difficult time controlling five of Iraq's eighteen provinces, and perhaps 12 million of its 26.8 million people. Iran is surely concerned about other retaliatory responses, including air attacks and even embargos. This is why Iran is somewhat careful to limit its activities and cover its tracks. It might perceive itself to be more secure from retaliatory air attack with a nuclear deterrent, but Israel's nuclear deterrent did not save it from rocket attack in the recent fighting in Lebanon. And from what is known about U.S. Cold War military planning for war against the Soviet Union, and for that matter possible conflict with China today, large nuclear retaliatory forces do not deter the United States from planning large scale conventional air operations against nuclear-armed countries.

Iran's leaders might also perceive that actual conventional attacks on its neighbors would carry less risk than in the past, due to possession of a nuclear deterrent. But counterattacks on its homeland is only one cost of such a gambit. Iran's conventional military offensive capability is not very great, and it would take enormous investments to improve them much. U.S. military spending is currently nearly three times Iran's total GDP, and ninety times Iran's defense effort.[10] Saudi Arabia might be able to defend itself without U.S. help, but we know from the 1991 Iraqi invasion of Kuwait that the kingdom and the United States have cooperated to assure that U.S. reinforcements can reach Saudi Arabia very quickly. Though tiny countries such as Kuwait and the Gulf sheikdoms cannot hope to defend themselves against Iran on their own, reinforcement with high-technology U.S. military forces would assure that Iran's offensive forces could not conquer these countries, and there again preparations have already been made to enable rapid U.S. reinforcement. And, for the foreseeable future, it seems very likely that considerable U.S. forces will be based in the Gulf states and the adjacent waters. Even if Iran's leaders somehow feel safe at home, the forces they dispatch abroad would surely be destroyed, and they likely understand this very well as they have had a box seat at two U.S. conventional wars in the region, and seen much of their own surface fleet sunk by the United States.

Direct Threats from Iran

A second possible use of Iran's nuclear weapons is bald nuclear coercion—especially against nonnuclear neighbors. Nuclear coercion, even against the weak, has certain risks, so it is hard to guess what Iranian interest would be worth such a gambit. In a drive for Gulf hegemony, Iran might demand that those of its neighbors who are close to the United States should weaken these ties—throw out U.S. forces, deny them ports of call and landing rights, destroy prepositioned equipment sites, and cease importing U.S. weapons. Less plausibly, Iran might demand that other oil producing states agree with its own views at any given time about how much oil to pump, or what to charge for it, though this

does not seem worth a nuclear crisis. It is worth noting that, since the end of World War II, no nuclear power has found a way to use nuclear threats to achieve offensive strategic objectives.

These gambits are unlikely to work, and the United States and its allies can act to forestall them. During the Cold War, the United States offered the protection of its nuclear deterrent forces to many allies who did not possess nuclear weapons—every NATO member state except Britain and France. The United States promised that if NATO were to be attacked by the Soviet Union with nuclear weapons, it would respond. Indeed, NATO strategy called for the employment of nuclear weapons in the event of a successful Soviet conventional invasion of NATO states. The United States made this commitment in spite of virtual nuclear parity with the Soviet Union. The United States risked annihilation to secure its interests in Europe.

The United States has, at least since the late 1970s, perceived itself through Democratic and Republican administrations to have a very strong interest in the security of Persian Gulf countries. It is likely that the United States would offer the Gulf Arab countries a nuclear "guarantee." Given that U.S. strategic nuclear forces today are vastly more powerful than anything Iran is likely to be able to deploy, the United States runs less risk in offering such an assurance than it did during the Cold War, and Iran would face very grave risks if it challenged them. Indeed, given U.S. nuclear advantages, Iran would be running the risk of a preemptive U.S. nuclear strike against Iranian forces, in the event that it began to alert these forces to add credibility to its threat. Put bluntly, to be a nuclear-armed state is to be a nuclear target.

Would a state such as Saudi Arabia be willing to count on the U.S. nuclear guarantee? Would it be willing to stand up to an Iranian threat, and risk the possibility that Iran might not be deterred? This is impossible to know. But, Saudi Arabia would know one thing: if it succumbed to Iran's blandishments once, and severed its connections to the United States, it essentially would become a satellite of Iran, and there would be no end to Iran's demands.

Iran and Nonstate Actors

Since the September 11, 2001, attacks on the United States, many have been concerned that nuclear weapons could fall into the hands of terrorists. One way this could occur, it is feared, would be for a state with a weapons program to give or sell one to a terrorist group. Such action seems unlikely in the case of Iran, or any state, because it serves no strategic purpose, invites retaliation, and cannot be controlled. It is perhaps the most self-destructive thing that any nation-state can do.

What strategic purpose, other than pure destruction, could such an action serve? A single nuclear weapon exploded in the United States, or any other state, would be a truly horrible event. But it would not destroy the existence of that state, or destroy its political power. And it would enrage that state, and no doubt cause extraordinary efforts to discover, and punish, the source of the attack.

If the weapon is tracked back to the source, the source country will be blamed. It will be blamed not only by the victim, but by other states, terrified by the implications of the action. The victim surely will try to punish the supplier, and it is likely that this punishment would involve nuclear strikes. Iran or any other nuclear weapons provider might hope to avoid detection, but they could only hope—they could not count on it. The characteristics of the explosion may provide some indications of the origin of the weapon.[11] Moreover, once the explosion occurs, intelligence collected and either ignored or misunderstood prior to the event will be reviewed in light of the event, and may have new meaning. Additionally, there are not all that many potential sources of a nuclear weapon—wherever an explosion occurs one can be sure that intelligence would quickly focus on nuclear problem states such as North Korea, Iran, and Pakistan. Indeed, these states

are so likely to end up in the spotlight for a terrorist use of a nuclear weapon, they probably have an interest in stopping *any* conspiracies of this kind that they discover.

Once a weapon is supplied to the nonstate actor, the supplying state has no guarantee that it will be used for the original agreed purpose. The nonstate actor may have promised to attack Israel, but instead may attack France, or the United States. Alternatively, that actor may simply be a middleman, and sell or trade the device to someone else. The risks cannot be controlled by the supplying state.

Iran and Israel

It is occasionally suggested that Iran in particular, because of its leaders' undisguised hatred for the state of Israel, and quite open assertions that the Middle East would be better off if Israel disappeared, might act to make their fantasies a reality. Iran could use its future nuclear weapons to annihilate the state of Israel, unconcerned about Israeli nuclear retaliation because Iran is a large country that would somehow survive a nuclear exchange with Israel, while Israel is a small country that would be entirely destroyed.

A few fission weapons would horribly damage the state of Israel, and a few fusion weapons would surely destroy it. But neither kind of attack could reliably shield Iran from a devastating response. Israel has had years to work on developing and shielding its nuclear deterrent. It is generally attributed with as many as 200 fission warheads, deliverable by several different methods, including Intermediate Range Ballistic Missile[s].[12] Were Iran to proceed with a weapons program, Israel would surely improve its own capabilities. Though Iran's population is large, and much of it is dispersed, about a quarter of Iranians (over fifteen million people) live in eight cities conservatively within range of Israel's Jericho II missile.[13] Much of Iran's economic capacity is also concentrated in these cities.[14] Nuclear attacks on these cities, plus some oil industry targets, would destroy Iran as a functioning society and prevent its recovery. There is little in the behavior of the leaders of revolutionary Iran that suggests they would see this as a good trade.

A premise of the foregoing fears is that Iran is led by religious fanatics, who might be more interested in the next world than this one. The current president of Iran, Mahmoud Ahmadinejad, has made statements that have caused observers to doubt his risk aversion and his grasp on reality. It is important to note, however, that in Iran's governing structure, the president does not have much influence over security policy. This belongs to the Supreme Leader Ayatollah Khamenei. Though its implications are much disputed, he has issued a *fatwa* against the development, production, stockpiling, and use of nuclear weapons.[15] This suggests awareness that nuclear weapons are particularly destructive and terrible. Iran's religious leaders have in the past shown themselves sensitive to costs. The founder of Iran's revolution, Ayatollah Khomeini, ceased the war with Iraq in the 1980s when he determined that the costs were too great.[16] By modern standards these costs were high, perhaps half a million dead. But those casualties pale against the casualties of a nuclear exchange with Israel. And Iran's suffering in a nuclear exchange with Israel would pale against its likely suffering in an exchange with the United States.

Mahmoud Ahmadinejad is nevertheless a worrying figure. He has denied that the Jewish Holocaust is a proven fact. He has said, or implied, that Israel should disappear from the map of the Middle East. In the first instance he denies a horror for world Jewry. In the second, he promises a new horror for the Jews, and given Israel's nuclear capabilities, a horror for Iranians as well if his own country were involved. What we cannot know is whether these observations are offered to produce a certain emotional effect, or whether he understands the implications of his utterances and believes and accepts them. Fortunately, few predict that Iran can acquire nuclear weapons soon, which gives time to assess and monitor

Ahmadinejad's actual strategic influence in Iran, and to discredit him in Iran and in the wider world by regularly pointing out the very grave risks that his ideas hold for his country. Iranians will have a chance to reconsider this man's leadership abilities. He came in with a vote; he can go out the same way. The time in office of Iranian presidents is fixed in any case—limited to two four-year terms.

Other Issues Resulting from a Nuclear-Armed Iran

A final set of concerns about a nuclear-armed Iran arise not from what Iran would or would not do from the point of view of considered strategy, but from a mixed bag of concerns about inadequate Iranian resources, organizational incompetence, and political decentralization. These concerns are not trivial, but even those who raise them do not advocate preventive war to avoid them, which helps put the risks in context.[17]

The first problem is the risk that, due to their relative poverty and inexperience, new nuclear states, such as Iran, will be unable or unwilling to develop the secure retaliatory forces necessary for a stable deterrent relationship. Iran's nuclear force could be small, vulnerable to attack, and lacking secure command and control. Such a force could attract preemption by a neighbor. Or, fearing preemption by a neighbor, Iran could adopt "hair-trigger" alert postures, or due to poor command and control, a fearful Iran might in a crisis inadvertently launch a nuclear weapon. These are all valid concerns, but many of these problems would be in Iran's hands to solve.

Precisely because even a single nuclear explosion is so destructive, Iran does not need a particularly large nuclear force to deter nuclear attacks by other nuclear states. If Iran's secondary purpose is to discourage further any effort to conquer Iran and change the government, then the state attempting to do that will inevitably present lucrative proximate targets for Iranian nuclear weapons. To deter its neighbors, or invaders, Iran does not need particularly long-ranged survivable systems—short-range mobile missiles should be sufficient and these are the easiest to hide.

Iran's most reasonable strategy is to disperse and hide its small force as best it can, and keep it quiet so that foreign intelligence means cannot attack it. This means eschewing dangerous alert postures, first-strike doctrines, and the like. Dispersal, secrecy, stealth, and communications security are the means to to survival, though they may present some command and control issues, and some nuclear security issues. There is no reason in principle, however, why a state such as Iran cannot use multiple-key arrangements to ensure against the unauthorized launch of its weapons.

Analysts of nuclear weapons organizations, however, fairly point to the fact that states do not always base their nuclear weapons in reasonable ways. And they do not necessarily confine their objectives to basic deterrence. Iran may decide that it wants a first-strike capability versus its neighbors, such as Israel. Such a dream is probably unachievable, but Iran might attempt to develop such a capability. This would set up an unstable strategic relationship between the two countries, and any crises would include an element of great risk, as one or the other became tempted to preempt. In the U.S.-Soviet case, these problems ultimately lead the two sides to ensure that some piece of their nuclear forces would likely survive an exchange to visit a horrible retaliation, and thus deter the other's first-strike temptations. These risks also led them to become quite cautious in their political competition, but there were hair-raising episodes along the way, and there is no reason to rule out similar events in the case of Iran.

On the other hand, it is virtually impossible for Iran to achieve a first-strike capability versus the United States. Any risks that Iran took in its basing mode and alert posture to get ready for a first strike against Israel could easily make it more vulnerable to a first strike from the United States. Spending its nuclear forces on Israel would leave Iran politically and militarily vulnerable to a huge U.S. retaliation. By striking first, it would have legitimated a U.S. nuclear attack, while simultaneously weakening its own deterrent with the weapons it had expended. The United States is the greater threat to Iran because it is much more powerful than Israel, and has actual strategic objectives in the Gulf. It is strategically reasonable for Iran to focus its deterrent energies on the United States, which it can only influence with a secure retaliatory force, capable of threatening U.S. forces and interests in the region.

A final potential problem in Iran is the apparent decentralization of power in the country. Iran essentially has two military organizations: the "professional" military, and the Revolutionary Guard Corps. The latter is ideologically motivated, secretive, and involved in assisting armed groups abroad in Iraq and Lebanon. Many fear that the latter would end up in control of the weapons, or at least with considerable access to them. Given the nature of this organization, some of its members might be willing to do things that the higher political authorities in the state would not choose to do. They might give the weapons away, or use them without authorization. It is impossible to know whether this would occur in Iran. The Revolutionary Guards are generally considered to be very loyal to the Supreme Leader, the ultimate political authority.[18] This should work against renegade behavior. Iran is dedicating considerable national resources to nuclear energy, and if it pursued its current path through to a complete weapons program, it will have devoted many more resources. It is likely, though not guaranteed, that Iran's leaders will take care to put the weapons under the control of people they trust to obey their orders. All states having relations with Iran have an interest in this matter. Nuclear powers must make clear to Iran that its nuclear weapons would be a state responsibility. It will not matter to others whether an Iranian nuclear weapon was employed or exported by "rogue" elements within the state. Even nonnuclear powers can convey this message to Iran, letting Iran know that such an excuse would not win Iran any diplomatic cover. Iran must also be carefully watched for signs of sloppy control practices, and if they appear, other states must make these practices a primary issue in their relations with Iran.

Regional Nuclear Proliferation and Risks to the Non-Proliferation Treaty

States in range of Iran's nuclear weapons will reasonably wish to take measures to protect themselves against nuclear coercion and nuclear attack. Iran's neighbors have three policy options to ensure themselves against a nuclear-armed Iran. They can choose to appease Iran comprehensively; they can find a nuclear guarantor; they can build their own nuclear weapons. Though elements of these three policies could be combined, one will tend to dominate.

Most countries will decline to appease Iran, if they have another plausible option, because most nation-states enjoy their autonomy and do not wish to give it up. Comprehensive appeasement is the road to ruin; one set of concessions to a demanding Iran could easily lead to another, until the state in question loses the ability to recover any shred of sovereignty. Comprehensive appeasement will likely only prove preferable to states facing a disastrous war, or disastrous defeat, with no hope of survival. Historically, this sort of behavior is generally only found among the very weak, and typically when they lack any other option.

The most important choice is whether states will seek their own nuclear weapons, or seek the protection of another nuclear power, if that protection is offered. That said, only a few states in the Middle East and Persian Gulf have the resources to attempt their own autonomous nuclear weapons programs. I have argued above that the United States likely would offer protec-

tion to regional states in order to protect its interests in the Persian Gulf from Iran. It also may offer such protection in order to forestall a spasm of nuclear proliferation in the region. The policies of the United States, and to a lesser extent the principal European states and the European Union, will be the most decisive determinant of whether or not Iran's nuclear programs are emulated.

At this time, and for the foreseeable future, four regional powers can be considered candidate nuclear competitors with Iran: Israel (already a nuclear-armed state), Egypt, Saudi Arabia, and Turkey.

Israel depends on the United States for its advanced conventional weaponry, but it is unwilling to count on any state for its immediate defense. Israel has had a nuclear weapons program for a very long time, though it declines to discuss the matter publicly. Open sources estimate a stockpile of two hundred weapons. Israel is believed to be able to deliver weapons by ballistic missile and by aircraft, and perhaps by submarine launched cruise missile. It seems to have taken care to produce a secure second-strike capability. In the face of an open Iranian program, Israel may be tempted to go public with its own program.

Though Iran is quite vulnerable to nuclear attack today, Israel might intensify its preparations to ensure that Iran understands just how dangerous nuclear threats toward Israel would be. Not many Israeli nuclear weapons would need to survive an attempted Iranian first strike to ruin Iran forever. Open improvements in Israeli nuclear capabilities, especially if accompanied by extensive public rhetoric, would likely raise security and prestige concerns among its neighbors. The United States would be wise to urge Israel to refrain from strong nuclear declarations, unless Iran's own public declarations about its nuclear capability demand a response.

Egypt would be concerned for reasons of both prestige and security if Iran was to become a nuclear weapons state, and Israel was to become an open nuclear power. Egypt at one time had an active nuclear energy research program, and there was concern that it could become a nuclear weapons [state]. It has the technological and scientific expertise and has recently announced a new civilian nuclear energy program.[19] Absent active U.S. diplomacy, and strategic guarantees, Egypt probably would follow suit in developing nuclear weapons. Egypt faces a number of barriers, however. First, it is highly dependent on the United States for conventional weaponry. The United States surely would suspend this relationship if Egypt decided to pursue nuclear weapons. This would be quite unsettling to Egypt's internal politics. Second, Egypt is a poor country; foreign economic assistance would also dry up if Egypt decided to go nuclear. Third, given that Israel is already a nuclear weapons state, and Iran is well ahead of Egypt, Egypt would go through a period of both conventional and nuclear vulnerability as it attempted to produce nuclear weapons. Egypt could choose to accept all these risks and costs, but it seems more plausible that the United States and the European Union could find a package of assurances and incentives that would be acceptable to Egypt.

Saudi Arabia would face similar, though stronger temptations, than Egypt. Saudi Arabia is arguably the other "great power" of the Persian Gulf region, and thus a natural competitor with Iran. With the demise of Iraq, it is the undisputed leader of the Arab states in the Gulf, and thus a rival to an Iran trying to expand its sphere of influence. Due to their proximity, Iran and Saudi Arabia are vulnerable to one another's conventional military power. Saudi Arabia likely views itself as the protector of Sunni Arabs from Shia Arabs, and from Shia Iran.

Saudi Arabia does not, however, have a developed nuclear science and technology effort. And it does not have the other industrial capabilities needed to support a nuclear weapons program and associated delivery systems. Saudi Arabia would thus take quite a long time to develop its own nuclear forces, and like Egypt, would be vulnerable in the interval. They would have to rely on an external guarantee, and the guarantor probably would not want to be a party to any nuclear program. With its wealth, however, it cannot be ruled out that the Saudis would simply try to buy nuclear weapons. They would need more than a few to compete with an Iranian program, and they would need delivery systems. Pakistan seems the only possible source, but it is under a great deal of scrutiny. Pakistan would face enormous pressure not to transfer complete weapons to another party. Finally, Saudi Arabia does have good reason to believe that outsiders are committed to its security. The United States and other great powers have extensive economic and military interests in maintaining Saudi security. The United States has demonstrated its commitment in many ways, including war. The Saudis are accustomed to security cooperation with the United States. A U.S. guarantee likely would prove the most attractive option for Saudi Arabia.

Turkey also will be concerned, for security and prestige reasons, about a nuclear weapons capability in neighboring Iran. Turkey's economic, scientific, and engineering capabilities probably make it more capable of going nuclear than either Egypt or Saudi Arabia. Turkey's calculation will be affected by other political interests, however. Turkey is a member of NATO, a nuclear alliance, and thus already enjoys a nuclear guarantee by the United States. Dozens of tactical nuclear weapons are based in Turkey, and some of Turkey's aircraft are wired to deliver these weapons, which could be turned over to them under circumstances determined by the United States, and based on long-standing procedures agreed within NATO. This relationship would be jeopardized were Turkey to embark on its own independent nuclear weapons program. Turkey also aspires to membership in the European Union. Though the Europeans have been only moderately encouraging, it seems likely that the EU would discourage an independent Turkish nuclear effort. Conversely, it seems possible that the EU might become more accommodating of Turkey's effort to join the EU if that helped discourage a Turkish nuclear program.

In sum, a nuclear Iran creates risks of additional nuclear proliferation in the Persian Gulf and Middle East regions. At the same time, these risks will be affected by the U.S. response. If the United States behaves consistent with its past interpretation of its regional interests and global interests, then it can mute the incentives of three of the four states in question to acquire nuclear weapons. This is not a sure thing, of course, and the United States will need to show leadership and sagacity. That said, it looks as if the kinds of policies recommended in this paper in the event of an Iranian nuclear weapons capability are similar to what the United States, its allies, and other Asian powers are doing in response to the North Korean nuclear weapons test. The United States and its allies have demonstrated their solidarity; North Korea has been warned not to export its nuclear weapons; and the United Nations has instituted a sanctions regime, which effectively legalizes searches of North Korean ships, planes, trucks, and railroad cars for nuclear contraband.

If Iran ultimately does get nuclear weapons, this will surely further damage the NPT. Insofar as Iran will have launched and developed its program under the cover of the NPT, member states will lose confidence that the system actually protects them in any way. Many member states with the capacity to build their own nuclear weapons will want to move themselves closer to an ability to do so in the event that any of their neighbors defect from the treaty. They will want to be months rather than years away from their own nuclear weapons. If some do this, then all may wish to do so. Thus the warning time that the treaty mechanisms provide to other members that regions are turning dangerous—warning that could be used for preventive diplomacy— will be shortened. If actual widespread and rapid proliferation then occurs in the Persian Gulf and Middle East, then the treaty obviously will have suffered a major failure.

Alternatively, Iran's weapons success will cause some member states of the NPT to demand even more aggressively than they already do that the entire treaty be renegotiated, with much stricter constraints on the technologies that non-nuclear weapon member states can pursue. This is a double-edged sword, because the nonnuclear weapon states will want a reopened negotiation to place further limits on the existing nuclear weapons states. This will make for a tense, and perhaps fruitless, negotiation. Foresight about all these difficulties will, however, provide an extra incentive for the advanced countries to discourage regional nuclear emulation of Iran.

Conclusion

A nuclear-armed Iran is not a trivial problem— for its neighbors or the United States. Indeed, Iran itself would be entering a difficult new period in its history. It would be better by far for Iran to forgo those technology development initiatives that would allow it to make a decision to become a nuclear weapons state. But current diplomatic efforts may fail, and the question arises as to whether preventive war dominates a strategy of containment and deterrence. This choice can only be considered if a strategy of containment is elucidated, and its odds of success assessed. Should Iran become a nuclear power, both the immediate strategic risks and the proliferation risks can be addressed with a reinvigorated commitment of U.S. power to stability and security in the Persian Gulf and the Middle East. Such a commitment is reasonable given U.S. strategic interests in the region. The United States should seek the help of outside partners in Europe and elsewhere in making this commitment. The United States can and should make it clear to Iran that the overt or covert use of its nuclear weapons, for blackmail or for war, would put Iran in the gravest danger of nuclear retaliation. The United States should similarly explain to regional actors why it is willing to make this commitment. Both the United States and regional actors may wish to reinforce this commitment with security agreements and some visible military preparations. At the same time, it will be necessary for the United States to forgo any future efforts to replace the Iranian regime. This would run nuclear risks that neither the United States, nor other great powers, nor regional powers will wish to run.

The strategy of deterrence and containment has worked for the United States before; there is no reason why it cannot work again. Relative to Iran, the United States and its likely allies have vastly superior material capabilities, a far more favorable situation than the in Cold War. In a confrontation with the United States, Iran would run risks of complete destruction, and it cannot threaten the United States with comparable damage.

Bismarck said of preventive war that it was like committing suicide out of fear of death. A preventive war versus Iran might not be suicidal, but it will definitely hurt. The United States and its allies have many military and diplomatic cards to play to manage the dangers posed by a nuclear-armed Iran. That said, a replay of the Cold War competition in the Persian Gulf is not a happy outcome. Though I think it is preferable to preventive war, far better would be a diplomatic solution. Since it is unlikely that economic pressure alone will bring diplomatic success, it would be wise to offer Iran a package of incentives more consistent with its apparent concerns than has been offered thus far. If Iran were to decline such an offer, this clarification of its purposes would assist the ultimate diplomacy of containment and deterrence.

NOTES

1. Jeffrey J. Schott, Institute for International Economics, "Economic Sanctions, Oil, and Iran," Testimony before the Joint Economic Committee, U.S. Congress, Hearing on "Energy and the Iranian Economy," July 25, 2006, available online at http://www.iie.com/publications/papers/paper.cfm?ResearchID=649.

2. Lionel Beehner, "What Sanctions Mean for Iran's Economy," Council on Foreign Relations Background Paper, May 2006, available online at http://www.cfr.org/publication/10590/what_sanctions_mean_for_irans_economy.html?

3. Flynt Leverett, "The Race for Iran," *New York Times*, June 20, 2006.

4. Austin Long and Whitney Raas, "Osirak Redux? Assessing Israeli Capabilities to Destroy Iranian Nuclear Facilities," April 2006, SSP Working Paper, available online at http://web.mit.edu/ssp/Publications/working_papers/wp_06-1.pdf.

5. For example, two hundred fighter bombers could easily deliver four hundred precision guided weapons against four hundred aim points. Given the U.S. naval and air presence in the Persian Gulf, this rather limited attack could probably be launched with little reinforcement.

6. Thomas A. Keaney and Eliot A. Cohen, *Gulf War Air Power Survey Summary Report* (Washington, D.C.: Government Printing Office, 1993), Figure 5, "Coalition Air Strikes by Day Against Iraqi Target Sets," p. 13 (numbers estimated from graph).

7. The recent Israeli experience in Lebanon is relevant. Neither the Israeli Air Force nor the powerful counterbattery attacks of the Israeli Army's artillery could prevent Hezbollah from launching a hundred or more artillery rockets into northern Israel almost every night. Given the length of the Iran/Iraq border, it seems likely that Iran could infiltrate small units into Iraq to raid bases and truck convoys. At this moment, Iran likely has agents in Southern Iraq, and has sufficiently strong relationships with Shiite militias that some of these militias might assist Iran. Finally, Iran's

intelligence on the location and strength of coalition forces is likely very good. It would not be surprising if Iran had precise coordinates for many of these potential targets, and spotters close to these targets, both of which would improve the performance of its otherwise inaccurate long range artillery rockets.

8. Robert Lowe and Claire Spencer, eds., *Iran, Its Neighbors and the Regional Crises, A Middle East Programme Report* (London: Royal Institute of International Affairs, 2006), pp. 6, 8–12; See also Vali Nasr, "When the Shiites Rise," *Foreign Affairs* 85 (July/August 2006): 58–74, esp. 66–68. Ray Takeyh, "A Profile in Defiance, Being Mahmoud Admadinejad," *National Interest*, no. 83 (Spring 2006): pp. 16–21 makes the point that the new Iranian president and his coterie of Iraq war veterans seem more religious, more nationalistic, and more confrontational than others in the Iranian political elite, but that they are only one faction.

9. *The World Factbook*, U.S. Central Intelligence Agency, available online at https://www.cia.gov/cia/publications/factbook/geos/ir.html, accessed Sept[ember] 25, 2006.

10. *The Military Balance 2006* (London: International Institute for Strategic Studies, and Routledge, 2006), pp. 18, 187.

11. William Dunlop and Harold Smith, "Who Did It? Using International Forensics to Detect and Deter Nuclear Terrorism," *Arms Control Today*, October 2006, available online at http://www.armscontrol.org/act/2006_10/CVR Forensics.asp, accessed October 29, 2006.

12. *The Military Balance 2006*, p. 191.

13. For population concentrations see, "World Urbanization Prospects: The 2005 Revision Population Database," "Iran," U.N. Population Division, available online at http://esa.un.org/unup, accessed 23 September 2006. Jericho II range estimates by Austin Long.

14. Perhaps a third of Iranian manufacturing industry is concentrated in or near Tehran, Karaj, and Isfahan alone. See "Table 7.9, Manufacturing Establishments by Legal Status and Ostan: 1381," Statistical Centre of Iran, available online at http://www.sci.org.ir/portal/faces/public/sci_en/sci_en.selected-data/sci_en.yearbookdata, accessed September 29, 2006.

15. Mark Fitzpatrick, "Assessing Iran's Nuclear Program," *Survival* 48, no. 3 (Autumn 2006): 13.

16. Graham E. Fuller, "War and Revolution in Iran," *Current History* (February 1989): 81–100. "In basic terms, Khomeini faced a stark choice between pursuing an increasingly unattainable revolutionary victory over Iraq and the survival of the Islamic Revolution itself" (p. 81).

17. Scott D. Sagan, "How to Keep the Bomb from Iran," *Foreign Affairs* 85 (September/October 2006): 45–59. Sagan raises many of the concerns outlined here. These concerns lead him to advise a focused diplomatic effort to discourage Iran from proceeding with its enrichment program. He explicitly concludes, however, that preventive war is not an appropriate answer to the Iranian program. Implicitly, therefore, he accepts that however problematical a nuclear Iran might be, these risks do not exceed those associated with a preventive war.

18. Jim Walsh, "Iran and the Nuclear Issue: Negotiated Settlement or Escalation?" Testimony before the Subcommittee on Federal Financial Management, Government Information and International Security, Committee on Homeland Security and Governmental Affairs, United States Senate, July 20, 2006, Washington, D.C.

19. For an excellent review of the nuclear potential of Egypt, Turkey, and Saudi Arabia, see Wyn Q. Bowen and Joanna Kidd, "The Nuclear Capabilities and Ambitions of Iran's Neighbors," in *Getting Ready for a Nuclear-Ready Iran*, Henry Sokolski and Patrick Clawson, eds. (Carlyle Barracks, Penn.: U.S. Army

War College, Strategic Studies Institute, 2005), pp. 51–88, available online at www.strategic studiesinstitute.army.mil/. See also William Wallis and Roula Khalaf, "Speculation after Egypt Revives Nuclear Plans," *Financial Times*,

September 25, 2006, available online at http://www.ft.com/cms/s/6e01b312-4cba-11db-b03c-0000779e2340.html, accessed October 29, 2006.

ROBERT J. LIEBER AND AMATZIA BARAM

Containment Breach

Preventing nuclear war between Iran and Israel would be more difficult than it ever was to avoid a nuclear confrontation between the United States and the Soviet Union. Here's why.

A number of influential policymakers and foreign policy analysts appear much too complacent regarding the prospects of a nuclear-armed Iran. Former CENTCOM Commander Gen. John Abizaid has argued that "[d]eterrence will work with Iran," and former Deputy Director of National Intelligence Thomas Fingar, one of the authors of the 2007 National Intelligence Estimate on Iran's nuclear capabilities, has voiced similar opinions.

Deterrence in the Middle East, they argue, could be just as stable as it was between the United States and the USSR during the Cold War. "Israel's massive nuclear force will deter Iran from ever contemplating using or giving away its own (hypothetical) weapon," wrote Fareed Zakaria in the Oct. 12 edition of *Newsweek*. "Deterrence worked with madmen like Mao, and with thugs like Stalin, and it will work with the calculating autocrats of Tehran."

But this historical analogy is dangerously misconceived. In reality, defusing an Israeli-Iranian nuclear standoff will be far more difficult than averting nuclear war during the Cuban missile crisis. This is true even if those Iranians with their fingers on the nuclear trigger are not given to messianic doomsday thinking. Here are five factors that will make an Israeli-Iranian nuclear confrontation potentially explosive.

Communication and trust. The October 1962 negotiations that settled the Cuban missile crisis were conducted through a fairly effective, though imperfect, communication system between the United States and Russia. There was also a limited degree of mutual trust between the two superpowers. This did not prevent confusion and suspicion, but it did facilitate the rivals' ability to understand the other's side and eventually resolve the crisis.

Israel and Iran, however, have no such avenues for communication. They don't even have embassies or fast and effective back-channel contacts—and, what's more, they mistrust each other completely. Israel has heard Iranian leaders—and not just President Mahmoud Ahmadinejad—call for its destruction. Meanwhile, Iranian leaders remain prone to paranoid and conspiratorial views of the outside world, especially Israel and the United States. In any future Iranian-Israeli crisis, each side could easily misinterpret

From *Foreign Policy* (Dec. 22, 2009).

the other's moves, leading to disaster. A proxy war conducted by Iran through Hezbollah or Hamas against Israel could quickly lead to a series of escalating threats.

Goals. The Soviets wanted to extend their power and spread Communism—they never pledged the annihilation of America. Iranian leaders, however, have called for Israel to be "wiped off the map of the Middle East." After the street protests that followed the June presidential election, Iran has entered into chronic instability. In a moment of heightened tension and urgent need for popular support, an Iranian leader could escalate not only rhetoric but action.

There is a strong precedent in the Middle East of such escalation leading to war. Arab threats to destroy any Jewish state preceded a massive invasion of the new Israeli state in May 1948. In May and June 1967, Egypt's President Gamal Abd al-Nasser loudly proclaimed his intent to "liberate Palestine" (i.e., Israel in its 1949 borders), and moved his panzer divisions to Israel's border. The result was the Six Day War.

Command and control. In 1962, the two superpowers possessed sophisticated command-and-control systems securing their nuclear weapons. Both also employed effective centralized decision-making systems. Neither may be the case with Iran: Its control technology will be rudimentary at first, and Tehran's decision-making process is relatively chaotic. Within Iran's byzantine power structure, the Islamic Revolutionary Guard Corps (IRGC) mounts an army and navy of its own alongside the regular army and navy, and internal differences within the regime over nuclear diplomacy are evidence of conflicting lines of authority. Recent events suggest that the IRGC, allied with Ahmadinejad, has increasingly infringed on the authority of the supreme leader, Ayatollah Ali Khamenei. As a result, no one can be certain how decisions are made and who makes them.

Mutual deterrence. Both the United States and USSR had second-strike capability made credible by huge land masses. They possessed hardened missile silos scattered throughout the countryside, large air forces equipped with nuclear bombs, and missile-launching submarines. In the Middle East, Iran stretches across a vast 636,000 square miles, against Israel's (pre-1967) 8,500 square miles of territory. This point was made by ex-president Hashemi Rafsanjani in 2001, who noted, "Israel is much smaller than Iran in land mass, and therefore far more vulnerable to nuclear attack." If this is the way an Iranian *pragmatist* thinks, how are the hardliners thinking?

In contrast, by 1962, the two superpowers implicitly recognized the logic of mutually assured destruction. And yet, they still came relatively close to war—in John F. Kennedy's words, the risk of a nuclear conflict was "between one out of three and even." When Iran goes nuclear, the huge disparity in size will pose a psychological obstacle for its recognition of mutual deterrence. Even assuming the United States promises Israel a retaliatory nuclear umbrella, Iran will doubt U.S. resolve. The mullahs will be tempted to conclude that with Israel gone, the United States would see no point in destroying Iran. Given the criticism leveled today against President Harry Truman for using the bomb against Japanese civilians in World War II, what are the chances of American retaliation against Iran, especially if the Islamic Republic has not attacked the United States?

Crisis instability. In view of the above dangers, if and when a grave crisis does erupt, Israel would be tempted to strike first in order to prevent an Iranian nuclear attack, which would devastate its urban core. Iran will be well aware of Israel's calculations and, in the early years of becoming a nuclear power, will have a smaller and probably more vulnerable nuclear arsenal. This will give it, in turn, strong incentives to launch its own preemptive strike.

The implications of a nuclear-armed Iran go well beyond the risks of an Iranian-Israeli war. Once Iran is a nuclear power, the Middle East is likely to enter a fast-moving process of nuclear proliferation. Until now, most Arab governments have not made an effort to match Israel's nuclear arsenal. However, they perceive Iran's nuclear weapons as a real strategic threat. A Middle East where more and more states have nuclear arms, known to experts as a saturated multiplayer environment, will present an almost insurmountable challenge for deterrence calculations by regional or external powers, and a still greater risk of serious instability. Contrary to the wishful thinking of some analysts that the possession of nuclear weapons could make Iran more cautious, a nuclear Iran will likely be emboldened. It could press Hezbollah to be more aggressive in Lebanon, flex its muscles in the Persian Gulf, and step up its challenges against U.S. forces in the region.

If diplomacy and sanctions fail to prevent Iran from going nuclear, Israel will be caught on the horns of an acute existential dilemma not of its own making. If Israel does not act, it will face a future in which it will live under a nuclear sword of Damocles wielded by a state that has called for its destruction. If it does act in the face of what are, after all, probabilities rather than certainties, Israel must expect a serious conventional war that would include attacks from Iran's proxies Hamas and Hezbollah and an escalation in international terrorism, all in exchange for an uncertain degree of success. Contrary to the assessments of those who foresee a best case scenario of stable deterrence, a nuclear-armed Iran will usher in a new era of instability in the Middle East—with consequences that nobody can accurately predict, much less contain.

ANDREW H. KYDD AND BARBARA F. WALTER

The Strategies of Terrorism

Terrorism often works. Extremist organizations such as al-Qaida, Hamas, and the Tamil Tigers engage in terrorism because it frequently delivers the desired response. The October 1983 suicide attack against the U.S. Marine barracks in Beirut, for example, convinced the United States to withdraw its soldiers from Lebanon.[1] The United States pulled its soldiers out of Saudi Arabia two years after the terrorist attacks of September 11, 2001, even though the U.S. military had been building up its forces in that country for more than a decade.[2] The Philippines recalled its troops from Iraq nearly a month

early after a Filipino truck driver was kidnapped by Iraqi extremists.[3] In fact, terrorism has been so successful that between 1980 and 2003, half of all suicide terrorist campaigns were closely followed by substantial concessions by the target governments.[4] Hijacking planes, blowing up buses, and kidnapping individuals may seem irrational and incoherent to outside observers, but these tactics can be surprisingly effective in achieving a terrorist group's political aims.

Despite the salience of terrorism today, scholars and policymakers are only beginning to understand how and why it works. Much has been written on the origins of terror, the motivations of terrorists, and counterterror responses, but little has appeared on the strategies terrorist organizations employ and the conditions under which

From *International Security* 31, no. 1 (Summer 2006): 49–80.

these strategies succeed or fail. Alan Krueger, David Laitin, Jitka Maleckova, and Alberto Abadie, for example, have traced the effects of poverty, education, and political freedom on terrorist recruitment.[5] Jessica Stern has examined the grievances that give rise to terrorism and the networks, money, and operations that allow terrorist organizations to thrive.[6] What is lacking, however, is a clear understanding of the larger strategic games terrorists are playing and the ways in which state responses help or hinder them.

Effective counterstrategies cannot be designed without first understanding the strategic logic that drives terrorist violence. Terrorism works not simply because it instills fear in target populations, but because it causes governments and individuals to respond in ways that aid the terrorists' cause. The Irish Republican Army (IRA) bombed pubs, parks, and shopping districts in London because its leadership believed that such acts would convince Britain to relinquish Northern Ireland. In targeting the World Trade Center and the Pentagon on September 11, al-Qaida hoped to raise the costs for the United States of supporting Israel, Saudi Arabia, and other Arab regimes, and to provoke the United States into a military response designed to mobilize Muslims around the world. That so many targeted governments respond in the way that terrorist organizations intend underscores the need for understanding the reasoning behind this type of violence.

In this article we seek answers to four questions. First, what types of goals do terrorists seek to achieve? Second, what strategies do they pursue to achieve these goals? Third, why do these strategies work in some cases but not in others? And fourth, given these strategies, what are the targeted governments' best responses to prevent terrorism and protect their countries from future attacks?

The core of our argument is that terrorist violence is a form of costly signaling. Terrorists are too weak to impose their will directly by force of arms. They are sometimes strong enough, however, to persuade audiences to do as they

wish by altering the audience's beliefs about such matters as the terrorist's ability to impose costs and their degree of commitment to their cause. Given the conflict of interest between terrorists and their targets, ordinary communication or "cheap talk" is insufficient to change minds or influence behavior. If al-Qaida had informed the United States on September 10, 2001, that it would kill 3,000 Americans unless the United States withdrew from Saudi Arabia, the threat might have sparked concern, but it would not have had the same impact as the attacks that followed. Because it is hard for weak actors to make credible threats, terrorists are forced to display publicly just how far they are willing to go to obtain their desired results.

There are five principal strategic logics of costly signaling at work in terrorist campaigns: (1) attrition, (2) intimidation, (3) provocation, (4) spoiling, and (5) outbidding. In an attrition strategy, terrorists seek to persuade the enemy that the terrorists are strong enough to impose considerable costs if the enemy continues a particular policy. Terrorists using intimidation try to convince the population that the terrorists are strong enough to punish disobedience and that the government is too weak to stop them, so that people behave as the terrorists wish. A provocation strategy is an attempt to induce the enemy to respond to terrorism with indiscriminate violence, which radicalizes the population and moves them to support the terrorists. Spoilers attack in an effort to persuade the enemy that moderates on the terrorists' side are weak and untrustworthy, thus undermining attempts to reach a peace settlement. Groups engaged in outbidding use violence to convince the public that the terrorists have greater resolve to fight the enemy than rival groups, and therefore are worthy of support. Understanding these five distinct strategic logics is crucial not only for understanding terrorism but also for designing effective antiterror policies.[7]

The article is divided into two main sections. The first discusses the goals terrorists pursue and examines the forty-two groups currently on the U.S. State Department's list of foreign terrorist organizations (FTOs).[8] The second section develops the costly signaling approach to terrorism, analyzes the five strategies that terrorists use to achieve their goals, discusses the conditions in which each of these strategies is likely to be successful, and draws out the implications for the best counterterror responses.

The Goals of Terrorism

For years the press has portrayed terrorists as crazy extremists who commit indiscriminate acts of violence, without any larger goal beyond revenge or a desire to produce fear in an enemy population. This characterization derives some support from statements made by terrorists themselves. For example, a young Hamas suicide bomber whose bomb failed to detonate said, "I know that there are other ways to do jihad. But this one is sweet—the sweetest. All martyrdom operations, if done for Allah's sake, hurt less than a gnat's bite!"[9] Volunteers for a suicide mission may have a variety of motives—obtaining rewards in the afterlife, avenging a family member killed by the enemy, or simply collecting financial rewards for their descendants. By contrast, the goals driving terrorist organizations are usually political objectives, and it is these goals that determine whether and how terrorist campaigns will be launched.

We define "terrorism" as the use of violence against civilians by nonstate actors to attain political goals.[10] These goals can be conceptualized in a variety of ways. Individuals and groups often have hierarchies of objectives, where broader goals lead to more proximate objectives, which then become specific goals in more tactical analyses.[11] For the sake of simplicity, we adopt the common distinction between goals (or ultimate desires) and strategies (or plans of action to attain the goals).

Although the ultimate goals of terrorists have varied over time, five have had enduring importance: regime change, territorial change, policy change, social control, and status quo maintenance. Regime change is the overthrow of a government and its replacement with one led by the terrorists or at least one more to their liking.[12] Most Marxist groups, including the Shining Path (Sendero Luminoso) in Peru have sought this goal. Territorial change is taking territory away from a state either to establish a new state (as the Tamil Tigers seek to do in Tamil areas of Sri Lanka) or to join another state (as Lashkar-e Tayyiba would like to do by incorporating Indian Kashmir into Pakistan). Policy change is a broader category of lesser demands, such as al-Qaida's demand that the United States drop its support for Israel and corrupt Arab regimes such as Saudi Arabia. Social control constrains the behavior of individuals, rather than the state. In the United States, the Ku Klux Klan sought the continued oppression of African Americans after the Civil War. More recently, antiabortion groups have sought to kill doctors who perform abortions to deter other doctors from providing this service. Finally, status quo maintenance is the support of an existing regime or a territorial arrangement against political groups that seek to change it. Many right-wing paramilitary organizations in Latin America, such as the United Self-Defense Force of Colombia, have sought this goal.[13] Protestant paramilitary groups in Northern Ireland supported maintenance of the territorial status quo (Northern Ireland as British territory) against IRA demands that the territory be transferred to Ireland.[14]

Some organizations hold multiple goals and may view one as facilitating another. For instance, by seeking to weaken U.S. support for Arab regimes (which would represent a policy change by the United States), al-Qaida is working toward the overthrow of those regimes (or regime change). As another example, Hamas aims to drive Israel out of the occupied territories (territorial change) and then to overthrow it (regime change).

A cross section of terrorist organizations listed in Table 8.1 illustrates the range of goals

TABLE 8.1

FOREIGN TERRORIST ORGANIZATIONS AND THEIR GOALS

Name	Ultimate Goals	RC	TC	PC	SC	SQM
Abu Nidal Organization	Destroy Israel; establish Palestinian state	X	X			
Abu Sayyaf Group	Secede from Philippines	X	X			
Al-Aqsa Martyrs' Brigade	Destroy Israel; establish Palestinian state	X	X			
Ansar al-Islam	Evict United States from Iraq; establish Islamic state	X		X		
Armed Islamic Group	Establish Islamic state in Algeria	X				
Asbat al-Ansar	Establish Islamic state in Lebanon	X				
Aum Shinrikyo	Seize power in Japan; hasten the Apocalypse	X				
Basque Fatherland and Liberty (ETA)	Secede from Spain		X			
Communist Party of the Philippines/New People's Army	Establish Communist state in Philippines	X				
Continuity Irish Republican Army	Evict Britain from Northern Ireland; unite with Eire		X			
Al-Gama'a al-Islamiyya (Islamic Group)	Establish Islamic state in Egypt	X				
Hamas (Islamic Resistance Movement)	Destroy Israel; establish Palestinian Islamic state	X	X			
Harakat ul-Mujahidin	Evict India from Kashmir; unite with Pakistan	X	X			
Hezbollah (Party of God)	Originally: evict Israel from Lebanon; now: destroy Israel and establish Palestinian Islamic state	X	X			
Islamic Jihad Group	Establish Islamic state in Uzbekistan; reduce U.S. influence	X		X		
Islamic Movement of Uzbekistan	Establish Islamic state in Uzbekistan	X				
Jaish-e-Mohammed (Army of Mohammed)	Evict India from Kashmir; unite with Pakistan		X			
Jemaah Islamiya	Establish Islamic state in Indonesia	X				
Al-Jihad (Egyptian Islamic Jihad)	Establish Islamic state in Egypt	X				
Kahane Chai (Kach)	Expand Israel		X			
Kongra-Gel (formerly Kurdistan Workers' Party)	Secede from Turkey		X			
Lashkar-e Tayyiba (Army of the Righteous)	Evict India from Kashmir; unite with Pakistan		X			
Lashkar i Jhangvi	Establish Islamic state in Pakistan	X				
Liberation Tigers of Tamil Eelam	Secede from Sri Lanka		X			
Libyan Islamic Fighting Group	Establish Islamic state in Libya	X				
Moroccan Islamic Combatant Group	Establish Islamic state in Morocco	X				
Mujahedin-e Khalq Organization	Overthrow Iranian government	X				
National Liberation Army	Establish Marxist government in Colombia	X				

(continued)

TABLE 8.1 *(continued)*

Name	Ultimate Goals	RC	TC	PC	SC	SQM
Palestine Liberation Front	Destroy Israel; establish Palestinian state	X	X			
Palestinian Islamic Jihad	Destroy Israel; establish Palestinian state	X	X			
Popular Front for the Liberation of Palestine	Destroy Israel; establish Palestinian state	X	X			
Popular Front for the Liberation of Palestine— General Command	Destroy Israel; establish Palestinian state	X	X			
Al-Qaida	Establish Islamic states in Middle East; destroy Israel; reduce U.S. influence	X	X	X		
Al-Qaida in Iraq (Zarqawi group)	Evict United States from Iraq; establish Islamic state	X		X		
Real Irish Republican Army	Evict Britain from Northern Ireland; unite with Eire		X			
Revolutionary Armed Forces of Colombia	Establish Marxist state in Colombia	X				
Revolutionary Nuclei (formerly Revolutionary People's Struggle)	Establish Marxist state in Greece	X				
Revolutionary Organization 7 November	Establish Marxist state in Greece	X				
Revolutionary People's Liberation Party/Front	Establish Marxist state in Turkey	X				
Salafist Group for Call and Combat	Establish Islamic state in Algeria	X				
Shining Path (Sendero Luminoso)	Establish Marxist state in Peru	X				
United Self-Defense Forces of Colombia	Preserve Colombian state					X
Total		31	19	4	0	1

NOTE: RC: regime change; TC: territorial change; PC: policy change; SC: social control; and SQM: status quo maintenance. Coding of goals is the authors'.

SOURCE: Office of Counterterrorism, U.S. Department of State, "Foreign Terrorist Organizations," fact sheet, October 11, 2005.

and their relative frequency. Of the forty-two groups currently designated as FTOs by the U.S. State Department, thirty-one seek regime change, nineteen seek territorial change, four seek policy change, and one seeks to maintain the status quo.[15] The list is neither exhaustive nor representative of all terrorist groups, and it does not reflect the frequency of goals in the universe of cases. None of the FTOs appear to pursue social control, but some domestic groups, which are by definition not on the list, are more interested in this goal.[16] What Table 8.1 reveals, however, is the instrumental nature of terrorist violence and some of the more popular political objectives being sought.

The Strategies of Terrorist Violence

To achieve their long-term objectives, terrorists pursue a variety of strategies. Scholars have suggested a number of typologies of terrorist strategies and tactics over the years. In a pathbreaking early analysis of terrorism, Thomas Thornton offered five proximate objectives: morale building, advertising, disorientation (of the target population), elimination of opposing forces, and provocation.[17] Martha Crenshaw also identifies advertising and provocation as proximate objectives, along with weakening the government, enforcing obedience in the population, and outbidding.[18] David Fromkin argues that provocation is *the* strategy of terrorism.[19] Edward Price writes that terrorists must delegitimize the regime and impose costs on occupying forces, and he identifies kidnapping, assassination, advertising, and provocation as tactics.[20] Although these analyses are helpful in identifying strategies of terrorism, they fail to derive them from a coherent framework, spell out their logic in detail, and consider best responses to them.

A fruitful starting point for a theory of terrorist strategies is the literature on uncertainty, conflict, and costly signaling. Uncertainty has

long been understood to be a cause of conflict. Geoffrey Blainey argued that wars begin when states disagree about their relative power, and they end when states agree again.[21] James Fearon and other theorists built upon this insight and showed that uncertainty about a state's willingness to fight can cause conflict.[22] If states are unsure what other states will fight for, they may demand too much in negotiations and end up in conflict. This uncertainty could reflect a disagreement about power, as Blainey understood, or a disagreement over resolve, willpower, or the intensity of preferences over the issue. The United States and North Vietnam did not disagree over their relative power, but the United States fatally underestimated North Vietnamese determination to achieve victory.

Uncertainty about trustworthiness or moderation of preferences can also cause conflict. Thomas Hobbes argued that if individuals mistrust each other, they have an incentive to initiate an attack rather than risk being attacked by surprise.[23] John Herz, Robert Jervis, and others have developed this concept in the international relations context under the heading of the security dilemma and the spiral model.[24] States are often uncertain about each other's ultimate ambitions, intentions, and preferences. Because of this, anything that increases one side's belief that the other is deceitful, expansionist, risk acceptant, or hostile increases incentives to fight rather than cooperate.

If uncertainty about power, resolve, and trustworthiness can lead to violence, then communication on these topics is the key to preventing (or instigating) conflict. The problem is that simple verbal statements are often not credible, because actors frequently have incentives to lie and bluff. If by saying "We're resolved," the North Vietnamese could have persuaded the United States to abandon the South in 1965, then North Vietnam would have had every incentive to say so even if it was not that resolute. In reality, they had to fight a long and costly war to prove their point. Similarly, when Mikhail Gorbachev wanted to reassure the West and end the Cold War, verbal

Target of Persuasion

Subject of Uncertainty		Enemy	Own Population
	Power	attrition	intimidation
	Resolve		outbidding
	Trustworthiness	spoiling	provocation

Figure 8.4. Strategies of Terrorist Violence

declarations of innocent intentions were insufficient, because previous Soviet leaders had made similar statements. Instead, real arms reductions, such as the 1987 Intermediate-Range Nuclear Forces Treaty, were necessary for Western opinion to change.

Because talk is cheap, states and terrorists who wish to influence the behavior of an adversary must resort to costly signals.[25] Costly signals are actions so costly that bluffers and liars are unwilling to take them.[26] In international crises, mobilizing forces or drawing a very public line in the sand are examples of strategies that less resolved actors might find too costly to take.[27] War itself, or the willingness to endure it, can serve as a forceful signal of resolve and provide believable information about power and capabilities.[28] Costly signals separate the wheat from the chaff and allow honest communication, although sometimes at a terrible price.

To obtain their political goals, terrorists need to provide credible information to the audiences whose behavior they hope to influence. Terrorists play to two key audiences: governments whose policies they wish to influence and individuals on the terrorists' own side whose support or obedience they seek to gain.[29] The targeted governments are central because they can grant concessions over policy or territory that the terrorists are seeking. The terrorists' domestic audience is also important, because they can

provide resources to the terrorist group and must obey its edicts on social or political issues.

Figure 8.4 shows how the three subjects of uncertainty (power, resolve, and trustworthiness) combine with the two targets of persuasion (the enemy government and the domestic population) to yield a family of five signaling strategies. These strategies form a theoretically cohesive set that we believe represents most of the commonly used strategies in important terrorist campaigns around the world today.[30] A terrorist organization can of course pursue more than one strategy at a time. The September 11 terrorist attacks, for example, were probably part of both an attrition strategy and a provocation strategy. By targeting the heart of the United States' financial district, al-Qaida may have been attempting to increase the cost of the U.S. policy of stationing soldiers in Saudi Arabia. But by targeting prominent symbols of American economic and military power, al-Qaida may also have been trying to goad the United States into an extreme military response that would serve al-Qaida's larger goal of radicalizing the world's Muslim population. The challenge for policymakers in targeted countries is to calibrate their responses in ways that do not further any of the terrorists' goals.

Below we analyze the five terrorist strategies in greater detail, discuss the conditions under which each is likely to succeed, and relate these conditions to the appropriate counterterrorism strategies.

Attrition: A Battle of Wills

The most important task for any terrorist group is to persuade the enemy that the group is strong and resolute enough to inflict serious costs, so that the enemy yields to the terrorists' demands.[31] The attrition strategy is designed to accomplish this task.[32] In an attrition campaign, the greater the costs a terrorist organization is able to inflict, the more credible its threat to inflict future costs, and the more likely the target is to grant concessions. During the last years of the British Empire, the Greeks in Cyprus, Jews in Palestine, and Arabs in Aden used a war of attrition strategy against their colonizer. By targeting Britain with terrorist attacks, they eventually convinced the political leadership that maintaining control over these territories would not be worth the cost in British lives.[33] Attacks by Hezbollah and Hamas against Israel, particularly during the second intifada, also appear to be guided by this strategy. In a letter written in the early 1990s to the leadership of Hamas, the organization's master bomb maker, Yahya Ayyash, said, "We paid a high price when we used only sling-shots and stones. We need to exert more pressure, make the cost of the occupation that much more expensive in human lives, that much more unbearable."[34]

Robert Pape presents the most thorough exposition of terrorism as a war of attrition in his analysis of suicide bombing.[35] Based on a data set of all suicide attacks from 1980 to 2003 (315 in total), Pape argues that suicide terrorism is employed by weak actors for whom peaceful tactics have failed and conventional military tactics are infeasible because of the imbalance of power. The strategy is to inflict costs on the enemy until it withdraws its occupying forces: the greater the costs inflicted, the more likely the enemy is to withdraw. Pape asserts that terrorists began to recognize the effectiveness of suicide terrorism with the 1983 Hezbollah

attack against U.S. Marines in Beirut that killed 241 people. Since then, suicide terrorism has been employed in nationalist struggles around the world.

CONDITIONS FAVORABLE TO ATTRITION A war of attrition strategy is more effective against some targets than others. Three variables are likely to figure in the outcome: the state's level of interest in the issue under dispute, the constraints on its ability to retaliate, and its sensitivity to the costs of violence.

The first variable, the state's degree of interest in the disputed issue, is fundamental. States with only peripheral interests at stake often capitulate to terrorist demands; states with more important interests at stake rarely do. The United States withdrew from Lebanon following the bombing of the marine barracks because it had only a marginal interest in maintaining stability and preventing Syrian domination of that country. In that case, the costs of the attack clearly outweighed the U.S. interests at stake. Similarly, Israel withdrew from southern Lebanon in 2000 because the costs of the occupation outstripped Israel's desire to maintain a buffer zone in that region. In contrast, the United States responded to the September 11 attacks by launching offensive wars in Afghanistan and Iraq rather than withdrawing U.S. troops from the region, as al-Qaida demanded (though U.S. troops did ultimately leave Saudi Arabia for Iraq). Similarly, Israel is unlikely to withdraw from East Jerusalem, much less allow itself to become an Islamic state as Hamas has demanded.

The second variable, constraints on retaliation, affects the costs paid by the terrorists for pursuing a war of attrition. Terrorist organizations almost always are weaker than the governments they target and, as a result, are vulnerable to government retaliation. The more constrained the government is in its use of force, the less costly an attrition strategy is, and the longer the terrorists can hold out in the hopes of achieving their goal. For instance, the Israelis have the military means to commit genocide against the Palestinian people or to expel them to surrounding Arab countries. Israel, however, depends for its long-term survival on close ties with Europe and the United States. Western support for Israel would plummet in response to an Israeli strategy designed to inflict mass casualties, making such a strategy prohibitively costly. This constraint makes a war of attrition strategy less costly (and more attractive) for the Palestinians.

Democracies may be more constrained in their ability to retaliate than authoritarian regimes. Pape finds that suicide bombers target democracies exclusively and argues that this is in part because of constraints on their ability to strike back.[36] Capable authoritarian regimes are able to gather more information on their populations than democracies and can more easily round up suspected terrorists and target those sympathetic to them. They are also less constrained by human rights considerations in their interrogation and retaliation practices.[37]

The ease with which a terrorist organization can be targeted also influences a country's ability to retaliate forcefully. Terrorist organizations such as al-Qaida that are widely dispersed, difficult to identify, or otherwise hard to target are at an advantage in a war of attrition because their enemies will have difficulty delivering punishment. Israel has, through superior intelligence gathering, been able to assassinate top members of Hamas's leadership at will, including its founder and spiritual leader, Sheik Ahmed Yassin, as well as his successor, Abdel Aziz Rantisi. The United States, by contrast, has been unable to locate Osama bin Laden and his top deputy, Ayman al-Zawahiri.

The third variable is a target's cost tolerance. Governments that are able to absorb heavier costs and hold out longer are less inviting targets for an attrition strategy. Terrorist organizations are likely to gauge a target's cost tolerance based on at least two factors: the target's regime type and the target's past behavior toward other terrorists. Regime type is important because democracies may be less able to tolerate the pain-

ful effects of terrorism than non-democracies. Citizens of democracies, their fears stoked by media reports and warnings of continued vulnerability, are more likely to demand an end to the attacks. In more authoritarian states, the government exerts more control over the media and can disregard public opinion to a greater extent. The Russian government's heavy-handed response to hostage situations, for example, suggests a higher tolerance for casualties than a more fully democratic government would have. Additionally, because terrorist organizations operate more freely in democracies and politicians must interact with the public to maintain political support, terrorists have an easier time targeting prominent individuals for assassination. Of four leaders assassinated by terrorists in the past quarter century—Indira Gandhi, Rajiv Gandhi, Yitzak Rabin, and Anwar Sadat—three were leaders of democracies.

Among democratic states, sensitivity to costs may vary with the party in power. When more dovish parties are in charge, the target may be perceived to have lower cost tolerances than if a more hawkish party were at the helm. The dove-hawk dimension may correlate with the left-right dimension in domestic politics, leading left-wing parties to be more likely to grant terrorist demands. This traditional divide between peace and security has characterized Israeli politics for years. Labor Party Prime Minister Ehud Barak was elected on a platform of withdrawing Israeli forces from Lebanon and making peace with the Palestinians; in contrast, Likud Party Prime Minister Ariel Sharon was elected on a platform of meeting terrorists with military force. Hoping for greater concessions, terrorists may preferentially attack dovish parties.

The number of prior concessions made to other terrorists is also likely to influence perceptions of the target's cost tolerance. Governments that have already yielded to terrorist demands are more likely to experience additional terrorist attacks. Evidence abounds that terrorists explicitly consider the prior behavior of states and are encouraged by signs of weakness. Israel's precipitous withdrawal from southern Lebanon in May 2000 convinced Hamas that the Israeli leadership's resolve was weakening and encouraged Hamas leaders to initiate the second intifada in September 2000.[38] Israelis fear the same inference will be drawn from their withdrawal from Gaza. A Hamas leader interviewed in October 2005 declared, "When we took up arms and launched [the second intifada], we succeeded in less than five years to force the Israelis to withdraw from the Gaza Strip. This fulfilled everyone's dream. I think we have to benefit from this experience by applying it accordingly to the West Bank and other occupied areas."[39] The past behavior of a targeted government, therefore, also provides important information to terrorist groups about its likely future behavior and the success of this particular strategy.

Perhaps the most important example of a terrorist group pursuing an attrition strategy is al-Qaida's war with the United States. In a November 2004 broadcast, bin Laden boasted, "We gained experience in guerilla and attritional warfare in our struggle against the great oppressive superpower, Russia, in which we and the mujahidin ground it down for ten years until it went bankrupt, and decided to withdraw in defeat. . . . We are continuing to make America bleed to the point of bankruptcy."[40] Al-Qaida's goal—policy change—is well suited to an attrition strategy. Bin Laden has frequently argued that the United States lacks the resolve to fight a long attritional war, as in his February 1996 declaration of jihad:

> Where was this false courage of yours when the explosion in Beirut took place in 1983 A.D.? You were transformed into scattered bits and pieces; 241 soldiers were killed, most of them Marines. And where was this courage of yours when two explosions made you leave Aden in less than twenty-four hours!
>
> But your most disgraceful case was in Somalia; where, after vigorous propaganda about the power of the U.S. and its post–cold war leadership of the new world order, you moved tens of thousands of international forces, including twenty-

eight thousand American soldiers, into Somalia. However, when tens of your soldiers were killed in minor battles and one American pilot was dragged in the streets of Mogadishu, you left the area in disappointment, humiliation, and defeat, carrying your dead with you. Clinton appeared in front of the whole world threatening and promising revenge, but these threats were merely a preparation for withdrawal. You had been disgraced by Allah and you withdrew; the extent of your impotence and weaknesses became very clear.[41]

Although difficult to prove, it also appears that bin Laden believed that he and his organization would be hard to target with counterattacks, making a war of attrition strategy even more appealing. In 2001 the Taliban was on the verge of eliminating armed resistance in northern Afghanistan; and, as a landlocked country, Afghanistan must have seemed relatively invulnerable to a U.S. invasion. The United States had bombed al-Qaida camps before to no effect. Even if the United States invaded, Afghanistan was both costly and difficult to conquer, as the Soviets discovered in the 1980s. In the end, of course, the Taliban would have been well advised to insist that the September 11 attacks be delayed until the Northern Alliance was defeated, but the latter's dramatic success with U.S. help was perhaps difficult to anticipate.

BEST RESPONSES TO ATTRITION There are at least five counterstrategies available to a state engaged in a war of attrition. First, the targeted government can concede inessential issues in exchange for peace, a strategy that we believe is frequently pursued though rarely admitted.[42] In some cases, the terrorists will genuinely care more about the disputed issue and be willing to outlast the target. In such cases, concessions are likely to be the state's best response. Other potential challengers, however, may perceive this response as a sign of weakness, which could lead them to launch their own attacks. To reduce the damage to its reputation, the target can vigorously fight other wars of attrition over issues it cares more deeply about, thus signaling a willingness to bear costs if the matter is of sufficient consequence.

Second, where the issue under dispute is important enough to the targeted state that it does not want to grant any concessions, the government may engage in targeted retaliation. Retaliation can target the leadership of the terrorist group, its followers, their assets, and other objects of value. Care must be taken, however, that the retaliation is precisely targeted, because the terrorist organization could simultaneously be pursuing a strategy of provocation. A harsh, indiscriminate response might make a war of attrition more costly for the terrorists, but it would also harm innocent civilians who might then serve as willing recruits for the terrorists. The Israeli policy of assassination of terrorist leaders is shaped by this concern.

Third, a state can harden likely targets to minimize the costs the terrorist organization can inflict. If targeted governments can prevent most attacks from being executed, a war of attrition strategy will not be able to inflict the costs necessary to convince the target to concede. The wall separating Israel from the West Bank and Gaza is a large-scale example of this counterstrategy. The United States has been less successful in hardening its own valuable targets, such as nuclear and chemical plants and the container shipping system, despite the creation of the Department of Homeland Security.[43] Protecting these types of targets is essential if one seeks to deter additional attacks and discourage the use of attrition.

Fourth, states should seek to deny terrorists access to the most destructive weapons, especially nuclear and biological ones. Any weapon that can inflict enormous costs will be particularly attractive to terrorists pursuing a war of attrition. The greater the destruction, the higher the likelihood that the target will concede increasingly consequential issues. Particular attention should be placed on securing Russian stockpiles of fissile material and on halting the spread of uranium enrichment technology to Iran and North Korea. No other country has as much material under so little government control as Russia, and Iran and North Korea are vital because of the links both countries have to terrorist organizations.[44]

Finally, states can strive to minimize the psychological costs of terrorism and the tendency people have to overreact. John Mueller has noted that the risks associated with terrorism are actually quite small; for the average U.S. citizen, the likelihood of being a victim of a terrorist attack is about the same as that of being struck by light[n]ing.[45] Government public education programs should therefore be careful not to overstate the threat, for this plays into the hands of the terrorists. If Americans become convinced that terrorism, while a deadly problem, is no more of a health risk than drunk driving, smoking, or obesity, then al-Qaida's attrition strategy will be undercut. What the United States should seek to avoid are any unnecessary costs associated with wasteful and misguided counterterror programs. The more costs the United States inflicts on itself in the name of counterterrorism policies of dubious utility, the more likely a war of attrition strategy is to succeed.

Intimidation: The Reign of Terror

Intimidation is akin to the strategy of deterrence, preventing some undesired behavior by means of threats and costly signals.[46] It is most frequently used when terrorist organizations wish to overthrow a government in power or gain social control over a given population. It works by demonstrating that the terrorists have the power to punish whoever disobeys them, and that the government is powerless to stop them.

Terrorists are often in competition with the government for the support of the population. Terrorists who wish to bring down a government must somehow convince the government's defenders that continued backing of the government will be costly. One way to do this is to provide clear evidence that the terrorist organization can kill those individuals who continue to sustain the regime. By targeting the government's more visible agents and supporters, such as mayors, police, prosecutors, and pro-regime citizens, terrorist organizations demonstrate that they have the ability to hurt their opponents and that the government is too weak to punish the terrorists or protect future victims.

Terrorists can also use an intimidation strategy to gain greater social control over a population. Terrorists may turn to this strategy in situations where a government has consistently refused to implement a policy a terrorist group favors and where efforts to change the state's policy appear futile. In this case, terrorists use intimidation to impose the desired policy directly on the population, gaining compliance through selective violence and the threat of future reprisals. In the United States, antiabortion activists have bombed clinics to prevent individuals from performing or seeking abortions, and in the 1960s racist groups burned churches to deter African Americans from claiming their civil rights. In Afghanistan, the Taliban beheaded the principal of a girls school to deter others from providing education for girls.[47]

An intimidation strategy can encompass a range of actions—from assassinations of individuals in positions of power to car bombings of police recruits, such as those carried out by the Zarqawi group in Iraq. It can also include massacres of civilians who have cooperated with the government or rival groups, such as the 1957 massacre at Melouza by the National Liberation Front during the Algerian war for independence.[48] This strategy was taken to an extreme by the Armed Islamic Group in Algeria's civil war of the 1990s. In that war, Islamist guerrillas massacred thousands of people suspected of switching their allegiance to the government. Massacres were especially common in villages that had once been under firm rebel control but that the army was attempting to retake and clear of rebels. Stathis Kalyvas argues that these conditions

pose extreme dilemmas for the local inhabitants, who usually wish to support whoever will provide security, but are often left exposed when the government begins to retake an area but has not established effective control.[49]

CONDITIONS FAVORABLE TO INTIMIDATION
When the goal is regime change, weak states and rough terrain are two factors that facilitate intimidation. James Fearon and David Laitin argue that civil wars are likely to erupt and continue where the government is weak and the territory is large and difficult to traverse. These conditions allow small insurgent groups to carve out portions of a country as a base for challenging the central government.[50] Intimidation is likely to be used against civilians on the fault lines between rebel and government control to deter individuals from supporting the government.

When the goal is social control, weak states again facilitate intimidation. When the justice system is too feeble to effectively prosecute crimes associated with intimidation, people will either live in fear or seek protection from non-state actors such as local militias or gangs. Penetration of the justice system by sympathizers of a terrorist group also facilitates an intimidation strategy, because police and courts will be reluctant to prosecute crimes and may even be complicit in them.

BEST RESPONSES TO INTIMIDATION
When the terrorist goal is regime change, the best response to intimidation is to retake territory from the rebels in discrete chunks and in a decisive fashion. Ambiguity about who is in charge should be minimized, even if this means temporarily ceding some areas to the rebels to concentrate resources on selected sections of territory. This response is embodied in the "clear-and-hold strategy" that U.S. forces are employing in Iraq. The 2005 National Strategy for Victory in Iraq specifically identifies intimidation as the "strategy of our enemies."[51] The proper response, as

Secretary of State Condoleezza Rice stated in October 2005, "is to clear, hold, and build: clear areas from insurgent control, hold them securely, and build durable national Iraqi institutions."[52] If rebels control their own zone and have no access to the government zone, they will have no incentive to kill the civilians they control and no ability to kill the civilians the government controls. In this situation, there is no uncertainty about who is in control; the information that would be provided by intimidation is already known. The U.S. military developed the clear-and-hold strategy during the final years of U.S. involvement in Vietnam. A principal strategy of the Vietcong was intimidation—to prevent collaboration with the government and build up control in the countryside. In the early years of the war, the United States responded with search and destroy missions, essentially an attrition strategy. Given that the insurgents were not pursuing an attrition strategy, and were not particularly vulnerable to one, this initial counterstrategy was a mistake. Clear-and-hold was the more appropriate response because it limited the Vietcong's access to potential targets and thus undercut its strategy.[53]

Clear-and-hold has its limitations. It is usually impossible to completely deny terrorists entry into the government-controlled zones. In 2002 Chechen terrorists were able to hold a theater audience of 912 people hostage in the heart of Moscow, and 130 were killed in the operation to retake the building. The Shining Path frequently struck in Lima, far from its mountain strongholds. In such situations, a more effective counterstrategy would be to invest in protecting the targets of attacks. In most states, most of the time, the majority of state agents do not need to worry about their physical security, because no one wants to harm them. However, certain state agents, such as prosecutors of organized crime, are more accustomed to danger, and procedures have been developed to protect them. These procedures should be applied to election workers, rural officials and police, community activists, and any individual who plays a visible role in

the support and functioning of the embattled government.

When the terrorist goal is social control, the best response is strengthening law enforcement. This may require more resources to enable the government to effectively investigate and prosecute crimes. More controversial, it may mean using national agencies such as the Federal Bureau of Investigation to bypass local officials who are sympathetic to the terrorist group and investigating law enforcement agencies to purge such sympathizers if they obstruct justice. The state can also offer additional protection to potential targets and increase penalties for violence against them. For instance, the 1994 federal Freedom of Access to Clinic Entrances Act, passed in the wake of the 1993 killing of a doctor at an abortion clinic in Florida, prohibits any violence designed to prevent people from entering such clinics.

Provocation: Lighting the Fuse

A provocation strategy is often used in pursuit of regime change and territorial change, the most popular goals of the FTOs listed by the State Department. It is designed to persuade the domestic audience that the target of attacks is evil and untrustworthy and must be vigorously resisted.

Terrorist organizations seeking to replace a regime face a significant challenge: they are usually much more hostile to the regime than a majority of the state's citizens. Al-Qaida may wish to topple the House of Saud, but if a majority of citizens do not support this goal, al-Qaida is unlikely to achieve it. Similarly, if most Tamils are satisfied living in a united Sri Lanka, the Tamil Tigers' drive for independence will fail. To succeed, therefore, a terrorist organization must first convince moderate citizens that their government needs to be replaced or that independence from the central government is the only acceptable outcome.

Provocation helps shift citizen support away from the incumbent regime. In a provocation strategy, terrorists seek to goad the target government into a military response that harms civilians within the terrorist organization's home territory.[54] The aim is to convince them that the government is so evil that the radical goals of the terrorists are justified and support for their organization is warranted.[55] This is what the Basque Fatherland and Liberty group (ETA) sought to do in Spain. For years, Madrid responded to ETA attacks with repressive measures against the Basque community, mobilizing many of its members against the government even if they did not condone those attacks. As one expert on this conflict writes, "Nothing radicalizes a people faster than the unleashing of undisciplined security forces on its towns and villages."[56]

David Lake argues that moderates are radicalized because government attacks provide important information about the type of leadership in power and its willingness to negotiate with more moderate elements.[57] Ethan Bueno de Mesquita and Eric Dickson develop this idea and show that if the government has the ability to carry out a discriminating response to terrorism but chooses an undiscriminating one, it reveals itself to be unconcerned with the welfare of the country's citizens. Provocation, therefore, is a way for terrorists to force an enemy government to reveal information about itself that then helps the organization recruit additional members.[58]

CONDITIONS FAVORABLE TO PROVOCATION

Constraints on retaliation and regime type are again important in determining when provocation is successful. For provocation to work, the government must be capable of middling levels of brutality. A government willing and able to commit genocide makes a bad target for provocation, as the response will destroy the constituency the terrorists represent. At the opposite pole, a government so committed to human rights and the rule of law that it is incapable of inflicting indiscriminate punishment also makes a bad target, because it cannot be provoked. Such

a government might be an attractive target for an attrition strategy if it is not very good at stopping attacks, but provocation will be ineffective.

What explains why a government would choose a less discriminating counterstrategy over a more precise one? In some instances, a large-scale military response will enhance the security of a country rather than detract from it. If the target government is able to eliminate the leadership of a terrorist organization and its operatives, terrorism is likely to cease or be greatly reduced even if collateral damage radicalizes moderates to some extent. A large-scale military response may also enhance the security of a country, despite radicalizing some moderates, if it deters additional attacks from other terrorist groups that may be considering a war of attrition. Target governments may calculate that the negative consequences of a provocation strategy are acceptable under these conditions.

Domestic political considerations are also likely to influence the type of response that the leadership of a target state chooses. Democracies may be more susceptible to provocation than nondemocracies. Populations that have suffered from terrorist violence will naturally want their government to take action to stop terrorism. Unfortunately, many of the more discriminating tools of counterterrorism, such as infiltrating terrorist cells, sharing intelligence with other countries, and arresting individuals, are not visible to the publics these actions serve to protect. Bueno de Mesquita has argued that democratic leaders may have to employ the more public and less discriminating counterterror strategies to prove that their government is taking sufficient action against terrorists, even if these steps are provocative.[59] Pressure for a provocative counterresponse may also be particularly acute for more hard-line administrations whose constituents may demand greater action.[60] Counterstrategies, therefore, are influenced in part by the political system from which they emerge.

The United States in September 2001 was ripe for provocation, and al-Qaida appears to have understood this. The new administration of

George W. Bush was known to be hawkish in its foreign policy and in its attitude toward the use of military power. In a November 2004 video-tape, bin Laden bragged that al-Qaida found it "easy for us to provoke this administration."[61] The strategy appears to be working. A 2004 Pew survey found that international trust in the United States had declined significantly in response to the invasion of Iraq.[62] Similarly, a 2004 report by the International Institute for Strategic Studies found that al-Qaida's recruitment and fundrais-ing efforts had been given a major boost by the U.S. invasion of Iraq.[63] In the words of Shibley Telhami, "What we're seeing now is a disturbing sympathy with al-Qaida coupled with resent-ment toward the United States."[64] The Bush administration's eagerness to overthrow Sad-dam Hussein, a desire that predated the Sep-tember 11 attacks, has, in the words of bin Laden, "contributed to these remarkable results for al-Qaida."[65]

BEST RESPONSES TO PROVOCATION   The best response to provocation is a discriminating strat-egy that inflicts as little collateral damage as pos-sible. Countries should seek out and destroy the terrorists and their immediate backers to reduce the likelihood of future terror attacks, but they must carefully isolate these targets from the general population, which may or may not be sympathetic to the terrorists.[66] This type of dis-criminating response will require superior intel-ligence capabilities. In this regard, the United States' efforts to invest in information-gathering abilities in response to September 11 have been underwhelming. Even the most basic steps, such as developing a deeper pool of expertise in the regional languages, have been slow in coming.[67] This stands in contrast to U.S. behavior during the Cold War, when the government sponsored research centers at top universities to analyze every aspect of the Soviet economic, military, and political system. The weakness of the U.S. intelligence apparatus has been most clearly revealed in the inability of the United States to

eliminate bin Laden and al-Zawahiri, and in the United States' decision to invade Iraq.[68] Faulty U.S. intelligence has simultaneously protected al-Qaida leaders from death and led to the destruc-tion of thousands of Muslim civilians—exactly the response al-Qaida was likely seeking.

Spoiling: Sabotaging the Peace

The goal of a spoiling strategy is to ensure that peace overtures between moderate leaders on the terrorists' side and the target government do not succeed.[69] It works by playing on the mistrust between these two groups and succeeds when one or both parties fail to sign or implement a settlement. It is often employed when the ulti-mate objective is territorial change.

Terrorists resort to a spoiling strategy when relations between two enemies are improving and a peace agreement threatens the terrorists' more far-reaching goals. Peace agreements alarm terrorists because they understand that moder-ate citizens are less likely to support ongoing violence once a compromise agreement between more moderate groups has been reached. Thus, Iranian radicals kidnapped fifty-two Americans in Tehran in 1979 not because relations between the United States and Iran were becoming more belligerent, but because three days earlier Iran's relatively moderate prime minister, Mehdi Bazargan, met with the U.S. national security adviser, Zbigniew Brzezinski, and the two were photographed shaking hands. From the perspec-tive of the radicals, a real danger of reconciliation existed between the two countries, and violence was used to prevent this.[70] A similar problem has hampered Arab-Israeli peace negotiations, as well as talks between Protestants and Catholics in Northern Ireland.

A spoiling strategy works by persuading the enemy that moderates on the terrorists' side can-not be trusted to abide by a peace deal. When-ever two sides negotiate a peace agreement, there is uncertainty about whether the deal is self-enforcing. Each side fears that even if it hon-ors its commitments, the other side may not, catapulting it back to war on disadvantageous terms. Some Israelis, for example, feared that if Israel returned an additional 13 percent of the West Bank to the Palestinians, as mandated by the 1998 Wye accord, the Palestinian Authority would relaunch its struggle from an improved territorial base. Extremists understand that moderates look for signs that their former enemy will violate an agreement and that targeting these moderates with violence will heighten their fears that they will be exploited. Thus terrorist attacks are designed to persuade a targeted group that the seemingly moderate opposition with whom it negotiated an agreement will not or cannot stop terrorism, and hence cannot be trusted to honor an agreement.

Terrorist acts are particularly effective during peace negotiations because opposing parties are naturally distrustful of each other's motives and have limited sources of information about each other's intentions. Thus, even if moderate leaders are willing to aggressively suppress extremists on their side, terrorists know that isolated violence might still convince the target to reject the deal. A reason for this is that the targeted group may not be able to readily observe the extent of the crackdown and must base its judgments primarily on whether terrorism occurs or not. Even a sincere effort at self-policing, therefore, will not necessarily convince the targeted group to proceed with a settlement if a terrorist attack occurs.

CONDITIONS FAVORABLE TO SPOILING Terrorists pursuing a spoiling strategy are likely to be more successful when the enemy perceives moderates on their side to be strong and therefore more capable of halting terrorism.[71] When an attack occurs, the target cannot be sure whether moderates on the other side can suppress their own extremists but choose not to, or are weak and lack the ability to stop them. Israelis, for example, frequently questioned whether Yasser Arafat was simply unable to stop terrorist attacks against Israel or was unwilling to do so. The

weaker the moderates are perceived to be, the less impact a terrorist attack will have on the other side's trust, and the less likely such an attack is to convince them to abandon a peace agreement.

The Israeli-Palestinian conflict, and in particular the Oslo peace process, has been plagued by spoilers. On the Palestinian side, Hamas's violent attacks coincided with the ratification and implementation of accords—occasions when increased mistrust could thwart progress toward peace. Hamas also stepped up its attacks prior to Israeli elections in 1996 and 2001, in which Labor was the incumbent party, in an effort to persuade Israeli voters to cast their votes for the less cooperative and less trusting hard-line Likud Party.[72] Terrorism was especially effective after Arafat's 1996 electoral victory, when it became clear to the Israelis that Arafat was, at the time, a popular and powerful leader within the Palestinian community.[73] This in turn suggested to the Israelis that Arafat was capable of cracking down aggressively on terrorist violence but was unwilling to do so, a sign that he could not be trusted to keep the peace.

BEST RESPONSES TO SPOILING When mutual trust is high, a peace settlement can be implemented despite ongoing terrorist acts and the potential vulnerabilities the agreement can create. Trust, however, is rarely high after long conflicts, which is why spoilers can strike with a reasonable chance that their attack will be successful. Strategies that build trust and reduce vulnerability are, therefore, the best response to spoiling.

Vulnerabilities emerge in peace processes in two ways. Symmetric vulnerabilities occur during the implementation of a deal because both sides must lower their guard. The Israelis, for example, have had to relax controls over the occupied territories, and the Palestinians were obligated to disarm militant groups. Such symmetric vulnerabilities can be eased by third-party monitoring and verification of the peace implementation process. Monitoring can help reduce uncertainty regarding the behavior of the parties. Even better, third-party enforcement of the deal can make reneging more costly, increasing confidence in the deal and its ultimate success.[74]

Vulnerabilities can also be longer term and asymmetric. In any peace deal between Israel and the Palestinians, the ability of the Palestinians to harm Israel will inevitably grow as Palestinians build their own state and acquire greater military capabilities. This change in the balance of power can make it difficult for the side that will see an increase in its power to credibly commit not to take advantage of this increase later on. This commitment problem can cause conflicts to be prolonged even though there are possible peace agreements that both sides would prefer to war.[75]

The problem of shifting power can be addressed in at least three ways. First, agreements themselves can be crafted in ways that limit the post-treaty shift in power. Power-sharing agreements such as that between the Liberals and Conservatives to create a single shared presidency in Colombia in 1957 are one example of this. Allowing the defeated side to retain some military capabilities, as Confederate officers were allowed to do after the surrender at Appomattox, is another example.[76] Second, peace settlements can require the side about to be advantaged to send a costly signal of its honorable intentions, such as providing constitutional protections of minority rights. An example is the Constitutional Law on National Minorities passed in Croatia in 2002, which protects the right of minorities to obtain an education in their own language. Finally, parties can credibly commit to an agreement by participating in international institutions that insist on the protection of minority rights. A government that is willing to join the European Union effectively constrains itself from exploiting a minority group because of the high costs to that government of being ejected from the group.

Outbidding: Zealots versus Sellouts

Outbidding arises when two key conditions hold: two or more domestic parties are competing for leadership of their side, and the general population is uncertain about which of the groups best represents their interests.[77] The competition between Hamas and Fatah is a classic case where two groups vie for the support of the Palestinian citizens and where the average Palestinian is uncertain about which side he or she ought to back.

If citizens had full information about the preferences of the competing groups, an outbidding strategy would be unnecessary and ineffective; citizens would simply support the group that best aligned with their own interests. In reality, however, citizens cannot be sure if the group competing for power truly represents their preferences. The group could be a strong and resolute defender of the cause (zealots) or weak and ineffective stooges of the enemy (sellouts). If citizens support zealots, they get a strong champion but with some risk that they will be dragged into a confrontation with the enemy that they end up losing. If citizens support sellouts, they get peace but at the price of accepting a worse outcome than might have been achieved with additional armed struggle. Groups competing for power have an incentive to signal that they are zealots rather than sellouts. Terrorist attacks can serve this function by signaling that a group has the will to continue the armed struggle despite its costs.

Three reasons help to explain why groups are likely to be rewarded for being more militant rather than less. First, in bargaining contexts, it is often useful to be represented by an agent who is more hard-line than oneself. Hard-line agents will reject deals that one would accept, which will force the adversary to make a better offer than one would get by representing oneself in the negotiations.[78] Palestinians might therefore prefer Hamas as a negotiating agent with Israel because it has a reputation for resolve and will reject inferior deals.

Second, uncertainty may also exist about the type of adversary the population and its competing groups are facing. If the population believes there is some chance that their adversary is untrustworthy (unwilling to compromise under any condition), then they know that conflict may be inevitable, in which case being represented by zealots may be advantageous.[79]

A third factor that may favor outbidding is that office-holding itself may produce incentives to sell out. Here, the problem lies with the benefits groups receive once in office (i.e., income and power). Citizens fear that their leaders, once in office, may betray important principles and decide to settle with the enemy on unfavorable terms. They know that holding office skews one's preferences toward selling out, but they remain unsure about which of their leaders is most likely to give in. Terrorist organizations exploit this uncertainty by using violence to signal their commitment to a cause. Being perceived as more extreme than the median voter works to the terrorists' benefit because it balances out the "tempering effect" of being in office.

An interesting aspect of the outbidding strategy is that the enemy is only tangentially related to the strategic interaction. In fact, an attack motivated by outbidding may not even be designed to achieve any goal related to the enemy, such as inducing a concession or scuttling a peace treaty. The process is almost entirely concerned with the signal it sends to domestic audiences uncertain about their own leadership and its commitment to a cause. As such, outbidding provides a potential explanation for terrorist attacks that continue even when they seem unable to produce any real results.

CONDITIONS FAVORABLE TO OUTBIDDING Outbidding will be favored when multiple groups are competing for the allegiance of a similar demographic base of support. In Peru, the 1970s saw the development of a number of leftist groups seeking to represent the poor and indigenous

population. When the military turned over power to an elected government in 1980, the Shining Path took up an armed struggle to distinguish itself from groups that chose to pursue electoral politics.[80] It also embarked on an assassination campaign designed to weaken rival leftist groups and intimidate their followers. When organizations encounter less competition for the support of their main constituents, outbidding will be less appealing.

BEST RESPONSES TO OUTBIDDING One solution to the problem of outbidding would be to eliminate the struggle for power by encouraging competing groups to consolidate into a unified opposition. If competition among resistance groups is eliminated, the incentive for outbidding also disappears. The downside of this counterstrategy is that a unified opposition may be stronger than a divided one. United oppositions, however, can make peace and deliver, whereas divided ones may face greater structural disincentives to do so.

An alternative strategy for the government to pursue in the face of outbidding is to validate the strategy chosen by nonviolent groups by granting them concessions and attempting to satisfy the demands of their constituents. If outbidding can be shown to yield poor results in comparison to playing within the system, groups may be persuaded to abandon the strategy. As in the case of the Shining Path, this may require providing physical protection to competing groups in case the outbidder turns to intimidation in its competition with less violent rivals. In general, any steps that can be taken to make the non-outbidding groups seem successful (e.g., channeling resources and government services to their constituents) will also help undermine the outbidders. The high turnout in the December 2005 Iraqi election in Sunni-dominated regions may indicate that outbidding is beginning to fail in the communities most strongly opposed to the new political system.[81]

Conclusion

Terrorist violence is a form of costly signaling by which terrorists attempt to influence the beliefs of their enemy and the population they represent or wish to control. They use violence to signal their strength and resolve in an effort to produce concessions from their enemy and obedience and support from their followers. They also attack both to sow mistrust between moderates who might want to make peace and to provoke a reaction that makes the enemy appear barbarous and untrustworthy.

In this article, we have laid out the five main goals terrorist organizations seek and the five most important terrorist strategies, and we have outlined when they are likely to be tried and what the best counterstrategies might look like. What becomes clear in this brief analysis is that a deeper study of each of the five strategies is needed to reveal the nuanced ways in which terrorism works, and to refine responses to it. We conclude by highlighting two variables that will be important in any such analysis, and by a final reflection on counterterror policies that are strategically independent or not predicated on the specific strategy being used.

The first variable is information. It has long been a truism that the central front in counterinsurgency warfare is the information front. The same is true in terrorism. Costly signaling is pointless in the absence of uncertainty on the part of the recipient of the signal. Attrition is designed to convince the target that the costs of maintaining a policy are not worth the gains; if the target already knew this, it would have ceded the issue without an attack being launched. Provocation is designed to goad the target into retaliating indiscriminately (because it lacks information to discriminate), which will persuade the population that the target is malevolent (because it is uncertain of the target's intentions). The other strategies are similarly predicated on uncertainty, intelligence, learning, and communi-

nication. Thus, it bears emphasizing that the problem of terrorism is not a problem of applying force per se, but one of acquiring intelligence and affecting beliefs. With the right information, the proper application of force is comparatively straightforward. The struggle against terrorism is, therefore, not usefully guided by the metaphor of a "war on terrorism" any more than policies designed to alleviate poverty are usefully guided by the metaphor of a "war on poverty" or narcotics policy by a "war on drugs." The struggle against terrorism can more usefully be thought of as a struggle to collect and disseminate reliable information in environments fraught with uncertainty.

The second important variable is regime type. Democracies have been the sole targets of attritional suicide bombing campaigns, whereas authoritarian regimes such as those in Algeria routinely face campaigns by rebel groups pursuing an intimidation strategy. Democracies also seem to be more susceptible to attrition and provocation strategies. This type of variation cries out for deeper analysis of the strengths and weakness of different regime types in the face of different terrorist strategies. Our analysis suggests that democracies are more likely to be sensitive to the costs of terrorist attacks, to grant concessions to terrorists so as to limit future attacks, to be constrained in their ability to pursue a lengthy attritional campaign against an organization, but also to be under greater pressure to "do something." This does not mean that all democracies will behave incorrectly in the face of terrorist attacks all the time. Democratic regimes may possess certain structural features, however, that make them attractive targets for terrorism.

Finally, we realize that our discussion is only a beginning and that further elaboration of each of the strategies and their corresponding counterstrategies awaits future research. We also understand that not all counterterrorism policies are predicated on the specific strategy terrorists pursue. Our analysis is at the middling level of strategic interaction. At the tactical level are all the tools of intelligence gathering and target defense that make sense no matter what the terrorist's strategy is. At the higher level are the primary sources of terrorism such as poverty, education, international conflict, and chauvinistic indoctrination that enable terrorist organizations to operate and survive in the first place. Our aim in this article has been to try to understand why these organizations choose certain forms of violence, and how this violence serves their larger purposes. The United States has the ability to reduce the likelihood of additional attacks on its territory and citizens. But it will be much more successful if it first understands the goals terrorists are seeking and the underlying strategic logic by which a plane flying into a skyscraper might deliver the desired response.

NOTES

1. Thomas L. Friedman, "Marines Complete Beirut Pullback: Moslems Move In," *New York Times*, February 27, 2004.

2. Don Van Natta Jr., "The Struggle for Iraq: Last American Combat Troops Quit Saudi Arabia," *New York Times*, September 22, 2003.

3. James Glanz, "Hostage Is Freed after Philippine Troops Are Withdrawn from Iraq," *New York Times*, July 21, 2004.

4. Robert A. Pape, *Dying to Win: The Strategic Logic of Suicide Terrorism* (New York: Random House, 2005), p. 65.

5. Alan B. Krueger and David D. Laitin, "Kto Kogo? A Cross-Country Study of the Origins and Targets of Terrorism," Princeton University and Stanford University, 2003; Alan B. Krueger and Jitka Maleckova, "Education, Poverty, and Terrorism: Is There a Causal Connection?" *Journal of Economic Perspectives*, Vol. 17, No. 4 (November 2003), pp. 119–144; and Alberto Abadie, "Poverty, Political Freedom, and the Roots of Terrorism," Faculty Research Working Papers Series, RWP04-043 (Cambridge, Mass.: John F. Kennedy School of Government, Harvard University, 2004).

6. Jessica Stern, *Terror in the Name of God: Why Religious Militants Kill* (New York: Ecco-HarperCollins, 2003).

7. Of course, terrorists will also be seeking best responses to government responses. A pair of strategies that are best responses to each other constitutes a Nash equilibrium, the fundamental prediction tool of game theory.

8. Office of Counterterrorism, U.S. Department of State, "Foreign Terrorist Organizations," fact sheet, October 11, 2005, http://www.state.gov/s/ct/rls/fs/3719.htm.

9. Quoted in Nasra Hassan, "An Arsenal of Believers: Talking to the 'Human Bombs,'" *New Yorker*, November 19, 2001, p. 37.

10. For discussion of differing definitions of terrorism, see Alex P. Schmid and Albert J. Jongman, *Political Terrorism: A New Guide to Actors, Authors, Concepts, Data Bases, Theories, and Literature* (New Brunswick, N.J.: Transaction, 1988), pp. 1–38. We do not focus on state terrorism because states face very different opportunities and constraints in their use of violence, and we do not believe the two cases are similar enough to be profitably analyzed together.

11. For the distinction between goals and strategies, see David A. Lake and Robert Powell, eds., *Strategic Choice and International Relations* (Princeton, N.J.: Princeton University Press, 1999), especially chap. 1.

12. On revolutionary terrorism, see Martha Crenshaw Hutchinson, "The Concept of Revolutionary Terrorism," *Journal of Conflict Resolution*, Vol. 16, No. 3 (September 1972), pp. 383–396; Martha Crenshaw Hutchinson, *Revolutionary Terrorism: The FLN in Algeria, 1954–1962* (Stanford, Calif.: Hoover Institution Press, 1978); and H. Edward Price Jr., "The Strategy and Tactics of Revolutionary Terrorism," *Comparative Studies in Society*

and History, Vol. 19, No. 1 (January 1977), pp. 52–66.

13. This group has recently surrendered its weapons.

14. Some analysts argue that many terrorist organizations have degenerated into little more than self-perpetuating businesses that primarily seek to enhance their own power and wealth, and only articulate political goals for rhetorical purposes. See, for example, Stern, *Terror in the Name of God*, pp. 235–236. This suggests that power and wealth should be considered goals in their own right. All organizations, however, seek power and wealth to further their political objectives, and these are better viewed as instrumental in nature.

15. A difficult coding issue arises in determining when a group is a nonstate actor engaged in status quo maintenance and when it is simply a covert agent of the state. Some death squads were linked to elements in the armed forces, yet were not necessarily responsive to the chief executive of the country. Others were tied to right-wing parties and are more clearly nonstate, unless that party is the party in power. See Bruce D. Campbell and Arthur D. Brenner, eds., *Death Squads in Global Perspective: Murder with Deniability* (New York: Palgrave Macmillan, 2002).

16. The Taliban, which is not listed, does pursue social control; and the Israeli group Kach, which seeks to maintain the subordinate status of Palestinians in Israel and eventually to expel them, may also be considered to seek it. The Memorial Institute for the Prevention of Terrorism maintains a database of terrorist organizations that includes more than forty groups based in the United States. Some of these can be considered to seek social control, such as the Army of God, which targets doctors who provide abortions. See http://www.tkb.org.

17. Thomas Perry Thornton, "Terror as a Weapon of Political Agitation," in Harry Eckstein,

ed., *Internal War: Problems and Approaches* (London: Free Press of Glencoe, 1964), p. 87.

18. Martha Crenshaw, "The Causes of Terrorism," *Comparative Politics*, Vol. 13, No. 4 (July 1981), pp. 379–399.

19. David Fromkin, "The Strategy of Terrorism," *Foreign Affairs*, Vol. 53, No. 4 (July 1975), pp. 683–698.

20. Price, "The Strategy and Tactics of Revolutionary Terrorism," pp. 54–58. Other related discussions include Paul Wilkinson, "The Strategic Implications of Terrorism," in M.L. Sondhi, ed., *Terrorism and Political Violence: A Sourcebook* (New Delhi: Har-anand Publications, 2000); Paul Wilkinson, *Terrorism and the Liberal State* (New York: New York University Press, 1986), pp. 110–118; and Schmid and Jongman, *Political Terrorism*, pp. 50–59.

21. Geoffrey Blainey, *The Causes of War*, 3d ed. (New York: Free Press, 1988), p. 122.

22. James D. Fearon, "Rationalist Explanations for War," *International Organization*, Vol. 49, No. 3 (Summer 1995), pp. 379–414; and Robert Powell, "Bargaining Theory and International Conflict," *Annual Review of Political Science*, Vol. 5 (June 2002), pp. 1–30.

23. Thomas Hobbes, *Leviathan* (New York: Penguin, [1651] 1968), pp. 184.

24. John H. Herz, "Idealist Internationalism and the Security Dilemma," *World Politics*, Vol. 2, No. 2 (January 1950), pp. 157–180; Robert Jervis, *Perception and Misperception in International Politics* (Princeton, N.J.: Princeton University Press, 1976); Robert Jervis, "Cooperation under the Security Dilemma," *World Politics*, Vol. 30, No. 2 (January 1978), pp. 167–214; and Charles L. Glaser, "The Security Dilemma Revisited," *World Politics*, Vol. 50, No. 1 (October 1997), pp. 171–202.

25. Andrew H. Kydd, *Trust and Mistrust in International Relations* (Princeton, N.J.: Princeton University Press, 2005).

26. John G. Riley, "Silver Signals: Twenty-five Years of Screening and Signaling," *Journal*

of Economic Literature, Vol. 39, No. 2 (June 2001), pp. 432–478.

27. James D. Fearon, "Signaling Foreign Policy Interests: Tying Hands vs. Sunk Costs," *Journal of Conflict Resolution*, Vol. 41, No. 1 (February 1977), pp. 68–90.

28. Dan Reiter, "Exploring the Bargaining Model of War," *Perspectives on Politics*, Vol. 1, No. 1 (March 2003), pp. 27–43; and Robert Powell, "Bargaining and Learning While Fighting," *American Journal of Political Science*, Vol. 48, No. 2 (April 2004), pp. 344–361.

29. Rival terrorist or moderate groups are also important, but terrorism is not often used to signal such groups. Sometimes rival groups are targeted in an effort to eliminate them, but this violence is usually thought of as internecine warfare rather than terrorism. The targeted government may also be divided into multiple actors, but these divisions are not crucial for a broad understanding of terrorist strategies.

30. This list is not exhaustive. In particular, it omits two strategies that have received attention in the literature: advertising and retaliation. Advertising may play a role in the beginning of some conflicts, but it does not sustain long-term campaigns of terrorist violence. Retaliation is a motivation for some terrorists, but terrorism would continue even if the state did not strike at terrorists, because terrorism is designed to achieve some goal, not just avenge counterterrorist attacks.

31. Per Baltzer Overgaard, "The Scale of Terrorist Attacks as a Signal of Resources," *Journal of Conflict Resolution*, Vol. 38, No. 3 (September 1994), pp. 452–478; and Harvey E. Lapan and Todd Sandler, "Terrorism and Signaling," *European Journal of Political Economy*, Vol. 9, No. 3 (August 1993), pp. 383–398.

32. J. Maynard Smith, "The Theory of Games and Evolution in Animal Conflicts," *Journal of Theoretical Biology*, Vol. 47 (1974), pp. 209–211; John J. Mearsheimer, *Conventional*

Deterrence (Ithaca, N.Y.: Cornell University Press, 1983), pp. 33–35; and James D. Fearon, "Bargaining, Enforcement, and International Cooperation," *International Organization*, Vol. 52, No. 2 (Spring 1998), pp. 269–305.

33. Bernard Lewis, "The Revolt of Islam," *New Yorker*, November 19, 2001, p. 61.

34. Quoted in Hassan, "An Arsenal of Believers," p. 38.

35. Robert A. Pape, "The Strategic Logic of Suicide Terrorism," *American Political Science Review*, Vol. 97, No. 3 (August 2003), pp. 343–361; and Pape, *Dying to Win*.

36. Pape, *Dying to Win*, p. 44. Krueger and Laitin also find that targets of terrorism tend to be democratic. See Krueger and Laitin, "Kto Kogo?"

37. The U.S. program of extraordinary rendition, for example, is an effort to evade the restrictions usually faced by democracies by outsourcing the dirty work.

38. Debate Goes On Over Lebanon Withdrawal, *Haaretz*, May 23, 2001; and Daoud Kuttab, "The Lebanon Lesson," *Jerusalem Post*, May 25, 2000.

39. Interview with Mahmoud Khalid al-Zahar, *Al Jazeera*, October 22, 2005.

40. Osama bin Laden, *Messages to the World: The Statements of Osama bin Laden*, trans. James Howarth, ed. Bruce Lawrence (London: Verso, 2005), pp. 241–242.

41. Osama bin Laden, "Declaration of War against the Americans Occupying the Land of the Two Holy Places," *Al-Quds Al-Arabi*, August 1996, http://www.pbs.org/newshour/terrorism/international/fatwa_1996.html.

42. Peter C. Sederberg, "Conciliation as Counterterrorist Strategy," *Journal of Peace Research*, Vol. 32, No. 3 (August 1995), pp. 295–312.

43. Stephen Flynn, *America the Vulnerable: How Our Government Is Failing to Protect Us from Terrorism* (New York: HarperCollins, 2004).

44. Graham T. Allison, Owen R. Coté Jr., Richard A. Falkenrath, and Steven E. Miller, *Avoiding*

Nuclear Anarchy: Containing the Threat of Loose Russian Nuclear Weapons and Fissile Material (Cambridge, Mass.: MIT Press, 1996); and Graham Allison, *Nuclear Terrorism: The Ultimate Preventable Catastrophe* (New York: Times Books, 2004).

45. John Mueller, "Six Rather Unusual Propositions about Terrorism," *Terrorism and Political Violence*, Vol. 17, No. 4 (Winter 2005), pp. 487–505.

46. The literature on deterrence is vast. See, for example, Thomas C. Schelling, *Arms and Influence* (New Haven, Conn.: Yale University Press, 1966); and Christopher H. Achen and Duncan Snidal, "Rational Deterrence Theory and Comparative Case Studies," *World Politics*, Vol. 41, No. 2 (January 1989), pp. 143–169.

47. Noor Khan, "Militants Behead Afghan Principal for Educating Girls," *Boston Globe*, January 5, 2006.

48. Crenshaw Hutchinson, "The Concept of Revolutionary Terrorism," p. 390.

49. Stathis N. Kalyvas, "Wanton and Senseless? The Logic of Massacres in Algeria," *Rationality and Society*, Vol. 11, No. 3 (August 1999), pp. 243–285.

50. James D. Fearon and David D. Laitin, "Ethnicity, Insurgency, and Civil War," *American Political Science Review*, Vol. 97, No. 1 (February 2003), pp. 75–90.

51. United States National Security Council, *National Strategy for Victory in Iraq* (Washington, D.C.: White House, November 2005), p. 7.

52. Secretary of State Condoleezza Rice, "Iraq and U.S. Policy," testimony before the U.S. Senate Committee on Foreign Relations, October 19, 2005, 109th Cong., 1st sess., http://www.foreign.senate.gov/testimony/2005/RiceTestimony051019.pdf.

53. See Lewis Sorley, *A Better War: The Unexamined Victories and the Final Tragedy of America's Last Years in Vietnam* (New York: Harcourt, 1999). This thesis is not without controversy. See Matt Steinglass, "Vietnam and Victory," *Boston Globe*, December 18, 2005.

54. Fromkin, "The Strategy of Terrorism."

55. Crenshaw, "The Causes of Terrorism," p. 387; and Price, "The Strategy and Tactics of Revolutionary Terrorism," p. 58.

56. Paddy Woodworth, "Why Do They Kill? The Basque Conflict in Spain," *World Policy Journal*, Vol. 18, No. 1 (Spring 2001), p. 7.

57. David A. Lake, "Rational Extremism: Understanding Terrorism in the Twenty-first Century," *Dialog-IO*, Vol. 56, No. 2 (Spring 2002), pp. 15–29.

58. Ethan Bueno de Mesquita and Eric S. Dickson, "The Propaganda of the Deed: Terrorism, Counterterrorism, and Mobilization," Washington University and New York University, 2005. Bueno de Mesquita and Dickson also argue that government violence lowers economic prosperity, which favors extremists in their competition with moderates.

59. Ethan Bueno de Mesquita, "Politics and the Suboptimal Provision of Counterterror," *International Organization* [Vol. 61, No. 1 (Winter 2007), pp. 9–36].

60. On the other hand, more dovish regimes might feel political pressure to take strong visible actions, whereas a regime with hawkish credentials could credibly claim that it was pursuing effective but nonvisible tactics. For a similar logic, see Kenneth A. Schultz, "The Politics of Risking Peace: Do Hawks or Doves Deliver the Olive Branch?" *International Organization*, Vol. 59, No. 1 (Winter 2005), pp. 1–38.

61. Bin Laden, *Messages to the World*, pp. 241–242.

62. Pew Research Center for the People and the Press, Pew Global Attitudes Project: Nine-Nation Survey, "A Year after the Iraq War: Mistrust of America in Europe Ever Higher, Muslim Anger Persists," March 16, 2004.

63. See International Institute for Strategic Studies, *Strategic Survey, 2003/4: An Evalua-*

tion and Forecast of World Affairs (London: Routledge, 2005).

64. Quoted in Dafna Linzer, "Poll Shows Growing Arab Rancor at U.S.," *Washington Post*, July 23, 2004.

65. Bob Woodward, *Plan of Attack* (New York: Simon and Schuster, 2004), pp. 21–23; and bin Laden, *Messages to the World*, pp. 241–242.

66. A program of economic and social assistance to these more moderate elements would provide counterevidence that the target is not malicious or evil as the terrorist organizations had claimed.

67. Farah Stockman, "Tomorrow's Homework: Reading, Writing, and Arabic," *Boston Globe*, January 6, 2006.

68. For an analysis of obstacles to innovation in U.S. intelligence agencies, see Amy B. Zegart, "September 11 and the Adaptation Failure of U.S. Intelligence Agencies," *International Security*, Vol. 29, No. 4 (Spring 2005), pp. 78–111.

69. Stephen John Stedman, "Spoiler Problems in Peace Processes," *International Security*, Vol. 22, No. 2 (Fall 1997), pp. 5–53.

70. Lewis, "The Revolt of Islam," p. 54.

71. Andrew H. Kydd and Barbara F. Walter, "Sabotaging the Peace: The Politics of Extremist Violence," *International Organization*, Vol. 56, No. 2 (Spring 2002), pp. 263–296.

72. Claude Berrebi and Esteban F. Klor, "On Terrorism and Electoral Outcomes: Theory and Evidence from the Israeli-Palestinian Conflict," Princeton University and Hebrew University of Jerusalem, 2004.

73. Kydd and Walter, "Sabotaging the Peace," pp. 279–289.

74. Barbara F. Walter, *Committing to Peace: The Successful Settlement of Civil Wars* (Princeton, N.J.: Princeton University Press, 2002); and Holger Schmidt, "When (and Why) Do Brokers Have to Be Honest? Impartiality and Third-Party Support for Peace Implementation after Civil Wars, 1945–1999," Georgetown University, 2004.

75. Fearon, "Rationalist Explanations for War"; James D. Fearon, "Commitment Problems and the Spread of Ethnic Conflict," in David A. Lake and Donald Rothchild, eds., *The International Spread of Ethnic Conflict: Fear, Diffusion, and Escalation* (Princeton, N.J.: Princeton University Press, 1998); and Robert Powell, "The Inefficient Use of Power: Costly Conflict with Complete Information," *American Political Science Review*, Vol. 98, No. 2 (May 2004), pp. 231–241.

76. As part of the terms of surrender, Confederate officers were allowed to keep their side-arms and personal property (including their horses) and return home.

77. For the most extensive treatment of terrorism and outbidding, see Mia Bloom, *Dying to Kill: The Allure of Suicide Terrorism* (New York: Columbia University Press, 2005). See also Stuart J. Kaufman, "Spiraling to Ethnic War: Elites, Masses, and Moscow in Moldova's Civil War," *International Security*, Vol. 21, No. 2 (Fall 1996), pp. 108–138.

78. Abhinay Muthoo, *Bargaining Theory with Applications* (Cambridge: Cambridge University Press, 1999), p. 230.

79. Rui J.P. de Figueiredo Jr. and Barry R. Weingast, "The Rationality of Fear: Political Opportunism and Ethnic Conflict," in Barbara F. Walter and Jack Snyder, eds., *Civil Wars, Insecurity, and Intervention* (New York: Columbia University Press, 1999), pp. 261–302.

80. James Ron, "Ideology in Context: Explaining Sendero Luminoso's Tactical Escalation," *Journal of Peace Research*, Vol. 38, No. 5 (September 2001), p. 582.

81. Dexter Filkins, "Iraqis, Including Sunnis, Vote in Large Numbers on Calm Day," *New York Times*, December 16, 2005.

DAVID KILCULLEN

From *The Accidental Guerrilla: Fighting Small Wars in the Midst of a Big One*

The Accidental Guerrilla

America . . . goes not abroad in search of monsters to destroy. . . . She well knows that by once enlisting under other banners than her own, were they even the banners of foreign independence, she would involve herself, beyond the power of extrication, in all the wars of interest and intrigue, of individual avarice, envy, and ambition, which assume the colors and usurp the standard of freedom. The fundamental maxims of her policy would insensibly change from liberty to force. The frontlet upon her brows would no longer beam with the ineffable splendor of freedom and independence; but in its stead would soon be substituted an imperial diadem, flashing in false and tarnished lustre the murky radiance of dominion and power. She might become the dictatress of the world: she would be no longer the ruler of her own spirit.

—John Quincy Adams, U.S. secretary of state, Address on the Anniversary of Independence (July 4, 1821)

In April 2001, five months before 9/11, I was studying at the Australian Defence College, attending a year-long course in strategy and national security policy for military officers and civilian offi-

From David Kilcullen, *The Accidental Guerrilla: Fighting Small Wars in the Midst of a Big One* (Oxford: Oxford University Press, 2009), Chap. 1.

cials. One morning, we received a distinguished American visitor, a retired general who spent much of his two-hour lecture talking about how ground warfare was disappearing.

The future threat environment, he said, would involve high-tech air and maritime campaigns, peace operations like Kosovo or Bosnia, humanitarian missions like Somalia, or stabilization missions like Sierra Leone or East Timor. Maritime conflict might arise with China over Taiwan, or with North Korea over its nuclear program,[1] and there was a slight possibility of the occasional brief, lopsided land conflict against a technologically and tactically unequal adversary, like the 1991 Gulf War. But serious ground combat was increasingly unlikely, he said.

The second half of the twentieth century had seen the United States achieve unprecedented dominance in conventional warfare through precision air and maritime strike, satellite- and sensor-based intelligence, and high-speed communications: a high-tech, network-based "system of systems." Any rational adversary would see the writing on the wall, eschew warfare as an instrument of policy, and instead choose to compete with the West in ideological or economic terms, since confronting us directly on the field of battle would be suicidal, as any potential enemy would know. Even if, through miscalculation or sheer stupidity, our enemies did fight us, U.S. military prowess was such that their defeat would be swift and decisive. The key challenge for Western militaries was therefore to keep up with the extremely fast pace of technological development being set by the United

States, the so-called revolution in military affairs. This would allow allies to contribute ground forces for relatively frequent but low-intensity peacekeeping interventions, while contributing "niche" air and maritime assets to round out U.S. forces in the highly unlikely event of a major conflict. Large-scale, long-term ground combat operations? Not so much.

One of my Air Force classmates had the temerity to point out that in fact, many wars were currently going on around the world—95 at the turn of the twenty-first century, according to one count—and almost all of these were land wars. It seemed that, in fact, ground combat was not becoming a thing of the past at all; around the world millions of people were engaged in it. True, technologically advanced democracies did not seem to be directly involved, except in conflict resolution or mitigation roles, but could we count on this always being so? Warfare seemed to be a phenomenon of the developing world, occurring within states or between ethnic or religious groups in parts of Asia and Africa. Nevertheless, didn't the large number of ongoing internal and ethnic conflicts invalidate our distinguished guest's view that war was disappearing?

Well, said the general, internal or ethno-religious conflicts weren't really wars, and civil wars didn't count under the classical definition of war either. War, formally declared, as a means for furthering policy objectives, was *organized violence between states*, in which the outcome was decided through the clash of armed forces on the battlefield, and this type of war *was* disappearing. The other conflicts we were seeing around the world arose from internal unrest, ethno-sectarian violence, narco-terrorism, or state fragility. Though we might choose to be involved in stabilizing or ending them, these would be interventions of choice, not wars of necessity, and our activities could not really be classed as "warfighting" but would be "military operations other than war."

Another classmate asked about the book *Chao Xian Zhan* (*Unrestricted Warfare*), published two years earlier by senior colonels Qiao Liang and Wang Xiangsui of the Chinese People's Liberation Army.[2] She pointed out that this book's key argument was that Western countries, particularly the United States, had created a trap for themselves by their very dominance of conventional warfare. Confronting the United States in direct conventional combat would indeed be folly, but rather than eschewing conflict, other countries or even nonstate actors could defeat the superpower through ignoring Western-defined rules of "conventional" war, instead applying what the authors called the "principle of addition": combining direct combat with electronic, diplomatic, cyber, terrorist, proxy, economic, political, and propaganda tools to overload, deceive, and exhaust the U.S. "system of systems." She emphasized that the authors advocated computer network attack, "lawfare" that exploited legal loopholes, economic warfare, attacking the viability of major corporations and financial institutions, media manipulation and deception, and urban guerrilla warfare.

Indeed, in an interview with *Zhongguo Qingnian Bao* (the official newspaper of the Chinese Communist Party Youth League), subsequently translated by the CIA's Foreign Broadcast Information Service, one of the authors, Colonel Qiao, said that "the first rule of unrestricted warfare is that there are no rules, with nothing forbidden."[3] Qiao said strong countries would not use "unrestricted warfare" against weak countries because "strong countries make the rules while rising ones break them and exploit loopholes. . . . The United States breaks [UN rules] and makes new ones when these rules don't suit [its purposes], but it has to observe its own rules or the whole world will not trust it."[4] Didn't this perhaps suggest, my colleague asked the general, that land warfare would continue into the new century? Rather than disappearing, might it change its character in response to the Western dominance of one particular high-technology *über-blitzkrieg* style of fighting that had become conventional orthodoxy but was not the only conceivable approach? Might our very dominance of this style of warfare have created an entirely new, but perhaps equally dangerous class of threats?

"Hmmm . . . no, I wouldn't really worry about that, if I were you," said the general, with a breezy, dismissive wave of the hand. United States dominance of conventional combat and precision strike would be enough to negate such new threats, reducing them to nuisance value only.

Listening to these exchanges, thinking back to my experience on operations during the preceding five years in Cyprus, Lebanon, Bougainville, Papua New Guinea, and East Timor—and remembering the Arabs, that night in the hills of West Java in 1996—I remember scratching my head and wondering what I was missing. Whether they admit it or not, most field officers think generals and politicians are wildly out of touch with reality, so I was prepared to cut this particular general some slack just on principle. But still, it felt as if there was more to this little difference of opinion than the normal generation gap.

Odd though it now seems, there was nothing particularly unusual before 9/11 about this "end of history" view of warfare. Some people saw as faintly ridiculous the notion that Western democracies would ever again deliberately initiate a war or that, even if one did break out, the West would be anything other than rapidly and sweetly victorious. Some took the same view as the general. Some emphasized the need to preserve technological superiority and a conventional war-fighting "capability edge" for deterrent purposes. Others focused on a crop of new security threats—people smuggling, narcotics trafficking, epidemic disease, natural disaster, climate change, poverty, state failure, terrorism, and civil unrest—many of which were internal and non-state-based, and related to *human* security (the welfare of individuals and groups in society) rather than *national* security (which, classically defined, focuses on the survival and political interests of states).[5]

At the same time, some thinkers were arguing that hybrid warfare, "a mixture of phenomena" involving a shifting combination of armed and unarmed, military and nonmilitary, state and nonstate, internal and international, and violent and nonviolent means would be the most common form of twenty-first-century conflict.[6] Like the authors of *Chao Xian Zhan*, these theorists saw the "principle of addition" and the complexity and many-sidedness of modern conflict (what Qiao and Wang called its "omni-directionality") as conceptual keys. In the "viscous medium" of ground combat, with its fear, hatred, chaos, and friction, the difficult but essential task of integrating military and civilian actions into a viable political strategy, under the arc-light scrutiny of the international media, would be critical: tactical virtuosity or operational art alone would count for little. Western countries would seek to master, control, and prevent violence, would uphold international norms (which, of course, they had themselves established in their own interests), and would tend to focus on preventing and ending conflicts started by others, preserving the status quo, rather than initiating wars themselves as an instrument of policy.

One of the best-considered expositions of this argument, known as counter war theory, came from Brigadier-General Loup Francart of the French army, a highly innovative strategist whose 1999 book *Maîtriser la violence: Une option stratégique* argued that in the twenty-first century, ground forces would mainly be required to intervene in extremely complex conditions of state failure and in humanitarian or peacekeeping environments, where law and order were compromised and state institutional frameworks were lacking.[7] Such forces would have to uphold the law of armed conflict (such as the Geneva Conventions) in the face of adversaries who ignored it, and Western countries would be seeking to control or end violence rather than, as in traditional warfare, to achieve policy ends *through* violence. This approach could be considered a "counterwar strategy," where the key threat to be mastered would be the conflict environment itself, rather than a particular armed enemy.[8]

It turns out, of course, that ground warfare is far from a thing of the past for Western democracies. Eight years after 9/11, with wars in Iraq and

Afghanistan and many other conflicts going on worldwide, the persistence of warfare on land into the twenty-first century is hardly a matter of dispute. And while human security, hybrid warfare, and counterwar strategy have certainly proven extremely important in today's complex operations, the notion that Western political leaders would never again initiate conflict preemptively or for policy reasons has proven spectacularly ill founded, while ground combat ("conventional"—that is, bound by the set of conventions favored by the current establishment, i.e., the West—or outside it and therefore "unconventional") has proven all too common, intense, and protracted. It would require another entire and rather different book to fully explore these issues, which remain hotly contentious: even analysts who follow them for a living are conceptually divided, and thinkers like Rupert Smith have done a better job in examining these questions than I could.[9] Instead, this [discussion] merely seeks to provide a context for * * * case studies of Afghanistan, Iraq, and other conflicts * * *. To do so, it lays out four ways to think about the threat, examines the risk of terrorism and approaches to managing it, and explores the implications for international security.

The Twenty-First Century Security Environment

HYBRID WARFARE What, then, are the key features of the threat environment? In general terms, we can begin by affirming the empirical validity of the hybrid warfare construct: today's conflicts clearly combine new actors with new technology and new or transfigured ways of war, but the old threats also remain and have to be dealt with at the same time and in the same space, stressing the resources and overloading the systems of western militaries. The "principle of addition" described almost a decade ago by Qiao and Wang clearly applies.

New actors include insurgent groups operating across international boundaries like Jema'ah Islamiyah (JI), Lashkar e-Tayyiba (LeT), and the Afghan Taliban; global terrorist networks with unprecedented demographic depth like Hizballah and al Qa'ida; and tribal and regional groups with postmodern capabilities but premodern structures and ideologies like some Iraqi insurgents. The new actors include gangs in Latin America and elsewhere whose levels of lethal capability and social organization are fast approaching those traditionally seen in insurgencies.[10] They also include "micro-actors with massive impact"[11]—like the eight terrorists who killed 191 commuters from 17 countries in the Madrid train bombings of March 11, 2004, spectacularly swaying Spain's general elections three days later and prompting its pull-out from Iraq. There are also armed commercial entities like security contractors and private military companies, and local and communitarian militias of various kinds.[12] In the maritime domain, the resurgence of piracy threats in the South China Sea and off the Horn of Africa suggests the existence of new and extremely well-armed and capable threat groups.

New technology includes new communications and media tools, high-lethality individual weapons, nanoengineering, robotics, and new kinds of explosives and munitions. New ways of war include Internet-enabled terrorism, transnational guerrilla warfare, and the emergence of an insurgent media marketplace. These have overlapped in the proliferation of weapons of mass destruction via networks like that of A. Q. Khan, which was ostensibly non-state-based (though Khan subsequently claimed that his relationship with the government of Pakistan was in fact very close).[13] And all of this exists alongside robust conventional and nuclear threats from traditional state-based adversaries. States still invade states, as Russia showed in its invasion of Georgia in August 2008, Israel in its invasion of Lebanon in 2006, Ethiopia in Somalia in 2007, and, of course, the West in Iraq and Afghanistan after 9/11.

Post-1945 institutions like the World Bank, the International Monetary Fund, the nuclear nonproliferation treaty regime, and the United

Nations have proven ill suited to the current environment, leading to widespread calls for reform. Some thinkers have questioned whether the "1945 rules-based order" still applies.[14] The United States, with national security institutions developed mainly under the Truman administration,[15] has struggled to adapt these institutions to post-9/11 threats. As the distinguished Singaporean diplomat and scholar Kishore Mahbubani has argued, policies like the invasion of Iraq, diplomatic unilateralism, comparative neglect of the Israel-Palestine peace process, extraordinary renditions, detention facilities like Guantanamo Bay, "water-boarding," and domestic surveillance have created the impression that the United States has walked away from the global rule-set that Washington and its key allies created after 1945. As noted earlier, Qiaø Liang predicted in 1999 that America "has to observe its own rules or the whole world won't trust it." This perceived breach of trust has indeed proven very harmful to America's reputation and wider interests, as well as to the functioning of the broader international system. In particular, events since 9/11 have exposed the limits of the utility of force as an international security tool, while as the eminent strategist Sir Michael Howard points out, framing the problem as a "war on terror" has tended to militarize key aspects of foreign policy.[16] I will discuss this issue in detail below, but first I will lay out a mental framework for thinking about the environment.

FOUR WAYS TO THINK ABOUT THE ENVIRONMENT As this discussion highlights, today's threat environment is nothing if not complex, ambiguous, dynamic, and multifaceted, making it impossible to describe through a single model. So this section examines the environment via four frameworks which, taken together, give a fuller picture of the threat, its characteristics, and its implications than could one framework alone. The four models are the *Globalization Backlash* thesis, the *Globalized Insurgency* model, the *Islamic Civil War* theory, and the *Asymmetric*

Warfare model. These are neither exhaustive nor mutually exclusive, but together they form a basis for the case studies that follow.

MODEL I: A BACKLASH AGAINST GLOBALIZATION The dozens of colonial insurgencies and guerrilla wars of the 1940s, 1950s, and 1960s—the conflicts Khrushchev called "wars of national liberation" in January 1961—seem in retrospect part of a pattern of "wars of decolonization." Between 1944 and about 1982,[17] almost all the old European empires crumbled, subject peoples gained their independence through armed or unarmed struggle, and the newly independent countries faced forbidding development and security challenges. Though each colonial conflict had some unique characteristics, all followed roughly similar pathways and contributed to a larger metapattern of conflict, fully visible only in retrospect. The threat environment within which the former colonial powers, the new postcolonial states, their internal constituents, and the broader security system operated was colored by this larger pattern, and by the proxy rivalry—global in scope and extremely intense at times—between the Soviet Union and the Western world.

The globalization backlash thesis suggests that, likewise, we may look back on today's conflicts as a series of "wars of globalization," in which each conflict differs but all follow similar pathways in response to one key driver, globalization, and in which a backlash against globalization provides the organizing principle for many conflicts. Globalization (a technology-enabled process of improved communications and transportation that enables the freer movement of goods, people, money, technology, ideas, and cultures across and within international borders) has prompted the emergence of a Western-dominated world culture, an interdependent world economy, and a global community of business, political, and intellectual elites. This is the world so insightfully described in economic terms in Thomas Friedman's 2005 book *The World Is Flat*, as a combination of "levelers" like personal computers, the Internet, open-sourcing, outsourcing, off-shoring, and streamlining of supply chains, along with a mutually reinforcing convergence between them.[18] Even the most avid apostles of globalization hesitate to suggest that its effects have been uniformly positive: indeed, most acknowledge that it has created a class of global haves and have-nots, and simultaneously (through globalized news media) has made the have-nots very aware of what they are missing, of how the other half lives, thus creating tension and anger through perceived "relative deprivation." Even beyond its uneven economic effects, the globalization process has thus also prompted a political and cultural backlash, often violent, against the extension of Western political and cultural influence, the disruptive effects of modernization and global integration, and the failure of markets to self-regulate in a way that protects the interests of people outside "core" countries. Such diverse figures as John Ralston Saul,[19] Paul Collier,[20] Thomas P. M. Barnett,[21] and Usama bin Laden,[22] among others, have commented on this. This globalization backlash has six principal implications for the international security environment.

First, traditional societies across the world have experienced the corrosive effects of globalization on deeply held social, cultural, and religious identities—sparking violent antagonism to Western-led modernization and its preeminent symbol: perceived U.S. cultural and economic imperialism. This antagonism takes many forms; at the nation-state level it includes reflexive anti-Americanism, economic and cultural protectionism, and a tendency to "balance" against U.S. policy initiatives or (conversely) to free ride on America's coattails. At the nonstate level, antagonism ranges from politicized but relatively benign cultural phenomena: one example, at the most benign end of the spectrum, is the slow food movement, which originally emerged as the Arcigola organization, a protest against globalized food culture prompted by the opening of a McDonalds franchise in Rome in 1986.[23] More violent examples include antiglobalization

attacks by activists like those who sabotaged the Seattle meeting of the World Trade Organization in November 2001 or disrupted the Davos forum in 2007.[24] It also involves violent internal conflict between communities divided by their response to globalization (as in parts of Indonesia and Africa); the persecution of minorities associated with globalization processes (such as Filipino immigrant workers in parts of the Middle East); and ultimately full-scale civil war and international terrorism.

Second, globalization, by its very openness, affords its opponents unprecedented access to its tools: the Internet, cellphones, and satellite communications, electronic funds transfer, ease of international movement and trade. Globalization has also prompted the proliferation of low-cost, high-lethality individual weapons systems like assault rifles, portable antiaircraft missiles, rocket launchers, mines, and extremely powerful blast munitions such as thermobarics.[25] Consequently, the opponents of globalization—from environmental activists to G8 protestors to AQ operatives—are paradoxically among the most globalized and networked groups on the planet, and the most adept at using globalization's instruments against it. Unlike traditional societies, which embody a xenophobic "antiglobalization" focus, some of these actors serve a vision of "counter-globalization"—a world that is just as globalized as today but (as in the AQ model of a global caliphate, discussed below) is organized along radically different lines. This is an extremely important distinction to which I shall return later, since the first group opposes globalization and seeks to insulate or defend itself from globalization's effects (and thus has a fundamentally defensive focus), whereas the second seeks to hijack and exploit globalization to attack and ultimately control the West (a basically offensive outlook). These groups have different interests, and one of them (the "counterglobalizers" like AQ) tends to exploit and manipulate the other (the "antiglobalizers," of which there are hundreds of local examples worldwide). This pattern was highlighted by Akbar S. Ahmed, whose 2007 book *Journey into Islam: The Crisis of Globalization* presented a compelling and detailed account of interactions with Islamic scholars and students across the Muslim world during field research in 2006–2007, demonstrating the destabilizing effects of globalized communications and extremist ideology.[26]

Third, globalization has connected geographically distant groups who previously could not coordinate their actions (for example, connecting insurgent and terrorist groups in different countries or connecting radicals in remote areas, such as Pakistan's Federally Administered Tribal Areas [FATA], with people originally from there who now live in immigrant communities in the West). This unprecedented connectivity means that widely spaced and disparate micro-actors can aggregate their effects, to achieve outcomes disproportionate to the size and sophistication of their networks. It also means that ungoverned, undergoverned, or poorly controlled areas (such as the FATA, the Sulu and Sulawesi seas between Indonesia, Malaysia, and the Philippines, the Sahara desert in North Africa, or the triborder area in Latin America), which used to be significant for local governments but less relevant to regional security, now hold international importance as potential safe havens and points of origin for terrorist and insurgent attacks on many points of vulnerability in the international system.

Fourth, the diversity and diffusion of globalized media makes what public relations specialists call "message unity"—a single consistent message across multiple audiences—impossible for democratic governments and open societies. Concepts such as "the international media" are less relevant now than even a decade ago, since they treat media organizations as actors or interest groups to be influenced, whereas in fact under globalized conditions the media space is a domain, an ecosystem, or even a battlespace, filled with dozens of independent, uncoordinated, competing, and conflicting entities rather than a single actor or audience. This is because the

modern media space is very different from a traditional broadcast media system (such as a traditional newspaper or television network) in which a few media producers develop, own, and deliver content to many consumers, and yet also different from a web-based system (like early internet forms of "new media" such as blogs and online journals) where many content producers interact with relatively few consumers. Rather, the new social network–based media (such as content-sharing applications like Facebook, MySpace, or YouTube) allow enormous numbers of people to become both consumers and producers of media content, shifting rapidly and seamlessly between these roles, sharing and producing information, and thus developing multiple sources of information, almost all of them outside the control of governments and media corporations.[27]

This carries consequences for Western governments—pursuing unpopular policies in the teeth of negative media coverage is harder, and state-based information agencies such as the State Department's R Bureau (the much-reduced successor to the United States Information Agency, which the Clinton administration abolished in 1999) have less leverage in this atomized and privatized media marketplace. But the atomization of the media also creates a profoundly new and different space in which individuals can communicate and form social/information networks that are innately free, democratic, non-state-based, and founded on personal choice. Even repressive societies like China, Iran, Burma, and parts of the Middle East now have enormous difficulty in suppressing information and preventing communication between their citizens and the wider world. Globalized information systems therefore, on balance, favor freedom but also carry new and sometimes poorly understood risks.

Fifth, as noted, the uneven pace and spread of globalization has created haves and have-nots; the so-called gap countries[28] in Africa, the Middle East, Latin America, and parts of Southeast and

Northeast Asia have benefited far less from globalization than core regions of western Europe and North America, while Paul Collier's "bottom billion" has suffered far more than people in those regions.[29] Some gap countries (Burma, North Korea, Syria, Iran, Somalia, or Pakistan) are actually or potentially what successive U.S. administrations have described as "rogue states," or else are safe havens for terrorist activity. But the United States has neither the mandate nor the resources to police or directly administer the world's undergoverned areas, nor would the American people be likely to support such a strategy. Indeed, trying to control and integrate every area of undergoverned or ungoverned space in the world could be seen as an aggressive attempt to bring about further globalization (thus increasing the backlash against it), as a coyly veiled bid for world domination, or as a means of formalizing an American role as a surrogate world government: a role that neither Americans nor others would be likely to accept. Hence a policy of international cooperation and low-profile support for legitimate and effective governance through local authorities, building effective and legitimate local allies, is likely to be a more viable response.

The final, obvious implication is that globalization is inherently a phenomenon over which governments have little control. As the financial crisis of 2008 demonstrated, large shifts in the global economy, and the well-being of millions of people, are set by market forces and individual choices exercised through the connectivity that globalization enables. This means that even though globalization has obvious negative security effects, governments have great difficulty in attempting to channel or stop it. Thus the antimodernization backlash within traditional societies, and the existence of networked counterglobalizers like AQ who exploit it, will probably be a long-standing trend regardless of Western policies.

This last observation relates to the second model for the environment: global insurgency.

MODEL 2: A GLOBALIZED INSURGENCY   The global insurgency thesis suggests that the "War on Terrorism" is best understood as an extremely large-scale, transnational globalized insurgency, rather than as a traditional terrorism problem. This model argues that by definition, AQ and the broader *takfiri* extremist movement it seeks to lead are insurgents (members of "an organized movement that aims at overthrowing the political order within a given territory, using a combination of subversion, terrorism, guerrilla warfare and propaganda").[30] According to this way of thinking, defining such groups via their use of a certain tactic—terrorism (which they share with every other insurgent movement in history)—is less analytically useful than defining them in terms of their strategic approach. Like other insurgents but unlike a classical terrorist organization (which draws its effectiveness from the motivation and cohesion of a small number of people in clandestine cells), AQ draws its potency from the depth of its demographic base (the world's 1.2 billion Sunni Muslims) and its ability to intimidate, co-opt, or mobilize that base for support. And as I shall show, AQ applies the same standard four tactics (provocation, intimidation, protraction, and exhaustion) used by all insurgents in history, though with far greater scope and ambition.

This implies that the best-fit conceptual framework to deal with AQ is counterinsurgency rather than conventional warfare or traditional counterterrorism. Like other counterinsurgencies, the civilized world's confrontation with *takfiri* extremism is therefore population-centric—that is, its key activities relate to protecting the world's Muslim population from AQ intimidation and manipulation, countering extremist propaganda, marginalizing insurgent movements, and meeting the Muslim population's legitimate grievances through a tailored, situation- and location-specific mix of initiatives that are mostly nonmilitary. Killing or capturing terrorists is a strictly secondary activity, because it is ultimately defensive (keeping today's terrorists at bay) rather than decisive (preventing future terrorism). Conversely, programs that address the underlying conditions that terrorists exploit (thus preventing another crop of terrorists from simply replacing those we kill or capture today) are ultimately decisive. Clearly, like any military or law enforcement strategy, countering AQ requires *both* the kill/capture of current terrorists *and* programs to counter their ideology and address the underlying conditions they exploit. These efforts are complementary (addressing both the supply and demand sides of the equation) rather than opposite choices. Still, and perhaps counterintuitively for some, activities to kill and capture terrorists seem (and are) offensive at the tactical level but are in fact strategically defensive, because they contain the problem rather than resolving it. This approach would differ very substantially from traditional counterterrorism, which is enemy-centric, focusing on disrupting and eliminating terrorist cells themselves rather than on controlling the broader environment in which they operate.

But although it is an insurgency, the *takfiri* extremist movement differs in key ways from a traditional insurgency because of its scale. Unlike other insurgents, the "given territory" in which AQ seeks to operate is the entire globe, and the "political order" it seeks to overthrow is the political order within the entire Muslim world and the relationship between the world's Muslim population (the *ummah*) and the rest of world society. This, again, has major implications for international security.

First, the unprecedented scale and ambition of this insurgent movement, and the unparalleled connectivity and aggregation effect it has achieved through access to the tools of globalization, renders many traditional counterinsurgency approaches ineffective. For example, traditional "hearts and minds" approaches are directed at winning the support of the population in a territory where insurgents operate. But under conditions of globalized insurgency, the world's entire Muslim population, and the populations of most Western countries, are a target of enemy propaganda and hence a potential focus for informa-

tion operations. But such a large and diverse target set is, by definition, not susceptible to traditional locally tailored hearts-and-minds activities, and the difficulty in achieving message unity (noted earlier) undercuts such attempts anyway. Likewise, traditional counterinsurgency uses improved governance and legitimacy to build alliances with local communities and marginalize insurgents; in a globalized insurgency, this approach may work at a local level with people in a given insurgent operating area, but may still have little impact on remote sources of insurgent support (such as Internet-based financial support or propaganda support from distant countries).

This implies the need for unprecedented international cooperation in managing the terrorism threat. Since 9/11, such cooperation has in fact been excellent (especially in areas such as transportation security and terrorist financing). United States leadership has been central to this effort, but international support for U.S. initiatives has waned substantially since the immediate post-9/11 period, largely as a result of international partners' dissatisfaction with U.S. unilateralism, perceived human rights abuses, and the Iraq War. This implies that America's international reputation, moral authority, diplomatic weight, persuasive ability, cultural attractiveness, and strategic credibility—its "soft power"—is not some optional adjunct to military strength. Rather, it is a critical enabler for a permissive operating environment—that is, it substantially reduces the friction and difficulty involved in international leadership against threats like AQ— and it is also the prime political component in countering a globalized insurgency. This in turn implies the need for greater balance between the key elements (diplomatic, informational, military, and economic) of national power.

In this context, it is important to clearly understand the role AQ plays. I describe its "military" strategy in the next section, but its organizational strategy is worth examining here. Al Qa'ida acts as "inciter-in-chief,"[31] or as Ayman al-Zawahiri describes it, *al talia al ummah*, the "vanguard of the *ummah*," a revolutionary party that seeks to build mass consciousness through provocation and spectacular acts of "resistance" to the existing world order. It works through regional affiliates (AQ in Iraq, AQ in the Arabian Peninsula, AQ-Maghreb, Groupe salafiste pour la prédication et le combat, Jema'ah Islamiyah, Abu Sayyaf Group, etc.) to co-opt and aggregate the effects of multiple, diverse local actors in more than 60 countries. It is this ability to aggregate and point all the players in one direction (via propaganda, technical assistance, broad strategic direction, and occasional direct guidance) that gives AQ its strength. This implies that a strategy which I described in 2004 as one of "disaggregation," cutting the links between AQ central leadership and among its local and regional allies and supporters, may be more successful than policies that lump all threats into the single undifferentiated category of "terrorists."

Fundamental to counterinsurgency is an ability to undercut the insurgents' appeal by discrediting their propaganda, exposing their motives, and convincing at-risk populations to voluntarily reject insurgent co-option and intimidation. In the context of a globalized insurgency this translates into diplomatic initiatives that undercut AQ credibility on issues like Israel/Palestine, Kashmir, Chechnya, Afghanistan, and Iraq. This cannot simply be "spin": it demands genuine attempts to address legitimate grievances. This in turn implies political initiatives to construct credible and legitimate alternatives for the world's Muslim population, instead of the current limited choice between support for AQ or "collaboration" with the West. In this context, the Amman Message initiative of King Abdullah II of Jordan is an extremely important first step, bringing together religious and political leaders from across the Islamic world to condemn AQ's heretical *takfiri* ideology.[32] Muslim initiatives of this kind exist, though they often receive little attention in the West. Being local and indigenous, they are much more powerful and credible than Western initiatives: the role of counterpropaganda efforts, wherever feasible, should be to support and amplify such Muslim initiatives rather than to generate competing Western messages. This also implies the need for counterpropaganda capabilities (discussed below) to discredit AQ and inoculate at-risk populations—including immigrant populations in the West—against AQ's appeal.

The final major implication is that an indirect, highly localized approach—working by, with, or through genuine alliances and local partnerships wherever possible—would probably be much more successful than a policy of direct U.S. intervention. This is because many governments in the world rightly resent U.S. interference in their internal affairs or cannot, because of domestic public opinion, accept direct U.S. counterterrorism assistance, making overtly U.S.-controlled or -funded approaches unacceptable. On the other hand, virtually every government in the world has an interest in protecting itself against domestic terrorism and extremist subversion. This implies that wherever possible, Western countries should seek to build genuine partnerships with local governments and civil society networks, operate behind the scenes, avoid large-scale commitment of U.S. combat forces, support locally devised initiatives, and apply diplomatic suasion (rather than force) to modify local government behavior. There is thus a trade-off between effectiveness and control: local initiatives afford less control but carry greater likelihood of success. In military terms, countering globalized insurgency therefore looks less like traditional single-country counterinsurgency and much more like a very robust aid, information, and foreign assistance program, supported by diplomatic initiatives, stabilization operations, and foreign internal defense (FID), with troops deployed only where absolutely needed.

Local governments are likewise fundamental to the third way of thinking about the threat: as a civil war within Islam.

MODEL 3: A CIVIL WAR WITHIN ISLAM   The Islamic civil war thesis suggests that the current turmoil within the Islamic world, along with the spillover of violence from Muslim countries into the international community via globalized insurgency and terrorism, arises from a civil war within Islam. There are several variants of this model, but all see AQ and its associated *takfiri* terrorist movements primarily as a response to a series of internal dynamics within the Muslim world: a youth bulge, corrupt and oppressive governments, a dysfunctional relationship between the sexes that limits the human capacity of societies by denying productive roles to half the population, a deficit of democracy and freedom of expression, economies dependent on oil but unable to provide fulfilling employment to an increasingly educated but alienated young male population, and a generalized *anomie* and sense of being victimized by a vaguely-defined "West." As a group of prominent Arab and Muslim scholars have shown in successive editions of the United Nations *Arab Human Development Report*, these dynamics have created enormous potential for unrest, and a well of grievances into which movements like AQ can tap.[33] This suggests that although it uses the West as a target of convenience, the real threat from AQ and the broader *takfiri* movement is to the status quo in Muslim countries, through activities directed initially at overthrowing existing political and religious structures in the Islamic world, and only then turning to remake the relationship between the *ummah* and the rest of global society. Again perhaps counterintuitively, this theory would imply that AQ terrorist violence is not fundamentally directed at the West, but rather *uses* attacks on Western countries and exploits their responses in order to further its real objective: gaining ascendancy over the Islamic world. What we are witnessing, this model suggests, is a battle for the soul of Islam, a violent competition for control over one-eighth of the world's population.

Both Faisal Devji, in *Landscapes of the Jihad*, and Akbar Ahmed, in *Islam under Siege*, advanced variations on this approach.[34] Ayman al-Zawahiri, identified as the principal AQ planner and ideologue,[35] also expressed this thinking in a statement shortly after 9/11. He outlined a two-phase strategy: in the first phase, AQ would focus on the greater Middle East: "this spirit of *jihad* would . . . turn things upside down in the region and force the U.S. out of it. This would be followed by the earth-shattering event, which the West trembles at: the establishment of an Islamic caliphate in Egypt."[36] Only after the success of this first stage, that is, the destruction of the current political order in the Muslim world, would the second stage begin, using the caliphate as a launching pad against the West, to remake the world order with the Muslim world in a dominant position. "If God wills it, such a state . . . could lead the Islamic world in a *jihad* against the West. It could also rally the world Muslims around it. Then history would make a new turn, God willing, in the opposite direction against the empire of the United States and the world's Jewish government."[37] A related document, the "General Guide to the Struggle of Jema'ah Islamiyah" (Pedoman Umum Perjuangan Jema'ah Islamiyah; PUPJI), issued by AQ's Southeast Asian ally Jema'ah Islamiyah (JI) in 2001, suggests similar strategic thinking. This document declares JI's objectives to be the establishment of an Islamic state in Indonesia, only then to be followed by the creation of a pan-Islamic state in Southeast Asia (*daula Islamiya nusantara*) covering Malaysia, Indonesia, the Philippines, southern Thailand, and Singapore. Only once this superstate was created would JI's aim become the establishment of a global pan-Islamic caliphate.[38]

Some analysts have focused on the threat to the West implied by what some extremists call the "caliphate concept." But, as advocates of the Islamic civil war thesis would argue, it is clear that the *takfiri* aim is first to overthrow and control power structures in the Muslim world, and only then to turn against the West. They might argue that if ever an extremist coalition should succeed in gaining control of the Middle East, it would have its hands full simply governing and controlling that area, though (like the Iranian Revolution, discussed below) such a revolution would also export violence and radicalism and thus destabilize the rest of the world. They might also argue, with strong justification in my view, that these statements—Zawahiri's after 9/11 and PUPJI—represent a snapshot of terrorist thinking that has been well and truly overtaken by events (as I shall show). In any case, the Islamic civil war thesis suggests that the primary threat of takfirism is against stability in the Arab world and the broader Muslim community worldwide, and only secondarily against Western governments and populations. By intervening directly against AQ, this theory suggests, we have not only waded into someone else's domestic dispute but have also treated AQ as a peer competitor worthy of our top priority and full attention, thus immensely increasing AQ's credibility and clout in its struggle for ascendancy over the *ummah*.

A second variant of the Islamic civil war thesis focuses on the Shi'a revival, a process cogently described by Vali Nasr, which involves, first, the rise of Shi'a theocracy under the banner of the Iranian Islamic Revolution and Ayatollah Khomeini's ideology of *vilayet-e faqih*, and second, the empowerment of the Iraqi Shi'a majority as a side-effect of the fall of Saddam Hussein.[39] This revival, resulting in the emergence of a so-called Shi'a Crescent from Iran to Lebanon, is deeply disruptive of established power structures in the Muslim world, especially in countries (such as Kuwait, Saudi Arabia, Lebanon, several Gulf states, and Pakistan) that have substantial but politically disenfranchised Shi'a minorities, some of whom (as in Saudi Arabia's Eastern Province) happen to live atop extremely large oil and gas reserves, making political instability in these areas a global concern. As Patrick Cockburn has shown, the importance of Iraqi Shi'a political and insurgent leaders like Muqtada al-Sadr cannot be fully grasped without reference to this pattern of Shi'a empowerment and its disruptive effect both on the established, Sunni-dominated order in Ba'athist Iraq and on the existing Shi'a religious and political establishment that has emerged since the fall of Saddam Hussein.[40] In a real sense, in Shi'a Iraq since 2003 we have been witnessing a violent internal social revolution as

well as an insurgency against occupation. Likewise, Hizballah, as a Shi'a organization that embodies elements of terrorist, insurgent, propaganda, charity, and social work, with a global reach, profound political influence in the Levant, and a client-proxy relationship with the Iranian regime, is a non-state instance of expanding Shi'a influence. Hizballah's good military showing in the 2006 war with Israel led the Israeli government's Winograd Commission to conclude that Hizballah had significantly strengthened since 2000, and that the Israeli Defense Force was simply not prepared to deal with its increased threat and capabilities.[41] Leading Hizballah scholar Andrew Exum, writing just after the war, suggested that its performance was such that "enemies of the United States will likely seek to emulate Hizballah's perceived successes in southern Lebanon."[42]

A third element of the Islamic civil war thesis is the geopolitical rise of Iran in its own right, as a powerful nation-state, nuclear threshold power, and potential regional hegemon, sitting in a geostrategically unassailable position astride the Gulf, the Caucasus, Central Asia, and Afghanistan, with a large population, long coastline, and enormous, rugged territory; an economy benefiting from increased world oil prices; increasing regional influence; a blossoming alliance of convenience with the Taliban in Afghanistan; and the potential to have a satellite buffer-state in southern Iraq. Again, this increase in Iranian influence is threatening and destabilizing to regional players like the Gulf Cooperation Council countries and particularly Saudi Arabia, though some Saudi analysts have concluded that the threat is overdrawn. For example, the Riyadh-based Saudi National Security Assessment Project concluded in September 2006 that

the Shi'a will attain more rights, but a full "revival" is not possible due to demographic, economic, and military challenges. Globally, Shi'a are outnumbered by more than five to one, and in the Middle East they are a clear minority. Economically, Iran lacks the strength to further its self-proclaimed ambitions or Shi'a movements elsewhere. While a major power, Iran's oil might doesn't match its rhetoric. Any military confrontation between Iran and its neighbors will bring in the U.S., and the acquisition of nuclear weapons will prompt other regional powers to do the same. There will be no hegemon in the Middle East, but instead a balance of power among the two or three leading countries in the region.[43]

This process of turmoil and internal conflict within the Islamic world has four major implications.

The first relates to American strategic choices. Immediately after 9/11, U.S. leaders opted for an activist policy of direct intervention in the Muslim world, recognizing that instability and conflict within Islam could spill over to harm the West in general and the United States in particular. The invasion of Afghanistan, the active promotion of democracy, women's rights, and governance reform in the Muslim world, and the subsequent invasion and occupation of Iraq can all be seen as enacting this approach. Likewise, the establishment of several Joint Interagency Task Forces (JIATFs) to project military power and civilian development assistance into unstable regions (all Muslim, like the Horn of Africa, the trans-Sahel, and the southern Philippines) and, more recently, a focus on Israel/Palestine via the Annapolis Conference are further instances of a policy that could be characterized as one of "direct intervention." This policy sought to fundamentally restructure the Islamic world, to remove the perceived causes of extremism. The direct intervention approach was very understandable, given the need to be seen to do something after the immense provocation of the 9/11 attacks, but its results (the strategic, moral, and material costs of the Iraq War, the failure of the Middle East democratization agenda, widespread American unpopularity, loss of credibility, a crisis of confidence among Western allies in the Muslim world, and a boost to AQ recruitment and support) have proven contrary to U.S. interests, at least in the short term.

One possible alternative would have been a containment policy, seeking to prevent the bleed-out of violence and instability from the Islamic world into the rest of global society, while encouraging and supporting Muslim leaders to resolve the internal turmoil within Islam on their own terms. This, too, would have carried severe risks, not least the possibility that authoritarian regimes in the Middle East would have seen the West as weak and continued oppressing their populations anyway. Moreover, given the integration of Muslim populations in almost every Western country and the globalization-enabled connectivity noted earlier, one could argue that the "Islamic world" simply cannot be quarantined from the rest of global society and left to stew in its own juice, as some "separationists" have suggested.[44] Indeed, we could regard direct intervention and separationism as opposite extremes along a spectrum of engagement. * * * [T]here is a strong case for adopting a policy of balanced response that makes limited use of intervention within a context of continuous engagement and a broader containment approach.

A second obvious implication is that, under current conditions, the United States is fighting against all parties to this civil war at once. Iran and AQ are natural opponents, as are Shi'a communitarian militias and Sunni rejectionist insurgents in Iraq, and Iran and the Taliban were enemies before 9/11. But Western powers are currently fighting all sides, partly (according to this theory) because the West has stepped into the middle of an internal conflict, prompting all players to turn against our intervention as if we were outsiders interfering in a violent domestic dispute. Partly, however, the fact that Western countries find ourselves fighting all sides arises because we have been insufficiently agile in distinguishing different and contradictory forms of Islamic extremism from each other, and have failed to listen to Muslim allies—like King Abdullah II of Jordan, or former president Abdurrahman Wahid of Indonesia—who understand the problem and its potential solutions in much greater and more nuanced detail than Westerners ever could. In some cases, we have fought enemies we had no need to fight, and have chosen to fight simultaneously enemies we could have fought in sequence. We have, in other words, signally failed to follow Frederick Hartmann's strategic principle of "conservation of enemies," which states that although enmity is a permanent feature in international relations, successful powers must avoid making, or simultaneously engaging, more enemies than absolutely necessary.[45]

A further implication is that we are failing to fully exploit the ideological and interest-based differences between our opponents (cleavages akin to the Cold War Sino-Soviet split). These differences exist not only between Shi'a and Sunni groups, but within *takfiri* movements, which, because of their extreme intolerance of even slightly differing points of view, have a strong tendency to fragment along ideological fault-lines into ever smaller and more fanatical groups.[46] As I have argued elsewhere, the *takfiri* extremist enemy is naturally vulnerable to a disaggregation approach that seeks to turn factions against each other and disrupt the overall effects of extremism.[47] But our tendency to lump all threats together under the banner of a "global war on terrorism" tends to have the opposite effect, unifying these disparate groups in the face of a common external foe, through a fusion mechanism that sociologists call "primary group cohesion" * * *.

A final observation: there is a certain amount of irrationality in our Iran policy, arising in part from the experiences of the U.S. Embassy hostage crisis in [Tehran] in 1979–1980, so vividly described in Mark Bowden's 2007 book *Guests of the Ayatollah*.[48] There is baggage on both sides, of course: some Iranians remember the U.S.-led overthrow of the Mossadeq government in 1953 with equally vivid bitterness,[49] while others, opposed to the current regime, blame America for the revolution of 1979. This baggage sometimes makes American policy-makers reluctant to accept the historical and geopolitical fact of Iran's importance in its region, and hence the underlying legitimacy of Iran's long-term aspirations to play a regional role, including in Afghanistan and Iraq. Of course, the United States and the rest of the international community have a clear interest in ensuring that Iran plays a constructive role in these countries, rather than its current highly destructive and destabilizing one. Still, it seems clear that distinguishing Iran, as a country, from the clericalist regime in Tehran and from the Iranian people it oppresses is fundamental to developing an effective Iran policy. The youthfulness of Iran's population, and Iranians' widespread dissatisfaction with the only regime many of them have ever known, are key advantages for the United States. But lack of diplomatic representation in Tehran, along with limited willingness to engage in discussion with Iran's leadership group—engagement that would of course have to be backed by force and international consensus, and addressing the broadest possible range of issues in partnership with other Muslim allies—severely limits U.S. options and restricts situational awareness. This makes it harder to clearly discern the Iranian role in an Islamic civil war, or to formulate viable policy responses to it.

MODEL 4: ASYMMETRIC WARFARE This model examines the security environment functionally rather than politically, from the standpoint of military capability. This theory argues that the underlying strategic logic of terrorism, insurgency, internal conflict, and unconventional warfare arises from a fundamental mismatch (or asymmetry) between U.S. military capabilities and those of the rest of the world. As noted, the United States currently possesses a degree of military superiority in conventional capability that is unprecedented in world history. No other country, or combination of countries, could expect to take on the United States in a conventional force-on-force engagement with any prospect of victory. This is underlined by the enormous scale of American defense spending: according to recent unclassified estimates, the U.S. defense budget accounted for 54.5 percent of total global defense spending in 2007, with the other 45.5

percent representing every other country on Earth combined.[50] In mid-2008, counting supplemental budget allocations for the Iraq War, the U.S. defense budget is approaching 70 percent of total global defense spending. This unparalleled investment in conventional military capability has created an asymmetry between U.S. capabilities and those of virtually all other actors (friendly or otherwise) in the international security environment, with five major implications, as follows.

First, under these conditions, regardless of ideology, any rational adversary is likely to fight the United States using nonconventional means. These may include propaganda and subversion, terrorist attacks, guerrilla warfare, weapons of mass destruction, or attempts to drag conventional forces into protracted engagements for little strategic gain, so as to exhaust the American people's political support for a conflict. Given overwhelming U.S. conventional superiority, and contrary to the pre-9/11 conventional wisdom embodied in the insouciant attitude of the general who visited my class in 2001, it turns out that adversaries do not give up the armed struggle under these conditions: rather, any smart enemy goes unconventional; and most enemies are likely to continue doing so, until we demonstrate the ability to prevail in irregular conflicts such as those we are currently engaged in. This may mean that, like Bill Murray's character in the movie *Groundhog Day*, we are doomed to live this day over and over again until we get it right: we may have to keep on fighting these types of wars until we win one.

The second implication of this massive asymmetry is that because its military superiority gives the United States the capability to destroy any other nation-state on the face of the earth, belief in the fundamentally benign intent of the United States becomes a critical factor in other countries' strategic calculus. Intelligence threat assessments typically examine the twin factors of *capability* and *intent,* focusing on capability because intent is subject to much more rapid and unpredictable change. But the destructive capability of the United States is so asymmetrically huge vis-à-vis every other nation on Earth that it poses what international relations theorists call a "security dilemma." Unless other countries can be assured of America's benign intent, they must rationally treat the United States as a potential threat and take steps to balance and contain American power or defend themselves against it. And efforts to improve U.S. military capacity, which American leaders may see as defensive, may therefore have a negative overall effect on U.S. national security because of the responses they generate. Again, this reflects Qiao Liang's insight that unless other countries trust the United States (that is, unless they believe it will follow its own self-imposed rule-set), the whole basis of international cooperation tends to be compromised. Thus the widely observed phenomenon of countries "bandwagoning" or engaging in balancing behavior against the United States, along with countries seeking nonconventional means of attack and defense, may not necessarily indicate hostile intent on these countries' part but rather it may simply be a rational response to overwhelming U.S. conventional military capability. Nor is such anti-American behavior necessarily a sign that the United States is doing something wrong: rather, it may simply be an inherent structural aspect of a unipolar global system, a security dilemma representing an inbuilt pattern that would have occurred whichever nation found itself in this position. Such thinking might suggest that American primacy, like the primacy of any other nation beyond certain limits that other nations find acceptable, could be inherently destabilizing of the global system and thus harmful to America's own interests. It also suggests that assuring other nations that the United States will exercise its power responsibly, sparingly, virtuously, and in accordance with international norms is therefore not an optional luxury or a sign of moral flaccidity. Rather, it is a key strategic requirement to prevent this previously noted adversarial "balance-of-power" response to the unprecedented scale of American military might. American power must be matched by American virtue,[51] or it will ultimately harm both the United States and the global system.

Third, however, the efforts of insurgents and terrorists since 9/11 may in fact have already put an end, through unconventional and asymmetric means, to the much-bruited military superiority of the United States, showing the way to all future adversaries and leaving Western powers with fabulously capable and appallingly expensive militaries that are precisely adapted to exactly the wrong kind of war. The post–Cold War era of unparalleled U.S. military power may have been a passing phase: AQ might indeed turn out to be, as Zawahiri called it, the vanguard of a new era of conflict. This is the analytical line taken by the historian Andrew Bacevich. In September 2006, the performance of Islamic militias and insurgents in the Palestinian Territories and Iraq, along with Hizballah's achievement in fighting Israel to a standstill (noted earlier) led Bacevich to describe a new "Islamic Way of War" that incorporates a "panoply of techniques employed to undercut the apparent advantages of high-tech conventional forces. The methods employed do include terrorism—violence targeting civilians for purposes of intimidation—but they also incorporate propaganda, subversion, popular agitation, economic warfare, and hit-and-run attacks on regular forces, either to induce an overreaction or to wear them down."[52] He concluded that

in Iraq, the world's only superpower finds itself mired in a conflict that it cannot win. History's mightiest military has been unable to defeat an enemy force of perhaps 20,000 to 30,000 insurgents equipped with post–World War II vintage assault rifles and anti-tank weapons. In Gaza and southern Lebanon, the Middle East's mightiest military also finds itself locked in combat with adversaries that it cannot defeat. Despite weeks of bitter fighting, the IDF's Merkava tanks, F-16 fighter-bombers, and missile-launching unmanned aerial vehicles failed to suppress, much less eliminate, the armed resistance of Hamas and Hezbollah. What are we to make of this? How is it that the

seemingly weak and primitive are able to frustrate modern armies only recently viewed as all but invincible? What do the parallel tribulations–and embarrassments—of the United States and Israel have to tell us about war and politics in the twenty-first century? In short, what's going on here? The answer to that question is dismayingly simple: *the sun has set on the age of unquestioned Western military dominance. Bluntly, the East has solved the riddle of the Western Way of War.* In Baghdad and in Anbar Province as at various points on Israel's troubled perimeter, the message is clear: methods that once could be counted on to deliver swift decision no longer work.[53]

I would go somewhat further than Bacevich, to suggest that the tendency toward hybrid forms of warfare combining terrorism, insurgency, propaganda, and economic warfare to sidestep Western conventional capability is not solely an Arab or Muslim phenomenon. It may be that groups like AQ, Hamas, and Hizballah have been pioneers in applying this method. But as we have seen, Chinese analysts published a study into unrestricted warfare over a decade ago, several far-left and extreme environmentalist groups are believed to have studied AQ methods,[54] and at least two other countries (in Latin America and Southeast Asia) have adopted tactical concepts that seek to exploit asymmetric advantages against the United States and turn our very superiority in conventional war-fighting against us.

A key adversary advantage in confronting U.S. conventional superiority is asymmetry of cost. Currently, the United States is spending in excess of $400 million *per day* in Iraq, a level of spending (drawn entirely from supplemental allocations and therefore representing unforecast and borrowed funds) that is clearly unsustainable over the long-duration commitment demanded by effective counterinsurgency campaigns, which often take decades.[55] By contrast, adversaries deliberately adopt low-cost methods in order to sustain their operations over a longer time period than America can, for an acceptable cost. For example, the 9/11 Commission estimated that the 9/11 attacks cost AQ between $400,000 and $500,000, plus the cost of training the 19 hijackers in the United States prior to the attack.[56] This would make the 9/11 attacks the most expensive terrorist attack in history. But when one considers that the attacks inflicted a direct cost of $27.2 *billion* on the United States,[57] and that subsequent operations in the "War on Terrorism" have cost about $700 billion to mid-2008,[58] it is clear that the cost of the attack to America has vastly outweighed its costs to AQ, and that the cost of America's subsequent response has even further dwarfed, by several orders of magnitude, what AQ spent on the attacks. This should give us pause, especially against the background of the 2008 financial crisis which many analysts have described as the worst since the Great Depression.

Another key aspect of asymmetry is the mismatch between military and nonmilitary elements of U.S. national power. United States military capability not only overshadows the capabilities of all other world militaries combined, it also dwarfs U.S. civilian capabilities. As an example, there are 1.68 million uniformed personnel in the U.S. armed forces.[59] By comparison, taking diplomatic capacity as a surrogate metric for other forms of civilian capability, the State Department employs about 6,000 foreign service officers, while the U.S. Agency for International Development (USAID) has about 2,000.[60] In other words, the Department of Defense is about 210 times larger than USAID and State combined, in personnel terms. (In budgetary terms, the mismatch is far greater, on the order of 350:1.) This represents a substantial asymmetry, particularly when it is realized that the typical size ratio between armed forces and diplomatic/aid agencies for other Western democracies is between 8 and 10:1 (compared to 210:1 in the case of the United States). The overwhelming size and capacity of the U.S. armed forces therefore has a distorting effect on U.S. national power and on America's ability to execute international security programs that balance military with nonmilitary elements of national power.

Even within the armed forces, there is a substantial mismatch between the capabilities needed for the current international security environment and those actually present in the U.S. military inventory. This is starkest in terms of the lack of capacity for stabilization and reconstruction operations, and for counterinsurgency or FID. The vast majority of defense capability is oriented to conventional war-fighting, while even within Special Operations Forces the primary focus is on direct action (killing or capturing key enemy personnel) rather than on capabilities that support an indirect, military assistance approach. At a higher level of abstraction, the resources available for land operations (including both army and marine ground forces and the air and maritime assets from all services that support them) are substantially overstretched by comparison to resources for conventional air and maritime war-fighting, which are far more expensive but much less likely to be called on. Thus the U.S. military exhibits both a capability mismatch and an asymmetry of capacity.

Despite all this, the U.S. government has enduring requirements to meet alliance obligations, deal with the potential for conventional adversaries, and hedge against the threat of major theater conflict. And because capabilities for irregular or unconventional conflict are much cheaper to acquire than those for conventional conflict, and require less hardware and industrial capacity, they are paradoxically less likely to be developed. This is because, through the "military-industrial complex," a substantial portion of the American economy, and numerous jobs in almost every congressional district, are linked to the production of conventional war-fighting capacity. It takes factories, jobs, and industrial facilities to build battleships and bombers, but aid workers, linguists, and Special Forces operators are vastly cheaper and do not demand the same industrial base. So shifting spending priorities onto currently unconventional forms of warfare would cost jobs and votes in the congressional districts of the very people who control that spending. This makes it structurally difficult for the United States fundamentally to reorient its military capabilities away from conventional war-fighting or to divert a significant proportion of defense spending into civilian capacity. Hence, absent a concerted effort by the nation's leadership in both the executive and legislative branches, the pattern of asymmetric warfare, with the United States adopting a basically conventional approach but being opposed by enemies who seek to sidestep American conventional power, is likely to be a long-standing trend.

INTEGRATING THE FOUR PERSPECTIVES Which is it then? Is the security environment best understood as a backlash against globalization (a technological-economic model of the environment), a global insurgency (a political-strategic model), a civil war within Islam (a geopolitical model), or an asymmetric response to Western conventional superiority (a military-functional model)? Or does some other paradigm—the clash of civilizations, Islamo-fascism, fourth-generation warfare, or something else again—explain the environment better than these four models? The answer, from my point of view, is that all four models explain some aspects of the environment but not others: they are all partial explanations: we have yet to stumble on some kind of unified field theory that fully explains current conflicts. It is also, perhaps, simply too early to tell. These four conceptual frameworks should therefore be seen neither as exhaustive (there are other convincing explanations) nor as mutually exclusive (there is no need to posit one as "correct" and the others as false). Rather, they offer a set of conceptual lenses that can be applied, with judgment and care, to make sense of events and to inform our understanding of field data. * * *

The Accidental Guerrilla

Because of al Qa'ida's role in several ongoing conflicts and the influence of terrorism threats in current American security thinking it is essential, before considering specific case[s], that we rightly understand AQ's strategy and tactics. As will become obvious, a realistic appraisal of the AQ threat, and a rational policy response to it, depends on a sound understanding of AQ methods and objectives—including, particularly, a solid grasp of what I call the *accidental guerrilla syndrome* of AQ interaction with local allies—an understanding that has been somewhat scantly expressed in Western public pronouncements to date.

AQ MILITARY STRATEGY I have already explored what one might call AQ's "organizational strategy": its desire to become the leading player in a loose coalition of *takfiri* extremist movements, to become the vanguard of the world's Muslim population, the *ummah*, and to act as a propaganda hub and center of excellence from which other movements can draw expertise, while exploiting their actions and aggregating their effects into a unified propaganda offensive against the United States and the broader international community. As noted, the leading counterterrorism analyst Michael Scheuer has emphasized that AQ sees itself as the "inciter-in-chief," not the "commander-in-chief": it seeks to provoke a global uprising against the world order and sustain that uprising over decades, in order to ultimately transform the relationship between the *ummah* and the rest of global society;[61] but it does not seek to directly control or systematically command the other movements within this coalition. Also as noted, AQ seeks to use the tools of globalization to aggregate the effects of diverse actors separated in time and space—to create a powerful movement whose efforts can be seen as akin to those of an extremely widespread globalized insurgency rather than a traditional terrorist movement.[62] So AQ's organizational strategy essentially boils down to creating a global *takfiri* coalition with AQ at its head.

Al Qa'ida's military strategy on the other hand, appears to be aimed at bleeding the United States to exhaustion and bankruptcy, forcing America to withdraw in disarray from the Muslim world so that its local allies collapse, and simultaneously to use the provoking and alienating effects of U.S. intervention as a form of provocation to incite a mass uprising within the Islamic world, or at least to generate and sustain popular support for AQ. In a statement released in late 2004, Usama bin Laden outlined this strategic approach as follows:

> All that we have mentioned has made it easy to provoke and bait this [U.S.] Administration. All we have to do is to send two *mujahidin* to the furthest point East to raise a cloth on which is written al-Qaeda, in order to make the [U.S.] generals race there to cause America to suffer human, economic and political losses without achieving for it anything of note . . . so we are continuing this policy of bleeding America to the point of bankruptcy. Allah willing and nothing is too great for Allah.[63]

Other AQ statements have indicated a strategic intent to provoke America into actions across the Muslim world that will destroy its credibility and that of the "apostate" regimes it supports, inciting the *ummah* to rise up and reject these regimes, create a neo-Salafist caliphate, restore Islam to its rightful place within the Islamic world, and then launch an offensive *jihad* to subjugate all non-Muslim peoples, in accordance with Muhammad's command to "fight them until they say 'There is no God but Allah'" (*aha-dith* al-Bukhari . . . and Muslim . . .). From this it can be seen that AQ's strategy is fundamentally one of bleeding the United States to exhaustion, while simultaneously using U.S. reaction to incite a mass uprising within the Islamic world. Al Qa'ida itself sees its own function primarily as a propaganda hub and incitement mechanism, mobilizing the *ummah* and provoking Western actions that alienate the Muslim world, in order to further this strategy.

AQ TACTICS In support of this strategy, AQ applies four basic tactics that are standard for any insurgent movement, as follows.

PROVOCATION Insurgents throughout history have committed atrocities, carrying out extremely provocative events to prompt their opponents to react (or overreact) in ways that harm their interests. This may involve provoking government forces into repressive actions that alienate the population or provoking one tribal, religious, ethnic, or community group into attacking another in order to create and exploit instability. Al Qa'ida or groups allied to it have carried out numerous provocation attacks. For example, on September 1, 2004, Chechen and Arab Islamist terrorists loyal to Shamil Basayev seized School Number One in Beslan, a town in North Ossetia in Russia's North Caucasus region, taking 1,100 primary school children and adults hostage and holding them under lethally abusive conditions for several days before a rescue attempt by Russian security services. Ultimately, 334 people, including 161 children, were killed, and hundreds more were injured in this horrendous atrocity, which appears to have been partly designed to provoke conflict between North Ossetia and the neighboring North Caucasus republic of Ingushetia.[64] Similarly, AQ in Iraq bombed the al-Askariya shrine in Samarra on February 22, 2006, an attack on one of the two holiest shrines in Shi'a Islam, and one that was designed to provoke a major backlash by Shi'a Iraqis against the Iraqi Sunni community. * * * [T]his attempt at provocation was highly successful.[65] Perhaps the most obvious example of a provocation attack is 9/11 itself, which was designed to provoke a massive U.S. retaliation and prompt a spontaneous uprising of the *ummah*. While the worldwide uprising failed to occur, subsequent U.S. actions could be seen as playing into the hands of this AQ provocation agenda.

INTIMIDATION Insurgents seek to prevent local populations from cooperating with governments or coalition forces by publicly killing those who collaborate, intimidating others who might seek to work with the government, and co-opting others. This dynamic was highlighted by the classical insurgency theorist Bernard B. Fall, who served in the French Resistance in the World War II; he wrote in 1965 that

> any sound revolutionary warfare operator (the French underground, the Norwegian underground, or any other anti-Nazi European underground) most of the time used small-war tactics—not to destroy the German army, of which they were thoroughly incapable, but to establish a competitive system of control over the population. Of course, in order to do this, here and there they had to kill some of the occupying forces and attack some of the military targets. But above all they had to kill their own people who collaborated with the enemy.[66]

As Fall notes, insurgents also intimidate government forces (especially police and local government officials) in order to force them into defensive actions that alienate the population or to deter them from taking active measures against the insurgents. Likewise, AQ and its allies have mounted terrorist attacks with the intention of intimidating Western countries and forcing them to cease their support of U.S.-led interventions in Iraq (such as the Madrid bombings of 2004, already noted, and the kidnapping of Filipino contractors in the same year, which successfully knocked Spain and the Philippines out of the coalition).[67] More recently, on July 7, 2008, Pakistan-based militants associated with the Taliban and the Haqqani network (both AQ allies at different times) mounted a car bombing aimed at the Indian Embassy in Kabul that killed 41 people and injured more than 100, probably in order to intimidate Indian diplomatic and

development personnel working on construction projects in Afghanistan, including the Kunar road program * * *. Another classic example was the attack by AQ in Iraq on the United Nations compound in Baghdad on August 19, 2003, which killed the UN secretary general's special representative, Sergio Vieira de Mello, along with 21 members of his staff, and forced the UN to withdraw its 600 personnel from Iraq less than a month later.[68]

PROTRACTION Insurgents seek to prolong the conflict in order to exhaust their opponents' resource, erode the government's political will, sap public support for the conflict, and avoid losses. Typically, insurgents react to government countermeasures by going quiet (reducing activity and hiding in inaccessible terrain or within sympathetic or intimidated population groups) when pressure becomes too severe. They then emerge later to fight on. This is one reason why an enemy-centric approach to counterinsurgency is often counterproductive: it tends to alienate and harm the innocent population, who become caught up in the fighting or suffer "collateral" damage, but does little harm to the enemy, who simply melt away when pressure becomes too great. Likewise, AQ and its affiliates have repeatedly gone quiet and drawn out the conflict when threatened, only to reemerge later. The classic example of this was Usama bin Laden's escape from Afghanistan, with key leadership cadres and a small number of core supporters, after the failure of U.S. and Northern Alliance forces to cut off his withdrawal after the battle of Tora Bora in December 2001.[69] He then established a new sanctuary in Pakistan but remained quiet for a lengthy period of regrouping before emerging with new operations in 2003.[70]

EXHAUSTION Finally, exhaustion is an insurgent tactic that seeks to impose costs on the opponent government, overstress its support system, tire its troops, and impose costs in terms of lives, resources, and political capital, in order to convince that government that continuing the war is not worth the cost. For example, during the Soviet-Afghan war, working with the Afghan insurgents, U.S. officials analyzed the Soviet warfighting system looking for weak links and vulnerabilities and then sought to overstress and overburden that system to cause it to collapse. In Iraq, the insurgents ambush and attack convoys and aircraft, so that each vehicle has to be fitted with expensive protective equipment—armor that alienates our forces from the population—and electronic countermeasures, and so that every activity takes much longer and costs much more effort, while carrying greater risk of death or injury. This imposes what Clausewitz called "friction" on a counterinsurgent force, and ultimately causes the government and the domestic population to cease supporting the war. As noted, an exhaustion strategy of this type is precisely the approach AQ adopted and bin Laden outlined in 2004.

AL QA'IDA: FROM EXPEDITIONARY TO GUERRILLA TERRORISM The 9/11 attacks are an example of what we might call "expeditionary terrorism." Al Qa'ida formed the team for the attacks in one country, assembled them in another, ran the logistics and financial support for the operation out of a third, and then clandestinely inserted the team across international borders to attack its target. They infiltrated 19 people into the United States: essentially, an expeditionary raiding approach.[71]

Contrast this with the Madrid bombing in 2004 or the London 7/7 bombing in 2005. In the latter case, rather than smuggling 19 people *in*, AQ openly brought one person *out*: Mohammed Sidique Khan, who traveled by ordinary commercial airliner on his own passport to Pakistan for briefing and training prior to the attack. He then returned to the UK and formed the attack team inside that country, using British nationals.[72] Unlike 9/11, where AQ formed a team remotely and inserted it covertly to the target, in the 7/7 bombings the organization grew the team

close to its target: not a true "home-grown" terrorism event, but rather a guerrilla approach that allowed AQ to sidestep the improved transportation security measures and international border controls put in place after 9/11 to defeat expeditionary-style terrorism.

Contrary to popular belief, most terrorist incidents since 9/11 have *not* been purely home-grown but have drawn on sponsorship, support, or guidance from AQ.[73] And as the 7/7 example shows, the expeditionary model now coexists alongside a guerrilla model in which local clandestine cells are recruited and trained in the target country.[74] Some cells are directly linked to AQ, while others receive training from AQ affiliates, or are inspired by AQ propaganda. There is a trend toward smaller, looser networks that are less capable, but also less predictable and harder to detect, than the more sophisticated networks of the pre-9/11 period.[75]

This suggests that AQ is agile in its operational approach, and willing to change and adapt as the situation develops. Before 9/11, as shown during the Harmony project[76] (an effort by the Combating Terrorism Center at West Point to translate and analyze a cache of AQ documents captured in Afghanistan in 2001), there was intense debate within the AQ leadership about the wisdom of the 9/11 attacks and the likelihood of a mass uprising as a result. In the immediate aftermath of 9/11, the mass uprising failed to occur, and expeditionary-style terrorism became more difficult, so the new guerrilla model emerged. Both now coexist, along with a reinvigorated AQ central leadership that is increasingly capable of planning and controlling attacks, and a population across large parts of the Muslim world (including Muslim populations in the West) that has been alienated by Western actions in Iraq, Afghanistan, and elsewhere and thus provides a recruiting base for guerrilla-style terrorism and a receptive audience for AQ propaganda.

This new model is extremely important in considering the accidental guerrilla syndrome, and this is an appropriate place to examine it in more detail.

THE ACCIDENTAL GUERRILLA SYNDROME * * *

I first began to notice the accidental guerrilla syndrome in the mid-1990s in West Java. But I did not come up with a name for it until 10 years later, after a conversation one afternoon on the Afghan-Pakistan frontier. With my State Department colleague Virginia Palmer, a former Africa hand with a wealth of field experience across Africa and Asia, I had been visiting Pakistan's FATA, which run for 1,200 kilometers along the Afghan-Pakistan frontier.

Virginia and I were working in the FATA with the Pakistan government, doing a detailed review of civil administration, economic development, and military policy on the frontier * * *. Our job was to assess the situation and report on how effectively Pakistan was employing the $100 million per month (at the time—the amount is greater now) the United States was providing in aid to the Pakistani government. We were traveling with a small escort from the Khyber Rifles, a regiment of the paramilitary Frontier Corps. The escort commander was a young Punjabi major, a city boy from Lahore who now found himself up in the mountains commanding a unit of people whose language he didn't speak and whose culture, history, and outlook were distinctly different from his own. One afternoon, when we were eating together, after a long hot day in the hills, and discussing the latest developments with al Qa'ida, I used the term "foreign fighters." He said, "You know, we Punjabis are the foreigners here on the frontier. Al Qa'ida has been here 25 years, their leaders have married into the tribes, they have children and businesses here, they've become part of local society. It's almost impossible for outsiders, including the Pakistan army, to tell the terrorists apart from anybody else in the tribal areas, except by accident." By *accident*. His word resonated in my mind, and I realized I now had a name for the phenomenon I had long recognized.

This Pakistani officer described a syndrome that is easily summed up, though extremely hard to counter: AQ moves into remote areas, creates alliances with local traditional communities, exports violence that prompts a Western intervention, and then exploits the backlash against that intervention in order to generate support for its *takfiri* agenda. Al Qa'ida's ideology tends to lack intrinsic appeal for traditional societies, and so it draws the majority of its strength from this backlash rather than from genuine popular support. * * * [T]his phenomenon [appears] in Iraq, Afghanistan, Pakistan, and elsewhere. [I]t is worth laying out the theory—the mechanism by which, I hypothesize, the accidental guerrilla emerges—as a starting point for [further] analysis.

Based on field observation in several theaters of the "War on Terrorism" since 2001, I theorize that the accidental guerrilla emerges from a cyclical process that takes place in four stages: infection, contagion, intervention, and rejection.

In detail, the four phases can be described as follows.

During the *infection* phase, AQ or an associated movement establishes a presence within a remote, ungoverned, or conflict-affected area. I use a medical analogy advisedly here, because just as a virus or bacterium is more easily able to affect a host whose immune system is compromised or to superinfect an existing wound, so *takfiri* groups opportunistically exploit existing breakdowns in the rule of law, poor governance, or preexisting conflict. Terrorist infection is thus part of the social pathology of broader societal breakdown, state weakness, and humanitarian crisis.

In this initial phase, the *takfiri* group establishes local cells, support systems, intelligence and information-gathering networks, and local alliances. It often seeks some form of tacit agreement or loose pact with the regime in the country at large (as did AQ in the 1980s in Pakistan, in the 1990s in the Sudan, and in Afghanistan before 9/11) and also seeks to build relationships with local tribes and community leaders, often through processes of intermarriage and shared business interests. The group may establish its own businesses, run front companies, or operate in partnership (or competition) with local criminal or business syndicates. It may establish training camps, education or ideological indoctrination centers, recruiting and logistics bases, transportation systems, centers for the production of counterfeit documentation, headquarters camps, media production facilities, and caches of equipment and supplies.

Importantly, the establishment of this type of safe haven is often met with resistance from the local people, who rightly regard AQ and similar externally motivated *takfiri* groups as alien outsiders who do not have local people's interests at heart. Al Qa'ida typically responds with a mixture of co-optation and intimidation: killing local community leaders (especially tribal elders and moderate religious leaders) who oppose their domination; establishing alliances by marriage, sometimes forced, with local women; bribing or killing government representatives who interfere; arbitrating local disputes; funneling money into the local economy; and establishing an uneasy ascendancy over the area. Although

AQ may appear secure in the safe haven, in fact it lacks intrinsic appeal to the local community, and there is always a dispossessed section of the local elite that is eager to regain its lost authority, and a disgruntled segment of the population who have had loved ones killed or harmed by the *takfiri* terrorists but feel too intimidated to act against the interlopers on their own.

In the second phase, *contagion*, the extremist group's influence spreads, and it begins to affect the country at large, other countries in the same region, and in some cases (enabled by the tools of globalization discussed earlier) other regions in the world, either directly through terrorist activity or "virtually" through propaganda and media influence. This is a critical stage in the process, since without it the terrorist presence in a given area would be unlikely to attract international attention or to present a threat to the world community at large, hence the next stage (intervention) would not occur. If not for his ability to spread contagion via globalization

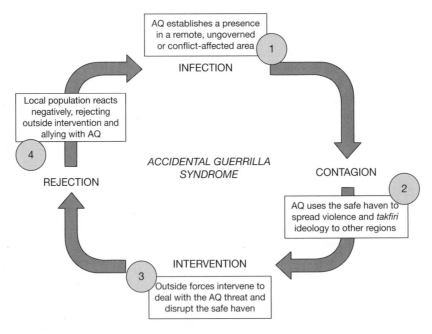

Figure 8.5. The Accidental Guerrilla Syndrome

pathways, Usama bin Laden, for example, would be simply one in a long line of charismatic extremist fugitive leaders who have hidden out in remote mountain areas and waged guerrilla warfare against local authorities. Hassan i-Sabah, the Old Man of the Mountains, is perhaps the archetype,[77] while others since the mid-nineteenth century include Imam Shamil in the Caucasus,[78] Mullah Powindah, Mirza Ali Khan (the Fakir of Ipi), Ajab Khan Afridi in the Hindu Kush, and Mohammed Abdullah Hassan (the Mad Mullah) in Somalia.[79] What makes the modern phenomenon different, and justifies a global response, is the potential for contagion: the bleed-out of violence to interconnected areas, the intersection between extremist ideology and weapons of mass destruction, and the global propaganda and destabilization effect of terrorist presence. Yet * * * the "cure" may be worse than the disease in this case, especially if it involves large-scale, overt, unilateral or heavy-handed Western military intervention.

In the third phase, *intervention*, external authorities begin to take action against the extremist presence, prompted by the ideological contagion or spread of subversion and violence emerging from the area. This phase may take several forms: intervention may be undertaken by the local (national or provincial) government only, by regional powers, or by the wider international community. Likewise, intervention may initially be nonviolent, applying aid and development measures and health, education, or governance extension programs. (This nonviolent approach usually does not last, because extremists react violently to the presence of external aid or governance workers, who then need to be protected by police or the military, so that violent clashes begin to occur.) Intervention may be episodic and short-term in nature, applying a "repetitive raiding" approach in the manner of a classical or colonial punitive expedition, or may adopt a long-term "persistent presence" approach.[80] It may be low-profile or highly public and overt. Finally and most important, it may

involve only local indigenous personnel or may be based on foreign presence (noting that, as our Khyber Rifles escort commander pointed out in 2006, the definition of "foreigner" is elastic, derives from local perceptions, and can include someone from a different provincial or cultural area as well as someone from another country). In other words, there are many forms of intervention, and choosing how to intervene—ideally in such a way as to minimize local backlash—is just as critical as deciding whether to intervene in the first place.

I have noted that during the initial stage of development of an extremist presence, there is usually a local opposition to the terrorist group (albeit often cowed, impotent, or intimidated). But during the intervention phase, the entire local dynamic shifts. The presence of the intervening outsiders causes local groups to coalesce in a fusion response, closing ranks against the external threat. This reaction is lessened if the intervention is slower, less violent, more locally based, or lower in profile. But a high-profile, violent, or foreign-based intervention tends to increase support for the *takfiri* terrorists, who can paint themselves as defenders of local people against external influence. Such an intervention also creates grievances, alienation, and a desire for revenge when local people are killed or are dishonored by the intervening outsiders' presence. Due to the dynamic of "balanced opposition," * * * local people in tribal societies will always tend to side with closer against more distant relatives, with local against external actors, and with coreligionists against people of other faiths. In this sense, although the terrorists may have been seen as outsiders until this point, their identity as such has been not fixed but "contingent": as soon as foreigners or infidels appear in the area, by comparison the terrorists are able to paint themselves as relative locals and opportunistically draw on local loyalties for support. The completely understandable (and necessary) imperative for the international community to intervene and prevent extremist contagion can thus act as a provocation, causing the next stage in the process: rejection.

Again, I use a medical analogy advisedly here. The *rejection* phase looks a lot like a social version of an immune response in which the body rejects the intrusion of a foreign object, even one (such as a pin in a broken bone or a stent in a blocked blood vessel) that serves an ultimately beneficial purpose. Societal antibodies recognize the intrusion as a foreign body, emerge to attack the intervening presence, and attempt to drive it out. This is the phase in which local people begin to become accidental guerrillas, fighting alongside extremist forces not because they support the *takfiri* ideology but because they oppose outside interference in their affairs, because they are rallied to support local tribal or community interests, or because they are alienated by heavy-handed actions of the intervening force. The more the *takfiri* group can paint itself as similar to the local people and the more it can appear as their defender against outsiders, the stronger this phenomenon becomes. A loose coalition of local groups emerges to defend local interests against outside attack and, unless local communities are carefully co-opted and won over by the government, the intervening force can end up fighting the whole of local society, when its original intent was to rescue local people from the exploitative presence of the extremist group.

The implications of the accidental guerrilla syndrome are far-reaching, and dealing effectively with it is likely to require a radical rethinking of some key Western policies, strategies, and attitudes. * * *

NOTES

1. This was the month of the EP3 surveillance plane incident, and U.S.-Korean relations were also at a low point. For a discussion of the China incident, see Congressional Research Service, *China–U.S. Aircraft Collision Incident of April 2001: Assessments and Policy Implications*, October 10, 2001; http://opencrs.cdt.org/document/RL30946.

2. Qiao Liang and Wang Xiangsui, *Unrestricted Warfare* (Beijing: PLA Literature and Arts Publishing House, February 1999).

3. Foreign Broadcast Intercept Service (FBIS), translation of interview, June 28, 1999, www.fbis.gov, document no. OW2807114599.

4. Ibid.

5. I am grateful to Dr Janine Davidson of George Mason University for bringing this key distinction to my attention during collaborative work in 2005–2006.

6. I am indebted to Assistant Professor Erin Simpson of the U.S. Marine Corps Staff College and Harvard University for this terminology. See Erin Simpson, "Thinking about Modern Conflict: Hybrid Wars, Strategy, and War Aims" (paper presented to the annual meeting of the Midwest Political Science Association, Chicago, April 7–11, 2005); www.people.fas.harvard.edu/~esimpson/papers/hybrid.pdf.

7. Loup Francart, *Maitriser la violence: Une option strategique* (Paris: Institut de stratégie comparée, 1999). For an English translation of some key concepts from this work see Loup Francart (a brigadier general in the French Army) and Jean-Jacques Party, "Mastering Violence: An Option for Operational Military Strategy," *Naval War College Review* 53, 3 (summer 2000): 144–84.

8. For an insightful discussion of these issues, see Michael Evans, "From Kadesh to Kandahar: Military Theory and the Future of War," *Naval War College Review* 53, 3 (summer 2003) 132–150; http://findarticles.com/p/articles/mi_moJIW/is_3_56/ai_105210224/print?tag=artBody;colr.

9. See Rupert Smith, *The Utility of Force: The Art of War in the Modern World* (New York: Knopf, 2007).

10. I am indebted to Lieutenant Colonel (retd) Bob Killebrew for this insight and for an

understanding of the sophistication and importance of modern gang structures and activities in this context. Killebrew, personal communications, March–June 2008.

11. I am indebted for this formulation to Ambassador Hank Crumpton, formerly U.S. coordinator for counterterrorism, who headed the CIA's intervention in Afghanistan in the immediate aftermath of 9/11.

12. John Lancaster and Kamran Khan, "Musharraf Named in Nuclear Probe: Senior Pakistani Army Officers Were Aware of Technology Transfers, Scientist Says," *Washington Post* Foreign Service, Tuesday, February 3, 2004, A13; www.washingtonpost.com/ac2/wp-dyn/A6884-2004Feb2.

13. See Kishore Mahbubani, *The New Asian Hemisphere: The Irresistible Shift of Global Power to the East* (New York: Public Affairs, 2008).

14. For a detailed discussion of these trends see Peter W. Singer, *Corporate Warriors: The Rise of the Privatized Military Industry*, Cornell Studies in Security Affairs (Ithaca, N.Y.: Cornell University Press, 2003) and Stephen Armstrong, *War Plc: The Rise of the New Corporate Mercenary* (New York: Faber & Faber, 2008).

15. The Truman administration (1945–1952) oversaw the establishment of most American security agencies, including the U.S. Air Force, the RAND Corporation, the CIA, the National Security Agency, National Security Council, National Intelligence Council, National Science Foundation, National Aeronautics and Space Administration, and indeed the Department of Defense itself.

16. Michael Howard, "What's in a Name? How to Fight Terrorism," *Foreign Affairs* (January–February 2002).

17. This somewhat arbitrary timeline begins with the conflicts in Greece, Indonesia, Palestine, and elsewhere that sparked as World War II ended and concludes with the fall of Ian Smith's white minority government to ZANLA/ZIPRA insurgents in Rhodesia in 1982, an event that brought down the final curtain on European empire in Africa.

18. Thomas L. Friedman, *The World Is Flat: A Brief History of the 21st Century* (New York: Farrar, Straus and Giroux, 2005).

19. John Ralston Saul, *Democracy and Globalization* (lecture series at the University of New South Wales, Sydney, January 1999); www.abc.net.au/specials/saul/default.htm.

20. Paul Collier, *The Bottom Billion: Why the Poorest Countries Are Failing and What Can Be Done about It* (New York: Oxford University Press, 2007).

21. Thomas P. M. Barnett, *The Pentagon's New Map* (New York: Putnam, 2004).

22. See bin Laden's statement of September 2007, which railed against a series of globalization-related grievances, discussed at www.dissidentvoice.orgz/2007/09/bin-laden-a-lefty/.

23. See the biography of Carlo Petrini, founder of the slow food movement; www.regione.piemonte.it/lingue/english/pagine/cultura/approfondimenti/16_petrini_eng.pdf.

24. For a listing of antiglobalization protest actions by such groups, see the Actions Against Globalization website archive: www.nadir.org/nadir/initiativ/agp/free/action07.html.

25. Thermobaric munitions combine explosive material and oxidants at the molecular level so that, unlike conventional explosives that rely on atmospheric oxygen to function correctly, they produce a sustained and deeply destructive blast wave even in confined spaces like tunnels, buildings, subways, and streets. Their use in conflicts in Chechnya, Afghanistan, and elsewhere has proven extremely effective, with gruesome results.

26. Akbar S. Ahmed, *Journey into Islam: The Crisis of Globalization* (Washington, D.C.: Brookings Institution Press, 2007).

27. I am indebted for these ideas to discussions at the Allen and Company Sun Valley Conference, Sun Valley, Idaho, July 10, 2008.

28. See Barnett, *Pentagon's New Map*.

29. Collier, *Bottom Billion*.

30. This is a modified form of the official U.S. Defense Department definition of insurgency. See Field Manual (FM) 3-24, *Counterinsurgency* (2006); www.fas.org/irp/doddir/army/fm3-24.pdf.

31. I am indebted for this formulation to Michael Scheuer, "Coalition Warfare, Part II: How Zarqawi Fits into Bin Laden's World Front," *Jamestown Terrorism Focus*, April 29, 2005; www.jamestown.org/news_details.php?news_id=109#.

32. See the official website of the Amman Message: http://ammanmessage.com/index.php?option=com_content&task=view&id=13&Itemid=27.

33. See United Nations Development Program, *Arab Human Development Report Series* (2001, 2002, 2003, 2004, and 2005); www.undp.org/arabstates/ahdr.shtml.

34. See Faisal Devji, *Landscapes of the Jihad: Militancy, Morality, Modernity* (Ithaca, N.Y.: Cornell University Press, 2005), and Akbar Ahmed, *Islam under Siege: Living Dangerously in a Post-honor World* (London: Polity, 2003).

35. See "The Operations Man: Ayman al-Zawahiri," *Estimate*, September 21, 2001, http://www.theestimate.com/public/092101_profile.html.

36. Ayman al-Zawahiri, "Knights under the Prophet's Banner," *Al-Sharq al-Awsat*, December 2, 2001.

37. Ibid.

38. See Abuza, *Zachary: 2004 NBR Analysis: Muslims, Politics and Violence in Indonesia: An Emerging Islamist-Jihadist Nexus?* (Seattle: National Bureau of Asian Research, 2004). For a slightly different interpretation, see also *Jema'ah Islamiyah in Southeast Asia: Damaged but Still Dangerous*, ICG Asia Report no. 863 (New York: International Crisis Group, August 26, 2003).

39. Vali S. Nasr, *The Shia Revival: How Conflicts within Islam Will Shape the Future* (New York: Norton, 2006).

40. Patrick Cockburn, *Muqtada: Muqtada al-Sadr, the Shia Revival, and the Struggle for Iraq* (London: Scribner, 2008).

41. See David Horovitz, "Editor's Notes: A Searing Indictment," *Jerusalem Post*, May 4, 2007.

42. Andrew M. Exum, *Hizballah at War: A Military Assessment*, Policy Focus no. 63 (Washington, D.C.: Washington Institute for Near East Policy, December 2006); www.washingtoninstitute.org/pubPDFs/PolicyFocus63.pdf.

43. See Nawaf Obaid, *A Shia Crescent and the Shia Revival: Myths and Realities* (Riyadh: Saudi National Security Assessment Project, September 27, 2006); E:2006_09_27_Iran_Project_Phase_A_Brief.pdf.

44. See, for example, the discussion of the separationist Robert Spencer's views: www.amnation.com/vfr/archives/006854.html.

45. Frederick H. Hartmann, *The Conservation of Enemies: A Study in Enmity* (Westport, Conn.: Greenwood Press, 1982).

46. For a detailed discussion of this tendency, see Mary R. Habeck, *Knowing the Enemy: Jihadist Ideology and the War on Terror* (New Haven, Conn.: Yale University Press, 2006).

47. See David Kilcullen, "Countering Global Insurgency," *Journal of Strategic Studies* 28, 4 (August 2005): 597–617.

48. See Mark Bowden, *Guests of the Ayatollah: The Iran Hostage Crisis: The First Battle in America's War with Militant Islam* (New York: Grove Press, 2007).

49. For a description of these events, see Kermit Roosevelt, *Countercoup: The Struggle for the Control of Iran* (New York: McGraw-Hill, 1979), and Stephen Kinzer, *All the Shah's Men: An American Coup and the Roots of Middle East Terror* (New York: Wiley, 2003).

50. See www.globalsecurity.org/military/world/spending.htm for current figures.

51. I am indebted to Ambassador Henry Crumpton, former coordinator for counterterrorism, for this insight.

52. Andrew Bacevich, "The Islamic Way of War," *American Conservative*, September 11, 2006;

www.amconmag.com/2006/2006_09_11/cover.html.

53. Ibid.

54. See, for example, the website of the Earth Liberation Front: www.earthliberationfront.com/elf_news.htm.

55. Discussion with senior civil service official responsible for finance and budgeting in Iraq, July 2007.

56. National Commission on Terrorist Attacks on the United States, *The 9/11 Commission Final Report* (Washington, D.C.: U.S. Government, 2004), chap. 5; http://govinfo.library.unt.edu/911/report/911Report_Ch5.htm.

57. Robert Looney, "Economic Costs to the United States Stemming from the 9/11 Attacks," *Strategic Insights* 1, 6 (August 2002); www.ccc.nps.navy.mil/si/augo2/homeland.asp.

58. Congressional Research Service, *The Cost of Iraq, Afghanistan, and Other Global War on Terror Operations since 9/11*, Report to Congress no. RL33110, updated June 23, 2008; www.fas.org/sgp/crs/natsec/RL33110.pdf.

59. Compiled from figures in *The Military Balance* 2007 (London: International Institute for Strategic Studies, 2007), 15–50.

60. Compiled from U.S. State Department and U.S. Agency for International Development, *Congressional Budget Justification* 2007 (Washington, D.C.: State Department, 2006), table 9; http://www.state.gov/s/d/rm/rls/cbj/2007/.

61. Scheuer, "Coalition Warfare."

62. Kilcullen, "Countering Global Insurgency."

63. Usama bin Laden, statement of November 1, 2004.

64. See Lawrence Uzzell, "Could the Beslan Tragedy Have Been Avoided?" [Jamestown Institute] *North Caucasus Weekly*, September 8, 2004; www.jamestown.org/chechnya_weekly/article.php?issue_id=3062.

65. Robert Worth, "Blast Destroys Shrine in Iraq, Setting Off Sectarian Fury," *New York Times*, February 22, 2006.

66. Bernard B. Fall, "The Theory and Practice of Insurgency and Counterinsurgency," *Naval War College Review* 51, 1 (winter 1998): 46–57 (first published April 1965).

67. Sheldon W. Simon, "Philippines Withdraws from Iraq and JI Strikes Again," *Comparative Connections* 6, 3 (October 2004): n.p.; www.ciaonet.org/olj/cpc/cpc_octo4/cpc_octo4f.pdf.

68. Sharon Otterman, "Iraq: Ongoing Attacks," *Council on Foreign Relations Backgrounder*, August 21, 2003; www.cfr.org/publication.html?id=7685.

69. For detailed accounts of these events, see Gary Berntsen, *Jawbreaker: The Attack on bin Laden and Al Qaeda* (New York: Crown, 2005), and Sean Naylor, *Not a Good Day to Die* (New York: Penguin, 2005).

70. See Peter Bergen, "The Long Hunt for Osama," *Atlantic Monthly*, October 2004, vol. 294.

71. National Commission on Terrorist Attacks on the United States, *9/11 Commission Final Report*, chap. 5.

72. Intelligence and Security Committee, *Report into the London Terrorist Attacks on 7 July 2005* (London: HMSO, May 2006).

73. Bruce Hoffman, Washington director, RAND Corporation, personal communication, July 6, 2006.

74. David Kilcullen, "Counterinsurgency *Redux*," *Survival* 48, 4 (winter 2006–7): 111–30.

75. U.S. Department of State, *Country Reports on Terrorism* 2005 (Washington, D.C.: Government Printing Office, 2005), chap. 2; www.state.gov/s/ct/rls/crt/2005/64332.htm.

76. See Joe Felter et al., *Harmony and Disharmony: Exploiting al Qa'ida's Organizational Vulnerabilities* (West Point, N.Y.: Combating Terrorism Center, February 2006); http://cisac.stanford.edu/publications/harmony_and_disharmony_exploiting_alqaidas_organizational_vulnerabilities/.

77. See Bernard Lewis, *The Assassins: A Radical Sect within Islam* (New York: Basic Books, 2002).

78. See Nicholas Griffin, *Caucasus: Mountain Men and Holy Wars* (New York: Thomas Dunne Books, 2003).

79. Mullah Powindah, the Mahsud leader, led a guerrilla war against British rule in the Tochi valley over decades in the nineteenth century. The Fakir of Ipi, Mirza Ali Khan, waged guerrilla war against the British throughout the 1930s and 1940s and only reconciled with the state of Pakistan in 1954. Ajab Khan Afridi was responsible for the 1923 kidnapping (and release) of Molly Ellis, daughter of a British officer in the Kohat garrison of the North-West Frontier Province, prompting an enormous manhunt, and hid out in the Hindu Kush for decades; he eventually died in his sleep. The Mad Mullah, Mohammed Abdullah Hassan, led a guerrilla movement against the British in Somaliland between the 1890s and 1920.

80. I am indebted to Lieutenant Colonel Chris Cavoli for the terms "repetitive raiding" and "persistent presence."

GARETH EVANS

When Is It Right to Fight?

Some wars will always have to be fought. National interest will demand it, or our common humanity will compel it. But every generation of political leaders seems to have to relearn that war, whatever the justice of the cause for which it is fought, is always ugly, always destructive, always the source of immense human pain and misery, and almost always produces unintended results. As professional soldiers often seem to know better than civilians, the decision to go to war should never be made lightly or cavalierly, with disregard for the evidence which might justify it, or inattention to its possible consequences. And it should never be made with indifference to the formal rules of international law, such as they are, that ban or allow the use of military force.

The trouble is that, as we look out on the world around us, those rules seem to be in serious disarray, their application erratic and their interpretation contested. Not for the first time in history, we have something approaching a crisis of confidence in the reality and relevance of the global legal order. There is growing cynicism and scepticism about the bindingness, and indeed even the existence, of the international rules authorising military action. Too many states are seen as making up the rules as they go along, going to war when they should not, and not going to war when they should.

There is concern, above all, about the way in which one state, the United States—and the power in the world with by far the most capacity to do so—has seemed to want singlehandedly to rewrite the rule book. What is challenged above all is the notion, asserted in the lead up to the attack on Iraq in 2003, that the right to act in self-defence, without need for prior UN Security Council approval, extends without check to situations where the threatened attack is neither actual nor imminent—and where the reacting country remains, in effect, the sole judge of whether there is a real threat at all. This led Secretary-General

From *Survival* 46, no. 3 (Autumn 2004): 59–82.

Kofi Annan to sound the alarm in the strongest possible terms in his address to the General Assembly on 23 September 2003: if states "reserve the right to act unilaterally, or in ad hoc coalitions"—without waiting for agreement in the Security Council—"[t]his logic represents a fundamental challenge to the principles on which, however imperfectly, world peace and stability have rested for the last fifty-eight years."[1]

The Secretary-General's concern prompted him at the same time to establish a High Level Panel on Threats, Challenges and Change, consisting of some very distinguished and well-known statesmen and women—and me—to advise him by the end of the year on how the international system might respond to the new security environment.[2] Our task is a daunting one: to evaluate the threats, old and new, to both state security and human security that the world will confront in the decades ahead; to identify appropriate policy responses; and to recommend necessary and desirable institutional changes. But it will also be to address what UK Foreign Secretary Jack Straw has been calling "the jurisprudence issue": the status and application of the most fundamental international rules of all, those determining when it is right to fight.

A Crisis in the International Legal Order?

The United Nations was created in 1945 above all else "to save succeeding generations from the scourge of war, which twice in our lifetime has brought untold sorrow to mankind."[3] And the detailed terms of the Charter appeared to deliver on that Preamble rhetoric. The use of force was subjected to the rule of law in a much clearer way than had ever previously been attempted, including in the ill-fated League of Nations Covenant, and the law was backed with a system of collective security much more potentially effective than anything that had gone before, with the centrepiece a Security Council empowered to deal

forcefully with acts of aggression and threats to the peace. The sense was very real, and for good reason, that international relations had at last emerged from a centuries-old jungle, and that a new age of international law had dawned.

The Charter made absolutely clear in Article 2(4) that all UN member states "shall refrain in their international relations from the threat or use of force against the territorial integrity or political independence of any state, or in any other manner inconsistent with the Purposes of the United Nations." It allowed only two exceptions to the prohibition on the use of force in international law: self-defence under Article 51, and military measures authorised by the Security Council in response to "any threat to the peace, breach of the peace or act of aggression" (under Chapter VII, and by extension for regional organisations in Chapter VIII).

While the Security Council's power to approve force in acting "to maintain or restore international peace and security" was left effectively open-ended, the traditional right of self-defence was spelt out in Article 51 in terms that are very far from open-ended, and in fact linked back to the Security Council:

> Nothing in the present Charter shall impair the inherent right of individual or collective self-defence if an armed attack occurs against a Member of the United Nations, until the Security Council has taken measures necessary to maintain international peace and security. Measures taken by members in the exercise of this right of self-defence shall be immediately reported to the Security Council.

But it was one thing to create a new legal order, quite another to make it work as intended. The founders of this new order were not naïve, recognising as Adlai Stevenson said at the time, that "[e]verything depends on the active participation, pacific intentions and good faith of the Big Five."[4] And the mutual hostility among the five permanent members themselves which very soon emerged, to be sustained throughout the Cold War years, certainly did threaten to bring the whole edifice down. For 44 years, until 1989, states repeatedly used military force against others (by one count 200 times and by another 680 times),[5] and a great many of these occasions could not begin to be explained or justified as self-defence under Article 51, although that fig-leaf was regularly relied upon.

But a paralysed Security Council passed very few Chapter VII resolutions, and there was only one large-scale collective military action responding to a breach of the peace—Korea in 1950, during the Soviet Union's misjudged period of absence from the Council. The order that prevailed was essentially a new variation on an old balance of power theme: one in which "each superpower would refrain from attacking the essential interests of the other, but would be freed to use force at will in its own sphere of influence."[6] That force was used repeatedly, particularly in Central and Eastern Europe and in Latin America and the Caribbean.

The irony is that some of the very few cases of military action to generate almost universal condemnation as indefensible intrusions on state sovereignty were ones that today might be regarded as permissible examples of "humanitarian intervention," or intervention for human protection purposes, although they were justified this way only partly or not at all by the intervening countries at the time: India's invasion of East Pakistan in 1971 (in the context of West Pakistan's brutal suppression of Bengalis) and Vietnam's invasion of Cambodia in 1978 (in the context of the Khmer Rouge's genocidal brutality toward its own people) were both claimed, implausibly, to be cases of national self-defence, but that did nothing to dilute the criticism.[7]

Through all this, the UN security system managed to stay afloat, playing a reasonably significant role at least in defusing and managing conflict. "Good offices" diplomacy contributed to the peaceful abatement of some 25% of the post-1945 conflicts.[8] And peacekeeping, a role invented by the Secretariat—involving the verification, monitoring and supervision of ceasefire and broader peace agreements—proved crucial

in reducing the risk of a number of further wars, especially in South Asia and the Middle East.[9] But it is hard to argue that the new international legal order promised by the Charter was, for the duration of the Cold War, under anything but stress.

All that changed dramatically after the Berlin Wall came down in 1989. The removal of a major source of ideological and great power conflict liberated the UN to play the global security role its founders intended, as became immediately apparent with the response to Iraq's invasion of Kuwait in 1991. Expectations were reinforced by UN-organised or authorised military deployments in the former Yugoslavia, Somalia and Haiti. The average number of resolutions passed in a year went from 15 to 60, or from a resolution a month to a resolution a week. Ninety-three percent (247 out of 267) of all Chapter VII resolutions of the Council were passed between 1990 and 2002. Before 1989 the Council applied sanctions twice; since then it has imposed them 15 times.[10]

Whether all this activity was effective is another question: certainly in relation to interventions for human protection purposes, too often what happened—not least in Somalia in 1993, Rwanda in 1994 and Bosnia in 1995—was too little too late, misconceived, poorly resourced, poorly executed, or all of the above. And of course in Kosovo in 1999, in what was arguably a very strong case for intervention, a divided Security Council was bypassed completely. But there was reason to believe that step by step, painful and disappointing as so much of the process was, a new and much more responsive international legal order was falling into place.

The high-water mark, in terms of both commitment to collective security institutions and a willingness to adapt them to deal with new kinds of threats, probably came with the unanimous Security Council resolution on 12 September 2001, immediately after the attacks on the twin towers and the Pentagon, accepting that Article 51 self-defence extended to using force against non-state terrorist organisations as well as "those responsible for aiding, supporting or harbouring the perpetrators, organizers and sponsors of . . . acts" of terrorism. This was followed two weeks later by the adoption of mandatory global controls to prevent the financing of terrorism and the recruiting of terrorists.[11] Confidence in the flexibility of the UN system, and its capacity to deliver, was strong.

But now the wheel has turned again, and maybe even more seriously than in the Cold War years. The decision of the US, and its coalition allies, to go to war in Iraq in March 2003 in defiance not only of one or more threatened vetoes, but of the clear and overwhelming majority of the members of the Security Council, was a watershed of a wholly different, and more disconcerting kind. Three different kinds of challenges to the international legal order are involved, all of them serious.

First, to the extent that the invasion of Iraq was based on a claim of anticipatory self-defence more far-reaching than any previously asserted, Article 51 has been stretched beyond endurance. Secondly, to the extent that the invasion was based on claims of threats to international peace and security sufficient under Chapter VII to justify Security Council authorisation, but with those claims poorly argued and the Council eventually bypassed, the credibility of the whole Charter system has again been frontally challenged. And thirdly, to the extent that the invasion was based on Saddam Hussein's record of tyranny over his own people—but again, poorly and inconsistently argued, and with the Council bypassed—we have seen almost choked at birth what many were hoping was an emerging new norm justifying intervention on the basis of the principle of "responsibility to protect."

I want to explore these issues in more detail, and then to make some suggestions as to how, in this very difficult environment, we might nonetheless go about consolidating or rebuilding an international legal order that *will* be capable of meeting the challenges of the twenty-first century. But first, it is necessary to address those who would say at the outset that this whole enterprise is misconceived.

Faced with all the stops and starts and tumult I have described, and the way in which the Security Council has been used, misused and bypassed not only during the desolate Cold War years but over the more hopeful years since, some voices—the most strident of them Professor Michael Glennon, writing in *Foreign Affairs*[12] last year—are going so far as to claim that there are simply no rules any more, that the whole UN Charter "edifice [has come] crashing down." Glennon argues that the reality of US power and the failure of the Security Council structure to reflect it should be frankly recognised and that, in any attempt in the future to recreate a body of international law governing the use of force in all its manifestations, "what the design should look like must be a function of what it can look like."

There is a lofty analytical response to this line of argument, for example, that offered by a commentator in a recent issue of the *American Journal of International Law* when he says "Glennon raises, but hardly resolves, law's most profound epistemological issue, namely the effect of deviance on the authority of norms."[13] I have to confess that my own response is a little more visceral. I find Michael Glennon's position to be deeply alarming, might-is-right realism dressed up as international law analysis, and am very much in sympathy with Thomas Franck's trenchant response:

> What, then, is the proper role for the lawyer? Surely, it is to stand tall for the rule of law. What this entails is self-evident . . . When the politicians seek to bend the law, the lawyers must insist that they have broken it . . . When the powerful are tempted to discard the law, the lawyer must ask whether someday, if our omnipotence wanes, we may not need the law. Lawyers who do that may even be called traitors. But those who do not are traitors to their calling.

The search for an orderly, principled system of international law and practice on conflict is almost as old as conflict itself. There is always a choice, when confronted with the unhappy reality that governments don't always behave as we hope they might, of raising your sights or lowering them: the tragedy of intellectualising failure in the way that those like Glennon do, is that it encourages so many to lower sights when the acute need is to raise them.

But that is only the beginning of the necessary answer. We have to satisfy ourselves that the rules we have are up to meeting the threats we now have to face, and that they are in fact capable of being applied. So what is to be said about the present status and workability of the Article 51 rule on self-defence, and the general competence of the Security Council to authorise the use of force under Chapter VII?

Do We Have to Hand the Legal Tools We Need?

Article 51 and Anticipatory Self-Defence

It has long been accepted, both as a matter of customary international law predating Article 51 and international practice since, that notwithstanding the language of the article referring only to the right arising "if an armed attack occurs," the right of self-defence extends beyond an actual attack to an imminently threatened one. Provided there is credible evidence of such an imminent threat, and the threatened state has no obvious alternative recourse available, there is no problem—and never has been—with that state, without first seeking Security Council approval, using military force "preemptively." If an army is mobilising, its capability to cause damage clear and its hostile intentions unequivocal, nobody has ever seriously suggested that you have to wait to be fired upon. In this sense, what has been described generically as "anticipatory self-defence" has always been legal.

The problem arises with another kind of anticipatory self-defence: when the threat of attack is claimed to be real, but there is no credible reason to believe it is imminent, and where—as linguistic purists insist—the issue accordingly is not preemption but *prevention*. (The English language seems to be unique in having two different words here—"preemption" to describe responses to imminent threats, and "prevention" for non-imminent ones: that luxury, however, cherished though it may be by policy aficionados who happen to be native English speakers, seems to have done far more to confuse than clarify the debate for everyone else, who tend to use the words, if at all, interchangeably.) The classic non-imminent threat situation is early stage acquisition of weapons of mass destruction [WMD] by a state presumed to be hostile—the case that was made against Iraq by Israel in justifying its strike on the half-built Osirak reactor in 1981, and the case that the US tried to make against Iraq before March 2003.

The problem here is not with the principle of military action against non-imminent threats as such. It is perfectly possible to imagine real threats which are not imminent—including the nightmare scenario combining rogue states, WMD and terrorists. The problem boils down to whether or not there is credible evidence of the reality of the threat in question (taking into account, as always, both capability and specific intent); whether the military attack response is the only reasonable one in all the circumstances; and—crucially—who makes the decision. The question is not whether preventive military action can ever be taken: it is entirely within the scope of the Security Council's powers under Chapter VII to authorise force if it is satisfied a case has been made (and the Council and others these days are quite properly giving increased attention, in relation to both WMD proliferation and terrorism, to circumstances in which such cases might be made). The question is whether military action in response to non-imminent threats can ever be taken *unilaterally*.

This is the question on which the US has led with its chin, and generated a storm of continuing international controversy in the lead up to the 2003 Iraq war, even though, in the event, it did not formally rely on Article 51. First there was President George W. Bush's "axis of evil" State of the Union address in January 2002, in which he declared that the US "will not permit the world's most dangerous regimes to threaten us with the world's most destructive weapons";[14] then, five months later at West Point, his assertion that "we must take the battle to the enemy, disrupt his plans, and confront the worst threats before they emerge";[15] then in September 2002 the release of the National Security Strategy, arguing for a broadening of the "concept of imminent threat to the capabilities and objectives of today's adversaries" and stating that "there is a compelling case for taking anticipatory action to defend ourselves, even if uncertainty remains as to the time and place of the enemy's attack."[16]

This was all too much even for Henry Kissinger, not normally a dedicated booster of international law or reluctant user of US power, who wrote in a *Washington Post* column on 16 September 2002:

> As the most powerful nation in the world, the United States has a special unilateral capacity to implement its convictions. But it also has a special obligation to justify its actions by principles that transcend the assertions of preponderant power. It cannot be in either the American national interest or the world's interest to develop principles that grant every nation an unfettered right of preemption against its own definition of threats to its security.

The biggest problem with extending the scope of unilateral self-defence action under Article 51 in the way contemplated by the Bush administration is that it utterly fails to acknowledge that what is sauce for the goose is sauce for the gander, legitimising the prospect of preventive strikes in any number of volatile regions, starting with the Middle East, South and East Asia. To undermine so comprehensively the norm of non-intervention on which any system of global order must be painstakingly built is to invite a slide into anarchy. We would be living in

a world where the unilateral use of force would be the rule, not the exception.

But even short of doomsday scenarios of this kind, the wrong-headedness of carrying out, threatening or even just hinting at unilateral preventive strikes is readily apparent. To the extent that the attack on Iraq can be characterised as such a strike, it does not seem to have done much so far—even before the recent disastrous revelations about the humiliation and abuse of Iraqi prisoners—to advance the cause of a democratic Greater Middle East. To the extent that North Korea was meant to be cowed by the prospect of such action, the effort seems to have been spectacularly counterproductive, generating a rush to acquire as fast as possible, as the best deterrent to such a strike, the very nuclear weapons whose potential acquisition was what prompted the unilateral sword-waving in the first place. Similar reasoning may be prompting Iran's foot-dragging in responding to the international demand to terminate its suspect nuclear programmes. Of course, any serious challenge to US dominance by anyone will be a long time coming, but history is replete with examples of over-exuberant military power eventually being countered by defensive alliances with aspirations of their own.

More prosaically, if a threat is real but not imminent, and there is, by definition, time to address it, there is every reason to believe that with an appropriate policy strategy, mobilising other international players as appropriate, and inspiring rather than alienating those whose support is needed, that threat can be deterred or contained, resolved by persuasion or negotiation, or reduced by the socialisation of the actors concerned. Recognising the inherent horror and hugely uncertain consequences of going to war, statecraft has always been about avoiding war if security objectives can possibly be guaranteed in other ways. But as Arthur Schlesinger Jr has put it, President Bush has repudiated the strategy that won the Cold War, replacing "a policy that aimed at peace through the prevention of war by a policy aimed at peace through preventive war."[17]

Chapter VII and External Threats

When a state poses a threat to other states, or individuals outside its borders, Chapter VII of the UN Charter fully empowers the Security Council to take any coercive action at all, including ultimately military action, that it deems "necessary to maintain or restore international peace and security." It doesn't matter whether the threat involves a "threat to the peace, breach of the peace or act of aggression"; whether it is occurring now, or in the imminent future or in the distant future; or whether it is constituted by an act or an omission; or whether it is constituted by the state's own actions or by non-state actors it harbours or supports.

Nor does it matter whether the threat is constituted by an actual or potential act of violence, or simply a challenge to the Council's authority. If the Security Council decides that a state is not acting in compliance with previous resolutions and for that reason alone, by putting the credibility of the Council's decisions at risk it is posing a "threat to the peace"—whatever other kind of threat that state may or may not constitute—the Council is fully entitled to make that judgement and act accordingly.

And the options available to the Council extend, at its complete discretion, to authorising or endorsing the use of force by blue helmets, Multinational Forces, "coalitions of the willing" or individual states, as well as endorsing (sometimes after the event) military action by regional organisations operating under Chapter VIII; for example, the Economic Community of West African States (ECOWAS) in Liberia and Sierra Leone.

While there is always the practical problem of ensuring that action follows decision, and what might be described as the Hotspur question in relation to the actual supply of authorised military resources ("I can call spirits from the vasty deep" . . . "But will they come?"),[18] there is, in short, no doubt about the legal capacity of the Security Council to declare effectively anything it wants to a threat to international peace and security, and to authorise military action accordingly.

Usually the only question—a huge one politically, but not legally—is how the unquestioned authority of the Council should be exercised, when the Charter offers no detailed criteria, when states see their interests so differently, and when some states exercise so much more influence than others. There is growing acceptance that, as the Secretary-General said last September, that there may need to be "early authorisation of coercive measures to address certain types of threats—for instance, terrorist groups armed with weapons of mass destruction." He suggested, very gently, that Security Council members "may need to begin a discussion on the criteria" for such early authorisation—this problem is addressed below.[19]

There may of course be a legal issue in a given case—as, notoriously, with Iraq last year—as to whether the Security Council has actually authorised the use of force at all, or whether some further resolution is necessary to accomplish that. As a former Attorney General and longstanding senior Cabinet lawyer, I am not entirely unfamiliar with the delicate task of commissioning or delivering opinions which somehow have to accommodate legal conscience with perceived political necessity. And no doubt there is much to be said—and has been said, by Adam Roberts[20] among others—for the "presumption of continuity" of those earlier Security Council resolutions requiring Iraq's full and complete disarmament and implying dire consequences if it didn't.

But even in my finest full-wigged days I don't think I could have managed to persuade myself, or anyone else, that either Resolution 687 back in April 1991, or Resolution 1441 as late as November 2002, or any resolution in between, actually in themselves authorised the use of force (in the way that Resolution 678 clearly did for the 1990 Gulf War); or that they required anything other than further resort to the Council before force could be used; or that they could possibly be construed as explicit enough in their terms to override the obvious reality that the current votes for force, vetoes quite apart fell conspicuously short of a majority.

Chapter VII and Internal Threats

While the UN Charter is as clear as it possibly could be on the question of external threats, it is much less clear about the right of collective action against a state when the only threat involved is to those within it—the issue of so-called humanitarian intervention. Article 2(7) expressly prohibits intervention "in matters which are essentially within the jurisdiction of any state," but this is in tension with language elsewhere acknowledging individual human rights, and with a mass of law and practice over the last few decades which have set real conceptual limits on claims of untrammelled state sovereignty, not least the Genocide Convention.[21]

What is clear is that the Security Council can always authorise Chapter VII military action against a state if it is prepared to declare that the situation, however apparently internal in character, does in fact amount to a "threat to international peace and security"—as it did for example in Somalia, and eventually Bosnia, in the early 1990s. With no higher authority to gainsay it, threats to international peace and security are what the Security Council says they are. But more often than not, even in shocking situations like Rwanda in 1994, it has declined to initiate or authorise any enforcement action at all. And that has led to a willingness, in cases where necessity seemed to demand, to bypass the Council, as in Kosovo in 1999, in ways that—if repeated—can't help but diminish its authority.

The need to actually mean it when we say "never again" after each Cambodia, or Rwanda, or Srebrenica—to respond quickly and forcefully to "gross and systematic violations of human rights that affect every precept of our common humanity," as Kofi Annan described the issue to the General Assembly in his 2000 Millennium

Report[22]—is in constant tension with desire of sovereign states not to see a diminution of their sovereign authority. The tenacity of that attachment can be seen to this day in the reluctance that has been evident in the Security Council to take on and hold to account Sudan for its contribution to the horrors continuing to unfold in Darfur.

It was to try to resolve this tension between the claims of state sovereignty and individual rights that the Canadian government sponsored the International Commission on Intervention and State Sovereignty (ICISS), which I co-chaired with the Secretary-General's Special Adviser on Africa, Mohamed Sahnoun, and which produced its report, *The Responsibility to Protect* in 2001.[23] The most groundbreaking contribution of the report was its characterisation of the central issue not as the "right" of anybody to intervene, but rather, the responsibility of the international community to act to protect a state's people when the state itself abdicated that responsibility, either through ill-will or incapacity. The ICISS spelt it out in the form of two critical principles. The primary responsibility for the protection of a state's own people must lie with the state itself. But where a population is suffering serious harm, as a result of internal war, insurgency, repression or state failure, and the state in question is unwilling or unable to halt or avert it, the principle of nonintervention should lead to a larger principle, that of the international responsibility to protect.

We had no doubt that the proper authority to authorise action in these circumstances was the Security Council, but had to face the problem that the Council has not always acted as it should in the face of conscience-shocking violations of humanity. Our bottom line was that the task was not to find alternatives to the Security Council, but to make the Security Council work better. And that led us specifically to formulate a set of criteria for military action, which we argued strongly should be accepted at least informally as guidelines by the Security Council and hopefully could ultimately become so embedded in practice that they assumed the status of customary international law.

In this respect, in order to maximise the chances of reaching consensus when the next Rwanda, or Kosovo—or Darfur—came along, the ICISS deliberately made the threshold criterion for coercive intervention very tough. The argument was that unless the bar is set very high and tight, excluding less than catastrophic forms of human-rights abuse, *prima facie* cases for the use of military force could be made across half the world. So we proposed that the trigger condition for intervention in these internal cases should be narrowly confined to two kinds of situation involving serious and irreparable harm to human beings in progress or imminent: either large-scale loss of life due to deliberate state action, inaction or inability to act; or large-scale "ethnic cleansing" carried out not only by killing, but forced expulsion, acts of terror or rape.

The "responsibility to protect" principles were quietly gaining momentum in the academic and political debate, albeit rather submerged by the preoccupations with terrorism and WMD that emerged after 11 September. But it has to be said that they have been rather thrown off course by the emergence of the argument in relation to last year's invasion of Iraq—as other rationales in terms of bombs and terrorists dropped away— that it was Saddam's murderous tyrannising of his own people that made him a suitable case for humanitarian intervention treatment. The argument was a very strong one a decade and more ago, when Saddam was massacring Kurds in the late 1980s and southern Shi'ites in the early 1990s—as the world in both cases looked steadfastly the other way—but it had much less application in recent years, when no such catastrophe was occurring or imminent and, awful as it was, the Iraqi regime's behaviour was not much worse than a score or two of others.[24]

It had all the appearance of a convenient rationalisation rather than genuine motivation, and certainly looked that way to those concerned, for good reasons or bad, about the potential over-reach of the humanitarian intervention principle. Was Robert Mugabe to be the next case for military treatment, the ostensible rationale for the enterprise being not his current onslaught on democracy and human rights, but the slaughters in Matabeleland in the 1980s?

The net result of all this was that an emerging international norm of real potential utility was once again struggling for acceptance. Those of us fighting to get the responsibility-to-protect principle recognised had to face all over again the argument, after Iraq, that any formalisation of the principle would, in the long tradition of *missions civilisatrices*, only encourage those who were all too inclined to misuse it.

How Do We Rebuild an International Legal Order?

So, what is the task ahead for those of us who do want to raise our sights, not lower them; who want to reverse the trend toward unilateralism rather than collective action in the use of force; who are appalled at the indifference being shown to, as Kofi Annan described them, "the principles on which, however imperfectly, world peace and stability have rested"[25] for the last six decades; who want to see a new consensus emerge, in the context of internal threats to human security, not only as to when states should not go to war, but when they should; and who, above all, want to recreate the kind of confidence in the role and judgement of the Security Council that will lead to a dramatically reduced inclination to bypass it on the part of those capable of doing so?

Four steps, I think, are involved. The first is simply to recognise the full range of security threats with which any credible contemporary international legal order has to deal. They include the most traditional of all concerns, attacks by states employing conventional weapons, whether actual, imminently threatened or possible. They certainly include attacks by states employing weapons of mass destruction, whether actual, imminently threatened or just possible. They must include the so-called new threats, in particular attacks—employing any class of weapons—by non-state actors supported by a state or operating in a failed state environment, whether those attacks be actual, imminently threatened or possible. They must also include attacks perpetrated or allowed by a state on its own people, again whether that violence be actual, imminently threatened or merely possible. And security threats should also be seen as constituted by persistent breach of UNSC resolutions putting at risk the credibility of the enforcement system.

The second step is to acknowledge that we do already have to hand all the legal tools and rules we need to properly manage every one of these security threats. When it comes to authorising the use of force, we don't need new rules, any modification of the existing rules or any new rule-making or rule-applying institutions. In the case of rules, Article 51 and Chapter VII, properly applied, between them enable us to fully respond—reactively, preemptively or preventively—to protect the national interest, the collective international interest and the intra-state human interest. And to do so when it comes to actual attacks of any kind, imminently threatened attacks of any kind, possible future attacks of any kind, and necessary measures to enforce the implementation of Security Council resolutions.

When it comes to rule-making and applying institutions, the Security Council's role can certainly be supplemented by that of the regional or sub-regional organisations recognised under Chapter VIII of the Charter, subject to their seeking at least subsequent authorisation from the Security Council. And there may be a role still for the General Assembly acting in Emergency Special Session under the "Uniting for Peace" procedure: it is quite possible, for example, had the Kosovo issue been tested there in 1999, that majority support would have been forthcoming. But, apart from the case of legitimate self-defence in response to actual or imminent attack, there simply is no better or more appropriate body than the UN Security Council to authorise military action.

Whatever its failings in terms of the contemporary representativeness and legitimacy of its composition, particularly so far as the five veto-wielding permanent members are concerned, the Security Council is the only body we have, or are ever likely to have, fully empowered to act in security matters on behalf of the only organisation we have, or are ever likely to have, with effectively universal membership. As the ICISS put it, with succinct and I hope impressive clarity, "The task is not to find alternatives to the Security Council as a source of authority, but to make the Security Council work better than it has."[26]

The third step is to recognise that, as a global community responding to security threats, we have to do much better at *prevention* than we have, to avoid so far as possible the issue of the use of military force ever having to arise. What this means in all the different contexts we have been addressing is a vast subject in itself. But for the purposes of illustration, let me take the critically important case of nuclear weapons, and what might more usefully be done than simply threatening certain unpalatable regimes with annihilation if they don't immediately give up whatever weapons capability they might have.[27]

The basic need here is to develop new and tougher universal rules that, on both the supply and demand side, prevent proliferation the old-fashioned way, through the hard diplomatic work of negotiating legal regimes and then putting appropriate resources into enforcing them: something that has not been happening, and (on the evidence of the break-up in disarray on 7 May 2004 of the latest Preparatory Committee meeting for next year's planned NPT Review Conference) is depressingly unlikely to happen any time soon. On the supply side the kind of measures that need to be worked on include tighter regulation of internal fuel-cycle activities for Nuclear Non-Proliferation Treaty (NPT) members; more stringent export control systems for NPT members; prohibitions on painless withdrawal from the NPT; effective interdiction measures able to be lawfully applied against non-NPT members and non-state actors; negotiation of a fissile material cut-off treaty; improved protective security and destruction regimes for fissile and other dangerous materials; and improved multilateral intelligence capability.

On the demand side, we need to fully understand the range of reasons states seek to acquire WMD, in particular nuclear weapons—to acknowledge that more often than not the motivation is not inherently aggressive, but related to considerations like perceived defensive security needs, national prestige and domestic political pressures—and for the "haves" to respond in ways that reduce the incentives of the "have-nots" to acquire. Those ways, in turn, include giving security assurances in appropriate cases; not testing or further developing new classes of nuclear weapons; not applying systematic double standards in accepting acquisition of nuclear weapons by some countries but not others; not applying double standards in condemning or reacting to proliferation activity; getting serious about arms reduction; and making a serious commitment to the elimination objective in Article VI of the NPT (something that all the existing nuclear powers, including Britain and France, have steadfastly refused to do).

The fourth and final step we need to take if we are to rebuild an effective international legal order for the twenty-first century is to recognise the acute need for better process in determining the proper application of the existing rules governing the use of force. By process here I don't mean the kind of institutional innovations proposed from time to time which may be conceptually attractive but are wildly unfeasible in practice—for example, the suggestion of Allen Buchanan and Robert Keohane that the Security Council appoint an impartial independent commission which would evaluate preventive uses of force after the event, applying sanctions if the empirical claims made before the event proved to be untrue.[28]

What is necessary, and I believe rather more realistically achievable, is for there to be much more attention paid—not only in academic discourse but in actual operational decision-making—to the group of principles which have to be satisfied if any decision to use military force is to be not just legal, but *legitimate*. The distinction between legality and legitimacy first came into prominence in this context with the argument of the Sweden-sponsored Kosovo Commission in 1999 that the NATO invasion may not have been legal, in the absence of Security Council approval, but it was—taking into account and balancing out some 14 "threshold" and "contextual" principles—legitimate.[29]

The distinction—if it can be operationalised, with criteria of legitimacy simplified, standardised and commonly accepted—is an important one. The effectiveness of the global collective security system, as with any other legal order, depends ultimately not only on the legality of decisions, but the common perception of their legitimacy—their being made on solid evidentiary grounds, for the right reasons, morally as well as legally. While it is obviously optimal for any military action to be both unquestionably legal under international law and more or less universally accepted as legitimate (as was the case, for example, with the 1991 Gulf War), it is fair to suggest that military action which is technically illegal but widely perceived to be legitimate (as with Kosovo in 1999) does far less damage than action which is generally perceived to be neither legal nor legitimate (Iraq in 2003).

A corollary of this argument is that if there is a widespread perception that action is illegitimate, making it formally legal won't do anything to change that—and may in fact do even more damage to the reputation of the legalising body. This was very much France's argument in the context of the Iraq debate, and—as some say about Wagner's music—it wasn't as bad as it sounds: that the credibility of the Security Council would be put even more at risk by endorsing action widely seen around the world as unjustified than it would by being ignored and bypassed altogether.

A further corollary of the argument may be that legitimacy helps breed legality. If there is general confidence that Security Council decisions on the use of force *will* be made for the right reasons, giving attention to the full range of threats with which major countries are currently preoccupied, having regard to the weight of the evidence, applying appropriate threshold and prudential criteria, and with the power of veto not being exercised capriciously, then those who are currently tempted to bypass the system will be much less tempted to do so—or, perhaps equally importantly, will be at much greater risk of embarrassment if they do so act.

Five Criteria of Legitimacy

My proposal is straightforward: that the Security Council, whenever considering whether to authorise the use of military force in the exercise of its powers under Chapter VII of the UN Charter, should always address—whatever other considerations it may take into account—at least the following five basic criteria of legitimacy:

Seriousness of threat: Is the threatened harm to state or human security of a kind, and sufficiently clear and serious, to *prima facie* justify the use of military force?

Proper purpose: Is it clear that the primary purpose of the proposed military action is to halt or avert the threat in question, whatever other purposes or motives may be involved?

Last resort: Has every non-military option for meeting the threat in question been considered, with reasonable grounds for believing lesser measures will not succeed?

Proportional means: Is the scale, duration and intensity of the proposed military action the minimum necessary to meet the threat in question?

Balance of consequences: Is there a reasonable chance of the military action being successful in meeting the threat in question, with the consequences of action not likely to be worse than the consequences of inaction?

The immediate intellectual origins of these criteria lie in a recommendation of the ICISS in its *The Responsibility to Protect* report: the context there was the specific one of "humanitarian intervention" in response to internal threats, but what we described there as "threshold" and "prudential" criteria can easily be expressed in the more generalised form given here.

Obviously the ICISS recommendations owed something, in turn, to the general approach of the Kosovo Commission before it. Even more obviously, their ultimate intellectual origins lie in the whole tradition, and vast literature, of "just war" theory. But that said, it is very important to emphasise that the criteria here argued for are intended to reflect universal values and not in any way be culture or religion specific. To the extent that I have scanned the literature on this subject,[30] I am not aware of anything to contradict this. Certainly many conversations over recent years with colleagues from different cultural and religious traditions, particularly Islam, have persuaded me that there is absolutely nothing incompatible there with the principles here espoused, and much to support them.

I would hope that these criteria are sufficiently simple, relevant and compelling to be employed by any policymakers anywhere—at a national as well as intergovernmental level—in any context when they are deciding whether it is right to fight. But my immediate proposal is that these criteria, or guidelines, however else they are used, be systematically discussed and applied whenever the Security Council is making any determination under Chapter VII as to whether it is appropriate to use military force in response to any "threat to the peace, breach of the peace or act of aggression" (Article 39). They would apply whether the threat is external or internal; whether the issue is the "right to react" or the "responsibility to protect"; or whether the threat is constituted by armies marching, WMD acquisition, terrorism or tribal machetes.

The criteria should also be regarded as relevant when the Security Council is considering its response to a claimed act of self-defence under Article 51, or the question of use of force by a regional organisation under Chapter VIII. They also have potential application, should the occasion ever arise, to any "Uniting for Peace" or similar resolution that might be considered by the General Assembly.

I am not proposing that the five criteria be embodied in the Charter or in any formal treaty—that would be much too tall an order to contemplate—only that they be adopted, informally if necessary, and applied by the Security Council in its deliberations. If they did win general support they might at some stage be embodied in a General Assembly declaratory resolution: this, and their regular application in practice, would over time enhance their prospect of being considered rules of customary international law.

It is of course possible to go into much more detail in drafting these criteria, particularly the crucial first one, asking, "Is the threatened harm to state or human security of a kind, and sufficiently clear and serious, to *prima facie* justify the use of military force?" I have already noted how, when the context is internal threats, the ICISS argued that the "just cause" threshold should be very narrowly confined, with the bar set high and tight, limited to situations of large-scale killing or ethnic cleansing, actual or apprehended.[31]

External threat and self-defence situations are much more variable, and it may be that there is nothing much to be gained by attempts at further refinement. What matters is that the question be asked, and given a rational and credible answer. In all these cases—as we are now acutely aware in the aftermath of the Iraq war—a great deal ultimately depends on the quality of the evidence. Actual behaviour is one thing, merely threatened behaviour is something else: to establish a threat, plausible evidence of both capability and intent to cause harm is required. (In this respect, an actual cross-border invasion, as with Iraq in 1991, is the easiest case to establish. By contrast, making a plausible case based on the *possibility of non-imminent* supply of *possibly* possessed weapons of mass destruction to international terrorists with whom a regime has *possible* links, as with Iraq in 2003, is about as hard as it gets.)

There have been quite a number of references by the Secretary-General and others over recent years to the possible utility of a set of guidelines or criteria of this kind. Prompted initially by the UK in the late 1990s, and later by the ICISS in 2001, there has already been some discussion within the Security Council about the pros and cons of going down this path, at least in the context of humanitarian intervention, in response to internal threats. Beyond that, the debate on criteria has not moved much beyond the stage of occasional footnote suggestions and throwaway single lines in speeches. It is to be hoped that, perhaps in the context of the work of the High Level Panel, that debate can now seriously start.

However they might ultimately be drafted, and whatever the form in which they might be adopted, the point of adopting these five criteria of legitimacy (and having them being seen to be applied) would I hope be clear. Nobody, least of all me, suggests that there is any push-button predictability about the kind of answers one will get when one puts the five questions I am suggesting: opinions will always differ, just as national interests will differ, and it is hardly unknown for interests to influence opinions. In betting on Security Council deliberations—or for that matter almost any governmental or intergovernmental process—objectivity, as we say in Australia,[32] is not normally the first horse you would back.

But, as someone who has spent a fair number of years in and around these kinds of deliberations, I am a firm believer that good process produces, if not always optimal, at least better outcomes. If the process demands that criteria have to be systematically discussed, it is much more difficult to duck, weave, fudge, dissimulate and simply ignore critical issues: colleagues will ask harder questions, and even the press will sometimes start asking the right questions. At the end of the day strong arguments will look stronger and weak arguments weaker, and these appearances do matter. Putting it succinctly, the point of adopting and applying the five criteria of legitimacy is not to guarantee that the objectively best outcome will always prevail: it is to maximise the possibility of achieving Security Council consensus on when it is appropriate or not to go to war; to maximise international support for whatever the Security Council decides; and to minimise the possibility of individual member states bypassing or ignoring the Security Council.

And if we can achieve any of that, we really will be well on the way to building an international legal order that, despite all the challenges which continue to buffet it, will give us some grounds for optimism that we are not forever condemned to repeat the mistakes of the past, going to war when we should not, and not going to war—to protect our fellow human beings from catastrophe—when we should. Judging when it is right, and not right, to fight is just about the hardest call that anyone in high public office is ever called upon to make. But the stakes are huge, and one has to nurture the hope that good leaders, if not always born, can—with good process added to basically sound law and institutions—at least be made.

NOTES

1. Speech of 23 September 2003, http://www.un .org/webcast/ga/58/statements/sg2eng030923 .htm.

2. The High Level Panel, announced by the Secretary-General on 4 November 2003 and due to report to him by 1 December 2004, comprises Anand Panyarachun (Chair), Robert Badinter, Joao Clemente Baena Soares, Gro Harlem Bruntdland, Gareth Evans, Mary Chinery-Hesse, David Hannay, Enrique Iglesias, Amre Moussa, Sadako Ogata, Satish Nambiar, Yevgeny Primakov, Qian Qichen, Nafis Sadiq, Salim Salim and Brent Scowcroft.

3. Charter of the United Nations, Preamble, http://www.un.org/aboutun/charter/.

4. Address to the Chicago Bar Association, June 1945, quoted in Stephen C. Schlesinger, *Act of Creation: The Founding of the United Nations*, (Boulder, CO: Westview, 2003), p. 261.

5. The figure of 200 is cited by Thomas M. Franck in "Some Observations on the I.C.J.'s Procedural and Substantive Innovations," *American Journal of International Law*, vol. 81, no. 1, 1987, pp. 116–121. He notes that customary norms of nonintervention are "adhered to, at best, only by some states, in some instances, and have been ignored . . . with impunity in at least two hundred cases." Herbert K. Tillema ("Risks of Battle and the Deadliness of War: International Armed Conflicts," paper presented to the International Studies Association, San Diego, 16–29 April 1996, and quoted elsewhere) counts 690 "overt military interventions" during roughly the same period. The disparity between the two is at least in part accounted for by the inclusion in the latter of interventions sanctioned by the state in which intervention occurred, interventions into non-fully-autonomous states, interventions justified under the terms of Article 51, as well as cases of UN-sanctioned interventions. Neither figure was derived with thresholds for casualties, as most counts of interstate war are.

6. Thomas M. Franck, "What Happens Now? The United Nations after Iraq," *American Journal of International Law*, vol. 97, no. 3, 2003.

7. International Commission on Intervention and State Sovereignty (ICISS), *The Responsibility to Protect: Supplementary Volume*, Essay 4, "Interventions Before 1990," pp. 49–68; see www.iciss-ciise.gc.ca for the full text of both Report and Supplementary Volume.

8. Adapted from "International Crisis Behavior" (ICB) dataset (updated through 2001: http:// www.cidcm.umd.edu/icb/), from Michael Brecher and Jonathan Wilkenfeld, *A Study of Crisis* (Ann Arbor, MI: University of Michigan Press, 2000).

9. The most sophisticated quantitative research on peacekeeping suggests that, all things being equal, the deployment of peacekeepers reduces the risk of another war by 70% to 85%. Virginia Fortna, "Peace Operations: Futile or Vital?," paper commissioned by the United Nations Foundation for the work of the High-Level Panel on Threats, Challenges and Change, January 2004.

10. Figures in Peter Wallensteen and Patrik Johansson, "Security Council Decisions in Perspective," in David Malone, ed., *The UN Security Council: From the Cold War to the 21st Century*, (Boulder, CO: Lynne Rienner, 2004), and David Cortright and George A. Lopez, *The Sanctions Decade: Assessing UN Strategies in the 1990s* (Boulder, CO: Lynne Rienner, 2000).

11. Franck, "What Happens Now?"

12. Michael J. Glennon, "Why the Security Council Failed," *Foreign Affairs*, May–June 2003, pp. 16–35.

13. Tom J. Farer, "The Prospect for International Law and Order in the Wake of Iraq," *American Journal of International Law*, vol. 97, no. 3.

14. President Delivers State of the Union Address, 29 January 2002 http://www.whitehouse.gov/news/releases/2002/01/20020129-11.html.

15. President Bush Delivers Graduation Speech at West Point, http://www.whitehouse.gov/news/releases/2002/06/20020601-3.html.

16. National Security Strategy of the United States of America, http://www.whitehouse.gov/nsc/nss.html.

17. "Eyeless in Gaza," *New York Review of Books*, 23 October 2003.

18. Shakespeare, *Henry IV Part I*, Glendower and Hotspur (3.1).

19. Speech of 23 September 2003, http://www.un.org/webcast/ga/58/statements/sg2eng030923.htm.

20. Adam Roberts, "Law and the Use of Force After Iraq," *Survival*, vol. 45 no. 2, summer 2003. Roberts makes clear his own reservations about the limits of "continuing author-ity" as a justification for the actual U.S. invasion of Iraq in 2003, stating, inter alia, that the argument was undermined by "the doubtful quality of the evidence that Iraq still possessed weapons of mass destruction in significant quantities." See p. 44 and the exchange of letters in *Survival*, vol. 45, no. 4, winter 2003–4, pp. 229–31.

21. See http://www.unhchr.ch/html/menu3/b/p_genoci.htm.

22. http://www.un.org/millennium/sg/report/full.htm.

23. The Commission's members were Gareth Evans and Mohamed Sahnoun (Co-Chairs), Gisele Cote-Harper, Lee Hamilton, Michael Ignatieff, Vladimir Lukin, Klaus Naumann, Cyril Ramaphosa, Fidel Ramos, Cornelio Sommaruga, Eduardo Stein and Ramesh Thakur. It consulted comprehensively over a full year, meeting in Asia and Africa as well as North America and Europe, and holding roundtables and other consultations in Latin America, the Middle East, Russia and China. The ICISS report, with its large supplementary research volume, is available on www.iciss-ciise.gc.ca.

24. See Gareth Evans, "Humanity Did Not Justify This War," *Financial Times*, 15 May 2003; Kenneth Roth, "War in Iraq: Not a Humanitarian Intervention," *Human Rights Watch World Report 2004*.

25. Speech of 23 September 2003.

26. International Commission on Intervention and State Sovereignty (ICISS), *The Responsibility to Protect*, 2001, p. 49, para 6.14. Text available at www.iciss-ciise.gc.ca.

27. Compare the argument for differential treatment—culminating in the application of non-Security Council endorsed military force if necessary—against certain "closed societ[ies] with no effective internal opposition," in Lee Feinsten and Anne-Marie Slaughter, "The Duty to Prevent" (*Foreign Affairs*, January/February 2004), and my commentary at the American Society of International Law Conference, Washington,

DC, 1 April 2004, "Uneasy Bedfellows: 'The Responsibility to Protect' and Feinstein-Slaughter's 'Duty to Prevent,'" accessible at http://www.crisisweb.org/home/index.cfm?id =2560&1=1.

28. Allen Buchanan and Robert O. Keohane, "The Preventive Use of Force: A Cosmopolitan Institutional Proposal," *Ethics in International Affairs*, Ja[n]uary 2004.

29. *Kosovo Report*, Independent International Commission on Kosovo, Co-chairs Richard Goldstone and Carl Tham, Oxford, 2000.

30. For example, Sohail Hashmi, "Interpreting the Islamic Ethics of War and Peace," in Sohail Hashmi, ed., *Islamic Political Ethics*

(Princeton, NJ: Princeton University Press 2002); Oliver P. Ramsbotham, "Islam, Christianity and Forcible Humanitarian Intervention," *Ethics and International Affairs*, vol. 12, 1998. I am indebted for these and other references and input to ICG Research Analyst Dan Vexler.

31. ICISS, *The Responsibility to Protect*, pp. 32–34, paras 4.18–27.

32. A former populist Premier of NSW, Jack Lang, gave future Prime Minister Paul Keating what he once told me was a formative piece of advice: "In any horse race, son, always back the one called Self Interest. He'll be the only one trying."

MARTHA FINNEMORE

From *The Purpose of Intervention: Changing Beliefs about the Use of Force*

Changing Norms of Humanitarian Intervention

Since the end of the cold war states have increasingly come under pressure to intervene militarily and, in fact, *have* intervened militarily to protect citizens other than their own from humanitarian disasters. Recent efforts by NATO to protect Albanian Kosovars in Yugoslavia from ethnic cleansing, efforts to alleviate starvation and establish some kind of political order in Somalia, endeavors to enforce protected areas for Kurds and no-fly zones over Shiites in Iraq,

From Martha Finnemore, *The Purpose of Intervention: Changing Beliefs about the Use of Force* (Ithaca, N.Y., and London: Cornell University Press, 2003), Chap. 3.

and the huge UN military effort to disarm parties and rebuild a state in Cambodia are all instances of military action whose primary goal is not territorial or strategic but humanitarian.

Realist and neoliberal theories do not provide good explanations for this behavior. The interests these theories impute to states are geostrategic or economic or both, yet many or most of these interventions occur in states of negligible geostrategic or economic importance to the intervenors. Thus no obvious national interest is at stake for the states bearing the burden of the military intervention in most if not all these cases. Somalia is, perhaps, the clearest example of military action undertaken in a state of little or no strategic or economic importance to the principal intervenor. Similarly, in Cambodia, the states that played central roles in the UN military action were, with the exception of China, not states that had any obvious geostrategic interests there by 1989; China, which did have a geostrategic interest, bore little of the burden of intervening. Realism and neoliberalism offer powerful explanations of the Persian Gulf War but have little to say about the extension of that war to Kurdish and Shiite protection through the enforcement of UN Resolution 688. The United States, France, and Britain have been allowing abuse of the Kurds for centuries. Why they should start caring about them now is not clear.

The recent pattern of humanitarian interventions raises the issue of what interests intervening states could possibly be pursuing. In most of these cases, the intervention targets are insignificant by any usual measure of geostrategic or economic interest. Why, then, do states intervene? This [discussion] argues that the pattern of intervention cannot be understood apart from the changing normative context in which it occurs. Normative context is important because it shapes conceptions of interest and gives purpose and meaning to action. It shapes the rights and duties states believe they have toward one another, and it shapes the goals they value, the means they believe are effective and legitimate to obtain those goals, and the political costs and benefits attached to different choices.

* * * I examine the role of humanitarian norms in shaping patterns of humanitarian military intervention over the past 180 years and the ways those norms have changed over time creating new patterns of intervention behavior. Three factors, in particular, have changed. Who is human has changed, that is, who can successfully claim humanitarian protection from strong states has changed. In the nineteenth century, only white Christians received protection; mistreatment of other groups did not evoke the same concern. By the end of the twentieth century, however, most of the protected populations were non-white, non-Christian groups. How we intervene has changed. Humanitarian intervention now must be multilateral in order to be acceptable and legitimate. Since 1945 states have con-

sistently rejected attempts to justify unilateral interventions as "humanitarian"; in the nineteenth century, however, they were accepted. Our military goals and definitions of "success" have also changed. Powerful states in the nineteenth century could simply install a government they liked as a result of these operations. Today we can only install a process, namely, elections. Given that elections often do not produce humane and just leaders (despite occasional attempts to manipulate them to do so), this may not be a particularly functional change, but it is a necessary one in the current international normative context.

By "humanitarian intervention" I mean deploying military force across borders for the purpose of protecting foreign nationals from man-made violence. Interventions to protect foreign nationals from natural disasters are excluded from the analysis. I am interested in the changing purpose of force, and, in such cases, militaries are not using force but are deployed in a completely consensual manner for their logistical and technical capabilities. Similarly interventions to protect a state's *own* nationals from abuse are excluded in this analysis. Although international legal scholars once categorized such interventions as humanitarian, these do not present the same intellectual puzzles about interests since protecting one's own nationals is clearly connected to conventional understandings of national interest.[1]

The analysis proceeds in five parts. The first shows that realist and neoliberal approaches to international politics do not provide good explanations of humanitarian intervention as a practice, much less how they have changed over time, because the interests they emphasize do not seem to correlate with these interventions. A more inductive approach that attends to the role of normative and ethical understandings can remedy this by allowing us to problematize interests and the way they change. In the second section I demonstrate that change has, indeed, occurred by examining humanitarian intervention practices in the nineteenth century and inducing a sketch of the norms governing behavior in that period from both the military actions taken and the way leaders spoke of them. Among the findings is the sharply circumscribed understanding of who was "human" and could successfully claim protection from powerful states. The third section traces the expansion of this definition of "humanity" by examining efforts to abolish slavery, the slave trade, and colonization. Although these were not the only arenas in which people fought to expand the West's definition of "humanity," they were important ones that involved military coercion, and thus they provide insight into intermediate stages in the evolution of links between humanitarian claims and military action. The fourth section briefly reviews humanitarian intervention as a state practice since 1945, paying particular attention to non-cases, that is, cases where humanitarian action could or should have been claimed but was not. These cases suggest that sovereignty and self-determination norms trumped humanitarian claims during the cold war, a relationship that no longer holds with consistency. They further suggest that unilateral intervention, even for humanitarian purposes, is normatively suspect in contemporary politics and that states will work hard to construct multilateral coalitions for this purpose. [I conclude] by comparing the goals or end states sought by intervenors in the nineteenth century versus the twentieth and [argue] that contemporary intervention norms contain powerful contradictions that make "success" difficult to achieve, not for material or logistical reasons but for normative ones.

Understanding Humanitarian Action

Humanitarian intervention looks odd from conventional perspectives on international politics because it does not conform to the conceptions of interest that they specify. Realists would expect to see some geostrategic or political advantage to be gained by intervening states. Neoliberals might emphasize economic or trade advantages for intervenors. These are hard to find in most post-1989 cases. The 1992–93 U.S. action in Somalia was a clear case of intervention without obvious interests. Economically Somalia was insignificant to the United States. Security interests are also hard to find. The United States had voluntarily given up its base at Berbera in Somalia, because advances in communications and aircraft technology made it obsolete for the communications and refueling purposes it once served. Further, the U.S. intervention in that country was not carried out in a way that would have furthered strategic interests. If the United States truly had had designs on Somalia, it should have welcomed the role of disarming the clans. It did not. The United States resisted UN pressure to "pacify" the country as part of its mission. In fact, U.S. officials were clearly and consistently interested not in controlling any part of Somalia but in getting out of the country as soon as possible— sooner, indeed, than the UN would have liked. That some administration officials opposed the Somalia intervention on precisely the grounds that no vital U.S. interest was involved underscores the realists' problem.

The massive intervention under UN auspices to reconstruct Cambodia in the early 1990s presented similar anomalies. Like Somalia, Cambodia was economically insignificant to the intervenors and, with the cold war ended, was strategically significant to none of the five powers on the Security Council except China, which bore very little of the intervention burden. Indeed, U.S. involvement appears to have been motivated by domestic opposition to the return of the Khmers Rouges on moral grounds—another anomaly for these approaches—rather than by geopolitical or economic interests. Kosovo and Bosnia touched the security interests of the major intervenor, the United States, only derivatively in that those states are in Europe. However, events in these places did not prompt intervention from major European powers, whose interests would presumably be much more involved, despite much U.S. urging. These targets are outside the NATO alliance and hence trigger none of that alliance's security guarantees; in both cases, moreover, intervention served no strong domestic constituency and was militarily and politically risky.

Liberals of a more classical and Kantian type might argue that these interventions were motivated by an interest in promoting democracy and liberal values. After all, the UN's political blueprint for reconstructing these states after intervention has occurred is a liberal one. However, these arguments run afoul of the evidence. The United States consistently refused to take on the state building and democratization mission in Somalia, which liberal arguments would have expected to have been at the heart of U.S. efforts. Similarly the UN stopped short of authorizing an overthrow of Saddam Hussein in Iraq in 1991, even when this was militarily possible and was supported by many in the U.S. armed forces. The United Nations, NATO, and especially the United States have emphasized the humanitarian rather than democratizing nature of these interventions, both rhetorically and in their actions on the ground.

None of these realist or liberal approaches provides an answer to the question: "What interests are intervening states pursuing?" A generous interpretation would conclude that realism and liberalism simply are not helpful in understanding these interventions, since the specification of interests is outside their analysis. To the extent that these approaches *do* specify interests, however, those specifications appear wrong in these cases.

The failure of these approaches leads me to adopt another method of analysis. Lacking any good alternative explanation that casts doubt on them, I take the intervenors' humanitarian claims seriously and try to untangle what, exactly, they mean by "humanitarian intervention," what makes those claims compelling to states, and what constraints exist on this kind of behavior. When intervenors claim humanitarian motives, I want to know what it means to them to be "humanitarian"—what action does that entail (or not entail). I want to know what kinds of claims prompt a humanitarian intervention (and what claims do not). I want to know the extent to which and the ways in which "humanitarianism" competes with (or complements) other kinds of incentives states might have to intervene (or not to intervene). This last point is important. Although there have been a rash of interventions since 1989 that look particularly altruistic, all interventions are prompted by a mixture of motivations in some way. Even if the principal decision maker had only one consideration in mind (which is unlikely), the vast number of people involved in these operations, often people from different intervening states, bring different motivations to bear on the intervention as it unfolds. Humanitarian motivations will interact differently with other state goals, depending on how humanitarian action is defined and what other kinds of goals states have. These definitions may change over time. For example, antidemocratic human rights abusers have now been defined as threats to international peace and security, which might explain why many more humanitarian interventions were undertaken in the 1990s than in any previous ten-year period.[2]

The empirical evidence presented here consistently points to the interwoven and interdependent character of norms that influence international behavior. Humanitarianism—its influence and definition—is bound up in other normative changes, particularly sovereignty norms and human rights norms. Mutually reinforcing and consistent norms appear to strengthen one another; success in one area (such as abolishing slavery) strengthens and legitimates new claims in logically and morally related norms (such as human rights and humanitarian intervention). The relationship identified here between slavery, sovereignty, and humanitarian intervention suggests the importance of viewing norms not as individual "things" floating atomistically in some international social space but rather as part of a highly structured social context. It may make more sense to think of a fabric of interlocking and interwoven norms rather than to think of individual norms concerning a specific issue, as current scholarship, my own included, has been inclined to do. Change in one set of norms may open possibilities for, and even logically or ethically require changes in, other norms and practices. Without attending to these relationships, we will miss the larger picture.[3]

Humanitarian Intervention in the Nineteenth Century

Before the twentieth century virtually all instances of military intervention to protect people other than the intervenor's own nationals involved protection of Christians from the Ottoman Turks.[4] In at least four instances during the nineteenth century European states used humanitarian claims to influence Balkan policy in ways that would have required states to use force—the Greek War for Independence (1821–27); in Syria/ Lebanon (1860–61); during the Bulgarian agitation of 1876–78; and in response to the Armenian massacres (1894–1917). Although not all these instances led to a full-scale military intervention, the claims made and their effects on policy in the other cases shed light on the evolution and influence of humanitarian claims during this period. I give a brief account of each incident below, highlighting commonalities and change.

GREEK WAR FOR INDEPENDENCE (1821-27) Russia took an immediate interest in the Greek insurrection and threatened to use force against the Turks as early as the first year of the war. In part its motivations were geostrategic; Russia had been pursuing a general strategy of weakening the Ottomans and consolidating control in the Balkans for years. But the justifications Russia offered were largely humanitarian. Russia had long seen itself as the defender of Orthodox Christians under Turkish rule. Atrocities, such as the wholesale massacres of Christians and sale of women into slavery, coupled with the Sultan's order to seize the Venerable Patriarch of the

Orthodox Church after mass on Easter morning, hang him and three Archbishops, and then have the bodies thrown into the Bosphorus, formed the centerpiece of Russia's complaints against the Turks and the justification of its threats of force.[5]

Other European powers, with the exception of France, opposed intervention largely because they were concerned that weakening Turkey would strengthen Russia.[6] However, although the governments of Europe seemed little affected by these atrocities, significant segments of their publics were. A Philhellenic movement had spread throughout Europe, especially in the more democratic societies of Britain, France, and parts of Germany. The movement drew on two popular sentiments: the European identification with the classical Hellenic tradition and the appeal of Christians oppressed by the Infidel. Philhellenic aid societies in Western Europe sent large sums of money and even volunteers, including Lord Byron, to Greece during the war. Indeed, it was a British Captain Hastings who commanded the Greek flotilla that destroyed a Turkish squadron off Salona and provoked the decisive battle at Navarino.[7] Russian threats of unilateral action against the Sultan eventually forced the British to become involved, and in 1827 the two powers, together with Charles X of France in his capacity as "Most Christian King," sent an armada that roundly defeated Ibrahim at Navarino in October 1827.

It would be hard to argue that humanitarian considerations were the only reason to intervene in this case; geostrategic factors were also very important. However, humanitarian disasters were the catalyst for intervention, galvanizing decision makers and powerful domestic elites. Humanitarianism also provided the public justification for intervention, and the episode is revealing about humanitarian intervention norms in several ways. First, it illustrates the circumscribed definition of who was "human" in the nineteenth-century conception. Massacring Christians was a humanitarian disaster; massacring Muslims was not. There were plenty of atrocities on both sides in this conflict. Many of the massacres of Christians by Ottomans were in response to previous massacres of Muslims at Morea and elsewhere in April 1821. For example, Greek Christians massacred approximately eight thousand Turkish Muslims in the town of Tripolitza in 1821. In all, about twenty thousand Muslims were massacred during the war in Greece without causing concern among the Great Powers. Since, under the law of the Ottoman Empire, the Christian Patriarch of Constantinople was responsible for the good behavior of his flock, his execution was viewed justified on grounds of these atrocities against Muslims.[8] The European Powers, however, were impressed only by the murder of Christians and less troubled about the fact that the initial atrocities of the war were committed by the Christian insurgents (admittedly after years of harsh Ottoman rule). The initial Christian uprising at Morea "might well have been allowed to burn itself out 'beyond the pale of civilization'"; it was only the wide-scale and very visible atrocities against Christians that put the events on the agenda of major powers.[9]

Second, intervening states, particularly Russia and France, placed humanitarian factors together with religious considerations at the center for their continued calls for intervention and application of force. As will be seen in other nineteenth-century cases, religion was important in both motivating humanitarian action and defining who is human. Notions about Christian charity supported general humanitarian impulses, but specific religious identifications had the effect of privileging certain people over others. In this case Christians were privileged over Muslims. Elsewhere, as later in Armenia and Bulgaria, denominational differences within Christianity appear important both in motivating action and in restraining it.

Third, the intervention was multilateral. The reasons in this case were largely geostrategic (restraining Russia from temptation to use this intervention for other purposes), but, as subsequent discussion will show, multilateralism as a characteristic of legitimate intervention becomes increasingly important.

Fourth, mass publics were involved. Not only did public opinion influence policy making in a diffuse way, but publics were organized transnationally in ways that strongly foreshadow humanitarian activity by nongovernmental organizations (NGOs) in the late twentieth century. Philhellenism was a more diffuse movement than the bureaucratized NGOs we have now, but the individual Philhellenic societies communicated across national borders and these groups were able to supply both military and financial aid directly to partisans on the ground, bypassing their governments.

LEBANON/SYRIA (1860–61) In May 1860 conflict between Druze and Maronite populations broke out in what is now Lebanon but at the time was Syria under Ottoman rule. Initial rioting became wholesale massacre of Maronite populations, first by the Druze and later by Ottoman troops. The conflict sparked outrage in the French popular press. As early as 1250, Louis IX signed a charter with the Maronite Christians in the Levant guaranteeing protection as if they were French subjects and, in effect, making them part of the French nation. Since then, France had styled itself as the "protector" of Latin Christians in the Levant. Napoleon III thus eagerly supported military intervention in the region at least in part to placate "outraged Catholic opinion" at home. Russia was also eager to intervene, and Britain became involved in the intervention to prevent France and Russia from using the incident to expand.[10]

On August 3, 1860, the six Great Powers (Austria, France, Britain, Prussia, Russia, and Turkey) signed a protocol authorizing the dispatch of twelve thousand European troops to the region to aid the Sultan in stopping violence and establishing order. A letter from the French foreign minister, Thouvenal, to the French ambassador in Turkey stressed that "the object of the mission is to assist stopping, by prompt and energetic measures, the effusion of blood, and [to put] an end to the outrages committed against

Christians, which cannot remain unpunished." The protocol further emphasized the lack of strategic and political ambitions of the Powers acting in this matter.[11]

France supplied half of the twelve thousand troops immediately and dispatched them in August 1860. The other states sent token warships and high-ranking officers but no ground troops, which meant that, in the end, the six thousand French troops were the sum total of the intervention force. The French forces received high marks for their humanitarian conduct while in the region, putting a stop to the fighting and helping villagers to rebuild homes and farms. They left when agreement was reached among the Powers for Christian representation in the government of the region.[12]

This case repeats many of the features of the Greek intervention. Again, saving Christians was central to the justification for intervention. Public opinion seems to have some impact, this time on the vigor with which Napoleon pursued an interventionist policy. The multilateral character of the intervention was different, however, in that there was multilateral consultation and agreement on the intervention plan but execution was essentially unilateral.

THE BULGARIAN AGITATION (1876-78) In May 1876 Ottoman troops massacred unarmed and poorly organized agitators in Bulgaria. A British government investigation put the number killed at twelve thousand with fifty-nine villages destroyed and an entire church full of people set ablaze after they had already surrendered to Ottoman soldiers. The investigation confirmed that Ottoman soldiers and officers were promoted and decorated rather than punished for these actions.[13] Accounts of the atrocities gathered by American missionaries and sent to British reporters began appearing in British newspapers in mid-June. The reports inflamed public opinion, and protest meetings were organized throughout the country, particularly in the North where W. T. Stead and his

paper, the *Northern Echo*, were a focus of agitation.[14]

The result was a split in British politics. Prime Minister Disraeli publicly refused to change British policy of support for Turkey over the matter, stating that British material interests outweighed the lives of Bulgarians.[15] However, Lord Derby, the Conservative foreign secretary, telegraphed Constantinople that "any renewal of the outrages would be more fatal to the Porte than the loss of a battle."[16] More important, former prime minister Gladstone came out of retirement to oppose Disraeli on the issue, making the Bulgarian atrocities the centerpiece of his anti-Disraeli campaign.[17] Although Gladstone found a great deal of support in various public circles, he did not have similar success in government. The issue barely affected British policy. Disraeli was forced to carry out the investigation mentioned above, and did offer proposals for internal Ottoman reforms to protect minorities—proposals Russia rejected as being too timid.[18]

Russia was the only state to intervene in the wake of the Bulgarian massacres. The treaty that ended the Crimean War was supposed to protect Christians under Ottoman rule. Russia justified her threats of force on the basis of Turkey's violation of these humanitarian guarantees. In March 1877 the Great Powers issued a protocol reiterating demands for the protection of Christians in the Ottoman Empire guaranteed in the 1856 treaty ending the Crimean War. After Constantinople rejected the protocol, Russia sent in troops in April 1877. Russia easily defeated the Ottoman troops and signed the Treaty of San Stefano, which created a large independent Bulgarian state—an arrangement that was drastically revised by the Congress of Berlin.

As in the previous cases, saving Christians was an essential feature of this incident, and Gladstone and Russia's justifications for action were framed in this way. However, military action in this case was not multilateral; Russia intervened unilaterally and, although other powers worried about Russian opportunism and how Russian actions might alter the strategic balance in the region, none said that the intervention was illegitimate or unacceptable because it was unilateral. Public opinion and the media, in particular, were powerful influences on the politics of this episode. Transnational groups, mostly church and missionary groups, were a major source of information for publics in powerful states about the atrocities being committed. These groups actively worked to get information out of Bulgaria and into the hands of sympathetic media outlets in a conscious attempt to arouse public opinion and influence policy in ways that resemble current NGO activist tactics. Although public opinion was not able to change British policy in this case, it was able to make adherence to that policy much more difficult for Disraeli in domestic terms.

ARMENIA (1894–1917) The Armenian case offers some interesting insights into the scope of Christianity requiring defense by European powers in the last century. Unlike the Orthodox Christians in Greece and Bulgaria and the Maronites in Syria, the Armenian Christians had no European champion. The Armenian Church was not in communion with the Orthodox Church, hence Armenian appeals had never resonated in Russia; the Armenians were not portrayed as "brothers" to the Russians as were the Bulgarians and other Orthodox Slavs. Similarly, no non-Orthodox European state had ever offered protection nor did they have historical ties as the French did with the Maronites. Thus many of the reasons to intervene in other cases were lacking in the Armenian case.

That the Armenians were Christians, albeit of a different kind, does seem to have had some influence on policy. The Treaty of Berlin explicitly bound the Sultan to carry out internal political reforms to protect Armenians, but the nature, timing, and monitoring of these provisions were left vague and were never enforced. The Congress of Berlin ignored an Armenian petition for an arrangement similar to that set up in Lebanon following the Maronite massacres (a Christian governor under Ottoman rule). Gladstone took up the matter in 1880 when he returned to power but dropped it when Bismarck voiced opposition.[19]

The wave of massacres against Armenians beginning in 1894 was far worse than any of the other atrocities examined here in terms of both the number killed or the brutality of their executions. Nine hundred people were killed and twenty-four villages burned in the Sassum massacres in August 1894. After this the intensity increased. Between fifty thousand and seventy thousand were killed in 1895. In 1896 the massacres moved into Constantinople where, on August 28–29, six thousand Armenians were killed in the capital.[20]

These events were well known and highly publicized in Europe.[21] Gladstone came out of retirement yet again to denounce the Ottomans and called Abd-ul-Hamid the "Great Assassin." French writers denounced him as "the Red Sultan." The European powers demanded an inquiry, which produced extensive documentation of "horrors unutterable, unspeakable, unimaginable by the mind of man" for European governments and the press.[22] Public opinion pressed for intervention, and both Britain and France used humanitarian justifications to threaten force. However, neither acted. Germany by this time was a force to be reckoned with, and the Kaiser was courting Turkey. Russia was nervous about nationalist aspirations in the Balkans generally and had no special affection for the Armenians, as noted above. Their combined opposition made the price of intervention higher than either the British or French were willing to pay.[23]

These four episodes are suggestive in several ways. They make it very clear that humanitarian intervention is not new in the twentieth century. The role played by what we now call "transnational civil society" or NGOs is also not new. There certainly were far fewer of these organizations and the networks of ties were much thinner, but they did exist and have influence even 180 years ago.

These episodes also say something about the relationship of humanitarian goals to other foreign-policy goals in the period. Humanitarian action was never taken when it jeopardized other articulated goals or interests of a state. Humanitarians were sometimes able to mount considerable pressure on policy makers to act contrary to stated geostrategic interests, as in the case of Disraeli and the Bulgarian agitation, but they never succeeded. Humanitarian claims did succeed, however, in creating new interests and new reasons for states to act where none had existed. Without the massacre of Maronites in Syria, France would almost certainly not have intervened. It is less clear whether there would have been intervention in the Greek War for Independence or in Bulgaria without humanitarian justifications for such interventions. Russia certainly had other reasons to intervene in both cases, but Russia was also the state that identified most with the Orthodox Christians being massacred. Whether the humanitarian claims from fellow Orthodox Christians alone would have been sufficient for intervention without any geostrategic issues at stake is impossible to know. The role of humanitarian claims in these cases thus seems to be constitutive and permissive rather than determinative. Humanitarian appeals created interests where none previously existed and provided legitimate justifications for intervention that otherwise might not have been taken; however, they certainly did not require intervention or override alliance commitments or realpolitik understandings of national security and foreign policy making.

Humanitarian intervention in the nineteenth century could be implemented in a variety of ways. Action could be multilateral, as in the case of Greek independence, unilateral, as when Russia intervened in Bulgaria, or some mixture of the two, as in Lebanon/Syria where intervention was planned by several states but execution was unilateral. As shown below, this variety of forms for intervention changes over time. Specifically the unilateral option for either the planning or execution of humanitarian intervention appears to have disappeared in the twentieth century, and multilateral options have become more elaborate and institutionalized.

Finally, and perhaps most significant, intervenors found reasons to identify with the victims of humanitarian disasters in some important and exclusive way. The minimal rationale for such identification was that the victims to be protected by intervention were Christians; there were no instances of European powers considering intervention to protect non-Christians. Pogroms against Jews did not provoke intervention. Neither did Russian massacres of Turks in Central Asia in the 1860s.[24] Neither did mass killings in China during the Taiping Rebellion against the Manchus.[25] Neither did mass killings by colonial rulers in their colonies.[26] Neither did massacres of Native Americans in the United States. Often a more specific identification or social tie existed between intervenor and intervened, as between the Orthodox Slav Russians and the Orthodox Slav Bulgarians. In fact, as the Armenian case suggests, the lack of an intense identification may contribute to inaction.

Over time, these exclusive modes of identification changed in European powers. People in Western states began to identify with non-Western populations during the twentieth century with profound political consequences, among them a greater tendency to undertake humanitarian intervention. Longer-standing identifications with Caucasians and Christians continue to be strong. That non-Christians and non-whites are now sometimes protected does not mean that their claims are equally effective as those of Christians and whites. But that their claims are entertained at all, and that these people are sometimes protected, is new. It is not the fact of humanitarian behavior that has changed but its focus. The task at hand is to explain how extending and deepening this identification to other groups changed humanitarian intervention.

The Expansion of "Humanity" and Sovereignty

The expansion of "humanity" between the nineteenth and late twentieth centuries drives much of the change we see in humanitarian intervention behavior, both directly and indirectly. It does this directly by creating identification with and legitimating normative demands by people who previously were invisible in the politics of the West. It contributes to change indirectly through the role it plays in promoting and legitimating new norms of sovereignty, specifically anticolonialism and self-determination. These changes in understandings about humanity and sovereignty obviously do much more than change humanitarian intervention. They alter the purpose of force broadly in world politics, changing the way people think about legitimate and effective uses of state coercion in a variety of areas. Understandings that shape social purpose do not exist, after all, in a vacuum. Social purpose is formed by a dense web of social understandings that are logically and ethically interrelated and, at least to some degree, mutually supporting. Thus changes in one strand of this web tend to have wide effects, causing other kinds of understandings to adjust. Social psychological mechanisms, such as cognitive dissonance, contribute to this process, but so, too, do institutional processes. People who are confronted with the fact that they hold contradictory views will try to adjust their beliefs to alleviate dissonance between them. Similarly lawyers and judges recognize "logical coherence" as a powerful standard for arbitrating between competing normative claims within the law; norms that no longer "fit" within the larger normative fabric of understandings are likely to be rejected in judicial processes and lose the support of associated social institutions.[27]

Like humanitarian intervention, slavery and colonialism were two large-scale activities in which state force intersected with humanitarian claims in the nineteenth century. In many ways slavery was the conceptual opposite of humanitarian intervention: It involved the use of state force to deny and suppress claims about humanitarian need rather than to provide protection. The effort to stamp out the slave trade raises cross-border humanitarian issues that reveal the limits in when states would use force and provides an interesting comparison with our intervention cases. Colonialism connects views about humanity with understandings about legitimate sovereignty and political organization. Colonialism was justified initially, in part, as a humane form of rule. The West was bringing the benefits of civilization to those in need. Decolonization involved turning this understanding of "humane" politics on its head, and the sovereignty norms that emerged from that struggle are extremely important to the subsequent practices of humanitarian intervention. If, indeed, changes in understandings about "humanity" have broad, interrelated effects, we should expect to see these transformed understandings reshaping states' policies and their use of force in dealing with colonialism.

ABOLITION OF SLAVERY AND THE SLAVE TRADE
The abolition of slavery and the slave trade in the nineteenth century were essential to the universalization of "humanity." European states generally accepted and legalized both slavery and the slave trade in the seventeenth and eighteenth centuries, but by the nineteenth century these same states proclaimed these practices "repugnant to the principles of humanity and universal morality."[28] Human beings previously viewed as beyond the edge of humanity—as being property—came to be viewed as human, and with that status came certain, albeit minimal, privileges and protections. For example, states did use military force to suppress the slave trade. Britain was particularly active in this regard and succeeded in having the slave trade labeled as piracy, thus enabling Britain to seize and board ships sailing under non-British flags that were suspected of carrying contraband slaves.[29]

Although in some ways this is an important case of a state using force to promote humanitarian ends, the fashion in which the British framed and justified their actions also speaks to the limits of humanitarian claims in the early to mid-nineteenth century. First, the British limited their military action to abolishing the *trade* in slaves, not slavery itself. No military intervention was undertaken on behalf of endangered Africans in slavery as it had been on behalf of endangered white Christians. Further, although the British public and many political figures contributed to a climate of international opinion that viewed slavery with increasing distaste, the abolition of slavery as a domestic institution of property rights was accomplished in each state where it had previously been legal without other states intervening militarily.[30] Moreover, the British government's strategy for ending the slave trade was to label such trafficking as piracy, which in turn meant the slaves were "contraband," that is, still property. The British justified their actions on the basis of Maritime Rights governing commerce. The practices of slavery and slaveholding themselves did not provoke the same reaction as Ottoman abuse of Christians. This may be because the perpetrators of the humanitarian violations were "civilized" Christian nations (as opposed to the infidel Turks).[31] Another reason was probably that the targets of these humanitarian violations were black Africans, not "fellow [i.e., white] Christians" or "brother Slavs." Thus it appears that by the 1830s black Africans had become sufficiently "human" that enslaving them was illegal inside Europe, but enslaving them outside Europe was only distasteful. One could keep them enslaved if one kept them at home, within domestic borders. Abuse of Africans did not merit military intervention inside another state.

Slavery itself was thus never the cause of military intervention, and, although trade in slaves did provoke some military action, it was limited in both scope and justification. The abolition of slavery was accomplished in most of the world

through either domestic mechanisms (sometimes violent ones, as in the United States) or through the transnational advocacy networks that have been described elsewhere or by both these means.[32] Once accomplished, however, the equality norms that defeated slavery norms fed back into later decisions about humanitarian intervention in interesting ways. For example, accusations of racism aimed at Western states that had provided much more attention and aid to Bosnia than Somalia in the early 1990s were important factors in mobilizing support for the intervention in Somalia, particularly from the U.S. government.[33]

COLONIZATION, DECOLONIZATION, AND SELF-DETERMINATION Justifications for both colonization and decolonization offer additional lenses through which to examine changing understandings of who is "human" and how these understandings shape uses of force. Both processes—colonization and its undoing—were justified, at least in part, in humanitarian terms. However, the understanding of what constituted humanity was different in the two episodes in ways that bear on the current investigation of humanitarian intervention norms.

The vast economic literature on colonization often overlooks the strong moral dimension that many of the colonizers perceived and articulated. Colonization was a crusade. It would bring the benefits of civilization to the "dark" reaches of the earth. It was a sacred trust, the white man's burden, and was mandated by God that these Europeans venture out to parts of the globe unknown to them, bringing what they understood to be a better way of life to the inhabitants there. Colonization for the missionaries and those driven by social conscience was a humanitarian undertaking of huge proportions and, consequently, of huge significance.

Colonialism's humanitarian mission was of a particular kind, however. The mission of colonialism was to "civilize" the non-European world—to bring the "benefits" of European social, political, economic, and cultural arrangements to Asia, Africa, and the Americas. Until these peoples were "civilized" they remained savages, barbarians, less than human. Thus, in a critical sense, the core of the colonial humanitarian mission was to *create* humanity where none had previously existed. Non-Europeans became human in European eyes by becoming Christian, by adopting European-style structures of property rights, by embracing European-style territorial political arrangements, by entering the growing European-based international economy.[34]

Decolonization also had strong humanitarian justifications.[35] By the mid-twentieth century normative understandings about humanity had shifted. Humanity was no longer something one could create by bringing civilization to savages. Rather, humanity was inherent in individual human beings. It had become universalized and was not culturally dependent as it was in earlier centuries. Asians and Africans were now viewed as having human "rights," and among these was the right to determine their own political future—the right to self-determination.

Like other major normative changes, the rise of human rights norms and decolonization are part of a larger, interrelated set of changes in the international normative web. Norms do not just evolve; they coevolve. Those studying norm change generally, and decolonization and slavery specifically, have noted several features of this coevolutionary process. The first, as indicated above, comes from international legal scholars who have emphasized the power of logical coherence in creating legitimacy in normative structures.[36] Norms that fit logically with other powerful norms are more likely to become persuasive and to shape behavior. Thus changes in core normative structures (in this case, changes toward recognition of human equality within Europe) provided an ethical platform from which activists could work for normative changes elsewhere in society and a way to frame their appeals that would be powerful. Mutually reinforcing and logically consistent norms appear to be harder to attack and to have an advantage in the normative contestations that occur in social life. In this sense, logic internal to norms themselves shapes their development and, consequently, shapes social change.

Applied to decolonization, the argument would be that the spread of these decolonization norms is the result, at least to some extent, of their "fit" within the logical structure of other powerful preexisting European norms. As liberal beliefs about the "natural" rights of man spread and gained power within Europe, they influenced Europe's relationship with non-European peoples in important ways. The egalitarian social movements sweeping the European West in the eighteenth and nineteenth centuries were justified with universal truths about the nature and equality of human beings. These notions were then exported to the non-European world as part of the civilizing mission of colonialism. Once people begin to believe, at least in principle, in human equality, there is no logical limit to the expansion of human rights and self-determination.[37]

The logical expansion of these arguments fueled attacks on both slavery and colonization. Slavery, more blatantly a violation of these emerging European norms, came under attack first. Demands for decolonization came more slowly and had to contend with the counter claims for the beneficial humanitarian effects of European rule. However, logic alone could not dismantle these institutions. In both cases former slaves and Western-educated colonial elites were instrumental in change. Having been "civilized" and Europeanized, they were able to use Europe's own norms against these institutions. These people undermined the social legitimacy of both slave holders and colonizers simply by being exemplars of "human" non-Europeans who could read, write, worship, work, and function in Western society. Their simple existence undercut the legitimacy of slavery and colonialism within a European framework of proclaimed human equality.

Another feature that channels contemporary normative coevolution is the rational-legal structure in which it is embedded. Increasingly since the nineteenth century international normative understandings have been codified in international law, international regimes, and the mandates of formal international organizations. To the extent that legal processes operate, the logical coherence processes described above will be amplified, since law requires explicit demonstrations of such logical fit to support its claims. International organizations, too, can amplify the power of new normative claims if these are enshrined in their mandates, structure, or operating procedures. For example, the United Nations played a significant role in the decolonization process and the consolidation of anticolonialism norms. Self-determination norms are proclaimed in the UN Charter, but the organization also contained Trusteeship machinery and one-state-one-vote voting structures that gave majority power to the weak, often formerly colonized states, all of which contributed to an international legal, organizational, and normative environment that made colonial practices increasingly illegitimate and difficult to carry out.[38]

Humanitarian Intervention since 1945

Unlike humanitarian intervention practices in the nineteenth century, virtually all the instances in which claims of humanitarian intervention have been made in the post-1945 period concern military action on behalf of non-Christians, non-Europeans, or both. Cambodia, Somalia, Bosnian Muslims, Kurds in Iraq, Albanian Muslims in Kosovo all fit this pattern. The "humanity" worth protecting has widened as a result of the normative changes described above. However, humanitarian intervention practices have also become more limited in a different dimension: Intervening states often shied away from humanitarian claims during the cold war when they could have made them. One would think that states would claim the moral high ground in their military actions whenever it was at all credible, and strong humanitarian claims were certainly credible in at least three cases: India's

intervention in East Pakistan in the wake of massacres by Pakistani troops; Tanzania's intervention in Uganda toppling the Idi Amin regime; and Vietnam's intervention in Cambodia ousting the Khmers Rouges. Amin and Pol Pot were two of the most notorious killers in a century full of infamous brutal leaders. If states could use humanitarian claims anywhere, it should have been in these cases, yet they did not. In fact, India initially claimed humanitarian justifications on the floor of the United Nations but quickly retracted them, expunging statements from the UN record. Why?

The argument here is that this reluctance stems not from norms about what is "humanitarian" but from norms about legitimate intervention. Although the scope of who qualifies as human has widened enormously and the range of humanitarian activities that states routinely undertake has expanded, norms about intervention have also changed, albeit less drastically. Humanitarian military intervention now must be *multilateral* to be legitimate; without multilateralism, claims of humanitarian motivation and justification are suspect.[39] As we saw in the nineteenth century, multilateralism is not new; it has often characterized humanitarian military action. However, states in the nineteenth century still invoked and accepted humanitarian justifications even when intervention was unilateral (for example, Russia in Bulgaria during the 1870s, and, in part, France in Lebanon). That did not happen in the twentieth century nor has it happened in the twenty-first century. Without multilateralism, states will not and apparently cannot successfully claim humanitarian justification.[40]

The move to multilateralism is not obviously dictated by the functional demands of intervention or military effectiveness. Certainly multilateralism had (and has) important advantages for states. It increases the transparency of each state's actions to others and so reassures states that opportunities for adventurism and expansion will not be used. It can be a way of sharing costs and thus be cheaper for states than unilateral action. However, multilateralism carries with it significant costs of its own. Cooperation and coordination problems involved in such action, an issue political scientists have examined in detail, can make it difficult to sustain multilateral action.[41] Perhaps more important, multilateral action requires the sacrifice of power and control over the intervention. Further, it may seriously compromise the military effectiveness of those operations, as recent debates over command and control in UN military operations suggest.

There are no obvious efficiency reasons for states to prefer either multilateral or unilateral intervention to achieve humanitarian ends. Each type of intervention has advantages and disadvantages. The choice depends, in large part, on perceptions about the political acceptability and political costs of each, which, in turn, depend on the normative context. As is discussed below, multilateralism in the present day has become institutionalized in ways that make unilateral intervention, particularly intervention not justified as self-defense, unacceptably costly, not in material terms but in social and political terms. A brief examination of these "non-cases" of humanitarian intervention and the way that states debated and justified these actions provides some insight into the normative fabric of contemporary intervention and the limitations these impose on humanitarian action.

UNILATERAL INTERVENTIONS IN HUMANITARIAN DISASTERS[42] a. India in East Pakistan (1971). Pakistan had been under military rule by West Pakistani officials since partition. When the first free elections were held in November 1970, the Awami League won 167 out of 169 parliamentary seats reserved for East Pakistan in the National Assembly. The Awami League had not urged political independence for the East during the elections but did run on a list of demands concerning one-man-one-vote political representation and increased economic autonomy for the East. The government in the West viewed the Awami League's electoral victory as a threat. In the wake of these electoral results, the government in Islamabad decided to postpone the convening of the new National Assembly indefinitely, and in March 1971 the West Pakistani army started killing unarmed civilians indiscriminately, raping women, burning homes, and looting or destroying property. At least one million people were killed, and millions more fled across the border into India.[43] Following months of tension, border incidents, and increased pressure from the influx of refugees, India sent troops into East Pakistan. After twelve days the Pakistani army surrendered at Dacca, and the new state of Bangladesh was established.

As in many of the nineteenth-century cases, the intervenor here had an array of geopolitical interests. Humanitarian concerns were not the only reason, or even, perhaps, the most important reason, to intervene. However, this is a case in which intervention could be justified in humanitarian terms, and initially the Indian representatives in both the General Assembly and the Security Council did articulate such a justification.[44] These arguments were widely rejected by other states, including many with no particular interest in politics on the subcontinent. States as diverse as Argentina, Tunisia, China, Saudi Arabia, and the United States all responded to India's claims by arguing that principles of sovereignty and noninterference should take precedence and that India had no right to meddle in what they all viewed as an "internal matter." In response to this rejection of its claims, India retracted its humanitarian justifications, choosing instead to rely on self-defense to defend its actions.[45]

b. Tanzania in Uganda (1979). This episode began as a straightforward territorial dispute. In the autumn of 1978 Ugandan troops invaded and occupied the Kagera salient—territory between the Uganda-Tanzania border and the Kagera River in Tanzania.[46] On November 1 Amin announced annexation of the territory. Nyerere considered the annexation tantamount to an act of war and, on November 15, launched an offensive from the south bank of the Kagera River. Amin, fearing defeat, offered to withdraw from the occupied territories if Nyerere would promise to cease support for Ugandan dissidents and agree not to attempt to overthrow his government. Nyerere refused and made explicit his intention to help dissidents topple the Amin regime. In January 1979 Tanzanian troops crossed into Uganda, and, by April, these troops, joined by some Ugandan rebel groups, had occupied Kampala and installed a new government headed by Yusef Lule.

As in the previous case, there were nonhumanitarian reasons to intervene; but if territorial issues were the only concern, the Tanzanians could have stopped at the border, having evicted Ugandan forces, or pushed them back into Uganda short of Kampala. The explicit statement of intent to topple the regime seems out of proportion to the low-level territorial squabble. However, humanitarian considerations clearly compounded other motives in this case. Tesón makes a strong case that Nyerere's intense dislike of Amin's regime and its abusive practices influenced the scale of the response. Nyerere had already publicly called Amin a murderer and refused to sit with him on the Authority of the East African Community.[47] Tesón also presents strong evidence that the lack of support or material help for Uganda in this intervention from the UN, the Organization of African Unity (OAU), or any state besides Libya suggests tacit international acceptance of what otherwise would have been universally condemned as international aggression because of the human rights record of the target state.[48]

Despite evidence of humanitarian motivations, Tanzania never claimed humanitarian justification. In fact, Tanzania went out of its way to disclaim responsibility for the felicitous humanitarian outcome of its actions. It claimed only that it was acting in response to Amin's invasion and that its actions just happened to coincide with a revolt against Amin inside Uganda. When Sudan and Nigeria criticized Tanzania for interfering in another state's internal affairs in violation of the OAU charter, it was the new Ugandan regime that invoked humanitarian justifications for Tanzania's actions. The regime criticized the critics, arguing that members of the OAU should not "hide behind the formula of non-intervention when human rights are blatantly being violated."[49]

c. Vietnam in Cambodia (1979). In 1975 the Chinese-backed Khmers Rouges took power in Cambodia and launched a policy of internal "purification" entailing the atrocities and genocide now made famous by the 1984 movie *The Killing Fields*. This regime, under the leadership of Pol Pot, was also aggressively anti-Vietnamese and engaged in a number of border incursions during the late 1970s. Determined to end this border activity, the Vietnamese and an anti–Pol Pot army of exiled Cambodians invaded the country in December 1978, succeeded in routing the Khmers Rouges by January 1979, and installed a sympathetic government under the name People's Republic of Kampuchea (PRK).

Again, humanitarian considerations may not have been central to Vietnam's decision to intervene, but humanitarian justifications would seem to have offered some political cover to the internationally unpopular Vietnamese regime. However, like Tanzania, the Vietnamese made no appeal to humanitarian justifications. Instead, they argued that they were only helping the Cambodian people to achieve self-determination against the neo-colonial regime of Pol Pot, which had been "the product of the hegemonistic and expansionist policy of the Peking authorities."[50] Even if Vietnam *had* offered humanitarian justifications for intervention, indications are that other states would have rejected them. A number of states mentioned Pol Pot's appalling human rights violations in their condemnations of Vietnam's action but said, nonetheless, that these violations did not entitle Vietnam to intervene. During the UN debate no state spoke in favor of the right to unilateral humanitarian intervention, and several states (Greece, the Netherlands,

Yugoslavia, and India) that had previously supported humanitarian intervention arguments in the UN voted for the resolution condemning Vietnam's intervention.[51]

MULTILATERAL INTERVENTION IN HUMANITARIAN DISASTERS   To be legitimate in contemporary politics, humanitarian intervention must be multilateral. The cold war made such multilateral efforts politically difficult to orchestrate, but, since 1989, several large-scale interventions have been carried out claiming humanitarian justifications as their raison d'être. All have been multilateral. Most visible among these have been the following:

- the U.S., British, and French efforts to protect Kurdish and Shiite populations inside Iraq following the Gulf War;
- the United Nations Transitional Authority in Cambodia (UNTAC) mission to end civil war and to reestablish a democratic political order in Cambodia;
- the large-scale U.S. and UN effort to end starvation and to construct a democratic state in Somalia;
- deployment of UN and NATO troops to protect civilian, especially Muslim, populations primarily from Serbian forces in Bosnia;
- NATO's campaign to stop the ethnic cleansing of Albanian Muslims in the province of Kosovo, Yugoslavia.

Although these efforts have attracted varying amounts of criticism concerning their effectiveness, their legitimacy has received little or no criticism. Further, and unlike their nineteenth-century counterparts, all have been organized through standing international organizations—most often the United Nations. Indeed, the UN Charter has provided the normative framework in which much of the normative contestation over intervention practices has occurred since 1945. Specifically, the Charter enshrines two principles that at times conflict. On the one hand, Article 2 preserves states' sovereign rights as the organiz-ing principle of the international system. The corollary is a near-absolute rule of nonintervention. On the other hand, Article 1 of the Charter emphasizes human rights and justice as a fundamental mission of the United Nations, and subsequent UN actions (among them, the adoption of the Universal Declaration of Human Rights) have strengthened this claim. Gross humanitarian abuses by states against their own citizens, like those discussed [here,] bring these two central principles into conflict.

In this struggle between principles, the balance seems to have shifted since the end of the cold war, and humanitarian claims now frequently trump sovereignty claims. States still may not respond to humanitarian appeals, but they do not hesitate because they think such intervention will be denounced internationally as illegitimate. A brief look at the "non-case" of Rwanda illustrates this. Contemporary humanitarian intervention norms do more than just "allow" intervention. The Genocide Convention actually makes action mandatory. Signatories must stop genocide, defined as "acts committed with intent to destroy, in whole or in part, a national, ethnical, racial or religious group."[52] Although the failure of the West to respond to the Rwandan genocide in 1994 shows that humanitarian claims must compete with other interests states have as they weigh the decision to use force, the episode also reveals something about the normative terrain on which these interventions are debated. In contrast to the cold war cases, no significant constituency was claiming that intervention in Rwanda for humanitarian purposes would have been illegitimate or an illegal breach of sovereignty. States did not fear the kind of response India received when it intervened in East Pakistan. France, the one state to intervene (briefly and with multilateral authorization) was criticized not because the intervention was illegitimate but because its actions aided the *génocidaires* rather than the victims.[53] States understood very well that legally and ethically this case required intervention, and because they did not want to intervene for other reasons, they had to work hard to suppress information and to avoid the word "genocide" in order to sidestep their obligations.[54] When the killing was (conveniently) over, the American president, Bill Clinton, actually went to Rwanda and apologized for his administration's inaction. While the Rwandan case can be viewed pessimistically as a case where ethics were ignored and states did what was convenient, it also reveals that states understood and publicly acknowledged a set of obligations that certainly did not exist in the nineteenth century and probably not during most of the cold war. States understood that they had not just a right but a duty to intervene in this case. That the Americans apologized substantiates this.[55]

In addition to a shift in normative burdens to act, intervention norms now place strict requirements on the ways humanitarian intervention can be carried out. Humanitarian intervention must be multilateral when it occurs. It must be organized under multilateral, preferably UN, auspices or with explicit multilateral consent. Further, it must be implemented with a multilateral force if at all possible. Specifically the intervention force should contain troops from "disinterested" states, usually middle-level powers outside the region of conflict—another dimension of multilateralism not found in nineteenth-century practice.

Contemporary multilateralism thus differs from the multilateral action of the nineteenth century. The latter was what John Ruggie might call "quantitative" multilateralism and only thinly so.[56] Nineteenth-century multilateralism was strategic. States intervened together to keep an eye on one another and to discourage adventurism or exploitation of the situation for nonhumanitarian gains. Multilateralism was driven by shared fears and perceived threats, not by shared norms and principles. States did not even coordinate and collaborate extensively to achieve their goals. Military deployments in the nineteenth century may have been contemporaneous, but they were largely separate; there was virtually no joint planning or coordination of operations. This follows logically from the nature of multi-lateralism, since strategic surveillance of one's partners is not a shared goal but a private one.

Recent interventions exhibit much more of what Ruggie calls the "qualitative dimension" of multilateralism. They are organized according to, and in defense of, "generalized principles" of international responsibility and the use of military force, many of which are codified in the UN Charter, in UN Declarations, and in the UN's standard operating procedures. These principles emphasize international responsibilities for ensuring human rights and justice, and dictate appropriate procedures for intervening such as the necessity of obtaining Security Council authorization for action. They also require that intervening forces be composed not just of troops of more than one state but of troops from disinterested states other than Great Powers—not a feature of nineteenth-century action.

Contemporary multilateralism is deeply political and normative, not just strategic. It is shaped by shared notions about when use of force is legitimate and appropriate. Contemporary legitimacy criteria for use of force, in turn, derive from these shared principles, articulated most often through the UN, about consultation and coordination with other states before acting and about multinational composition of forces. U.S. interventions in Somalia and Haiti were not multilateral because the United States needed the involvement of other states for military or strategic reasons. The United States was capable of supplying the forces necessary and, in fact, did supply the lion's share. No other Great Power was particularly worried about U.S. opportunism in these areas so none joined the action for surveillance reasons. These interventions were multilateral for political and normative reasons. To be legitimate and politically acceptable, the United States needed UN authorization and international participation for these operations. Whereas Russia, France, and Britain tolerated one another's presence in operations to save Christians from the infidel Turk, the United States had to beg other states to join it for a humanitarian operation in Haiti.

Multilateral norms create political benefits for conformance and costs for nonconforming action. They create, in part, the structure of incentives states face. Realists or neoliberal institutionalists might argue that in the contemporary world multilateral behavior is efficient and unproblematically self-interested because multilateralism helps to generate political support for intervention both domestically and internationally. However, this argument only begs the question: *Why* is multilateralism necessary to generate political support? It was not necessary in the nineteenth century. Indeed, multilateralism, as currently practiced, was inconceivable in the nineteenth century. As discussed earlier, nothing about the logic of multilateralism itself makes it clearly superior to unilateral action. Each action has advantages and costs to states, and the costs of multilateral intervention have become abundantly clear in recent UN operations. One testament to the power of these multilateral norms is that states adhere to them even when they know that doing so compromises the effectiveness of the mission. Criticisms of the UN's ineffectiveness for military operations are widespread. That UN involvement continues to be a central feature of these operations, despite the UN's apparent lack of military competence, underscores the power of multilateral norms.[57]

Multilateralism legitimizes action by signaling broad support for the actor's goals. Intervenors use it to demonstrate that their purpose in intervening is not merely self-serving and particularistic but is joined in some way to community interests that other states share.[58] Making this demonstration is often vital in mustering international support for an intervention, as India discovered, and can be crucial in generating domestic support as well. Conversely, failure to intervene multilaterally creates political costs. Other states and domestic constituencies both start to question the aims and motives of intervenors when others will not join and international organizations will not bless an operation. These benefits and costs flow not from material features of the intervention but from the expec-tations that states and people in contemporary politics share about what constitutes legitimate uses of force. Perceptions of illegitimacy may eventually have material consequences for intervenors, but the motivations for imposing those costs are normative.

Both realist and neoliberal analyses fail to ask where incentives come from. They also fail to ask where interests come from. A century ago the plight of non-white, non-Christians was not an "interest" of Western states, certainly not one that could prompt the deployment of troops. Similarly, a century ago, states saw no interest in multilateral authorization, coordination, and use of troops from "disinterested" states. The argument here is that these interests and incentives have been constituted socially through state practice and the evolution of shared norms through which states act.

Conclusion

Humanitarian intervention practices are not new. They have, however, changed over time in some systemic and important ways. First, the definition of who qualifies as human and is therefore deserving of humanitarian protection by foreign governments has changed. Whereas in the nineteenth century European Christians were the sole focus of humanitarian intervention, this focus has been expanded and universalized such that by the late twentieth century all human beings were treated as equally deserving in the international normative discourse. In fact, states are very sensitive to charges that they are "normatively backward" and still privately harbor distinctions. When Boutros-Ghali, shortly after becoming Secretary-General, charged that powerful states were attending to disasters in white, European Bosnia at the expense of non-white, African Somalia, the United States and other states became defensive, refocused attention, and ultimately launched a full-scale intervention in Somalia before acting in Bosnia.

Second, although humanitarian intervention in the nineteenth century was frequently multilateral, it was not necessarily so. Russia, for example, claimed humanitarian justifications for its intervention in Bulgaria in the 1870s; France was similarly allowed to intervene unilaterally, with no companion force to guard against adventurism. Other states did not contest, much less reject, these claims despite the fact that Russia, at least, had nonhumanitarian motives for intervening. They did, however, reject similar claims by India in the twentieth century. By the twentieth century, not only did multilateralism appear to be necessary to claim humanitarian justifications but sanction by the United Nations or some other formal organization was required. The United States, Britain, and France, for example, went out of their way to find authority in UN resolutions for their protection of Kurds in Iraq.

These changes have not taken place in isolation. Changes in humanitarian intervention behavior are intimately connected with other sweeping changes in the normative fabric that have taken place over the past two centuries. Who counts as human has changed, not just for intervention but in all arenas of social life—slavery, colonialism, but also political participation generally at all levels and in most parts of the world. Similarly multilateralism norms are by no means specific to, or even most consequential for, intervention behavior. As Ruggie and his colleagues have amply documented, these norms pervade virtually all aspects of interstate politics, particularly among the most powerful Western states (which are also the most likely and most capable intervenors).[59] The related proliferation of formal institutions and the ever-expanding use of these rational-legal authority structures to coordinate and implement international decision making are also generalized phenomena. These trends have clear and specific impacts on contemporary humanitarian interventions but are also present and powerful in a wide variety of areas of world politics.[60] These interconnections should not surprise us. Indeed, they are to be expected given both the social psychological and institutional mechanisms at work to resolve normative paradoxes and the ways that these extend normative changes to logically and ethically related areas of social life. Changes as fundamental as the ones examined here, namely, changes in who is human and in the multilateral and rational-legal structure of politics, are logically connected to a vast range of political activity and appear again in other cases of intervention * * *.

NOTES

1. Scholars of international law have increasingly made the distinction I make here and have reserved the term "humanitarian intervention" for military protection of foreign citizens, as I do, in order to follow changing state practice. See Anthony Clark Arend and Robert J. Beck, *International Law and the Use of Force: Beyond the UN Charter Paradigm* (New York: Routledge, 1993), esp. chap. 8; and Fernando Tesón, *Humanitarian Intervention: An Inquiry into Law and Morality* (Dobbs Ferry, N.Y.: Transnational, 1988).

2. For more on the way that respect for human rights has become an integral part of contemporary definitions of "security" and how this was accomplished, most visibly at the UN in the 1970s during the anti-apartheid movement, see Audie Klotz, "Norms Reconstituting Interests: Global Racial Equality and U.S. Sanctions against South Africa," *International Organization* 49, no. 3 (summer 1995): 451–78; Michael Barnett, "Bringing in the New World Order: Liberalism, Legitimacy, and the United Nations," *World Politics* (July 1997): 526–51; and Michael Barnett and Martha Finnemore, "The Politics, Power, and Pathologies of International Organizations," *International Organization* 53, no. 4 (1999): 699–732.

3. That the regimes literature, which brought norms back into the study of international politics in the 1980s, defined norms in issue-specific terms probably influenced this

orientation in the scholarship. Arguments about interrelationships between norms and the nature of an overarching social normative structure have been made by sociological institutionalists, legal scholars, and, to a lesser extent, scholars of the English school like Gerrit Gong in his discussion of standards of "civilisation" (Gerrit Gong, *The Standard of "Civilisation" in International Society* [Oxford: Clarendon, 1984]). See the discussion of the content of the world polity in George Thomas, John Meyer, Francisco Ramirez and John Boli, eds., *Institutional Structure: Constituting State, Society, and the Individual* (Newbury Park, Calif.: Sage, 1987), esp. chap. 1; John Boli and George M. Thomas, eds., *Constructing World Culture: International Nongovernmental Organizations since 1875* (Stanford: Stanford University Press, 1999), esp. chaps. 1–2 and the conclusion. On the kinds of norm relationships that contribute to legitimacy and fairness, see Thomas M. Franck, *The Power of Legitimacy among Nations* (New York: Oxford University Press, 1990); Thomas M. Franck, *Fairness in International Law and Institutions* (New York: Oxford University Press, 1995); and Gong, *The Standard of "Civilisation."*

4. Intervention in the Boxer Rebellion in China (1898–1900) is an interesting related case. I omit it from the analysis here because the primary goal of intervenors was to protect their own nationals, not the Chinese. But the intervention did have the happy result of protecting a large number of mostly Christian Chinese from slaughter.

5. J. A. R. Marriott, *The Eastern Question: An Historical Study in European Diplomacy* (Oxford: Clarendon, 1917), 183–85. Atrocities continued through the more than five years of the conflict and fueled the Russian claims. Perhaps the most sensational of these were the atrocities Egyptian troops committed under Ibrahim when they arrived to quell the Greek insurrection in 1825 for the Sultan (to whom they were vassals). Egyptian troops

began a process of wholesale extermination of the Greek populace, apparently aimed at recolonization of the area by Muslims. This fresh round of horrors was cited by European powers for their final press toward a solution.

6. France had a long-standing protective arrangement with eastern Christians, as described below, and had consistently favored armed intervention (*Cambridge Modern History*, 10:193).

7. William St. Clair, *That Greece Might Still Be Free* (London: Oxford University Press, 1972), 81; C. W. Crawley, *The Question of Greek Independence* (New York: Fertig, 1973), 1; *Cambridge Modern History*, 10:180, 196. In addition to St. Clair, two other sources on the Philhellenic movement are Douglas Dakin, *British and American Philhellenes during the War of Greek Independence, 1821–1833* (Thessaloniki, 1955); and Theophilus C. Prousis, *Russian Society and the Greek Revolution* (DeKalb: Northern Illinois University Press, 1994).

8. Eric Carlton, *Massacres: An Historical Perspective* (Aldershot, Hants., England: Scolar, 1994), 82. Marriott, *The Eastern Question*, 183; *Cambridge Modern History*, 10:178–83.

9. *Cambridge Modern History*, 10:178–79.

10. R. W. Seton-Watson, *Britain in Europe, 1789 to 1914* (New York: Macmillan, 1937), 419–21; Marc Trachtenberg, "Intervention in Historical Perspective," in *Emerging Norms of Justified Intervention*, ed. Laura W. Reed and Carl Kaysen (Cambridge, Mass.: American Academy of Arts and Sciences, 1993), 23.

11. Louis B. Sohn and Thomas Buergenthal, *International Protection of Human Rights* (Indianapolis: Bobbs-Merrill, 1973), 156–60.

12. A. L. Tiwabi, *A Modern History of Syria* (London: Macmillan, 1969), 131; Seton-Watson, *Britain in Europe*, 421.

13. Mason Whiting Tyler, *The European Powers and the Near East, 1875–1908* (Minneapolis: University of Minnesota Press, 1925), 66 n.; Seton-Watson, *Britain in Europe*, 519–20;

Marriott, *The Eastern Question*, 291–92; *Cambridge Modern History*, 12:384.

14. Seton-Watson, *Britain in Europe*, 519.

15. Mercia Macdermott, *A History of Bulgaria, 1393–1885* (New York: Praeger, 1962), 280.

16. *Cambridge Modern History*, 12:384.

17. Tyler, *European Powers and the Near East*, 70. Gladstone even published a pamphlet on the subject, *The Bulgarian Horrors and the Question of the East*, which sold more than two hundred thousand copies. Seton-Watson, *Britain in Europe*, 519; Marriott, *The Eastern Question*, 293.

18. Macdermott, *History of Bulgaria*, 277; Tyler, *European Powers and the Near East*, 21.

19. *Cambridge Modern History*, 12:415–17; Marriott, *The Eastern Question*, 349–51.

20. Of course, these events late in the nineteenth century were only the tip of the iceberg. More than a million Armenians were killed by Turks during World War I, but the war environment obviates discussions of military intervention.

21. Indeed, there were many firsthand European accounts of the Constantinople massacres since execution gangs even forced their way into the houses of foreigners to execute Armenian servants (*Cambridge Modern History*, 12:417).

22. The quotation is from Lord Rosebery as cited in *Cambridge History of British Foreign Policy*, 3:234.

23. *Cambridge Modern History*, 12:417–18; Sohn and Buergenthal, *International Protection of Human Rights*, 181.

24. For more on this topic, see Stanford J. Shaw and Ezel Kural Shaw, *History of the Ottoman Empire and Modern Turkey*, vol. 2, *Reform, Revolution, and Republic: The Rise of Modern Turkey* (Cambridge: Cambridge University Press, 1977).

25. Christopher Hibbert, *The Dragon Wakes: China and the West, 1793–1911* (Newton Abbot, Devon, England: Reader's Union, 1971). Hibbert estimates that the three-day massacre in Nanking alone killed more than one hundred thousand people (*The Dragon Wakes*, 303).

26. In one of the more egregious incidents of this kind the Germans killed sixty-five thousand indigenous inhabitants of German Southwest Africa (Namibia) in 1904. See Barbara Harff, "The Etiology of Genocides," in *Genocide and the Modern Age: Etiology and Case Studies of Mass Death*, ed. Isidor Wallimann and Michael N. Dobkowski (New York: Greenwood, 1987), 46, 56.

27. For more social psychological underpinnings, see Alice Eagly and Shelly Chaiken, *The Psychology of Attitudes* (Fort Worth, Tex.: Harcourt Brace Jovanovich, 1993). For more on logical coherence in law, see Franck, *The Power of Legitimacy*, esp. chap. 10.

28. Quotation comes from the Eight Power Declaration concerning the Universal Abolition of the Trade in Negroes, signed February 8, 1815, by Britain, France, Spain, Sweden, Austria, Prussia, Russia, and Portugal; quoted in Leslie Bethell, *The Abolition of the Brazilian Slave Trade* (Cambridge: Cambridge University Press, 1970), 14.

29. Bethell, *Abolition of the Brazilian Slave Trade*, chap. 1. In 1850 Britain went so far as to fire on and board ships in Brazilian ports to enforce anti-slave-trafficking treaties (Bethell, *Abolition of the Brazilian Slave Trade*, 329–31). One might argue that such action was a violation of sovereignty and thus qualifies as military intervention, but, if so, they were interventions of a very peripheral kind. Note, too, that British public opinion on abolition of the slave trade was not uniform. See Chaim D. Kaufmann and Robert A. Pape, "Explaining Costly International Moral Action: Britain's Sixty-Year Campaign against the Atlantic Slave Trade," *International Organization* 53, no. 4 (1999): 631–68.

30. The United States is a possible exception. One could argue that the North intervened militarily in the South to abolish slavery. Such an argument would presume that (a) there were always two separate states such

that the North's action could be understood as "intervention," rather than civil war, and (b) that abolishing slavery rather than maintaining the Union was the primary reason for the North's initial action. Both assumptions are open to serious question. (The Emancipation Proclamation was not signed until 1863 when the war was already half over.) Thus, although the case is suggestive of the growing power of a broader conception of "humanity," I do not treat it in this analysis.

31. For an extended treatment of the importance of the categories "civilized" and "barbarian" on state behavior in the nineteenth century, see Gong, *The Standard of "Civilisation."*

32. Margaret Keck and Kathryn Sikkink, *Activists beyond Borders* (Ithaca, N.Y.: Cornell University Press, 1998), chap. 2; James Lee Ray, "The Abolition of Slavery and the End of International War," *International Organization* 43, no. 3 (1989): 405–39.

33. See Boutros-Ghali's comment in the July 22, 1992, Security Council meeting. Rep. Howard Wolpe made a similar comment in the House Africa Subcommittee hearings on June 23, 1992, about double standards in policy toward Bosnia and Somalia. The black caucus became galvanized around this "double standard" issue and became a powerful lobbying force in the administration, and its influence was felt by General Colin Powell, then chairman of the Joint Chiefs of Staff, among others. For details of the U.S. decision-making process on Somalia, see John G. Sommer, *Hope Restored? Humanitarian Aid in Somalia, 1990–1994* (Washington, D.C.: Refugee Policy Group, 1994). For a discussion of Boutros-Ghali and Wolpe, see Sommer, *Hope Restored?* 22 n. 63; for a discussion of Powell, see 30 n. 100.

34. Gerrit Gong provides a much more extensive discussion of what "civilization" meant to Europeans from an international legal perspective. See Gong, *The Standard of "Civilisation."* Uday Mehta investigates the philosophical underpinnings of colonialism in Lockean liberalism and the strategies aimed at the systematic political exclusion of culturally dissimilar colonized peoples by liberals professing universal freedom and rights. One of these strategies was civilizational infantilization; treating peoples in India, for example, like children allowed liberals to exclude them from political participation and, at the same time, justified extensive tutelage in European social conventions in the name of civilizing them and preparing them for liberal political life (Uday S. Mehta, "Liberal Strategies of Exclusion," *Politics and Society* 18 [1990]: 427–54).

Of necessity this very abbreviated picture of colonialism obscures the enormous variety in European views of what they were doing. Some social reformers and missionaries no doubt had far more generous notions of the "humanity" of the non-Europeans they came in contact with and treated them with respect. For more racist participants in the colonialist project, no amount of Christian piety or Europeanization would ever raise these non-Europeans to a level of humanity comparable to that of Europeans. My goal in this sketch is to emphasize the effort to create humanity, so that readers will see the connections with decolonization.

35. To reiterate, I am making no claims about the causes of decolonization. These causes were obviously complex and have been treated extensively in the vast literature on the subject. I argue only that humanitarian norms were central in the justification for decolonization.

36. For an excellent exposition, see Franck, *The Power of Legitimacy*, esp. chap. 10.

37. Neta Crawford, "Decolonization as an International Norm: The Evolution of Practices, Arguments, and Beliefs," in *Emerging Norms of Justified Intervention*, ed. Laura Reed and Carl Kaysen (Cambridge, Mass.: American Academy of Arts and Sciences, 1993), 37–61 at 53; Neta Crawford, *Argument and Change*

in World Politics: Ethics, Decolonization, and Humanitarian Intervention (New York: Cambridge University Press, 2002). David Lumsdaine makes a similar point about the expanding internal logic of domestic welfare arguments that led to the creation of the foreign aid regime in his *Moral Vision in International Politics: The Foreign Aid Regime, 1949–1989* (Princeton, N.J.: Princeton University Press, 1993).

38. Crawford, "Decolonization as an International Norm," 37–61; Crawford, *Argument and Change in World Politics;* Michael Barnett, "The United Nations and the Politics of Peace: From Juridical Sovereignty to Empirical Sovereignty," *Global Governance* 1 (1995): 79–97.

39. Other authors have noted a similar trend in related areas. David Lumsdaine discusses the role of multilateral versus bilateral giving of foreign aid in his *Moral Vision in International Politics.*

40. An interesting exception that proves the rule is the U.S. claim of humanitarian justifications for its intervention in Grenada. First, the human beings to be protected by the intervention were not Grenadians but U.S. nationals. Protecting one's own nationals can still be construed as protecting national interests and is therefore not anomalous or of interest analytically in the way that state action to protect nationals of *other* states is. Second, the humanitarian justification offered by the United States was widely rejected in the international community, which underscores the point made here that states are generally suspicious of unilateral humanitarian intervention. See the discussion in Tesón, *Humanitarian Intervention,* 188–200; and Arend and Beck, *International Law and the Use of Force,* 126–28.

The apparent illegitimacy of unilateral humanitarian intervention is probably related to two broad issues that cannot be treated adequately in this limited space, namely, the expansion of multilateralism as a practice and the strengthening of juridical sovereignty norms, especially among weak states. On multilateralism, see John Ruggie, ed., *Multilateralism Matters* (New York: Columbia University Press, 1993). Concerning the strengthening of sovereignty norms among weak states, see Stephen D. Krasner, *Structural Conflict* (Berkeley: University of California Press, 1985). For an empirical demonstration of the increased robustness of sovereign statehood as a political form in the periphery, see David Strang, "Anomaly and Commonplace in European Political Expansion: Realist and Institutional Accounts," *International Organization* 45, no. 2 (spring 1991): 143–62.

41. Significantly, those who are more optimistic about solving these problems and about the utility of multilateral action rely on norms and shared social purpose to overcome these problems. Norms are an essential part both of regimes and multilateralism in the two touchstone volumes on these topics. See Stephen D. Krasner, ed., *International Regimes* (Ithaca, N.Y.: Cornell University Press, 1983); and Ruggie, *Multilateralism Matters.*

42. These synopses are drawn, in large part, from Tesón, *Humanitarian Intervention,* chap. 8; Michael Akehurst, "Humanitarian Intervention," in *Intervention in World Politics,* ed. Hedley Bull (Oxford: Clarendon, 1984), 95–118; and Arend and Beck, *International Law and the Use of Force,* chap. 8.

43. Estimates of the number of refugees vary wildly. The Pakistani government put the number at two million; the Indian government claimed ten million. Independent estimates have ranged from five to nine million. See Tesón, *Humanitarian Intervention,* 182, including n. 163 for discussion.

44. See ibid., 186 n. 187, for the text of a General Assembly speech by the Indian representative articulating this justification. See also Akehurst, "Humanitarian Intervention," 96.

45. Akehurst concludes that India actually had prior statements concerning humanitarian justifications deleted from the Official Record of the UN ("Humanitarian Intervention," 96–97).

46. Amin attempted to justify this move by claiming that Tanzania had previously invaded Ugandan territory.

47. Tesón, *Humanitarian Intervention*, 164.

48. Ibid., 164–67.

49. As quoted in Akehurst, "Humanitarian Intervention," 99.

50. As quoted ibid., 97 n. 17.

51. One reason for the virtual absence of humanitarian arguments in this case, compared to the Tanzanian case, may have been the way the intervention was conducted. Tanzania exerted much less control over the kind of regime that replaced Amin, making the subsequent Ugandan regime's defense of Tanzania's actions as "liberation" less implausible than were Vietnam's claims that it, too, was helping to liberate Cambodia by installing a puppet regime that answered to Hanoi.

52. The definition in Article 2 of the 1948 Genocide Convention lists the following specific acts as included in the term "genocide": "(a) Killing members of the group; (b) Causing serious bodily or mental harm to members of the group; (c) Deliberately inflicting on the group conditions of life calculated to bring about its physical destruction in whole or in part; (d) Imposing measures intended to prevent births within the group; (e) Forcibly transferring children of the group to another group" (Convention on the prevention and punishment of the crime of genocide, Adopted by Resolution 260 (III) A of the United Nations General Assembly on December 9, 1948. Available at http://www.unhchr.ch/html/menu3/b/p _genoci.htm).

53. For particularly damning accounts, see Philip Gourevitch, *We Wish to Inform You That Tomorrow We Will Be Killed with Our Families* (New York: Farrar, Straus and Giroux, 1998), chap. 11; and Samantha Power, *"A Problem from Hell": America and the Age of Genocide* (New York: Basic Books, 2002), chap. 10.

54. The suppression of a cable from the United Nations Assistance Mission in Rwanda (UNAMIR) commander in Kigali, Dallaire, to his superiors at the Department of Peace Operations in New York (then run by Kofi Annan) was a scandal when it was uncovered. See Gourevitch, *We Wish to Inform You*; Michael Barnett, *Eyewitness to a Genocide: The United Nations and Rwanda* (Ithaca, N.Y.: Cornell University Press, 2002); Michael Barnett, "The UN Security Council, Indifference, and Genocide and Rwanda," *Cultural Anthropology* 12, no. 4 (1997): 551–78; *Frontline* documentary, "The Triumph of Evil," and accompanying website at www.pbs.org/wgbh/ pages/shows/frontline/evil. The U.S. administration's attempts to avoid "the G word" would have been comical if they did not have such tragic effects. See the *Frontline* documentary, "The Triumph of Evil," and interviews with James Woods and Tony Marley at www.pbs .org/wgbh/pages/shows/frontline/evil.

55. Samantha Power would probably be unimpressed with this change. She argues that the United States has known about virtually every genocide in the twentieth century and never acted to stop any of them. I do not dispute her claim; rather, we are investigating a different question. Power wants to know why the United States has not acted to stop genocide; I want to know why the United States has done any humanitarian intervention at all. See Power, *"A Problem from Hell."*

56. John G. Ruggie, "Multilateralism: The Anatomy of an Institution," in Ruggie, *Multilateralism Matters*, 6. Ruggie's edited volume provides an excellent analysis of the sources and power of multilateral norms generally.

57. Contemporary multilateralism is not, therefore, "better" or more efficient and effective than the nineteenth-century brand. I contend only that it is different. This difference in multilateralism poses a particular challenge

to neoliberal institutionalists. These scholars have sophisticated arguments about why international cooperation should be robust and why it might vary across issue areas. They cannot, however, explain these qualitative changes in multilateralism, nor can they explain changes in the amount of multilateral activity over time without appealing to exogenous variables (like changes in markets or technology).

58. For a more generalized argument about the ways international organizations enjoy legitimacy of action because they are able to present themselves as guardians of community interests as opposed to self-seeking states, see Michael N. Barnett and Martha Finnemore, *The Power and Pathologies of International Organizations* (Ithaca, N.Y.: Cornell University Press, forthcoming).

59. Ruggie, *Multilateralism Matters*.

60. Barnett and Finnemore, "The Politics, Power, and Pathologies of International Organizations"; Barnett and Finnemore, *The Power and Pathologies of International Organizations*.

9 International Political Economy

Economic issues are critical to understanding international relations in the twenty-first century. In the first selection here, a classic from U.S. Power and the Multinational Corporation *(1975), Princeton University's Robert Gilpin concisely discusses the relationship between economics and politics. He examines the three basic conceptions of political economy (liberalism, radicalism, and mercantilism), comparing their perspectives on the nature of economic relations, actors, and goals of economic relations; their theories of change; and how they characterize the relationship between economics and politics.*

International economic institutions play a key role in the liberal economy. Helen V. Milner, of Princeton University, examines the impact of these institutions— the IMF, World Bank, and World Trade Organization—on developing countries. She finds mixed economic outcomes, leading her to explore possible explanations. Martin Wolf, in his 2004 book Why Globalization Works, *responds to critics of neoliberal economic globalization. In this book chapter, he asks whether human welfare is rising. He finds that never before have so many individuals enjoyed such high standards of living. The poorest countries have not been hurt by the effects of economic liberalization, they have just failed to participate in it.*

Having an abundance of natural resources has been traditionally viewed as a key to economic development. Yet, scholars increasingly refer to a "resource curse." In their article, Macartan Humphreys, Jeffrey D. Sachs, and Joseph E. Stiglitz explain how resource abundance can cause instability, violence, dictatorship, and poverty.

In the last selection, Nobel Prize–winning economist Joseph Stiglitz explains how the recent global financial crisis was "Made in the USA" with excesses in the financial sector and inadequate regulation, then exported around the world. A seismic shift in the global political economy has occurred, Stiglitz argues in this excerpt from his book Freefall: America, Free Markets, and the Sinking of the World Economy *(2010).*

ROBERT GILPIN

The Nature of Political Economy

The international corporations have evidently declared ideological war on the "antiquated" nation state. . . . The charge that materialism, modernization and internationalism is the new liberal creed of corporate capitalism is a valid one. The implication is clear: the nation state as a political unit of democratic decision-making must, in the interest of "progress," yield control to the new mercantile mini-powers.[1]

While the structure of the multinational corporation is a modern concept, designed to meet the requirements of a modern age, the nation state is a very old-fashioned idea and badly adapted to serve the needs of our present complex world.[2]

These two statements—the first by Kari Levitt, a Canadian nationalist, the second by George Ball, a former United States undersecretary of state—express a dominant theme of contemporary writings on international relations. International society, we are told, is increasingly rent between its economic and its political organization. On the one hand, powerful economic and technological forces are creating a highly interdependent world economy, thus diminishing the traditional significance of national boundaries. On the other hand, the nation-state continues to command men's loyalties and to be the basic unit of political decision making. As one writer has put the issue, "The conflict of our era is between ethnocentric nationalism and geocentric technology."[3]

Ball and Levitt represent two contending positions with respect to this conflict. Whereas

From Robert Gilpin, *U.S. Power and the Multinational Corporation* (New York: Basic Books, 1975), Chap. 1.

Ball advocates the diminution of the power of the nation-state in order to give full rein to the productive potentialities of the multinational corporation, Levitt argues for a powerful nationalism which could counterbalance American corporate domination. What appears to one as the logical and desirable consequence of economic rationality seems to the other to be an effort on the part of American imperialism to eliminate all contending centers of power.

Although the advent of the multinational corporation has put the question of the relationship between economics and politics in a new guise, it is an old issue. In the nineteenth century, for example, it was this issue that divided classical liberals like John Stuart Mill from economic nationalists, represented by Georg Friedrich List. Whereas the former gave primacy in the organization of society to economics and the production of wealth, the latter emphasized the political determination of economic relations. As this issue is central both to the contemporary debate on the multinational corporation and to the argument of this study, this chapter analyzes the three major treatments of the relationship between economics and politics—that is, the three major ideologies of political economy.

The Meaning of Political Economy

The argument of this study is that the relationship between economics and politics, at least in the modern world, is a reciprocal one. On the one hand, politics largely determines the framework of economic activity and channels it in directions intended to serve the interests of dominant groups; the exercise of power in all its forms is a major determinant of the nature of an economic system. On the other hand, the economic process itself tends to redistribute power and wealth; it transforms the power relationships among groups. This in turn leads to a transformation of the political system, thereby giving rise to a new structure of economic relationships. Thus, the dynamics of international relations in the modern world is largely a function of the reciprocal interaction between economics and politics.

First of all, what do I mean by "politics" or "economics"? Charles Kindleberger speaks of economics and politics as two different methods of allocating scarce resources: the first through a market mechanism, the latter through a budget.[4] Robert Keohane and Joseph Nye, in an excellent analysis of international political economy, define economics and politics in terms of two levels of analysis: those of structure and of process.[5] Politics is the domain "having to do with the establishment of an order of relations, a structure. . . ."[6] Economics deals with "short-term allocative behavior (i.e., holding institutions, fundamental assumptions, and expectations constant). . . ."[7] Like Kindleberger's definition, however, this definition tends to isolate economic and political phenomena except under certain conditions, which Keohane and Nye define as the "politicization" of the economic system. Neither formulation comes to terms adequately with the dynamic and intimate nature of the relationship between the two.

In this study, the issue of the relationship between economics and politics translates into that between wealth and power. According to this statement of the problem, economics takes as its province the creation and distribution of wealth; politics is the realm of power. I shall examine their relationship from several ideological perspectives, including my own. But what is wealth? What is power?

In response to the question, What is wealth?, an economist-colleague responded, "What do you want, my thirty-second or thirty-volume answer?" Basic concepts are elusive in economics, as in any field of inquiry. No unchallengeable definitions are possible. Ask a physicist for his definition of the nature of space, time, and matter, and you will not get a very satisfying response. What you will get is an *operational* definition, one which is usable: it permits the physicist to build an intellectual edifice whose foundations would crumble under the scrutiny of the philosopher.

Similarly, the concept of wealth, upon which the science of economics ultimately rests, cannot be clarified in a definitive way. Paul Samuelson, in his textbook, doesn't even try, though he provides a clue in his definition of economics as "the study of how men and society *choose* . . . to employ *scarce* productive resources . . . to produce various commodities . . . and distribute them for consumption."[8] Following this lead, we can say that wealth is anything (capital, land, or labor) that can generate future income; it is composed of physical assets and human capital (including embodied knowledge).

The basic concept of political science is power. Most political scientists would not stop here; they would include in the definition of political science the purpose for which power is used, whether this be the advancement of the public welfare or the domination of one group over another. In any case, few would dissent from the following statement of Harold Lasswell and Abraham Kaplan:

> The concept of power is perhaps the most fundamental in the whole of political science: the political process is the shaping, distribution, and exercise of power (in a wider sense, of all the deference values, or of influence in general.)[9]

Power as such is not the sole or even the principal goal of state behavior. Other goals or values constitute the objectives pursued by nation-states: welfare, security, prestige. But power in its several forms (military, economic, psychological) is ultimately the necessary means to achieve these goals. For this reason, nation-states are intensely jealous of and sensitive to their relative power position. The distribution of power is important because it profoundly affects the ability of states to achieve what they perceive to be their interests.

The nature of power, however, is even more elusive than that of wealth. The number and variety of definitions should be an embarrassment to political scientists. Unfortunately, this study cannot bring the intradisciplinary squabble to an end. Rather, it adopts the definition used by Hans Morgenthau in his influential *Politics among Nations*: "man's control over the minds and actions of other men."[10] Thus, power, like wealth, is the capacity to produce certain results.

Unlike wealth, however, power can not be quantified; indeed, it cannot be overemphasized that power has an important psychological dimension. Perceptions of power relations are of critical importance; as a consequence, a fundamental task of statesmen is to manipulate the perceptions of other statesmen regarding the distribution of power. Moreover, power is relative to a specific situation or set of circumstances; there is no single hierarchy of power in international relations. Power may take many forms— military, economic, or psychological—though, in the final analysis, force is the ultimate form of power. Finally, the inability to predict the behavior of others or the outcome of events is of great significance. Uncertainty regarding the distribution of power and the ability of the statesmen to control events plays an important role in international relations. Ultimately, the determination of the distribution of power can be made only in retrospect as a consequence of war. It is precisely for this reason that war has had, unfortunately, such a central place in the history of international relations. In short, power is an elusive concept indeed upon which to erect a science of politics.

* * *

The distinction * * * between economics as the science of wealth and politics as the science of power is essentially an analytical one. In the real world, wealth and power are ultimately joined.

This, in fact, is the basic rationale for a political economy of international relations. But in order to develop the argument of this study, wealth and power will be treated, at least for the moment, as analytically distinct.

To provide a perspective on the nature of political economy, the next section of the chapter will discuss the three prevailing conceptions of political economy: liberalism, Marxism, and mercantilism. Liberalism regards politics and economics as relatively separable and autonomous spheres of activities; I associate most professional economists as well as many other academics, businessmen, and American officials with this outlook. Marxism refers to the radical critique of capitalism identified with Karl Marx and his contemporary disciples; according to this conception, economics determines politics and political structure. Mercantilism is a more questionable term because of its historical association with the desire of nation-states for a trade surplus and for treasure (money). One must distinguish, however, between the specific form mercantilism took in the seventeenth and eighteenth centuries and the general outlook of mercantilistic thought. The essence of the mercantilistic perspective, whether it is labeled economic nationalism, protectionism, or the doctrine of the German Historical School, is the subservience of the economy to the state and its interests—interests that range from matters of domestic welfare to those of international security. It is this more general meaning of mercantilism that is implied by the use of the term in this study.

* * *

Three Conceptions of Political Economy

The three prevailing conceptions of political economy differ on many points. Several critical differences will be examined in this brief comparison. (See Table 9.1.)

TABLE 9.1			
COMPARISON OF THE THREE CONCEPTIONS OF POLITICAL ECONOMY			
	Liberalism	*Marxism*	*Mercantilism*
Nature of economic relations	Harmonious	Conflictual	Conflictual
Nature of the actors	Households and firms	Economic classes	Nation-states
Goal of economic activity	Maximization of global welfare	Maximization of class interests	Maximization of national interest
Relationship between economics and politics	Economics *should* determine politics	Economics *does* determine politics	Politics determines economics
Theory of change	Dynamic equilibrium	Tendency toward disequilibrium	Shifts in the distribution of power

The Nature of Economic Relations

The basic assumption of liberalism is that the nature of international economic relations is essentially harmonious. Herein lay the great intellectual innovation of Adam Smith. Disputing his mercantilist·predecessors, Smith argued that international economic relations could be made a positive-sum game; that is to say, everyone could gain, and no one need lose, from a proper ordering of economic relations, albeit the distribution of these gains may not be equal. Following Smith, liberalism assumes that there is a basic harmony between true national interest and cosmopolitan economic interest. Thus, a prominent member of this school of thought has written, in response to a radical critique, that the economic efficiency of the sterling standard in the nineteenth century and that of the dollar standard in the twentieth century serve "the cosmopolitan interest in a national form."[11] Although Great Britain and the United States gained the most from the international role of their respective currencies, everyone else gained as well.

Liberals argue that, given this underlying identity of national and cosmopolitan interests in a free market, the state should not interfere with economic transactions across national boundaries. Through free exchange of commodities, removal of restrictions on the flow of investment, and an international division of labor, everyone will benefit in the long run as a result of a more efficient utilization of the world's scarce resources. The national interest is therefore best served, liberals maintain, by a generous and cooperative attitude regarding economic relations with other countries. In essence, the pursuit of self-interest in a free, competitive economy achieves the greatest good for the greatest number in international no less than in the national society.

Both mercantilists and Marxists, on the other hand, begin with the premise that the essence of economic relations is conflictual. There is no underlying harmony; indeed, one group's gain is another's loss. Thus, in the language of game theory, whereas liberals regard economic relations as a nonzero-sum game, Marxists and mercantilists view economic relations as essentially a zero-sum game.

The Goal of Economic Activity

For the liberal, the goal of economic activity is the optimum or efficient use of the world's scarce resources and the maximization of world welfare. While most liberals refuse to make value judgments regarding income distribution, Marxists and mercantilists stress the distributive effects of economic relations. For the Marxist the distribution of wealth among social classess is central; for the mercantilist it is the distribution of employment, industry, and military power among nation-states that is most significant Thus, the goal of economic (and political) activity for both Marxists and mercantilists is the redistribution of wealth and power.

The State and Public Policy

These three perspectives differ decisively in their views regarding the nature of the economic actors. In Marxist analysis, the basic actors in both domestic and international relations are economic classes; the interests of the dominant class determine the foreign policy of the state. For mercantilists, the real actors in international economic relations are nation-states; national interest determines foreign policy. National interest may at times be influenced by the peculiar economic interests of classes, elites, or other subgroups of the society; but factors of geography, external configurations of power, and the exigencies of national survival are primary in determining foreign policy. Thus, whereas liberals speak of world welfare and Marxists of class interests, mercantilists recognize only the interests of particular nation-states.

Although liberal economists such as David Ricardo and Joseph Schumpeter recognized the importance of class conflict and neoclassical liberals analyze economic growth and policy in terms of national economies, the liberal emphasis is on the individual consumer, firm, or entrepreneur. The liberal ideal is summarized in the view of Harry Johnson that the nation-state has no meaning as an economic entity.[12]

Underlying these contrasting views are differing conceptions of the nature of the state and public policy. For liberals, the state represents an aggregation of private interests: public policy is but the outcome of a pluralistic struggle among interest groups. Marxists, on the other hand, regard the state as simply the "executive committee of the ruling class," and public policy reflects its interests. Mercantilists, however, regard the state as an organic unit in its own right: the whole is greater than the sum of its parts. Public policy, therefore, embodies the national interest or Rousseau's "general will" as conceived by the political élite.

The Relationship between Economics and Politics; Theories of Change

Liberalism, Marxism, and mercantilism also have differing views on the relationship between economics and politics. And their differences on this issue are directly relevant to their contrasting theories of international political change.

Although the liberal ideal is the separation of economics from politics in the interest of maximizing world welfare, the fulfillment of this ideal would have important political implications. The classical statement of these implications was that of Adam Smith in *The Wealth of Nations*.[13] Economic growth, Smith argued, is primarily a function of the extent of the division of labor, which in turn is dependent upon the scale of the market. Thus he attacked the barriers erected by feudal principalities and mercantilistic states against the exchange of goods and the enlargement of markets. If men were to multiply their wealth, Smith argued, the contradiction between political organization and economic rationality had to be resolved in favor of the latter. That is, the pursuit of wealth should determine the nature of the political order.

Subsequently, from nineteenth-century economic liberals to twentieth-century writers on economic integration, there has existed "the dream . . . of a great republic of world commerce, in which national boundaries would cease to have any great economic importance and the web of trade would bind all the people of the world in the prosperity of peace."[14] For liberals the long-term trend is toward world integration, wherein functions, authority, and loyalties will be transferred from "smaller units to larger ones; from states to federalism; from federalism to supranational unions and from these to superstates."[15] The logic of economic and technological development, it is argued, has set mankind on an inexorable course toward global political unification and world peace.

In Marxism, the concept of the contradiction between economic and political relations was enacted into historical law. Whereas classical liberals—although Smith less than others—held that the requirements of economic rationality *ought* to determine political relations, the Marxist position was that the mode of production does in fact determine the superstructure of political relations. Therefore, it is argued, history can be understood as the product of the dialectical process—the contradiction between the evolving techniques of production and the resistant sociopolitical system.

Although Marx and Engels wrote remarkably little on international economics, Engels, in his famous polemic, *Anti-Duhring*, explicitly considers whether economics or politics is primary in determining the structure of international relations.[16] E. K. Duhring, a minor figure in the German Historical School, had argued, in contradiction to Marxism, that property and market relations resulted less from the economic logic of capitalism than from extraeconomic political factors: "The basis of the exploitation of man by man was an historical act of force which created an exploitative economic system for the benefit of the stronger man or class."[17] Since Engels, in his attack on Duhring, used the example of the unification of Germany through the Zollverein or customs union of 1833, his analysis is directly relevant to this discussion of the relationship between economics and political organization.

Engels argued that when contradictions arise between economic and political structures, political power adapts itself to the changes in the balance of economic forces; politics yields to the dictates of economic development. Thus, in the case of nineteenth-century Germany, the requirements of industrial production had become incompatible with its feudal, politically fragmented structure. "Though political reaction was victorious in 1815 and again in 1848," he argued, "it was unable to prevent the growth of large-

scale industry in Germany and the growing participation of German commerce in the world market."[18] In summary, Engels wrote, "German unity had become an economic necessity."[19]

In the view of both Smith and Engels, the nation-state represented a progressive stage in human development, because it enlarged the political realm of economic activity. In each successive economic epoch, advances in technology and an increasing scale of production necessitate an enlargement of political organization. Because the city-state and feudalism restricted the scale of production and the division of labor made possible by the Industrial Revolution, they prevented the efficient utilization of resources and were, therefore, superseded by larger political units. Smith considered this to be a desirable objective; for Engels it was an historical necessity. Thus, in the opinion of liberals, the establishment of the Zollverein was a movement toward maximizing world economic welfare;[20] for Marxists it was the unavoidable triumph of the German industrialists over the feudal aristocracy.

Mercantilist writers from Alexander Hamilton to Frederich List to Charles de Gaulle, on the other hand, have emphasized the primacy of politics; politics, in this view, determines economic organization. Whereas Marxists and liberals have pointed to the production of wealth as the basic determinant of social and political organization, the mercantilists of the German Historical School, for example, stressed the primacy of national security, industrial development, and national sentiment in international political and economic dynamics.

In response to Engels's interpretation of the unification of Germany, mercantilists would no doubt agree with Jacob Viner that "Prussia engineered the customs union primarily for political reasons, in order to gain hegemony or at least influence over the lesser German states. It was largely in order to make certain that the hegemony should be Prussian and not Austrian that Prussia continually opposed Austrian entry into the Union, either openly or by pressing for a customs union tariff lower than highly protectionist

Austria could stomach."[21] In pursuit of this strategic interest, it was "Prussian might, rather than a common zeal for political unification arising out of economic partnership, (that) . . . played the major role."[22]

In contrast to Marxism, neither liberalism nor mercantilism has a developed theory of dynamics. The basic assumption of orthodox economic analysis (liberalism) is the tendency toward equilibrium; liberalism takes for granted the existing social order and given institutions. Change is assumed to be gradual and adaptive—a continuous process of dynamic equilibrium. There is no necessary connection between such political phenomena as war and revolution and the evolution of the economic system, although they would not deny that misguided statesmen can blunder into war over economic issues or that revolutions are conflicts over the distribution of wealth; but neither is inevitably linked to the evolution of the productive system. As for mercantilism, it sees change as taking place owing to shifts in the balance of power; yet, mercantilist writers such as members of the German Historical School and contemporary political realists have not developed a systematic theory of how this shift occurs.

On the other hand, dynamics is central to Marxism; indeed Marxism is essentially a theory of social *change*. It emphasizes the tendency toward *dis*equilibrium owing to changes in the means of production, and the consequent effects on the everpresent class conflict. When these tendencies can no longer be contained, the sociopolitical system breaks down through violent upheaval. Thus war and revolution are seen as an integral part of the economic process. Politics and economics are intimately joined.

Why an International Economy?

From these differences among the three ideologies, one can get a sense of their respective explanations for the existence and functioning of the international economy.

An interdependent world economy constitutes the normal state of affairs for most liberal economists. Responding to technological advances in transportation and communications, the scope of the market mechanism, according to this analysis, continuously expands. Thus, despite temporary setbacks, the long-term trend is toward global economic integration. The functioning of the international economy is determined primarily by considerations of efficiency. The role of the dollar as the basis of the international monetary system, for example, is explained by the preference for it among traders and nations as the vehicle of international commerce.[23] The system is maintained by the mutuality of the benefits provided by trade, monetary arrangements, and investment.

A second view—one shared by Marxists and mercantilists alike—is that every interdependent international economy is essentially an imperial or hierarchical system. The imperial or hegemonic power organizes trade, monetary, and investment relations in order to advance its own economic and political interests. In the absence of the economic and especially the political influence of the hegemonic power, the system would fragment into autarkic economies or regional blocs. Whereas for liberalism maintenance of harmonious international market relations is the norm, for Marxism and mercantilism conflicts of class or national interests are the norm.

* * *

NOTES

1. Kari Levitt, "The Hinterland Economy," *Canadian Forum* 50 (July–August 1970): 163.
2. George W. Ball, "The Promise of the Multinational Corporation," *Fortune*, June 1, 1967, p. 80.
3. Sidney Rolfe, "Updating Adam Smith," *Interplay* (November 1968): 15.
4. Charles Kindleberger, *Power and Money: The Economics of International Politics and the Politics of International Economics* (New York: Basic Books, 1970), p. 5.

5. Robert Keohane and Joseph Nye, "World Politics and the International Economic System," in *The Future of the International Economic Order: An Agenda for Research*, ed. C. Fred Bergsten (Lexington, Mass.: D. C. Heath, 1973), p. 116.

6. Ibid.

7. Ibid., p. 117.

8. Paul Samuelson, *Economics: An Introductory Analysis* (New York: McGraw-Hill, 1967), p. 5.

9. Harold Lasswell and Abraham Kaplan, *Power and Society: A Framework for Political Inquiry* (New Haven: Yale University Press, 1950), p. 75.

10. Hans Morgenthau, *Politics among Nations* (New York: Alfred A. Knopf), p. 26. For a more complex but essentially identical view, see Robert Dahl, *Modern Political Analysis* (Englewood Cliffs, N.J.: Prentice-Hall, 1963).

11. Kindleberger, *Power and Money*, p. 227.

12. For Johnson's critique of economic nationalism, see Harry Johnson, ed., *Economic Nationalism in Old and New States* (Chicago: University of Chicago Press, 1967).

13. Adam Smith, *The Wealth of Nations* (New York: Modem Library, 1937).

14. J. B. Condliffe, *The Commerce of Nations* (New York: W. W. Norton, 1950), p. 136.

15. Amitai Etzioni, "The Dialectics of Supranational Unification" in *International Political Communities* (New York: Doubleday, 1966), p. 147.

16. The relevant sections appear in Ernst Wangerman, ed., *The Role of Force in History: A Study of Bismarck's Policy of Blood and Iron*, trans. Jack Cohen (New York: International Publishers, 1968).

17. Ibid., p. 12.

18. Ibid., p. 13.

19. Ibid., p. 14.

20. Gustav Stopler, *The German Economy* (New York: Harcourt, Brace and World, 1967), p. 11.

21. Jacob Viner, *The Customs Union Issue*, Studies in the Administration of International Law and Organization, no. 10 (New York: Carnegie Endowment for International Peace, 1950), pp. 98–99.

22. Ibid., p. 101.

23. Richard Cooper, "Eurodollars, Reserve Dollars, and Asymmetrics in the International Monetary System," *Journal of International Economics* 2 (September 1972): 325–44.

HELEN V. MILNER

Globalization, Development, and International Institutions: Normative and Positive Perspectives

Introduction

At the conclusion of World War II, several international institutions were created to manage the world economy and prevent another Great Depression. These institutions include the International Monetary Fund (IMF), the International Bank for Reconstruction and Development (now called the World Bank), and the General Agreement on Tariffs and Trade (GATT), which was expanded and institutionalized into the World Trade Organization (WTO) in 1995. These institutions have not only persisted for over five decades, but they have also expanded their mandates, changed their missions, and increased their membership. They have, however, become highly contested. As Stiglitz notes, "International bureaucrats—the faceless symbols of the world economic order—are under attack everywhere. . . . Virtually every major meeting of the International Monetary Fund, the World Bank and the World Trade Organization is now the scene of conflict and turmoil."[1]

Their critics come from both the left and right wings of the political spectrum. Anti-globalization forces from the left see them as instruments for the domination of the developing countries by both the rich countries or the forces of international capitalism. Critics from the right view these institutions as usurping the role of the market

From *Perspectives on Politics* 3, no. 4 (Dec. 2005): 833–854. Some of the author's notes have been omitted.

and easing pressures on developing states to adopt efficient, market-promoting policies. These debates often occur in a highly ideological and polemical fashion; they would benefit from being more informed by social science. By reviewing some of the recent social science literature, this essay addresses three questions: what has been the impact of these institutions on the developing countries, why have they had this impact, and what should be their role in the development process.

Conventional wisdom in international and comparative political economy has held that international institutions, like the IMF, World Bank, and WTO (and its predecessor, the GATT), have been largely beneficial for the countries in them. These institutions, it is claimed, constrain the behavior of the most powerful countries and provide information and monitoring capacities that enable states to cooperate.[2] All states involved are better off with these institutions than otherwise. Recently, however, evidence has mounted that these institutions may not be so beneficial for the developing countries.

Discerning the impact of these institutions requires that one address difficult counterfactual questions.[3] Would the developing countries have been better off if these institutions had not existed? Would resources for aid and crisis management have been as plentiful or more so if they had not existed? Would globalization have occurred as fast and extensively, or even faster and deeper, if these international institutions had not been present? Counterfactuals cannot be answered directly because they presume a situation which did not occur and rely on speculation about what this hypothetical world would have been like.[4] Researchers can only make indirect counterfactual speculations. First, longitudinal comparison asks whether a developing country performed as well before it joined the institution (or participated in its programs) as after it did so. This enables the researcher to hold constant many characteristics of the country that do not change over time. Second, cross-sectional comparison asks if countries belonging to the institution (or participating in its programs) fare better or worse than those countries who do not. These comparisons are usually not enough. Part of the problem of knowing what the "right" counterfactual is depends on why countries join. Selection bias arises if the countries are joining or participating for nonrandom reasons which are not held constant. If countries choose to participate only under certain conditions, then the counterfactual experiment must correct for this or its results are likely to be biased. Because selection bias can arise from both observed and unobserved factors, correcting for selection effects is not straightforward. Little of the research on these international institutions addresses all of these methodological issues.

Assessing the impact of these institutions involves addressing this counterfactual. But recent normative scholarship claims that answering this counterfactual is not enough for assessing their role. It proposes different standards for evaluation and raises the contentious question of what standard one should use to assess the responsibility of these institutions for the developing countries. This debate involves the extent of moral obligations that the rich countries and the institutions they created have regarding the poor countries, ranging from a limited "duty of assistance" to a cosmopolitan striving for equality. Combining normative and empirical scholarship may be unusual, but it may be fruitful. As Beitz claims, "reflection about reform of global governance is well advanced in other venues, both academic and political, almost never with the benefit of the moral clarity that might be contributed by an articulate philosophical conception of global political justice."[5]

* * *

The Role of the International Economic Institutions

The roles of the three main institutions have changed over time; in addition, their membership has become nearly universal. All of these institutions were created by the victors in World War II and were intended to help them avoid another global depression. Part of the problem for these institutions lies in their legacy. They were designed to help the developed countries create a cooperative and stable world economy in a nonglobalized world.

The IMF was established to support the fixed exchange rate system created at the Bretton Woods Conference in 1944; its role was to aid countries that were experiencing difficulties in maintaining their fixed exchange rate by providing them with short term loans. It was a lender of last resort and a provider of funds in crisis, enabling countries to avoid competitive devaluations. Ensuring a stable international monetary system to promote trade and growth was its central mission. From an initial membership of 29 countries, it has become almost universal with 184 members.

With the collapse of the Bretton Woods fixed exchange rate system in the early 1970s, this role changed. The IMF dealt less with the developed countries and more with the developing ones. It provided long and short term loans at below-market interest rates for countries in all sorts of economic difficulty, making it less distinct from the World Bank. It began attaching increasing numbers of conditions to those loans ("conditionality"), negotiating with countries to make major changes in their domestic policies and institutions. Promoting economic growth as well as resolving specific crises became its mission, which meant that ever more countries became involved in these so-called structural adjustment programs. Indeed, as Vreeland notes, in 2000 alone the IMF had programs with sixty countries, or more than one-third of the developing world. These changes made the IMF more similar to the World Bank.

Formed after World War II, the Bank concentrated mostly on reconstruction and later on development; in 1960, with the formation of the International Development Association (IDA), the Bank moved further toward economic development programs.[6] Many countries over the years have received both IMF and World Bank loans, often simultaneously.[7] The World Bank also gives interest-free loans and grants (similar to foreign aid) to the poorest developing countries. This aid has been heavily used in Africa; indeed, in 2003, 51 percent of it went to sub-Saharan Africa. This overlap of missions, proliferation of adjustment loans, and expansion of conditionality are central issues today.

The WTO's central mission has been to promote trade liberalization by fostering negotiations among countries to reciprocally lower their trade barriers and providing information about countries' trade policies. Membership in the GATT/WTO has grown importantly over the years, from a mere 23 in 1947 to 146 countries in 2003.[8] Like the IMF and World Bank, the GATT was originally a negotiating forum for the developed countries; its impact on the developing countries has grown slowly over time. The liberalization of trade policy has become an accepted doctrine for most developing countries; barriers in the developing world have fallen significantly since 1980.[9] In addition, the WTO's mission has increasingly involved the connections between domestic policies and trade barriers. With significant lowering of tariffs and quotas, many domestic policies such as intellectual property laws, environmental policy, domestic subsidies, and tax laws, are now seen to affect trade flows

and hence to reside within the WTO's jurisdiction. As with conditionality in the monetary domain, the attack on trade barriers has increasingly brought this international institution into contact with domestic politics.

The GATT/WTO system has sponsored numerous trade negotiation rounds over the past fifty years. The most recently concluded negotiations, called the Uruguay Round, ended in late 1994 with the debut of the WTO and accords lowering trade barriers and extending agreements into other areas such as intellectual property and foreign investment. This system relies on reciprocity, attempting to balance countries' gains and losses. The WTO is now conducting the new Doha Round of trade negotiations, which is intended to address the problems of the developing countries more directly.

The Experience of the Developing Countries

Debate over these institutions has arisen from the seeming lack of progress in the developing world. Except for the World Bank, the original and primary mission of these institutions was not promoting growth in the developing world. Nevertheless, since the change in their roles from the 1970s onward, they have increasingly been judged by their impact on the poor. Fairly or not, the question has been whether these institutions have fostered development.[10]

Each of these institutions has promoted the adoption of market-friendly policies, and part of the reaction against them has been connected to these policies. "The widespread recourse of indebted developing countries to structural adjustment loans from the Bretton Woods institutions in the aftermath of the debt crisis of the early 1980s played a pivotal role in the redefinition of trade and industrialization strategies. Prominent among the conditions attached to these loans was the liberalization of policies towards trade and FDI (foreign direct investment). This was in line with the rising influence of pro-market economic doctrines during this period. Under these structural adjustment programs, there was a significant increase in the number of cases of trade and investment liberalization in many developing countries."[11]

But concerns abound over whether trade and capital market liberalization, privatization, deregulation, austerity, and the other elements of the so-called Washington Consensus that these institutions advocated promote development in poor countries. If one looks solely at the economic side, progress has been mixed in many developing countries. As Easterly concludes, "there was much lending, little adjustment, and little growth in the 1980s and 1990s" in the developing world.[12] Annual per capita growth for the developing countries averaged 0 percent for the years from 1980 to 1998, whereas from 1960–1979 their growth had averaged about 2.5 percent annually.[13] Poverty remains very high, with roughly 20 percent of the world's population living on less than a dollar a day and more than 45 percent on less than two dollars a day.[14] Because of these conditions, some 18 million people a year die of easily preventable causes, many of them children.[15] A sizable number of these countries were worse off economically in 2000 than they were in the 1980. World Bank data indicate, for instance, that per capita income was lower in 1999 in at least nine countries (for which we have data) than in 1960: Haiti, Nicaragua, Central African Republic, Chad, Ghana, Madagascar, Niger, Rwanda, and Zambia.[16] From 1980 to 2002, twenty countries experienced a decrease in their human development indexes, which include more than just economic growth.[17]

Since 1980 the world's poorest countries have done worse economically than the richest.[18] In the 1980s the high income countries of the Organisation for Economic Co-operation and Development (OECD) grew at 2.5 percent annually and in the 1990s at 1.8 percent; the developing countries grew at 0.7 percent and 1.7 percent, respectively.[19] Moreover, if one excludes East Asia where the growth was extraordinary (5.6 percent in the 1980s and 6.4 percent in the 1990s), the developing countries grew much more slowly than the developed ones. Thus, they have been falling further behind the rich countries, increasing the gap between the two. As Lant Pritchett has shown, over the period 1820 to 1992 the divergence in incomes between the world's rich and poor has grown enormously.[20] In 1820 the richest country had three times the income that the poorest did; in the early 1990s this number was thirty.[21] Much of this divergence is due to the rich countries' rapid growth.[22]

Economic crises among the developing countries have also proliferated after the 1970s. In addition, the debt problems of many developing countries have increased. "Total debt of developing countries increased until 1999 and then stabilized at about $3 trillion as of last year [that is, 2003]. Furthermore, while debt has declined as a proportion of GDP, it remains high at some 40 percent, and the ratio of debt to exports at 113 percent. More importantly, the net resource transfer—the resources available for use after paying interest—has been negative in recent years for all regions. These magnitudes suggest that it is difficult to consider current levels of debt sustainable and helping growth."[23]

The performance of the developing countries has not been uniformly poor, however. From 1960 to 2000, life expectancy increased from 46 to 63 years in the developing world. Child mortality rates were halved in the same period, as were illiteracy rates.[24] Poverty as a percentage of the developing countries' populations has declined recently.[25] Including China, where the declines have been enormous, the percentage of people in the developing countries living on the poverty threshold of $1 a day has fallen from over 28 percent in 1990 to below 22 percent in 2000.[26] The percentage living on $2 a day in the developing world also fell from 61 percent to 54 percent in this period.[27] Unfortunately, the absolute numbers of the desperately poor have not fallen much, if at all, because of high growth population rates.[28]

The developing countries have also upgraded their role in the world economy. They now are producers and exporters of manufactures and not primarily of primary products. In 2000, about 64 percent of low and middle income countries' exports were manufactures, while only 10 percent were agriculture, and their share of world trade in manufactures rose over this period from 9 percent to 26 percent.[29] Especially in East and South Asia, the developing economies have become tightly integrated into the world production and trading system led by multinational corporations. This increase in the value-added and the diversification of developing countries' production and trade has been a boon for many.

This mixed record of economic outcomes has raised questions about the impact of these international economic institutions. But one must pose the counterfactual to assess their impact: would the performance of these countries have been better, the same, or even worse had these institutions not existed?

Theories about the Functions and Benefits of International Institutions

Many international relations scholars have argued that countries should benefit from these institutions. States rationally decide to join them; therefore, they join only if the net benefits are greater than those offered by staying out of the organization. Membership is voluntary. The net utility derived from joining could be negative, but less negative than that incurred by remaining outside the institution. As Gruber has argued, if the most powerful states define the alternatives open to the developing countries and set up multilateral institutions, the developing countries can be better off by joining them than staying outside, but worse off than if the institutions never existed.[30] The rush lately by all countries to join these institutions suggests that developing countries have found them to be more beneficial than the alternative of staying out, but it

does not moot the question of whether they would be better of without any of these multilateral institutions in the first place. Four reasons are often theorized for the existence of these institutions: (1) constraining the great powers, (2) providing information and reducing transaction costs, (3) facilitating reciprocity, and (4) promoting reform in domestic politics.

Constraining the Great Powers

International institutions may exert a constraint on the underlying anarchy of the international system. They make the use of force and power by states to achieve their goals less likely; the rules, norms, and procedures established by these institutions replace to some extent the pursuit of national interest by power. Most importantly, as Ikenberry claims, they help to harness the behavior of the most powerful states.[31] By creating and complying with these institutions, the Great Powers, or hegemon, can reassure other states that they will not take advantage of them. The strongest bind themselves to a set of norms and rules that the other states voluntarily agree to accept.

Evidence for this effect is mixed. As the WTO points out, "trade is likely to expand and be more profitable under conditions of certainty and security as to the terms of market access and the rules of trade—precommitment around a set of rules also diminishes the role of power and size in determining outcomes."[32] This motivation is important in trade where countries with large markets, and hence market power, can use this to obtain more favorable trading arrangements in bilateral negotiations with smaller countries.

Nevertheless, critics maintain that developing countries have not gained much from the GATT trade rounds; most of the gains have gone to developed countries. Some scholars even allege that the trade rounds have allowed the developed countries to exploit the developing ones by engaging them in unfair agreements. As Stiglitz says, "previous rounds of trade negotiations [in the GATT/

WTO] had protected the interests of the advanced industrial countries—or more accurately, special interests within those countries—without concomitant benefits for the lesser developed countries."[33] The unbalanced outcome of the recent Uruguay trade round is an important issue. "Several computable general equilibrium models have shown that the Uruguay Round results disproportionately benefit developed country gross domestic products (GDPs) compared to developing countries, and that some developing countries would actually suffer a net GDP loss from the Uruguay Round—at least in the short run."[34]

Developing countries have raised concerns about the equity of the outcome of this and other rounds. "With hindsight, many developing country governments perceived the outcome of the Uruguay Round to have been unbalanced. For most developing countries (some did gain), the crux of the unfavourable deal was the limited market access concessions they obtained from developed countries in exchange for the high costs they now realize they incurred in binding themselves to the new multilateral trade rules."[35] Others note that asymmetric outcomes are an intrinsic part of the GATT/WTO bargaining process. "[Trade] rounds have been concluded through power-based bargaining that has yielded asymmetrical contracts favoring the interests of powerful states. The agenda-setting process (the formulation of proposals that are difficult to amend), which takes place between launch and conclusion, has been dominated by powerful states; the extent of that domination has depended upon the extent to which powerful countries have planned to use their power to conclude the round."[36]

The counterfactual one must pose is the following: without the GATT or WTO would the developing countries be better off if they had to negotiate bilaterally with the large, rich countries? Multilateralism seems well suited to giving the developing countries a better outcome than would such bilateral negotiations.[37] "Multilateralism ensures transparency, and provides protection—however inadequate—against the asymmetries of power and influence in the international community."[38] It may not only place some constraints on the behavior of the large, developed countries, but it may also encourage developing countries to realize their common interests and counterbalance the rich countries. By giving them more political voice than otherwise, institutions like the WTO may enhance their capacity to influence outcomes.

Evidence of the constraining power of the IMF or World Bank is less apparent. Decisions in the IMF and World Bank are taken by weighted voting, with the rich countries—and especially the United States—having the lion's share of votes. Since the end of the fixed exchange rate system in the early 1970s, these institutions have basically collected funds from the developed countries and private capital markets to give to the developing ones under increasing conditions. Conditionality has been designed by these institutions with the tacit support of the developed countries, and it has been negotiated with the poor ones. Since the late 1970s few, if any, developed countries have not been subject to IMF programs; only the developing world has. Article IV of the IMF charter requires surveillance of all members and discussion of the problems in their fiscal and monetary policies, but since the late 1970s, de facto this has not applied to the developed countries.[39] The IMF has remarked on its own inefficacy: "Nowhere is the difficulty of conducting surveillance more apparent than in the relations between the IMF and the major industrial countries. Effective oversight over the policies of the largest countries is obviously essential if surveillance is to be uniform and symmetric across the membership, but progress in achieving that goal has been slow and hesitant."[40] It is difficult to argue that the IMF and World Bank constrain the exercise of power by the developed countries. Indeed, these multilateral institutions may enhance the capacity of the rich countries to collectively enforce their will on the poor countries, as Rodrik argues.[41]

Does their existence change the behavior of the rich? Without the two institutions, would the developed countries lend or donate as much as they do now? Does multilateral lending and aid substitute for or complement bilateral giving? Would the least well-off and the most politically insignificant countries be left to fend for themselves if they ran into economic crises, should the World Bank and IMF not exist? And would the terms of any aid or loans given bilaterally be worse for these countries than they are now? Evidence exists that bilateral aid tends to be more oriented toward the political and economic interests of donors than is multilateral aid.[42] Some critics of the IMF and World Bank claim that countries would experience fewer crises since they would be more attentive to their financial situation in the absence of the moral hazard presented by the existence of these multilateral organizations.[43] Others scholars have demonstrated that the distribution of aid and loans even with these institutions is weighted toward the economically better off and the politically more important developing countries.[44] For instance, Stone shows that in lending to the transition countries the IMF gave more and imposed lighter conditions on those states with stronger political ties to the United States.[45] Further, he shows how this political process undermines the credibility of the IMF's position and induces the recipient countries to ignore its conditionality. His research, however, does not really address the question of whether the IMF's presence affected the overall amount of lending or the allocation of those loans, relative to a situation where the Fund did not exist. These counterfactuals are essential for addressing questions about these multilateral institutions, but they are difficult to assess.

Providing Information and Reducing Transaction Costs

Following New Institutionalism theories, some argue that a major reason for these institutions is the lowering of transaction costs and the provision of information to facilitate multilateral cooperation in an anarchic world. As Keohane writes, international institutions "facilitate agreements by raising the anticipated costs of violating others' property rights, by altering transaction costs through clustering of issues, and by providing reliable information to members. [They] are relatively efficient institutions, compared to the alternative of having a myriad of unrelated agreements, since their principles, rules, and institutions create linkages among issues that give actors incentives to reach mutually beneficial agreements."[46] For him, international institutions also reduce uncertainty by monitoring the member states' behavior and allowing decentralized enforcement through reciprocity strategies.[47]

Scholars such as Anne Krueger have suggested just such an informational role for the IMF and World Bank.[48] Surveying and reporting on the policy behavior of member countries, providing information about the likelihood of crises, and being a repository of expert information are key roles for these institutions. The Meltzer Commission also emphasizes this role, and the most severe critics on the right imply that the IMF and World Bank should give up all roles except monitoring and providing expert information to member states. Others have noted the expertise role of the IFIs. "The World Bank is widely recognized to have exercised power over development policies far greater than its budget, as a percentage of North/South aid flows, would suggest because of the expertise it houses. . . . This expertise, coupled with its claim to "neutrality" and its "apolitical" technocratic decision-making style, have given the World Bank an authoritative voice with which it has successfully dictated the content, direction, and scope of global development over the past fifty years."[49]

The WTO has also been seen as an information-provision institution. It monitors and reports on the compliance of states with the commitments they have made to each other. This task reassures other member countries and domestic publics about the behavior of their political leaders, making cooperation more likely and sustainable.[50]

Informational arguments suggest that all states gain from participation in such institutions.[51] This mutual gain explains the voluntary participation of states in these multilateral forums. The expectation would be that developing countries join largely for these informational benefits, but there remains the issue of who provides what information for whose benefit. Are the developing countries providing more information than otherwise? Are the principal beneficiaries private investors in the developing countries or in the developed world, other domestic groups, or the institutions themselves? Do the IMF and World Bank provide developing countries with useful information about other members or with expertise that would otherwise be unavailable? These empirical questions have not been examined much.

One central complaint against the IMF and World Bank is that the policy advice they give (especially the "Washington Consensus" advice) has been unhelpful, if not detrimental, since it failed to take into account the circumstances of the developing countries.[52] The claim is that the policy expertise given (or imposed via conditionality) has not been beneficial. For instance, Stiglitz, Bhagwati, and others have all criticized the IMF for pushing the developing countries into opening their capital markets.[53] They have argued that little, if any, economic evidence or theory supports this, the consequences have been negative for most countries, and the main beneficiaries have been private investors in the developed world. As Stiglitz writes, "the [main] problem is that the IMF (and sometimes the other international economic organizations) presents as received doctrines propositions and policy recommendations for which there is not widespread agreement; indeed, in the case of capital market liberalization, there was scant evidence in support and a massive amount of evidence against."[54] Even the advice to open their economies to

trade has not been unquestioned. Economic analysis shows that the impact of trade openness on economic growth can be positive but also insignificant.[55]

Easterly's book is also an indictment of the economic policy prescriptions of the Bank and Fund. Each chapter shows how the prevailing wisdom guiding economic policy prescriptions in the IFIs has either been proven wrong or never been attempted to be proven right or wrong. As he concludes, "in part II, we saw that the search for a magic formula to turn poverty into prosperity failed . . . Growth failed to respond to any of these formulas . . ."[56]

Vreeland's book supports these claims about the failed policy advice of the IMF. His research shows that IMF programs lower economic growth and redistribute income away from the most needy; the impact of conditionality is to retard development. As he concludes, this result means that either the IMF's policy prescriptions are incorrect or economic growth and poverty reduction are not the goals of the IMF. Stone's findings counter these; he shows that IMF programs do reduce inflation and return greater macroeconomic stability but only when they are not interfered with by political factors. Thus, even the informational value of the international institutions has been questioned.

Facilitating Reciprocity

International institutions facilitate reciprocity strategies among countries in an anarchic environment. Cooperation in anarchy relies on reciprocity, but more cooperation can be sustained if it need not require simultaneous and perfectly balanced exchanges. "International regimes can be thought of in part as arrangements that facilitate nonsimultaneous exchange."[57] Bagwell and Staiger have developed the most rigorous claims about the importance of reciprocity for the international trading system.[58] If countries are sizable economic actors in world markets, then they can use trade policy to manipulate their terms of trade and gain advantages over their trading partners. If these big countries set trade policy unilaterally, they will arrive at an inefficient outcome, sacrificing the gains to be had from mutual trade liberalization. Reciprocity enhanced by the WTO's rules and monitoring can provide a context in which these big countries can achieve more efficient, cooperative outcomes. The main function of international institutions is to make reciprocity credible and feasible.

In the case of the large, rich countries in world trade this motivation seems apparent. The United States, European Union and Japan have used the GATT/WTO to enforce reciprocity strategies and lower their trade barriers. However, there is little evidence that this reciprocity has extended to the developing world. Many developing countries did not join the WTO until recently; most of the developing country members did not reciprocally liberalize their trade in the trade rounds.

> In the period until the launch of the Uruguay Round and the formation of the WTO, only the industrial countries were meaningful participants in multilateral trade negotiations. They bargained amongst themselves to reduce trade barriers, while developing countries were largely out of this process and had few obligations to liberalize. The latter availed themselves of the benefits of industrial country liberalization, courtesy of the Most Favored Nation (MFN) principle, but that defined pretty much the limits of their contribution to or benefits from the General Agreement on Tariffs and Trade (GATT). Industrial countries were content with this arrangement, in part because it alleviated the pressure on them to liberalize sensitive sectors such as agriculture and clothing, but perhaps more importantly because the markets of developing countries were not at that stage sufficiently attractive.[59]

This situation is not unexpected. Theories about the value of reciprocity in trade depend on the assumption that the country is a large trader (that is, it can affect prices); for most developing countries, this is not a realistic assumption.[60] "Countries with small markets are just not attractive enough for larger trading partners to engage in meaningful reciprocity negotiations."[61] The 100 largest developing countries (excluding the transition economies) accounted for 29 percent of total world exports in 2003; the United States alone accounted for 10 percent, the EU (excluding intra-EU trade) for 15 percent and Japan for 6.5 percent.[62]

In addition, many of the developing countries received preferential access to developed countries' markets, as noted above. Ironically, this access has reduced their interest in reciprocal multilateral liberalization since it simply reduces their preference margins.[63] "The problem with granting preferential access in goods trade as the payoff to small and poor countries is that it is counterproductive and even perverse. Although preferential access does provide rents in the short run, the empirical evidence suggests that preferences do not provide a basis for sustaining long-run growth.[64] In addition, preferences create an incentive for recipients to have more protectionist regimes.[65] For most of the developing world then, ensuring reciprocity has not been a main function of the trade regime.[66]

Facilitating Reform in Domestic Politics

Some scholars have speculated that joining an international institution and publicly agreeing to abide by its rules, norms, and practices has important domestic political consequences. It can help domestic leaders to alter policies at home that they otherwise would not be able to do. It can help them lock in "good" policies (that is, ones that enhance general welfare) and resist pressures by special interests to adopt "bad" policies (that is, ones that benefit special interests only). Or it can help domestic leaders to activate interest groups to counterbalance other groups' pressures and thus introduce different policies than otherwise.

Several logics exist to support these claims. For some, once leaders join an institution it becomes hard for them to violate its practices since leaders who do so tarnish their international reputations and are less capable of making new agreements; their publics lose from this and are more likely to evict the leader, making noncompliance more costly than otherwise.[67] Others argue that domestic publics receive signals from the monitoring of international institutions and that when the institution sounds a violation alarm, some domestic groups hear this and know their leaders are probably giving in to special interests and become more likely to vote them out of office.[68] For others the key is that achieving cooperative agreements with other countries brings advantages for some domestic groups that otherwise would not be involved in a change of policy; once their interests are engaged through the multilateral process, they can become strong proponents for policy change at home.[69]

Evidence for this binding effect is not extensive in the trade area. Mattoo and Subramanian, for instance, show that the poorest countries (roughly a third of all countries) have not used the WTO to make commitments. "For a vast majority of the poor and small countries, both the proportion of [tariff] bindings in the industrial sector is small and the wedge between actual and committed tariffs is large, indicating that countries have given themselves a large margin of flexibility to reverse their trade policies without facing adverse consequences in the WTO."[70]

Moreover, as others have noted, many of the developing countries chose to liberalize their trade regimes unilaterally.[71] That is, they decided to open their markets before joining the WTO; membership in the WTO was not necessary for them to liberalize. Once they liberalized, however, membership then became more important; it helped to prevent the raising of trade barriers.

The domestic political consequences of IMF and World Bank membership may be important but little research addresses this directly. Vreeland notes that countries underwent IMF programs out of choice as much as necessity.

Governments were using the IMF to produce changes in policies that they desired, but unfortunately, these changes did not produce economic growth or poverty reduction. His analysis demonstrates that the programs were used instead to promote the welfare of capital owners, who tend to be the richest groups in developing countries and thus may have further hurt developing countries. Stone's analysis also shows that compliance with the IMF has been variable, and that, especially for important borrowers, domestic binding or compliance has been low. In sum, we do not know what the overall domestic effect of IMF and World Bank membership on countries has been.

Four Sources of the Problems with International Institutions

If the WTO, IMF, and World Bank do not provide the benefits for developing countries that scholars predict they might, what could explain this? Four claims have been advanced. Some argue that these institutions have minimal impact. Others argue that they are captured by either the powerful rich countries or by private producers and investors and so do not focus on the interests of the poor countries. Finally, the problems may lie with the internal organization and dynamics of the institutions themselves and the failure of the member countries to monitor their behavior.

1. NO IMPACT It may be that these institutions had little or no impact on the developing countries. Their fate could be far more sensitive to other forces, such as globalization and domestic politics.

Because of technological innovation, reduced communications and transportation costs, and policy changes, the developing countries have been increasingly exposed to the world economy.[72] But the capacity of the IMF and World Bank has not grown proportionately, and thus, they are less able to help, especially at times of crisis. "The IFIs seek to fulfill their role of technical and financial support, but the relative size of their financing remains low. They constitute only about 19 per cent of total debt outstanding by developing countries, and only 13 per cent among middle-income countries."[73] The developing countries have thus experienced increasing globalization while the IFIs capacity has not kept up with the rising demand for funds.

The debate over the impact of globalization on the developing countries is too vast to join here, but suffice it to say that many scholars have argued that globalization is having a large effect on such countries (whether it is positive or negative is much debated).[74] Globalization, however, is not disconnected from the WTO, World Bank, and IMF. These institutions were intended to help manage the process of integrating the developing economies into the world one. Nevertheless, the larger point is that globalization may have done more to affect these countries than these international institutions.

Others have attributed the outcomes of the developing countries to their own domestic problems. Political instability, corruption, civil war, lack of the rule of law, and authoritarianism are viewed as the bigger sources of their problems. Recent research touting the importance of domestic political institutions supports this line of argument. Without institutions that protect private property rights for broad segments of the population, growth is unlikely.[75] In this view, reforming domestic institutions is a first priority to promote sustained growth.[76] To the extent that the international institutions have advanced such institutional reform, they have helped the developing world. To the degree they have permitted developing nations to avoid or postpone such domestic change, they have hurt their prospects for development. From this perspective, it is essential not to attribute too much impact to the three international economic institutions. Much as realists in international relations maintain, these institutions may be more epiphenomenal; whatever impact they have, if any, is derived from their role in some larger political or economic structure.

2. CAPTURE BY THE POWERFUL DEVELOPED COUNTRIES For many scholars, Realists and others, these institutions were created by and for the interests of the large, rich countries. They were established at American initiative during its hegemony following World War II. American and European dominance in these organizations has been sealed by their sizable market power and their de facto control over the institutions' operations. Serving the interests of the advanced industrial nations has meant either that the interests of the poor countries were at best neglected and at worst damaged. "There are thus serious problems with the current structure and processes of global governance. Foremost among these is the vast inequality in the power and capacity of different nation states. At the root of this is the inequality in the economic power of different nations. The industrialized countries have far higher per capita incomes, which translates into economic clout in negotiations to shape global governance. They are the source of much-needed markets, foreign investments, financial capital, and technology. The ownership and control of these vital assets gives them immense economic power. This creates a built-in tendency for the process of global governance to be in the interests of powerful players, especially in rich nations."[77] In this view, the international institutions have not helped much since they are oriented to promote the interests of the developed countries.

This bias operates in a number of ways in each organization. World Bank aid has been questioned. It has been heavily used in sub-Saharan Africa, but this region has done least well. Scholars have argued that this aid has been used to prop up authoritarian governments and to continue with failed policies longer than they otherwise could have.[78] The link between the amount of aid a country received and its growth rate remains disputed; many find that aid alone has no significant impact on economic growth.[79] But aid flows have not been allocated to the neediest countries. Studies show that donor interests, both economic and foreign policy ones, often dictate which countries receive what aid, and when.[80] Countries with poor governments and policies may for other reasons receive large allocations of aid; the priorities of rich donors may undermine the developmental impact of aid.

According to other scholars, policy recommendations the developing countries were given reflected the experiences and interests of the rich countries. Trade liberalization promoted by the WTO and IMF occurred too quickly and without (enough) concern for finding alternative means for the poor countries to fund their budgets and develop social safety nets. For others, the problem is more how the agenda is set and how negotiating power is distributed. In the WTO, Steinberg shows the enormous power of the rich countries. "The secretariat's bias in favor of great powers has been largely a result of who staffs it and the shadow of power under which it works. From its founding until 1999, every GATT and WTO Director-General was from Canada, Europe, or the United States, and most of the senior staff of the GATT/WTO secretariat have been nationals of powerful countries. Secretariat officials' . . . actions have usually been heavily influenced or even suggested by representatives of the most powerful states. For example . . . the package of proposals that became the basis for the final stages of negotiation in the Uruguay Round . . . was largely a collection of proposals prepared by and developed and negotiated between the EC and the United States."[81]

IMF and World Bank conditionality programs mandating capital market liberalization, privatization and governmental austerity programs often ran aground because the developing countries did not have the financial or legal institutions to support such policies. These policies might work in the context of the developed world where these institutions existed. An example of this is Russia, which Stiglitz and Stone discuss in detail. They show that American government officials pushed the IMF to loan and continue loaning large sums to Russia, that the IMF promoted policy changes that the Russian political economy could not handle, and finally

that American pressure undercut the ability of the IMF to induce Russia to reform. "The officials who applied Washington Consensus policies failed to appreciate the social context of the transition economies";[82] privatization in the absence of a legal framework of corporate governance only helped cause economic and political problems. Stone, who presents a more optimistic picture of the IMF largely because his central focus is on reducing inflation and not increasing growth or equality, shows that American influence on the IMF is pervasive and pernicious. In the Russian case, for instance, he claims that the IMF made some mistakes (for example, in advising capital market liberalization in 1996, which was pushed by the Americans) but that most of the problems came not from IMF advice but from Russia's failure to listen to the IMF. American pressure on the IMF and support for Russia were largely to blame for this outcome; Russian politicians knew that the IMF would never carry out their threats since the United States would never let them. Stone's identification of the credibility problems that big country interference with the IMF engenders is a novel and subtle mechanism for rich country influence on the developing world.

Pressure from the rich countries has been seen as causing the international institutions at times to provide unhelpful advice as well as to shift the agenda and negotiating outcomes away from those favorable to the developing world. Bhagwati notes that "the rush to abandon controls on capital flows . . . was hardly a consequence of finance ministers and other policy makers in the developing countries suddenly acknowledging the folly of their ways. It reflected instead external pressures . . . from both the IMF and the U.S. Treasury."[83] Thacker shows that the United States exerts a great deal of influence over which countries get IMF loans.[84] Countries voting similarly to the United States in the United Nations do better at the IMF. The literature on foreign aid also suggests that a country's relationship to powerful sponsors makes a difference. Countries tend to get more aid from all sources the more ties they have to powerful, rich countries, especially the once-colonial powers. Loans, aid, and advice may respond to the pressures of the most powerful developed countries, while trade agreements may promote the agendas and interests of these rich countries, but are these effects more or less likely when multilateral institutions exist than when these relations must be negotiated bilaterally?

3. CAPTURE BY PRIVATE PRODUCERS AND INVESTORS Some have argued that the mission of the WTO, IMF, and World Bank have been increasingly dominated by the interests of private producers and investors.[85] Sometimes their influence over these institutions operates through the power of the United States and European governments, and other times it operates independently or even at cross purposes from the developed countries' interests. The impression given is that these commercial and financial interests have hijacked the agenda of these institutions and have turned them into enforcers of open access to the markets of the poor countries. Furthermore, globalization has increased the influence of these private actors. "The governance structure of the global financial system has also been transformed. As private financial flows have come to dwarf official flows, the role and influence of private actors such as banks, hedge funds, equity funds and rating agencies has increased substantially. As a result, these private financial agencies now exert tremendous power over the economic policies of developing countries, especially the emerging market economies."[86]

Stiglitz claims that "financial interests have dominated the thinking at the IMF, [and] commercial interests have had an equally dominant role at the WTO."[87] Even Bhagwati, who holds one of the most positive views about globalization, indicts the "Wall Street-U.S. Treasury complex" for many of the undesirable policies promoted by the international institutions and resultant problems they created for the developing countries.[88] Is there strong evidence for this? One area that many scholars have pointed to is

the WTO's promotion of trade-related aspects of intellectual property rights (TRIPs), especially in drugs and pharmaceuticals. As Bhagwati claims, "the multinationals have, through their interest-driven lobbying, helped set the rules in the world trading, intellectual property, aid and other regimes that are occasionally harmful to the interest of the poor countries."[89] He notes that a key example of this harmful effect has been in intellectual property protection where "the pharmaceutical and software companies muscled their way into the WTO and turned it into a royalty-collection agency because the WTO can apply trade sanctions."[90] He goes on to describe how the industries lobbied to get their views onto the American trade policy agenda and then used the United States government to force this onto the WTO and the developing countries.[91]

The impact of private actors seems most well-documented in the case of the IMF. Gould's research, for example, shows that the number and nature of conditionality in the IMF have responded increasingly to private investors. Their influence has grown because such investors play such a prominent role in international financing. As she claims,

> many of the controversial changes in the terms of Fund conditionality agreements reflect the interests and preferences of supplementary financiers. The Fund often provides only a fraction of the amount of financing that a borrowing country needs in order to balance its payments that year and implement the Fund's recommended program. Both the Fund and the borrower rely (often explicitly) on outside financing to supplement the Fund's financing. This reliance gives the supplementary financiers some leverage over the design of Fund programs. The supplementary financiers, in turn, want to influence the design of Fund programs because these programs help them ensure that borrowers are using their financing in the ways they prefer.[92]

Perhaps international economic institutions like the IMF, World Bank, and WTO are a means for private actors to affect policies in the developing countries, particularly when globalization is high. Scholars "have pointed out that liberal international regimes improve the bargaining power of private investors vis-à-vis governments and other groups in society."[93] Again, the counterfactual deserves consideration: would the developing countries have been more or less subject to the pressure of private capital if these institutions had not existed?

4. INTERNAL DYSFUNCTIONS AND FAILURE OF ACCOUNTABILITY Some scholars have been sensitive to the internal dynamics of the institutions themselves. They claim these organizations have developed their own internal logics, which may not serve the interests of the poor (or rich) countries. Effective control over them by either the advanced industrial countries or the developing ones may be difficult; long chains of delegation allow them much slack and make adequate monitoring of their behavior costly.[94] Principal-agent models suggest such outcomes are especially likely when multiple principals (that is, countries) try to control a single agent (that is, the institution); in these situations, the ability of the bureaucracy to play off different countries' interests and to avoid monitoring is maximized. Unlike the previous explanations that treated international institutions as mere servants of either powerful states or private producers and investors, this claim gives the organizations broad independence and wide latitude for autonomous action.

Vaubel has been one of the foremost proponents of this view.[95] He produces evidence showing that bureaucratic incentives within the IMF and other international institutions lead to policies and practices inappropriate for their stated purposes. Concerns over career advancement and budget size induce actors within these agencies to focus on making loans and giving aid, but not on monitoring the results. Giving more loans and aid is always preferred to giving fewer, and recipients know this and use it to extract more. "If both institutions [that is, the IMF and World Bank] are left to themselves, they will likely revert to internal bureaucratic politics determining loans. The act of making loans will be rewarded rather than the act of helping the poor in each country."[96]

As noted by Barnett and Finnemore, the IR literature has tended to take a benign view of international organizations, viewing them as instruments for facilitating cooperation and making efficient agreements.[97] But "IOs often produce undesirable and even self-defeating outcomes repeatedly, without punishment much less dismantlement . . . In this view, decisions are not made after a rational decision process but rather through a competitive bargaining process over turf, budgets, and staff that may benefit parts of the organization at the expense of overall goals."[98] For instance, they point to the case of the World Bank: "Many scholars and journalists, and even the current head of the World Bank, have noticed that the bank has accumulated a rather distinctive record of 'failures' but continues to operate with the same criteria and has shown a marked lack of interest in evaluating the effectiveness of its own projects."[99] A series of internal problems could be responsible thus for the performance of these institutions vis-à-vis the developing countries.

These four problems are not exclusive or exhaustive. Enumerating them is important. Figuring out which problems affect which institutions seems important and understudied. Moreover, the type of reform desired depends on the problem. For example, Stone recommends further insulation of the IMF from the pressures of the donors, especially the United States. He wants the IMF to be more like an independent central bank. Insulation is desirable if the main problem is that they are too easily pressured by the rich countries or by private investors. Stiglitz, among others, however, has the opposite view. He thinks they should be more transparent and open to developing-country influence. Studies of bureaucracy in general see insulation as necessary, if undesirable, outside influences are strong and leaders are tempted to yield to them; but they see insulation as the problem itself if the bureaucracy's unaccountability and standard operating procedures are the failings. If the IMF's problem results mainly from its own internal organization and logic, then further insulation is only going to worsen the problem. Without further systematic evidence about the sources of these institutions' main problems in delivering benefits, to the developing countries, reform proposals may do more harm than good.

In sum, today's international economic institutions seem to be falling short of the goals that theories expect of them, and the reasons seem numerous. The current state of our knowledge does not warrant advocating the abolition of these international institutions, however. They appear to provide some benefits to the poor countries over the most likely counterfactual scenarios. But they probably could be reformed to provide even greater benefits.

*　*　*

Conclusions: What Is to Be Done?

What do we know about the impact of the major international economic institutions, the IMF, World Bank, and the WTO, on the developing countries? Have these institutions improved the lives of the poor in these countries? Have they made the developing countries better off than they would have been in the absence of these global institutions? Is this counterfactual the appropriate standard to evaluate them by? What is the moral obligation of the rich countries and their international institutions to the poor ones? Should the institutions be reformed to better fulfill their "duty of assistance" to the poor? Or is a better standard for their evaluation one that asks whether the institutions could be reformed at low cost to the rich countries so that they would provide more benefits to the poor ones?

How do normative and positive analyses together shed light on these institutions?

In terms of the four major functions that theories of international institutions identify, these three global institutions seem to have failed to live up to the expectations of these theories in their impact on the developing countries. They have had a difficult time constraining the large, developed countries; most of the time these countries have bargained hard to maximize their advantage vis-à-vis the developing nations. Perhaps they have left the developing countries better off than if they had to negotiate bilaterally for access to trade, aid, and loans, but it seems as if these institutions could have bargained less hard with the developing countries at little cost to themselves or the developed countries and thus provided more benefits for the poor.

The IMF, World Bank, and WTO have certainly helped provide monitoring and information. But the monitoring and information provision have been asymmetric; it is the developing countries that are monitored and provide more information than otherwise. This action, however, may make the developed countries and private investors more likely to trade with, invest in, and provide loans to the poor countries, but the terms of these agreements have often imposed multiple and powerful conditions on the developing countries that may have impeded their growth.

Facilitating reciprocity has been a central function attributed to international institutions. For these three organizations, reciprocity vis-à-vis the developing world has not been a central mission; trade agreements have often been very asymmetric and the aid and lending programs are one way. Finally, the ability to alter domestic politics by creating support or locking it in for reform has been less studied, but seems to clearly have had an impact. The impact of the international institutions on the developing countries and their domestic situation has been powerful but not always benign.

The difficulties faced by the international institutions in providing benefits for the developing countries have arisen from at least four sources. It may be the case that globalization has simply overwhelmed these institutions and that their impact is minor compared to other factors, especially with a large and open world economy, and it is likely that domestic weaknesses account for part of their poor performance. But their problems may also lie in the pressures exerted by the large, developed countries and private producers and investors. Both of these groups have shaped the functioning of the WTO, IMF, and World Bank. The powerful, rich countries have bargained hard within these institutions to advance their own interests. Private producers and investors have directly and indirectly affected the performance of the institutions through their central role in the world economy. All of these institutions were established to support and facilitate private trade and capital flows, not to supplant them. Finally, one cannot overlook the claim that part of the problems arises from the internal organization and procedures of the institutions themselves. Making loans and imposing conditions may be more important for career advancement than measuring the impact of these activities on the developing nations.

Positive, empirical research asks the question of whether the developing world would have been better or worse off with the presence of these international institutions than without them. The evidence suggests that even though problems abound with the institutions, one cannot rule out the counterfactual: without these institutions many developing countries could be worse off as they faced bilateral negotiations with the most powerful countries. Thus, advocating their abolition is premature.

Nevertheless, one has to ask if this question is the right one. Arguments from one stream of moral philosophers imply that it is not. Cosmopolitan versions of global distributive justice see this question as insufficient. They propose one ask whether these institutions could be reformed at low cost to the wealthy countries to provide more benefits to the poor. Are these institutions the best feasible ones that could help the developing countries without imposing large costs on the developed ones?

By many accounts, the answer is negative. A number of feasible and low cost reforms could be enacted that would render these institutions much more helpful to the poor at limited cost to the rich. Pogge makes such a case for the WTO.[100] By the standards posed in global distributive justice arguments, reforming the international institutions is imperative. Interestingly, normative and positive analyses sometimes agree; some international economists such as Bhagwati and Stiglitz propose similar reforms.

In addition to policy implications, several ramifications for future research arise from the arguments surveyed here. Pogge's point about the "nationalist" research agenda in the field is salient. His prescription that we include more international factors in research on the sources of poverty and economic and political development is not unfamiliar and seems a worthy one. Including global factors and their interactions with domestic ones in comparative studies is an important step that cannot be emphasized enough.

The field would benefit from more research on the actual effects of international institutions, rather than debates about whether they are autonomous agents. More empirical research on the ways in which these institutions function and on the forces that prevent them from functioning as our theories predict is essential. This is particularly the case vis-à-vis the developing countries, many of whom do not have the capacity to evaluate the impact of these institutions on their fortunes. "Identifying who gains and who loses from existing policies is important both to determine the need for policy change and to build support for such change. For example, documenting how specific OECD policies hurt the poor both at home and in developing countries can have a powerful effect on mobilizing support for welfare improving reforms. . . . Building coalitions with NGOs and other groups that care about development is vital in generating the political momentum that is needed to improve access in sensitive sectors and improve the rules of the game in the WTO."[101] Generating greater academic knowledge thus may contribute vastly to producing better policy and outcomes, which may be a moral imperative given the grave problems of the developing countries.

NOTES

1. Stiglitz 2002, 3.
2. For example, Keohane 1984; Ikenberry 2001.
3. Counterfactuals are defined as "subjunctive conditionals in which the antecedent is known . . . to be false" (Tetlock and Belkin 1996, 4). A critical issue is how can one know what would have happened if the antecedent was false, that is, if factor X, which was present, had not been present. This problem of cotenability, identified by Elster (1978) early on, remains crucial: counterfactuals require connecting principles that sustain but do not require the conditional claim, and these connecting principles must specify all else that would have to be true for the false conditional claim to have been true.
4. Tetlock and Belkin 1996.
5. Beitz 2005, 26.
6. In fiscal 2003, IBRD provided loans totaling $11.2 billion in support of 99 projects in 37 countries. In 2003, the grant arm of the Bank, the International Development Association (IDA), provided $7.3 billion in financing for 141 projects in 55 low-income countries (World Bank *Annual Report* 2004).
7. In the fourteen years between 1980 and 1994, Ghana received nineteen adjustment loans from the IMF and World Bank; Argentina, fifteen; Peru, eight; and Zambia, twelve (Easterly 2001a, 104–5).
8. WTO, World Trade Report 2003.
9. Studies show that WTO membership by developing countries has had little, if any, impact on the level of either their trade flows or their trade barriers (Rose 2002; Rose 2004; Milner with Kubota 2005; Subramanian and Wei 2003; Özden and Reinhardt 2002; Özden and Reinhardt 2004). Many developing countries were members of the GATT but retained very high trade barriers.
10. Defining development itself is an issue. Sen (2000) provides an excellent discussion and a rationale for a broad conception.
11. International Labor Organization 2004, 33.
12. Easterly 2001a, 102–3.
13. Easterly 2001b; Easterly 2001a, 101.
14. Chen and Ravaillon 2005, table 2.
15. Pogge 2002, 2.
16. This data from World Bank WDI 2003 is measured in 1995 $ using the chain method. Using constant dollar purchasing power parity data from the World Bank, the number of countries whose GNP per capita was lower in 2000 than in 1975 rises to 37, most in Africa, then Latin America and the Middle East. Even this calculation is likely to understate the problem; the worst off countries are most likely not to have any data, for example, Afghanistan, North Korea, Yemen, and Somalia.
17. UNDP 2004, 132.
18. Easterly 2001a, 60.
19. World Bank 2004, 43.
20. Pritchett 1997.
21. Easterly 2001a, 62.
22. The debate over whether inequality is falling or rising is too extensive to reproduce here. The answer depends on how it is measured (for example, Sala-i-Martin 2002a and Sala-i-Martin 2002b).
23. Loser 2004, 2.
24. UNDP 2004, 129.
25. Pogge and Reddy (2005) dispute these poverty figures, claiming they understate absolute poverty greatly.
26. World Bank 2004, 46. Even excluding China, this ratio fell from 27 percent to 23 percent. China joined the IMF and World Bank in

1980 and used their facilities often for the first fifteen years or so. It acceded to the WTO in 2003.

27. World Bank 2004, 46.

28. See Aisbett (2005) for a discussion of different interpretations of the data on globalization and poverty.

29. World Bank 2004, 40.

30. Gruber 2000.

31. Ikenberry 2001.

32. WTO 2003, xviii.

33. Stiglitz 2002, 61.

34. Steinberg 2002, 366.

35. ILO 2004, 33.

36. Steinberg 2002, 341.

37. If the large countries compete for access to the small countries' markets in a bilateral system, the small may find advantages. The recent Mercosur negotiations with the EU for a PTA have had an impact on the US position in its negotiations with the Mercosur countries for the Free Trade Area of the Americas.

38. ILO 2004, 6.

39. It is not clear that the IMF would tolerate some of the recurrent practices of the developed countries; many have run persistent government budget and current account deficits of a magnitude that the IMF condemns in the developing countries.

40. Boughton 2001, 135–36.

41. Rodrik 1996.

42. For example, Maizels and Nissanke 1984; Lumsdaine 1993; Milner 2004.

43. For example, Meltzer 2000. Moral hazard is a situation in which doing something for someone changes their incentives to help themselves. The common example is home insurance; when owners have insurance that fully replaces their house, they may be less attentive to making sure it does not burn down.

44. For example, Alesina and Dollar 2000.

45. Stone 2002.

46. Keohane 1984, 97.

47. These arguments tend to overlook the distributional effects of institutions, and to focus on the mutual gains from cooperation within the institution. See Martin and Simmons 1998.

48. Krueger 1998.

49. Barnett and Finnemore 1999, 709–10.

50. For example, Mansfield, Milner and Rosendorff 2002; Milner, Rosendorff and Mansfield, 2004.

51. Keohane is ambivalent, arguing throughout much of the book that membership is voluntary and rational, meaning members should be better off than otherwise if they join and remain. But in his final chapter, he notes that these institutions reflect the interests of the rich countries, and that while the poor countries gain from them, they might gain more if they were reformed (1984, 256).

52. "Many critics of the IMF's handling of the Asian financial crises have argued that the IMF inappropriately applied a standardized formula of budget cuts plus high interest rates to combat rapid currency depreciation without appreciating the unique and local causes of this depreciation. These governments were not profligate spenders, and austerity policies did little to reassure investors, yet the IMF prescribed roughly the same remedy that it had in Latin America. The result, by the IMF's later admission, was to make matters worse" (Barnett and Finnemore 1999, 721).

53. Stiglitz 2002, chap. 3; Bhagwati 2004, 204.

54. Stiglitz 2002, 220.

55. For example, Sachs and Warner 1995; Frankel and Romer 1999; Rodriguez and Rodrik 2001; UNCTAD 2004.

56. Stiglitz 2002, 143.

57. Keohane 1984, 129.

58. Bagwell and Staiger 2002.

59. Mattoo and Subramanian 2004, 6.

60. Mattoo and Subramanian (2004) survey 62 small and poor countries, which account for about one-third of the world's total countries but they individually account for less than 0.05 percent of world trade, and collectively for only 1.1 percent of global trade. China is the only developing country that

has a significant share of the world market; its share of world exports has risen from less than 1 percent in 1980 to 6 percent in 2003.

61. Mattoo and Subramanian 2004, 11.

62. WTO, International Trade Statistics, 2004.

63. Mattoo and Subramanian 2004, 19.

64. Romalis 2003.

65. Özden and Reinhardt 2004.

66. The IMF and World Bank do not seem to play much of a role in enforcing reciprocity. As noted before, they obtain their funds and mandates from the developed countries and do their lending and aid giving in the developing world. The symmetric treatment of rich and poor countries is not evident.

67. E.g., McGillivray and Smith 2000.

68. For example, Mansfield, Milner and Rosendorff 2002.

69. For example, Gilligan 1997; Bailey, Goldstein and Weingast 1997.

70. Mattoo and Subramanian 2004, 11.

71. For example, Milner with Kubota 2005.

72. Their trade dependence has grown significantly from approximately 50 percent in 1960 to over 80 percent in 2000, or nearly a 60 percent increase, for the about 80 developing countries accounting for more than 70 percent of world population.

73. UNCTAD, Ext Debt #24, 2004, 2.

74. For example, Rodrik 1997; Kaufman and Segura-Ubiergo 2001; Adsera and Boix 2002; Mosley 2003.

75. For example, Acemoglu, Johnson, and Robinson 2001; Acemoglu, Johnson, and Robinson 2002; Rodrik, Subramanian, and Trebbi 2002; Easterly and Levine 2002.

76. For example, Acemoglu, Johnson, and Robinson 2001; Acemoglu, Johnson, and Robinson 2002; Rodrik, Subramanian, and Trebbi 2002; Easterly and Levine 2002. The causes of differential growth may lie in international politics. The way in which the great powers colonized the developing countries centuries ago is strongly related to their growth prospect now. It is not easy to disentangle domestic and international factors.

77. ILO, 2004, 76.

78. For example, Bueno de Mesquita and Root 2002; Van de Walle 2001.

79. For example, Burnside and Dollar 2000; Easterly 2003.

80. For example, Schraeder et al. 1998; McKinlay and Little 1977; McKinlay and Little 1978; Alesina and Dollar 2000.

81. Steinberg 2002, 356.

82. Stiglitz 2002, 160.

83. Bhagwati 2004, 204.

84. Thacker 1999.

85. The articles of agreement of the IBRD and the IMF give as one of their main purposes the promotion of private foreign investment in the developing countries. So it is not a surprise that the two institutions are susceptible to pressures from private investors.

86. ILO 2004, 35.

87. Stiglitz 2002, 216.

88. Bhagwati 2004, 205.

89. Bhagwati 2004, 182.

90. Bhagwati 2004, 182.

91. Chaudhuri, Goldberg, and Jia (2003) show in a sophisticated counterfactual analysis that in a key segment of the pharmaceuticals market in India, the losses to Indian consumers are far greater than the increased profits of foreign producers from the introduction of TRIPs.

92. Gould 2004, ch8, p. 1. For Gould, supplementary financiers are both public and private actors.

93. Keohane 1984, 253.

94. For example, Vreeland 2003, 157.

95. Vaubel 1986; Vaubel 1996.

96. Easterly 2001a, 290.

97. Barnett and Finnemore 1999, 701.

98. Barnett and Finnemore 1999, 701, 717.

99. Barnett and Finnemore 1999, 723.

100. Pogge 2002, 162.

101. Hoekman 2002, 26.

REFERENCES

Acemoglu, Daron, Simon Johnson, and James Robinson. 2001. The colonial origins of comparative development: An empirical investigation. *American Economic Review* 91 (5): 1369–1401.

Acemoglu, Daron, Simon Johnson, and James Robinson. 2002. Reversal of fortune: Geography and institutions in the making of the modern world income distribution. *Quarterly Journal of Economics* 117 (4): 1231–94.

Adsera, Alicia, and Carles Boix. 2002. Trade, democracy and the size of the public sector: The political underpinnings of openness. *International Organization* 56 (2): 229–62.

Aisbett, Emma. 2005. Why are the critics so convinced that globalization is bad for the poor? *National Bureau of Economic Research Working Paper* 11066.

Alesina, Alberto, and David Dollar. 2000. Who gives foreign aid to whom and why? *Journal of Economic Growth* 5(1): 33–63.

Bagwell, Kyle, and Robert W. Staiger. 2002. *The economics of the world trading system.* Cambridge: MIT Press.

Bailey, Michael A., Judith Goldstein, Barry R. Weingast. 1997. The institutional roots of American trade policy: Politics, coalitions, and international trade. *World Politics* 49(3): 309–338.

Barnett, Michael N., and Martha Finnemore. 1999. The politics, power, and pathologies of international organizations. *International Organization* 53 (4): 699–732.

Barry, Brian M. 1995. *Justice as impartiality.* Oxford: Oxford University Press.

Beitz, Charles R. 1979. *Political theory and international relations.* Princeton: Princeton University Press.

———. 1999. International liberalism and distributive justice: A survey of recent thought. *World Politics* 51(2): 269–96.

———. 2000. Rawls's law of peoples. *Ethics* 110(4): 669–696.

———. 2005. Cosmopolitanism and global justice. *The Journal of Ethics* 9 (1–2): 11–27.

Bhagwati, Jagdish. 2004. *In defense of globalization.* New York: Oxford University Press.

Bird, Graham, and Dane Rowlands. 2001. IMF Lending: How is it affected by economic, political and institutional factors? *Policy Reform* 4 (3): 243–70.

Blake, Michael. 2001. Distributive justice, state coercion and autonomy. *Philosophy and Public Affairs* 30 (3): 257–95.

Boughton, James M. 2001. *Silent revolution: The International Monetary Fund 1979–1989.* Washington, DC: IMF.

Buchanan, Allen. 2000. Rawls's law of peoples: Rules for a vanished Westphalian world. *Ethics* 110 (4): 697–721.

Bueno de Mesquita, Bruce, and Hilton Root, eds. 2002. *Governing for prosperity.* New Haven: Yale University Press.

Burnside, Craig, and David Dollar. 2000. Aid, policies and growth. *American Economic Review* 90(4): 847–68.

Caney, Simon. 2001. International distributive justice. *Political Studies* 49 (4): 974–97.

Chaudhuri, Shubham, Pinelopi Goldberg, and Panle Jia. 2003. Estimating the effects of global patent protection for pharmaceuticals: A case study of fluoroquinolones in India. Unpublished manuscript.

Chen, Shaohua, and Martin Ravaillon. 2005. How have the world's poorest fared since the early 1980s? World Bank Staff Paper 3341.

Cullity, Garrett. 1994. International aid and the scope of kindness. *Ethics* 105 (1): 99–127.

Elster, Jon. 1978. *Logic and society: Contradictions and possible worlds.* New York: John Wiley.

Easterly, William. 2001a. *The elusive quest for growth: Economists' adventures and misadventures in the tropics.* Cambridge: MIT Press.

———. 2001b. The lost decades: Developing countries' stagnation in spite of policy reform, 1980–1998. *Journal of Economic Growth* 6 (2): 135–57.

———. 2003. Can foreign aid buy growth? *Journal of Economic Perspectives* 17 (3): 23–48.

Easterly, William, and Ross Levine. 2002. Tropics, germs and crops: How endowments influence economic development. National Bureau of Economic Research Working Paper 9106.

Frankel, Jeffrey A., and David Romer. 1999. Does trade cause growth? *American Economic Review* 89 (3): 379–99.

Gilligan, Michael J. 1997. *Empowering exporters.* Ann Arbor, MI: University of Michigan Press.

Gould, Erica R. 2004. Money talks: The International Monetary Fund, conditionality and supplementary financiers. Unpublished manuscript.

Grant, Ruth W., and Robert O. Keohane. 2005. Accountability and abuses of power in world politics. *American Political Science Review* 99 (1): 29–43.

Gruber, Lloyd. 2000. *Ruling the world: Power politics and the rise of supranational institutions.* Princeton: Princeton University Press.

Hoekman, Bernard. 2002. Economic development and the WTO after Doha. World Bank Policy Research Working Paper 2851.

Ikenberry, G. John. 2001. *After victory: Institutions, strategic restraint, and the rebuilding of order after major wars.* Princeton: Princeton University Press.

International Labor Organization. 2004. *A fair globalization: Creating opportunities for all.* Geneva: International Labor Office.

Kaufman, Robert R., and Alex Segura-Ubiergo. 2001. Globalization, domestic politics, and social spending in Latin America: A time-series cross-section analysis, 1973–97. *World Politics* 53 (4): 553–87.

Keohane, Robert O. 1984. *After hegemony: Cooperation and discord in the world political economy.* Princeton: Princeton University Press.

Krueger, Anne O. 1998. Whither the World Bank and the IMF? *Journal of Economic Literature* 36 (4): 1983–2020.

Kuper, Andrews. 2004. *Democracy beyond borders: Justice and representation in global institutions.* New York: Oxford University Press.

Loser, Claudio M. 2004. External debt sustainability: Guidelines for low- and middle-income countries. G-24 Discussion Paper Series 26. Geneva.

Lumsdaine, David Halloran. 1993. *Moral vision in international politics: The foreign aid regime, 1949–1989.* Princeton: Princeton University Press.

Macedo, Stephen. 2004. What self-governing peoples owe to one another: Universalism, diversity and the law of peoples. *Fordham Law Review* 72 (5): 1721–38.

Maizels, Alfred, and Machiko K. Nissanke. 1984. Motivations for aid to developing countries. *World Development* 12 (9): 879–900.

Mansfield, Edward D., Helen V. Milner, and B. Peter Rosendorff. 2002. Why democracies cooperate more: Electoral control and international trade agreements. *International Organization* 56 (3): 477–514.

Martin, Lisa, and Beth Simmons. 1998. Theories and empirical studies of international institutions. *International Organization* 52 (4): 729–57.

Mattoo, Aaditya, and Arvind Subramanian. 2004. The WTO and the poorest countries: The stark reality. IMF Working Paper 04/81.

McGillivray, Fiona, and Alastair Smith. 2000. Trust and cooperation through agent specific punishments. *International Organization* 54 (4): 809–24.

McKinlay, Robert D, and Richard Little. 1977. A foreign policy model of US bilateral aid allocation. *World Politics* 30 (1): 58–86.

———. 1978. A foreign policy model of the distribution of British bilateral aid, 1960–70. *British Journal of Political Science* 8 (3): 313–31.

Meltzer, Alan. 2000. Report of the international financial institutions advisory commission. Meltzer Commission. Washington, DC.

Milner, Helen V. 1998. Rationalizing politics: The emerging synthesis of international, American, and comparative politics. *International Organization* 52 (4): 759–86.

———. 2004. Why multilateralism? Foreign aid and domestic principal-agent problems. Unpublished manuscript.

Milner, Helen V., with Keiko Kubota. 2005. Why the move to free trade? Democracy and trade policy in the developing countries, 1970–1999. *International Organization* 59 (1): 107–43.

Milner, Helen V., B. Peter Rosendorff, and Edward Mansfield. 2004. International trade and domestic politics: The domestic sources of international trade agreements and organizations. *The impact of international law on international cooperation.* Eyal Benvenisti and Moshe Hirsch, eds. Cambridge, UK: Cambridge University Press.

Mosley, Layna. 2003. *Global capital and national governments.* New York: Cambridge University Press.

Nagel, Thomas. 2005. The problem of global justice. *Philosophy and Public Affairs.* 33 (2): 113–47.

Özden, Çaglar, and Eric Reinhardt. 2002. The perversity of preferences: GSP and developing countries trade policies, 1976–2000. World Bank Working Papers 2955.

Özden, Çaglar, and Eric Reinhardt. 2004. First do no harm: The effect of trade preferences on developing country exports. World Bank Research Paper.

Pogge, Thomas W. 2002. *World poverty and human rights.* Cambridge, UK: Polity.

Pogge, Thomans, and Sanjay Reddy. 2005. How *not* to count the poor. Forthcoming in *Measuring global poverty,* Sudhir Anand and Joseph Stiglitz, eds. Oxford: Oxford University Press.

Pritchett, Lant. 1997. Divergence, big time. *Journal of Economic Perspectives* 11 (3): 3–17.

Rawls, John. 1999. *The law of peoples; with, The idea of public reason revisited.* Cambridge: Harvard University Press.

Risse, Mathias. 2004a. Does the global order harm the poor? Unpublished manuscript, Harvard University, John F. Kennedy School of Government.

———. 2004b. What we owe to the global poor. *Journal of Ethics* 9 (1/2): 81–117.

Rodriguez, Francisco, and Dani Rodrik. 2001. Trade policy and economic growth: A skeptic's guide to the cross-national evidence. *NBER macroeconomics annual 2000.* Ben S. Bernancke and Kenneth Rogoff. Cambridge: MIT Press for NBER: 261–325.

Rodrik, Dani. 1996. Why is there multilateral lending? In *Annual World Bank conference on development economics, 1995,* ed. Michael Bruno and Boris Pleeskovic, 167–93. Washington, DC: International Monetary Fund.

———. 1997. *Has globalization gone too far?* Washington, DC: Institute for International Economics.

———. 2000. Development strategies for the next century. Paper prepared for the conference on "Developing Economies in the Twenty-First Century," Ciba, Japan, January 26–27. http://ksghome.harvard.edu/~.drodrik.academic.ksg/.

Rodrik, Dani, Arvind Subramanian, and Francesco Trebbi. 2002. Institutions rule: The primacy of institutions over geography and integration in economic development. National Bureau of Economic Research Working Paper 9305.

Romalis, John. 2003. Would rich country trade preferences help poor countries grow? Evidence from the generalized system of preferences. Manuscript. http://gsbwww.uchicago.edu/fac/john.romalis/research/.

Rose, Andrew K. 2002. Do WTO members have a more liberal trade policy? National Bureau of Economic Research Working Paper 9347.

———. 2004. Do we really know that the WTO increases trade? *American Economic Review* 94(1): 98–114.

Sachs, Jeffrey, and Andrew Warner. 1995. Economic reform and the process of global integration. *Brookings Papers on Economic Activity* (1): 1–118.

Sala-i-Martin, Xavier. 2002a. The world distribution of income (estimated from individual country distributions). NBER working paper #8933.

———. 2002b. The disturbing "rise" of global income inequality. NBER Working Paper 8904.

Schraeder, Peter J., Stephen W. Hook, and Bruce Taylor. 1998. Clarifying the foreign aid puzzle: A comparison of American, Japanese, French and Swedish aid flows. *World Politics* 50 (2): 294–323.

Sen, Amartya. 2000. *Development as freedom.* New York: Alfred A. Knopf.

Singer, Peter. 1972. Famine, affluence, and morality. *Philosophy & Public Affairs* 1 (3): 229–243.

———. 2002. *One world: The ethics of globalization.* New Haven: Yale University Press.

Steinberg, Richard. 2002. In the shadow of law or power? Consensus-based bargaining and outcomes in the in the GATT/WTO. *International Organization* 56 (2): 339–74.

Stiglitz, Joseph E. 2002. *Globalization and its discontents.* New York: W. W. Norton.

Stone, Randall W. 2002. *Lending credibility: The International Monetary Fund and the post-communist transition.* Princeton: Princeton University Press.

Subramanian, Arvind, and Shang-Jin Wei. 2003. The WTO promotes trade, strongly but unevenly. National Bureau of Economic Research Working Paper 10024.

Tetlock, Philip E., and Aaron Belkin, eds. 1996. *Counterfactual thought experiments in world politics: Logical, methodological, and psychological perspectives.* Princeton: Princeton University Press.

Thacker, Strom Cronan. 1999. The high politics of IMF lending. *World Politics* 52 (1): 38–75.

United Nations Conference on Trade and Development (UNCTAD). 2004. *Trade and poverty.* Geneva: UNCTAD.

UNDP. 2004. *Human development report 2004.* New York: UNDP.

Van de Walle, Nicolas. 2001. *African economies and the politics of permanent crisis, 1979–1999.* New York: Cambridge University Press.

Vaubel, Roland. 1986. A public choice approach to international organization. *Public Choice* 51 (1): 39–57.

———. 1996. Bureaucracy at the IMF and the World Bank: A comparison of the evidence. *World Economy* 19 (2): 195–210.

Vreeland, James Raymond. 2003. *The IMF and economic development.* New York: Cambridge University.

World Bank. 2002. *World development indicators.* Washington, DC: World Bank.

———. 2003. *Annual report 2003.* Washington, DC: World Bank.

———. 2004. *Annual report 2004.* Washington, DC: World Bank.

———. 2004. *Global economic prospects.* Washington, DC: World Bank.

World Trade Organization. 2003. *World trade report 2003.* Geneva: World Trade Organization.

———. 2004. *International trade statistics.* Geneva: World Trade Organization.

MARTIN WOLF

From *Why Globalization Works*

* * *

Chapter 9

Incensed about Inequality

> Globalization has dramatically increased inequality between and within nations, even as it connects people as never before. A world in which the assets of the 200 richest people are greater than the combined income of the more than 2bn people at the other end of the economic ladder should give everyone pause.
>
> —Jay Mazur, president of the Union of Needletrades, Industrial and Textile Employees.[1]

—Jay Mazur is not alone. Ignacio Ramonet has written on similar lines, in *Le Monde Diplomatique*, that:

> the dramatic advance of globalization and neoliberalism . . . has been accompanied by an *explosive growth in inequality* and a return of mass poverty and unemployment. The very opposite of everything which the modern state and modern citizenship is supposed to stand for.
>
> The net result is a *massive growth in inequality.* The United States, which is the richest country in the world, has more than 60 million poor. The world's foremost trading power, the European Union, has over 50 million. In the United States, 1 percent of the population owns 39 percent of the country's wealth. Taking the planet as a whole, the combined wealth of the 358 richest people (all of them dollar billionaires) is greater than the total annual income of 45 percent of the world's poorest inhabitants, that is, 2.6bn people.[2]

Let us, for a moment, ignore the assumption that the number of poor (how defined?) in two of the richest regions in the world tells one anything about global inequality, or about poverty for that matter, or even about inequality within the U.S. and the European Union. Let us also ignore the comparison between the *assets* of one group of people, the richest, and the *incomes* of another, the poor, which is a comparison of apples and oranges. (In order to obtain the permanent incomes of the rich, one would need to divide the value of their assets by at least twenty.) These absurdities merely make Ramonet's diatribe representative of the empty rhetoric of many critics of globalization. But the questions that underlie his remarks need to be tackled. Here are seven propositions that can be advanced about what has happened in the age of so-called neoliberal globalization over the past two decades.

First, the ratio of average incomes in the richest countries to those in the poorest has continued to rise.

Second, the absolute gap in living standards between today's high-income countries and most developing countries has also continued to rise.

Third, global inequality among individuals has risen.

From *Why Globalization Works* (New Haven, Conn., and London: Yale University Press, 2004), 138–172. Some of the author's notes have been omitted.

Fourth, the number of people in extreme poverty has risen.

Fifth, the proportion of people in extreme poverty in the world's population has also risen.

Sixth, the poor of the world are worse off not just in terms of incomes, but in terms of a wide range of other indicators of human welfare.

Seventh, income inequality has risen in every country and particularly in countries most exposed to international economic integration.

In the rest of this chapter I will consider what we know about these propositions and how the answers relate to international economic integration. Before examining them, however, we need to ask what matters to us. Most of the debate has been either about whether inequality has risen between the world's rich and poor or about whether the number of people in income poverty has risen. But critics of globalization have themselves often rightly argued that there is more to life than income. What is most important must be the living standards of the poor, not just in terms of their incomes, narrowly defined, but in terms of their health, life expectancy, nourishment and education.

Equally, we need to understand that rises in inequality might occur in very different ways. Three possibilities come to mind at once: a rise in incomes of the better off, at the expense of the poor; a rise in the incomes of the better off, with no effects on the welfare of the poor; or rises in incomes of the better off that, in various ways, benefit the poor, but not by proportionately as much as they benefit the better off. It seems clear that the first of these is malign, the second desirable, unless the welfare of the better off counts for nothing, and the third unambiguously desirable, though one might wish more of the gains to accrue to the poor. True egalitarians would differ on these judgements, of course. Indeed, an extreme egalitarian might take the view that a world in which everybody was an impoverished subsistence farmer would be better than the world we now have, because it would be less unequal. Most people—including, I imagine, many protesters against globalization—would

regard this as crazy. Few are that egalitarian. Most people are not even as egalitarian as the late philosopher John Rawls, who argued that inequality was permissible only to the extent that it benefited the poor.

We need to be equally careful in considering the role of globalization in relation to inequality and poverty. International economic integration may affect global inequality in several different ways. Here are a few possibilities: it may increase inequality by lowering the incomes of the poor; it may raise the incomes of the better off, without having any impact on the incomes of the poor; it may raise the incomes of the poor by proportionately less than it raises the incomes of the better off; or it may raise the incomes of the poor by proportionately more than it raises those of the better off. Only the first is unambiguously bad, but all of the first three would be associated with increasing inequality. Yet both of the last two mean higher living standards for the poor.

Again, it may not be globalization, as such, that delivers these outcomes, but a combination of globalization with non-globalization. Globalization may raise incomes of globalizers, while non-globalization lowers the incomes of non-globalizers. Then an era of globalization may be associated with rising inequality that is caused not by globalization, but by its opposite, the refusal (or inability) of some countries to participate.

The most important questions to bear in mind in the discussions below are, therefore, these. Is human welfare, broadly defined, rising? Is the proportion of humanity living in desperate misery declining? If inequality is rising, are the rich profiting at the expense of the poor? Is globalization damaging the poor or is it rather non-globalization that is doing so? To answer all these questions, one must start at the beginning, with economic growth.

Economic Growth and Globalization

In the mid-1970s I was the World Bank's senior divisional economist on India during the country's worst post-independence decade. After a spurt of growth in the early phase of its inward-looking development, growth in incomes per head had ground virtually to a halt. Hundreds of millions of people seemed, as a result, to be mired in hopeless and unending poverty. In a book published in 1968, a well-known environmentalist doomsayer, Paul Ehrlich, had written the country off altogether.[3] For a young man from the UK, work in India as an economist was both fascinating and appalling: so much poverty; so much frustration; so much complacency. Yet I was convinced then, as I am now, that, with perfectly feasible policy changes, this vast country could generate rapid rates of economic growth and reductions in poverty. No iron law imposed levels of real output (and so real incomes) per head at only 10 percent of those in high-income countries.

Since those unhappy days, India has enjoyed the fruit of two revolutions: the green revolution, which transformed agricultural productivity; and a liberalizing revolution, which began, haltingly, under Rajiv Gandhi's leadership, in the 1980s and then took a "great leap forward" in 1991, in response to a severe foreign exchange crisis, under the direction of one of the country's most remarkable public servants, Manmohan Singh, the then finance minister. Slowly, India abandoned the absurdities of its pseudo-Stalinist "control raj" in favor of individual enterprise and the market. As a result, between 1980 and 2000, India's real GDP per head more than doubled. Stagnation has become a thing of the past.

India was not alone. On the contrary, it was far behind a still more dynamic and even bigger liberalizing country—China, which achieved a rise in real incomes per head of well over 400 percent between 1980 and 2000. China and India, it should be remembered, contain almost two-fifths of the world's population. China alone

contains more people than Latin America and sub-Saharan Africa together. Many other countries in east and south Asia have also experienced rapid growth. According to the 2003 *Human Development Report* from the United Nations Development Programme, between 1975 and 2001, GDP per head rose at 5.9 percent a year in east Asian developing countries (with 31 percent of the world's population in 2000). The corresponding figure for growth of GDP per head for south Asia (with another 22 percent of the world's population) was 2.4 percent a year. Between 1990 and 2001, GDP per head rose at 5.5 percent a year in east Asia, while growth rose to 3.2 percent a year in south Asia.

Never before have so many people—or so large a proportion of the world's population—enjoyed such large rises in their standards of living. Meanwhile, GDP per head in high-income countries (with 15 percent of the world's population) rose by 2.1 percent a year between 1975 and 2001 and by only 1.7 percent a year between 1990 and 2001. This then was a period of partial convergence: the incomes of poor developing countries, with more than half the world's population, grew substantially faster than those of the world's richest countries.

This, in a nutshell, is why Mazur and the many people who think like him are wrong. Globalization has not increased inequality. It has reduced it, just as it has reduced the incidence of poverty. How can this be, critics will demand? Are absolute and proportional gaps in living standards between the world's richest and poorest countries not rising all the time? Yes is the answer. And is inequality not rising in most of the world's big countries? Yes, is again the answer. So how can global inequality be falling? To adapt Bill Clinton's campaign slogan, it is the growth, stupid. Rapid economic growth in poor countries with half the world's population has powerful effects on the only sort of inequality which matters, that among individuals. It has similarly dramatic effects on world poverty. The rise of Asia is transforming the world, very much for the better. It is the "Asian drama" of our times, to plagiarize the title of a celebrated work by a Nobel-laureate economist, the late Gunnar Myrdal.

What, the reader may ask, has this progress to do with international economic integration? In its analysis of globalization, published in 2002, the World Bank divided seventy-three developing countries, with aggregate population, in 1997, of 4 billion (80 percent of all people in developing countries), into two groups: the third that had increased ratios of trade to GDP, since 1980, by the largest amount and the rest.[4] The former group, with an aggregate population of 2.9 billion, managed a remarkable combined increase of 104 percent in the ratio of trade to GDP. Over the same period, the increase in the trade ratio of the high-income countries was 71 percent, while the "less globalized" two-thirds of countries in the sample of developing countries experienced a decline in their trade ratios.

The average incomes per head of these twenty-four globalizing countries rose by 67 percent (a compound rate of 3.1 percent a year) between 1980 and 1997. In contrast, the other forty-nine countries managed a rise of only 10 percent (a compound rate of 0.5 percent a year)

in incomes per head over this period. As Table 9.2 shows, these more globalized countries did not have particularly high levels of education in 1980. At that time, they were also a little poorer, as a group, than the rest. Subsequently, the new globalizers, as the World Bank calls them, cut their import tariffs by 34 percentage points, on average, against 11 percentage points for the other group. They also achieved a better reading on the rule of law than the others. The World Bank's conclusion is that, "as they reformed and integrated with the world market, the 'more globalized' developing countries started to grow rapidly, accelerating steadily from 2.9 percent in the 1970s to 5 percent in the 1990s."[5]

While what the Bank says is both true and important, it should be observed that its notion of a group of twenty-four countries is something of a fiction. China and India contain, between them, 75 percent of the group's combined population. With Brazil, Bangladesh, Mexico, the Philippines, and Thailand, one has 92 percent of the group's population. Moreover, Asian countries dominate: they make up 85 percent of the population of this group of globalizing countries.

TABLE 9.2		
CHARACTERISTICS OF MORE GLOBALIZED AND LESS GLOBALIZED DEVELOPING ECONOMIES *(POPULATION-WEIGHTED AVERAGE)*		
Socioeconomic characteristics	*More globalized (24)*	*Less globalized (49)*
Population, 1997 (billions)	2.9	1.1
Per-capita GDP, 1980	$1,488	$1,947
Per-capita GDP, 1997	$2,485	$2,133
Compound annual growth rate of GDP per head, 1980–1997	3.1%	0.5%
Rule of law index, 1997 (world average=0)	−0.04	−0.48
Average years primary schooling, 1980	2.4	2.5
Average years primary schooling, 1997	3.8	3.1
Average years secondary schooling, 1980	0.8	0.7
Average years secondary schooling, 1997	1.3	1.3
Average years tertiary schooling, 1980	0.08	0.09
Average years tertiary schooling, 1997	0.18	0.22

SOURCE: World Bank, *Globalization, Growth & Poverty: Building an Inclusive World Economy* (Washington, DC: World Bank, 2002), Table 1.1.

What then do we learn from the success of the countries picked out as globalizers by the World Bank? We can say, with confidence, that the notion that international economic integration necessarily makes the rich richer and the poor poorer is nonsense. Here is a wide range of countries that increased their integration with the world economy and prospered, in some cases dramatically so. A subtler question, to which we shall return in subsequent chapters, is precisely what policies relatively successful developing countries have followed. Critics are right to argue that success has not required adoption of the full range of so-called neo-liberal policies—privatization, free trade, and capital-account liberalization. But, in insisting upon this point, critics are wilfully mistaking individual policy trees for the market-oriented forest. What the successful countries all share is a move towards the market economy, one in which private property rights, free enterprise and competition increasingly took the place of state ownership, planning and protection. They chose, however haltingly, the path of economic liberalization and international integration. This is the heart of the matter. All else is commentary.

If one compares the China of today with the China of Mao Zedong or the India of today with the India of Indira Gandhi, the contrasts are overwhelming. Market forces have been allowed to operate in ways that would have been not just unthinkable but criminal a quarter of a century ago. Under Mao, economic freedom had been virtually eliminated. Under the Indian control system, no significant company was allowed to produce, invest, or import without government permission. From this starting-point, much of the most important liberalization was, necessarily and rightly, internal. Given where it was in the 1970s, liberalizing agriculture alone started China on the path towards rapid development. Similarly, eliminating the more absurd controls on industry permitted an acceleration in Indian economic growth. In both cases then these initial reforms and the abundance of cheap and hardworking labor guaranteed accelerated growth.

Yet in neither case can the contribution of economic integration be ignored. This is spectacularly true of China. The volume of China's exports grew at 13 percent a year between 1980 and 1990 and then at 11 percent between 1990 and 1999. Between 1990 and 2000 the ratio of trade in goods to Chinese GDP, at market prices, jumped from 33 to 44 percent, an extraordinarily high ratio for such a large economy. The ratio of merchandise trade to output of goods in the economy rose from 47 percent to 66 percent over the same period.[6] In 2001, China's gross merchandize exports of $266 billion amounted to 4.3 percent of the world total, up from a mere 0.7 percent in 1977.[7] By that year, China was the world's sixth largest merchandise exporter (including intra-European Union trade in the total), just behind the UK, but already ahead of Canada and Italy. Meanwhile, private capital flows into China jumped from 3 percent of GDP in 1990 to 13 percent in 2000. By 2001, the stock of inward foreign direct investment in China was $395 billion, 6 percent of the world's total, up from $25 billion in 1990. In 2000, inward direct investment financed 11 percent of the giant's gross fixed capital formation, while foreign affiliates generated 31 percent of China's manufacturing sales and, more astonishingly, 50 percent of its exports.[8] It is possible to argue that China's dramatic economic growth somehow had nothing to do with its headlong rush into the global market economy. But it would be absurd to do so.

India's integration was much less spectacular. So, not coincidentally, was its growth. Yet here, too, the change was palpable. India's volume of merchandise exports fell in the 1980s, which contributed mightily to the foreign exchange crisis that brought to an end its overwhelmingly inward-looking liberalization of the 1980s. But export volume rose at 5.3 percent a year between 1990 and 1999, after external liberalization had begun. India's share in world merchandise exports had fallen from 2.1 percent in 1951 to a low of 0.4 percent in 1980. But by 2001 this share was modestly back up, to 0.7 percent, putting it in thirtieth place globally. Between 1990 and

2000, the share of trade in goods also rose from 13 to 20 percent of GDP. India did achieve a significant success in exports of commercial services (particularly software). By 2001, its exports of such services were $20 billion, almost half as much as its $44 billion in merchandise exports. Its share in world exports of commercial services was 1.4 percent, double its share in exports of goods, while its rank in the world was nineteenth, though even here it was behind China's exports of $33 billion (2.3 percent of the world total). India also lagged in openness to inward direct investment, which only reached $3.4 billion in 2001. But even this was close to revolutionary in a country that had, for decades, discouraged all inward FDI. In 1990, the total stock of inward FDI was a mere $1.7 billion. By 2001, it had reached $22 billion. The 1990s were, in all, India's most economically successful post-independence decade. They were also the decade in which the country liberalized both internal and external transactions and increased its integration into the global economy. An accident? Hardly.

Now consider an even more fascinating example in the Bank's list of globalizing economies—Bangladesh, certainly the poorest sizeable country in the world in the 1970s and, as I remember well, almost universally deemed a hopeless case. Even this country has benefited from international economic integration. The GDP per head of Bangladesh rose at 2.3 percent a year between 1975 and 2001, generating a 60 percent rise in real income per head over more than a quarter of a century. Between 1990 and 2001, GDP per head grew considerably faster, at 3.1 percent a year, as the economy opened. In 1975, Bangladesh's real GDP per head (measured at purchasing power parity) was roughly half that of sub-Saharan Africa. By 2000, its real GDP per head was close to the average level of sub-Saharan Africa. In the 1980s, Bangladesh's volume of merchandise exports barely rose. In the 1990s, it rose at a remarkable 15 percent a year. Between 1990 and 2000, the ratio of exports to GDP jumped from 18 to 32 percent. The volume of trade also grew 6 percentage points a year faster than GDP in the

decade. Bangladesh did not suddenly become a magnet for foreign direct investment. That is hardly surprising, since it has been ranked bottom of seventy-five countries in the cost of corruption.[9] But the stock of inward direct investment did reach $1.1 billion by 2001, up from $150 million in 1990. Even for Bangladesh, international economic integration has paid off. It is only a start. But it is, at least, that.

If a successful move to the market, including increasing integration in the world economy, explains the success stories of the past two decades, what explains the failures, that is, those which have failed to take advantage of the opportunities for global economic integration? Failure to develop has involved a complex interplay of institutions, endowments and policies.

Emphasis on institutions and their evolution has, quite properly, become a dominant focus of analysts of development. It is discovered, not surprisingly, that poor performers have corrupt, predatory or brutal governments or, sometimes even worse, no government at all, but rather civil war among competing warlords.[10] The failure of the state to provide almost any of the services desperately needed for development is at the root of the African disaster. This reflects both the artificiality of the states and the weak—if not non-existent—sense of moral responsibility of Africa's "big men." Mobutu's Zaire was perhaps the most catastrophic example. But he was also one of many. Today, Robert Mugabe's destruction of once-prosperous Zimbabwe is almost equally horrifying.[11] An even more depressing case is that of sub-Sahara's giant, Nigeria. Today, Nigeria's GDP per head, at PPP, is the same as it was in 1970, despite three decades of abundant oil revenues, all of which has been wasted in foolish public spending and capital flight. The proportion of Nigeria's population in extreme poverty (real incomes of less than a dollar a day, at PPP) has doubled over this period. The élite has been predatory in the extreme: in 2000, the top 2 percent had the same income as the bottom 55 percent.[12] Much of Nigeria's wealth has been squirrelled away abroad. Alas, Nigeria is merely an extreme case. It is estimated that about 40 percent of Africa's private wealth was held overseas by 1990. But bad governments have also failed to provide the infrastructure on which development depends. As a result, African countries trade even less with one another and the rest of the world than would be predicted from their adverse locations.[13]

The second obstacle to development is a country's natural endowments. There is much evidence that location in the tropics is a handicap, though whether this is only via the impact on the evolution of countries' institutions, or independently, remains controversial. The probability is that it is a bit of both. Debilitating diseases have long been rife in the tropics. But it is also true that colonial regimes tended to create predatory institutions in their tropical possessions. Distance from the sea is also a handicap and particularly being landlocked. The disadvantages faced by the landlocked—a natural form of protection against foreign trade—also underline the costs of non-globalization.[14]

Endowments enter into development in another way, as resources. Natural resources, especially mineral wealth, seem to be an obstacle, not a spur, to economic development. This "resource curse" has many dimensions: resources tend to corrupt politics, turning it into a race to seize the incomes produced by resources, often generating debilitating civil wars; they generate unstable terms of trade, because prices of natural resources or agricultural commodities fluctuate widely; and they produce a high real exchange rate that, among other things, hinders development of internationally competitive manufacturing.

Data on real GDP per head show that developing countries with few natural resources grew two to three times faster between 1960 and 1990 than countries with abundant natural resources. The World Bank demonstrates that no fewer than forty-five countries experienced "unsustained growth" over the past four decades: they matched their 1999 level of real income per head in a previous decade, many as far back as the 1960s. All but six of these countries possess "point-source

natural resources"—oil or minerals. Nigeria is one example of a country ruined by an abundance of oil. Angola is another: its GDP per head is lower today than it was in 1960.[15] So much, by the way, for the view that what countries need for successful development is more aid. If foreign resources were all that was needed to make a country rich, Angola and Nigeria would not be in the state they are in.

Even where natural resources do not generate corrupt, rent-seeking societies, they can be an obstacle to sustained development. In the postwar era, the most successful route to development seems to have been via the export of labor-intensive manufactures, the route on which China has followed Hong Kong, Singapore, Taiwan, and South Korea. The success of developing countries with exports of manufactures has been astonishing: in 1980 only 25 percent of the merchandise exports of developing countries were manufactures. By 1998, this had risen to 80 percent. The old view in which developing countries exported commodities in return for manufactures is entirely outmoded. Today, they are just as likely to export manufactures (and services, too, since their share in total exports of developing countries has risen to 17 percent, from 9 percent in the early 1980s) in return for commodities.[16]

The path of manufactures offers a number of significant advantages. World markets for manufactures, while not free, have been relatively open and dynamic. Markets for agricultural commodities have either been slow-growing and price-insensitive (as for the classic tropical commodities—cocoa, tea, and coffee), highly protected in the world's most important markets (as for temperate agricultural commodities), or both (as for sugar). Manufactures also offer a natural ladder up the chain of comparative advantage. A country that has specialized in natural-resource exports will find it hard to shift into competitive manufactures as it must break into world markets after having already achieved quite high real wages and, correspondingly, must do so at relatively high levels of productivity. Since there is learning-by-doing (and other spillovers) in manufacturing, achieving this transition to exports of manufactures can be tricky at relatively high-wages. The transition can be thwarted altogether by policies of blanket protection used, as they were in Argentina and other resource-rich countries, to spread resource rents to a politically influential working class. The task is not hopeless: the U.S. itself is an example of such a transition, successfully completed a century or so ago. More recently, Chile has had great success with a path based on commodity exports.

A final aspect of resources is human resources, both latent and overt. Under latent resources are the underlying cultural and behavioural assumptions of a society—its software, so to speak. Under overt human resources is the level of education achieved by the population. It cannot be altogether an accident that the most successful region of the world, after Europe and the British offshoots in the New World, is east Asia, long home to sophisticated agrarian states, with established bureaucratic cultures and developed mercantile traditions. From this point of view, sub-Saharan Africa has been doubly handicapped, long isolated from Eurasia, still enveloped in tribal traditions and lacking a sizeable number of highly educated people at the time of independence, when many mistakes were made.

Finally, there are policies. If all that mattered were endowments and institutions, one would never have seen sudden take-offs by some countries in response to policy changes. But the rapid growth of South Korea and Taiwan in the 1960s only followed a move to realistic exchange rates and export promotion. The mistakes repeatedly made by other countries have included overvalued real exchange rates, often used to suppress the inflationary consequences of fiscal imprudence (as in Zimbabwe today), creation of corrupt and incompetent public sector monopolies in vital areas, such as electric power generation and distribution or marketing of export commodities; and high and variable protection against imports, often via corruption-fuelling controls. How much these mistakes matter tends to depend on a country's comparative advantage. If a country possesses a supply of very cheap and highly motivated labor, as China does today, it seems easier to survive mistakes (and institutional failings) that would cripple an Argentina or a Mexico. Nevertheless, it was only after a series of reforms that China began to integrate into the world economy. Countries without China's human resources must try even harder to get policy right.

Growth and Inequality

Now what does the performance of those who have succeeded in growing through economic integration mean for inequality? Inequality is a measure of relative incomes. If the average real incomes of poor countries containing at least half of the world's population have been rising faster than those of the relatively rich, inequality among countries, weighted by population, will have fallen. This will be true even if the ratio of the incomes of the world's richest to the world's poorest countries and the absolute gaps in average incomes per head between rich countries and almost all developing countries have risen (as they have).

These two points may need a little explanation. First, compare, say, the U.S. with China. Between 1980 and 2000, according to the World Bank, Chinese average real incomes rose by about 440 percent. Over the same period, U.S. average real incomes per head rose by about 60 percent. The ratio of Chinese real incomes per head, at purchasing power parity, to those of the U.S. rose, accordingly, from just over 3 percent in 1980 to just under 12 percent in 2000. This is a big reduction in relative inequality. But the absolute gap in real incomes between China and the U.S. rose from $20,600 to $30,200 per head (at PPP). The reason is simple: since China's standard of living was, initially, about a thirtieth of that of the U.S. the absolute gap could have remained constant only if China's growth had been thirty times faster than that of the U.S. That would have been impossible. If China continues to grow faster than the U.S. however, absolute gaps will ultimately fall, as happened with Japan in the 1960s and 1970s.

Second, while the *ratio* of the average incomes per head in the richest country to those in the world's least successful countries is rising all the time, the *proportion* of the world's population living in the world's poorest countries has, happily, been falling. Thirty years ago, China and India were among the world's poorest countries. Today, the poorest seems to be Sierra Leone, a country with a population of only 5 million. China's average real income per head is now some ten times higher than Sierra Leone's. The largest very poor country today is Nigeria, with a population of 127 million in 2000 and a real income, at PPP, just a fortieth of that of the U.S. (and a fifth of China's). Again, this means that rising ratios between the average incomes of the world's richest and poorest countries are consistent with declining inequality among countries, weighted by their populations. Moreover, it is also perfectly possible for inequality to have risen in every single country in the world (as Mazur alleges, wrongly) while global inequality has fallen. Unless the increase in inequality among individuals within countries offsets the reduction in population-weighted inequality among countries, not only inequality among (population-weighted) countries, but also inequality among individuals will have declined.

Andrea Boltho of Oxford University and Gianni Toniolo of Rome University have computed population-weighted inequality among forty-nine countries that contain 80 percent of the world's population, back to 1900. To compute their measure of inequality, the gini coefficient, the authors weight the average income, at purchasing power parity (in order to compare standards of living), of each country by its population.[17] They conclude that inequality among countries, weighted in this way, reached its maximum in 1980, at a value of 0.54, but has fallen by 9 percent since then, to 0.50, a level not seen since some six decades ago. This decline in inequality among countries, weighted by their population size, is exactly what one would expect.

The reason for weighting distribution among countries by population is that it is people who matter, not countries. Then the right thing to do must be to take account of changes in distribution of income within countries as well. A paper by François Bourguignon and Christian Morrison, for the World Bank, has attempted this heroic task for 1820 to 1992. As Figure 9.1 shows, they reach five significant conclusions.

First, global inequality among individuals rose progressively, from 1820 to a peak in 1980.

Second, all the increase in global inequality over those 160 years was the result of increases in inequality *among* countries, not *within* them. Within-country inequality was, they estimate (albeit roughly), lower in 1980 than 1820.

Third, back in 1820, only 13 percent of the inequality of individuals was determined by differences in the average prosperity among countries. By 1980, however, just over 60 percent of inequality among individuals was determined by differences in the average prosperity of countries. In the words of the authors, "differences in country economic growth rates practically explain all the increase in world inequality."[18] By 1980, the most important determinant of one's prosperity was not one's class or profession, but where one lived.

Fourth, inequality within countries reached a peak in 1910, subsequently fell to a trough in 1960 and then started to rise, modestly, once again.

Finally, because of a fall in inequality among countries, which offset a modest rise in inequality within them, global inequality among individuals fell, at last, between 1980 and 1992.

The most important conclusion then is that, since the beginning of the nineteenth century, changes in inequality among the world's individuals have been driven by changes in the relative wealth of nations. In particular, the steeply rising inequality among the people of the world in the nineteenth and first half of the twentieth century was driven by the divergent performance of Europe and the British offshoots, on the one hand, and Asia, on the other. What matters then is relative rates of economic growth over extended periods. Consequently, Asia's improved growth

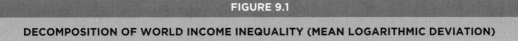

FIGURE 9.1

DECOMPOSITION OF WORLD INCOME INEQUALITY (MEAN LOGARITHMIC DEVIATION)

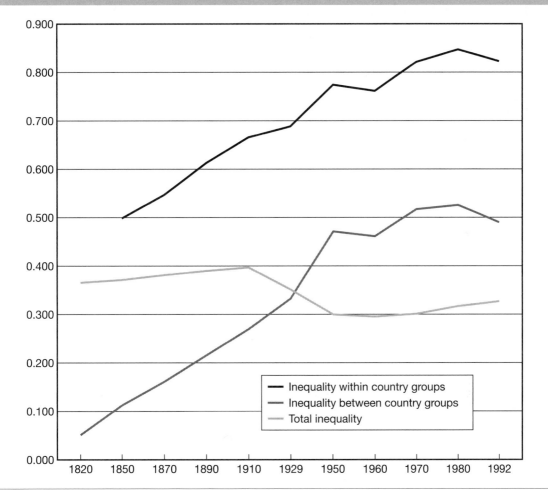

Inequality within country groups
Inequality between country groups
Total inequality

SOURCE: François Bourguignon and Christian Morrison, "Inequality among World Citizens," *American Economic Review*, Vol. 92, No. 4 (September 2002), pp. 727–44.

performance, and especially that of the Asian giants, has started to reverse this picture of rising inequality over the past two decades.

This World Bank study suffers from two defects: to take the analysis so far back, it had to rely on highly limited, indeed sketchy, data; and it ended in 1992, at the beginning of yet another decade of rapid growth in Asia, not least in China.

More recent studies, on similar lines, remedy these defects. These are by another group of three authors at the World Bank, by Surjit Bhalla, formerly a World Bank economist, and by Xavier Sala-I-Martin of Columbia University (see Figure 9.2). All three reach a very similar conclusion: global inequality among households, or individuals, peaked in the 1970s, whereupon it started to

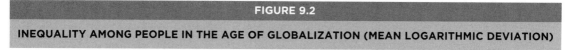

FIGURE 9.2

INEQUALITY AMONG PEOPLE IN THE AGE OF GLOBALIZATION (MEAN LOGARITHMIC DEVIATION)

SOURCE: Xavier Sala-I-Martin, "The World Distribution of Income (Estimated from Individual Country Distributions)" (May 2002, mimeo), Table 8.

fall. This decline happened not because of greater equality within countries, but because of greater population-weighted equality among them.

The three World Bank authors found, for example, that income inequality increased within high-income countries between 1980 and 1995, but fell quite sharply, world-wide, from its peak in 1965–9. This happened entirely because of reductions in (population-weighted) inequality among countries. Bhalla's results are similar, but even stronger. Global inequality in 2000 was lower, he argues, than at any time since 1910. It had fallen from its peak in 1980 by 5 percent (on the gini-coefficient measure). He agrees that inequality rose among people living in high-income countries after 1980, though it was well below levels in 1960. Inequality had fallen sharply among the people of the developing countries, with China and India included, but not with these two giants excluded. Finally, Professor Sala-I-Martin concludes that global inequality peaked in the 1970s (in 1978, to be precise). Between then and 1998, he, too, found inequality had fallen by 5 percent (also on the gini-coefficient measure). It fell substantially more, however, on some of the other measures (see Figure 9.2).

Others contest this relatively sunny picture of global interpersonal inequality in the age of globalization. Perhaps the most important challenge has come from other World Bank researchers. Branko Milanovic, in particular, has written an influential paper, assessing what he calls "true world income distribution" for 1988 and 1993. The important difference between this study (as well as Bank analyses of changes in global poverty, to which I will turn below) and the studies cited above is that it ignores data from national accounts. It relies, instead, only on household surveys of income and expenditure. This has advantages: surveys include home consumption, which is important for poor people in poor countries, and exclude undistributed profits and increases in inventories, which do not affect the current welfare of a population. But it also has a significant disadvantage: the level and rate of rise of spending in such surveys frequently bear little relation to figures in national accounts. This is worrying. National accounts may be flawed, but they do have the virtue of being self-checking, since they are put together from independent evidence on output, income and expenditure. No comparable internal checks can be made on surveys of household incomes and spending.

Milanovic concluded from the evidence he uses that inequality rose substantially between 1988 and 1993. Measured by the gini coefficient, the rise was from 0.63 to 0.66 (a remarkably large 5 percent jump over such a short period). He also concludes that "The most important contributors were: rising urban–rural differences in China, and slow growth of rural purchasing-power adjusted incomes in South Asia, compared to several large developed market economies."[19] The results, though significantly different from those of the other researchers cited above, do at least support them in one respect. Milanovic concludes that "the difference between countries' mean incomes . . . is the most important factor behind world inequality. It explains between 75 and 88 percent of overall inequality" (depending on the measure used).[20] Milanovic also comes up with a number of additional statistics: the richest 1 percent of people in the world receive as much (in PPP terms) as the bottom 57 percent; and an American with the average income of the bottom decile (the bottom 10 percent) is better off than two-thirds of the world's people.

Milanovic's conclusion that inequality increased sharply over five years was, subsequently, the basis of an influential article in *The Economist* newspaper by Robert Wade of the London School of Economics.[21] But are his results both credible and meaningful? A part of the answer is that this was an exceptional period, which makes the results more credible but less meaningful. Chinese economic growth slowed at the time of the Tiananmen Square massacre in 1989. Similarly, India suffered an economic crisis in 1991. Thus Milanovic's analysis was, accidentally, timed to coincide with the one period in the last two decades of the twentieth century when the two giant developing countries were growing quite modestly. Even Sala-I-Martin found that global inequality rose between 1986 and 1989, before falling, once again, after 1990 (see Figure 9.2). It would, for this reason, be dangerous to generalize from an analysis that covers this period. All the same, the size of the increase in inequality estimated by Milanovic is remarkable. According to Bhalla, the relative incomes of the high-income countries would need to rise by 27 percent to generate a 5 percent increase in global income inequality (measured by the gini coefficient). That simply did not happen. So the question of credibility remains.

Milanovic's data indicate, for example, that there was no increase in rural incomes in China between 1988 and 1993. National accounts give quite a different picture. So what is going on? A part of the answer, as suggested above, is that average household incomes and spending generally rise much more slowly in surveys of household income and expenditure than in national accounts. To take a significant example, the survey data relied upon by two authoritative World Bank researchers for their estimates of changes in absolute poverty between 1987 and 1999 show a rise in real consumption in developing countries of just 11 percent.[22] Over the same period, observes Bhalla, national accounts data (converted with PPP exchange rates) show rises in average real incomes of 24 percent and in consumption of 21 percent. This is not some small discrepancy—it is a yawning chasm.

Bhalla also observes that, between 1987 and 1998, the ratio of average incomes in surveys of incomes to those in national accounts fell from 56 to 46 percent in east Asia, from 75 to 62 percent in south Asia and from 69 to 63 percent in sub-Saharan Africa. For consumption surveys, the ratio of averages fell from 82 to 81 percent in east Asia, 73 to 56 percent in south Asia and 125 to 115 percent in sub-Saharan Africa. On similar lines, Milanovic shows that, for Africa, average household income/expenditure in the surveys he used was 79 percent of levels in national accounts in 1988, but only 70 percent by 1993. For Asia, the ratio fell more modestly, from 61 to 59 percent. Nevertheless, in Milanovic's study, growth in average incomes, between 1988 and 1993, in the developing regions with the largest number of poor people was lower than in national accounts (at PPP): 49 percent, against 54 percent, for Asia,

and 19 percent, against 33 percent for sub-Saharan Africa. This, in turn, must be a part of the explanation for the discrepancy between Milanovic's results and those of researchers who use national accounts.

How then is one to explain this discrepancy between the growth shown in surveys and the growth shown in national accounts? Logically, there are three alternatives.

The first is that the surveys are correct in their estimate of the level of consumption and incomes, in which case economic growth has been far slower in many important developing countries than we have believed. The national accounts are not reliable estimates, but propaganda. The second possibility is that both national accounts and the surveys are correct, for what they cover. This would be possible if virtually all the spending (and income) under-recorded in the surveys was by (and of) the rich *and* if the true share of the rich in both incomes and spending in the economy was also rising rapidly. This would mean that in many developing countries income and spending were becoming more unequal, more quickly, than the standard estimates of inequality suggest. The third possibility is that household surveys have become ever less reliable as a way of estimating the rise in real incomes and spending over time (though they still remain all we have if we want to calculate changes in the distribution of income and spending over time).

The first possibility seems hugely implausible. If we did reject national accounts data for economic growth, we would be left with no idea of what has been going on in developing countries. Moreover, while there are questions about national accounts data, notably for China, they are probably the most carefully constructed national data in any country. This leaves the second and third possibilities. We cannot, on the evidence we now have, distinguish between them. In other words, either countries have been becoming more unequal more quickly than all the evidence suggests (because of rapid increases in unrecorded incomes and spending of the rich) or the household surveys themselves are unreliable.

This is not, however, the only difficulty. Converting incomes at average PPP exchange rates will itself create important distortions because the consumption of tradable goods and non-tradable services will vary across households. In general, the poor in developing countries will consume more of the former and the rich more of the latter. Every visitor from the west to a developing country must have been struck by the ability of the prosperous to employ hordes of servants, long vanished in the west, even though they cannot afford the latest high-technology machinery. If this were taken into account, the income distribution, properly measured at PPP, would be more unequal than the measured income distribution at domestic relative prices. The reverse side of this is that, in rapidly growing countries, the prices of services rise in relation to those of goods. If the poor consume goods more intensively than the rich, then they gain more from growth than the rich do. Thus, while the initial income distribution would be more unequal than calculations at domestic relative prices suggest, it would also be becoming more equal more quickly than they suggest. This reinforces the assumption that the poor are likely to have benefited substantially from growth in rapidly growing developing countries.

The bottom line is that it is plausible that inequality among individuals across the world has been falling over the past two decades, because of the relatively rapid growth of the Asian giants. This is consistent with rising inequality within many countries, rising relative gaps between the average incomes of the richest and very poorest countries, and increasing absolute gaps between the average incomes in the high-income countries, on the one hand, and virtually all developing countries, on the other. But the latter simply shows the tyranny of history. By 1980, inequality among countries was so large that it was impossible for absolute gaps to close, until there was much greater convergence of relative incomes.

Yet this ignores the fact that a great many countries have not enjoyed rapid growth, most notably in Africa, but also, to a lesser extent, in Latin America, the Middle East and, in the 1990s,

the countries in transition from communism, especially the former Soviet Union. In the 1990s, for example, according to the Human Development Report, fifty-four countries, with 12 percent of the world's population, had negative growth rates in real incomes per head, while another seventy-one countries, with 26 percent of the world's population, had growth of between zero and 3 percent a year in real incomes per head.[23] Similarly, in the World Bank's study of globalization, countries containing 1.1 million people had virtually stagnant real incomes between 1980 and 1997 (see Table 9.2). While the poor performance of so many countries may not have prevented global income distribution from improving (though it will tend to do so once China's average incomes rise above the world average), it has certainly had a significant impact on the scale and regional distribution of world poverty. To that topic, just as vexed as income distribution, we now turn.

Growth and Poverty

On all measures, global inequality rose until about the early 1980s. Since then, it appears, inequality among individuals has declined as a result of the rapid growth of much of Asia and, above all, China. But it is also important to understand what drove the long-term trend towards global inequality over almost two centuries. It is the consequence of the dynamic growth that spread, unevenly, from the UK in the course of the nineteenth and twentieth centuries. In the process a growing number of people became vastly better off than any one had ever been before, but few can have become worse off. Such dynamic growth is bound to be uneven. Some regions of the world proved better able to take advantage of the new opportunities for growth, because of superior climates, resources and policies. In just the same way, some parts of countries, particularly huge countries such as China or India, are today better able to take advantage of new opportunities than others. To bemoan the resulting increase in inequality is to bemoan the growth itself. It is to

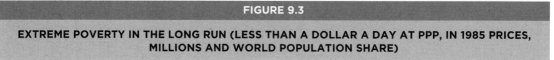

FIGURE 9.3

EXTREME POVERTY IN THE LONG RUN (LESS THAN A DOLLAR A DAY AT PPP, IN 1985 PRICES, MILLIONS AND WORLD POPULATION SHARE)

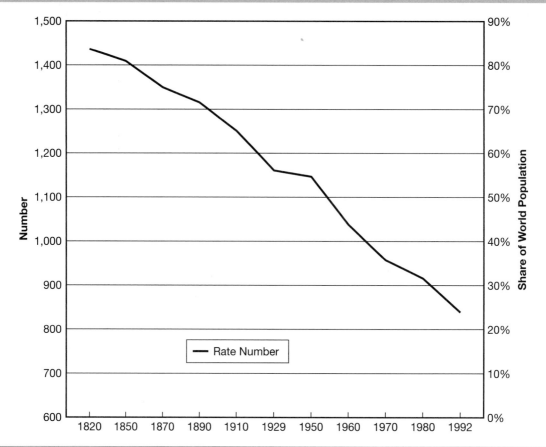

SOURCE: François Bourguignon and Christian Morrison, "Inequality among World Citizens," *American Economic Review*, Vol. 92, No. 4 (September 2002), pp. 727–44.

argue that it would be better for everybody to be equally poor than for some to become significantly better off, even if, in the long run, this will almost certainly lead to advances for everybody.

For this reason, it makes more sense to focus on what has happened to poverty than to inequality. Again, the statistical debate is a vexed one. But some plausible conclusions can be reached.

The World Bank has, for some time, defined extreme poverty as an income of a dollar a day at

1985 international prices (PPP). Bourguignon and Morrison also used that figure in an analysis of extreme poverty since 1820, on the same lines as their analysis of inequality (see Figure 9.3).[24] It comes to three intriguing conclusions. First, the number of desperately poor people rose from about 900 million in 1820 to a peak of from 1.3 to 1.4 billion between 1960 and 1980, before falling, modestly, to just under 1.3 billion in 1992. Second, the proportion of the world's population living on

TABLE 9.3

INCOME POVERTY, BY REGION (MILLIONS OF PEOPLE LIVING ON LESS THAN $1.08 A DAY AT 1993 PPP)

Regions	1987	1990	1999
East Asia and Pacific	418	486	279
(Excluding China)	114	110	57
China	304	376	222
Europe and Central Asia	1	6	24
Latin America and Caribbean	64	48	57
Middle East and North Africa	9	5	6
South Asia	474	506	488
Sub-Saharan Africa	217	241	315
Total	1,183	1,292	1,169
Total, excluding China	880	917	945

SOURCES: World Bank, *World Development Report 2000/2001: Attacking Poverty* (Washington, DC: World Bank, 2000), Table 1.1, and World Bank, *Global Economic Prospects and the Developing Countries 2003: Investing to Unlock Global Opportunities* (Washington, DC: World Bank, 2003), Table 1.9.

less than a dollar a day fell dramatically, over time, from over 80 percent in 1820, a time when living on the margins of subsistence was the norm, to about two-thirds at the beginning of the twentieth century, to close to 50 percent by 1950, then 32 percent in 1980 and, finally, 24 percent by 1992. The contrast between rising numbers and falling proportions of the world's population in extreme poverty reflects the race between higher output and rising population, particularly in poor countries. In 1820, the world's population was a little over a billion. By 1910 it was 1.7 billion and by 1992 it had risen to 5.5 billion.

Again, the results from Bourguignon and Morrison are cause for qualified optimism. From being universal, extreme poverty has become, if not rare, the affliction of less than a quarter of a vastly increased human population. But, again, it is necessary to look more closely at what has happened in the supposed period of globalization, the years since 1980. Here, the authoritative voice is that of the World Bank, the institution whose "dream is a world without poverty."[25] The numbers in Tables

9.3 and 9.4 come from two recent World Bank publications.[26] They reach the following conclusions.

First, the number of people in extreme poverty fell from 1.18 billion in 1987 to 1.17 billion in 1999, but not before jumping upwards to 1.29 billion in 1990, underlining the extent to which the 1988–93 period chosen by Milanovic was exceptional.

Second, enormous declines in the number of people in extreme poverty have occurred in dynamic east Asia, from 486 million in 1990 to 279 million in 1999, including China, and from 114 million to 57 million, excluding China. In China itself, the decline, between 1990 and 1999, was from 376 million to 222 million. Rapid growth reduces poverty dramatically. This remains today, as it has been for two centuries, an abiding truth.

Third, the number of people in extreme poverty fell very modestly in south Asia between 1990 and 1999, while it rose sharply in eastern Europe and central Asia (the former Soviet empire) and, above all, sub-Saharan Africa, from 217 million in 1987 to 241 million in 1990, and then 315 million in 1999.

TABLE 9.4		
REGIONAL INCIDENCE OF INCOME POVERTY (SHARE OF PEOPLE LIVING ON LESS THAN $1.08 A DAY AT 1993 PPP, IN REGIONAL POPULATIONS, PERCENT)			
Regions	*1987*	*1990*	*1999*
East Asia and Pacific	26.6	30.5	15.6
(Excluding China)	23.9	24.2	10.6
China	27.8	33.0	17.7
Europe and Central Asia	0.2	1.4	5.1
Latin America and Caribbean	15.3	11.0	11.1
Middle East and North Africa	4.3	2.1	2.2
South Asia	44.9	45.0	36.6
Sub-Saharan Africa	46.6	47.4	49.0
Total	28.3	29.6	23.2
Total, excluding China	28.5	28.5	25.0
World total	23.7	24.6	19.5

SOURCES: World Bank, *World Development Report 2000/2001: Attacking Poverty*, Table 1.1, and World Bank, *Global Economic Prospects 2003*, Table 1.9.

Fourth, the regional incidence of poverty fell dramatically in east Asia, from 30.5 percent of the population in 1990 to just 15.6 percent in 1999. Excluding China, it fell from 24.2 to 10.6 percent. In China, it fell from 33 percent of the population to just under 18 percent over nine years. This was, without doubt, the most rapid reduction in the incidence of extreme poverty anywhere, ever.

Fifth, the incidence of poverty also fell sharply in south Asia (dominated by India) in the 1990s, from 45.0 percent of the population in 1990 to 36.6 percent in 1999. But it rose sharply in eastern Europe and central Asia and also increased in sub-Saharan Africa, from 47.4 percent of the population to 49.0 percent.

As with the numbers of inequality, so with those on poverty, controversy abounds. In the optimistic corner are, once again, Bhalla and Sala-I-Martin. A comparison between their results and those of the World Bank for the number of people in absolute poverty over the 1990s (on slightly different definitions) appears in Figure 9.4. All three show substantial declines between 1990

and the end of the decade. But the World Bank's is a 9.5 percent decline over nine years; Sala-I-Martin has one of 13.1 percent over eight years; and Bhalla one of 25.6 percent over ten years.

What is one to make of these discrepancies? As Sala-I-Martin notes, the difference between his results and those of the World Bank, after some adjustments, are not large.[27] The big discrepancy is with the results of Bhalla. The most important source of those differences seems to be his use of national accounts data for the growth in average incomes and spending, along with household surveys for distribution of income and spending, against the Bank's use of surveys for both.

The implication of this difference is shown most clearly for what is, in many ways, the most surprising single case: India. For in India, as we know, real incomes per head rose by around a half in the 1990s yet the number of people in extreme poverty appears, on the World Bank data, to have fallen quite modestly. In south Asia, as a whole, dominated by India, it fell only from 506 million to 488 million between 1990 and

FIGURE 9.4

THE FALL IN NUMBERS IN EXTREME POVERTY IN THE 1990S (MILLIONS)

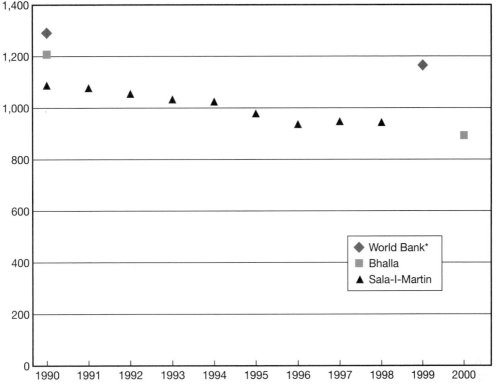

*To make these data roughly comparable, those chosen are as follows: for the World Bank, the $1.08 poverty line, at 1993 PPP, which appears to apply to consumption; for Bhalla, a $1.30 poverty line, at 1993 prices and, for Sala-I-Martin, his consumption poverty rates (applied to world population, to derive levels) for a dollar a day (probably at 1993 PPP).

SOURCES: World Bank, *Global Economic Prospects and the Developing Countries 2003: Investing to Unlock Global Opportunities* (Washington, DC: World Bank, 2003), Table 1.9; Surjit S. Bhalla, *Imagine There's No Country: Poverty, Inequality and Growth in the Era of Globalization* (Washington, DC: Institute for International Economics, 2002), Table 9.1; and Sala-I-Martin, "The World Distribution of Income (Estimated from Individual Country Distributions)" (May 2002, mimeo), Table 3A.

1999. This, Bhalla suggests, does not look very plausible. Since the latter figure is 42 percent of all the people in extreme poverty in the world, any significant error in calculating it is bound to create equally significant mistakes in the totals.

One thing we do know is that between 1987 and 1998 the proportion of the consumption shown in national accounts covered by the household surveys fell from 73 percent to only 56 percent in south Asia. It looks then as though the surveys missed a great deal of the rise in consumption in these countries. Moreover, as Bhalla points out, surveys of wages and unemployment in India indicate rises in rural wages that are far more consistent with consumption figures in the national accounts than in the household surveys of expenditure. In addition, India's official estimate of the poverty rate in 1999 (at a threshold rate of $1.25 a day, at PPP, in 1993 prices, which is higher than the Bank's $1.08 and should generate a significantly higher number of poor people) was 26 percent, or 260 million. Yet the Bank apparently calculates this figure, on its own lower threshold, at around 360 million. It also calculates the level of poverty, on the Indian government's $1.25 line, at 470 million, which is 210 million more than the Indian government does itself. The government's estimates are themselves at the high end. Other estimates—from the respected National Council for Applied Economic Research, for example—give far lower numbers still for the population in extreme poverty in India, at 150 million in 1999.[28]

In short, there are good reasons to believe that the Bank has overestimated the number of people in extreme poverty – and underestimated its decline. If that is not so, then it must surely mean that the increase in inequality in India since the early 1990s has been very large indeed. That is logically possible, since so many of the poor live in the most backward states, such as Uttar Pradesh and Bihar. But it is not what India's own data show. One may not wish to go as far as Bhalla, who argues that the proportion of the developing world's population below $1.25 a day (at 1993 PPP) fell from 44 percent in 1980 to 13 percent in 2000. But the decline in poverty in India, and so the world, may well be substantially greater than the Bank suggests.

This, needless to say, is not universally accepted. Professors Thomas Pogge and Sanjay Reddy, also of Columbia University, like Professor Sala-I-Martin, argue that the Bank's numbers, if not necessarily too optimistic, are unsoundly based. They suggest, in particular, that this admittedly heroic attempt to compare poverty across the globe with the use of one measuring rod ($1.08 a day at PPP, in 1993 prices) is fundamentally flawed, in three ways. First, the international poverty line used by the Bank "fails to meet elementary requirements of consistency." As a result, "the Bank's poverty line leads to meaningless poverty estimates." Second, "the Bank's poverty line is not anchored in any assessment of the basic resource requirements of human beings." And third, "the poverty estimates currently available are subject to massive uncertainties because of their sensitivity to the values of crucial parameters that are estimated on the basis of limited data or none at all."[29]

Let us grant most of this. It is evident that converting national data with PPP exchange rates that are themselves both averages for economies and variable from year to year is a rough-and-ready procedure, to put it mildly. Equally, the dollar-a-day line is both inherently arbitrary and bound to mean different things in different countries. It is also true, as Pogge and Reddy argue, that PPP adjustments, which are largely for the relative price of non-tradable services, will create large, and growing, mismeasurement of the real incomes of the poor, since the latter consume commodities more intensively than the better off. That could well justify higher poverty lines. At the same time, it might mean that the rate of decline in poverty is higher than estimated by the Bank, since relative prices of commodities normally fall in fast-growing countries.

The big question, however, is whether it would be easy to do better. Pogge and Reddy suggest that the exercise should be conducted in terms not of arbitrary levels of income, but of capabilities—"calories and essential nutrients." They argue that "the income persons need to avoid poverty at some particular time and place can then be specified in terms of the least expensive locally available set of commodities containing the relevant characteristics needed to achieve the elementary human capabilities."[30] This sounds, straightforward. In fact, long experience suggests that reaching agreement on such poverty levels across countries is nigh on impossible.

Pogge and Reddy provide a warning. All poverty estimates are inherently arbitrary. Certainly, there is no good reason to believe in anybody's estimates of the levels of poverty at any moment.

Trends are another matter. It is certain that the share of those in extreme (absolute, as opposed to relative) income poverty in the world's population has fallen enormously over the last two centuries, a decline that has, equally certainly, continued since 1980. It is almost equally certain that the numbers in extreme income poverty fell in east Asia over the past few decades and particularly over the past two. That is likely, though less certain, for India. Encouragingly, both China and India show enormous declines in estimates of numbers in extreme poverty on their different national measures (about 100 million for India, between 1980 and 2000, and 220 million for China, between 1978 and 1999, despite large increases in population in both countries over this period). Given these changes in east and south Asia, it is plausible, though not certain, that numbers in absolute income poverty declined world-wide. What is more than merely plausible is the proposition that, where numbers in extreme poverty have declined, the cause has been accelerated growth. This is as true of regions within countries (especially where mobility is hindered, as in China) as among them.

Poverty and Human Welfare

In the absence of any of the internationally comparable measures of capabilities that Pogge and Reddy call for, one has to look at other supporting evidence. It is here that we find unambiguous good news. For it is clear that human welfare has improved greatly in recent decades.[31] As an independent analyst, Indur Goklany, persuasively argues, it is possible, in addition, for people to enjoy better health and longer lives, at lower incomes, than before.[32] This is the result of technological and organizational improvements that have come from the world's rich countries. In 1913, life expectancy at birth in the U.S. was fifty-two years. U.S. GDP per head, at PPP, was then about 50 percent higher than China's would be in 2000, and 150 percent higher than India's.[33] Yet,

in 2000, life expectancy in China was seventy and in India sixty-three. In 1900, Sweden seems to have had the world's highest life expectancy, at fifty-six. In 2000, only very poor countries, mostly in Africa, had life expectancy as low as (or lower than) this. As Goklany shows, the curve relating life expectancy to average GDP per head has shifted upwards over time. Similarly, the curve relating infant mortality to incomes has shifted downwards over time. Much the same desirable pattern can be observed for the relationship between other indicators of human welfare and income.

In the developing world as a whole, life expectancy rose by four months each year after 1970, from fifty-five years in 1970 to sixty-four years in 2000. It rose from forty-nine in 1970 to sixty-two in south Asia and from fifty-nine to sixty-nine in east Asia. Tragically, life expectancy fell in thirty-two countries in the 1990s, mostly because of the AIDS epidemic, or the gross incompetence (or worse) of governments, as in North Korea and Zimbabwe. It also fell because of western hysteria about DDT, which removed the only effective way of controlling that dreadful curse, malaria. Improvements in life expectancy have meant a decline in global inequality as well. In 1950, average life expectancy in developing countries was two-thirds of the levels in high-income countries (forty-four and sixty-six years of age, respectively). By 2000, it was 82 percent (sixty-four and seventy-eight).

Meanwhile, in the developing world as a whole, infant mortality rates have fallen from 107 per thousand in 1970 to eighty-seven in 1980 and fifty-eight in 2000. In east Asia, the region with the fastest-growing economy, they have fallen from fifty-six in 1980 to thirty-five in 2000. In south Asia, infant mortality fell from 119 in 1980 to seventy-three in 2000. In sub-Saharan Africa progress was, once again, slower. But infant mortality fell even there, from 116 in 1980 to ninety-one in 2000.

Losing a child must inflict the sharpest grief human beings can suffer. The decline in infant mortality is thus a tremendous blessing in itself.

So, too, is the rise in life expectancy. But these improvements also mean that it makes sense to invest in education. The world increasingly produces smaller families with much better-educated children. On average, adult literacy in developing countries rose from 53 percent in 1970 to 74 percent in 1998. By 2000, adult male illiteracy was down to 8 percent in east Asia, though it was still 30 percent in sub-Saharan Africa and (a real scandal this) 34 percent in south Asia. Adult female illiteracy was more widespread than that for men, but was also improving. Between 1990 and 2000, female illiteracy fell from 29 percent to 21 percent in east Asia. In south Asia, it fell from 66 percent to 57 percent (an even worse scandal than the low rate for men), while in sub-Saharan Africa it fell from 60 to 47 percent. Illiteracy is much lower among the young. This guarantees that rates will continue to fall, as time passes.

The reduction in fertility rates has also been remarkable. In the developing world as a whole, births per woman (the fertility rate) have fallen from 4.1 in 1980 to 2.8 in 2000. In east Asia, the fertility rate, down from 3.0 to 2.1, is already at close to the replacement rate. In Latin America, the fertility rate has fallen from 4.1 to 2.6. Even in south Asia it has fallen from 5.3 in 1980 to 3.3 in 2000. Again, progress has been slowest in sub-Saharan Africa, where the birth rate has only fallen from 6.6 in 1980 to 5.2 in 2000. But, in all, these reductions tell us of improved control by women of their fertility, of fewer children with more parental investment in each and of far stronger confidence that children will survive to maturity. The demographic transition that is now under way in the developing world is immensely encouraging. It is also an indication— as well as a source—of rising welfare.

Now, let us look at hunger. Growth in food production has substantially outpaced that of population. Between 1961 and 1999, the average daily food supply per person increased 24 percent globally. In developing countries, it rose by 39 percent, to 2,684 calories. By 1999, China's average daily food supply had gone up 82 percent, to 3,044 calories, from a barely subsistence level of 1,636 in 1961. India's went up by 48 percent to 2,417 calories, from 1,635 calories in 1950–1. According to estimates by the United Nations Food and Agricultural Organization, the average active adult needs between 2,000 and 2,310 calories per person. Thus the developing-country food supply has gone, on average, from inadequate to adequate. Hunger persists. But the FAO estimates that the number of people suffering from chronic undernourishment fell from 920 million in 1969–71 to 790 million in 1997–9, or from 35 to 17 percent of the population of developing countries. Trends in sub-Saharan Africa, the continent that did not grow, were far worse. Between 1979–81 and 1997–9, the share of the population that was undernourished declined from 38 to 34 percent, but absolute numbers, in a rapidly growing population, rose from 168 million to 194 million.[34]

Now, turn to what has become one of the most controversial indicators: child labor. One would expect that more prosperous parents, with fewer children, who are also expected to live longer, would wish to see their children being educated rather than at work. So, happily, it has proved. The proportion of children aged ten to fourteen in the labor force has, according to the World Bank, fallen from 23 percent in all developing countries in 1980 to 12 percent in 2000. The fall in east Asia has, once again, been astonishing, from 26 to 8 percent. In south Asia, it has fallen from 23 to 15 percent. In sub-Saharan Africa, the decline has been less impressive, from 35 to 29 percent. China's transformation has been breathtaking, with a fall from 30 percent in 1980 to just 8 percent in 2000. In lagging India, the fall was from 21 to 12 percent. Thus, just as one would expect, countries whose economies have done well in the era of globalization have been ones in which parents have chosen to withdraw their children from the labor force. Parents have never put their children to work out of indifference or malevolence, but only out of necessity.

Finally, let us remember some of the other features of the last two decades: the worldwide shift to democracy, however imperfect; the disappearance of some of the worst despotisms in history; the increase in personal economic opportunity in vast swathes of the world, notably China and India; and the improving relative position of women almost, although not quite, everywhere.

All these are very encouraging trends. People in developing countries and, particularly, in the fast-growing ones are enjoying longer and healthier lives than before. They are better fed and better educated. They treat their fewer children better. All these good things have not happened only because of rising incomes. Learning from the high-income countries has helped. Developing countries are reaching higher levels of social progress at lower levels of income than the high-income countries of today. But, as one would expect, social progress has been greatest where incomes have risen fastest. It remains "the growth, stupid."

Inequality within Countries

If Mazur was wrong about global inequality, is he at least right about inequality within countries? For, as I have argued above, it is perfectly possible that globalization has worsened income distribution within every country, while improving it in the world as a whole. But has it done so? The answer is: up to a point. To be more precise, one needs to look at what has happened within developing and high-income countries separately.

Inequality within Developing Countries

Inequality has increased among what the World Bank calls the "new globalizers," its twenty-four countries with an aggregate population of close to 3 billion people, but only because of China.[35] The widening of inequality in China over the past two decades, almost entirely because of growing inter-regional inequality, was, however, inevitable, for four reasons: first, the distribution of incomes in Mao Zedong's gigantic prison was at least highly equal; second, the

growth has been driven, since the initial surge in rural incomes, after abolition of the communes, by integration into the world economy, which has been dominated by the coastal regions of the country; third, in a country as enormous as China, as in the world as a whole, any imaginable growth process is certain to be regionally uneven (as is also becoming increasingly evident in India); and, last but not least, the Chinese authorities have done their best to limit migration from the rural hinterland to the booming coast. Thus, in many ways, today's China replicates, on a smaller scale, what has happened in the world as a whole over the past two decades. The reason for the growing internal inequality is, as it has been at the world level, the rising gap between the living standards of regions (countries) that are integrating successfully into the world economy and regions (countries) that are not. The poorest regions (countries) were not hurt by globalization. They just failed to be part of it. The challenge for China (as for the world) is to improve the ability of these lagging regions to participate, not to accept the clamour from some critics to separate itself from the world economy (hardly likely, as it happens).

If we look at other globalizing developing countries, we find they are as likely to have an improved distribution of income as a worsening one. David Dollar and Aart Kraay, in an already well-known paper, have argued that trade helps growth and that the poor tend to share in equal proportions with the rich in any rise in subsequent incomes. The paper, based on an analysis of 137 countries, finds that the poorest 20 percent of the population does, on average, share equally in growth.[36] This, interestingly, is a contradiction of a previously accepted idea, originally proposed by the Nobel-laureate Simon Kuznets, that inequality rises initially with growth, before declining once again. Bhalla, in his subsequent analysis, argues that in fact Kuznets was right and Dollar and Kraay are wrong. The evidence continues to suggest modest widening in inequality in growing economies.[37]

But note that, even if the Kuznets hypothesis were true, growth would still be very much better for the poor than stagnation all round.

What seems clear is that the poor do share in growth. Viet Nam is an interesting example. Of the poorest 5 percent of households in 1992–3, some 98 percent had higher incomes six years later. Similar declines in income poverty were observed in Uganda in the 1990s.[38] Two qualifications, however, need to be made about this story. First, even if the poor do share equally in any proportionate increase in incomes, as Dollar and Kraay argue, the absolute increase in incomes they enjoy depends on their initial share. This is one sense in which growth can be more, or less, "pro-poor." Second, whether or not the poor share more or less equally in the benefits of the faster growth stimulated by greater trade depends on a country's comparative advantage. This is particularly important in understanding the contrasting experience with the moves towards outward-looking policies of the east Asian tigers and Latin American countries.

Standard theory (and experience) suggests that liberalization is good for the incomes of the relatively abundant factor of production. In east Asia, initial comparative advantage was based on cheap labor. One would expect international integration to be especially good for the relative incomes of the poor—and, on the whole, it was. Latin America is, however, a land-abundant continent with relatively high wages and a history of protection aimed at distributing income from the agricultural sector to the industrial working class. In these cases, one would expect liberalization to create greater inequality. The negative impact on the wages of the unskilled in Latin America has also probably been exacerbated by the entry of China and the rest of east Asia into the world economy.

Inequality within High-Income Countries

Let us turn, then, from the developing countries to the high-income countries. Here there seems to be less ambiguity: inequality has risen in most high-income countries. Where it has not risen, unemployment has tended to increase instead. In these countries, moreover, changes in inequality tend to be driven by changes in relative wages, while in developing countries wage-earners, especially in the modern sector, tend to be an élite. Widening of gaps in relative pay between the skilled and unskilled was substantial in the U.S. and UK in the 1980s and early 1990s. In the U.S. in particular, "the widening has been severe enough that lower-skilled groups had no gain and probably a slight loss, in real pay, over the whole quarter century 1973–98, this despite a healthy growth of real earnings for the labor force as a whole."

This pattern of rising relative pay between skilled and unskilled workers does not seem to apply to other important high-income countries, however, such as Germany, France, Italy and Japan, at least for full-time workers. But when one takes work hours and unemployment into account, the same applies. Unskilled workers were more likely to be unemployed or to work part-time. As a result, from the mid-1980s to the mid-1990s, twenty out of twenty-one members of the Organization for Economic Co-operation and Development experienced a rise in inequality, largely because of rising inequality of labor earnings.[39]

If these are the facts, what are the causes? Logically, there could be several, some that work via the demand for labor and others that work on the supply. These include: trade, particularly rising imports of labor-intensive manufactures, partly as a result of growing outsourcing by multinational companies; a general growth in competition, eroding the monopoly position of industries (such as steel and automobile manufacture) that have, historically, granted large wage premia to trade-union-organized unskilled and semi-skilled labor; laws and other social and economic changes that have weakened the bargaining position of trades unions; technology, particularly skill-biased technological change or, less technically, innovations which raise the relative demand for skilled labor; a failure of the education system to improve the supply of skilled labor with sufficient speed; and immigration of unskilled labor.

Trade, reinforced by immigration, is then one of a number of possible explanations for the growth in inequality or, more precisely, the declining relative position of unskilled workers in high-income countries. Some would further argue that trade has caused the skill-bias in technical change—to save on what is, by world standards, relatively expensive unskilled labor, companies have developed technologies that save on its use. But, even if this were not true, a well-known economic theorem, the Stolper-Samuelson theorem, named after its two inventors, argues that prices of factors of production, including wages of labor, will be equalized in trade.[40] If so, since unskilled labor is enormously abundant in the world and a far higher proportion of that labor is engaged—actually and potentially—in the world economy than ever before, the wages of such labor in the high-income countries are bound to fall, relatively if not absolutely. To put this point more brutally, the working people of the high-income countries have historically benefited from the monopoly of their countries in manufacturing. Now, however, they are in competition with the unskilled of the world, with potentially devastating results.

I will return to some of these points in the next chapter, when considering the impact of trade, more narrowly. At this point, one must note that there are a number of powerful assumptions underlying the applicability of the Stolper-Samuelson theorem. Among others, productive efficiency must be the same in all countries, which is not. Moreover, if this theorem applied, there would have been an improvement in the terms of trade (a reduction in the price of labor-intensive imports relative to exports), followed by a switch in methods of production towards those that use what had become redundant unskilled labor more intensively, everywhere. Yet, as Jagdish Bhagwati of Columbia University and others have argued, neither seems to have hap-

pened since the early 1980s. Particularly striking is the shift to greater use of skilled labor in almost every industry. This suggests to most observers that skill-biased technological change has been the dominant forces. Professors Lindert and Williamson summarize the broad consensus among economists on the rise in inequality in the U.S. (where the rise has been particularly large) that somewhere between 15 percent and a third is due to trade.[41]

The bottom line then is that the increased inequality in high-income countries over the past two decades may have been caused, in modest part, by increased exports from the developing world. Even so, two essential qualifications must be made.

First, if this has been the case, it is the result of an economic process that has benefited both the exporting countries *and* the importing countries as a whole. The right response is to help those adversely affected by low-wage imports, through retraining, improved education, generalized wage subsidies for low-wage labor and, if all else fails, simple transfers of income. It would be immoral for rich countries to deprive the poor of the world of so large an opportunity for betterment merely because they are unable to handle sensibly and justly the distribution of the internal costs of a change certain to be highly beneficial overall.

Second, remember above all that this upheaval in the high-income countries is part of a benign broadening of global prosperity. Bhalla has a particularly telling way of illustrating this. He defines the global middle class as those earning between $3,650 and $14,600 a year, at PPP, in 1993 prices. On his analysis, in 1960, some 64 percent of all the middle-class people in the world lived in the high-income countries. Today, this is down to 17 percent, with 51 percent living in Asia, the Middle East and North Africa, up from just 6 percent in 1960 and 16 percent in 1980. Only the most selfish westerners can complain about a transformation that has brought so much to so many so quickly.

Conclusion

Let us return then to the propositions with which this exploration of growth, poverty and inequality began. Here they are, together with what we now know.

First, the ratio of average incomes in the richest countries to those in the very poorest has continued to rise in the age of globalization. Response: correct.

Second, the absolute gap in living standards between today's high-income countries and the vast proportion of developing countries has continued to rise. Response: also correct and inevitably so, given the starting-point two decades ago.

Third, global inequality among individuals has risen. Response: false. Global inequality among individuals has, in all probability, fallen since the 1970s.

Fourth, the number of people in extreme income poverty has also risen. Response: probably false. The number of people in extreme poverty may well have fallen since 1980, for the first time in almost two centuries, because of the rapid growth of the Asian giants.

Fifth, the proportion of people in extreme poverty in the world's population has also risen. Response: false. The proportion of the world's population in extreme poverty has certainly fallen.

Sixth, the poor of the world are worse off not just in terms of incomes, but in terms of a wide range of indicators of human welfare and capability. Response: unambiguously false. The welfare of humanity, judged by life expectancies, infant mortality, literacy, hunger, fertility, and the incidence of child labor has improved enormously. It has improved least in sub-Saharan Africa, partly because of disease and partly because of the continent's failure to grow.

Seventh, income inequality has risen in every country and particularly in countries most exposed to international economic integration. Response: false. Income inequality has not risen in most of the developing countries that have integrated with the world economy, though it has risen in China. Inequality has apparently risen in the high-income countries, but the role of globalization in this change is unclear and, in all probability, not decisive.

We can also make some propositions of our own. Human welfare, broadly defined, has risen. The proportion of humanity living in desperate misery is declining. The problem of the poorest is not that they are exploited, but that they are almost entirely unexploited: they live outside the world economy. The soaring growth of the rapidly integrating developing economies has transformed the world for the better. The challenge is to bring those who have failed so far into the new web of productive and profitable global economic relations.

NOTES

1. "Labor's New Internationalism," *Foreign Affairs*, Vol. 79, January–February 2000.

2. Ignacio Ramonet, *Le Monde Diplomatique*, May 1998. Cited in Xavier Sala-I-Martin, "The Myth of Exploding Income Inequality in Europe and the World," in Henryk Kierzkowski (ed.), *Europe and Globalization* (Basingstoke: Palgrave Macmillan, 2002), p. 11.

3. Paul Ehrlich, *The Population Bomb* (New York: Ballantine Books, 1968).

4. World Bank, *Globalization, Growth & Poverty: Building an Inclusive World Economy* (Washington, DC: 2002), Table 1.1, p. 34.

5. *Ibid.*, p. 36.

6. These data are from World Bank, *World Development Indicators 2002* (Washington, DC: World Bank, 2002).

7. World Trade Organization, *International Trade Statistics 2002* (Geneva: WTO, 2002), and T. N. Srinivasan, *Eight Lectures on India's Economic Reforms* (New York: Oxford University Press, 2000), p. 73, for the data on China in the 1970s and a comparison between China and India.

8. United Nations Conference on Trade and Development, *World Investment Report 2002: Transnational Corporations and Export Competitiveness* (New York: United Nations, 2002).

9. World Economic Forum, *The Global Competitiveness Report 2001–02* (New York: Oxford University Press, 2002).

10. See, on the role of government, particularly chapter 5, above.

11. See, on this, Johan Norberg's splendid tract, *In Defence of Global Capitalism* (Timbro, 2001), pp. 102 and, more generally, 98–113.

12. See, for example, Xavier Sala-I-Martin and Arvind Subramanian, "Addressing the Natural Resource Curse: An Illustration from Nigeria," May 2003, mimeo.

13. See World Bank, *Globalization, Growth & Poverty*, pp. 38–40.

14. A study that brought out the benefits of trade by focusing on natural barriers of distance is: Jeffrey Frankel and David Romer, "Does Trade Cause Growth?," *American Economic Review*, June 1999.

15. See, on the role of resources in development, World Bank, *World Development Report 2003: Sustainable Development in a Dynamic World: Transforming Institutions, Growth and Quality of Life* (New York: Oxford University Press, for the World Bank, 2003), pp. 148–56.

16. See World Bank, *Globalization, Growth & Poverty*, pp. 32–3.

17. Data come from Angus Maddison, *Monitoring the World Economy, 1820–1992* (Paris: Development Centre of the Organization for Economic Co-operation and Development, 1995 and 1998) and the International Monetary Fund's *World Economic Outlook*. See Andrea Boltho and Gianni Toniolo, "The Assessment: The Twentieth Century—Achievements, Failures, Lessons," *Oxford Review of Economic Policy*, Vol. 15, No. 4 (Winter 1999), pp. 1–17, Table 4.

18. Bourguignon and Morrison, "Inequality among World Citizens," p. 733.

19. Milanovic, "True World Income Distribution," Abstract.

20. *Ibid.*, p. 51.

21. Robert Wade, "Winners and Losers," *The Economist*, 26 April 2001. Professor Wade also cites another World Bank study, using the same data sets: Yuri Dikhanov and Michael Ward, "Measuring the Distribution of Global Income," World Bank, 2000, mimeo.

22. Shaohua Chen and Martin Ravallion, "How Did the World's Poorest Fare in the 1990s?," World Bank, Washington, DC, 2000, mimeo. This discrepancy between surveys and national accounts is discussed at length by Bhalla, *Imagine There's No Country*, pp. 78–87 and chapter 7.

23. See United Nations Development Programme, *Human Development Report 2003: Millennium Development Goals: A Compact among Nations to End Human Poverty* (New York: Oxford University Press, for the United Nations Development Programme, 2003), p. 40.

24. Bourguignon and Morrison, "Inequality among World Citizens," Table 1.

25. Cynics might suppose this is the Bank's nightmare. Fortunately for the Bank, though not for the world, poverty seems most unlikely to be eliminated in the near future, particularly since richer societies tend to define their poverty lines upwards, more or less *pari passu.*

26. Poverty lines are defined as $1.08 a day at 1993 PPP.

27. Professor Sala-I-Martin discusses those discrepancies in section 3D of his paper, "The World Distribution of Income."

28. See on this debate, Bhalla, *Imagine There's No Country*, chapter 7, World Bank, *Global Economic Prospects*, pp. 32–3, and Martin Ravallion, "The Debate on Globalization, Poverty and Inequality: Why Measurement Matters," World Bank, no date, www.worldbank.org.

29. See Thomas W. Pogge and Sanjay G. Reddy, "Unknown: The Extent, Distribution and Trend of Global Income Poverty," 16 July 2003, mimeo, pp. 1–2.

30. *Ibid.*, p. 12.

31. Where not otherwise indicated, data in this section come from World Bank, *World*

Development Indicators 2002 (Washington, DC: World Bank, 2002).

32. Indur M. Goklany, "The Globalization of Human Well-Being," Policy Analysis No. 447, Cato Institute, Washington, DC, 22 August 2002.

33. Maddison, *The World Economy*.

34. The data from the FAO are cited in *ibid.*, p. 7.

35. World Bank, *Globalization, Growth and Poverty*, p. 48.

36. David Dollar and Aart Kraay, "Growth Is Good for the Poor," Policy Research Working Paper No. 2587 (Washington, DC: World Bank, 2001).

37. Bhalla, *Imagine There's No Country*, pp. 36–46. Bhalla argues that the conclusion of Dollar and Kraay is biased by the inclusion of central and eastern Europe (including the former Soviet Union), where a huge widening in inequality coincided with a fall in incomes. This tends to make the elasticity of the incomes of the poor with respect to rising average incomes, in the sample as a whole, closer to unity (i.e. the falling shares in income of the eastern European poor as income falls is interpreted in the pooled cross-section regression as a rising share as income rises).

38. World Bank, *Globalization, Growth & Poverty*, pp. 49–50.

39. See Jean-Marc Burniaux, Thai-Thanh Dang, Douglas Fore, Michael Forster, Mario Mira d'Ercole and Howard Oxley, "Income Distribution and Poverty in Selected OECD Countries," OECD Economics Department Working Paper 189, Paris, OECD, March 1998, www.oecd.org.

40. Wolfgang Stolper and Paul A. Samuelson, "Protection and Real Wages," *Review of Economic Studies*, Vol. 9 (1941), pp. 58–73.

41. Lindert and Williamson, "Does Globalization Make the World More Unequal?," p. 33.

MACARTAN HUMPHREYS, JEFFREY D. SACHS, AND JOSEPH E. STIGLITZ

What Is the Problem with Natural Resource Wealth?

There is a curious phenomenon that social scientists call the "resource curse" (Auty 1993). Countries with large endowments of natural resources, such as oil and gas, often perform *worse* in terms of economic development and good governance than do countries with fewer resources. Paradoxically, despite the prospects

From Macartan Humphreys, Jeffrey D. Sachs, and Joseph E. Stiglitz, eds., *Escaping the Resource Curse* (New York: Columbia University Press, 2007), Chap. 1.

of wealth and opportunity that accompany the discovery and extraction of oil and other natural resources, such endowments all too often impede rather than further balanced and sustainable development.

On the one hand, the *lack* of natural resources has not proven to be a fatal barrier to economic success. The star performers of the developing world—the Asian Tigers (Hong Kong, Korea, Singapore, and Taiwan)—all achieved booming export industries based on manufactured goods and rapid economic growth *without* large natural resource reserves. On the other hand, many natural resources–rich countries have struggled to generate self-sustaining economic takeoff and growth and have even succumbed to deep economic crises (Sachs and Warner 1995). In country after country, natural resources have helped to raise living standards while failing to produce self-sustaining growth. Controlling for structural attributes, resource-rich countries grew less rapidly than resource-poor countries during the last quarter of the twentieth century. Alongside these growth failures are strong associations between resource wealth and the likelihood of weak democratic development (Ross 2001), corruption (Sala-i-Martin and Subramanian 2003), and civil war (Humphreys 2005).

This generally bleak picture among resource-rich countries nonetheless masks a great degree of variation. Some natural resource–rich countries have performed far better than others in resource wealth management and long-term economic development. Some 30 years ago, Indonesia and Nigeria had comparable per capita incomes and heavy dependencies on oil sales. Yet today, Indonesia's per capita income is four times that of Nigeria (Ross 2003). A similar discrepancy can be found among countries rich in diamonds and other nonrenewable minerals akin to oil and gas. For instance, in comparing the diamond-rich countries of Sierra Leone and Botswana, one sees that Botswana's economy has grown at an average rate of 7 percent over the past 20 years while Sierra Leone has plunged into civil strife, its gross domestic product (GDP) per capita actually dropping 37 percent between 1971 and 1989 (World Bank Country Briefs).

The United Nation's Human Development Index illustrates the high degree of variation in well-being across resource-rich countries (Human Development Report 2005). This measure summarizes information on income, health, and education across countries worldwide. Looking at this measure, we find that Norway, a major oil producer, ranks at the very top of the index. Other relatively high-ranking oil-producing countries include Brunei, Argentina, Qatar, United Arab Emirates, Kuwait, and Mexico. Yet, many oil-producing countries fall at the other extreme. Among the lowest ranked countries in the world are Equatorial Guinea, Gabon, The Republic of Congo, Yemen, Nigeria, and Angola. Chad comes in close to the bottom at 173 out of 177.

Variation in the effects of resource wealth on well-being can be found not only across countries but also *within* them. Even when resource-rich countries have done fairly well, they have often been plagued by rising inequality—they become rich countries with poor people. Approximately half the population of Venezuela—the Latin American economy with the most natural resources—lives in poverty; historically, the fruits of the country's bounty accrued to a minority of the country's elite (Weisbrot et al. 2006). This reality presents yet another paradox. At least in theory, natural resources can be taxed without creating disincentives for investment. Unlike in the case of mobile assets—such as capital, where high taxes can induce capital to exit a country—oil is a nonmovable commodity. Since tax proceeds from the sale of oil can be used to create a more egalitarian society, one could expect less, not more, inequality in resource-rich countries. In reality, however, this is rarely the case.

The perverse effects of natural resources on economic and political outcomes in developing states give rise to a wide array of difficult policy questions for governments of developing countries and for the international community. For instance, should Mexico privatize its state-run oil companies? Should the World Bank help finance the development of oil in Chad; if so, under what conditions? Should the international community have "allowed" Bolivia and Ecuador to mortgage future oil revenues to support deficit spending during the recessions they faced in the past decade? Should Azerbaijan use its oil revenues to finance a reduction in taxes or should it put the money into a stabilization fund? Should Nigeria offer preferential exploration rights to China rather than requiring open competitive bidding in all blocks? Should Sudan use the proceeds from oil sales to support oil-producing regions or spread the wealth more evenly across different regions?

*   *   *

* * * [L]et us begin our study with an examination of the origins of the resource curse—why does oil and gas wealth often do more harm than good? The basic paradox calls for an explanation, one that will allow countries to do something to undo the resource curse. Fortunately, over the past decade, research by economists and political scientists has done much to enhance our understanding of the issues.

Where Does the Resource Curse Come From?

To understand the natural resource paradox we need first a sense of what makes natural resource wealth different from other types of wealth. Two key differences stand out. The first is that unlike other sources of wealth, natural resource wealth does not need to be produced. It simply needs to be extracted (even if there is often nothing simple about the extraction process). Since it is not a result of a production process, the generation of natural resource wealth can occur quite independently of other economic processes that take place in a country; it is, in a number of ways, "enclaved."[1] For example, it can take place without major linkages to other industrial sectors and it can take place without the participation of large segments of the domestic labor force. Natural resource extraction can thus also take place quite independently of other political processes; a government can often access natural resource wealth regardless of whether it commands the cooperation of its citizens or effectively controls institutions of state. The second major feature stems from the fact that many natural resources—oil

and gas in particular—are nonrenewable. From an economic aspect, they are thus less like a source of income and more like an asset.

These two features—the detachment of the oil sector from domestic political and economic processes and the nonrenewable nature of natural resources—give rise to a large array of political and economic processes that produce adverse effects on an economy. One of the greatest risks concerns the emergence of what political scientists call "rent-seeking behavior." Especially in the case of natural resources, a gap—commonly referred to as an economic *rent*—exists between the value of that resource and the costs of extracting it. In such cases, individuals, be they private sector actors or politicians, have incentives to use political mechanisms to capture these rents. Rampant opportunities for rent-seeking by corporations and collusion with government officials thereby compound the adverse economic and political consequences of natural resource wealth.

Unequal Expertise

The first problems arise even before monies from natural resource wealth make it into the country. Governments face considerable challenges in their dealings with international corporations, which have great interest and expertise in the sector and extraordinary resources on which to draw. Since oil and gas exploration is both capital and (increasingly) technologically intensive, extracting oil and gas typically requires cooperation between country governments and experienced international private sector actors. In many cases, this can produce the unusual situation in which the buyer—the international oil company—actually knows more about the value of the good being sold than the seller—the government of the resource-rich country. Companies can, in such instances, be in very strong bargaining positions relative to governments. The challenge for host countries is to find ways to contract with the international corporations in a manner that also gives them a fair deal. If, of course, there are large numbers of corporations that have the requisite knowledge, competition should be able to eliminate the rents associated with expertise, thereby allowing the resource-rich country to receive a larger fraction of the resource's market value. But countries cannot always rely on the existence of such competition.

"Dutch Disease"

Once a contract has been negotiated and the money begins to flow in, new problems arise. In the 1970s, the Netherlands discovered one of these problems. Following the discovery of natural gas in the North Sea, the Dutch found that their manufacturing sector suddenly started performing more poorly than anticipated.[2] Resource-rich countries that similarly experience a decline in preexisting domestic sectors of the economy are now said to have caught the "Dutch disease" (Ebrahim-[z]adeh 2003). The pattern of the "disease" is straightforward. A sudden rise in the value of natural resource exports produces an appreciation in the real exchange rate. This, in turn, makes exporting non–natural resource commodities more difficult and competing with imports across a wide range of commodities almost impossible (called the "spending effect"). Foreign exchange earned from the natural resource meanwhile may be used to purchase internationally traded goods, at the expense of domestic manufacturers of the goods. Simultaneously, domestic resources such as labor and materials are shifted to the natural resource sector (called the "resource pull effect"). Consequently, the price of these resources rises on the domestic market, thereby increasing the costs to producers in other sectors. All in all, extraction of natural resources sets in motion a dynamic that gives primacy to two domestic sectors—the natural resource sector and the nontradables sector, such as the construction industry—at the expense of more traditional export sectors. In the Dutch case, this was manufacturing; in developing countries, this tends to be agriculture. Such dynamics appear to occur widely, whether in the context of Australian gold booms in the nineteenth century, Colombian coffee in the 1970s, or the looting of Latin America's gold and silver by sixteenth-century Spanish and Portuguese imperialists.

Globally, these shifts can have adverse effects on the economy through several channels. Any shift can be costly for an economy, as workers need to be retrained and find new jobs, and capital needs to be readjusted. Beyond this, the particular shifts induced by the Dutch disease may have other adverse consequences. If the manufacturing sector is a long-term source of growth—for example, through the generation of new technologies or improved human capacity—then the decline of this sector will have adverse growth consequences (Sachs and Warner 2001). Another channel is through income distribution—if returns to export sectors such as agriculture or manufacturing are more equitably distributed than returns to the natural resource sector, then this sectoral shift can lead to a rise in inequality. In any case, the Dutch disease spells trouble down the road—when activities in the natural resource sector eventually slow down, other sectors may find it very difficult to recover.

Volatility

The Dutch disease problem arises because of the *quantity* of oil money coming in; other problems arise because of the *timing* of the earnings. Earnings from oil and gas production, if viewed as a source of income, are highly volatile. The volatility of income comes from three sources: the variation over time in rates of extraction, the variability in the timing of payments by corporations to states, and fluctuations in the value of the natural resource produced. As an example of the first two sources of variability consider figure 9.5, which shows one projection for Chad's earnings from the sale of oil over the period 2004–2034. We see a sharp rise, followed by a rapid decline, a second rise, and a second decline. This pattern emerges from two distinct sources. The first is the variation over time in the rate of extraction. A

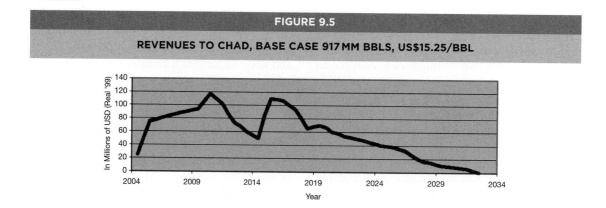

FIGURE 9.5

REVENUES TO CHAD, BASE CASE 917 MM BBLS, US$15.25/BBL

SOURCE: Based on estimates presented in the World Bank Inspection Panel (2000).

typical pattern is to have a front-loading of extraction rates since production volumes tend to reach a peak within the first few years of production and then gradually descend until production stops. In practice, risks exist in Chad—as in Nigeria and elsewhere—that this volatility will be compounded further by interruptions that result from political instability in the country and in producing regions. The second major source of volatility derives from the nature of the agreement between the producing companies and the government. In the Chad case, the oil consortium was exempted from taxes on earning for the first years of production. Since taxes constitute a major source of government earnings, the eventual introduction of taxes should provide a major boost to Chad's earnings.

The third major source of volatility—not even accounted for in Figure 9.6—arises from the highly volatile nature of oil and gas prices. The figure presented by the World Bank is based on prices of $15.25 a barrel, a number that now appears hopelessly out of date. Figure 9.6 shows the price of oil over the past 20 years. Note that while there is a very clear upward trend over these years, the variation around this trend is very great with week on week changes of plus or minus 5 to 10 percent relatively common.

There are a number of difficulties with a highly volatile income source. Most obvious is the fact that longer term planning is rendered difficult by great uncertainty over future financing, especially as a result of fluctuations in the value of the commodity. Even when the volatility is not associated with uncertainty, with capital market imperfections, volatility in receipts often translates into volatility in expenditure. The result can be high levels of expenditure in good years followed by deep cuts in bad years. These in turn lead to "boom–bust cycles." All too often, the benefits in the good years are transitory whereas the problems generated during the bad years endure.

The magnitude of these fluctuations can be increased by international lending. When times are good (prices and output are high), the country borrows from abroad, exacerbating the boom. But when prices fall, lenders demand repayment, forcing expenditure reductions which increase the magnitude of the downturn. On some occasions, most famously in the oil price booms of the 1970s, several oil states mortgaged their futures by borrowing against booming oil revenues, only to end up in debt crisis when oil prices fell in the early 1980s. Mexico, Nigeria, and Venezuela typified the oil-debt boom and bust. This is not quite as irrational as it seems. Most poor countries are rationed in international borrowing, and may be

FIGURE 9.6

ALL COUNTRIES SPOT PRICE FOB WEIGHTED BY ESTIMATED EXPORT VOLUME (US $/BBL)

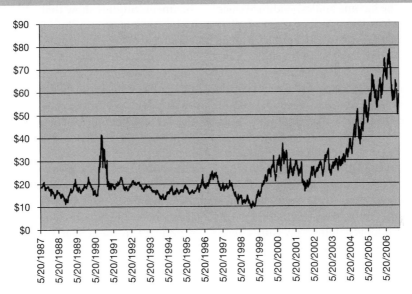

unable to borrow to secure financing for infra-structure needed for growth. Oil can serve as collateral, or at least as an informal guarantee (since the oil earnings are easy to identify and direct toward debt servicing). Thus, an oil boom, either through higher prices or quantities, can unleash not only a higher cash flow but also increased access to international loans. If the infrastructure investments are indeed high economic priorities, it might make sense to borrow against future oil earnings in this way. However, that "if" has been a big one, since much international borrowing has been wasted or stolen, and international capital inflows have been subject to panic and sharp reversals, often throwing the borrowing countries into a deep debt crisis. This is true for non-oil as well as oil states, but the very nature of natural resource endowments makes resource-rich countries even more susceptible to this dynamic.

Living Off Your Capital

A new set of problems arises once governments start spending their earnings. Because oil and gas resources are nonrenewable, any consumption of revenues from sales should be viewed as a consumption of capital rather than a consumption of income. If all revenues are consumed in each period, then the value of the country's total capital declines. Ignoring extraction costs, an optimal strategy involves converting most of the natural resource stock into financial assets, investing the assets in a diversified portfolio and treating the interest on the financial assets as income. * * * In principle, the portfolio composition problem can be fully separated from the expenditure decision. It may be optimal to convert oil below the ground into gold, apartment buildings, dollars, or some other assets above the ground. Indeed doing so—for example, by selling oil rights on futures markets—could entirely remove the income volatility associated with natural resources. Similarly, complete privatization of oil rights (with up-front payments) might—in perfectly functioning markets—serve a similar role. It turns out, however, that the implicit price governments pay for this conversion of a risky natural resource asset into a financial asset is extremely high, so that in general governments would be ill-advised to do so.[3]

In practice, the income and expenditure sides get linked. International advisers often emphasize that the country is not *wealthier* as a result of resource extraction; it has just changed the composition of its asset base. But this argument has only limited resonance. In practice, along with access to capital stock and rising income comes pressure to spend sooner rather than later. This pressure comes from many sources. As discussed [later], politicians with an uncertain hold on power have an incentive to spend sooner rather than to leave opportunities on the table for future political opponents. And their incentives are greater if spending can help ensure that they will remain in power longer. Other pressures may arise from populations demanding rapid and visible improvements in welfare or from constituents demanding favors in return for political support. Particularly compelling arguments can be made for the use of the resources (or even borrowing against future resources) when the economy is operating below full capacity and a small amount of pump priming will have large effects on national income. International Monetary Fund (IMF) rules of budgetary stringency make little sense in this context.

The far more difficult cases arise when a government has a worthwhile project that entails drawing on significant domestic resources. It can be tempting to use oil revenues to cover the costs of domestic resource mobilization. But unless paired with other policies, this approach would likely give rise to currency appreciation, reducing jobs elsewhere in the economy. The net benefits might be negative. Nevertheless, if a government can use resource wealth to cover foreign exchange needs while mobilizing domestic tax revenue to finance the domestic component, such investments can still enable growth *without* exchange rate appreciation. Indeed, * * * in many cases, high levels of investment in the short run may be optimal, but the pressure to spend even beyond the optimum may still be very great.

Insufficient Investments in Education

Along with overconsumption comes underinvestment. Studies show that education as a form of investment especially suffers in resource-rich countries (Gylfason 2001). When states start relying on natural resource wealth, they seem to forget the need for a diversified and skilled workforce that can support other economic sectors once resource wealth has dried up. As a result, the share of national income spent on education declines, along with secondary school enrollment and the expected years of schooling for girls. While the costs of such declines might not be felt in the short term, as capital-intense activities take up a larger share of national production, their effects are likely to become more significant in the longer run as soon as economies start trying to diversify.

It is possible to understand this bias in terms of the nature of the sources of wealth. When a country's wealth depends on investments in manufacturing or other productive activities, human capital investment is an essential part of wealth creation. When a country's wealth arises from an endowment of natural resources, however, investment in a skilled workforce is not necessary for the realization of current income. Without a focus on wealth creation, or sustainability, insufficient attention will be paid to investments in human capital (or other productive investments).

Beyond these economic and financial concerns, a series of political dynamics associated with oil and gas dependence can exacerbate adverse economic effects. As mentioned earlier, oil-dependent economies, for example, are considerably more likely to have limited political freedoms, to be governed by nondemocratic regimes, to have higher levels of corruption, and to suffer from civil wars within their boundaries. Evidence suggests that natural resource dependency causes these outcomes through a variety of mechanisms, as described in the following sections.

Spoliation

Higher levels of corruption present the most obvious political risk that can arise from large holdings of natural resources. The short run availability of large financial assets increases the opportunity for the theft of such assets by political leaders. Those who control these assets can use that wealth to maintain themselves in power, either through legal means (e.g., spending in political campaigns) or coercive ones (e.g., funding militias). By some accounts, corruption is a hallmark of the oil business itself.[4] But oil and gas dependence can also affect corruption indirectly. As discussed later, the presence of oil and gas wealth can produce weak state structures that make corrupt practices considerably easier for government officials. These risks are also likely to be exacerbated if the growth of the oil and gas sector is associated with a concentration of bureaucratic power, which increases the difficulty of securing transparency and other constraints on those in power. Not surprisingly, statistical studies that seek to account for variation in levels of corruption across different countries find that natural resource dependence is a strong predictor (Leite and Weidmann 1999).

Corruption related to natural resources takes many forms. International mining and oil companies that seek to maximize profits find that they can lower the costs of obtaining resources more easily by obtaining the resources at below market value—by bribing government officials—than by figuring out how to extract the resources more efficiently. In other cases, the natural resource is sold to domestic firms at below full value, with government officials either getting a kickback or an ownership share. In practice, the risks of corruption in resource-rich environments are very large and the costs of such corruption to the national economy are enormous. By some accounts, for example, Nigeria's president Abacha was responsible for the theft of as much as US$3 billion (Ayittey 2006).

Weak, Unaccountable States

Although one might expect that the added resources available to states from oil and gas revenues might make them stronger, there are a number of reasons why, paradoxically, it can make them weaker (Karl 1997). States that are able to generate revenue from the sale of oil and gas are less reliant on citizens, which can result in weak linkages between governments and citizens. When citizens are untaxed they sometimes have less information about state activities and, in turn, may demand less of states. Even if they disapprove of state action, they lack the means to withdraw their financial support from states. As a result, states have less need to engage with civilians. Moreover, in relying on external income sources rather than on domestic revenue, states have less of a need to develop a bureaucratic apparatus to raise revenue (Fearon and Laitin 2003). The need to collect taxes is widely thought to have contributed to the emergence of strong state and even democratic institutions in many Western countries (Ross 2004). The *lack* of reliance on tax revenue in favor of reliance on external sources of revenue is thus thought to hinder the development of effective states in many resource-rich developing countries (Moore 1998).

Further, since a resource-rich country's revenue is largely independent of the strength and success of the overall economy, the government of the resource-rich country has less of a need to engage in activities that support the economy. Without a broad support base in the economy, a government can instead invest its earnings in an oppressive capacity. Doing so does not, however, produce strong states. The structures that result are often not resilient and indeed, the capacity of repression can be turned against the incumbent. Even if such a strategy is successful at protecting leaders, it will not necessarily produce the capacity needed to engage productively with the national economy. * * *

Threats to Democracy

The adverse political effects associated with high levels of corruption and weak states ultimately have consequences for the political system itself. Countries rich in natural resources—in particular, in oil and gas—are less likely to have democratic political systems. Specifically, nondemocratic oil states are less likely to become democratic than states that do not export oil. This relationship has been found in cross-national studies that relate the discovery of oil in a given period to democratic changes over the coming decades (Tsui 2005). In effect, access to oil wealth can allow leaders to successfully repress or co-opt their oppositions, and thus avoid having to relinquish power through electoral competition.

These adverse political effects of oil are not just a problem for developing countries; such patterns have even been seen within the United States. One recent study examined the relationship between oil and coal production within each of the American states over the period 1929 to 2002 and related this to gubernatorial turnover. The study found that a 1 percent increase in state dependence on these resources is associated with a rise of approximately half a percent in the governor's margin of victory in these states (Goldberg et al. 2005). Overall, at least three features of oil dependent states help to explain the relationship between natural resource dependence and the lack of democratization (Ross 2001). First, governments do not feel the same pressures to exchange political power for the rights to tax, since they can raise their revenues from other sources. Second, they can invest in coercive capacity that can be used to quell threats to their political power. Finally, citizens in these states are less likely to undergo the transformative effects of industrializing countries that have been associated with demands for democratization elsewhere.

Grievances in Producing Regions

The production of natural resources is liable to give rise to various types of political frustrations within a country and especially in producing regions. The extraction process itself may result in forced out-migration, new in-migration, and, with attendant population pressures, environmental pollution or degradation. Even if such changes to local conditions are minimal, resource-rich regions may feel that they have a particular claim on resource wealth and may be aggrieved if they see the wealth leaving their region and benefiting others. Such complaints have been raised in oil regions including Cabinda in Angola, Doba in Chad, and even in the small island of Principe in Sao Tome and Principe. * * *

Military Challenges to Governments

Oil exporters spend much more on their militaries even in the absence of civil war—between 2 and 10 times more. In the most difficult cases, the resource curse results not only in militarization but also in civil war. Civil wars are, statistically speaking, more likely to occur in oil-rich states (Humphreys 2005). Indeed, some oil-rich states such as Angola, Colombia, or Sudan have had civil wars within their borders for decades on end. There are a number of reasons for this. If oil and gas wealth accrues to political leaders simply by virtue of the fact that they maintain nominal control of a state, this increases the incentives of nonstate actors to attempt to capture the state in order to benefit from the resource wealth, often through the use of violence (Collier and Hoeffler 2000; Fearon and Laitin 2003). This can lead to secessionist bids in some countries—sometimes aided by the grievances that arise in producing regions—or to attempts to topple the central government outright, as, for example, in the Republic of Congo (Englebert and Ron 2004). These incentives are all the stronger if the resource-rich state has weak capacity and lacks legitimacy. Because of the major international interest in these resources, outside actors—states, as well as corporations—may have an interest then in supporting threats to a central government in anticipation of special relations with the new regime. Foreign powers have often meddled shamelessly in the politics of oil-producing countries to try to maintain a hold on oil resources and revenue flows. The CIA-backed coup in Iran in 1953 is the most famous example (Gasiorowski 1987).

Political and Economic Interactions

There are strong interactions between the economic problems discussed in the first part of this section and the political problems discussed in the second. Even in democracies, when governments privatize natural resources they often receive less than their full market value. Firms in extractive industries care first and foremost about minimizing what they have to pay for access to the resources. They therefore seek to ensure that the deals are structured in a way that benefits them over the government. Often, this is achieved through political action such as campaign contributions and other forms of public–private alliances. Moreover, while selling access to natural rents is seen as a relatively easy way to reduce budget deficits, the possibilities for shortsighted deals and complicity in rent-seeking abound. Various administrations in the United States have, at times, practically given away natural resources to raise additional budgetary funds. Ronald Reagan, for example, designed a "fire sale" of oil leases, rapid auctions that resulted in a significant depression in the prices government received. Corporations in the extractive industries also have an incentive to limit transparency, to make it more difficult for citizens to see how much their government is getting in exchange for sale of the country's resources. In most cases, such corporations have an incentive to limit government regulations that would restrict environmental damage or that would force corporations to pay for the cost of the damage they inflict.[5]

What to Do?

* * * [We] assume throughout that both countries and companies can and should do some-thing to more effectively and fairly develop oil resources. We assume in particular that governments are willing to take sometimes bold and difficult steps to try to succeed where most states have failed. If states are unable or unwilling to take such steps, then the best solution may well be to leave the oil and gas in the ground. The fact is that oil in the ground is a nonwasting asset.[6] Although leaving oil in the ground means that interest is forgone, the ground just might be the safest place for the asset, especially if there exists the risk that governments may use revenue for their purposes rather than for the good of society, as has happened so often already. In such cases, the people may benefit *some*, but clearly not as much as if the money were spent in ways that were directly intended to enhance their well-being. A judgment call is required, and not solely by the government of the host country, which often lacks the political will necessary to postpone extraction of natural resource reserves. In addition to governments and international corporations, civil society and the international community play an important role in influencing the extraction of natural resources. If the orientation of a government is such that there are likely to be few benefits to the people, then domestic groups and the international community should provide no help for extraction. Plausibly, the prospects of the money being used better later are greater than the prospects today, and so patience may be what is required.

Assuming, however, that a government is willing to take some of the difficult measures, what can be done? * * * The first question that a country faces is: should the government get involved at all, or can the problem of extraction be left entirely in the hands of the private sector? Joseph Stiglitz * * * argues that privatization is not the panacea that some advocates suggest;[7] rather, privatization can lead to a considerable loss of value for a state without necessarily resolving either the micro problems of good management or the macroeconomic problems that plague oil- and gas-rich countries. * * * [O]ptimal auctions/contractual relationships are markedly different from those commonly employed, largely because of the political economy factors discussed earlier.

Some level of engagement with the private sector is, however, generally unavoidable and can be highly productive. * * * In most cases, competitive bidding is likely to be the best way to offer drilling rights; not only does it generally fetch the highest bidding price, but it also can protect the country from corrupt dealings. * * *

As we have seen, however, once oil and gas monies start coming into a country, new problems arise. * * * A country's optimal expenditure path depends on how well it can balance the adverse macroeconomic consequences of large inflows of foreign exchange earnings with the need to invest in other sectors in order to achieve higher growth rates in the long run. * * * The optimal investment strategy might involve much higher levels of front-loaded expenditure than many analysts suggest. A problem arises, however, in that—for any given optimal expenditure path, whether or not it is front loaded—there will generally exist political pressures to spend too much too soon. * * * Some solutions to this problem can be found in the deployment of Natural Resource Funds, but only if these funds actually alter the incentives facing political actors. Incentives can be influenced in at least three key ways: by broadening the set of actors who play a role in expenditure decisions; by giving these actors a way to make commitments to particular expenditure paths; and by making it costly for them to deviate later from earlier decisions.

* * *

* * * Plaguing all well-meaning prescriptions, however, is the problem that the resource curse is such that many individuals in governments and in the private sector fare quite well in the short run when resources are misused. Even if such behavior does not benefit them in the long run, changing this behavior unilaterally may be too costly in the absence of reform by other actors. The challenge is to find ways to alter the incentives facing these actors to make it in their interest to do a better job. * * * [T]his can be done only if greater light is shed on the industry so that publics are provided with much better information with which to evaluate the choices of their political leaders. Absent changes to the structure of oil and gas politics that can ensure much greater access to information about how deals are made, who gets what, and how resources are managed by incumbents, the lost opportunities that we see on a daily basis in oil- and gas-rich countries are set to continue for a long time to come.

NOTES

1. Natural resource extraction is therefore sometimes referred to by social scientists as "enclaved" (Hirschman 1958; Seers 1964).
2. See "The Dutch Disease" (1977).
3. Bonus (up-front) payments can be viewed as a loan from the corporation to the government; but the interest rate on this loan is the cost to capital of the corporation, which is typically much, much higher than the rate at which government can borrow.
4. In one testimony before French magistrates, the former Africa manager of Elf Aquitaine argued that "All international oil companies have used kickbacks since the first oil shock of the 1970s to guarantee the companies' access to oil." ("Oil Firm ELF" 2001).
5. They even have an incentive to restrict the use of accounting frameworks (like green GDP) that would call attention to the costs of resource depletion and environmental degradation. During the Clinton administration, there was an attempt to develop and implement green GDP accounting, but congressional pressure, especially from coal mining states, led to a cutoff of funding. There is a vicious circle: extractive industries have an incentive to maintain political systems or administrations which allow them to have greater voice.

6. According to Hotelling (1931), in perfectly functioning markets, on average, prices of natural resources will increase— in an amount just sufficient to offset the loss of interest. In such perfectly functioning markets, it would pay for those with high extraction costs to leave their resources in the ground; global efficiency would, for instance, focus current extraction on the low cost producers (probably in the Middle East).

7. For a recent study that argues in favor of privatization of the oil sector, see Weinthal and Luong (2006).

REFERENCES

Auty, R. 1993. *Sustaining Development in Mineral Economies: The Resource Curse Thesis.* London: Routledge.

Ayittey, G. B. N. 2006. "Nigeria's Struggle with Corruption." Testimony before the Committee on International Relations' Subcommittee on Africa, Global Human Rights and International Operations House Sub-Committee on Africa, U.S. House of Representatives, May 18, Washington, DC.

Collier, P. and A. Hoeffler. 2000. "Greed and Grievance in Civil Wars." Working Paper, World Bank. WPS 2000–18.

"The Dutch Disease." 1977. *The Economist,* November 26: 82–83.

Ebrahim-zadeh, C. 2003. "Back to Basics: Dutch Disease. Too Much Wealth Managed Unwisely." *Finance and Development* 40(1): 50–51.

Englebert, P. and J. Ron. 2004. "Primary Commodities and War: Congo-Brazzaville's Ambivalent Resource Curse." *Comparative Politics* 37(1): 61–81.

Fearon, J. D. and D. Laitin. 2003. "Ethnicity, Insurgency, and Civil War." *American Political Science Review* 97(1): 75–91.

Gasiorowski, M. 1987. "The 1953 Coup d'Etat in Iran." *International Journal of Middle East Studies* 19(3): 261–86.

Goldberg, E., E. Wibbels, and E. Mvukiyehe. 2005. "Lessons from Strange Cases: Democracy, Development, and the Resource Curse in the U.S. States, 1929–2002." Paper presented at the 2005 meeting of the American Political Science Association.

Gylfason, T. 2001. "Natural Resources, Education, and Economic Development." *European Economic Review* 45(4–6): 847–59.

Hirschman, A. O. 1958. *The Strategy of Economic Development.* New Haven: Yale University Press.

Hotelling, H. 1931. "The Economics of Exhaustible Resources." *Journal of Political Economy* 39(2): 137–75.

Human Development Report. 2005. http://hdr. undp.org/reports/global/2005/ (accessed July 15, 2006).

Humphreys, M. 2005. "Natural Resources, Conflict and Conflict Resolution." *Journal of Conflict Resolution* 49: 508–37.

Karl, T. L. 1997. *The Paradox of Plenty: Oil Booms and Petro-States.* Berkeley: University of California Press.

Leite, C. and J. Weidmann. 1999. "Does Mother Nature Corrupt?" Working Paper, IMF.

Moore, M. 1998. "Death without Taxes: Democracy, State Capacity, and Aid Dependence in the Fourth World." In *The Democratic Developmental State*, M. Robinson and G. White, eds. Oxford: Oxford University Press, pp. 84–124.

"Oil Firm ELF Accused of Bribing African Officials." 2001. Inter-Press Service, November 22.

Ross, M. 2001. "Does Oil Hinder Democracy?" *World Politics* 53(3): 326–61.

Ross, M. 2003. "Nigeria's Oil Sector and the Poor." Prepared for the UK Department for International Development.

Ross, M. 2004. "Does Taxation Lead to Representation?" *British Journal of Political Science* 34: 229–49.

Sachs, J. and A. M. Warner. 1995. "Natural Resource Abundance and Economic Growth." NBER Working Paper No. 5398.

Sachs, J. and A. M. Warner. 2001. "The Curse of Natural Resources." *European Economic Review* 45(4–6): 827–38.

Sala-i-Martin, X. and A. Subramanian. 2003. "Addressing the Natural Resource Curse: An Illustration from Nigeria." NBER Working Paper No. 9804.

Seers, D. 1964. "The Mechanism of an Open Petroleum Economy." *Social and Economic Studies* 13: 233–42.

Tsui, K. 2005. "More Oil, Less Democracy? Theory and Evidence from Crude Oil Discoveries." http://are.berkeley.edu/courses/envres_seminar/KTsuijobmarketpaper.pdf.

Weinthal, E. and P. Luong. 2006. "Combating the Resource Curse: An Alternative Solution to Managing Mineral Wealth." *Perspectives on Politics* 4(1): 35–53.

Weisbrot, M., L. Sandoval, and D. Rosnick. 2006. *Poverty Rates in Venezuela: Getting the Numbers Right.* Center for Economic and Policy Research.

World Bank Country Briefs. http://web.worldbank.org (accessed June 15, 2006).

JOSEPH E. STIGLITZ

From *Freefall: America, Free Markets, and the Sinking of the World Economy*

The Making of a Crisis

The only surprise about the economic crisis of 2008 was that it came as a surprise to so many. For a few observers, it was a textbook case that was not only predictable but also predicted. A deregulated market awash in liquidity and low interest rates, a global real estate bubble, and skyrocketing subprime lending were a toxic combination. Add in the U.S. fiscal and trade deficit and the corresponding accumulation in China of huge reserves of dollars—an unbalanced global economy—and it was clear that things were horribly awry.

What *was* different about this crisis from the multitude that had preceded it during the past quarter century was that this crisis bore a "Made in the USA" label. And while previous crises had been contained, this "Made in the USA" crisis spread quickly around the world. We liked to think of our country as one of the engines of global economic growth, an exporter of sound economic policies—not recessions. The last time the United States had exported a major crisis was during the Great Depression of the 1930s.

The basic outlines of the story are well known and often told. The United States had a housing bubble. When that bubble broke and housing prices fell from their stratospheric levels, more and more homeowners found themselves "underwater." They owed more on their mortgages than what their homes were valued. As they lost their homes, many also lost their life savings and their dreams for a future—a college education for their children, a retirement in comfort. Americans had, in a sense, been living in a dream.

From Joseph E. Stiglitz, *Freefall: America, Free Markets, and the Sinking of the World Economy* (New York: W. W. Norton, 2010), Chaps. 1, 8. Some of the author's notes have been omitted.

The richest country in the world was living beyond its means, and the strength of the U.S. economy, and the world's, depended on it. The global economy needed ever-increasing consumption to grow; but how could this continue when the incomes of many Americans had been stagnating for so long?[1] Americans came up with an ingenious solution: borrow and consume as if their incomes *were* growing. And borrow they did. Average savings rates fell to zero—and with many rich Americans saving substantial amounts, that meant poor Americans had a large negative savings rate. In other words, they were going deeply into debt. Both they and their lenders could feel good about what was happening: they were able to continue their consumption binge, not having to face up to the reality of stagnating and declining incomes, and lenders could enjoy record profits based on ever-mounting fees.

Low interest rates and lax regulations fed the housing bubble. As housing prices soared, homeowners could take money out of their houses. These mortgage equity withdrawals—which in one year hit $975 billion, or more than 7 percent of GDP (gross domestic product, the standard measure of the sum of all the goods and services produced in the economy)—allowed borrowers to make a down payment on a new car and still have some equity left over for retirement. But all of this borrowing was predicated on the risky assumption that housing prices would continue to go up, or at least not fall.

The economy was out of kilter: two-thirds to three-quarters of the economy (of GDP) was housing related: constructing new houses or buying contents to fill them, or borrowing against old houses to finance consumption. It was unsustainable—and it wasn't sustained. The breaking of the bubble at first affected the worst mortgages (the subprime mortgages, lent to low-income individuals), but soon affected all residential real estate.

When the bubble popped, the effects were amplified because banks had created complex products resting on top of the mortgages. Worse still, they had engaged in multibillion-dollar bets with each other and with others around the world. This complexity, combined with the rapidity with which the situation was deteriorating and the banks' high leverage (they, like households, had financed their investments by heavy borrowing), meant that the banks didn't know whether what they owed to their depositors and bondholders exceeded the value of their assets. And they realized accordingly that they couldn't know the position of any other bank. The trust and confidence that underlie the banking system evaporated. Banks refused to lend to each other—or demanded high interest rates to compensate for bearing the risk. Global credit markets began to melt down.

At that point, America and the world were faced with both a financial crisis and an economic crisis. The economic crisis had several components: There was an unfolding residential real estate crisis, followed not long after by problems in commercial real estate. Demand fell, as households saw the value of their houses (and, if they owned shares, the value of those as well) collapse and as their ability—and willingness—to borrow diminished. There was an inventory cycle—as credit markets froze and demand fell, companies reduced their inventories as quickly as possible. And there was the collapse of American manufacturing.

There were also deeper questions: What would replace the unbridled consumption of Americans that had sustained the economy in the years before the bubble broke? How were America and Europe going to manage their restructuring, for instance, the transition toward a service-sector economy that had been difficult enough during the boom? Restructuring was inevitable—globalization and the pace of technology demanded it—but it would not be easy.

The Story in Short

While the challenges going forward are clear, the question remains: How did it all happen? This is not the way market economies are *supposed* to work. Something went wrong—badly wrong.

There is no natural point to cut into the seamless web of history. For purposes of brevity, I begin with the bursting of the tech (or dot-com) bubble in the spring of 2000—a bubble that Alan Greenspan, chairman of the Federal Reserve at that time, had allowed to develop and that had sustained strong growth in the late 1990s. Tech stock prices fell 78 percent between March 2000 and October 2002. It was hoped that these losses would not affect the broader economy, but they did. Much of investment had been in the high-tech sector, and with the bursting of the tech stock bubble this came to a halt. In March 2001, America went into a recession.

The administration of President George W. Bush used the short recession following the collapse of the tech bubble as an excuse to push its agenda of tax cuts for the rich, which the president claimed were a cure-all for any economic disease. The tax cuts were, however, not designed to stimulate the economy and did so only to a limited extent. That put the burden of restoring the economy to full employment on monetary policy. Accordingly, Greenspan lowered interest rates, flooding the market with liquidity. With so much excess capacity in the economy, not surprisingly, the lower interest rates did not lead to more investment in plant and equipment. They worked—but only by replacing the tech bubble with a housing bubble, which supported a consumption and real estate boom.

The burden on monetary policy was increased when oil prices started to soar after the invasion of Iraq in 2003. The United States spent hundreds of billions of dollars importing oil—money that otherwise would have gone to support the U.S. economy. Oil prices rose from $32 a barrel in March 2003 when the Iraq war began to $137 per barrel in July 2008. This meant that Americans were spending $1.4 billion per day to import oil (up from $292 million per day before the war started), instead of spending the money at home. Greenspan felt he could keep interest rates low because there was little inflationary pressure, and without the housing bubble that the low interest rates sustained and the consumption boom that the housing bubble supported, the American economy would have been weak.

In all these go-go years of cheap money, Wall Street did not come up with a good mortgage product. A good mortgage product would have low transaction costs and low interest rates and would have helped people manage the risk of homeownership, including protection in the event their house loses value or borrowers lose their job. Homeowners also want monthly payments that are predictable, that don't shoot up without warning, and that don't have hidden costs. The U.S. financial markets didn't look to construct these better products, even though they are in use in other countries. Instead, Wall Street firms, focused on maximizing their returns, came up with mortgages that had high transaction costs and variable interest rates with payments that could suddenly spike, but with no protection against the risk of a loss in home value or the risk of job loss.

Had the designers of these mortgages focused on the ends—what we actually wanted from our mortgage market—rather than on how to maximize *their* revenues, then they might have devised products that would have *permanently* increased homeownership. They could have "done well by doing good." Instead their efforts produced a whole range of complicated mortgages that made them a lot of money in the short run and led to a slight *temporary* increase in homeownership, but at great cost to society as a whole.

The failings in the mortgage market were symptomatic of the broader failings throughout the financial system, including and especially the banks. There are two core functions of the banking system. The first is providing an efficient payments mechanism, in which the bank facilitates transactions, transferring its depositors' money to those from whom they buy goods and services. The second core function is assessing and managing risk and making loans. This is related to the first core function, because if a bank makes poor credit assessments, if it gambles recklessly, or if it puts too much money into risky ventures that default, it can no longer make good on its promises to return depositors' money. If a bank does its job well, it provides money to start new businesses and expand old businesses, the economy grows, jobs are created, and at the same time, it earns a high return—enough to pay back the depositors with interest and to generate competitive returns to those who have invested their money in the bank.

The lure of easy profits from transaction costs distracted many big banks from their core functions. The banking system in the United States and many other countries did not focus on lending to small and medium-sized businesses, which are the basis of job creation in any economy, but instead concentrated on promoting securitization, especially in the mortgage market.

It was this involvement in mortgage securitization that proved lethal. In the Middle Ages, alchemists attempted to transform base metals into gold. Modern alchemy entailed the transformation of risky subprime mortgages into AAA-rated products safe enough to be held by pension funds. And the rating agencies blessed what the banks had done. Finally, the banks got directly involved in gambling—including not just acting as middlemen for the risky assets that they were creating, but actually holding the assets. They, and their regulators, might have thought that they had passed the unsavory risks they had created on to others, but when the day of reckoning came—when the markets collapsed—it turned out that they too were caught off guard.

Parsing Out Blame

As the depth of the crisis became better understood—by April 2009 it was already the longest recession since the Great Depression—it was natural to look for the culprits, and there was plenty of blame to go around. Knowing who, or at least what, is to blame is essential if we are to reduce the likelihood of another recurrence and if we are to correct the obviously dysfunctional aspects of today's financial markets. We have to be wary of too facile explanations: too many begin with the excessive greed of the bankers.

That may be true, but it doesn't provide much of a basis for reform. Bankers acted greedily because they had incentives and opportunities to do so, and that is what has to be changed. Besides, the basis of capitalism is the pursuit of profit: should we blame the bankers for doing (perhaps a little bit better) what everyone in the market economy is supposed to be doing?

In the long list of culprits, it is natural to begin at the bottom, with the mortgage originators. Mortgage companies had pushed exotic mortgages on to millions of people, many of whom did not know what they were getting into. But the mortgage companies could not have done their mischief without being aided and abetted by the banks and rating agencies. The banks bought the mortgages and repackaged them, selling them on to unwary investors. U.S. banks and financial institutions had boasted about their clever new investment instruments. They had created new products which, while touted as instruments for managing risk, were so dangerous that they threatened to bring down the U.S. financial system. The rating agencies, which should have checked the growth of these toxic instruments, instead gave them a seal of approval, which encouraged others—including pension funds looking for safe places to put money that workers had set aside for their retirement—in the United States and overseas, to buy them.

In short, America's financial markets had failed to perform their essential societal functions of managing risk, allocating capital, and mobilizing savings while keeping transaction costs low. Instead, they had created risk, misallocated capital, and encouraged excessive indebtedness while imposing high transaction costs. At their peak in 2007, the bloated financial markets absorbed 41 percent of profits in the corporate sector.

One of the reasons why the financial system did such a poor job at managing risk is that the market mispriced and misjudged risk. The "market" badly misjudged the risk of defaults of subprime mortgages, and made an even worse mistake trusting the rating agencies and the investment banks when they repackaged the sub-prime mortgages, giving a AAA rating to the new products. The banks (and the banks' investors) also badly misjudged the risk associated with high bank leverage. And risky assets that normally would have required substantially higher returns to induce people to hold them were yielding only a small risk premium. In some cases, the seeming mispricing and misjudging of risk was based on a smart bet: they believed that if troubles arose, the Federal Reserve and the Treasury would bail them out, and they were right.

The Federal Reserve, led first by Chairman Alan Greenspan and later by Ben Bernanke, and the other regulators stood back and let it all happen. They not only claimed that they couldn't tell whether there was a bubble until after it broke, but also said that even if they had been able to, there was nothing they could do about it. They were wrong on both counts. They could have, for instance, pushed for higher down payments on homes or higher margin requirements for stock trading, both of which would have cooled down these overheated markets. But they chose not to do so. Perhaps worse, Greenspan aggravated the situation by allowing banks to engage in ever-riskier lending and encouraging people to take out variable-rate mortgages, with payments that could—and did—easily explode, forcing even middle-income families into foreclosure.

Those who argued for deregulation—and continue to do so in spite of the evident consequences—contend that the costs of regulation exceed the benefits. With the global budgetary and real costs of this crisis mounting into the trillions of dollars, it's hard to see how its advocates can still maintain that position. They argue, however, that the real cost of regulation is the stifling of innovation. The sad truth is that in America's financial markets, innovations were directed at circumventing regulations, accounting standards, and taxation. They created products that were so complex they had the effect of both increasing risk and information asymmetries. No wonder then that it is impossible to trace any sustained increase in economic growth

(beyond the bubble to which they contributed) to these financial innovations. At the same time, financial markets did not innovate in ways that would have helped ordinary citizens with the simple task of managing the risk of homeownership. Innovations that would have helped people and countries manage the other important risks they face were actually resisted. Good regulations could have redirected innovations in ways that would have increased the efficiency of our economy and security of our citizens.

Not surprisingly, the financial sector has attempted to shift blame elsewhere—when its claim that it was just an "accident" (a once-in-a-thousand-years storm) fell on deaf ears.

Those in the financial sector often blame the Fed for allowing interest rates to remain too low for too long. But this particular attempt to shift blame is peculiar: what other industry would say that the reason why its profits were so low and it performed so poorly was that the costs of its inputs (steel, wages) were too low? The major "input" into banking is the cost of its funds, and yet bankers seem to be complaining that the Fed made money too cheap! Had the low-cost funds been used well, for example, if the funds had gone to support investment in new technology or expansion of enterprises, we would have had a more competitive and dynamic economy.

* * *

Greenspan and others, in turn, have tried to shift the blame for the low interest rates to Asian countries and the flood of liquidity from their excess savings.[2] Again, being able to import capital on better terms should have been an advantage, a blessing. But it is a remarkable claim: the Fed was saying, in effect, that it can't control interest rates in America anymore. Of course, it can; the Fed *chose* to keep interest rates low, partly for reasons that I have already explained.

In what might seem an outrageous act of ingratitude to those who rescued them from their deathbed, many bankers blame the government—biting the very hand that was feeding them. They blame the government for not having stopped them—like the kid caught stealing from the candy store who blamed the storeowner or the cop for looking the other way, leading him to believe he could get away with his misdeed. But the argument is even more disingenuous because the financial markets had *paid* to get the cops off the beat. They successfully beat back attempts to regulate derivatives and restrict predatory lending. Their victory over America was total. Each victory gave them more money with which to influence the political process. They even had an argument: deregulation had led them to make more money, and money was the mark of success. Q.E.D.

Conservatives don't like this blaming of the market; if there is a problem with the economy, in their hearts, they know the true cause must be government. Government wanted to increase household ownership, and the bankers' defense was that they were just doing their part. Fannie Mae and Freddie Mac, the two private companies that had started as government agencies, have been a particular subject of vilification, as has the government program called the Community Reinvestment Act (CRA), which encourages banks to lend to underserved communities. Had it not been for these efforts at lending to the poor, so the argument goes, all would have been well. This litany of defenses is, for the most part, sheer nonsense. AIG's almost $200 billion bailout (that's a big amount by any account) was based on derivatives (credit default swaps)—banks gambling with other banks. The banks didn't need any push for egalitarian housing to engage in excessive risk-taking. Nor did the massive overinvestment in commercial real estate have anything to do with government homeownership policy. Nor did the repeated instances of bad lending around the world from which the banks have had to be repeatedly rescued. Moreover, default rates on the CRA lending were actually comparable to other areas of lending—showing that such lending, if done well, does not pose greater risks. The most telling point though is that Fannie Mae and Freddie Mac's mandate was for "conforming loans,"

loans to the middle class. The banks jumped into subprime mortgages—an area where, at the time, Freddie Mac and Fannie Mae were not making loans—without any incentives from the government. The president may have given some speeches about the ownership society, but there is little evidence that banks snap to it when the president gives a speech. A policy has to be accompanied by carrots and sticks, and there weren't any. * * * Later on, years after the private sector had invented the toxic mortgages * * * the privatized and under-regulated Fannie Mae and Freddie Mac decided that they too should join in the fun. Their executives thought, Why couldn't they enjoy bonuses akin to others in the industry? Ironically, in doing so, they helped save the private sector from some of its own folly: many of the securitized mortgages wound up on their balance sheet. Had they not bought them, the problems in the private sector arguably would have been far worse, though by buying so many securities, they may also have helped fuel the bubble.[3]

* * * [F]iguring out what happened is like "peeling an onion": each explanation raises new questions. In peeling back the onion, we need to ask, Why did the financial sector fail so badly, not only in performing its critical social functions, but even in serving shareholders and bondholders well? Only executives in financial institutions seem to have walked away with their pockets lined—less lined than if there had been no crash, but still better off than, say, the poor Citibank shareholders who saw their investments virtually disappear. The financial institutions complained that the regulators didn't *stop* them from behaving badly. But aren't firms supposed to behave well on their own? * * * I * * * give a simple explanation: flawed incentives. But then we must push back again: Why were there flawed incentives? Why didn't the market "discipline" firms that employed flawed incentive structures, in the way that standard theory says it should? The answers to these questions are complex but include a flawed system of corporate governance, inadequate enforcement of competition laws, and imperfect information and an

inadequate understanding of risk on the part of the investors.

While the financial sector bears the major onus for blame, regulators didn't do the job that they should have done—ensuring that banks don't behave badly, as is their wont. Some in the less regulated part of the financial markets (like hedge funds), observing that the worst problems occurred in the highly regulated part (the banks), glibly conclude that regulation is the problem. "If only they were unregulated like us, the problems would never have occurred," they argue. But this misses the essential point: The reason why banks are regulated is that their failure can cause massive harm to the rest of the economy. The reason why there is less regulation needed for hedge funds, at least for the smaller ones, is that they can do less harm. The regulation did not cause the banks to behave badly; it was deficiencies in regulation and regulatory enforcement that failed to prevent the banks from imposing costs on the rest of society as they have repeatedly done. Indeed, the one period in American history when they have not imposed these costs was the quarter century after World War II when strong regulations were effectively enforced: it can be done.

＊　＊　＊

Market Failures

Today, after the crash, almost everyone says that there is a need for regulation—or at least for more than there was before the crisis. Not having the necessary regulations has cost us plenty: crises would have been less frequent and less costly, and the cost of the regulators and regulations would be a pittance relative to these costs. Markets on their own evidently fail—and fail very frequently. There are many reasons for these failures, but two are particularly germane to the financial sector: "agency"—in today's world scores of people are handling money and making decisions on behalf of (that is, as agents of) others—and the increased importance of "externalities."

The agency problem is a modern one. Modern corporations with their myriad of small shareholders are fundamentally different from family-run enterprises. There is a separation of ownership and control in which management, owning little of the company, may run the corporation largely for its own benefit. There are agency problems too in the process of investment: much was done through pension funds and other institutions. Those who make the investment decisions—and assess corporate performance—do so not on their behalf but on behalf of those who have entrusted their funds to their care. All along the "agency" chain, concern about performance has been translated into a focus on *short-term returns*.

With its pay dependent not on long-term returns but on stock market prices, management naturally does what it can to drive up stock market prices—even if that entails deceptive (or creative) accounting. Its short-term focus is reinforced by the demand for high quarterly returns from stock market analysts. That drive for short-term returns led banks to focus on how to generate more fees—and, in some cases, how to circumvent accounting and financial regulations. The innovativeness that Wall Street ultimately was so proud of was dreaming up new products that would generate more income in the short term for its firms. The problems that would be posed by high default rates from some of these innovations seemed matters for the distant future. On the other hand, financial firms were not the least bit interested in innovations that might have helped people keep their homes or protect them from sudden rises in interest rates.

In short, there was little or no effective "quality control." Again, in theory, markets are supposed to provide this discipline. Firms that produce excessively risky products would lose their reputation. Share prices would fall. But in today's dynamic world, this market discipline broke down. The financial wizards invented highly risky products that gave about normal returns for a while—with the downside not apparent for years. Thousands of money managers boasted that they could "beat the market," and there was a ready population of shortsighted investors who believed them. But the financial wizards got carried away in the euphoria—they deceived themselves as well as those who bought their products. This helps explain why, when the market crashed, they were left holding billions of dollars' worth of toxic products.

Securitization, the hottest financial-products field in the years leading up to the collapse, provided a textbook example of the risks generated by the new innovations, for it meant that the relationship between lender and borrower was broken. Securitization had one big advantage, allowing risk to be spread; but it had a big disadvantage, creating new problems of imperfect information, and these swamped the benefits from increased diversification. Those buying a mortgage-backed security are, in effect, lending to the homeowner, about whom they know nothing. They trust the bank that sells them the product to have checked it out, and the bank trusts the mortgage originator. The mortgage originators' incentives were focused on the quantity of mortgages originated, not the quality. They produced massive amounts of truly lousy mortgages. The banks like to blame the mortgage originators, but just a glance at the mortgages should have revealed the inherent risks. The fact is that the bankers *didn't want to know.* Their incentives were to pass on the mortgages, and the securities they created backed by the mortgages, as fast as they could to others. In the Frankenstein laboratories of Wall Street, banks created new risk products (collateralized debt instruments, collateralized debt instruments squared, and credit default swaps * * * without mechanisms to manage the monster they had created. * * *

EXTERNALITIES The bankers gave no thought to how dangerous some of the financial instruments were to the rest of us, to the large externalities that were being created. In economics, the technical term *externality* refers to situations where a market exchange imposes costs or benefits on others who aren't party to the exchange. If you are trading on your own account and lose your money, it doesn't really affect anyone else. However, the financial system is now so intertwined and central to the economy that a failure of one large institution can bring down the whole system. The current failure has affected everyone: millions of homeowners have lost their homes, and millions more have seen the equity in their homes disappear; whole communities have been devastated; taxpayers have had to pick up the tab for the losses of the banks; and workers have lost their jobs. The costs have been borne not only in the United States but also around the world, by billions who reaped no gains from the reckless behavior of the banks.

When there are important agency problems and externalities, markets typically fail to produce efficient outcomes—contrary to the widespread belief in the efficiency of markets. This is one of the rationales for financial market regulation. The regulatory agencies were the last line of defense against both excessively risky and unscrupulous behavior by the banks, but after years of concentrated lobbying efforts by the banking industry, the government had not only stripped away existing regulations but also failed to adopt new ones in response to the changing financial landscape. People who didn't understand why regulation was necessary—and accordingly believed that it was unnecessary—became regulators. The repeal in 1999 of the Glass-Steagall Act, which had separated investment and commercial banks, created ever larger banks that were too big to be allowed to fail. Knowing that they were too big to fail provided incentives for excessive risk-taking.

In the end, the banks got hoisted by their own petard: The financial instruments that they used to exploit the poor turned against the financial markets and brought them down. When the bubble broke, most of the banks were left holding enough of the risky securities to threaten their very survival—evidently, they hadn't done as good a job in passing the risk along to others as they had thought. This is but one of many ironies that have marked the crisis: in Greenspan and Bush's attempt to minimize the role of government in the economy, the government has assumed an unprecedented role across a wide swath—becoming the owner of the world's largest automobile company, the largest insurance company, and (had it received in return for what it had given to the banks) some of the largest banks. A country in which socialism is often treated as an anathema has socialized risk and intervened in markets in unprecedented ways.

These ironies are matched by the seeming inconsistencies in the arguments of the International Monetary Fund (IMF) and the U.S. Treasury before, during, and after the East Asian crisis—and the inconsistencies between the policies then and now. The IMF might claim that it believes in market fundamentalism—that markets are efficient, self-correcting, and accordingly, are best left to their own devices if one is to maximize growth and efficiency—but the moment a crisis occurs, it calls for massive government assistance, worried about "contagion," the spread of the disease from one country to another. But contagion is a quintessential externality, and if there are externalities, one can't (logically) believe in market fundamentalism. Even after the multibillion-dollar bailouts, the IMF and U.S. Treasury resisted imposing measures (regulations) that might have made the "accidents" less likely and less costly—because they believed that markets fundamentally worked well on their own, even when they had just experienced repeated instances when they didn't.

The bailouts provide an example of a set of inconsistent policies with potentially long-run consequences. Economists worry about incentives—one might say it is their number-one preoccupation. One of the arguments put forward by many in the financial markets for not helping mortgage owners who can't meet their repayments is that it gives rise to "moral hazard"—that is, incentives to repay are weakened if mortgage owners know that there is some chance they will be helped out if they don't repay.

Worries about moral hazard led the IMF and the U.S. Treasury to argue vehemently against bailouts in Indonesia and Thailand—setting off a massive collapse of the banking system and exacerbating the downturns in those countries. Worries about moral hazard played into the decision not to bail out Lehman Brothers. But this decision, in turn, led to the most massive set of bailouts in history. When it came to America's big banks in the aftermath of Lehman Brothers, concerns about moral hazard were shunted aside, so much so that the banks' officers were allowed to enjoy huge bonuses for record losses, dividends continued unabated, and shareholders and bondholders were protected. The repeated rescues (not just bailouts, but ready provision of liquidity by the Federal Reserve in times of trouble) provide part of the explanation of the current crisis: they encouraged banks to become increasingly reckless, knowing that there was a good chance that if a problem arose, they would be rescued. * * *

Agency issues and externalities mean that there is a role for government. If it does its job well, there will be fewer accidents, and when the accidents occur, they will be less costly. When there are accidents, government will have to help in picking up the pieces. But how the government picks up the pieces affects the likelihood of future crises—and a society's sense of fairness and justice. Every successful economy—every successful society—involves both government and markets. There needs to be a balanced role. It is a matter not just of "how much" but also of "what." During the Reagan and both Bush administrations, the United States lost that balance—doing too little then has meant doing too much now. Doing the wrong things now may mean doing more in the future.

RECESSIONS One of the striking aspects of the "free market" revolutions initiated by President Ronald Reagan and Prime Minister Margaret Thatcher of England was that perhaps the most important set of instances when markets fail to yield efficient outcomes was forgotten: the repeated episodes when resources are not fully utilized. The economy often operates below capacity, with millions of people who would like to find work not being able to do so, with episodic fluctuations in which more than one out of twelve can't find jobs—and numbers that are far worse for minorities and youth. The official unemployment rate doesn't provide a full picture: Many who would like to work full-time are working part-time because that's the only job they could get, and they are not included in the unemployment rate. Nor does the rate include those who join the rolls of the disabled but who would be working if they could only get a job. Nor does it include those who have been so discouraged by their failure to find a job that they give up looking. This crisis though is worse than usual. With the broader measure of unemployment, by September 2009 more than one in six Americans who would have liked to have had a full-time job couldn't find one, and by October, matters were worse. While the market is self-correcting—the bubble eventually burst—this crisis shows once again that the correction may be slow and the cost enormous. The cumulative gap between the economy's actual output and potential output is in the trillions.

Who Could Have Foreseen the Crash?

In the aftermath of the crash, both those in the financial market and their regulators claimed, "Who could have foreseen these problems?" In fact, many critics had—but their dire forecasts were an inconvenient truth: too much money was being made by too many people for their warnings to be heard.

I was certainly not the only person who was expecting the U.S. economy to crash, with global consequences. New York University economist Nouriel Roubini, financier George Soros, Morgan Stanley's Stephen Roach, Yale University housing expert Robert Shiller, and former Clinton Council of Economic Advisers/National Economic Coun-

cil staffer Robert Wescott all issued repeated warnings. They were all Keynesian economists, sharing the view that markets were not self-correcting. Most of us were worried about the housing bubble; some (such as Roubini) focused on the risk posed by global imbalances to a sudden adjustment of exchange rates.

But those who had engineered the bubble (Henry Paulson had led Goldman Sachs to new heights of leverage, and Ben Bernanke had allowed the issuance of subprime mortgages to continue) maintained their faith in the ability of markets to self-correct—until they *had* to confront the reality of a massive collapse. One doesn't have to have a Ph.D. in psychology to understand why they wanted to pretend that the economy was going through just a minor disturbance, one that could easily be brushed aside. As late as March 2007, Federal Reserve Chairman Bernanke claimed that "the impact on the broader economy and financial markets of the problems in the subprime market seems likely to be contained."[4] A year later, even after the collapse of Bear Stearns, with rumors swirling about the imminent demise of Lehman Brothers, the official line (told not only publicly but also behind closed doors with other central bankers) was that the economy was already on its way to a robust recovery after a few blips.

* * *

Indeed, anyone looking closely at the American economy could easily have seen that there were major "macro" problems as well as "micro" problems. As I noted earlier, our economy had been sustained by an unsustainable bubble. Without the bubble, aggregate demand—the sum total of the goods and services demanded by households, firms, government, and foreigners—would have been weak, partly because of the growing inequality in the United States and elsewhere around the world, which shifted money from those would have spent it to those who didn't.

For years, my Columbia colleague Bruce Greenwald and I had drawn attention to the further problem of a *global* lack of aggregate demand—the total of all the goods and services that people throughout the world want to buy. In the world of globalization, global aggregate demand is what matters. If the sum total of what people around the world want to buy is less than what the world can produce, there is a problem—a weak global economy. One of the reasons for weak global aggregate demand is the growing level of reserves—money that countries set aside for a "rainy day."

Developing countries put aside hundreds of billions of dollars in reserves to protect themselves from the high level of global volatility that has marked the era of deregulation, and from the discomfort they feel at turning to the IMF for help. The prime minister of one of the countries that had been ravished by the global financial crisis of 1997 said to me, "We were in the class of '97. We learned what happens if you don't have enough reserves."

The oil-rich countries too were accumulating reserves—they knew that the high price of crude was not sustainable. For some countries, there was another reason for reserve accumulation. Export-led growth had been lauded as the best way for developing countries to grow; after new trade rules under the World Trade Organization took away many of the traditional instruments developing countries used to help create new industries, many turned to a policy of keeping their exchange rates competitive. And this meant buying dollars, selling their own currencies, and accumulating reserves.

These were all good reasons for accumulating reserves, but they had a bad consequence: there was insufficient global demand. A half trillion dollars, or more, was being set aside in these reserves every year in the years prior to the crisis. For a while, the United States had come to the rescue with debt-based profligate consumption, spending well beyond its means. It became the world's consumer of last resort. But that was not sustainable.

THE GLOBAL CRISIS   This crisis quickly became global—and not surprisingly, as nearly a quarter of U.S. mortgages had gone abroad. Unintentionally, this helped the United States: had foreign institutions not bought as much of its toxic instruments and debt, the situation here might have been far worse. But first the United States had exported its deregulatory philosophy—without that, foreigners might not have bought so many of its toxic mortgages. In the end, the United States also exported its recession. This was, of course, only one of several channels through which the American crisis became global: the U.S. economy is still the largest, and it is hard for a downturn of this magnitude not to have a global impact. Moreover, global financial markets have become closely interlinked—evidenced by the fact that two of the top three beneficiaries of the U.S. government bailout of AIG were foreign banks.

In the beginning, many in Europe talked of decoupling, that they would be able to maintain growth in their economies even as America went into a downturn: the growth in Asia would save them from a recession. It should have been apparent that this too was just wishful thinking. Asia's economies are still too small (the entire consumption of Asia is just 40 percent of that of the United States), and their growth relies heavily on exports to the United States. Even after a massive stimulus, China's growth in 2009 was some 3 to 4 percent below what it had been before the crisis. The world is too interlinked; a downturn in the United States could not but lead to a global slowdown. * * *

While Europe's financial institutions suffered from buying toxic mortgages and the risky gambles they had made with American banks, a number of European countries grappled with problems of their own design. Spain too had allowed a massive housing bubble to develop and is now suffering from the near-total collapse of its real estate market. In contrast to the United States, however, Spain's strong banking regulations have allowed its banks to withstand a much bigger trauma with better results—though, not surprisingly, its overall economy has been hit far worse.

The United Kingdom too succumbed to a real estate bubble. But worse, under the influence of the city of London, a major financial hub, it fell into the trap of the "race to the bottom," trying to do whatever it could to attract financial business. "Light" regulation did no better there than in the United States. Because the British had allowed the financial sector to take on a greater role in their economy, the cost of the bailouts was (proportionately) even greater. As in the United States, a culture of high salaries and bonuses developed. But at least the British understood that if you give taxpayer money to the banks, you have to do what you can to make sure they use it for the purposes intended—for more loans, not for bonuses and dividends. And at least in the U.K., there was some understanding that there had to be accountability—the heads of the bailed-out banks were replaced—and the British government demanded that the taxpayers get fair value in return for the bailouts, not the giveaways that marked both the Obama and Bush administrations' rescues.

Iceland is a wonderful example of what can go wrong when a small and open economy adopts the deregulation mantra blindly. Its well-educated people worked hard and were at the forefront of modern technology. They had overcome the disadvantages of a remote location, harsh weather, and depletion of fish stocks—one of their traditional sources of income—to generate a per capita income of $40,000. Today, the reckless behavior of their banks has put the country's future in jeopardy.

I had visited Iceland several times earlier in this decade and warned of the risks of its liberalization policies. This country of 300,000 had three banks that took on deposits and bought assets totaling some $176 billion, eleven times the country's GDP.[5] With a dramatic collapse of Iceland's banking system in the fall of 2008, Iceland became the first developed country in more than thirty years to turn to the IMF for help. Iceland's banks had, like banks elsewhere, taken

on high leverage and high risks. When financial markets realized the risk and started pulling money out, these banks (and especially Landsbanki) lured money from depositors in the U.K. and Netherlands by offering them "Icesaver" accounts with high returns. The depositors foolishly thought that there was a "free lunch": they could get higher returns without risk. Perhaps they also foolishly thought their own governments were doing their regulatory job. But, as everywhere, regulators had largely assumed that markets would take care of themselves. Borrowing from depositors only postponed the day of reckoning. Iceland could not afford to pour hundreds of billions of dollars into the weakened banks. As this reality gradually dawned on those who had provided funds to the bank, it became only a matter of time before there would be a run on the banking system; the global turmoil following the Lehman Brothers collapse precipitated what would in any case have been inevitable. Unlike the United States, the government of Iceland knew that it could not bail out the bondholders or shareholders. The only questions were whether the government would bail out the Icelandic corporation that insured the depositors, and how generous it would be to the foreign depositors. The U.K. used strong-arm tactics—going so far as to seize Icelandic assets using anti-terrorism laws—and when Iceland turned to the IMF and the Nordic countries for assistance, they insisted that Icelandic taxpayers bail out U.K. and Dutch depositors even beyond the amounts the accounts had been insured for. On a return visit to Iceland in September 2009, almost a year later, the anger was palpable. Why should Iceland's taxpayers be made to pay for the failure of a private bank, especially when foreign regulators had failed to do their job of protecting their own citizens? One widely held view for the strong response from European governments was that Iceland had exposed a fundamental flaw in European integration: "the single market" meant that any European bank could operate in any country. Responsibility for regulation was put on the "home" country. But if the home country failed to do its job, citizens in other countries could lose billions. Europe didn't want to think about this and its profound implications; better to simply make little Iceland pick up the tab, an amount some put at as much as 100 percent of the country's GDP.

As the crisis worsened in the United States and Europe, other countries around the world suffered from the collapse in global demand. Developing countries suffered especially, as remittances (transfers of money from family members in developed countries) fell and capital that had flowed into them was greatly diminished—and in some cases reversed. While America's crisis began with the financial sector and then spread to the rest of the economy, in many of the developing countries—including those where financial regulation is far better than in the United States—the problems in the "real economy" were so large that they eventually affected the financial sector. The crisis spread so rapidly partly because of the policies, especially of capital and financial market liberalization, the IMF and the U.S. Treasury had foisted on these countries—based on the same free market ideology that had gotten the United States into trouble. But while even the United States finds it difficult to afford the trillions in bailouts and stimulus, corresponding actions by poorer countries are well beyond their reach.

THE BIG PICTURE Underlying all of these symptoms of dysfunction is a larger truth: the world economy is undergoing seismic shifts. The Great Depression coincided with the decline of U.S. agriculture; indeed, agricultural prices were falling even before the stock market crash in 1929. Increases in agricultural productivity were so great that a small percentage of the population could produce all the food that the country could consume. The transition from an economy based on agriculture to one where manufacturing predominated was not easy. In fact, the economy only resumed growing when the New Deal kicked

in and World War II got people working in factories.

Today the underlying trend in the United States is the move away from manufacturing and into the service sector. As before, this is partly because of the success in increasing productivity in manufacturing, so that a small fraction of the population can produce all the toys, cars, and TVs that even the most materialistic and profligate society might buy. But in the United States and Europe, there is an additional dimension: globalization, which has meant a shift in the locus of production and comparative advantage to China, India, and other developing countries.

Accompanying this "microeconomic" adjustment are a set of macroeconomic imbalances: while the United States should be saving for the retirement of its aging baby-boomers, it has been living beyond its means, financed to a large extent by China and other developing countries that have been producing more than they have been consuming. While it is natural for some countries to lend to others—some to run trade deficits, others surpluses—the pattern, with poor countries lending to the rich, is peculiar and the magnitude of the deficits appear unsustainable. As countries get more indebted, lenders may lose confidence that the borrower can repay—and this can be true even for a rich country like the United States. Returning the American and global economy to health will require the restructuring of economies to reflect the new economics and correcting these global imbalances.

We can't go back to where we were before the bubble broke in 2007. Nor should we want to. There were plenty of problems with that economy—as we have just seen. Of course, there is a chance that some new bubble will replace the housing bubble, just as the housing bubble replaced the tech bubble. But such a "solution" would only postpone the day of reckoning. Any new bubble could pose dangers: the oil bubble helped pushed the economy over the brink. The longer we delay in dealing with the underlying problems, the longer it will be before the world returns to robust growth.

*   *   *

From Global Recovery to Global Prosperity

*   *   *

A New Global Economic Order: China and America

The current crisis is so deep and so disturbing that things will change, whether leaders strive to make it happen or not. The most profound changes may concern the sometimes difficult relationship between the United States and China. China has a long way to go before it surpasses the United States in GDP—in "purchasing power parity," reflecting differences in costs of living, it is still about one-half that of the United States—and even further before it approaches the U.S. income per capita—it is about one-eighth.[6] But still, China has been achieving some impressive records. The year 2009 saw it likely becoming the world's largest merchandise exporter, car producer, and manufacturer more generally. It also earned the dubious distinction of outpacing the United States in carbon emissions to become the leader in the world. Its growth, while slower than it was before the crisis, remains markedly higher than that of the United States, by 7 percentage points a year (in 2009, the difference was more like 10 percent), and at that rate the gap in GDP is cut in half every ten years. Moreover, well within the next quarter century, China is likely to become the dominant economy in Asia, and Asia's economy is likely to be larger than that of the United States.

Though China's economy is still so much smaller than the United States', the U.S. imports far more from China than it exports, and these large trade imbalances have generated growing tensions as U.S. unemployment mounts. The relationship may be symbiotic—China helps finance America's massive fiscal deficits, without China's inexpensive goods the standard of living of many Americans might be markedly lower, and America provides the markets for China's ever-growing supply—but in the Great Recession, the focus is on jobs. Most Americans don't understand the principles of comparative advantage—that each country produces the goods that it is *relatively* good at; and they find it difficult to grasp that the United States may have lost its comparative advantage in many areas of manufacturing. If China (or any other country) is outcompeting the United States, they believe it *has to be* because they are doing something unfairly: manipulating exchange rates or subsidizing their products or selling products below costs (which is called "dumping").

The crisis has, in fact, turned everything topsy-turvy. America is being accused of massive and unfair subsidies (to its banks and auto companies). A loan from the Fed at close to zero interest rate to a large corporation that would have to pay a very high interest rate on the open market—if it could get financing at all—too can be viewed as a massive subsidy. Maintaining low interest rates is one of the critical ways that countries "manage" their exchange rate (when interest rates are low, capital flows out of the country to places where it can get a higher return), and many in Europe believe that the United States is using the low exchange rate to get a competitive advantage.

While both the United States and China have imposed protectionist actions (the United States, partly in response to union pressure, China, partly as a matter of retaliation and partly as an element of its development strategy), * * * the extent is limited. But as I noted earlier, there is a recognition that *something* needs to be done about global imbalances, of which the U.S.-China trade imbalance is the most important component.

In the short run, America may find it easier to adjust than China. China needs to consume more, but it is hard to induce households to consume more when they face high levels of uncertainty. China's problems arise less, however, from a high household savings rate than from the fact that household income is a smaller fraction of GDP than in most other countries. Low wages ensure high profits, and there is little pressure to distribute the profits. The result is that enterprises (both public and private) retain a large fraction of their income. But changing the distribution of income in any country is difficult.

China's growth model has been driven by supply: profits are reinvested, increasing production far faster than consumption, and the difference is exported. The model has worked well—creating jobs in China and keeping prices low in the rest of the world—but the crisis has highlighted a flaw in the model. In this downturn, it has been hard for China to export the surplus; over the longer run, as its share of many manufactured goods has increased, it will be difficult for it to maintain its growth rate. This would be true even if there were no protectionist responses in many of its trading partners—there are only so many television sets and other consumption goods that those in the West can buy—but not surprisingly, as China has demonstrated its prowess not just in low-skill manufactured goods but across a wide range of products, protectionist stridency has increased.

Many in China realize that they will have to change their growth strategy—providing more support for small and medium-sized enterprises, for instance, through creating more local and regional banks. Such enterprises are, in most countries, the basis of job growth. Job growth will lead to higher wages, and this will shift the distribution of income in ways that will support more domestic consumption. Some of the apparent corporate profits arise from China's failure to charge appropriately for natural resources (including land). In effect, the corporations were given these assets, which really belong to the people; if, for instance, they auctioned off those resources, the revenues would generate a hefty income. If China captured the return on these assets for all of its people, it would have more revenues to finance health, education, and retirement benefits, and this would reduce some of the need for high household savings.

While this new growth strategy may seem sensible, there are powerful political forces arrayed against it: the large enterprises and their officials, for instance, enjoy the current system, and they hope that it can somehow be made sustainable. Those same political forces will also oppose allowing China's exchange rate to appreciate, which would both decrease the competitiveness of China's exports and increase the real wages of its workers. Those in the West who argue for the need for large banks and other large enterprises provide succor to these New Industrialists. China, they contend, needs equally large firms (sometimes called "national champions") to compete globally. It is too soon to know how this struggle will play out.

China's stimulus package—one of the largest in the world (relative to the size of the country)[7]—reflected these tensions in economic policy. Much of the money went to infrastructure and to help "green" the economy. A new high-speed railroad system may have an impact on China analogous to that of the construction of the intercontinental railroad in the post–Civil War United States. It may help forge a stronger national economy, as economic geography changes almost overnight. The stimulus package also provided explicit encouragement for consumption, especially in the rural sector, and especially to buy products that face marked declines in sales abroad. It also provided for rapid increases in expenditure on rural health and education. At the same time, there were efforts to strengthen certain key sectors, like automotive and steel. The government argued that it is simply trying to "rationalize" production—increasing efficiency—but critics worry that these efforts might exacerbate the problems of excess supply and/or might reduce effective competition. This would increase corporate profits and lower real wages, exacerbating the problem of underconsumption.

* * *

But inside China, there is growing reluctance to increase its lending to the U.S. government, where returns remain low and risk high. There are alternatives—China can invest in real assets in America. But when China has tried to do so, it has sometimes met resistance (as when it tried to buy Unocal, a relatively small American oil company, most of whose assets were actually in Asia). The United States allowed China to buy its highest-polluting car, the Hummer, as well as IBM's laptop division, which became Lenovo. While America is seemingly open to investments in many areas, it has had a broad notion of sectors that are critical for national security and are to be protected from such investments, and this risks undermining the fundamental principles of globalization: America told developing countries that they must open up their markets to foreign ownership as part of the basic rules of the game.

If China sells significant amounts of the dollars it holds in reserves, it will lead to a further appreciation of its currency (the RMB) against the dollar, which will, in turn, improve America's bilateral trade balance with China. It is likely to do less, however, than one might hope for the U.S. overall trade deficit—America will just buy its textiles from some other developing country. However, it will mean that China will take a big loss on its remaining massive holdings of U.S. T-bills and other dollar-denominated assets.

To some, it appears that China is caught between a rock and a hard place. If it moves out of the dollar, it takes massive losses on its reserves and exports. If it stays in the dollar, it postpones the losses on the reserves, but adjustment may eventually have to come in any case. The worry about the loss of sales is perhaps exaggerated: China is currently providing "vendor" finance—that is, it provides the money to those who buy its goods. Instead of lending to America to buy its goods, it can lend to those in other parts of the world—as it is increasingly doing—or even to its own citizens.

A New Global Reserve System

Concerned about its holdings of dollars, in March 2009 the head of China's central bank lent support to a long-standing idea: creation of a global reserve currency. Keynes pushed the idea some seventy-five years ago, and it was part of his original conception for the IMF. Additionally, support for this idea has come from another quarter—a UN commission of experts on the restructuring of the global financial and economic system, which I chaired.

Developing countries, *China foremost*, today hold trillions of dollars in reserves—money they can draw upon in the event of a crisis, such as the Great Recession. [Earlier], I emphasized that this crisis exposed the problem of a global insufficiency of aggregate demand. Sadly, *so far*, neither the U.S. administration nor the G-20 has even begun to discuss this underlying problem—let alone take action. Annual emissions of a new global reserve currency would mean that countries would no longer have to set aside part of their current income as protection against global volatility—instead, they could set aside the newly issued "money." This would thereby increase global aggregate demand and strengthen the global economy.

There are two other important reasons for this initiative. The first is that the present system is unstable. Currently, countries hold dollars to provide confidence to their currency and country as a kind of insurance against the vicissitudes of the global marketplace. As more and more dollars are held by foreigners in their reserves, there is greater and greater anxiety about America's increasing indebtedness abroad.

There is another reason why the current system contributes to instability. If some countries insist on having a trade surplus (exporting more than they import) in order to build up reserves, other countries have to have trade deficits; the sum of the surpluses must equal the sum of the deficits. But trade deficits can be a problem—countries with persistent trade deficits are more likely to face an economic crisis—and countries have worked hard to get rid of them. If one country gets rid of its trade deficit, then some other country's deficit must rise (if the surplus countries don't change their behavior), so trade deficits are like a hot potato. In recent years, most countries have learned how to avoid deficits, with the result that the United States has become the "deficit of last resort." In the long run, America's position is clearly untenable. Creating a global reserve currency with annual emissions would provide a buffer. A country could run a small trade deficit and still build up its reserves, because of the allocation of new global reserve currency that it receives. As investors see reserves build up, they would gain confidence.

*   *   *

A good reserve currency needs to be a good store of value—a stable currency—but the dollar has been highly volatile and is likely to remain so. Already, many smaller countries have moved much of their reserves out of dollars, and even China is reported to have a quarter or more of its reserves in other currencies. The question is not whether the world will move away from the dollar reserve system altogether, but whether it does it thoughtfully and carefully. Without a clear plan the global financial system would become even more unstable.

*   *   *

Already, there are initiatives to create regional reserve arrangements. The Chiang Mai Initiative in East Asia allows countries to exchange their reserves; in response to the crisis, they increased the size of the program by 50 percent. The world may move to a two- (or three-) currency system, with both the dollar and euro in use. But such a system could be even more unstable than the current one. For the world, it might mean that if the euro is expected to gain relative to the dollar, countries would start to shift their holdings into euros. As they do this, the euro strengthens, reinforcing their beliefs—until some event, a political or economic disturbance, starts the reverse process. For Europe, it would pose a special problem, since countries in the European Union have constraints on their ability to run fiscal deficits to offset weak demand.

The dollar-based global reserve system is fraying, but efforts to create an alternative are only just beginning. Central bankers have at last learned the basic lesson of wealth management—diversification—and for years many have been moving reserves out of the dollar. In 2009, the G-20 agreed to a large ($250 billion) issuance of special drawing rights (SDRs), which are a kind of global reserve currency created by the IMF. But the SDRs have strong limitations. They are allocated to countries on the basis of their IMF "quotas" (their effective share holdings)—with the United States getting the largest piece. But the United States obviously has no need to hold reserves, since it can simply print dollar bills. The system would work far better if the reserve emissions were allocated to countries that otherwise would be expanding their reserves; alternatively, new global reserve emissions could go to poor countries needing assistance.

It would be even better if the new system was designed to discourage trade surpluses. The United States hectors China about its surplus, but in current arrangements there are strong incentives for countries to maintain reserves, and to run surpluses to add to reserves. Those countries that had large reserves fared far better in this crisis than those without adequate reserves. In a well-designed global reserve system, countries with persistent surpluses would have their reserve currency allocation diminished, and this, in turn, would encourage them to maintain a better balance. A well-designed global reserve system could go further in stabilizing the global economy, for if more of the global reserve currency were issued when global growth was weak, it would encourage spending—with a concomitant increase in growth and employment.

With support from the United States, a new global reserve system can be quickly achieved. The question is whether and when the Obama administration will realize how much the United States, and the world, have to gain. The risk is that America will bury its head in the sand. The world will be moving away from the dollar-based reserve system. Without an agreement on the creation of a new global reserve system, the world is likely to move out of the dollar and into a multiple-currency reserve system, producing global financial instability in the short term and a regime more unstable than the current system in the long term.

The crisis will almost surely mark a change in the global economic and political order. America's power and influence will be diminished; China's increased. Even before the crisis, a global reserve system depending on one country's currency seemed out of synch with twenty-first-century globalization—but it seems especially so given the vagaries of the dollar and the U.S. economics and politics.

Toward a New Multilateralism

Out of the disaster of the Great Depression and the Second World War, a new global order emerged and a new set of institutions were created. That framework worked for many years but increasingly became unsuited for managing the evolving global economic system. The current crisis has brought into full view its limitations. But just as the United States tried to muddle through in the domestic arena, attempting largely to re-create the world as it was before the crisis, so too in the international arena. In the aftermath of the last global crisis ten years ago, there was much discussion of reforms in the

"global financial architecture." There was a suspicion that those who wished to maintain the status quo (including those from the U.S. and other Western financial markets who benefited from the way things were working, and their allies in government) used grandiose language to cover up their true agenda: people would talk and talk and talk, until the crisis was over, and with the end of the crisis would come the end of the resolve to do anything. In the years following the 1997–1998 crisis, little was done—obviously, much too little to prevent an even grander crisis. Will this happen once again?

The United States should, in particular, do what it can to strengthen multilateralism—which means democratizing, reforming, and funding the IMF and the World Bank so that developing countries find less need to turn to bilateral support in times of need (whether from China, Russia, or Europe). It must turn away from protectionism and the bilateral trade agreements of the Bush era. These undermine the multilateral trading system that so many have worked so hard to create over the past sixty years. The United States should help design a new coordinated global financial regulatory system, without which these markets are at risk of fragmentation, and support the new global reserve system described earlier. Without these efforts global financial markets risk a new era of instability and the world a continued era of economic weakness. More broadly, the United States needs to support and strengthen the international rule of law—without which none of this is possible.

During the years of American triumphalism, between the fall of the Berlin Wall and the fall of Lehman Brothers, the United States did not use its power and influence to shape globalization in a way that was fair, especially to developing countries. Its economic policy was based less on principles than on its own self-interest—or more accurately, the desires and aversions of the special interest groups that have played, and will continue to play, such a key role in shaping economic policy. Not only has Europe been more vocal in articulating the concerns of the poor in developing countries, but many of the European countries have actually put their money where their mouth is. During the Bush years, America often did what it could to undermine multilateralism.

America's economic hegemony will no longer be taken for granted in the way that it was. If America wishes to have the respect of others, if it wishes to exercise the influence that it once did, it will have to earn it not just by its words but by its actions, both by the examples that it sets at home—including the way it treats those who are disadvantaged—and by what it does abroad.

The global economic system has not worked as many had hoped. Globalization has led to unprecedented prosperity for many, but in 2008 it helped transmit the U.S. recession to countries around the world—to those that had managed well their financial systems (far better than the United States) and to those that had not, to those that had gained enormously by globalization and to those that had benefited less. Not surprisingly, those countries that were most open, most globalized, were hit the worst. Free market ideology underlay many of the institutions and agreements that provided the framework for globalization; just as these ideas had been the basis for the deregulation that played such a big role in the creation of the current crisis, they underpinned the capital and financial market liberalization that played such a big role in the rapid spread of the crisis around the world.

This [discussion] has shown how the crisis is likely to change the global economic order, including the global balance of economic power—and how certain key reforms, including the creation of a new global reserve system, can help restore global prosperity and stability. * * *

NOTES

1. From 2000 to 2008, real median household income (that is, adjusting for inflation) decreased by almost 4 percent. At the end of the last expansion, in 2007, incomes were still some 0.6 percent below the level attained before the end of the previous expansion, in 2000. See U.S. Census Bureau, "Income, Poverty, and Health Insurance Coverage in the United States: 2008," *Current Population Reports,* September 2009, available at http://www.census.gov/prod/2009pubs/p60-236.pdf.

2. Alan Greenspan, "The Fed Didn't Cause the Housing Bubble," *Wall Street Journal,* March 11, 2009, p. A15.

3. Freddie Mac purchased a total of $158 billion, or 13 percent, of all subprime and Alt-A securities created in 2006 and 2007, and Fannie Mae purchased an additional 5 percent. The biggest suppliers of the securities to Fannie and Freddie included Countrywide Financial Corp. of Calabasas, California, as well as Irvine, California–based New Century Financial Corp. and Ameriquest Mortgage Co., lenders that either went bankrupt or were forced to sell themselves. Fannie and Freddie were the biggest buyers of loans from Countrywide, according to the company. See Jody Shenn, "Fannie, Freddie Subprime Spree May Add to Bailout," *Bloomberg.com,* September 22, 2009.

4. Statement of Ben S. Bernanke, Chairman, Board of Governors of the Federal Reserve System, before the Joint Economic Committee, U.S. Congress, Washington, DC, March 28, 2007.

5. Willem H. Buiter and Anne Sibert, "The Icelandic Banking Crisis and What to Do about It: The Lender of Last Resort Theory of Optimal Currency Areas," Centre for Economic Policy Research (CEPR) Policy Insight 26, October 2008, available at http://www.cepr.org/pubs/PolicyInsights/PolicyInsight26.pdf.

6. At current exchange rates, China's GDP is $7,916 billion, and the United States' is $14,462 billion. The GDP per capita for China, at $5,962, is one-eighth that of the United States, which is $46,859. International Monetary Fund, *World Economic Outlook* database, April 2009, available at http://www.imf.org/

external/pubs/ft/weo/2009/01/weodata/index .aspx.

7. In November 2008, China announced a two-year stimulus package of $586 billion, approximately 14 percent of China's GDP. An equivalently sized U.S. stimulus would require $2 trillion. See Xinhua News Agency, "China's 4 Trillion Yuan Stimulus to Boost Economy, Domestic Demand," November 9, 2008, available at http://news.xinhuanet. com/english/2008-11/09/content_10331324. htm.

10 Transnational Issues

Arising out of the interconnectedness of globalization, transnational issues have become part of the global agenda—issues of population, disease, the environment, and human rights. Among the issues that have been affected by globalization is health. William Easterly, former World Bank economist and critic, examines two disturbing paradoxes in his chapter from The White Man's Burden *(2006). Foreign aid has done much to improve health around the world, yet policy makers have been glacially slow to respond to AIDS. Cheaper alternatives aimed at preventing AIDS could actually save lives, yet policy makers have focused on expensive AIDS treatment.*

In many transnational issues, the rights and responsibilities of the individual, the state, and the international community may be incompatible or even diverge. On the issue of human rights, many scholars have argued in favor of enforcement of a universal definition of human rights. These are human rights applicable across all peoples and all cultures. Other writers think that the notion of a universality of human rights is but an illusion. Cambridge University's Amartya Sen suggests that there is a great diversity of human rights experiences among both Western and non-Western cultures. The application of Western human rights standards across cultures may be problematic.

When human rights are violated, what is the proper response of the international community? Transnational activist groups have pushed for criminal trials of perpetrators of atrocities and for truth commissions to expose wrongdoers to public shame, relying on arguments that echo the thinking of constructivist international relations theorists. But states find that it is sometimes necessary to bargain with powerful human rights abusers, giving them amnesties in exchange for stepping down from power. Jack Snyder and Leslie Vinjamuri evaluate the effectiveness of these approaches, arguing in favor of a pragmatic "logic of consequences" against the activists' normative "logic of appropriateness" and cathartic "logic of emotions." Kathryn Sikkink's The Justice Cascade *(forthcoming) in the Norton Series in World Politics offers a detailed rebuttal from a constructivist standpoint.*

But health and human rights are not the only transnational issues where interests may vary. Does a couple have the right of unlimited procreation when resources are limited? Do the rights of the individual take precedence over the right of the community in the use of land and natural resources? Garrett Hardin in his pathbreaking article, published in 1968, posits in unequivocal terms that the pursuit of individual interests may not necessarily lead to the common good. Strategies to address that "tragedy" are delineated in stark, yet profound, ways.

WILLIAM EASTERLY

The Healers: Triumph and Tragedy

> Oh tear-filled figure who, like a sky held back grows heavy above the landscape of her sorrow. . . .
> —Rainer Maria Rilke, "O Lacrimosa,"
> translated by Stephen Mitchell, 1995

In 1989, a team of field researchers in southern Uganda, near the Tanzanian border, stumbled on an older man living by himself in a thatched hut. The man himself was incoherent, but neighbors told his story: his wife and eight children had all died of AIDS. Asked about the man's future, villagers said, "He will not marry again."

Fourteen years later, I am sitting in a health clinic in Soweto, South Africa, talking to a sad young woman named Constance. Constance tells me she is HIV-positive and is too sick to work to support her three children. Even when she is feeling better, she cannot find a job. The father of her children is also unemployed, and she rarely sees him. Constance didn't tell her mother that she is HIV-positive, for fear that her mother

From *The White Man's Burden: Why the West's Efforts to Aid the Rest Have Done So Much Ill and So Little Good* (New York: Penguin, 2006), 238–263.

and stepfather would eject her and her children from the household. She says her stepfather complains bitterly about her not working and not contributing to the maintenance of her children. Left unspoken between us is Constance's fate, and the fate of her three children when she succumbs to AIDS.

Southern Uganda was one of the places where AIDS first appeared in the early 1980s, but in the years since then, the epidemic has spread to most of southern and eastern Africa. South Africa is the most recent casualty of its spread. Thirty percent of pregnant women in their twenties test HIV-positive in South African antenatal clinics.

A third of the adult population is now HIV-positive in Botswana, Lesotho, Swaziland, and Zimbabwe. In other eastern and southern African countries, between 10 and 25 percent of the adult population is HIV-positive. AIDS is spreading also to African countries outside of the

"AIDS corridor," which now runs from Ethiopia to South Africa. In Africa as a whole, there are 29 million HIV-positive people. Tragedies like that of the man in southern Uganda and Constance have happened many times over the past decades, and will happen many more times in the future. More than 2 million people in Africa died from AIDS in 2002. Their places in the epidemic were taken by the 3.5 million Africans newly infected in 2002.

AIDS gets attention. Celebrities and statesmen—ranging from Bill Clinton and Nelson Mandela to Bono and Ashley Judd—call for action. The anti-globalization activists also focus on AIDS. Oxfam calls for access to life-saving drugs for AIDS patients in Africa. American activists at international AIDS conferences (such as American health secretary Tommy Thompson at a conference in Barcelona in 2002) shout down anyone not responding with sufficient alacrity, *pour encourager les autres*.

The foreign aid doyens have also woken up to the problem. The actors include the UN agency UNAIDS, the World Bank's multicountry program to fight AIDS in Africa, the World Health Organization's Commission on Macroeconomics and Health, and the Global Fund to Fight AIDS, TB, and Malaria.

In his 2003 State of the Union Address, President George W. Bush announced the release of fifteen billion dollars in foreign aid to fight AIDS. The initiative was passed by Congress, and Bush signed it into law on May 27, 2003.

It is great that public figures are publicizing the needs of AIDS victims. Many people feel compassion in the face of the death sentence of millions of HIV-positive people in Africa, and in the face of fear that the epidemic will keep spreading.

Yet behind this recent Western attention to AIDS is a tale of two decades of neglect, prevarication, incompetence, and passivity by all those same political actors and aid agencies. By the time researchers found the incoherent victim in southern Uganda in 1989, and even years before that, the West had all the information it needed to predict (and virtually every expert did predict) that AIDS would kill tens of millions of people worldwide, above all in Africa, if nothing was done.

Paradox of Evil and the White Man's Burden

Scholars of religion talk about the paradox of evil, which says you cannot have all three of the following conditions hold: (1) a benevolent God; (2) an all-knowing and all-powerful God; and (3) evil things happening to good people. If you have (1) and (2), then why would God (3) let bad things happen to good people?

Similarly, in the White Man's Burden, you cannot have all the following hold: (1) the White Man's Burden is acting in the interests of the poor in the Rest; (2) the White Man's Burden is effective at resolving poor people's problems; and (3) lots of bad things, whose prevention was affordable, are happening to poor people. If (3) happens, then either (1) or (2) must not hold. Religion is a matter of faith in an invisible Supreme Being, so the contradictions inherent in the Paradox of Evil are more easily tolerated by true believers. Foreign aid is not a faith-based area, however. It is a visible policy with visible dollars meant to help visible people.

The breakdown of the aid system on AIDS is a good test case of the paradox of evil in foreign aid. It reflects how out of touch were the Planners at the top with the tragedy at the bottom, another sign of the weak power of the intended beneficiaries. It shows how ineffective Planners are at making foreign aid work. It is hard to imagine anything more in the interest of the poor than preventing the spread of a fatal disease. Today, the Western aid community has finally woken up to AIDS. Now that community has moved from inaction to ineffective action. Aid for AIDS still appears mismatched to the choices of the poor.

Health Triumphs

The failure on AIDS is all the more striking when we consider that health is he area where foreign aid has enjoyed its most conspicuous successes.[1] Maybe the part of the White Man's Burden that addresses disease offers a more hopeful picture than the malfunctioning bureaucracy in other areas. The healers are working on an issue where the needs and wants of the poor were more obvious—they don't want to die—and so feedback is less critical. The outcomes are more observable, as deaths tend to get noticed by others.

The successes may tell us about the ability of aid agencies to be effective when they have narrow, monitorable objectives that coincide with the poor's needs and with political support in the rich countries for an uncontroversial objective like saving lives. As the previous chapters argue, areas with visible individual outcomes are more likely to put Searchers in charge—in contrast to the power of Planners in areas where nobody can be held individually accountable, such as economic growth. I also hypothesize that Searchers are more likely to succeed at their narrow goals than the Planners are to succeed at their more general goals.

A vaccination campaign in southern Africa virtually eliminated measles as a killer of children. Routine childhood immunization combined with measles vaccination in seven southern African nations starting in 1996 virtually eliminated measles in those countries by 2000. A national campaign in Egypt to make parents aware of the use of oral rehydration therapy from 1982 to 1989 cut childhood deaths from diarrhea by 82 percent over that period. A regional program to eliminate polio in Latin America after 1985 has eliminated it as a public health threat in the Americas. The leading preventable cause of blindness, trachoma, has been cut by 90 percent in children under age ten in Morocco since 1997, thanks to a determined effort to promote surgery, antibiotics, face washing, and environmental cleanliness. Sri Lanka's commitment to preventing maternal deaths during childbirth has cut the rate of maternal mortality from 486 to 24 deaths per 100,000 births over the last four decades. A program to control tuberculosis in China cut the number of cases by 40 percent between 1990 and 2000. Donors collabourated on a program to wipe out river blindness in West Africa starting in 1974, virtually halting the transmission of the disease. Eighteen million children in the twenty-country area of the program have been kept safe from river blindness since the program began. An international effort eradicated smallpox worldwide. Another partnership among aid donors contributed to the near eradication of guinea worm in twenty African and Asian countries where it was endemic. Beginning in 1991, a program of surveillance, house spraying, and environmental vector control halted transmission of Chagas' disease in Uruguay, Chile, and large parts of Paraguay and Brazil. Worldwide, as we see in chapter 3, infant mortality in poor countries has fallen and life expectancy has increased.

Many of these programs benefited from donor funding and technical advice. In Egypt's fight against childhood diarrhea, for example, it was a grant from USAID and technical advice from the World Health Organization (WHO). In China's campaign against tuberculosis, it was a World Bank loan and WHO advice. In Morocco, the drug company Pfizer donated antibiotics to fight trachoma. Although the aid agencies have not calculated the aid impact in a scientifically rigorous way, the broad facts support the belief that aid was effective in many of the above health interventions. Alas, instead of expanding success in the many health areas where it had triumphed, the international health community was going to get bogged down in its equivalent of Vietnam: AIDS.

The Coming Storm

The health successes make the failure on AIDS stand out even more. As with any contagious disease, early action is far more effective than later action. A bucket of water is enough to put out a campfire; it takes more to put out a forest fire.

On the plus side, it was the West that solved the scientific problem of what caused AIDS, making prevention efforts possible. Unfortunately, this knowledge did not translate into effective prevention in Africa.

The World Bank advertises that it is now the "world's single largest funder of AIDS programs" (the same claim is made by the World Health Organization and by the U.S. Agency for International Development). The World Bank doesn't mention that it did a total of one project dedicated to AIDS before 1993 (an eight-million-dollar loan to Mobutu in Zaire in 1988). The World Bank today endorses the WHO calculation that Africa needs one billion dollars a year in AIDS-prevention spending. Yet over the entire period 1988–99, the World Bank spent fifteen million dollars a year on all AIDS projects in Africa. In 1992, a World Bank study noted that the Bank "has done little to initiate prevention in countries in which the risk of spread is high."

Why did the West not act more vigorously early on in the AIDS crisis? Was it because people didn't know how bad the crisis would become, because action was ineffective, or simply because it took millions of deaths to make it a headline issue worth responding to?

The defense that the West didn't know is not credible. As long ago as 1986, AIDS in Africa was attracting international attention. On October 27, 1986, an article in the *Times* of London said: "A catastrophic epidemic of AIDS is sweeping across Africa. . . . the disease has already infected several millions of Africans, posing colossal health problems to more than 20 countries. . . . 'Aids has become a major health threat to all Africans and prevention and control of infection . . . must become an immediate public health priority for all African countries,' says report published in a leading American scientific journal."

Signs of the coming epidemic appeared even earlier. A sample of prostitutes in Butare, Rwanda, in 1983 found that 75 percent were infected. A later study by the group that reported this statistic dated the general awareness that Central Africa was at risk for the spread of AIDS back to 1983 as well.[2]

The World Bank did its first AIDS strategy report in 1988. The report said the crisis was urgent. It presciently detected "an environment highly conducive to the spread of HIV" in many African countries. It noted that the epidemic was far from reaching its full potential and that "the AIDS epidemic in Africa is an emergency situation and appropriate action must be undertaken now."[3] Yet the effort at the time was underwhelming: the World Bank made a grant of one million dollars to the World Health Organization (WHO) in the 1988/1989 fiscal year to fight AIDS.

A 1992 World Bank retrospective on the 1988 strategy damns it with faint praise: "In view of the 1988 decision to deal with AIDS using existing resource levels and the small PHN [Population, Health, and Nutrition] staff that has had to handle a steadily increasing work program, we conclude that the agenda in the 1988 Strategy Paper has been reasonably well implemented."[4]

The World Bank's 1993 World Development Report, whose theme was health, notes that "At present, most national AIDS programs are inadequate, despite international attention and the significant effort by WHO to help design and implement plans for controlling AIDS." Translation: it's the WHO's fault.

An article in 1991 in the World Bank/IMF quarterly magazine predicted that thirty million people would be infected worldwide by the year 2000 if nothing was done.[5] The actual figure would turn out to be forty million, but the point is: more than a decade ago many knew that a catastrophic epidemic was under way.

The 1992 World Bank study, while noting the lack of progress, did sound the obligatory refrain that progress was under way, not least because "countries have been informed of the Bank's increasing attention to AIDS."

The World Bank itself was directing the tiny flows of AIDS financing to "currently affected countries," while "little has been done by the

Bank to prevent AIDS in less affected countries with a high potential for spread." The 1992 report closed with the curious admonition that "AIDS should not be allowed to dominate the Bank's agenda on population, health, and nutrition issues in Africa." Raising this issue early in the epidemic is strange, when an ounce of prevention *is* worth a pound of cure. Now AIDS work has crowded out treatment of other equally lethal threats to Africans because its spread was not averted. The best way to have kept AIDS from "dominating the Bank's agenda" was to have prevented its spread.

Perhaps we can better understand the aid community's difficulties on prevention if we realize that prevention was not very visible to the rich-country public. Although insiders knew that a horrific AIDS crisis was brewing in Africa in the late 1980s and early 1990s, this attracted little attention from Western media or politicians. Part of the problem was probably that aid agencies didn't know what to do to address the crisis, but the above examples show little evidence that they were searching for answers. Only *after* a truly massive number of people were infected with HIV did AIDS gain the sufficient level of visibility for action.

Not Following Your Own Advice

By 1998, the World Bank had done ten stand-alone AIDS projects. Researcher Julia Dayton was hired by the Bank to analyze its programs.[6]

Dayton found that only half of the fifty-one World Bank projects with AIDS components promoted condom use or financed condom purchases. To understand this omission, consider another Dayton finding: almost none of the fifty-one projects did any economic analysis of what an effective AIDS interventions was.

Dayton also found that World Bank country teams were missing in action on AIDS. AIDS was already reaching epidemic levels in Côte d'Ivoire, Haiti, Kenya, and Zambia in the 1990s.

The World Bank's Country Assistance Strategy Documents in the 1990s for those countries did not describe HIV prevalence or transmission, recommend STD. or HIV/AIDS-prevention or care, or in fact analyze HIV/AIDS at all. Ironically for aid agencies that often are trying to do everything, "everything" sometimes leaves out some high priorities.

Day of Judgment

Shortly after Dayton's report was issued, the World Bank produced another AIDS report. The World Bank Africa vice-president wrote in the introduction to this 2000 report that "AIDS is completely preventable." He gave a prediction that "those who look back on this era will judge our institution in large measure by whether we recognized this wildfire that is raging across Africa for the development threat that it is, and did our utmost to put it out. They will be right to do so."[7] He could have spared us the use of the future tense.

The World Bank did produce a Monitoring and Evaluation Operations Manual, prepared jointly by UNAIDS and the World Bank.[8] The manual sensibly warns that "the more complex an M&E system, the more likely it is to fail." It then spends fifty-two pages laying out its extremely complex M&E system. This includes the ten-step M&E program (step 3: "NAC [National AIDS Councils] and stakeholders engage in an intensive participatory process to build ownership and buy-in, particularly for the overall M&E system and programme monitoring"). There is also the list of thirty-four indicators (none of which involves monitoring "core transmitters"), the nineteen-point terms of reference for the M&E consultant to the NAC, and the "summary terms of reference for specialized programme activity monitoring entity." The accepted scientific standard for any program evaluation, the randomized controlled trial, did not make it into the manual.

The Kitty Genovese Effect

Winston Moseley killed Kitty Genovese, a twenty-eight-year-old bar manager, in Queens, New York, in 1964. Her murder is the first news story I remember from my childhood. As Moseley first stabbed Kitty, neighbors heard her screams but didn't call the police. Moseley drove away and then came back and stabbed her some more, till she died. Police later identified thirty-eight neighbors who saw or heard part of the attack. The eyewitnesses' failure to call police became a symbol of the callousness of urban America. I think my mother showed me the newspaper to illustrate the wickedness of big-city folks.

The last thing I want to do is defend such bad Samaritans, but economists point out that the callousness of each individual was not as great as their group behavior suggests. All the neighbors agreed that saving Kitty's life would have been worthwhile. Outraged commentators pointed out that only one out of those thirty-eight people had to call the police, but that was exactly the problem. Calling the police would have had some cost to the individual, who may later have had to testify and may have feared retribution from the associates of the killer. Each of the thirty-eight people might have been willing to bear this cost to save Kitty's life, but preferred that someone else make the call. With so many witnesses to the scene, each person calculated a high probability that someone else *would* make the call and save Kitty. Therefore, each person did nothing. If there had been only one witness, and if that person had known he was the only witness, he would have been more likely to call the police.

The Kitty Genovese effect is another plausible example of the problem of collective responsibility I mention in chapter 5, which leads to bureaucratic inaction. Each development agency is one among many responsible for solving crises in the poor countries. Each agency may altruistically care about the poor. Suppose that action by one agency will be enough to solve a problem, and all agencies will share in the glory of the triumph; it is difficult to tell which agency's effort made the difference. If effort is costly and diverts resources away from other organizational goals, each agency will prefer that some other agency make the effort. The more agencies that could act, the less likely that action will occur.

The Genovese effect can also operate within aid bureaucracies. Each department might wish that results happen, but would prefer that some other department achieve them, with glory for all. Departments then get into the game of shifting responsibility for difficult tasks onto other departments, which drives the leaders of even the most results-oriented agency insane.

Action does become more likely as the status quo deteriorates due to inaction. The crisis could eventually become big enough to outweigh the option of waiting for someone else to act. In the Kitty Genovese example, a neighbor did eventually call the police. Kitty was dead by then.

A story like this could help account for the long period of inaction on the AIDS crisis, until the crisis was so severe that finally aid agencies acted.

Orphans in the Storm

Mary Banda, about sixty-five, lives in Lusaka, Zambia.[9] Five of her eight children have died from AIDS. In Zambia, adult children usually care for their aged parents. AIDS reversed the equation for Mary Banda. Instead of her children caring for her, she is caring for eight orphaned grandchildren, ranging in age from six to twenty.

Mbuya (Grandmother) Banda doesn't get much help from her three surviving children. One of her children is in South Africa, and Mbuya hasn't heard from her. Her youngest daughter is unmarried and unemployed. Her remaining daughter is married, but does not work; her husband can only sporadically find work. She comes around with a bag of mealie meal (cornmeal) every now and then.

The biggest problem is finding food for the orphans. Mrs. Banda sells groundnuts by the road, and grows a little maize, sweet potato, and greens. It is never quite enough. Only two of the children are in school, where they are sometimes refused entry because they lack fees, shoes, and uniforms.

When her children became sick from AIDS, she tried traditional healers as well as the hospital. Mary Banda believes her children died from witchcraft—a sign of the need to adjust to local conditions with prevention messages. Her four deceased daughters were businesswomen buying secondhand clothes in Lusaka and exchanging them for groundnuts in the villages, and then reselling the groundnuts in Lusaka. She believes villagers jealous of their success bewitched her daughters through their feet. She blames her son's death on witchcraft from jealous-rivals after his work promoted him. She wishes her children had seen a witchdoctor to get preventive medicine to put on their feet.

Discussion of African beliefs in witchcraft is taboo in aid agencies, as nobody wants to reinforce ill-informed stereotypes. Unfortunately, political correctness gets in the way of making policy, as conventional public health approaches may not work if people *do* believe that witchcraft causes illness and turn to traditional healers. Americans and Europeans also believed in witches when they were at similar levels of income as Africa (and many Americans still do today; hence the spiritualism section at the Barnes & Noble bookstore in Greenwich Village—one of the intellectual capitals of the United States—is three times the size of the science section). Moreover, many American evangelicals believe divine intervention can cure illness.

Beliefs in invisible malign forces in Africa are not so surprising when a virus visible only to scientists is killing previously healthy young people. Princeton political scientist and ethnographer Adam Ashforth documented the widespread belief in Soweto, South Africa, that witchcraft causes many symptoms of illness, including symptoms similar to AIDS.[10] AIDS-prevention efforts would do much better to work with traditional healers on fighting HIV transmission than to ignore beliefs in witchcraft because of political sensitivities.

Mrs. Banda speaks for her generation of Mbuyas: "I'm an old woman who's suffering. When I was young, I never thought such cruel things could happen. When I think about it, I pray and cry, but I don't like to cry because it'll upset the children."

At least Mrs. Banda's grandchildren have her to care for them. A group even more unlucky is Lusaka's growing population of street children. AIDS orphans with no one to care for them are on the street. The manager of a shelter for abandoned kids, Rodgers Mwewa, noticed the increase in orphaned children coming into Lusaka. The traditional extended-family system of caring for children is breaking down because too many of its adult members are dead. "HIV is destroying families and family bonds," says Mwewa.[11]

The street children don't live long: cars frequently hit them, they get into fights, and they resort to petty crime, drugs, or sniffing glue. They are beaten up by the police. Worst of all, the children sell themselves for sex, and thus sooner or later acquire the HIV virus that killed their parents.

Less anecdotal evidence confirms that orphans in Africa face a rough road. The less orphans can rely on family, the worse off they are. Princeton University scholars Anne Case, Christine Paxson, and Joseph Ableidinger found in a study of orphans in ten African countries that orphans who live with unrelated adults get less schooling than orphans who live with nonparental relatives, who themselves get less schooling than children living with their parents. These effects show up even as discrimination within the household. For example, an orphan living with her aunt and uncle typically gets less schooling than her cousin, the aunt and uncle's child.[12]

Africa's AIDS crisis is leaving a generation of undereducated, undernourished, underparented orphans who will soon be adults. As if Africa's development crisis weren't bad enough for the current generation, the orphans of AIDS complicate development even more.

Treating the Sick

Now that twenty-nine million people in Africa are HIV-positive, compassion would call for treating the sick, right? Yet pity is not always a reliable guide to action. By a tragic irony, compassion is driving the fight against AIDS in Africa in a direction that may cost more lives than it saves. It is political suicide in rich countries to question AIDS treatment. Too bad—what should matter is what helps the poor the most, not what sells politically in rich countries. This political pressure led Planners to fixate on the goal of treatment even when the costs were so prohibitive that it diverted money from cheaper actions that Searchers had found to save many more lives.

The Western aid community is now installing a gold-plated barn door after the horse has been stolen. Foreign aid programs are now starting to finance the "triple-drug cocktail" known as highly active antiretroviral therapy (HAART), which has dramatically lowered AIDS mortality in the West. All of the actors described earlier signed on to financing AIDS treatment. The UN General Assembly Special Session passed a resolution calling for AIDS treatment. This used to be impossible for low-income African AIDS patients, because of high drug prices (ten thousand dollars a year per patient). However, competition from a growing number of generic HIV/AIDS drugs has cut prices, which are now as low as $304 per year per patient.[13] This caused leaders of international aid agencies, such as former WHO director-general GrÖ Harlem Brundtland, to ask, "Does anyone deserve to be sentenced to certain death because she or he cannot access care that costs less than two dollars a day?" The WHO started a "3 by 5" campaign to get three million HIV-positive patients on antiretroviral therapy by the end of 2005.

Saving lives is not so simple. First of all, the focus on drug prices understates the expense and difficulty of treatment. Three hundred and four dollars is just the price of the first-line therapy drugs per year. The population first needs to be tested to see who is HIV-positive. Patients need to have their viral load tested to see if they should start taking drugs and, after taking them, if the drugs are working to decrease the viral load. The drugs are toxic, with potentially severe side effects. Health workers need to adjust the combination of drugs when side effects are too extreme. Patients need counseling and monitoring to make sure they are taking the medicine (if there is less than full adherence to treatment, the virus builds up resistance to the drugs). Patients also need treatment for the opportunistic infections that afflict AIDS sufferers. So treatment is more expensive than just the cost of the drugs. The World Health Organization is working with a figure of $1,500 per year per patient for delivering treatment to prolong the life of an AIDS patient by one year. Even if the WHO can drive down the price of the drugs further, the cost per year would still be $1,200. Other experts use similar figures.[14] But is even this number too high to justify giving a person another year of life?

The advocates for treatment stress the universal human right for HIV-positive patients to have access to life-saving health care, no matter what the cost. This is a great ideal, but a utopian one. There are also other ideals—first of all, prevention of the further spread of AIDS. And what about the universal human right for health care for other killer diseases, freedom from starvation, and access to clean water? Who chose the human right of universal treatment of AIDS over the other human rights? A non-utopian approach would make the tough choices to spend foreign aid resources in a way that reached the most people with their most urgent needs.

Poor people have many other needs besides AIDS treatment. The total amount of foreign aid for the world's approximately three billion poor people is only about twenty dollars per person per year. Is the money for AIDS treatment going to be "new money" or will it come from these already scarce funds? President Bush's 2005 budget proposal increased funding for the American AIDS program (especially treatment), but cut money for child health and other global health priorities by nearly a hundred million dollars (later reversed after protests).[15]

Bush's cut in other health spending was particularly unfortunate when two and a half times as many Africans die from other preventable diseases as die from AIDS. These diseases include measles and other childhood illnesses, respiratory infections, malaria, tuberculosis, diarrhea, and others. Worldwide, in 2002 there were 15.6 million deaths from these causes, as opposed to 2.8 million deaths from AIDS.[16]

A well-established public health principle is that you should save lives that are cheap to save before you save lives that are more expensive to save. That way you save many more lives using the scarce funds available. Prevention and treatment of these other diseases cost far less than AIDS treatment.

Granting life through prevention of AIDS itself costs far less than AIDS treatment. A years' supply of condoms to prevent HIV infection costs about fourteen dollars. In a 2002 article in *The Lancet*, Andrew Creese from the World Health Organization and co-authors estimated that AIDS-prevention interventions such as condom distribution, blocking mother-to-child transmission, and voluntary counseling and testing could cost as little as one to twenty dollars per year of life saved, and twenty to four hundred dollars per HIV infection averted (even though this study may overstate the confidence that these things always work). Other studies come up with similar estimates.[17]

Then there are other diseases for which Searchers have found cheap interventions (although we have seen that the Planners' domination of aid often interferes with making these things work). The medicines that cure TB cost about ten dollars per case of the illness. A package of interventions designed to prevent maternal and infant deaths costs less than three dollars

per person per year. Worldwide, three million children die a year because they are not fully vaccinated, even though vaccines cost only pennies per dose. One in four people worldwide suffers from intestinal worms, though treatments cost less than a dollar per year. A full course of treatment for a child suffering even from drug-resistant malaria costs only about one dollar. In fact, Vietnam, a relatively poor country, reduced deaths from malaria by 97 percent from 1991 to 1997 with a campaign that included bed nets and antimalarial drugs.[18] A bed net program in Tanzania also reduced mortality significantly.[19] (The availability of such cheap remedies makes it all the more tragic that malaria is still so widespread—we are back to the second tragedy of the world's poor.)

Overall, the World Bank estimates the cost per year for a variety of health interventions like these to range from five to forty dollars, compared with the fifteen-hundred-dollar cost of prolonging the life of an AIDS patient by a year with antiretroviral treatment. The $4.5 billion the WHO plans to spend on antiretroviral treatment for one more year of life for three million could grant between seven and sixty years of additional life for five times that many people—fifteen million. For the HIV-positive patients themselves, you could reach many more of them to prolong their lives by treating the opportunistic infections, especially TB, that usually kill AIDS victims.

Other researchers come up with similar numbers. For example, Harvard economics professor Michael Kremer noted in an article in the *Journal of Economic Perspectives* in 2002: "for every person treated for a year with antiretroviral therapy, 25 to 110 Disability Adjusted Life Years could be saved through targeted AIDS prevention efforts or vaccination against easily preventable diseases."

A group of health experts wrote in the prestigious medical journal *The Lancet* in July 2003 about how 5.5 million child deaths could have been prevented in 2003, lamenting that "child survival has lost its focus." They blamed in part the "levels of attention and effort directed at preventing the small proportion of child deaths due to AIDS with a new, complex, and expensive intervention."[20]

The WHO expects the added years of life for AIDS patients from antiretroviral treatment to be only three to five years—not exactly a miracle cure.[21] The United Nations Population Division in 2005 similarly estimated that the added years of life from antiretroviral treatment to be a median of 4.5 years.[22] After that, resistance to the first-line treatment (the one with the cheap drugs, which is all that is on the table in Africa, outside of South Africa) builds up and full-blown AIDS sets in. Other estimates are even more pessimistic. The average length of effectiveness of the first-line treatment in Brazil, which has a large-scale treatment program, has been only fourteen months.[23]

The big question is whether poor Africans themselves would have chosen to spend scarce funds on prolonging some lives with AIDS treatment, as opposed to saving many lives with other health interventions. Would the desperately poor themselves, such as those on an income of one dollar a day, choose to spend fifteen hundred dollars on antiretroviral treatment? Should the West impose its preferences for saving AIDS victims instead of measles victims just because it makes the West feel better?

Path of Least Resistance

Getting a complex AIDS and development crisis under control just by taking a pill is irresistible to politicians, aid agencies, and activists. We see here again one bias toward observable actions by aid agencies. The activists' cause plays well in the Western media because the tragedy of AIDS victims even has a villain—the international drug companies that were reluctant to lower the price on life-saving drugs—which makes mobilization for the cause even easier.

AIDS treatment is another example of the SIBD syndrome—rich-country politicians want to convince rich-country voters that "something is being done" (SIBD) about the tragic problem of AIDS in Africa. It is easier to achieve SIBD catharsis if politicians and aid officials treat people who are already sick, than it is to persuade people with multiple sexual partners to use condoms to prevent many more people from getting the disease. Alas, the poor's interests are sacrificed to political convenience. When the U.S. Congress passed Bush's fifteen-billion-dollar AIDS program (known as the President's Emergency Plan for AIDS Relief, or PEPFAR) in May 2003, it placed a restriction that no more than 20 percent of the funds be spent on prevention, while 55 percent was allocated for treatment.[24]

In a fit of religious zealotry, Congress also required organizations receiving funds to publicly oppose prostitution. This eliminates effective organizations that take a pragmatic and compassionate approach to understanding the factors that drive women into prostitution. Programs that condemn prostitutes are unlikely to find a receptive audience when they try to persuade those prostitutes to avoid risky behavior.

To make things even worse, the religious right in America is crippling the funding of prevention programs to advocate their own imperatives: abstain from sex or have sex only with your legally married spouse. Studies in the United States find no evidence that abstinence programs have any effect on sexual behavior of young people, except to discourage them from using condoms.[25] The evangelists' message has not convinced American youth, so the evangelists want to export it to African youth. Moreover, devout women who follow the sex-within-marriage mantra are still at risk if their husbands have sex with other partners without using condoms before or during their marriage. The religious right threatens NGOs that aggressively market condoms with a cutoff of official aid funds, on the grounds that those NGOs are promoting sexual promiscuity. Pushed by the religious right, Congress mandated that at least one third of the already paltry PEPFAR prevention budget go for abstinence-only programs.

The Vatican is also pushing its followers to oppose condom distribution in Africa because of religious doctrine that forbids the use of birth control.[26] These religious follies are one of the most extreme examples of rich peoples' preferences in the West trumping what is best for the poor in the Rest.

While prevention is tied up in religious knots, everyone seems to agree on treatment. The gay community, a group usually not identified with the religious right, is also emphasizing treatment. Activist groups such as ACT UP helped along the push for treatment—in their Web site for the 2002 Barcelona AIDS conference, they mentioned "treatment" eighteen times, but didn't mention "prevention" once.[27] Why do we have a well-publicized Treatment Access Coalition when there is no Prevention Access Coalition? Why didn't the WHO have a "3 by 5" campaign intended to *prevent* three million new cases of AIDS by the end of 2005? The activists have been only too successful in focusing attention on treatment instead of prevention. A LexisNexis search of articles on AIDS in Africa in *The Economist* over the previous two years found eighty-eight articles that mentioned "treatment" but only twenty-two that mentioned "prevention."

Instead of spending ten billion dollars on treatment over the next three years, money could be spent on preventing AIDS from spreading from the 28 million HIV-positive Africans to the 644 million HIV-negative Africans. Thailand has successfully implemented prevention campaigns targeting condom use among prostitutes, increasing condom usage from 15 percent to 90 percent and reducing new HIV infections dramatically. Senegal and Uganda have apparently also had success with vigorous prevention campaigns promoted by courageous political leaders (although the Ugandan government is now backing off from condom promotion under pressure from religious leaders).

If money spent on treatment went instead to effective prevention, between three and seventy-five new HIV infections could be averted for every extra year of life given to an AIDS patient. Spending AIDS money on treatment rather than on prevention makes the AIDS crisis *worse*, not better. If we consider that averting an HIV infection gives many extra years of life to each individual, then the case for prevention instead of treatment gets even stronger. For the same money spent giving one more year of life to an AIDS patient, you could give 75 to 1,500 years of additional life (say fifteen extra years for each of five to one hundred people) to the rest of the population through AIDS prevention.

We should ask the aid agencies why they want to put this much money now into the treatment of AIDS for twenty-nine million people when the same money spent to prevent the spread of HIV might have spared many of the twenty-nine million from infection. This past negligence is *not* an argument for or against any particular direction of action today—we must move forward from where we are now. But it does show how politicians and aid bureaucrats react passively to dramatic headlines and utopian ideals rather than according to where the small aid budget will benefit the most people. Is this what poor people themselves would choose to spend the money on?

Trade-offs

It is the job of economists to point out trade-offs; it is the job of politicians and Planners to deny that trade-offs exist. AIDS campaigners protest that AIDS treatment money is "new money" that would have been otherwise unavailable, but that just begs the question of where new money is best spent. Why are there not campaigns to spread even further the successful campaigns against children's diarrhea, where a given amount of money—raised from the same sources—would reach many more people than money for AIDS treatment?

The utopian reaction is that the West will spend "whatever it takes" to cover *all* the health programs described above. This was the approach taken by the WHO Commission on Macroeconomics and Health in 2001. This commission recommended that rich countries spend an additional twenty-seven billion dollars on health in poor countries by 2007, which at the time was more than half of the world's foreign aid budget to poor countries. They ramp this number up to forty-seven billion dollars by 2015, of which twenty-two billion would be for AIDS. The commission's report was influential in gaining adherents for AIDS treatment in poor countries.

In an obscure footnote to the report, the commission notes that people often asked it what its priorities would be if only a lower sum were forthcoming, but it says it was "ethically and politically" unable to choose. The most charitable view is that this statement is the commission's strategy to get the money it wants. Otherwise, this refusal to make choices is inexcusable Public policy is the science of doing the best you can with limited resources—it is dereliction of duty for professional economists to shrink from confronting trade-offs. Even when you get new resources, you still have to decide where they would be best used.

If you want priorities and trade-offs, you can get them in the WHO itself. The WHO's 2002 World Health Report contains the following common sense: "Not everything can be done in all settings, so some way of setting priorities needs to be found. The next chapter identifies costs and the impact on population health of a variety of interventions, as the basis on which to develop strategies to reduce risk."[28]

The next chapter in the WHO report actually states that money spent on educating prostitutes saves between one thousand and one hundred times more lives than the same amount of money spent on antiretroviral treatment.[29]

Getting back to the WHO Commission on Macroeconomics and Health, the commission's sum, according to its own assumptions, did not eliminate all avoidable deaths in the poor countries. These sums, not to mention total foreign aid, are paltry relative to all the things that the world's three billion desperately poor people need. The commission *did* place some limit on what it thought rich countries were willing to spend to save lives in poor countries. *Everybody* places limits on what they spend on health. Even in rich countries, people could maximize their chances of catching killer diseases early enough for treatment by, say, having a daily MRI. Nobody, except possibly Woody Allen, actually does this, because it's too costly relative to the expected gain in life and relative to other things that rich people would like to spend money on. Virtually nobody was advocating AIDS treatment in Africa when the drug cocktail cost more than ten thousand dollars per year. Everybody, except political campaigners, knows that money, whether "new" or "old," is limited.

A political campaigner giving a graphic description of AIDS patients dying without life-saving drugs is hard to resist, making the trade-offs described earlier seem coldhearted. But money should not be spent according to what the West considers the most dramatic kind of suffering. Others with other diseases have their own chronicles of suffering. The journalist Daniel Bergner describes the relentless wailing of mothers in Sierra Leone who have lost a child to measles, the wailing that never stopped in a village during a measles epidemic. The high fever of measles stirs up intestinal worms, which spill out from the children's noses. Sores erupt inside their mouths. The parents in desperation pour kerosene down the children's throats. The graves of the dead children lie behind their parents' huts, mounds of dirt covered by palm branches.[30]

Take also the small baby dying in his mother's arms, tortured by diarrhea, which can be prevented so easily and cheaply with oral rehydration therapy. *Many* deaths can be prevented more cheaply than treating AIDS, thus reaching many more suffering people on a limited aid budget. Nobody asks the poor in Africa whether they would like to see most "new" money spent on

AIDS treatment as opposed to the many other dangers they face. The questions facing Western AIDS campaigners should not be "Do they deserve to die?" but "Do we deserve to decide who dies?"

Constance, the HIV-positive mother from Soweto whom I mention at the beginning of this chapter, had an interesting perspective on priorities. When I asked her to name Soweto's biggest problem, she did not say AIDS or lack of antiretroviral treatment. She said, "No jobs." Finding a way to earn money to feed herself and her children was a more pressing concern for her than her eventual death from AIDS.

The more sophisticated way to deny that tradeoffs exist is to insist that each part of the budget is necessary for everything else to work. When asked to choose between guns and butter, the canny politician insists that guns are necessary to protect the butter. In the AIDS field, strategic responses gave us the mantra "prevention is impossible without treatment." The proposition rests on the plausible reasoning that people will not come forward to be tested (most HIV-positive Africans do not know they are HIV-positive) unless there is hope of treatment. Some bits of evidence support this intuition, but the notion has not really been subjected to enough empirical scrutiny. Moreover, it is also plausible, and there is also a little evidence, to support the idea that treatment makes prevention more difficult. There is evidence that people in rich countries engaged in riskier sexual behavior *after* HAART became available.[31] Prevention campaigns did work in Senegal, Thailand, and Uganda without being based on treatment. Finally, there remains the risk that treatment with imperfect adherence will result in emergence of resistant strains of HIV, so that treatment itself will sow the seeds of its own downfall.[32]

Dysfunctional Health Systems

Admittedly, these trade-offs are oversimplified. Cost-effectiveness analysis—which compares different health interventions according to their estimated benefits (years of lives saved) and costs (drugs, medical personnel, clinics, hospitals)—gives us these numbers. This is the mainstream approach in the international public health field. Many of the advocates for treatment, such as Grö Harlem Brundtland and WHO staff, buy into this approach. They just fail to follow the logic through to the conclusion that you could save many more lives spending on other health interventions—including AIDS prevention—with what they propose to spend on AIDS treatment.

Lant Pritchett of Harvard's Kennedy School and Jeffrey Hammer and Deon Filmer of the World Bank criticize these cost-effectiveness calculations for the oversimplifications they are. Just because it costs a dollar to treat a person's illness, it doesn't follow that giving a dollar to the national health system will result in treating that person. We have already seen what a difficult time international aid planners have in getting even simple interventions to work.

Despite the health successes noted earlier, Filmer, Hammer, and Pritchett talk about "weak links in the chain" that leads from the donors dollar to the person's treatment. The second tragedy of the world's poor means that many effective interventions are not reaching the poor because of some of the follies of Planners mentioned in previous chapters.

Because of the insistence on working through governments, funds get lost in patronage-swollen national health bureaucracies (not to mention international health bureaucracies). In countries where corruption is as endemic as AIDS, health officials often sell aid-financed drugs on the black market. Studies in Cameroon, Guinea, Tanzania, and Uganda estimated that 30 to 70 percent of government drugs disappeared before reaching the patients. In one low-income country, a crusading journalist accused the ministry of health of misappropriating fifty million dollars in aid funds. The ministry issued a rebuttal: the journalist had irresponsibly implied that the fifty million dollars had gone AWOL in a single year, whereas they had actually misappropriated the money over a *three-year* period.

I have heard from multiple sources of AIDS money disappearing before it reached any real or potential victims. In Cameroon, the World Bank lent a large amount for AIDS, which the health ministry handed out to local AIDS committees. Critics allege there was virtually no monitoring and no controls and are not quite sure what the local committees did, except for vaguely defined "AIDS sensitization." In one alleged case, a local committee chair threw a large party for his daughter's wedding under the category of "AIDS sensitization."

Many doctors, nurses, and other health workers are poorly trained and poorly paid. The AIDS treatment campaigners are oblivious to these harsh realities of medical care in poor countries. The worst part about the heartfelt plea for money for AIDS treatment is that it will save many fewer lives than campaigners promise.

Of course, similar arguments would also weaken the case for the allegedly more cost effective health interventions on illnesses such as diarrhea, malaria, and measles. They do not work everywhere as well as they should, as the rest of this book makes clear. But this complication does not strengthen the argument for funding AIDS treatment in Africa. The cheap interventions have some successes, as noted earlier. They are cheap because they are simpler for Searchers to find ways to administer—a measles vaccination has to happen only at one given point just for each child. A bed net impregnated with insecticide has to be handed out just once to each potential malaria victim, along with the information on how to use it, then impregnated again periodically.

The treatment of AIDS with drugs is vastly more complicated and depends on many more "links in the chain": refrigeration, lab tests, expert monitoring and adjusting therapy if resistance and toxic side effects emerge, and educating the patient on how to take the drug. In Europe and North America, 20 to 40 percent of AIDS patients do not take their drugs as prescribed. Resistance will emerge if there are lapses from the correct regimen. Even with good

intentions, government bureaucrats currently do a poor job making sure that drug supply matches demand in each locale. Unfortunately for the patients, it is critical that AIDS treatment not be interrupted by drug shortages (critical both for effectiveness and for preventing resistant strains from developing). A 2004 article in the *Journal of the American Medical Association*, while generally positive about treatment in developing countries, sounded some concerns:

> Finally, how will the tens of thousands of health care professionals required for global implementation of HIV care strategies be trained, motivated, supervised, resourced, and adequately reimbursed to ensure the level of care required for this complex disease? To scale up antiretroviral therapy for HIV without ensuring infrastructure, including trained practitioners, a safe and reliable drug delivery system, and simple but effective models for continuity of care, would be a disaster, leading to ineffective treatment and rapid development of resistance.[33]

Even doing the huge amount of testing required to find out who is HIV-positive and eligible for treatment would likely overwhelm health budgets and infrastructure in poor countries.

The tardy response to the AIDS crisis has meant that it has built up to an unbearable tragedy—to the point that it's now too late to save many millions of lives. Spending money on a mostly futile attempt to save all the lives of this generation of AIDS victims will take money away from saving the lives of the next generation, perpetuating the tragedy. The political lobby for treatment doesn't mention that no amount of treatment will stop the crisis. The only way to stop the threat to Africans and others is *prevention*, no matter how unappealing the politics or how uncomfortable the discussion about sex. The task is to save the next generation before it is again too late.

Let's commend the campaigners wanting to spend money on AIDS treatment in Africa for their dedication and compassion. But could they redirect some of that compassion to where it will do the most good?

Feedback and Idealism Again

Why did the health system fail on AIDS when foreign aid successes are more common in public health than in other areas? The AIDS crisis was less susceptible to feedback, and the interests of the poor were not coincident with rich-country politics. The necessary actions were in the area of prevention, which doesn't involve just taking a pill or getting a shot, as in many of the other successes. The donors showed shamefully little interest in researching the sexual behavior that causes AIDS to spread or in which prevention strategies work to change that behavior. Donors should have asked, "How many people have we prevented from becoming HIV-positive?"

A patient who is already HIV-positive is a highly visible target for help—a lot more visible than someone who is going to get infected in the future but doesn't yet know it. The rich-country politicians and aid agencies get more PR credit for saving the lives of sick patients, even if the interests of the poor would call for saving them from getting sick in the first place. This again confirms the prediction that aid agencies skew their efforts toward visible outcomes, even when those outcomes have a lower payoff than less visible interventions.

The politicians and aid agencies didn't have the courage to confront the uncomfortable question of how to change human sexual behavior. The AIDS failure shows that the bureaucratic healers too often settle for simply handing out pills.

Heroes

The AIDS disaster in Africa features many ineffective bureaucrats and few energetic rescuers. But there are a few heroes. A group called HIVSA works in Soweto, South Africa, helping people like Constance. Its energetic director, Steven Whiting, was formerly an affluent interior designer. He stumbled on the AIDS issue by chance when he got the contract to renovate the headquarters of the Perinatal HIV Research Unit at the largest hospital in Soweto. He was so moved by what he saw there that he decided to quit his job and devote his efforts full time to fighting AIDS.

HIVSA does the little things that make a difference. It provides the drug nevirapine to block transmission of the HIV virus from mothers to newborns. Doctors give just one dose during labor, an intervention that is highly cost effective compared with other AIDS treatments. To follow up, HIVSA provides infant formula to HIV-positive new mothers, since breast-feeding can also transmit the HIV virus to newborns. Less tangibly, HIVSA provides support groups meeting in health clinics throughout Soweto to help HIV-positive mothers confront the stigma of HIV and their many other problems. (One hint of such problems: the signs all over the clinics announcing that no guns are allowed inside the clinics.) When the mothers visit the clinics, they get a free meal and nutritional supplements. Mothers and HIVSA staff work in community gardens attached to each clinic to provide food. HIVSA staff are almost all from the Soweto community and are HIV-positive.

Constance has problems that are overwhelming, but her most recent baby was born HIV-negative, thanks to nevirapine. HIVSA's free meals, nutritional supplements, and emotional support make her life a little more bearable.

If only all the West's efforts at fighting AIDS were so constructive at giving the poor victims what they want and need. The West largely ignored AIDS when it was building up to a huge humanitarian crisis, only to focus now on an expensive attempt at treatment that neglects the prevention so critical to stop the disaster from getting even worse.

SNAPSHOT: PROSTITUTES FOR PREVENTION

Prostitutes in Sonagachi, the red-light district of Calcutta, India, form a world unto themselves. Social norms about female sexual behavior in India are such that prostitution carries an even larger stigma in India than elsewhere. Cut off from the wider world, prostitutes have their own subculture, with an elite of madams and pimps. As in any subculture, its members strive for status. Prostitutes who aspire to greater status attain it most commonly by attracting long-term clients.

Many well-intentioned bureaucrats have tried to help the prostitutes by "rescuing" them and taking them to shelters to be trained in another profession, such as tailoring. However, sex work pays a lot better than tailoring, and former prostitutes face harassment and discrimination in the outside world. Hence, most "rescued" women returned to prostitution. But the advent of the AIDS epidemic in India and the well-known role of prostitutes in spreading AIDS caused increased concern about these failures.

Dr. Smarajit Jana, head of the All India Institute of Hygiene and Public Health, had another idea in 1992. He and his team would learn the subculture of the prostitutes and work with it to fight AIDS.

They formed a mutually respectful relationship with the madams, pimps, prostitutes, and clients. They noted the class system within Sonagachi. By trial and error, and with feedback from the prostitutes, Dr. Jana and his team hit upon a strategy for fighting AIDS. The strategy was awfully simple in retrospect: they trained a group of twelve prostitutes to educate their fellow workers about the dangers of AIDS and the need to use condoms. The peer educators wore green medical coats when they were engaged in their public health work, and they attained greater status in Sonagachi. Condom use in Sonagachi increased dramatically. By 1999, HIV incidence in Sonagachi was only 6 percent, compared with 50 percent in other red-light districts in India.

The project had other, unexpected consequences. The increased confidence of the peer educators and the media attention on the success of prevention efforts led the community to aspire to greater things. The prostitutes formed a union to campaign for legalization of prostitution and a reduction in police harassment, and to organize festivals and health fairs. Dr. Jana's approach based on feedback from the intended beneficiaries succeeded when so many other AIDS prevention programs had failed.

NOTES

1. Center for Global Development, "Millions Saved: Proven Successes in Global Health," Washington, D.C., 2004.

2. Bekki J. Johnson and Robert S. Pond, "AIDS in Africa: A Review of Medical, Public Health, Social Science, and Popular Literature," MISEORE, Campaign Against Hunger and Disease in the World (Episcopal Organization for Development Cooperations), Aachen, West Germany, 1988.

3. World Bank, Africa Technical Department, "Acquired Immune Deficiency Syndrome (AIDS): The Bank's Agenda for Action in Africa," October 24, 1988.

4. Jean-Louis Lamboray and A. Edward Elmendorf, "Combatting AIDS and Other Sexually Transmitted Diseases in Africa: A Review of the World Bank's Agenda for Action," World Bank Discussion Paper no. 181, Africa Technical Department, 1992, p. 29.

5. Jill Armstrong, "Socioeconomic Implications of AIDS in Developing Countries," *Finance and Development* 28, no. 4 (December 1991): 14–17.

6. Julia Dayton, "World Bank HIV/AIDS Interventions: Ex-ante and Ex-post Evaluation," World Bank discussion paper no. 389, Washington, D.C., 1998, p. 9.

7. World Bank, Africa Region, "Intensifying Action against HIV/AIDS in Africa: Responding to a Development Crisis," 2000.

8. http://www.worldbank.org/afr/aids/map/me_manual.pdf.

9. This story comes from Emma Guest, *Children of AIDS: Africa's Orphan Crisis*, London: Pluto Press, 2001.

10. Adam Ashforth, *Witchcraft, Violence, and Democracy in South Africa*, Chicago: University of Chicago Press, 2005, pp. 8–10.

11. Guest, *Children of AIDS*, pp. 144–47.

12. Anne Case, Christina Paxson, and Joseph Ableidinger, "The Education of African Orphans," Princeton University mimeograph, 2003, http://www.wwsprinceton.edu/%7Erpds/Downloads/case_paxson_education_orphans.pdf.

13. WHO/UNAIDS, "Report on the Methods Used to Estimate Costs of Reaching the WHO Target of '3 by 5,'" February 10, 2004, p. 6.

14. Andrew Cresse, Katherine Floyd, Anita Alban, Lorna Guiness, "Cost-effectiveness of HIV/AIDS Interventions in Africa: A Systematic Review of the Evidence," *The Lancet* 359 (2002): 1635–42; Lilani Kumaranayarake, "Cost-Effectiveness and Economic Evaluation of HIV/AIDS-Related Interventions: The State of the Art," in *International AIDS Economics Network, State of the Art: AIDS and Economics*, HIV/AIDS Policy Project, www.iaen.org/conferences/stateofepidemic.php., 2002.

15. http://www.interaction.org/advocacy/budget_request_05.html, FY2005 Foreign Operations Budget Request Summary and Analysis.

16. WHO, World Health Report 2003, Annex 2.

17. See, for example, Emiko Masaki, Russell Green, Fiona Greig, Julia Walsh, and Malcolm Potts, "Cost-Effectiveness of HIV Prevention versus Treatment for Resource-Scarce Countries: Setting Priorities for HIV/AIDS Management," Bay Area International Group, School of Public Health, University of California at Berkeley, 2002.

18. http://www.massiveeffort.org/html/success_stories_vietnam.html, http://rbm.who.int/cmc_upload/0/000/017/025/vietnam-ettling.pdf.

19. Salim Abdulla, Joanna Armstrong Schellenberg, Rose Nathan, Oscar Mukasa, Tanya Marchant, Tom Smith, Marcel Tanner, Christian Lengeler, "Impact on Malaria Morbidity of a Programme Supplying Insectide-Treated Nets in Children Aged Under Two Years in Tanzania: Community Cross-Sectional Study," *British Medical Journal*, 322 (February 3, 2001): 270–73.

20. Gareth Jones, Richard W. Steketec, Robert E. Black, Zulfiqar A. Bhutta, Saul S. Morris, and the Beliagio Child Survival Study Group, "How Many Child Deaths Can We Prevent This Year?" *The Lancet* 362 (2003): 65–71.

21. WHO/UNAIDS, "Report on the Methods Used to Estimate Costs of Reaching the WHO Target of '3 by 5,'" February 10, 2004.

22. United Nations Population Division (UNDP), "World Population Prospects," 2004 revision, 2005, p. 22.

23. David Canning, "The Economics of HIV/AIDS Treatment and Prevention in Developing Countries," Harvard School of Public Health, mimeograph, 2005, in *Journal of Economic Perspectives*.

24. Center for Health and Gender Equity and Sexuality, Information and Education Council of the United States, "The U.S. Global AIDS Strategy: Politics, Ideology, and the Global AIDS Epidemic," May 2003.

25. Human Rights Watch, "The Less They Know, the Better: Abstinence-Only HIV/AIDS Programs in Uganda," *Human Rights Watch* 17, no. 4a (March 2005).

26. Helen Epstein, "God and the Fight against AIDS," *New York Review of Books*, April 28, 2005.

27. Barcelona AIDS Conference Reports, "President Bush Is Killing People with AIDS by Lack of Leadership," http://www.actupny.org/reports/bcn/Bcnbush AUpr.html.

28. WHO, World Health Report 2002, "Reducing Risks, Promoting Healthy Life," Geneva, 2002, p. 92.

29. Ibid., pp. 123, 132.

30. Daniel Bergner, *In the Land of Magic Soldiers: A Story of White and Black in West Africa*, New

York: Farrar, Straus, & Giroux, 2003, pp. 66–68.

31. Dr. Stan Lehman and colleagues, CDC, presentation at XIII International AIDS Conference, Durban, South Africa, 2000.

32. Warren Stevens, Steve Kaye, and Tumani Corrah, "Antiretroviral Therapy in Africa,"

British Medical Journal 328 (January 31, 2004): 280–82.

33. Merle A. Sande and Allan Ronald, "Treatment of HIV/AIDS: Do the Dilemmas Only Increase?" *Journal of the American Medical Association* 292, no. 2 (July 14, 2004): 267.

AMARTYA SEN

Universal Truths: Human Rights and the Westernizing Illusion

My students seem to be very concerned and also very divided on how to approach the difficult subject of human rights in non-Western societies. Is it right, the question is often asked, that non-Western societies should be encouraged and pressed to conform to "Western values of liberty and freedom"? Is this not cultural imperialism? The notion of human rights builds on the idea of a shared humanity. These rights are not derived from citizenship of any country, or membership of any nation, but taken as entitlements of every human being. The concept of universal human rights is, in this sense, a uniting idea. Yet the subject of human rights has ended up being a veritable battleground of political debates and ethical disputes, particularly in their application to non-Western societies. Why so?

From *Harvard International Review* 20, no. 3 (Summer 1998): 40–43. This article is a revised version of the Commencement Address given at Bard College on May 24, 1997. Related arguments were presented in Professor Sen's Morgenthau Memorial Lecture ("Human Rights and Asian Values") at the Carnegie Council on Ethics and International Affairs on May 1, 1997, and published by the Carnegie Council.

A Clash of Cultures?

The explanation for this is sometimes sought in the cultural differences that allegedly divide the world, a theory referred to as the "clash of civilizations" or a "battle between cultures." It is often asserted that Western countries recognize many human rights, related for example to political liberty, that have no great appeal in Asian countries. Many people see a big divide here. The temptation to think in these regional and cultural terms is extremely strong in the contemporary world.

Are there really such firm differences on this subject in terms of traditions and cultures across the world? It is certainly true that governmental spokesmen in several Asian countries have not only disputed the relevance and cogency of universal human rights, they have frequently done this disputing in the name of "Asian values," as a contrast with Western values. The claim is that in the system of so-called Asian values, for example in the Confucian system, there is greater emphasis on order and discipline, and less on rights and freedoms.

Many Asian spokesmen have gone on to argue that the call for universal acceptance of human rights reflects the imposition of Western values on other cultures. For example, the censorship of the press may be more acceptable, it is argued, in Asian society because of its greater emphasis on discipline and order. This position was powerfully articulated by a number of governmental spokesmen from Asia at the Vienna Conference on Human Rights in 1993. Some positive things happened at that conference, including the general acceptance of the importance of eliminating economic deprivation and some recognition of social responsibility in this area. But on the subject of political and civil rights the conference split through the middle, largely on regional lines, with several Asian governments rejecting the recognition of basic political and civil rights. In this argument, the rhetoric of "Asian values" and their differences from Western priorities played an important part.

If one influence in separating out human rights as specifically "Western" comes from the pleading of governmental spokesmen from Asia, another influence relates to the way this issue is perceived in the West itself. There is a tendency in Europe and the United States to assume, if only implicitly, that it is in the West—and only in the West—that human rights have been valued from ancient times. This allegedly unique feature of Western civilization has been, it is assumed, an alien concept elsewhere. By stressing regional and cultural specificities, these Western theories of the origin of human rights tend to reinforce, rather inadvertently, the disputation of universal human rights in non-Western societies. By arguing that the valuing of toleration, of personal liberty, and of civil rights is a particular contribution of Western civilization, Western advocates of these rights often give ammunition to the non-Western critics of human rights. The advocacy of an allegedly "alien" idea in non-Western societies can indeed look like cultural imperialism sponsored by the West.

Modernity as Tradition

How much truth is there in this grand cultural dichotomy between Western and. non-Western civilizations on the subject of liberty and rights? I believe there is rather little sense in such a grand dichotomy. Neither the claims in favor of the specialness of "Asian values" by governmental spokesmen from Asia, nor the particular claims for the uniqueness of "Western values" by spokesmen from Europe and America can survive much historical examination and critical scrutiny.

In seeing Western civilization as the natural habitat of individual freedom and political democracy, there is a tendency to extrapolate backwards from the present. Values that the European Enlightenment and other recent developments since the eighteenth century have made common and widespread are often seen, quite arbitrarily, as part of the long-run Western heritage, experienced in the West over millennia. The concept of universal human rights in the broad general sense of entitlements of every human being is really a relatively new idea, not to be much found either in the ancient West or in ancient civilizations elsewhere.

There are, however, other ideas, such as the value of toleration, or the importance of individual freedom, which have been advocated and defended for a long time, often for the selected few. For example, Aristotle's writings on freedom and human flourishing provide good background material for the contemporary ideas of human rights. But there are other Western philosophers (Plato and St. Augustine, for example) whose preference for order and discipline over freedom was no less pronounced than Confucius' priorities. Also, even those in the West who did emphasize the value of freedom did not, typically, see this as a fight of all human beings. Aristotle's exclusion of women and slaves is a good illustration of this nonuniversality. The defenses of individual freedom in Western tradition did exist but took a limited and contingent form.

Confucius and Co.

Do we find similar pronouncements in favor of individual freedom in non-Western traditions, particularly in Asia? The answer is emphatically yes. Confucius is not the only philosopher in Asia, not even in China. There is much variety in Asian intellectual traditions, and many writers did emphasize the importance of freedom and tolerance, and some even saw this as the entitlement of every human being. The language of freedom is very important, for example, in Buddhism, which originated and first flourished in South Asia and then spread to Southeast Asia and East Asia, including China, Japan, Korea, and Thailand. In this context it is important to recognize that Buddhist philosophy not only emphasized freedom as a form of life but also gave it a political content. To give just one example, the Indian emperor Ashoka in the third century bce presented many political inscriptions in favor of tolerance and individual freedom, both as a part of state policy and in the relation of different people to each other. The domain of toleration, Ashoka argued, must include everybody without exception.

Even the portrayal of Confucius as an unmitigated authoritarian is far from convincing. Confucius did believe in order, but he did not recommend blind allegiance to the state. When Zilu asks him how to serve a prince, Confucius replies, "Tell him the truth even if it offends him"—a policy recommendation that may encounter some difficulty in contemporary Singapore or Beijing. Of course, Confucius was a practical man, and he did not recommend that we foolhardily oppose established power. He did emphasize practical caution and tact, but also insisted on the importance of opposition. "When the [good] Way prevails in the state, speak boldly and act boldly. When the state has lost the Way, act boldly and speak softly," he said.

The main point to note is that both Western and non-Western traditions have much variety within themselves. Both in Asia and in the West, some have emphasized order and discipline, even as others have focused on freedom and tolerance. The idea of human rights as an entitlement of every human being, with an unqualified universal scope and highly articulated structure, is really a recent development; in this demanding form it is not an ancient idea either in the West or elsewhere. But there are limited and qualified defenses of freedom and tolerance, and general arguments against censorship, that can be found both in ancient traditions in the West and in cultures of non-Western societies.

Islam and Tolerance

Special questions are often raised about the Islamic tradition. Because of the experience of contemporary political battles, especially in the Middle East, the Islamic civilization is often portrayed as being fundamentally intolerant and hostile to individual freedom. But the presence of diversity and variety within a tradition applies very much to Islam as well. The Turkish emperors were often more tolerant than their European contemporaries. The Mughal emperors in India, with one exception, were not only extremely tolerant, but some even theorized about the need for tolerating diversity. The pronouncements of Akbar, the great Mughal emperor in sixteenth century India, on tolerance can count among the classics of political pronouncements, and would have received more attention in the West had Western political historians taken as much interest in Eastern thought as they do in their own intellectual background. For comparison, I should mention that the Inquisitions were still in full bloom in Europe as Akbar was making it a state policy to tolerate and protect all religious groups.

A Jewish scholar like Maimonides in the twelfth century had to run away from an intolerant Europe and from its persecution of Jews for the security offered by a tolerant Cairo and the patronage of Sultan Saladin. Alberuni, the Iranian mathematician, who wrote the first general book on India in the early eleventh century, aside from translating Indian mathematical treatises into Arabic, was among the earliest of anthropological theorists in the world. He noted and protested against the fact that "depreciation of foreigners . . . is common to all nations towards each other." He devoted much of his life to fostering mutual understanding and tolerance in his eleventh-century world.

Authority and Dissidence

The recognition of diversity within different cultures is extremely important in the contemporary world, since we are constantly bombarded by oversimplified generalizations about "Western civilization, . . . Asian values," "African cultures," and so on. These unfounded readings of history and civilization are not only intellectually shallow, they also add to the divisiveness of the world in which we live. Boorishness begets violence.

The fact is that in any culture people like to argue with each other, and often do. I recollect being amused in my childhood by a well-known poem in Bengali from nineteenth century Calcutta. The poet is describing the horror of death, the sting of mortality. "Just think," the poem runs, "how terrible it would be on the day you die / Others will go on speaking, and you will not be able to respond." The worst sting of death would appear to be, in this view, the inability to argue, and this illustrates how seriously we take our differences and our debates.

Dissidents exist in every society, often at great risk to their own security. Western discussion of non-Western societies is often too respectful of authority—the governor, the Minister, the military leader, the religious leader. This "authoritarian bias" receives support from the fact that Western countries themselves are often represented, in international gatherings, by governmental officials and spokesmen, and they in turn seek the views of their "opposite numbers" from other countries.

The view that Asian values are quintessentially authoritarian has tended to come almost exclusively from spokesmen of those in power and their advocates. But foreign ministers, or government officials, or religious leaders do not have a monopoly in interpreting local culture and values. It is important to listen to the voices of dissent in each society.

National and Cultural Diversity

To conclude, the so-called "Western values of freedom and liberty," sometimes seen as an ancient Western inheritance, are not particularly ancient, nor exclusively Western in their antecedence. Many of these values have taken their full form only over the last few centuries. While we do find some anticipatory components in parts of the ancient Western traditions, there are other such anticipatory components in parts of non-Western ancient traditions as well. On the particular subject of toleration, Plato and Confucius may be on a somewhat similar side, just as Aristotle and Ashoka may be on another side.

The need to acknowledge diversity applies not only between nations and cultures, but also within each nation and culture. In the anxiety to take adequate note of international diversity and cultural divergences, and the so-called differences between "Western civilization," "Asian values," "African culture," and so on, there is often a dramatic neglect of heterogeneity within each country and culture. "Nations" and "cultures" are not particularly good units to understand and analyze intellectual and political differences. Lines of division in commitments and skepticism do not run along national boundaries—they criss-cross at many different levels. The rhetoric of cultures, with each "culture" seen in largely homogenized terms, can confound us politically as well as intellectually.

JACK SNYDER AND LESLIE VINJAMURI

Trials and Errors: Principle and Pragmatism in Strategies of International Justice

Advocacy groups such as Human Rights Watch and Amnesty International have made a historic contribution to the cause of international human rights by publicizing the need to prevent mass atrocities such as war crimes, genocide, and widespread political killings and torture.[1] However, a strategy that many such groups favor for achieving this goal—the prosecution of perpetrators of atrocities according to universal standards—risks causing more atrocities than it would prevent, because it pays insufficient attention to political realities.[2] Recent international criminal tribunals have utterly failed to deter subsequent abuses in the former Yugoslavia and Central Africa. Because tribunals, including the International Criminal Court (ICC), have often been unable to gain the active cooperation of powerful actors in the United States and in countries where abuses occur, it is questionable whether this strategy will succeed in the long run unless it is implemented in a more pragmatic way.

Amnesties, in contrast, have been highly effective in curbing abuses when implemented in a credible way, even in such hard cases as El Salvador and Mozambique. Truth commissions, another strategy favored by some advocacy groups, have been useful mainly when linked to amnesties, as in South Africa. Simply ignoring the question of punishing perpetrators—in effect, a de facto amnesty—has also succeeded in ending atrocities when combined with astute politi-

cal strategies to advance political reforms, as in Namibia.

The shortcomings of strategies preferred by most advocacy groups stem from their fundamentally flawed understanding of the role of norms and law in establishing a just and stable political order. Like some scholars who write about the transformative impact of such groups, these advocates believe that rules of appropriate behavior constitute political order and consequently that the first step in establishing a peaceful political order is to lobby for the universal adoption of just rules.[3] We argue that this reverses the sequence necessary for the strengthening of norms and laws that will help prevent atrocities.

Justice does not lead; it follows. We argue that a norm-governed political order must be based on a political bargain among contending groups and on the creation of robust administrative institutions that can predictably enforce the law. Preventing atrocities and enhancing respect for the law will frequently depend on striking politically expedient bargains that create effective political coalitions to contain the power of potential perpetrators of abuses (or so-called spoilers).[4] Amnesty—or simply ignoring past abuses—may be a necessary tool in this bargaining. Once such deals are struck, institutions based on the rule of law become more feasible.[5] Attempting to implement universal standards of criminal justice in the absence of these political and institutional preconditions risks weakening norms of justice by revealing their ineffectiveness and hindering necessary political bargaining. Although we agree that the ultimate goal is

From *International Security* 28, no. 3 (Winter 2003/04): 5–44. Some of the authors' notes have been omitted.

to prevent atrocities by effectively institutionalizing appropriate standards of criminal justice, the initial steps toward that goal must usually travel down the path of political expediency.

∗   ∗   ∗

Three Logics of Action

The social psychologist Tory Higgins posits three different logics whereby a person may decide on the rightness of a choice of action: whether it follows right principles, whether it leads to the right outcome, and whether it feels right given the person's current emotional state.[6] These correspond to the logics of appropriateness, consequences, and emotions that we argue reflect the prevailing range of views on justice for perpetrators of atrocities.

These logics are ideal types. The strategies adopted by real political actors inevitably include a mix of these elements, as do those advocated by scholars. For example, human rights "norms entrepreneurs" argue not only that following their prescriptions is morally right; they also claim that these principles are grounded in a correct empirical theory of the causes of behavior and will therefore lead to desirable outcomes.[7] Thus, even arguments based on the logic of appropriateness usually also make claims about consequences.[8] Conversely, proponents of the logic of consequences might argue that bargains based on the expediency of power and interest are often a necessary precondition for creating coalitions and institutions that will strengthen norms in the long run. For example, in September 2002, the United Nations administrator for Afghanistan, Lakhdar Brahimi, resisted calls from outgoing Human Rights Commissioner Mary Robinson to investigate war crimes by key figures in the UN-backed government of Afghanistan's Hamid Karzai on the grounds that such investigations would undercut progress toward peace and stability.[9] In

short, all three logics are concerned with reducing the chance of future atrocities, and consequently it is justifiable to compare the validity of their empirical claims.[10]

The Logic of Appropriateness

Martha Finnemore and Kathryn Sikkink, leading social scientific scholars studying human rights, adopt a social constructivist definition of a norm as "a standard of appropriate behavior for actors with a given identity."[11] Norms, for them, imply a moral obligation that distinguishes them from other kinds of rules. In this constructivist view, norms do more than regulate behavior; they mold the identities of actors, define social roles, shape actors' understanding of their interests, confer power on authoritative interpreters of norms, and infuse institutions with guiding principles.[12] In this sense, norms— and discourse about what norms ought to be— help to constitute social reality. Powerful states and social networks matter, too, but principled ideas and arguments often animate their actions. In that sense, world society is what its norms make of it.

According to this perspective, norms entrepreneurs attempt to persuade others to accept and adhere to new norms; targets of persuasion respond with arguments and strategies of their own.[13] Persuasion may work through any of several channels, including logical arguments about consistency with other norms and beliefs that the target already adheres to, arguments from legal precedent, and emotional appeals.[14] Once persuasion has succeeded in establishing a norm within a social group, norms entrepreneurs seek to promote conformity with the norm by "naming and shaming" violators, to use the terminology of constructivist theorists and human rights activists.[15]

Thomas Risse and Sikkink note that the early stages of convincing a recalcitrant actor to adopt certain norms may include "instrumental adaptation" and "strategic bargaining."[16] In this scenario, a powerful community of states and nongovernmental organizations (NGOs) seeks to persuade the rights-abusing state to change its ways by arguing on the merits, but they may also take coercive measures, such as threatening to cut off aid.[17] In response, the state may begin to pay lip service to the norm, but do nothing to change its behavior. Nonetheless, Risse and Sikkink argue, this is a key first step: It traps the state into allowing rights monitors to verify the behavior of the rights-abusing state, and it forces the state to justify its actions in terms of the norm.[18] The logic of appropriateness, though stretched in this usage, retains a central position even in this rather coercive mechanism of normative change.

Finnemore and Sikkink conceive of the process of normative change as a three-stage "cascade." First, norms entrepreneurs use their organizational platforms to call attention to issues by naming, interpreting, and dramatizing them. Second, once these entrepreneurs achieve widespread success in their campaign of persuasion, a tipping process pushes the norm toward universal acceptance as international organizations, states, and transnational networks jump on the bandwagon. This occurs in part because of these actors' concern to safeguard their reputation and legitimacy, and in part because processes of socialization, institutionalization, and demonstration effects convince people that the rising norm is a proper one. In the third stage, the logic of appropriateness is so deeply imbued in law, bureaucratic rules, and professional standards that people and states conform unquestioningly out of conviction and habit.[19]

Constructivist social scientists have written little that directly applies the logic of appropriateness to the study of judicial accountability for war crimes or genocide.[20] Nonetheless, NGOs and legalists advocating war crimes tribunals implicitly hold to the constructivist theory. These activists assume that efforts to change the prevailing pattern of social behavior should begin with forceful advocacy for generalized rules embodied in principled institutions, such as courts.

Proponents of war crimes prosecutions have long been prone to exaggerate the centrality of rule following in ordering world politics. Judith Shklar, for example, in discussing the post–World War II Nuremberg and Japanese war crimes trials charged some of their proponents with excessive, apolitical legalism, which she defined as "the ethical attitude that holds that moral conduct is to be a matter of rule following, and moral relationships to consist of duties and rights determined by rules."[21] Contemporary activists argue that handing down indictments and holding trials strengthen legal norms even when perpetrators are hard to arrest and convict. Many of them favor generalizing norms through such measures as universal jurisdiction for prosecuting war crimes and crimes against humanity.[22] They also encourage setting up judicial institutions that embody the norm of accountability, such as the ICC, even when its short-term effect is to reduce the chance that a powerful, skeptical actor such as the United States will cooperate with the implementation of the norm.[23]

In the realm of international criminal justice, the logic of appropriateness generates several predictions. First, as norms of criminal accountability for war crimes and other violations of international humanitarian and human rights law begin to cascade, the notion of individual responsibility should gain international momentum. Local actors, not just proponents in the advanced liberal democracies, should increasingly blame atrocities on individuals (e.g., specific Serbian leaders), not collectivities (e.g., the Serbian ethnic group as a whole).

Second, if the vast majority of individuals worldwide accept the basic principles of the laws of war and prohibitions against genocide and torture, then prevailing practices will tip in favor of a universal system of international criminal justice. In this view, changes in behavior follow the adoption of new beliefs about appropriate standards of behavior. We argue, in contrast, that the prevailing pattern of political power and institutions shapes behavior in ways that are difficult to change simply through normative persuasion. For example, an extensive survey commissioned by the International Committee of the Red Cross (ICRC) shows that large majorities of people in powerful democracies and in conflict-ridden developing countries agree that it is wrong to target civilians for attack or to engage in indiscriminate military practices that result in widespread civilian slaughter.[24] The vast majority of those polled, however, were not participating as fighters in the conflicts. Respondents who said they were participants or who identified with one side expressed significant reservations about the laws of war. The ICRC report finds that "the more conflicts engage and mobilize the population," as in Israel and Palestine, "and the more committed the public is to a side and its goals, the greater the hatred of the enemy and the greater the willingness to breach whatever limits there exist in war."[25] Moreover, "weak defenders feel they can suspend the limits in war in order to do what is necessary to save or protect their communities."[26] Despite the convergence on abstract principles, these data imply that one person's terrorist is often another's freedom fighter.

Third, as the norm is embodied in legal institutions such as the war crimes tribunals for Yugoslavia and Rwanda and the ICC, it should begin to have some deterrent effect.[27] We argue, however, that deterrence depends on the predictable ability to enforce the law coercively, which often falls short in countries where abuses take place. When enforcement power is weak, pragmatic bargaining may be an indispensable tool in getting perpetrators to relinquish power and desist from their abuses. Moreover, perpetrators of mass crimes can sometimes be indispensable allies in efforts to bring peace to war-torn states. For example, the 2001–02 U.S. war against the terrorist-harboring Taliban would have been infeasible without the self-interested participation of the Afghan Northern Alliance, whose own leadership was earlier responsible for horrendous crimes in the Afghan civil war in the 1990s.

In such circumstances, legalists need to exercise prosecutorial discretion: A crime is a crime, but not all crimes must be prosecuted.[28] Such choices, however, risk putting judges and lawyers in charge of decisions that political leaders are better suited to make. For example, the investigations of the International Criminal Tribunal for Yugoslavia (ICTY) have complicated a peace settlement between the Macedonian government and ethnic Albanian former guerrillas accused of committing atrocities.[29] The settlement granted these rebels an amnesty except for crimes indictable by the international tribunal. The ICTY's decision to investigate rebel atrocities led the guerrillas to destroy evidence of mass graves, creating a pretext for hard-line Slavic Macedonian nationalists to renew fighting in late November 2001 and to occupy Albanian-held terrain.[30]

In sum, the logic of appropriateness and the theory of norms cascades capture the mind-set and strategies of advocates of international criminal accountability. This social constructivist theory of normative change, however, fundamentally misunderstands how norms gain social force. As a result, legalist tactics for strengthening human rights norms can backfire when institutional and social preconditions for the rule of law are lacking. In an institutional desert, legalism is likely to be either counterproductive or simply irrelevant.

The Logic of Consequences

Drawing on the work of James March and Johan Olsen, Finnemore and Sikkink distinguish between the logic of appropriateness and the logic of consequences.[31] Whereas Finnemore and Sikkink place the former at the center of their analysis, our approach emphasizes the latter. The logic of consequences assumes that actors try to achieve their objectives using the full panoply of material, institutional, and persuasive resources at their disposal. Norms may facilitate or coordinate actors' strategies, but actors will follow rules and promote new norms only insofar as they are likely to be effective in achieving substantive ends, such as a reduction in the incidence of atrocities.

If norms are to shape behavior and outcomes, they must gain the support of a dominant political coalition in the social milieu in which they are to be applied. The coalition must establish and sustain the institutions that will monitor and sanction compliance with the norms. Strategies that underrate the logic of consequences—and thus hinder the creation of effective coalitions and institutions—undermine normative change.

This perspective has important implications for rethinking strategies of international criminal justice. Sporadic efforts by international actors to punish violations in turbulent societies are unlikely to prevent further abuses. Deterrence requires neutralizing potential spoilers, strengthening a coalition that supports norms of justice in the society, and improving the domestic administrative and legal institutions that are needed to implement justice predictably over the long run. Meeting these requirements must take precedence over the objective of retroactive punishment when those goals are in conflict. Where human rights violators are too weak to derail the strengthening of the rule of law, they can be put on trial. But where they have the ability to lash out in renewed violations to try to reinforce their power, the international community faces a hard choice: either commit the resources to contain the backlash or offer the potential spoilers a deal that will leave them weak but secure. Efforts to prosecute individuals for crimes must also be sensitive to the impact of these efforts on relations between dominant groups in a future governing coalition. Where trials threaten to create or perpetuate intracoalition antagonisms in a new government, they should be avoided.

To serve as a bridge between lawlessness and norm-governed social relations, pragmatic bargaining needs to have a consistent rationale.[32] It must be part of an integrated normative vision, not an arbitrary departure from the rules. Toward that end, international norms should stipulate that decisions to prosecute past abuses must consider the consequences for the strengthening of

the rule of law. When a decision to prosecute cannot pass that test, a simple decision not to prosecute may sometimes suffice. When the bargaining situation demands it, however, granting a formal amnesty may sometimes be necessary. Amnesty should therefore be recognized as a legitimate tool when it serves the broader interest in establishing the rule of law.

Legal efforts to override domestic amnesties, however, have eroded their credibility. For example, despite President Carlos Menem's pardon of military officers convicted of crimes committed during Argentina's "dirty war" of 1976–83, both houses of Argentina's Congress voted in August 2003 to annul the laws that had barred the prosecution of military officers for human rights violations.[33] Other efforts to override amnesties come from international sources. For example, the Chilean military's self-amnesty did not protect former President Augusto Pinochet from legal action in a British court initiated by a Spanish judge under the doctrine of universal jurisdiction for crimes against humanity. The statute of the ICC fails to guarantee that amnesties will be respected.[34]

According to the logic of consequences, decisions about prosecution should be weighed in light of their effects on the strengthening of impartial, law-abiding state institutions. In the immediate aftermath of a state's transition to democracy, such institutions may already be capable of bringing rights abusers to trial, as for example, in Greece following the collapse of the junta in 1974. However, in transitional countries that are rich in potential spoilers and poor in institutions, such as contemporary Indonesia, the government may need to gain spoilers' acquiescence to institutional reforms, especially the professionalization of police and military bureaucracies and the development of an impartial legal system. In these cases, decisions to try members of the former regime should be weighed against the possibly adverse effects on the strengthening of institutions. Trials may be advantageous if they can be conducted efficiently, strengthen public understanding of the rule of law, add to the institutional capacities of domestic courts, assist in discrediting rights abusers, help to defuse tensions between powerful groups in society, and produce no backlash from spoilers. Where these conditions are absent, punishment for the abuses of the former regime may be a dangerous misstep and should be a low priority.

In short, the logic of consequences generates the following empirical predictions: When a country's political institutions are weak, when forces of reform there have not won a decisive victory, and when potential spoilers are strong, attempts to put perpetrators of atrocities on trial are likely to increase the risk of violent conflict and further abuses, and therefore hinder the institutionalization of the rule of law.

The Logic of Emotions

A third approach to dealing with past atrocities and preventing their recurrence reflects the logic of emotions. Scholars and advocates suggest that eliminating the conditions that breed atrocities depends on achieving an emotional catharsis in the community of victims and an acceptance of blame by the perpetrators. Without an effort to establish a consensus on the truth about past abuses, national reconciliation will be impossible, as resentful groups will continue to use violence to express their emotions. For these reasons, proponents of truth commissions stress the importance of encouraging perpetrators to admit responsibility for their crimes, sometimes in exchange for amnesty.[35]

Some proponents of the logic of emotions speak in the language of psychotherapy.[36] Others ground their arguments in evolutionary biology, claiming that the emotional aspects of reconciliation are central to social cohesion. For example, an important study by William Long and Peter Brecke contends that successful civil war settlements tend to go through a trajectory that starts with truth telling and limited justice, culminates in an emotionally salient call for a new relationship between former enemies, and

sometimes accomplishes a redefinition of social identities.[37] One problem with their research design, however, is the difficulty of knowing whether the emotional theater of reconciliation is causally central to establishing peace or whether it is mainly window dressing that makes political bargaining and amnesties more palatable to the public.

* * *

Short-Term Effects of Trials, Truth Commissions, and Amnesties

In this section, we review the empirical claims of different approaches to international justice and evaluate them in light of recent evidence. * * *

Trials

Advocates of legal accountability make three claims regarding the effectiveness of trials. First, trials send a strong signal to would-be perpetrators of atrocities that they will be held individually accountable for their actions. Human Rights Watch claims, for example, that "justice for yesterday's crimes supplies the legal foundation needed to deter atrocities tomorrow."[38] Second, trials strengthen the rule of law by teaching both elites and masses that the appropriate means of resolving conflict is through impartial justice. This helps to consolidate democracy in postconflict and postauthoritarian states.[39] Third, trials emphasize the guilt of particular individuals and thereby defuse the potential for future cycles of violence between ethnic groups.

Proponents contend that both domestic and international trials can promote these positive ends if domestic legal systems are sound. International trials underscore that atrocities violate universal standards of justice and engage public opinion worldwide. Some observers argue, however, that domestic trials are likely to have a greater impact on attitudes in the country where the abuses took place.[40] Mixed tribunals under the joint aegis of international and local judges, held in the country where the crimes occurred, aim to accomplish both goals, dispensing justice locally while maintaining international standards and oversight. Mixed tribunals are intended to help build the institutional capacity of local judiciaries and thereby strengthen the rule of law.

Truth Commissions

We also evaluate the claim that truth telling about past abuses, especially through a truth commission, makes a significant contribution to reconciling former enemies, promoting social reintegration in a newly democratic state, and reducing the likelihood of further atrocities.[41]

Amnesties

According to the logic of consequences, trials may provoke a violent backlash from still-powerful criminals, making norms seem ineffectual and thus undermining respect for human rights norms.[42] The stronger the indicted parties, the greater the risk of backlash. Only a decisive military victory over the criminal parties can remove this danger. In the absence of a decisive victory, a formal amnesty is likely to be a necessary first step in the process of consolidating peace, the rule of law, and democracy. Sometimes a de facto amnesty—that is, doing nothing about whether to hold trials—may serve the same purpose. This is especially true of divided societies where prosecutions not only risk backlash from spoilers but also threaten to further cleavages between groups whose cooperation is critical to future governance. In addition, an effective institutional apparatus—above all, a strong, competent state—is needed to enforce norms of justice in a predictable manner that carries deterrent force.

Testing the Strategies of Justice

To assess the effects of these three strategies of justice, we examined thirty-two cases of civil wars between 1989 and 2003. We chose this period because calls for postconflict justice became more common and more politically efficacious after the Cold War. We used Freedom House and Polity rankings of democracy and civil liberties to establish a rough measure of democracy, the rule of law, and human rights standards in our cases and to assess how trends in these indicators correlate with the strategy of justice used in each case.[43]

We find that various strategies of justice have been used in cases in which human rights abuses were reduced, peace was secured, and the degree of democracy was substantially improved. Successful cases, as measured in this broad way, include three cases of trials and truth commissions that do not include amnesty (East Timor, the former Yugoslavia except Macedonia, and Peru); one case of amnesty only (Mozambique, though Macedonia might yet prove to be in this category); one case of de facto amnesty (Namibia), two cases of amnesty plus a truth commission (El Salvador and South Africa), one case of de facto amnesty plus a truth commission (Guatemala), and one case of a truth commission only (Sri Lanka, but for part of the conflict only).

This metric, however, is a blunt instrument that has three significant shortcomings. First, it does not credit the short-term successes of amnesties in stopping the fighting (e.g., Macedonia, Angola, and the Chittagong Hills conflict in Bangladesh). Second, it does not get at the counterfactual of what would have happened if trials had been pursued (e.g., Afghanistan). Third, it fails to address whether the consolidation of peace happened despite the complicating effects of trials or because of them (e.g., the former Yugoslavia).

We assess these more subtle issues of causality in reviewing a number of the post-1989 civil wars below. We also comment in passing on some international wars and some problems of domestic strife from the pre-1989 period. Our analysis yields three findings. First, trials tend to contribute to the ending of abuses only when spoiler groups are weak and the domestic infrastructure of justice is already reasonably well established before trials begin. In other words, trials work best when they are needed least.

Second, the capacity of truth commissions to promote reconciliation is far more limited than their proponents suggest. Truth commissions contribute to democratic consolidation only when a prodemocracy coalition holds power in a fairly well institutionalized state. Absent those conditions, truth commissions can have perverse effects, sometimes exacerbating tensions and at other times providing public relations smoke screens for regimes that continue to abuse rights. Apparent successes of truth commissions are better attributed to the effects of the amnesties that accompany them.

Third, amnesties, whether formal or de facto, can help to pave the way for peace. Like tribunals, however, amnesties require effective political backing and strong institutions to enforce their terms. Indeed, the point of granting an amnesty should be to create the political preconditions for the strengthening of law-abiding state institutions.

Trials Held by International Tribunals

Evidence from recent cases casts doubt on the claims that international trials deter future atrocities, contribute to consolidating the rule of law or democracy, or pave the way for peace. Since 1989, two international criminal tribunals have convened: the ICTY (Yugoslavia) and the ICTR (Rwanda). In neither case did their trials deter subsequent atrocities or contribute to bringing peace in the region. Indeed, in the former case, the democratization and pacification of the Yugoslav successor states likely occurred despite the tensions provoked by the tribunal and not because of it. More generally, neither the Yugoslavia nor the Rwanda tribunals has had a demonstrable

effect on reducing atrocities globally or on altering the calculations of combatants in conflicts in East Timor, Chechnya, Sierra Leone, or other war sites.

YUGOSLAVIA Two years after the 1993 UN resolution creating the ICTY, Bosnian Serb forces massacred thousands of civilians in Srebrenica, Bosnia. Even after the tribunal began to convict war criminals in May 1997, paramilitaries under the direction of Serbian President Slobodan Milosevic committed mass war crimes in Kosovo in 1999. The tribunal's case against Milosevic notes that he ignored Western diplomats' face-to-face warnings that he would be prosecuted if he failed to stop Serbian abuses in Kosovo.[44]

Some proponents of trials argue that the ICTY discouraged anti-Serb violence in Kosovo and forced war criminals to abandon the use of tactics that received particular scrutiny from prosecutors, including mass detentions or concentration camps.[45] Critics, however, contend that the ICTY merely induced the perpetrators to hide evidence of their crimes—for example, removing bodies from mass graves and avoiding the use of written documents to distribute orders.

Rather than individualizing guilt, the ICTY seems to have reinforced ethnic cleavages.[46] For example, many Serbs have complained that the tribunal unfairly targets Serbs, while many Croats have argued that their group has been unfairly singled out. Once ethnic groups are polarized by intergroup violence, it generally takes a decisive change in strategic circumstances and political institutions, not just the invocation of legal norms, to convince people to think in terms of individual rather than group responsibility.[47]

Survey results suggest that there has been a public relations backlash against the ICTY in Serbian areas. In a survey conducted by the National Democratic Institute for International Affairs in February 2002, only 22 percent of respondents in Republika Srpska approved its adoption of a law on cooperation with The Hague.[48] For Serbia, the same survey revealed that virtually every "significant leader and party in the governing coalition" had suffered a drop in image with the exception of Milosevic and his Socialist Party. Milosevic had gained modest support because of the local perception that his trial in The Hague was unjust.[49] A November 2002 survey revealed that 40 percent of Serbs felt that the next president of Serbia should not hand over indicted Serbs to the ICTY; 18 percent thought that all cooperation with the ICTY should be suspended; 22 percent favored continued cooperation; and 13 percent sought additional cooperation.[50] Moreover, 47 percent of Serbs preferred a Serbian president who would try suspected war criminals only in Yugoslav courts. Serbs under thirty years of age were no more likely to favor cooperating with the ICTY (40 percent) than pursuing investigations in Yugoslav courts only (40 percent).[51]

The Serbian public's acquiescence to the ICTY has been based on expediency, not conviction. For example, in an April 2002 survey, 44 percent of Serbs said they thought cooperating with the ICTY would help obtain European Union membership for Serbia, while another 22 percent doubted this; 36 percent felt that cooperation with the ICTY would help obtain U.S. aid, while 22 percent were skeptical. In contrast, only 20 percent were convinced that cooperation with the ICTY was "morally right," and only 10 percent saw the ICTY as the best way to serve justice.[52]

* * *

* * * [H]owever, the worst backlash fears of skeptics appear to have been exaggerated. Earlier, for example, Milosevic continued to negotiate the Serbian withdrawal from Kosovo under relentless NATO air attacks despite his simultaneous indictment by The Hague tribunal.[53] In part, such backlash effects have been limited because prudent politicians have not pushed trials past the point that might have provoked violent opposition. Where trials do threaten to undermine public order, authorities typically

proceed with extreme caution. After the signing of the 1995 Dayton peace accords on Bosnia, for example, the ICTY's activities alienated both the Croats and the Serbs and diminished their inclination to proceed with the process of implementing peace. When the tribunal sought to arrest prominent Bosnian Serb war criminals such as former Bosnian Serb President Radovan Karadzic and Gen. Ratko Mladic, Bosnian Serb President Biljana Plavsic threatened to withdraw support for the peace accords and warned that "massive civil and military unrest would result in the Republika Srpska which might well prove uncontrollable by the civil authorities."[54] The states providing UN peacekeeping forces took the danger of a Serb backlash seriously, and as a result, Karadzic and Mladic remained at large while lesser criminals were tried at The Hague.

Similarly, the fear of retaliation against NATO's KFOR peacekeeping mission in Kosovo led the ICTY to keep secret the indictment of Albanians suspected of killing Serb civilians in 1999.[55] Despite the indictment of Milosevic, significant Western pressure to have him extradited to The Hague was delayed until after he had ceased to be a serious force in local politics. This kind of anticipatory self-restraint masks potential evidence for the backlash hypothesis. Where this self-restraint has abated, it has followed, not led, events on the ground.

* * *

RWANDA The deterrent effect of the ICTR has likewise been unimpressive. Proponents claim that the tribunal may have helped to neutralize the Hutu Power movement's agenda of Tutsi extermination following the massacre of some 800,000 Tutsis and Hutu moderates in 1994.[56] However, this was mainly accomplished by the military victory of the Tutsi-led Rwanda Patriotic Front (RPF) armed forces, not by later trials. In fact, the work of the tribunal, which meets in Arusha, Tanzania, has been largely invisible to the Rwandan population. Critics claim that the tribunal, which was tasked only with collecting information pertaining to the year in which the genocide occurred, has been ill suited to presenting a coherent account of the events leading to the genocide.[57]

Evaluated on a regional basis, claims that the Arusha tribunal has deterred further crimes are unsustainable. Some perpetrators of the genocide rearmed in the refugee camps of eastern Congo, leading to military intervention on Congolese territory by the RPF in 1996 and again in 1998. These and other battles in Congo's civil war have led to deaths numbering in the millions, involving widespread atrocities against civilians.[58] Meanwhile in nearby Burundi, fighting between the Tutsi military and Hutu rebels, including atrocities against civilians, has continued sporadically since 1993.

The ICTR has done little to strengthen domestic institutions or to enhance the protection of political and civil liberties in Rwanda. Holding the tribunal in Tanzania created little opportunity for spillover effects for Rwanda's weak judicial institutions. The new government of Rwanda decided to hold domestic trials of those individuals who were not turned over to the international tribunal. Disputes over the tribunal's lack of a death penalty and its limits on pretrial detention derailed its cooperation with these domestic forums. The government of Rwanda felt that the ICTR was more concerned with due process and the rights of the accused than it was with holding leaders of the genocide accountable.

Domestic Trials

We find that domestic trials have only a marginal effect on the deterrence of subsequent abuses and the peaceful consolidation of democracy, and sometimes they may even be counterproductive. Where legal institutions are weak, domestic trials typically lack independence from political authorities, fail to dispense justice, and sometimes even fail to protect the security of trial participants. In states where the postatrocity regime retains autocratic features, rulers have sometimes used trials to legitimate their power over domestic opponents or gain international legitimacy through the veneer of legality (as in Cambodia and Indonesia). In other states with weak judicial institutions, trials have largely languished amid a lack of political will or sheer bureaucratic incapacity (as in Ethiopia and Rwanda). In contrast, trials are most effective in cases where legal institutions are already fairly well established, and therefore where the demonstration effect of trials is least needed. In a number of cases, for example, domestic trials have taken place well after rights-respecting democratic regimes were firmly installed (as in Germany and Poland in the 1990s, or in Greece after the fall of the junta in 1974).

These problems are especially acute when the new regime is the result of a negotiated settlement with still-powerful perpetrators of atrocities, but such problems confound trials even in cases where reformers have won military or political victories. We begin with a discussion of several cases where reformers were victorious, yet holding trials remained fraught with political complications.

ARGENTINA Following the collapse of the military junta that led Argentina to defeat in the 1982 Falklands War, five of the junta's leaders were convicted during the 1980s for their crimes in the regime's "dirty war" against domestic political opponents between 1976 and 1983. Activists pressed for more extensive prosecutions. Arguably, these trials were unnecessary to deter future crimes, because the junta's methods were already thoroughly discredited by their defeat in the Falklands War, their disastrous stewardship of the economy, and the widespread publicity about "disappearances" and rights abuses. Nonetheless, pressure for these trials from human rights advocates and victims' families risked provoking disturbances or even a coup attempt by unreconciled elements of the officer corps. Even sympathetic analysts agree that demands to expand the scope of the trials played into the military's hand and created a backlash among moderate opinion in favor of curtailing the trials.[59] Ultimately, President Menem pardoned even the five convicted generals in 1989, but in 2003 Argentine President Nestor Kirchner pushed for the cases to be reopened. In August 2003, the Argentine Congress overturned the laws that had granted amnesty for human rights abuses.[60]

ETHIOPIA After the 1991 defeat of Ethiopia's brutal Dergue regime in a civil war, the new government sought to put perpetrators of atrocities on trial. Over time, however, new political cleavages and economic dilemmas came to preoccupy the semidemocratic regime. Ethiopia's poorly institutionalized court system became bogged down in the vast task of collecting evidence against thousands of potential defendants.[61] The government's interest in prosecutions waned. In 2001, after some convictions and much fruitless activity, the court began releasing defendants for lack of evidence.[62]

RWANDA Despite the military victory of the RPF, the new Tutsi-dominated regime in Rwanda was too weak at the local level to protect those who would participate in prosecutions of perpetrators of genocide. "Especially outside the Rwandan capital city of Kigali, magistrates, prosecutors, court clerks, and witnesses worried that their lives would be endangered if they took part in genocide prosecutions in national courts," says Jennifer Widner. "Over three hundred survivors, scheduled to testify as witnesses, were murdered between 1994 and 1997, and paralysis set in. Without security," she notes, "officials and citizens feared to take the steps required to build the rule of law."[63]

Thousands of detainees swamped Rwanda's justice system. Trained legal personnel for the local trials were lacking. Formal domestic trials eventually gave way to a process based on a traditional form of local community justice, the *gacaca*. International human rights groups have contested the legality and prudence of this traditional model, arguing that it does not provide adequate protection for witnesses. Instead of spending millions on an international tribunal, some observers have argued that a better strategy for strengthening the rule of law would have been to provide much greater international support for institutionalizing a better judicial process within Rwanda.[64]

KOSOVO After NATO's 1999 military defeat of the Serbs in Kosovo, ethnic tensions between Kosovar Albanians and Kosovar Serbs remained high, making Kosovo an important test case to evaluate the claim that war crimes trials can defuse tensions between groups by individualizing guilt. In this tense setting, the United Nations Mission in Kosovo (UNMIK) mounted local trials, while the ICTY tried higher-level suspects in The Hague. The trials in Kosovo, however, exacerbated ethnic tensions. Local Albanian judicial officials were heavily biased in their prosecution of several Serb suspects apprehended by KFOR in the summer and fall of 1999.[65] Amid continuing ethnic unrest, Kosovo Serbs detained for war crimes in Mitrovica went on hunger strikes in early 2000. An October 2001 National Democratic Institute poll revealed that 89 percent of Kosovo Serbs felt that local courts would not resolve disputes with members of another ethnicity fairly.[66]

To improve procedural standards and address Serbian criticisms, UNMIK gave international judges and prosecutors a majority voice in these trials. The reconstituted courts reversed eight of eleven prior convictions.[67] This internationalization of local trials may have bolstered legal standards, but it revealed the incapacity of trials to socialize local elites into accepting the rule of law. Rather than eliciting local support, retrials outraged local judges.[68]

War crimes trials in Kosovo have had little deterrent value, as interethnic violence has continued since NATO's victory. Local judicial officials failed to adequately prosecute those responsible for two notorious attacks against Kosovo Serbs. In 1999, fourteen Serb farmers were gunned down south of Pristina, and in 2001, eleven Serbs riding civilian buses were killed and forty others injured.[69] Between January and May of 2000, there were ninety-five murders in Kosovo, twenty-six of them among the tiny Serb population. The violence decreased by 2002, primarily because much of the Serb population had fled. The trial and conviction in July 2003 of four former members of the Kosovo Liberation Army, however, sparked a new wave of violence against the international police and judiciary amid claims that the UNMIK trials were biased against Kosovar Albanians.[70]

* * *

Truth Commissions

Truth commissions have most often been the choice of states whose stability depends on the cooperation of still-powerful potential spoilers. We find that truth commissions are most likely to be useful when they provide political cover for amnesties, and when they help a strong, reformist coalition to undertake the strengthening of legal institutions as part of a strategy based on the logic of consequences.

Eleven of the thirteen states that convened truth commissions terminated their civil wars through negotiated settlements.[71] Only in Ethiopia and Peru did the new government pursue a truth commission following a decisive victory. In Ethiopia, however, the objective of the commission was to produce information that the state would use in subsequent trials. In the remaining eleven cases, no one group had enough power to impose war crimes trials on its competitors. International truth commissions have likewise served to manage rather than alter the existing balance of power. In El Salvador and East Timor, the United Nations preferred truth commissions to a more confrontational strategy of international war crimes trials.

EL SALVADOR, GUATEMALA, AND HAITI Often states keep truth commissions on a short leash because of the anticipated backlash from potential spoilers. Following the release of the truth commission's report in El Salvador in 1993, for example, the government issued an amnesty that proved critical in securing support for the peace process from key actors. In Guatemala, where the primary purpose of the truth commission was to confer a degree of legitimacy on the government and to minimize the potential for a backlash, the truth commission's report in 1999 did not name names. Despite this compromise, the commission's project director, Bishop Juan Gerardi Conedera, was murdered two days after the release of the report.[72]

Even in the face of threats from spoilers, truth commissions have sometimes produced good results, but only when a reformist political coalition fosters improvements in institutional underpinnings of democracy. In El Salvador, for example, the truth commission contributed to democratic consolidation by investigating the role of the judiciary in past abuses and recommending reforms intended to bring the judicial branch into conformity with international standards. Its report charged that the judiciary had covered up evidence of atrocities and failed to cooperate with the commission's investigations. The report recommended extensive reforms, including the reduction in power of the supreme court and the creation of laws protecting the rights of defendants. While the government rejected the commission's call for the resignation of a long list of members of the judiciary, a reformist ruling coalition implemented some of its recommendations.[73] In contrast, Haiti lacked political support for its truth commission's recommendations for judicial reform, which failed to bear fruit.

SOUTH AFRICA As in El Salvador, the presence of a reformist political coalition in South Africa made possible the successes of the truth commission that heard testimony on political crimes of the apartheid era. Despite the very different circumstances that surrounded the granting of amnesty in South Africa and El Salvador, in each of these cases, a truth commission provided political cover for this controversial policy. Although amnesty minimizes the backlash from past perpetrators, truth commissions also need to worry about backlash from those who are demanding sterner justice. In South Africa, the truth-telling aspect of the Truth and Reconciliation Commission provoked the anger of some relatives who watched revealed perpetrators walk free.[74] Truth commission staff in Haiti refrained from making the names of perpetrators public for fear that this would lead to random acts of retaliation.[75] However, well-designed truth commissions in the future might be able to minimize such resentments. James Gibson's survey research shows that South Africans consider amnesty to be necessary, but unfair. This perceived unfairness could be mitigated, according to the survey's findings, if victims' families had a voice in truth commission proceedings, if perpetrators' apologies were perceived to be sincere, and if victims were financially compensated.[76]

* * *

Amnesties

Amnesties were negotiated following eleven of the civil wars that have ended since 1989. Some were combined with truth commissions, as in South Africa, El Salvador, and the original plan for Sierra Leone in 1999. In other cases, such as Namibia and Afghanistan, the new government did not grant an official amnesty, but the demand for war crimes trials either did not surface or was effectively deferred. Many of these amnesties or de facto amnesties helped to shore up peace and an improved human rights situation. The evidence suggests, however, that amnesties, like tribunals, require effective political backing and strong institutions to enforce their terms. Indeed, the point of giving an amnesty should be to create

the political preconditions for the strengthening of law-abiding state institutions. Amnesties are likely to succeed only if they are accompanied by political reforms that curtail the power of rights abusers, and if they can be effectively enforced.

NAMIBIA In some cases, doing nothing has been a viable strategy for consolidating peace. For example, Namibia's durable peace settlement was not disturbed by the failure to prosecute crimes that had been committed by both sides in the war. Indeed, the terms of the postconflict transition were negotiated before the international human rights movement began to emphasize war crimes trials. As result, the question of accountability for atrocities was left off the agenda, with no apparent ill effects.

MOZAMBIQUE In Mozambique, peace has been sustained since the signing of a 1992 accord, which provided that neither party had to take public responsibility for crimes committed during the country's civil war. At the outset of the peace talks, each side insisted that the other be held accountable for its misdeeds. A negotiating stalemate resulted. To break the logjam, mediators from the St. Egidio Catholic Church organization suggested that the sides grant each other an amnesty. The Mozambican parliament followed up with a grant of amnesty for "crimes against the state" to speed reconciliation.[77]

EL SALVADOR An amnesty helped to gain the cooperation of key actors in implementing Salvador's successful peace accord. To end the civil war, moderate conservatives in the business community eagerly supported the provisions of a UN-brokered agreement to completely reconstruct the country's army, police, and other governmental institutions. These economic elites had realized during the course of the war that they could no longer make money through coffee production with repressive control of labor, and instead sought to take advantage of the trend toward economic globalization by expanding *maquiladora* light manufacturing exports. This meant turning their back on their former allies in the right-wing death squads and making peace with the leftist rebels.[78]

An amnesty for crimes committed during the war helped to seal this deal for institutional transformation, which was grounded in an iron-clad political and economic logic, whatever its shortcomings from the standpoint of backward-looking justice. The conservative government granted the amnesty as a defensive move following the release of reports by a truth commission and an ad hoc commission on crimes committed during the civil war, which called for the discharge of several military officers and the resignation of a number of judges. Contrary to proponents' claim that truth commissions shore up peace by reconciling former enemies, the Salvadoran government viewed the release of these reports as a dangerous provocation. The military, the defense minister, and the supreme court all denounced the reports as biased. Three days after the truth commission report was released, the president proclaimed the amnesty, and two officers convicted of murdering Jesuit priests were freed. Although 55 percent of the public opposed the amnesty and 77 percent favored punishing those who had committed crimes, the decision for amnesty was crucial in gaining the cooperation of the military, the judiciary and, more generally, the government in subsequent stages of the peace process. ARENA, the governing party, argued for the amnesty on the grounds that forgetting was critical to reconciliation.[79]

SIERRA LEONE AND IVORY COAST

In both Sierra Leone and Ivory Coast, rebels were offered amnesty and key posts in the new government. Neither situation proved to be stable. In Sierra Leone, the Lomé accords gave an amnesty to the still powerful RUF leader, Foday Sankoh, and put him in charge of diamond mining in the new gov-

ernment. Far from being reconciled to peace and the rule of law, the RUF saw the accord as a step toward entrenching their practices of domination and plunder. When this view of the settlement was challenged, Sankoh's rebels renewed their violence against the government and civilians.

In Ivory Coast, when France attempted to settle the civil war by proposing that rebels be given key government posts, protesters thronged the streets and sporadic fighting continued. Despite this result, in July 2003 the government of Ivory Coast announced plans for a new amnesty. These cases underscore the importance of removing perpetrators from positions of arbitrary power as the price of gaining amnesty.

MACEDONIA

In Macedonia, an amnesty covering certain crimes committed by ethnic Albanian rebels was an essential component of the 2001 peace settlement that dampened conflict after the post-Kosovo fighting. This amnesty did not, however, cover crimes under the purview of the ICTY. The tribunal's subsequent investigations in Macedonia created a pretext for Slavic Macedonian nationalists to resume fighting ethnic Albanian former guerrillas accused of committing atrocities, which nearly caused the settlement to unravel.[80]

* * *

AFGHANISTAN

Afghanistan stands out as a case where de facto amnesty has been the dominant strategy of justice in an international environment that is hostile to such a policy. Despite the political utility of amnesty, recent international legal developments call the credibility of offers of amnesty or de facto amnesty into question. The ICC lacks provisions that explicitly guarantee the sanctity of domestic amnesties. Advocates continue to suggest overturning amnesties. To date, however, efforts to move forward with war crimes trials for Afghanistan have been rebuffed. UN Human Rights Commissioner

Mary Robinson pressed Afghanistan's interim government to set up a truth commission with no amnesty powers to investigate crimes not only of the Taliban, but also of the earlier regimes whose members once again secured high positions in Hamid Karzai's interim government. Lakhdar Brahimi, UN special representative for Afghanistan, was successful in persuading the international community that pressing for war crimes investigations would undermine his efforts to institute peace.

* * *

In short, these cases show that amnesty can be an indispensable tool in reaching peace settlements when perpetrators remain strong. Moreover, amnesty per se does not appear to be incompatible with the subsequent consolidation of peace. In implementing an amnesty, however, it is important to make sure that perpetrators are removed from office or that the institutional setting of politics is so fundamentally altered that a return to the ways of the past is unfeasible.

Effects on Longer-Term Evolution of Global Norms and Institutions

Even if the short-term benefits of war crimes trials are dubious, advocates of strict, legal accountability argue that bringing suspected war criminals to trial strengthens global norms and institutions of justice over the long term. The demonstration effect of the first post-Nuremberg international war crimes trials and those for the former Yugoslavia did indeed seem to set off a chain reaction in Rwanda, East Timor, Sierra Leone, and Cambodia. At the same time, activists and jurists pursued innovations in domestic courts, most notably Belgium's, designed to try individuals under the principle of universal jurisdiction. This wave of activity

also included the ratification of the multilateral treaty creating a permanent International Criminal Court, which came into force in July 2002.

Despite what might seem like an increasingly institutionalized "norms cascade" in the area of international criminal justice, we are skeptical of these claims. Dismayed by the constraints that these legalistic developments place on pragmatic bargaining, states have engaged in an effective, ongoing effort to rein in this trend toward supranational justice. Rather than supplanting the norm of sovereignty and bolstering the norm of human rights and individual accountability, the norm of justice has mutated in directions that recognize the right of states, especially powerful states, to exert control over the terms of justice. One reason for the strength of this countertrend is that states are often correct in acting on a prudent logic of consequences rather than a narrow logic of legal appropriateness.

* * *

The interaction of the strategies of states and advocates of universal justice, however, sometimes creates unintended consequences. Pressed by principled activists and vocal public opinion, democratic leaders often pay lip service to human rights principles and accountability for crimes. These leaders over-promise but underdeliver because they suspect that their publics' underlying preferences are similar to their own: that is, they do not really want to bear the costs and risks that a policy of forceful, unbending application of universal principles would produce. As a result, policies and institutions of humanitarian justice are "designed to fail."[81] Skeptical pragmatists who are required to carry out the policies mandated by legalistic advocates constrain implementing institutions with inadequate resources, support, and authority. Thus, NATO refused to arrest known war criminals for the ICTY.[82] The International Criminal Court may be headed for a similar fate.

* * *

Conclusion

In recent years the world has witnessed rampant human rights abuses. Preventing such disasters is one of the most important issues on the international agenda. Legalism, focusing on the universal enforcement of international humanitarian law and persuasion campaigns to spread benign human rights norms, offers one strategy for accomplishing this. We find, however, that evidence from recent experience offers little support for the central empirical assumptions that underpin this approach. Trials do little to deter further violence and are not highly correlated with the consolidation of peaceful democracy.

In contrast, the empirical hypotheses underpinning pragmatism and the logic of consequences fare better. Amnesties or other minimal efforts to address the problem of past abuses have often been the basis for durable peaceful settlements. The main positive effect of truth commissions has probably been to give political cover to amnesties in transitional countries with strong reform coalitions. The international criminal justice regime should permit the use of amnesties when spoilers are strong and when the new regime can use an amnesty to decisively remove them from power. Deciding what approach to adopt in a particular case requires political judgment. Consequently, decisions to prosecute should be taken by political authorities, such as the UN Security Council or the governments of affected states, not by judges who remain politically unaccountable.

Nonetheless, purely pragmatic approaches are inadequate if they do not address the long-term goal of institutionalizing the rule of law in conflict-prone societies. Opportunistic "deals with the devil" are at best a first step toward removing spoilers from positions of power so that institutional transformation can move forward. Institution building must begin with the strengthening of general state capacity and then move on to regularize the rule of law more deeply. Both amnesties and trials require effective state institutions and political coalitions to enforce them. Without those conditions, neither approach is likely to succeed. Above all, external pressure and assistance should be targeted on future-oriented tasks such as human rights training of police and military personnel, improved human rights monitoring of field operations, reform of military finances and military justice, and punishment of new abuses once the reforms are in place.

In cases where legal accountability is not barred by the danger of backlash from spoilers, trials should be carried out through local justice institutions in ways that strengthen their capacity, credibility, and legitimacy. When international jurists must get involved, we favor mixed international-domestic tribunals, such as the one in Sierra Leone. Above all, choices about punishment of past abuses must be made through the application of resolutely forward-looking criteria designed to avert atrocities and secure human rights, not backward-looking strategies based on rigid rule following or on what "feels right."

NOTES

1. Ann Marie Clark, *Diplomacy of Conscience: Amnesty International and Changing Human Rights Norms* (Princeton, N.J.: Princeton University Press, 2001). We address violations of both international human rights law, which applies to all people at all times, and international humanitarian law, which concerns the actions of combatants during military conflict. For details, see Geoffrey Best, *War and Law since 1945* (Oxford: Clarendon, 1994); and Roy Gutman and David Rieff, eds., *Crimes against War: What the Public Should Know* (New York: W.W. Norton, 1999).

2. On proposals for international tribunals, see Neil J. Kritz, "Coming to Terms with Atrocities: A Review of Accountability Mechanisms for Mass Violations of Human Rights," *Law and Contemporary Problems* (Duke University School of Law), Vol. 59, No. 4 (Autumn 1996),

pp. 127–152; Martha Minow, *Between Vengeance and Forgiveness: Facing History after Genocide and Mass Violence* (Boston: Beacon, 1998), pp. 24–51; as well as the numerous publications by Human Rights Watch, Amnesty International, and the Coalition for International Justice. See also the sources cited in the balanced critical commentary by Gary Jonathan Bass, *Staying the Hand of Vengeance: The Politics of War Crimes Tribunals* (Princeton, N.J.: Princeton University Press, 2000), pp. 284–310.

3. Martha Finnemore and Kathryn Sikkink, "International Norm Dynamics and Political Change," *International Organization*, Vol. 52, No. 4 (Autumn 1998), pp. 887–917, especially p. 898, Table 1; and Kenneth Roth, "The Case for Universal Jurisdiction," *Foreign Affairs*, Vol. 80, No. 5 (September 2001), pp. 150–154. Roth is director of Human Rights Watch.

4. Stephen John Stedman, "Spoiler Problems in Peace Processes," *International Security*, Vol. 22, No. 2 (Fall 1997), pp. 5–53.

5. On institutionalization of the rule of law as a precondition for successful human rights promotion, see Tonya Putnam, "Human Rights and Sustainable Peace," in Stephen John Stedman, Donald Rothchild, and Elizabeth Cousens, eds., *Ending Civil Wars: The Implementation of Peace Agreements* (New York: Lynne Rienner, 2002), pp. 237–271; and Michael Ignatieff, *Human Rights as Politics and Idolatry*, ed. Amy Gutmann (Princeton, N.J.: Princeton University Press, 2001), pp. 25, 40.

6. E. Tory Higgins, "Making a Good Decision: Value from Fit," *American Psychologist*, Vol. 55, No. 11 (November 2000), pp. 1217–1230; and Christopher Camacho, E. Tory Higgins, and Lindsay Luger, "Moral Value Transfer from Regulatory Fit: 'What Feels Right *Is* Right' and 'What Feels Wrong *Is* Wrong,'" *Journal of Personality and Social Psychology*, Vol. 84, No. 3 (March 2003), pp. 498–510.

7. Finnemore and Sikkink, "International Norm Dynamics and Political Change," pp. 896–899.

8. See William F. Schulz, *In Our Own Best Interest: How Defending Human Rights Benefits Us All* (Boston: Beacon, 2001). Schultz is the executive director of Amnesty International USA. On a philosophical plane, see Thomas Nagel, "War and Massacre," in Samuel Scheffer, ed., *Consequentialism and Its Critics* (Oxford: Oxford University Press, 1988), p. 60.

9. John F. Burns, "Political Realities Impeding Full Inquiry into Afghan Atrocity," *New York Times*, August 29, 2002.

10. Finnemore and Sikkink, "International Norm Dynamics and Political Change," pp. 910–914.

11. Ibid., p. 881.

12. Ibid., p. 913; more generally, see Alexander Wendt, *Social Theory of International Politics* (Cambridge: Cambridge University Press, 1999).

13. Finnemore and Sikkink, "International Norm Dynamics and Political Change," p. 914.

14. Ibid., pp. 912–913.

15. Margaret Keck and Kathryn Sikkink, *Activists beyond Borders: Transnational Advocacy Networks in International Politics* (Ithaca, N.Y.: Cornell University Press, 1998), pp. 16–25.

16. Thomas Risse and Kathryn Sikkink, "The Socialization of International Human Rights Norms into Domestic Practice," in Risse, Stephen C. Ropp, and Sikkink, eds., *The Power of Human Rights: International Norms and Domestic Change* (Cambridge: Cambridge University Press, 1999), pp. 5, 11–12.

17. Keck and Sikkink, *Activists beyond Borders*, pp. 23–24.

18. Risse and Sikkink, "The Socialization of International Human Rights Norms into Domestic Practice," pp. 25–28, 34–35.

19. Finnemore and Sikkink, "International Norm Dynamics and Political Change," pp. 904–905.

20. Ellen Lutz and Kathryn Sikkink, "International Human Rights Law and Practice,"

International Organization, Vol. 54, No. 3 (Summer 2000), pp. 633–651, especially p. 644; Kathryn Sikkink, *The Justice Cascade* (Norton forthcoming).

21. Judith N. Shklar, *Legalism: Law, Morals, and Political Trials* (Cambridge, Mass.: Harvard University Press, 1964), p. 1; see also Ruti Teitel, "Bringing the Messiah through the Law," in Carla Hesse and Robert Post, eds., *Human Rights in Political Transitions: Gettysburg to Bosnia* (New York: Zone Books, 1999).

22. Roth, "The Case for Universal Jurisdiction."

23. For historical background, see Lawrence Weschler, "Exceptional Cases in Rome: The United States and the Struggle for an ICC," pp. 85–111, and David J. Scheffer, "The U.S. Perspective on the ICC," pp. 115–118, both in Sarah B. Sewall and Carl Kaysen, eds., *The United States and the International Criminal Court* (New York: Rowman and Littlefield, 2000).

24. Greenberg Research, *The People on War Report: ICRC Worldwide Consultation on the Rules of War* (Geneva: International Committee of the Red Cross, October 1999), http://www.icrc.org/web/eng/siteeng0.nsf/iwpList74/B1C2D1622A51A9F4C1256C550043C232.

25. Ibid., p. 32.

26. Ibid., p. 33.

27. Neil J. Kritz, "War Crime Trials: Who Should Conduct Them—and How?" in Belinda Cooper, ed., *War Crimes: The Legacy of Nuremberg* (New York: TV Books, 1999), pp. 168–182.

28. Roth, "The Case for Universal Jurisdiction," p. 153.

29. "Macedonia Bolsters Albanian Rights: After Constitutional Change, Amnesty Is Declared for Former Rebels," *International Herald Tribune*, November 17–18, 2001.

30. Timothy Garton Ash, "Is There a Good Terrorist?" *New York Review of Books*, November 29, 2001, pp. 30–33; and "Macedonia Is Seeking Control of Land Harboring Ex-Rebels," *New York Times*, November 26, 2001, p. A11.

31. [James G.] March and [Johan P.] Olsen, *Rediscovering Institutions[: The Organizational Basis of Politics* (New York: Free Press, 1989)], chap. 2.

32. For a different solution to this same problem, see Ruti G. Teitel, *Transitional Justice* (New York: Oxford University Press, 2000).

33. "Argentina Faces Its Past," Human Rights Watch, Monthly Update, August 2003, http://hrw.org/update/2003/08/#1.

34. If the ICC decided to prosecute despite a domestic amnesty, the UN Security Council could defer the indictment for one-year renewable periods if it determined that hearings would threaten peace and security. Regarding the prosecution of current officeholders, a 2003 ruling by the International Court of Justice invoked the doctrine of sovereign immunity in holding that a Belgian court could not try the Congolese foreign minister, Yerodia Ndombasi, for the 1998 killings of ethnic Tutsis because representatives of foreign governments are entitled to diplomatic immunity. More generally, Putnam, "Human Rights and Sustainable Peace," notes that, according to Yoram Dinstein and Mala Tabory, the permissibility of a recommendation for amnesty in a civil war "follows from Article 6(5) of the Additional Protocol to the Geneva Convention of 12 August 1949, and Relating to the Protection of Victims of Non-International Armed Conflict (Protocol II)." Dinstein and Tabory, eds., *War Crimes in International Law* (The Hague: Martinus Nijhoff, 1996), p. 319.

35. Elizabeth Kiss, "Moral Ambition Within and Beyond Political Constraints: Reflections on Restorative Justice," pp. 216–230, and Martha Minow, "The Hope for Healing: What Can Truth Commissions Do?" pp. 235–260, in Robert I. Rotberg and Dennis Thompson, eds., *Truth v. Justice: The Morality of Truth Commissions* (Princeton, N.J.: Princeton University Press, 2000).

36. Vanessa Pupavac, "Therapeutic Governance: Psycho-Social Intervention and Trauma Risk Management," *Disasters*, Vol. 25, No. 4 (December 2001), pp. 358–372.

37. William J. Long and Peter Brecke, *War and Reconciliation: Reason and Emotion in Conflict Resolution* (Cambridge, Mass.: MIT Press, 2003), especially p. 31.

38. See the Human Rights Watch website on international criminal justice, October 2003, http://www.hrw.org/justice/about.php.

39. Kritz, "War Crime Trials"; and Teitel, *Transitional Justice*, pp. 28–30.

40. José E. Alvarez, "Crimes of States/Crimes of Hate: Lessons from Rwanda," *Yale Journal of International Law*, Vol. 24, No. 2 (Summer 1999), pp. 365–483.

41. Kritz, "Coming to Terms with Atrocities"; and Minow, *Between Vengeance and Forgiveness*.

42. For a normative discussion of amnesties and some historical examples, see W. James Booth, "The Unforgotten: Memories of Justice," *American Political Science Review*, Vol. 95, No. 4 (December 2001), pp. 783–785.

43. Using standard databases, we reviewed the following cases: Afghanistan, Angola, Bangladesh, Bosnia, Burundi, Cambodia, Chad, Colombia, Congo/Zaire, Croatia, East Timor, El Salvador, Ethiopia, Guatemala, Haiti, Indonesia, Iraq, Israel/Palestine, Ivory Coast, Kosovo, Liberia, Macedonia, Namibia, Northern Ireland, Peru, Russia/Chechnya, Rwanda, Sierra Leone, South Africa, Sri Lanka (Tamils and Janatha Vimukthi Peramuna [People's Liberation Front]), and Turkey/Kurds. For a table listing the justice strategies and outcomes of these cases, see Jack Snyder and Leslie Vinjamuri, "Principle and Pragmatism in Strategies of International Justice," paper delivered at the annual meeting of the American Political Science Association, Philadelphia, Pennsylvania, August 28–31, 2003. Data are drawn from MIT Cascon System for Analyzing International Conflict Database, July 2003, http://mit.edu/cascon; State Failure: Internal Wars and Failures of Governance, 1955–2001 Database (University of Maryland), July 2003, http://www.cidcm.umd.edu/inscr/stfail/sftable.htm; Project Ploughshares' Armed Conflicts Report 2002 Database, July 2003, http://www.ploughshares.ca/CONTENT/ACR/ACR00/ACR00.html; Dan Smith, "Counting Wars: The Research Implications of Definitional Decisions," paper presented at the annual meeting of the Uppsala Conflict Data Conference, Uppsala, Norway, June 8–9, 2001; R. Williams Ayres, VINC Project (Violent, Intrastate Nationalist Conflicts), July 2003, http://facstaff.uindy.edu/?bayres/vinc.htm; Freedom House, *Freedom in the World 2003: The Annual Survey of Political Rights and Civil Liberties*, August 2003, http://www.freedomhouse.org/research/index.htm; and Michael W. Doyle and Nicholas Sambanis, "Cases of Internal War and Peacebuilding Outcomes since 1944," in "International Peacebuilding: A Theoretical and Quantitative Analysis," August 22, 2000, American Political Science Association, p. 49, Table 1, http://www.worldbank.org/research/conflict/papers/peacebuilding/pbapsr_finalv4.pdf.

44. On the testimony of former British Member of Parliament Paddy Ashdown, see Marlise Simons, "Briton Gives Testimony on Warning to Milosevic," *New York Times*, March 17, 2002, p. 7.

45. Comments made by Aryeh Neier at a conference at Bard College, "Accounting for Atrocities," Annandale-on-Hudson, New York, October 5–6, 1998.

46. For a more positive view, see José E. Alvarez, "Rush to Closure: Lessons of the Tadic Judgment," *Michigan Law Review*, Vol. 96, No. 7 (June 1998), pp. 2031–2113; and Payam Akhavan, "Beyond Impunity: Can International Criminal Justice Prevent Future Atrocities?" *American Journal of International Law*, Vol. 95, No. 1 (January 2001), p. 16.

47. Chaim Kaufmann, "Possible and Impossible Solutions to Ethnic Civil Wars," *International Security*, Vol. 20, No. 4 (Spring 1996), pp. 136–175.

48. "A Survey of Voter Attitudes in B&H, Summary Report," National Democratic Institute for International Affairs, Bosnia and Herzegovina, May 31, 2002, p. 21.

49. "Serbia: Reform Constituency Shrinks," Results of the Nationwide Survey Conducted by Greenberg Quinlan Rosner Research, NDI, June 2002, p. 1.

50. International Republican Institute, November 2002 Serbian National Survey, Rob Autry and Gene Ulm, Public Opinion Strategies, slide 48.

51. Ibid., slide 50.

52. "Serbia: Reform Constituency Shrinks," p. 2.

53. For other Yugoslav examples, see Akhavan, "Beyond Impunity," p. 14.

54. Plavsic letter to Secretary-General Kofi Annan, January 2, 1997, Appendix B, in Human Rights Watch, *Bosnia and Hercegovina: The Unindicted—Reaping the Rewards of "Ethnic Cleansing,"* Vol. 9, No. 1 (D) (January 1997), p. 71.

55. Misha Glenny, "Trials' Political and Financial Costs Questioned," *Times* (London), February 14, 2002, p. 15; see also "Special Report: Balkan War Crimes," *Economist,* February 9, 2002, p. 25.

56. International Crisis Group, "International Criminal Tribunal for Rwanda: Justice Delayed," *Africa Report,* June 7, 2001, pp. 7–8.

57. Ibid., pp. 8, 27; and Alvarez, "Crimes of States/ Crimes of Hate," pp. 365–483.

58. Sarah Kenyon Lischer, "Collateral Damage: Humanitarian Assistance as a Cause of Conflict," *International Security,* Vol. 28, No. 1 (Summer 2003), pp. 79–109.

59. Carlos Nino, *Radical Evil on Trial* (New Haven, Conn.: Yale University Press, 1996), p. 116.

60. For a critique of Kirchner's proposal, see Jackson Diehl, "Revisionist Justice in Argentina," *Washington Post,* September 1, 2003, p. A25.

61. By 1998, Freedom House had raised Ethiopia's rating on political rights and on civil rights to level 4 ("partly free"), on par with such countries as Armenia, Russia, and Senegal. Freedom House, *Freedom in the World,* *1998–99* (New York: Freedom House, 1998), pp. 182–184; and John Harbeson, "Elections and Democratization in Post-Mengistu Ethiopia," in Krishna Kumar, ed., *Postconflict Elections, Democratization, and International Assistance* (Boulder, Colo.: Lynne Rienner, 1998), pp. 111–132.

62. Yacob Haile-Mariam, "The Quest for Justice and Reconciliation: The International Criminal Tribunal for Rwanda and the Ethiopian High Court," *Hastings International and Comparative Law Review,* Vol. 22, No. 4 (Summer 1999), pp. 667–745; and Todd Howland, "Learning to Make Proactive Human Rights Interventions Effective: The Carter Center and Ethiopia's Office of the Special Prosecutor," *Wisconsin International Law Journal,* Vol. 18, No. 2 (Spring 2000), p. 407.

63. Jennifer Widner, "Courts and Democracy in Postconflict Transitions: A Social Scientist's Perspective on the African Case," *American Journal of International Law,* Vol. 95, No. 1 (January 2001), Symposium: State Reconstruction after Civil Conflict, pp. 67–68.

64. Alvarez, "Crimes of States/Crimes of Hate, pp. 365–483.

65. International Crisis Group, "Finding the Balance: The Scales of Justice in Kosovo," ICG Balkans Report No. 134, September 12, 2002, p. 20.

66. National Democratic Institute, "Public Opinion Poll," by PRISM Market, Media, and Social Research, November 2001, cited in ICG, "Finding the Balance," p. 25.

67. Organization for Security and Co-operation in Europe, Mission in Kosovo, *Kosovo's War Crimes Trials: A Review,* September 2002, pp. 10–11, 48.

68. "Decision to Acquit Serb for Kosovan War Crimes Absurd," Agence France-Presse, January 30, 2001, cited in International Crisis Group, "Finding the Balance," p. 21.

69. Ibid., p. 24.

70. Arben Qirezi, "Kosovo: KLA Trial Backlash," Institute for War and Peace Reporting, Pristina, Kosovo, August 1, 2003.

71. Note that plans to pursue a truth commission in Sierra Leone followed the 1999 negotiated settlement but not the 2000 British intervention that led to the defeat of the RUF.

72. Priscilla B. Hayner, *Unspeakable Truths: Confronting State Terror and Atrocity* (New York: Routledge, 2001), p. 244.

73. Ibid., pp. 101–105.

74. James L. Gibson and Amanda Gouws, "Truth and Reconciliation in South Africa: Attributions of Blame and the Struggle over Apartheid," *American Political Science Review*, Vol. 93, No. 3 (September 1999), pp. 501–518.

75. Hayner, *Unspeakable Truths*, pp. 123.

76. James L. Gibson, "Truth, Justice, and Reconciliation: Judging the Fairness of Amnesty in South Africa," *American Journal of Political Science*, Vol. 46, No. 3 (July 2002), pp. 540–556.

77. Ibid., p. 187.

78. William Stanley, *The Protection Racket State: Elite Politics, Military Extortion, and Civil War in El Salvador* (Philadelphia: Temple University Press, 1996), pp. 218–255; and Elisabeth Wood, *Forging Democracy from Below: Insurgent Transitions in South Africa and El Salvador* (Cambridge: Cambridge University Press, 2000). For a similar point regarding the Guatemala settlement, see Mark Peceny and William Stanley, "Liberal Social Reconstruction and the Resolution of Civil Wars in Central America," *International Organization*, Vol. 55, No. 1 (Winter 2001), pp. 171–175.

79. Margaret Popkin, "El Salvador: A Negotiated End to Impunity?" in Naomi Roht-Arriaza, ed., *Impunity and Human Rights in International Law and Practice* (New York: Oxford University Press, 1995), pp. 198–217.

80. "Macedonia Bolsters Albanian Rights, After Constitutional Change, Amnesty Is Declared for Former Rebels," *International Herald Tribune*, November 17–18, 2001.

81. On the concept of institutions designed to fail, see Terry Moe, "The Politics of Bureaucratic Structure," in John E. Chubb and Paul E. Peterson, eds., *Can the Government Govern?* (Washington, D.C.: Brookings, 1989), pp. 267–329, especially p. 326.

82. Richard Holbrooke, *To End a War* (New York: Random House, 1998), p. 339.

GARRETT HARDIN

The Tragedy of the Commons

The population problem has no technical solution; it requires a fundamental extension in morality.

At the end of a thoughtful article on the future of nuclear war, Wiesner and York[1] concluded that: "Both sides in the arms race are . . . confronted by the dilemma of steadily increasing military power and steadily decreasing national security. *It is our considered professional judgment that this dilemma has no technical solution.* If the great powers continue to look for solutions in the area of science and technology only, the result will be to worsen the situation."

I would like to focus your attention not on the subject of the article (national security in a nuclear world) but on the kind of conclusion they reached, namely that there is no technical

From *Science* 162, no. 3859 (Dec. 13, 1968): 1243–1248.

solution to the problem. An implicit and almost universal assumption of discussions published in professional and semipopular scientific journals is that the problem under discussion has a technical solution. A technical solution may be defined as one that requires a change only in the techniques of the natural sciences, demanding little or nothing in the way of change in human values or ideas of morality.

In our day (though not in earlier times) technical solutions are always welcome. Because of previous failures in prophecy, it takes courage to assert that a desired technical solution is not possible. Wiesner and York exhibited this courage; publishing in a science journal, they insisted that the solution to the problem was not to be found in the natural sciences. They cautiously qualified their statement with the phrase, "It is our considered professional judgment. . . ." Whether they were right or not is not the concern of the present article. Rather, the concern here is with the important concept of a class of human problems which can be called "no technical solution problems," and, more specifically, with the identification and discussion of one of these.

It is easy to show that the class is not a null class. Recall the game of tick-tack-toe. Consider the problem, "How can I win the game of tick-tack-toe?" It is well known that I cannot, if I assume (in keeping with the conventions of game theory) that my opponent understands the game perfectly. Put another way, there is no "technical solution" to the problem. I can win only by giving a radical meaning to the word "win." I can hit my opponent over the head; or I can drug him; or I can falsify the records. Every way in which I "win" involves, in some sense, an abandonment of the game, as we intuitively understand it. (I can also, of course, openly abandon the game—refuse to play it. This is what most adults do.)

The class of "No technical solution problems" has members. My thesis is that the "population problem," as conventionally conceived, is a member of this class. How it is conventionally conceived needs some comment. It is fair to say that most people who anguish over the population problem are trying to find a way to avoid the evils of overpopulation without relinquishing any of the privileges they now enjoy. They think that farming the seas or developing new strains of wheat will solve the problem—technologically. I try to show here that the solution they seek cannot be found. The population problem cannot be solved in a technical way, any more than can the problem of winning the game of tick-tack-toe.

What Shall We Maximize?

Population, as Malthus said, naturally tends to grow "geometrically," or, as we would now say, exponentially. In a finite world this means that the per capita share of the world's goods must steadily decrease. Is ours a finite world?

A fair defense can be put forward for the view that the world is infinite; or that we do not know that it is not. But, in terms of the practical problems that we must face in the next few generations with the foreseeable technology, it is clear that we will greatly increase human misery if we do not, during the immediate future, assume that the world available to the terrestrial human population is finite. "Space" is no escape.[2]

A finite world can support only a finite population; therefore, population growth must eventually equal zero. (The case of perpetual wide fluctuations above and below zero is a trivial variant that need not be discussed.) When this condition is met, what will be the situation of mankind? Specifically, can Bentham's goal of "the greatest good for the greatest number" be realized?

No—for two reasons, each sufficient by itself. The first is a theoretical one. It is not mathematically possible to maximize for two (or more) variables at the same time. This was clearly stated by von Neumann and Morgenstern,[3] but the principle is implicit in the theory of partial differential equations, dating back at least to D'Alembert (1717–1783).

The second reason springs directly from biological facts. To live, any organism must have a source of energy (for example, food). This energy is utilized for two purposes: mere maintenance and work. For man, maintenance of life requires about 1600 kilo-calories a day ("maintenance calories"). Anything that he does over and above merely staying alive will be defined as work, and is supported by "work calories" which he takes in. Work calories are used not only for what we call work in common speech; they are also required for all forms of enjoyment, from swimming and automobile racing to playing music and writing poetry. If our goal is to maximize population it is obvious what we must do: We must make the work calories per person approach as close to zero as possible. No gourmet meals, no vacations, no sports, no music, no literature, no art. . . . I think that everyone will grant, without argument or proof, that maximizing population does not maximize goods. Bentham's goal is impossible.

In reaching this conclusion I have made the usual assumption that it is the acquisition of energy that is the problem. The appearance of atomic energy has led some to question this assumption. However, given an infinite source of energy, population growth still produces an inescapable problem. The problem of the acquisition of energy is replaced by the problem of its dissipation, as J. H. Fremlin has so wittily shown.[4] The arithmetic signs in the analysis are, as it were, reversed; but Bentham's goal is still unobtainable.

The optimum population is, then, less than the maximum. The difficulty of defining the optimum is enormous; so far as I know, no one has seriously tackled this problem. Reaching an acceptable and stable solution will surely require more than one generation of hard analytical work—and much persuasion.

We want the maximum good per person; but what is good? To one person it is wilderness, to another it is ski lodges for thousands. To one it is estuaries to nourish ducks for hunters to shoot; to another it is factory land. Comparing one good with another is, we usually say, impossible because goods are incommensurable. Incommensurables cannot be compared.

Theoretically this may be true; but in real life incommensurables *are* commensurable. Only a criterion of judgment and a system of weighting are needed. In nature the criterion is survival. Is it better for a species to be small and hide-able, or large and powerful? Natural selection commensurates the incommensurables. The compromise achieved depends on a natural weighting of the values of the variables.

Man must imitate this process. There is no doubt that in fact he already does, but unconsciously. It is when the hidden decisions are made explicit that the arguments begin. The problem for the years ahead is to work out an acceptable theory of weighting. Synergistic effects, nonlinear variation, and difficulties in discounting the future make the intellectual problem difficult, but not (in principle) insoluble.

Has any cultural group solved this practical problem at the present time, even on an intuitive level? One simple fact proves that none has: there is no prosperous population in the world today that has, and has had for some time, a growth rate of zero. Any people that has intuitively identified its optimum point will soon reach it, after which its growth rate becomes and remains zero.

Of course, a positive growth rate might be taken as evidence that a population is below its optimum. However, by any reasonable standards, the most rapidly growing populations on earth today are (in general) the most miserable. This association (which need not be invariable) casts doubt on the optimistic assumption that the positive growth rate of a population is evidence that it has yet to reach its optimum.

We can make little progress in working toward optimum poulation size until we explicitly exorcize the spirit of Adam Smith in the field of practical demography. In economic affairs, *The Wealth of Nations* (1776) popularized the "invisible hand," the idea that an individual who "intends only his own gain," is, as it were, "led by an invisible hand to promote . . . the public interest."[5] Adam Smith did not assert that this was invariably true, and perhaps neither did any of his followers. But he contributed to a dominant tendency of thought that has ever since interfered with positive action based on rational analysis, namely, the tendency to assume that decisions reached individually will, in fact, be the best decisions for an entire society. If this assumption is correct it justifies the continuance of our present policy of laissez-faire in reproduction. If it is correct we can assume that men will control their individual fecundity so as to produce the optimum population. If the assumption is not correct, we need to reexamine our individual freedoms to see which ones are defensible.

Tragedy of Freedom in a Commons

The rebuttal to the invisible hand in population control is to be found in a scenario first sketched in a little-known pamphlet[6] in 1833 by a mathematical amateur named William Forster Lloyd (1794–1852). We may well call it "the tragedy of the commons," using the word "tragedy" as the philosopher Whitehead used it[7]: "The essence of dramatic tragedy is not unhappiness. It resides in the solemnity of the remorseless working of things:" He then goes on to say, "This inevitableness of destiny can only be illustrated in terms of human life by incidents which in fact involve unhappiness. For it is only by them that the futility of escape can be made evident in the drama."

The tragedy of the commons develops in this way. Picture a pasture open to all. It is to be expected that each herdsman will try to keep as many cattle as possible on the commons. Such an arrangement may work reasonably satisfactorily for centuries because tribal wars, poaching, and disease keep the numbers of both man and beast well below the carrying capacity of the land. Finally, however, comes the day of reckoning, that is, the day when the long-desired goal of social stability becomes a reality. At this point, the inherent logic of the commons remorselessly generates tragedy.

As a rational being, each herdsman seeks to maximize his gain. Explicitly or implicitly, more or less consciously, he asks, "What is the utility *to me* of adding one more animal to my herd?" This utility has one negative and one positive component.

1) The positive component is a function of the increment of one animal. Since the herdsman receives all the proceeds from the sale of the additional animal, the positive utility is nearly +1.

2) The negative component is a function of the additional overgrazing created by one more animal. Since, however, the effects of overgrazing are shared by all the herdsmen, the negative utility for any particular decision-making herdsman is only a fraction of –1.

Adding together the component partial utilities, the rational herdsman concludes that the only sensible course for him to pursue is to add another animal to his herd. And another; and another. . . . But this is the conclusion reached by each and every rational herdsman sharing a commons. Therein is the tragedy. Each man is locked into a system that compels him to increase his herd without limit—in a world that is limited. Ruin is the destination toward which all men rush, each pursuing his own best interest in a society that believes in the freedom of the commons. Freedom in a commons brings ruin to all.

Some would say that this is a platitude. Would that it were! In a sense, it was learned thousands of years ago, but natural selection favors the forces of psychological denial.[8] The individual benefits as an individual from his ability to deny the truth even though society as a whole, of which he is a part, suffers. Education can counteract the natural tendency to do the wrong thing, but the inexorable succession of generations requires that the basis for this knowledge be constantly refreshed.

A simple incident that occurred a few years ago in Leominster, Massachusetts, shows how perishable the knowledge is. During the Christmas shopping season the parking meters downtown were covered with plastic bags that bore tags reading: "Do not open until after Christmas. Free parking courtesy of the mayor and city council." In other words, facing the prospect of an increased demand for already scarce space, the city fathers reinstituted the system of the commons. (Cynically, we suspect that they gained more votes than they lost by this retrogressive act.)

In an approximate way, the logic of the commons has been understood for a long time, perhaps since the discovery of agriculture or the invention of private property in real estate. But it is understood mostly only in special cases which are not sufficiently generalized. Even at this late date, cattlemen leasing national land on the western ranges demonstrate no more than an ambivalent understanding, in constantly pressuring federal authorities to increase the head count to the point where overgrazing produces erosion and weed-dominance. Likewise, the oceans of the world continue to suffer from the survival of the philosophy of the commons. Maritime nations still respond automatically to the shibboleth of the "freedom of the seas." Professing to believe in the "inexhaustible resources of the oceans," they bring species after species of fish and whales closer to extinction.[9]

The National Parks present another instance of the working out of the tragedy of the commons. At present, they are open to all, without limit. The parks themselves are limited in extent—there is only one Yosemite Valley—whereas population seems to grow without limit. The values that visitors seek in the parks are steadily eroded. Plainly, we must soon cease to treat the parks as commons or they will be of no value to anyone.

What shall we do? We have several options. We might sell them off as private property. We might keep them as public property, but allocate the right to enter them. The allocation might be on the basis of wealth, by the use of an auction system. It might be on the basis of merit, as defined by some agreed-upon standards. It might be by lottery. Or it might be on a first-come, first-served basis, administered to long queues. These, I think, are all the reasonable possibilities. They

are all objectionable. But we must choose—or acquiesce in the destruction of the commons that we call our National Parks.

Pollution

In a reverse way, the tragedy of the commons reappears in problems of pollution. Here it is not a question of taking something out of the commons, but of putting something in—sewage, or chemical, radioactive, and heat wastes into water; noxious and dangerous fumes into the air; and distracting and unpleasant advertising signs into the line of sight. The calculations of utility are much the same as before. The rational man finds that his share of the cost of the wastes he discharges into the commons is less than the cost of purifying his wastes before releasing them. Since this is true for everyone, we are locked into a system of "fouling our own nest," so long as we behave only as independent, rational, free-enterprisers.

The tragedy of the commons as a food basket is averted by private property, or something formally like it. But the air and waters surrounding us cannot readily be fenced, and so the tragedy of the commons as a cesspool must be prevented by different means, by coercive laws or taxing devices that make it cheaper for the polluter to treat his pollutants than to discharge them untreated. We have not progressed as far with the solution of this problem as we have with the first. Indeed, our particular concept of private property, which deters us from exhausting the positive resources of the earth, favors pollution. The owner of a factory on the bank of a stream—whose property extends to the middle of the stream—often has difficulty seeing why it is not his natural right to muddy the waters flowing past his door. The law, always behind the times, requires elaborate stitching and fitting to adapt it to this newly perceived aspect of the commons.

The pollution problem is a consequence of population. It did not much matter how a lonely

American frontiersman disposed of his waste. "Flowing water purifies itself every 10 miles," my grandfather used to say, and the myth was near enough to the truth when he was a boy, for there were not too many people. But as population became denser, the natural chemical and biological recycling processes became overloaded, calling for a redefinition of property rights.

How to Legislate Temperance?

Analysis of the pollution problem as a function of population density uncovers a not generally recognized principle of morality, namely: *the morality of an act is a function of the state of the system at the time it is performed.*[10] Using the commons as a cesspool does not harm the general public under frontier conditions, because there is no public; the same behavior in a metropolis is unbearable. A hundred and fifty years ago a plainsman could kill an American bison, cut out only the tongue for his dinner, and discard the rest of the animal. He was not in any important sense being wasteful. Today, with only a few thousand bison left, we would be appalled at such behavior.

In passing, it is worth noting that the morality of an act cannot be determined from a photograph. One does not know whether a man killing an elephant or setting fire to the grassland is harming others until one knows the total system in which his act appears. "One picture is worth a thousand words," said an ancient Chinese; but it may take 10,000 words to validate it. It is as tempting to ecologists as it is to reformers in general to try to persuade others by way of the photographic shortcut. But the essen[c]e of an argument cannot be photographed: it must be presented rationally—in words.

That morality is system-sensitive escaped the attention of most codifiers of ethics in the past. "Thou shalt not . . ." is the form of traditional ethical directives which make no allowance for particular circumstances. The laws of our society follow the pattern of ancient ethics, and therefore are poorly suited to governing a complex, crowded, changeable world. Our epicyclic solution is to augment statutory law with administrative law. Since it is practically impossible to spell out all the conditions under which it is safe to burn trash in the back yard or to run an automobile without smog-control, by law we delegate the details to bureaus. The result is administrative law, which is rightly feared for an ancient reason—*Quis custodiet ipsos custodes?*—"Who shall watch the watchers themselves?" John Adams said that we must have "a government of laws and not men." Bureau administrators, trying to evaluate the morality of acts in the total system, are singularly liable to corruption, producing a government by men, not laws.

Prohibition is easy to legislate (though not necessarily to enforce); but how do we legislate temperance? Experience indicates that it can be accomplished best through the mediation of administrative law. We limit possibilities unnecessarily if we suppose that the sentiment of *Quis custodiet* denies us the use of administrative law. We should rather retain the phrase as a perpetual reminder of fearful dangers we cannot avoid. The great challenge facing us now is to invent the corrective feedbacks that are needed to keep custodians honest. We must find ways to legitimate the needed authority of both the custodians and the corrective feedbacks.

Freedom to Breed Is Intolerable

The tragedy of the commons is involved in population problems in another way. In a world governed solely by the principle of "dog eat dog"—if indeed there ever was such a world—how many children a family had would not be a matter of public concern. Parents who bred too exuberantly would leave fewer descendants, not more, because they would be unable to care adequately for their children. David Lack and others have found that such a negative feedback demonstrably controls the fecundity of birds.[11] But men are not birds, and have not acted like them for millenniums, at least.

If each human family were dependent only on its own resources; *if* the children of improvident parents starved to death; *if,* thus, overbreeding brought its own "punishment" to the germ line—*then* there would be no public interest in controlling the breeding of families. But our society is deeply committed to the welfare state,[12] and hence is confronted with another aspect of the tragedy of the commons.

In a welfare state, how shall we deal with the family, the religion, the race, or the class (or indeed any distinguishable and cohesive group) that adopts overbreeding as a policy to secure its own aggrandizement?[13] To couple the concept of freedom to breed with the belief that everyone born has an equal right to the commons is to lock the world into a tragic course of action.

Unfortunately this is just the course of action that is being pursued by the United Nations. In late 1967, some 30 nations agreed to the following[14]:

> The Universal Declaration of Human Rights describes the family as the natural and fundamental unit of society. It follows that any choice and decision with regard to the size of the family must irrevocably rest with the family itself, and cannot be made by anyone else.

It is painful to have to deny categorically the validity of this right; denying it, one feels as uncomfortable as a resident of Salem, Massachusetts, who denied the reality of witches in the 17th century. At the present time, in liberal quarters, something like a taboo acts to inhibit criticism of the United Nations. There is a feeling that the United Nations is "our last and best hope," that we shouldn't find fault with it; we shouldn't play into the hands of the archconservatives. However, let us not forget what Robert Louis Stevenson said: "The truth that is suppressed by friends is the readiest weapon of the enemy." If we love the truth we must openly deny the validity of the Universal Declaration of Human Rights, even though it is promoted by the United Nations. We should also join with Kingsley Davis[15] in attempting to get Planned Parenthood-World Population to see the error of its ways in embracing the same tragic ideal.

Conscience Is Self-Eliminating

It is a mistake to think that we can control the breeding of mankind in the long run by an appeal to conscience. Charles Galton Darwin made this point when he spoke on the centennial of the publication of his grandfather's great book. The argument is straightforward and Darwinian.

People vary. Confronted with appeals to limit breeding, some people will undoubtedly respond to the plea more than others. Those who have more children will produce a larger fraction of the next generation than those with more susceptible consciences. The difference will be accentuated, generation by generation.

In C. G. Darwin's words: "It may well be that it would take hundreds of generations for the progenitive instinct to develop in this way, but if it should do so, nature would have taken her revenge, and the variety *Homo contracipiens* would become extinct and would be replaced by the variety *Homo progenitivus*."[16]

The argument assumes that conscience or the desire for children (no matter which) is hereditary—but hereditary only in the most general formal sense. The result will be the same whether the attitude is transmitted through germ cells, or exosomatically, to use A. J. Lotka's term. (If one denies the latter possibility as well as the former, then what's the point of education?) The argument has here been stated in the context of the population problem, but it applies equally well to any instance in which society appeals to an individual exploiting a commons to restrain himself for the general good—by means of his conscience. To make such an appeal is to set up a selective system that works toward the elimination of conscience from the race.

Pathogenic Effects of Conscience

The long-term disadvantage of an appeal to conscience should be enough to condemn it; but has serious short-term disadvantages as well. If we ask a man who is exploiting a commons to desist "in the name of conscience," what are we saying to him? What does he hear?–not only at the moment but also in the wee small hours of the night when, half asleep, he remembers not merely the words we used but also the nonverbal communication cues we gave him unawares? Sooner or later, consciously or subconsciously, he senses that he has received two communications, and that they are contradictory: (i) (intended communication) "If you don't do as we ask, we will openly condemn you for not acting like a responsible citizen"; (ii) (the unintended communication) "If you *do* behave as we ask, we will secretly condemn you for a simpleton who can be shamed into standing aside while the rest of us exploit the commons."

Everyman then is caught in what Bateson has called a "double bind." Bateson and his co-workers have made a plausible case for viewing the double bind as an important causative factor in the genesis of schizophrenia.[17] The double bind may not always be so damaging, but it always endangers the mental health of anyone to whom it is applied. "A bad conscience," said Nietzsche, "is a kind of illness."

To conjure up a conscience in others is tempting to anyone who wishes to extend his control beyond the legal limits. Leaders at the highest level succumb to this temptation. Has any President during the past generation failed to call on labor unions to moderate voluntarily their demands for higher wages, or to steel companies to honor voluntary guidelines on prices? I can recall none. The rhetoric used on such occasions is designed to produce feelings of guilt in noncooperators.

For centuries it was assumed without proof that guilt was a valuable, perhaps even an indispensable, ingredient of the civilized life. Now, in this post-Freudian world, we doubt it.

Paul Goodman speaks from the modern point of view when he says: "No good has ever come from feeling guilty, neither intelligence, policy, nor compassion. The guilty do not pay attention to the object but only to themselves, and not even to their own interests, which might make sense, but to their anxieties."[18]

One does not have to be a professional psychiatrist to see the consequences of anxiety. We in the Western world are just emerging from a dreadful two-centuries-long Dark Ages of Eros that was sustained partly by prohibition laws, but perhaps more effectively by the anxiety-generating mechanisms of education. Alex Comfort has told the story well in *The Anxiety Makers*[19]; it is not a pretty one.

Since proof is difficult, we may even concede that the results of anxiety may sometimes, from certain points of view, be desirable. The larger question we should ask is whether, as a matter of policy, we should ever encourage the use of a technique the tendency (if not the intention) of which is psychologically pathogenic. We hear much talk these days of responsible parenthood; the coupled words are incorporated into the titles of some organizations devoted to birth control. Some people have proposed massive propaganda campaigns to instill responsibility into the nation's (or the world's) breeders. But what is the meaning of the word responsibility in this context? Is it not merely a synonym for the word conscience? When we use the word responsibility in the absence of substantial sanctions are we not trying to browbeat a free man in a commons into acting against his own interest? Responsibility is a verbal counterfeit for a substantial *quid pro quo*. It is an attempt to get something for nothing.

If the word responsibility is to be used at all, I suggest that it be in the sense Charles Frankel uses it.[20] "Responsibility," says this philosopher, "is the product of definite social arrangements." Notice that Frankel calls for social arrangements—not propaganda.

Mutual Coercion Mutually Agreed Upon

The social arrangements that produce responsibility are arrangements that create coercion, of some sort. Consider bank-robbing. The man who takes money from a bank acts as if the bank were a commons. How do we prevent such action? Certainly not by trying to control his behavior solely by a verbal appeal to his sense of responsibility. Rather than rely on propaganda we follow Frankel's lead and insist that a bank is not a commons; we seek the definite social arrangements that will keep it from becoming a commons. That we thereby infringe on the freedom of would-be robbers we neither deny nor regret.

The morality of bank-robbing is particularly easy to understand because we accept complete prohibition of this activity. We are willing to say "Thou shalt not rob banks," without providing for exceptions. But temperance also can be created by coercion. Taxing is a good coercive device. To keep downtown shoppers temperate in their use of parking space we introduce parking meters for short periods, and traffic fines for longer ones. We need not actually forbid a citizen to park as long as he wants to; we need merely make it increasingly expensive for him to do so. Not prohibition, but carefully biased options are what we offer him. A Madison Avenue man might call this persuasion; I prefer the greater candor of the word coercion.

Coercion is a dirty word to most liberals now, but it need not forever be so. As with the four-letter words, its dirtiness can be cleansed away by exposure to the light, by saying it over and over without apology or embarrassment. To many, the word coercion implies arbitrary decisions of distant and irresponsible bureaucrats; but this is not a necessary part of its meaning. The only kind of coercion I recommend is mutual coercion, mutually agreed upon by the majority of the people affected.

To say that we mutually agree to coercion is not to say that we are required to enjoy it, or even to pretend we enjoy it. Who enjoys taxes? We all grumble about them. But we accept compulsory taxes because we recognize that voluntary taxes would favor the conscienceless. We institute and (grumblingly) support taxes and other coercive devices to escape the horror of the commons.

An alternative to the commons need not be perfectly just to be preferable. With real estate and other material goods, the alternative we have chosen is the institution of private property coupled with legal inheritance. Is this system perfectly just? As a genetically trained biologist I deny that it is. It seems to me that, if there are to be differences in individual inheritance, legal possession should be perfectly correlated with biological inheritance—that those who are biologically more fit to be the custodians of property and power should legally inherit more. But genetic recombination continually makes a mockery of the doctrine of "like father, like son" implicit in our laws of legal inheritance. An idiot can inherit millions, and a trust fund can keep his estate intact. We must admit that our legal system of private property plus inheritance is unjust—but we put up with it because we are not convinced, at the moment, that anyone has invented a better system. The alternative of the commons is too horrifying to contemplate. Injustice is preferable to total ruin.

It is one of the peculiarities of the warfare between reform and the status quo that it is thoughtlessly governed by a double standard. Whenever a reform measure is proposed it is often defeated when its opponents triumphantly discover a flaw in it. As Kingsley Davis has pointed out,[21] worshippers of the status quo sometimes imply that no reform is possible without unanimous agreement, an implication contrary to historical fact. As nearly as I can make out, automatic rejection of proposed reforms is based on one of two unconscious assumptions: (i) that the status quo is perfect; or (ii) that the choice we face is between reform and no action; if the proposed reform is imperfect, we presumably should take no action at all, while we wait for a perfect proposal.

But we can never do nothing. That which we have done for thousands of years is also action. It also produces evils. Once we are aware that the status quo is action, we can then compare its discoverable advantages and disadvantages with the predicted advantages and disadvantages of the proposed reform, discounting as best we can for our lack of experience. On the basis of such a comparison, we can make a rational decision which will not involve the unworkable assumption that only perfect systems are tolerable.

Recognition of Necessity

Perhaps the simplest summary of this analysis of man's population problems is this: the commons, if justifiable at all, is justifiable only under conditions of low-population density. As the human population has increased, the commons has had to be abandoned in one aspect after another.

First we abandoned the commons in food gathering, enclosing farm land and restricting pastures and hunting and fishing areas. These restrictions are still not complete throughout the world.

Somewhat later we saw that the commons as a place for waste disposal would also have to be abandoned. Restrictions on the disposal of domestic sewage are widely accepted in the Western world; we are still struggling to close the commons to pollution by automobiles, factories, insecticide sprayers, fertilizing operations, and atomic energy installations.

In a still more embryonic state is our recognition of the evils of the commons in matters of pleasure. There is almost no restriction on the propagation of sound waves in the public medium. The shopping public is assaulted with mindless music, without its consent. Our government is paying out billions of dollars to create supersonic transport which will disturb 50,000 people for every one person who is whisked from coast to coast 3 hours faster. Advertisers muddy the airwaves of radio and television and pollute the view of travelers. We are a long way from outlawing the commons in matters of pleasure. Is this because our Puritan inheritance makes us view pleasure as something of a sin, and pain (that is, the pollution of advertising) as the sign of virtue?

Every new enclosure of the commons involves the infringement of somebody's personal liberty. Infringements made in the distant past are accepted because no contemporary complains of a loss. It is the newly proposed infringements that we vigorously oppose; cries of "rights" and "freedom" fill the air. But what does "freedom" mean? When men mutually agreed to pass laws against robbing, mankind became more free, not less so. Individuals locked into the logic of the commons are free only to bring on universal ruin; once they see the necessity of mutual coercion, they become free to pursue other goals. I believe it was Hegel who said, "Freedom is the recognition of necessity."

The most important aspect of necessity that we must now recognize, is the necessity of abandoning the commons in breeding. No technical solution can rescue us from the misery of overpopulation. Freedom to breed will bring ruin to all. At the moment, to avoid hard decisions many of us are tempted to propagandize for conscience and responsible parenthood. The temptation must be resisted, because an appeal to independently acting consciences selects for the disappearance of all conscience in the long run, and an increase in anxiety in the short.

The only way we can preserve and nurture other and more precious freedoms is by relinquishing the freedom to breed, and that very soon. "Freedom is the recognition of necessity"— and it is the role of education to reveal to all the necessity of abandoning the freedom to breed. Only so, can we put an end to this aspect of the tragedy of the commons.

NOTES

1. J. B. Wiesner and H. F. York, *Sci. Amer.* 211 (No. 4), 27 (1964).

2. G. Hardin, *J. Hered.* 50, 68 (1959); S. von Hoernor, *Science* 137, 18 (1962).

3. J. von Neumann and O. Morgenstern, *Theory of Games and Economic Behavior* (Princeton Univ. Press, Princeton, N.J., 1947), p. 11.

4. J. H. Fremlin, *New Sci.*, No. 415 (1964), p. 285.

5. A. Smith, *The Wealth of Nations* (Modern Library, New York, 1937), p. 423.

6. W. F. Lloyd, *Two Lectures on the Checks to Population* (Oxford Univ. Press, Oxford, England, 1833), reprinted (in part) in *Population, Evolution, and Birth Control*, G. Hardin, Ed. (Freeman, San Francisco, 1964), p. 37.

7. A. N. Whitehead, *Science and the Modern World* (Mentor, New York, 1948), p. 17.

8. G. Hardin, Ed. *Population, Evolution, and Birth Control* (Freeman, San Francisco, 1964), p. 56.

9. S. McVay, *Sci. Amer.* 216 (No. 8), 13 (1966).

10. J. Fletcher, *Situation Ethics* (Westminster, Philadelphia, 1966).

11. D. Lack, *The Natural Regulation of Animal Numbers* (Clarendon Press, Oxford, 1954).

12. H. Girvetz, *From Wealth to Welfare* (Stanford Univ. Press, Stanford, Calif., 1950).

13. G. Hardin, *Perspec. Biol. Med.* 6, 366 (1963).

14. U. Thant, *Int. Planned Parenthood News*, No. 168 (February 1968), p. 3.

15. K. Davis, *Science* 158, 730 (1967).

16. S. Tax, Ed., *Evolution after Darwin* (Univ. of Chicago Press, Chicago, 1960), vol. 2, p. 469.

17. G. Bateson, D. D. Jackson, J. Haley, J. Weakland, *Behav. Sci.* 1, 251 (1956).

18. P. Goodman, *New York Rev. Books* 10(8), 22 (23 May 1968).

19. A. Comfort, *The Anxiety Makers* (Nelson, London, 1967).

20. C. Frankel, *The Case for Modern Man* (Harper, New York, 1955), p. 203.

21. J. D. Roslansky, *Genetics and the Future of Man* (Appleton-Century-Crofts, New York, 1966), p. 177.

Credits

Bull, Hedley. "Does Order Exist in World Politics?" From *The Anarchical Society*, pp. 23–26, 32, 37–39, 49–50 (1977). From *The Anarchical Society: A Study of Order in World Politics*, 2d ed. Copyright © 1977 by Hedley Bull. Reprinted by permission of Columbia University Press and Palgrave Macmillan.

Clausewitz, Carl von. "War as an Instrument of Policy." From *On War* (Routledge, 1962; Penguin, 1968), pp. 402–410. © 1968 Penguin Group. Reprinted by permission.

Doyle, Michael W. "Liberalism and World Politics." From *American Political Science Review* 80, no. 4 (December 1986): 1151–1169. Copyright © 1986 by American Political Science Association. Reprinted with the permission of Cambridge University Press.

Easterly, William. "The Healers: Triumph and Tragedy," "Snapshot: Prostitutes for Prevention." From *The White Man's Burden: How The West's Efforts to Aid the Rest Have Done So Much Ill and So Little Good.* by William Easterly, copyright © 2006 by William Easterly. Used by permission of The Penguin Press, a division of Penguin Group (USA) Inc.

Evans, Gareth. "When Is It Right to Fight?" From *Survival* 46, no. 3 (Autumn 2004): 59–81. © Crisis Group. Reprinted by permission.

Fearon, James D. "Rationalist Explanations for War," *International Organization* 49, no. 3 (Summer 1995): 379–414. © 1995 by the IO Foundation and the Massachusetts Institute of Technology. Reprinted by permission.

Finnemore, Martha. "Changing Norms of Humanitarian Intervention." From *The Purpose of Intervention: Changing Beliefs about the Use of Force*, 2003, pp. 52–84. Reprinted by permission of Columbia University Press.

Fortna, Virginia Page. From *Does Peacekeeping Work? Shaping Belligerents' Choices after Civil War* (Princeton: Princeton University Press, 2008), pp. 1–4, 172–179. Reprinted by permission of Princeton University Press.

Gilpin, Robert. "The Nature of Political Economy." From *U.S. Power and the Multinational Corporation: The Political Economy of Foreign Direct Investment*, pp. 20–33. Copyright © 1975 by Basic Books, Inc. Reprinted by permission of Basic Books, a member of Perseus Books Group.

Hardin, Garrett. From "The Tragedy of the Commons," *Science* 162 (Dec. 13, 1968): 1243–1248. Reprinted with permission from AAAS.

Humphreys, Macartan, Jeffrey D. Sachs, and Joseph E. Stiglitz. From *Escaping the Research Curse*. Chapter 1: "What Is the Problem with Natural Resource Wealth?" 2007 pp. 1–14. Reprinted by permission of Columbia University Press.